Lecture Notes in Computer Science 3951

Commenced Publication in 1973
Founding and Former Series Editors:
Gerhard Goos, Juris Hartmanis, and Jan van Leeuwen

Aleš Leonardis   Horst Bischof
Axel Pinz (Eds.)

Computer Vision – ECCV 2006

9th European Conference on Computer Vision
Graz, Austria, May 7-13, 2006
Proceedings, Part I

 Springer

Volume Editors

Aleš Leonardis
University of Ljubljana
Faculty of Computer and Information Science
Visual Cognitive Systems Laboratory
Trzaska 25, 1001 Ljubljana, Slovenia
E-mail: alesl@fri.uni-lj.si

Horst Bischof
Graz University of Technology
Institute for Computer Graphics and Vision
Inffeldgasse 16, 8010 Graz, Austria
E-mail: bischof@icg.tu-graz.ac.at

Axel Pinz
Graz University of Technology
Institute of Electrical Measurement and Measurement Signal Processing
Schießstattgasse 14b, 8010 Graz, Austria
E-mail: Axel.Pinz@tugraz.at

Library of Congress Control Number: 2006924180

CR Subject Classification (1998): I.4, I.3.5, I.5, I.2.9-10

LNCS Sublibrary: SL 6 – Image Processing, Computer Vision, Pattern Recognition, and Graphics

ISSN   0302-9743
ISBN-10   3-540-33832-2 Springer Berlin Heidelberg New York
ISBN-13   978-3-540-33832-1 Springer Berlin Heidelberg New York

Springer is a part of Springer Science+Business Media

springer.com

© Springer-Verlag Berlin Heidelberg 2006
Printed in Germany

Typesetting: Camera-ready by author, data conversion by Scientific Publishing Services, Chennai, India
Printed on acid-free paper   SPIN: 11744023   06/3142   5 4 3 2 1 0

Preface

These are the proceedings of the 9th European Conference on Computer Vision (ECCV 2006), the premium European conference on computer vision, held in Graz, Austria, in May 2006.

In response to our conference call, we received 811 papers, the largest number of submissions so far. Finally, 41 papers were selected for podium presentation and 151 for presentation in poster sessions (a 23.67% acceptance rate).

The double-blind reviewing process started by assigning each paper to one of the 22 area chairs, who then selected 3 reviewers for each paper. After the reviews were received, the authors were offered the possibility to provide feedback on the reviews. On the basis of the reviews and the rebuttal of the authors, the area chairs wrote the initial consolidation report for each paper. Finally, all the area chairs attended a two-day meeting in Graz, where all decisions on acceptance/rejection were made. At that meeting, the area chairs responsible for similar sub-fields thoroughly evaluated the assigned papers and discussed them in great depth. Again, all decisions were reached without the knowledge of the authors' identity. We are fully aware of the fact that reviewing is always also subjective, and that some good papers might have been overlooked; however, we tried our best to apply a fair selection process.

The conference preparation went smoothly thanks to several people. We first wish to thank the ECCV Steering Committee for entrusting us with the organization of the conference. We are grateful to the area chairs, who did a tremendous job in selecting the papers, and to more than 340 Program Committee members and 220 additional reviewers for all their professional efforts. To the organizers of the previous ECCV 2004 in Prague, Vaclav Hlaváč, Jiří Matas and Tomáš Pajdla for providing many insights, additional information, and the superb conference software. Finally, we would also like to thank the authors for contributing a large number of excellent papers to support the high standards of the ECCV conference.

Many people showed dedication and enthusiasm in the preparation of the conference. We would like to express our deepest gratitude to all the members of the involved institutes, that is, the Institute of Electrical Measurement and Measurement Signal Processing and the Institute for Computer Graphics and Vision, both at Graz University of Technology, and the Visual Cognitive Systems Laboratory at the University of Ljubljana. In particular, we would like to express our warmest thanks to Friedrich Fraundorfer for all his help (and patience) with the conference software and many other issues concerning the event, as well as Johanna Pfeifer for her great help with the organizational matters.

February 2006

Aleš Leonardis,
Horst Bischof,
Axel Pinz

Organization

Conference Chair

Axel Pinz   Graz University of Technology, Austria

Program Chairs

Horst Bischof   Graz University of Technology, Austria
Aleš Leonardis   University of Ljubljana, Slovenia

Organization Committee

Markus Brandner	Local Arrangements	Graz Univ. of Technology, Austria
Friedrich Fraundorfer	Local Arrangements	Graz Univ. of Technology, Austria
Matjaž Jogan	Tutorials Chair	Univ. of Ljubljana, Slovenia
Andreas Opelt	Local Arrangements	Graz Univ. of Technology, Austria
Johanna Pfeifer	Conference Secretariat	Graz Univ. of Technology, Austria
Matthias Rüther	Local Arrangements	Graz Univ. of Technology, Austria
Danijel Skočaj	Workshops Chair	Univ. of Ljubljana, Slovenia

Conference Board

Hans Burkhardt   University of Freiburg, Germany
Bernard Buxton   University College London, UK
Roberto Cipolla   University of Cambridge, UK
Jan-Olof Eklundh   Royal Institute of Technology, Sweden
Olivier Faugeras   INRIA, Sophia Antipolis, France
Anders Heyden   Lund University, Sweden
Bernd Neumann   University of Hamburg, Germany
Mads Nielsen   IT University of Copenhagen, Denmark
Tomáš Pajdla   CTU Prague, Czech Republic
Giulio Sandini   University of Genoa, Italy
David Vernon   Trinity College, Ireland

Area Chairs

Michael Black   Brown University, USA
Joachim M. Buhmann   ETH Zürich, Switzerland

Rachid Deriche — INRIA Sophia Antipolis, France
Pascal Fua — EPFL Lausanne, Switzerland
Luc Van Gool — KU Leuven, Belgium & ETH Zürich, Switzerland
Edwin Hancock — University of York, UK
Richard Hartley — Australian National University, Australia
Sing Bing Kang — Microsoft Research, USA
Stan Li — Chinese Academy of Sciences, Beijing, China
David Lowe — University of British Columbia, Canada
Jirí Matas — CTU Prague, Czech Republic
Nikos Paragios — Ecole Centrale de Paris, France
Marc Pollefeys — University of North Carolina at Chapel Hill, USA
Long Quan — HKUST, Hong Kong, China
Bernt Schiele — Darmstadt University of Technology, Germany
Amnon Shashua — Hebrew University of Jerusalem, Israel
Peter Sturm — INRIA Rhône-Alpes, France
Chris Taylor — University of Manchester, UK
Bill Triggs — INRIA Rhône-Alpes, France
Joachim Weickert — Saarland University, Germany
Daphna Weinshall — Hebrew University of Jerusalem, Israel
Andrew Zisserman — University of Oxford, UK

Program Committee

Motilal Agrawal	Stan Birchfield	Octavia Camps
Jörgen Ahlberg	Laure Blanc-Feraud	David Capel
Miguel Alemán-Flores	Nicolas P. de la Blanca	Barbara Caputo
Yiannis Aloimonos	Volker Blanz	Stefan Carlsson
Amir Amini	Rein van den Boomgaard	Vicent Caselles
Arnon Amir	Patrick Bouthemy	Tat-Jen Cham
Elli Angelopoulou	Richard Bowden	Mike Chantler
Adnan Ansar	Edmond Boyer	Francois Chaumette
Helder Araujo	Yuri Boykov	Rama Chellappa
Tal Arbel	Francois Bremond	Tsuhan Chen
Antonis Argyros	Thomas Breuel	Dmitry Chetverikov
Karl Astrom	Lisa Brown	Ondrej Chum
Shai Avidan	Michael Brown	James Clark
Vemuri Baba	Thomas Brox	Bob Collins
Subhashis Banerjee	Alfred Bruckstein	Dorin Comaniciu
Aharon Bar-Hillel	Andres Bruhn	Tim Cootes
Kobus Barnard	Roberto Brunelli	Joao Costeira
Joao Pedro Barreto	Antoni Buades	Daniel Cremers
Chiraz Ben Abdelkader	Michael Burl	Antonio Criminisi
Marie-Odile Berger	Brian Burns	James Crowley
Marcelo Bertalmio	Darius Burschka	Kristin Dana
Ross Beveridge	Aurelio Campilho	Kostas Daniilidis

Trevor Darrell
James W. Davis
Fernando DelaTorre
Herve Delingette
Frank Dellaert
Frederic Devernay
Michel Dhome
Sven Dickinson
Zachary Dodds
Ondrej Drbohlav
Mark S. Drew
Zoran Duric
Pinar Duygulu
Charles Dyer
Alexei Efros
Jan-Olof Eklundh
James Elder
Ahmed Elgammal
Mark Everingham
Aly Farag
Paolo Favaro
Ronald Fedkiw
Michael Felsberg
Rob Fergus
Cornelia Fermüller
Vittorio Ferrari
Frank P. Ferrie
James Ferryman
Mario Figueiredo
Graham Finlayson
Bob Fisher
Patrick Flynn
Wolfgang Förstner
Hassan Foroosh
David Forsyth
Friedrich Fraundorfer
Daniel Freedman
Andrea Fusiello
Xiang Gao
Nikolas Gebert
Yakup Genc
Guido Gerig
Jan-Mark Geusebroek
Christopher Geyer
Georgy Gimel'farb

Joshua Gluckman
Jacob Goldberger
Dmitry Goldgof
Venu Govindaraju
Etienne Grossmann
Frederic Guichard
Yanlin Guo
Allan Hanbury
Horst Haussecker
Eric Hayman
Tamir Hazan
Martial Hebert
Bernd Heisele
Anders Heyden
R. Andrew Hicks
Adrian Hilton
Jeffrey Ho
Tin Kam Ho
David Hogg
Ki-Sang Hong
Anthony Hoogs
Joachim Hornegger
Kun Huang
Slobodan Ilic
Atsushi Imiya
Sergey Ioffe
Michael Isard
Yuri Ivanov
Allan D. Jepson
Hailin Jin
Peter Johansen
Nebojsa Jojic
Mike Jones
Fredrik Kahl
J.K. Kamarainen
Chandra Kambhamettu
Yoshinari Kameda
Kenichi Kanatani
Qifa Ke
Daniel Keren
Renaud Keriven
Benjamin Kimia
Ron Kimmel
Nahum Kiryati
Josef Kittler

Georges Koepfler
Vladimir Kolmogorov
Pierre Kornprobst
Jana Kosecka
Danica Kragic
Kiriakos Kutulakos
InSo Kweon
Shang-Hong Lai
Ivan Laptev
Erik Learned-Miller
Sang Wook Lee
Bastian Leibe
Christophe Lenglet
Vincent Lepetit
Thomas Leung
Stephen Lin
Michael Lindenbaum
Jim Little
Yanxi Liu
Alex Loui
Brian Lovell
Claus Madsen
Marcus Magnor
Shyjan Mahamud
Atsuto Maki
Tom Malzbender
R. Manmatha
Petros Maragos
Sebastien Marcel
Eric Marchand
Jorge Marques
Jose Luis Marroquin
David Martin
Aleix M. Martinez
Bogdan Matei
Yasuyuki Matsushita
Iain Matthews
Stephen Maybank
Helmut Mayer
Leonard McMillan
Gerard Medioni
Etienne Memin
Rudolf Mester
Dimitris Metaxas
Krystian Mikolajczyk

Majid Mirmehdi
Anurag Mittal
J.M.M. Montiel
Theo Moons
Philippos Mordohai
Greg Mori
Pavel Mrázek
Jane Mulligan
Joe Mundy
Vittorio Murino
Hans-Hellmut Nagel
Vic Nalwa
Srinivasa Narasimhan
P.J. Narayanan
Oscar Nestares
Heiko Neumann
Jan Neumann
Ram Nevatia
Ko Nishino
David Nister
Thomas O'Donnell
Masatoshi Okutomi
Ole Fogh Olsen
Tomáš Pajdla
Chris Pal
Theodore Papadopoulo
Nikos Paragios
Ioannis Pavlidis
Vladimir Pavlovic
Shmuel Peleg
Marcello Pelillo
Francisco Perales
Sylvain Petitjean
Matti Pietikainen
Filiberto Pla
Robert Pless
Jean Ponce
Rich Radke
Ravi Ramamoorthi
Deva Ramanan
Visvanathan Ramesh
Ramesh Raskar
Christopher Rasmussen
Carlo Regazzoni
James Rehg

Paolo Remagnino
Xiaofeng Ren
Tammy Riklin-Raviv
Ehud Rivlin
Antonio Robles-Kelly
Karl Rohr
Sami Romdhani
Bodo Rosenhahn
Arun Ross
Carsten Rother
Nicolas Rougon
Mikael Rousson
Sebastien Roy
Javier Sanchez
Jose Santos-Victor
Guillermo Sapiro
Radim Sara
Jun Sato
Yoichi Sato
Eric Saund
Hanno Scharr
Daniel Scharstein
Yoav Y. Schechner
Otmar Scherzer
Christoph Schnörr
Stan Sclaroff
Yongduek Seo
Mubarak Shah
Gregory Shakhnarovich
Ying Shan
Eitan Sharon
Jianbo Shi
Ilan Shimshoni
Ali Shokoufandeh
Kaleem Siddiqi
Greg Slabaugh
Cristian Sminchisescu
Stefano Soatto
Nir Sochen
Jon Sporring
Anuj Srivastava
Chris Stauffer
Drew Steedly
Charles Stewart
Tomáš Suk

Rahul Sukthankar
Josephine Sullivan
Changming Sun
David Suter
Tomáš Svoboda
Richard Szeliski
Tamas Sziranyi
Hugues Talbot
Tieniu Tan
Chi-keung Tang
Xiaoou Tang
Hai Tao
Sibel Tari
Gabriel Taubin
Camillo Jose Taylor
Demetri Terzopoulos
Ying-li Tian
Carlo Tomasi
Antonio Torralba
Andrea Torsello
Panos Trahanias
Mohan Trivedi
Emanuele Trucco
David Tschumperle
Yanghai Tsin
Matthew Turk
Tinne Tuytelaars
Nuno Vasconcelos
Olga Veksler
Svetha Venkatesh
David Vernon
Alessandro Verri
Luminita Aura Vese
Rene Vidal
Markus Vincze
Jordi Vitria
Julia Vogel
Toshikazu Wada
Tomáš Werner
Carl-Fredrik Westin
Yonatan Wexler
Ross Whitaker
Richard Wildes
Chris Williams
James Williams

Lance Williams
Richard Wilson
Lior Wolf
Kwan-Yee K. Wong
Ming Xie
Yasushi Yagi
Hulya Yalcin

Jie Yang
Ming-Hsuan Yang
Ruigang Yang
Jingyi Yu
Ramin Zabih
Changshui Zhang
Zhengyou Zhang

Cha Zhang
Song-Chun Zhu
Todd Zickler
Michael Zillich
Larry Zitnick
Lilla Zöllei
Steven Zucker

Additional Reviewers

Vitaly Ablavsky
Jeff Abrahamson
Daniel Abretske
Amit Adam
Gaurav Aggarwal
Amit Agrawal
Timo Ahonen
Amir Akbarzadeh
H. Can Aras
Tamar Avraham
Harlyn Baker
Patrick Baker
Hynek Bakstein
Olof Barr
Adrien Bartoli
Paul Beardsley
Isabelle Bégin
Ohad Ben-Shahar
Møarten Björkman
Mark Borg
Jake Bouvrie
Bernhard Burgeth
Frédéric Cao
Gustavo Carneiro
Nicholas Carter
Umberto Castellani
Bruno Cernuschi-Frias
Ming-Ching Chang
Roland Chapuis
Thierry Chateau
Hong Chen
Xilin Chen
Sen-ching Cheung
Tat-Jun Chin
Mario Christhoudias

Chi-Wei Chu
Andrea Colombari
Jason Corso
Bruce Culbertson
Goksel Dedeoglu
David Demirdjian
Konstantinos Derpanis
Zvi Devir
Stephan Didas
Miodrag Dimitrijevic
Ryan Eckbo
Christopher Engels
Aykut Erdem
Erkut Erdem
Anders Ericsson
Kenny Erleben
Steven Eschrich
Francisco Estrada
Ricardo Fabbri
Xiaodong Fan
Craig Fancourt
Michela Farenzena
Han Feng
Doug Fidaleo
Robert Fischer
Andrew Fitzhugh
Francois Fleuret
Per-Erik Forssén
Ben Fransen
Clement Fredembach
Mario Fritz
Gareth Funka-Lea
Darren Gawely
Atiyeh Ghoreyshi
Alvina Goh

Leo Grady
Kristen Grauman
Ralph Gross
Nicolas Guilbert
Abdenour Hadid
Onur Hamsici
Scott Helmer
Yacov Hel-Or
Derek Hoiem
Byung-Woo Hong
Steve Hordley
Changbo Hu
Rui Huang
Xinyu Huang
Camille Izard
Vidit Jain
Vishal Jain
Christopher Jaynes
Kideog Jeong
Björn Johansson
Marie-Pierre Jolly
Erik Jonsson
Klas Josephson
Michael Kaess
Rahul Khare
Dae-Woong Kim
Jong-Sung Kim
Kristian Kirk
Dan Kushnir
Ville Kyrki
Pascal Lagger
Prasun Lala
Michael Langer
Catherine Laporte
Jean-Marc Lavest

Albert Law
Jean-Pierre Lecadre
Maxime Lhuillier
Gang Li
Qi Li
Zhiguo Li
Hwasup Lim
Sernam Lim
Zicheng Liu
Wei-Lwun Lu
Roberto Lublinerman
Simon Lucey
Gian Luca Mariottini
Scott McCloskey
Changki Min
Thomas Moeslund
Kooksang Moon
Louis Morency
Davide Moschini
Matthias Mühlich
Artiom Myaskouvskey
Kai Ni
Michael Nielsen
Carol Novak
Fredrik Nyberg
Sang-Min Oh
Takahiro Okabe
Kenki Okuma
Carl Olsson
Margarita Osadchy
Magnus Oskarsson
Niels Overgaard
Ozge Ozcanli
Mustafa Ozuysal
Vasu Parameswaran
Prakash Patel
Massimiliano Pavan
Patrick Perez
Michael Phelps

Julien Pilet
David Pisinger
Jean-Philippe Pons
Yuan Quan
Ariadna Quattoni
Kevin Quennesson
Ali Rahimi
Ashish Raj
Ananath Ranganathan
Avinash Ravichandran
Randall Rojas
Mikael Rousson
Adit Sahasrabudhe
Roman Sandler
Imari Sato
Peter Savadjiev
Grant Schindler
Konrad Schindler
Robert Schwanke
Edgar Seemann
Husrev Taha Sencar
Ali Shahrokni
Hong Shen
Fan Shufei
Johan Skoglund
Natalia Slesareva
Jan Sochman
Jan Erik Solem
Jonathan Starck
Jesse Stewart
Henrik Stewenius
Moritz Stoerring
Svetlana Stolpner
Mingxuan Sun
Ying Sun
Amir Tamrakar
Robby Tan
Tele Tan
Donald Tanguay

Leonid Taycher
Ashwin Thangali
David Thirde
Mani Thomas
Tai-Peng Tian
David Tolliver
Nhon Trinh
Ambrish Tyagi
Raquel Urtasun
Joost Van-de-Weijer
Andrea Vedaldi
Dejun Wang
Hanzi Wang
Jingbin Wang
Liang Wang
Martin Welk
Adam Williams
Bob Woodham
Stefan Wörz
Christopher Wren
Junwen Wu
Wen Wu
Rong Yan
Changjiang Yang
Qing-Xiong Yang
Alper Yilmaz
Jerry Yokono
David Young
Quan Yuan
Alan Yuille
Micheal Yurick
Dimitrios Zarpalas
Guoying Zhao
Tao Zhao
Song-Feng Zheng
Jie Zhu
Loe Zhu
Manli Zhu

Sponsoring Institutions

Advanced Computer Vision, Austria
Graz University of Technology, Austria
University of Ljubljana, Slovenia

Table of Contents – Part I

Tracking and Motion

Multiview Geometry and 3D Reconstruction

Statistical Models and Visual Learning

Low-Level Vision, Image Features

3D Reconstruction and Multi-view Geometry

Table of Contents – Part II

Energy Minimization

Tracking and Motion

Poster Session II

Tracking and Motion

Multiview Geometry and 3D Reconstruction

Statistical Models and Visual Learning

Low-Level Vision, Image Features

Face/Gesture/Action Detection and Recognition

Segmentation and Grouping

Object Recognition, Retrieval and Indexing

Segmentation

Table of Contents – Part III

Face/Gesture/Action Detection and Recognition

Segmentation and Grouping

Visual Tracking

Table of Contents – Part IV

Face Detection and Recognition

Illumination and Reflectance Modelling

Poster Session IV

Tracking and Motion

Face/Gesture/Action Detection and Recognition

Segmentation and Grouping

Low-Level Vision, Segmentation and Grouping

TextonBoost: Joint Appearance, Shape and Context Modeling for Multi-class Object Recognition and Segmentation

Jamie Shotton[2], John Winn[1], Carsten Rother[1], and Antonio Criminisi[1]

[1] Microsoft Research Ltd., Cambridge, UK
{jwinn, carrot, antcrim}@microsoft.com
[2] Department of Engineering,
University of Cambridge
jdjs2@cam.ac.uk

Abstract. This paper proposes a new approach to learning a discriminative model of object classes, incorporating appearance, shape and context information efficiently. The learned model is used for automatic visual recognition and semantic segmentation of photographs. Our discriminative model exploits novel features, based on textons, which jointly model shape and texture. Unary classification and feature selection is achieved using shared boosting to give an efficient classifier which can be applied to a large number of classes. Accurate image segmentation is achieved by incorporating these classifiers in a conditional random field. Efficient training of the model on very large datasets is achieved by exploiting both random feature selection and piecewise training methods.

High classification and segmentation accuracy are demonstrated on three different databases: i) our own 21-object class database of photographs of real objects viewed under general lighting conditions, poses and viewpoints, ii) the 7-class Corel subset and iii) the 7-class Sowerby database used in [1]. The proposed algorithm gives competitive results both for highly textured (e.g. grass, trees), highly structured (e.g. cars, faces, bikes, aeroplanes) and articulated objects (e.g. body, cow).

1 Introduction

This paper investigates the problem of achieving automatic detection, recognition and segmentation of object classes in photographs. Precisely, given an image, the system should automatically partition it into semantically meaningful areas each labeled with a specific object class. The challenge is to handle a large number of both structured and unstructured object classes, while modeling their variabilities. Our focus is not only the accuracy of segmentation and recognition, but also the efficiency of the algorithm, which becomes particularly important when dealing with large image collections.

At a local level, the *appearance* of an image patch leads to ambiguities in its class label. For example, a window can be part of a car, a building or an aeroplane. To overcome these ambiguities, it is necessary to incorporate longer

A. Leonardis, H. Bischof, and A. Pinz (Eds.): ECCV 2006, Part I, LNCS 3951, pp. 1–15, 2006.

range information such as the spatial configuration of the patches on an object (the object *shape*) and also *contextual* information from the surrounding image. To achieve this we construct a discriminative model for labeling images which exploits all three types of information: appearance, shape and context.

Related work. Whilst the fields of object recognition and segmentation have been extremely active in recent years, many authors have considered these two tasks separately. For example, recognition of particular object classes has been achieved using the constellation models of Fergus et al. [2], the deformable shape models of Berg et al. [3] and the texture models of Winn et al. [4]. None of these methods leads to a pixel-wise segmentation of the image. Conversely, other authors have considered only the segmentation task, e.g. [5, 6].

Joint detection and segmentation of a *single* object class has been achieved by several authors [7, 8, 9]. Typically, these approaches exploit a global shape model and are therefore unable to cope with arbitrary viewpoints or severe occlusion. Additionally, only highly structured object classes are addressed.

A similar task as addressed in this paper was considered in [10] where a classifier was used to label regions found by automatic segmentation. However such segmentations often do not correlate with semantic objects. Our solution to this problem is to perform segmentation and recognition in the same unified framework rather than in two separate steps. Such a unified approach has been presented in [11] where only text and faces are recognized and at a high computational cost. Konishi and Yuille [12] label images using a unary classifier and hence do not achieve spatially coherent segmentations.

The most similar work to ours is that of He et al. [1] which incorporate region and global label features to model shape and context in a Conditional Random Field. Their work uses Gibbs sampling for both the parameter learning and label inference and is therefore limited in the size of dataset and number of classes which can be handled efficiently. Our focus on the speed of training and inference allows us to use larger datasets with many more object classes. We currently handle 21 classes (compared to the seven classes of [1]) and it would be tractable to train our model on even larger datasets than presented here.

Our contributions in this paper are threefold. First, we present a discriminative model which is capable of fusing shape, appearance and context information to recognize efficiently the object classes present in an image, whilst exploiting edge information to provide an accurate segmentation. Second, we propose features, based on textons, which are capable of modeling object shape, appearance and context. Finally, we demonstrate how to train the model efficiently on a very large dataset by exploiting both boosting and piecewise training methods.

The paper is structured as follows. In the next section we describe the image database used in our experiments. Section 3 introduces the high-level model, a Conditional Random Field, while section 4 presents our novel low-level image features and their use in constructing a boosted classifier. Experiments, performance evaluation and conclusions are given in the final two sections.

2   Image Databases

Our object class models are learned from a set of labeled training images. In this paper we consider three different labeled image databases. Our own database[1] is composed of 591 photographs of the following 21 object classes: building, grass, tree, cow, sheep, sky, aeroplane, water, face, car, bike, flower, sign, bird, book, chair, road, cat, dog, body, boat (fig. 1). The training images were hand-labeled with

Fig. 1. The labeled image database. A selection of images in our 21-class database and their corresponding ground-truth annotations. Colors map uniquely to object class labels. All images are approximately 320×240 pixels.

the assigned colors acting as indices into the list of object classes. Note that we consider completely general lighting conditions, camera viewpoint, scene geometry, object pose and articulation. Our database is split randomly into roughly 45% training, 10% validation and 45% test sets, while ensuring approximately proportional contributions from each class.

Note that the ground-truth labeling of the 21-class database contains pixels labeled as 'void'. These were included both to cope with pixels that do not belong to a database class, and to allow for a rough and quick hand-segmentation which does not align exactly with the object boundaries. Void pixels are ignored for both training and testing.

For comparison with previous work we have also used the 7-class Corel database subset (where images are 180×120 pixels) and the 7-class Sowerby database (96×64 pixels) used in [1]. For those two databases the numbers of images in the training and test sets are exactly as for [1].

3   A Conditional Random Field Model of Object Classes

We use a Conditional Random Field (CRF) model [13] to learn the conditional distribution over the class labeling given an image. The use of a Conditional Random Field allows us to incorporate shape, texture, color, location and edge cues in a single unified model. We define the conditional probability of the class labels $\mathbf{c}$ given an image $\mathbf{x}$ as

$$\log P(\mathbf{c}|\mathbf{x}, \boldsymbol{\theta}) = \sum_i \overbrace{\psi_i(c_i, \mathbf{x}; \boldsymbol{\theta}_\psi)}^{\text{shape−texture}} + \overbrace{\pi(c_i, \mathbf{x}_i; \boldsymbol{\theta}_\pi)}^{\text{color}} + \overbrace{\lambda(c_i, i; \boldsymbol{\theta}_\lambda)}^{\text{location}}$$

$$+ \sum_{(i,j)\in\mathcal{E}} \overbrace{\phi(c_i, c_j, \mathbf{g}_{ij}(\mathbf{x}); \boldsymbol{\theta}_\phi)}^{\text{edge}} - \log Z(\boldsymbol{\theta}, \mathbf{x}) \qquad (1)$$

---

[1] Publicly available at http://research.microsoft.com/vision/cambridge/recognition/

where $\mathcal{E}$ is the set of edges in the 4-connected grid, $Z(\boldsymbol{\theta}, \mathbf{x})$ is the partition function, $\boldsymbol{\theta} = \{\boldsymbol{\theta}_\psi, \boldsymbol{\theta}_\pi, \boldsymbol{\theta}_\lambda, \boldsymbol{\theta}_\phi\}$ are the model parameters, and i and j index nodes in the grid (corresponding to positions in the image).

Shape-texture potentials. The shape-texture potentials ψ use features selected by boosting to represent the shape, texture and appearance context of the object classes. These features and the boosting procedure used to perform feature selection while training a multi-class logistic classifier are described in section 4. We use this classifier directly as a potential in the CRF, so that

$$\psi_i(c_i, \mathbf{x}; \boldsymbol{\theta}_\psi) = \log \widetilde{P}_i(c_i | \mathbf{x}) \qquad (2)$$

where $\widetilde{P}_i(c_i | \mathbf{x})$ is the normalized distribution given by the classifier using learned parameters $\boldsymbol{\theta}_\psi$.

Edge potentials. The pairwise edge potentials ϕ have the form of a contrast sensitive Potts model [14],

$$\phi(c_i, c_j, \mathbf{g}_{ij}(\mathbf{x}); \boldsymbol{\theta}_\phi) = -\boldsymbol{\theta}_\phi^T \mathbf{g}_{ij}(\mathbf{x}) \delta(c_i \neq c_j). \qquad (3)$$

In this work, we set the edge feature $\mathbf{g}_{ij}$ to measure the difference in color between the neighboring pixels, as suggested by [15], $\mathbf{g}_{ij} = [\exp(-\beta \|x_i - x_j\|^2), 1]^T$ where x_i and x_j are three-dimensional vectors representing the color of the ith and jth pixels. Including the unit element allows a bias to be learned, to remove small, isolated regions. The quantity β is set (separately for each image) to $(2\langle \|x_i - x_j\|^2 \rangle)^{-1}$, where $\langle \cdot \rangle$ averages over the image.

Color potentials. Capture the color distribution of the instances of a class in a *particular image*. This choice is motivated by the fact that, whilst the distribution of color across an entire class of objects is broad, the color distribution across one or a few instances of the class is typically compact. Hence the parameters $\boldsymbol{\theta}_\pi$ are learned separately for each image (and so this learning step needs to be carried out at test time). This aspect of the model captures the more precise image-specific appearance that a solely class-specific recognition system cannot.

Color models are represented as mixtures of Gaussians (GMM) in color space where the mixture coefficients depend on the class label. The conditional probability of the color of a pixel x is given by

$$P(x|c) = \sum_k P(k|c) \mathcal{N}(x \mid \bar{x}_k, \Sigma_k) \qquad (4)$$

where k is a random variable representing the component the pixel is assigned to, and $\bar{x}_k$ and Σ_k are the mixture mean and variance respectively. Notice that the mixture components are shared between different classes and only the coefficients depend on the class label, making the model much more efficient to learn than a separate GMM for each class. For a particular pixel x_i we compute a fixed soft assignment to the mixture components $P(k|x_i)$.[2] Given this assignment, we choose our color potential to have the form

$$\pi(c_i, x_i; \boldsymbol{\theta}_\pi) = \log \sum_k \boldsymbol{\theta}_\pi(c_i, k) P(k|x_i) \tag{5}$$

where parameters $\boldsymbol{\theta}_\pi$ act as a probability lookup-table; see (8).

Location potentials. capture the weak dependence of the class label on the absolute location of the pixel in the image. The potential takes the form of a look-up table with an entry for each class and pixel location,

$$\lambda_i(c_i, i; \boldsymbol{\theta}_\lambda) = \log \boldsymbol{\theta}_\lambda(c_i, \hat{i}). \tag{6}$$

The index $\hat{i}$ is the normalized version of the pixel index i, where the normalization allows for images of different sizes; e.g. if the image is mapped onto a canonical square then $\hat{i}$ indicates the pixel position within this canonical square.

3.1 Learning the CRF Parameters

Ideally, we would learn the model parameters by maximizing the conditional likelihood of the true class labels given the training data. This can be achieved using gradient ascent, and computing the gradient of the likelihood with respect to each parameter, requiring the evaluation of marginals over the class labels for each training image. Exact computation of these marginals is intractable due to the complexity of the partition function $Z(\mathbf{x}, \boldsymbol{\theta})$ in (1). Instead, we approximated the label marginals by the mode, i.e. the most probable labeling, computed as discussed later in this section. This choice of approximation was made because the size of our datasets limited the time available to estimate marginals. Using this approximation, conjugate gradient ascent did converge but unfortunately the learned parameters gave poor results (almost no improvement on unary classification alone).

Given these problems with directly maximizing the conditional likelihood, we decided to use a method based on *piecewise training* [16] instead. Piecewise training involves dividing the CRF model into pieces, each of which is trained independently. As discussed in [16], this training method minimizes an upper bound on the log partition function. However, this bound is generally an extremely loose one and performing parameter training in this way leads to problems with overcounting during inference in the combined model. Modifying piecewise training to incorporate fixed powers can compensate for overcounting. It can be shown that this leads to an approximate partition function of similar form of that used in [16], except that it is no longer an upper bound on the true partition function. Optimal selection of those powers is an area of active research. In this work, we added power parameters for the location and color potentials and optimized them discriminatively.

---

[2] A soft assignment was seen to give a marginal improvement over a hard assignment, at negligible extra cost.

Each of the potential types is therefore trained separately to produce a normalized model. For the shape-texture potentials, we simply use the parameters learned during boosting. For the location potentials, we train the parameters by maximizing the likelihood of the normalized model containing just that potential and raising the result to a fixed power w_λ (specified in section 5) to compensate for overcounting. Hence, the location parameters are learned using

$$\boldsymbol{\theta}_\lambda(c_i, \hat{i}) = \left(\frac{N_{c,\hat{i}} + \alpha_\lambda}{N_{\hat{i}} + \alpha_\lambda} \right)^{w_\lambda} \tag{7}$$

where $N_{c,\hat{i}}$ is the number of pixels of class c at normalized location $\hat{i}$ in the training set, $N_{\hat{i}}$ is the total number of pixels at location $\hat{i}$ and α_λ is a small integer (we use $\alpha_\lambda = 1$) corresponding to a weak Dirichlet prior on $\boldsymbol{\theta}_\lambda$.

At test time the color parameters are learned for each image in a piecewise fashion using Iterative Conditional Modes, similar to [15]. First a class labeling $\mathbf{c}^\star$ is inferred and then the color parameters are updated using

$$\boldsymbol{\theta}_\pi(c_i, k) = \left(\frac{\sum_i \delta(c_i = c_i^\star) P(k|x_i) + \alpha_\pi}{\sum_i P(k|x_i) + \alpha_\pi} \right)^{w_\pi}. \tag{8}$$

Given this new parameter setting, a new class labeling is inferred and this procedure is iterated [15]. The Dirichlet prior parameter α_π was set to 0.1, and the power parameter is w_π. In practice, $w_\pi = 3$, fifteen color components and two iterations of this procedure gave good results. Because we are training in pieces, the color parameters do not need to be learned for the training set.

Learning the edge potential parameters $\boldsymbol{\theta}_\phi$ by maximum likelihood was also attempted. Unfortunately, the lack of alignment between object edges and label boundaries in the roughly labeled training set forced the learned parameters to tend towards zero. Instead, the values of the only two contrast-related parameters were manually selected to minimize the error on the validation set.

3.2   Inference in the CRF Model

Given a set of parameters learned for the CRF model, we wish to find the most probable labeling $\mathbf{c}^\star$; i.e. the labeling that maximizes the conditional probability (1). The optimal labeling is found by applying the alpha-expansion graph-cut algorithm of [14] (note that our energy is *regular*). In our case the initial configuration is given by the mode of the unary potentials, though the MAP solution was not in practice sensitive to this initialization.

4   Boosted Learning of Shape, Texture and Context

The most important part of the CRF energy is the unary potential, which is based on a novel set of features which we call *shape filters*. These features are capable of capturing shape, texture and appearance context jointly. We describe shape filters next, together with the process for automatic feature selection.

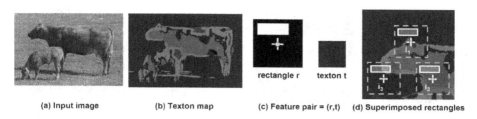

| (a) Input image | (b) Texton map | (c) Feature pair = (r,t) | (d) Superimposed rectangles |

Fig. 2. Shape filter responses and appearance context. (**a, b**) An image and its corresponding texton map (colors map uniquely to texton indices). (**c**) A rectangle mask r (white) is offset from the center (yellow cross), and paired with a texton index t which here maps to the blue color. (**d**) As an example, the feature response $v(i, r, t)$ is calculated at three positions in the texton map (zoomed). If A is the area of r, then in this example $v(i_1, r, t) \approx A$, $v(i_2, r, t) \approx 0$, and $v(i_3, r, t) \approx A/2$. For this feature where t is a 'grass' texton, our algorithm learns that points i (such as i_1) belonging to 'cow' regions tend to produce large counts $v(i, r, t)$, and hence exploits the contextual information that 'cow' pixels tend to be surrounded by 'grass' pixels.

Textons. Efficiency demands compact representations for the range of different appearances of an object. For this we utilize *textons* [17] which have been proven effective in categorizing materials [18] as well as generic object classes [4]. A dictionary of textons is learned by convolving a 17-dimensional filter bank[3] with all the training images and running K-means clustering (using Mahalanobis distance) on the filter responses. Finally, each pixel in each image is assigned to the nearest cluster center, thus providing the *texton map* (see fig. 2(a,b)).

Shape filters. Consist of a set of N_R rectangular regions whose four corners are chosen at random within a fixed bounding box covering about half the image area. For a particular texton t, the feature response at location i is the count of instances of that texton under the offset rectangle mask (see fig. 2(c,d)). These filter responses can be efficiently computed over a whole image with integral images [19] (K for each image, where K is the number of textons).

Shape filters with their pairing of rectangular masks and textons can be seen as an extension of the features used in [19]. Our features are sufficiently general to allow us to *learn* automatically shape and context information, in contrast to techniques such as Shape Context [20] which utilize a hand-picked shape descriptor. Figure 2 illustrates how shape filters are able to model appearance-based context. Modeling shape is demonstrated for a toy example in fig. 3.

Joint Boosting for unary classification. A multi-class classifier is learned using an adapted version of the Joint Boosting algorithm of [21]. The algorithm iteratively builds a strong classifier as a sum of 'weak classifiers', simultaneously

---

[3] The filter bank used here is identical to that in [4], consisting of scaled Gaussians, x and y derivatives of Gaussians, and Laplacians of Gaussians. The Gaussians are applied to all three color channels, while the remaining filters only to the luminance. The perceptually uniform CIELab color space is used.

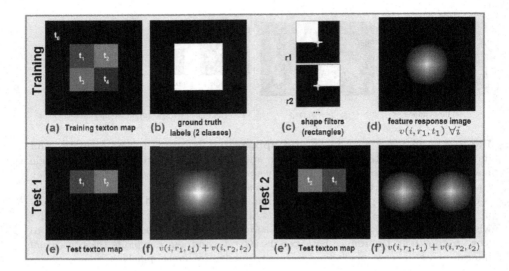

Fig. 3. Capturing local shape information. This toy example illustrates how our *shape filters* capture relative positions of textons. (**a**) Input texton map. (**b**) Input binary ground-truth label map (e.g. foreground=white, background=black). (**c**) Example rectangle masks (r_1 and r_2). (**d**) The feature response image $v(i, r_1, t_1)$ shows a positive response within the foreground region and zero in the background. An identical response image is computed for feature (r_2, t_2). Boosting would pick both these features as discriminative. (**e**) A test input with textons t_1 and t_2 in the *same* relative position as that of training. (**f**) Illustration that the two feature responses *reinforce* each other. (**e'**) A second test with t_1 and t_2 swapped. (**f'**) The summed feature responses do not reinforce, giving a weaker signal for classification. Note (**f**) and (**f'**) are illustrative only since boosting actually combines thresholded feature responses.

selecting discriminative features. Each weak classifier is a decision stump based on a thresholded feature response, and is *shared* between a set of classes, allowing a single feature to help classify several classes at once. The sharing of features between classes allows for classification with cost sub-linear in the number of classes, and also leads to improved generalization.

The learned 'strong' classifier is an additive model of the form $H(c_i) = \sum_{m=1}^{M} h_m(c_i)$, summing the classification confidence of M weak classifiers. This confidence value can be reinterpreted as a probability distribution over c_i using the softmax transformation $\widetilde{P}_i(c_i|\mathbf{x}) = \frac{\exp(H(c_i))}{\sum_{c_i'} \exp(H(c_i'))}$ [22].

Each weak-learner is a decision stump of the form

$$h(c_i) = \begin{cases} a\delta(v(i, r, t) > \theta) + b & \text{if } c_i \in N \\ k_{c_i} & \text{otherwise} \end{cases} \quad (9)$$

with parameters $(a, b, \{k_c\}_{c \notin N}, \theta, N, r, t)$ and where $\delta(\cdot)$ is a 0-1 indicator function. The r and t indices together specify the shape filter feature (rectangle mask and texton respectively), with $v(i, r, t)$ representing the corresponding feature response at position i. For those classes that share this feature ($c_i \in N$), the weak learner gives $h(c_i) \in \{a + b, b\}$ depending on the comparison of $v(i, r, t)$ to a threshold θ. For each class not sharing the feature ($c_i \notin N$) there is a constant k_{c_i} that ensures asymmetrical sets of positive and negative training examples do not adversely affect the learning procedure.

The boosting algorithm iteratively minimizes an error function which unfortunately requires an expensive brute-force search over the sharing set N, the features (r and t), and the thresholds θ. Given these parameters, a closed form solution exists for a, b and $\{k_c\}_{c \notin N}$. The set of all possible sharing sets is exponentially large, and so we employ the quadratic-cost greedy approximation of [21]. To speed up the minimization over features we employ the random feature selection procedure described below. Optimization over $\theta \in \Theta$ for a discrete set Θ can be made efficient by careful use of histograms of feature responses.

Sub-sampling and random feature selection for training efficiency. The considerable memory and processing requirements make training on a per-pixel basis impractical. Computational expense is reduced by calculating filter responses on a $\Delta \times \Delta$ grid (either 3×3 for the smaller databases or 5×5 for the largest database). The shape filter responses themselves are still calculated at full resolution to enable per-pixel accurate classification at test time.

One consequence of this sub-sampling is that a small degree of shift-invariance is learned. On its own, this would lead to inaccurate segmentation at object boundaries. However, when applied in the context of the CRF, the edge and color potentials come into effect to locate the object boundary accurately.

Even with sub-sampling, exhaustive searching over all features (pairs of rectangle and texton) at each round of boosting is prohibitive. However, our algorithm examines only a fraction $\tau \ll 1$ of features, randomly chosen at each round

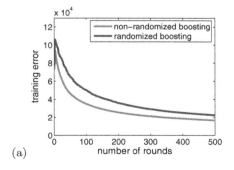
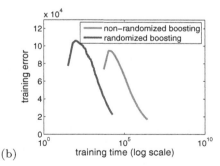

(a)　　　　　　　　　　　　　　　(b)

Fig. 4. Effect of random feature selection on a toy example. (a) Training error as a function of the number of rounds (axis scales are unimportant). (b) Training error as function of time. Randomization makes learning two orders of magnitude faster here, with very little increase in training error for the same number of rounds. The peak in error in the first few rounds is due to an artefact of the learning algorithm.

(see [23]). All our results use $\tau = 0.003$ so that, over several thousand rounds, there is high probability of testing all features at least once.

To analyze the effect of random feature selection, we compared the results of boosting on a toy data set of ten images with ten rectangle masks, 400 textons, and $\tau = 0.003$. The results in fig. 4 show that using random feature selection improves the training time by several orders of magnitude whilst having only a small impact on the training error.

5   Results and Comparisons

Boosting accuracy. Fig. 5(a) illustrates the effect of training the boosted classifier in isolation, i.e. separately from the CRF. As expected, the error decreases (non-linearly) as the number of weak classifiers increases. Furthermore, fig. 5(b) shows the accuracy of classification with respect to the validation set, which after about 5000 rounds flattens out to a value of approximately 73%.

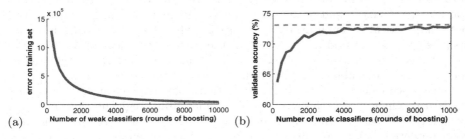

Fig. 5. Error plots. Training error **(a)** and accuracy on the validation set **(b)** as function of the number of weak classifiers. While the training error decreases almost to zero, the validation set accuracy rises to a maximum of about 73%.

The boosting procedure takes 42 hours for 5000 rounds on the 21-class training set of 276 images on a 2.1 Ghz machine with 2GB memory. Without random feature selection, the training time would be around 14000 hours. Note that due to memory constraints, the training integral images had to be computed on-the-fly which slowed the learning down by at least a factor two.

Object class recognition and segmentation. This section presents results for the full CRF model on our 21-class database. Our unoptimized implementation takes approximately three minutes to segment each test image. The majority of this time is spent evaluating all the $\widetilde{P}_i(c_i|\mathbf{x})$ involving a few thousand weak-classifier evaluations. Evaluating those potentials on a $\Delta \times \Delta$ grid (with $\Delta = 5$) produces almost as good results in about twenty-five seconds per test image.

Example results of simultaneous recognition and segmentation are shown in fig. 6. The figure shows both the original photographs and the color-coded output labeling. Note for instance that despite large occlusions, bicycles are recognized and segmented correctly, and large variations in the appearance of grass and road

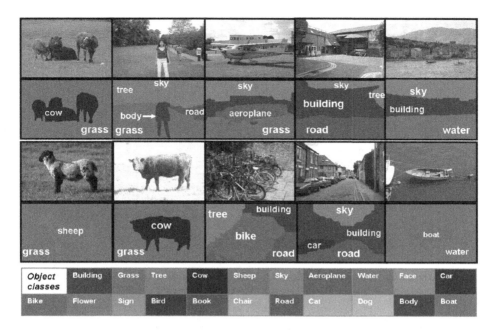

Fig. 6. Some example results. Above, original images with corresponding color-coded output object-class maps. Below, color-coding legend for the 21 object classes. For clarity, textual labels have also been superimposed on the result object maps.

Fig. 7. Some examples where recognition works less well. Input test images with corresponding color-coded output object-class maps. Note that even when recognition fails segmentation may still be quite accurate.

are correctly modeled. In order to better understand the behavior of our algorithm we also present some examples which work less well, in fig. 7. In fig. 7(a,d) despite the recognition of the central figure being incorrect, the segmentation is still accurate. For cases like these, the algorithm of [24] could be used to refine the class labeling. In fig. 7(e) the entire image is incorrectly recognized due to lack of similar examples of water in the training data, a typical drawback of discriminative learning.

True class \ Inferred class	building	grass	tree	cow	sheep	sky	aeroplane	water	face	car	bike	flower	sign	bird	book	chair	road	cat	dog	body	boat
building	**61.6**	4.7	9.7	0.3		2.5	0.6	1.3	2.0	2.6	2.1		0.6	0.2	4.8		6.3	0.4		0.5	
grass	0.3	**97.6**	0.5								0.1									1.3	
tree	1.2	4.4	**86.3**	0.5		2.9	1.4	1.9	0.8	0.1							0.1		0.2	0.1	
cow		30.9	0.7	**58.3**					0.9	0.4				0.4	4.2					4.1	
sheep	16.5	25.5	4.8	1.9	**50.4**										0.6		0.2				
sky	3.4	0.2	1.1			**82.6**		7.5									5.2				
aeroplane	21.5	7.2				3.0	**59.6**	8.5													
water	8.7	7.5	1.5	0.2		4.5		**52.9**		0.7	4.9			0.2	4.2		14.1	0.4			
face	4.1		1.1						**73.5**	7.1							8.4		0.4	0.2	5.2
car	10.1		1.7							**62.5**	3.8			5.9	0.2		15.7				
bike	9.3		1.3							1.0	**74.5**			2.5		3.9	5.9		1.6		
flower		6.6	19.3	3.0								**62.8**			7.3		1.0				
sign	31.5	0.2	11.5	2.1		0.5		6.0		1.5		2.5	**35.1**		3.6	2.7	0.8	0.3		1.8	
bird	16.9	18.4	9.8	6.3	8.9	1.8		9.4						**19.4**			4.6	4.5			
book	2.6		0.6						0.4				2.0		**91.9**					2.4	
chair	20.6	24.8	9.6	18.2	0.2					3.7					1.9	**15.4**	4.5		1.1		
road	5.0	1.1	0.7					3.4	0.3	0.7	0.6		0.1	0.1	1.1		**86.0**			0.7	
cat	5.0		1.1	8.9					0.2	2.0					0.6		28.4	**53.6**	0.2		
dog	29.0	2.2	12.9	7.1				9.7							8.1		11.7		**19.2**		
body	4.6	2.8	2.0	2.1	1.3	0.2			6.0	1.1					9.9		1.7	4.0	2.1	**62.1**	
boat	25.1		11.5			3.8		30.6		2.0	8.6		6.4	5.1			0.3				**6.6**

Fig. 8. Accuracy of segmentation for the 21-class database. Confusion matrix with percentages row-normalized. Overall pixel-wise accuracy 72.2%.

Quantitative evaluation. Figure 8 shows the confusion matrix obtained by applying our algorithm to the test image set. Accuracy values in the table are computed as percentage of image pixels assigned to the correct class label, ignoring pixels labeled as void in the ground-truth. The overall classification accuracy is 72.2%; random chance would give $1/21 = 4.76\%$, and thus our results are about 15 times better than chance. For comparison, the boosted classifier alone gives an overall accuracy of 69.6% and so the color, edge and location potentials increase the accuracy by 2.6%. This seemingly small numerical improvement corresponds to a large perceptual improvement (cf. fig. 10). The parameter settings, learned against the validation set, were $M = 5000$ rounds, $N_t = 400$ textons, edge potential parameters $\boldsymbol{\theta}_\phi = [45, 10]^T$, and location potential power $w_\lambda = 0.1$.

The greatest accuracies are for classes which have low visual variability and many training examples (e.g. grass, book, tree, road, sky and bicycle) whilst the lowest accuracies are for classes with high visual variability and fewer training examples (e.g. boat, chair, bird, dog). We expect more training data to boost considerably the recognition accuracy for those difficult classes. Additionally, using features with better lighting invariance properties would help considerably.

Let us now focus on some of the largest mistakes in the confusion matrix to gather some intuition on how the algorithm may be improved. Structured objects such as aeroplanes, chairs, signs, boats are sometimes incorrectly classified as buildings. Perhaps this kind of problem may be fixed by a part-based modeling approach. For example, detecting windows and roofs should resolve many such ambiguities. Furthermore, objects such as cows, sheep and chairs (benches) which in training are always seen sitting on grass do get confused with grass.

Table 1. Comparison of segmentation/recognition accuracy and efficiency

	Accuracy		Speed (Train/Test)	
	Sowerby	Corel	Sowerby	Corel
This paper – Full CRF model	88.6%	74.6%	5h/10s	12h/30s
This paper – Unary classifier only	85.6%	68.4%		
He et al. – mCRF model [1]	89.5%	80.0%	Gibbs	Gibbs
He et al. – unary classifier only	82.4%	66.9%		

Fig. 9. Example results on the Corel and Sowerby databases. A different set of object class labels and thus different color-coding is used here. Textual labels are superimposed for clarity.

This latter effect is probably due to inaccuracies in the manual ground-truth labeling where pixels belonging to such classes are often labeled as grass near the boundary.

Comparison with existing methods. To assess how much the shape and context modeling help with recognition we have compared the accuracy of our system against the framework of [4], i.e. given a (manually) selected region, assign one single class label to it and then measure classification accuracy. On the 21-class database, our algorithm achieves 70.5% region-based recognition accuracy beating our implementation of [4] which achieves 67.6% using 5000 textons and their Gaussian class models. Moreover, the significant advantages of our proposed algorithm are that: i) no regions need to be specified manually, ii) a pixel-wise labeling (segmentation) of the image is obtained.

We have also compared our results with those of He et al [1] on their Corel and Sowerby databases, as shown in table 1 and fig. 9. For both models we show the results of the unary classifier alone as well as results for the full model. For the Sowerby database the parameters were set as $M = 6500$, $K = 250$, $\boldsymbol{\theta}_\phi = [10, 2]^T$, and $w_\lambda = 2$. For the Corel database, all images were first automatically color and intensity normalized and the training set was augmented by applying random affine intensity changes to give the classifier improved invariance to illumination. The parameters were set as $M = 5000$, $K = 400$, $\boldsymbol{\theta}_\phi = [20, 2]^T$, and $w_\lambda = 4$.

Our method gives comparable or better (with unary classifier alone) results than [1]. However, the careful choice of efficient features and learning techniques,

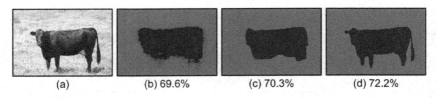

(a)   (b) 69.6%   (c) 70.3%   (d) 72.2%

Fig. 10. Effect of different model potentials. The original input image (**a**) and the result from the boosted classifier alone (**b**), with no explicit spatial coherency; brighter pixels correspond to lower entropy of the unary potentials. (**c**) Results for the CRF model without color modeling, i.e. omitting term π in (1), and (**d**) for the full CRF model. Segmentation accuracy figures are given over the whole dataset. Observe the marked improvement in perceived segmentation accuracy of the full model over the boosted classifier alone, despite a seemingly small numerical improvement.

and the avoidance of inefficient Gibbs sampling enables our algorithm to scale much better with the number of training images *and* object classes. Incorporating *semantic* context information as [1] is likely to improve our performance.

The effect of different model potentials. Figure 10 shows results for variations of our model with different potentials included. It is evident that imposing spatial coherency (c) as well as an image dependent color model (d) improves the results considerably. The percentage accuracies in fig. 10 show that each term in our model captures essential information from the training set. Note that the improvement given by the full model over just the unary classifiers, while numerically small, corresponds to a significant increase in perceived accuracy (compare fig. 10b with 10d) since the object contour is accurately delineated.

6   Conclusions

This paper has presented a new discriminative model for efficient recognition and simultaneous semantic segmentation of objects in images. We have: i) introduced new features which capture simultaneous appearance, shape and context information, ii) trained our model efficiently by exploiting both boosting and piecewise training techniques, iii) achieved efficient labeling by a combination of integral image processing and feature sharing. The result is an accurate algorithm which recognizes and locates a large number of object classes in photographs.

In the future we hope to integrate explicit *semantic* context information such as in [1] to improve further the classification accuracy. We are also interested in learning object parts (for structured objects) and their spatial arrangement. While we currently capture shape and thereby some implicit notion of objects 'parts', an explicit treatment of these would better model structured objects.

Acknowledgements. The authors would like to thank Florian Schroff, Roberto Cipolla, Andrew Blake and Andrew Zisserman for their invaluable help.

References

1. He, X., Zemel, R.S., Carreira-Perpiñán, M.A.: Multiscale conditional random fields for image labeling. Proc. of IEEE CVPR (2004)
2. Fergus, R., Perona, P., Zisserman, A.: Object class recognition by unsupervised scale-invariant learning. In: CVPR'03. Volume II. (2003) 264–271
3. Berg, A.C., Berg, T.L., Malik, J.: Shape matching and object recognition using low distortion correspondences. In: CVPR. (2005)
4. Winn, J., Criminisi, A., Minka, T.: Categorization by learned universal visual dictionary. Int. Conf. of Computer Vision (2005)
5. Kumar, S., Herbert, M.: Discriminative fields for modeling spatial dependencies in natural images. In: NIPS. (2004)
6. Borenstein, E., Sharon, E., Ullman, S.: Combining top-down and bottom-up segmentation. In: Proceedings IEEE workshop on Perceptual Organization in Computer Vision, CVPR 2004. (2004)
7. Winn, J., Jojic, N.: LOCUS: Learning Object Classes with Unsupervised Segmentation. Proc. of IEEE ICCV. (2005)
8. Kumar, P., Torr, P., Zisserman, A.: Obj cut. Proc. of IEEE CVPR. (2005)
9. Leibe, B., Schiele, B.: Interleaved object categorization and segmentation. In: BMVC'03. Volume II. (2003) 264–271
10. Duygulu, P., Barnard, K., de Freitas, N., Forsyth, D.: Object recognition as machine translation: Learning a lexicon for a fixed image vocabulary. ECCV (2002)
11. Tu, Z., Chen, X., Yuille, A.L., Zhu, S.: Image parsing: Unifying segmentation, detection, and recognition. In: CVPR. (2003)
12. Konishi, S., Yuille, A.L.: Statistical cues for domain specific image segmentation with performance analysis. In: CVPR. (2000)
13. Lafferty, J., McCallum, A., Pereira, F.: Conditional random fields: Probabilistic models for segmenting and labeling sequence data. In: ICML. (2001)
14. Boykov, Y., Jolly, M.P.: Interactive graph cuts for optimal boundary and region segmentation of objects in n-d images. Proc. of IEEE ICCV. (2001)
15. Rother, C., Kolmogorov, V., Blake, A.: Interactive foreground extraction using iterated graph cuts. ACM Transactions on Graphics (SIGGRAPH'04). (2004)
16. Sutton, C., McCallum, A.: Piecewise training of undirected models. In: 21st Conference on Uncertainty in Artificial Intelligence. (2005)
17. Leung, T., Malik, J.: Representing and recognizing the visual appearance of materials using three-dimensional textons. IJCV **43** (2001) 29–44
18. Varma, M., Zisserman, A.: A statistical approach to texture classification from single images. International Journal of Computer Vision: Special Issue on Texture Analysis and Synthesis **62** (2005) 61–81
19. Viola, P., Jones, M.: Rapid object detection using a boosted cascade of simple features. In: CVPR01. (2001) I:511–518
20. Belongie, S., Malik, J., Puzicha, J.: Shape matching and object recognition using shape contexts. PAMI **24** (2002) 509–522
21. Torralba, A., Murphy, K., Freeman, W.: Sharing features: efficient boosting procedures for multiclass object detection. Proc. of IEEE CVPR (2004) 762–769
22. Friedman, J., Hastie, T., Tibshirani, R.: Additive logistic regression: a statistical view of boosting. Technical report, Dept. of Statistics, Stanford University. (1998)
23. Baluja, S., Rowley, H.A.: Boosting sex identification performance. In: AAAI. (2005) 1508–1513
24. Kumar, S., Hebert, M.: A hierarchical field framework for unified context-based classification. In: ICCV05. (2005) II: 1284–1291

Weakly Supervised Learning of Part-Based Spatial Models for Visual Object Recognition

David J. Crandall and Daniel P. Huttenlocher

Cornell University, Ithaca, NY 14850, USA
{crandall, dph}@cs.cornell.edu

Abstract. In this paper we investigate a new method of learning part-based models for visual object recognition, from training data that only provides information about class membership (and not object location or configuration). This method learns both a model of local part appearance and a model of the spatial relations between those parts. In contrast, other work using such a weakly supervised learning paradigm has not considered the problem of simultaneously learning appearance and spatial models. Some of these methods use a "bag" model where only part appearance is considered whereas other methods learn spatial models but only given the output of a particular feature detector. Previous techniques for learning both part appearance and spatial relations have instead used a highly supervised learning process that provides substantial information about object part location. We show that our weakly supervised technique produces better results than these previous highly supervised methods. Moreover, we investigate the degree to which both richer spatial models and richer appearance models are helpful in improving recognition performance. Our results show that while both spatial and appearance information can be useful, the effect on performance depends substantially on the particular object class and on the difficulty of the test dataset.

1 Introduction

We consider the weakly supervised learning problem for object class recognition, in which we are given a set of positive exemplars that each contain at least one instance of a given object class, and a set of negative exemplars that generally do not contain instances of that class. We use an undirected graphical model (or Markov random field) representation scheme, where nodes of the graph correspond to local image regions that represent object parts, and edges connect pairs of nodes whose relative locations are constrained using a Gaussian model. This type of graphical model has recently been used for object class recognition by a number of researchers including [2, 5, 7, 8]. We use graphical structures that have small maximal clique sizes thus allowing for efficient exact discrete inference. Such structures include trees, star graphs and low tree-width fans (a generalized form of star graph with a central clique rather than a single central node).

We develop a new weakly supervised learning procedure for such models and demonstrate its performance for star-graph models (used in [7]) and fan models

A. Leonardis, H. Bischof, and A. Pinz (Eds.): ECCV 2006, Part I, LNCS 3951, pp. 16–29, 2006.

(used in [2]). Our learning method achieves better detection performance than these previous techniques on some common datasets. We formulate the learning problem as that of simultaneously estimating models of part appearance and spatial relationships between parts. This type of combined estimation approach has been used in previous *supervised* learning methods, where training data is labeled with part locations (e.g. [2, 5, 11]). However previous work on weakly supervised learning has generally solved a *data association* problem, where a feature detector is first run and then detected features are selected in order to form spatial relational models (e.g., [6, 7, 8]). We briefly discuss this related work in the following section. In contrast, our approach uses an EM procedure that iteratively improves both the appearance and spatial models. This procedure is computationally feasible due to the form of the underlying graphical models, which have small cliques and Gaussian spatial relational terms.

1.1   Related Work

The work presented here most closely relates to two current lines of research, both of which are concerned with learning probabilistic models of part appearance and spatial relations. The first line of research involves approaches that simultaneously estimate appearance and spatial parameters from training data using a maximum likelihood formulation (e.g, [2, 5, 11]). However these methods all rely on supervised learning procedures for which individual part locations are marked in the training data. The second line of related research involves approaches that require only weak supervision, where part locations are not provided in training (e.g, [6, 7, 8, 14]). However these methods can be viewed as learning spatial models given fixed appearance models, because particular feature detectors are first run to locate interest points. The subsequent learning process then involves forming a model that provides a consistent association to these detected features.

A number of other recent object class recognition techniques are also relevant to our approach, especially work on learning bag models. These models are collections of features or parts that do not explicitly include spatial information (e.g., [13, 3, 12]). Such models can still capture limited spatial information such as relative sizes of parts, and some fragment-based models encode information about overlap of parts at different scales [10]. Among these learning techniques there again is a dichotomy between those that are highly supervised but do not require feature detection (e.g., [13]) and those that rely on feature detectors to solve a data association problem (e.g., [3]). Both [10] and [12] are weakly supervised and do not use feature detectors, making them most similar to the approach we take here, although they do not explicitly model spatial relations.

2   Form of the Model

We use the undirected graphical model (Markov random field) framework in [2, 5, 7] where an object model $\Theta = (A, S)$ consists of appearance templates $A = (a_1, \ldots, a_m)$ for each part, and Gaussian spatial constraints $S = \{s_{ij}\}$

defined between certain pairs of parts. One can think of an underlying graph $G = (V, E)$ with a node $v_i \in V$ for each part and a corresponding appearance template a_i. A random variable l_i specifies the location of each part in some configuration space, and $L = (l_1, \ldots, l_m)$ denotes the overall configuration of an object with m parts (i.e., locations for all of the parts). An undirected edge $e_{ij} \in E$ corresponds to each pair of parts v_i and v_j for which there is a Gaussian constraint s_{ij} on the relative locations of those parts. The particular form of the appearance models a_i and the pairwise spatial constraints s_{ij} are described further below. Examples of some learned models are shown in Figure 2.

We now briefly turn to two important properties of these models. First, the likelihood of seeing an image given a configuration L of the model factors into a term for the background and a product over the individual parts of the model. That is, we assume the appearance of the parts is independent. Second, the prior probability of a configuration L, for a given model Θ, factors into a product of functions over maximal cliques (recall that a clique is a fully connected subset of nodes) of the graph,

$$P(L|\Theta) = \prod_C \Psi_C(L_C), \tag{1}$$

where each $C \subset V$ is a maximal clique, L_C denotes the location parameters corresponding to the vertices $v_i \in C$, and Ψ_C is some (non-negative) function of the location parameters. The utility of this factorization depends on the maximal cliques being small, as it allows the prior to be factored into a product of terms that are each over relatively small state spaces L_C rather than the full state space L. For instance in the case of trees (or star-graphs) the cliques are only size 2.

Taken together these two properties make it possible to efficiently compute the exact likelihood of an image x_n for a given model Θ, with a discrete set of possible locations L,

$$P(x_n|\Theta) = \sum_L P(x_n|\Theta, L)P(L|\Theta). \tag{2}$$

The precise running time is $O(mh^c)$ for a model with m parts, h possible locations per part, and where c is the size of the largest subset C. For Gaussian models this time can be reduced to $O(mh^{c-1})$ using the approximation methods in [5].

It is also common to use the maximizing configuration L^* to approximate (2) rather than summing over all values of L. This configuration is the maximum *a posteriori* location for a given model and image (the MAP estimate),

$$\arg \max_L P(L|x_n, \Theta) \tag{3}$$

Using the distance transform techniques introduced in [5] this MAP estimate can also be computed in $O(mh^{c-1})$ time. For clique sizes $c \leq 3$ these algorithms are quite fast in practice, using conservative pruning heuristics that guarantee the correct answer. While these fast inference procedures have previously been used for detection and localization, [2, 5, 7] here we use them as part of an unsupervised learning procedure that simultaneously estimates appearance and spatial parameters from training data.

2.1   Appearance Model

We use a simple oriented edge appearance template (as in [2]). Let I be the output of an oriented edge detector, so that at each pixel p, $I(p)$ has a value u indicating that either no edge is present or that there is an edge at one of a small fixed number of possible orientations. We model the appearance of the part i by an appearance template a_i. Let $f_i(p)[u]$ denote the probability that pixel $p \in a_i$ has value u. We assume these probabilities are independent given the location of the template.

As is common, we assume that the likelihood of an image given a particular model, as a function of location, is the product of two terms: one for absence of the model and one for presence of the model. When the model is absent we simply assume an independent background probability $b[u]$ for each pixel, yielding $\prod_p b[I(p)]$. When the model is present we assume that the individual part appearances are independent. Thus for a configuration L where the templates do not overlap,

$$p(I|\Theta, L) = \prod_p b[I(p)] \prod_{v_i \in V} g_i(I, l_i), \tag{4}$$

where

$$g_i(I, l_i) = \prod_{p \in T} \frac{f_i(p)[I(p + l_i)]}{b[I(p + l_i)]}. \tag{5}$$

Each term in g_i is the ratio of the foreground and background probabilities for a pixel that is covered by template a_i. In equation (4) the denominator of g_i cancels out the background model contribution for pixels that are under a part.

As long as we only consider configurations L without overlapping parts this likelihood is a true probability distribution over images (i.e., it integrates to one). When parts overlap it becomes an approximation, since evidence is overcounted for pixels under multiple templates. In [1] a patchworking operation was used that averages the probabilities of overlapping templates in computing $P(I|\Theta, L)$ in order to eliminate overcounting. We follow that approach here. However, to make computation tractable, we only apply this more accurate method to evaluating the likelihood of the best configuration L^* and not to the optimization used to estimate L^*.

2.2   Spatial Model

We use the fan models proposed in [2] because they include both bag models (e.g., [13]) and star-graph models (e.g., [7]) as special cases. A k-fan is a graph with a central clique of k reference nodes, with the remaining $m - k$ non-reference nodes connected to all k reference nodes but to none of the other non-reference nodes. Figure 1 illustrates the structure of 1- and 2-fan models. A 1-fan has a single reference node, with all other nodes connected to that node but not to one another. In other words a 1-fan is a star-graph with a single central node, or equivalently, a tree of depth 1. A 2-fan replaces the single node in the center with a pair of nodes. These two reference nodes are connected to one another and to all the non-reference nodes, but there are no edges between non-reference nodes. When $k = m - 1$ the fan structure is a complete graph. At the other extreme, when $k = 0$ there are no edges, corresponding to a bag model with no spatial constraints between the parts.

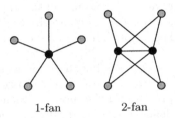

1-fan   2-fan

Fig. 1. Example 1- and 2-fans with reference nodes shown in black

Let $R = \{v_1, \ldots, v_k\}$ be the reference parts of a k-fan and $L_R = (l_1, \ldots, l_k)$ be a particular configuration of these reference parts. Let $\overline{R}$ be the non-reference parts, $\overline{R} = V - R$. The spatial prior for a k-fan can be written in terms of conditional distributions as,

$$P(L|\Theta) = P(L_R|\Theta) \prod_{v_i \in \overline{R}} P(l_i|\Theta, L_R). \tag{6}$$

In this form it is apparent that the location of each non-reference part is independent when conditioned on the root parts.

For small k, this factorization meets our criterion in equation (1) of being a product over small cliques. This can be seen explicitly in the joint form,

$$P(L|\Theta) = \frac{\prod_{v_i \in \overline{R}} P(l_i, L_R|\Theta)}{P(L_R|\Theta)^{n-(k+1)}}. \tag{7}$$

where the denominator can be viewed as a normalization term based on the choice of reference set R.

For a Gaussian model the marginal distribution of any subset of variables is itself Gaussian. If μ_R and Σ_R are the mean and covariance for the locations of the reference parts then the marginal distribution of the reference parts together with one non-reference part v_i is given by the Gaussian with mean and covariance,

$$\mu_{i,R} = \begin{bmatrix} \mu_i \\ \mu_R \end{bmatrix}, \quad \Sigma_{i,R} = \begin{bmatrix} \Sigma_i & \Sigma_{iR} \\ \Sigma_{Ri} & \Sigma_R \end{bmatrix}. \tag{8}$$

These can be used to define the full spatial prior in terms of the above expressions for $P(L|\Theta)$.

3   Weakly Supervised Learning

Given a set of positive exemplar images, $D = (x_1, \ldots, x_N)$, each of which contains at least one instance of the object, it is customary to find a model Θ that maximizes the likelihood of the data,

$$\Theta^* = \arg\max_{\Theta} p(D|\Theta) = \arg\max_{\Theta} \prod_{n=1}^{N} P(x_n|\Theta).$$

In searching over possible models, evaluating $P(x_n|\Theta^t)$ for a particular model Θ^t and image x_n involves summing over the discrete space of possible model configurations for that image,

$$P(x_n|\Theta^t) = \sum_{L} P(x_n|\Theta^t, L)P(L|\Theta^t).$$

As we saw in Section 2, this can be solved efficiently because the model factors according to equations (1) and (4).

Maximum likelihood estimation problems that involve such hidden parameters can be solved using an expectation maximization (EM) algorithm, where a given model Θ^t is used to estimate values of the hidden variables L, which are then used to estimate an improved model Θ^{t+1}. In the current setting, there are two important characteristics that make EM particularly simple. First, both $P(x_n|\Theta^t)$ and corresponding optimal values of the location variable L_n^{t*} can be computed efficiently. In other settings such computations are often intractable, and much effort is devoted to finding good approximations that can be computed efficiently. Second, in our case we do not have a prior for the parameters Θ of the model (i.e., we are using a uniform prior over these parameters). In many applications of EM the prior over the parameters plays an important role in the optimization.

For a given model Θ^t, an optimal set of location parameters L_n^{t*} can be estimated for each image x_n either by computing the expected value of the location parameters or by computing the MAP estimate, as described for equations (2) and (3) above. For a given model Θ^t and image x_n, the MAP estimate of location can be interpreted as the best configuration of the model in the image. On the other hand the expectation might not correspond to any good configuration, if for example there are several instances of an object in the image. Given this natural interpretation of the maximizing configuration, we use the MAP estimate rather than the expected value for L_n^{t*}.

Given the set D of positive exemplar training images and a candidate model Θ^t we estimate the likelihood of the data given the model $P(D|\Theta^t)$ using the MAP location parameters L_n^{t*} for each image $x_n \in D$. Using these best locations, a new maximum likelihood model Θ^{t*} can easily be estimated using the supervised training procedures in [5, 2]. To summarize, we have described a straightforward EM procedure for estimating the model Θ^* that maximizes the likelihood of the training data D, given some initial model $\Theta^0 = (A^0, S^0)$. We now discuss how to learn an initial model from weakly supervised training data.

4   Learning an Initial Model

The EM approach to learning object models described in the previous section requires an initial model $\Theta^0 = (A^0, S^0)$. Since EM is a local search technique, it is important to start with a reasonable initial model. Our approach is to compute a large set of candidate appearance templates that seem promising based only upon how well they individually discriminate between the positive and negative training data. Then we examine the configurations of those templates in the positive training data to both choose which candidates to include in the initial appearance model A^0 and to define an initial spatial model S^0.

4.1   Candidate Patch Models

As in [10, 12], our approach is to first generate a large set of potential appearance template models and then determine how well each such patch predicts the positive training examples compared to how well it predicts the negative training examples. Thus in addition to the positive exemplars D used for training the overall model, we also consider negative exemplars $\overline{D} = (\overline{x}_1, \ldots, \overline{x}_M)$, and we rank a given template a_i by the ratio of the likelihoods of the positive and negative training data,

$$\frac{P(D|a_i)}{P(\overline{D}|a_i)}. \tag{9}$$

We use the appearance templates discussed in Section 2.1 that specify the probability of an edge at each of several orientations at each pixel in the template. For the experiments in this paper, four quantized edge orientations were used: north-south, east-west, northeast-southwest, and northwest-southeast. Our initial set of candidate templates consists of patches drawn at random from the positive training images, sampled uniformly from several patch sizes and from all image locations such that the patches are contained within the image boundaries. We use three patch sizes: 12×12, 24×24, and 48×48 pixels. For the experiments reported in this paper we use approximately 100,000 initial patches. The edges in each patch are dilated in both the spatial and edge orientation dimensions in order to generalize the initial template from a single training example. We use a dilation radius of 2.5 pixels in the spatial dimension and 45 degrees in the orientation dimension.

To improve the quality of the templates, we employ a simple EM procedure, similar to the one discussed in Section 3 for learning the overall models. This procedure only maximizes the likelihood of the positive training data $P(D|a_i)$ rather than the ratio in (9), however in practice we observe that this also increases the ratio (and halts the optimization loop if it does not).

More formally, we are interested in maximizing

$$P(D|a_i) = \prod_n P(x_n|a_i)$$

where

$$P(x_n|a_i) = \sum_l P(x_n|a_i, l) \approx \max_l P(x_n|a_i, l).$$

As above, we use the maximizing location because it specifies the best location of the template in each image, whereas computing an expected location might not correspond to any one particular good match. For a given model a_i^t at iteration t we compute the maximizing location $l_{i,n}^{t*}$ for each image x_n. The resulting set of locations for the positive exemplars D can then be used to estimate an optimal template using the supervised learning procedure discussed above. The process is iterated until the likelihood ratio for the patch stops improving.

This optimization procedure is performed for each initial template. Due to the redundancy in the selection of the initial patches, there is generally considerable similarity between many of the resulting templates. However we do not attempt to cluster or otherwise collapse templates at this stage. All the resulting templates are ranked according to the likelihood ratio in (9). Templates with a low ratio are poor predictors of the positive exemplars over the negative exemplars, so patches with ratios below a threshold (e.g. 1.0) are discarded. All other templates are retained as candidate parts.

4.2   Pairwise Location of Candidate Patches

The previous step generates a very large set (e.g. tens of thousands) of candidate patches. It still remains to select some subset of these patches and to build an initial spatial model. In both selecting among patches and in modeling spatial relationships we want to take location information into account. For instance, it could be that a given template appears in both the positive and negative training examples, but in the positive examples it always appears at a particular location relative to other templates, making it a potentially predictive part of a model.

The simplest spatial relations are between pairs of patches, so we consider all pairs of candidate patches and form a Gaussian model of the relative patch locations $s_{ij} = (\mu_{ij}, \Sigma_{ij})$ for each pair. This is again a simple supervised learning procedure because for each template a_i and image x_n we have previously estimated the best location $l_{i,n}^*$. The mean and covariance of a Gaussian model of relative pairwise location are readily estimated by considering these locations for all the positive training images D and a given pair of templates.

Together with the appearance templates these spatial models yield a pairwise model $\theta_{ij} = (a_i, a_j, s_{ij})$ for each (unordered) pair of templates. These are just simple two-node instances of our more general models. For instance the likelihood of the training data given a model is just

$$P(D|\theta_{ij}) = \prod_n \sum_{l_i, l_j} P(x_n|a_i, l_i) P(x_n|a_j, l_j) P(l_i, l_j|s_{ij}). \qquad (10)$$

This serves as a natural measure of the quality of a pair. As we have before, we approximate this using the maximizing parameter values l_i^*, l_j^* rather than summing over the parameters. In practice, we have found that the estimated locations for the parts can be noisy. In order to prevent the disproportionate influence of far outliers, we consider only the 90% of samples that best fit the spatial model $s_{i,j}$ (i.e., we compute a trimmed mean and covariance).

Some objects have two or more distinct parts that are similar in appearance. Examples include the two wheels of a bicycle and the two eyes of a human face. For these objects, the maximizing locations $l_{i,n}^*$ for a given patch a_i may correspond to one part in some images and another part in other images. As a result, the relative displacement between two patches may be a multimodal distribution to which it makes little sense to fit a Gaussian model. In these cases we have found it is better to fit a model to the strongest mode and ignore the rest of the distribution. The underlying idea is that with the high degree of redundancy in the patches, it is not necessary at this stage to explicitly handle patches that match at multiple locations. In practice, we handle this case by fitting a mixture of Gaussian model with a small number of mixture components when a single Gaussian is not a good a good fit. We then choose the highest-likelihood mixture component and use the mean and covariance of that component as the model of the pairwise relative location.

4.3   Initial k-Fan Model

We use a greedy procedure to construct an initial k-fan model for a given k. First consider the case of a 1-fan, in which cliques of the model are just the pairs constructed in the previous section. We exhaustively consider all the candidate patches identified in Section 4.1 as possible root parts (a 1-fan has just a single root part). For a given such choice of root part, a_r, we consider all other parts a_i, $i \neq r$, in order of their quality, ranked by the likelihood of the data given the pairwise model θ_{ri} in (10). Considering the pairs in this order, if a given part a_i does not overlap any of the other parts thus far in the model, then that part is added to the model. In practice a small degree of overlap is allowed. This greedy process continues until there are either no more parts left to add, or until some pre-determined maximal number of parts is reached. The result of this process is a set of parts for a potential model with root a_r. When repeated for each possible root part, a large set of candidate 1-fan models is generated.

This process differs only slightly for references sets of size $k > 1$. We consider all k-tuples of candidate patches rather than all singletons as possible reference sets. For each such reference set we as above greedily form a single model, where for a fixed reference set R all non-reference patches are considered in order, and added only if they do not overlap patches already in the model. The ordering in this case is determined according to the product of the pairwise scores in (10) for all the pairs of a reference patches with the current candidate patch, rather than just a single such score. Let θ_R denote the best model selected in this greedy fashion for each reference set R.

Each potential model θ_R (one corresponding to each possible choice of reference node) is scored in order to select one as the best initial model. Ideally we would like to use the likelihood of the positive exemplars given the model $P(D|\theta_R)$. However it is costly to evaluate this for the tens of thousands of candidate models. Instead we use a simple approximation: the product of all the individual part likelihoods and the product of the spatial priors for each connected pair of parts,

$$\prod_n \left(\prod_{v_i \in V_R} P(x_n | a_i, l^*_{i,n}) \prod_{(v_i, v_j) \in E_R} P(l^*_{i,n}, l^*_{j,n} | s_{ij}) \right), \tag{11}$$

where V_R and E_R are the set of nodes and edges of the model θ_R. Note that in the case of a 1-fan this quantity is the same as the true likelihood, because all the cliques are pairs of nodes. For other fan models, however, the true spatial prior is approximated as a product of pairwise spatial priors.

Finally we choose the model that maximizes (11). While the parts of this model form the initial appearance templates A^0, it is still necessary to create the initial Gaussian spatial models S^0 because the greedy model formation process considers only pairwise spatial models. This is done using the same simple supervised learning procedure by which the pairwise models were formed in Section 4.2 only now the true cliques of the k-fan model are considered rather than just pairs. This results in the initial model $\Theta^0 = (A^0, S^0)$ that is then improved using the EM procedure described previously in Section 3.

5 Experimental Results

In our first set of experiments, we applied our weakly supervised learning method to the image sets of the Caltech database [6]. Each of these image sets consists of 800 positive images and 800 negative (background) images, except for the faces set which contains 435 positive images. The positive and negative datasets were partitioned so that half of the images were used for training and the other half were held out for testing. Positive images were scaled so that object size was approximately uniform across the set of images. In these experiments we learned models that were limited to six parts, to facilitate comparison with earlier methods that also used six parts. Table 1 presents the results of these experiments, and compares the equal-ROC detection accuracy of our method to other recently reported results. The results are directly comparable because the image data and experimental protocol are identical across all of these tests. Figure 2 shows examples of the models that were learned for some of the Caltech object classes.

These results show that our weakly supervised learning method performs substantially better than the supervised results presented in [2], in which models

Table 1. Results of detection experiment on CalTech image set

		0-fan	1-fan	2-fan	Results from literature
Motorbikes	unsupervised	**96.7%**	**98.6%**	**98.6%**	92.5% [6], 97.3% [7]
	supervised [2]	96.5%	97.0%	97.0%	
Airplanes	unsupervised	**90.3%**	**94.3%**	**95.0%**	90.2% [6], 93.6% [7]
	supervised [2]	90.5%	91.3%	93.3%	
Faces	unsupervised	**86.0%**	**98.0%**	**98.2%**	96.4% [6], 90.3% [7]
	supervised [2]	98.2%	98.2%	98.2%	
Cars (rear view)	unsupervised	**88.9%**	**94.4%**	**94.4%**	90.3% [6], 87.7% [7]

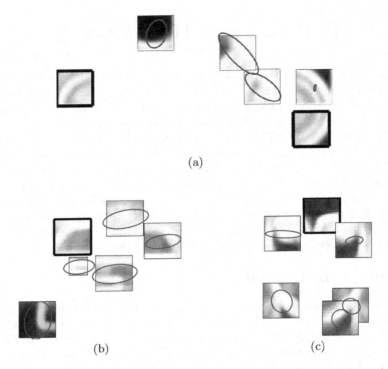

(a)

(b)   (c)

Fig. 2. Some models produced by our weakly supervised learning technique: (a) 2-fan motorbike model, (b) 1-fan rear-view car model, and (c) 1-fan face model. Reference parts are shown with a thick border. The spatial covariance with respect to these reference parts is illustrated with an ellipse. For simplicity, each template shows only the overall probability of an edge rather than the probability of each orientation.

were learned using hand-labeled locations for each part in each image. This is an encouraging result, as one might expect that carefully hand- labeled data would yield better performance. The results also show that our unsupervised learning method produces better results than previous techniques that use a fixed set of feature detectors rather than simultaneously learning part appearance and spatial models [6, 7].

The results in Table 1 show that the detection accuracy for all classes increases substantially between the 0-fan models and the 1-fan models. There was also some improvement as k increased from 1 to 2 for the airplanes, but little or no improvement for the other classes. This suggests that for some objects and image sets, increasing the degree of spatial constraint (i.e. increasing k) in the object model improves detection performance whereas for other objects and image sets additional spatial information provides little or no benefit. In part this is due to the fact that the positive versus negative images in this database are highly different from one another, making it unnecessary to use spatial relationships to distinguish positive from negative.

Table 2. Results of detection experiment on Graz bicycle image set

	0-fan	1-fan	2-fan
6 parts	79.0%	81.0%	81.0%
25 parts	80.0%	84.0%	84.0%

Table 3. Results of detection experiment on motorbikes, with bicycles as background images

	0-fan	1-fan	2-fan
6 parts	83.3%	88.1%	88.8%
25 parts	84.3%	89.3%	90.1%

We also tested the detection accuracy of the models learned by our unsupervised algorithm on the non-normalized version of the Caltech imageset, in which scale is not known. As in [2], we did this by applying the models at several different scales on each image and choosing the scale having the highest-likelihood detection. The equal-ROC points for the 0-fan and 1-fan models in this setting were 94.3% and 97.0% for motorbikes, 88.3% and 90.7% for airplanes, 85.7% and 98.0% for faces, and 86.0% and 93.5% for cars, respectively.

We also considered two more challenging datasets. The first of these is the Graz bicycle image set [9], consisting of 150 images with bicycles and 150 negative images. Unlike the Caltech data, many of the negative images in this set are similar to the positive images. The second is a hybrid set using the Caltech motorbike images as the positive images and the Graz bicycle data as the negative images. This is particularly challenging because many of the local features such as wheels and handlebars are quite similar between these two classes. As before, the images were partitioned into separate training and testing sets, and positive images were rescaled so that the object width was approximately uniform.

Table 2 presents the results of the experiments using the Graz bicycles data, showing equal-ROC detection results for 0-, 1- and 2-fan models consisting of 6 and of 25 parts. We considered the effect of adding more parts to the model because approaches that use a bag model generally use large numbers of features or "parts" (e.g., [4, 13, 3]). The results show that both increasing the number of parts and increasing the degree of spatial constraint improve the performance. These results still do not quite achieve the accuracy of bag models on this dataset; for instance [4] report an equal-ROC rate of 88.0% and [9] report one of 86.5%, but they come closer than any other spatial models we are aware of.

Table 3 presents the results of the experiments using the Caltech motorbike data with the Graz bicycle images as the negative test images. Again this table shows equal-ROC detection results for 0-, 1- and 2-fan models consisting of 6 and 25 parts. The most pronounced result is that for this data increasing k from 0 to 2 increased the equal-ROC detection results by about 6 percentage points (i.e., in going from a bag model with no explicit spatial constraints to a model with a moderate amount of spatial constraint).

The running time of the entire unsupervised learning process is approximately 24 hours on a small cluster of 20 Pentium III nodes. Note that the majority of this processing time is spent performing the correlations between the training images and the tens of thousands of candidate part templates. The results of this part of the process can be cached and reused when learning models for different values of k. Once the correlation computation has been performed, learning a new model requires approximately 1 hour on a single Pentium III node. Once a model has been learned, the average time required to localize an object in an image is approximately 0.1 seconds for a 0-fan, 0.3 seconds for a 1-fan, and 2.5 seconds for a 2-fan.

6   Summary

We have introduced a weakly supervised method of learning undirected graphical models for object class recognition. This method simultaneously estimates both part appearance and spatial relations between parts. In contrast, existing weakly supervised methods for learning these kinds of models rely on feature detectors rather than learning both appearance and spatial models from the data. Our method uses previously developed efficient inference and supervised learning algorithms to develop a simple and effective EM procedure. We have shown that our method produces better detection results on some standard datasets than are obtained by state-of-the art methods for learning such spatial models. We have also shown that for some problems, spatial information seems to be quite important in achieving high accuracy.

Our results, together with results of some other recent research, raise interesting questions about the role of feature detection in object class recognition. For bag models, with no explicit spatial information, very good detection performance is obtained both using feature detection (e.g., [4]) and by methods that do not use features (e.g., [13]). On the other hand, for spatial models such as the one used here, better results seem to be obtained by methods that do not use feature detection. Two recent papers have demonstrated improved object detection results by not using feature detectors [2, 7]. In this paper we further demonstrate that better object detection results can be obtained by also not using features in the learning process, and instead learning appearance models together with spatial models. Another interesting set of open questions is raised by the fact that bag models currently perform better than spatial models for most common datasets. Our results suggest that this may partly be due to the datasets, but it remains to better characterize what aspects of bag models versus spatial models seem to account for these differences.

References

1. Y. Amit and A. Trouve. Pop: Patchwork of parts models for object recognition. Technical report, The University of Chicago, April 2005.
2. D.J. Crandall, P.F. Felzenszwalb, and D.P. Huttenlocher. Spatial priors for part-based recognition using statistical models. In *IEEE Conference on Computer Vision and Pattern Recognition*, pages 10–17, 2005.

3. C. Dance, J. Willamowski, L. Fan, C. Bray, and G. Csurka. Visual categorization with bags of keypoints. In *European Conference on Computer Vision*, 2004.
4. Gyuri Dorko and Cordelia Schmid. Object class recognition using discriminative local features. Technical report, INRIA Grenoble, September 2005.
5. P.F. Felzenszwalb and D.P. Huttenlocher. Efficient matching of pictorial structures. In *IEEE Conference on Computer Vision and Pattern Recognition*, pages II:66–73, 2000.
6. R. Fergus, P. Perona, and A. Zisserman. Object class recognition by unsupervised scale-invariant learning. In *IEEE Conference on Computer Vision and Pattern Recognition*, 2003.
7. R. Fergus, P. Perona, and A. Zisserman. A sparse object category model for efficient learning and exhaustive recognition. In *IEEE Conference on Computer Vision and Pattern Recognition*, pages 380–387, 2005.
8. S. Ioffe and D.A. Forsyth. Probabilistic methods for finding people. *International Journal of Computer Vision*, 43(1):45–68, 2001.
9. A. Opelt, M. Fussenegger, A. Pinz, and P. Auer. Weak hypotheses and boosting for generic object detection and recognition. In *European Conference on Computer Vision*, pages 71–84, 2004.
10. E. Sali S. Ullman and M. Vidal-Naquet. A fragment-based approach to object representation and classification. In *4th International Workshop on Visual Form, IWVF4*, 2001.
11. H. Schneiderman and T. Kanade. Probabilistic formulation for object recognition. In *IEEE Conference on Computer Vision and Pattern Recognition*, 1998.
12. T. Serre, L. Wolf, and T. Poggio. A new biologically motivated framework for robust object recognition. In *IEEE Conference on Computer Vision and Pattern Recognition*, 2005.
13. J. Winn, A. Criminisi, and T. Minka. Object categorization by learned universal visual dictionary. In *IEEE International Conference on Computer Vision*, 2005.
14. W. Zhang, B. Yu, D. Samaras, and G. Zelinsky. Object class recognition using multiple layer boosting with heterogeneous features. In *IEEE Conference on Computer Vision and Pattern Recognition*, 2005.

Hyperfeatures – Multilevel Local Coding for Visual Recognition

Ankur Agarwal and Bill Triggs

GRAVIR-INRIA-CNRS, 655 Avenue de l'Europe, Montbonnot 38330, France
{Ankur.Agarwal, Bill.Triggs}@inrialpes.fr
http://www.inrialpes.fr/lear/people/{agarwal, triggs}

Abstract. Histograms of local appearance descriptors are a popular representation for visual recognition. They are highly discriminant and have good resistance to local occlusions and to geometric and photometric variations, but they are not able to exploit spatial co-occurrence statistics at scales larger than their local input patches. We present a new multilevel visual representation, 'hyperfeatures', that is designed to remedy this. The starting point is the familiar notion that to detect object parts, in practice it often suffices to detect co-occurrences of more local object fragments – a process that can be formalized as comparison (*e.g.* vector quantization) of image patches against a codebook of known fragments, followed by local aggregation of the resulting codebook membership vectors to detect co-occurrences. This process converts local collections of image descriptor vectors into somewhat less local histogram vectors – higher-level but spatially coarser descriptors. We observe that as the output is again a local descriptor vector, the process can be iterated, and that doing so captures and codes ever larger assemblies of object parts and increasingly abstract or 'semantic' image properties. We formulate the hyperfeatures model and study its performance under several different image coding methods including clustering based Vector Quantization, Gaussian Mixtures, and combinations of these with Latent Dirichlet Allocation. We find that the resulting high-level features provide improved performance in several object image and texture image classification tasks.

1 Introduction

Local codings of image appearance based on invariant descriptors are a popular representation for visual recognition [40, 39, 3, 30, 12, 26, 27, 11, 36, 22, 13]. The image is treated as a loose collection of quasi-independent local patches, robust visual descriptors are extracted from these, and a statistical summarization or aggregation process is used to capture the statistics of the resulting set of descriptor vectors and hence quantify the image appearance. There are many variants. Patches can be selected at one or at many scales, and either densely, at random, or sparsely according to local informativeness criteria [19, 23]. There are many kinds of local descriptors, which can incorporate various degrees of resistance to common perturbations such as viewpoint changes, geometric deformations, and photometric transformations [43, 30, 39, 32, 33]. Aggregation can be done in different ways, either over local regions to make higher-level local descriptors, or globally to make whole-image descriptors.

A. Leonardis, H. Bischof, and A. Pinz (Eds.): ECCV 2006, Part I, LNCS 3951, pp. 30–43, 2006.

The simplest example is the 'texton' or 'bag-of-features' approach. This was initially developed for texture analysis (*e.g.* [31, 29]), but turns out to give surprisingly good performance in many image classification and object recognition tasks [44, 12, 11, 36, 22, 13]. Local image patches or their feature vectors are coded using vector quantization against a fixed codebook, and the votes for each codebook centre are tallied to produce a histogram characterizing the distribution of patches over the image or local region. Codebooks are typically constructed by running clustering algorithms such as k-means over large sets of training patches. Soft voting into several nearby centres can be used to reduce aliasing effects. More generally, EM can be used to learn a mixture distribution or a deeper latent model in descriptor space, coding each patch by its vector of posterior mixture-component membership probabilities or latent variable values.

1.1 Hyperfeatures

The main limitation of local coding approaches is that they capture only the first order statistics of the set of patches (within-patch statistics and their aggregates such as means, histograms, *etc.*), thus ignoring the fact that inter-patch statistics such as co-occurrences are important for many recognition tasks. To alleviate this, several authors have proposed methods for incorporating an additional level of representation that captures pairwise or neighbourhood co-occurrences of coded patches [37, 41, 42, 3, 26].

This paper takes the notion of an additional level of representation one step further, generalizing it to a generic method for creating multi-level hierarchical codings. The basic intuition is that image content should be coded at several levels of abstraction, with the higher levels being spatially coarser but (hopefully) semantically more informative. Our approach is based on the local histogram model (*e.g.* [37, 42]). At each level, the image is divided into local regions with each region being characterized by a descriptor vector. The base level contains raw image descriptors. At higher levels, each vector is produced by coding (*e.g.* vector quantizing) and locally pooling the finer-grained descriptor vectors from the preceding level. For instance, suppose that the regions at a particular level consist of a regular grid of overlapping patches that uniformly cover the image. Given an input descriptor vector for each member of this grid, the descriptors are vector quantized and their resulting codes are used to build local histograms of code values over (say) 5×5 blocks of input patches. These histograms are evaluated at each point on a coarser grid, so the resulting upper level output is again a grid of descriptor vectors (local histograms). The same process can be repeated at higher levels, at each stage taking a local set of descriptor vectors from the preceding level and returning its coded local histogram vector. We call the resulting higher-level features **hyperfeatures**. The codebooks are learned in the usual way, using the descriptor vectors of the corresponding level from a set of training images. To promote scale-invariant recognition, the whole process also runs at each layer of a conventional multi-scale image pyramid, so there is actually a pyramid, not a grid of descriptor vectors at each level of the hyperfeature hierarchy[1]. The hyperfeature construction process is illustrated in fig. 1.

---

[1] Terminology: 'layer' denotes a standard image pyramid layer, i.e. the same image at a coarser scale; 'level' denotes the number of folds of hyperfeature (quantize-and-histogram) local coding that have been applied, with each transformation producing a different, higher-level 'image' or 'pyramid'.

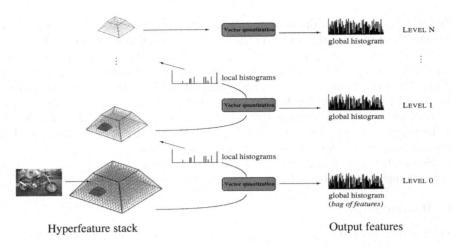

Hyperfeature stack   Output features

Fig. 1. Constructing a hyperfeature stack. The 'level 0' (base feature) pyramid is constructed by calculating a local image descriptor vector for each patch in a multiscale pyramid of overlapping image patches. These vectors are vector quantized according to the level 0 codebook, and local histograms of codebook memberships are accumulated over local position-scale neighbourhoods (the smaller darkened regions) to make the level 1 feature vectors. The process simply repeats itself at higher levels. The level l to $l+1$ coding is also used to generate the level l output vectors – global histograms over the whole level-l pyramid. The collected output features are fed to a learning machine and used to classify the (local or global) image region.

Our main claim is that hyperfeature based coding is a natural feature extraction framework for visual recognition. In particular, the use of vector quantization coding followed by local histogramming of membership votes provides an effective means of integrating higher order spatial relationships into texton style image representations. The resulting spatial model is somewhat 'loose' – it only codes nearby co-occurrences rather than precise geometry – but for this reason it is robust to spatial misalignments and deformations and to partial occlusions, and it fits well with the "spatially weak / strong in appearance" philosophy of texton representations. The basic intuition is that despite their geometric weakness, *in practice* simple co-occurrences of characteristic object fragments are often sufficient cues to deduce the presence of larger object parts, so that as one moves up the hyperfeature hierarchy, larger and larger assemblies of parts are coded until ultimately one codes the entire object. Owing to their loose, agglomerative nature, hyperfeature stacks are naturally robust to occlusions and feature extraction failures. Even when the top level object is not coded successfully, substantial parts of it are captured by the lower levels of the hierarchy and the system can still cue recognition on these.

1.2 Previous Work

The hyperfeature representation has several precursors. Classical 'texton' or 'bag of features' representations are global histograms over quantized image descriptors – 'level 0' of the hyperfeature representation [31, 29]. Histograms of quantized 'level 1' features have also been used to classify textures and to recognize regularly textured objects [37, 42] and a hierarchical feature-matching framework for simple second level features has been developed [25].

Hyperfeature stacks also have analogies with multilevel neural models such as the neocognitron [18], Convolutional Neural Networks (CNN) [28] and HMAX [38]. These are all multilayer networks with alternating stages of linear filtering (banks of learned convolution filters for CNN's and of learned 'simple cells' for HMAX and the neocognitron) and nonlinear rectify-and-pool operations. The neocognitron activates a higher level cell if atleast one associated lower level cell is active. In CNN's the rectified signals are pooled linearly, while in HMAX a max-like operation ('complex cell') is used so that only the dominant input is passed through to the next stage. The neocognitron and HMAX lay claims to biological plausibility whereas CNN is more of an engineering solution, but all are convolution based and typically trained discriminatively. In contrast, although hyperfeatures are still bottom-up, they are essentially a descriptive statistics model not a discriminative one: training is completely unsupervised and there are no convolution weights to learn for hyperfeature extraction, although the object classes can still influence the coding indirectly via the choice of codebook. The basic nonlinearity is also different: exemplar comparison by nearest neighbour lookup – or more generally nonlinear codings based on membership probabilities of latent patch classes – followed by a comparatively linear accumulate-and-normalize process for hyperfeatures, *versus* linear convolution filtering followed by simple rectification for the neural models.

The term 'hyperfeatures' itself has been used to describe combinations of feature position with appearance [14]. This is very different from its meaning here.

2   Base Features and Image Coding

The hyperfeature framework can be used with a large class of underlying image coding schemes. This section discusses the schemes that we have tested so far. For simplicity we describe them in the context of the base level (level 0).

2.1   Image Features

The 'level 0' input to the hyperfeature coder is a base set of local image descriptors. In our case these are computed on a dense grid – in fact a multiscale pyramid – of image patches. As patch descriptors we use SIFT-like gradient orientation histograms, computed in a manner similar to [30] but using a normalization that is more resistant to image noise in nearly empty patches. (SIFT was not originally designed to handle patches that may be empty). The normalization provides good resistance to photometric transformations, and the spatial quantization within SIFT provides a pixel or two of robustness to spatial shifts. The input to the hyperfeature coder is thus a pyramid of 128-D SIFT descriptor vectors. But other descriptors could also be used (*e.g.* [34, 4]).

Hyperfeature models based on sparse (*e.g.* keypoint based [12, 11, 26, 33]) feature sets would also be possible but they are not considered here, in part for simplicity and space reasons and in part because recent work (*e.g.* [22]) suggests that dense representations will outperform sparse ones.

2.2   Vector Quantization and Gaussian Mixtures

Vector quantization is a simple and widely-used method of characterizing the content of image patches [29]. Each patch is coded by finding the most similar patch in a dictionary of reference patches and using the index of this patch as a label. Here we use nearest neighbour coding based on Euclidean distance between SIFT descriptors, with a vocabulary learned from a training set using a clustering algorithm similar to the mean shift based on-line clusterer of [22]. The histograms have a bin for each centre (dictionary element) that counts the number of patches assigned to the centre. In the implementation, a sparse vector representation is used for efficiency.

Although vector quantization turns out to be very effective, abrupt quantization into discrete bins does cause some aliasing. This can be reduced by **soft vector quantization** – softly voting into the centers that lie close to the patch, *e.g.* with Gaussian weights. Taking this one step further, we can fit a probabilistic **mixture model** to the distribution of training patches in descriptor space, subsequently coding new patches by their vectors of posterior mixture-component membership probabilities. In §4 we test hard vector quantization (VQ) and diagonal-covariance Gaussian mixtures (GM) fitted using Expectation-Maximization. The GM codings turn out to be more effective.

2.3   Latent Dirichlet Allocation

VQ and mixture models are flexible coding methods, but capturing fine distinctions often requires a great many centres. This brings the risk of fragmentation, with the patches of an object class becoming scattered over so many label classes that it is difficult to learn an effective recognition model for it. 'Bag of words' text representations face the same problem – there are many ways to express a given underlying 'meaning' in either words or images. To counter this, one can attempt to learn deeper latent structure models that capture the underlying semantic "topics" that generated the text or image elements. This improves learning because each topic label summarizes the 'meaning' of many different 'word' labels.

The simplest latent model is Principal Components Analysis ('Latent Semantic Analysis' *i.e.* linear factor analysis), but in practice statistically-motivated nonlinear approaches such as Probabilistic Latent Semantic Analysis (pLSA) [20] perform better. There are many variants on pLSA, typically adding further layers of latent structure and/or sparsifying priors that ensure crisper distinctions [8, 9, 24, 7]. Here we use **Latent Dirichlet Allocation (LDA)** [5]. LDA models document words as samples from sparse mixtures of topics, where each topic is a mixture over word classes. More precisely: the gamut of possible topics is characterized by a learned matrix β of probabilities for each topic to generate each word class; for each new document a palette of topics (a sparse multinomial distribution) is generated from a Dirichlet prior; and for each word in the document a topic is sampled from the palette and a word class is sampled from the topic. Giving each word its own topic allows more variety than sharing a single fixed mixture of topics across all words would, while still maintaining the underlying coherence of the topic-based structure. In practice the learned values of the Dirichlet parameter α are small, ensuring that the sampled topic palette is sparse for most documents.

In our case – both during learning and use – the visual 'words' are represented by VQ or GM code vectors and LDA functions essentially as a locally adaptive nonlinear dimensionality reduction method, re-coding each word (VQ or GM vector) as a vector of posterior latent topic probabilities, conditioned on the local 'document' model (topic palette). The LDA 'documents' can be either complete images or the local regions over which hyperfeature coding is occurring. Below we use local regions, which is slower but more discriminant. Henceforth, "coding" refers to either VQ or GM coding, optionally followed by LDA reduction.

3   Constructing Hyperfeatures

The hyperfeature construction process is illustrated in figure 1. At level 0, the image (more precisely the image pyramid) is divided into overlapping local neighbourhoods, with each neighbourhood containing a number of image patches. The co-occurrence statistics within each local neighbourhood $\mathcal{N}$ are captured by vector quantizing or otherwise nonlinearly coding its patches and histogramming the results over the neighbourhood. This process converts local patch-level descriptor vectors (image features) to spatially coarser but higher-level neighbourhood-level descriptor vectors (local histograms). It works for any kind of descriptor vector. In particular, it can be repeated recursively over higher and higher order neighbourhoods to obtain a series of increasingly high level but spatially coarse descriptor vectors.

Let $\mathcal{F}^{(l)}$ denote the hyperfeature pyramid at level l, (x, y, s) denote position-scale coordinates within a feature pyramid, $d^{(l)}$ denote the feature or codebook/histogram dimension at a level l, and $\mathcal{F}^{(l)}_{ixys}$ denote the level-l descriptor vector at (x, y, s) in image i. During training, a codebook or coding model is learned from all features (all i, x, y, s) at level l. In use, the level-l codebook is used to code the level-l features in some image i, and these are pooled spatially over local neighbourhoods $\mathcal{N}^{(l+1)}(x, y, s)$ to make the hyperfeatures $\mathcal{F}^{(l+1)}_{ixys}$. The complete algorithm for VQ coding on N levels is summarized in figure 2.

For vector quantization, coding involves a single global clustering for learning, followed by local histogramming of class labels within each neighbourhood for use. For GM, a global mixture model is learned using EM, and in use the mixture component membership probability vectors of the neighbourhood's patches are summed to get the code vector. If LDA is used, its parameters α, β are estimated once over all training im-

---

1. $\forall (i, x, y, s)$, $\mathcal{F}^{(0)}_{ixys} \leftarrow$ base feature at point (x, y), scale s in image i.
2. For $l = 0, \ldots, N$:
   - If learning, cluster $\{\mathcal{F}^{(l)}_{ixys} \mid \forall (i, x, y, s)\}$ to obtain a codebook of $d^{(l)}$ centres in this feature space.
   - $\forall i$:
     - If $l < N$, $\forall (x, y, s)$ calculate $\mathcal{F}^{(l+1)}_{ixys}$ as a $d^{(l)}$ dimensional local histogram by accumulating votes from $\mathcal{F}^{(l)}_{ix'y's'}$ over neighbourhood $\mathcal{N}^{(l+1)}(x, y, s)$.
     - If global descriptors need to be output, code $\mathcal{F}^{(l)}_i$ as a $d^{(l)}$ dimensional histogram $\mathcal{H}^{(l)}_i$ by globally accumulating votes for the $d^{(l)}$ centers from all (x, y, s).
3. Return $\{\mathcal{H}^{(l)}_i \mid \forall i, l\}$.

Fig. 2. The hyperfeature coding algorithm

ages, and then used to infer topic distributions over each neighbourhood independently, *i.e.* each neighbourhood is a separate 'document' with its own LDA context.

In all of these schemes, the histogram dimension is the size of the codebook or GM/LDA basis. The neighbourhoods are implemented as small trapezoids in scale space, as shown in figure 1. This shape maintains scale invariance and helps to minimize boundary losses, which cause the pyramids to shrink in size with increasing level. The size of the pooling region at each level is a parameter. The effective region size should grow with the level – otherwise the same information is re-encoded each time, which tends to cause rapid saturation and suboptimal performance.

4   Experiments on Image Classification

To illustrate the discriminative capabilities of hyperfeatures, we present image classification experiments on three datasets: a 4 class object dataset based on the "Caltech 7" [15] and "Graz" [35] datasets that was used for the European network PASCAL's "Visual Object Classes Challenge" [10]; the 10 class KTH-TIPS texture dataset [16]; and the CRL-IPNP dataset of line sketches used for picture naming in language research [1]. The PASCAL dataset contains 684 training and 689 test images, which we scale to a maximum resolution of 320×240 pixels. The texture dataset contains 450 training and 360 test images over 10 texture classes, mostly 200×200 pixels. The CRL-IPNP dataset consists of 360 images of 300×300 pixels which we divide into two classes, images of people and others. As base level features we used the underlying descriptor of Lowe's SIFT method – local histograms of oriented image gradients calculated over 4×4 blocks of 4×4 pixel cells [30][2]. The input pyramid had a scale range of 8:1 with a spacing of $1/3$ octave and patches sampled at 8 pixel intervals, giving a total of 2500-3000 descriptors per image. For the pooling neighbourhoods $\mathcal{N}$, we took volumes of $3 \times 3 \times 3$ patches in (x, y, s) by default, increasing these in effective size by a factor of $2^{1/3}$ (one pyramid layer) at each hyperfeature level.

The final image classifications were produced by training soft linear one-against-all SVM classifiers independently for each class over the global output histograms collected from the active hyperfeature levels, using SVM-light [21] with default settings.

Effect of multiple levels. Figure 3 presents DET[3] curves showing the influence of hyperfeature levels on classification performance for the PASCAL dataset. We used GM coding with a 200 center codebook at the base level and 100 center ones at higher levels. Including higher levels gives significant gains for 'cars' and especially 'motorbikes', but little improvement for 'bicycles' and 'people'. The results improve up to level 3 (*i.e.* using the hyperfeatures from all levels 0–3 for classification), except for 'people' where level 1 is best. Beyond this there is overfitting – subsequent levels introduce more noise than information. We believe that the difference in behaviour between classes can be attributed to their differing amounts of *structure*. The large appearance variations in the 'person'

---

[2] But note that this is tiled densely over the image with no orientation normalization, not applied sparsely at keypoints and rotated to the dominant local orientation as in [30].

[3] DET curves plot miss rate *vs.* false positive rate on a log-log scale – the same information as a ROC curve in more visible form. Lower values are better.

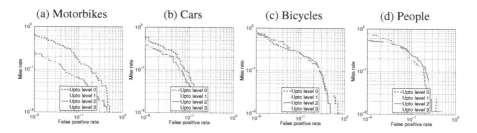

| (a) Motorbikes | (b) Cars | (c) Bicycles | (d) People |

Fig. 3. Detection Error Trade-off curves for the classes of the PASCAL dataset. Up to a certain level, including additional levels of hyperfeatures improves the classification performance. For the motorbike, car and bicycle classes the best performance is at level 3, while for the person class it is at level 1 (one level above the base features). The large gain on the motorbike (a $5\times$ reduction in false positives at fixed miss rate) and car classes suggests that local co-occurrence structure is quite informative, and is captured well by hyperfeatures.

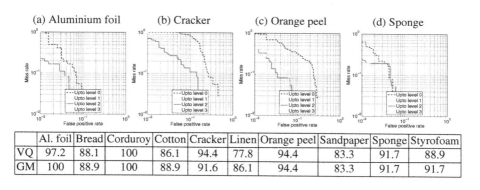

| (a) Aluminium foil | (b) Cracker | (c) Orange peel | (d) Sponge |

	Al. foil	Bread	Corduroy	Cotton	Cracker	Linen	Orange peel	Sandpaper	Sponge	Styrofoam
VQ	97.2	88.1	100	86.1	94.4	77.8	94.4	83.3	91.7	88.9
GM	100	88.9	100	88.9	91.6	86.1	94.4	83.3	91.7	91.7

Fig. 4. *Top:* Detection Error Trade-off curves for 4 of the 10 classes from the KTH-TIPS dataset, using a mixture of 100 Gaussians at each level. Including hyperfeatures improves the classification performance for every texture that is poorly classified at level 0, without hurting that for well-classified textures. The aluminium and sponge classes are best classified by including 3 levels of hyperfeatures, and cracker and orange peel by using 2 levels. *Bottom:* One-vs-rest classification performance (hit rate) at the equal error point for the 10 classes of this dataset, using hard vector quantization (VQ) and a diagonal Gaussian mixture model learned by EM (GM). Each class uses its optimal number of hyperfeature levels. GM performs best on average.

class leave little in the way of regular co-occurrence statistics for the hyperfeature coding to key on, whereas the more regular geometries of cars and motorbikes are captured well, as seen in figure 3(a) and (b). Different coding methods and codebook sizes have qualitatively similar evolutions the absolute numbers can be quite different (see below).

The results on the KTH-TIPS texture dataset in fig. 4 (top) lead to similar conclusions. For 4 of the 10 classes the level 0 performance is already near perfect and adding hyperfeatures makes little difference, while for the remaining 6 there are gains (often substantial ones) up to hyperfeature level 3. The texture classification performance at

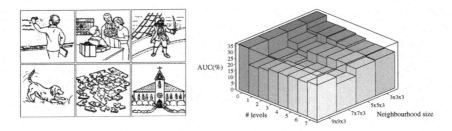

Fig. 5. *Left:* Sample positive (people) and negative (object/scene) pictures from the CRL-IPNP dataset. *Right:* Average miss rates on the positive class for different pooling neighbourhood sizes and different numbers of hyperfeature levels. For a 3x3x3 neighbourhood (in x, y, s), 5 levels of hyperfeatures are best, but the best overall performance is achieved by 7x7x3 neighbourhoods with 3 levels of hyperfeatures.

equal error rates for VQ[4] and GM coding is shown in fig. 4 (bottom). GM is better on average. Overall, its mean hit rate of 91.7% at equal error is slightly better than the 90.6% achieved by the bank of filters approach in [17] – a good result considering that in these experiments relatively few centres, widely spaced samples and only a linear SVM were used. (Performance improves systematically with each of these factors).

On the CRL-IPNP dataset, we find that 4 or 5 levels of hyperfeatures give the best performance, depending on the size of the pooling regions used. See fig. 5.

Coding methods and hyperfeatures. Fig. 6 (left half) shows average miss rates (1 − Area Under ROC Curve) on the PASCAL dataset, for different coding methods and numbers of centers. The overall performance depends considerably on both the coding method used and the codebook size (number of clusters / mixture components / latent topics), with GM coding dominating VQ, the addition of LDA always improving the results, and performance increasing whenever the codebook at any level is expanded. On the negative side, learning large codebooks is computationally expensive, especially for GM and LDA. GM gives much smoother codings than VQ as there are no aliasing artifacts, and its partition of the descriptor space is also qualitatively very different – the Gaussians overlap heavily and inter-component differences are determined more by covariance differences than by centre differences. LDA seems to be able to capture canonical neighbourhood structures more crisply than VQ or GM, presumably because it codes them by selecting a sparse palette of topics rather than an arbitrary vector of codes. If used to reduce dimensionality, LDA may also help simply by reducing noise or overfitting associated with large VQ or GM codebooks, but this can not be the whole

---

[4] At the base level of the texture dataset, we needed to make a manual correction to the SIFT VQ codebook to work around a weakness of codebook creation. Certain textures are homogeneous enough to cause all bins of the SIFT descriptor to fire about equally, giving rise to a very heavily populated "uniform noise" centre in the middle of SIFT space. For some textures this centre receives nearly all of the votes, significantly weakening the base level coding and thus damaging the performance at all levels. The issue can be resolved by simply deleting the rogue centre (stop word removal). It does not occur either at higher levels or for GM coding.

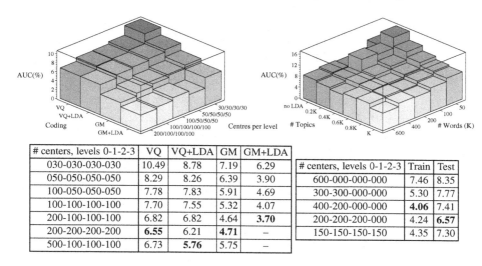

# centers, levels 0-1-2-3	VQ	VQ+LDA	GM	GM+LDA
030-030-030-030	10.49	8.78	7.19	6.29
050-050-050-050	8.29	8.26	6.39	3.90
100-050-050-050	7.78	7.83	5.91	4.69
100-100-100-100	7.70	7.55	5.32	4.07
200-100-100-100	6.82	6.82	4.64	**3.70**
200-200-200-200	**6.55**	6.21	**4.71**	–
500-100-100-100	6.73	**5.76**	5.75	–

# centers, levels 0-1-2-3	Train	Test
600-000-000-000	7.46	8.35
300-300-000-000	5.30	7.77
400-200-000-000	**4.06**	7.41
200-200-200-000	4.24	**6.57**
150-150-150-150	4.35	7.30

Fig. 6. Average miss rates on the PASCAL objects test set. *Left (plot and table):* Miss rates for different codebook sizes and coding methods. Larger codebooks always give better performance. GM coding outperforms VQ coding even with significantly fewer centres, and adding LDA consistently improves the results. The LDA experiments use the same number of topics as VQ/GM codebook centres, so they do not change the dimensionality of the code, but they do make it sparser. *Top right:* For the LDA method, performance improves systematically as both code centres (here VQ) and LDA topics are added. *Bottom right:* For a fixed total number of centers (here VQ ones), performance improves if they are distributed relatively evenly across several levels (here 3 levels, with the inclusion of a 4th reducing the performance): adding higher level information is more useful than adding finer-grained low level information.

story as LDA performance continues to improve even when there are more topics than input centres. (*c.f.* fig. 6 top right.)

Given that performance always improves with codebook size, one could argue that rather than adding hyperfeature levels, it may be better to include additional base level features. To study this we fixed the total coding complexity at 600 centres and distributed the centres in different ways across levels. Fig. 6 (bottom right) shows that spreading centres relatively evenly across levels (here up to level 3) improves the results, confirming the importance of higher levels of abstraction.

5   Object Localization

One advantage of hyperfeatures is that they offer a controllable tradeoff between locality and level of abstraction: higher level features accumulate information from larger image regions and thus have less locality but potentially more representational power. However, even quite high-level hyperfeatures are still local enough to provide useful object-region level image labeling. Here we use this for bottom-up localization of possible objects of interest. The image pyramid is tiled with regions and in each region we build a "mini-pyramid" containing the region's hyperfeatures (*i.e.* the hyperfeatures

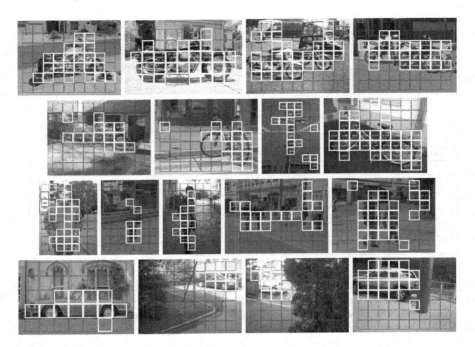

Fig. 7. Object localization in the PASCAL dataset [10] by classifying local image regions using hyperfeatures. Each row shows examples of results using one of the four independent classifiers, each being trained to classify foreground regions of its own class against the combined set of all other regions – background regions and foregrounds from other classes. An image region is labeled as belonging to the object class if the corresponding SVM returns a positive score. Each region is classified independently – there is no attempt to enforce spatial coherence.

of all levels, positions and scales whose support lies entirely within the region). The resulting region-level hyperfeature histograms are then used to learn a local region-level classifier for each class of interest. Our goal here is simply to demonstrate the representational power of hyperfeatures, not to build a complete framework for object recognition, so the experiments below classify regions individually without any attempt to include top-down or spatial contiguity information.

The experiments shown here use the bounding boxes provided with the PASCAL dataset as object masks for foreground labeling[5]. The foreground labels are used to train linear SVM classifiers over the region histograms, one for each class with all background and other-class regions being treated as negatives. Fig. 7 shows results obtained by using these one-against-all classifiers individually on the test images. Even though

---

[5] This labeling is not perfect. For many training objects, the bounding rectangles contain substantial areas of background, which are thus effectively labeled as foreground. Objects of one class also occur unlabeled in the backgrounds of other classes and, *e.g.*, instances of people sitting on motorbikes are labeled as 'motorbike' not 'person'. In the experiments, these imperfections lead to some visible 'leakage' of labels. We would expect a more consistent foreground labeling to reduce this significantly.

true \ estimated	motorbike	cycle	person	car	background
motorbike	**41.02**	17.58	10.03	18.02	13.34
cycle	20.17	**42.21**	14.66	6.51	16.45
person	9.81	13.67	**55.71**	6.43	14.39
car	18.32	4.56	6.19	**63.00**	7.93
background	7.48	13.66	15.99	19.09	**43.78**
true proportion	20.62	9.50	3.52	4.71	61.65

true \ est.	motorbike	cycle	person	car
motorbike	**69.34**	45.17	19.79	35.76
cycle	49.82	**63.56**	26.08	14.43
person	27.01	35.37	**65.84**	19.54
car	52.43	12.43	10.39	**77.30**
background	16.36	19.81	19.46	23.46
negative	**22.98**	**25.81**	**19.74**	**25.07**

Fig. 8. Confusion matrices for region level labeling. Four two-class linear SVM region classifiers are trained independently, each treating regions from the background and from other classes as negatives. *Left:* A classical confusion matrix for the classifiers in winner-takes-all mode with negative best scores counting as background. The final row gives the population proportions, *i.e.* the score for a random classifier. *Right:* Each column gives entries from the pairwise confusion matrix of the corresponding classifier used alone (independently of the others), with the negative true-class scores (final row) broken down into scores on each other class and on the background. (NB: in this mode, the assigned class labels are not mutually exclusive).

each patch is treated independently, the final labellings are coherent enough to allow the objects to be loosely localized in the images. The average accuracy in classifying local regions over all classes is 69%. This is significantly lower than the performance for classifying images as a whole, but still good enough to be useful as a bottom-up input to higher-level visual routines. Hyperfeatures again add discriminative power to the base level features, giving an average gain of 4–5% in classification performance. Figure 8 shows the key entries of the combined and the two-class confusion matrices, with negatives being further broken down into true background patches and patches from the three remaining classes.

6 Conclusions and Future Work

We have introduced 'hyperfeatures', a new multilevel nonlinear image coding mechanism that generalizes – or more precisely, iterates – the quantize-and-vote process used to create local histograms in texton / bag-of-feature style approaches. Unlike previous multilevel representations such as convolutional neural networks and HMAX, hyperfeatures are optimized for capturing and coding local appearance patches and their co-occurrence statistics. Our experiments show that the introduction of one or more levels of hyperfeatures improves the performance in many classification tasks, especially for object classes that have distinctive geometric or co-occurrence structures.

Future work. The hyperfeature idea is applicable to a wide range of problems involving part-based representations. In this paper the hyperfeature codebooks have been trained bottom-up by unsupervised clustering, but more discriminative training methods should be a fruitful area for future investigation. For example image class labels could usefully be incorporated into the learning of latent topics. We also plan to investigate more general LDA like methods that use local context while training. One way to do this is to formally introduce a "region" (or "subdocument") level in the word–topic–document hierarchy. Such models should allow us to model contextual information at several different levels of support, which may be useful for object detection.

Acknowledgments

We would like to thank the European projects LAVA and PASCAL for financial support, and Diane Larlus, Frederic Jurie, Gyuri Dorko and Navneet Dalal for comments and code. We are also thankful to Andrew Zisserman and Jitendra Malik for providing feedback on this work. Our experiments make use of code derived from C. Bouman's *Cluster* [6] for fitting Gaussian mixtures, D. Blei's implementation of LDA [5], and T. Joachim's SVM-Light [21]. See [2] for extra details on this work.

References

1. Center for Research in Language, International Picture Naming Project. Available from http://crl.ucsd.edu/ aszekely/ipnp/index.html.
2. A. Agarwal and B. Triggs. Hyperfeatures – Multilevel Local Coding for Visual Recognition. Technical report, INRIA Rhône Alpes, 2005.
3. S. Agarwal, A. Awan, and D. Roth. Learning to detect objects in images via a sparse, part-based representation. *PAMI*, 26(11):1475–1490, November 2004.
4. A. Berg and J. Malik. Geometric Blur for Template Matching. In *Int. Conf. Computer Vision & Pattern Recognition*, 2001.
5. D. Blei, A. Ng, and M. Jordan. Latent Dirichlet Allocation. *Journal of Machine Learning Research*, 3:993–1022, 2003.
6. C. A. Bouman. Cluster: An unsupervised algorithm for modeling Gaussian mixtures. Available from http://www.ece.purdue.edu/~bouman, April 1997.
7. W. Buntine and A. Jakaulin. Discrete principal component analysis. Technical report, HIIT, 2005.
8. W. Buntine and S. Perttu. Is multinomial pca multi-faceted clustering or dimensionality reduction? *AI and Statistics*, 2003.
9. J. Canny. Gap: A factor model for discrete data. In *ACM Conference on Information Retrieval (SIGIR)*, Sheffield, U.K., 2004.
10. Visual Object Classes Challenge. The PASCAL Object Recognition Database Collection. Available at www.pascal-network.org/challenges/VOC.
11. G. Csurka, C. Bray, C. Dance, and L. Fan. Visual categorization with bags of keypoints. In *European Conf. Computer Vision*, 2004.
12. G. Dorko and C. Schmid. Object class recognition using discriminative local features. Technical report, INRIA Rhône Alpes, 2005.
13. L. Fei-Fei and P. Perona. A bayesian hierarchical model for learning natural scene categories. In *Int. Conf. Computer Vision & Pattern Recognition*, 2005.
14. A. Ferencz, E. Learned-Miller, and J. Malik. Learning Hyper-Features for Visual Identification. In *Neural Information Processing Systems*, 2004.
15. R. Fergus and P. Perona. The Caltech database. Available at www.vision.caltech.edu/html-files/archive.html.
16. M. Fritz, E. Hayman, B. Caputo, and J.-O. Eklundh. The KTH-TIPS database. Available at www.nada.kth.se/cvap/databases/kth-tips.
17. M. Fritz, E. Hayman, B. Caputo, and J.-O. Eklundh. On the Significance of Real-World Conditions for Material Classification. In *European Conf. Computer Vision*, 2004.
18. K. Fukushima. Neocognitron: a self organizing neural network model for a mechanism of pattern recognition unaffected by shift in position. *Biol. Cybernetics*, 36(4):193–202, 1980.
19. C. Harris and M. Stephens. A Combined Corner and Edge Detector. In *Alvey Vision Conference*, pages 147–151, 1988.

20. T. Hofmann. Probabilistic Latent Semantic Analysis. In *Proc. of Uncertainty in Artificial Intelligence*, Stockholm, 1999.
21. T. Joachims. Making large-Scale SVM Learning Practical. In *Advances in Kernel Methods - Support Vector Learning*. MIT-Press, 1999.
22. F. Jurie and B. Triggs.   Creating Efficient Codebooks for Visual Recognition.   In *Int. Conf. Computer Vision*, 2005.
23. T. Kadir and M. Brady. Saliency, Scale and Image Description. *Int. J. Computer Vision*, 45(2):83–105, 2001.
24. M. Keller and S. Bengio. Theme-Topic Mixture Model for Document Representation. In *PASCAL Workshop on Learning Methods for Text Understanding and Mining*, 2004.
25. G. Lang and P. Seitz. Robust Classification of Arbitrary Object Classes Based on Hierarchical Spatial Feature-Matching. *Machine Vision and Applications*, 10(3):123–135, 1997.
26. S. Lazebnik, C. Schmid, and J. Ponce. Affine-Invariant Local Descriptors and Neighborhood Statistics for Texture Recognition. In *Int. Conf. Computer Vision*, 2003.
27. S. Lazebnik, C. Schmid, and J. Ponce. Semi-local Affine Parts for Object Recognition. In *British Machine Vision Conference*, volume volume 2, pages 779–788, 2004.
28. Y. LeCun, F.-J. Huang, and L. Bottou. Learning Methods for Generic Object Recognition with Invariance to Pose and Lighting. In *CVPR*, 2004.
29. T. Leung and J. Malik.   Recognizing Surfaces Using Three-Dimensional Textons.   In *Int. Conf. Computer Vision*, 1999.
30. D. Lowe.   Distinctive Image Features from Scale-invariant Keypoints. *Int. J. Computer Vision*, 60, 2:91–110, 2004.
31. J. Malik and P. Perona. Preattentive texture discrimination with early vision mechanisms. *J. Optical Society of America*, A 7(5):923–932, May 1990.
32. K. Mikolajczyk and C. Schmid.   A performance evaluation of local descriptors.   *IEEE Trans. Pattern Analysis & Machine Intelligence*, 27(10), 2005.
33. K. Mikolajczyk, T. Tuytelaars, C. Schmid, A. Zisserman, J. Matas, F. Schaffalitzky, T. Kadir, and L. Van Gool. A comparison of affine region detectors. *IJCV*, 65(1/2), 2005.
34. G. Mori and J. Malik.   Recognizing Objects in Adversarial Clutter: Breaking a Visual CAPTCHA. In *Int. Conf. Computer Vision & Pattern Recognition*, 2003.
35. A. Opelt, M. Fussenegger, A. Pinz, and P. Auer. The Graz image databases. Available at http://www.emt.tugraz.at/~pinz/data/.
36. A. Opelt, M. Fussenegger, A. Pinz, and P. Auer. Weak hypotheses and boosting for generic object detection and recognition. In *European Conf. Computer Vision*, 2004.
37. J. Puzicha, T. Hofmann, and J. Buhmann. Histogram Clustering for Unsupervised Segmentation and Image Retrieval. *Pattern Recognition Letters*, 20:899–909, 1999.
38. M. Riesenhuber, T., and Poggio. Hierarchical Models of Object Recognition in Cortex. *Nature Neuroscience*, 2:1019–1025, 1999.
39. F. Schaffalitzky and A. Zisserman. Viewpoint invariant texture matching and wide baseline stereo. In *Int. Conf. Computer Vision*, pages 636–643, Vancouver, 2001.
40. B. Schiele and J. Crowley. Recognition without Correspondence using Multidimensional Receptive Field Histograms. *Int. J. Computer Vision*, 36(1):31–50, January 2000.
41. B. Schiele and A. Pentland.   Probabilistic Object Recognition and Localization.   In *Int. Conf. Computer Vision*, 1999.
42. C. Schmid. Weakly supervised learning of visual models and its application to content-based retrieval. *Int. J. Computer Vision*, 56(1):7–16, 2004.
43. C. Schmid and R. Mohr. Local Grayvalue Invariants for Image Retrieval. *IEEE Trans. Pattern Analysis & Machine Intelligence*, 19(5):530–534, 1997.
44. M. Varma and A. Zisserman.   Texture Classification: Are filter banks necessary?   In *Int. Conf. Computer Vision & Pattern Recognition*, 2003.

Riemannian Manifold Learning for Nonlinear Dimensionality Reduction

Tony Lin[1,*], Hongbin Zha[1], and Sang Uk Lee[2]

[1] National Laboratory on Machine Perception,
Peking University, Beijing 100871, China
{lintong, zha}@cis.pku.edu.cn
[2] School of Electrical Engineering,
Seoul National University, Seoul 151-742, Korea
sanguk@ipl.snu.ac.kr

Abstract. In recent years, nonlinear dimensionality reduction (NLDR) techniques have attracted much attention in visual perception and many other areas of science. We propose an efficient algorithm called Riemannian manifold learning (RML). A Riemannian manifold can be constructed in the form of a simplicial complex, and thus its intrinsic dimension can be reliably estimated. Then the NLDR problem is solved by constructing Riemannian normal coordinates (RNC). Experimental results demonstrate that our algorithm can learn the data's intrinsic geometric structure, yielding uniformly distributed and well organized low-dimensional embedding data.

1 Introduction

In visual perception, a human face image of size of 64×64 pixels is often represented by a vector in a 4096-dimensional space. Obviously, the 4096-dimensional vector space is too large to allow any efficient image processing. A typical way to avoid this "curse of dimensionality" problem [1] is to use dimensionality reduction techniques. Classical linear methods, such as Principal Component Analysis (PCA) [2] and Multidimensional Scaling (MDS) [3], can only see flat Euclidean structures, and fail to discover the curved and nonlinear structures of the input data. Previous nonlinear extensions of PCA and MDS, including Autoencoder Neural Networks [4], SOM [5], Elastic Nets [6], GTM [7], and Principal Curves [8], suffer from the difficulties in designing cost functions and training too many free parameters, or are limited in low-dimensional data sets. In recent years some nonlinear manifold learning techniques have been developed, such as Isomap [9, 10], LLE [11], Laplacian Eigenmaps [12, 13], Hessian Eigenmaps [14], SDE [15], manifold charting [16], LTSA [17], diffusion maps [18]. Due to their nonlinear nature, geometric intuition and computational practicability, these nonlinear manifold learning techniques have attracted extensive attention

---

* This work was supported by NSFC (60302005), NSFC (60333010), NKBRP (2004CB318005) and FANEDD (200038), China.

A. Leonardis, H. Bischof, and A. Pinz (Eds.): ECCV 2006, Part I, LNCS 3951, pp. 44–55, 2006.

of the researchers from different disciplines. The basic assumption is that the input data lie on or close to a smooth low-dimensional manifold [19].

Each manifold learning algorithm attempts to preserve a different geometrical property of the underlying manifold. Local approaches (e.g. LLE [11], Laplacian Eigenmaps [12], LTSA [17]) aim to preserve the local geometry of the data. They are also called spectral methods, since the low dimensional embedding task is reduced to solving a sparse eigenvalue problem under the unit covariance constraint. However, due to this imposed constraint, the aspect ratio is lost and the global shape of the embedding data can not reflect the underlying manifold. In contrast, global approaches like Isomap [9] attempt to preserve metrics at all scales and therefore give a more faithful embedding. However, Isomap, or isometric mapping, can be only applied to intrinsically flat manifolds, e.g. 2D developable surfaces (cylinders, cones, and tangent surfaces). Conformal mapping [10, 20] appears to be a promising direction.

We propose a general framework called Riemannian manifold learning (RML). The problem is formulated as constructing local coordinate charts for a Riemannian manifold. The most widely used is the Riemannian normal coordinates (RNC) chart. In [21] Brun et al. presented a method for manifold learning directly based on the concept of RNC. In order to calculate the geodesic directions, high sampling density is required and the second order polynomial interpolation is computationally expensive. In this paper, we propose a more efficient method to calculate RNC. The basic idea is to preserve geodesic distances and directions only in a local neighborhood. We also describe a novel method for estimating intrinsic dimension of a Riemannian manifold. Our method is derived by reconstructing the manifold in the form of an simplicial complex, whose dimension is determined as the maximal dimension of its simplices.

2   Mathematical Preliminaries

In this section we briefly review some basic concepts of Riemannian geometry [22]. A bijective map is called a homeomorphism if it is continuous in both directions. A (topological) manifold M of dimension m is a Hausdorff space for which every point has a neighborhood U homeomorphic to an open set V of R^m with $\phi : U \to V \subset R^m$. (U, ϕ) is called a local coordinate chart. An atlas for M means a collection of charts $\{(U_\alpha, \phi_\alpha) | \alpha \in J\}$ such that $\{U_\alpha | \alpha \in J\}$ is an open cover of M. A manifold M is called a differential manifold if there is an atlas of M, $\{(U_\alpha, \phi_\alpha) | \alpha \in J\}$, such that for any $\alpha, \beta \in J$, the composite $\phi_\alpha \phi_\beta^{-1} : \phi_\beta(U_\alpha \cap U_\beta) \to R^m$ is differentiable of class C^∞. A differential manifold M endowed with a smooth inner product (called Riemannian metric) $g(u, v)$ or $\langle u, v \rangle$ on each tangent space $T_p M$ is called a Riemannian manifold (M, g).

An exponential map $exp_p(v)$ is a transform from a tangent vector $v \in T_p M$ into a point $q \in \gamma \subset M$ such that $dist(p, q) = ||v|| = \langle v, v \rangle^{1/2}$, where γ is the unique geodesic traveling through p such that its tangent vector at p is v. A geodesic is a smooth curve which locally join their points along the shortest path.

All the geodesics passing through p are called radial geodesics. The local coordinates defined by the chart (U, exp_p^{-1}) are called Riemannian Normal Coordinates (RNC) with center p. Note that the RNC mapping preserves the distances on radial geodesics. A simple example is paring an orange, which maps a sphere onto a plane, while the distances on the great circles of the sphere are preserved.

3   Manifold Assumption

Most manifold learning algorithms [9, 11, 19] assume that a set of image data may generate a low-dimensional manifold in a high-dimensional image space. Here we present a simple geometric imaging model (shown in Fig. 1) for human face images to clarify this assumption. Varying poses and lighting conditions are considered in this model, as they are two important factors in face detection and recognition. The model may be adapted to image data of other objects (e.g. cars), if similar imaging conditions are encountered.

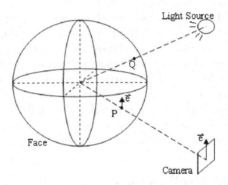

Fig. 1. A geometric imaging model for human face images

We model the head of a human as a unit sphere S^2, where the frontal hemisphere is the human face. Different poses are obtained by moving the camera, as the human face is kept in stationary. The focal length is assumed to be unchanged in the imaging process. We also assume that the distance from the camera to the face is fixed, so the face images have similar scales. Commonly, the center axis of the camera is set to passing through the center of the sphere. The camera is allowed to have some degree of planar rotations. The lighting is simply modeled with a point light source far away from the sphere. Under these variations, this set of face images generates a 5-dimensional manifold, which is homeomorphic to

$$M = \{PQe | P \in S^2, Q \in S^2, e \in S^1\},$$

where P and Q are two intersection points on S^2 by the center axis of the camera and the lighting ray, and e is a unit vector to show the planar rotation angle of the camera. This representation is just a simple extension of the parametric representation of a surface, $r = r(u, v)$, where (u, v) are two varying parameters. If the lighting variation is ignored, a 3-dimensional manifold may be generated:

$$M' = \{Pe | P \in S^2, e \in S^1\}.$$

This is called a circle bundle on a sphere, which is one of the simplest tangent bundles. This manifold can be visualized as the earth running in its circular orbit in the 4-dimensional space-time.

4   Manifold Reconstruction

The m-manifold M generated from a set of data points in R^n is modeled with an approximating simplicial complex, whose dimension serves as a reliable estimation of the intrinsic dimension of M. Our manifold reconstruction is a simplified version of Freedman's method [23], which involves a computationally expensive optimization for convex hulls.

The key to the reconstruction problem from unstructured sample points is to recover the edge connections within a local neighborhood. The neighborhood of one point $p \in M$, denoted $NBD(p)$, is defined as the K nearest points to p. K is often set as $c \times m'$, where c is a constant number between 2 and 5, and m' is an initial estimation of the intrinsic dimension m. Then we select k $(1 \leq k \leq K)$ edge points from the K neighbors, such that the edge connections are built between p and each edge point. Note that the number of edge points, k, is varying with p. A point q is said to be an edge point of p if no other point r separates p and q by the normal plane passing through r and perpendicular to the line (p, r). Formally, the edge point set of point p is defined as

$$EP(p) = \{q \in NBD(p) \mid \langle p - r, q - r \rangle \geq 0, \text{ any } r \in NBD(p)\}.$$

It is easy to show that by this definition, the angle between any two adjacent edges is acute or right, while obtuse angles are prohibited. This property guarantees to yield well-shaped simplices, which are basic building blocks to construct the target simplicial complex. The underlying reason for this property is explained by a simple example shown in Fig. 2. It is often believed that the 1D reconstruction in (b) is much better than the 2D reconstruction in (c). These points are more likely to be sampled from a 1D curve, rather than a 2D surface. The width of the 2D complex in (c) is too small and thus can be ignored. In fact, any thin rope in the physical world can be modeled as a 1D curve by ignoring its radius. This definition of an edge point permits edge connections like (b) while (c) is prohibited.

Simplices in each dimension are constructed by grouping adjacent edges. For example, if (p, q) is an edge and r is any other point, a triangle (p, q, r) is generated when there are two edges (p, r) and (q, r). This procedure repeats from low-dimensional to high-dimensional, until there are no new simplices generated. The target simplicial complex is composed of all the simplices. The dimension of the complex is a good estimate of the intrinsic dimension of M.

Fig. 2. Reconstruction of five points sampled from a curve. (a) Unorganized points. (b) 1D reconstruction. (c) 2D reconstruction.

5 Manifold Charting

Manifold charting consists of two steps: (1) Compute the tangent space and set up a Cartesian coordinate system; (2) Use Dijkstra's algorithm to find single-source shortest paths, and calculate the Riemannian Normal Coordinates (RNC) for each end point of the shortest paths.

In principle, the base point p for a RNC chart may be freely selected. Here we choose the base point close to the center of the input data. For each candidate point, the maximal geodesic distance (called geodesic radius) is computed using Dijkstra's algorithm. One point with the minimal geodesic radius is the optimal base point.

A local coordinate chart is set up by computing the tangent space $T_p M$:

$$x_0 + \text{span}\{x_1 - x_0, \ldots, x_m - x_0\},$$

where $\{x_0, x_1, \ldots, x_m\}$ are $(m + 1)$ geometrically independent edge points (or nearest neighbors) of p. Any point on the tangent space can be represented as

$$x_0 + \sum_{i=1}^{m} \lambda_i (x_i - x_0).$$

An orthonormal frame, denoted $(p \, ; e_1, \ldots, e_m)$, is computed from the vectors $\{x_1 - x_0, \ldots, x_m - x_0\}$ by using the Gram-Schmidt orthogonalization.

Then the Dijkstra's algorithm [24] is exploited to find single-source shortest paths in the graph determined by the simplicial complex. Each time a new shortest path is found, we compute the RNC of the end point on this path. If the end point q is an edge point of p, we directly compute the projection of q, denoted $q' \in R^m$, onto the tangent space frame $(p \, ; e_1, \ldots, e_m)$ by solving the following least squares problem

$$\min_{X \in R^m} \left\| q - \left(p + \sum_{i=1}^{m} x_i e_i \right) \right\|^2,$$

where $X = (x_1, x_2, \ldots, x_m)$ are the projection coordinates of q' in the tangent space. The RNC of q is given by

$$\frac{\|q - p\|_{R^n}}{\|X\|_{R^m}} X \,,$$

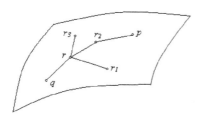

Fig. 3. An example illustrating how to compute the RNC of q. In this case, q is not an edge point of the base point p.

since the RNC preserves the distances on each radial geodesic, which is approximated by the corresponding shortest path.

If the end point $q \in M \subset R^n$ is not an edge point of p, the RNC of q (denoted q') is computed by solving a quadratically constrained linear least squares problem. Let point r be the previous point on the shortest path from p to q. Let $\{r_1, \ldots, r_k\}$ be the edge points (or nearest neighbors if needed) of r, whose RNCs have been computed. The number of these points, k, is required to be larger than or equal to m in order to guarantee the constrained least squares problem to be correctly solved. (One exception may occur at the beginning of the Dijkstra's algorithm, when k is less than m. In this case, point q is treated as an edge point of p to compute its RNC.) Fig. 3 shows such an example with $k = 3$. The basic idea is that we want to preserve the angles in the neighborhood of r, while keeping the geodesic distance from q to r unchanged. This leads to the following linear least squares problem

$$\cos\theta = \frac{\langle q - r, r_i - r \rangle}{\|q - r\| \cdot \|r_i - r\|} \approx \cos\theta' = \frac{\langle q' - r', r_i' - r' \rangle}{\|q' - r'\| \cdot \|r_i' - r'\|}, \quad i = 1, 2, \ldots, k$$

with a quadratic constraint

$$\|q - r\| = \|q' - r'\|,$$

where q', r', and r_i' are the RNCs of q, r, and r_i. Our goal is to compute $q' \in R^m$.

We get the following linear least squares problem with quadratic constraints [25]:

$$\min_{x \in R^m} \|A_{k \times m} x_{m \times 1} - b_{k \times 1}\|^2 \text{ subject to } \|x_{m \times 1}\|^2 = \alpha^2 \ (k \geq m).$$

This problem can be solved by the following Lagrange multipliers optimization

$$\phi(x, \lambda) = \|b - Ax\|^2 + \lambda(\|x\|^2 - \alpha^2) = (b^T - x^T A^T)(b - Ax) + \lambda(x^T x - \alpha^2).$$

Setting the gradient of this function with respect to x (and not λ) equal to zero yields the equation

$$\frac{\partial\phi}{\partial x} = -2A^T b + 2A^T Ax + 2\lambda x = 0,$$

which has the solution

$$x = (A^T A + \lambda I)^{-1} A^T b$$

provided the inverse of $(A^T A + \lambda I)$ exists. Substituting this result into the constraint $\|x\|^2 = \alpha^2$, we have

$$\psi(\lambda) = b^T A (A^T A + \lambda I)^{-2} A^T b - \alpha^2 = 0.$$

Let $A = U \Sigma V^T$ be the singular value decomposition of A. Then our constraint equation becomes

$$
\begin{aligned}
\psi(\lambda) = 0 &= b^T U \Sigma V^T (V \Sigma^T U^T U \Sigma V^T + \lambda I)^{-2} V \Sigma^T U^T b - \alpha^2 \\
&= b^T U \Sigma V^T (V (\Sigma^T \Sigma + \lambda I) V^T)^{-2} V \Sigma^T U^T b - \alpha^2 \\
&= b^T U \Sigma V^T (V (\Sigma^T \Sigma + \lambda I) V^T V (\Sigma^T \Sigma + \lambda I) V^T)^{-1} V \Sigma^T U^T b - \alpha^2 \\
&= b^T U \Sigma (\Sigma^T \Sigma + \lambda I)^{-2} \Sigma^T U^T b - \alpha^2.
\end{aligned}
$$

Letting $\beta = U^T b$, we get

$$\psi(\lambda) = \sum_{i=1}^{m} \frac{\beta_i^2 \sigma_i^2}{(\sigma_i^2 + \lambda)^2} - \alpha^2 = 0.$$

It is easy to verify that $\psi(\lambda)$ decrease from ∞ to $-\alpha^2$ as λ goes from $-\sigma_m^2$ to ∞. We can use Newton's method to find the root λ. A good initial value for λ is zero, and the objective function vanishes to zero very fast.

Notice that the RNC of one data point can be efficiently computed in a local neighborhood, not involving any global optimization.

6   Experimental Results

First we test our dimension estimation method on four data sets [9, 11]: Swiss roll data, Isomap face data, LLE face data, and ORL face data. The number of the nearest neighbors, K, is set to 7, 8, 12, and 12, respectively. Table 1 shows the numbers of simplices in each dimension. Recall that the dimension of a complex is the maximal dimension of its simplices. For instance, the complex generated from Swiss roll data is composed of 1357 2D simplices, while no 3D simplices are contained in this complex. Therefore, the estimated dimension for Swiss roll

Table 1. Numbers of simplices in each dimension

Dim.	0	1	2	3	4	5	6	7	8	9	10
Swiss roll	1000	1800	1357	0							
Isomap	698	2337	5072	3782	751	0					
LLE		1965	6177	22082	40500	40384	19726	2820	0		
ORL		400	3011	11048	30602	91575	304923	932544	2261383	3674580	2835000 0

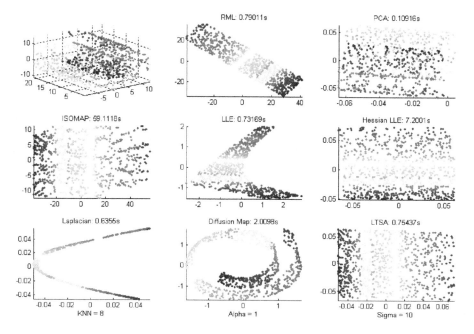

Fig. 4. Comparison results of Swiss Roll

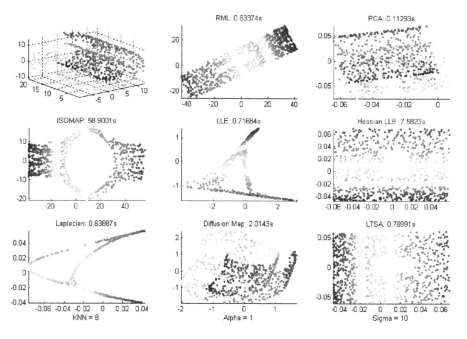

Fig. 5. Comparison results of Swiss Hole

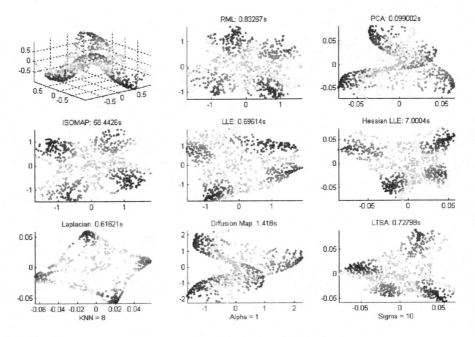

Fig. 6. Comparison results of Twin Peaks

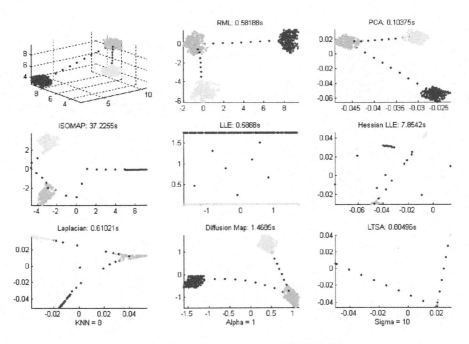

Fig. 7. Comparison results of 3D Clusters

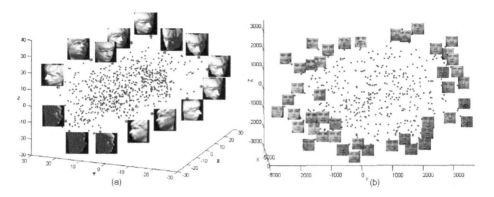

Fig. 8. Three-dimensional embedding: (a) Isomap face data; (b) ORL face data

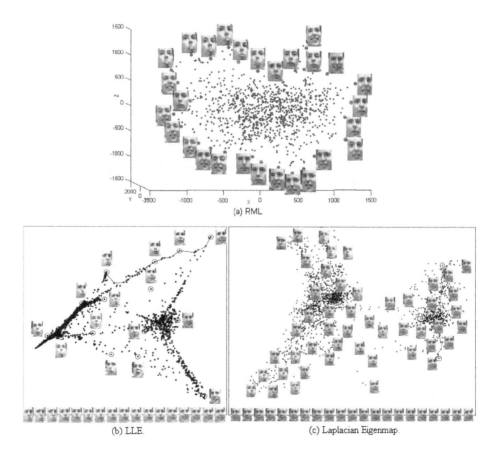

Fig. 9. Comparison results of LLE face data

is 2. Notice that our estimation for the Isomap face dataset is 4, though it is rendered with 3 parameters (one for lighting and two for pose). Several other methods [26] reported similar estimates of about 4 dimension.

Second, four sets of synthetic data from the MANI demo (http://www.math. umn.edu/~wittman/mani/) and the above three sets of face data are used to illustrate the behavior of our manifold learning algorithm RML. For synthetic data, several other competing algorithms (PCA, Isomap, LLE, HLLE, Laplacian Eigenmaps, Diffusion maps, LTSA) are compared and the results are shown in Fig. 4-7. RML outperforms other algorithms by correctly learning the nonlinear geometry of each data set. Both RML and Isomap have metric-preserving properties, e.g. intrinsically mapping Swiss Roll data onto a 2D Rectangle region. However, Isomap fails on Swiss Hole. In general, LTSA and HLLE consistently perform better than other spectral methods, though they cannot preserve the original metrics of each data set. The running speed of RML is less than one second, which is comparable to that of LLE, Laplacian Eigenmaps, and LTSA. Often HLLE and Diffusion maps spend several seconds, while Isomap needs one minute. Fig. 8-9 show the embedding results of three sets of face data. In contrast to LLE [11] and Laplacian Eigenmaps [13], RML yields embedding results that are uniformly distributed and well organized.

7   Conclusion

We presented a RNC-based manifold learning method for nonlinear dimensionality reduction, which can learn intrinsic geometry of the underlying manifold with metric-preserving properties. Experimental results demonstrate the excellent performance of our algorithm on synthetic and real data sets. The algorithm should find a wide variety of potential applications, such as data analysis, visualization, and classification.

References

1. Donoho, D.: High-Dimensional Data Analysis: The Curses and Blessings of Dimensionality. Mathematical Challenges of the 21st Century. American Mathematical Society, Los Angeles, CA (2000)
2. Jolliffe, I.: Principal Component Analysis. Springer-Verlag, New York (1989)
3. Cox, T., Cox, M.: Multidimensional Scaling. Chapman & Hall, London (1994)
4. Bourlard, H., Kamp, Y.: Auto-association by multilayer perceptrons and singular value decomposition. Biological Cybernetics **59** (1988) 291–294
5. Erwin, E., Obermayer, K., Schulten, K.: Self-organizing maps: Ordering, convergence properties and energy functions. Biological Cybernetics **67** (1992) 47–55
6. Durbin, R., Willshaw, D.: An analogue approach to the travelling salesman problem using an elastic net method. Nature **326** (1987) 689–691
7. Bishop, C., Svenson, M., Williams, C.: Gtm: The generative topographic mapping. Neural Computation **10** (1998) 215–234
8. Hastie, T., Stuetzle, W.: Principal curves. J. American Statistical Association **84** (1989) 502–516

9. Tenenbaum, J., Silva, V.d., Langford, J.: A global geometric framework for nonlinear dimensionality reduction. Science **290** (2000) 2319–2323
10. Silva, V., Tenenbaum, J.: Global versus local methods in nonlinear dimensionality reduction. Advances in Neural Information Processing Systems, MIT Press (2003)
11. Roweis, S., Saul, L.: Nonlinear dimensionality reduction by locally linear embedding. Science **290** (2000) 2323–2326
12. Belkin, M., Niyogi, P.: Laplacian eigenmaps for dimensionality reduction and data representation. Neural Computation **15** (2003) 1373–1396
13. He, X., Yan, S., Hu, Y., Niyogi, P., Zhang, H.: Face recognition using laplacianfaces. IEEE Trans. Pattern Analysis and Machine Intelligence **27** (2005) 328–340
14. Donoho, D., Grimes, C.: Hessian eigenmaps: New tools for nonlinear dimensionality reduction. Proc. National Academy of Science (2003) 5591–5596
15. Weinberger, K., Saul, L.: Unsupervised learning of image manifolds by semidefinite programming. Proc. CVPR (2004) 988–995
16. Brand, M.: Charting a manifold. Advances in Neural Information Processing Systems, MIT Press (2003)
17. Zhang, Z., Zha, H.: Principal manifolds and nonlinear dimensionality reduction via tangent space alignment. SIAM Journal on Scientific Computing **26** (2004) 313–338
18. Nadler, B., Lafon, S., Coifman, R., Kevrekidis, I.: Diffusion maps, spectral clustering and reaction coordinates of dynamical systems. (submitted to Journal of Applied and Computational Harmonic Analysis)
19. Seung, H., Lee, D.: The manifold ways of perception. Science **290** (2000) 2268–2269
20. Sha, F., Saul, L.: Analysis and extension of spectral methods for nonlinear dimensionality reduction. Proc. Int. Conf. Machine Learning, Germany (2005)
21. Brun, A., Westin, C.F., Herberthson, M., Knutsson, H.: Fast manifold learning based on riemannian normal coordinates. Proc. 14th Scandinavian Conf. on Image Analysis, Joensuu, Finland (2005)
22. Jost, J.: Riemannian Geometry and Geometric Analysis. 3rd edn. Springer (2002)
23. Freedman, D.: Efficient simplicial reconstructions of manifolds from their samples. IEEE Trans. Pattern Analysis and Machine Intelligence **24** (2002) 1349–1357
24. Cormen, T., Leiserson, C., Rivest, R., Stein, C.: Introduction to Algorithms. MIT Press, Cambridge (2001)
25. Golub, G., Loan, C.: Matrix Computations. 3rd edn. Jonhs Hopkins Univ. (1996)
26. Levina, E., Bickel, P.: Maximum likelihood estimation of intrinsic dimension. Advances in Neural Information Processing Systems, MIT Press (2004)

Controlling Sparseness in Non-negative Tensor Factorization

Matthias Heiler and Christoph Schnörr

Computer Vision, Graphics, and Pattern Recognition Group,
Department of Mathematics and Computer Science,
University of Mannheim, 68131 Mannheim, Germany
{heiler, schnoerr}@uni-mannheim.de

Abstract. Non-negative tensor factorization (NTF) has recently been proposed as sparse and efficient image representation *(Welling and Weber, Patt. Rec. Let., 2001)*. Until now, sparsity of the tensor factorization has been empirically observed in many cases, but there was no systematic way to control it. In this work, we show that a sparsity measure recently proposed for non-negative *matrix* factorization *(Hoyer, J. Mach. Learn. Res., 2004)* applies to NTF and allows precise control over sparseness of the resulting factorization. We devise an algorithm based on sequential conic programming and show improved performance over classical NTF codes on artificial and on real-world data sets.

1   Introduction and Related Work

Non-negative tensor factorization (NTF) has recently been proposed as sparse and efficient image representation [1, 2, 3]. Compared to non-negative *matrix* factorization (NMF) [4, 5], which has also been used for image modeling [6], tensor factorization offers some advantages due to the fact that spacial and temporal correlations are accounted for more accurately than in NMF where images and videos are treated as vectors [7]. In particular, it has been reported that compared to NMF tensor factorization shows a greater degree of sparsity, clearer separation of image parts, better recognition rates, and a tenfold increased compression ratio [3].

From a data analysis viewpoint, NTF is attractive because it usually allows for a *unique decomposition* of a data set into factors. In contrast, while NMF will be unique up to permutation and scaling under some conditions, there are realistic scenarios where additive factors are not separated into independent factors but pollute the whole image basis with "ghost artifacts" [8]. This is not the case with NTF: Under mild conditions, which are usually satisfied by real-world data, tensor factorization is unique [9, 10].

However, until now it was not possible to exercise *explicit sparsity control* with NTF. This differs from NMF where very efficient sparsity control was introduced in [11]. The main problem is that current algorithms for NTF [2] are often variations of general nonlinear programming codes that can be very fast

A. Leonardis, H. Bischof, and A. Pinz (Eds.): ECCV 2006, Part I, LNCS 3951, pp. 56–67, 2006.

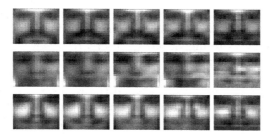

Fig. 1. Sparse NTF face model. MIT CBCL faces are factorized ($k = 10$) and re-constructed using sparsity-control for horizontal factors u_1 (see text). The min-sparsity constraints were 0.0, 0.2, 0.4, 0.6, 0.8 (from left to right). Starting from $s_i^{\min} = 0.4$ re-constructions look increasingly generic and individual features disappear.

as long as sparsity constraints are absent [12, 13]. With additional sparsity constraints the corresponding *projected gradient descent* algorithm [11] can converge slowly. This aggravates with NTF where individual factors interact in a more complicated way.

For sparsity controlled NMF, approaches from convex programming and global optimization [14] have thus been proposed [15]. In this work, we build on such ideas to allow for *fully sparsity-controlled NTF models* and study the behavior of the resulting model on artificial data and on databases of real-world images.

Overview. After this introduction we discuss the sparsity-controlled NTF problem in Sec. 2. In Sec. 3 we provide a practical algorithm to solve the problem. We validate it empirically in Sec. 4 before we summarize our paper in Sec. 5.

Notation. We represent image data as tensor of order 3, e.g., $V \in \mathbb{R}_+^{d_1 \times d_2 \times d_3}$ denotes d_3 images of size $d_1 \times d_2$. We are not concerned about the transformation properties of V, so this simplified 3-way array notation is sufficient. The factorization is given by vectors $u_i^j \in \mathbb{R}^{d_i}$, where $j = 1, \ldots, k$ indexes k independent vectors. Where convenient, we omit indices of the factors, e.g., $u_i \in \mathbb{R}^{d_i \times k}$ is the matrix of k factors corresponding to index i, and u alone is the ordered set of such matrices.

2 The NTF Optimization Problem and Sparseness

In this section we formally state the NTF optimization problem in its original form and extended by sparseness constraints.

2.1 Original NTF Model

The NTF optimization problem admits the general form

$$\min_{u_i^j \in \mathbb{R}^{d_i}} \quad \|V - \sum_{j=1}^{k} \bigotimes_{i=1}^{3} u_i^j\|_F^2 \tag{1}$$

$$\text{s.t.} \quad 0 \leq u_i^j.$$

Here, image volume V is approximated by the sum of k rank-1 tensors that are outer products $u_1^j \otimes u_2^j \otimes u_3^j$. By using outer products with additional factors $u_i^j, i > 3$, this generalizes to higher-order tensors. In this work, however, we are concerned with image volumes only.

It is instructive to compare NTF with the more widespread NMF model: In NMF, image data is first vectorized, and the resulting non-negative matrix $V \in \mathbb{R}_+^{m \times d_3}$, $m = d_1 \cdot d_2$, is then factorized as the product of two non-negative matrices $W \in \mathbb{R}_+^{m \times k}$ and $H \in \mathbb{R}_+^{k \times d_3}$. In short, one optimizes

$$\min_{W,H} \quad \|V - WH\|_F^2$$
$$\text{s.t.} \quad 0 \leq W, H. \tag{2}$$

It is clear that the vectorized representation does not take into account the spatio-temporal correlations of image data or video. In contrast, the NTF analogon to basis images are rank-one matrices $u_1^j \otimes u_2^j$ that nicely represent correlations along the x and y direction of the image plane. The price to pay is that with NTF basis images are no longer arbitrary: The rank one restriction rules out, e.g., basis images with diagonal structures.

2.2 Sparsity-Constrained NTF

It has early been reported that NTF codes tend do be *sparse*, i.e., many entries of the u_i^j equal zero [1]. Especially for pattern recognition applications, sparsity is a key property since it relates directly to learnability [16, 17] and is biologically well motivated [18]. Sparsity also seems to act as a strong prior for *localized image representations* [11]. Such representations are desirable since they naturally focus on *parts* and thus are potentially *more robust against occlusion or noise* than are their global counterparts.

Thus, the following sparseness measure has been suggested for NMF [11]:

$$\text{sp}(x) := \frac{1}{\sqrt{n} - 1} \left(\sqrt{n} - \frac{\|x\|_1}{\|x\|_2} \right). \tag{3}$$

It assigns to each vector[1] $x \in \mathbb{R}^n \setminus \{0\}$ a real number within $[0, 1]$ where $\text{sp}(x) = 0$ corresponds to a uniform vector with $x_i = const > 0, \forall i$, and $\text{sp}(x) = 1$ corresponds to a vector with a single non-zero element. Since $\text{sp}(x)$ is not affected by multiplicative factors, i.e., $c > 0 \Rightarrow \forall x : \text{sp}(x) = \text{sp}(c \cdot x)$, and varies continuously between the two boundary cases it serves as a convenient and expressive sparsity measure. Empirically, it has been observed that extending (2) by sparseness constraints can lead to considerably improved non-negative basis functions which are more localized and allow easier semantic interpretation [11, 15].

---

[1] Where convenient, we will also use $\text{sp}(M) \in \mathbb{R}^n$ for matrices $M \in \mathbb{R}^{m \times n}$. Then, sparsity is measured for each column of M and the results are stacked into a vector.

Thus, it is desirable to extend (1) by similar sparsity-controlling constraints, leading to the problem

$$
\begin{aligned}
\min_{u_i^j \in \mathbb{R}^{d_i}} \quad & \|V - \sum_{j=1}^{k} \bigotimes_{i=1}^{3} u_i^j\|_F^2 \\
\text{s.t.} \quad & 0 \leq u_i \\
& s_i^{\min} \leq \mathrm{sp}(u_i) \leq s_i^{\max}.
\end{aligned}
\tag{4}
$$

The parameters $s_i^{\min}$ and $s_i^{\max}$ are real numbers in $[0, 1]$ specified by the user for a given application. We propose solvers for (4) in Sec. 3 and validate the model on artificial and on real-world data in Sec. 4.

3   Solving Sparsity-Constrained NTF

In this section, we develop an algorithm for solving problem (4). The basic building block of our method are *second order cone programs* (SOCPs) which we introduce in Sec. 3.1. In Sec. 3.2 we propose an algorithm that dually and alternately optimizes sparseness and reconstruction quality of the tensor approximation.

3.1   Sparsity and Second Order Cones

From an optimization viewpoint, it is important to note that (3) models a *second order conic set* [19]. The second order standard cone $\mathcal{L}^{n+1} \subset \mathbb{R}^{n+1}$ is the convex set:

$$
\mathcal{L}^{n+1} := \left\{ \begin{pmatrix} x \\ t \end{pmatrix} = (x_1, \ldots, x_n, t)^\top \ \middle| \ \|x\|_2 \leq t \right\}.
\tag{5}
$$

As second order cones are useful in modeling a range of applications and are computationally convenient at the same time, they gave rise to the framework of second order cone programming [19]. In SOCP one considers problems with conic constraints that admit the general form

$$
\begin{aligned}
\inf_{x \in \mathbb{R}^n} \quad & f^\top x \\
\text{s.t.} \quad & \begin{pmatrix} A_i x + b_i \\ c_i^\top x + d_i \end{pmatrix} \in \mathcal{L}^{n+1}, \qquad i = 1, \ldots, m.
\end{aligned}
\tag{6}
$$

Being convex problems, efficient and robust solvers for SOCPs exist in software [20, 21, 22]. Furthermore, additional linear constraints and, in particular, the condition $x \in \mathbb{R}_+^n$ are admissible, as they are special cases of constraints of the form (6).

Considering the sparseness function (3) it has been pointed out [15] that the set of non-negative vectors $x \geq 0$ no sparser than $s \in [0, 1]$ is given by the second order cone

$$
C(s) := \left\{ x \in \mathbb{R}^n \ \middle| \ \begin{pmatrix} x \\ \frac{1}{c_{n,s}} e^\top x \end{pmatrix} \in \mathcal{L}^{n+1} \right\}, \qquad c_{n,s} := \sqrt{n} - (\sqrt{n} - 1)s.
\tag{7}
$$

In this light, we can rewrite (4) as

$$\min_{u_i^j} \quad \|V - \sum_{j=1}^{k} \bigotimes_{i=1}^{3} u_i^j\|_F^2 \tag{8}$$
$$\text{s.t.} \quad u_i^j \in (\mathbb{R}_+^{d_i} \cap C(s_i^{\max})) \setminus C(s_i^{\min}), \quad j = 1, \dots, k.$$

This notation makes explicit that the constraints consist of a *convex* part $u_i^j \in \{\mathbb{R}_+^{d_i} \cap C(s_i^{\max})\}$ and a *reverse-convex* part $u_i^j \notin C(s_i^{\min})$. The two fundamental challenges to address are thus, first, the non-convex objective function, and, second, the reverse-convex min-sparsity constraint.

3.2   The Sparsity Maximization Algorithm (SMA)

We use two strategies to cope with the basic challenges in problem (8): First, to address the non-convexity of the objective function, we apply an *alternate minimization approach* where only one component u_i, $i \in \{1, 2, 3\}$, is optimized at a time while the other two components are held constant. The resulting objective function is convex quadratic in each step. Alternate minimization is very popular with NMF, NTF, and similar models and seems to perform well in experiments [1, 2, 3, 4, 5, 6, 13, 15]. Note that for problems where memory is not a major concern, *joint* optimizations of pairs or triplets of the u_i components may offer performance benefits, especially toward the end of an optimization [5, 23]. For our sparsity maximization-approach, however, we will remain with the more memory efficient and simpler scheme of strict alternate minimization.

To deal with the second challenge, the reverse-convex min-sparsity constraint, we adopt an approach from global optimization [24]: Given a current estimate for u_i we compute the maximally sparse approximation subject to the constraint that the reconstruction error does not deteriorate, and, dually, given a maximally sparse approximation we minimize the reconstruction error subject to the constraint that the min-sparsity constraint may not be violated.

Let us assume that within the alternate minimization approach ("outer loop") we optimize component u_i, while the components $\bar{I} := \{1, 2, 3\} \setminus \{i\}$ remain fixed. Then the target function $f(V, u) := \|V - \sum_{j=1}^{k} \bigotimes_{i=1}^{3} u_i^j\|_F^2$ can be written as $f(V, u_i) = \|\text{vec}(V) - U\text{vec}(u_i)\|_2^2$, where U is a sparse matrix containing the corresponding entries u_i, $i \in \bar{I}$, that are not currently optimized.

Initialization. We start with any u_i that obeys the constraints of (8). A simple way to obtain such an initialization is to first solve the problem ignoring the min-sparsity constraint, i.e.,

$$\min_{u_i} \quad f(V, u_i) \tag{9}$$
$$\text{s.t.} \quad u_i^j \in \mathbb{R}_+^{d_i} \cap C(s_i^{\max}), \quad j = 1, \dots, k$$

which is a SOCP that reads in standard form

$$\min_{u_i, z} \quad z$$

$$\text{s.t.} \quad 0 \leq u_i$$

$$\begin{pmatrix} \text{vec}(V) - U\text{vec}(u_i) \\ z \end{pmatrix} \in \mathcal{L}^{kd_i+1} \tag{10}$$

$$\begin{pmatrix} u_i^j \\ (c_{d_i, s_i^{\max}})^{-1} e^\top u_i^j \end{pmatrix} \in \mathcal{L}^{d_i+1}, \quad j = 1, \ldots, k.$$

The resulting u_i can then be projected on the boundary of the min-sparsity cone. Accuracy is of no concern in this step, so simple element-wise exponentiation followed by normalization

$$\pi(u_i^j) \propto \frac{(u_i^j)^t}{\|(u_i^j)^t\|_2} \tag{11}$$

with suitable parameter t, yields a feasible initialization.

Step one. In the first step we maximize worst-case sparsity subject to the constraint that reconstruction accuracy may not deteriorate:

$$\max_{u_i} \quad \min_j \text{sp}(u_i^j)$$

$$\text{s.t.} \quad u_i^j \in \mathbb{R}_+^{d_i} \cap C(s_i^{\max}), \quad j = 1, \ldots, k \tag{12}$$

$$f(V, u_i) \leq f(V, \bar{u}_i),$$

where $\bar{u}_i$ is the estimate for u_i before sparsity maximization. Problems similar to (12) have been solved using cutting plane methods, however, such solvers seem to perform well for small to medium-sized problems only [24, 14]. For the large scale problems common in computer vision and machine learning, we must content ourselves with a local solution obtained by *linearization* of the sparsity cone around the current estimate $\bar{u}_i$. The resulting problem is a SOCP:

$$\max_{u_i, z} \quad z \tag{13a}$$

$$\text{s.t.} \quad u_i^j \in \mathbb{R}_+^{d_i} \cap C(s_i^{\max}), \quad j = 1, \ldots, k \tag{13b}$$

$$f(V, u_i) \leq f(V, \bar{u}_i) \tag{13c}$$

$$z \leq \text{sp}(\bar{u}_i^j) + \langle \nabla \text{sp}(\bar{u}_i^j), u_i^j - \bar{u}_i^j \rangle, \quad j = 1, \ldots, k. \tag{13d}$$

Note that $\text{sp}(x)$ is convex, so the linearization (13) is valid in the sense that min-sparsity will never decrease in step one.

Step two. In the second step we improve the objective function while paying attention not to violate the min-sparsity constraints. Given the sparsity-maximized estimate $\bar{u}_i$ we solve the SOCP

$$\min_{u_i} \quad f(V, u_i) \tag{14a}$$

$$\text{s.t.} \quad u_i^j \in \mathbb{R}_+^{d_i} \cap C(s_i^{\max}), \quad j = 1, \ldots, k \tag{14b}$$

$$\|u_i^j - \bar{u}_i^j\|_2 \leq \min_{q \in C(s_i^{\min})} \|q - \bar{u}_i^j\|_2, \quad j = 1, \ldots, k \tag{14c}$$

Algorithm 1. The sparsity maximization algorithm in pseudocode

1: initialize all u_i^j using eqn. (10) and (11), set $\bar{u} \leftarrow u$
2: **repeat**
3:    **for** $i = 1$ to 3 **do**
4:       **repeat**
5:          $u_{\text{old}} \leftarrow u$
6:          $\bar{u}_i \leftarrow$ solution of (13)
7:          $u_i \leftarrow$ solution of (14)
8:       **until** $|f(V, u_i) - f(V, u_{\text{old},i})| \leq \epsilon$
9:    **end for**
10: **until** no improvement found in loop 3–9

which is straightforward to translate to standard form. Note that constraints (14c) make sure that the resulting u_i^j will not enter the min-sparsity cone. In effect, the reverse-convex min-sparsity constraint is translated in (14) into a convex proximity constraint. This is similar to *trust region* approaches common in nonlinear programming.

Termination. After the second step we check whether $f(V, u_i)$ improved more than ϵ. If it did we jump to step one, otherwise we switch in the outer loop to a different factor i. The whole algorithm is outlined in Alg. 1.

3.3   Convergence Properties

Regarding termination of Alg. 1, we assert:

Proposition 1. *The SMA algorithm (Alg. 1) terminates in finite time for any sparsity-constrained NTF problem.*

Proof (sketch). For lack of space, we omit technicalities and note that:

- Step 1 consists of solving three convex programs and subsequent projections. These operations will terminate in polynomial time.
- Any current estimate u is a feasible point for the convex programs (polynomial time) in the inner loop (steps 6 and 7). Thus, with each iteration of the inner loop the objective value $f(V, u)$ can only decrease or remain constant.
- Since $f(V, u)$ is bounded from below, the inner loop will eventually terminate (step 8).
- And so will the outer loop (step 10) for the same reason.   □

The algorithm conveniently converges on a stationary point if the constraints are *regular*. Following [24] we call constraints regular if their gradients are linearly independent and if removing one would allow for a new optimum with lower objective value. From a practical viewpoint, this means that in particular we assume $s_i^{\min} < s_i^{\max}$, i.e., the interior of the feasible set is not empty.

Proposition 2. *Under regular sparsity constraints, Alg. 1 converges on a stationary point of problem (4).*

Proof. The first order optimality conditions for problem (4) read:

$$-\frac{\partial L}{\partial u_i^*} \in N_{Q_i}(u_i^*), \tag{15a}$$

$$G_i(u_i^*) \in \mathbb{R}_+^k, \tag{15b}$$

$$\lambda_i^* \in R_-^k, \tag{15c}$$

$$\langle \lambda_i^*, u_i^* \rangle = 0, \tag{15d}$$

where i runs from 1 to 3. Here,

$$L(u, \lambda_1, \lambda_2, \lambda_3) = f(V, u) + \sum_{i=1}^{3} \lambda_i^\top G_i(u_i) \tag{16}$$

is the Lagrangean of the problem and

$$G_i(u_i) = \left(\|u_i^1\|_2 - (c_{d_i, s_i^{\min}})^{-1} \|u_i^1\|_1, \cdots, \|u_i^k\|_2 - (c_{d_i, s_i^{\min}})^{-1} \|u_i^k\|_1 \right)^\top \tag{17}$$

encodes the min-sparsity constraints: $G_i(u_i)$ is non-negative if the min-sparsity constraints on u_i are adhered to. Finally, N_{Q_i} in (15a) is the normal cone [25] to the convex set $R_+^{d_i \times k} \cap C(s_i^{\max})$, $i = 1, \ldots, 3$.

Now assume the algorithm converged (Prop. 1) on a point $\tilde{u}$. Because $\mathrm{sp}(\cdot)$ is convex and the constraints are regular we find that (13d) is locally equivalent to $z \leq \mathrm{sp}(\tilde{u}_i)$. In fact, $z = s_i^{\min}$ because the min-sparsity constraint is active for some vector $\tilde{u}_i^j$: Otherwise we could remove the constraint without changing the objective value of the solution.

Overall, we find that the solution to (13) satisfies

$$\begin{aligned} \max_{z, u_i \in Q_i} \quad & z, \\ \text{s.t.} \quad & z = \min_i \mathrm{sp}(u_i), \\ & 0 \leq f(V, u_i) - f(V, \tilde{u}_i), \\ & G_i(u_i) \in \mathbb{R}_+^k. \end{aligned} \tag{18}$$

Then the solution obeys the corresponding first order condition

$$-\frac{\partial}{\partial u_i} \left(\hat{\lambda}_{fi} f(V, u_i) + \langle \hat{\lambda}_{ui}, G_i(u_i) \rangle \right) \in N_{Q_i}(u_i^*) \tag{19}$$

which is equivalent to (15). □

3.4 Practical Considerations

The SOCP problems (13) and (14) are sparse but can become very large. Solvers with support for sparse matrices are crucial[2]. In applications where the convex max-sparsity constraints are not used, i.e., only min-sparsity constraints are specified, quadratic programming (QP) solvers can be used instead of SOCP solvers. Commercial QP solvers are usually highly optimized and may be faster than their SOCP counterparts.

---

[2] In our experiments we used MOSEK 3.2.1.8 [22].

4   Experiments

In this section we show that our optimization framework works robustly in practice. A comparison demonstrates that explicit sparsity-control leads to improved performance. Our results validate that sparsity-controlled NTF can be a useful model in real applications.

4.1   Ground Truth Experiment

To validate our approach we created an artificial data set with known ground truth. Specifically, we used three equally-sized factors u_i with $d_i = 10$ and all entries zero except for the entries shown in Fig. 2(a). We computed $V = u_1 \otimes u_2 \otimes u_3 + |\nu|$, where $\nu \sim \mathcal{N}(0, 0.5)$ was i.i.d. Gaussian noise.

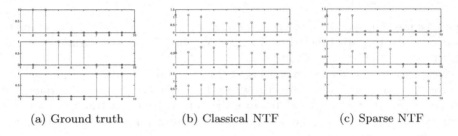

(a) Ground truth   (b) Classical NTF   (c) Sparse NTF

Fig. 2. Ground truth experiment. We created an artificial data set with known factors u_i (Fig. 2(a)). We added noise (see text) and used NTF to recover the factors from $V = u_1 \otimes u_2 \otimes u_3 + |\nu|$. While the NTF model without sparsity constraints failed (Fig. 2(b)), sparsity-controlled NTF successfully recovered the factors (Fig. 2(c)).

We found that over 10 repeated runs the classical NTF model without sparsity constraints was not able to recover any of the factors (Fig. 2(b)). In contrast, sparsity-controlled NTF with $s_i^{\min} = 0.55$ yielded useful results in all 10 repeated runs (Fig. 2(c)).

We conclude that in the presence of noise, sparsity constraints are crucial to successfully recover sparse factors. Further, we find that at least with the simple data set above the sparsity maximization algorithm converged on the correct factorization in 10 out of 10 repeated runs.

4.2   Face Detection

For the face detection problem, impressive results are reported in [3] where NTF without sparsity constraints clearly outperformed NMF recognition rates on the MIT CBCL face data set [26]. We demonstrate in this section that performance can further be improved by using sparsity-constrained NTF.

In our experiments we used the original training and test data sets provided by CBCL [26]. In this data sets, especially the test data set is very imbalanced:

Table 1. Recognition performance of sparse NTF codes. We trained a SVM on a subset of the MIT CBCL face detection data set (see text). Features were raw pixels, a NMF basis, and a NTF basis with different min-sparsity constraints. We compared area under ROC for the MIT training data (first row), the MIT test data set (second row) and recognition accuracy for a balanced test data set with 50% face samples (last row). NTF with a relatively strong min-sparsity constraint $s_1^{\min} = 0.8$ performs best.

feature	pixels	NMF	NTF	NTF	NTF	NTF	NTF	**NTF**	NTF
$s_1^{\min}$			0.0	0.3	0.4	0.6	0.7	**0.8**	0.9
ROC (trai)	0.997	0.995	1.000	1.000	0.997	0.997	0.994	**1.000**	0.991
ROC (test)	0.817	0.817	0.835	0.822	0.789	0.830	0.822	**0.860**	0.821
ACC-50 (test)	0.611	0.667	0.753	0.600	0.702	0.743	0.728	**0.761**	0.719

A trivial classificator returning "non-face" for all input would obtain 98% accuracy. For this reason, we consider the *area under the ROC curve* as a more suitable performance measure. We thus trained radial-basis function SVMs on small subsets (250 samples only) of the CBCL training data set. To determine the SVM and kernel parameters, we used 5-fold crossvalidation on the training data. For the resulting SVM we determined the area under the ROC on the test data set. In addition, we also created a data set ACC-50 consisting of all 472 positive samples in the test data set as well as of 472 randomly chosen negative test samples.

We compared the following feature sets:

1. the $19 \times 19 = 361$ raw image pixels as found in the CBCL data set,
2. coefficients for 10 NMF basis functions determined on a subset of the faces in the training data set,
3. coefficients for 10 NTF basis functions determined on a subset of the faces in the training data set using different values of the min-sparsity constraint on u_1. Reconstructions using these features are shown in Fig. 1. Note that the NTF basis corresponds to an about 10-fold higher compression ratio than the NMF basis.

The results are summarized in Tab. 1: NMF and raw pixel values perform similar in this experiment. NTF yields improved results, which is consistent with [3]. Best results are obtained with NTF with strong sparsity constraint ($s_1^{\min} = 0.8$).

5   Conclusions

We extended the non-negative tensor factorization model for images [1, 2, 3] by explicit sparseness constraint [11]. We found that compared to unconstrained NTF the extended model can be more robust against noise (Sec. 4.1) and the corresponding image codes can be more efficient for recognition, especially when training data is scarce (Sec. 4.2).

From an optimization point of view, we devised an algorithm based on sequential conic programming (Sec. 3.2) which has desirable convergence properties (Sec. 3.3) and works well in practice (Sec. 4). Because the algorithm's basic building blocks are convex programs, we believe the model could further be extended by additional convex constraints taking into account prior knowledge about the specific problem at hand, while still remaining in the sequential convex programming framework.

References

1. M. Welling and M. Weber, "Positive tensor factorization," *Pattern Recog. Letters*, vol. 22, no. 12, pp. 1255–1261, 2001.
2. A. Shashua and T. Hazan, "Non-negative tensor factorization with applications to statistics and computer vision," in *Proc. of ICML*, 2005.
3. T. Hazan, S. Polak, and A. Shashua, "Sparse image coding using a 3D non-negative tensor factorization," in *Proc. of ICCV*, 2005.
4. J. Shen and G. W. Israël, "A receptor model using a specific non-negative transformation technique for ambient aerosol," *Atmospheric Environment*, vol. 23, no. 10, pp. 2289–2298, 1989.
5. P. Paatero and U. Tapper, "Positive matrix factorization: A non-negative factor model with optimal utilization of error estimates of data values," *Environmetrics*, vol. 5, pp. 111–126, 1994.
6. D. D. Lee and H. S. Seung, "Learning the parts of objects by non-negative matrix factorization," *Nature*, vol. 401, pp. 788–791, Oct. 1999.
7. A. Shashua and A. Levin, "Linear image coding for regression and classification using the tensor-rank principle," in *Proc. of CVPR*, 2001.
8. D. Donoho and V. Stodden, "When does non-negative matrix factorization give a correct decomposition into parts?," in *Adv. in NIPS*, vol. 17, 2004.
9. J. B. Kruskal, "Three-way arrays: Rank and uniqueness of trilinear decompositions, with application to arithmetic complexity and statistics," *Linear Algebra and its Applications*, vol. 18, pp. 95–138, 1977.
10. N. D. Sidiropoulos and R. Bro, "On the uniqueness of multilinear decompositions of N-way arrays," *J. of Chemometrics*, vol. 14, pp. 229–239, 2000.
11. P. O. Hoyer, "Non-negative matrix factorization with sparseness constraints," *J. of Mach. Learning Res.*, vol. 5, pp. 1457–1469, 2004.
12. D. D. Lee and H. S. Seung, "Algorithms for non-negative matrix factorization," in *Adv. in NIPS*, 2000.
13. M. Chu, F. Diele, R. Plemmons, and S. Ragni, "Optimality, computations, and interpretation of nonnegative matrix factorizations." submitted to SIAM J. Mat. Anal. Appl., 2004. www4.ncsu.edu:8030/~mtchu/Research/Papers/nnmf.pdf.
14. R. Horst and H. Tuy, *Global Optimization*. Springer, Berlin, 1996.
15. M. Heiler and C. Schnörr, "Learning non-negative sparse image codes by convex programming," in *Proc. of ICCV*, 2005.
16. N. Littlestone and M. Warmuth, "Relating data compression, learnability, and the Vapnik-Chervonenkis dimension," tech. rep., Univ. of Calif. Santa Cruz, 1986.
17. R. Herbrich and R. C. Williamson, "Algorithmic luckiness," *J. of Mach. Learning Res.*, vol. 3, pp. 175–212, 2002.
18. B. A. Olshausen and D. J. Field, "Sparse coding with an overcomplete basis set: A strategy employed by V1?," *Vision Research*, vol. 37, pp. 3311–3325, Dec. 1997.
19. M. S. Lobo, L. Vandenberghe, S. Boyd, and H. Lebret, "Applications of second-order cone programming," *Linear Algebra and its Applications*, 1998.

20. J. F. Sturm, *Using SeDuMi 1.02, a Matlab toolbox for optimization over symmetric cones (updated version 1.05)*. Department of Econometrics, Tilburg University, Tilburg, The Netherlands, 2001.
21. H. Mittelmann, "An independent benchmarking of SDP and SOCP solvers.," *Math. Programming, Series B*, vol. 95, no. 2, pp. 407–430, 2003.
22. MOSEK ApS, Denmark, *The MOSEK optimization tools version 3.2 (Revision 8) User's manual and reference*, 2005.
23. A. M. Buchanan and A. W. Fitzgibbon, "Damped Newton algorithms for matrix factorization with missing data," in *CVPR05*, vol. 2, pp. 316–322, 2005.
24. H. Tuy, "Convex programs with an additional reverse convex constraint," *J. of Optim. Theory and Applic.*, vol. 52, pp. 463–486, Mar. 1987.
25. R. Rockafellar and R.-B. Wets, *Variational Analysis*, vol. 317 of *Grundlehren der math. Wissenschaften*. Springer, 1998.
26. CBCL, "CBCL face database #1." MIT Center For Biological and Computational Learning, http://cbcl.mit.edu/software-datasets, 2000.

Conditional Infomax Learning: An Integrated Framework for Feature Extraction and Fusion

Dahua Lin[1] and Xiaoou Tang[1,2]

[1] Dept. of Information Engineering,
The Chinese University of Hong Kong, Hong Kong, China
dhlin4@ie.cuhk.edu.hk
[2] Microsoft Research Asia, Beijing, China
xitang@microsoft.com

Abstract. The paper introduces a new framework for feature learning in classification motivated by information theory. We first systematically study the information structure and present a novel perspective revealing the two key factors in information utilization: class-relevance and redundancy. We derive a new information decomposition model where a novel concept called class-relevant redundancy is introduced. Subsequently a new algorithm called Conditional Informative Feature Extraction is formulated, which maximizes the joint class-relevant information by explicitly reducing the class-relevant redundancies among features. To address the computational difficulties in information-based optimization, we incorporate Parzen window estimation into the discrete approximation of the objective function and propose a Local Active Region method which substantially increases the optimization efficiency. To effectively utilize the extracted feature set, we propose a Bayesian MAP formulation for feature fusion, which unifies Laplacian Sparse Prior and Multivariate Logistic Regression to learn a fusion rule with good generalization capability. Realizing the inefficiency caused by separate treatment of the extraction stage and the fusion stage, we further develop an improved design of the framework to coordinate the two stages by introducing a feedback from the fusion stage to the extraction stage, which significantly enhances the learning efficiency. The results of the comparative experiments show remarkable improvements achieved by our framework.

1 Introduction

Pattern recognition in a high dimensional space, such as face recognition, is a challenging problem due to the difficulties brought by "the curse of dimensionality". Hence, it is crucial to extract a compact set of features to describe the samples so that the classification can be performed efficiently and robustly in a feature space of much lower dimension.

In the literatures of learning, feature extraction has been studied extensively. PCA[1] and LDA[2][3][4] are among the most popular algorithms. The former finds a subspace best preserving the sample variations, while the latter seeks a feature space where the ratio between the between-class scattering and the

A. Leonardis, H. Bischof, and A. Pinz (Eds.): ECCV 2006, Part I, LNCS 3951, pp. 68–82, 2006.

within-class scattering is maximized. Though some improved variants[5][6] are proposed, the fundamental limitation of PCA and LDA are yet to be solved: they are solely based on the second order statistical moments, thus may not work well in the practical cases where the distributions are nongaussian.

To break the limitation, we need a method which does not rely on parametric assumptions on the sample distribution. The intrinsic relationship between information theory and pattern recognition, established by the well known Fano's inequality[7], inspires a new way to the feature learning. In the past decade, many works have been done to apply information theory to the learning problems. Some [8][9][10][11] use infomax principle for sequential feature selection. However, they only concern the information conveyed by each individual feature without considering their relation, thus often produce feature sets with a large amount of redundancy. Some improved feature selection algorithms[12][13][14] try to tackle the problem by taking the diversity among the features into consideration. Nonetheless, the criteria of these methods are based on either heuristic rules without convincing justification or some very loose approximations. Hence, the improvement achieved is not significant.

So far the use of information theory in pattern recognition is basically restricted to the feature selection due to two difficulties: 1) No rigorous theory is available to study the inter-feature relation and how the relation affects the performance of the whole feature set; 2) The evaluation of entropy and mutual information incurs great computational difficulties in the optimization. Recently, Torkkola et al.[15][16] propose an infomax feature extraction method to learn a joint set of orthogonal features based on Renyi entropy. However, it suffers from the following drawbacks: 1) The Renyi approximation is not sufficiently justified and what effects it brings to the solution is unclear; 2) It is based on density estimation in a multi-dimensional space, which is computationally expensive and not robust; 3) It does not account for the inter-feature relations.

In this paper, to address the two difficulties, we first systematically investigate the structure of information conveyed by the feature set and present an information decomposition model. It shows that the effectiveness of the feature set is influenced by two key factors: the class relevance and the inter-feature redundancy. As a novel approach, our model also points out that *the redundancy can be factorized into class-relevant and irrelevant ingredients* and introduces the concept *class-relevant redundancy* with theoretically well-founded formulation. We then derive the *Conditional Informative Feature Extraction* algorithm which maximizes the information conveyed by the whole feature set by explicitly reducing the class-relevant redundancies. To attack the computational difficulty, we couple the discrete approximation with the 1D Parzen window technique and further propose a *Local Active Region method*, which substantially reduces the computational cost from $O(n^2)$ to $O(n)$ and thus enables large-scale application of the method.

We also develop the Bayesian Feature fusion algorithm to effectively utilize the feature set by incorporating Laplacian sparse prior and Multivariate logistic regression into the Bayesian MAP formulation, where the features are adaptively weighted. Considering that the separate treatment of feature extraction and fusion incurs inefficiency, we finally improve the framework architecture to coordinate the two stages by introducing a feedback from the fusion stage to the extraction stage. By the new design, both the learning efficiency and the effectiveness of the resultant feature set are greatly enhanced.

2   Conditional Informative Feature Extraction

2.1   Problem Formulation and Features

Consider a multiclass classification problem: the training set consists of n samples from C classes, which is denoted by $\{(\mathbf{x}_i, c_i)\}_{i=1}^n$, where $\mathbf{x}_i \in \mathcal{X}$ is a d-dimensional vector representing the i-th sample, c_i is its class label. For discrimination, we extract a set of features, denoted by $F = \{y^{(1)}, y^{(2)}, \ldots, y^{(m)}\}$. Each feature is a functional: $y^{(t)} : \mathcal{X} \to R$, which maps a sample vector to a scalar. For each sample $\mathbf{x}$, all the m feature values constitute a feature vector, denoted by $\mathbf{y}(\mathbf{x}) = \left[y^{(1)}(\mathbf{x}), y^{(2)}(\mathbf{x}), \ldots, y^{(m)}(\mathbf{x}) \right]^T$. For succinctness, we denote the features for the i-th training sample by $\mathbf{y}_i = [y_i^{(1)}, y_i^{(2)}, \ldots, y_i^{(m)}]^T$.

Linear features are the most widely used features in the literature owning to its simplicity and effectiveness. Each linear feature is parameterized by a projection vector $\mathbf{w}$ subject to $\|\mathbf{w}\| = 1$, and the feature value for the sample $\mathbf{x}$ can be extracted by $y = \mathbf{w}^T \mathbf{x}$. In the cases where the sample distribution is highly nongaussian, linear features are insufficient to classify the samples well. To tackle the difficulty, we can extract nonlinear features by kernelization, where a nonlinear mapping ϕ is employed to map the original vector space to a Hilbert space of much higher dimension. Each feature can be regarded as a projection of such mapping. Assume that the projection vector in the Hilbert space can be expanded by $\mathbf{w}^\phi = \sum_{i=1}^n a_i \phi(\mathbf{x}_i)$, then with the kernel trick, the feature value can be computed by $y = \mathbf{a}^T [k(\mathbf{x}, \mathbf{x}_1), \ldots, k(\mathbf{x}, \mathbf{x}_n)]^T$, where $\mathbf{a} = [a_1, \ldots, a_n]$ is the vector of expansion coefficients.

2.2   The Information Maximization Principle

In information theory, the *entropy* of a random feature $\mathbf{y}$, denoted by $H(\mathbf{y})$, contains two-fold meanings: 1) $H(\mathbf{y})$ measures the uncertainty on $\mathbf{y}$, 2)$H(\mathbf{y})$ represents the total information conveyed by $\mathbf{y}$. Based on the notion that information stems from uncertainty, the mutual information $I(\mathbf{x}; \mathbf{y})$ is defined by $I(\mathbf{x}; \mathbf{y}) = H(\mathbf{x}) - H(\mathbf{x}|\mathbf{y})$, which indicates that the information delivered from $\mathbf{x}$ to $\mathbf{y}$ equals the reduction of uncertainty of $\mathbf{y}$ when $\mathbf{x}$ is known. [7] gives a comprehensive treatment to the concepts of information theory.

Intuitively, when we know more about the classes, we can classify the objects more accurately. This rationale leads to the *infomax principle* for feature learning, which advocates to learn features by maximizing the mutual information between the features and the classes. The principle is validated theoretically by Fano's inequality[7]

$$P(\hat{c} \neq c) \geq \frac{H(\mathbf{y}|c) - 1}{\log C} = \frac{H(c) - I(\mathbf{y}; c) - 1}{\log C}, \tag{1}$$

where $\hat{c}$ is the decision made based on the feature vector $\mathbf{y}$, c is the true underlying class. This inequality relates the lower bound of the Bayes error to the mutual information between the features and the classes. Vasconcelos[10] reinforces the relation by showing that: *The infomax solution is near optimal in the minimum Bayes error sense.*

2.3   The Information Decomposition and the Conditional Objective

Since each sample is usually described by multiple features, there may exist some relations between the features. How do the inter-feature relations affect the process of information utilization? To answer this question, we first study the structure of the joint information by examining the two-feature case.

$$H(y^{(1)}) = I(y^{(1)}; c) + H(y^{(1)}|c) \tag{2}$$

$$H(y^{(2)}) = I(y^{(2)}; c) + H(y^{(2)}|c) \tag{3}$$

$$H(y^{(1)}y^{(2)}) = I(y^{(1)}y^{(2)}; c)$$
$$+ H(y^{(1)}y^{(2)}|c) \tag{4}$$

$$H(y^{(1)}y^{(2)}) = H(y^{(1)}) + H(y^{(2)})$$
$$- I(y^{(1)}; y^{(2)}) \tag{5}$$

$$I(y^{(1)}y^{(2)}; c) = I(y^{(1)}; c) + I(y^{(2)}; c)$$
$$- [I(y^{(1)}; y^{(2)}) - I(y^{(1)}; y^{(2)}|c)] \tag{6}$$

Fig. 1. The important formulas characterizing the information structure

Suppose we have two features $y^{(1)}$ and $y^{(2)}$ to represent the samples. Then the information carried by $y^{(1)}$ and $y^{(2)}$ are $H(y^{(1)})$ and $H(y^{(2)})$ respectively. The information conveyed by the joint set of two features is $H(y^{(1)}y^{(2)})$. Based on information theory, we deduce the formulas given in fig.1, which characterize the relations between these quantities and those between information and classification. Though they are simple, however, careful analysis of them leads us to an insightful perspective on the information structure:

1) Eq.(2-4) indicate that the information conveyed by the features consists of two parts: the class-relevant part $I(y; c)$ and the irrelevant part $H(y|c)$. Only the former contributes to classification.

2) Eq.(5) gives another view: when two features are used, the joint information of the feature set would be less than the sum of information conveyed by individual features due to the redundancy, which is measured by the mutual information between the two features.

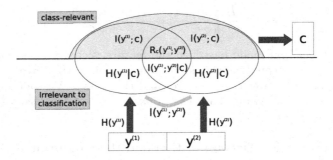

Fig. 2. Illustration of Joint Information Decomposition

3) Eq.(6) combines the class-relevance factor and the redundancy factor to depict the information structure: the class-relevant information conveyed by the joint set is equal to the sum of the individual class-relevant information delivered by $y^{(1)}$ and $y^{(2)}$ minus the *class-relevant redundancy*. For conciseness, we denote it by $R_c(y^{(1)}; y^{(2)}) = I(y^{(1)}; y^{(2)}) - I(y^{(1)}; y^{(2)}|c)$, then Eq.(6) can be rewritten as

$$I(y^{(1)}y^{(2)}; c) = I(y^{(1)}; c) + I(y^{(2)}; c) - R_c(y^{(1)}; y^{(2)}). \qquad (7)$$

The fig.2 illustrates the two-feature information decomposition model and gives a clear picture to the information structure.

The Eq.(7) can be generalized to the case of multiple features with mathematical induction. It results in the following theorem:

Theorem 1. *Assume that* $\forall i \neq j, k_1, k_2, \ldots \notin \{i, j\}$ $I(y^{(i)}; y^{(j)}|y^{(k_1)}, y^{(k_2)}, \ldots) = I(y^{(i)}; y^{(j)})$ *and* $I(y^{(i)}; y^{(j)}|c, y^{(k_1)}, y^{(k_2)}, \ldots) = I(y^{(i)}; y^{(j)}|c)$, *then*

$$I(\mathbf{y}; c) = I(y^{(1)}y^{(2)} \cdots y^{(m)}; c) = \sum_{t=1}^{m} I(y^{(t)}; c) - \sum_{t=1}^{m-1} \sum_{u=t+1}^{m} R_c(y^{(t)}; y^{(u)}). \qquad (8)$$

The theorem states that when the communication of any two features is not affected by other features, the joint class-relevant information equals the sum of the individual feature information minus the total pairwise redundancies. We can rewrite Eq.(8) by

$$I(\mathbf{y}; c) = \sum_{t=1}^{m} \left[I(y^{(t)}; c) - \sum_{u=1}^{t-1} R_c(y^{(u)}; y^{(t)}) \right]. \qquad (9)$$

This form enables us to extract features sequentially, given that $t - 1$ features are extracted, the t-th feature can be extracted by optimizing the *Conditional Informative Objective* as

$$\theta_t = \underset{\theta_t}{\mathrm{argmax}} \left\{ I(y^{(t)}; c) - \sum_{u=1}^{t-1} R_c(y^{(u)}; y^{(t)}) \right\}, \qquad (10)$$

where θ is the parameter for the t-th feature. Accordingly, the feature extraction algorithm based on Eq.(10) is called *Conditional Informative Feature Extraction*.

Discussion

The significance of the information decomposition model lies in three aspects:

First, it is the first work to present an insightful view into the composition of information with a classification context, where two key factors: *class-relevance* and *inter-feature redundancy* are revealed and analyzed with solid theoretical foundation.

Second, a novel concept called *class-relevant redundancy* is introduced, which serves a key role in the information-oriented classification. This concept reflects the compound influence of class-relevance and redundancy, which has not been discussed in previous literatures.

Third, Eq.(8) integrates the two factors to form an approximation of joint information with the second-order interactions taken into account. The condition when the approximation is exact is also given. This formulation on one hand explicitly exploits the redundancies among features, which plays an important role in learning, on the other hand ignores the higher-order interactions which will lead to exponentially increasing complexity. In this sense, it achieves a good trade-off between the accuracy and the complexity.

3   The Efficient Optimization

According to the Asymptotic Equipartition Property[7], when a reasonably large set of samples are available, the entropy can be approximated by the sample mean as

$$H(y) = -\int_{\mathcal{R}} p(y) \log(p(y)) dy = -E\left\{\log(p(y))\right\} \approx -\frac{1}{n} \sum_{i=1}^{n} \log(p(y)). \quad (11)$$

To evaluate $p(y)$, we apply the nonparametric Parzen window technique instead of relying on any parametric assumptions that are often violated in practical cases. Here, we use a Gaussian kernel, defined by $\phi(r) = (2\pi\sigma^2)^{-\frac{1}{2}} \exp(-\frac{r^2}{2\sigma^2})$, and σ controls the width of the kernel. Then the approximation is given by

$$p(y) \approx \frac{1}{n} \sum_{i=1}^{n} \phi(y - y_i) \quad (12)$$

In the following text, we try to unveil the underlying working mechanism of conditional infomax learning by studying the terms in the objective function given in Eq.(10).

1) Class-relevant Information. From Eq.(11) and Eq.(12), we have

$$I(y^{(t)}; c) = \frac{1}{n} \sum_{i=1}^{n} \left\{ \log \sum_{j:c_j=c_i} \frac{1}{n_k} \phi(y_i^{(t)} - y_j^{(t)}) - \log \sum_{j=1}^{n} \frac{1}{n} \phi(y_i^{(t)} - y_j^{(t)}) \right\}. \quad (13)$$

We observe two types of terms: the terms representing the interactions between the samples in the same class gathered together by log-sum, and the terms representing the interactions between any pair of samples accumulated by negative log-sum. Considering that $\phi(y_i^{(t)}, y_j^{(t)})$ increases when $y_i^{(t)}$ and $y_j^{(t)}$ become closer, maximizing such an objective will agglomerate the feature values from the same class and disperse those from different classes. In this sense, the optimization process pursues a feature space beneficial to discrimination.

2) Redundancy. We have discussed that $I(y^{(u)}; y^{(t)})$ represents the inter-feature redundancy between $y^{(u)}$ and $y^{(t)}$. In the evaluation of the joint distribution $p(y^{(u)}, y^{(t)})$, we employ the parzen window technique with an isotropic 2D gaussian kernel, which can be expressed as $\phi(y^{(u)}y^{(t)}) = \phi(y^{(u)})\phi(y^{(t)})$. Then we have

$$I(y^{(u)}; y^{(t)}) = \frac{1}{n}\sum_{i=1}^{n} \log \frac{\frac{1}{n}\sum_{j=1}^{n} \phi(y_i^{(t)} - y_j^{(t)})\phi(y_i^{(u)} - y_j^{(u)})}{\left[\frac{1}{n}\sum_{j=1}^{n} \phi(y_i^{(t)} - y_j^{(t)})\right]\left[\frac{1}{n}\sum_{j=1}^{n} \phi(y_i^{(u)} - y_j^{(u)})\right]}. \quad (14)$$

We find that the unit of the formula is "normalized" correlation between the kernel values for feature $y^{(u)}$ and $y^{(t)}$. Considering that the inter-sample relationship are characterized by the kernel values, and the correlation is a typical measurement of similarity, the redundancy is actually represented by the similarity between the inter-sample relations induced by the two features.

To further clarify how it affects the optimization, we introduce the affinity coefficients $\lambda_{ij}^{(u)} = \frac{\phi(y_i^{(u)} - y_j^{(u)})}{\sum_{j=1}^{n} \phi(y_i^{(u)} - y_j^{(u)})}$, which reflects the affinity between the sample i and j in the u-th feature space. Then Eq.(14) can be simplified to be

$$I(y^{(u)}; y^{(t)}) = \frac{1}{n}\sum_{i=1}^{n}\left\{ \log \sum_{j=1}^{n} \lambda_{ij}^{(u)}\phi(y_i^{(t)} - y_j^{(t)}) - \log \sum_{j=1}^{n} \frac{1}{n}\phi(y_i^{(t)} - y_j^{(t)}) \right\}. \quad (15)$$

We can see that the formula assigns heavy weights on the sample-pairs which are close in the u-th feature space. Therefore minimizing the redundancy will encourage these pairs of samples go farther from each other, thus to create an inter-sample relationship in the t-th feature space, which are distinct from that in the u-th feature space.

As discussed before, some part of the total redundancy is irrelevant to classification, we need to subtract the term $I(y^{(u)}; y^{(t)}|c)$ to compensate its effect. Similar analysis can be applied to this term.

3) Derivative. The analysis above shows that all the terms in the objective function can be written in the following form:

$$f(y^{(t)}) = \pm \sum_{i=1}^{n} \log \sum_{j=1}^{n} \omega_{ij}\phi(y_i^{(t)} - y_j^{(t)}), \quad (16)$$

where ω_{ij} are some coefficients dependent on the specific term. For the terms with $\sum_{j:c_j=c_i}$, they can be expressed by Eq.(16) by setting $\omega_{ij} = 0$ when $c_j \neq c_i$.

When $\phi(\cdot)$ is an even function, the derivative w.r.t the feature values is derived as follows

$$\frac{\partial f}{\partial y_i^{(t)}} = \pm \sum_{k=1}^{n} \left[\frac{\omega_{ik}}{\sum_{j=1}^{n} \omega_{ij}\phi(y_i^{(t)} - y_j^{(t)})} + \frac{\omega_{ki}}{\sum_{j=1}^{n} \omega_{kj}\phi(y_k^{(t)} - y_j^{(t)})} \right] \psi(y_i^{(t)} - y_k^{(t)}).$$

(17)

With the derivatives given, we can use stochastic gradient descent to optimize the objective function.

3.1   Local Active Region Method

As shown in fig.3, both the potential and the force attenuates drastically as the distance increases. This observation implies that the interactions within a certain region centered at each sample dominates the objective function, which we call "Local Active Region". As a consequence, we can approximate the objective function and its derivative by retaining only the terms reflecting the interactions with the local regions.

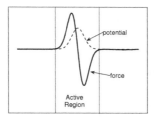

Fig. 3. The potential and the force

Retrieving the neighborhood of every sample is computationally expensive, especially when the sample number is large. Fortunately, we are handling the feature values in a 1-D space, therefore it is feasible to partition the whole value-range into small sections. Here we propose a simple scheme to establish the neighborhoods: suppose the minimum and maximum value of the current feature are y_{min} and y_{max} respectively. Then we divide the range $[y_{min}, y_{max}]$ into sub-sections. The feature values of all samples are categorized into one of the sub-sections. For each sample, the samples residing in the same sub-section constitute its neighborhood. To attain a satisfactory level of accuracy and robustness, the section length is determined so that the average number of samples in each section is about 5.

By employing the simplified way to build neighborhood and discarding the non-neighboring interactions, the time complexity is reduced from $O(n^2)$ to $O(n)$. Such a great improvement in computational efficiency makes the large scale application of infomax learning feasible. Moreover, our algorithm has two important advantages: 1) The Parzen window estimation is performed in 1D and 2D spaces instead of a multidimensional space such as in MMI[15][16], thus it is robust and accurate. 2) The system with only local interactions favors the preservation of local consistency and hence effectively reduces the risk of overfitting.

4   Bayesian Feature Fusion with Sparse Prior

After obtaining the set of features, a question arise naturally: how to combine the features to give the final decision? In many literatures, it is a typical approach to directly compute the Euclidean distance in the feature space, and classify a sample to the nearest class. Though simple, these methods neglect the different contributions of different features thus fails to optimally utilize the features.

In our framework, we assign different weights to different features and evaluate the dissimilarities between samples in the following weighted form:

$$d(\mathbf{y}_i, \mathbf{y}_j) = \sum_{t=1}^{m} b_t \left(y_i^{(t)} - y_j^{(t)} \right)^2. \tag{18}$$

It is known that to achieve a good generalization capability, it is crucial to control the model complexity in order to prevent over-fitting, thus it is desirable to reduce the redundant components by giving a sparse estimating on the coefficients. It has been shown[17] that the Laplacian prior is favorable to sparse estimation.

$$p(\mathbf{b}) \propto \exp \left(\alpha \sum_{t=1}^{m} |b_t| \right). \tag{19}$$

Considering the discriminant learning context, we employ the multivariate logistic regression model to give the conditional likelihood of $\mathbf{b} = [b_1, \ldots, b_m]^T$ as follows

$$p(\mathbf{y}_1, \ldots, \mathbf{y}_n | \mathbf{b}) \propto \prod_{i=1}^{n} p(c_i | \mathbf{y}_i; \mathbf{b}) = \prod_{i=1}^{n} \frac{\exp\left(-d(\mathbf{y}_i, \mathbf{m}_{c_i}) \right)}{\sum_{k=1}^{C} \exp\left(-d(\mathbf{y}_i, \mathbf{m}_k) \right)}, \tag{20}$$

where $\mathbf{m}_k$ is the mean vector of the k-th class. By incorporating Laplacian prior and logistic likelihood into the Bayesian MAP learning formulation, we have

$$\mathbf{b} = \operatorname*{argmax}_{\mathbf{b}} p(\mathbf{y}_1, \ldots, \mathbf{y}_n | \mathbf{b}) p(\mathbf{b}). \tag{21}$$

A well balance can be achieved between the sparsity and the discriminative power in the learning process. The optimization can be accomplished by Sparse Regression[17][18] proposed by Figueiredo et al.

5   The Integrated Framework for Feature Learning

Traditionally, there are two typical paradigms for feature learning: one first generates a large pool of simple features and then selects a subset from it[8][11][12], while the other directly learns discriminant features from the raw representation and then combines them[1][2][19][15]. They both suffers from a limitation: due to the separate treatment of the two stages, the feature extracted or selected in the 1st stage may not be useful in the fusion or decision stage. Though we can

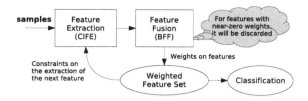

Fig. 4. The Architecture of the Integrated Framework

tackle the problem by extracting a sufficiently large set in the first step, it will inevitably incur considerable waste.

To achieve high efficiency while guaranteeing sufficient expressive power in the feature set, we develop a new framework to coordinate the two stages so that they can intimately cooperate. The whole procedure is introduced as follows:

---

1. Initialize an empty feature set $F \leftarrow \{\}$.
2. Learn the first feature $y^{(1)}$ by the infomax principle; $F \leftarrow F \cup \{y^{(1)}\}$.
3. Repeat the following steps until the stop criterion is met:
   (a) Extract the feature $y^{(t)}$ with the redundancy evaluated on F.
   (b) Add the new feature: $F \leftarrow F \cup \{y^{(t)}\}$.
   (c) Optimize the fusion weights **b**.
   (d) Discard the features with weights smaller than ϵ.

In each step of iteration, we keep monitoring the value of Eq.(8) and stop the loop when the objective function keeps basically unchanged for several iterations.

In the framework, the results of fusion stage are fed back to the extraction stage in order that the extractor can make use of it to evaluate the redundancies based on the fused set and produce an complementary feature as illustrated in fig.4. By eliminating the inactive features, the extractor can find new features adapted to the true demand of the fusion stage without being affected by the unused features, otherwise, the feature set will be gradually filled by the obsolete features and mislead the optimization process by the redundancy terms, thus seriously hinder the effective renewal.

6   Experiments

6.1   A Toy Problem

First, we design a toy problem to give an intuitive insight to the relation between class-relevant information and feature learning in pattern recognition as illustrated in Figure 5. In this experiment, two classes of Gaussian distributed samples are randomly generated, with each class having 500 samples. We extract a series of 1D features by linearly projecting the samples onto 64 different directions. The results clearly show that the class-relevant information, which is the difference between the total entropy and the class conditional entropy, closely

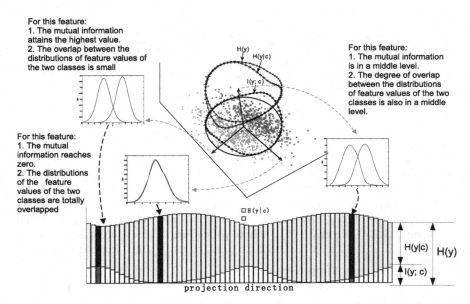

Fig. 5. The Toy Problem. The figure illustrates the relationship between information and feature distribution. The upper part shows a 2D feature space and the 1D distributions of feature values along 3 different directions. The lower part shows the values of the entropy, class-conditional entropy, and mutual information for the features along 64 consecutive directions.

relates to discrimination. From the figure, we can see that for the features with large information values, the distributions of the feature values of the two classes are well separated, while for the features with information values approximating zero, the distributions of the feature values are basically overlapped so that it is difficult to distinguish one class from the other based on that feature. Though the example is simple, it sufficiently exhibits the strong connections between information and classification.

6.2   Face Recognition

Experiment Settings. Face recognition problems is a challenging pattern recognition problem in computer vision, which is a good testbed to evaluate the practical performance of the feature extraction algorithms. To thoroughly test the algorithms, we compare our algorithms with other representative algorithms in face recognition literatures on three standard face databases: FERET[20], XM2VTS[21] and PURDUE AR[22]. To examine the generalization capabilities, for each database, we divide the selected samples into three disjoint datasets: the training set, the gallery set, and the probe set. The training set is for learning the features in the training stage. In the testing stage, every sample in the probe set is compared with each sample in the gallery set, and classified to the person whose gallery sample is most close to it in the feature space. We employ the

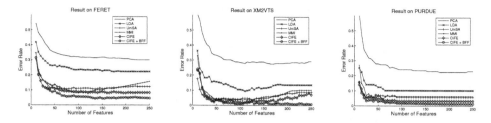

Fig. 6. The Face Recognition Performances for Linear Features

Table 1. The Best Performances of algorithms with Linear Features

Error rate	PCA	LDA	UniSA	MMI	CIFE	CIFE+BFF
FERET	0.299	0.175	0.087	0.079	0.065	0.044
XM2VTS	0.275	0.095	0.037	0.034	0.017	0.007
PURDUE	0.235	0.148	0.057	0.052	0.031	0.022

error rates to measure the performance of the algorithms. In detail, for FERET, we use all the 295 persons with $3 - 4$ samples for each person to form the training set, which has totally 995 samples. We then select another 800 persons for testing, where the gallery is composed of 800 (fa) samples from different persons, and the probe set is composed of 800 (fb) samples; For XM2VTS, the face images from 295 persons are captured in 4 different sessions. We assign the 295×3 samples captured in the session $1, 2, 3$ to the training set, the 295 samples from the session 1 to the client set, and the 295 samples from the session 4 to the probe set; For PURDUE, there are 90 persons who have the samples captured in all the 26 different conditions. We select 6 samples from each person with diverse expressions and illumination conditions to the training set, a sample captured in normal condition to the gallery set, and another 6 samples captured in different conditions to the probe set. The samples with extreme lighting condition and occlusion are not used in the experiment.

All face images are pre-processed. For each image, we first align it by affine transform to fix the positions of the eye centers and the mouth center, and crop it to the size of 64×72, and then perform histogram equalization to normalize the pixel values. After that, we use a mask to eliminate the background pixels. The remaining 4114 pixels are scanned in order to form the original vector representation of the face. To enhance efficiency and robustness, we use PCA to reduce the dimension and suppress the noise. 99% of the variational energy is preserved in the principal subspace after dimension reduction.

Linear Features. We compare our algorithms with other representative algorithms for feature extraction including PCA[1], LDA[2], Unified Subspace Analysis(UniSA)[4], Maximum Mutual Information(MMI) Algorithm proposed by Torkkola[15]. To clarify the contributions of different components of the framework, we test our algorithms in two different configurations. In a sim-

Table 2. The Best Performances of algorithms with Kernelized Features

Error rate	Kernels	PCA	LDA	UniSA	MMI	CIFE	CIFE+BFF
FERET	Poly 2	0.266	0.162	0.062	0.055	0.042	0.032
	Poly 4	0.267	0.150	0.051	0.052	0.042	0.027
	Sigmoid	0.271	0.142	0.057	0.051	0.037	0.022
	Gauss	0.265	0.134	0.051	0.055	0.032	0.017
XM2VTS	Poly 2	0.264	0.078	0.017	0.034	0.014	0.003
	Poly 4	0.264	0.075	0.017	0.014	0.014	0.013
	Sigmoid	0.254	0.085	0.017	0.014	0.014	0.003
	Gauss	0.258	0.064	0.014	0.007	0.000	0.000
PURDUE	Poly 2	0.241	0.139	0.056	0.035	0.022	0.017
	Poly 4	0.224	0.122	0.044	0.039	0.020	0.011
	Sigmoid	0.220	0.131	0.043	0.041	0.020	0.009
	Gauss	0.222	0.128	0.044	0.033	0.015	0.007

ple configuration, we merely use the Conditional Infomax Feature Extraction (CIFE) to extract features and simply use the Euclidean distance in the feature space to measure the dissimilarities between samples. In a full-functional configuration (CIFE + BFF), we further incorporate the Bayesian Feature Fusion scheme and follow the whole procedure of the integrated framework. The results obtained using different numbers of features are illustrated in Figure 6 and the best results for each algorithm are reported in the Table 1. We can see from the results that the algorithms based on infomax principle outperforms other ones. The CIFE consistently achieves better accuracies than the MMI. By incorporating the Maximum Information Fusion and dynamically discarding the obsolete features, both the accuracy and the robustness of the framework are further enhanced.

Kernelized Features. We also investigate the performances of the algorithms for nonlinear features based on their kernelized versions. The results are given in Table 2. The results of nonlinear feature extraction further validates the effectiveness of our framework. Moreover, we can see that with the adaptive weighting scheme employed, the CIFS + BFF framework has a desirable property that the performance will not degrade with the increasing of the feature numbers as in conventional approaches. The results also confirm the observation in previous works that kernelization can lead to better performance in real data, where the distributions are often nongaussian. By combining the kernel learning and infomax learning and incorporating an effective fusion stage, our framework achieves near perfect classification performance in all the 3 databases.

7   Conclusion

We have presented a novel information-theoretical perspective on the supervised learning and carefully studied the two key factors: class-relevance and redundancy. We introduced a new framework effectively unifying two novel algorithms:

Conditional Informative Feature Extraction and Bayesian Feature Fusion. The results of extensive experiments have sufficiently demonstrated the superiority of our framework over other state-of-the-art approaches.

Acknowledgement

The work described in this paper was fully supported by grants from the Research Grants Council of the Hong Kong Special Administrative Region and a joint grant (N_CUHK409-03) from HKSAR RGC and China NSF. The work was done in The Chinese University of Hong Kong.

References

1. M. Turk, A. Pentland: Eigenfaces for Recognition. J. Cognitive Neuroscience **3**(1) (1991) 71–86
2. P. N. Belhumeur, J. P. Hespanha, D. J. Kriegman: Eigenfaces vs. Fisherfaces: Recognition Using Class Specific Linear Projection. IEEE Trans. on PAMI **19**(7) (1997) 711–720
3. K. Etemad, R. Chellappa: Discriminant Analysis for Recognition of Human Face Images. J. Opt. Soc. Am. **14**(8) (1997) 1724–1733
4. X. Wang, X. Tang: A Unified Framework for Subspace Face Recognition. IEEE Trans. on PAMI **26**(9) (2004) 1222–1228
5. R.P.W. Duin, R. Haeb-Umbach: Multiclass Linear Dimension Reduction by Weighted Pairwise Fisher Criteria. IEEE Trans. on PAMI **23**(7) (2001) 762–766
6. M. Loog, R.P.W. Duin: Linear Dimensionality Reduction via a Heteroscedastic Extension of LDA: The Chernoff Criterion. IEEE Trans. on PAMI **26**(6) (2004) 732–739
7. T. M. Cover, J. A. Thomas: Elements of Information Theory. John Wiley Sons, Inc. (1991)
8. Y. Yang, J. O. Pedersen: A Comparative Study on Feature Selection in Text Categorization. In: ICML'97. (1997)
9. N. Kwak, C. Choi: Input Feature Selection by Mutual Information Based on Parzen Window. IEEE Trans. on PAMI **24**(12) (2002) 1667–1671
10. N. Vasconcelos: Feature Selection by Maximum Marginal Diversity. In: NIPS'02. (2002)
11. Y. Wu, A. Zhang: Feature Selection for Classifying High-Dimensional Numerical Data. In: CVPR'04. (2004)
12. H. Peng, F. Long, C. Ding: Feature Selection Based on Mutual Information Criteria of Max-Dependency, Max-Relevance, and Min-Redundancy. IEEE Trans. on PAMI **27**(8) (2005) 1226–1238
13. P. Mitra, C.A. Murthy, S.K. Pal: Unsupervised Feature Selection Using Feature Similarity. IEEE Trans. on PAMI **24**(3) (2002) 301–312
14. N. Vasconcelos, M. Vasconcelos: Scalable Discriminant Feature Selection for Image Retrieval and Recognition. In: CVPR'04. (2004)
15. K. Torkkola, W. M. Campbell: Mutual Information in Learning Feature Transformations. In: ICML'00. (2000)
16. K. Torkkola: Feature Extraction by Non-Parametric Mutual Information Maximization. J. Machine Learning Research (2003) 1415–1438

17. M.A.T. Figueiredo: Adaptive Sparseness for Supervised Learning. IEEE Trans. on PAMI **25**(9) (2003) 1150–1159
18. B. Krishnapuram, A.J. Hartemink, L. Carin, M.A.T. Figueiredo: A Bayesian Approach to Joint Feature Selection and Classifier Design. IEEE Trans. on PAMI **26**(9) (2004) 1105–1111
19. A. Hyvarinen, E. Oja: Independent Component Analysis: Algorithms and Applications. Neural Networks **13**(4-5) (2000) 411–430
20. P. J. Phillips, H. Moon, S. A. Rizvi, P. J. Rauss: The FERET Evaluation Methodology for Face-Recognition Algorithms. IEEE Trans. PAMI **22**(10) (2000) 1090–1104
21. K. Messer, J. Matas, J. Kittler, J. Luettin, G. Maitre: XM2VTSDB: The Extended M2VTS Database. In: Proc. of Int.l Conf. Audio- and Video-based Person Authentication. (1999)
22. A.M. Martinez, R. Benavente: The AR Face Database. CVC Technical Report 24, Purdue University (1998)

Degen Generalized Cylinders and Their Properties

Liangliang Cao[1], Jianzhuang Liu[1], and Xiaoou Tang[1,2]

[1] Department of Information Engineering, The Chinese University of Hong Kong,
Hong Kong, China
{llcao, jzliu, xtang}@ie.cuhk.edu.hk
[2] Microsoft Research Asia, Beijing, China
xitang@microsoft.com

Abstract. Generalized cylinder (GC) has played an important role in computer vision since it was introduced in the 1970s. While studying GC models in human visual perception of shapes from contours, Marr assumed that GC's limbs are planar curves. Later, Koenderink and Ponce pointed out that this assumption does not hold in general by giving some examples. In this paper, we show that straight homogeneous generalized cylinders (SHGCs) and tori (a kind of curved GCs) have planar limbs when viewed from points on specific straight lines. This property leads us to the definition and investigation of a new class of GCs, with the help of the surface model proposed by Degen for geometric modeling. We call them Degen generalized cylinders (DGCs), which include SHGCs, tori, quadrics, cyclides, and more other GCs into one model. Our rigorous discussion is based on projective geometry and homogeneous coordinates. We present some invariant properties of DGCs that reveal the relations among the planar limbs, axes, and contours of DGCs. These properties are useful for recovering DGC descriptions from image contours as well as for some other tasks in computer vision.

1 Introduction

A generalized cylinder (GC) is a solid obtained by sweeping a planar region along an axis. The planar region is called the cross section of the GC and is not necessarily circular or constant. The axis can also be curved in space. This model was at first proposed by Binford in 1971 [1], and has received extensive attention and become popular in computer vision in the past three decades. Because of their ability to represent objects explicitly and their object-centered coordinate frames derivable from image data, GCs have been applied to shape recovery [2], [3], [4], [5], [6], object modelling [7], [8], [9], [10], model-based segmentation and detection [11], [12], modelling tree branches in computer graphics [13], and designing robot vision systems [14].

From previous work on the study of the properties and recovery of GCs, we can roughly divide GCs into two groups: GC with straight axes and GCs with curved axes. In what follows, we call them straight GCs and curved GCs, respectively. Most of the work considers GCs in single views. Straight homogeneous generalized cylinders (SHGCs) are the most important subset of straight GCs, whose sweeping axes are straight and whose cross sections are scaled along the axes. SHGCs were first defined by Shafer and Kanade [15], and then studied extensively by many researchers [2], [4], [6], [11], [12], [16], [17], [18].

A. Leonardis, H. Bischof, and A. Pinz (Eds.): ECCV 2006, Part I, LNCS 3951, pp. 83–94, 2006.

Compared with SHGCs, less work on curved GCs has been done. The difficulty is mainly due to two facts: the projection of the axis of a curved GC may not be necessarily the axis of its 2D contours [19], and the angle between the axis and the cross section in the image no longer keeps constant [20]. To interpolate the axis of a curved GC in scattered data, Shani and Ballard proposed an iterative solution of minimizing the torsion of the axis [10]. In [5], Sayd et al. presented a scheme to recover a constrained subset of curved GCs with circular and constant cross sections. Ulupinar and Nevatia focused on a subset of GCs whose axes are planar curves[1] and normal to the constant cross sections [21]. Zerroug and Nevatia studied the invariants and quasi-invariants of a subset of GCs with planar curved axes and with circular (not necessarily constant) cross sections [22]. In [9], Gross considered GCs with planar curved axes or with circular cross sections, and presented an algorithm to recover the GCs using image contours and reflectance information.

The analysis of the previous work on SHGCs and curved GCs is explicitly separate, focusing on special classes of GCs. In this paper, starting from the discussion of the conditions when SHGCs and tori (a kind of curved GCs) have planar limbs, we define and study a new class of GCs, with the help of the surface model proposed by Degen for geometric modeling [23], [24]. We call them Degen generalized cylinders (DGCs), which include SHGCs, tori, quadrics, cyclides, and more other GCs into one model. Our rigorous discussion is based on projective geometry and homogeneous coordinates. We present some invariant properties of DGCs that reveal the relations among the planar limbs, axes, and contours of DGCs. We also discuss how the proposed properties can be used for recovering DGC descriptions from image contours, and for generating good initializations for a new 3D deformable DGC model in 3D data fitting and segmentation.

2   Planar Limbs and View Directions

This section discusses two classes of GCs that have planar limbs when viewed from specific directions. These GCs with the property of planar limbs are the motivation of our work.

In this paper, image contours are referred to as the projections of *contour generators* that are curves in space. There are two kinds of contour generators: *limbs* and *edges* [6]. Limb points are the points where the surface turns smoothly away from the observer, and edge points are those where the surface orientation is discontinuous. A limb is sometimes called a rim [25], viewpoint-dependent edge, or virtual edge [26].

Although a curve in 3D space can be formed freely, its projected contours cannot keep all the information of its 3D shape. Fig. 1 shows such a limitation. From the projection of a curve, one cannot judge whether it is planar or not in 3D space. To guess the ability of human vision on recovering 3D information from contours, Stevens assumed that one tends to interpret the 2D projection of a space curve as the projection of a planar curve [27], [28]. We can see this tendency from the projections in Fig. 1 if the space curve is not shown. In differential geometry, the torsion of a planar curve is zero, which was used by Shani and Ballard as the minimization criterion to recover 3D curved axes [10].

---

[1] A planar curve is a curve lying on a plane in space.

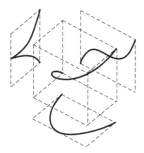

Fig. 1. 2D Projections unable to fully describe the 3D information of the space curve

Marr also assumed that limbs are planar in human visual interpretation. With this assumption and other constraints, Marr showed that human beings always interpret the projected surface as part of a GC; limbs being planar is a basic assumption in the study of reconstructing object surfaces in Marr's fundamental vision theory [25].

However, this assumption does not hold generally as pointed out by Koenderink [29]. He showed that the contour of a torus, which is a curved GC, is often the projection of a non-planar limb. Later Ponce and Chelberg revealed that even SHGCs cannot possess planar limbs from all viewing directions [16]. Fig. 2 gives such an example, where the bold black curves are the intersection of a plane and the GC's surface. From the two viewing directions, the limbs in Fig. 2(a) are planar, but the limbs in Fig. 2(b) are not. Now we discuss in what conditions SHGCs and tori can have planar limbs.

We use the similar notation and the coordinate system as those in [6] and [16]. Suppose that the axis of a SHGC coincides with the z-axis as shown in Fig. 3. The surface of a SHGC can be represented in the polar coordinate system by

$$\mathbf{x}(z, \theta) = \rho(\theta)r(z)\cos\theta\mathbf{i} + \rho(\theta)r(z)\sin\theta\mathbf{j} + z\mathbf{k} \tag{1}$$

where $z \in [a, b]$, $\theta \in [0, 2\pi]$, and ρ defines the reference cross section on the x-y plane, and r defines the scaling sweeping rule of the SHGC. Let $\mathbf{v}$ be the viewing direction, and $\mathbf{n}$ be the normal vector to the surface at the points on a limb. Then according to the definition of limbs, we have the relation

$$\mathbf{v} \cdot \mathbf{n} = 0. \tag{2}$$

Proposition 1. *A SHGC has planar limbs when the viewing direction is normal to the axis of the SHGC under orthographic projection.*

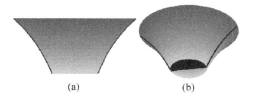

(a)   (b)

Fig. 2. (a) Planar limbs. (b) Non-planar limbs

Proof. Assume the viewing direction is given by its spherical coordinate (α, β) (see Fig. 3). Then

$$\mathbf{v} = \sin\beta\cos\alpha\mathbf{i} + \sin\beta\sin\alpha\mathbf{j} + \cos\beta\mathbf{k}. \tag{3}$$

With (2), Ponce [6] proved that points on a limb satisfy

$$\rho^2 r'\cos\beta = [\rho(\theta)\cos(\theta-\alpha) + \rho'(\theta)\sin(\theta-\alpha)]\sin\beta. \tag{4}$$

When $\mathbf{v}$ is normal to $\mathbf{k}$, $\beta = 90°$. Hence

$$\rho(\theta)\cos(\theta-\alpha) + \rho'(\theta)\sin(\theta-\alpha) = 0, \tag{5}$$

which implies a function θ of α only (independent of z), i.e., $\theta = f(\alpha)$. We can write the limb equation as

$$\begin{aligned}
\mathbf{l}(z) &= \mathbf{x}(z, f(\alpha)) \\
&= r(z)\rho(f(\alpha))(\cos f(\alpha)\mathbf{i} + \sin f(\alpha)\mathbf{j}) + z\mathbf{k} \\
&= r(z)\mathbf{u}(\alpha) + z\mathbf{k},
\end{aligned} \tag{6}$$

where $\mathbf{u}(\alpha) = \rho(f(\alpha))(\cos f(\alpha)\mathbf{i} + \sin f(\alpha)\mathbf{j})$. From (6),

$$\mathbf{l}''(z) = r''(z)\mathbf{v}(\alpha) \tag{7}$$
$$\mathbf{l}'''(z) = r'''(z)\mathbf{v}(\alpha) \tag{8}$$
$$\mathbf{l}''(z) \times \mathbf{l}'''(z) = \mathbf{0}. \tag{9}$$

Hence $\mathbf{l}'(z) \times \mathbf{l}''(z) \times \mathbf{l}'''(z) = \mathbf{0}$, which indicates that the limb is a planar curve, because the torsion of a planar curve is equal to zero [30]. □

Although a torus (a curved GC) does not belong to the class of SHGCs, it also has planar limbs when viewed from specific directions. Note that the axis of a torus is a circle inside the torus.

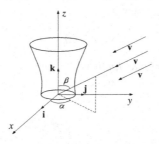

Fig. 3. The coordinate system with a SHGC and the viewing direction $\mathbf{v}$

Proposition 2. *A torus has planar limbs while viewed from a point where the line through the point and the torus center is orthogonal to the torus axis.*

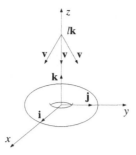

Fig. 4. A torus with the viewpoint at the z-axis

Proof. Without loss of generality, we assume that the axis of the torus is located on the x-y plane, the center of it coincides with the origin, and the viewpoint is at $l\mathbf{k}$, as shown in Fig. 4. Then the surface of the torus can be parameterized by [31]

$$\mathbf{x}(z,\theta) = (R - r\cos z)\cos\theta\mathbf{i} + (R - r\cos z)\sin\theta\mathbf{j} + r\sin z\mathbf{k}. \tag{10}$$

The normal to the surface is given by

$$\begin{aligned}
\mathbf{n}(z,\theta) &= \frac{\partial\mathbf{x}}{\partial z} \times \frac{\partial\mathbf{x}}{\partial\theta} \\
&= -r\cos z(R - r\cos z)\cos\theta\mathbf{i} - r\cos z(R - r\cos z)\sin\theta\mathbf{j} \\
&\quad + (R + r\sin z)(R - r\cos z)\mathbf{k}.
\end{aligned} \tag{11}$$

The viewing direction from $l\mathbf{k}$ to the surface is

$$\mathbf{v}(z,\theta) = \mathbf{x}(z,\theta) - l\mathbf{k}. \tag{12}$$

Substituting $\mathbf{v}$ in (12) and $\mathbf{n}$ in (11) into (2) yields

$$rl\sin z + Rr\cos z - Rr\sin z - r^2 + Rl = 0, \tag{13}$$

which implies a function z of l only (independent of θ). i.e., $z = g(l)$. Thus we can write the limb equation as

$$\mathbf{l}(\theta) = \mathbf{x}(g(l),\theta) = (R - r\cos g(l))(\cos\theta\mathbf{i} + \sin\theta\mathbf{j}) + r\sin g(l)\mathbf{k}. \tag{14}$$

It is easy to show

$$\mathbf{l}'(\theta) \times \mathbf{l}''(\theta) \times \mathbf{l}'''(\theta) = \mathbf{0}. \tag{15}$$

Thus the limb is planar since its torsion is zero. □

3 DGCs in Homogeneous Coordinates

We have shown that SHGCs and tori have planar limbs when viewed from some specific directions. There are also other curved GCs sharing the same property. This property leads us to the investigation of DGCs. For mathematical convenience, we will mainly use homogeneous coordinates and projective geometry in the following discussion of DGCs.

3.1 Homogeneous Coordinates

Homogeneous coordinates are used in projective geometry [32]. They are a useful tool in computer vision and graphics. Points in homogeneous coordinates are represented by vectors $\mathbf{p} = (w, x, y, z)^T \in \mathbb{R}^4 \setminus \{(0, 0, 0, 0)^T\}$. The w, x, y, z are called homogeneous coordinates of $\mathbf{p}$. $\mathbf{p}$ and $\rho\mathbf{p}$ with $\rho \in \mathbb{R} \setminus \{0\}$ define the same point. Given a point $\mathbf{p} = (w, x, y, z)^T$ with $w \neq 0$ in homogeneous coordinates, its corresponding point $\bar{\mathbf{p}}$ in Cartesian coordinates is

$$\bar{\mathbf{p}} = (\bar{x}, \bar{y}, \bar{z})^T = (\frac{x}{w}, \frac{y}{w}, \frac{z}{w})^T. \tag{16}$$

If $w = 0$, the point $(0, x, y, z)$ stands for a point at *infinity* (called an *ideal point*).

Orthogonal projection can be treated as a special case of perspective projection when the viewpoint is at infinity. Thus under perspective projection, Proposition 1 states that a SHGC has planar limbs when the viewpoint is at infinity and the viewing direction is normal to the axis of the SHGC.

Using homogeneous coordinates, points on a straight line $\mathbf{L}$ can be represented by

$$\mathbf{L} = \alpha\mathbf{a} + \beta\mathbf{b}, \tag{17}$$

where $\alpha, \beta \in \mathbb{R}$ and $\mathbf{a}, \mathbf{b}$ are two independent points in the projective space. In what follows, we denote the line $\mathbf{L}$ by $\mathbf{a} \wedge \mathbf{b}$. Similarly, points on a plane $\mathbf{P}$ can be represented by

$$\mathbf{P} = \alpha\mathbf{a} + \beta\mathbf{b} + \gamma\mathbf{c} \tag{18}$$

where $\alpha, \beta, \gamma \in \mathbb{R}$ and $\mathbf{a}, \mathbf{b}, \mathbf{c}$ are three independent points. We denote the plane $\mathbf{P}$ by $\mathbf{a} \wedge \mathbf{b} \wedge \mathbf{c}$. Therefore, a curve $\mathbf{C}(s)$ is planar if it can be written in this form

$$\mathbf{C}(s) = p_1(s)\mathbf{a} + p_2(s)\mathbf{b} + p_3(s)\mathbf{c}. \tag{19}$$

To verify whether a curve is planar or not, this way is more convenient than calculating the torsion of the curve in Cartesian coordinates.

3.2 Degen Surfaces

Degen proposed a novel surface model for geometric modelling in [23] and [24]. We call those surfaces *Degen surfaces*. They cover a wide range of curved surfaces such as those showed in Fig. 5. A Degen surface is parameterized by the following equation in homogeneous coordinates

$$\mathbf{X}(u, v) = \alpha(u)\mathbf{a} + \beta(u)\mathbf{b} + \gamma(v)\mathbf{c} + \delta(v)\mathbf{d} = \mathbf{p}(u) + \mathbf{q}(v), \tag{20}$$

where $\mathbf{p}(u) = \alpha(u)\mathbf{a} + \beta(u)\mathbf{b}$, $\mathbf{q}(v) = \gamma(v)\mathbf{c} + \delta(v)\mathbf{d}$, $u \in [u_1, u_2]$, $v \in [v_1, v_2]$, $\mathbf{a}, \mathbf{b}, \mathbf{c}, \mathbf{d}$ are independent, and $\alpha, \beta, \gamma, \delta$ are certain functions. The two straight lines $\mathbf{a} \wedge \mathbf{b}$ and $\mathbf{c} \wedge \mathbf{d}$ are called the axes of the Degen surface.

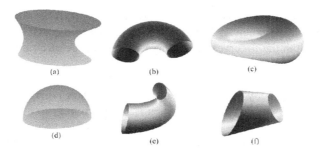

Fig. 5. Some examples of Degen Surfaces including SHGCs(a), an open torus(b), a cyclide(c), a quadric(d), and more other GCs (e,f), respectively

3.3 DGCs

Before defining DGCs, we show that SHGCs and tori can be represented in the form of Degen surfaces in homogeneous coordinates. The parameterized surface of a SHGC in homogeneous coordinates is simply

$$\mathbf{X}(u,v) = (1, \rho(u)r(v)\cos u, \rho(u)r(v)\sin u, v)^T, \tag{21}$$

where the z and θ in (1) are replaced by u and v, respectively. Then $\mathbf{X}(u,v) = \mathbf{p}(u) + \mathbf{q}(v)$ with

$$\mathbf{p}(u) = (0, \rho(u)\cos u, \rho(u)\sin u, 0)^T \tag{22}$$

$$\mathbf{q}(v) = \frac{1}{r(v)}(1, 0, 0, v)^T. \tag{23}$$

Furthermore

$$\mathbf{p}(u) = \rho(u)(\cos u)\mathbf{a} + \rho(u)(\sin u)\mathbf{b} \tag{24}$$

$$\mathbf{q}(v) = \frac{1}{r(v)}\mathbf{c} + \frac{v}{r(v)}\mathbf{d} \tag{25}$$

with $\mathbf{a} = (0,1,0,0)^T, \mathbf{b} = (0,0,1,0)^T, \mathbf{c} = (1,0,0,0)^T, \mathbf{d} = (0,0,0,1)^T$.

Similarly, replacing the z and θ in (10) with u and v, respectively, we can show that a torus belongs to a Degen surface by

$$\mathbf{p}(u) = \frac{1}{R - r\cos u}(1/r, 0, 0, \sin u)^T = \frac{1}{r(R - r\cos u)}\mathbf{a} + \frac{\sin u}{R - r\cos u}\mathbf{b} \tag{26}$$

$$\mathbf{q}(v) = \frac{1}{r}(0, \cos v, \sin v, 0)^T = \frac{\cos v}{r}\mathbf{c} + \frac{\sin v}{r}\mathbf{d}, \tag{27}$$

with $\mathbf{a} = (1,0,0,0)^T, \mathbf{b} = (0,0,0,1)^T, \mathbf{c} = (0,1,0,0)^T, \mathbf{d} = (0,0,1,0)^T$.

Definition 1. *On a Degen surface with the parametrization of* $\mathbf{X}(u,v)$*, when* $v = v_0$ *is fixed, the curve* $\mathbf{C}_1(u) = \mathbf{X}(u, v_0)$ *is called a u-curve; when* $u = u_0$ *is fixed, the curve* $\mathbf{C}_2(v) = \mathbf{X}(u_0, v)$ *is called a v-curve.*

In the above examples, the u-curves of a SHGC are $(0, \rho(u)\cos u, \rho(u)\sin u, 0)^T + \mathbf{q}(v_0)$, which are closed when $u \in [0, 2\pi]$; the v-curves of the SHGC are $\mathbf{p}(u_0) + \frac{1}{r(v)}(1, 0, 0, v)^T$. Both the u-curves and v-curves of a torus are circles, which are also closed.

On a Degen surface with $u \in [u_1, u_2]$, $v \in [v_1, v_2]$, the family of u-curves $\{\mathbf{C}_1(u) = \mathbf{X}(u, v_0) \mid v_0 \in [v_1, v_2]\}$ covers the whole surface. Thus a Degen surface can be seen as a surface obtained by sweeping a u-curve when v_0 varies from v_1 to v_2. If the u-curve is closed, the region bounded by it can be regarded as the cross section of a GC. Note that all the u-curves and v-curves are planar as stated in Lemma 1 in Section 4.

Definition 2. *A Degen generalized cylinder (DGC) is a solid bounded by a Degen surface* $\mathbf{X}(u, v) = \alpha(u)\mathbf{a} + \beta(u)\mathbf{b} + \gamma(v)\mathbf{c} + \delta(v)\mathbf{d}$ *with closed u-curves, or closed v-curves, or both. The axes of the DGC are the two straight lines* $\mathbf{a} \wedge \mathbf{b}$ *and* $\mathbf{c} \wedge \mathbf{d}$.

Obviously, the surface of a DGC is a Degen surface. However, a Degen surface with neither u-curves nor v-curves closed does not form a DGC. Fig. 6 gives such an example. The Degen surfaces showed in Fig. 5 form six DGCs if the cross sections are considered as regions instead of curves.

It should be emphasized that a conventional GC has only one axis and the axis of a conventional curved GC is a curve. It is often more difficult to recover curved axes than to recover straight axes.

4   Properties of DGCs

In this section, we present the properties of DGCs that are useful for some computer vision tasks.

Proposition 3. *The axis of a SHGC coincides with one of the two axes of the DGC that is the corresponding representation of the SHGC in homogeneous coordinates. Another axis of the DGC is a line at infinity.*

Proof. When a SHGC is written as (1), its axis is the z-axis (Fig. 3). The same SHGC can be represented in the form of a DGC as in (21)–(25). One axis of the DGC is $\mathbf{c} \wedge \mathbf{d}$, i.e., a line passing through $(1, 0, 0, 0)^T$ and $(0, 0, 0, 1)^T$, which denotes the z-axis in homogeneous coordinates. Another axis of the DGC is a line at infinity, which passes through the two ideal points $\mathbf{a} = (0, 1, 0, 0)^T$ and $\mathbf{b} = (0, 1, 0, 0)^T$. $\square$

It is also easy to find the two axes of a torus when it is represented in the form of a DGC. Suppose a torus in Euclidean geometry is expressed by (10). From (26) and (27), we

Fig. 6. A Degen surface with neither u-curves nor v-curves closed

see that one axis of the torus is $\mathbf{a} \wedge \mathbf{b}$ with $\mathbf{a} = (1, 0, 0, 0)^T$ and $\mathbf{b} = (0, 0, 0, 1)^T$, which is the z-axis in homogeneous coordinates. Another axis is $\mathbf{c} \wedge \mathbf{d}$ with $\mathbf{c} = (0, 1, 0, 0)^T$ and $\mathbf{d} = (0, 0, 1, 0)^T$, which is a line through the two ideal points $\mathbf{c}$ and $\mathbf{d}$ at infinity.

As pointed out in Propositions 1 and 2, both SHGCs and tori have planar limbs when viewed from the special directions. Now we show that all DGCs have this property. At first, we give two lemmas that are proved in [23].

Lemma 1. *All the u-curves and v-curves of a DGC are planar.*

Lemma 2. *All the tangent planes on a u-curve $\mathbf{X}(u, v_0)$ (v-curve $\mathbf{X}(u_0, v)$, respectively) pass through the same point $\gamma'(v_0)\mathbf{c} + \delta'(v_0)\mathbf{d}$ ($\alpha'(u_0)\mathbf{a} + \beta'(u_0)\mathbf{b}$, respectively).*

Proposition 4. *A DGC has planar limbs when viewed from points on its two axes $\mathbf{a} \wedge \mathbf{b}$ and $\mathbf{c} \wedge \mathbf{d}$, and the planar limbs are u-curves and v-curves.*

Proof. From Lemma 2, we know that all the tangent planes on a u-curve $X(u, v_0)$ pass through the point $\gamma'(v_0)\mathbf{c} + \delta'(v_0)\mathbf{d}$. All such points with different values of v_0 lie on the axis $\mathbf{c} \wedge \mathbf{d}$. Therefore, if the DGC is observed from one of the points, the viewing directions must lie on these tangent planes at points on the u-curves. Thus the u-curve becomes a limb of the DGC. By Lemma 1, the limb is planar. Similarly, the DGC has planar limbs when observed from points on another axis $\mathbf{a} \wedge \mathbf{b}$. $\square$

Proposition 5. *For any two contour points from the same u-curve (v-curve, respectively), the tangents to the contours at the two points intersect on the projection of the axis $\mathbf{c} \wedge \mathbf{d}$ ($\mathbf{a} \wedge \mathbf{b}$, respectively).*

Proof. From Lemma 2, all the tangent planes of the u-curve (v-curve, respectively) meet at the same point on the axis $\mathbf{c} \wedge \mathbf{d}$ ($\mathbf{a} \wedge \mathbf{b}$, respectively). Since the tangent plane at a point of the limb is projected onto the tangent at the corresponding point on the contour generated by the limb [33], this proposition holds. $\square$

Fig. 7 illustrates this invariant property. Note that when a DGC is a SHGC, one axis becomes the axis of the SHGC (Proposition 3). Thus the SHGC's invariant property stated in Lemma 4 in Ponce et al.'s work [6] becomes a special case of Proposition 5.

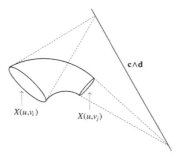

Fig. 7. Illustration of Proposition 5

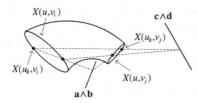

Fig. 8. Illustration of Proposition 6

Definition 3. *Let* $\mathbf{X}(u, v_i)$ *and* $\mathbf{X}(u, v_j)$ *be two u-curves of a DGC. Two points* $\mathbf{X}(u_k, v_i)$ *and* $\mathbf{X}(u_k, v_j)$ *on the two u-curves define a line of correspondence from the two u-curves. Let* $\mathbf{X}(u_m, v)$ *and* $\mathbf{X}(u_n, v)$ *be two v-curves of a DGC. Two points* $\mathbf{X}(u_m, v_q)$ *and* $\mathbf{X}(u_n, v_q)$ *on the two v-curves define a line of correspondence from the two v-curves.*

Proposition 6. *All the lines of correspondence from any two u-curves (v-curves, respectively) of a DGC intersect at the same point on the axis* $\mathbf{c} \wedge \mathbf{d}$ *(* $\mathbf{a} \wedge \mathbf{b}$ *, respectively).*

Proof. Let $\mathbf{X}(u, v_i)$ and $\mathbf{X}(u, v_j)$ be two u-curves as shown in Fig. 8, the line of correspondence passing through the two points $\mathbf{X}(u_k, v_i)$ and $\mathbf{X}(u_k, v_j)$ can be expressed as

$$\mathbf{X}(u_k, v_i) + \lambda \mathbf{X}(u_k, v_j), \quad \lambda \in \mathbb{R}. \tag{28}$$

When $\lambda = -1$,

$$\begin{aligned}
\mathbf{X}(u_k, v_i) - \mathbf{X}(u_k, v_j) &= [\mathbf{p}(u_k) + \mathbf{q}(v_i)] - [\mathbf{p}(u_k) + \mathbf{q}(v_j)] \\
&= \mathbf{q}(v_i) - \mathbf{q}(v_j) \\
&= [\gamma(v_i) - \gamma(v_j)]\mathbf{c} + [\delta(v_i) - \delta(v_j)]\mathbf{d}, \tag{29}
\end{aligned}$$

which is a point on the axis $\mathbf{c} \wedge \mathbf{d}$. Since this point is independent of u_k, all such lines from the two u-curves intersect at this point. In the same way, we can also prove that the proposition is true for the lines of correspondence from two v-curves. $\quad\square$

From Proposition 6, we can obtain a corollary, the geometry of which is illustrated in Fig. 9. The proof is omitted due to space limitation.

Corollary 1. *In the general case, the two axes* $\mathbf{a} \wedge \mathbf{b}$ *and* $\mathbf{c} \wedge \mathbf{d}$ *of a DGC can be determined from a pair of u-curves and a pair of v-curves of the DGC.*

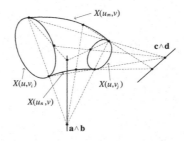

Fig. 9. Illustration of Corollary 1

5   Conclusions

GCs have been used in many applications of computer vision. Previous work on GCs focuses on relatively narrow sets of GCs. In this paper, we have proposed a new set of GCs, called Degen generalized cylinders (DGCs). DGCs cover a wide range of GCs, including SHGCs, tori, quadrics, cyclides, and more other GCs into one unified model. We have presented a number of properties existing in DGCs. Our rigorous discussion is based on homogeneous coordinates in projective geometry, which is more general than Euclidean geometry. The invariant properties of DGCs reveal the relations among the planar limbs, axes, and contours of DGCs. These properties can be used for recovering DGC descriptions from image contours, representing GCs in computer vision and graphics, and modeling surface warping in 3D animation.

Acknowledgments

The authors would like to thank the anonymous reviewers for their useful comments. This work is supported by RGC Research Direct Grant 2050369, CUHK.

References

1. Binford, T.: Visual perception by computer. IEEE Conf. Systems and Control (1971)
2. Sato, H., Binford, T.: Finding and recovering SHGC objects in an edge image. CVGIP: Graphical Model and Image Processing **57**(3) (1993) 346–358
3. Dhome, M., Glachet, R., Lapreste, J.: Recovering the scaling function of a SHGC from a single perspective view. IEEE Proc. Computer Vision and Pattern Recognition (1992) 36–41
4. Ulupinar, F., Nevatia, R.: Shape from contour: Straight homogeneous generalized cylinders and constant cross-section generalized cylinders. IEEE Trans. Pattern Analysis and Machine Intelligence **17**(2) (1995) 120–135
5. Sayd, P. Dhome, M., Lavest, J.: Recovering generalized cylinders by monocular vision. Object Representation in Computer Vision II (1996) 25–51
6. Ponce, J., Chelberg, D., Mann, W.: Invariant properties of straight homogeneous generalized cylinders and their contours. IEEE Trans. Pattern Analysis and Machine Intelligence **11**(9) (1989) 951–966
7. O'Donnell, T. Boult, T., Fang, X., Gupta, A.: The extruded generalized cylinder: A deformable model for object recovery. Proc. IEEE Conf. Computer Vision and Pattern Recognition (1994) 174 – 181
8. O'Donnell, T., Dubuisson-Jolly, M.P., Gupta, A.: A cooperative framework for segmentation using 2-D active contours and 3-D hybrid models as applied to branching cylindrical structures. Proc. Int'l Conf. Computer Vision (1998) 454 – 459
9. Gross, A.D.: Analyzing generalized tubes. Proc. SPIE Conf. Intelligent Robots and Computer Vision XIII: 3D Vision, Product **2354** (1994)
10. Shani, U., Ballard, D.H.: Splines as embeddings for generalized cylinders. Computer Vision, Graphics, and Image Processing (CVGIP) **27**(2) (1984) 129–156
11. Zerroug, M., Nevatia, R.: Segmentation and recovery of SHGCS from a real intensity image. European Conf. Computer Vision (1994) 319–330
12. Gross, A.D., Boult, T.E.: Recovery of SHGCs from a single intensity view. IEEE Trans. Pattern Analysis and Machine Intelligence **18**(2) (1996) 161–180

13. Bloomenthal, J.: Modeling the mighty maple. Proc. SIGGRAPH '85 **19**(3) (1985)
14. Brooks, R. A., R.G., Binford, T.O.: The ACRONYM model-based vision system. Proc. of 6th Int'l Joint Conf. Artificial Intelligence (1979) 105–113
15. Shafer, S., Kanade, T.: The theory of straight homogeneous generalized cylinders and a taxonomy of generalized cylinders. Technical Report, Carnegie Mellon Universit (1983)
16. Ponce, J., Chelberg, D.: Finding the limbs and cusps of generalized cylinders. Int'l Journal of Computer Vision **1** (1987) 195–210
17. Ulupinar, F., Nevatia, R.: Perception of 3-D surfaces from 2-D contours. IEEE Trans. Pattern Analysis and Machine Intelligence **15**(1) (1993) 3–18
18. Ulupinar, F., Nevatia, R.: Recovery of 3-D objects with multiple curved surfaces from 2-D contours. Artificial Intelligence **67**(1) (1994) 1–28
19. P.J.Giblin, B.B.Kimia: Transitions of the 3D medial axis under a one-parameter family of deformations. European Conf. Computer Vision (2002) 718–724
20. Zerroug, M., Nevatia, R.: Three-dimensional descriptions based on the analysis of the invariant and quasi-invariant properties of some curved-axis generalized cylinders. IEEE Trans. Pattern Analysis and Machine Intelligence **18**(3) (1996) 237–253
21. Ulupinar, F., Nevatia, R.: Recovering shape from contour for constant cross section generalized cylinders. Proc. IEEE Conf. Computer Vision and Pattern Recognition (1991) 674–676
22. Zerroug, M., Nevatia, R.: Quasi-invariant properties and 3-D shape recovery of non-straight, non-constant generalized cylinders. Proc. IEEE Conf. Computer Vision and Pattern Recognition (1993) 96–103
23. Degen, W.L.F.: Nets with plane silhouettes. Proc. IMA Conf. the Mathematics of Surfaces V (1994) 117–133
24. Degen, W.L.F.: Conjugate silhouette nets. Curve and surface design: 99 (2000) 37–44
25. Marr, D.: Vision: A Computational Investigation into the Human Representation and Processing of Visual Information. Henry Holt Company (1982)
26. Zhu, Q.: Virtual edges, viewing faces, and boundary traversal in line drawing representation of objects with curved surfaces. Int'l J. Computers and Graphics **15**(2) (1991) 161–173
27. Stevens, K.: The visual interpretation of surface contours. Artificial Intelligence **17**(1-3) (1981) 47–73
28. Stevens, K.: Implementation of a theory for inferring surface shape from contours. MIT AI Memo-676 (1982)
29. Koenderink, J.: What does the occluding contour tell us about solid shape? Perception **13** (1984) 321–330
30. Carmo, D.: Differential geometry of curves and surfaces. Englewood Cliffs, N.J. : Prentice Hal (1976)
31. Marsh, D.: Applied Geometry for Computer Graphics and CAD. Springer Undergraduate Mathematics Series. Springer (1999)
32. E.A.Maxwell: General Homogeneous Coordinates in Space of Three Dimensions. Cambridge University Press (1951)
33. Ulupinar, F., Nevatia, R.: Shape from contour: Straight homogeneous generalized cones. Proc. Int'l Conf. Pattern Recognition (1990) 582–586

Geodesics Between 3D Closed Curves Using Path-Straightening

Eric Klassen[1] and Anuj Srivastava[2]

[1] Department of Mathematics, Florida State University, Tallahassee, FL 32306
[2] Department of Statistics, Florida State University, Tallahassee, FL 32306

Abstract. In order to analyze shapes of continuous curves in $\mathbb{R}^3$, we parameterize them by arc-length and represent them as curves on a unit two-sphere. We identify the subset denoting the closed curves, and study its differential geometry. To compute geodesics between any two such curves, we connect them with an arbitrary path, and then iteratively straighten this path using the gradient of an energy associated with this path. The limiting path of this path-straightening approach is a geodesic. Next, we consider the shape space of these curves by removing shape-preserving transformations such as rotation and re-parametrization. To construct a geodesic in this shape space, we construct the shortest geodesic between the all possible transformations of the two end shapes; this is accomplished using an iterative procedure. We provide step-by-step descriptions of all the procedures, and demonstrate them with simple examples.

1 Introduction

In recent years, there has been an increasing interest in analyzing shapes of objects. This research is motivated in part by the fact that shapes of objects form an important feature for characterizing them, with applications in recognition, tracking, and classification. For instance, shapes of boundaries of objects in images can be used to short-list possible objects present in those images. Also, shape has been used as a feature in image retrieval [14, 4, 6]. Shape analysis in image=based applications is often restricted to shapes of planar curves [19, 11, 8]; these curves can come, for example, from the boundaries of objects in 2D images. Shapes have also been used for medical diagnosis using non-invasive imaging techniques. Shapes, or growths of shapes, are often used to determine normailty/abnormalty of anatomical parts in computational anatomy [5]. A fundamental tool, central to any differential-geometric analysis of shapes, is the construction of a geodesic path path between any two given shapes in a pre-determined shape space. This tool can lead to a full statistical analysis – computation of means, covariances, tangent-space probability models – on shape spaces. As an example, the construction of geodesics and their use in statistical analysis of shapes of 2D curves is demonstrated in [8].

Although analysis of planar curves are useful in certain image understanding problems, a more general issue is to study and compare shapes of objects in 3D. Since most objects of interest are 3D objects, and 3D observations of objects

A. Leonardis, H. Bischof, and A. Pinz (Eds.): ECCV 2006, Part I, LNCS 3951, pp. 95–106, 2006.

using laser scans are becoming readily available, an important goal is to analyze shapes of two-dimensional surfaces in $\mathbb{R}^3$. In particular, given surfaces of two objects, the task is to quantify differences between their shapes. A differential-geometric analysis of shapes of surfaces, akin to the analysis of planar curves discussed above, remains a difficult and an unsolved problem. To our knowledge, there is no explicit method in the literature for computing geodesic between 3D closed curves. Several approximate methods have been pursued over the last few years. For example, the papers [16, 15] use histograms of distances on surfaces to represent and compare objects. Another approximate approach that has been suggested in recent years is to represent surfaces with a finite number of level curves, and then compare shapes of surfaces by comparing shapes of corresponding level curves [18]. Since these level curves can potentially be 3D curves [2], this approach requires a technique for comparing shapes of closed curves in $\mathbb{R}^3$. However, past research on geometric treatment of shapes of curves was restricted mainly to planar curves and a similar differential-geometric approach for comparing shapes of closed, continuous curves in $\mathbb{R}^3$ is not present in the literature, to the best of our knowledge.

In this paper, we present a differential-geometric technique for constructing geodesic paths between shapes of arbitrary two closed, continuous curves in $\mathbb{R}^3$. Given two curves p_0 and p_1, our basic approach is to: (i) define a shape space of all parameterized, closed curves in $\mathbb{R}^3$, (ii) construct an initial path connecting p_0 and p_1 in this space, and (iii) iteratively straighten this path until it becomes a geodesic path. This iteration is performed to minimize an energy associated with a path, and flows that minimize that energy are called *path-straightening* flows [9, 10], and more recently in [3, 13]. This methodology is quite different from the approach used in [8] where a shooting method was used to find geodesic paths between shapes. In a shooting method, one searches for a tangent direction at the first shape such that a geodesic *shot* in that direction reaches the target shape in a unit time. This search is based on adjusting the shooting direction in such a way that the miss function, defined as an extrinsic distance between the shape reached and the target shape, goes to zero. Intuitively, a path-straightening flow is expected to perform better than a shooting method for the following reasons:

1. While shooting, in principle, one can get stuck in a local minima of the miss function that is bounded away from zero. In other words, the resulting geodesic may not reach the target shape. In the path-straightening method, by construction, the geodesic always reaches the target shape.
2. Since the shooting is performed using numerical techniques, i.e. using numerical gradient of the miss function, these iterations can become unstable if the manifold is sharply curved near the target shape. A path-straightening approach, on the other hand, is numerically more stable as it uses the gradient of path length.

We will develop a path-straightening approach to computing geodesics in $\mathcal{C}$, the space of all closed curves in $\mathbb{R}^3$. Here we do not take into account the shapes of these curves, and the fact that many curves have the same shape. In future, we will define a shape space, as a quotient space of $\mathcal{C}$, and derive algorithms for computing geodesics between elements of this shape space.

The rest of this paper is organized as follows. In Section 2, we present a representation of closed curves, and analyze the geometry of $\mathcal{C}$, the space of such curves. Section 3 presents a formal discussion on the construction of path-straightening flows on $\mathcal{C}$, followed by algorithms for computer implementations in Section 4. Section 5 presents some illustrative examples on computing geodesic paths in $\mathcal{C}$. The paper ends with a summary in Section 6.

2   Geometry of Shapes and Shape Spaces

In this section we introduce a geometric representation of curves that underlies our construction of geodesics and the resulting analysis of shapes.

2.1   Representations of Closed Curves

Let $p : [0, 2\pi] \mapsto \mathbb{R}^3$ be a curve of length 2π, parameterized by the arc length. In this paper we will assume p to be piecewise C^1. For $v(s) \equiv \dot{p}(s) \in \mathbb{R}^3$, we have $\|v(s)\| = 1$ for all $s \in [0, 2\pi)$, in view of the arc-length parametrization. Here $\| \cdot \|$ denotes the Euclidean norm in $\mathbb{R}^3$. Note that the restriction to arc-length parametrization can be relaxed, as is done in [12], resulting in elastic-string models, but is not pursued in this paper. The function v is called the *direction function* of p and itself can be viewed as a curve on the unit sphere $\mathbb{S}^2$, i.e. $v : [0, 2\pi] \mapsto \mathbb{S}^2$. Shown in Figure 1(a) is an illustration of this idea where a closed curve p on $\mathbb{R}^3$ is represented by a curve v in $\mathbb{S}^2$. We will use the direction function v to represent the curve p . Let $\mathcal{P}$ be the set of all such direction functions, $\mathcal{P} = \{v | v : [0, 2\pi] \mapsto \mathbb{S}^2\}$. Since we are interested in *closed* curves, we establish that set as follows. Define a map $\phi : \mathcal{P} \mapsto \mathbb{R}^3$ by $\phi(v) = \int_0^{2\pi} v(s) ds$, and define $\mathcal{C} = \phi^{-1}(0) \equiv \{v \in \mathcal{P} | \phi(v) = 0\}$ $\subset \mathcal{P}$. It is easy to see that $\mathcal{C}$ is the set of all closed curves in $\mathbb{R}^3$. In the next section we will study the geometry of $\mathcal{C}$ in order to develop tools for shape analysis.

First, we introduce some notation for studying geometry of $\mathbb{S}^2$. Recall that geodesics on $\mathbb{S}^2$ are great circles, and we have analytical expressions for computing them. The geodesic on $\mathbb{S}^2$ starting at a point $x \in \mathbb{S}^2$ in the tangent direction $a \in T_x(\mathbb{S}^2)$ is given by:

$$\chi_t(x; a) = \cos(t\|a\|)x + \frac{\sin(t\|a\|)}{\|a\|}a \ . \tag{1}$$

χ_t will be used frequently in this paper to denote geodesics, or great circles, on $\mathbb{S}^2$. Another item that we need relates to the rotation of tangent vectors on $\mathbb{S}^2$. Let x_1 and x_2 be two elements in $\mathbb{S}^2$, and let a be a tangent to $\mathbb{S}^2$ at x_1. Then, a vector defined as:

$$\pi(a; x_1, x_2) = \begin{cases} a - (2(a \cdot x_2)/(\|x_1 + x_2\|^2))(x_1 + x_2) & \text{if } x_1 \neq -x_2 \\ -a & \text{if } x_1 = -x_2 \end{cases} \tag{2}$$

is the rotation of a to x_2 so that it is now tangent to $\mathbb{S}^2$ at x_2. Here, $(a \cdot b)$ denotes the Euclidean inner product of $a, b \in \mathbb{R}^3$. $\pi(\cdot, x_1, x_2) : T_{x_1}(\mathbb{S}^1) \mapsto T_{x_2}(\mathbb{S}^1)$ is a rotation map that takes a tangent vector from x_1 to x_2; in differential geometry this is also called the *parallel transport* along the geodesic from x_1 to x_2.

2.2   Geometry of $\mathcal{C}$

To develop a geometric framework for analyzing elements of $\mathcal{C}$, we would like understand its tangent bundle and to impose a Riemannian structure on it. First, we focus on the set $\mathcal{P}$. On any point $v \in \mathcal{P}$, what form does a tangent f to $\mathcal{P}$ takes? This tangent f can be derived by constructing a one-parameter flow passing through v, and by computing its velocity at v. Since v is also a curve on $\mathbb{S}^2$, the tangent f can also be viewed as a field of vectors tangent to $\mathbb{S}^2$ on v. This idea is illustrated pictorially in Figure 1(b). We will interchangeably refer to f as a tangent vector on $\mathcal{P}$ and a tangent vector field on points along $v \subset \mathbb{S}^2$. The space of all such tangent vectors, denoted by $T_v(\mathcal{P})$, is given by: $T_v(\mathcal{P}) = \{f | f : [0, 2\pi] \mapsto \mathbb{R}^3, (f(s) \cdot v(s)) = 0, \forall s\}$. $f(s)$ and $v(s)$ are vectors in $\mathbb{R}^3$. Let $f \in T_v(\mathcal{P})$ be a vector field on v such that it is also tangent to $\mathcal{C}$. It can be shown that f satisfies $\int f(s)ds = 0$. That is,

$$T_v(\mathcal{C}) = \{f | f : [0, 2\pi] \mapsto \mathbb{R}^3, \forall s, (f(s) \cdot v(s)) = 0, \int_0^{2\pi} f(s)ds = 0\} . \quad (3)$$

To see that, let $\alpha(t)$ be a path in $\mathcal{C}$ such that $\alpha(0) = v$. Since $\alpha(t) \in \mathcal{C}$, we have $\int_0^{2\pi} \alpha(t)(s)ds = 0$, for all t. Taking the derivative with respect to t and setting $t = 0$, we get $\int_0^{2\pi} \dot{\alpha}(0)(s)ds = 0$. For every tangent vector f at v there is a corresponding flow α, such that $f = \dot{\alpha}(0)$, and therefore, this property is satisfied by all tangent vectors.

Riemannian Structure: To impose a Riemannian structure on $\mathcal{P}$, we will assume the following inner product on $T_v(\mathcal{P})$: for $f, g \in T_v(\mathcal{P})$, $\langle f, g \rangle = \int_0^{2\pi} (f(s) \cdot g(s))ds$.

Consider the linear mapping $d\phi_v : T_v(\mathcal{P}) \mapsto \mathbb{R}^3$ defined by $d\phi_v(f) = \int_0^{2\pi} f(s)ds$. Similar to the argument in [13], it can be shown that $d\phi_v$ is surjective,

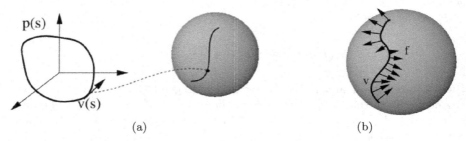

(a)   (b)

Fig. 1. (a): A closed curve in $\mathbb{R}^3$ is denoted by a curve on $\mathbb{S}^2$. (b): For a curve v on $\mathbb{S}^2$, f is vector field to $\mathbb{S}^2$ on v.

as long as $v([0, 2\pi))$ is not contained in a one-dimensional subspace of $\mathbb{R}^3$, and therefore $\mathcal{C}$ is a co-dimension three submanifold of $\mathcal{P}$. The adjoint of $d\phi_v$, $d\phi_v^*$: $\mathbb{R}^3 \to T_v(\mathcal{P})$ is the unique linear transformation with the property that for all $f \in T_v(\mathcal{P})$ and $w \in \mathbb{R}^3$, $(d\phi_v(f) \cdot w) = \langle f, d\phi_v^*(w) \rangle$. Mathematically, this adjoint is given by $d\phi_v^*(w) \equiv f$ such that $f(s) = w - (w \cdot v(s))v(s)$. In other words, $d\phi_v^*$ takes a vector w in $\mathbb{R}^3$ and forms a tangent vector-field on v by making w perpendicular to $v(s)$ for all s (or by projecting w onto the tangent space $T_{v(s)}(\mathbb{S}^2)$ for each s). This formula makes explicit the role of v in definition of $d\phi_v^*$.

With this framework, we develop tools for projecting $v \in \mathcal{P}$ into $\mathcal{C}$. Also, we derive a mechanism for projecting $f \in T_v(\mathcal{P})$ into $T_v(\mathcal{C})$. For details we refer to a larger paper [7].

3 Path-Straightening Flows in $\mathcal{C}$

Now we present our approach for constructing geodesic flows on $\mathcal{C}$. This approach is based on the use of path-straightening flows. That is, we connect the two given shapes by an arbitrary path in $\mathcal{C}$, and then iteratively straighten it, or shorten it, using a gradient approach till we reach a fixed point. The fixed point of this iterative procedure becomes the desired geodesic path. In this section we present formal mathematical ideas, followed by computer implementations in the next section.

For any two closed curves, denoted by v_0 and v_1 in $\mathcal{C}$, we are interested in finding a geodesic path between them in $\mathcal{C}$. Our approach is to start with any path $\alpha(t)$ connecting v_0 and v_1. That is $\alpha : [0, 1] \mapsto \mathcal{C}$ such that $\alpha(0) = v_0$ and $\alpha(1) = v_1$. Then, we iteratively "straighten" α till it achieves a local minimum of the energy: $E(\alpha) \equiv \frac{1}{2} \int_0^1 (\frac{d\alpha}{dt}(t) \cdot \frac{d\alpha}{dt}(t)) dt$. It can be shown that a local minimum of E is a geodesic on $\mathcal{C}$. However, it is possible that there are multiple geodesics between a given pair of curves, and a local minimum of E may not correspond to the shortest of all geodesics. Therefore, this approach has the limitation that it finds a geodesic between a given pair but may not reach the shortest geodesic. One can use certain stochastic techniques to increase the probability of reaching the shortest geodesic but these are not explored in this paper.

Let $\mathcal{H}$ be the set of all paths in $\mathcal{C}$, parameterized by $t \in [0, 1]$, and $\mathcal{H}_0$ be the subset of $\mathcal{H}$ of paths that start at v_0 and end at v_1. The tangent spaces of $\mathcal{H}$ and $\mathcal{H}_0$ are: $T_\alpha(\mathcal{H}) = \{w| \ \forall t \in [0, 1], w(t) \in T_{\alpha(t)}(\mathcal{C})\}$, where $T_{\alpha(t)}(\mathcal{C})$ is as specified in Eqn. 3, and $T_\alpha(\mathcal{H}_0) = \{w \in T_\alpha(\mathcal{H})|w(0) = w(1) = 0\}$. To understand this space, consider a path $\alpha \in \mathcal{H}_0$ and an element $w \in T_\alpha(\mathcal{H}_0)$. Recall that for any t, $\alpha(t)$ is also a curve on $\mathbb{S}^2$, which in turn corresponds to a closed curve in $\mathbb{R}^3$. Now, w is path of vector fields such that for any $t \in [0, 1]$, $w(t)$ is a tangent vector field restricted to the curve $\alpha(t)$ on $\mathbb{S}^2$. That is, $w(t)(s)$ is a vector tangent to $\mathbb{S}^2$ at the point $\alpha(t)(s)$. Furthermore, $\int_0^{2\pi} w(t)(s) ds = 0$ for all $t \in [0, 1]$. Our study of paths on $\mathcal{H}$ requires the use of covariant derivatives and integrals of vector fields along these paths.

Definition 1 (Covariant Derivative, [1](pg. 309)). *For a given path* $\alpha \in \mathcal{H}$ *and a vector field* $w \in T_\alpha(\mathcal{H})$, *one defines the covariant derivative of* w *along* α *to be the vector field obtained by projecting* $\frac{dw}{dt}(t)$ *onto the tangent space* $T_{\alpha(t)}(\mathcal{C})$, *for all* t. *It is denoted by* $\frac{Dw}{dt}$.

Similarly, a vector field $u \in T_\alpha(\mathcal{H})$ is called the *covariant integral* of w along α if the covariant derivative of u is w, i.e. $\frac{Du}{dt} = w(t)$.

To make $\mathcal{H}$ a Riemannian manifold, we use the Palais metric [17]: for w_1, $w_2 \in T_\alpha(\mathcal{H})$, $\langle\langle w_1, w_2 \rangle\rangle = \langle w_1(0), w_2(0) \rangle + \int_0^1 \langle \frac{Dw_1}{dt}(t), \frac{Dw_2}{dt}(t) \rangle \, dt$, where Dw/dt denotes the vector field along α which is the covariant derivative of w. With respect to the Palais metric, $T_\alpha(\mathcal{H}_0)$ is a closed linear subspace of $T_\alpha(\mathcal{H})$, and $\mathcal{H}_0$ is a closed subspace of $\mathcal{H}$.

Our goal is to find a minimizer of E in $\mathcal{H}_0$, and we will use a gradient flow to minimize E. Therefore, we wish to find the gradient of E in $T_\alpha(\mathcal{H}_0)$. To do this, we first find the gradient of E in $T_\alpha(\mathcal{H})$ and then project it into $T_\alpha(\mathcal{H}_0)$.

Theorem 1. *The gradient vector of* E *in* $T_\alpha(\mathcal{H})$ *is given by a vector field* q *such that* $\frac{Dq}{dt} = \frac{d\alpha}{dt}$ *and* $q(0) = 0$. *In other words,* q *is the covariant integral of* $\frac{d\alpha}{dt}$ *with zero initial value at* $t = 0$.

Proof: Refer to a more detailed paper [7].

Given $\frac{d\alpha}{dt}$, the vector field q is obtained using numerical techniques for covariant integration, as described in the next section. Next, we want to project tangent field $q \in T_\alpha(\mathcal{H})$ to the space $T_\alpha(\mathcal{H}_0)$.

Definition 2 (Covariantly Constant). *A vector field* w *along the path* α *is called covariantly constant if* Dw/dt *is zero at all points on* α.

Definition 3 (Geodesic). *A path is called a geodesic if its velocity vector field is covariantly constant. That is,* α *is a geodesic if* $\frac{D}{dt}(\frac{d\alpha}{dt}) = 0$ *for all* t.

Definition 4 (Covariantly Linear). *A vector field* w *along the path* α *is called covariantly linear if* Dw/dt *is a covariantly constant vector field.*

Lemma 1. *The orthogonal complement of* $T_\alpha(\mathcal{H}_0)$ *in* $T_\alpha(\mathcal{H})$ *is the space of all covariantly linear vector fields* w *along* α.

Definition 5 (Parallel Translation). *A vector field* u *is called the forward parallel translation of a tangent vector* $w \in T_{\alpha(0)}(\mathcal{C})$, *along* α, *if and only if* $u(0) = w$ *and* $\frac{Du(t)}{dt} = 0$ *for all* $t \in [0, 1]$.

Similarly, u *is called the backward parallel translation of a tangent vector* $w \in T_{\alpha(1)}(\mathcal{C})$, *along* α, *when for* $\tilde{\alpha}(t) \equiv \alpha(1 - t)$, u *is the forward parallel translation of* w *along* $\tilde{\alpha}$.

It must be noted that parallel translations, forward or backward, lead to vector fields that are covariantly constant.

According to Lemma 1, to project the gradient q into $T_\alpha(\mathcal{H}_0)$, we simply need to subtract off a covariantly linear vector field which agrees with q at $t = 0$ and $t = 1$. Clearly, the correct covariantly linear field is simply $t\tilde{q}(t)$, where $\tilde{q}(t)$ is the covariantly constant field obtained by parallel translating $q(1)$ backwards along α. Hence, we have proved following theorems.

Theorem 2. *Let* $\alpha : [0,1] \mapsto \mathcal{C}$ *be a path,* $\alpha \in \mathcal{H}_0$. *Then, with respect to the Palais metric:*

1. *The gradient of the energy function* E *on* $\mathcal{H}$ *is the vector field* q *along* α *satisfying* $q(0) = 0$ *and* $\frac{Dq}{dt} = \frac{d\alpha}{dt}$.
2. *The gradient of the energy function* E *restricted to* $\mathcal{H}_0$ *is* $w(t) = q(t) - t\tilde{q}(t)$, *where* q *is the vector field defined in the previous item, and* $\tilde{q}$ *is the vector field obtained by parallel translating* $q(1)$ *backwards along* α.

Theorem 3. *For a given pair* v_0, $v_1 \in \mathcal{C}$, *a critical point of* E *on* $\mathcal{H}_0$ *is a geodesic on* $\mathcal{C}$ *connecting* v_0 *and* v_1.

4   Computer Implementations

In this section, we provide step-by-step details for different procedures mentioned in the last section. In particular, we provide algorithms for: (i) finding the direction vector representation of a given closed curve p, (ii) given any two closed curves, v_0 and v_1, initializing a path α connecting them in $\mathcal{C}$, (iii) computing the velocity vector $\frac{d\alpha}{dt}$ for a given path α, (iv) computing the covariant derivative q of $\frac{d\alpha}{dt}$, (v) computing the backward parallel transport $\tilde{q}$ of $q(1)$, and (vi) updating the path α along the gradient direction given by the vector field w. We explain these procedures one by one next.

1. **Direction Function Representation of closed curves:** The first computational step in our analysis is to find an element of $\mathcal{C}$ for a given 3D curve. Let $x_i \in \mathbb{R}^3$, $i = 1, \ldots, m$ be a given order set of samples on a 3D curve. and we want to re-sample this curve using n uniform samples as follows:

   Subroutine 1 (Uniform Re-sampling of Curve)
   > *set* $x_{m+1} = x_1$
   > *compute* $\rho_i = \|x_{i+1} - x_i\|$, $i = 1, \ldots, m$
   > *while standard-deviation(*$\{\rho_i\}$*)* $> \epsilon$
   > $s_i = \sum_{j=1}^{i} \rho_j$, $i = 1, \ldots, m$
   > $t = ([1:n]/n)s_m$
   > $k_j = \mathrm{argmin}_i(s_i \geq t_j)$, $j = 1, \ldots, n$
   > $y_1 = x_1$
   >   *for* $j = 1, \ldots, n - 1$
   > $y_{j+1} = ((t_j - x_{k_j-1})x_{k_j+1} + (x_{k_j} - t_j)x_{k_j})/(x_{k_j+1} - x_{k_j})$
   > $w_j = y_{j+1} - y_j$, *and* $v_j = \frac{w_j}{\|w_j\|}$, $\rho_j = \|w_j\|$,
   >   *end* j
   >   *set* $m = n$ *and* $x = y$.
   > *end while*
   > *project* v *into* $\mathcal{C}$

   Shown in Figure 2 is an example. The given curve with $m = 200$ is shown in the left panel; it is re-sampled repeatedly for $n = 30$ with results shown

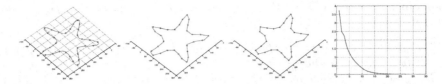

Fig. 2. Resampling the piecewise-linear curve formed by the given set of points using Subroutine 1. Right: evolution of standard deviation of distances between resampled points.

in next two panels. To show that points become increasingly uniform, we show the standard deviation of ρ_js at every iteration. A standard deviation of zero implies that the points are uniformly spaced.

2. **Initialize the path α:** Given v_0 and v_1 in $\mathcal{C}$, we want to form a path $\alpha : [0, 1] \mapsto \mathcal{C}$ such that $\alpha(0) = v_0$ and $\alpha(1) = v_1$. There are several ways of doing this. One is to form 3D coordinates p_0 and p_1, respectively, associated with the two shapes, and connect $p_0(s)$ and $p_1(s)$ linearly, for all s, using $p_t(s) = tp_1(s) + (1 - t)p_0(s)$. The intermediate curves are neither uniformly sampled nor closed. We can use Subroutine 1 to re-sample them uniformly and to close them. The other idea is to use the fact that $v_0(s), v_1(s) \in \mathbb{S}^2$, and construct a path in $\mathbb{S}^2$ from one point to another, parameterized by t. We summarize this idea in the following subroutine.

Subroutine 2 (Initialize a path α)
> *for all $s \in [0, 2\pi]$*
>> *define $\theta(s) = \cos^{-1}(v_0(s) \cdot v_1(s))$*
>> *define $f(s) = v_1(s) - (v_0(s) \cdot v_1(s))v_0(s)$, and $f(s) = \theta(s)f(s)/\|f(s)\|$.*
> *end s*
> *for all $t \in [0, 1]$*
>> *for all $s \in [0, 2\pi)$*
>>> *define $\alpha(t)(s) = \chi_1(v_0(s); f(s))$*
>> *end s*
>> *project $\alpha(t)$ into $\mathcal{C}$*
> *end t*

In case $v_0(s)$ and $v_1(s)$ are antipodal points on $\mathbb{S}^2$, and thus $f(s) = 0$, one can arbitrarily choose a path connecting them on the sphere. That is, choose any $f(s) \in T_{v_0(s)}(\mathbb{S}^1)$ of length $\theta(s)$. This situation rarely occurs in practical situations.

3. **Vector Field $\frac{d\alpha}{dt}$:** In order to compute the gradient of E in $T_\alpha(\mathcal{H})$, we first need to compute the path velocity $\frac{d\alpha}{dt}$. For a continuous path $\frac{d\alpha}{dt}(t)$ automatically lies in $T_{\alpha(t)}(\mathcal{C})$, but in the discrete case one has to ensure this property using additional steps. This process uses the approximation $x'(t) \approx (x(t) - x(t - \epsilon))/\epsilon$, modified to account for the nonlinearity of $\mathcal{C}$. Let the interval $[0, 1]$ be divided into k uniform bins. The procedure for computing $\frac{d\alpha}{dt}$ at these discrete times is summarized next.

Subroutine 3 (Computation of $\frac{d\alpha}{dt}$ along α)

    for $\tau = 1, \ldots, k$

        for all $s \in [0, 2\pi)$

$$\theta(s) = k \cos^{-1}(\alpha(\tfrac{\tau}{k})(s) \cdot \alpha(\tfrac{\tau-1}{k})(s))$$

$$f(s) = -\alpha(\tfrac{\tau-1}{k})(s) + (\alpha(\tfrac{\tau-1}{k})(s) \cdot \alpha(\tfrac{\tau}{k})(s))\alpha(\tfrac{\tau}{k})(s)$$

$$\tfrac{d\alpha}{dt}(\tfrac{\tau}{k})(s) = \theta(s)f(s)/\|f(s)\|.$$

        end s

        project $\frac{d\alpha}{dt}(\frac{\tau}{k})$ into $T_{\alpha(\frac{\tau}{k})}(\mathcal{C})$

    end τ.

Now we have a vector field $\frac{d\alpha}{dt} \in T_\alpha(\mathcal{H})$ along a given path $\alpha \in \mathcal{H}$.

4. **Computation of Vector field q:** We seek a vector field q such that $q(0) = 0$ and $\frac{Dq}{dt} = \frac{d\alpha}{dt}$. In other words, q is the covariant integral of the vector field $\frac{d\alpha}{dt}$.

Subroutine 4 (Covariance Integration of $\frac{d\alpha}{dt}$ to form q)

    for $\tau = 0, 1, 2, \ldots, k - 1$,

        for all s

            define $q^{\|}(\frac{\tau}{k})(s) = \pi(q(\frac{\tau}{k})(s); \alpha(\frac{\tau}{k})(s), \alpha(\frac{\tau+1}{k})(s))$.

            (π is defined in Eqn. 2)

            set $q(\frac{\tau+1}{k})(s) = \frac{1}{k}\frac{d\alpha}{dt}(\frac{\tau+1}{k})(s) + q^{\|}(\frac{\tau}{k})(s)$.

        end s

    end τ

$q^{\|}(\frac{\tau}{k})$ is the parallel transport of $q(\frac{\tau}{k})$ from $T_{\alpha(\frac{\tau}{k})}(\mathcal{C})$ to $T_{\alpha(\frac{\tau+1}{k})}(\mathcal{C})$. This subroutine results in the gradient vector field $\{q(\frac{\tau}{k}) \in T_{\alpha(\frac{\tau}{k})}(\mathcal{C}) | \tau = 1, \ldots, k\}$.

5. **Covariant Vector Field $\tilde{q}$:** Given $q(1)$, we need to find a vector field $\tilde{q}$ along the path α in $\mathcal{C}$ that is the backward parallel transport of $q(1)$. We have already computed the points $\alpha(0), \alpha(1/k), \alpha(2/k), \ldots, \alpha(1)$. Each $\alpha(\frac{\tau}{k})$ is an element of $\mathcal{C}$, i.e. it is a curve on $\mathbb{S}^2$. We will perform the backward parallel transport iteratively, as follows.

Subroutine 5 (Backward Parallel Transport)

    set $\tilde{q}(1) = q(1)$

    let $l = (\langle q(1), q(1)\rangle)^{1/2}$

    for $\tau = k - 1, k - 2, \ldots, 3, 2$

        for all $s \in [0, 2\pi)$

            $\tilde{q}(\frac{\tau}{k})(s) = \pi(\tilde{q}(\frac{\tau+1}{k})(s); \alpha(\frac{\tau+1}{k})(s), \alpha(\frac{\tau}{k})(s))$

        end s

        project $\tilde{q}(\frac{\tau}{k})$ into $T_{\alpha(\frac{\tau}{k})}(\mathcal{C})$

        let $l_1 = (\langle \tilde{q}(\frac{\tau}{k}), \tilde{q}(\frac{\tau}{k})\rangle)^{1/2}$

        set $\tilde{q}(\frac{\tau}{k}) = \tilde{q}(\frac{\tau}{k})l/l_1$;

    end τ

6. **Gradient of E:** With the computation of q and $\tilde{q}$ along the path α, the gradient vector field of E is given by: for any $\tau \in \{0, 1, \ldots, k\}$ and $s \in [0, 2\pi)$

$$w(\tfrac{\tau}{k})(s) \equiv (q(\tfrac{\tau}{k})(s) - (\tfrac{\tau}{k})\tilde{q}(\tfrac{\tau}{k})(s)) \quad \in T_{\alpha(\frac{\tau}{k})(s)}(\mathbb{S}^2) \; . \tag{4}$$

7. **Update in Gradient Direction:** Now that we have computed the gradient vector field w on the current path α, we update this path in the direction given by w: for $\tau = 1, 2, \ldots, k$ and $s \in [0, 2\pi)$,

$$\alpha(\frac{\tau}{k})(s) = \chi_1(\alpha(\frac{\tau}{k})(s); w(\frac{\tau}{k})(s)) \, . \tag{5}$$

Now we summarize the algorithm to compute a geodesic path between any two given closed curves in $\mathbb{R}^3$. We assume that the curves are available in form of sampled points on these curves.

Algorithm 1 (Find a geodesic between two curves in $\mathcal{C}$)

1. *Compute the representations of each curve in $\mathcal{C}$ using Subroutine 1. Denote these elements by v_0 and v_1, respectively.*
2. *Initialize a path α between v_0 and v_1 using Subroutine 2.*
3. *Compute the velocity vector field $\frac{d\alpha}{dt}$ along the path α using Subroutine 3.*
4. *Compute the covariant integral of $\frac{d\alpha}{dt}$, denoted by q, using Subroutine 4. If $\sum_{\tau=1}^{k} \langle \frac{d\alpha}{dt}(\tau), \frac{d\alpha}{dt}(\tau) \rangle$ is small, then stop. Else, continue to the next step.*
5. *Compute the backward parallel transport of the vector $q(1)$ along α using the Subroutine 5.*
6. *Compute the full gradient vector field of the energy E along the path α, denoted by w, using Eqn. 4.*
7. *Update α using Eqn. 5. Return to Step 3.*

The desired geodesic path is given by the resulting α, and its length is given by $d_{\mathcal{C}}(v_0, v_1) = \sum_{\tau=1}^{k} (\langle \frac{d\alpha}{dt}(\frac{\tau}{k}), \frac{d\alpha}{dt}(\frac{\tau}{k}) \rangle)^{1/2}$. For a later use, we highlight $\frac{d\alpha}{dt}(0)$ as the initial velocity vector in $T_{\alpha(0)}(\mathcal{C})$ that generates the geodesic at $\alpha(0)$.

5 Experimental Results

In this section we describe some computer experiments for generating geodesic paths between shapes in $\mathcal{C}$. Let the two curves of interest be: $p_0(t) = (a\cos(t), b\sin(t), c\sqrt{b^2 - a^2\sin^2(t)})$, and $p_1(t) = (a(1 + \cos(t)), \sin(t), 2\sin(t/2))$, and we want to compute a geodesic path between them in $\mathcal{C}$. Shown in Figure 3 are the

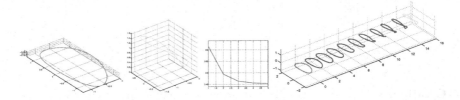

Fig. 3. The two shapes used in computing geodesic path, evolution of the energy E during path-straightening, and a view of that geodesic in $\mathbb{R}^3$

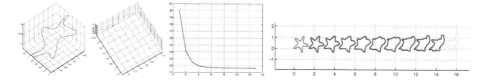

Fig. 4. Geodesic Computation: The two curves in $\mathcal{C}$, evolution of E as Algorithm 1 proceeds, and a view of the resulting geodesic path

results. The first two panels show the two curves. The first curve is an example of a *bicylinder* and the second one is an example of a *Viviani* curve. We apply Algorithm 1 on these two curves to generate a geodesic path between them. The third panel shows the evolution of the energy E during the iterations in Algorithm 1. The last panel shows a view of the resulting geodesic path in $\mathbb{R}^3$.

Shown in Figure 4 is another example, where the two end shapes (left two panels), evolution of the energy (middle), and a view of the final geodesic path (right) are displayed.

6   Summary

We have presented a differential geometric approach to studying shapes of closed curves in $\mathbb{R}^3$. The main tool presented in this study is the construction of geodesic paths between arbitrary two curves on an appropriate space of closed curves. This construction is based on path-straightening, i.e. we construct an initial path between those two curves, and iteratively straighten it using the gradient of the energy E. The limit point of this procedure is a geodesic path. We have presented step-by-step procedures for computing these geodesics, and have illustrated them using simple examples.

Acknowledgements

This research was supported in part by grants ARO W911NF-04-1-0268, ARO W911NF-04-1-0113, and CCF-0514743.

References

1. W. M. Boothby. *An Introduction to Differential Manifolds and Riemannian Geometry.* Academic Press, Inc., 1986.
2. A. M. Bronstein, M.M. Bronstein, and R. Kimmel. Three-dimensional face recognition. *International Journal of Computer Vision*, 64(1):5–30, 2005.
3. G. Dziuk, E. Kuwert, and R. Schatzle. Evolution of elastic curves in R^n: existence and computation. *SIAM J. Math. Anal*, 33:1228–1245, 2002.
4. J. P. Eakins, K. Shields, and J. Boardman. ARTISAN – a shape retrieval system based on boundary family indexing. In *Storage and Retrieval for Still Image and Video Databases IV. Proceedings SPIE*, volume 2670, pages 17–28, 1996.

5. U. Grenander and M. I. Miller. Computational anatomy: An emerging discipline. *Quarterly of Applied Mathematics*, LVI(4):617–694, 1998.
6. M. M. Kazhdan. *Shape Representations and Algorithms for 3D Model Retrieval.* PhD thesis, Computer Science, Princeton, April 2004.
7. E. Klassen and A. Srivastava. A path-straightening method for finding geodesics in shape spaces of closed curves in $\mathbb{R}^3$. *SIAM Journal of Applied Mathematics*, page in review, 2005.
8. E. Klassen, A. Srivastava, W. Mio, and S. Joshi. Analysis of planar shapes using geodesic paths on shape spaces. *IEEE Patt. Analysis and Machine Intell.*, 26(3):372–383, March, 2004.
9. J. Langer and D. A. Singer. Curve straightening and a minimax argument for closed elastic curves. *Topology*, 24:75–88, 1985.
10. J. Langer and D. A. Singer. Curve straightening in Riemannian manifolds. *Ann. Global Anal. Geom.*, 5:133–150, 1987.
11. P. W. Michor and D. Mumford. Riemannian geometries on spaces of plane curves. *Journal of the European Mathematical Society*, to appear, 2005.
12. W. Mio and A. Srivastava. Elastic string models for representation and analysis of planar shapes. In *Proc. of IEEE Computer Vision and Pattern Recognition*, 2004.
13. W. Mio, A. Srivastava, and E. Klassen. Interpolation by elastica in Euclidean spaces. *Quarterly of Applied Mathematics*, LXII(2):359–378, June 2004.
14. F. Mokhtarian, S. Abbasi, and J. Kittler. Efficient and robust shape retrieval by shape content through curvature scale space. In *Proceedings of First International Conference on Image Database and MultiSearch*, pages 35–42, 1996.
15. M. Novotni and R. Klein. A geometric approach to 3D object comparison. In *International Conference on Shape Modeling and Applications*, pages 167–175, 2001.
16. R. Osada, T. Funkhouser, B. Chazelle, and D. Dobkin. Matching 3D models with shape distributions. In *International Conference on Shape Modeling and Applications*, pages 154–166, 2001.
17. R. S. Palais. Morse theory on Hilbert manifolds. *Topology*, 2:299–340, 1963.
18. C. Samir, A. Srivastava, and M. Daoudi. Human face recognition using 2D facial curves. In *International Conference on Acoustic, Speech, and Signal Processing (ICASSP)*, May, 2006.
19. L. Younes. Optimal matching between shapes via elastic deformations. *Journal of Image and Vision Computing*, 17(5/6):381–389, 1999.

Robust Homography Estimation from Planar Contours Based on Convexity

Alberto Ruiz[1], Pedro E. López de Teruel[2], and Lorenzo Fernández[2]

[1] Dept. Informática y Sistemas, University of Murcia
[2] Dept. Tecnología e Ingeniería de Computadores, University of Murcia
aruiz@um.es, {pedroe, lfmaimo}@ditec.um.es

Abstract. We propose a homography estimation method from the contours of planar regions. Standard projective invariants such as cross ratios or canonical frames based on hot points obtained from local differential properties are extremely unstable in real images suffering from pixelization, thresholding artifacts, and other noise sources. We explore alternative constructions based on global convexity properties of the contour such as discrete tangents and concavities. We show that a projective frame can be robustly extracted from arbitrary shapes with at least one appreciable concavity. Algorithmic complexity and stability are theoretically discussed and experimentally evaluated in a number of real applications including projective shape matching, alignment and pose estimation. We conclude that the procedure is computationally efficient and notably robust given the ill-conditioned nature of the problem.

1 Introduction

The homography relating two perspective views of a plane is a fundamental geometric entity in many computer vision applications. Instead of conventional estimation methods based on explicit point or line correspondences, we are interested in robust and efficient homography estimation from the *contours* of two views of a given planar region with arbitrary shape. Using this transformation we can solve several related problems including shape recognition and matching, object alignment, spatial pose location (given additional information about the camera parameters), robot guidance from conventional signs (e.g. arrows), image rectification and camera calibration.

For instance, Figs. 1.a-b show two views of a well-known geographical feature. Using the homography relating the two views we could verify that the aerial image effectively corresponds to the lake in the map, the cities in the map can be located on the image, and we can even compute the 3D position and orientation of the camera in the reference frame induced by the map.

These natural shapes lack distinguished points or lines; at a given resolution they can be considered just as irregular silhouettes in which small details are neither reliable nor relevant. Furthermore, contours extracted from real images suffer from pixelization, thresholding artifacts, and other unavoidable noise sources, specially in low resolution views with large slant (Fig. 1.c).

A. Leonardis, H. Bischof, and A. Pinz (Eds.): ECCV 2006, Part I, LNCS 3951, pp. 107–120, 2006.
© Springer-Verlag Berlin Heidelberg 2006

(a)   (b)

(c)

Fig. 1. Real world shapes. (a-b) Two views of Lake Geneva. (c) Noisy contours of traffic plate symbols extracted from a video sequence.

In noisy contours the differential properties of curves (required for computation of lines, inflection points, cusps, and other local projective invariants) are destroyed. Cross-ratio constructions are also very sensitive to noise and must be used with caution. Contour smoothing and noise filtering do not completely solve this problem: noise is inhomogeneously transmitted in different regions of the contour due to the nonlinear effects of perspective imaging. Analytical models (e.g. polygonal approximations, implicit polynomials, *snakes*, etc.) may even destroy valuable features for contour alignment. Certain modeling techniques may be adequate for specific shapes (e.g. straight line approximations for essentially polygonal contours, etc.), but contour recognition in general conditions is precisely one of our main goals. In consequence, in this paper all contours will be represented and manipulated in its "raw" form as closed and possibly irregularly spaced polylines without self-intersections.

Some of the first approaches to shape recognition under perspective imaging conditions were based on more or less *ad hoc* constructions [1]. Later, the application of projective geometry [2, 3, 4] to computer vision clarified enormously the field, but the emphasis was mainly in estimation of 3D structure from explicit point or line correspondences in multiple images.

Projective contour analysis under real world, noisy conditions has received comparably less attention. Most of the proposed solutions for curve matching are based on differential properties [5, 6, 7, 8, 9] or in specific contour models [10, 11], which cannot be directly used over low quality images The projective geometry of multiple views of curves has been studied in [12]. Invariant signatures based on rays have been proposed in [13] to retrieve shapes in a database of trademarks. Application of contour matching to visual servoing using snakes is described in [14], where weak perspective estimates, point redistribution, and projective correction steps are iterated until convergence. An approach based on image moments is reported in [15]. A curious and completely different idea is proposed in [16], where a linear program can be established on the homography entries, with constraints given by region bounds. This method admits partial occlusions but requires at least two contours to avoid trivial solutions. In addition to shape recognition, contour alignment has been used in other applications including camera calibration [17] and structure and motion recovery [18, 19].

Contour matching under similar or affine transformations (e.g. weak perspective) is a notably easier problem [20, 21, 22]. For instance, robust affine alignment can be based on shape covariance equalization and Fourier analysis. Unfortunately, this kind of approaches cannot be directly extended to full perspective images due to the essentially nonlinear laws of image formation. While small shapes can frequently be acceptably modeled by affine transformations, such kind of weak perspective approximation is only valid for shape recognition. Accurate alignment and pose estimation can only be achieved from true projective homographies containing information about both the focal length and the distance to the object.

Our goal is a simple, efficient, and robust method for homography estimation from arbitrary contours. In the rest of the paper we will discuss a number of geometric constructions, essentially based on convexity, which can be used to compute a projectively invariant reference frame.

2   Robust Projective Invariants

The homography relating two projective views of a plane is completely characterized by at least four corresponding points (or lines) [2]. However, two corresponding contours only impose (if differential or local properties are discarded) an ordering on the possible point correspondences. Distances between points along the contour may drastically expand or shrink in different views. We are interested in a projective reference frame that can be constructed using 'global' invariant geometric properties of the curve, avoiding local properties. The construction must be tolerant to a reasonable amount of noise in the curve locations.

A promising property is convexity. The convex hull of a figure is preserved under projective transformations if the whole shape is in front of the camera (otherwise objects are split across the horizon; we consider *quasi-affine* transformations [2, ch. 21], [23]). In this work we assume that the admissible contours are completely contained in the image, without occlusions. In such conditions, and in contrast with curvature-based invariants, the global convexity properties of a figure can only be destroyed by large amounts of noise. This kind of region

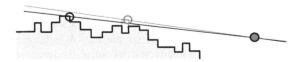

Fig. 2. The discrete tangent with respect to a external point (but not the point of contact) is reasonably robust against contour perturbations

convexity invariance seems to be a minimal and reasonable requirement. If 'large' concavities disappear contour matching becomes unsolvable in practice.

Closely related to convexity, tangency is also projectively preserved. While ordinary curve tangents, based on differential properties, are not robust, 'discrete' tangency with respect to external points or regions is a much more stable geometric construction (Fig. 2). Note that the specific point of contact *is not* a robust projective invariant (it may slide along the tangent line).

2.1 Polygon Tangency and Convex Hull Computation

The points of contact of the tangents to a polygon are contained in its convex hull, which can be efficiently computed using Melkman's algorithm for polylines with no self-intersections [24]. This method sequentially processes each of the polyline vertices. At each stage, the algorithm determines and stores on a double-ended queue those vertices that form the ordered hull for all polyline vertices considered so far. Each new vertex satisfies one of two conditions (Fig. 3): either (1) it is inside the currently constructed hull, and can be ignored; or (2) it is outside the current hull, and becomes a new hull vertex extending the old

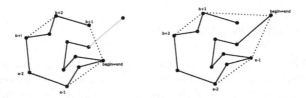

Fig. 3. Illustration of one step in Melkman's convex hull algorithm

hull. However, in case (2), vertices that are on the list for the old hull, may become interior to the new hull, and need to be discarded before adding the new vertex to the new list. Each vertex can be inserted on the deque at most twice (once at each end) and the elements on the deque can be removed at most once. Each of these events has constant time, providing a linear execution order.

2.2 Contour Pairs

To illustrate a simple example of convexity based invariants we will consider first the easiest situation. Given a *pair* of closed, disjoint coplanar contours, the four tangent lines to both contours is an eight d.o.f. projective invariant which completely determines the homography relating two views (Fig. 4).

This idea can be immediately applied to planar objects with at least two holes (e.g. the shape "B"), but obviously we are actually interested in the more general case of simple contours without holes. In principle, this method could be applied to figures with at least two clear concavities (which, together with the

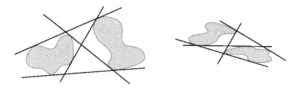

Fig. 4. Four invariant lines from a contour pair

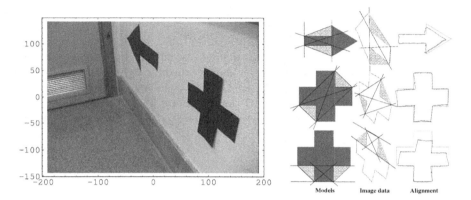

Fig. 5. Alignment using a pair of concavities

convex hull, are also projectively invariant). For example, Fig. 5 illustrates this idea for projective alignment of signs in a robot guidance application [25] [1].

Alignment is acceptable despite the bad quality of the signals, which are loosely glued to the wall. As shown in the last row, alignment quality strongly depends on the chosen pair of concavities: we must try all combinations and return the best match. Homography computation from the corresponding lines becomes ill conditioned if the contours in the pair are too close, or too separated, or their sizes are disparate.

In any case, this method is in general not robust since concavities are actually defined by *open* contours with extremes that may slide along the convex hull. The bitangent contact points induced by the concavities, which could in principle be used to define a projective reference frame, are also unstable. In the next section we propose a more robust and general alignment method.

3   Single Concavity

Under ideal conditions a smooth concavity defines at least four invariant points (Fig. 6.a) which specify a projective reference frame [5, 6] (the points supporting

---

[1] In this particular example polygonal models could directly provide candidate lines or vertices for matching. However, the proposed model is completely general and only the raw contours are required for alignment.

the concavity base line (bitangent) and the inflection points or the points of contact of tangents). However, these points are not stable in most real, noisy situations, and may even be not defined (Fig. 6.b).

(a)   (b)

Fig. 6. Invariant points specified by a concavity

Consider instead projective frames defined essentially by discrete tangents. Disregarding local curvature, a convex shape can only reduce the 8 degrees of freedom of an arbitrary homography to 4, namely the angle/position of contact of four lines enclosing the shape (Fig. 7 (left)). Therefore, a *smooth* convex shape can robustly specify neither projective nor affine (6 d.o.f.) reference frames.

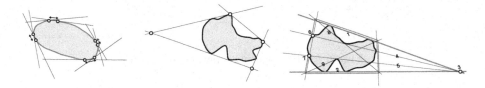

Fig. 7. Using only tangencies a convex shape can only fix 4 d.o.f. in a homography (left). Projective frame completely fixed using 4 (center) and 2 concavities (right).

We need some appreciable concavities (or straight line fragments) in the shape in order to constrain the remaining degrees of freedom of the projectivity with additional tangencies. The bitangent of a concavity is a robust invariant in the sense of Sect. 2 (clearly, its stability increases with the distance between the contact points). A convex shape with four or more concavities trivially defines one or more projective frames (Fig. 7 (center)). The bitangents are efficiently computed as a side effect of the convex hull algorithm. Interestingly, taking advantage of tangents to the concavities and intersections with the convex hull only two of them are actually required to define a projective frame (Fig. 7 (right)). Of course, many other alternative constructions can be conceived; practical considerations suggest that the most stable one (following the ideas exposed in Section 4) should be used in each situation.

We are interested in the minimal requirements in a smooth shape for robust estimation of a projective transformation. It can be easily proved that a single concavity is sufficient. The idea is to set up a projective frame with one side on the bitangent, the other three sides tangent to the convex hull of the figure, and with both diagonals tangent to the concavity (Fig. 8).

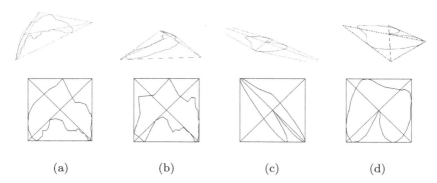

(a)   (b)   (c)   (d)

Fig. 8. Projective frame from a single concavity. (a) and (b) are the contours of the two views of the lake in Fig. 1. (c) and (d) illustrate the dependence of the construction on the desired cross ratio of the intersections of the diagonal (c) = 0.36, (d)=0.01.

3.1   Existence and Uniqueness of the Construction

We outline an informal existence argument. Given the convex hull of the shape and the convex hull of the concavity we can set an 'initial', extremely distorted projective frame with diagonals 'including', but not touching, the concavity (Fig. 9.a), with two points extremely close and three sides nearly collinear. If the base extremes move closer to the shape, the diagonals will eventually touch the concavity, since we can always set up another extremely distorted frame intersecting the concavity (Fig. 9.b). Note that to achieve the desired double tangency the positions of the extremes are not independent from each other; there is a one-parameter family of solutions.

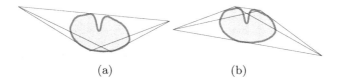

(a)   (b)

Fig. 9. The diagonals of a projective frame can always be tangent to a concavity

The bitangent fixes one d.o.f. in the projective frame in addition to the previous four shown in Fig. 7 (left), and two more d.o.f.'s can be fixed by making the two diagonals of the projective frame tangent to the concavity. Uniqueness can be achieved by eliminating the remaining d.o.f. with a predetermined cross-ratio in the intersections of one diagonal and the convex hull (Fig. 8.c-d)

3.2   Algorithmic Complexity

In contrast with the two (or more) concavities case, where the projective reference frame can be directly constructed from the immediately available bitangents, working with a single concavity requires some search. We recommend the following algorithm. From an arbitrary starting point k in the bitangent (Fig. 10) we compute the tangent t to the concavity and the intersections a and b. The chosen cross-ratio fixes the opposite corner q in the frame[2]. From the tangents from q to the convex hull we obtain the intersections c and d.

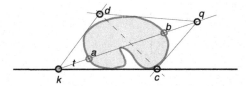

Fig. 10. Projective frame construction (see text)

Now we have only two possibilities: either the diagonal cd crosses the concavity, or not (the case shown in the figure). Given a k_{right} close enough to the left contact point of the bitangent (remember that the exact location of this point is not reliable) this diagonal will intersect the concavity (Fig. 11.a). Alternatively a k_{left} sufficiently far from the shape induces a diagonal that will not touch the concavity (Fig. 11.b). From the starting k_{left} and k_{right} positions we perform a binary search for the solution k^* with a cd diagonal tangent to the concavity (in practice, tangency can be acceptable if the diagonal intersects the convex-hull of the concavity in two points sufficiently close).

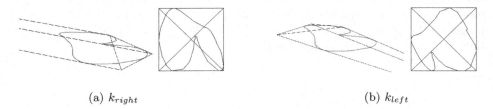

(a) k_{right} (b) k_{left}

Fig. 11. The two cases in the binary search of the concavity double tangency (see text)

In our experiments the projective frame is computed in a search process taking about 10 steps. Each tentative frame construction takes linear time with respect to polyline size and no polyline transformation, smoothing or preprocessing must be performed in the search, so the algorithm is extremely efficient. The overall computation time is negligible in relation to the image processing tasks required to extract the contours.

The construction becomes ill-conditioned when the contact points of the bitangent are very close (the concavity is nearly a hole) and when the concavity is too deep or too flat (three points in the reference become nearly collinear). In this paper we focus on constructions using a single concavity, even if the shapes have more than one, in order to evaluate the most adverse situation.

---

[2] We must check that q is in the correct side (the horizon is not 'crossed'), since some extreme k positions are incompatible with a frontal view.

3.3   Shape Similarity

A planar curve can be described by a continuous function $f : (0,1) \in \mathbb{R} \to \mathbb{C}$. A reasonable similarity measure for closed contours is the mean squared distance between 'homologous points': $d(f,g) = \int_0^1 (|f(t) - g(t)|^2 dt$. From the Parseval theorem this can be immediately computed in the frequency domain provided that the parameterization of both curves is consistent (normalization of the starting point involves a simple modification of the phase of the spectral coordinates). The desired Fourier coefficients of a closed polyline with arbitrarily spaced knots can be efficiently computed without need of resampling using the technique proposed in [20, Appendix]. The canonical version of a shape (projectively normalized by transforming the reference frame to the unit square) can be characterized by its low frequency coordinates. However, precise error alignment must be computed in the reference frame of the views.

4   Robustness Analysis

The proposed projective frame is built using only global properties of the shape. Local projective invariants, extremely sensitive to noise, are avoided. Therefore, it is expected that homography estimations based on it are robust against moderated amounts of noise. In this section we suggest a theoretical, rigorous approach to the study of the stability of the above construction and also describe a more practical stability assessment method used in our experiments.

For simplicity we quantify the level of noise in the imaging process (including acquisition, color thresholding or edge extraction and linking) by a single magnitude ϵ defined as the *maximum* distance from a true point in the 'ideal' contour and the corresponding 'corrupt' point (e.g., in certain cases ϵ could be related to pixel size). Therefore, the true shape lies inside a tolerance band around the observed contour. From this band we can compute the extreme constructions and report the *worst case* alignment situation for a given level of noise (Fig 12).

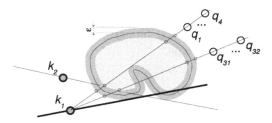

Fig. 12. Possible constructions induced by noise level ϵ (only a few points are shown)

An alternative, empirical approach is based on repeated computation of the projective frame from contour perturbations of at most size ϵ and report the distribution of alignment errors. Stability can be also assessed by alignment of the shape with a perturbed version of itself. Since we must go (loosely speaking) through the canonical frame and return, this kind of self alignment error is related to the quality of the shape for homography estimation.

A more practical stability measure can be directly derived from the own structure of the construction. The vertices of the projective frame are intersections of discrete tangent lines whose points of contact have error as large as ϵ (Fig. 13). Even if the rest of the construction is noiseless, a certain intersection x will have an uncertainty $\Delta x = S\epsilon$, where $S = \overline{px}/\overline{pc}$.

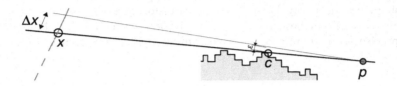

Fig. 13. Stability of a polygon tangent

The overall stability of the frame is in some sense dominated by the worst ingredient in the construction, so, for instance, an approximate unstability measure is the maximum 'error amplification' ratio S of all tangents.

5   Experiments

Fig. 14 shows the quality of the alignment of the lake contours, including the alignment error E (measured in normalized MSE distance $\times 1000$), and the simple unstability measure S ($\times 10$) of the constructions explained above. Observe that shape (a) is less stable ($S = 7.9$) than (b) ($S = 4.4$), as intuitively expected from the lengths and angles of the constructed frames. Even though the contours have been extracted with low precision and from completely unrelated sources, the proposed global procedure is still able to satisfactorily align both shapes directly from the raw available polylines. Note that alternative methods based on identification of homologous points or lines would require some kind of intelligent interpretation of the shape.

Fig. 14. Alignment of the lake shapes in Fig 1

Fig. 15. Some frames in real-time alignment of a smooth shape (see text)

Fig. 15 shows real time alignment of a smooth, handwritten 'B' shape in a video sequence taken by a camera which moves freely in space. The first frame is the target and the rest are some illustrative views, most of them specifically selected with perturbations in the contour to demonstrate the robustness of the method. The full video sequence and additional demonstrations can be downloaded from the web page `http://ditec.um.es/contour`. Alignment is also acceptable on significantly reduced polylines (Fig. 16).

Fig. 16. Alignment on reduced polylines

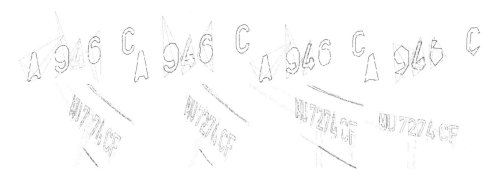

Fig. 17. Symbol recognition

Fig. 17 shows some examples of traffic plate symbol recognition for increasing noise levels, caused again by the tolerance in polyline reduction. (In this case an affine model is sufficient for shape recognition in views with small slant.)

Finally, Fig. 18 illustrates the estimation of camera pose [2] in a video sequence using the alignment homographies obtained from a smooth contour. We assume that the camera parameters are known.

Fig. 18. Estimated 3D camera trajectory

6   Conclusions and Future Work

This paper proposes a novel projectively invariant representation of planar contours based on global convexity properties. We have shown that a canonical frame can be efficiently extracted from shapes with at least one appreciable concavity, using a remarkably simple geometric construction working from raw, irregularly sampled polylines. The stability of the reference frame has been formally studied and the maximum error amplification ratio has been proposed as a pragmatic measure of shape quality for projective alignment. Our experiments indicate that the homographies estimated by this method are surprisingly accurate even for considerable noise levels. In such extreme conditions alternative methods based on finding correspondences of local properties such as hot points, straight lines or conic approximations produce unacceptable results.

The method can be applied to image-model homography estimation, shape normalization and recognition, and even pose localization (given some knowledge of camera parameters). All these tasks can be performed in real time: the construction has linear algorithmic complexity with respect to the number of polyline knots, so the computational effort required by homography estimation is negligible in relation to the rest of low-level image processing stages.

This work can be extended in several directions. First, self-consistency tests must be implemented to avoid ill-conditioned configurations (for instance, contours with very small concavities). Alignments produced by extreme projective transformations should also be automatically detected and rejected. Second, a characterization of admissible occlusions (those which do not disturb the construction of the projective frame) would be very attractive for applications in cluttered environments. Finally, a theoretical model of alignment degradation should be rigorously developed in terms of noise level and some appropriate stability measure of the projective frame.

Acknowledgments

The authors would like to thank the anonymous reviewers for their useful suggestions. This work has been supported by the Spanish MCYT grants DPI2001-0469-C03-01 and TIC2003-08154-C06-03.

References

1. Pizlo, Z., Rosenfeld, A.: Recognition of planar shapes from perspective images using contour-based invariants. Computer Vision, Graphics, and Image Processing **56**(3) (1992) 330–350
2. Hartley, R., Zisserman, A.: Multiple View Geometry in Computer Vision. 2 edn. Cambridge University Press (2004)
3. Faugeras, O., Luong, Q.T., Papadopoulo, T.: The Geometry of Multiple Images. MIT Press (2001)
4. Mundy, J., Zisserman, A.: Appendix – Projective geometry for machine vision. In: Geometric Invariances in Computer Vision, MIT Press (1992)
5. Rothwell, C.A., Zisserman, A., Forsyth, D.A., Mundy, J.L.: Canonical frames for planar object recognition. In: Proc. 2nd European Conference on Computer Vision, Santa Margherita Ligure, Italy, (1992) 757–772
6. Carlsson, S., Mohr, R., Moons, T., Morin, L., Rothwell, C., Diest, M.V., Gool, L.V., Veillon, F., Zissermann, A.: Semi-local projective invariants for the recognition of smooth plane curve. IJCV **19**(3) (1996) 211–236
7. Salden, A., Haar, B., Viergever, R.: Affine and projective differential geometric invariants of space curves. In: Baba Vemuri, ed., Geometric Methods in Computer Vision II, SPIE. (1993)
8. Zisserman, A., Blake, A., Rothwell, C., Van Gool, L., Van Diest, M.: Eliciting qualitative structure from image curve deformations. In: Proc. 4th IEEE ICCV. (1993) 340–345
9. Weiss, I.: Noise resistant invariants of curves. IEEE PAMI **15**(9) (1993) 943–948
10. Lei, Z., Blane, M.M., Cooper, D.B.: 3L fitting of higher degree implicit polynomials. In: Proc. 3rd IEEE WACV, Sarasota (USA) (1996)
11. Tarel, J., Civi, H., Cooper, D.B.: Pose estimation of free-form 3D objects without point matching using algebraic surface models. In: Proc. 1st IEEE Workshop on Model-Based 3D Image Analysis, Mumbai (India) (1998) 13–21
12. Schmid, C., Zisserman, A.: The geometry and matching of curves in multiple views. In: Proc. 5th ECCV, Freiburg (Germany) (1998) 394–409
13. Startchik, S., Milanese, R., Pun, T.: Projective and photometric invariant representation of planar disjoint shapes. Image and Vision Comp. **16**(9-10) (1998) 713–723
14. Chesi, G., Malis, E., Cipolla, R.: Collineation estimation from two unmatched views of an unknown planar contour for visual servoing. In: Proc. 10th BMVC, Nottingham (UK) (1999)
15. Sato, J., Cipolla, R.: Extracting group transformations from image moments. Computer Vision and Image Understanding **73**(1) (1999) 29–42
16. Basri, R., Jacobs, D.: Projective alignment with regions. PAMI **23**(5) (2001) 519–527
17. Mendonca, P., Wong, K., Cipolla, R.: Camera pose estimation and reconstruction from image profiles under circular motion. In: Proc. 6th ECCV, Dublin (Ireland) (2000) 864–877
18. Wong, K., , Cipolla, R.: Structure and motion from silhouettes. In: Proc. 8th IEEE ICCV, Vancouver (Canada) (2001) 217–222
19. Cipolla, R., Giblin, P.: Visual Motion of Curves and Surfaces. Cambridge University Press (2000)
20. Arbter, K., Snyder, W., Burkhardt, H., Hirzinger, G.: Application of affine-invariant fourier descriptors to recognition of 3D objects. PAMI **12**(7) (1990) 640–647

21. Startchik, S., Milanese, R., Rauber, C., Pun, T.: Planar shape databases with affine invariant search. In: Proc. 1st Int. Workshop on Image Databases and Multimedia Search, Amsterdam (Netherlands) (1996)
22. Vinther, S., Cipolla, R.: Object model acquisition and recognition using 3D affine invariants. In: Proc. 4th BMVC, Guilford (UK) (1993) 369–378
23. Stolfi, J.: Oriented Projective Geometry. Academic Press, Boston (1991)
24. Melkman, A.: On-line construction of the convex hull of a simple polygon. Information Processing Letters **25** (1987) 11–12
25. López-de-Teruel, P.E., Ruiz, A., Fernández, L.: Geobot: A high level visual perception architecture for autonomous robots. In: Proc. 4th IEEE ICVS, New York (USA) (2006)

Detecting Instances of Shape Classes That Exhibit Variable Structure

Vassilis Athitsos[1], Jingbin Wang[2], Stan Sclaroff[2], and Margrit Betke[2]

[1] Siemens Corporate Research, Princeton, NJ 08540, USA
[2] Computer Science Department, Boston University, Boston, MA 02215, USA

Abstract. This paper proposes a method for detecting shapes of variable structure in images with clutter. The term "variable structure" means that some shape parts can be repeated an arbitrary number of times, some parts can be optional, and some parts can have several alternative appearances. The particular variation of the shape structure that occurs in a given image is not known a priori. Existing computer vision methods, including deformable model methods, were not designed to detect shapes of variable structure; they may only be used to detect shapes that can be decomposed into a fixed, a priori known, number of parts. The proposed method can handle both variations in shape structure and variations in the appearance of individual shape parts. A new class of shape models is introduced, called Hidden State Shape Models, that can naturally represent shapes of variable structure. A detection algorithm is described that finds instances of such shapes in images with large amounts of clutter by finding globally optimal correspondences between image features and shape models. Experiments with real images demonstrate that our method can localize plant branches that consist of an a priori unknown number of leaves and can detect hands more accurately than a hand detector based on the chamfer distance.

1 Introduction

This paper introduces a detection algorithm that is explicitly designed for a large category of shape classes where existing detection methods are not applicable: shape classes that exhibit variable structure. The term "variable structure" is used to characterize shape classes with the following properties:

- Some shape parts can be repeated an arbitrary number of times, like the teeth in the hair combs of Fig. 1.
- Some shape parts may be missing. For example, in the rightmost branch shown on Fig. 1, one of the leaves on the right side of the branch is missing.
- Some parts can appear in alternative ways. For example, in the hand shapes shown on Fig. 1, a finger can appear totally extended, partially bent, or completely bent.

Natural, biological and man-made objects may have variable structures that result in large differences in shape. Blood vessels in the retina, airway ducts in the lung, and dendrites are examples of biological objets with variable structure. Detecting and recognizing such objects is important for tasks like diagnosing diseases of the retina or detecting nodules in the lung. Roadways and waterways in aerial images are also examples of object classes with variable structure.

A. Leonardis, H. Bischof, and A. Pinz (Eds.): ECCV 2006, Part I, LNCS 3951, pp. 121–134, 2006.

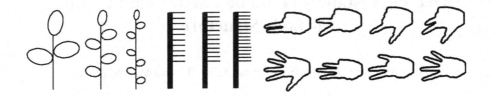

Fig. 1. Three shape classes that exhibit variable structure: branches with leaves, hair combs, and hand contours. Such classes can be naturally modeled with a Hidden State Shape Model (HSSM).

In order to model shape classes of variable structure, we introduce Hidden State Shape Models (HSSMs), a generalization of Hidden Markov Models (HMMs) [1]. Using HSSMs, shapes can be detected in polynomial time, even in the presence of a significant amount of clutter. We describe an algorithm that performs detection-by-registration, and finds globally optimal correspondences between the HSSM model and image features. In experiments with real images, our method localizes branches of leaves with 79% accuracy, without prior knowledge of the number of leaves, and our method detects and recognizes hand shapes with higher accuracy than a method based on the chamfer distance.

2 Related Work

A large amount of literature in computer vision addresses the issue of detecting deformable shapes in images. Shock graphs [2] and FORMS [3] can be used for fitting deformable models to silhouettes extracted from images, but these methods are sensitive to segmentation errors that change the topological properties of silhouettes. Such errors are frequent in the presence of noise and clutter. Another family of deformable models are active contours [4] and active shape models [5]. However active contours and active shapes cannot be used for automatically detecting deformable shapes in an image, unless a good initial alignment between the model and the image is provided.

Graphical models can be used to detect deformable shapes automatically, without requiring an initial guess [6, 7, 8]. When the graphical model is a sequence of parts, or a tree, Dynamic Programming (DP) can be used to find a globally optimal registration between the model and a set of possible shape part locations, even in the presence of clutter [9, 10, 11, 12, 13]. A limitation of DP is that it cannot capture cyclical dependencies between shape parts. Graphical models using iterative inference can capture such dependencies, at the cost of not guaranteeing a globally optimal solution [6, 7, 8].

The main difference between the method we introduce in this paper and all abovementioned methods is that our method can be used for modeling and detection of shape classes that exhibit *variable* structure. We should stress that "structure variation" is not synonymous with "deformation." Objects can be totally rigid and still exhibit variable structure, like the hair combs in Fig. 1. Deformable model methods [2, 3, 4, 5, 6, 7, 8, 9, 10, 11, 12, 13] can model deformations of individual shape parts and deformations in the spatial arrangements between shape parts; they cannot capture structure variations, like the possibility that a shape part may be repeated an arbitrary number of times. Our method, in addition to modeling deformations, is explicitly designed to model variable structure.

Using existing deformable model methods [2, 3, 4, 5, 6, 7, 8, 9, 10, 11, 12, 13], the only way one can model a shape class of variable structure is by exhaustively defining one deformable model for each fixed structure that is a legal structure for that shape class. However, such an approach can quickly become computationally intractable. For example, in the branch images shown in Fig. 1, a unique fixed structure is determined by specifying the number of leaves, and then specifying, for each leaf, if it occurs on the left or the right side of the stem. Thus, the number of possible fixed structures is exponential to the number of leaves, and any of the approaches in [2, 3, 4, 5, 6, 7, 8, 9, 10, 11, 12, 13] would require exponential time to detect such a shape class. In contrast, our method captures such shape variability with a *single* model, and thus provides polynomial-time detection.

The HSSM models that we introduce in this paper are a generalization of HMMs [1]. HMMs have been used for shape modeling in previous work [14, 15, 16]. However, in those methods, HMMs are used to recognize shapes, and object detection is required as preprocessing. Traditional HMMs [14, 15, 16] cannot be used for object detection in clutter, even for objects with fixed structure. Our method extends HMMs in a way that overcomes this limitation.

Complex and variable-structure shapes can also be modeled with shape grammars. Lindenmayer systems (L-systems) have been used successfully in computer graphics for generating realistic images of biological shapes [17]. A generic shape grammar is used in [11] for the task of low-level image segmentation and grouping. In [18] a shape grammar is used to improve the accuracy of rectangle detection in images. The main difference between the proposed method and the methods described in [17, 11, 18] is that our method, in addition to modeling shape classes of variable structure, also addresses the issue of detecting specific shape classes in cluttered images.

3   Modeling Shapes with HSSMs

First we introduce formal definitions and notation. Then, in Section 3.2, we provide an example of how an HSSM can be used to model a shape. In Section 3.3 we discuss how HSSMs are related to HMMs.

3.1   Terminology and Notation

At a high level, in order to design an HSSM for a specific shape class we need to perform two steps: first, specify a set of states, where each state corresponds to a shape part. Second, specify some cost functions, that can be used to evaluate how well a sequence of image features matches a sequence of states. More formally, an HSSM is defined by specifying the following elements:

1. A set of N states $\mathbb{S} = S_1, \ldots, S_N$.
2. A transition cost function A. $A(S_i, S_j)$ is a non-negative real number that represents the cost of transitioning from state S_i to state S_j.

3. An observation cost function B. $B(S_i, F_k)$ is a non-negative real number that represents the cost corresponding to observing feature F_k at state S_i.
4. A feature transition cost function D. $D(S_i, F_k, S_j, F_l)$ is a non-negative real number that represents the cost associated with consecutively matching feature F_k to state S_i and feature F_l to state S_j. This feature transition cost function is an important difference between an HSSM model and a classical HMM model, as explained in Sec. 3.3.
5. An initial cost function I. $I(S_i)$ is a non-negative real number that represents the cost corresponding to state S_i being the initial state of the shape. If S_i is not a legal initial state, then $I(S_i) = \infty$.
6. A subset $\mathbb{E} \subset \mathbb{S}$ of legal end states for the shape.

Given a test image J, we assume that, using some feature extraction method, a set of K features $\mathbb{F} = \{F_1, \ldots, F_K\}$ has been extracted. For example each F_i can correspond to an edge pixel, and F_i can store the location and orientation of that edge pixel.

A registration between the HSSM and the set $\mathbb{F}$ of image features is denoted as $R_{\mathbb{Q},\mathbb{O}} = ((Q_1, O_1), \ldots, (Q_T, O_T))$, where $\mathbb{Q} = (Q_1, \ldots, Q_T)$ is a sequence of T states (each $Q_i \in \mathbb{S}$), and $\mathbb{O} = (O_1, \ldots, O_T)$ is a sequence of T observations (each $O_i \in \mathbb{F}$). The pair (Q_i, O_i), which represents the i-th step of the registration, consists of the model being in state Q_i (where $Q_i = S_j$ for some j) and the corresponding feature at that step being O_i (where $O_i = F_k$ for some k). Intuitively, a registration specifies which image features correspond to which shape parts.

The cost $C(R_{\mathbb{Q},\mathbb{O}})$ of registration $R_{\mathbb{Q},\mathbb{O}}$ is defined as follows:

$$C(R_{\mathbb{Q},\mathbb{O}}) = I(Q_1) + \sum_{i=1}^{T} B(Q_i, O_i) + \sum_{i=1}^{T-1} A(Q_i, Q_{i+1})$$

$$+ \sum_{i=1}^{T-1} D(Q_i, O_i, Q_{i+1}, O_{i+1}) . \tag{1}$$

We define an operation $\oplus$ that takes a registration $R_{\mathbb{Q},\mathbb{O}} = ((Q_1, O_1), \ldots, (Q_T, O_T))$ and a state-feature pair (Q, O) and returns a new registration that is the result of appending (Q, O) to the end of R:

$$R_{\mathbb{Q},\mathbb{O}} \oplus (Q, O) = ((Q_1, O_1), \ldots, (Q_T, O_T), (Q, O)) . \tag{2}$$

We define a registration $R_{\mathbb{Q},\mathbb{O}} = ((Q_1, O_1), \ldots, (Q_T, O_T))$ to be a *total registration* if $Q_T \in \mathbb{E}$, i.e., if the last state of the registration is a legal end state for the HSSM.

Suppose we are given a shape modeled as an HSSM, a registration length $T_{\max}$, and a set $\mathbb{F}$ of features extracted from image J. Detecting the shape in image J consists of finding the globally optimal total registration R_{opt}, i.e., the registration among all possible total registrations $R_{\mathbb{Q},\mathbb{O}}$ with length $T_{\max}$ that minimizes $C(R_{\mathbb{Q},\mathbb{O}})$. Although the set of all possible total registrations is exponential in $T_{\max}$, the algorithm described in Sec. 4 finds a globally optimal total registration in polynomial time, using DP.

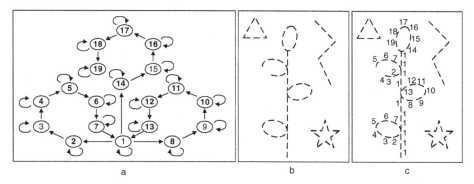

Fig. 2. An HSSM model of the branch class. a). The states of the model, and the allowed transitions out of each state. State S_1 models the stem, states $S_2, \dots, S_7$ model the left-side leaves, states $S_8, \dots, S_{13}$ model the right-side leaves, states $S_{14}, \dots, S_{19}$ model the top leaf. b). An edge image, containing a branch and some "clutter" objects. Each line and arc segment stand for an image feature. c). An example registration of the model with the image features: state labels are shown next to the features they were matched with. Note that the "clutter" features are not assigned to any state.

3.2 An Example

Consider the class of branch shapes shown in Fig. 1. Fig. 2a displays the state topology of an HSSM model for this class. We actually use this model in the experiments, to detect branches of leaves. In Sec. 5 we quantitatively define the cost functions associated with this model. In the next paragraphs we describe at an intuitive level what we want to capture with the model topology and the cost functions.

In the model, the stem is modeled as a straight line, and the leaves are modeled as hexagons. From the input image we extract oriented edge pixels (Fig. 2b). State S_1 models the stem. We expect stem features to have an upright orientation, and observation cost $B(S_1, F_i)$ penalizes for deviations from that orientation. Similarly, the six states corresponding to each leaf have low observation costs for features whose orientations are similar to the orientations expected to be observed at those states.

The state transition cost $A(S_i, S_j)$ is set to zero for all the legal state transitions shown in Fig. 2a, and to infinity for all other transitions. The initial cost $I(S_1)$ for state S_1 is zero, and the initial cost for all other states is infinity. The feature transition cost function $D(S_i, F_k, S_j, F_l)$ reflects the expectation that, if we match state S_i with feature F_k and then we make the transition from state S_i to state S_j, then the feature F_l matched to state S_j should appear in a position near F_k, and the direction of the vector connecting F_k to F_l should be compatible with the transition from S_i to S_j.

Fig. 2c shows an example registration of the model shown in Fig. 2a with the edge image shown in Fig. 2b. We should stress that the model shown in Fig. 2a is simply one of many possible models for the class of branch shapes shown in Fig. 1. For example, one could instead design leaf detectors, and model each leaf with a single state. The image features that would be matched to that state would correspond to locations where the detector response exceeds a threshold, and the observation cost of each feature would depend on the detector response at that feature location.

3.3   Relation to HMMs

HSSMs are a superclass of HMMs. An HMM is a special case of an HSSM, in which:

- Feature transition cost function D is set to zero.
- Function $A(S_i, S_j)$ is the negative logarithm of the transition probability of moving from state S_i to state S_j.
- Function $B(S, F)$ is the negative logarithm of the probability of observing feature F while at state S.
- Function $I(S)$ is the negative logarithm of the probability of S being the initial state.

Overall, if functions A, B, D and I are defined to be negative log likelihoods, then the HSSM model becomes probabilistic, and it provides a generative model that describes how to stochastically generate a set of image features given a shape class. At the same time, if the underlying probability distributions are not available, we can easily create HSSMs by constructing cost functions either manually or automatically. In our experiments we found it straightforward and intuitive to define those functions manually, as described in Sec. 5.

HMMs are typically used to recognize temporal sequences of observations. The traditional Viterbi algorithm employed in HMMs [1] optimally assigns a state to each observation, but relies on two key assumptions: first, that the observations are ordered (temporal sequences of observations are naturally ordered based on the time in which they were observed), and second, that each observation should be matched with the model. In our setting, we cannot use the standard Viterbi algorithm because neither of those two assumptions holds. The set $\mathbb{F}$ of features is an *unordered* set of observations, and only a subset of those observations may actually match the model, since many (possibly most) observations will correspond to clutter.

Since our system does not know a priori the order in which features must be registered, we need a feature transition cost function to evaluate different possible orderings. This function models the fact that, given two consecutive states S_i and $S_{i'}$, we may have two features F_k and $F_{k'}$ such that $B(S_i, F_k)$ and $B(S_{i'}, F_{k'})$ are very low, but the features F_k and $F_{k'}$ are located so far from each other or have some other combined property that makes them a really bad choice for consecutively matching S_i and $S_{i'}$. Fig. 3 illustrates an example.

4   Optimal Registration in Clutter

Suppose that we are given an HSSM model, a registration length $T_{\max}$, and a set $\mathbb{F}$ of features extracted from image J. We want to find a globally optimal total registration R_{opt}. In this section we describe how to find R_{opt} in polynomial time, using a modified version of the Viterbi algorithm.

As is typical in DP methods, we solve our problem by breaking it up into many subproblems whose solutions are related to each other. In particular, we define $W(i, j, k)$ to be the registration $R_{\mathbb{Q},\mathbb{O}}$ that achieves the smallest cost $C(R_{\mathbb{Q},\mathbb{O}})$ under the following constraints:

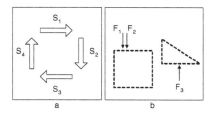

Fig. 3. An illustration of the need for a feature transition cost function. A square is modeled with four states, $S_1, \ldots, S_4$, as shown on the left. Suppose that $B(S_i, F_k)$ compares the edge orientation at F_k with the orientation corresponding to state S_i. Consider features F_1, F_2, F_3, shown on the right. Without a feature transition cost function, registration $((S_1, F_1), (S_1, F_2))$ is as good as registration $((S_1, F_1), (S_1, F_3))$, since F_1, F_2, and F_3 have the same orientation. The feature transition cost function D can penalize the transition from (S_1, F_1) to (S_1, F_3), since F_3 is so far from F_1.

1. The length of $R_{Q,O}$ is j.
2. $Q_j = S_i$. That is, the last state Q_j of $R_{Q,O}$ is state S_i.
3. $O_j = F_k$. That is, the last feature O_j of $R_{Q,O}$ is feature F_k.

If $j = 1$, then $W(i, j, k) = ((S_i, F_k))$. For $j > 1$, assume that we have already computed $W(i', j - 1, k')$ for every $i' \in \{1, \ldots, N\}$ and $k' \in \{1, \ldots, K\}$, where N is the number of states and K is the number of features. Then, $W(i, j, k)$ can be found easily as follows: first, for notational convenience, for every i', k', we define registration $V(i', k', i, j, k)$ as:

$$V(i', k', i, j, k) = W(i', j - 1, k') \oplus (S_i, F_k) . \tag{3}$$

Now, $W(i, j, k)$ is simply the $V(i', k', i, j, k)$ for which the cost $C(V(i', k', i, j, k))$ is minimized:

$$W(i, j, k) = \mathrm{argmin}_{V(i', k', i, j, k)} C(V(i', k', i, j, k)) . \tag{4}$$

Suppose that we have computed $W(i, j, k)$ for every combination of i, j, k. We want to find the globally optimal total registration R_{opt}, i.e., the total registration $R_{Q,O}$ with the lowest cost $C(R_{Q,O})$. First we define the set $\mathbb{W}$ of all registrations $W(i, T_{\mathrm{max}}, k)$ that are total, meaning that their last state is a legal end state:

$$\mathbb{W} = \{W(i, T_{\mathrm{max}}, k) | S_i \in \mathbb{E}\} . \tag{5}$$

The globally optimal total registration R_{opt} is simply the registration in $\mathbb{W}$ with the lowest cost:

$$R_{\mathrm{opt}} = \mathrm{argmin}_{R_{Q,O} \in \mathbb{W}} C(R_{Q,O}) . \tag{6}$$

Registration R_{opt} describes the optimal way to align the HSSM with the observed image features. It specifies where the shape is in the image, and also it specifies the actual structure of the shape, and the location of each individual shape part.

4.1 Complexity

In the worst case, to determine $W(i, j, k)$ for a specific combination of i, j, k we need to evaluate KN possible registrations $V(i', k', i, j, k)$, where K is the number of image features and N is the number of model states. Each of these possible registrations can be evaluated in constant time assuming that, for every i, j, k, when we compute $W(i, j, k)$ we save the cost $C(W(i, j, k))$ in an array $U(i, j, k)$. Then,

$$C(V(i', k', i, j, k)) = U(i', j - 1, k') + A(S_{i'}, S_i)$$
$$+ D(S_{i'}, F_{k'}, S_i, F_k) + B(S_i, F_k) .$$

There are $O(KT_{max}N)$ possible combinations of i, j, k. Therefore, the worst case cost of computing $W(i, j, k)$ for every combination of i, j, k is $O(K^2 T_{max} N^2)$ operations. This cost is polynomial to all terms, which is much more efficient than the brute force method of simply evaluating every one of the exponentially many possible registrations between the model and the set of image features.

The complexity can be further reduced if we can impose some additional constraints. Constraints can be imposed in three different ways:

- By restricting the set of allowed state transitions. This restriction significantly reduces the number of registrations $V(i', k', i, j, k)$ that need to be evaluated in order to find $W(i, j, k)$, by requiring that $S_{i'}$ can be legally succeeded by S_i.
- By restricting the set of allowed feature transitions. If such a restriction is available, it can be used so that, when $W(i, j, k)$ is computed, the system only evaluates registrations $V(i', k', i, j, k)$ such that $F_{k'}$ can be legally succeeded by F_k.
- By restricting, for each state, the set of features that can legally be matched to that state. Then, $W(i, j, k)$ is evaluated only if F_k can be legally matched to S_i.

In the HSSM models used in our experiments we implemented two of those restrictions: first, there are at most four legal transitions for every state. Second, we do not allow a transition between any features f_k and f_l if the distance between f_k and f_l exceeds a threshold. With these two restrictions, the time complexity of the registration process is reduced from $O(K^2 T_{max} N^2)$ to $O(KT_{max}N)$.

5   Implementation

Given a shape class of variable structure, there are several alternative ways to set up an HSSM model for that class. For example, one can define specific detectors for individual shape parts and use the results of those detectors as features [10, 13]. For the implementation used in our experiments, we opted for a simpler solution, where every feature F is simply the location of an edge pixel. We denote with $L(F)$ the location of F, and with $\theta(F)$ the edge orientation of F, where the range of $\theta(F)$ is $[0, 2\pi)$.

Each state S simply models a line segment with orientation $\theta(S)$. To determine how well a feature F matches state S, we simply measure the difference between their orientations. We will denote with $\Delta(\theta_1, \theta_2)$ the angle between orientations θ_1 and θ_2. The range of $\Delta(\theta_1, \theta_2)$ is limited to $[0, \frac{\pi}{2}]$. Based on this notation, we define the observation cost function B between state S and feature F as follows:

$$B(S, F) = \Delta(\theta(S), \theta(F)) \tag{7}$$

In all the models used for the experiments we set the transition cost function A to zero for state transitions that we define as legal, and to infinity for state transitions that we define as illegal. Every state is allowed to make a transition to itself. The observation transition cost function $D(S_i, F_k, S_j, F_l)$ depends on the difference in position and orientation between F_k and F_l. More formally, we denote by $V(\theta)$ the two-dimensional unit vector with orientation θ. Given a weight α that balances position and orientation information, the observation transition cost function $D(S_i, F_k, S_j, F_l)$ is defined as:

$$D(S_i, F_k, S_j, F_l) = \|\frac{L(F_l) - L(F_k)}{\|L(F_l) - L(F_k)\|} - V(\theta(S_j))\| +$$
$$\alpha |\Delta(\theta(S_i), \theta(S_j)) - \Delta(\theta(F_k), \theta(F_l))| . \tag{8}$$

Note that these definitions make the resulting HSSM models invariant to translation, since we do not use absolute feature location in any of the cost functions; we only use, in function D, relative feature location with respect to the location of the previous feature. The HSSM models used in the experiments are dependent on scale and orientation. We obtain the optimal value for α using a validation set, disjoint from the set of test images.

6 Experiments

We have evaluated our method on the task of object localization in two datasets of real images containing shapes of variable structure. The first dataset consists of 100 images of branches of leaves, and the second dataset consists of 353 hand images (Figs. 4, 5, 6). The task of object localization can be summed up as follows: the system knows that there is a single object of the desired class in the image, and the goal is to successfully locate the object and identify the orientation and shape of the object.

In order to provide quantitative measures of accuracy, we will use the following terms to describe accuracy on a particular image:

- "Correct recognition": the system has found the shape at the correct location and orientation, has correctly estimated the number of shape parts, and has correctly registered each shape part.
- "Correct localization": the system has identified the correct object location and orientation. In particular, for the branches we require that 75% of the stem be registered correctly, and for hand images we require that the 75% of the palm edges be registered correctly. We allow incorrect estimation of the number and/or location of some shape parts, and incorrect registration of some shape parts.
- "Incorrect localization": the method failed to find the correct object location and orientation.

Figs. 4, 5, 6 illustrate the meaning of each of these terms with example images.

Exhaustive search was used to identify the orientation that gave the best registration score. For each image, eight different orientations were applied, sampled uniformly in the range from 0 to 2π. With respect to the scale of the object, we assume that $T_{\max}$ is known. The values used for $T_{\max}$ were from the set $\{200, 250, 300, 350, 400, 450, 500\}$.

The test images were 120×160 pixels. All images were converted to grayscale, no color information was available to the algorithm. Edges were extracted using a Canny edge detector. There were between 2000 and 4000 edge pixels extracted from each image. In the HSSMs used for these experiments we did not allow transitions between features that were more than five pixels away. It took about 5-6 minutes to process each image (including trying all eight orientations), with a C++ implementation, on an Opteron 2.0GHz processor. The memory size of the program was under 400MB.

6.1   Experiments on Branch Localization

We constructed an HSSM model for branches of leaves, where leaves occur at the left and right side of the stem (Fig. 2). We then registered the model with 100 real images

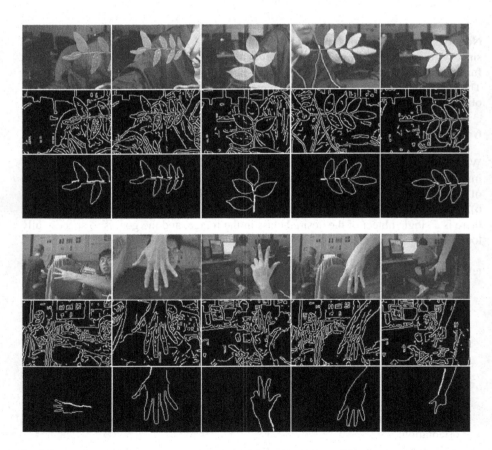

Fig. 4. Examples of "correct recognition" on images of branches of leaves (top half) and hand images (bottom half). For each test image, we show the actual image, the corresponding edge image, and the edge pixels registered to the HSSM model.

of branches. The intention of this experiment was to illustrate that our method extracts useful information from heavily cluttered edge images, and can be a useful complement to other sources of information, like color, motion, and background modeling.

Figs. 4, 5, 6 show example results of our method, and Table 1 provides a quantitative evaluation. In 79% of the images our method produced correct localization. Registration was correct in 43% of the images. We find these results promising, given that we only used edge information. Incorporating color information and more descriptive features, like shape context [19] and SIFT features [20], should greatly improve registration accuracy. Such enhancements remain a topic for future investigation.

6.2 Experiments on Hand Localization

We also applied our method to the problem of localizing hands in grayscale images using only edge information. We compared the detection and recognition accuracy of our method to results obtained using both the chamfer distance [21], and the modified chamfer distance (denoted here as chamfer distance + orientations) that takes edge orientations into account and was used in [22] for hand localization.

The class of hand contours that we modeled in this experiment is defined as follows: the back of the palm is visible, the camera viewing direction is perpendicular to the palm surface, and each of the five fingers can be either fully extended or fully hidden. Since each of the five fingers can appear in two different ways, for the chamfer distance we used $2^5 = 32$ fixed-structure models, so as to represent all valid fixed structures. In contrast, a single HSSM was sufficient for modeling the entire range of variations.

We tested our method on 353 real images of hands, from seven different subjects. Figs. 4, 5, 6 show example results, and Table 1 quantitatively compares our method to the chamfer distance. For detection and recognition based on the chamfer distance, "correct localization" means that best response was obtained at the correct position

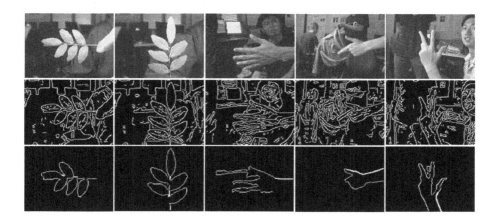

Fig. 5. Example images of branches and hands where the HSSM had "correct localization" but not "correct recognition." For each test image, we show the actual image, the corresponding edge image, and the edge pixels registered to the HSSM model.

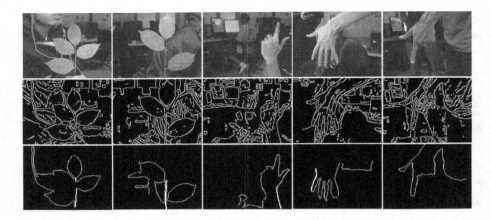

Fig. 6. Example images of branches and hands where the result was labeled as "incorrect". For each test image, we show the actual image, the corresponding edge image, and the edge pixels registered to the HSSM model.

Table 1. Results of HSSM on images of branches and hands,as measured on 100 images of branches of leaves and 353 hand images. For hand images, we also show results using two version of the chamfer distance. Note that "correct recognition" is a subcase of "correct localization." Under each method we indicate the number of orientations at which the method was applied.

dataset:	branches	hands		
method:	HSSM	HSSM	chamfer distance + orientations	chamfer distance
number of orientations:	8	8	72	72
correct recognition	43.0%	33.7%	21.8%	4.0%
correct localization	79.0%	59.5%	54.6%	35.2%
incorrect localization	21.0%	40.5%	45.4%	64.8%

(up to a displacement of half the size of the palm) and orientation (up to 45 degrees). "Correct recognition" means that, in addition to obtaining correct localization, the best response was obtained by the correct fixed-structure model.

To ensure a fair comparison to our method, the scale of the hand was available to the chamfer distance. For each image, brute-force search for the smallest chamfer distance was conducted over all pixel locations, 72 orientations, and all 32 models. Hand localization using the chamfer distance took about 15 seconds/image.

As seen in Table 1, our method was more accurate than the results obtained using either variant of the chamfer distance, in terms of both correct localization and correct recognition. At the same time, we consider the accuracy reported here as the "lower bound" on hand pose matching accuracy with our approach, since color features, motion, etc. could be added to further improve localization and recognition rates. We deliberately did not include these additional features, so that edge-based matching performance vs. the chamfer distance could be directly tested and compared.

7   Discussion and Future Work

We have described a novel method for detecting shapes of variable structure in cluttered images, using the proposed HSSM models. A globally optimal registration can be found in polynomial time, using Dynamic Programming. The HSSM models used in our experiments can be registered with a cluttered image using only easy-to-extract, low level features like edge pixel locations and orientations.

So far we have evaluated our method in a localization setting, where the system knows that there is exactly one object of interest, and the system tries to find the best registration hypothesis for that object. However, our method can also be applied in a more classical detection setting, where the system does not know a priori if there are zero, one, or multiple instances of an object. Fig. 7 shows some preliminary results for multiple instance detection. Those results correspond to the two highest scoring registrations found using the proposed registration algorithm.

Fig. 7. Preliminary results illustrating the ability of our method to detect multiple objects in the same image. Two branches and two hands are detected successfully, by using, for each input image, the two highest scoring registrations found by the proposed registration algorithm.

In this paper, a registration is constrained to be a linearly ordered set of feature-state pairs. However, dynamic programming algorithms can also efficiently produce registrations that are tree-ordered [10, 13]. Such registrations are more appropriate for branching shapes like waterways, dendrites, and blood vessels. We are interested in extending our method to handle such cases.

It is interesting to note that our method operates in a strictly bottom-up way, and the resulting global registration is simply the result of many local decisions. We expect that pairing our method with top-down mechanisms can significantly reduce false matches. We also believe that the accuracy of the method can be greatly improved by applying machine learning methods to optimize the cost functions, and to identify the most discriminative features for each state of the HSSM model. We are currently working on incorporating such methods into our framework.

Acknowledgments

This research was supported in part through NSF grants IIS 0329009, IIS 0308213, IIS-0093367, EIA 0202067, EIA 0326483, and ONR grant N00014-03-1-0108.

References

1. Rabiner, L.R.: A tutorial on hidden markov models and selected applications in speech recognition. In: Proc. of the IEEE. Volume 77:2. (1989) 257–286
2. Sebastian, T.B., Klein, P.N., Kimia, B.B.: Recognition of shapes by editing shock graphs. In: ICCV. (2001) 755–762
3. Zhu, S.C., Yuille, A.L.: FORMS: a flexible object recognition and modeling system. IJCV **20** (1996) 187–212
4. Kass, M., Witkin, A., Terzopoulos, D.: Snakes: Active contour models. IJCV **1** (1988) 321–331
5. Cootes, T.F., Taylor, C.J., Cooper, D.H., Graham, J.: Active shape models - their training and application. CVIU **61** (1995) 38–59
6. Coughlan, J.M., Ferreira, S.J.: Finding deformable shapes using loopy belief propagation. In: ECCV. Volume 3. (2002) 453–468
7. Sigal, L., Isard, M., Sigelman, B.H., Black, M.J.: Attractive people: Assembling loose-limbed models using non-parametric belief propagation. In: NIPS. (2003)
8. Zhang, J., Collins, R., Liu, Y.: Representation and matching of articulated shapes. In: CVPR. Volume 2. (2004) 342–349
9. Amini, A.A., Weymouth, T.E., Jain, R.C.: Using dynamic programming for solving variational problems in vision. PAMI **12** (1990) 855–867
10. Felzenszwalb, P.F., Huttenlocher, D.P.: Pictorial structures for object recognition. IJCV **61** (2005) 55–79
11. Felzenszwalb, P.F.: Representation and Detection of Shapes in Images. PhD thesis, MIT (2003)
12. Geiger, D., Gupta, A., Costa, L.A., Vlontzos, J.: Dynamic programming for detecting, tracking, and matching deformable contours. PAMI **17** (1995) 294–302
13. Ioffe, S., Forsyth, D.A.: Probabilistic methods for finding people. IJCV **43** (2001) 45–68
14. He, Y., Kundu, A.: 2-D shape classification using Hidden Markov Model. PAMI **13** (1991) 1172–1184
15. Arica, N., Yarman-Vural, F.T.: A shape descriptor based on circular Hidden Markov Model. In: ICPR. (2000) 1924–1927
16. Bicego, M., Murino, V.: Investigating Hidden Markov Models' capabilities in 2D shape classification. PAMI **26** (2004) 281–286
17. Prusinkiewicz, P., Lindenmayer, A.: The algorithmic beauty of plants. Springer-Verlag New York, Inc., New York, NY, USA (1990)
18. Han, F., Zhu, S.C.: Bottom-up/top-down image parsing by attribute graph grammar. In: ICCV. (2005) 1778–1785
19. Belongie, S., Malik, J., Puzicha, J.: Shape matching and object recognition using shape contexts. PAMI **24** (2002) 509–522
20. Lowe, D.G.: Distinctive image features from scale-invariant keypoints. IJCV **60** (2004) 91–110
21. Barrow, H.G., Tenenbaum, J.M., Bolles, R.C., Wolf, H.C.: Parametric correspondence and chamfer matching: Two new techniques for image matching. In: IJCAI. (1977) 659–663
22. Thayananthan, A., Stenger, B., Torr, P.H.S., Cipolla, R.: Shape context and chamfer matching in cluttered scenes. In: CVPR. (2003) 127–133

Direct Solutions for Computing Cylinders from Minimal Sets of 3D Points

Christian Beder and Wolfgang Förstner

Institute for Photogrammetry,
Bonn University, Germany
{beder, wf}@ipb.uni-bonn.de

Abstract. Efficient direct solutions for the determination of a cylinder from points are presented. The solutions range from the well known direct solution of a quadric to the minimal solution of a cylinder with five points. In contrast to the approach of G. Roth and M. D. Levine (1990), who used polynomial bases for representing the geometric entities, we use algebraic constraints on the quadric representing the cylinder. The solutions for six to eight points directly determine all the cylinder parameters in one step: (1) The eight-point-solution, similar to the estimation of the fundamental matrix, requires to solve for the roots of a 3rd-order-polynomial. (2) The seven-point-solution, similar to the six-point-solution for the relative orientation by J. Philip (1996), yields a linear equation system. (3) The six-point-solution, similar to the five-point-solution for the relative orientation by D. Nister (2003), yields a ten-by-ten eigenvalue problem. The new minimal five-point-solution first determines the direction and then the position and the radius of the cylinder. The search for the zeros of the resulting 6th order polynomials is efficiently realized using 2D-Bernstein polynomials. Also direct solutions for the special cases with the axes of the cylinder parallel to a coordinate plane or axis are given. The method is used to find cylinders in range data of an industrial site.

1 Introduction

This paper presents direct solutions for estimating circular cylinders from range data both for unconstrained cylinders as well as for cylinders being parallel to a coordinate axis or a coordinate plane. Especially it provides an efficient direct solution for the estimation of a cylinder from the minimum number of five points.

1.1 Motivation

Cylinders play a central role in the representation of the geometry of man made structures such as industrial plants [2, 17], architectures or orthopedy [19]. As-built reconstruction as well as reverse engineering often rely on dense range data. Segmenting point clouds into basic geometric primitives such as planes, cylinders, cones and spheres often is a first step for object recognition.

A. Leonardis, H. Bischof, and A. Pinz (Eds.): ECCV 2006, Part I, LNCS 3951, pp. 135–146, 2006.

Such segmentation may use different methods. Classical segmentation methods are based on local surface properties mainly depending on the local orientation and curvature thus address free form surfaces. These algorithms start from an initial surface description, mostly from triangular meshes, cf. the overview of [12] and of [8] where also the detection of breakline is addressed. Hence cylinders are not addressed explicitly. Tensor voting [16] may be used to achieve the transition from the raw 3D-point cloud to an initial surface description.

In case objects are known to consist of basic geometric primitives this knowledge may immediately be used for the segmentation. Random sample consensus (RANSAC) [4, 5] is a commonly applied technique due to its ease in implementation and efficiency to cope with large percentage of outliers. Basic prerequisite for RANSAC is a direct solution for the parameters of the geometric primitive. Roth and Levine [14] collect polynomial bases for extracting geometric primitives from range data. However, general cylinders do not have a simple basis, for which classical direct estimation schemes would work.

Most approaches to extract cylinders from range data use the information about the surface normal. The Gaussian image of the surface, i. e. the mapping of the surface normals to the unit sphere, is a great circle which may be found by RANSAC [2], clustering [19] or Hough-transform [17]. The so-called Blaschke-image of the surface, i. e. the mapping of the surfaces' tangent planes into the projective space $(\mathbf{n}, d)$ with unit normals and distances, eases the identification of multiple primitives [11].

Both analysis methods, surface segmentation as well as cylinder extraction using normals presume the neighborhood relations between the measured points are established. We want to provide direct methods for cylinder extraction which can work on the original 3D-point cloud. As a general cylinder has five degrees of freedom, four for the axis and one for the radius, one needs at least five points to determine the parameters. To our knowledge, no direct solution has been published hitherto in spite of various attempts to express the cylinder constraints on the quadric parameters [18]. As the solution is much more involving than the direct solutions for quadrics we also present solutions with more points, which allows to balance computing time and samples required in RANSAC. Moreover, as in many cases the 3D-data may easily be referred to the plumbline and horizontal and vertical cylinders are quite common we also present the solutions for cylinders with such special orientations.

1.2   General Setup

A cylinder can be described by 5 parameters, the 4 parameters for the axis and one for the radius.

In case the cylinder axis is parallel to one coordinate plane, e. g. in case it is horizontal, the number of parameters reduces to 4, the 3 parameters for the axis and the radius.

In case the cylinder axis is parallel to a coordinate axis, we only need 3 parameters, 2 for the position of the axis and one for the radius. If we do not know the coordinate axis, we might check all three.

Table 1. Number of parameters for a cylinder (boldface), presented algorithms with maximum number of solutions. The maximum number of solutions for the five point algorithm is not known.

cylinder	# points + (# solutions)
general	**5** (?), 6 (10), 7 (1), 8 (3), 9 (1)
parallel to plane	**4** (3)
parallel to line	**3** (1)

Each point on the surface yields one constraint. Therefore we have the cases collected in table 1. The number of solutions for the presented algorithms is also given, where we know it. Note, that this number is only an algebraic property of the algorithm and an unique solution is easily obtained for all of the non-minimal cases.

The paper is organized as follows: In section 2 we present direct solutions for cylinders being parallel to an axis or a plane. These results will be be used for the solutions for cylinders with general orientation in section 3, where we present algorithms from 9 down to 5 points. Section 4 shows experiments and results for finding general cylinders in 3D-point-clouds.

2   Cylinders Parallel to Coordinate Axes or Planes

2.1   Cylinder Parallel to an Axis

Without restriction we may assume the axis is parallel to the Z-axis. Then the cylinder is given by

$$(X - s)^2 + (Y - t)^2 - r^2 = 0$$

The cylinder has 3 unknown parameters. The classical solution (cf. [1]) uses the substitution $u = s^2 + t^2 - r^2$. Then the the three parameters s, t and u can be determined from the following three equations

$$X_i^2 + Y_i^2 - 2X_i s - 2Y_i t + u = 0 \qquad i = 1, 2, 3 \tag{1}$$

linear in the parameters, which can be written as

$$\begin{bmatrix} 2X_1 & 2Y_1 & -1 \\ 2X_2 & 2Y_2 & -1 \\ 2X_3 & 2Y_3 & -1 \end{bmatrix} \begin{bmatrix} s \\ t \\ u \end{bmatrix} = \begin{bmatrix} X_1^2 + Y_1^2 \\ X_2^2 + Y_2^2 \\ X_3^2 + Y_3^2 \end{bmatrix} \tag{2}$$

The parameter r can be determined from $r = \sqrt{s^2 + t^2 - u}$.

2.2   Cylinder Parallel to a Plane

A cylinder parallel to a given plane is described by 4 parameters. Therefore we need four points X_i.

Without restriction we may assume the cylinder is parallel to the XY-plane. Then we may describe the cylinder as a reference cylinder parallel to the X-axis

$$(Y' - s)^2 + (Z' - t)^2 - r^2 = 0$$

rotated around the Z axis by some angle κ. Then we first determine a direction $[\cos\kappa, \sin\kappa, 0] = [a, b, 0]$ such that the four points lie on a circle.

The four rotated points are $\boldsymbol{X}'_i = R\boldsymbol{X}_i$ thus

$$\boldsymbol{X}'_i = \begin{bmatrix} aX_i + bY_i \\ -bX_i + aY_i \\ Z_i \end{bmatrix} \qquad a^2 + b^2 = 1$$

Similar to (1) we obtain the constraint $Y'^2_i + Z'^2_i - 2Y'_i s - 2Z'_i t + (s^2 + t^2 - r^2) = 0$ or expanding the rotation

$$(-bX_i + aY_i)^2 + Z_i^2 - 2(-bX_i + aY_i)s - 2Z_i t + (s^2 + t^2 - r^2) = 0$$

For the four points we therefore get the linear system

$$\begin{bmatrix} (-bX_1 + aY_1)^2 + Z_1^2 & -2(-bX_1 + aY_1) & -2Z_1 & 1 \\ (-bX_2 + aY_2)^2 + Z_2^2 & -2(-bX_2 + aY_2) & -2Z_2 & 1 \\ (-bX_3 + aY_3)^2 + Z_3^2 & -2(-bX_3 + aY_3) & -2Z_3 & 1 \\ (-bX_4 + aY_4)^2 + Z_4^2 & -2(-bX_4 + aY_4) & -2Z_4 & 1 \end{bmatrix} \begin{bmatrix} 1 \\ s \\ t \\ u \end{bmatrix} = \begin{bmatrix} 0 \\ 0 \\ 0 \\ 0 \end{bmatrix}$$

The 4×4-matrix is singular if the four points are co-circular. The determinant is cubic in a and b, however only containing monomials $[a^3, a^2b, ab^2, b^3, a, b]$. Together with the constraint $a^2 + b^2 = 1$ we obtain 6 solutions for a and b, which pairwise differ by a factor -1, thus represent the same cylinder. Thus we may obtain up to 3 solutions.

An example would be three points in a horizontal triangle and a fourth point not in that height. Then we have three cylinders parallel to the three sides of that triangle.

3 General Cylinders

3.1 Representation of a Cylinder

The cylinder is a special 3D-quadric, representable as symmetric and homogeneous matrix C for the surface points with homogeneous coordinates $\mathbf{X}$

$$\mathbf{X}^\mathsf{T} C \mathbf{X} = 0 \tag{3}$$

which fulfills the constraint, that there exists a plane, so that all points $\mathbf{X}$ on the cylinder projected on that plane are co-circular. If this plane is without loss of generality the XY-plane, this condition can be expressed by

$$(X' - s)^2 + (Y' - t)^2 - r^2 = 0 \tag{4}$$

for some s, t and r, or in terms of the cylinder representation

$$C' = \lambda \begin{bmatrix} D' & d' \\ d'^\mathsf{T} & -r^2 \end{bmatrix}$$

with

$$D' = \begin{bmatrix} 1 & 0 & 0 \\ 0 & 1 & 0 \\ 0 & 0 & 0 \end{bmatrix} \quad \text{and} \quad d' = \begin{bmatrix} -s \\ -t \\ 0 \end{bmatrix}$$

Because the projection plane is in general unknown, one has to allow a spatial motion

$$M = \begin{bmatrix} R & t \\ \mathbf{0}^\mathsf{T} & 1 \end{bmatrix}$$

to be applied, so that one obtains the general cylinder as

$$\begin{aligned} \mathsf{C} &= M^{-T} \mathsf{C}' M^{-1} \\ &= \lambda \begin{bmatrix} RD'R^\mathsf{T} & -RD'R^\mathsf{T}t + Rd' \\ -t^\mathsf{T}RD'R^\mathsf{T} + d'^\mathsf{T}R^\mathsf{T} & t^\mathsf{T}RD'R^\mathsf{T}t - 2t^\mathsf{T}Rd' - r^2 \end{bmatrix} = \begin{bmatrix} D & d \\ d^\mathsf{T} & d \end{bmatrix} \end{aligned}$$

3.2 Constraints on the Parameters of a Cylinder

One immediately observes, that the matrix D is singular and has two identical eigenvalues, which can be expressed algebraically (cf. [3], p. 254) by the ten equations

$$|D| = 0 \tag{5}$$

$$2DD^\mathsf{T}D - \mathrm{tr}DD^\mathsf{T}D = \underset{3\times 3}{0} \tag{6}$$

Note that the second equations yield only 6 independent constraints due to symmetry. Further one can see, that

$$Dd = \lambda^2 RD'R^\mathsf{T}(-RD'R^\mathsf{T}t + Rd') = \lambda d$$

thus d is an eigenvector of D yielding the additional three constraints

$$[d]_\times Dd = \mathbf{0} \tag{7}$$

and one finally arrives at ten linear independent algebraic constraints (5), (6) and (7).

We now exploit these constraints stepwise.

3.3 Solutions with 9, 8, 7, and 6 Points

Solution with 9 points. If one has given 9 points $\mathbf{X}_i, i = 1, ..., 9$ on the cylinder, the constraint (3) is sufficient to solve the problem using a simple singular value decomposition of the homogeneous equation system

$$\mathsf{A} \, \mathrm{vech}\mathsf{C} = [\mathrm{vech}^\mathsf{T}(\mathbf{X}_i\mathbf{X}_i^\mathsf{T})] \, \mathrm{vech}\mathsf{C} = \mathbf{0}$$

in the ten unknown elements of C (cf. [7], p. 563).

Solution with 8 points. If only 8 points are given, the nullspace resulting from the singular value decomposition of the homogeneous matrix A imposed by constraint (3) is two-dimensional. The solution is thus known to be

$$C = xC_1 + C_2$$

for some scalar x, where the two matrices C_i result from the nullspace of A. Analogous to the well-known 7-point-algorithm for computing the fundamental matrix (cf. [7], p. 264), one picks any of the ten constraints (e.g. (5)), which are all polynomials of degree three in x and solves for the roots yielding up to three solutions.

Solution with 7 points. Again constraint (3) is used to compute the now three-dimensional nullspace, in which the solution is found:

$$C = xC_1 + yC_2 + C_3$$

Following the approach of [13], x and y can be found using the ten constraints (5), (6) and (7), which are all polynomials of degree three in x and y. More specifically the ten polynomials are written as homogeneous equation system in the monomials

$$N \begin{bmatrix} x^3 & x^2y & xy^2 & y^3 & x^2 & xy & y^2 & x & y & 1 \end{bmatrix}^\mathsf{T} = 0$$

The unknowns x and y are found uniquely as the 8th and 9th element of the right zero-eigenvector of N via singular value decomposition.

Solution with 6 points. Using only 6 points the nullspace of the homogeneous equation system imposed by (3) is four-dimensional:

$$C = xC_1 + yC_2 + zC_3 + C_4 \tag{8}$$

The three coefficients are obtained similar to [15]. To do this, observe, that the ten constraints (5), (6) and (7) are cubic polynomials in x, y and z. Ordering the 20 monomials of up to 3rd degree in graded reverse lexicographic order and partitioning them into two vectors of size ten, one gets

$$\boldsymbol{q} = \begin{bmatrix} x^3 & x^2y & x^2z & xy^2 & xyz & xz^2 & y^3 & y^2z & yz^2 & z^3 \end{bmatrix}^\mathsf{T}$$

$$\boldsymbol{r} = \begin{bmatrix} x^2 & xy & xz & y^2 & yz & z^2 & x & y & z & 1 \end{bmatrix}^\mathsf{T}$$

The ten constraints are now expressible as

$$N \begin{bmatrix} \boldsymbol{q} \\ \boldsymbol{r} \end{bmatrix} = \begin{bmatrix} N_1 & N_2 \end{bmatrix} \begin{bmatrix} \boldsymbol{q} \\ \boldsymbol{r} \end{bmatrix} = N_1\boldsymbol{q} + N_2\boldsymbol{r} = 0$$

and it follows, that

$$\boldsymbol{q} = -N_1^{-1}N_2\boldsymbol{r} = B\boldsymbol{r}$$

Also observe, that the first six elements of $\boldsymbol{q}$ are a multiple of the first six elements of $\boldsymbol{r}$. Combining this and denoting with $\boldsymbol{B}_{1:6,:}$ the first six rows of B, one obtains the condition

$$\boldsymbol{q} = \begin{bmatrix} \boldsymbol{B}_{1:6,:} \\ \begin{bmatrix} I_{3\times3} & \boldsymbol{0}_{3\times3} & \boldsymbol{0}_{3\times1} & \boldsymbol{0}_{3\times2} \\ \boldsymbol{0}_{1\times3} & \boldsymbol{0}_{1\times3} & 1 & \boldsymbol{0}_{1\times3} \end{bmatrix} \end{bmatrix} \boldsymbol{r} = F\boldsymbol{r} = x\boldsymbol{r}$$

Obviously r is an eigenvector of F and one obtains up to ten solutions with the 7th, 8th and 9th elements of these vectors being the unknown parameters to be fed into (8).

3.4   Solution with 5 Points

To our knowledge the strategy taken thus far does not carry over to the minimal case of 5 given points. We were unable to find enough linear independent constraints. Therefore we chose a different path.

1. First, the direction of the cylinder axis is determined, leading to a 6-th degree polynomial in the direction parameters a and b
2. Second, the position of the cylinder axis across this direction and the radius are determined, leading to a linear equation system.

Determination of the direction of the cylinder axis. The direction of cylinder axis is determined by a rotation such that the cylinder axis is the Z-axis. Then all rotated points, when projected into the XY-plane are co-circular.
Using quaternions, this rotation can be represented as

$$R(a,b) = \frac{1}{1+a^2+b^2} \begin{bmatrix} 1+a^2-b^2 & 2ab & 2b \\ 2ab & 1-a^2+b^2 & -2a \\ -2b & 2a & 1-a^2-b^2 \end{bmatrix}$$

as the quaternion $\mathbf{q} = (1, [a, b, 0]) = (1, \mathbf{r}\tan\phi/2)$ represents a general rotation around a horizontal axis $\mathbf{r}$ with angle ϕ. Only angles $\phi \leq 90°$ are relevant in our context, thus $a^2 + b^2 \leq 1$.
All 5 points $\mathbf{X}_i$ are then transformed according to $\mathbf{X}'_i(a,b) = R(a,b)\mathbf{X}_i$ leading to

$$\begin{bmatrix} X'_i(a,b) \\ Y'_i(a,b) \\ Z'_i(a,b) \end{bmatrix} = \frac{1}{1+a^2+b^2} \begin{bmatrix} X_i a^2 - X_i b^2 + 2Y_i ab + 2Z_i b + X_i \\ -Y_i a^2 + Y_i b^2 + 2X_i ab - 2Z_i a + Y_i \\ -Z_i a^2 - Z_i b^2 + 2Y_i a - 2X_i b + Z_i \end{bmatrix}$$

The projection of all 5 $\mathbf{X}'_i$ into the $X'Y'$-plane must be co-circular and therefore obey equation (4). Using the substitution $u = s^2+t^2-r^2$, this can be formulated as homogeneous equation system

$$\begin{bmatrix} X_1'^2(a,b) + Y_1'^2(a,b) & -2X_1'(a,b) & -2Y_1'(a,b) & 1 \\ X_2'^2(a,b) + Y_2'^2(a,b) & -2X_2'(a,b) & -2Y_2'(a,b) & 1 \\ X_3'^2(a,b) + Y_3'^2(a,b) & -2X_3'(a,b) & -2Y_3'(a,b) & 1 \\ X_4'^2(a,b) + Y_4'^2(a,b) & -2X_4'(a,b) & -2Y_4'(a,b) & 1 \\ X_5'^2(a,b) + Y_5'^2(a,b) & -2X_5'(a,b) & -2Y_5'(a,b) & 1 \end{bmatrix} \begin{bmatrix} 1 \\ s \\ t \\ u \end{bmatrix} = H(a,b) \begin{bmatrix} 1 \\ s \\ t \\ u \end{bmatrix} = 0$$
(9)

Each of the five 4×4-submatrices of $H(a,b)$ must therefore be singular, i.e. have a zero determinant. The numerators of this five determinants are bivariate polynomials of 6-th degree in the two variables a and b, hence are expressible as

$$p_l(a,b) = \begin{bmatrix} 1 & a & a^2 & a^3 & a^4 & a^5 & a^6 \end{bmatrix} G_l \begin{bmatrix} 1 & b & b^2 & b^3 & b^4 & b^5 & b^6 \end{bmatrix}^T = 0, \quad l = 1, ..., 5 \quad (10)$$

Their common roots need to be calculated in order to obtain the cylinder axis direction.

Determination of position and radius. Having computed a set of common roots, i.e. the cylinder axis directions, for each solution the translation and radius of the cylinder must be computed. Therefore one either solves the homogeneous equation system (9), or, more efficiently, selects three arbitrary rows and converts it into the linear equation system (2), however referring to the rotated points $\mathbf{X}'$ yielding the remaining cylinder parameters.

Finding the common roots of the 6-th order polynomials. For finding the common roots of the 6-th order polynomials (10) we use an interval method (cf. [9]) like [10] did in the univariate case. More specifically we use an approach using Bernstein polynomials (cf. [6]), to track down the roots of the bivariate polynomials. First the polynomials are transformed, so that all roots are inside the unit box $[0,1] \times [0,1]$. Since rotation of the cylinder axis by $180°$ does not change the cylinder, all roots are found inside the box $[-1,1] \times [-1,1]$ and therefore by a simple variable substitution the coefficients become

$$\overline{G} = \mathbf{\Gamma} G \mathbf{\Gamma}^{\mathsf{T}} \tag{11}$$

with

$$\mathbf{\Gamma}_{ij} = \begin{cases} \binom{j}{i}(-1)^{j-i}2^i & \text{if } i \leq j \\ 0 & \text{otherwise} \end{cases}$$

Next the polynomials are transformed into the Bernstein basis by

$$B = \mathbf{\Phi}^{-1}\overline{G}\mathbf{\Phi}^{-\mathsf{T}} \tag{12}$$

with

$$\mathbf{\Phi}_{ij} = \begin{cases} \binom{6}{j}\binom{6-j}{i-j}(-1)^{i-j} & \text{if } i \geq j \\ 0 & \text{otherwise} \end{cases}$$

One property of this Bernstein coefficients B is, that their minima and maxima yield a lower and upper bound on the polynomial in the unit box. Therefore bounds on equation (10) in the box $[-1,1] \times [-1,1]$ are given by

$$\min B \leq p([-1,1],[-1,1]) \leq \max B$$

so that one can easily decide for each polynomial, if there is any root in the interval of interest by checking, if there exists positive and negative coefficients.

To track down the roots, the intervals need to be bisected and the Bernstein coefficients of the polynomials, that have the roots of the bisected interval inside the unit box, must be computed. Fortunately there is a much more efficient method than applying equations (11) and (12). The two sets of Bernstein coefficients of the bisection are computable using the following dynamic programming algorithm: For the bisection along the x-axis the coefficients starting with ${}^{x_1}B^{(0)} = B$ are updated sequentially according to

$$ {}^{x_1}B_{ij}^{(k)} = \begin{cases} \dfrac{{}^{x_1}B_{i-1,j}^{(k-1)} + {}^{x_1}B_{ij}^{(k-1)}}{2} & \text{if } i > k \\ {}^{x_1}B_{ij}^{(k-1)} & \text{otherwise} \end{cases} \qquad k = 1, ..., 7$$

yielding the new set of coefficients $^{x_1}\boldsymbol{B} = {}^{x_1}\boldsymbol{B}^{(7)}$ representing the polynomial having the roots inside the left hand side subinterval put into the unit interval. The coefficients $^{x_2}\boldsymbol{B}$ of the right hand side subinterval are obtained during this computation using the fact, that

$$^{x_2}\boldsymbol{B}_{ij} = {}^{x_1}\boldsymbol{B}_{7j}^{(8-i)}$$

The computation of the bisection along the y-axis is completely symmetric, i.e. starting with $^{y_1}\boldsymbol{B}^{(0)} = \boldsymbol{B}$ the coefficients are sequentially updated according to

$$^{y_1}\boldsymbol{B}_{ij}^{(k)} = \begin{cases} \dfrac{^{y_1}\boldsymbol{B}_{i,j-1}^{(k-1)} + {}^{y_1}\boldsymbol{B}_{ij}^{(k-1)}}{2} & \text{if } j > k \\ ^{y_1}\boldsymbol{B}_{ij}^{(k-1)} & \text{otherwise} \end{cases} \qquad k = 1, ..., 7$$

$$^{y_2}\boldsymbol{B}_{ij} = {}^{y_1}\boldsymbol{B}_{i7}^{(8-j)}$$

Putting everything together the roots of the five polynomials are found as follows: First the Bernstein coefficients for each polynomial are computed. Then the intervals are alternating bisected along the x- and the y-axis. By checking signs of the Bernstein coefficients it is decided, if each of the five polynomials has a possible root inside the subintervals. If this is the case, the search is continued inside this subinterval. Note, that the size of the subintervals and therefore the accuracy of the roots decreases exponentially. A final single Gauss-Newton update may be applied to further increase the accuracy of the roots.

4   Experiments

4.1   Finding Cylinders with RANSAC

The value of direct solutions for computing cylinders from minimal sets of 3D-points is, that the RANSAC-algorithm for robust estimation needs a direct solution from as few data as possible to be efficient. In [7], p. 104, the number of its iterations is given by $N = \log{(1-p)}/\log{(1-(1-\epsilon)^s)}$ where p is the error probability, ϵ is the proportion of outliers and s is the size of the sample. As discussed above, the complexity of the algorithm and thus the running time per sample increases with decreasing sample size s. Therefore the sample size must be carefully engineered with respect to the expected proportion of outliers in the data. If few outliers are expected, the 9-point-solution is fast and easy and the additional running time due to more RANSAC-iterations is negligible. If on the other hand many outliers are expected, the 5-point-solution will increase the overall running time. All intermediate solutions may be useful, too, depending on the speed of the implementations and the expected number of outliers in the data.

To find all cylinders contained in a 3D-point-cloud, we proceed as follows: Repeatedly a set of five points is sampled at random from the set of points and the cylinders going through this five points are computed. For each of this cylinders the points lying on its surface are counted and the one cylinder is retained, that has most supporting points on its surface. If the number of supporting points is to low, the process is stopped and the cylinder is removed. Otherwise the cylinder is kept, the supporting points are removed from the point-cloud and the whole process is iterated.

4.2   Results

The efficiency of the root-finder. The performance of the five-point-method mainly depends on the efficiency for finding the common roots of the five polynomial equations yielding the axis direction of the cylinder. In figure 1, left, the logarithm of the sum of the five squared polynomials is shown for a typical point configuration. The standard Gauss-Newton-Method for finding the four roots would search this cost function.

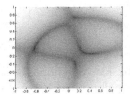 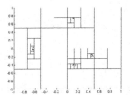

Fig. 1. Left: Logarithm of the sum of the five squared polynomials for a typical point configuration. The minima of this function would be searched with the standard Gauss-Newton-Method. Right: The bisections required with the Bernstein-Method for tracking down the roots of the same five polynomials as depicted in the figure left.

The approach using Bernstein-polynomials is much more efficient than this. The bisections required for the previous example polynomials are shown in figure 1, right. Obviously the quality of the bounds is essential for the efficiency of the approach. As seen in figure 1, right, the required bisection for that special example are very good. To quantify the quality, the area searched by the algorithm in each iteration is analyzed. For the method to be efficient, this area must decrease exponentially. As seen in figure 2, left, this is the case, as the logarithm of the average search area for random point configurations is shown to decrease linearly.

Number of solutions. Another crucial point for the efficiency of the RANSAC-procedure is the number of solutions, that are found by the algorithm. The maximum number of different solutions for this problem is not known. Due to the ambiguity of the rotation parameters (a, b) it must be less or equal 18. This is because two 6-th degree polynomials in general may have up to 36 real solutions and the two quaternions $(1, a, b, 0)$ and $(1, -a/(a^2 + b^2), -b/(a^2 + b^2, 0))$ rotate

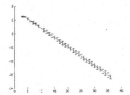 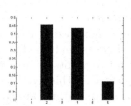

Fig. 2. Left: Logarithm of the average area considered by the root finder (with standard deviation) against the search depth for random point configurations. Right: Histogram of the number of solutions.

the same axis into the Z-axis. In our experiments the number of solutions was always 2, 4 or 6, though.

In figure 2, right, the histogram of the number of solutions for random point configurations is shown. The average number of solutions was 3.3.

Experiment with real data. Finally the performance of the algorithm on real data is shown. In figure 3, left, a 3D point cloud comprising of about 170.000 points is depicted. It was taken by a laser scanner at an industrial site containing several pipes. Figure 3, right, shows the cylinders, that were extracted from this point cloud.

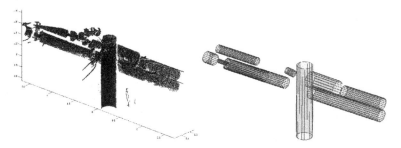

Fig. 3. Left: 3D point cloud obtained by a laser-scanner at an industrial site (courtesy of G.Vosselman and T.Rabbani). Right: Extracted cylinders.

5   Conclusion

We have presented direct solutions for determining the parameters of cylinders from surface points, which are to our knowledge new except for the 9-point-method. The five-point algorithm for circular straight cylinders has been efficiently realized using Bernstein polynomials and tested on synthetic and real range data. There are still some open problems:

- The maximum number of solutions is unknown.
- The critical configurations are unknown.
- It needs to be investigated under which constraints the other solutions, with 6 and more points, are more efficient.

References

1. F. L. Bookstein. Fitting conic sections to scattered data. *CGIP*, 9(1):56–71, 1979.
2. T. Chaperon and F. Goulette. Extracting cylinders in full 3d data using a random sampling method and the gaussian image. In *Proceedings of the Vision Modeling and Visualization Conference*, pages 35–42, 2001.
3. O. Faugeras. *Three-Dimensional Computer Vision: A Geometric Viewpoint*. MIT Press, 1993.
4. M. A. Fischler and R. C. Bolles. Random sample consensus: a paradigm for model fitting with applications to image analysis and automated cartography. *Commun. ACM*, 24(6):381–395, 1981.

5. M. A. Fischler and R. C. Bolles. A RANSAC-based approach to model fitting and its application to finding cylinders in range data. In *IJCAI81*, pages 637–643, 1981.
6. J. Garloff and A. P. Smith. Solution of systems of polynomial equations by using bernstein expansion. In G. Alefeld, S. Rump, J. Rohn, and T. Yamamoto, editors, *Symbolic Algebraic Methods and Verification Methods*. Springer, 2001.
7. R. Hartley and A. Zisserman. *Multiple View Geometry in Computer Vision*. Cambridge University Press, 2000.
8. H. Hoppe, T. DeRose, T. Duchamp, M. Halstead, H. Jin, J. McDonald, J. Schweitzer, and W. Stuetzle. Piecewise smooth surface reconstruction. In *SIGGRAPH '94: Proceedings of the 21st annual conference on Computer graphics and interactive techniques*, pages 295–302, New York, NY, USA, 1994. ACM Press.
9. R. Martin, H. Shou, I. Voiculescu, A. Bowyer, and Guojin Wang. Comparison of interval methods for plotting algebraic curves. *Comput. Aided Geom. Des.*, 19(7):553–587, 2002.
10. D. Nistér. An efficient solution to the five-point relative pose problem. *IEEE Trans. Pattern Anal. Mach. Intell.*, 26(6):756–777, 2004.
11. M. Peternell, H. Pottmann, and T. Steiner. Hough transform and Laguerre geometry for the recognition and reconstruction of special 3D shapes. Technical Report 100, Institute of Geometry, April 2003.
12. S. Petitjean. A survey of methods for recovering quadrics in triangle meshes. *ACM Comput. Surv.*, 34(2):211–262, 2002.
13. J. Philip. A non-iterative algorithm for determining all essential matrices corresponding to five point pairs. *Photogrammetric Record*, 15(88):589–599, 1996.
14. G. Roth and M. D. Levine. Segmentation of geometric signals using robust fitting. In *Int. Conference on Pattern Recognition*, pages 826–831, 1990.
15. H. Stewenius, C. Engels, and D. Nister. Recent developments on direct relative orientation. *ISPRS Journal*, 2006. to appear.
16. C.K. Tang and G. Medioni. Curvature-augmented tensor voting for shape inference from noisy 3d data. *PAMI*, 24(6):858–864, June 2002.
17. G. Vosselman, B. G. H. Gorte, G. Sithole, and T. Rabbani. Recognising structure in laser scanner point clouds. In *International Archives of Photogrammetry, Remote Sensing and Spatial Information Sciences*, volume 46, pages 33–38, 2004.
18. N. Werghi, R.B. Fisher, C. Robertson, and A.P. Ashbrook. Faithful recovering of quadric surfaces from 3d range data. In *Second International Conference on 3-D Imaging and Modeling3DIM99*, pages 280–289, 1999.
19. S. Winkelbach, R. Westphal, and T. Gösling. Pose estimation of cylindrical fragments for semi-automatic bone fracture reduction. In Bernd Michaelis and Gerald Krell, editors, *DAGM-Symposium*, volume 2781 of *Lecture Notes in Computer Science*, pages 566–573. Springer, 2003.

Estimation of Multiple Periodic Motions from Video

Alexia Briassouli and Narendra Ahuja

Beckman Insitute, University of Illinois, Urbana-Champaign,
405 N Matthews, Urbana, IL, 61801
{briassou, ahuja}@vision.ai.uiuc.edu

Abstract. The analysis of periodic or repetitive motions is useful in many applications, both in the natural and the man-made world. An important example is the recognition of human and animal activities. Existing methods for the analysis of periodic motions first extract motion trajectories, e.g. via correlation, or feature point matching. We present a new approach, which takes advantage of both the frequency and spatial information of the video. The 2D spatial Fourier transform is applied to each frame, and time-frequency distributions are then used to estimate the time-varying object motions. Thus, multiple periodic trajectories are extracted and their periods are estimated. The period information is finally used to segment the periodically moving objects. Unlike existing methods, our approach estimates multiple periodicities simultaneously, it is robust to deviations from strictly periodic motion, and estimates periodicities superposed on translations. Experiments with synthetic and real sequences display the capabilities and limitations of this approach. Supplementary material is provided, showing the video sequences used in the experiments.

1 Introduction

Periodic motion characterizes the motion of humans and animals, as well as many man-made objects [1]. This paper presents a new approach to the analysis of multiple periodic motions in a video sequence. The primary motivation and intuition lie in the observation that repetitive patterns have distinct frequency space signatures. If these signatures can be extracted, then they can be used to enhance the more common, spatial domain analysis of the video sequence. This synergy between periodic motion and frequency space representations has been surprisingly underexploited.

The main parts of the proposed approach are as follows. (1) Through a process called μ-propagation, the periodic changes in object motions are converted into a proportional variation in frequency (Sec. 4). This results in a frequency-modulated (FM) signal with time-varying frequencies. (2) Time-frequency distributions (TFDs) are used to estimate the time-varying frequencies, and the periods present in them are estimated via spectral analysis methods (Sec. 3, 4). (3) Once all the periods in the video sequence are estimated, each object is

A. Leonardis, H. Bischof, and A. Pinz (Eds.): ECCV 2006, Part I, LNCS 3951, pp. 147–159, 2006.

segmented (Sec. 5) by matching each frame with frames at displacements corresponding to its period (since an object is expected to re-appear in the same position after an integer number of periods).

1.1 Previous Work

The numerous methods for analyzing repetitive motions can be separated in two large categories: the first based on the analysis of feature correspondences, and the second category on region correlations.

Point Correspondence Methods: Much of the work on periodic motion estimation and analysis [2], [3] extracts the trajectories by tracking the position of reflective markers throughout the video. When manual intervention or the placement of markers are not possible, feature correspondences are used. However, varying illumination, or local occlusion lead to point feature detection and localization errors, making the point matching unreliable. Given the detected point features in each image, the large numbers of possible pairings also make them computationally forbidding for many applications.

Region Correspondences: Region based methods [4] find repetitions in interframe region correlations [5]. They avoid the sensitivity of point correspondences, but are still sensitive to non-constant illumination. Also, they detect "in position" periodicities, i.e. oscillating positions of the objects around the same pixel(s). They cannot detect periodicities superposed on other motions, such as translations (e.g. walking), without pre-processing. Pre-processing requires that each oscillating object is segmented in each frame [4], [6] and then aligned in successive frames, to detect periodicities.

1.2 Motivation

The proposed work is strongly motivated by the aforementioned frequency-compatible nature of periodic motion analysis, the limitations of the current, spatially based methods, and the potential advantages of combining the strengths of spatial and frequency based approaches. The advantages the frequency based methods [7], [8] introduce include the following. (1) Frequency-based approaches involve spatially global, instead of local, analysis. (2) There is no need for explicit feature matching (as in spatial methods). (3) Frequency domain analysis is robust to illumination changes: Fourier Transform (FT) based motion estimates are extracted from phase changes induced by motions, which are not as sensitive to illumination changes as spatial correlations [9]. (4) Efficient algorithms are available for FT computation.

1.3 Contributions

The major contributions of the proposed approach are: (1) Unlike previous work, it extracts multiple periodic motions. (2) Periodic trajectories are extracted simultaneously, not one at a time (Sec. 5). (3) It is robust to deviations from strict periodicity (Sec. 6). For example, (a) when the period is not truly constant, or

(b) when the magnitude of the velocity or displacement profile does not have the exact same value at each repetition, or (c) when object shape is not rigid, and all or some of the motion parameters fluctuate around some "mean" values, the effects of these deviations on the proposed approach are marginal (Sec. 9). (4) The computational cost is lower than that of the spatial methods, because (a) the FT computation is efficient, and (b) frame by frame processing is reduced to a few frame correlations for segmentation (Step (3) in Sec. 1). (5) It is an example for formulating joint spatial and frequency solutions to other problems.

2   Mathematical Formulation

Consider M periodically moving objects $s_i(\bar{r})$, $1 \leq i \leq M$, with no interobject occlusion, and a still background $s_b(\bar{r})$. In the spatial domain, frame 1 is $a(\bar{r}, 1) = s_b(\bar{r}) + \sum_{i=1}^{M} s_i(\bar{r}) + v_{noise}(\bar{r}, 1)$. The objects actually mask background areas [10], so a more accurate model is acquired by removing (setting to 0) the background in each frame[1]. Then, frame n $(1 \leq n \leq N)$ is $a(x, y, n) = \sum_{i=1}^{M} s_i(x - b_i^x(n), y - b_i^y(n)) + v_{noise}(x, y, n)$, where $\bar{b}_i(n) = [b_i^x(n), b_i^y(n)]$ represents the displacement of object i, $1 \leq i \leq M$ from frame 1 to n, $1 \leq n \leq N$. Its 2D FT is:

$$A(\omega_x, \omega_y, n) = \sum_{i=1}^{M} S_i(\omega_x, \omega_y) e^{-j(\omega_x b_i^x(n) + \omega_y b_i^y(n))} + V_{noise}(\omega_x, \omega_y, n). \qquad (1)$$

$A(\omega_x, \omega_y, n)$ has $b_i^x(n)$ and $b_i^y(n)$ as linear terms in its phase, and consequently it has a time-varying spectrum. The latter cannot be estimated via the 3D FFT, since the motion is not constant, as in [11]. Alternate methods are needed if we wish to estimate the periodicity in b_i^x and b_i^y from the spectral variations.

3   Short Term Fourier Transform

Non-stationary signals, i.e. signals with time-varying spectra, can be analyzed with time-frequency distributions (TFD's), which capture the variations of the frequency content of the signal with time [7]. We use the Short-Term Fourier Transform (STFT), which is the most common TFD [12]. The STFT captures the spectral variation with time by computing the FT of the local signal, by filtering it with an appropriate low-pass time function. The spectrum of the filtered signal represents the spectral content of the signal at that time instant. For a 1D signal $s(t)$, the STFT is defined as $STFT_s(t, \omega; h) \equiv \int_{-\infty}^{+\infty} s(\tau + t)h^*(\tau)e^{-j\omega\tau} d\tau$, where $h(t)$ is a lowpass function representing the "analysis window". There is an inherent tradeoff between time and frequency resolutions, depending on the window used: if $h(t)$ has higher values near the observation point t, the STFT estimates more local quantities. A window that is compact in time leads to higher

---

[1] In general, the background at each pixel can be estimated from the observed intensity distributions at each pixel, and its recognition as background will involve a statistical decision. We will omit the details of this step in this paper.

time resolution, whereas a window peaked in the frequency domain gives better frequency resolution.

4   Time-Varying Frequency Estimation

The time-varying frequency of the signal $A(\omega_x, \omega_y, n)$ in Eq. (1) can be estimated by applying the TFDs, which have been used for 1D signals [13]. They have also been used for motion estimation [14], but for horizontal or vertical projections of the video, i.e. 1D signals again. Here, we present a method that can estimate the 2D object motions without resorting to projections.

Consider frame $a(x, y, n)$. We construct an FM signal, whose 2D frequency is modulated by the time-varying displacements of the objects, via constant μ propagation [14]. Essentially, we estimate the 2D FT at a constant 2D "spatial frequency" $\bar{\mu} = [\mu_1, \mu_2]$, as follows:

$$A(\mu_1, \mu_2, n) = \sum_x \sum_y \sum_{i=1}^{M} [s_i(x - b_i^x(n), y - b_i^y(n)) + v_{noise}(x, y, n)] e^{j(\mu_1 x + \mu_2 y)}$$

$$= \sum_{i=1}^{M} S_i(\mu_1, \mu_2) e^{j\mu_1 b_i^x(n)} e^{j\mu_2 b_i^y(n)} + V_{noise}(\mu_1, \mu_2).$$

The frequencies $\omega_i(n) = \mu_1 b_i^x(n) + \mu_2 b_i^y(n)$ in $A(\mu_1, \mu_2, n)$ are extracted by applying TFDs to that signal. However, the motion appears in each $\omega_i(n)$ as a weighted sum of the horizontal and vertical displacements. This problem can be overcome simply, by estimating $A(\mu_1, \mu_2, n)$ at $\mu_1 = 0$ and $\mu_2 = 0$. This gives $\omega_i(n) = \mu_2 b_i^y(n)$ and $\omega_i(n) = \mu_1 b_i^x(n)$ respectively, so the horizontal and vertical displacements are separated.

Using TFD's, the multiple frequencies are represented by multiple ridges in the time-frequency plane, which show the power spectrum corresponding to each time and frequency instant. The peaks of these ridges give the dominant frequencies at each time n, leading to a multicomponent signal, consisting of the M time-varying frequencies $\omega_i(n)$, one for each object $1 \leq i \leq M$.

5   Multiple Period Detection and Estimation

We introduce a simple but efficient method for the recovery of the M different repetitive components of the object motions, that takes advantage of their periodic nature. At each frame n, we have M displacement values $b_1^x(n), ..., b_M^x(n)$ and $b_1^y(n), ..., b_M^y(n)$. For each object, the $b_i^x(n)$, $b_i^y(n)$ form periodic functions of time. We examine only the horizontal trajectories, since the same analysis can be applied to the vertical ones. For object i, $1 \leq i \leq M$, and time n, $1 \leq n \leq N$, we get the periodic signal $\bar{b}_i^x = [b_i^x(1), ..., b_i^x(N)]$, representing its motion over time. We sum the M signals $\bar{b}_i^x$ of all objects i at each instant n, to form the function $\bar{g}_x = [g^x(1), ..., g^x(N)] = \sum_{i=1}^{M} \bar{b}_i^x$, with values at each frame n ($1 \leq n \leq N$)

given by $g^x(n) = \sum_{i=1}^{M} b_i^x(n)$. The resulting 1D function $\bar{g}_x$ is a sum of periodic functions $\bar{b}_i^x$, with different periods T_i^x ($1 \leq i \leq M$). Traditional spectral analysis methods (e.g. the MUSIC algorithm) give the M frequencies ω_i^x ($1 \leq i \leq M$) of $\bar{g}_x$, and the corresponding periods $T_i^x = 1/\omega_i^x$. The details of the spectral analysis methods used are omitted, as they are beyond the scope of this paper, and well documented in the literature [15], [8].

5.1   Periodically Moving Object Extraction

Once the different periods are estimated, the moving objects can also be extracted: by correlating frames separated by an integer number of periods, we expect to get higher correlation values in the area of each periodically moving object. We have $b_i^x(n) = b_i^x(n + T_i^x)$, $b_i^y(n) = b_i^y(n + T_i^y)$ for object i. We consider $T_i^x = T_i^y = T_i$ for simplicity, but the same analysis can be applied when $T_i^x \neq T_i^y$. If T_j denotes the period of object j, at time $n' = n + T_j$ we have:

$$a(x, y, n') = \sum_{i=1}^{M} s_i(x - b_i^x(n'), y - b_i^y(n')) + v_{noise}(x, y, n')$$

$$= \sum_{i \neq j} s_i(x - b_i^x(n'), y - b_i^y(n')) + s_j(x - b_j^x(n'), y - b_j^y(n')) + v_{noise}(x, y, n')$$

since object j is in the same position in frames n and $n' = n + T_j$. Therefore, we can extract the j_{th} object by correlating frames n and $n' = n + T_j$: since only that object is expected to re-appear in the same position in those frames, the correlation values will be highest in the pixels in its area.

5.2   Object Extraction for Periodic Motion Superposed on Translation

As stated in Sec. 1, one of the main contributions of our method is the fact that it allows the estimation of periodic motions superposed on translations, such as walking. In these cases, the legs are moving periodically, but the moving entity is also translating. Correlation-based methods cannot deal with such motions, because of the shifting position of the periodically moving object. The time-varying trajectory $b(n)$, which is used to create the FM signal, is of the form $b(n) = \alpha \cdot n + b_P(n)$, where $1 \leq n \leq N$, α is a constant and $b_P(n)$ is the periodic component of the motion. The FM signal we create via μ-propagation is $z(n) = e^{j\mu(\alpha \cdot n + b_P(n))}$, with phase $\phi_z(n) = \mu(\alpha \cdot n + b_P(n))$. The TFDs estimate its frequency, i.e. the time-derivative of $\phi_z(n)$, $\omega_z(n) = \frac{\partial(j\mu(\alpha \cdot n + b_P(n)))}{\partial n} = j\mu\alpha n + \frac{\partial b_P(n)}{\partial n}$. Consequently, the translational component of the motion becomes a simple additive term, whereas the periodicity of $b_P(n)$ is retained in the extracted frequency. This allows us to deal with periodic motions superposed on translations, without needing to align the video frames.

The segmentation cannot be performed directly in terms of the periodic motion parameters, since the object has also translated. This difficulty can be easily overcome by estimating the "mean" translation between frames, via their

FT [9], [10]. If there are M objects in the sequence, where object i is displaced by $\bar{b}_i(n)$ from frame 1 to n, the ratio of the FTs of frame n (Eq. (1)) and frame 1 is $\phi_n(\bar{\omega}) = \frac{A(\bar{\omega},n)}{A(\bar{\omega},1)} = \sum_{i=1}^M \gamma_i(\bar{\omega}) e^{-j\bar{\omega}^T \bar{b}_i(n)} + \gamma_n(\bar{\omega})$, where $\gamma_i(\bar{\omega}) = \frac{S_i(\bar{\omega})}{A(\bar{\omega},1)}$, $\gamma_n(\bar{\omega},n) = \frac{V_{noise}(\bar{\omega},n)}{A_1(\bar{\omega})}$. Its inverse FT is:

$$\phi_n(\bar{r}) = \sum_{i=1}^M \gamma_i(\bar{r})\delta(\bar{r} - \bar{b}_i(n)) + \gamma_n(\bar{r},n), \tag{2}$$

so it has peaks at $\bar{r} = \bar{b}_i(n)$, for $1 \le i \le M$. Thus, the peaks of $\phi_n(\bar{r})$ estimate the "mean" translations $\bar{b}_i(n)$ of object centroids, between frames 1 and n.

6   Evaluation of the Robustness of the Estimates

Although many motions appearing in nature and in man-made applications have a repetitive form, they are not necessarily strictly periodic. In most cases, their period may fluctuate around a "mean period", and the peak displacement may exhibit similar deviations around a mean value. For the analysis here, we consider one object, and only the motion in the x-direction since the same applies to the y-direction. Consider an ideal periodic trajectory $x(t) = x(t + T)$, and a nearly periodic trajectory $x'(t) = x(t + T') + \epsilon_2$, where $T' = T + \epsilon_1$, $\epsilon_1 \sim \mathcal{N}(0, \sigma_1^2)$, $\epsilon_2 \sim \mathcal{N}(0, \sigma_2^2)$. The analysis will be carried out in continuous time, so the signal under examination is $A(\mu_1, 0, t) = S(\mu_1, 0, t)e^{j\mu_1 x(t)}$, with STFT $STFT'(t, \omega) = \int S(\mu_1, 0)e^{j\mu_1 x(t+\tau)}h^*(\tau)e^{-j\omega\tau}d\tau$. For a near-periodic trajectory $x'(t)$, the STFT is $STFT(t, \omega) = \int S(\mu_1, 0)e^{j\mu_1(x(t+\tau+T+\epsilon_1)+\epsilon_2)}h^*(\tau)e^{-j\omega\tau}d\tau$. The noise in the displacement period and peak magnitude introduce errors in the STFT, which is a random quantity. Its mean, w.r.t. the random quantities ϵ_1, ϵ_2, is $E_{\epsilon_1,\epsilon_2}[STFT'(t,\omega)] = E_{\epsilon_1}E_{\epsilon_2}[STFT'(t,\omega)] = E_{\epsilon_2}[e^{j\mu_1\epsilon_2}]E_{\epsilon_1}[F(\epsilon_1)]$, where $F(\epsilon_1) = S(\mu_1, 0)\int e^{j\mu_1 x(t+\tau+T+\epsilon_1)}h^*(\tau)e^{-j\omega\tau}d\tau$. Then:

$$E_{\epsilon_2}[e^{j\mu_1\epsilon_2}] = \frac{1}{\sqrt{2\pi}\sigma_2}\int_{-\Delta_2}^{\Delta_2} exp\left[-\frac{1}{2}\left(\frac{\epsilon_2^2}{\sigma_2^2} - 2j\mu_1\epsilon_2\right)\right]d\epsilon_2. \tag{3}$$

For $z = \frac{\epsilon_2}{\sigma_2} - j\mu_1\sigma_2$, Eq. (3) is $E_{\epsilon_2}[e^{j\mu_1\epsilon_2}] = \frac{e^{-\frac{1}{2}\mu_1^2\sigma_2^2}}{\sqrt{2\pi}}\int_{-\Delta_2/\sigma_2-jmu_1\sigma_2}^{\Delta_2/\sigma_2-j\mu_1\sigma_2} e^{-z^2/2}dz$. This integral can be estimated numerically, and it can be shown that for $\sigma_2 \to 0$, $E_{\epsilon_2}[e^{j\mu_1\epsilon_2}] \to 1$. This shows that the mean STFT, with respect to the displacement magnitude error ϵ_2, is unaffected by this noise. Essentially, the STFT estimator is unbiased with respect to ϵ_2, i.e. if this error is introduced in many realizations of the trajectory, the average value of the resulting "noisy" STFTs will be the same as the true STFT. This explains why the time-frequency distribution estimate (STFT) is robust to deviations from a "perfect" trajectory, where $\epsilon_2 = 0$. For the error in the trajectory period ϵ_1, we have:

$$E_{\epsilon_1}[F(\epsilon_1)] = \frac{1}{\sqrt{2\pi}\sigma_1}\int F(\epsilon_1)e^{-\epsilon_1^2/2\sigma_1^2}d\epsilon_1 = \frac{1}{\sqrt{2\pi}\sigma_1}\int h^*(\tau)e^{-j\omega\tau}A(\tau)d\tau, \tag{4}$$

for $A(\tau) = \frac{1}{\sqrt{2\pi}\sigma_1} \int_{-\Delta_1}^{\Delta_1} e^{j\mu_1 x(t+\tau+T+\epsilon_1)} e^{-\epsilon_1^2/2\sigma_1^2} d\epsilon_1$. For $\epsilon_1 = 0$, i.e. when T is constant, Eq. (4) gives the STFT of the ideal periodic signal. $A(\tau)$ depends on the form of $x(t)$, but $E_{\epsilon_1}[F(\epsilon_1)]$ in Eq. (4) is essentially the same as the STFT of $e^{j\mu_1 x(t)}$, except after the signal $x(t)$ has been "filtered" by the Gaussian function $e^{-\epsilon_1^2/2\sigma_1^2}$. This filtering behaves like a low pass function for the signal $x(t)$, since it is blurred by the Gaussian function. Eq. (4) will give the time-frequency power spectrum of this "filtered" signal, which will lead to correct frequency estimates, since the peaks in the spectrum will simply be spread out by the blurring process.

7 Experiments

Experiments are conducted both with synthetic and real sequences that contain multiple periodic motions. Most real sequences involve only nearly periodic motions, i.e., they contain many deviations from strict periodicity. **They can be seen in the supplementary material to this paper.** The goals of the experiments are: (1) To show that the proposed method can detect multiple periodic motions. (2) To show that the multiple periods can be estimated reliably. (3) To extract the periodically moving objects.

Synthetic Sequence - Two Objects: Experiments are conducted with a synthetic sequence, with horizontal motion (Fig. 1). We use μ-propagation [14] to estimate the STFT (Fig. 2(a)). The power spectrum of the STFT max (Fig. 2(b)) gives the correct periods present in the sequence (Fig. 2(c)).

Real Sequence - Walking: In this experiment we examine the case of periodic motion superposed on translation. We use the video of a person walking in parallel to the camera sensor: the human's body is translating to the left, but his legs and arms are performing repetitive motions (Fig. 3). The periods of his arms and legs are empirically found to be 5 by observing the video sequence. They are extracted correctly via the STFT, as Figs. 4 and 5 show. The mean

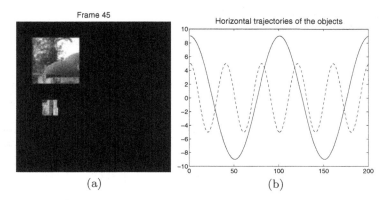

(a)   (b)

Fig. 1. (a) Frame 45 of synthetic sequence with two periodically moving objects. (b) Object velocities in the horizontal direction, as functions of time.

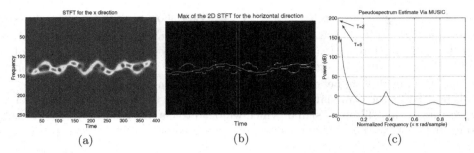

Fig. 2. Synthetic sequence: (a) STFT. (b) Max of the STFT. (c) The power spectrum of the TFD max gives the correct periods.

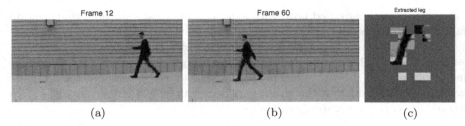

Fig. 3. Walking Sequence: (a) Frame 12. (b) Frame 60. (c) Segmentation of the periodically moving leg, shown in black. The deviation of the leg's motion from strict periodicity introduces blocking artifacts in the correlation process.

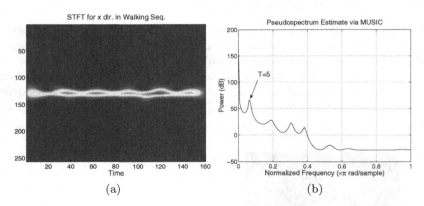

Fig. 4. Horizontal direction of Walking Sequence: (a) 2D STFT (b) The power spectrum for the horizontal direction correctly finds $T = 5$ for the leg motion

translation is then estimated to be 135 pixels via Eq. (2), and the image is shifted back to the same position in all frames. Finally, the periodically moving leg is extracted by correlating the shifted frame 60 with frame 12, corresponding to 3 periods, giving the result of Fig. 3(c).[2] In Fig. 3(c) we show only the segmented object (leg) area of the frame, shown on a larger scale than the original frames,

---

[2] The sequence has 80 frames and $T = 5$ so every 16 frames correspond to one period.

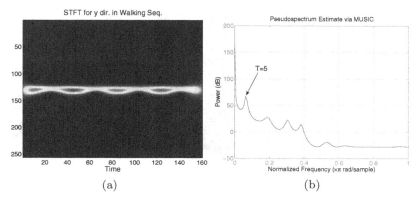

Fig. 5. Vertical direction of Walking Sequence: (a) 2D STFT (b) The PSD for the vertical direction correctly finds $T = 5$ for the arm motion

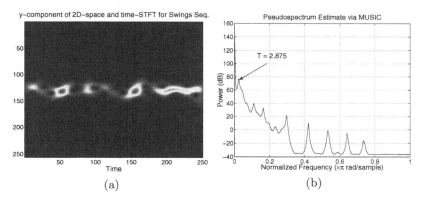

Fig. 6. Swings sequence, y direction: (a) STFT. (b) Power spectrum of the STFT. The period estimate $T = 2.875$ is close to the actual value $T = 2.5$.

for clarity. The leg is the black part of this figure, but parts of the background have also been extracted with it during the correlation process. This is because the leg's motion is not perfectly periodic, despite its strongly repetitive nature: it is not in precisely the same position after an integer number of periods, although it is very close to its original place, as Fig. 3(a),(c) show. Thus, the correlation process also extracts some of the background around the object (leg), because of these deviations from strict periodicity.

Real Sequence - Swings: This sequence shows two children on swings (Fig. 7(a)), moving with the same period, $T = 2.5$, but different phase, as they start off from different positions. In Fig. 6(a) we see that the STFT in the y-direction captures the repetitive motions in that direction. The power spectrum of the peaks of this TFD contains the periodicity information, as shown in Fig. 6(b): the period estimate $T = 2.875$ is quite close to its observed value

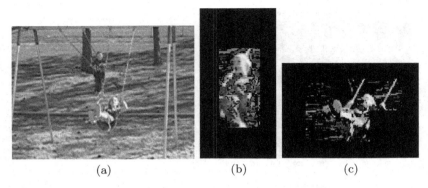

(a)   (b)   (c)

Fig. 7. Swings sequence: (a) Frame 10. Segmentation results for (b) boy (c) girl

(a)   (b)

Fig. 8. Jump-rope and dribbling sequence: (a) Frame 1 (b) Frame 10

of $T = 2.5$. It is used to correlate frames that are an integer number of periods apart, and thus segment the periodically moving children (Fig. 7(b), (c)). We show only the segmented object areas of the frame, on a larger scale than the original frames, for clarity. It should be noted that the method succeeds despite the fact that the children are non-rigid objects. Also, since they are non-rigid, the correlation is performed with large block sizes to account for the variations in their overall shape (e.g. legs folding or extending).

Real Sequence - Jump-Rope and Dribbling Sequence: In this experiment we used a sequence consisting of two different periodic motions: a girl with a jump rope, jumping in place next to a girl that is dribbling a basketball (Fig. 8). The empirically observed periods for the Jump-Rope sequence are $T_x = 4.5$ in the horizontal direction and $T_y = 8$ in the vertical direction, while in the Dribbling sequence, we have $T_x = 2.5$ and $T_y = 5$. As Fig. 9 shows, the estimated horizontal periods are $T = 2.5$ and $T = 5$, so the period of the x-movement for the dribbling is found correctly, while the jump-rope's horizontal period is estimated with a small error. This is expected, as the horizontal motion of the girl jumping is small and noisy, because of the random motion and occlusion introduced by her arms and the jump-rope. The dribbling of the ball is a more regular motion, so its period is found with better precision. Similarly, the periods of the motions in the y-direction are found to be $T = 5.4$ and $T = 7.8$ for the ball and the girl jumping, respectively. Again, they are estimated with good accuracy, although there are possible sources of errors, such as occlusion and non-rigidly moving

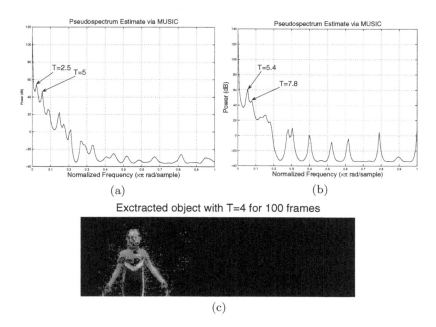

(a)   (b)

Exctracted object with T=4 for 100 frames

(c)

Fig. 9. Power spectral density of the 2D TFDs. (a) In the x-direction both periods are estimated correctly. (b) In the y-direction both periods are also estimated correctly. (c) The object with $T = 4$ in the x-direction extracted via spatial correlation.

objects (e.g. arms) in the sequence. Finally, using the estimated periods for the moving objects, we also extract the objects that undergo the corresponding repetitive motions. The segmentation of the jumping girl obtained via spatial correlation is shown in Fig. 9(c).

8   Evaluation Results

We quantitatively measure the performance of our method by estimating the errors in the period estimates and the segmentation (Table 1). The ground truth for the periods of the moving objects is obtained by empirically counting the repetitions of each motion in the sequence. The error e_T in the period estimates T_{est} is then given by the absolute difference of T_{est} and the ground truth T

Table 1. Errors in the Period Estimates and Object Segmentation for 2D Method

Video	e_T (x dir)	e_T (y dir)	e_S for object 1	e_S for object 2
Synthetic	0	0	0.235	0.121
Walking	0	0	0.255	0.27
Swings	0.3	-	0.37	0.443
Jump-rope and Dribbling	0.25	0.4	0.27	0.15

i.e. $e_T = |T_{est} - T|$. When there are many objects in the video, the error in the period estimate in each direction is the mean of their individual errors. The object segmentation ground truth is obtained by manually segmenting out each moving object $S_i(\bar{r})$ and the corresponding error e_S is given by the number of pixels where the extracted and actual objects differ, divided by the number of pixels in the real object area. The segmentation errors are related to the object's real size. They usually originate from blocking artifacts, introduced by the correlation. Since in some experiments there is periodic motion in only one direction or there is only one object, there are some blanks ("−") in the table.

9   Conclusions and Discussion

We have proposed a method for multiple periodic motion estimation that combines frequency and spatial data, to overcome many difficulties and shortcomings of existing purely spatial methods.

1. Our approach detects and estimates multiple periods in a video sequence simultaneously (Sec. 5), in contrast to the existing literature, where each periodic motion is analyzed separately, with the help of manual intervention.
2. The proposed approach can deal with motions that deviate from strict periodicity (Sec. 6), as the mean STFT error is zero. This is also shown in experiments, where the real sequences do not have perfectly periodic motions.
3. Our approach can also extract objects with periodic motion superposed on translation, such as walking (Sec. 5.2). Such motions cannot be analyzed without preprocessing in the existing literature.
4. Once the periods in the video are estimated, the periodically moving objects can be extracted via spatial correlation methods (Sec. 5.1). Since the periods have already been found, our segmentation is more reliable than those of spatial only methods.

References

1. Boyd, J., Little, J.: Motion from transient oscillations. In: Proceedings of the Conference on Computer Vision and Pattern Recognition, CVPR 2001. (2001)
2. Seitz, S., Dyer, C.R.: View-invariant analysis of cyclic motion. International Journal of Computer Vision 25 (1997) 231–251
3. Tsai, P., Shah, M., Keiter, K., Kasparis, T.: Cyclic motion detection for motion based recognition. Pattern Recognition 27 (1994) 1591–1603
4. Cutler, R., Davis, L.S.: Robust real-time periodic motion detection, analysis, and applications. IEEE Transactions on Pattern Analysis and Machine Intelligence 22 (2000) 781–796
5. Polana, R., Nelson, R.: Detection and recognition of periodic, nonrigid motion. International Journal of Computer Vision 23 (1997) 261–282
6. Lu, C., Ferrier, N.: Repetitive motion analysis: Segmentation and event classification. IEEE Transactions on Pattern Analysis and Machine Intelligence 26 (2004) 258 – 263

7. Cohen, L.: Time-frequency distributions-a review. Proceedings of the IEEE **77** (1989) 941–981

8. Pepin, M.P., Clark, M.P.: On the performance of several 2-d harmonic retrieval techniques. In: Signals, Systems and Computers, 1994. 1994 Conference Record of the Twenty-Eighth Asilomar Conference on. (Volume 1.) 254 –258

9. Briassouli, A., Ahuja, N.: Fusion of frequency and spatial domain information for motion analysis. In: ICPR 2004, Proceedings of the 17th International Conference on Pattern Recognition. Volume 2. (2004) 175–178

10. Chen, W., Giannakis, G.B., Nandhakumar, N.: A harmonic retrieval framework for discontinuous motion estimation. IEEE Transactions on Image Processing **7** (1998) 1242–1257

11. Kojima, A., Sakurai, N., Kishigami, J.I.: Motion detection using 3D-FFT spectrum. In: 1993 IEEE International Conference on Acoustics, Speech, and Signal Processing. Volume 5. (1993) 213–216

12. Czerwinski, R., Jones, D.: Adaptive short-time Fourier analysis. IEEE Signal Processing Letters **4** (1997) 42–45

13. Boashash, B.: Estimating and interpreting the instantaneous frequency of a signal - Part 1: Fundamentals. Proceedings of the IEEE **80** (1992) 520–538

14. Djurovic, I., Stankovic, S.: Estimation of time-varying velocities of moving objects by time-frequency representations. IEEE Transactions on Signal Processing **47** (1999) 493–504

15. Kay, S.M.: Modern Spectral Estimation, Theory and Applications. Prentice-Hall, Englewood Cliffs, NJ (1988)

Robust Multi-body Motion Tracking Using Commute Time Clustering

Huaijun Qiu and Edwin R. Hancock

Department of Computer Science, University of York
York, YO10 5DD, UK

Abstract. The presence of noise renders the classical *factorization method* almost impractical for real-world multi-body motion tracking problems. The main problem stems from the effect of noise on the shape interaction matrix, which looses its block-diagonal structure and as a result the assignment of elements to objects becomes difficult. The aim in this paper is to overcome this problem using graph-spectral embedding and the k-means algorithm. To this end we develop a representation based on the commute time between nodes on a graph. The commute time (i.e. the expected time taken for a random walk to travel between two nodes and return) can be computed from the Laplacian spectrum using the discrete Green's function, and is an important property of the random walk on a graph. The commute time is a more robust measure of the proximity of data than the raw proximity matrix. Our embedding procedure preserves commute time, and is closely akin to kernel PCA, the Laplacian eigenmap and the diffusion map. We illustrate the results both on the synthetic image sequences and real world video sequences, and compare our results with several alternative methods.

1 Introduction

Multi-body motion tracking is a challenging problem which arises in shape from motion, video coding, the analysis of movement and surveillance. One of the classical techniques is the *factorization method* of Costeira and Kanade [4]. The basic idea underpinning this method is to use singular value decomposition (SVD) to factorize the feature trajectory matrix into a motion matrix and a shape matrix. The shape interaction matrix is found by taking outer product of the right eigen-vector matrix, and can be used to identify the independently moving objects present. Gear [7] has developed a related method based on the reduced row echelon form of the matrix, and object separation is achieved using probabilistic analysis on a bipartite graph. Both methods work well in the ideal case when there is no noise (i.e. feature-point jitter) and outliers are not present. However, real-world image sequences are usually contaminated by the two types of noise. There have been several attempts to overcome this problem. For instance, Ichimura [9] has improved the *factorization method* by using a discriminant criterion to threshold-out the noise and outliers.

Rather than working with a matrix derived from the data, some researchers place the emphasis on the original data. Kanatani [10, 19, 18] developed a subspace separation method by incorporating dimension correction and model selection. Wu et al [21] argue that the subspaces associated with the different objects are not only distinct, but also orthogonal. They hence employ an orthogonal subspace decomposition method to

A. Leonardis, H. Bischof, and A. Pinz (Eds.): ECCV 2006, Part I, LNCS 3951, pp. 160–173, 2006.

separate objects. This idea is further extended by Fang et al who use independent sub-spaces [6] and multiple subspace inference analysis [5]. In addition to attempting to improve the behaviour of the factorization method under noise, there has been a considerable effort at overcoming problems such as degeneracy, uncertainty and missing data [8, 22].

The factorisation method is clearly closely akin to graph-spectral methods used in clustering, since it uses the eigenvector methods to determine the class-affinity of sets of points. In fact Weiss [20] has presented a unifying view of spectral clustering methods, and this includes the factorization method. There has been some dedicated effort devoted to solving the object separation problem using spectral clustering methods. Park et al [12] have applied a multi-way min-max cut clustering method to the shape interaction matrix. Here the shape-interaction matrix is used as a cluster indicator matrix and noise compensation is effected using a combination of spectral clustering and subspace separation methods.

In general graph theoretic clustering methods aim to locate clusters of nodes that minimize the cut or disassociation, while maximizing the association. One of the most successful methods is the normalised cut of Shi and Malik [16] which as been applied to image segmentation problems. Pavan and Pelillo [13] have shown how the performance of this method can be improved using a finer measure of cluster cohesion based on dominant-sets. In a recent paper Qiu and Hancock [14] have shown how commute time can be used to characterise the mutual affinity of nodes. The commute time is the expected time taken for a random walk to travel between two nodes and return. It is determined by the Green's function or pseudo inverse of the Laplacian matrix, and can hence be conveniently computed using the Laplacian spectrum.

The commute time has properties that can lead to clusters of nodes that increase both the dissociation and the association. A pair of nodes in the graph will have a small commute time value if one of three conditions is satisfied. The first of these is that they are close together, i.e. the length of the path between them is small. The second case is if the sum of the weights on the edges connecting the nodes is small. Finally, the commute time is small if the pair of nodes are connected by many paths. Hence, the commute time can lead to a finer measure of cluster cohesion than the simple use of edge-weight which underpins algorithms such as the normalized cut [16].

The aim in this paper is to explore whether an embedding based on commute time can be used to solve the problem of computing the shape-interaction matrix in a robust manner. We use the shape-interaction matrix Q as a data-proximity weight matrix, and compute the associated Laplacian matrix (the degree matrix minus the weight matrix). The aim is to embed feature points in a space that preserves commute time. The embedding co-ordinate matrix is found the premultiplying the transpose of the Laplacian eigenvector matrix by the inverse square-root of the eigenvalue matrix. Under the embedding nodes which have small commute time are close, and those which have a large commute time are distant. This allows us to separate the objects in the embedded subspace by applying simple k-means clustering. There are of course many graph-spectral embedding algorithms reported in the literature, and recent and powerful additions include kernel PCA [15], the Laplacian eigenmap [1] and the diffusion map [3]. We explore the relationship of the commute-time embedding to these alternatives.

2 Factorization Method Review

Suppose there are N objects moving independently in a scene and the movement is acquired by an affine camera as F frames. In each frame, P feature points are tracked and the coordinate of the ith point in the fth frame is given by (x_i^f, y_i^f). Let X and Y denote two $F \times P$ matrices constructed from the image coordinates of all the points across all of the frames satisfying: $X = \begin{bmatrix} x_1^1 & x_2^1 & \cdots & x_P^1 \\ x_1^2 & x_2^2 & \cdots & x_P^2 \\ \vdots & \vdots & \ddots & \vdots \\ x_1^F & x_2^F & \cdots & x_P^F \end{bmatrix}$ and $Y = \begin{bmatrix} y_1^1 & y_2^1 & \cdots & y_P^1 \\ y_1^2 & y_2^2 & \cdots & y_P^2 \\ \vdots & \vdots & \ddots & \vdots \\ y_1^F & y_2^F & \cdots & y_P^F \end{bmatrix}$. Each row in the two matrices above corresponds to a single frame and each column corresponds to a single point. The two coordinate matrices can be stacked to form the matrix $W = \begin{bmatrix} X \\ Y \end{bmatrix}_{2F \times P}$.

The W matrix can be factorized into a motion matrix M and a shape matrix S thus, $W_{2F \times P} = M_{2F \times r} \times S_{r \times P}$ where r is the rank of W ($r = 4$ in the case of W without noise and outliers). In order to solve the factorization problem, matrix W can be decomposed using SVD by $W = U \Sigma R^T$.

If the features from the same object are grouped together, then U, Σ and R will have a block-diagonal structure as $W = [U_1 \cdots U_N] \begin{bmatrix} \Sigma_1 & & \\ & \ddots & \\ & & \Sigma_N \end{bmatrix} \begin{bmatrix} R_1^T & & \\ & \ddots & \\ & & R_N^T \end{bmatrix}$ and the shape matrix for object k can be approximated by $S_k = B^{-1} \Sigma_k R_k^T$ where B is an invertible matrix that can be found from M.

In a real multi-body tracking problem, the coordinates of the different objects are potentially permuted into a random order. As a result it is impossible to correctly recover the shape matrix S_k without knowledge of the correspondence order. Since the eigenvector matrix V is related to the shape matrix, the shape interaction matrix was introduced by Costeira and Kanade [4] to solve the multi-body separation problem. The shape interaction matrix is

$$Q = RR^T = \begin{bmatrix} S_1^T \Sigma_1^{-1} S_1 & 0 & \cdots & 0 \\ 0 & S_2^T \Sigma_2^{-1} S_2 & \cdots & 0 \\ \vdots & \vdots & \ddots & 0 \\ 0 & 0 & \cdots & S_N^T \Sigma_N^{-1} S_N \end{bmatrix} \tag{1}$$

From Equation 1, the shape interaction matrix Q has the convenient properties that $Q(u, v) = 0$, if points u,v belong to different objects and $Q(u, v) \neq 0$, if points u,v belong to the same object. The matrix Q is also invariant to both the object motion and the selection of the object coordinate systems. This leads to a simple scheme for separating multi-object motions by permuting the elements of Q so that it acquires a block diagonal structure. In Costeira and Kanade's method [4] a greedy algorithm is used to permute the Q matrix into block diagonal form. An illustration is shown in Figure 1(a,b,c,d). This method works well only for the ideal case where is no noise and outliers are not present. In Figures 1 e and f we respectively show the effect of adding

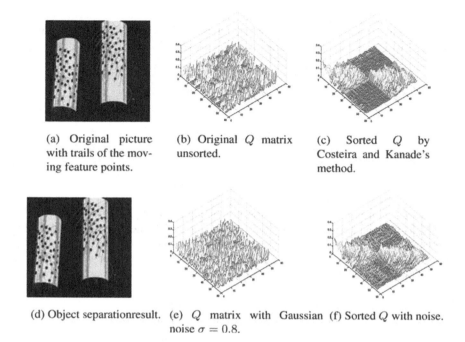

(a) Original picture with trails of the moving feature points.

(b) Original Q matrix unsorted.

(c) Sorted Q by Costeira and Kanade's method.

(d) Object separationresult.

(e) Q matrix with Gaussian noise $\sigma = 0.8$.

(f) Sorted Q with noise.

Fig. 1. A multi-body motion separation example using Costeira and Kanade's method

Gaussian noise to the Q matrix in 1(b) and the resulting permuted matrix. In the noisy case, the block structure is badly corrupted and object separation is almost impossible.

3   Robust Object Separation by Commute Time Clustering

In this section, we will show how the multi-body motion tracking problem can be posed as one of commute time embedding using the Q matrix. The method is motivated by the intuition that since the eigenvectors associated with the different objects span different subspaces, they can be embedded using a spectral method and separated using a simple clustering method.

3.1   Graph Laplacian, Heat Kernel, Green's Function and the Commute Time

Commute time is a concept from spectral graph theory that has close links with the graph Laplacian, the heat kernel and random walks on a graph. In the following sections, we show how to compute commute time and describe the relationships to the graph Laplacian and the heat kernel.

Graph Laplacian and Heat kernel. Let the weighted graph Γ be the triple (V, E, Ω), where V is the set of nodes, E is the set of arcs, and $\Omega = \{w_{u,v}, \forall (u, v) \in E\}$ is a set of weights associated with the edges. Further let $T = diag(d_v; v \in V(\Gamma))$ be the diagonal weighted degree matrix with $T_u = \sum_{v=1}^{n} w_{u,v}$ and A be the adjacency matrix. The un-normalized weighted Laplacian matrix is given by $L = T - A$ and the normalized weighted Laplacian matrix is defined to be $\mathcal{L} = T^{-1/2}LT^{-1/2}$, and has elements

$$\mathcal{L}_\Gamma(u,v) = \begin{cases} 1 & \text{if } u = v \\ -\frac{w_{u,v}}{\sqrt{d_u d_v}} & \text{if } u \neq v \text{ and } (u,v) \in E \\ 0 & \text{otherwise} \end{cases}$$

The spectral decomposition of the normalized Laplacian is $\mathcal{L} = \Phi'\Lambda'\Phi'^T$, where $\Lambda' = diag(\lambda'_1, \lambda'_2, ..., \lambda'_{|V|})$ is the diagonal matrix with the ordered eigenvalues as elements satisfying: $0 = \lambda'_1 \leq \lambda'_2 ... \leq \lambda'_{|V|}$ and $\Phi' = (\phi'_1|\phi'_2|....|\phi'_{|V|})$ is the matrix with the ordered eigenvectors as columns. The corresponding eigendecomposition of the un-normalized Laplacian matrix is $L = \Phi\Lambda\Phi^T$.

The heat equation associated with the graph Laplacian is given by $\frac{\partial \mathcal{H}_t}{\partial t} = -\mathcal{L}\mathcal{H}_t$ where $\mathcal{H}_t$ is the heat kernel and t is time. The solution of the heat-equation is found by exponentiating the Laplacian eigenspectrum i.e. $\mathcal{H}_t = \exp[-t\mathcal{L}] = \Phi' \exp[-t\Lambda']\Phi'^T$. The heat kernel is a $|V| \times |V|$ matrix, and for the nodes u and v of the graph Γ the element of the matrix is $\mathcal{H}_t(u,v) = \sum_{i=1}^{|V|} \exp[-\lambda'_i t]\phi'_i(u)\phi'_i(v)$.

Green's function: Now consider the discrete Laplace operator $\Delta = T^{-1/2}\mathcal{L}T^{1/2}$. The Green's function is the left inverse operator of the Laplace operator Δ, defined by $G\Delta(u,v) = I(u,v) - \frac{d_v}{vol}$, where $vol = \sum_{v \in V(\Gamma)} d_v$ is the volume of the graph. A physical interpretation of the Green's function is the temperature at a node in the graph due to a unit heat source applied to the external node. It is related with the heat kernel $\mathcal{H}_t$ in the following manner

$$G(u,v) = \int_0^\infty d_u^{1/2} \left(\mathcal{H}_t(u,v) - \phi'_1(u)\phi'_1(v)\right) d_v^{-1/2} dt \qquad (2)$$

Here ϕ'_1 is the eigenvector associated with the zero eigenvalue 0 and which has k-th element is $\phi'_1(k) = \sqrt{d_k/vol}$. Furthermore, the normalized Green's function $\mathcal{G} = T^{-1/2}GT^{1/2}$ is defined as (see [2] page 6(10)),

$$\mathcal{G}(u,v) = \sum_{i=2}^{|V|} \frac{1}{\lambda'_i}\phi'_i(u)\phi'_i(v) \qquad (3)$$

where λ' and ϕ' are the eigenvalue and eigenvectors of the normalized Laplacian $\mathcal{L}$. The corresponding un-normalized Green's function $\bar{G} = T^{-1}G = T^{1/2}\mathcal{G}T^{1/2}$ is given by $G(u,v) = \sum_{i=2}^{|V|} \frac{1}{\lambda_i}\phi_i(u)\phi_i(v)$. where λ and ϕ are the eigenvalue and eigenvectors of the un-normalized Laplacian L.

The normalized Green's function is hence the generalized inverse of the normalized Laplacian $\mathcal{L}$. Moreover, it is straightforward to show that $\mathcal{G}\mathcal{L} = \mathcal{L}\mathcal{G} = I - \phi'_1\phi'^T_1$, and as a result $(\mathcal{L}\mathcal{G})(u,v) = \delta(u,v) - \frac{\sqrt{d_u d_v}}{vol}$. From Equation 3, the eigenvalues of $\mathcal{L}$ and $\mathcal{G}$ have the same sign and $\mathcal{L}$ is positive semidefinite, and so $\mathcal{G}$ is also positive semidefinite. Since $\mathcal{G}$ is also symmetric(see [2] page 4), it follows that $\mathcal{G}$ is a kernel. The same applies to the un-normalized Green's function $\bar{G}$.

Commute Time: We note that the *hitting time* $O(u,v)$ of a random walk on a graph is defined as the expected number of steps before node v is visited, commencing from node u. The *commute time* $CT(u,v)$, on the other hand, is the expected time for the random walk to travel from node u to reach node v and then return. As a result $CT(u,v) = O(u,v) + O(v,u)$. The hitting time $O(u,v)$ is given by [2]

$$O(u,v) = \frac{vol}{d_v}G(v,v) - \frac{vol}{d_u}G(u,v)$$

where G is the Green's function given in equation 2. So, the commute time is given by

$$CT(u,v) = O(u,v) + O(v,u) = \frac{vol}{d_u}G(u,u) + \frac{vol}{d_v}G(v,v) - \frac{vol}{d_u}G(u,v) - \frac{vol}{d_v}G(v,u) \quad (4)$$

As a consequence of (4) the commute time is a metric on the graph. The reason for this is that if we take the elements of G as inner products defined in a Euclidean space, CT will become the norm satisfying: $\|x_i - x_j\|^2 = <x_i - x_j, x_i - x_j> = <x_i, x_i> + <x_j, x_j> - <x_i, x_j> - <x_j, x_i>$.

Substituting the spectral expression for the Green's function into the definition of the commute time, it is straightforward to show that

$$CT(u,v) = vol \sum_{i=2}^{|V|} \frac{1}{\lambda_i'} \left(\frac{\phi_i'(u)}{\sqrt{d_u}} - \frac{\phi_i'(v)}{\sqrt{d_v}} \right)^2 \quad (5)$$

In the un-normalized case, it becomes:

$$CT(u,v) = vol \sum_{i=2}^{|V|} \frac{1}{\lambda_i} (\phi_i(u) - \phi_i(v))^2 \quad (6)$$

3.2   Commute Time Embedding

Basics: Equation 5, can be re-written in the following form which makes the relationship between the commute time and the Euclidean distance between the components of the eigenvectors explicit

$$CT(u,v) = \sum_{i=2}^{|V|} \left(\sqrt{\frac{vol}{\lambda_i' d_u}} \phi_i'(u) - \sqrt{\frac{vol}{\lambda_i' d_v}} \phi_i'(v) \right)^2 \quad (7)$$

Hence, the embedding of the nodes of the graph into a vector space that preserves commute time has the co-ordinate matrix

$$\Theta = \sqrt{vol}\Lambda'^{-1/2}\Phi'^T T^{-1/2} \quad (8)$$

The columns of the matrix are vectors of embedding co-ordinates for the nodes of the graph. The term $T^{-1/2}$ arises from the normalisation of the Laplacian. If the commute time is computed from the un-normalised Laplacian, the corresponding matrix of embedding co-ordinates is

$$\Theta = \sqrt{vol}\Lambda^{-1/2}\Phi^T \tag{9}$$

The embedding is nonlinear in the eigenvalues of the Laplacian. This distinguishes it from principle components analysis (PCA) and locality preserving projection (LPP) which are both linear. As we will demonstrate in the next section, the commute time embedding is just kernel PCA [15] on the Green's function. Moreover, it can be viewed as Laplacian eigenmap since they actually are minimizing the same objective function.

The commute time embedding and Kernel PCA: Let us consider the un-normalized case above. Since the Green's function $\bar{G}$ is the pseudo-inverse of the Laplacian, it discards the zero eigenvalue and the corresponding eigenvector $\mathbf{1}$ of the Laplacian. The columns of the eigenvector matrix are orthogonal which means the eigenvector matrix Φ of $\bar{G}$ satisfies $\Phi^T \mathbf{1} = \mathbf{0}$. Hence, $\sqrt{vol}\Lambda^{-1/2}\Phi^T \mathbf{1} = \mathbf{0}$, and this means that the data is centred. As a result, the covariance matrix for the centred data is

$$C_f = \Theta\Theta^T = vol\Lambda^{-1/2}\Phi^T\Phi\Lambda^{-1/2} = vol\Lambda^{-1} = \Lambda_{\bar{G}} \tag{10}$$

and the kernel or Gram matrix is

$$K = \Theta^T\Theta = vol\Phi\Lambda^{-1/2}\Lambda^{-1/2}\Phi^T = vol\Phi\Lambda^{-1}\Phi^T = vol\bar{G} \tag{11}$$

which is just the Green's function multiplied by a constant. Hence, we can view the embedding as performing kernel PCA on the Green's function for the Laplacian.

The commute time embedding and the Laplacian eigenmap: In the Laplacian eigenmap [1] the aim is to embed a set of points with co-ordinate matrix $\bar{\mathbf{X}} = \{\bar{\mathbf{x}}_1, \bar{\mathbf{x}}_2, ..., \bar{\mathbf{x}}_n\}$ from a R^n space into a lower dimensional subspace R^m with the co-ordinate matrix $\mathbf{Z} = \{\mathbf{z}_1, \mathbf{z}_2, ..., \mathbf{z}_m\}$. The original data-points have a proximity weight matrix Ω with elements $\Omega_{u,v} = \exp[-||\bar{\mathbf{x}}_u - \bar{\mathbf{x}}_v||^2]$. The aim is to find the embedding that minimises the objective function $\epsilon = \sum_{u,v} ||\mathbf{z}_u - \mathbf{z}_v||^2 \Omega(u,v) = tr(\mathbf{Z}^T L \mathbf{Z})$ where Ω is the edge weight matrix of the original data $\bar{\mathbf{X}}$.

To remove the arbitrary scaling factor and to avoid the embedding undergoing dimensionality collapse, the constraint $\mathbf{Z}^T T \mathbf{Z} = I$ is applied. The embedding problem becomes $\mathbf{Z} = \arg\min_{\mathbf{Z}^T T \mathbf{Z} = I} tr(\mathbf{Z}^T L \mathbf{Z})$.

The solution is given by the lowest eigenvectors of the generalized eigen-problem

$$L\mathbf{Z} = \Lambda' T\mathbf{Z} \tag{12}$$

and the value of the objective function corresponding to the solution is $\epsilon^* = tr(\Lambda')$.

For the commute-time embedding the objective function minimised is

$$\epsilon' = \frac{\sum_{u,v} ||\mathbf{z}_u - \mathbf{z}_v||^2 \Omega(u,v)}{\sum_u \mathbf{z}_u^2 d_u} = tr(\frac{\mathbf{Z}^T L \mathbf{Z}}{\mathbf{Z}^T T \mathbf{Z}})$$

To show this, let $\mathbf{Z} = Y^T = (\sqrt{vol}\Lambda'^{-1/2}\Phi'^T T^{-1/2})^T$, we have

$$\epsilon' = tr(\frac{\sqrt{vol}\Lambda'^{-1/2}\Phi'^T T^{-1/2}LT^{-1/2}\Phi'\Lambda'^{-1/2}\sqrt{vol}}{\sqrt{vol}\Lambda'^{-1/2}\Phi'^T T^{-1/2}TT^{-1/2}\Phi'\Lambda'^{-1/2}\sqrt{vol}})$$
$$= tr(\frac{\Lambda'^{-1/2}\Phi'^T \mathcal{L}\Phi'\Lambda'^{-1/2}}{\Lambda'^{-1/2}\Phi'^T\Phi'\Lambda'^{-1/2}}) = tr(\frac{\Lambda'^{-1/2}\Lambda'\Lambda'^{-1/2}}{\Lambda'^{-1}}) = tr(\Lambda') = \epsilon^*$$

Hence, the commute time embedding not only aims to maintain proximity relationships by minimizing $\sum_{u,v}\|\mathbf{z}_u - \mathbf{z}_v\|^2 \Omega(u,v)$, but it also aims to assign large co-ordinates values to nodes (or points) with large degree (i.e. it maximizes $\sum_u \mathbf{z}_u^2 d_u$). Nodes with large degrees are the most significant in a graph since they have the largest number of connecting edges. In the commute time embedding, these nodes are furthest away from the origin and are hence unlikely to be close to one-another.

The commute time and the diffusion map: Finally, it is interesting to note the relationship with the diffusion map embedding of Lafon *et al* [3]. The method commences from the random walk on a graph which has transition probability matrix $P = T^{-1}A$, where A is the adjacency matrix. Although P is not symmetric, it does have a right eigenvector matrix Ψ, which satisfies the equation $P\Psi = \Lambda_P\Psi$.

Since $P = T^{-1}A = T^{-1}(T - L) = I - T^{-1}L$ and as result $(I - T^{-1}L)\Psi = \Lambda_P\Psi$, i.e. $T^{-1}L\Psi = (I - \Lambda_P)\Psi$, and as result $L\Psi = (I - \Lambda_P)T\Psi$, which is identical to Equation 12 if $\mathbf{Z} = \Psi$ and $\Lambda' = I - q\Lambda_P$. The embedding co-ordinate matrix for the diffusion map is $Y = \Lambda^t\Psi^T$, where t is real. For the embedding the diffusion distance between a pair of nodes is $D_t^2(u,v) = \sum_{i=1}^m (\lambda_P)_i^{2t}(\psi_i(u) - \psi_i(v))^2$. Clearly if we take $t = -1/2$ the diffusion map is equivalent to the commute time embedding and the diffusion time is equal to the commute time.

The diffusion map is designed to give a distance function that reflects the connectivity of the original graph or point-set. The distance should be small if a pair of points are connected by many short paths, and this is also the behaviour of the commute time. The advantage of the diffusion map or distance is that it has a free parameter t, and this may be varied to alter the properties of the map. The disadvantage is that when t is small, the diffusion distance is ill-posed. The reason for this is that according to the original definition of the diffusion distance for a random walk ($D_t^2(u,v) = \|p_t(u,\cdot) - p_t(v,\cdot)\|^2$), and as a result the distance between a pair of nodes depends on the transition probability between the nodes under consideration and all of the remaining nodes in the graph. As a result if t is small, then the random walk will not have propagated significantly, and the distance will depend only on very local information. There are also problems when t is large. When this is the case the random walk converges to its stationary state with $P^t = T/vol$ (a diagonal matrix), and this gives zero diffusion distance for all pairs of distinct nodes. So it is a critical to control t carefully in order to obtain useful embeddings.

Some embedding examples: [Figure 2 shows four synthetic examples of point- configurations (left-hand panel) and the resulting commute time embeddings (right-hand panel). Here we have computed the proximity weight matrix Ω by exponentiating the Euclidean distance between points. The main features to note are as follows. First, the embedded points corresponding to the same point-clusters are cohesive, being scattered

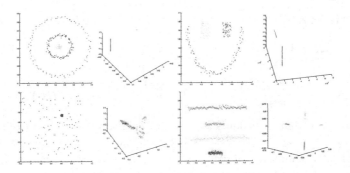

Fig. 2. Commute time embedding examples

around approximately straight lines in the subspace. Second, the clusters corresponding to different objects give rise to straight lines that are orthogonal.

Robustness of the commute time embedding: From Equation 9 we can see that the co-ordinates of the commute time embedding depend on the eigenvalues and eigenvectors of the Laplacian matrix. Hence, the stability of the embedding depends on the stability of the eigenvalue and eigenvector matrices. According to Weyl's theorem, the variation of the eigenvalues of a perturbed matrix is bounded by the maximum and the minimum eigenvalues of the perturbing matrix. However, the eigenvectors are less stable under perturbation. Despite this anticipated problem, the commute time matrix is likely to be relatively stable under perturbations in graph structure. According to Rayleigh's Principle in the theory of electrical networks, commute time can neither be increased by adding an edge or a node, nor decreased by deleting a single edge or a node. In fact, the impact of deleting or adding an edge or a node to the commute time between a pair of nodes is negligible if they are well connected. This property reduces the impact of outliers in motion tracking, since outliers are dissimilar to the object point-clusters.

3.3   Commute Times Applied to the Multi-body Motion Tracking Problem

Having discussed some of the properties of the commute time embedding, in this section we return to the issue of how it may be used for multi-body motion analysis. As we have already seen, the shape interaction matrix Q introduced in the factorization method is invariably contaminated by noise and this limits its effectiveness. Our aim is to use commute time as a shape separation measure. Specifically, we use the commute time to refine the block structure of the Q matrix and group the feature points into objects.

Object Separation Steps: The algorithm we propose for this purpose has the following steps:

1. Use the shape interaction matrix Q as the weighted adjacency matrix A and construct the corresponding graph Γ.
2. Compute the Laplacian matrix of graph Γ using $L = T - Q$.

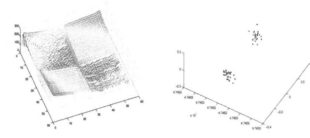

(a) Sorted commute time matrix.

(b) Clustered points in the
commute time subspace for
two objects.

Fig. 3. Multi-body motion separation re-casted as a commute time clustering problem

3. Find the eigenvalue matrix Λ and eigenvector matrix Φ of L using $L = \Phi\Lambda\Phi^T$.
4. Compute the commute time matrix CT using Λ and Φ from Equation 6.
5. Embed the commute time into a subspace of R^n using Equation 8 or 9.
6. Cluster the data points in the subspace using the k-means algorithm [11].

To illustrate the effectiveness of this method, we return to example used earlier in Section 2. First, in the ideal case, the Q matrix will have a zero value for the feature points belonging to different objects. As a result the graph Γ, constructed from Q, will have disjoint subgraphs corresponding to the nodes belonging to different objects. The partitions give rise to infinite commute times, and are hence unreachable by the random walk. However, when we add noise (Q with 0.8 Gaussian noise) and the clustering steps listed above we still recover a good set of objects (see Figure 1(d)). This is illustrated in Figure 3. Here, in Figure 3 sub-figure (a) shows the commute time matrix of graph Γ and sub-figure (b) shows the embedding in a 3D subspace. It is clear that the commute time matrix gives a good block-diagonal structure and the points are well clustered in the embedding space even when significant noise is present.

4 Experiments

In this section we conduct experiments with the commute time method on both synthetic data and real-world motion tracking problems. To investigate the robustness of the method, we add Gaussian noise to the data sets and compare the results with some classical methods.

4.1 Synthetic Data

Figure 4 shows a sequence of five consecutive synthetic images with 20 background points(green dots) and 20 foreground points(red dots) moving independently. We have added Gaussian noise of zero mean and standard deviation σ to the coordinates of these 29 points, and then cluster them into two groups.

We have compared our method with Costeira and Kanade's greedy algorithm [4], Ichimura's discrimination criterion method [9] and Kenichi's subspace separation

Fig. 4. Synthetic image sequence

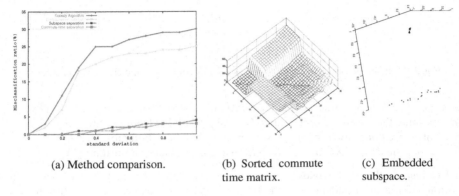

(a) Method comparison.   (b) Sorted commute   (c) Embedded
                                time matrix.   subspace.

Fig. 5. Synthetic data

method [10]. In Figure 5 we plot the average misclassification ratio over an increasing σ on the different algorithms. The results are based on an average of 50 trials for each method. From the figure, it is clear that our method performs significantly better than the greedy method and the discrimination criterion method. It also has a margin of advantage over the subspace separation method.

For an example with a Gaussian noise with $\sigma = 0.5$, the commute time matrix and the embedded subspace are shown in Figure 5(b) and 5(c) respectively. It is clear that even in the noise contaminated case, the commute time matrix still maintains a good block-diagonal structure. Moreover, under the embedding the points are easily separated.

4.2 Real-World Motion Tracking

In this section we experiment with the commute time method on real-world multi-body motion tracking problems. Figure 6 shows five real video sequences with the successfully tracked feature points using the commute time method. The full sequences can be found in the supplementary material web-site.

The first three rows are for the data used by Sugaya and Kanatani in [19, 18]. Here there is one moving object and a moving camera. A successful tracking method will separate the moving object from the moving background. The forth and fifth rows in Figure 6 are two video sequences captured using a Fuji-Film 2.0M camera(320×240 pixels). For each of sequence, we detected feature points using the KLT [17], and tracked the feature points using the commute time method. Due to the continuous loss of the feature points in the successive frames by the KLT algorithm, we use only ten frames each from the sequences with 117 and 116 feature points respectively. Compared to the data from Sugaya and Kanatani, we increase the number of detected moving objects from one to two, which makes the separation more difficult.

In the case of the forth row of Figure 6, our method not only separates the ducks correctly from the moving background, but it also separates the moving ducks from each other. The fifth row of Figure 6 is the most difficult one with two independently moving hands and a moving background. it also separates the wall from the floor correctly.

Fig. 6. Real-world video sequences and successfully tracked feature points

For the same sequences, we compared our results with Costeira and Kanade's greedy algorithm, Ichimura's discrimination criterion method, Kanatani's subspace separation method and Sugaya and Kanatani's multi-stage learning method. The comparison is shown in Table 1.

Table 1 lists the accuracies of different methods measured by the number of correctly classified points over the total number of points in percentage. The percentage is averaged over 50 trails for each method. From the table, it is clear that the greedy algorithm gives the worst results. The discrimination criterion method and the subspace separation method perform better due to their robustance to the noise. The multi-stage learning method delivers significantly better results due to its adaptive capabilities, but failed on our data. The failures are most pronounced when there are several moving ob-

Table 1. Separation accuracy for the sequences in Fig. 6

	A	B	C	D	E
Costeira-Kanade	60.3	71.3	58.8	45.5	30.0
Ichimura	92.6	80.1	68.3	55.4	47.2
Subspace Separation	59.3	99.5	98.9	80.6	67.2
Multi-stage Learning	100.0	100.0	100.0	93.7	81.5
Commute Time Separation	**100.0**	**100.0**	**100.0**	**100.0**	**100.0**

jects and an inconsistent moving background. Our method gives the best performance and achieves 100% accuracy.

5   Conclusion

In this paper, we have described how the multi-body motion tracking problem can be cast into a graph spectral setting using a commute time embedding method together with k-means clustering. The commute time is conveniently computed using the Laplacian eigensystem. We have shown how the commute time embedding is linked to kernel PCA, the Laplacian eigenmap and the diffusion map. We have compared our embedding method with a number of alternative tracking algorithms on both synthetic and real world data. Here it offers a convincing margin of improvement for noise-contaminated multi-body motion tracking.

Acknowledgements. The authors would like to thank João Costeira and Jared Jacobs for generously providing their data and code for this work.

References

1. M. Belkin and P. Niyogi. Laplacian eigenmaps for dimensionality reduction and data representation. *Neural Computation*, 15(6):1373–1396, 2003.
2. F.R.K. Chung and S.-T. Yau. Discrete green's functions. In *J. Combin. Theory Ser.*, pages 191–214, 2000.
3. R.R. Coifman, S. Lafon, A.B. Lee, M. Maggioni, B. Nadler, F. Warner, and S.W. Zucker. Geometric diffusions as a tool for harmonic analysis and structure definition of data: Diffusion maps. *National Academy of Sciences*, 102(21):7426–7431, 2005.
4. J. Costeira and T. Kanade. A multibody factorization method for independently moving objects. *IJCV*, 29(3):159 – 179, 1997.
5. Z. Fan, J. Zhou, and Y. Wu. Inference of multiple subspaces from high-dimensional data and application to multibody grouping. In *CVPR*, pages 661–666, 2004.
6. Z. Fan, J. Zhou, and Y. Wu. Multibody motion segmentation based on simulated annealing. In *CVPR*, pages 776–781, 2004.
7. C.W. Gear. Multibody grouping from motion images. *IJCV*, 29(2):130–150, 1998.
8. A. Gruber and Y. Weiss. Multibody factorization with uncertainty and missing data using the em algorithm. In *CVPR*, pages 707–714, 2004.
9. N. Ichimura. Motion segmentation based on factorization method and discriminant criterion. In *ICCV*, pages 600–605, 1999.

10. K. Kanatani. Motion segmentation by subspace separation and model selection. In *ICCV*, pages 301–306, 2001.
11. J. B. MacQueen. Some methods for classification and analysis of multivariate observations. In *Proceedings of the fifth Berkeley symposium on mathematical statistics and probability*, pages 281–297, 1967.
12. J. Park, H. Zha, and R. Kasturi. Spectral clustering for robust motion segmentation. In *ECCV*, pages 390–401, 2004.
13. M. Pavan and M. Pelillo. A new graph-theoretic approach to clustering and segmentation. In *CVPR03*, pages I: 145–152, 2003.
14. H. Qiu and E.R. Hancock. Image segmentation using commute times. In *BMVC*, pages 929–938, 2005.
15. B. Sch, A. Smola, and K. Muller. Nonlinear component analysis as a kernel eigenvalue problem. *Neural Computation*, 10:1299–1319, 1998.
16. J. Shi and J. Malik. Normalized cuts and image segmentation. *IEEE PAMI*, 22(8):888–905, 2000.
17. J. Shi and C. Tomasi. Good features to track. In *CVPR*, pages 593–600, 1994.
18. Y. Sugaya and K. Kanatani. Outlier removal for motion tracking by subspace separation. *IEICE Trans. INF and SYST*, E86-D(6):1095–1102, 2003.
19. Y. Sugaya and K. Kanatani. Multi-stage unsupervised learning for multi-body motion segmentation. *IEICE Trans. INF and SYST*, E87-D(7):1935–1942, 2004.
20. Y. Weiss. Segmentatoin using eigenvectors: a unifying view. In *ICCV.*, pages 975–982, 1999.
21. Y. Wu, Z. Zhang, T. S. Huang, and J. Y. Lin. Multibody grouping via orthogonal subspace decomposition. In *CVPR*, pages 252–257, 2001.
22. L. Zelnik-Manor and M. Irani. Degeneracies, dependencies and their implications in multi-body and multi-sequence factorizations. In *CVPR*, pages 287–293, 2003.

A Tuned Eigenspace Technique for Articulated Motion Recognition

M. Masudur Rahman and Antonio Robles-Kelly

National ICT Australia*, RSISE Bldg. 115, ANU, ACT 0200, Australia
Masud.Rahman@{rsise.anu.edu.au, nicta.com.au}
Antonio.Robles-Kelly@{anu.edu.au, nicta.com.au}

Abstract. In this paper, we introduce a tuned eigenspace technique so as to classify human motion. The method presented here overcomes those problems related to articulated motion and dress texture effects by learning various human motions in terms of their sequential postures in an eigenspace. In order to cope with the variability inherent to articulated motion, we propose a method to tune the set of sequential eigenspaces. Once the learnt tuned eigenspaces are at hand, the recognition task then becomes a nearest-neighbor search over the eigenspaces. We show how our tuned eigenspace method can be used for purposes of real-world and synthetic pose recognition. We also discuss and overcome the problem related to clothing texture that occurs in real-world data, and propose a background subtraction method to employ the method in out-door environment. We provide results on synthetic imagery for a number of human poses and illustrate the utility of the method for the purposes of human motion recognition.

1 Introduction

In computer vision and pattern recognition, there is a considerable body of work aimed at understanding and developing appearance-based methods. Appearance-based methods can cope with illumination, reflectance and pose effects based upon the appearance of the scene in the image. The bulk of this work focuses on using PCA to build a subspace representation of the scene which is then used for purposes of appearance-base object and pose recognition. Turk and Pentland [1] have shown how this PCA-based representation, called the eigenspace, can be used to perform face recognition. In a related development, Murase and Nayar [2] have performed object and pose recognition by projecting the views under study onto a basis formed by the eigenspace components. Kopp-Borotschnig *et al.* [3] have developed a method to recognise objects from ambiguous viewpoints using an active vision approach. Hall, Marshall and Martin [4] have shown how appearance models can be updated based upon addition and substraction of eigenspaces. Recently Schechtman and Irani [5] have introduced a behaviour-based similiarity measure which is computed from intensity information.

One of the main arguments levelled against these methods is that they are not robust to occlusion, shadows or background texture. Ohba and Ikeuchi [6] have proposed a method to cope with partially occluded objects by storing partial appearances of on

---

* National ICT Australia is funded by the Australian Governments Backing Australia's Ability initiative, in part through the Australian Research Council.

A. Leonardis, H. Bischof, and A. Pinz (Eds.): ECCV 2006, Part I, LNCS 3951, pp. 174–185, 2006.

an "eigenwindow". A mean eigenwindow method has also proposed by Rahman and Ishikawa[7] for reducing partial occlusion. Leonardis and Bischof [8] have shown how the coefficients of the eigenimages can be computed so as to cope with occlusion and segmentation. Black *et al.* [9] have used robust estimators to model structured noise and corruption. Yilmaz and Gokmen [10] have overcome problems related to illumination changes by applying the eigenspace representation to the edge images rather than the intensity values.

Despite effective, the methods above are prone to error due to texturing and articulated object variation such as the one present in human body motion. Thus, in this paper, we introduce a novel development of the appearance-based technique to recognise human motion. Here, we propose a tuned eigenspace so as to represent and recognise human posture and/or motion that has which considers dress-changes, pose variation, imaging noise and background clutter. We depart from the eigenspace technique of Murase and Nayar [2]. As mentioned earlier, this method makes use an eigenspace which is prone to variations in pose, dress-texture and clothing variation. Therefore, we generalise the eigenspace projection approach so that we can overcome these problems. In addition, we make use of a blurred edge image so as to solve to make the eigenspace projection robust to dress-texture variations. Further, in order to learn the eigenspace for a variety of human motions, we propose a mean posture matrix created from similar pose-windows. This is done by collecting similar poses from a particular subject and recovering the mean posture matrix. This mean posture matrix is then used to learn the eigenspace for the human motion under study. The eigenspace recovered from the mean posture matrix is what we called a tuned eigenspace. With these ingredients, the recognition of unobserved motions can be posed as a nearest neighbour search over the learnt tuned eigenspace. The study conducts a number of experiments for investigating the human dress-texture effect in the eigenspace and how the proposed method recovers it. Furthermore, We propose a background subtraction method in order to introduce this method in out-door application. We also compare our results with the conventional method.

2   Generating the Eigenspace

In order to develop a tuned eigenspace which can handle dress-texture and articulated human motion, we consider $P = \{p_1, p_2, \ldots, p_{|P|}\}$ successive views. Each of these views is, in practice, an image comprised by $M_{rows} \times N_{cols}$ pixels, where M_{rows} is the height and N_{rows} is the width of the image p_i. These pixels can be rearranged in a raster scan manner into a column vector of the form $x_p = [x_{1p}, x_{2p}, \ldots, x_{Np}]^T$, where $N \cong M_{rows} \times N_{cols}$. In the sake of simplicity, we assume that this vector is already normalised to unity, i.e., $\|x_p\| = 1$.

For a set $\mathcal{M}$ of different human motions of order M, we denote the vector x corresponding to the mth motion as x_p^m. For each motion, its image stream is sampled P times. These $P \times M$ images are collected into a single matrix X of the form $X = [x_1^1 - \hat{x} \mid x_2^1 - \hat{x} \mid \ldots \mid x_p^1 - \hat{x} \mid x_1^2 - \hat{x} \mid x_2^2 - \hat{x} \mid \ldots \mid x_p^2 - \hat{x} \mid \ldots \mid x_1^M - \hat{x} \mid x_2^M - \hat{x} \mid \ldots \mid x_P^M - \hat{x}]$, where $\hat{x}$ is the mean for the set of all vectors x_i^j, i.e.

$$\hat{\mathbf{x}} = \frac{1}{P \times M} \sum_{i=1}^{P} \sum_{j=1}^{M} \mathbf{x}_i^j \tag{1}$$

The matrix X contains $P \times M$ columns and N rows. For the matrix X, the covariance matrix C is defined by $\mathbf{C} = \mathbf{X}\mathbf{X}^T$.

We can use PCA [11], we can construct a subspace representation for the covariance matrix $\mathbf{C}$ as follows. Let $\lambda_1 \geq \lambda_2 \geq \lambda_3 \geq \ldots \geq \lambda_N$ be the N eigenvalues of the covariance matrix C arranged in decreasing order of rank. We can then select the first k eigenpairs, i.e. the eigenvectors $\boldsymbol{e}_i$ and eigenvalues λ_i such that $\lambda_1 \geq \lambda_2 \geq \ldots \geq \lambda_k$ so as to build a k-dimensional space which we denote the eigenspace of X. The image $\boldsymbol{x}_p^m$ is then projected into a point $\boldsymbol{g}_p^m$ in the eigenspace by the following equation

$$\boldsymbol{g}_p^m = [\boldsymbol{e}_1 \mid \boldsymbol{e}_2 \mid \ldots \mid \boldsymbol{e}_K]^T \boldsymbol{x}_p^m \tag{2}$$

For each motion, $\mid P \mid$ points, which correspond to each of the p_i successive observations in P, describe a trace in the eigenspace. Since a motion is smooth, these points conform a smooth curved line. This is called a motion line. If a motion starts and ends with the same pose, the motion line composes a closed loop, which is referred to as a motion trajectory hereafter. A global eigenspace is that which contains M motion loops so as to capture multiple motions.

3   Developing a Tuned Eigenspace

As mentioned in the previous section, a human posture is represented by a point in the eigenspace, projected making use of Equation 2. A motion is described by a set of successive points that can provide a motion line. For H subjects, the motion lines in the eigenspace, corresponding to a particular motion, should ideally coincide with one other. In practice, this is not the case. Therefore we compute a mean expression of the postures for every of the motions under study. In this way, we take into account a general pattern which is comprised by the mean over all the motion lines for the motion under study. The proposed eigenspace containing the mean expression is called a tuned eigenspace. Consider a set H of human motion subjects. Let $\boldsymbol{x}_p^{m,h}$ denote the image stream corresponding to the pth view of the motion indexed m, for the subject h. For the subject h, the matrix $\boldsymbol{X}$ becomes

$$X_h = [\boldsymbol{x}_{1,h}^1 \mid \boldsymbol{x}_{2,h}^1 \mid \ldots \mid \boldsymbol{x}_p^{1,h} \mid \boldsymbol{x}_1^{2,h} \mid \boldsymbol{x}_2^{2,h} \mid \ldots \mid \boldsymbol{x}_p^{2,h} \mid \ldots \mid \boldsymbol{x}_1^{M,h} \mid \boldsymbol{x}_2^{M,h} \mid \ldots \mid \boldsymbol{x}_p^{M,h}] \tag{3}$$

With the matrix X_h at hand, we define the matrix $\tilde{X} = [X_1 \mid X_2 \mid \ldots \mid \ldots \mid X_{|H|}]$, which can be regarded as a higher-order analogous of X. For every of the $\mid H \mid$ subjects, we can project the image stream $\boldsymbol{x}_p^{m,h}$ for the subject h into the point $\boldsymbol{g}_p^{m,h}$ of the tuned eigenspace making use of the expression $\boldsymbol{g}_p^{m,h} = [\tilde{\boldsymbol{e}}_1 \mid \tilde{\boldsymbol{e}}_2 \mid \ldots \mid \tilde{\boldsymbol{e}}_K]^T \boldsymbol{x}_p^{m,h}$, where $\tilde{\boldsymbol{e}}_i$ is the ith eigenvector of the covariance matrix $\tilde{C} = \tilde{X}\tilde{X}^T$. For the set H of subjects, we have $\mid H \mid$ such points, i.e., $\boldsymbol{g}_p^{m,h}$; $h = \{1, 2, \ldots, H\}$. Thus, the points in the tuned eigenspace are given by the average point $\overline{\boldsymbol{g}}_p^m = \frac{1}{H} \sum_{h=1}^{H} \boldsymbol{g}_p^{m,h}$, which captures the pth postures of a particular motion m learnt from a set H of subjects. The set of $\mid P \mid$ points

$\bar{g}_p^m | p = (1, 2, \ldots, P)$ defines a mean line for the motion m. Hence, in the paper, we call the mean motion line for the M motions a *global tuned eigenspace*.

4   Dress Texture

In order to employ the global tuned eigenspace for purposes of human motion recognition, motion representation should be generalised so as to be robust to dress-texture and clothe variations. The standard eigenspace technique, however, is prone to error due to the changes in appearance introduced by variations in clothes and dress-texture. Therefore, here we follow Yilmaz and Gokmen [10] and employ, to recover the eigenspace, edge images as an alternative to the gray-scale views. In contrast with their approach, we have used a blurred edge image so as to introduce a Gaussian kernel over the edge-image for our set of views. Thus, every of our views is comprised by a blurred edge image $E(x, y)$ computed from the original image $I(x, y)$, which is given by $E(x, y) = G_{\sigma 2}(x, y) * D(G_{\sigma 1}(x, y) * I(x, y))$.

Here $G_{\sigma 1}(x, y)$ is a Gaussian kernel with a standard deviation σ_1. The Gaussian kernel $G_{\sigma 1}(x, y)$ is convolved with the Image $I(x, y)$ in order to reduce random jitter and image noise. The resultant image is differentiated making use of differential operator D, which in our experiments is given by the Sobel operator. The differentiated images is, again, convolved with a Gaussian kernel whose standard deviation is σ_2.

5   Recognition Strategy

Our aim in this paper is to perform human motion recognition based upon the tuned eigenspace introduced in the previous sections. Consider an image containing a data view of an unknown human motion. We want to decide if that view belongs to any of the learnt motions and in the case it does belong to one of the learnt motion classes, relate it to the views that characterise the motion to which it belongs. Let p' denote the data view under consideration. The view p' is then projected onto a discrete point $g_{p'}^m$ in the learnt global tuned eigenspace. To perform recognition, we make use of the minimum Euclidean distance d_{p*}^{m*} in the learnt tuned eigenspace given by $d_{p*}^{m*} = min_{p \in P; m \in \mathcal{M}} \| g_{p'}^m - \bar{g}_{p'}^m \|$.

Thus, d_{p*}^{m*} is such that the nearest learned point in the eigenspace to our data point $g_{p'}^m$ is related to both, a particular motion $m \in \mathcal{M}$ and an observation $p \in P$. Therefore, our strategy of motion recognition does not rely only on the recognition of a particular view but on the mean for the learnt set of views. Furthermore, since we employ the Euclidean distance between the data point in the tuned eigenspace and the mean motion line, our recognition strategy can be viewed as the search over the mass-centres for the points in the eigenspace corresponding to the observations for every of the learnt motions.

6   Experimental Results

In this section, we conduct a number of experiments in order to verify the effectiveness of our method for purposes of human motion recognition. This section is divided into three parts. In the first of these, we perform recognition using a set of synthetic motion views rendered using camera rotations. We then provide results on real-world data for 6 cricket umpiring motions obtained from 5 persons. We conclude the section by conducting an extensive sensitivity study on dress-texture and its impact on our tuned eigenspace technique. Along these lines, we propose a background subtraction method to overcome background noise and jitter and perform experiments so as to evaluate the proposed method under various noise levels.

6.1 Synthetic Motion Representation and Recognition

We commence by providing results on synthetic imagery. Here, we have modelled synthetic motion by rotating the viewpoint. Since the positions of the subject under study and the camera are relative, this camera rotation procedure is equivalent to the appearance changes induced by subject position variation. We have used 3D Studio Max to create a set of four articulated motions in which the camera rotates about the vertical, sagittal and temporal axis of the subject under study. For each motion, we have used a subject with a different pose and rendered 120 frames rotating the camera in $4.5°$ degree intervals. In Figure 1, we show example views for our 3 different camera rotations. In

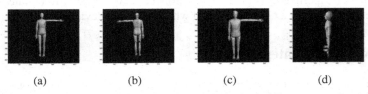

| (a) | (b) | (c) | (d) |

Fig. 1. Sample poses (out of a total of 120) obtained from the 3 different camera rotations about the subject under study

Figure 2, we show the four poses used in our experiments. The pose in the right-most panel of Figure 2 constitutes our data pose. The other three poses are used for purposes of learning the tuned eigenspace. It is worth noting that the position of the arm and hand of the subject vary in an articulated fashion. To learn this articulated variation of the subject's limb position, we have used 360 views, i.e. 120×3. We have then used a fourth sequence of 120 views of the same subject in a different pose as our data set.

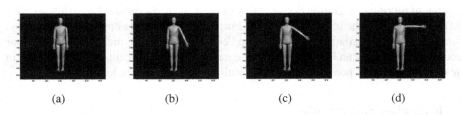

| (a) | (b) | (c) | (d) |

Fig. 2. (a), (b) and (c): Poses used to learn the tuned eigenspace; (d): Pose used to render our data views

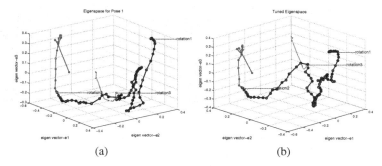

(a)   (b)

Fig. 3. Eigenspaces obtained from the articulated motions: (a) Eigenspaces of a single pose, and (b) tuned eigenspace obtained from 3 poses

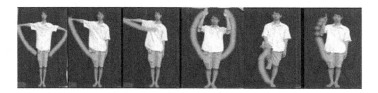

Fig. 4. Real world motions used in the experiment

For our recognition task, we consider a view to have been classified correctly if it corresponds to the point in the tuned eigenspace for the set of view in our learning set whose camera position is the same as that of the data view. This is, the rotation of the camera for the views in the learning set and that of the data view are the same. We have done this since the camera rotations along with hand movement give us various appearance-change. Therefore, for our synthetic data, the camera rotation and the pose determine the appearance. In our experiments, the recognition rate was of 99.3%. In other words, 118 views out of the 120 data views were classified correctly. An eigenspace obtained from 120 sample views is shown in Figure 3(a) and a tuned eigenspace generated from the three subject's poses is also shown in the Figure 3(b).

6.2   Human Motion Representation and Recognition

For our real-world experiments, we have employed 6 prominent actions $(M = 6)$ of an umpire arbitrating a cricket match, i.e. "wide", "no", "boundary", "over-boundary", "leg bye", and "out". Sample views for each of these are shown in Figure 4. The motions were captured using a digital video camera. For each motion, we have used 10 views, i.e. $(P = 10)$. For purposes of recognition, we have used the blurred edge images computed making use of the procedure introduced earlier in the paper. For our gaussian blurring, we have chosen $\sigma_1 = 0.30$ and $\sigma_2 = 2.0$. As a result, $P \times M = 60$ edge-images were used to learn our global eigenspace. In the left-hand panel of Figure 5(a) we show 10 successive images of the "wide" motion. Their blurred edge images are shown in the right-hand panel of the figure 5(b). A graphical representation of a global eigenspace is

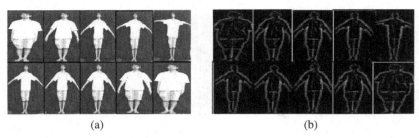

(a)   (b)

Fig. 5. (a) Sequential images of "wide motion" (a) Sobel-edge images

(a)   (b)

Fig. 6. Persons involved in performing the experiments. Models where background subtraction method is: (a) not employed, and (b) employed.

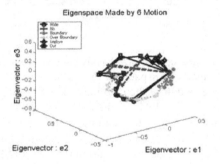

Fig. 7. A global eigenspace of 6 motions. Only 3 prominent dimensions are displayed.

shown in Figure 7. In the figure, individual motion trajectories are indicated by different colors/markers in the graph. Since all the motions start and end with an identical pose, i.e., a natural standing posture, every motion makes a closed loop. As a result,

the global eigenspace in Figure 7 contains 6 motion loops originating from a common point. In order to illustrate how the tuned eigenspace reflects the eigenspaces for each of the 6 motions, in Figure 8 we have plotted the motion trajectories in the eigenspace for individual motions. In the top row of Figure 8, we show the trajectories of the "wide" and "no" motions, respectively, for five subjects. These have been obtained using our method. It is worth noting that, despite the models all wear different clothes, this do not the recovered eigenspace. As a result, each motion trajectory is very similar to one another. We have also compared our results with those obtained using the method of Murase and Nayar [2]. In the bottom row of Figure 8, we show the results for the method in [2]. The motion trajectories are less congruent and show more variation than those recovered using our method.

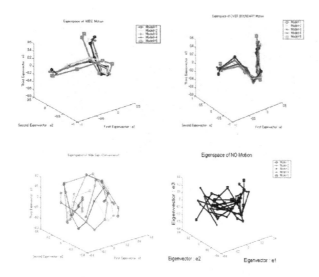

Fig. 8. Top row: comparison of motion trajectories obtained from 5 persons: Similar motion trajectories obtained from the proposed approach; Bottom row: Motion trajectories affected by the model's variations in the conventional method.

Table 1. Experimental results. MPM denotes mean posture matrix

Experiment	Training Set/MPM (Postures)	Testing Set (Postures)	Eigen Dimension	Recog. Rate (Average)
Human Motion	4 (240)	1(60)	6	87.5%
Dress	9(324)	1(36)	6	88.88%
Background	16(576)	51(36)	6	86.9%

6.2.1 Motion Recognition Using Tuned Eigenspaces

Since our method employed primarily 5 motions for recognizing human motions via posture recognition, a leave-one-out scheme is applied for selecting the image set. It means that we always choose 4 data sets for generating a tuned eigenspace and leave one data set for testing. A tuned eigenspace obtained from 4 data sets is shown in Figure 11(a). The obtained recognition results are shown in Table 1. We have obtained an average of 86.5% recognition rates where background issue were not considered. It is worth noting that the obtained motion recognition is 100%.

6.3 Special Experiment Considering Clothing Problem

We have further performed another experiment where the attention was focused in the clothing problem with a number of typical dressing schemes. In the experimental setup, we have used a camera for taking a video image of a turning motion (therefore $m = 1$) of a particular subject wearing 10 typical clothes. The dresses are shown in Figure 9. From the 10 different clothes, we have obtained $P = 360$ sampled views. For the com-

Fig. 9. Models used for investigating the clothing problem

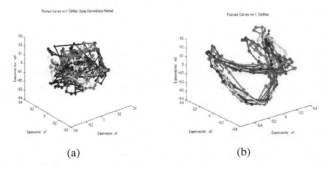

Fig. 10. Motion's trajectories with all of 10 dresses: (a) the conventional method, and (b) the proposed method

parison, the study employed a conventional method [2] where an original gray image was employed for generating an eigenspace. Figure 10 shows the closed motion trajectories generated from various clothes. Dress texture has made an undesirable effect by the conventional method, as shown in Figure 10(a) producing dissimilar motion trajectories, despite having identical models and motions. On the other hand, the motion loops are mutually quite similar using the proposed method as shown in Figure 10(b). For obtaining the recognition performance, we have employed the earlier mentioned leave-one-out scheme for selecting the tuned eigenspace. Therefore, 9 data set are used for training and one data set is always left for the testing. An average of 87% recognition rate is achieved for this particular data set as shown in Table 1.

6.4   Background Subtraction Method

A background subtraction method is applied in order to prove the effectiveness of the method. We have conducted an experiment employing 17 human models as shown in Figure 6(b). The motion categories and segmentation process were same as described in section 6.3. However, respective backgrounds have been subtracted automatically from the sampled images and silhouette images are obtained. Figure 12 shows the

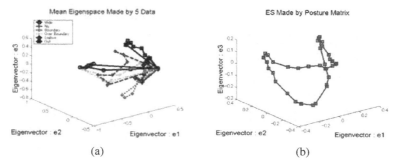

(a)   (b)

Fig. 11. Tuned eigenspace for the 5 data sets in Figure 6(a), and (b) 5 data sets in Figure 9

Fig. 12. Background subtraction method: (from left to right) original image, background subtracted image, segmented image and Sobel edge image

result of this subtraction method. Figures (from left to right) show an original image, background subtracted image, a segmented image containing human portion and the sobel-edge image. Once again, we have employed leave-one-out method for generating tuned eigenspace and obtaining the recognition results. The recognition results are listed in the Table 1.

6.5 Comparison Results

We have compared our results with the conventional method [2]where original images are used for generating the eigenspace. It is also mentioned that conventional method employed only one data sample obtained from the best search scheme for creating the eigenspace. Once again, the proposed method has employed earlier described image pre-processing techniques for overcoming the clothing and noise effect, and a posture matrix for creating a tuned eigenspace. Since we have employed a leave-one-out method for selecting the data sets for creating the tuned eigenspace, it confirms use of every image data either for training and/or testing. The comparisons are two manifold:representation of eigenspaces in the presence of clothing effects, model variations and appearance-change. The proposed method has always generated eigenspaces with similar pattern with respect to the motions. Therefore, an eigenspace of a particular motion can be used for testing the other models. The requirement of eigen dimensions were also reasonable in the proposed method as shown in Figure 14. In contradictory, eigenspace obtained form the conventional way have always been affected by the pre-

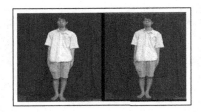

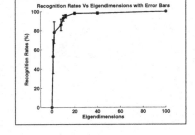

Fig. 13. Imaging noise used in the experiment. (left) Original image and (right) Image with 20% salt and pepper.

Fig. 14. Requirement of eigen dimensions. The error bars correspond to the standard error for the recognition rate.

ceding problems. Therefore, conventional method is not suitable for flexible object recognition. Consequently, poor recognition rates (i.e., 44.4% of using the data used in the experiment 6.2 and 42.1% from the data used in the experiment 6.3) have been achieved from the conventional method.

6.6   Noise Reduction

As stated earlier, double gaussian kernel are used mainly for reducing random noise and clothing texture effects. Therefore, our method is also effective under noisy image environments. We have made a comparison how the proposed method works under various noise levels. Figure 13 shows the noise level used in the experiment. We have used 20% salt and pepper noise to the images shown in the Figure 6(a) and they have used for creating eigenspaces and for the recognition. If we do not use the gaussian blurring, the posture recognition rate is shown always less than 70% even using the proposed method. Therefore, the pre-image processing techniques has provided us the noise reduction capability in a significant level.

7   Discussion and Conclusions

In this paper, we have introduced a novel appearance-based method for articulated motion recognition and illustrated its utility in recognition tasks. We have validated the proposed method in a number of ways using synthetic and real-world data. The proposed tuned eigenspace has the robustness to work under both, real human and articulated motions. Furthermore, the method also has the robustness to work under random imaging noise and background variations.

Acknowledgment

The authors are indebted with the Ishikawa Laboratory in the Control Engineering Department of the Kyushu Institute of Technology, Japan for facilitating them the real-world imagery used in the experimental section of this paper.

References

1. Turk, M.A., Pentland, A.P.: Face recognition using eigenfaces. In: International Conference on Computer Vision and Pattern Recognition. (1991) 586–591
2. Murase, H., Nayar, S.K.: Visual learning and recognition of 3-d objects from appearance. International Journal of Computer Vision **14**(5) (1995) 39–50
3. Kopp-Borotschnig, H., Paletta, L., Prantl, M., Pinz, A.: Appearance-based active object recognition. Image and Vision Computing **18**(9) (2000) 715–727
4. Hall, P., Marshall, D., Martin, R.: Merging and splitting eigenspace models. IEEE Transaction on Pattern Analysis Machine Intelligence **22**(9) (2000) 1042–1049
5. Shechtman, E., Irani, M.: Space–time behavioral correlation. In: Computer Vision and Pattern Recognition. (2005) I:405–412
6. Ohba, K., Ikeuchi, K.: Detectability, uniqueless and reliability of eigen windows for stable verifications of partially occluded objects. IEEE Transaction on Pattern Analysis Machine Intelligence **19** (1997) 1043–1047
7. Rahman, M.M., Ishikawa, S.: A robust recognition method for partially occluded/destroyed objects. In: Sixth Asian Conference on Computer Vision. (1996) 984–988
8. Leonardis, A., Bischof, H.: Robust recognition using eigenimages. Computer Vision and Image Understanding **78** (2000) 99–118
9. Black, M.J., Fleet, D.J., Yacoob, Y.: Robustly estimating changes in image appearance. Computer Vision and Image Understanding **78**(1) (2000) 8–31
10. Yilmaz, A., Gokmen, M.: Eigenhill vs. eigenface and eigenedge. Pattern Recognition (34) (2001) 181–184
11. Gonzalez, R.C., Wintz, P.: Digital Image Processing. Addison-Wesley Publishing Company Limited (1986)

Real-Time Non-rigid Shape Recovery Via Active Appearance Models for Augmented Reality

Jianke Zhu, Steven C.H. Hoi, and Michael R. Lyu

Department of Computer Science & Engineering,
Chinese University of Hong Kong,
Shatin, Hong Kong
{jkzhu, chhoi, lyu}@cse.cuhk.edu.hk

Abstract. One main challenge in Augmented Reality (AR) applications is to keep track of video objects with their movement, orientation, size, and position accurately. This poses a challenging task to recover non-rigid shape and global pose in real-time AR applications. This paper proposes a novel two-stage scheme for online non-rigid shape recovery toward AR applications using Active Appearance Models (AAMs). First, we construct 3D shape models from AAMs offline, which do not involve processing of the 3D scan data. Based on the computed 3D shape models, we propose an efficient online algorithm to estimate both 3D pose and non-rigid shape parameters via local bundle adjustment for building up point correspondences. Our approach, without manual intervention, can recover the 3D non-rigid shape effectively from either real-time video sequences or single image. The recovered 3D pose parameters can be used for AR registrations. Furthermore, the facial feature can be tracked simultaneously, which is critical for many face related applications. We evaluate our algorithms on several video sequences. Promising experimental results demonstrate our proposed scheme is effective and significant for real-time AR applications.

1 Introduction

1.1 Augmented Reality

The objective of Augmented Reality (AR) is to integrate virtual objects into real-world video sequences, enabling computer generated objects to be overlaid on the video in such a manner as to appear part of the viewed 3D scene. Recently, some well-known AR toolkits have been developed for AR applications [1]. Although these tools have facilitated the AR applications to obtain good registration data automatically and robustly, it is still a challenging and open issue to keep track of objects with their movement, orientation, size, and position accurately in AR applications. This critical requirement also results in an important problem, i.e., determining the position and orientation of an object, which plays an important role in many research areas such as robotics, computer vision, computer graphics.

A. Leonardis, H. Bischof, and A. Pinz (Eds.): ECCV 2006, Part I, LNCS 3951, pp. 186–197, 2006.

In the subsequent part we describe some recent advances of technologies for object tracking and shape recovery in the computer vision community. Along with the introduction of previous work, we provide the motivation and brief introduction of our work in this paper particularly for AR applications.

1.2 Previous Work and Motivation

L. Vacchetti et al. [2] proposed an efficient real-time solution for tracking rigid objects in 3D scene using a single camera. They demonstrated that the virtual glasses and masks can be added on to the head. Since they employed a rigid 3D model, the local facial feature was not able to be located and tracked. In addition, a few keyframes were required to make the tracker more robust. L. Vacchetti et al. pointed that it was very convenient to estimate the camera position from a single image in order to initialize the tracker and to recover the failure automatically. Active Appearance Models based approaches [3, 4, 5] provide a good solution to recover the 2D affine pose parameters along with the feature points from single image. Recently, researchers [6, 7, 8] have attempted to build the AAM with three dimensions.

P. Mittrapiyanumic [6] proposed two AAMs algorithms for rigid object tracking and pose estimation. The first method is to utilize two instances of AAM to track landmark points in a stereo pair of images and perform 3D reconstruction of the landmarks followed by 3D pose estimation. The second method, i.e., AAM matching algorithm, is an extension of the original AAM that incorporates the full six degrees of freedom pose parameters as part of the parameters for the minimization. The results showed that the accuracy in pose estimation of appearance based methods is better than the methods using the geometric approach. J. Ahlberg [7] proposed an approach using the 3D AAM for face and facial feature tracking, in which the depth information of 3D shape was acquired by fitting a generic model. In addition, the pose parameters were estimated from a motion tracker, then the shape model parameters were recovered by AAM fitting.

Jing Xiao et al. [8] proposed a non-rigid structure-from-motion algorithm that could be used to convert a 2D AAM into a 3D face model. They then described how a non-rigid structure-from-motion algorithm was able to be employed to compute the corresponding 3D shape models from a 2D AAM. Their method did not require 3D range data in [9] and also shared fast fitting speeds. They then showed how the 3D modes could be used to constrain the AAM so that it could only generate model instances, but also could be generated with the 3D modes. Their fast fitting algorithm mainly benefited from the projection-out method and Inverse Compositional update strategy, thus the Jacobi matrix was constant. However, the approximation that the shape Jacobi matrix was made orthogonal to the texture Jacobi matrix, was only valid for few texture modes. Only shape parameters were recovered iteratively, and the texture parameters were recovered linearly in one step. In addition, the recovered pose parameters were not accurate enough, mainly because the pose parameters were compensated by the shape variations. A weak perspective camera model was employed in order to decrease the computational cost, and the full perspective camera model was necessary for the common AR applications. These may limit their applications particularly for AR applications.

This paper presents a novel scheme of real-time non-rigid shape recovery via active appearance models for augmented reality applications. The rest of this paper is organized as follows. Section 2 reviews the AAM algorithm and describes an extended AAM matching algorithm which predicts shape directly from texture for improving the accuracy of AAM searching. Section 3 presents our proposed scheme. We first provide an overview of our scheme in the context of augmented reality applications in Section 3.1. Then Section 3.2 describes how to construct the 3D shape models based on the 2D AAM tracking results. Section 3.3 presents a novel and efficient algorithm for online estimation of 3D pose and non-rigid shape parameters simultaneously via local bundle adjustment. Section 3.4 gives our experimental results and the details of our experimental implementation. Section 4 discusses the critical requirements of real-time AR applications, several major differences of our proposed scheme compared with previous work, and the advantages of our scheme particularly for AR applications as well as the disadvantages and our future work. Section 5 sets out our conclusion.

2   An Extended AAM Matching Algorithm

The Active Appearance Models (AAMs) [3, 4, 5, 7] have been proven as a successful method for matching statistical models of appearance to new images. AAMs are taking the analysis-through-synthesis approach to the extreme. This approach has been successfully applied in numerous different applications. AAMs establish a compact parameterizations of object variability, as learned from a training set by estimating a set of latent variables. The modelled object properties are usually shape and pixel intensities. There are several modifications for the basic AAM algorithm [4]. One approach was the Direct Appearance Model (DAM) for improving the convergence speed and searching accuracy by predicting the shape directly from the texture [10].

The AAM matching algorithm tries to minimize the residual between the model and image $\mathbf{r} = \mathbf{g}_i - \mathbf{g}_m$, where $\mathbf{g}_i$ is the sampled image below model shape, and $\mathbf{g}_m$ is the model texture. During the DAM training phase, one learns the relationships

$$\delta\mathbf{t} = \mathbf{R_t r} \,,$$

$$\delta\mathbf{b_t} = \mathbf{R_g r} \,.$$

Instead of using a traditional approach for AAM matching in [3], we implement a modified AAM fitting algorithm for quicker convergency and better matching accuracy similar to the approach in [5]. The proposed iterative AAM matching algorithm which predicts shape directly from texture is given in Fig. 1.

In our experiments, the AAMs are built up with 140 still face images belonging to 20 individuals, seven images for each. Each image is manually labelled with 100 points. As shown in Fig. 2, the matching experiment is performed on an AAM with 14 shape parameters, 68 texture parameters, and 36335 color pixels.

The algorithm of AAM Matching
1. Generate texture vector $\mathbf{g}_m$ from model
2. Sample image below the model shape $\mathbf{g}_i$
3. Evaluate error vector $\mathbf{r} = \mathbf{g}_i - \mathbf{g}_m$ and error $\mathbf{E} = |\mathbf{r}|$
4. Compute displacements in pose $\delta\mathbf{t} = \mathbf{R_t r}$
5. Compute displacements in texture $\delta\mathbf{b_t} = \mathbf{R_g r}$
6. Update pose and texture parameters with initial $k = 1$
7. Transform the shape by the estimated parameters
8. Repeat step 1-3 to form a new error $\mathbf{E}'$
9. If $\mathbf{E}' < \mathbf{E}$ accept the new estimate, otherwise goto step 6 to try other k=0.5, 0.25, ...

Fig. 1. An extended AAM matching algorithm

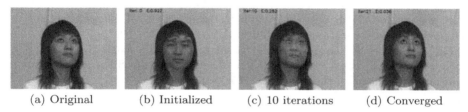

(a) Original   (b) Initialized   (c) 10 iterations   (d) Converged

Fig. 2. An example of our AAM fitting to a single image. The estimated errors are displayed in each case.

Fig 2 respectively show (a) the original single image, (b) the initialization of our AAM fitting, (c) the result after 10 iterations and the final converged result after 21 iterations. In each case the rendered model images and estimation errors are displayed in the figures.

3 Real-Time Non-rigid Shape Recovery for AR

3.1 Overview of Our Solution

Our scheme tries to attack the critical problems of pose and non-rigid shape recovery. Traditional techniques may be neither flexible and powerful enough for model representations nor efficient enough for real-time purposes. For tackling the challenges, we solve the problem by a two-stage scheme via AAM techniques:

- We acquire the 2D shape of objects using the AAM fitting algorithm described in Section 2 firstly, then construct the 3D shape basis offline based on the AAM fitting results.
- We estimate the 3D pose and 3D shape parameters online simultaneously via local bundle adjustment by building up the point correspondences between 2D and 3D.

The above proposed solution differs from the regular approach in [2] which estimated the pose of an object through point matching. To exploit the representational power of AAMs, instead of matching points between two frames, we propose a novel approach to setup the point correspondences between the 2D and 3D shape via AAM fitting to a single image. This procedure needs no manual initialization. The details of our approach are described as follows.

3.2   Offline Construction of 3D Shape Basis

Bregler et al. [11] proposed a solution for recovering 3D non-rigid shape models from image sequences. Their technique is based on a non-rigid model, where the 3D shape in each frame is a linear combination of a set of basis shapes. By analyzing the low rank of the image measurements, they proposed a factorization-based method that enforces the orthonormality constraints on camera rotations for reconstructing the non-rigid shape and motion. Torresani et al. [12] extended the method in [11] to initialize the optimization process. By using the extended AAM matching algorithm in Section 2, we first acquire the 2D shapes of objects. With the trained 2D shapes, we are able to construct the 3D shape basis due to the powerful representational capability of AAMs [8].

The 3D shape can be described as a set of key-frame basis $S_1, S_2, \cdots, S_m$. Each key-frame S_i is a $3 \times n$ matrix. The 3D shape of a specific configuration is a linear combination of the following basis set:

$$\mathbf{S} = \mathbf{S_0} + \sum_{i=1}^{m} p_i \mathbf{S_i} \qquad \mathbf{S}, \mathbf{S_i} \in R^{3 \times n}, p_i \in R \qquad (1)$$

where the coefficients p_i are the 3D shape parameters, and $\mathbf{S_i}$ are the 3D coordinates: $\mathbf{S} = \{\mathbf{M_1}, \mathbf{M_2}, \cdots, \mathbf{M_n}\}, \mathbf{M_i} \in R^{3 \times 1}$. Under a weak perspective projection, the n points of $\mathbf{S}$ are projected into 2D image points (u_i, v_i):

$$\begin{bmatrix} u_1 \ u_2 \cdots u_n \\ v_1 \ v_2 \cdots v_n \end{bmatrix} = \mathbf{R} \cdot (\sum_{i=0}^{m} p_i \mathbf{S_i}) + \mathbf{T} \qquad (2)$$

$\mathbf{R}$ contains the first 2 rows of the full 3D camera rotation matrix, and $\mathbf{T}$ is the camera translation. The scale of the projection is coded in $p_1, p_2, \cdots, p_m$. The camera translation $\mathbf{T}$ is eliminated by subtracting the mean of all 2D points, and henceforth one can assume that $\mathbf{S}$ is centered at the origin.

If the AAMs are tracked through a sequence of N images, 2D points of the AAM shape in each frame can be obtained. Let us add a temporal index to each 2D point, and denote the tracked points in frame t as (u_i^t, v_i^t). All points of AAM shape in all N images are stacked into one large measure $2N \times n$ matrix W. The number of 3D shape verities equals to the number of 2D AAM vertices n, it can be rewritten as follows:

$$W = \begin{bmatrix} u_1^1 \ u_2^1 \cdots u_n^1 \\ v_1^1 \ v_2^1 \cdots v_n^1 \\ \vdots \ \vdots \ \vdots \ \vdots \\ u_1^N \ u_2^N \cdots u_N^n \\ v_1^N \ v_2^N \cdots v_n^N \end{bmatrix} = \underbrace{\begin{bmatrix} \mathbf{R}_1 \ p_1^1\mathbf{R}_1 \cdots p_m^1\mathbf{R}_1 \\ \mathbf{R}_2 \ p_1^2\mathbf{R}_2 \cdots p_m^2\mathbf{R}_2 \\ \vdots \ \vdots \ \vdots \ \vdots \\ \mathbf{R}_N \ p_1^N\mathbf{R}_N \cdots p_m^N\mathbf{R}_N \end{bmatrix}}_{\mathbf{M}} \cdot \underbrace{\begin{bmatrix} \mathbf{S_0} \\ \mathbf{S_1} \\ \vdots \\ \mathbf{S_m} \end{bmatrix}}_{\mathbf{B}} \qquad (3)$$

where $\mathbf{M}$ is a $2N \times 3(m+1)$ scaled projection matrix and $\mathbf{B}$ is a $3(m+1) \times n$ shape matrix. In the noise-free case, $\mathbf{W}$ has a rank $r \leq 3(m+1)$, which can be factorized into the product of a $2N \times 3(m+1)$ matrix $\tilde{\mathbf{M}}$ and a $3(m+1) \times n$ matrix $\tilde{\mathbf{B}}$. This decomposition is not unique, which can be determined by a linear transformation. Any non-singular $3(m+1) \times 3(m+1)$ matrix $\mathbf{G}$ and its inverse could be inserted between $\tilde{\mathbf{M}}$ and $\tilde{\mathbf{B}}$. In addition, their product still remains equal to $\mathbf{W}$. Namely, we have the following equations

$$\mathbf{M} = \tilde{\mathbf{M}} \cdot \mathbf{G} \tag{4}$$

$$\mathbf{B} = \mathbf{G}^{-1} \cdot \tilde{\mathbf{B}} \tag{5}$$

where the corrective matrix $\mathbf{G}$ can be found by solving a least square optimization problem [11]. Thus, given 2D tracking data $\mathbf{W}$, a non-rigid 3D shape matrix with r degrees of freedom can be estimated, along with the corresponding camera rotations and configuration weights for each time frame.

In our experiments, we implement the AAM matching algorithm given in Section 2 and run it to fit the short video sequences of of 20 individuals (2678 frames in total). The training results are employed to construct the 3D shape basis in our experiments. Fig. 3 shows an example of the computed 3D mean shape modes of three views from AAM. Fig. 4 shows the first six 3D shape modes from an AAM.

Fig. 3. An example of 3D mean shape of three views $\mathbf{S_0}$

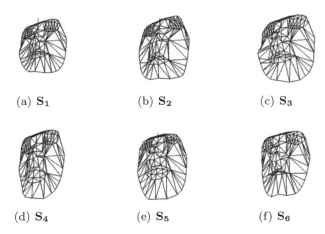

(a) $\mathbf{S_1}$ (b) $\mathbf{S_2}$ (c) $\mathbf{S_3}$

(d) $\mathbf{S_4}$ (e) $\mathbf{S_5}$ (f) $\mathbf{S_6}$

Fig. 4. An example of the first six 3D shape modes (a-f) from an AAM

3.3 Real-Time Non-rigid Shape and Pose Recovery for AR

To make it flexible and general for wide applications, we employ the perspective camera model, in which a 3D point $\mathbf{Q}$ is re-projected based on the 2D point $\mathbf{q}$:

$$\mathbf{q} = \mathbf{A}[\mathbf{R}|\mathbf{T}] \cdot \mathbf{Q}$$

where the camera rotation matrix $\mathbf{R}$ and the translation vector $\mathbf{T}$ estimated from the current frame are expressed in the object coordinate system, and $\mathbf{A}$ is the intrinsic camera matrix. The intrinsic parameters of the camera can be calculated offline. This does not require to be done precisely, and typically an approximate configuration is sufficient. Hence, we can assume the intrinsic parameters are fixed. Moreover, in order to allow some deformation, the rigid shape model is replaced by the 3D linear shape model. We now describe how to in real-time estimate the 3D pose parameters and non-rigid shape parameters simultaneously.

Given the constructed 3D shape basis via AAM training algorithm, we can build up the 2D-3D correspondences. Based on the established correspondences, an efficient way for estimating the parameters of camera position and the 3D shape coefficients can be turned into minimizing the re-projection error:

$$\min_{\mathbf{R},\mathbf{T},p} \rho\left(\mathbf{s}, \phi\left(\mathbf{A}[\mathbf{R}|\mathbf{T}], \mathbf{S}\right)\right) \tag{6}$$

Let $\mathbf{S} = \mathbf{S_0} + \sum_{i=1}^{m} p_i \mathbf{S_i}$, the optimization problem can be written as

$$\min_{\mathbf{R},\mathbf{T},p} \rho\left(\mathbf{s}, \phi\left(\mathbf{A}[\mathbf{R}|\mathbf{T}], \mathbf{S_0} + \sum_{i=1}^{m} p_i \mathbf{S_i}\right)\right) \tag{7}$$

with respect to the orientation and translation parameters $\mathbf{R}$ and $\mathbf{T}$, where

- ρ is the robust M-estimator [13] in consideration of outliers which can be given as follows:

$$\rho(u) = \left\{ \begin{array}{ll} \frac{\alpha^2}{6}[1 - (1 - (\frac{u}{\alpha})^2)^3], & |u| \leq \alpha \\ \frac{\alpha^2}{6}, & |u| > \alpha \end{array} \right. \tag{8}$$

- $\phi\left(\mathbf{A}[\mathbf{R}|\mathbf{T}], \mathbf{S_0} + \sum_{i=1}^{m} p_i \mathbf{S_i}\right)$ denotes the projection of 3D shape given the parameters $\mathbf{A}$, $\mathbf{R}$ and $\mathbf{T}$.

The above optimization procedure can converge quickly within a couple of iterations when it begins with a good initial estimation.

3.4 Experimental Results

The results of estimated 3D shapes of two individuals are depicted in Fig. 5, which are extracted from two video clips with total 300 frames. We can see that the 3D shapes are successfully fitted to the face image. The face deformation can be well described by 6 3D shape parameters, for example, fitting to different individuals with the same AAM model in Fig. 5(a-f). The algorithm can handle

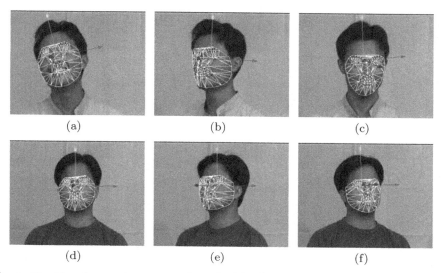

(a)   (b)   (c)

(d)   (e)   (f)

Fig. 5. Tracking faces using proposed method in the augmented video sequences, the axis in the displayed frames indicates the current 3D pose of tracked subject

large pose variations and displacements, as shown in Fig. 5(a,b,e,f). Fig. 5(a,c) revealed that the proposed approach can handle tilt pose, and Fig. 5(d-f) displayed the results which deal with out-of-plane rotation. In each result image, the axis indicates the current orientation and translation. Since the intrinsic and extrinsic camera matrices are computed, the virtual rigid and deformable objects can be inserted into the scene. Fig. 6 shows that a rigid virtual glasses and a deformable beard are added into the video sequences. From the results, we can observe that the beard can be deformed along with the expression changes. The added virtual objects are tightly overlaid on the subject. We use the results of previous frames as the initial values for the optimization, thus, only 3-4 iterations per frame required for AAM convergence. Since no relation with image information, the 3D pose and 3D shape parameters are computed efficiently.

Fig. 7 plots the re-projection error in the online non-rigid shape recovery step when varying number of 3D shape basis m. The experiment is performed on a video clip with 65 frames. As shown in Fig. 7, large error occurred only rigid

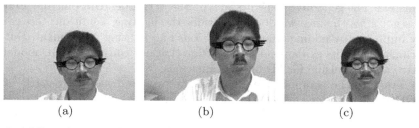

(a)   (b)   (c)

Fig. 6. Adding glasses and beard to the subject in the augmented video sequence, the beard is deformed along with the expression changes

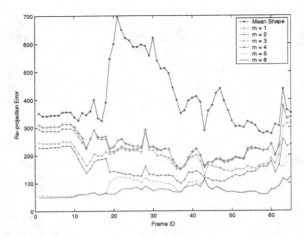

Fig. 7. The re-projection error with various number of 3D shape basis

shape is used for pose estimation, and the error reaches $700/100 = 7$ per point. The re-projection error decreases significantly when introducing the 3D linear shape model, additionally, it becomes smaller when **m** grows up. When six 3D shape basis are used, the average re-projection is below $100/100 = 1$ each point. However, large number of nonlinear parameters would affect the convergence speed of the object function, there is a trade-off between the accuracy and efficiency. Furthermore, large number of 3D shape basis may decreases the number of optimization iterations.

In order to demonstrate our proposed nonrigid shape and pose recovery approach is effective and promising for generating novel view and 3D facial animation purposes, we first map the recovered 3D nonrigid shape into high resolution mesh via interpolation [14], then render the novel views by mapping different texture and with different poses. Fig. 8(a) shows rendered enlarged novel view rotated from the current pose by 20° on Y-axis. Fig. 8(b) shows the experimental result by replacing face texture of a person with anther person. In the Fig. 8(b) , the top left one is the modelled person and the bottom left is the constructed 3D mesh in which 3D pose information is available; the top right one is the front face of the replaced person and the bottom right shows the generated results by replacing the texture using the built 3D model and 3D pose parameters. The generated view fits well on the 3D model. But one may find the skin is not smooth since we do not consider the lighting condition; this can be easily improved by adding smooth operations and lighting adjustment. But the experimental results can answer our question that our constructed 3D model are effective and promising for 3D facial animations.

We evaluate the computational cost of the proposed method on a Pentium III 1GHz CPU. It runs at 200ms per image of size 352×288. AAM fitting takes 40ms and 3D recovery step takes 74ms. The AAM with 10 shape parameters, 52 texture parameters. The non-rigid shape recovery step with 6 camera parameters and 6 3D shape parameters.

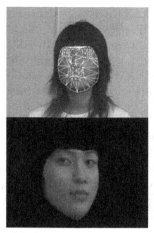
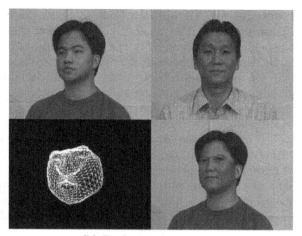

(a) Rendering novel view   (b) Replacing face texture

Fig. 8. Applications of non-rigid shape and pose recovery

4   Discussions

In this section, we discuss several major differences and advantages of our proposed scheme compared with previous work from several aspects in which we show that our proposed scheme is particularly flexible and powerful for augmented reality applications. Finally, we also mention the disadvantages and some improvements in our future work.

Rigid vs. Non-rigid. The prior model employed by L. Vacchetti et al. [2] is only for rigid objects or deformable objects with small variations. P. Mittrapiyanumic et al. [6] do not take full advantage of AAM's deformation power, the AAM is just used to estimated the 3D pose of rigid objects. The proposed method can deal with 3D deformation through introducing 3D linear shape models. In addition, large variation can be obtained by increasing the number of 3D shape basis. The facial feature can be located accurately by the power of AAM fitting, thus, the added virtual beard can be deformed with the facial expressions in Fig. 6. The novel view can be generated from the current view, even the facial texture of different individuals can be exchanged, as shown in Fig. 6 and Fig. 8. Additionally, the proposed approach provides a solution for building the 2D-3D correspondence from single image. Thus, the tracker can be initialized without manual intervention. In addition, the failure can be recovered automatically.

Offline vs. Online. Many methods [11, 12] have been presented for offline non-rigid shape recovery from image sequences through factorizing analysis on the 2D tracked points. Different from these approaches, our proposed method is able to work online by exploiting the 3D shape models that can be constructed offline effectively by using AAM tracking. This enables us to online acquire 3D non-rigid shape and pose which can be applicable for many AR applications.

Advantages for AR applications. In [8], the model and the fitting algorithm are person specific. The generic AAM is slower than the person specific AAM, but provides good accuracy in the case of large texture variations[15]. In addition, the inverse compositional update strategy is good for smooth shape, and not for the non smooth ones. The proposed extended AAM is a generic model with additive update method rather than person specific model with inverse compositional approach. Thus, it can handle large texture variations, fitting to different individuals. The weak-perspective model used in "Combined 2D+3D AAM" is not suitable for augmented reality applications, moreover, the optimization procedure of the algorithm is complicated. We optimize AAM and 3D pose parameters respectively. Virtual objects can be added to the scene by the estimated camera, orientations and translations information. In addition, the proposed approach is more flexible. The AAM fitting step can be replaced with other algorithms, such as Active Shape Models based approaches [13].

Disadvantages and Future Work. The proposed approach does not take full advantage of 3D information for speeding up AAM convergence. The accuracy of AAM fitting is critical to the 3D pose output. Large rotation may be compensated by the 3D linear mode, therefore, the estimated pose is not so accurate. In the future, problem mentioned above will be solved by training the 3D AAM with the aligned 3D shapes instead of 2D shapes.

5   Conclusions

In this paper we presented a novel scheme for non-rigid shape recovery in real-time augmented reality applications. Our scheme first builds the 3D shape models offline using an effective AAM algorithm. Given the constructed 3D shape models, an efficient online algorithm is suggested to estimate both the 3D pose and non-rigid shape parameters simultaneously. One of our main contributions is the introduction of 3D linear shape model to estimate the 3D pose parameters and non-rigid shape simultaneously via local bundle adjustment. Moreover, we suggested an updating scheme to predict the shape directly from texture that can improve the accuracy of AAM searching. The promising experimental results validate our proposed scheme is effective for real-time AR applications.

Acknowledgments. The work was fully supported by two grants: Innovation and Technology Fund ITS/105/03, and the Research Grants Council Earmarked Grant CUHK4205/04E.

References

1. Kato, H., Billinghurst, M.: Marker tracking and hmd calibration for a video-based augmented reality conferencing system. In: Proceedings of the 2nd IEEE and ACM International Workshop on Augmented Reality. (2004)
2. Vacchetti, L., Lepetit, V., Fua, P.: Stable real-time 3d tracking using online and offline information. IEEE Trans. PAMI **26** (2004)

3. Cootes, T., Edwards, G., Taylo, C.: Active appearance models. IEEE Trans. PAMI **23** (2001)
4. Cootes, T., Kittipanya-ngam, P.: Comparing variations on the active appearance model algorithm. (In: British Machine Vision Conference)
5. Stegmann, M., Ersboll, B., Larsen, R.: Fame-a flexible appearance modeling environment. IEEE Trans. Medical Imaging **22** (2003)
6. Mittrapiyanumic, P., DeSouza, G., Kak, A.: Calculating the 3d-pose of rigid-objects using active appearance models. In: Proceedings of the International Conference in Robotics and Automation. Volume 5. (2004) 5147–5152
7. Ahlberg, J.: Using the active appearance algorithm for face and facial feature tracking. In: Recognition, Analysis, and Tracking of Faces and Gestures in Real-Time Systems, 2001. Proceedings. IEEE ICCV Workshop on. (2001) 68–72
8. Xiao, J., Baker, S., Matthews, I., Kanade, T.: Real-time combined 2d+3d active appearance models. In: IEEE CVPR'2004. Volume 2. (2004) 535–542
9. Blanz, V., Vetter, T.: Face recognition based on fitting a 3d morphable model. IEEE Trans. PAMI **25** (2003)
10. Hou, X., S.Z., L., Zhang, H., Cheng, Q.: Direct appearance models. In: IEEE CVPR'2001. Volume 1. (2001) 828–833
11. C.Bregler, A.Hertzmann, H.Biermann: Recovering non-rigid 3d shape from image streams. In: IEEE CVPR'2000. Volume 2. (2000) 690–696
12. Torresani, L., Yang, D., Alexander, E., Bregler, C.: Tracking and modeling non-rigid objects with rank constraints. In: IEEE CVPR'01. Volume 1. (2001) 493–500
13. Medioni, G., Kang, S.B.: Emerging topics in computer vision. Prentice Hall (2004)
14. Nielson, G.: Scattered data modeling. IEEE Computer Graphics and Applications **13** (1993)
15. Gross, R., Matthews, I., Baker, S.: Generic vs. person specific active appearance models. In: British Machine Vision Conference. (2004)

A Fluid Motion Estimator for Schlieren Image Velocimetry

Elise Arnaud[1], Etienne Mémin[2], Roberto Sosa[3], and Guillermo Artana[3]

[1] Disi, Università di Genova, 16146 Genova, Italy
arnaud@disi.unige.it
[2] IRISA, Université de Rennes 1, 35 042 Rennes Cedex, France
memin@irisa.fr
[3] Facultad de Ingeniería, Universitad de Buenos Aires
Buenos Aires 1412, Argentina
{rsosa, gartana}@fi.uba.ar

Abstract. In this paper, we address the problem of estimating the motion of fluid flows that are visualized through a Schlieren system. Such a system is well known in fluid mechanics as it enables the visualization of unseeded flows. As the resulting images exhibit very low photometric contrasts, classical motion estimation methods based on the brightness consistency assumption (correlation-based approaches, optical flow methods) are completely inefficient. This work aims at proposing a sound energy based estimator dedicated to these particular images. The energy function to be minimized is composed of (a) a novel data term describing the fact that the observed luminance is linked to the gradient of the fluid density and (b) a specific div curl regularization term. The relevance of our estimator is demonstrated on real-world sequences.

1 Introduction

The ability to understand the complexities of fluid flow behavior has large implications in our daily lives and safety as their control and understanding is of the greatest importance in different applications ranging from aero or hydrodynamic studies (air conditioning, aircraft design, etc.) to environmental sciences (weather forecasting, climate predictions, flood disasters monitoring, etc.).

Flow visualization has been a powerful tool to depict flow features. Efforts to develop high-quality flow visualization techniques date back over a century. The analysis of the recorded images consisted firstly to a qualitative interpretation of the streak lines, leading overall global insight into the flow properties but lacking quantitative details on important parameters such as velocity fields or turbulence intensities. Point measurement tools such as hot wire probes or Laser Doppler Velocimetry have typically provided these details. As these probes give information only at the point where they are placed, simultaneous evaluations at different points require to dispose a very large number of probes and the evaluation of unsteady field (most of the flows are unsteady) is almost unachievable.

A. Leonardis, H. Bischof, and A. Pinz (Eds.): ECCV 2006, Part I, LNCS 3951, pp. 198–210, 2006.
© Springer-Verlag Berlin Heidelberg 2006

In an effort to avoid the limitations of these probes, the Particle Image Velocimetry (PIV), a non-intrusive diagnostic technique, has been developed in the last two decades. PIV enables obtaining velocity fields by seeding the flow with particles (e.g. dye, smoke, particles) and observing the motion of these tracers. An underlying assumption of PIV technique is that the motion of these particles follows the motion of the neighboring fluid. This condition is not always satisfied and requires to seed the flow with small sized tracers leading to an increase of the measurement difficulties. Moreover, some phenomena such as natural convection may be influenced by the large amount of seeding particles and the seeding may in return alter results. The setting up of the experiment, adjustment of the seeding concentration and other experimental procedures are in general tedious tasks in many large scale facilities. As a consequence this technique is mainly adapted for test in small closed loops wind tunnels.

Given the various complexities associated to the use of PIV, it is important to examine techniques that can be used to generate quantitative measurements of unseeded flows. The techniques that provide useful visualization images and, at the same time, yields high-quality quantitative data about the flow are of particular interest. In general, Shadowgraph, Schlieren and Interferometry fall into this category. These three techniques do not require flow seeding since they are based on index-of-refraction effects. One of the attractive capabilities of the Schlieren technique is that it can be implemented to undertake full scale measurements and outdoor experiments [1, 2].

The objective of this work is to analyze the ability of a dense motion estimator to extract velocity fields from Schlieren images of fluid flows. To date no satisfying technique exists to perform accurately such velocity measurements. The dense motion estimator we propose here relies on a data model specifically designed for such images. The devised data model has been elaborated on physical grounds. In addition to this constraint, we have also considered a div-curl smoothing function allowing the preservation of curl blobs.

2   Description of the Schlieren Technique

The Schlieren technique [3, 4] is an optical method used for fluid flow visualization. Contrary to standard visualization approaches, where a tracer (e.g. solid particle) is followed along the fluid motion or laser-Doppler systems, in which the frequency shift of scattered illumination from such a marker is measured, the Schlieren technique does not require any intrusion in the fluid and prevents any modifications of the considered flow. Such a technique is used to study density fields in transparent media, usually gases or liquids. A typical Schlieren system is described in figure 1. It is based on the fact that a light beam traveling initially in the z direction passing through a medium whose index of refraction varies in x and y direction undergoes a small deviation. For sake of simplicity, the figure 1 presents this phenomenon only in the yz plane. In that case, the light beam has been deviated by an angle α. The Schlieren system is basically a device to observe the angle α as a function of position in the xy plane (respectively

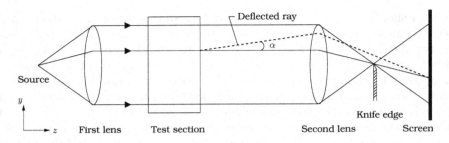

Fig. 1. Typical Schlieren system using lenses - figure from [3]

the angle in the xz plane). As the light beam deviation depends on the flow density variations, it can be demonstrated that the light pattern obtained with a Schlieren system is determined by the first derivative of the index of refraction such as [3]:

$$\mathbf{I(s)} = K \int \left(\frac{\partial \rho(x,y,z)}{\partial x} + \frac{\partial \rho(x,y,z)}{\partial y} \right) \, dz, \qquad (1)$$

where $\mathbf{I(s)}$ is the luminance value of pixel $\mathbf{s} = (x,y)$ and $\rho(x,y,z)$ denotes the density of the observed fluid at the physical point of 3d coordinates (x,y,z). The constant K depends on the focal f of the second lens, on the Gladstone-Dale constant C and on a_k, the size of the beam cut off by the knife-edge:

$$K = C \, \frac{f}{a_k}. \qquad (2)$$

As described by the equation (1), the Schlieren visualization integrates the quantity measured over the length of the light beam. As a consequence, this technique is well suited to the study of almost-2d fields, where no density variation is present in the test section. In that case, the light pattern can be expressed as:

$$\mathbf{I(s)} = K \, \Delta z \, \left(\frac{\partial \rho(x,y,z)}{\partial x} + \frac{\partial \rho(x,y,z)}{\partial y} \right), \qquad (3)$$

where Δz is the width of the region where the light beam is deflected (supposed small).

Since the Schlieren technique is non intrusive and does not require any seeding of particles, this visualization procedure enables studies either for laboratory tests or for full scale models in industrial applications. To illustrate this visualization technique, a sample of images are displayed in figure 2. In particular, figure 2(c) represents a typical image provided by Schlieren systems. Such systems are widely used in experimental fluid mechanics laboratories but to date no satisfying solution exists to analyze image sequences of this nature. Indeed, due to the absence of contrast, no image technique allowing a reliable quantitative evaluation of the visualized fluid flow motion is available. To the best of our knowledge, very few works [5, 6] have been carried out to estimate velocity fields from Schlieren images. All these works rely on correlation methods [4].

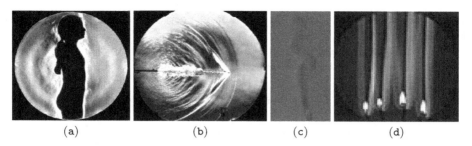

| (a) | (b) | (c) | (d) |

Fig. 2. Example of images obtained from a Schlieren system: (**a**) human thermal plume (image from [4]); (**b**) instantaneous image of bullet and blast (image from [4]); air flow; visualized flames with a color Schlieren system (here displayed in black and white)

These methods suffer from several limitations. Among them, one can cite the fact that the results are sensitive to the size of the correlation window support and the possible lack of spatial coherence of the resulting displacement field. We believe that the use of dense motion estimation using optical flow is an interesting alternative that has not been investigated for the Schlieren imagery. These methods, formalized as the minimization of an energy function, have been already successfully implemented for general fluid flow imagery. We have adapted one of these methods to the Schlieren technique. Nevertheless, before describing the proposed dedicated Schlieren energy function, a brief overview of classical dense motion estimator is given in the next section.

3   Related Works on Dense Motion Estimation

3.1   Standard Optical Flow Estimation

Dense estimation of the apparent motion aims at recovering a 2d displacement field $\mathbf{w}$ defined over the continuous plane domain S. The estimation is based on the knowledge of the luminance function at two consecutive instants denoted $\mathbf{I}(\mathbf{s}, t)$, $\mathbf{s} \in S$.

The most accurate techniques to address this problem are related to the Horn and Schunck (H&S) optical flow estimator [7, 8, 9, 10, 11]. Such estimators are formalized as the minimizer of an energy function H composed of a *data term* H_1 and a *regularization term* H_2. The first one describes a consistency assumption of the luminance function along a point trajectory. The standard brightness consistency assumption $\frac{d\mathbf{I}}{dt} = 0$ leads to consider the well-know optical flow constraint (OFC):

$$H_1(\mathbf{w}) = \int_S \phi_1 \left[\nabla \mathbf{I}(\mathbf{s}, t) \, . \, \mathbf{w}(\mathbf{s}) + \frac{\partial \mathbf{I}(\mathbf{s}, t)}{\partial t} \right] \, d\mathbf{s}, \tag{4}$$

where $\nabla \mathbf{I}$ accounts for the spatial gradient of the luminance function and $\mathbf{w}(\mathbf{s}) = (u(\mathbf{s}), v(\mathbf{s}))^T$ is the velocity at point $\mathbf{s}$. The penalty function ϕ_1 is often chosen as the L_2 norm but better results may be obtained using a robust function that attenuates the effects of areas that do not respect the brightness assumption [8, 9, 10].

The regularization term captures an *a priori* on the displacement field. A standard first-order spatial smoothness is usually considered:

$$H_2(\mathbf{w}) = \alpha \int_S \phi_2 \left[\|\nabla \mathbf{w}(\mathbf{s})\| \right] \, d\mathbf{s}, \tag{5}$$

where $\|\nabla \mathbf{w}(\mathbf{s})\| = \|\nabla \mathbf{u}(\mathbf{s})\| + \|\nabla \mathbf{v}(\mathbf{s})\|$ with an abuse of notation. Like ϕ_1, the penalty function ϕ_2 authorizes handling local deviations from the smoothness model. The parameter α balances the relative influence of both terms in the functional.

Facing large frame-to-frame displacements, the data term H_1 is not anymore relevant due to its differential nature. To tackle this problem, the brightness consistency assumption has to be expressed in an integrated way, according to the *displacement* $\mathbf{d}(\mathbf{s})$ from time t to $t + \Delta t$ instead of the *velocity* $\mathbf{w}(\mathbf{s})$. As we have:

$$\frac{d\mathbf{I}}{dt} = \lim_{\Delta t \to 0} \frac{\mathbf{I}(\mathbf{s} + \mathbf{d}(\mathbf{s}), t + \Delta t) - \mathbf{I}(\mathbf{s}, t)}{\Delta t} \quad \text{with} \quad \mathbf{d}(\mathbf{s}) = \mathbf{w}(\mathbf{s}) \, \Delta t, \tag{6}$$

by relaxing the constraint on the limit, the integrated version may be readily written as:

$$\mathbf{I}(\mathbf{s} + \mathbf{d}(\mathbf{s}), t + \Delta t) - \mathbf{I}(\mathbf{s}, t) = 0. \tag{7}$$

To circumvent the high nonlinearity of this form with respect to the displacement field, the solution consists in proceeding to successive linearizations around an increment field $d\mathbf{w}$. This is usually performed within a multiresolution scheme. A first-order linearization of the first term of (7) yields to the following new energy function (where the time increment Δt has been set to 1 for simplicity):

$$\mathcal{H}(d\mathbf{w}) = \int_S \phi_1 \left[\nabla \mathbf{I}(\mathbf{s} + \mathbf{w}(\mathbf{s}), t + 1) \cdot d\mathbf{w}(\mathbf{s}) + \mathbf{I}(\mathbf{s} + \mathbf{w}(\mathbf{s}), t + 1) - \mathbf{I}(\mathbf{s}, t) \right] \\ + \alpha \, \phi_2 \left[\|\nabla(\mathbf{w}(\mathbf{s}) + d\mathbf{w}(\mathbf{s}))\| \right] \, d\mathbf{s}. \tag{8}$$

For an interested reader, a state of the art of such techniques as well as their comparison can be found in [12, 13].

3.2 Dense Motion Analysis in Fluid Imagery

As detailed in [14], although estimators based on the energy function (8) have been used for the velocity estimation of fluid structures, the two main assumptions involved in this function are not well suited to that specific case.

First, the brightness consistency assumption involved in the data term is rarely valid for sequences of fluid flows. As a matter of fact, the observed luminance of a fluid structure may exhibits high spatio-temporal variations caused by temperature and pressure variations or due to its inherent deformable nature. The use of the fluid law of mass conservation (also called the *continuity equation*) as an alternative assumption applied to the evolution of the luminance function has originally been proposed in [15]. Denoting $\mathbf{v} = (u, v, w)$ the 3d velocity, the continuity equation reads:

$$\frac{\partial \rho}{\partial t} + \operatorname{div}(\rho \, \mathbf{v}) = 0, \tag{9}$$

where $\operatorname{div}(\mathbf{v}) = \frac{\partial u}{\partial x} + \frac{\partial v}{\partial y} + \frac{\partial w}{\partial z}$ denotes the divergence of the 3d velocity. Making a direct analogy between the density of a fluid particle and its luminance, this law has been integrated in some optical flow schemes [14, 16, 17]. Nevertheless, let us remark that apart from transmittance images [18], the use of the continuity equation remains an approximate constraint when applied to the image brightness. For Schlieren imagery we will show that an exact brightness variation model can be devised. This model will be detailed in the next section.

Secondly, concerning the regularization term, it can be demonstrated that a first order regularization is not adapted to fluid phenomena as it favors the estimation of velocity fields with low divergence and vorticity. A second order regularization can advantageously be consider as proposed in [19]:

$$H_2(\mathbf{w}) = \alpha \int_S \left[\|\nabla \operatorname{div}(\mathbf{w}(\mathbf{s}))\|^2 + \|\nabla \operatorname{curl}(\mathbf{w}(\mathbf{s}))\|^2 \right] \, d\mathbf{s}, \tag{10}$$

where $\operatorname{div}(\mathbf{w}) = \frac{\partial u}{\partial x} + \frac{\partial v}{\partial y}$ and $\operatorname{curl}(\mathbf{w}) = -\frac{\partial u}{\partial y} + \frac{\partial v}{\partial x}$ are respectively the divergence and the vorticity of the 2d field $\mathbf{w} = (u, v)$. To circumvent the difficulty of implementing second order smoothness constraint, this regularization term can be simplified - in a computational point of view – in two interleaved first-order div-curl regularizations based on two auxiliary variables ξ_1 and ξ_2 approximating the divergence and the vorticity of the flow [14]. Introducing the use of a robust penalty function instead of the quadratic function, we have:

$$\begin{aligned} H_2(\mathbf{w}, \xi_1, \xi_2) = \alpha \int_S \big[\quad & (\operatorname{div}(\mathbf{w}(\mathbf{s})) - \xi_1)^2 + \beta \, \phi_2[\|\nabla \xi_1\|] \\ + \, & (\operatorname{curl}(\mathbf{w}(\mathbf{s})) - \xi_2)^2 + \beta \, \phi_2[\|\nabla \xi_2\|] \, \big] \, d\mathbf{s}, \end{aligned} \tag{11}$$

where β is a positive regularization parameter.

4   Dense Estimator Dedicated to Schlieren Images

4.1   Data Term

To construct a relevant dense motion estimator for Schlieren image sequences, it is essential to take into account the physical properties of this fluid visualization method. In particular, as previously described, the light pattern at time t is deduced from the density of the fluid (eq. (3)). In case of an almost 2d flow, introducing the time variable, we have:

$$\mathbf{I}(\mathbf{s}, t) = K\Delta z \left(\frac{\partial \rho(x, y, z, t)}{\partial x} + \frac{\partial \rho(x, y, z, t)}{\partial y} \right). \tag{12}$$

From that expression, we can deduce:

$$\frac{d\mathbf{I}}{dt} = K \ \Delta z \ \underbrace{\left[\frac{\partial}{\partial x} \left(\frac{d\rho}{dt} \right) + \frac{\partial}{\partial y} \left(\frac{d\rho}{dt} \right) \right.}_{A} \underbrace{\left. - \nabla\rho.\frac{\partial \mathbf{v}}{\partial x} - \nabla\rho.\frac{\partial \mathbf{v}}{\partial y} \right]}_{B} \qquad (13)$$

where $\mathbf{v} = (u, v, w)$ is the 3D velocity. This expression can be modified relying on the continuity equation (9) which can be alternatively rewritten after simple manipulations as:

$$\frac{d\rho}{dt} + \rho \ \mathrm{div}(\mathbf{v}) = 0. \qquad (14)$$

This expression can be advantageously used in the first term A of equation (13). Using expression (12) we have:

$$A = - \ \rho \ \left(\frac{\partial \ \mathrm{div}(\mathbf{v})}{\partial x} + \frac{\partial \ \mathrm{div}(\mathbf{v})}{\partial y} \right) - \mathrm{div}(\mathbf{v}) \left(\frac{\partial \rho}{\partial x} + \frac{\partial \rho}{\partial y} \right) \qquad (15)$$

$$= - \ \rho \ \left(\frac{\partial \ \mathrm{div}(\mathbf{v})}{\partial x} + \frac{\partial \ \mathrm{div}(\mathbf{v})}{\partial y} \right) - \frac{\mathbf{I}}{K \ \Delta z} \ \mathrm{div}(\mathbf{v}). \qquad (16)$$

In order to simplify the second term B, let us assume that the two first components of the spatial gradient of the density are of the same order, i.e. $\frac{\partial \rho}{\partial x} \approx \frac{\partial \rho}{\partial y}$ with no local favored direction. This assumption does not necessary cancel the possibility that a global preferential direction for the pressure gradients may exist. It may be erroneous to associate directly the flow direction, or the favored pressure gradient direction, as the direction of the local fluid density gradients. Many flows of interest behave as incompressible flows and in these kinds of flows it can be admitted that the pressure gradients that drive the fluid flow may produce only negligible changes in the fluid density. The density field results in general from a complex interaction of the different coupled fields: temperature, pressure, buoyancy forces and velocity. As it is difficult to determine *a priori* a principal direction for the density gradients, it seemed to us reasonable to admit as a first approach that no direction for density gradients is preferential. Using this assumption, expression (12), and the fact that we are interested in this work on the dense motion estimation of mainly bidimensional fluid flows (i.e. inducing $\frac{\partial \rho}{\partial z} = 0$), we have:

$$B = - \frac{\mathbf{I}}{2 \ K \ \Delta z} \left(\frac{\partial u}{\partial x} + \frac{\partial v}{\partial x} + \frac{\partial u}{\partial y} + \frac{\partial v}{\partial y} \right). \qquad (17)$$

As a 2D fluid flow is considered, we can also suppose that the apparent 2D velocity is defined by the two first components of the 3D velocity i.e. $\mathbf{w} = (u, v)$. From that hypothesis, we can deduce that $\mathrm{div}(\mathbf{v}) = \mathrm{div}(\mathbf{w})$. Then:

$$A = - \ \rho \ \left(\frac{\partial \ \mathrm{div}(\mathbf{w})}{\partial x} + \frac{\partial \ \mathrm{div}(\mathbf{w})}{\partial y} \right) - \frac{\mathbf{I}}{K \ \Delta z} \ \mathrm{div}(\mathbf{w}) \qquad (18)$$

and

$$B = - \frac{\mathbf{I}}{2 \ K \ \Delta z} \left(\mathrm{div}(\mathbf{w}) + \frac{\partial v}{\partial x} + \frac{\partial u}{\partial y} \right). \qquad (19)$$

The evolution in time of the luminance is then governed by the expression:

$$\frac{d\mathbf{I}}{dt} = -\frac{3}{2}\,\mathbf{I}\,\mathrm{div}(\mathbf{w}) - \frac{1}{2}\,\mathbf{I}\,\left(\frac{\partial v}{\partial x} + \frac{\partial u}{\partial y}\right) - \rho\,K\,\varDelta z\,\left(\frac{\partial\,\mathrm{div}(\mathbf{w})}{\partial x} + \frac{\partial\,\mathrm{div}(\mathbf{w})}{\partial y}\right).$$
(20)

Finally, as for most flows studied through a Schlieren system, it can be demonstrated that $\mathrm{div}(\mathbf{v}) = 0$, i.e. $\mathrm{div}(\mathbf{w}) = 0$, the resulting equation reads:

$$\frac{d\mathbf{I}}{dt} + \frac{1}{2}\,\mathbf{I}\,\left(\frac{\partial v}{\partial x} + \frac{\partial u}{\partial y}\right) = 0.$$
(21)

In a similar manner as the standard optical flow estimation (§ 3.1), the expression (21) is not relevant for the estimation of large frame-to-frame displacements. An integrated version of this constraint has to be considered. Assuming that the velocity is constant between two instants t and $t+\varDelta t$, equation (21) is a first order differential equation at constant coefficient (equation of type $y'(t) - m\,y(t) = p$). Choosing $\mathbf{I}(\mathbf{s}, t)$ as the initial condition, and setting the time interval $\varDelta t$ to 1, the integrated for of the data model reads:

$$\mathbf{I}(\mathbf{s} + \mathbf{w}(\mathbf{s}), t + 1)\,\exp\left(\frac{1}{2}\frac{\partial\,v(\mathbf{s})}{\partial x} + \frac{1}{2}\frac{\partial\,u(\mathbf{s})}{\partial y}\right) - \mathbf{I}(\mathbf{s}, t) = 0.$$
(22)

To cope with the non linearity of this constraint regarding to the displacement field, a coarse to fine strategy has to be settled. A first-order linearization of the left term in eq. (22) is considered with respect to an increment field $d\mathbf{w}$. Removing the time index for sake of clarity and introducing the following notations $\mathbf{I}(.) = \mathbf{I}(., t)$; $\widetilde{\mathbf{I}}(.) = \mathbf{I}(., t+1)$, the Schlieren data term can be finally written as:

$$\mathcal{H}_1(d\mathbf{w}) = \int_S \phi_1\left[-\mathbf{I}(\mathbf{s}) + \exp(g(\mathbf{w}(\mathbf{s}))\left(\widetilde{\mathbf{I}}(\mathbf{s} + \mathbf{w}(\mathbf{s}))\right.\right.$$
$$\left.\left. + (\nabla\widetilde{\mathbf{I}}(\mathbf{s} + \mathbf{w}(\mathbf{s})) + \nabla g(\mathbf{w}(\mathbf{s}))\,\widetilde{\mathbf{I}}(\mathbf{s} + \mathbf{w}(\mathbf{s}))) \,.\, d\mathbf{w}(\mathbf{s}))\right)\right]\,d\mathbf{s},$$
(23)

where $g(\mathbf{w}(\mathbf{s})) = \frac{1}{2}\left(\frac{\partial\,v(\mathbf{s})}{\partial x} + \frac{\partial\,u(\mathbf{s})}{\partial y}\right)$.

4.2   Regularization Term

As for the regularization term, a second-order div-curl regularizer is considered as it enables the preservation of the fluid structures. To deal with the computational difficulties of second order smoothness functional implementation, the approach proposed in [14] is followed. This leads to a regularization term already described by equation (11). Writing this expression in terms of a function of a velocity field increment to be minimized, we have:

$$\mathcal{H}_2(d\mathbf{w}, \xi_1, \xi_2) = \alpha\int_S\left[\;(\mathrm{div}(\mathbf{w}(\mathbf{s}) + d\mathbf{w}(\mathbf{s})) - \xi_1)^2 + \beta\,\phi_2[\|\nabla\xi_1\|]\right.$$
$$\left. + (\mathrm{curl}(\mathbf{w}(\mathbf{s}) + d\mathbf{w}(\mathbf{s})) - \xi_2)^2 + \lambda\,\phi_2[\|\nabla\xi_2\|]\;\right]\,d\mathbf{s}.$$
(24)

This formulation has the very interesting property of allowing the introduction of an *a priori* information on the divergence and/or vorticity map. In particular, we have seen in the previous paragraph that in the studied experimental images, the divergence of the flow can be considered as null. Such a constraint has to be taken into account in the regularization term also. To that purpose, the term $\mathcal{H}_2$ is modified to consider a constrained minimization implemented through a Lagrangian optimization technique. The new regularization reads:

$$\mathcal{H}_2(d\mathbf{w}, \xi, \lambda) = \alpha \int_S \Big[\ (\text{curl}(\mathbf{w}(\mathbf{s}) + d\mathbf{w}(\mathbf{s})) - \xi)^2 + \beta \ \phi_2[\|\nabla\xi\|]$$
$$+ \ \lambda \ (\text{div}(\mathbf{w}(\mathbf{s}) + d\mathbf{w}(\mathbf{s})))^2 \ \Big] \ d\mathbf{s}, \tag{25}$$

where λ denotes the Lagrangian multiplier associated to the constraint $\text{div}(\mathbf{w}(\mathbf{s}) + d\mathbf{w}(\mathbf{s})) = 0$.

4.3   Minimization Issues

The incremental estimation of the dense displacement field is conducted through a multiresolution structure that consists in implementing an incremental estimation scheme on a pyramidal hierarchical representation of the image data. At a given resolution level, an incremental displacement field is computed considering that the main component of the displacement is known (supposed null at the coarsest level) and refined by solving:

$$\min_{d\mathbf{w}, \xi, \lambda} \mathcal{H}_1(d\mathbf{w}) + \mathcal{H}_2(d\mathbf{w}, \xi, \lambda) \tag{26}$$

where $\mathcal{H}_1$ and $\mathcal{H}_2$ are defined by equations (23,25). The minimization of the functional is considered through a direct discretization of $\mathcal{H}_1$ and $\mathcal{H}_2$. The different functions involved in the functional are discretized on the image lattice. A particular attention has been paid for the discretization of divergence and curl operator for which an uncentered discretization scheme has been used.

   The overall system is constituted by two main sets of variables that have to be estimated. The first one is the motion field $\mathbf{w}$, and the second set comprises the scalar field ξ. The estimation is conducted alternatively by minimizing $\mathcal{H}_1 + \mathcal{H}_2$ with respect to $d\mathbf{w}$, λ and ξ respectively. For the motion field, considering the curl estimate ξ as being fixed, the robust minimization with respect to $d\mathbf{w}$ is solved with an iteratively re-weighted least squares technique. This optimization is embedded in an efficient multi-parametric adaptive multigrid framework [10]. In turn, the motion field $d\mathbf{w}$ being fixed, the minimization of the cost function with respect to ξ is in fact equivalent to the minimization of $\mathcal{H}_2$ and is again conducted using an iteratively re-weighted least squares technique.

5   Experimental Results

In this section, experimental results are presented to highlight the relevance of our estimator. Two image sequences are studied. They both have been obtained

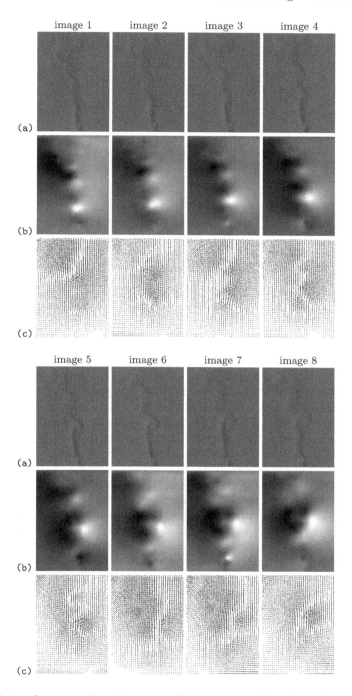

Fig. 3. Natural convection. Sequence of (a) images, (b) estimated vorticity maps and (c) estimated displacement fields.

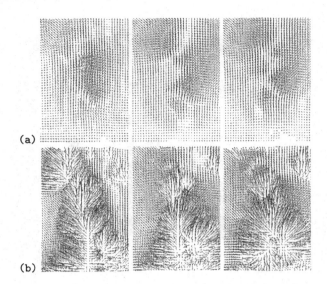

Fig. 4. Natural convection. Comparison between the estimated displacement fields obtained on images 2,3,4 with (a) our estimator and (b) the fluid dedicated estimator of Corpetti et al. [14].

in a laboratory of fluid mechanics [1]. The first experiment corresponds to a natural convection of a cylinder test in air at rest and the second one corresponds to a forced convection test of a heated cylinder immersed in a free airstream at room temperature. As it can be noticed on figures 3, 5, the obtained images are very difficult to analyze due to low brightness contrasts. It clearly appears that generic methods based on the brightness consistency assumption (correlation approaches, H&S methods) are hardly suited to these images.

The images obtained from the first experiment are shown on fig. 3, as well as the sequence of motion fields and vorticity maps obtained by a dense optical-flow estimator [14]. The difficulties of this sequence lie in the lack of luminance variations and in the large frame-to-frame displacements of the fluid structures. As it can be noticed on the vorticity maps, the emergence of a vortex has been well captured by our estimator, as well as the smaller structures. This result proves the validity of the Schlieren dedicated data term. The impact of the new regularization term (that forces the estimation of a flow with null divergence) is demonstrated on fig. 4. This figure presents a comparison between our method and an optical-flow estimator proposed in [14]. As it can be noticed on the

---

[1] The images have been obtained with a Schlieren system disposed in a Z configuration. It comprised two spherical mirrors of 35 cm in diameter and the light was cut off with two razor blades disposed in vertical and horizontal positions, thus density gradients in both directions could be detected. The parallel light rays traversed the test section of a low speed wind tunnel with windows in the test section of optical quality to avoid improper light deflections. The images were recorded on a monochromatic digital image camera of 12 bits that enabled fast frame acquisition.

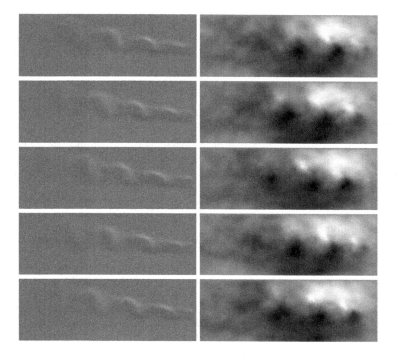

Fig. 5. Forced convection. Images 1, 5, 10, 15, 20 and associated estimated vorticity maps.

presented displacement fields, this latter generates a motion field with areas of high divergence that are not physically plausible.

The results obtained on the second experiment are shown on fig. 5. These results are displayed in terms of vorticity maps. These pictures show that the moving vertical structures of the fluid flows have been well recovered. We can see in particular the coherent displacement of the lower vortex and the vanishing due to dissipation of the upper vortices. The curl maps also highlight the temporal consistency of the recovered motion fields.

6   Conclusion

In this paper, we have presented a new method for the estimation of dense fluid motion fields dedicated to images obtained with a Schlieren system. The analysis of the Schlieren images is of great importance in the field of fluid mechanics since this system enables the visualization of unseeded flows. The proposed method is a minimization-based approach where the two terms involved in the cost function have been designed for these images. In particular, the data term has been deduced from the physical relation between the luminance function and the fluid density gradient. The very promising results have demonstrated the interest of using such an approach for the Schlieren image analysis. The following planned step is to validate our approach considering synthetic images produced by a Direct Numerical Simulation code. From this work, several perspectives can be investigated such as the study of 3D flows (using for example the Schlieren tomography [20]), and the design of dedicated algorithms to track the fluid structures.

References

1. Settles, G.S., Hackett, E.B., Miller, J.D., Weinstein, L.M.: Full-scale schlieren flow visualization. In: Flow Visualization VII. (1995) 2–13
2. Settles, G.S.: The penn state full-scale schlieren system. In: Int. Symp. on Flow Visualization. (2004)
3. Goldstein, R.J., Kuehn, T.H.: Optical systems for flow measurement: Shadowgraph, schlieren, and interferometric techniques. In: Fluid Mechanics Measurement. Taylor and Francis (1996) 451–508
4. Settles, G.S.: Schlieren and shadowgraph techniques: visualizing phenomena in transparent media. Springer-Verlag (2001)
5. Fu, S., Wu, Y., Kothari, R., Xing, H.: Flow visualization using thye negative-positive grid schlieren and its image analysis. In: Int. Symp. on Flow Visualization. (2000)
6. Kegerise, M.A., Settles, G.S.: Schlieren image-correlation velocimetry and its application to free-convection flows. In: Int. Symp. on Flow Visualization. (2000)
7. Horn, B., Schunck, B.: Determining optical flow. Artificial Intelligence **17** (1981) 185–203
8. Black, M., Anandan, P.: The robust estimation of multiple motions: Parametric and piecewise-smooth flow fields. CVIU **63** (1996) 75–104
9. Brox, T., Bruhn, A., Papenberg, N., Weickert, J.: High accuracy optical flow estimation based on a theory for warping. In: ECCV. (2004) 25–36
10. Mémin, E., Pérez, P.: Hierarchical estimation and segmentation of dense motion fields. IJCV **46** (2002) 129–155
11. Ruhnau, P., Kohlberger, T., Nobach, H., Schnörr, C.: Variational optical flow estimation for particle image velocimetry. In B. Ruck, A.L., Dopheide, eds.: Proc. Lasermethoden in der Strömungsmesstechnik. Karlsruhe (2004)
12. Barron, J., Fleet, D., Beauchemin, S.: Performance of optical flow techniques. IJCV **12** (1994) 43–77
13. Beauchemin, S., Barron, J.: The computation of optical flow. ACM Computing Survey **27** (1995) 433–467
14. Corpetti, T., Mémin, E., Pérez, P.: Dense estimation of fluid flows. PAMI **24** (2002) 365–380
15. Schunk, B.: The motion constraint equation for optical flow. In: ICPR. (1984) 20–22
16. Béréziat, D., Herlin, H., Younes, L.: A generalized optical flow constraint and its physical interpretation. In: CVPR. Volume 2. (2000) 487–492
17. Kohlberger, T., Mémin, E., Schnörr, C.: Variational dense motion estimation using the Helmholtz decomposition. In: Scale-Space. (2003)
18. Fitzpatrick, J.: The existence of geometrical density-image transformations corresponding to object motions. CVGIP **44** (1988) 155–174
19. Suter, D.: Motion estimation and vector splines. In: CVPR. (1994) 939–942
20. Agrawal, A., Butuk, N., Gollahalli, S., Griffin, D.: Three-dimensional rainbow schlieren tomography of a temperature field en gas flows. Applied Optics (1998)

Bilateral Filtering-Based Optical Flow Estimation with Occlusion Detection

Jiangjian Xiao, Hui Cheng, Harpreet Sawhney,
Cen Rao, and Michael Isnardi

Sarnoff Corporation
{jxiao, hcheng, hsawhney, crao, misnardi}@sarnoff.com

Abstract. Using the variational approaches to estimate optical flow between two frames, the flow discontinuities between different motion fields are usually not distinguished even when an anisotropic diffusion operator is applied. In this paper, we propose a multi-cue driven adaptive bilateral filter to regularize the flow computation, which is able to achieve the smoothly varied optical flow field with highly desirable motion discontinuities. First, we separate the traditional one-step variational updating model into a two-step filtering-based updating model. Then, employing our occlusion detector, we reformulate the energy functional of optical flow estimation by explicitly introducing an occlusion term to balance the energy loss due to the occlusion or mismatches. Furthermore, based on the two-step updating framework, a novel multi-cue driven bilateral filter is proposed to substitute the original anisotropic diffusion process, and it is able to adaptively control the diffusion process according to the occlusion detection, image intensity dissimilarity, and motion dissimilarity. After applying our approach on various video sources (movie and TV) in the presence of occlusion, motion blurring, non-rigid deformation, and weak textureness, we generate a spatial-coherent flow field between each pair of input frames and detect more accurate flow discontinuities along the motion boundaries.

1 Introduction

Optical flow estimation has been investigated by computer vision researchers for a long time [10, 12, 19, 3, 4, 11, 1, 6]. Given two input images, how to compute accurate optical flow is still challenging problem in computer vision especially when the images have severe occlusion and non-rigid motion. The basic idea of optical flow computation is maintaining the brightness constancy assumption, which relates the image gradient, ∇I, to the components u and v of the local optical flow. Since this is an ill-posed problem, some additional constraints are required to regularize the motion field during the flow estimation. From the well-known aperture phenomenon, a larger region of integration is more preferable to produce stable motion estimation but it may be more likely contain multiple motions in this region and cannot handle non-rigid deformation very well [4]. Therefore, the fundamental problem of optical flow estimation is still how to design an effective anisotropic smoothness regularizer, such that it not only maintains variable spatial coherence inside each piecewise-smooth region but also keeps accurate flow discontinuities at the motion boundaries.

A. Leonardis, H. Bischof, and A. Pinz (Eds.): ECCV 2006, Part I, LNCS 3951, pp. 211–224, 2006.

Currently, the most popular regularizers of optical flow estimation are the variational-based isotropic and/or anisotropic smoothness operators [10, 8, 2, 1, 6]. However, these techniques have two drawbacks. First, when the input images in the presence of occlusion, these methods cannot correctly handle the flow estimation for the occluded region, and the flow at those occluded regions appears over-smoothing or randomly dragging. Second, if the input images have large homogeneous colored regions, these methods will fail to produce correct flow vector inside those regions due to the poor texture and image gradient field. To overcome these two problems, some researchers propose parametric model or motion segmentation to break the optical flow field into several piecewise-smooth parts [4, 9, 13, 21, 20]. Unfortunately, due to the inherent limitation of the parametric model, these approaches cannot correctly handle the non-rigid scene, where the objects may have irregular deformation.

Aiming to solve those pre-mentioned problems, this paper combines the occlusion detection and an adaptive bilateral filter into a two-step updating variational framework to estimate a high-quality optical flow field between two input frames. In our approach, first we design an occlusion detector to identify the occluded areas, which effectively breaks the spatial coherence over the motion boundaries and makes it possible to produce accurate flow discontinuities. Then, based on this occlusion detector, a novel variational model is proposed where the occlusion detection and occlusion penalty are integrated into the model to explicitly handle the occlusion problem. Third, at the second updating step of the variational model, we substitute the traditional anisotropic filter by our multi-cue driven bilateral filter to deal with the incorrect (or missing) flow estimation of those occlusion regions. As a result, our approach effectively preserve motion discontinuities between the different motion fields and generate smoothly varying motion flow inside each piece of rigid or non-rigid motion field. Furthermore, in this paper we also illustrate the flexibility of integrating more constraints, such as the flow symmetric property, into our framework to compute more accurate optical flow.

The remainder of this paper is organized as follows. Section 2 discusses the existing variational model of optical flow computation and also illustrates how to convert the model into a two-step iteration with a convolution-based diffusion. Based on the new iteration model, Section 3 presents a novel optical flow framework integrated with the explicit occlusion term and a multi-cue driven bilateral filter. In Section 4, we demonstrate several results on various video sources in the presence of occlusion, motion blurring, non-rigid deformation, and weak texture conditions.

2   The Two-Step Variational Updating Model

According to the brightness constancy assumption, given two input images I_1 and I_2, the image brightness of a pixel at $\mathbf{x} = [x \ y]^T$ in I_1 should not be changed by the motion vector $\mathbf{u} = [u \ v]^T$, such that $I_1(\mathbf{x}) = I_2(\mathbf{x} + \mathbf{u})$ [10]. One direct solution of optical flow estimation is to minimize the following quadratic data energy functional over the image domain Ω, such that $E_d(\mathbf{u}) = \int_\Omega \left(I_1(\mathbf{x}) - I_2(\mathbf{x} + \mathbf{u}) \right)^2 d\mathbf{x}$. Since this data energy is differentiable, it can be approximated by the first order Taylor expansion

$$E_d(\mathbf{u}) = \int_\Omega \left(\nabla I^T \mathbf{u} + I_t\right)^2 d\mathbf{x}, \tag{1}$$

where ∇I is the average gradient of images I_1 and I_2, and I_t is the temporal derivative between I_1 and I_2. In order to avoid the aperture problem and suppress noise during optical flow estimation, a smoothness constraint should be added to regularize the optical flow gradient, $\nabla \mathbf{u}$. The most common smoothness term used in optical flow estimation is the edge-preserving anisotropic operator which can efficiently prevent flow to be smoothed over region boundaries [14, 15, 5, 1, 16]. Therefore, the new overall energy functional for optical flow minimization becomes

$$E(\mathbf{u}) = E_d(\mathbf{u}) + E_s(\nabla \mathbf{u}) = \int_\Omega \left(\left(\nabla I^T \mathbf{u} + I_t\right)^2 + \nabla \mathbf{u}^T D(\nabla I_1) \nabla \mathbf{u}\right) d\mathbf{x}$$
$$= \int_\Omega \left(e_d(\mathbf{u}) + e_s(\nabla \mathbf{u})\right) d\mathbf{x}, \tag{2}$$

where $e_d(\mathbf{u})$ is a data term corresponding to data energy $E_d(\mathbf{u})$, $e_s(\nabla \mathbf{u})$ is the smoothness term to smoothness energy $E_s(\nabla \mathbf{u})$, ∇I_1 is the image gradient of frame 1, and $D(\nabla I_1)$ is an anisotropic diffusion tensor defined by

$$D(\nabla I_1) = \frac{1}{\|\nabla I_1\|^2 + 2\nu^2}\left(\nabla I_1^\perp \nabla I_1^{\perp T} + \nu^2 \mathbf{1}\right), \tag{3}$$

where $\mathbf{1}$ is a 2×2 identity matrix, ν is a parameter to control the degree of isotropy smoothness, and $\nabla I_1^\perp$ is the vector perpendicular to ∇I_1. The diffusion tensor, $D(\nabla I_1)$, has two orthogonal eigenvectors: $\eta = \frac{\nabla I_1}{\|\nabla I_1\|}$ and $\xi = \eta^\perp = \frac{\nabla I_1^\perp}{\|\nabla I_1\|}$ with corresponding eigenvalues, λ_η and λ_ξ, as shown in Fig.1.

To obtain the minimal energy of Eq.2, we can apply Euler Lagrange equation to iteratively update the flow field $\mathbf{u}$ along the gradient descent direction, such that

$$\frac{\partial \mathbf{u}}{\partial \tau} = \mathbf{u}^\tau - \mathbf{u}^{\tau-1} = -\left(\frac{\partial e_d(\mathbf{u})}{\partial \mathbf{u}} - \operatorname{div}\left(\frac{\partial e_s(\nabla \mathbf{u})}{\partial \nabla \mathbf{u}}\right)\right)$$
$$= -\nabla I\left(\nabla I^T \mathbf{u} + I_t\right) + \operatorname{div}\left(D(\nabla I_1)\nabla \mathbf{u}\right), \tag{4}$$

where the optical flow $\mathbf{u}^\tau$ is the flow field at iteration step τ. From this equation, it is clear to see that since the data and smoothness terms are operating on different domains: $\mathbf{u}$ and $\nabla \mathbf{u}$, these two terms will keep separated after applying Euler Lagrange equation. Therefore, instead of updating $\mathbf{u}^\tau$ in one step, we divide the updating process into a two-step procedure, such that

$$\mathbf{u}^{\tau'} - \mathbf{u}^{\tau-1} = -\frac{\partial e_d(\mathbf{u})}{\partial \mathbf{u}} = -\nabla I\left(\nabla I^T \mathbf{u}^{\tau-1} + I_t\right), \tag{5}$$

$$\mathbf{u}^\tau - \mathbf{u}^{\tau'} = \operatorname{div}\left(\frac{\partial e_s(\nabla \mathbf{u})}{\partial \nabla \mathbf{u}}\right) = \operatorname{div}\left(D(\nabla I_1)\nabla \mathbf{u}^{\tau'}\right), \tag{6}$$

where the first step is updating the flow field to an intermediate result, $\mathbf{u}^{\tau'}$, by minimizing the data energy, and the second step is preforming an independent diffusion process

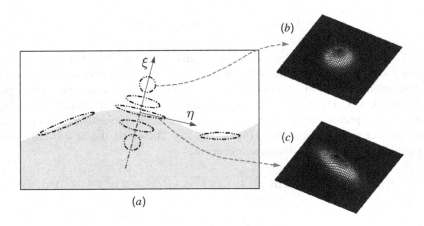

Fig. 1. (*a*) Given an image with two distinguished regions, one pair of eigenvectors, η and ξ, are shown for a pixel located at the region boundary. Depending on the diffusion tensor $\mathbf{T}$, the shape and size of the Gaussian kernel are varying at different locations. (*b*) The isotropic Gaussian kernel at the homogeneous region. (*c*) The anisotropic oriented Gaussian kernel at the region boundary.

on the estimated motion field $\mathbf{u}^{\tau'}$. One interesting point of this separation is that if we construct a structure tensor $\mathbf{T} = \lambda_\eta \eta \eta^T + \lambda_\xi \xi \xi^T$ and let $\mathbf{H} = \begin{bmatrix} \mathbf{u}_{xx}^{\tau'} & \mathbf{u}_{xy}^{\tau'} \\ \mathbf{u}_{yx}^{\tau'} & \mathbf{u}_{yy}^{\tau'} \end{bmatrix}$, then Eq.6 can be rewritten as $\mathbf{u}^\tau - \mathbf{u}^{\tau'} = \text{trace}(\mathbf{TH})$, and this diffusion equation can be further replaced by a 2D oriented Gaussian convolution [18], such that

$$\mathbf{u}^\tau = \mathbf{u}^{\tau'} * G(\mathbf{T}, \Delta\tau), \quad \text{where } G(\mathbf{T}, \Delta\tau) = \frac{1}{4\pi\Delta\tau} \exp\left(-\frac{\mathbf{x}^T \mathbf{T}^{-1} \mathbf{x}}{4\Delta\tau}\right), \quad (7)$$

and $\Delta\tau$ is the step length of iteration. If $\Delta\tau$ is set to more than 1, the size of the oriented Gaussian kernel becomes large and the diffusion process would be speeded up. Fig.1.*a* shows the variation of the Gaussian kernel at different locations due to its varied structure tensor, $\mathbf{T}$. Notice that the radii of the oriented Gaussian kernel also depend on the eigenvalues of $\mathbf{T}^{-1}$, which are $\frac{1}{\lambda_\eta}$ and $\frac{1}{\lambda_\xi}$. When the pixel $\mathbf{x}$ is located at the interior of a smooth region, $\|\nabla I_1\|$ is small and $\lambda_\xi \simeq \lambda_\eta \simeq \frac{1}{2}$, which is equivalent to applying an isotropic Gaussian kernel for the smoothing as shown in Fig.1.*b*. If the pixel is located at the sharp boundary between two segments, $\|\nabla I_1\|$ will be large and $\lambda_\xi \simeq 1 \gg \lambda_\eta \simeq 0$, which is equivalent to applying an oriented Gaussian kernel on the images as shown in Fig.1.*c*.

After separating the updating procedure into two steps, another interesting point is that we can substitute the original diffusion tensor by a more powerful, convolution-based diffusion filter in this variational framework, and this new filter may not be implemented by the traditional PDE iteration. Based on this motivation, the next section will show how to integrate a powerful, convolution-based bilateral filter into the flow estimation framework to achieve highly discontinuous flow field from two input images.

3 Highly Discontinuity-Persevering Optical Flow Estimation with Occlusion Detection

Even with the anisotropic diffusion term in the energy minimization function, the previous work still has difficulties to obtain highly discontinuous flow field due to the unclear occlusion process [19, 8, 1, 6, 16]. In [1, 16], the authors all point out that occlusion detection is critical for the motion estimation especially when the motion gap is large. However, the quality of occlusion detection and optical flow estimation at occluded regions are unsatisfactory in these papers due to the lack of the elaborate occlusion handling. In this section, we first exploit the natural property of the occlusion between two frames, and then provide an occlusion detector to identify the occlusion area. Based on the occlusion analysis, an explicit occlusion term is introduced into the variational framework to balance the data and occlusion energy. Furthermore, we substitute the traditional anisotropic diffusion tensor in the variational framework by a more flexible, multi-cue driven bilinear filter to preform more effective occlusion handling and produce more accurate optical flow field.

3.1 Occlusion Analysis and Detection

Fig.2 illustrates two kinds of occlusion happening in optical flow estimation. The first case is motion occlusion, where the occlusion generation is due to object motion and the occluded areas from two frames are not overlapped at the same location. The second case is mismatching where the occluded regions from different images are overlapped at the same position. The mismatching may happen under different conditions, such as object appearing/disappearing, shadow, color change, or large object deformation (shrinking or expanding), etc.

To detect such occlusion, one way is checking the consistency between the forward and backward flow. If the backward and forward flow is constant, the pixel will be

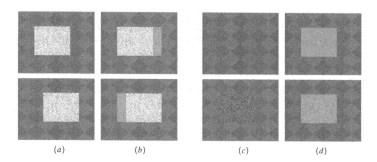

(a) (b) (c) (d)

Fig. 2. (a) The case of the motion occlusion, where a rectangle is moving from the left (the top frame) to the right side (the bottom frame). (b) The corresponding occluded areas of (a) are masked in red and the occluded areas locate at different positions due to the object's motion. (c) The case of mismatching, where the top is the first frame and a rectangle suddenly appears in the second frame (the bottom one). (d) The corresponding occluded areas of (c) are also masked in red, but in this case these occluded regions are overlapped at the same location.

Fig. 3. (*a*) The first input frame. (*b*) The second input frame. (*c*) The estimated optical flow using the traditional variational approach, where the flow of the weak-textured regions are dragged by the high gradient region boundaries (*Note: for comparison, please refer Fig.5.b*). (*d*) The zoomed image from the blue box in (*c*). (*e*) The dense flow field shown in color coded fashion where it is easy to see the dragging around the high gradient boundaries. (*f*) The color code map where the color represents the orientation of the vector and brightness stands for its magnitude. *Note: in* (*c*) *and* (*d*), *we also draw the flow vector using a line segment which starts from red and ends at green.*

considered as non-occluded [1]. However, this forward-backward matching may not be reliable for some cases, such as mismatching where the flow inside the both overlapping occluded regions may be zero as shown in Fig.2.$c - d$. As a result, this detector will not detect the error from forward and backward flow and it will calm such regions as non-occluded, which is contradictory to our analysis. In order to avoid such missing detection, we propose a simple but robust solution to detect the occlusion for the both cases by employing the squared image residue as

$$\rho(\mathbf{u}) = \begin{cases} 0 & \text{if } \left(I_1(\mathbf{x}) - I_2(\mathbf{x} + \mathbf{u})\right)^2 > \epsilon_I \\ 1 & \text{otherwise.} \end{cases} \tag{8}$$

where ϵ_I is a threshold to decide the occlusion, $\rho = 0$ means the pixel is occluded, and $\rho = 1$ denotes this pixel is visible in the both frames. To obtain a continuous function of $\rho(\mathbf{u})$ for PDE differentiation, a numerical approximation of the Heaviside function is used, such that

$$\rho(\mathbf{u}) = \frac{1}{2} + \frac{1}{\pi} \tan^{-1} \left(\left(I_1(\mathbf{x}) - I_2(\mathbf{x} + \mathbf{u})\right)^2 - \epsilon_I \right). \tag{9}$$

3.2 Energy Model with Occlusion Detection

One mishandling in the current variational model is trying to minimize the squared intensity error or data energy for every pixel regardless if the pixel is occluded or not. As a result, the warped image, $I_2(\mathbf{x} + \mathbf{u})$, has to perform incorrect deformation to fill the occluded area of frame $I_1(\mathbf{x})$ even though no corresponding pixel at I_2 can match the occluded pixel $\mathbf{x}$ at the first frame.

Fig.3 shows one example when a large occlusion between two images, this minimization will produce some serious distortion or dragging. In this example, there is a large motion difference between non-rigid foreground and the rigid background. Using the traditional framework, the weak-textured regions would be dragged to follow the movement of the high-gradient region boundaries. Another possible common case is when camera has apparent zooming or pan, a larger number of pixels should be occluded at the image boundary. If without correct occlusion handling, the energy of those pixels will be minimized to cause the serious distortion along the image boundary.

To fix these problems, we need to exclude the occluded pixels from the minimization process and add a corresponding penalty into the energy functional to balance occlusion and visibility. Therefore, our new energy model can be written as

$$E(\mathbf{u}) = \big(E_d(\mathbf{u}) + E_s(\nabla\mathbf{u})\big) \cdot \rho(\mathbf{u}) + \big(E_d{}^{oc} + E_s{}^{oc}(\nabla\mathbf{u})\big) \cdot \big(1 - \rho(\mathbf{u})\big), \quad (10)$$

where the first part of this equation is dealing with the energy of the non-occluded pixels and it includes two components, E_d and E_s, which correspond to the conventional data and smoothness energy similar to the model in the previous section. The second part of the equation is handling the energy of the occluded pixels, where $E_d{}^{oc}$ is occlusion energy and $E_s{}^{oc}$ is the smooth regulation for the occluded pixels. If the smooth processing of E_s and $E_s{}^{oc}$ are same, we can merge these two terms into one, such that

$$E(\mathbf{u}) = \big(E_d(\mathbf{u}) - E_d{}^{oc}\big) \cdot \rho(\mathbf{u}) + E_d{}^{oc} + E_s(\mathbf{u}),$$
$$= \int_\Omega \Big(\big(e_d(\mathbf{u}) - e_d{}^{oc}\big) \cdot \rho(\mathbf{u}) + e_d{}^{oc} + e_s(\nabla\mathbf{u})\Big) d\mathbf{x}, \quad (11)$$

where $e_d{}^{oc}$ is a constant occlusion penalty corresponding to the occlusion energy $E_d{}^{oc}$, $e_d(\mathbf{u})$ and $e_s(\nabla\mathbf{u})$ are data and smoothness terms same as Eq.2. From this equation, it is obvious when the occlusion penalty $e_d{}^{oc}$ increase, the occlusion detection will become more difficult and less pixels will be claimed as occluded. Therefore, a proper occlusion penalty will balance energies between the occlusion and data terms, and correctly locate the occlusion regions. In our experiment, we set $e_d{}^{oc} = \epsilon_I$, same as the occlusion detector threshold in Section 3.1.

Then, after applying Euler Lagrange equation, we can update the flow field by the two-step updating scheme as (Eq.5-7) becomes

$$\mathbf{u}^{\tau'} - \mathbf{u}^{\tau-1} = -\frac{\partial e_d(\mathbf{u})}{\partial \mathbf{u}}\rho(\mathbf{u}) - \big(e_d(\mathbf{u}) - e_d^{oc}\big)\frac{\partial \rho(\mathbf{u})}{\partial \mathbf{u}}, \quad (12)$$

$$\mathbf{u}^{\tau} - \mathbf{u}^{\tau'} = \operatorname{div}\left(\frac{\partial e_s(\nabla\mathbf{u})}{\partial \nabla\mathbf{u}}\right) \quad \text{or} \quad \mathbf{u}^{\tau} = \mathbf{u}^{\tau'} * G(\mathbf{T}, \Delta\tau), \quad (13)$$

where the first step is updating the flow field only based on the data and occlusion penalty, and the second step is performing diffusion process to suppress the noise and propagate the flow to non-textured region by either PDE updating or Gaussian convolution.

3.3 Occlusion Diffusion Using Multi-cue Driven Adaptive Bilateral Filter

Theoretically, the pixels at the occlusion area should not be assigned any flow vector since there is no correspondence available in the other frame. Nevertheless, in practice, the occluded pixels will be associated with certain motion flow by the diffusion operation in the variational model, and therefore the estimated flow at these areas will heavily depend on the diffusion process. Unfortunately, using the current variational-based anisotropic diffusion or oriented Gaussian smoothing, the diffusion process lacks the occlusion handling mechanism and also cannot distinguish the flow influence from different regions very well, which may produces serious distortion at the region boundaries.

Fig.4.a shows two kinds of mishandling of the current anisotropic diffusion on a simple example, where the cyan box is moving from the left to the right and the red region is occluded region similar to the Fig.2.b (To save space, we only show the first frame). In the first non-occluded case at pixel $\mathbf{x}_1$, an oriented Gaussian kernel is generated to perform diffusion process based on the diffusion tensor $D(\triangledown I_1)$. Even though this Gaussian kernel is stretched along the region boundary, the diffusion process will still convolute with a certain of flow information from the dissimilar regions to estimate its flow vector. Hence, the flow influence from the cyan region may dramatically distort the flow field in the white background region. In the second case, the pixel, $\mathbf{x}_2$, is located at the occluded region, similarly an oriented Gaussian kernel is generated as shown in Fig.4.a. However, if the occlusion gap is large, the radius of the oriented Gaussian kernel may not be possible to cover the size of occlusion area. Therefore, the only information convoluted for the flow estimation of pixel $\mathbf{x}_2$ is from the unreliable occluded region.

Therefore, in order to overcome these two mishandling, we need to redesign the diffusion process which can adaptively change the diffusion kernel's size and shape to minimize the flow influence from the inconsistent regions. In this section, we present an adaptive, multi-cue driven bilateral filter to block such incorrect flow influence between different regions and simultaneously infer the motion flow for the occluded regions from the surrounding non-occluded pixels. In Fig.4.b, one possible solution of Fig.4.a is given. In the both cases, the kernel size is adaptively changed and the kernel shape is truncated into two parts according to the occlusion detection and image intensity. The first part of these kernels is the support region marked as green where the motion information inside this region is used to estimate the flow vector for pixels $\mathbf{x}_i$. The remaining part of the kernels is the unsupport region and its information is discarded or reduced by certain weights during the flow estimation.

The original bilateral filter is introduced by Tomasi and Manduchi to preform a non-linear diffusion on image restoration [17], where two Gaussian kernels are stacked together such that

$$I'(\mathbf{x}_1) = \frac{1}{k(\mathbf{x}_1)} \int_{\Omega} I(\mathbf{x}) \cdot g_s(\mathbf{x} - \mathbf{x}_1) \cdot g_I\big(I(\mathbf{x}) - I(\mathbf{x}_1)\big) d\mathbf{x}, \qquad (14)$$

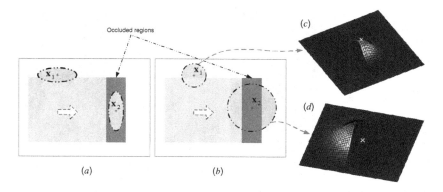

Fig. 4. Comparison between the variational-based anisotropic diffusion and our adaptive bilateral filter. Here the cyan box is moving from the left to the right side as indicated by the big yellow arrow. The red region is occluded region similar as the Fig.2.b (here we only show the first frame). (*a*) Two kinds of Mishandling for the pixel located near the region boundary and occluded area by using the variational-based anisotropic diffusion. (*b*) Employing our adaptive bilateral filter, the shape and size of the Gaussian kernel are adaptively changed for different cases and the optical flow is correctly estimated for the both cases. *Note: only the green area is used for the diffusion.* (*c*) and (*d*) are 3D visualization of the bilateral filter kernels where a green cross is marked at the kernel center.

where the normalize term $k(\mathbf{x}_1) = \int_\Omega g_s(\mathbf{x} - \mathbf{x}_1) \cdot g_I\big(I(\mathbf{x}) - I(\mathbf{x}_1)\big)d\mathbf{x}$, $I'(\mathbf{x}_1)$ is the output of the bilateral filter for pixel $\mathbf{x}_1$, $g_s(\cdot)$ and $g_I(\cdot)$ are two Gaussian functions for spatial and intensity domains respectively. Using the function $g_I(\cdot)$, the influence of the intensity-dissimilar pixels are effectively reduced. One can simplify Eq.14 by a convolution format such that

$$I' = I * G_s(\mathbf{x}, \sigma_s) * G_I(I, \sigma_I), \tag{15}$$

where $G_s(\sigma_s)$ is a Gaussian kernel on spatial domain $\mathbf{x}$ with variance σ_s, which corresponds to $g_s(\mathbf{x} - \mathbf{x}_1)$ of Eq.14. $G_I(\sigma_I)$ is another Gaussian kernel on intensity domain I with variance σ_I, which corresponds to $g_I\big(I(\mathbf{x}) - I(\mathbf{x}_1)\big)$ of Eq.14.

In our two-step optical flow estimation model, since the diffusion process is explicitly separated from the motion estimation step, we can simply substitute the oriented Gaussian filter in Eq.13 by our adaptive bilateral filter, such that

$$\mathbf{u}^\tau = \mathbf{u}^{\tau'} * G_s\big(\mathbf{x}, \sigma_s(\rho, \chi)\big) * G_I(I, \sigma_I) * G_\mathbf{u}(\mathbf{u}, \sigma_\mathbf{u}) * \rho. \tag{16}$$

Compared to the original bilateral filter (Eq.15), two additional convolution function are added. One is the occlusion function, ρ, which can fully disable the influence of the occluded region during the diffusion process. The other is a one dimensional Gaussian kernel, $G_\mathbf{u}$, to reduce the influence based on motion dissimilarity. Moreover, we also modify the spatial Gaussian kernel, G_s, which is able to adaptively change the kernel size by the occlusion function ρ and a varied occlusion region radius, χ, such that

$$\sigma_s(\rho, \pi)) = \begin{cases} \sigma_0 & \text{if } \rho = 1 \\ \sigma_0 + \frac{\chi}{3} & \text{if } \rho = 0 \end{cases}, \tag{17}$$

(a) (b)

(c) (d)

Fig. 5. (a) The estimated optical flow of Fig.3 using our approach, where the flow of the weak-textured regions are not dragged by the high gradient region boundaries any more. (b) The zoomed image from the blue box in (a). Compared to Fig.3.d, the flow vectors at the background region are not dragged by high gradient boundary any more. (c) Dense flow field. (d) The occluded areas in frame 1 (red regions).

where σ_0 is a default value of the kernel variance. When $\rho = 1$, the pixel is located at the non-occluded area where the estimated flow is reliable. With the convolution of the intensity kernel G_I and motion kernel $G_\mathbf{u}$, a small Gaussian kernel with $\sigma_s = \sigma_0$ is applied to preform diffusion as shown at position $\mathbf{x}_1$ in Fig.4.b, and the influence from the dissimilar pixels are efficiently reduced by G_I and $G_\mathbf{u}$. When $\rho = 0$, the pixel is occluded and the kernel size is increased by an additional term, $\frac{\chi}{3}$, where χ is an occlusion region radius function and it is pre-computed for each pixel after the occlusion detection step. With this new term, we can guarantee the radius of spatial kernel is always larger than the radius of the occluded region. Then employing the convolution of function $G_I * G_\mathbf{u} * \rho$, the flow influence from the unreliable occluded region is disabled, and the influence from the other dissimilar regions is also reduced according to the intensity and motion similarities. As a result, our adaptive bilateral filter can effectively collect the flow influence from the non-occluded, intensity and motion similar, surrounding regions to estimate correct flow vector for the occlude pixel as shown at position $\mathbf{x}_2$ in Fig.4.b.

Fig.5 shows the estimated flow field between frame Fig.3.*a* and 3.*b* by using our approach. Compared to the previous results in Fig.3.*c* − *e*, our approach correctly detects the occluded regions and effectively excludes these occluded pixels from the data minimization process to avoid the undesirable background dragging. Then, with the multi-cue bilateral filter, the motion flow for these occluded regions are inferred from the surrounding non-occluded pixels. As a result, the sharp motion discontinuities are obtained between different flow fields, and the non-rigid, continuous flow inside each flow fields are maintained as well.

4   Experiments and Evaluation

In the case of the optical flow is more than one pixel, a multi-scale pyramid [7] is necessary to be applied to avoid the minimization process trapped into a local minimum. After creating pyramids for two input reference frames, we start from the top level and iteratively update the flow field in two steps: first we estimate the flow vectors between the reference frame and the corresponding warped frame, then an adaptive bilateral diffusion process (Eq.16) is applied to correct the flow field and suppress the noise.

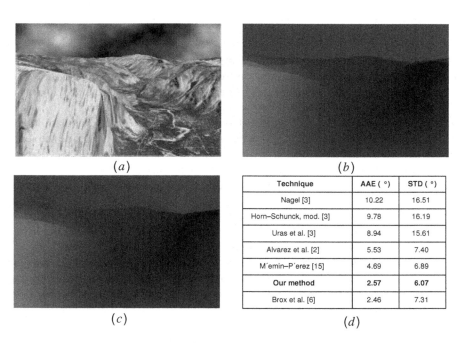

(*a*)   (*b*)

Technique	AAE (°)	STD (°)
Nagel [3]	10.22	16.51
Horn–Schunck, mod. [3]	9.78	16.19
Uras et al. [3]	8.94	15.61
Alvarez et al. [2]	5.53	7.40
M´emin–P´erez [15]	4.69	6.89
Our method	**2.57**	**6.07**
Brox et al. [6]	2.46	7.31

(*c*)   (*d*)

Fig. 6. (*a*) One frame from the Yosemite sequence with clouds. The occluded regions are masked in red, which hasn't been done in the literature. (*b*) The corresponding dense flow field of the ground truth. (*c*) Dense flow field of our result. (*d*) Comparison with the results from the literature with 100% density for the Yosemite sequence with clouds. AAE denotes average angular error and STD denotes standard deviation.

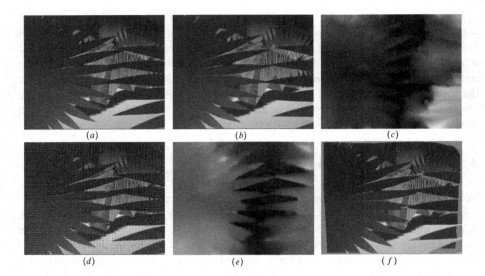

Fig. 7. (*a*) The first frame. (*b*) The second frame. (*c*) Dense flow field using the traditional approach. (*d*) The estimated optical flow in the first frame using our approach. (*e*) Dense flow field using our approach. (*f*) The occluded areas in frame 1 (red regions).

In order to evaluate our algorithm, we test our method on the synthetic data which has the ground truth. In Fig.6, we show our results for the well-known Yosemite with clouds sequence, and also compare them to the results from the literature. From the table of Fig.6.*d*, our results are slightly worse than the current best results [6] in this small motion case, but outperform the rest algorithms. The average computation time of this sequence is 4.03 sec/frame at 3.6GHz Intel Xeon CPU. For Yosemite sequence without clouds, the average angular error of our results is $1.57°$ with 100% density, which is also comparable to the most state-of-arts algorithms [3, 11, 6].

Beside this, we also test our algorithm in different real videos from movie or TV. In these videos, some non-rigid objects have serious deformation and large displacement of the moving objects produce severe occlusion and motion blurring as shown in Fig.7-8. Fig.7.*c* shows two frames from one cartoon video, "Tiger", where the leaves have large motion along different directions and some parts of the scene without texture. Using the traditional approach, the flow vectors of the background are dragged with the high-gradient boundaries and the motion discontinuities are not preserved very well along the leave boundaries as shown in Fig.7.*c*. In our results (Fig.7.*d* − *f*), we correctly detect the boundary occlusion and achieve more accurate motion discontinuities between the leaves and background regions. In Fig.8, we also show one result from Football TV. The first two images are the input frames. Our results (Fig.8.*d* − *f*) is apparently better than the traditional optical flow algorithm. Using our approach, we obtain more accurate and highly contrast motion discontinuities for this non-rigid, fast motion sequence with irregular occlusions.

Fig. 8. (*a*) The first frame. (*b*) The second frame. (*c*) Dense flow field using the traditional approach. (*d*) The estimated optical flow in the first frame using our approach. (*e*) Dense flow field using our approach. (*f*) The occluded areas in frame 1 (red regions).

5   Conclusion

In this paper, we present a novel variational-based framework to compute the optical flow for the video sequence in the presence of large occlusion and non-rigid motion. Our main contributions consist of: (1) We explicitly introduce an occlusion term into variational model to balance the data energy with occlusion handling process. (2) We initialize a two-step updating model for optical flow estimation, and further seamlessly integrate it with our multi-cue driven bilateral diffusion process to solve the occlusion mishandling of the previous approaches. Using our approach, the occluded regions are explicitly excluded from the optical flow computation, and our bilateral diffusion effectively infer the flow vectors for the occluded regions. After applying our approach on various video sources, the experiments show that our method can maintain piecewise spatial-coherent flow field for the rigid or non-rigid objects and also preserve accurate flow discontinuities along the motion boundaries simultaneously.

References

1. Alvarez, L., Deriche, R., Papadopoulo, T., Sanchez, J.: Symmetrical dense optical flow estimation with occlusion detection. In: European Conference on Computer Vision, Springer (2002) 721–735
2. Alvarez, L., Weickert, J., Sanchez, J.: Reliable estimation of dense optical flow fields with large displacements. International Journal of Computer Vision **39** (2000) 41–56
3. Barron, J., Fleet, D., Beauchemin, S.: Performance of optical flow techniques. International Journal of Computer Vision **12** (1994) 43–77

4. Black, M., Anandan, P.: The robust estimation of multiple motions: parametric and piecewise smooth flow fields. Computer Vision and Image Understanding **63** (1996) 75–104
5. Black, M., Sapiro, G., Marimont, D., Heeger, D.: Bobust anisotropic diffusion. IEEE Trans. on Image Processing **7** (1998) 421–432
6. Brox, T., Bruhn, A., Papenberg, N., Weickert, J.: High accuracy optical flow estimation based on a theory for warping. In: European Conference on Computer Vision, Springer (2004) 25–36
7. Burt, P., Adelson, E.: The laplacian pyramid as a compact image code. IEEE Trans. on Communications **31** (1983) 532–540
8. Deriche, R., Kornprobst, P., Aubert, G.: Optical-flow estimation while preserving its discontinuities: a variational approach. In: Asian Conference on Computer Vision. (1995) 290–295
9. Farneback, G.: Very high accuracy velocity estimation using orientation tensors, parametric motion, and simultaneous segmentation of the motion field. In: International Conference on Computer Vision. (2001) 171–177
10. Horn, B., Schunck, B.: Determining optical flow. Artificial Intelligence **17** (1981) 185–203
11. Ju, S., Black, M., Jepson, A.: Skin and bones: Multi-layer, locally affine, optical flow, and regularization with transparency. Computer Vision and Pattern Recognition (1996) 307–314
12. Lucas, B., Kanade, T.: An iterative image registration technique with an application to stereo vision. In: International Joint Conference on Artificial Intelligence. (1981) 674–679
13. Memin, E., Perez, P.: Hierarchical estimation and segmentation of dense motion fields. International Journal of Computer Vision **46** (2002) 129–155
14. Nagel, H., Enkelmann, W.: An inverstigation of smoothness constraints for the estimation of displacement vector fields from image sequences. IEEE Trans. on Pattern Analysis and Machine Intelligence **8** (1986) 565–593
15. Pernoa, P., Malik, J.: Scale-space and edge detection using anisotropic diffusion. IEEE Trans. on Pattern Analysis and Machine Intelligence **12** (1990) 629–639
16. Strecha, C., Fransens, R., Van Gool, L.: A probabilistic approach to large displacement optical flow and occlusion detection. In: Workshop on Statistical Methods in Video Processing. (2004) 71–82
17. Tomasi, C., Manduchi, R.: Bilateral filtering for gray and color images. In: International Conference on Computer Vision. (1998) 839–846
18. Tschumperle, D., Deriche, R.: Vector-valued image regularization with pde's: A common framework for different applications. In: Computer Vision and Pattern Recognition. (2003) 651–656
19. Weber, J., Marlik, J.: Bobust computation of optical flow in a multi-scale differential framework. International Journal of Computer Vision **2** (1994) 5–19
20. Xiao, J., Shah, M.: Accurate motion layer segmentation and matting. In: Computer Vision and Pattern Recognition. (2005) 698–703
21. Xiao, J., Shah, M.: Motion layer extraction in the presence of occlusion using graph cuts. IEEE Trans. on Pattern Analysis and Machine Intelligence **27** (2005) 1644–1659

Geometry and Kinematics with Uncertain Data

Christian Perwass, Christian Gebken, and Gerald Sommer

Institut für Informatik, CAU Kiel,
Christian-Albrechts-Platz 4, 24118 Kiel, Germany
{chp, chg, gs}@ks.informatik.uni-kiel.de

Abstract. In Computer Vision applications, one usually has to work with uncertain data. It is therefore important to be able to deal with uncertain geometry and uncertain transformations in a uniform way. The Geometric Algebra of conformal space offers a unifying framework to treat not only geometric entities like points, lines, planes, circles and spheres, but also *transformations* like reflection, inversion, rotation and translation. In this text we show how the uncertainty of all elements of the Geometric Algebra of conformal space can be appropriately described by covariance matrices. In particular, it will be shown that it is advantageous to represent uncertain transformations in Geometric Algebra as compared to matrices. Other important results are a novel pose estimation approach, a uniform framework for geometric entity fitting and triangulation, the testing of uncertain tangentiality relations and the treatment of catadioptric cameras with parabolic mirrors within this framework. This extends previous work by Förstner and Heuel from points, lines and planes to non-linear geometric entities and transformations, while keeping the linearity of the estimation method. We give a theoretical description of our approach and show exemplary applications.

1 Introduction

In Computer Vision one has to deal almost invariably with uncertain data. Appropriate methods to deal with this uncertainty do therefore play an important role. In this text we show how geometric entities and transformations can be described together with their uncertainty in a single, unifying mathematical framework, namely the Geometric Algebra of conformal space.

A particular advantage of the presented approach stems from the linear representation of geometric entities and transformations and from the fact that algebra operations are simply bilinear functions. This allows us to easily construct geometric constraints with the symbolic power of the algebra and then to equivalently express these constraints as multi-linear functions, such that the whole body of linear algebra can be applied. Solutions to many problems, like the estimation of the best line, plane, circle or sphere fit through a set of points, or the best rotation between two point sets (in a least-squares sense), reduces to the estimation of the null space of a matrix. Applying the so called Gauss-Helmert model, it is then also possible to evaluate the uncertainty of the estimated entity.

This text builds on previous works by Förstner et al. [1] and Heuel [2] where uncertain points, lines and planes were treated in a unified manner. The linear estimation of rotation operators in Geometric Algebra was previously discussed in [3], albeit without

A. Leonardis, H. Bischof, and A. Pinz (Eds.): ECCV 2006, Part I, LNCS 3951, pp. 225–237, 2006.

taking account of uncertainty. In [4] the description of uncertain circles and 2D-conics in Geometric Algebra was first discussed. The stratification of Euclidean, projective and affine spaces in Geometric Algebra, has been previously presented in [5]. In [6] the estimation of uncertain general operators was introduced.

In this text we present a number of new results and show how this method can be used in important applications of Computer Vision. We start out with a short introduction to Geometric Algebra. We then show how uncertain geometry and transformations can be represented in the algebra and discuss the error introduced when embedding Euclidean vectors in conformal space. Then we present the novel result that the uncertainty of transformations can be represented by linear subspaces, i.e. through a covariance matrix. Note that this is, for example, not possible for rotation matrices, since the sub-space of orthogonal matrices is not linear.

Next a number of applications of this methodology are presented. Firstly, estimation of geometric entities is discussed, where it is, for example, shown that triangulation of points and lines can be done in much the same way as the fitting of lines, planes, circles and spheres to a set of points. Next we present two variants of pose estimation, one of which estimates the pose of a known object given a set of projection rays. The corresponding constraint equation is quadratic in the components of the transformation operator, while not making any approximations of the operator. Later on we show how the estimation of projection rays from corresponding image points can be done via a matrix multiplication, for a projective and a catadioptric camera with parabolic mirror. The latter is, to the best of our knowledge, a new result, which makes pose estimation with catadioptric cameras mathematically as complex as pose estimation with projective cameras. Furthermore, we also show how uncertain geometric relations can be tested. This includes next to the test for the intersection of two lines, also tests for tangentiality of planes to circles and spheres.

2   Geometric Algebra

For a detailed introduction to Geometric Algebra see e.g. [7, 8]. Here we can only give a short overview. Geometric Algebra is an associative, graded algebra, whereby the algebra product is called *geometric product*. The Geometric Algebra over a n-dimensional vector space $\mathbb{R}^{p,q}$, with $n = p + q$ has dimension 2^n and is denoted by $\mathbb{G}(\mathbb{R}^{p,q})$ or simply $\mathbb{G}_{p,q}$. Here p denotes the number of basis elements of the vector space that square to $+1$ and q the number of basis elements that square to -1. If only one index is given, it denotes the number of positively squaring basis elements. Elements of different grade of the algebra can be constructed through the *outer product* of linearly independent vectors. For example, if $\{a_i\} \in \mathbb{R}^n$ are a set of k linearly independent vectors, then $A_{\langle k \rangle} := a_1 \wedge \ldots \wedge a_k$ is an element of $\mathbb{G}_n$ of grade k, which is called a *blade*, where $\wedge$ denotes the outer product. A general element of the algebra, called *multivector*, can always be expressed as a linear combination of blades of possibly different grades. Geometric entities are represented in the algebra through blades, while operators are typically represented by linear combinations of blades of different grades.

Geometric Algebra of Conformal Space. To combine projective geometry and kinematics we need to consider the Geometric Algebra of the (projective) *conformal space* of 3D-Euclidean space (cf. [7]). The embedding function $\mathcal{K}$ is defined as $\mathcal{K} : \boldsymbol{x} \in \mathbb{R}^3 \mapsto \boldsymbol{x} + \frac{1}{2}\boldsymbol{x}^2 \mathbf{e}_\infty + \mathbf{e}_o \in \mathbb{R}^{4,1}$. The basis of $\mathbb{R}^{4,1}$ can be written as $\{\mathbf{e}_1, \mathbf{e}_2, \mathbf{e}_3, \mathbf{e}_\infty, \mathbf{e}_o\}$, where $\mathbf{e}_i^2 = +1$, $\mathbf{e}_\infty^2 = \mathbf{e}_o^2 = 0$ and $\mathbf{e}_\infty \cdot \mathbf{e}_o = -1$. The various geometric entities that can be represented by blades in $\mathbb{G}_{4,1}$ are shown in table 1. In this table $\boldsymbol{X}, \boldsymbol{Y}, \boldsymbol{Z}, \boldsymbol{U}, \boldsymbol{V} \in \mathbb{R}^{4,1}$ are embeddings of points $\boldsymbol{x}, \boldsymbol{y}, \boldsymbol{z}, \boldsymbol{u}, \boldsymbol{v} \in \mathbb{R}^3$, respectively, and the $\mathbf{e}_{ij} \equiv \mathbf{e}_i \wedge \mathbf{e}_j$ etc. denote the algebra basis elements of an entity.

In particular, note that the elements *homogeneous point*, *line* and *plane* represent those elements that can also be expressed in the Geometric Algebra over projective space. For the homogeneous point, the element $\mathbf{e}_{o\infty}$ takes on the role of the homogeneous dimension.

Apart from representing geometric entities by blades, it is also possible to define operators in Geometric Algebra. The class of operators we are particularly interested in are *versors*. A versor $\boldsymbol{V} \in \mathbb{G}_n$ is a multivector that satisfies the following two conditions: $\boldsymbol{V}\widetilde{\boldsymbol{V}} = 1$ and for any blade $\boldsymbol{A}_{\langle k \rangle} \in \mathbb{G}_n$, $\boldsymbol{V}\,\boldsymbol{A}_{\langle k \rangle}\,\widetilde{\boldsymbol{V}}$ is also of grade k, i.e. a versor is *grade preserving*. The expression $\widetilde{\boldsymbol{V}}$ denotes the *reverse* of $\boldsymbol{V}$. The reverse operation changes the sign of the constituent blade elements depending on their grade, which has an effect similar to conjugation in quaternions. The most interesting versors for our purposes in conformal space are rotation operators (rotors), translation operators (translators) and scaling operators (dilators).

All of them share the property that they can be applied to all geometric entities in the same way. That is, it does not matter whether a blade $\boldsymbol{A}_{\langle k \rangle}$ represents a point, line, plane, circle or sphere. If $\boldsymbol{R}$ represents a rotation operations, then the rotated entity is always given by $\boldsymbol{R}\,\boldsymbol{A}_{\langle k \rangle}\,\widetilde{\boldsymbol{R}}$.

Table 1. Entities and their algebra basis. Note that the operators are mostly multivectors of mixed grade.

Entity	Grade	No.	Basis Elements
Point $\boldsymbol{X}$	1	5	$\mathbf{e}_1, \mathbf{e}_2, \mathbf{e}_3, \mathbf{e}_\infty, \mathbf{e}_o$
Homogen. Point $\boldsymbol{X} \wedge \mathbf{e}_\infty$	2	4	$\mathbf{e}_{1\infty}, \mathbf{e}_{2\infty}, \mathbf{e}_{3\infty}, \mathbf{e}_{o\infty}$
Point Pair $\boldsymbol{X} \wedge \boldsymbol{Y}$	2	10	$\mathbf{e}_{23}, \mathbf{e}_{31}, \mathbf{e}_{12}, \mathbf{e}_{1o}, \mathbf{e}_{2o}, \mathbf{e}_{3o}, \mathbf{e}_{1\infty}, \mathbf{e}_{2\infty}, \mathbf{e}_{3\infty}, \mathbf{e}_{o\infty}$
Line $\boldsymbol{X} \wedge \boldsymbol{Y} \wedge \mathbf{e}_\infty$	3	6	$\mathbf{e}_{23\infty}, \mathbf{e}_{31\infty}, \mathbf{e}_{12\infty}, \mathbf{e}_{1o\infty}, \mathbf{e}_{2o\infty}, \mathbf{e}_{3o\infty}$
Circle $\boldsymbol{X} \wedge \boldsymbol{Y} \wedge \boldsymbol{Z}$	3	10	$\mathbf{e}_{23\infty}, \mathbf{e}_{31\infty}, \mathbf{e}_{12\infty}, \mathbf{e}_{23o}, \mathbf{e}_{31o}, \mathbf{e}_{12o},$ $\mathbf{e}_{1o\infty}, \mathbf{e}_{2o\infty}, \mathbf{e}_{3o\infty}, \mathbf{e}_{123}$
Plane $\boldsymbol{X} \wedge \boldsymbol{Y} \wedge \boldsymbol{Z} \wedge \mathbf{e}_\infty$	4	4	$\mathbf{e}_{123\infty}, \mathbf{e}_{23o\infty}, \mathbf{e}_{31o\infty}, \mathbf{e}_{12o\infty}$
Sphere $\boldsymbol{X} \wedge \boldsymbol{Y} \wedge \boldsymbol{Z} \wedge \boldsymbol{U}$	4	5	$\mathbf{e}_{123\infty}, \mathbf{e}_{123o}, \mathbf{e}_{23o\infty}, \mathbf{e}_{31o\infty}, \mathbf{e}_{12o\infty}$
Reflection	1	4	$\mathbf{e}_1, \mathbf{e}_2, \mathbf{e}_3, \mathbf{e}_\infty$
Inversion	1	5	$\mathbf{e}_1, \mathbf{e}_2, \mathbf{e}_3, \mathbf{e}_\infty, \mathbf{e}_o$
Rotor $\boldsymbol{R}$	0,2	4	$1, \mathbf{e}_{23}, \mathbf{e}_{31}, \mathbf{e}_{12}$
Translator $\boldsymbol{T}$	0,2	4	$1, \mathbf{e}_{1\infty}, \mathbf{e}_{2\infty}, \mathbf{e}_{3\infty}$
Dilator $\boldsymbol{D}$	0,2	2	$1, \mathbf{e}_{o\infty}$
Motor $\boldsymbol{RT}$	0,2,4	8	$1, \mathbf{e}_{23}, \mathbf{e}_{31}, \mathbf{e}_{12}, \mathbf{e}_{1\infty}, \mathbf{e}_{2\infty}, \mathbf{e}_{3\infty}, \mathbf{e}_{123\infty}$
Gen. Rotor $\boldsymbol{T}\boldsymbol{R}\widetilde{\boldsymbol{T}}$	0,2	7	$1, \mathbf{e}_{23}, \mathbf{e}_{31}, \mathbf{e}_{12}, \mathbf{e}_{1\infty}, \mathbf{e}_{2\infty}, \mathbf{e}_{3\infty}$

Table 2. Tensor symbols for algebra operations and corresponding Jacobi matrices. Note that for tensors with two indices (i.e. matrices) we define the first index to denote the matrix row and the second index the matrix column.

Operation	Geometric Product	Outer Product	Inner Product	Reverse	Dual
Tensor Symbol	$\mathsf{G}^k{}_{ij}$	$\mathsf{O}^k{}_{ij}$	$\mathsf{N}^k{}_{ij}$	$\mathsf{R}^j{}_i$	$\mathsf{D}^j{}_i$
Jacobi Matrices	$\mathsf{G}(\mathsf{a}) := \mathsf{a}^i\,\mathsf{G}^k{}_{ij}$ $\bar{\mathsf{G}}(\mathsf{b}) := \mathsf{b}^j\,\mathsf{G}^k{}_{ij}$	$\mathsf{O}(\mathsf{a}) := \mathsf{a}^i\,\mathsf{O}^k{}_{ij}$ $\bar{\mathsf{O}}(\mathsf{b}) := \mathsf{b}^j\,\mathsf{O}^k{}_{ij}$	$\mathsf{N}(\mathsf{a}) := \mathsf{a}^i\,\mathsf{N}^k{}_{ij}$ $\bar{\mathsf{N}}(\mathsf{b}) := \mathsf{b}^j\,\mathsf{N}^k{}_{ij}$	$\mathsf{R} := \mathsf{R}^j{}_i$	$\mathsf{D} := \mathsf{D}^j{}_i$

Representation as Component Vectors. Let $\{E_i\}$ denote the 2^n-dimensional algebra basis of $\mathbb{G}_n$. Then a multivector $A \in \mathbb{G}_n$ can be written as $A = \mathsf{a}^i\,E_i$, where a^i denotes the ith component of a vector $\mathsf{a} \in \mathbb{R}^{2^n}$ and a sum over the repeated index i is implied. We will use this Einstein summation convention also in the following, i.e. $\mathsf{a}^i\,E_i \equiv \sum_i \mathsf{a}^i\,E_i$. If $B = \mathsf{b}^i\,E_i$ and $C = \mathsf{c}^i\,E_i$, then the components of C in the algebra equation $C = A \circ B$ can be evaluated via $\mathsf{c}^k = \mathsf{a}^i\,\mathsf{b}^j\,\mathsf{G}^k{}_{ij}$, where a summation over i and j is again implied. Such a summation of tensor indices is also called *contraction*. Here $\circ$ is a placeholder for an algebra product and $\mathsf{G}^k{}_{ij} \in \mathbb{R}^{2^n \times 2^n \times 2^n}$ is a tensor encoding this product.

The set of tensor symbols representing the various algebra operations, that we use in the following, is shown in table 2. This table also gives the symbolic abbreviations for the Jacobi matrices of the tensor contractions.

For example, the geometric product of multivectors $A, B \in \mathbb{G}_n$ can be written in terms of their component vectors $\mathsf{a}, \mathsf{b} \in \mathbb{R}^{2^n}$ as $\mathsf{a}^i\,\mathsf{b}^j\,\mathsf{G}^k{}_{ij} = \mathsf{G}(\mathsf{a})\,\mathsf{b} = \bar{\mathsf{G}}(\mathsf{b})\,\mathsf{a}$.

We can reduce the complexity of the tensor equations considerably by only using those components of multivectors that are actually needed. In the following we therefore refer to the minimum number of components as given in table 1, when talking about the component vector of a multivector.

3   Geometric Algebra with Uncertain Entities

In order to describe the uncertainty of multivectors, we need to expressed them as component vectors and algebra operations as tensor contractions.

Operations between Multivectors. We now give a short description of *error propagation* for operations between uncertain multivectors. This is based on the assumption that the uncertainty of a multivector can be modeled by a Gaussian distribution. Hence, the probability density function of a random multivector variable is fully described by a mean multivector and a covariance matrix. Using error propagation we can then evaluate the mean and covariance of a function of random multivector variables. In particular, this allows us to evaluate the mean and covariance of algebra products between multivector valued random variables. For a detailed introduction to error propagation see [9, 10].

We will denote a random variable by an underbar, its expectation or mean value by the symbol itself, the expectation operator by $\mathcal{E}$ and the covariance matrix of a random vector variable $\underline{\mathsf{a}}$ by $\Sigma_{\mathsf{a,a}}$. The cross-covariance matrix between two random variables $\underline{\mathsf{a}}$ and $\underline{\mathsf{b}}$, say, will be written as $\Sigma_{\mathsf{a,b}}$.

Let $\underline{A}, \underline{B} \in \mathbb{G}_n$ be two general random multivector variables and $\underline{a}, \underline{b} \in \mathbb{R}^{2^n}$ their component vectors. Furthermore, let $\underline{C} \in \mathbb{G}_n$ be given by $\underline{C} = \underline{A}\,\underline{B}$. It then follows that $\underline{c} = \mathsf{G}(\underline{a})\,\underline{b}$. Since we assume the random vector variables to have Gaussian probability density distributions, we would like to know the expectation value and covariance matrix of $\underline{C}$, given the expectation values and covariance matrices of $\underline{A}$ and $\underline{B}$. Error propagation yields,

$$\mathsf{c} = \mathsf{G}(\mathsf{a})\,\mathsf{b} \quad \text{and} \quad \Sigma_{\mathsf{c},\mathsf{c}} = \quad \bar{\mathsf{G}}(\mathsf{b})\,\Sigma_{\mathsf{a},\mathsf{a}}\,\bar{\mathsf{G}}(\mathsf{b})^{\mathsf{T}} + \mathsf{G}(\mathsf{a})\,\Sigma_{\mathsf{b},\mathsf{b}}\,\mathsf{G}(\mathsf{a})^{\mathsf{T}} \tag{1}$$
$$+ \bar{\mathsf{G}}(\mathsf{b})\,\Sigma_{\mathsf{a},\mathsf{b}}\,\mathsf{G}(\mathsf{a})^{\mathsf{T}} + \mathsf{G}(\mathsf{a})\,\Sigma_{\mathsf{b},\mathsf{a}}\,\bar{\mathsf{G}}(\mathsf{b})^{\mathsf{T}}.$$

Note that this equation is only an approximation. In the case of the geometric product, the exact expression for evaluating the mean of a product of two random variables is $\mathsf{c}^k = \mathsf{a}^i\,\mathsf{b}^j\,\mathsf{G}^k{}_{ij} + \Sigma_{\mathsf{a},\mathsf{b}}^{ij}\,\mathsf{G}^k{}_{ij}$. Furthermore, the exact expression for the covariance matrix $\Sigma_{\mathsf{c},\mathsf{c}}$ is the one given in equation (1) minus the term $(\Sigma_{\mathsf{a},\mathsf{b}}^{rs}\,\mathsf{G}^i{}_{rs})\,(\Sigma_{\mathsf{a},\mathsf{b}}^{rs}\,\mathsf{G}^j{}_{rs})$. That is, if $\underline{a}$ and $\underline{b}$ are statistically independent, then equation (1) is the exact expression for the error propagation in all algebra products.

The meaning of the term $\Sigma_{\mathsf{a},\mathsf{b}}^{ij}\,\mathsf{G}^k{}_{ij}$ can be understood when writing the cross-covariance matrix in terms of a singular value decomposition (SVD). Let $\{\mathsf{u}_n\}$ and $\{\mathsf{v}_n\}$ denote the set of left and right singular column vectors of $\Sigma_{\mathsf{a},\mathsf{b}}$, and let the $\{\sigma_n\}$ denote the corresponding set of singular values. Then $\Sigma_{\mathsf{a},\mathsf{b}} = \sum_n \sigma_n\,\mathsf{u}_n\,\mathsf{v}_n^{\mathsf{T}}$, and thus $\Sigma_{\mathsf{a},\mathsf{b}}^{ij}\,\mathsf{G}^k{}_{ij} = \sum_n \sigma_n\,\mathsf{u}_n^i\,\mathsf{v}_n^j\,\mathsf{G}^k{}_{ij}$. That is, the correction term $\Sigma_{\mathsf{a},\mathsf{b}}^{ij}\,\mathsf{G}^k{}_{ij}$ is a linear combination of the geometric products of corresponding left and right singular vectors of $\Sigma_{\mathsf{a},\mathsf{b}}^{ij}$. The order of magnitude of this correction is the sum of the singular values. Similarly, the order of magnitude of the correction to the covariance matrix is the square of the sum of the singular values.

Conformal Space. We want to work with uncertain geometric entities and operators in conformal space. However, the initial data we will be given, has almost invariably been measured in Euclidean space. We therefore have to embed the Euclidean data and its uncertainty in conformal space.

Let $\underline{a} \in \mathbb{R}^3$ be a Euclidean random vector variable with covariance matrix $\Sigma_{a,a}$, and let $\underline{A} \in \mathbb{R}^{4,1}$ be defined by $\underline{A} := \mathcal{K}(\underline{a})$. It may then be shown that $A = \mathcal{E}[\mathcal{K}(\underline{a})] = a + \frac{1}{2}a^2\,\mathbf{e}_\infty + \mathbf{e}_o + \frac{1}{2}\mathrm{tr}(\Sigma_{a,a})\,\mathbf{e}_\infty$. Note that by definition of the geometric product $a^2 \equiv \|a\|^2$. Typically the trace of $\Sigma_{a,a}$ is negligible compared to $\|a\|^2$, which leaves us with $A = \mathcal{K}(a)$. If we denote the Jacobi matrix of $\mathcal{K}$ evaluated at a by $\mathsf{J}_{\mathcal{K}}(a)$, then the error propagation equation for the covariance matrix can be written as $\Sigma_{A,A} = \mathsf{J}_{\mathcal{K}}(a)\,\Sigma_{a,a}\,\mathsf{J}_{\mathcal{K}}^{\mathsf{T}}(a)$. Denoting by $\mathrm{I} \in \mathbb{R}^{3\times 3}$ the identity matrix and by $\mathsf{a} \in \mathbb{R}^3$ the column component vector of a, the Jacobi matrix $\mathsf{J}_{\mathcal{K}}(a) \in \mathbb{R}^{5\times 3}$ is given by $\mathsf{J}_{\mathcal{K}}(a) = [\,\mathrm{I}\,\mathsf{a}\,0\,]^{\mathsf{T}}$.

From the definition of the conformal embedding function $\mathcal{K}$ it follows that $\mathcal{K}$ maps the Euclidean space onto a paraboloid in $\mathbb{R}^{4,1}$, the so called *horosphere* [11]. However, this implies that when we move a vector $A = \mathcal{K}(a)$ within the subspace spanned by its covariance matrix $\Sigma_{A,A}$, it will no longer exactly represent a point. In fact, the subspace spanned by $\Sigma_{A,A}$ is tangential to the horosphere at A. For small covariances of A this is still a good approximation. Furthermore, if we only need an affine point ($A \wedge \mathbf{e}_\infty$), then the quadratic component of A is removed and the corresponding covariance matrix gives an exact description of the uncertainty.

Depending on the application, it may or may not be necessary to express entities of the Geometric Algebra of conformal space in Euclidean terms. The only geometric entities that may be projected back directly into Euclidean space are points. However, if the goal is to test geometric relations, then a projection back into Euclidean space is not necessary.

Given a point in conformal space as $A = \alpha^1\,\mathbf{e}_1 + \alpha^2\,\mathbf{e}_2 + \alpha^3\,\mathbf{e}_3 + \alpha^\infty\,\mathbf{e}_\infty + \alpha^o\,\mathbf{e}_o$, the projection operation $\mathcal{K}^{-1}$ back into Euclidean space is given by $\mathcal{K}^{-1}(A) = a/\alpha^o$, where $a := \alpha^1\,\mathbf{e}_1 + \alpha^2\,\mathbf{e}_2 + \alpha^3\,\mathbf{e}_3$. That is, $\mathbf{e}_o$ takes on the function of the homogeneous dimension. If we again denote the component vector of a by a, then the corresponding Jacobi matrix $\mathsf{J}_{\mathcal{K}^{-1}}(A) \in \mathbb{R}^{3\times 5}$ is given by $\mathsf{J}_{\mathcal{K}^{-1}}(A) = \frac{1}{\alpha^o}\,[\,\mathsf{I}\ 0\ -\mathsf{a}/\alpha^o\,]$.

Blades and Operators. In this section we will show that covariance matrices can be used to describe the uncertainty of blades and operators in Geometric Algebra. The fundamental problem is, that while covariance matrices describe the uncertainty of an entity through a linear subspace, the subspace spanned by entities of the same type may not be linear.

For example, Heuel [2] describes the evaluation of general homographies, by writing the homography matrix H as a vector h and solving for it, given appropriate constraints. It is then also possible to evaluate a covariance matrix $\Sigma_{\mathsf{h},\mathsf{h}}$ for h. While this is fine for general homographies, Heuel also notes that it is problematic for constrained transformations like rotations, since the necessary constraints on h are non-linear. The basic problem here is that the subspace of vectors h that represent rotation matrices, is not linear. Hence, a covariance matrix for h is not well suited to describe the uncertainty of the corresponding rotation matrix.

The question therefore is, whether the representation of geometric entities and operators in Geometric Algebra allows for an uncertainty description via covariance matrices. For example, consider a line L, which may be represented in conformal space as $L = X \wedge Y \wedge \mathbf{e}_\infty$ (cf. table 1). The six components of L are the well known Plücker coordinates, which have to satisfy the Plücker condition in order to describe a line. In Geometric Algebra the Plücker condition is equivalent demanding that L is a blade, i.e. it can be factorized into the outer product of three vectors.

If we want to describe the uncertainty of a line L with a covariance matrix, the sum of the component vector of L with any component vector in the linear subspace spanned by the covariance matrix, has to satisfy the Plücker condition. Here we only want to motivate that such a linear subspace can exist. For that purpose suppose that the covariance matrix of X has rank 1 with eigenvector $D \in \mathbb{R}^{4,1}$ and Y is a point without uncertainty. If a scaled version of D is added to X, then the L changes according to the following equation.

$$(X + \alpha\,D) \wedge Y \wedge \mathbf{e}_\infty = X \wedge Y \wedge \mathbf{e}_\infty + \alpha\,(D \wedge Y \wedge \mathbf{e}_\infty), \qquad (2)$$

where $\alpha \in \mathbb{R}$. Thus any scaled version of $D \wedge Y \wedge \mathbf{e}_\infty$ can be added to L, such that their sum still satisfies the Plücker condition. Furthermore, $D \wedge Y \wedge \mathbf{e}_\infty$ is the eigenvector of the covariance matrix of L.

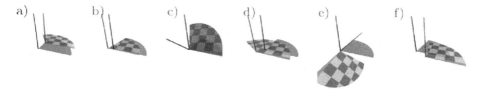

Fig. 1. Effect of adding each of the six eigenvectors of the covariance matrix of a rotor onto the rotor's component vectors. In each of the images, the darker rotor is the initial one.

Since rigid transformation operators also consist of blades, they inherit the same property. For example, a rotor representing a rotation about an arbitrary axis, can be generated by the geometric product of the dual of two planes, that intersect in a line. (If the planes are parallel they result in a translation operator.) The rotation axis is then this intersection line and the rotation angle is twice the angle between the planes. Using error propagation we can in this way construct an uncertain rotor. It turns out that the corresponding covariance matrix can be at most of rank six. The effect on the rotation operation when transforming such an uncertain rotor separately along the six eigenvectors of its covariance matrix is shown in figure 1.

Expressing uncertain transformation operations, like rotation and translation, through elements of the Geometric Algebra of conformal space, therefore offers an advantageous description compared to matrices, since the space of rotation matrices is not linear. In synthetic experiments presented in [6], it was shown that this results in a robust estimation of operators.

Furthermore, note that the sub-algebra of rotors for rotations about the origin, is isomorphic to the quaternion algebra and the sub-algebra of motors is isomorphic to the dual quaternions [12, 13]. Compared to quaternions and dual quaternions, the Geometric Algebra of conformal space allows us not only to describe the operators themselves, but also to apply them to any geometric entity that can be expressed in the algebra. In contrast, when using quaternions only points can be represented by pure quaternions (i.e. no scalar part), and in the dual quaternions only lines can be represented.

4   Applications

In this section we give a number of examples of how uncertain Geometric Algebra can be applied to various problem settings in Computer Vision. The type of problems can be roughly separated into three different categories: construction, estimation and the testing of geometric relations of uncertain entities. For example, given the uncertain optical center of a camera and an uncertain image point, we can construct the uncertain projection ray. On the other hand, given a number of such uncertain projection rays, which should all meet in one point, we can estimate that point and its uncertainty. Alternatively, we could also test the hypothesis that two projection rays meet.

Geometric Entity Estimation. A fundamental problem that often occurs is the evaluation of a geometric entity based on the measurement of a number of geometric entities of a different type. For example, suppose we want to find the line L that best fits a given set of points $\{X_n\}$. Additionally, we also want to obtain a covariance matrix for the estimated line. This can be achieved using the Gauss-Helmert (GH) model as described in [6, 2, 9, 10]. The GH-model allows us to evaluate a parameter vector with associated covariance matrix, given a set of data vectors with covariance matrices, a constraint function between data and parameter vectors and possibly a constraint function on the parameters alone. The resultant parameter vector is the solution to a system of linear equations that depends on the Jacobi matrices of the constraint functions, the data and the covariance matrices.

In terms of the GH-model, the parameters are the components l of the line L that is to be estimated, and the data vectors $\{\mathsf{x}_n\}$ are the component vectors of the points $\{X_n\}$. The constraint function $Q(X_n, L)$ between data and parameters has to be zero if a point lies on the line. The constraint function on the parameters alone $H(L)$ has to be zero if L does indeed represent a normalized line, i.e. l satisfies the Plücker condition and $\mathsf{l}^{\mathsf{T}}\,\mathsf{l} = 1$.

In this case $Q(X_n, L) = X_n \wedge L$, or $\mathsf{q}^k(\mathsf{x}_n, \mathsf{l}) = \mathsf{x}_n^i\,\mathsf{l}^j\,\mathsf{O}^k{}_{ij}$ and $H(L) = L\,\tilde{L} - 1$, or $\mathsf{h}^k(\mathsf{l}) = \mathsf{l}^{i_1}\,\mathsf{l}^j\,\mathsf{R}^{i_2}{}_j\,\mathsf{G}^k{}_{i_1 i_2} - \delta^k{}_1$, where $\delta^k{}_j$ is the Kronecker delta, and index 1 is assumed to be the index of the scalar component of the corresponding multivector. The Jacobi matrices of q are $\mathsf{Q}^k{}_{nj} = \mathsf{x}_n^i\,\mathsf{O}^k{}_{ij}$ and $\bar{\mathsf{Q}}^k{}_i = \mathsf{l}^j\,\mathsf{O}^k{}_{ij}$ and the Jacobi matrix of h is $\mathsf{H}^k{}_j = \mathsf{l}^{i_1}\,(\mathsf{R}^{i_2}{}_{i_1}\,\mathsf{G}^k{}_{ji_2} + \mathsf{R}^{i_2}{}_j\,\mathsf{G}^k{}_{i_1 i_2})$. With these definitions of the constraint functions and their Jacobi matrices, we can now apply the GH-model, to evaluate the best uncertain line that fits the given uncertain points.

Table 3 lists the constraint functions Q between geometric entities, that result in a zero vector if one geometric entity is completely contained within the other. For example, the constraint between two lines is only zero if the multivectors describe the same line up to scale. The constraint function H stays the same for all parameter types. Note in particular that instead of fitting a line to a set of points, we can also fit a point to a set of lines. This can, for example, be used for triangulation, where the best intersection of a set of projection rays has to be evaluated. Similarly, the best intersection line of a set of projective planes can found. In table 3, the symbols $\underline{\times}$ and $\overline{\times}$ denote the commutator and anti-commutator product, respectively, which are defined as $A \underline{\times} B = \frac{1}{2}(A\,B - B\,A)$ and $A \overline{\times} B = \frac{1}{2}(A\,B + B\,A)$.

Table 3. Constraints between data and parameters that are zero if the corresponding geometric entities are contained in one another

↓ Data, Parameter →	Point X	Line L	Plane P	Circle C	Sphere S
Points $\{Y_n\}$	$X \wedge Y_n$	$L \wedge Y_n$	$P \wedge Y_n$	$C \wedge Y_n$	$S \wedge Y_n$
Lines $\{K_n\}$	$X \wedge K_n$	$L \underline{\times} K_n$	$P \overline{\times} K_n$		
Planes $\{O_n\}$	$X \wedge O_n$	$L \overline{\times} O_n$	$P \underline{\times} O_n$		
Circles $\{B_n\}$	$X \wedge B_n$			$C \underline{\times} B_n$	$S \overline{\times} B_n$
Spheres $\{R_n\}$	$X \wedge R_n$			$C \overline{\times} R_n$	$S \underline{\times} R_n$

Pose Estimation. An important problem in Computer Vision is the estimation of the relative pose of two objects. The simplest instance of this problem is to find the unknown rigid body transformation M that maps a set of points $\{X_n\}$ into the set $\{Y_n\}$, i.e. $Y_n = M X_n \widetilde{M}$. Since $M \widetilde{M} = 1$, the constraint equation is $Q(Y_n, M) = M X_n - Y_m M$ and in this way gives a linear constraint on M. In terms of the parameter vectors this constraint can be written as $Q(y_n, m) = y_n^j m^r Q^k{}_{jr}$, with $Q^k{}_{rj} := (x_n^i G^k{}_{ri} - G^k{}_{jr})$ and thus an initial solution for m is given by the common right null space of $Q(y_n) = y_n^j Q^k{}_{jr}$ for all n (cf. [3]). When using the GH-model to estimate M and its covariance matrix, then the constraint on M alone is again $M \widetilde{M} - 1 = 0$. Experimental results of this method can be found in [6].

A more complicated, but also more interesting case of pose estimation is to fit a given set of model points onto a corresponding set of projection rays. This occurs, when we want to estimate the camera or object pose from a single view of a known object. Let L_n denote the projection ray of the transformed model point $M X_n \widetilde{M}$, where M denotes the unknown motor. Then the constraint equation is $Q(L_n, M) = L_n \wedge (M X_n \widetilde{M})$. This equation cannot be made linear in M, since $Q_n(l_n, m) = l_n^{k_1} m^{p_1} m^{q_2} Q^r{}_{n\,k_1\,p_1\,q_2}$, with

$$Q^r{}_{n\,k_1\,p_1\,q_2} = x_n^{p_2} G^{q_1}{}_{p_1 p_2} G^{k_2}{}_{q_1 q_2} O^r{}_{k_1 k_2}. \tag{3}$$

Thus we also cannot immediately obtain an initial estimate for m from a null space of Q. Nonetheless, we have a constraint equation for the evaluation of a motor, that is only quadratic in the components of the motor, without having made any approximations, like a small angle approximation.

We developed a robust method to evaluate an initial estimate for m using a geometric construction [14]. Alternatively, an initial estimate for m may be given through a tracking assumption. Once an initial estimate for m is known, $Q_n(l_n, m)$ may again be used in the GH-model approach. The constraint on M is $M \widetilde{M} - 1 = 0$, as before.

We tested this approach on synthetic data in the following way. First random model points were generated and transformed by a "true" rigid transformation. Then a covariance matrix was associated with each transformed model point and error vectors were added to the transformed model points according to their respective covariance matrices. Note that the error vectors were parallel to the image plane. These points were then projected onto a virtual camera. We then estimated the rigid transformation that best mapped the initial model points onto the noisy projection rays using the above described method. The results are shown in table 4. Here μ_r denotes the mean length of the error vectors added to the model points, and μ denotes the mean Euclidean distance between the projection rays and the model points transformed with the true, the initial estimate and the Gauss-Helmert (GH) estimate of the transformation, respectively. The σ columns give the corresponding standard deviations. The values shown are the mean of 800 runs with varying "true" transformations. It can be seen that the Gauss-Helmert approach always leads to good results, which are better than the estimate with the "true" and "initial" transformation. Note that since random vectors were added to the model points, the initially "true" transformation, need not anymore be the best solution.

Testing Uncertain Geometric Relations. Given uncertain geometric entities, a question like *"does point X lie on line L"* is not very useful, since the probability that this occurs for ideal points and lines is infinitesimal. We therefore follow the method described by Heuel and Förstner in [2, 1], who apply statistical hypothesis testing as described in [9].

Table 4. Results of pose estimation for a synthetic experiment

	True		Initial		GH	
μ_r	μ	σ	μ	σ	μ	σ
0.200	0.227	0.037	0.233	0.045	0.215	0.040
0.283	0.320	0.051	0.330	0.066	0.304	0.055
0.416	0.470	0.074	0.476	0.095	0.441	0.081

Table 5. Constraints between geometric entities that yield zero if they intersect in a single point

$\downarrow$ Entity $\rightarrow$	Line L	Circle C	Sphere S
Line K	$K^* \cdot L$	$(K^* \cdot C)^2$	$(K^* \cdot S)^2$
Circle B		$(B^* \cdot C)^2$	$(B^* \cdot S)^2$
Sphere R			$(R^* \cdot S)^2$

The basic idea is that the hypothesis H_0 "X *lies on* L" is tested against the hypothesis H_1 "X *does* not *lie on* L". In order to perform the hypothesis test, we need to fix the probability α that we reject H_0 even though it is true. Furthermore, we assume that a vector valued distance measure q with associated covariance matrix $\Sigma_{q,q}$ is given, which is zero if X is incident with line L. Then hypothesis H_0 can be rejected if $q^\mathsf{T} \Sigma_{q,q}^{-1} q > \chi^2_{1-\alpha;n}$, where $\chi^2_{1-\alpha;n}$ is the $(1-\alpha)$-quantile of the χ^2_n distribution for n degrees of freedom. Note that if $\Sigma_{q,q}$ is not of full rank, its pseudo-inverse can also be used in the above equation.

The distance measure Q for the containment of geometric entities is just given by the constraint equations of table 3. The covariance matrix $\Sigma_{q,q}$ can then be evaluated with equation (1) using the appropriate Jacobi matrices.

Furthermore, the distance measure Q for the intersection in a single point (not containment as in table 3) is given in table 5. Note that the relation between lines and circles and two circles is also zero, if the entities are co-planar. Also, note that if a plane and a sphere intersect in a single point, the plane is tangential to the sphere. That is, we can also test tangentiality in this way.

In terms of the component vectors we have, for example, for two lines $q^k(k, l) = k^i \, l^{j_2} \, D^{j_1}{}_i N^k{}_{j_1 j_2}$, with Jacobi matrices $Q^k{}_{j_2}(k) = k^i \, D^{j_1}{}_i N^k{}_{j_1 j_2}$ and $\bar{Q}^k{}_i(l) = l^{j_2} \, D^{j_1}{}_i N^k{}_{j_1 j_2}$, which can be used in equation (1) to evaluate $\Sigma_{q,q}$. For line and circle we have

$$q^s(k, c) = w^{r_1}(k, c)\, w^{r_2}(k, c)\, G^s{}_{r_1 r_2}, \qquad w^k(k, c) = k^i \, c^{j_2} \, D^{j_1}{}_i N^k{}_{j_1 j_2}. \qquad (4)$$

When evaluating the covariance matrix for q(k, c) one also has to include the cross-correlation part of equation (1) with cross-correlation matrix $\Sigma_{w,w}$ in the calculation.

Projective Camera. A central aspect of Computer Vision is the projection of points and lines onto the image plane of a projective camera and also the reconstruction of points and lines in 3D-space from their projections.

The projection of a point X onto the image plane P_A of a camera with optical center A can be evaluated as the intersection of the projective ray $A \wedge X \wedge \mathbf{e}_\infty$ with

Fig. 2. a) Projection on a parabolic mirror and b) its mathematical representation as stereographic projection

P_A. The projected point X_A is then given by $X_A = (A \wedge X \wedge e_\infty) \cdot P_A^*$. Note that this description of a camera is intimately related to the corresponding camera matrix as is shown in [15]. Using this formula we can immediately evaluate the projection of an uncertain point, whereby also an uncertainty of the camera basis can be accounted for. Note that the resultant projected point is an affine point as described in section 2.

Conversely, if we are given an uncertain image point X_A (as a standard point), and we would like to estimate the corresponding uncertain projection ray L, we can use the relation $L = A \wedge X_A \wedge e_\infty$. If we assume that A is a certain point, then this becomes, in terms of the component vectors, $l = K x_A$ and $\Sigma_{l,l} = K \Sigma_{x_A,x_A} K^T$, with

$$K^k{}_{i_2} = a^{i_1} e^{j_2}_\infty O^{j_1}{}_{i_1 i_2} O^k{}_{j_1 j_2}, \tag{5}$$

Note that $K \in \mathbb{R}^{6 \times 5}$, since x_A contains the five components of a standard point and l the six Plücker coordinates of the projective ray. An uncertain projection ray evaluated in this way may, for example, be used in the pose estimation approach described above.

Catadioptric Camera. We now show how the projection ray related to an image point in a catadioptric camera with a parabolic mirror can be constructed using Geometric Algebra. Figure 2a shows the basic setup of a catadioptric imaging system with a parabolic mirror. A light ray emanating from point X in the world that would pass through the focal point F of a parabolic mirror (shown with a half-transparent checkered texture), is reflected down at point X_M with direction parallel to the axis of the parabolic mirror. If below the mirror a projective camera is placed focused to infinity, then an image as shown in the figure is generated. Schematically we can replace the projective camera with an orthogonal one, and then obtain image point X_I from world point X.

In [16], Geyer and Daniilidis show that this type of image generation can mathematically be modeled as shown in figure 2b. The world point X is projected onto a unit sphere, centered on the focal point of the parabolic mirror, thus generating X_S. A stereographic projection of X_S then results in X_I', which lies on the plane bisecting the sphere perpendicular to the parabolic mirror's axis. Projecting X_I' parallel to the parabolic mirror's axis, then generates the same image point X_I as before.

We found that the stereographic projection of the latter method can be replaced by an inversion in the sphere centered on N with radius $\sqrt{2}$. This allows us to perform the following geometric construction using the Geometric Algebra of conformal space. Suppose we are given an image point X_I with an associated covariance matrix and we would like to evaluate the corresponding uncertain projection ray passing through the focal point of the parabolic mirror F and X_S. First of all, we can move X_I to X_I' without the need for error propagation. If S represents the inversion sphere centered on N with radius $\sqrt{2}$, then $X_S = S^* X_I' S^*$. The projection ray L is then given by $L = F \wedge e_\infty \wedge X_S = F \wedge e_\infty \wedge (S^* X_I' S^*)$. Again we can apply standard error propagation to obtain the covariance matrix of L.

If we assume that F and S are ideal, that is they are not regarded as uncertain entities, then L and its covariance matrix can be evaluated from X_I' via matrix multiplications using the corresponding component vectors. Let e_∞, f, s, l and x_I denote the component vectors of e_∞, F, S^*, L and X_I', respectively. Then $l = K\, x_I$ and $\Sigma_{l,l} = K\, \Sigma_{x_I,x_I}\, K^T$, where

$$K^r{}_{k_2} = f^{i_1}\, e_\infty^{i_2}\, s^{k_1}\, s^{l_2}\, G^{l_1}{}_{k_1 k_2}\, O^{j_1}{}_{i_1 i_2}\, G^{j_2}{}_{l_1 l_2}\, O^r{}_{j_1 j_2}. \tag{6}$$

Note that $K \in \mathbb{R}^{6 \times 5}$, since l contains the six Plücker coordinates of the projective ray and x_I the five components of a standard point in conformal space. Again, an uncertain projection ray evaluated in this way may be used in the pose estimation approach described above.

5 Conclusions

We have presented a unifying framework for the description of uncertain geometry and kinematics. It was shown that the Geometric Algebra of conformal space can be applied to many important applications of Computer Vision and can deal with the invariably occurring uncertainties of geometric entities and transformations, in an appropriate way.

A result of particular importance is that covariance matrices can appropriately represent the uncertainty of algebra entities that represent transformations. This is, for example, not possible for rotation matrices, since orthogonal matrices do not span a linear subspace.

Furthermore, a novel pose estimation approach was introduced, which is quadratic in the components of the transformation, without having made any approximations. A uniform framework for geometric entity fitting and triangulation and the testing of uncertain geometric relations was presented. Finally, the treatment of catadioptric cameras with parabolic mirrors within this framework was discussed. The main result here was that the construction of projection rays from image points, which is needed for pose estimation, can be achieved by a simple matrix multiplication for projective and catadioptric cameras.

We believe these results show that a combination of an algebraic description of geometric problems, with a linear algebra approach to their numerical solution, offers a valuable framework for the treatment of many Computer Vision applications.

References

1. Förstner, W., Brunn, A., Heuel, S.: Statistically testing uncertain geometric relations. In Sommer, G., Krüger, N., Perwass, C., eds.: Mustererkennung 2000. Informatik Aktuell, Springer, Berlin (2000) 17–26
2. Heuel, S.: Uncertain Projective Geometry. Volume 3008 of LNCS. Springer (2004)
3. Perwass, C., Sommer, G.: Numerical evaluation of versors with Clifford algebra. In Dorst, L., Doran, C., Lasenby, J., eds.: Applications of Geometric Algebra in Computer Science and Engineering, Birkhäuser (2002) 341–349
4. Perwass, C., Förstner, W.: Uncertain geometry with circles, spheres and conics. In Klette, R., Kozera, R., Noakes, L., Weickert, J., eds.: Geometric Properties from Incomplete Data. Volume 31 of Computational Imaging and Vision. Springer-Verlag (2006) 23–41
5. Rosenhahn, B., Sommer, G.: Pose estimation in conformal geometric algebra, part I: The stratification of mathematical spaces. Journal of Mathematical Imaging and Vision **22** (2005) 27–48
6. Perwass, C., Gebken, C., Sommer, G.: Estimation of geometric entities and operators from uncertain data. In: 27. Symposium für Mustererkennung, DAGM 2005, Wien, 29.8.-2.9.005. Number 3663 in LNCS, Springer-Verlag, Berlin, Heidelberg (2005)
7. Perwass, C., Hildenbrand, D.: Aspects of geometric algebra in Euclidean, projective and conformal space. Technical Report Number 0310, CAU Kiel, Institut für Informatik (2003)
8. Hestenes, D., Sobczyk, G.: Clifford Algebra to Geometric Calculus: A Unified Language for Mathematics and Physics. Reidel, Dordrecht (1984)
9. Koch, K.R.: Parameter Estimation and Hypothesis Testing in Linear Models. Springer (1997)
10. Mikhail, E., Ackermann, F.: Observations and Least Squares. University Press of America, Lanham, MD20706, USA (1976)
11. Li, H., Hestenes, D., Rockwood, A.: Generalized Homogeneous Coordinates for Computational Geometry. In: Geometric Computing with Clifford Algebras. Springer, Berlin, Heidelberg (2001) 27–59
12. Clifford, W.K.: Preliminary sketch of bi-quaternions. In: Proceedings of the London Mathematical Society. Volume 4. (1873) 381–395
13. Daniilidis, K.: Using the Algebra of Dual Quaternions for Motion Alignment. In: Geometric Computing with Clifford Algebras. Springer, Berlin, Heidelberg (2001) 489–500
14. Gebken, C., Perwass, C., Buchholz, S., Sommer, G.: A robust geometrical solution to pose estimation using geometric algebra. In: submitted to ECCV 2006. (2006)
15. Perwass, C.: Applications of Geometric Algebra in Computer Vision. PhD thesis, Cambridge University (2000)
16. Geyer, C., Daniilidis, K.: Catadioptric projective geometry. International Journal of Computer Vision (2001) 223–243

Euclidean Structure from $N \geq 2$ Parallel Circles: Theory and Algorithms

Pierre Gurdjos[1], Peter Sturm[2], and Yihong Wu[3]

[1] IRIT-TCI, UPS, 118 route de Narbonne,
31062 Toulouse, cedex 9, France
Pierre.Gurdjos@irit.fr
[2] PERCEPTION, INRIA Rhône-Alpes,
655, avenue de l'Europe, 38330 Montbonnot, France
Peter.Sturm@inrialpes.fr
[3] NLPR-IA, Chinese Academy of Sciences, P.O. Box 2728,
No. 95 East Road of Zhong Guan Cun, Beijing 100080, China
yhwu@nlpr.ia.ac.cn

Abstract. Our problem is that of recovering, in one view, the 2D Euclidean structure, induced by the projections of N parallel circles. This structure is a prerequisite for camera calibration and pose computation. Until now, no general method has been described for $N > 2$. The main contribution of this work is to state the problem in terms of a system of linear equations to solve. We give a closed-form solution as well as bundle adjustment-like refinements, increasing the technical applicability and numerical stability. Our theoretical approach generalizes and extends all those described in existing works for $N = 2$ in several respects, as we can treat simultaneously pairs of orthogonal lines and pairs of circles within a unified framework. The proposed algorithm may be easily implemented, using well-known numerical algorithms. Its performance is illustrated by simulations and experiments with real images.

1 Introduction

The roles played by quadrics and conics in recovering the Euclidean structure of a 3D world have been widely investigated in the computer vision literature [1][3][12][15][17][19]. More generally, it is now well-understood that the keys to Euclidean structures [6][11][13][14][17][19][23], in the considered d-dimensional space, are the identifications of *absolute* entities, typically *absolute* quadrics and conics, whose characteristics are to be left invariant under similarities in d-space. As an example, the absolute disk quadric envelope, introduced by Triggs in [22], encodes the complete Euclidean structure of the 3D space.

In the specific case of a 2D scene, located on some 3D supporting plane π, the image plane of a pinhole camera, to which is projected the scene, can be seen as a projective representation of π. Formally speaking, the 2D Euclidean structure of π is given by two (projected) *absolute* conjugate complex points, so-called (projected) circular points [5][18]. The circular points of π are, by definition, common to all of its circles. It is therefore not surprising that the issue of

A. Leonardis, H. Bischof, and A. Pinz (Eds.): ECCV 2006, Part I, LNCS 3951, pp. 238–252, 2006.

inferring metric properties about the camera and/or the scene, from projections of circular features has been considered, especially for camera calibration purposes [3][11][13][19][23]. Intrinsically, circular targets offer arguably interesting visual clues: they can be easily detected and fitted [7], even if partially occluded. It is nevertheless worth remembering that the sole knowledge of the 2D Euclidean structure of π w.r.t. one view is insufficient for calibrating the camera and recovering the 3D pose of π i.e., multiple views are required [20][22][24].

In this work, we are aiming at finding a closed-form solution to the problem of recovering such a 2D Euclidean structure, common to a family of parallel planes, from $N \geq 2$ projected unknown parallel circles. Until now, this only has been solved (in these terms) for $N = 2$. We emphasize the fact that circles may correspond to physical entities, like external parallels of a surface of revolution [6], but also to virtual ones e.g., the para-catadioptric projection of a line onto the mirror surface [2], the circular motion of a 3D point [11] or even the absolute conic [10, pp. 81-83], which makes this problem of broader interest.

Our theoretical approach, giving new geometrical insights, unifies and generalizes those described in prior works for $N = 2$ in several respects. We propose:

 – a rigorous formalism, based on the projective invariance of absolute signatures of degenerate circles and generalized eigenvalues of circle pencils;
 – a linear algorithm for $N \geq 2$ circles, that yields a closed-form solution and optimal (non-linear) refinements; it generalizes [14, p.60], by the ability of treating simultaneously pairs of orthogonal lines and pairs of circles.

2 Problem Statement and Proposed Interpretation

Our problem, so-called P_N, is that of recovering the Euclidean structure, common to a family of parallel planes, from N projected circles in one view, taken by an uncalibrated camera. By *projected circles*, we refer to conics of the image plane $\tilde{\pi}$, which are the projections of 3D *parallel circles* i.e., lying on parallel planes. Let h denote the world-to-image homography, mapping one of these plane, say π, to the image plane $\tilde{\pi}$. Since the pre-image $\mathcal{A} \equiv h^{-1}(\tilde{\mathcal{A}})$ of any projected circle $\tilde{\mathcal{A}}$ is always a circle in π, for the sake of simplicity, we will only consider as world circles, not all 3D parallel circles, but the corresponding coplanar circles of π. Hence, we restrict the terms circles to only refer *coplanar circles*.

To solve P_N, all we have at our disposal are the symmetric image matrices $\tilde{\mathbf{A}}_j \in \mathbb{R}^{3 \times 3}$ of $N \geq 2$ projections $\tilde{\mathcal{A}}_j$ of circles $\mathcal{A}_j$ of π, $j = 1..N$. The problem P_2 i.e., for $N = 2$, can be simply stated e.g., as in [6][11][23]. The Euclidean structure of π is encoded by its projected circular points $\tilde{\mathtt{I}} \equiv h(\mathtt{I})$, $\tilde{\mathtt{J}} \equiv h(\mathtt{J})$, where the circular points $\mathtt{I}$, $\mathtt{J}$ are, by definition [5][18], common to all circles, including the absolute conic. Hence, two projected circles have four points in common, among which is the point-pair $(\tilde{\mathtt{I}}, \tilde{\mathtt{J}})$. The other point-pair, denoted here by $(\tilde{\mathtt{G}}, \tilde{\mathtt{H}})$, consists of either real or conjugate complex points. Both point-pairs span real lines, namely the vanishing line $\tilde{\mathtt{L}}_\infty \equiv h(\mathtt{L}_\infty)$ and some "other" line $\tilde{\Delta} \equiv h(\Delta)$. The existing algorithms solving P_2 basically work as follows: (i) they compute the four common points of $\tilde{\mathcal{A}}_1$, $\tilde{\mathcal{A}}_2$; (ii) they pick up the projected circular point-pair $(\tilde{\mathbf{I}}, \tilde{\mathbf{J}})$. Regarding (ii), when the two obtained point-pairs are conjugate complex, it can be required to first determine which line is $\tilde{\mathbf{L}}_\infty$ i.e., is the line spanned by $(\tilde{\mathbf{I}}, \tilde{\mathbf{J}})$. These algorithms were designed to only deal with two circles and their extensions to multiple circles is clearly troublesome. Indeed, for $N > 2$, it is about estimating the common root of multiple degree-4 polynomials. Thus, the issue of finding a numerically stable closed-form solution is far from straightforward.

Consider a set of $N \geq 2$ projected circles. An elegant means of solving the problem P_N is to interpret all or some pairs of the set of projected circles as "generators" of pencils of conics [5][17][18]. This is the basic idea of the proposed work. Let us say that $(\tilde{\mathcal{A}}_1, \tilde{\mathcal{A}}_2)$ is one of these pairs, spanning the conic pencil $\{\tilde{\mathcal{A}}_1, \tilde{\mathcal{A}}_2\}$. This latter is the linear family of projected circles, with image matrices $\tilde{\mathbf{A}}(\tilde{\lambda}) \equiv \tilde{\mathbf{A}}_1 - \tilde{\lambda}\tilde{\mathbf{A}}_2$, where $\tilde{\mathbf{A}}$ is the image matrix of $\tilde{\mathcal{A}}$ and $\tilde{\lambda} \in \mathbb{C}$ is a parameter. It includes three *degenerate conics consisting of line-pairs*, whose parameters $\tilde{\lambda}_k$, $k = 1..3$, are the generalized eigenvalues of $(\tilde{\mathbf{A}}_1, \tilde{\mathbf{A}}_2)$. If $\tilde{\mathbf{p}} \in \mathbb{C}^3$ represents any of the four common points of $\tilde{\mathcal{A}}_1$ and $\tilde{\mathcal{A}}_2$, then the equation $\tilde{\mathbf{p}}^\top \tilde{\mathbf{A}}_1 \tilde{\mathbf{p}} = 0$ holds as well as $\tilde{\mathbf{p}}^\top \tilde{\mathbf{A}}_2 \tilde{\mathbf{p}} = 0$. Thus, taking any linear combination for one of the generalized eigenvalues λ_k, the equation $\tilde{\mathbf{p}}^\top (\tilde{\mathbf{A}}_1 - \tilde{\lambda}_k \tilde{\mathbf{A}}_2) \tilde{\mathbf{p}} = 0$ also holds. This means that the projected circular points $\tilde{\mathbf{I}}, \tilde{\mathbf{J}}$ lie on *all* the projected degenerate conics of the pencil, which so are projected *degenerate circles*. Therefore, by considering multiple projected circle-pairs, this reduces the problem of recovering $\tilde{\mathbf{I}}, \tilde{\mathbf{J}}$ to basically that of finding the (complex) intersection of a set of lines (cf. Fig. 1). A closed-form solution can then be obtained using a *linear algorithm* i.e., by solving an overdetermined system of linear equations.

This proposed interpretation will also allow us to exhibit interesting results. It can be shown that one of the degenerate members of the pencil $\{\tilde{\mathcal{A}}_1, \tilde{\mathcal{A}}_2\}$ is the projected degenerate circle $\widetilde{\Delta \mathbf{L}_\infty}$ i.e., consisting of the two lines $\tilde{\Delta}$ and $\tilde{\mathbf{L}}_\infty$, where $\tilde{\mathbf{L}}_\infty$ is the vanishing line of π. An important fact is that $\widetilde{\Delta \mathbf{L}_\infty}$ can always be distinguished from the other degenerate members, thanks to a discriminant invariant *absolute signature* (cf. §3.1). Because our algorithm requires to distinguish $\tilde{\mathbf{L}}_\infty$ from $\tilde{\Delta}$, in §4.3, we will put the emphasis on the roles played by the projections $\tilde{\mathbf{Z}}_1 = h(\mathbf{Z}_1)$ and $\tilde{\mathbf{Z}}_2 = h(\mathbf{Z}_2)$ of the so-called *limiting points* of the pencil $\{\tilde{\mathcal{A}}_1, \tilde{\mathcal{A}}_2\}$, whose image vectors correspond to two (identifiable) generalized eigenvectors of $(\tilde{\mathbf{A}}_1, \tilde{\mathbf{A}}_2)$. Specifically, we will be able to establish a general necessary and sufficient condition, cf. Propr. 1, depending on the relative positions of $\tilde{\mathbf{Z}}_1$, $\tilde{\mathbf{Z}}_2$ w.r.t. $\tilde{\Delta}$, for problem P_2 to be well-posed i.e., for the Euclidean structure to be recovered. In particular, we will show there exist enclosing but not concentric circle-pairs (as shown in Fig. 2) for which the condition holds, contrary to what was previously claimed in [11][23].

3   Some Projective and Euclidean Properties of Conics

Before going more into detail about our problem P_N, we state some properties of conics relevant to our work. General projective properties of conics and their envelopes can be found in standard textbooks, such as [18]. In this section, we restrict the term conics to only refer *coplanar conics*.

Throughout §3-§4, for the sake of simplicity, we will deal with two different 2D representations of a supporting plane, namely Euclidean and projective. The former can be seen as the world representation and the latter as the image representation. When referring to the vectors/matrices of entities w.r.t. the projective representation, we will systematically add the symbol ˜, like in (1). We ask the reader to keep in mind that $\mathbf{Q}$ and $\tilde{\mathbf{Q}}$ will represent the same entity $\mathcal{Q}$ until §5.1.

The dual notion of a (point) conic $\mathcal{Q}$, represented by the symmetric matrix $\mathbf{Q} \in \mathbb{R}^{3 \times 3}$, is the (line) conic envelope $\mathcal{Q}^*$, whose matrix is the adjugate matrix[1] $\mathbf{Q}^*$. The *projective matrix* $\tilde{\mathbf{Q}}$ of a conic $\mathcal{Q}$ is related to the *Euclidean matrix* $\mathbf{Q}$ of $\mathcal{Q}$ by the congruence:

$$\tilde{\mathbf{Q}} = s\mathbf{H}^{-\top}\mathbf{Q}\mathbf{H}^{-1}, \; s \neq 0, \tag{1}$$

where $\mathbf{H} \in \mathbb{R}^{3 \times 3}$ is the matrix of the Euclidean-to-projective homography.

3.1 Projectively Invariant Classification of Degenerate Conics

We let the reader dually restate the following results, by substituting point for line as well as envelope for locus, whenever the sans serif font is used.

A degenerate conic locus consists of either two lines M and N, with vectors $\tilde{\mathbf{m}}$ and $\tilde{\mathbf{n}}$, such that its matrix satisfies $\tilde{\mathbf{D}} \sim \tilde{\mathbf{m}}\tilde{\mathbf{n}}^{\top} + \tilde{\mathbf{n}}\tilde{\mathbf{m}}^{\top}$, or a repeated line M = N such that $\tilde{\mathbf{D}} \sim \tilde{\mathbf{m}}\tilde{\mathbf{m}}^{\top}$. If M $\neq$ N i.e., rank($\tilde{\mathbf{D}}$) = 2, then $\tilde{\mathbf{m}} \times \tilde{\mathbf{n}} \in \text{null}\,\tilde{\mathbf{D}}$.

We will now focus on degenerate conics $\mathcal{D}$, whose matrices $\tilde{\mathbf{D}}$ are real. They obey to a projectively invariant classification, thanks to the following properties.

For any singular $\tilde{\mathbf{D}} \in \mathbb{R}^{3 \times 3}$, define the **absolute signature** $\Sigma(\tilde{\mathbf{D}}) \equiv |\eta - \nu|$, where η and ν count the positive and negative eigenvalues of $\tilde{\mathbf{D}}$. As a corollary of Sylvester's inertia theorem [9, p. 403], it can be established that $\Sigma(\tilde{\mathbf{D}}) \equiv |\eta - \nu|$ is invariant under congruence transformations of $\tilde{\mathbf{D}}$, as is rank $\tilde{\mathbf{D}} \equiv \eta + \nu$, which entails that both the absolute signature and the rank of $\mathcal{D}$ are projectively invariant. It is then easy to show that:

$$\Sigma(\tilde{\mathbf{D}}) = \begin{cases} 0 \Leftrightarrow \{\tilde{\mathbf{m}}, \tilde{\mathbf{n}}\} = \{\tilde{\mathbf{x}}_1 + \tilde{\mathbf{x}}_2, \tilde{\mathbf{x}}_1 - \tilde{\mathbf{x}}_2\} & \text{iff M, N are } \textit{real} \text{ and } \textit{distinct} \\ 1 \Leftrightarrow \tilde{\mathbf{m}} = \tilde{\mathbf{n}} = \tilde{\mathbf{x}}_1 & \text{iff M = N is } \textit{real} \\ 2 \Leftrightarrow \{\tilde{\mathbf{m}}, \tilde{\mathbf{n}}\} = \{\tilde{\mathbf{x}}_1 + i\tilde{\mathbf{x}}_2, \tilde{\mathbf{x}}_1 - i\tilde{\mathbf{x}}_2\} & \text{iff M, N are } \textit{conjugate complex} \end{cases}$$

$$\text{where } \begin{bmatrix} \tilde{\mathbf{x}}_1 \; \tilde{\mathbf{x}}_2 \end{bmatrix} \equiv \mathbf{U}\mathbf{S}^{1/2} \begin{bmatrix} \mathbf{e}_1 \; \mathbf{e}_2 \end{bmatrix} \in \mathbb{R}^{3 \times 2} \tag{2}$$

involves the SVD [9, p. 70] $\mathbf{U}^{\top}\tilde{\mathbf{D}}\mathbf{V} = \text{diag}(s_1, s_2, 0) \equiv \mathbf{S}$, for orthogonal $\mathbf{U}$, $\mathbf{V} \in \mathbb{R}^{3 \times 3}$, with singular values $s_1 > s_2 \geq 0$, and $\mathbf{e}_1 \equiv (1, 0, 0)^{\top}$, $\mathbf{e}_2 \equiv (0, 1, 0)^{\top}$.

3.2 Euclidean Structure and Circular-Point Envelope

In the light of §3.1, the "absolute" degenerate conic that will be central regarding our problem is the **circular-point envelope IJ**, consisting of the circular point-pair. It encodes the Euclidean structure in 2D space, in much the same way as the degenerate absolute quadric envelope [21], encodes the Euclidean structure in 3D space. Thus, IJ is left invariant under 2D similarities.

---

[1] If $\mathbf{Q}$ is not degenerate, then $\mathbf{Q}^* \equiv \det(\mathbf{Q})\mathbf{Q}^{-1}$.

The only "tangent" that touches IJ at both circular points is L_∞, such that (3a) holds. The other "tangents" touch IJ at one circular point and are isotropic lines. An **isotropic line** is the complex line, denoted by C^I (resp. C^J), through a real finite point C and I (resp. J), with conjugate complex vectors $\tilde{x}_1 + i\tilde{x}_2$ (resp. $\tilde{x}_1 - i\tilde{x}_2$). They are *self-perpendicular lines*, satisfying (3b). *Perpendicular lines* M and N, with vectors $\tilde{m}$ and $\tilde{n}$, are conjugate w.r.t. IJ, satisfying (3c).

$$\tilde{C}_\infty^* \tilde{l}_\infty = 0_3, \tag{3a}$$

$$\tilde{x}_1^\top \tilde{C}_\infty^* \tilde{x}_2 = 0 \quad \text{and} \quad \tilde{x}_1^\top \tilde{C}_\infty^* \tilde{x}_1 - \tilde{x}_1^\top \tilde{C}_\infty^* \tilde{x}_2 = 0, \tag{3b}$$

$$\tilde{m}^\top \tilde{C}_\infty^* \tilde{n} = 0. \tag{3c}$$

Equations (3a), resp. (3b)-(3c), describe affine, resp. Euclidean, constraints on IJ, with rank-2 matrix $\tilde{C}_\infty^*$.

4 Linear Euclidean Constraints from $N \geq 2$ Circles

4.1 Treating Two Circles as Generators of a Pencil of Circles

As said before, interpreting all or some circle-pairs as generators of pencils of circles [5][18] offers an elegant means of extending the algorithm from $N = 2$ to $N > 2$ circles. The conic pencil $\{A_1, A_2\}$, with circle-pair (A_1, A_2) as generators, is the linear family of circles, with matrices of the form $\tilde{A}(\tilde{\lambda}) \equiv \tilde{A}_1 - \tilde{\lambda}\tilde{A}_2$. There are three degenerate circles in $\{A_1, A_2\}$, whose parameters $\tilde{\lambda}$ are the generalized eigenvalues of $(\tilde{A}_1, \tilde{A}_2)$.

In this work, we *only* consider non-intersecting generators[2]. As a consequence, any degenerate circles of $\{A_1, A_2\}$ have a real rank-2 matrix so can be classified and decomposed into lines, according to (2). Remind that the Euclidean structure of π is encoded by the circular-point envelope IJ, as explained in §3.2. The important fact is that a degenerate circle of $\{A_1, A_2\}$ is either an isotropic line-pair, through I and J, or a real line-pair, including L_∞. In the former case, we call it **point-circle**, yielding Euclidean constraints (3b) on the plane's structure IJ. In the latter, we call it **line-circle**, yielding, providing L_∞ is identified, affine constraints (3a). Identifying L_∞ is about distinguishing its vector in decomposition (2). As explained in [23], solving this ambiguity requires to study the relative position of A_1 and A_2.

4.2 Relative Positions of Two Circles and Generalized Eigenvalues

The issue of studying the different relative positions of A_1 and A_2 is now tackled by analysing the generalized eigenvalues [9, p. 375] of $(\tilde{A}_1, \tilde{A}_2)$, which are the three real solutions for $\tilde{\lambda}$ of the cubic equation $\det(\tilde{A}_1 - \tilde{\lambda}\tilde{A}_2) = 0$.

---

[2] Actually, the case of intersecting circles does not introduce major difficulties to be treated in the proposed framework, besides dealing with complex generalized eigenvalues. However, owing to lack of space, this could hardly be included here.

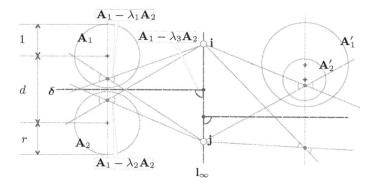

Fig. 1. The problem of finding the circular points may reduce to that of intersecting degenerate circles, consisting of line-pairs, with rank-2 matrices of the form $\mathbf{A}_1 - \lambda\mathbf{A}_2$

An interesting fact is that the generalized eigenvalues are projectively invariant as a set, up to a scale factor [16]. More precisely, if $\tilde{\mathbf{A}}_j = s_j\mathbf{H}^{-\top}\mathbf{A}_j\mathbf{H}^{-1}$, then $(\lambda, \mathbf{z})$ and $(\frac{s_2}{s_1}\lambda, \mathbf{Hz})$ are generalized eigen-pairs of $(\mathbf{A}_1, \mathbf{A}_2)$ and $(\tilde{\mathbf{A}}_1, \tilde{\mathbf{A}}_2)$, respectively. This allows us to introduce canonical matrices in order to simplify computations.

Let us attach some Euclidean representation to the 3D plane such that $\mathcal{A}_1$ and $\mathcal{A}_2$ have (Euclidean) matrices:

$$\mathbf{A}_1 = \begin{bmatrix} 1 & 0 & 0 \\ 0 & 1 & 0 \\ 0 & 0 & -1 \end{bmatrix}, \quad \mathbf{A}_2 = \begin{bmatrix} 1 & 0 & -d \\ 0 & 1 & 0 \\ -d & 0 & d^2 - r^2 \end{bmatrix}. \tag{4}$$

Thus, $\mathcal{A}_1$ is centred at the origin $\mathbf{0}$ and has radius 1; $\mathcal{A}_2$ is centred at point $(0, d)$, with $d \geq 0$, and has radius $r > 0$ (cf. Fig. 1).

We can specify all relative positions of $\mathcal{A}_1$, $\mathcal{A}_2$, using constraints on d and r. Circles **intersect** (i.e., at *two* real points) iff $d > |r - 1|$ *and* $d < r + 1$, or, equivalently, iff $\alpha < 0$, where:

$$\alpha \equiv (d - r + 1)(d - r - 1)(d + r - 1). \tag{5}$$

Regarding other cases, $\mathcal{A}_1$ and $\mathcal{A}_2$ are **tangent** iff $\alpha = 0$ and are **disjoint** i.e., not intersecting, iff $\alpha > 0$. Disjoint circles can be **separate** $(d > r + 1)$, **concentric** $(d = 0)$ or **enclosing but not concentric** $(d < |r - 1|)$.

What the generalized eigenvalues of $(\tilde{\mathbf{A}}_1, \tilde{\mathbf{A}}_2)$ ***tell us.*** We now explain how to recover d and r from the generalized eigenvalues of $(\tilde{\mathbf{A}}_1, \tilde{\mathbf{A}}_2)$ and, thus, how to determine the relative position of the generators $\mathcal{A}_1$, $\mathcal{A}_2$.

Let $\tilde{\boldsymbol{\lambda}}$, resp. $\boldsymbol{\lambda}$, denote the vector of generalized eigenvalues of $(\tilde{\mathbf{A}}_1, \tilde{\mathbf{A}}_2)$, resp. $(\mathbf{A}_1, \mathbf{A}_2)$, computed by MAPLE as:

$$\tilde{\boldsymbol{\lambda}} \sim \boldsymbol{\lambda} = \left(\frac{1 + r^2 - d^2 - \sqrt{\beta}}{2r^2}, \frac{1 + r^2 - d^2 + \sqrt{\beta}}{2r^2}, 1 \right)^\top, \quad \beta \equiv \alpha(d + r + 1). \tag{6}$$

Since we deal with non-intersecting generators, we have $\alpha \geq 0 \Rightarrow \beta \geq 0$. Therefore, all the λ's are real so all the degenerate circles have real matrices.

Now, consider the system of two equations obtained by expanding and simplifying $(\tilde{\lambda}_1 \pm \tilde{\lambda}_2)/\tilde{\lambda}_3$, in order to eliminate the scale factor in $\tilde{\boldsymbol{\lambda}}$. Then, solve it for d and r by only picking the positive values. We get:

$$\begin{cases} (\tilde{\lambda}_1 + \tilde{\lambda}_2)/\tilde{\lambda}_3 = (r^2 - d^2 + 1)/r^2 \\ (\tilde{\lambda}_1 - \tilde{\lambda}_2)/\tilde{\lambda}_3 = \sqrt{\beta}/r^2 \end{cases} \Leftrightarrow \begin{cases} d = \sqrt{\tilde{\lambda}_1\tilde{\lambda}_2(\tilde{\lambda}_1 - \tilde{\lambda}_3)(\tilde{\lambda}_2 - \tilde{\lambda}_3)}/|\tilde{\lambda}_1\tilde{\lambda}_2| \\ r = |\tilde{\lambda}_3|/\sqrt{\tilde{\lambda}_1\tilde{\lambda}_2} \end{cases} \quad (7)$$

Ordering the generalized eigenvalues. Since $\tilde{\lambda}_1$, $\tilde{\lambda}_2$ play symmetric roles in (7), do not distinguish them by using indifferently the notations $\tilde{\lambda}_+$ or $\tilde{\lambda}_-$. Moreover, denote by $\Sigma(\tilde{\lambda})$ the absolute signature $\Sigma(\tilde{\mathbf{A}}_1 - \tilde{\lambda}\tilde{\mathbf{A}}_2)$. Of course, let these notations also apply to the Euclidean representation.

After some symbolic computations, it can be stated that the degenerate circles satisfy, either $\Sigma(\lambda_+) = 2$ *and* $\Sigma(\lambda_-) = \Sigma(\lambda_3) = 1$ for concentric generators, or $\Sigma(\lambda_+) = \Sigma(\lambda_-) = 2$ *and* $\Sigma(\lambda_3) = 0$, otherwise. Thanks to invariance of the absolute signature, this eventually entails that:

$$\Sigma(\tilde{\mathbf{A}}_1 - \tilde{\lambda}_\pm\tilde{\mathbf{A}}_2) \geq 1 \geq \Sigma(\tilde{\mathbf{A}}_1 - \tilde{\lambda}_3\tilde{\mathbf{A}}_2). \quad (8)$$

The pair (d, r) ***as a double invariant of two circles.*** Assume that the $\tilde{\lambda}$'s in $\tilde{\boldsymbol{\lambda}}$ are sorted by decreasing order of absolute signatures such that (8) holds. As a result, d and r, given as functions (7) of the $\tilde{\lambda}$'s, are *projectively invariant*.

Therefore, given $(\tilde{\mathbf{A}}_1, \tilde{\mathbf{A}}_2)$, we can deduce the relative position of $\mathcal{A}_1$ and $\mathcal{A}_2$, by determining which constraint on d and r holds.

4.3   Recovering the Line at Infinity

After analysing their decompositions into lines according to (2), the set of three degenerate circles of the pencil are made up of:

- the rank-1 line-circle L^2_∞ twice and the point-circle $\mathsf{0}^\mathsf{I}\mathsf{0}^\mathsf{J}$ (concentric case),
- a rank-2 line-circle $\Delta\mathsf{L}_\infty$ and the point-circle $\mathsf{Z}^\mathsf{I}\mathsf{Z}^\mathsf{J}$ twice (tangent case),
- a rank-2 line-circle $\Delta\mathsf{L}_\infty$ and two distinct point-circles $\mathsf{Z}_c^\mathsf{I}\mathsf{Z}_c^\mathsf{J}$ (disjoint case),

where $\mathsf{0}$ is the origin. Points Z as well as line Δ will be specified in §4.3.

The issue is now to recover the line at infinity L_∞. The only relative positions that require investigations are cases of two non-concentric circles i.e., iff $d > 0$.

What the generalized eigenvectors of $(\tilde{\mathbf{A}}_1, \tilde{\mathbf{A}}_2)$ ***tell us.*** Assume $d > 0$. MAPLE computes the matrix of generalized eigenvectors associated with $\tilde{\boldsymbol{\lambda}}$ as:

$$\tilde{\mathbf{Z}} = \mathbf{HZ}\begin{pmatrix} \xi_1 & & \\ & \xi_2 & \\ & & \xi_3 \end{pmatrix}, \quad \mathbf{Z} = \begin{bmatrix} \frac{1+d^2-r^2+\sqrt{\beta}}{2d} & \frac{1+d^2-r^2-\sqrt{\beta}}{2d} & 0 \\ 0 & 0 & 1 \\ 1 & 1 & 0 \end{bmatrix}, \quad (9)$$

where ξ_1, ξ_2, ξ_3 are some non-zero scale factors.

The third column $\mathbf{z}_3$ of $\mathbf{Z}$ is the Euclidean vector of the centre of a line-circle ΔL_∞, with Euclidean matrix $\mathbf{A}(\lambda_3)$. Using (2), given that $\mathbf{l}_\infty \sim (0,0,1)^\top$, we have $\mathbf{A}(\lambda_3) \sim \mathbf{A}_1 - 1\mathbf{A}_2 \sim \mathbf{l}_\infty \boldsymbol{\delta}^\top + \boldsymbol{\delta} \mathbf{l}_\infty^\top$, where:

$$\boldsymbol{\delta} = (-2d, 0, 1 + d^2 - r^2)^\top. \tag{10}$$

$\boldsymbol{\delta}$ is the Euclidean vector of the **radical axis** Δ of $\{\mathcal{A}_1, \mathcal{A}_2\}$, which is the locus of points having equal powers w.r.t. both circles [5, pp. 95-96]. Note that when $d = 0$, we have $\boldsymbol{\delta} \sim \mathbf{l}_\infty$ so $\Delta L_\infty = L_\infty^2$ consists of the repeated line at infinity.

Vectors $\mathbf{z}_c$ ($c = 1, 2$) are the Euclidean vectors of the centres Z_c of point-circles $Z_c^I Z_c^J$, whose Euclidean matrices are $\mathbf{A}(\lambda_c)$. A point-circle $Z_c^I Z_c^J$ may be looked upon a "limiting circle" of the pencil with radius zero. For this reason, Z_c is called a **limiting point** of the pencil $\{\mathcal{A}_1, \mathcal{A}_2\}$ [5, p.97] (see Fig. 2). If $\mathcal{A}_1$, $\mathcal{A}_2$ are separate, then it is defined as the point included in every circle of $\{\mathcal{A}_1, \mathcal{A}_2\}$ located in each half-plane bounded by Δ. If $\mathcal{A}_1$, $\mathcal{A}_2$ are tangent, both limiting points coincide with the contact point Z. In any case, they are located on the line of the centres of the generators.

An important fact is that vectors $\mathbf{z}_1$, $\mathbf{z}_2$ satisfy $(\boldsymbol{\delta}^\top \mathbf{z}_1)(\boldsymbol{\delta}^\top \mathbf{z}_2) \leq 0$ i.e., that Z_1 and Z_2 either *lie on the radical axis Δ or are on opposite sides of* Δ. Since $(\mathbf{l}_\infty^\top \mathbf{z}_1)(\mathbf{l}_\infty^\top \mathbf{z}_2) > 0$, they also lie *on the same half-plane bounded by* L_∞.

5 Proposed Algorithms

5.1 Outline of the Linear Algorithm

We will now make again the distinction between the entities of π and their projections onto the image plane $\tilde{\pi}$, by adding $\tilde{\ }$ to the calligraphic letters denoting these latter. Thus, let us denote by $\tilde{\mathbf{A}}_j$, $j = 1..N$, the image matrices of the projections $\tilde{\mathcal{A}}_j$ of N circles $\mathcal{A}_j$ of π, onto the image plane $\tilde{\pi}$.

The proposed algorithm consists in "fitting" the projection $\widetilde{IJ}$ of the circular-point envelope IJ, using constraints (3a-3c), from the degenerate projected circles of the pencils $\{\tilde{\mathcal{A}}_1^q, \tilde{\mathcal{A}}_2^q\}$ spanned by Q selected pairs, $1 \leq q \leq Q \leq \frac{1}{2}N(N-1)$. To estimate the matrix $\tilde{\mathbf{C}}_\infty^*$ of $\widetilde{IJ}$ with a linear method, we substitute some regular symmetric matrix $\mathbf{X}$ for $\tilde{\mathbf{C}}_\infty^*$ in Eqs. (3a-3c). Hence, there are six unknowns, defined up to a scalar. The algorithm works as follows. We solve the equation system built by calling the procedure **AddLinearConstraint**(), as described in Procedure 1, for each of the Q matrix-pairs $(\tilde{\mathbf{A}}_1^q, \tilde{\mathbf{A}}_2^q)$. Basically, this procedure identifies the relative position of the corresponding circles in π and classifies the degenerate members of $\{\tilde{\mathcal{A}}_1^q, \tilde{\mathcal{A}}_2^q\}$, so as to yield equations (3a) and/or (3b).

Note that our solution generalizes that of Liebowitz [10, p.56][14, p.60], by the ability of also treating simultaneously pairs of projected orthogonal lines i.e., enabling us to add constraints (3c).

N=2 projected circles (exact solution). Given one pair $(\tilde{\mathbf{A}}_1^q, \tilde{\mathbf{A}}_2^q)$ we can obtain zero or one constraint (3a) and two constraints (3b). For problem P_2 to be well-posed so to get an exact solution, we need at least one constraint

(3a), ensuring that the property rank($\mathbf{X}$) = 2 holds, plus at least one constraint (3b). We have to discuss in which cases this can be achieved. Remind that the projected line-circle $\widetilde{L_\infty \Delta^q}$ can always be identified among the three degenerate circles of the pencil $\{\tilde{\mathcal{A}}_1^q, \tilde{\mathcal{A}}_2^q\}$ *but* there is an ambiguity in saying which line is $\tilde{L}_\infty$ (or, equivalently, the projected radical axis $\tilde{\Delta}^q$). Since, in the world plane, the limiting points Z_1^q, Z_2^q of a pencil $\{\mathcal{A}_1^q, \mathcal{A}_2^q\}$ either lie on, or are on both sides of, the radical axis Δ^q (cf. §4.3), we claim that (superscript q is omitted):

Proposition 1. *A necessary and sufficient condition for the projected limiting points $\tilde{Z}_1$, $\tilde{Z}_2$ to lie, in the image plane, on opposite sides of the projected radical axis $\tilde{\Delta}$ is that Z_1, Z_2 lie, in the world plane π, on the same half-plane bounded by the line $(\pi \cap \tilde{\pi}_F)$, which is the intersection of the principal plane[3] $\tilde{\pi}_F$ and π.*

Proof is omitted due to lack of space. Note that this proposition (see Fig. 2) could have been equivalently stated by using a condition for $\tilde{Z}_1$ and $\tilde{Z}_2$ to lie, in the image plane, on the same half-plane bounded by $\tilde{L}_\infty$.

In other words, we know exactly when P_2 is well-posed: the Euclidean structure can be recovered from two projected circles, providing the limiting points lie in front of the camera. This holds for all relative positions of two circles except for some, *not all*, cases of enclosing, non-concentric, circle-pairs. Clearly, there exist such pairs (see Fig. 2) from which $(\tilde{I}, \tilde{J})$ is recoverable, contrary to what was claimed in some previous works [11][23].

Procedure 1. SYS = **AddLinearConstraint**(SYS, $\tilde{A}_1$, $\tilde{A}_2$)

$[\ \tilde{\lambda},\ \tilde{Z}\ ]$ = **GeneralizedEig**($\tilde{A}_1, \tilde{A}_2$)
if all $\tilde{\lambda}$'s are real /* *non-interesecting circles only* */   then
  sort $\tilde{\lambda}$ and $\tilde{Z}$ to ensure $\Sigma(\tilde{A}(\tilde{\lambda}_k)) \geq \Sigma(\tilde{A}(\tilde{\lambda}_l))$ for $k \leq l$
  compute d and r using (7)
  if $d == 0$ /* *concentric circles* */   then
    $\tilde{l}_\infty = \tilde{A}_1 \tilde{z}_1$
    add equation (3a) to system SYS /* *affine constraint* */
    $[\ \tilde{x}_1,\ \tilde{x}_2\ ]$ = **LinesofRank2RealConic**($\tilde{A}_1 - \tilde{\lambda}_1 \tilde{A}_2$) /* $\Sigma == 2$ */
    add equation (3b) to system SYS /* *Euclidean constraint* */
  else
    if $d \geq |r - 1|$ /* *non-enclosing circles only* */   then
      $[\ l_0,\ l_1\ ]$ = **LinesofRank2RealConic**($\tilde{A}_1 - \tilde{\lambda}_3 \tilde{A}_2$) /* $\Sigma == 0$ */
      $l_\infty = l_{1-c}$, where $c \in \{0,1\}$ is such that $\frac{1}{\tilde{Z}_{31}\tilde{Z}_{32}}(l_c^\top \tilde{z}_1)(l_c^\top \tilde{z}_2) < 0$
      add equation (3a) to system SYS /* *affine constraint* */
    end if
    for $k \in \{1..2\}$ do
      $[\ \tilde{x}_1,\ \tilde{x}_2\ ]$ = **LinesofRank2RealConic**($\tilde{A}_k - \tilde{\lambda}_k \tilde{A}_2$) /* $\Sigma == 2$ */
      add equation (3b) to system SYS /* *Euclidean constraint* */
    end for
  end if
end if

---

[3] Containing the camera centre and parallel to the image plane.

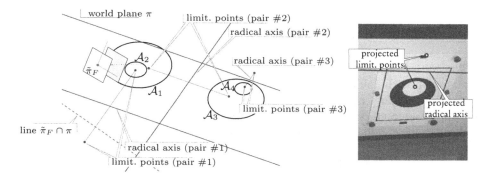

Fig. 2. Prop. 1 says that problem P_2 is ill-posed for enclosing pair #1 ($\mathcal{A}_1, \mathcal{A}_2$) but well-posed for separate pair #2 ($\mathcal{A}_1, \mathcal{A}_3$) and enclosing pair #3 ($\mathcal{A}_3, \mathcal{A}_4$). Right-hand, a real image of some enclosing pair, from which the projected circular points are recovered.

$N \geq 2$ projected circles (Least-Squares solutions). If $N \geq 2$, strictly speaking, this is an overdetermined problem of estimating parameters subject to an ancillary constraint, in our case $\det(\mathbf{X}) = 0$. Efficient and well-founded methods exist, e.g. [4]. However, we use a straightforward solution that consists in seeking a least-squares solution $\hat{\mathbf{X}}$, then imposing the ancillary constraint via a rank-2 approximation of $\hat{\mathbf{X}}$ by cancelling its smallest singular value.

It is worth noting that, once the circular point-envelope is recovered, a rectifying homography matrix $\mathbf{M}^{-1}$ can be computed [10, pp.55-56] from the SVD-like decomposition $\tilde{\mathbf{C}}^*_\infty = \mathbf{M} \operatorname{diag}(1,1,0) \mathbf{M}^\top$, where $\mathbf{M} \in \mathbb{R}^{3 \times 3}$ satisfies $\mathbf{M} \sim \mathbf{HS}$ for some 2D similarity $\mathbf{S} \in \mathbb{R}^{3 \times 3}$ of π. Since there are only 4 d.o.f. in $\tilde{\mathbf{C}}^*_\infty$, there are also only 4 d.o.f. in $\mathbf{M}$. Typically, by applying $\mathbf{M}^{-1}$ to the image, we get its metric rectification (e.g., as shown in Fig. 4).

5.2   Non-linear Algorithm Refinements

We also implemented a bundle adjustment style optimization of both, the rectified circles, and the plane-to-image homography. In addition, for every image point we estimate an associated point that lies exactly on the associated rectified circle. The cost function for the optimization is then the sum of squared distances between image points and corresponding points on circles, re-projected to the image via the homography.

Since rectification is defined up to a similarity transformation in the scene plane, we may fix 4 degrees of freedom in our parameterization. We implemented two approaches to do so. The first one is to parameterize the homography using 4 parameters [10]. The second one is to use 8 parameters for the homography (we simply fix H_{33} to a non-zero value, which is appropriate in our scenario), but to fix the centres of two of the circles to their initial positions.

Each circle $\mathcal{A}_c$ is naturally parameterized by its radius r_c and centre (x_c, y_c), and each point Q_{cp} on a circle is parameterized by an angle Θ_{cp}, with vector $\mathbf{Q}_{cp} = (x_c + r_c \cos \Theta_{cp}, y_c + r_c \sin \Theta_{cp}, 1)^\top$. The optimization problem is then:

$$\min_{\mathbf{H}, x_c, y_c, r_c, \Theta_{cp}} \sum_{c=1}^{N} \sum_{p=1}^{P} dist^2(\mathbf{q}_{cp}, \mathbf{H}\mathbf{Q}_{cp})$$

The initializations of the unknowns is rather trivial, given the results of a rectification with any of the method LINEAR. Note that the above cost function is identical in spirit to the one used in [8] for estimating ellipses that minimize the sum of squared distances to data points.

We use Levenberg-Marquardt for the optimization, and take advantage of the sparse structure of the Jacobian. The most complex step in each iteration is the inversion of a symmetric matrix of order $(4 + N)$. Typically, for simulated experiments similar to those in §6, with up to $N = 10$ circles and 50 points per circle, the optimization took (much) less than a second (see results in Tab. 1).

Table 1. RMS residuals of non-linear optimization. Average over 500 runs of the square roots of the average cost function value.

Circles	2	3	4	5	6	7	8	9	10
RMS	0.49	0.52	0.54	0.55	0.56	0.57	0.57	0.57	0.58

6   Experiments

Synthetic data. We are aiming here at assessing how accurately is fitted the Euclidean structure, given $N = 16$ unknown non-intersecting circles projected in one view. We investigate the link between the number $Q \in \{1, .., 25\}$ of randomly selected circle-pairs (among the 120 possible pairs) and several fitting errors. Fig. 3 shows the average values of these errors.

The synthetic scene, located on some world-plane π, consists of a 1500×1500 square area over which are spatially distributed the N circles, whose radii vary within $[25; 75]$. The camera is at a distance of about 2500, with randomly generated camera orientations, in terms of azimuth, elevation and swing angles varying within $[-60°; 60°]$. The simulated camera has a 512×512 pixel resolution and constant internal parameters. Each circle projects to an ellipse, sampled by S equally spaced pixels, where S roughly equals the ellipse perimeter. Gaussian noise of zero mean and standard deviation $\sigma = 1$ is added to the pixel (integer) coordinates.

Series of 500 tests are conducted for each of the following error criteria.

Let $\hat{\mathbf{C}}_\infty^*$ denote the estimated projected circular-point envelope $\tilde{\mathbf{C}}_\infty^*$, using our algorithm described in §5.1, both matrices being normalized to have unitary Frobenius norm. The "true" world-to-image homography $\mathbf{H}$, induced by the chosen Euclidean representation of π, must obey to the decomposition [20][24] $\mathbf{H} = \mathbf{KR}[\mathbf{e}_1 \mid \mathbf{e}_2 \mid \mathbf{t}]$, where $\mathbf{K} \in \mathbb{R}^{3 \times 3}$ is the calibration matrix, $\mathbf{R} \in \mathbb{R}^{3 \times 3}$ is a rotation such that $\mathbf{r}_3$ represents the normal to π w.r.t. the camera frame, and $\mathbf{t} \in \mathbb{R}^3$. Hence, the "true" matrix $\tilde{\mathbf{C}}_\infty^*$ satisfies $\mathbf{K}^{-1}\tilde{\mathbf{C}}_\infty^*\mathbf{K}^{-\top} \sim \mathbf{R}\,\mathrm{diag}(1,1,0)\mathbf{R}^\top$ i.e., its two nonzero singular values are equal. Referring to Fig. 3(a), two error

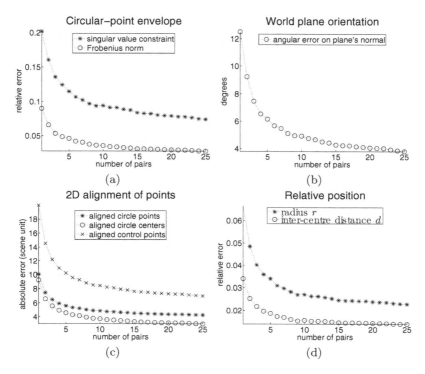

Fig. 3. Assessing the performance of the proposed method

criteria on $\hat{\mathbf{C}}^*_\infty$ are derived. We quantify, in a way, how $\hat{\mathbf{C}}^*_\infty$ is closed to the "true" $\tilde{\mathbf{C}}^*_\infty$: first, by computing the relative error $(\hat{s}_1 - \hat{s}_2)/\hat{s}_1$, where $\hat{s}_1 \geq \hat{s}_2 > \hat{s}_3 = 0$ are the singular values of $\mathbf{K}^{-1}\hat{\mathbf{C}}^*_\infty \mathbf{K}^{-\top}$, involving the "true" $\mathbf{K}$ (*"singular value constraint"*); second, by computing the error $||\hat{\mathbf{C}}^*_\infty - \tilde{\mathbf{C}}^*_\infty||_F$ (*"Frobenius norm"*). In Fig. 3(b), we quantify the error on the pose of π, by computing the *angular error on the normal to* π, that is $\arccos(\mathbf{r}_3^\top \hat{\mathbf{u}}_3)$, involving the "true" $\mathbf{r}_3$, where $\hat{\mathbf{u}}_3$ is the singular vector associated with $\hat{s}_3 = 0$.

Let $\hat{\mathbf{M}}^{-1}$ be the estimated rectifying homography, obtained from $\hat{\mathbf{C}}^*_\infty$ (cf. end of §5.1). In Fig. 3(c-d), we assess the accuracy of the 2D reconstruction by computing errors on the alignment between reconstructed of image points, via $\hat{\mathbf{M}}^{-1}$, and true world points. The alignment error is the sum of the squared residuals for all points, from the best Euclidean 2D mapping between reconstructed points and true points. Alignment errors have been computed for the circle points and circle centres as well as for a set of control points. Lastly, in Fig. 3(d), we compute the relative error on "normalized" radii and distances between centres, as defined by r and d in §4.2, of the (approximated) reconstructed circles.

These series of tests show the excellent performance of the proposed algorithm. The obtained solutions are unquestionably more stable when using multiple circles, much like using multiple points to fit a conic.

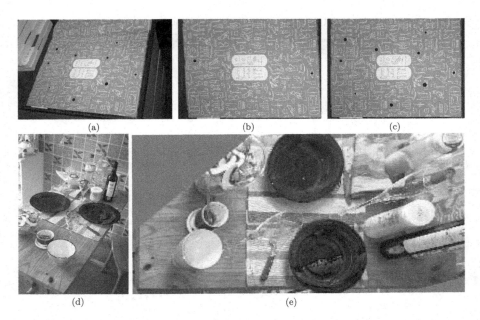

Fig. 4. Top: (a) 1536×1024 photograph of the endpaper of some comic book, with drawn hieroglyphs. (b) Image rectification from $N = 2$ (black-filled) circles ; (c) from $N = 9$ circles. Bottom: (d) 1536×1024 photograph of a table in a kitchen, (e) Image rectification (cropped) using $N = 6$ (blue) circles.

Real data. We illustrate the performance of the proposed algorithm by carrying out a metric rectification [10, §1.7.5] of an image i.e., by warping it to remove the perpespective distortion. The image in Fig.4 was captured using a CANON EOS 300D camera, with 1536×1024 image resolution.

7   Conclusion

We described a method for recovering the Euclidean structure of some observed world plane π, from $N \geq 2$ projected parallel circles. We suggested to state the problem as that of "fitting" the projected degenerate absolute conic of π, namely the projected circular-point envelope $\widetilde{IJ}$, to line-pairs, so-called projected line- and point-circles. These are the degenerate members of the conic pencil, spanned by all (or some) combinations of pairs of the whole set of projected circles. We showed that the degenerate members of the pencil can yield either affine or Euclidean linear constraints on the parameters of $\widetilde{IJ}$. Depending on the relative position of the corresponding circle-pair in π, we show exactly what these line-pairs are and which kind of constraints they will set on $\widetilde{IJ}$. Consequently, the problem is stated as that of solving a (possibly) overdetermined system of linear equations, so taking into account more than two projected circles.

We are convinced that the usefulness of the proposed formalism, through the interpretation of the geometrical nature of the degenerate members of conic pencils or quadric pencils, as reported in [17], might go beyond the scope of this work e.g., regarding calibration of catadioptric cameras [2], or even the problem of calibration from spheres [1].

References

1. M. Agrawal and L.S. Davis, "Camera calibration using spheres: A semi-definite programming approach," *ICCV*, vol. 2, pp. 782-791, 2003.
2. J. Barreto, General Central Projection Systems: Modeling, Calibration and Visual Servoing. Ph.D. Thesis. University of Coimbra. 2003.
3. Q. Chen, H. Wu and T. Wada, "Camera Calibration with Two Arbitrary Coplanar Circles," *ECCV*, vol. 3, pp. 521-532, 2004.
4. W. Chojnacki, M.J. Brooks, A. van den Hengel and D. Gawley, "A New Constrained Parameter Estimator for Computer Vision Applications," *IVC*, vol. 22(2), pp. 85-91, 2004.
5. J.-L. Collidge, *A Treatise on the Circle and the Sphere*. Oxford: Clarendon Press, 1916.
6. C. Columbo, A. Del Bimbo and F. Pernici, "Metric 3D Reconstruction and Texture Acquisition of Surfaces of Revolution from a Single Uncalibrated View," *PAMI*, vol. 27, no. 1, pp. 99-114, Jan. 2005.
7. A.W. Fitzgibbon, M. Pilu, and R.B. Fisher, "Direct Least Square Fitting of Ellipses," *PAMI*, vol. 21, no. 5, pp. 476-480, May 1999.
8. W. Gander, G.H. Golub and R. Strebel, "Fitting of Circles and Ellipsess," *BIT*, 34, pp.558-578, 1994.
9. G. Golub and C. Van Loan, *Matrix Computations*. Johns Hopkins University Press, 3rd edition, 1996.
10. R. Hartley and A. Zisserman, *Multiple View Geometry in Computer Vision*. Cambridge Univ. Press, 2nd edition, 2003.
11. G. Jiang, H.-T. Tsui, L. Quan, and A. Zisserman, "Single Axis Geometry by Fitting Conics," *ECCV*, vol. 1, pp. 537-550, May 2002.
12. K. Kanatani and W. Liu, "3D Interpretation of Conics and Orthogonality," *CVIU*, vol. 58, no. 3, pp. 286-301, Nov. 1993.
13. J.-S. Kim, P. Gurdjos and I.-S. Kweon, "Geometric and Algebraic Constraints of Projected Concentric Circles and Their Applications to Camera Calibration," *PAMI*, vol. 27, no. 4, pp. 637 - 642, April 2005.
14. D. Liebowitz, Camera Calibration and Reconstruction of Geometry from Images. Ph.D. Thesis University of Oxford. Trinity Term 2001.
15. S.D. Ma, "Conics-based Stereo, Motion estimation, and Pose Determination," *IJCV*, vol. 10, no. 1, pp. 7-25, Feb. 1993.
16. J.L. Mundy and A. Zisserman Eds., *Geometric Invariance in Computer Vision* MIT Press, 1992.
17. L. Quan, "Conic Reconstruction and Correspondence from Two Views," *PAMI*, vol. 18, no. 2, pp. 151-160, Feb. 1996.
18. J. Semple and G. Kneebone, *Algebraic Projective Geometry*. Oxford Classic Series, 1952, reprinted, 1998.
19. P. Sturm and L. Quan, "Affine Stereo Calibration," Technical Report LIFIA-29, LIFIA-IMAG, June 1995.

20. P. Sturm and S. Maybank, "On Plane-Based Camera Calibration: a General Algorithm, Singularities, Applications," *CVPR*, vol. 1, pp. 1432-1437, 1999.
21. B. Triggs, "Autocalibration and the Absolute Quadric," *CVPR*, pp. 609-614, 1997.
22. B. Triggs, "Autocalibration from Planar Scenes," *ECCV*, vol. 1, pp. 89-105, 1998.
23. Y. Wu, X. Li, F. Wu and Z. Wu, "Coplanar circles, Quasi-Affine Invariance and Calibration," *Image and Vision Computing*. To appear, 2004.
24. Z. Zhang, "A Flexible New Technique for Camera Calibration," *PAMI*, vol. 22, no. 11, pp. 1330-1344, Nov. 2000.

Overconstrained Linear Estimation of Radial Distortion and Multi-view Geometry

R. Matt Steele and Christopher Jaynes

Center for Visualization and Virtual Environments,
University of Kentucky, Lexington, Kentucky, USA

Abstract. This paper introduces a new method for simultaneous estimation of lens distortion and multi-view geometry using only point correspondences. The new technique has significant advantages over the current state-of-the art in that it makes more effective use of correspondences arising from any number of views. Multi-view geometry in the presence of lens distortion can be expressed as a set of point correspondence constraints that are quadratic in the unknown distortion parameter. Previous work has demonstrated how the system can be solved efficiently as a quadratic eigenvalue problem by operating on the normal equations of the system. Although this approach is appropriate for situations in which only a minimal set of matchpoints are available, it does not take full advantage of extra correspondences in overconstrained situations, resulting in significant bias and many potential solutions. The new technique directly operates on the initial constraint equations and solves the quadratic eigenvalue problem in the case of rectangular matrices. The method is shown to contain significantly less bias on both controlled and real-world data and, in the case of a moving camera where additional views serve to constrain the number of solutions, an accurate estimate of both geometry and distortion is achieved.

1 Introduction

Radial distortion introduces systematic error into the results of standard linear algorithms (e.g. the Eight Point Algorithm, Direct Linear Transform homography estimation, trifocal tensor estimation) that do not account for it. Many applications require wide-angle lenses, for which distortion can be quite severe. Although a priori modelling of lens distortion [1] can remedy the problem, some computer vision tasks, such as structure and motion recovery from uncalibrated video, preclude offline calibration by definition. Assumptions about the scene structure in order to perform online distortion estimation [2] are often undesirable, and can be error-prone.

Consequently, there has been significant work to obtain distortion estimates based only on image-to-image correspondences and the application of multi-view geometric constraints, that is, exactly the information available in uncalibrated video of an unknown scene. By insightful choice of distortion model, Fitzgibbon [3] is able to express the epipolar constraints for distorted correspondences

A. Leonardis, H. Bischof, and A. Pinz (Eds.): ECCV 2006, Part I, LNCS 3951, pp. 253–264, 2006.

as a quadratic eigenvalue problem (QEP). Solutions may be found via efficient and globally convergent algorithms, yielding an estimate for both the distortion and the epipolar geometry. Some information is lost, however, in multiplication by the transpose matrix in order to make the rectangular eigensystem square. One can see this is the case by noting that no matter how many correspondences are available, the square QEP will still allow multiple solutions. Even the correct choice out of the solutions, that is, the one that best minimizes re-projection error, suffers from a surprising amount of bias due to noise, even when many correspondences are available in a strong geometric configuration.

The standard answer to these deficiencies, refinement via bundle adjustment, can suffer from slow or unreliable convergence when an accurate initialization is unavailable. Consequently, a technique is sought which possesses the highly desirable efficiency and convergence properties of the square QEP while more efficiently exploiting the extra information in all matchpoints to obtain a more accurate estimate of distortion and multi-view geometry.

Section 2 of this paper presents such a technique. Rather than solving a square QEP, a rectangular QEP is constructed with one row for each available correspondence. The rectangular QEP does not have an exact solution, but an optimal approximation may be defined by seeking the closest perturbed eigensystem which does have an exact solution. With the help of results from [4], an efficient algorithm is presented which solves this problem. Building on this contribution, Section 2.3 presents a second, generalized algorithm which supports simultaneous solution of multiple, independent multi-view geometries while enforcing a single, global radial distortion model. Thus, not only are additional correspondences exploited, but also extra view pairs, which need not be interconnected by long-lived feature tracks. Section 3 compares the new algorithms to the previous square QEP method [3] on simulated and real data, revealing striking reductions in estimation variance, and especially bias.

1.1   Related Work

The work builds on a recent tradition of exploring how radial distortion estimation can occur simultaneously with the recovery of multi-view geometry [3, 5, 6]. This tradition is quite different from methods that estimate lens distortion offline [1] or techniques that combine a priori scene knowledge with the results of feature extraction such as plumb-line methods [2]. Instead, more recent efforts don't make assumptions beyond those required for traditional multi-view geometry estimation (e.g. the eight-point algorithm). Much of these efforts have emphasized the importance of simultaneous estimation of both a linear geometric model and the nonlinear distortion parameters. This is an improvement over other methods that have been designed for online radial distortion estimation [7] in that they must deal with each task independently. Independent estimation can lead to bias in the geometric estimate because distorted points are used.

Simultaneous estimation was first explored by Fitzgibbon as a hypothesis generator for RANSAC [3]. The technique was shown to be successful in providing better discrimination between outliers and inliers even in the presence of significant distortion. Because the radial component is computed simultaneously, the geometric estimate is no longer biased by unmodelled distortion.

In addition to the work of Fitzgibbon, more recent work has presented alternative direct methods of estimating lens distortion parameters without a priori knowledge of scene structure. These methods provide for graceful extension to overdetermined systems, but have other drawbacks. Lifting the correspondences into a higher-dimensional space [8] can allow the distorted epipolar mapping to be represented by linear matrix multiplication in the higher-dimensional space. The lifted matrix, however, has multiple unwanted degrees of freedom, and attempts to appropriately constrain the relationship have not yet been satisfactory. Deriving 1D radial correspondences from the original 2D correspondences allows estimation of a distortion-free multi-view geometry [6] which in turn supports direct estimates of the distortion model. The method requires, however, that all correspondences be constrained to lie on a single plane, or the camera motion be purely rotational.

In addition to work from computer vision, this paper draws on results from the numerical analysis community. Recent results lay the groundwork for an alternative solution based on solving an extended notion of the QEP, one in which the matrices are not square. The concept of pseudospectra, a generalization of eigenvalues for non-square matrices, is discussed and studied in [9]. A non-square analogue of the generalized eigenvalue problem is posed in [4] that builds on these results, and an algorithm is presented for the special case in which only a single, primary pseudoeigenvalue is sought. This line of inquiry informs our approach in solving the rectangular QEP that results from the formulation of the problem studied in this paper.

2   Problem Formulation

Assume that a camera in motion observes an arbitrary scene and that the radial distortion is fixed throughout the image sequence. Under these conditions, the goal is to simultaneously estimate pairwise epipolar relationships as well as the radial distortion coefficient λ. We denote 2D points observed in image i as $\mathbf{x} = (x, y)$ and their correspondences in image j as $\hat{\mathbf{x}}$. Following the notation of [3], each image point, $\mathbf{x}$, is said to arise from a radial distortion model applied to an underlying undistorted point, $\mathbf{p}$.

We shall denote by $\mathbf{F}_{ij}$ the *fundamental matrix* corresponding to the pair of images i and j. The task of this paper, given an image sequence and a set of n image pairings $(i_1 j_1, \ldots, i_n j_n)$ for the sequence, is to derive the fundamental matrices $(\mathbf{F}_{i_1 j_1}, \ldots, \mathbf{F}_{i_n j_n})$ for the view pairs, in addition to the distortion parameter λ governing the radial distortion of points observed in all images.

Traditionally, the eight-point-algorithm can be used to estimate $\mathbf{F}$ for any given pair in the image sequence [10, 11]. By assuming no distortion, a linear system can be derived that utilizes the epipolar constraint described by the fundamental matrix:

$$\hat{\mathbf{p}}^{\mathsf{T}} \mathbf{F} \mathbf{p} = 0 \tag{1}$$

The traditional eight-point algorithm requires either offline measurement of λ, an independent estimation of distortion using scene knowledge (e.g. plumb line methods), or restricting matchpoints to a central region of the image where distortion can be neglected. Each of these approaches has significant drawbacks. Offline estimation can be cumbersome and is impossible in the case of archival video. The use of scene knowledge to measure distortion (e.g. [2]) requires that the scene conforms to a priori constraints, and the feature extraction process is typically higher-level and more susceptible to failure than the low-level task at hand. Neglecting potential matchpoints near the periphery of the image is not desirable and can unnecessarily eliminate matchpoints arising from robust features. Many image sequences contain overlap primarily at the periphery of the image, and ignoring matchpoints from these regions leads to unstable estimation of camera geometry.

Given these problems, techniques that support simultaneous estimation of λ are of interest. Recently, Fitzgibbon [3] demonstrated that radial distortion can be cleanly incorporated into Equation 1 by developing a distortion model that only depends on $\mathbf{x}$ and $\hat{\mathbf{x}}$, the measured matchpoints:

$$\mathbf{p} = \frac{1}{1 + \lambda\|\mathbf{x}\|^2}\mathbf{x} \tag{2}$$

Given this division model of distortion, the epipolar constraint is:

$$(\hat{\mathbf{x}} + \lambda\hat{\mathbf{z}})^\mathsf{T} \mathbf{F} (\mathbf{x} + \lambda\mathbf{z}) = 0$$
$$\hat{\mathbf{x}}^\mathsf{T}\mathbf{F}\mathbf{x} + \lambda\left(\hat{\mathbf{z}}^\mathsf{T}\mathbf{F}\mathbf{x} + \hat{\mathbf{x}}\mathbf{F}\mathbf{z}\right) + \lambda^2\hat{\mathbf{z}}^\mathsf{T}\mathbf{F}\mathbf{z} = 0 \tag{3}$$

where $\mathbf{z}$ is $\begin{bmatrix} 0 & 0 & \|\mathbf{x}\|^2 \end{bmatrix}^\mathsf{T}$. Note that Equation 3 is comprised of four terms in $\mathbf{F}$, each possessing the same form as the traditional epipolar constraint.

2.1   The Quadratic Eigenvalue Problem for Estimating λ and $\mathbf{F}$

Simultaneous estimation of λ and $\mathbf{F}$ may be performed by formulating Equation 3 as a quadratic eigenvalue problem (QEP). The QEP is obtained by gathering the vector factors of $\mathbf{F}$, for each term, into a separate design matrix. The elements of $\mathbf{F}$ are extracted into vector $\mathbf{f}$ [3]. This procedure is identical to the method by which the traditional eight-point equations are obtained from Equation 1.

$$\left(\mathbf{D}_1 + \lambda\mathbf{D}_2 + \lambda^2\mathbf{D}_3\right)\mathbf{f} = 0 \tag{4}$$

Well-known techniques may be employed to solve this QEP for $\mathbf{f}$ and λ when the matrices are square [12]. These techniques cannot be directly applied, however, in the case where there are more than 9 correspondences, and the design matrices are consequently non-square.

In order to solve the QEP for such over-determined problems, Fitzgibbon [3] obtains the normal equations of Equation 4 through left-multiplication by $\mathbf{D}_1^\mathsf{T}$. This technique has the virtue of preserving the true solution in the noiseless case. Empirical results have shown, however, that in the presence of noise the solution to the normal equations suffers from bias and significant variance. Furthermore, the square problem arising from the normal equations admits 10 general solutions, of which 6, in practice, are real regardless of how overdetermined the system becomes. This is counter-intuitive as oftentimes scene geometry and other constraints should support only a single solution.

It may be surprising that the normal equations have proved so problematic, as they usually provide reasonably good results. For example, the standard eight-point algorithm's residual *is* minimized through the normal equations, specifically by computing the eigenvector with smallest-magnitude eigenvalue. This situation appears to parallel that of the QEP, but there is an important difference. In the eight-point algorithm, the normal equations are constructed from the transpose of the entire matrix factor of $\mathbf{f}$. In the QEP, however, λ is not known, and only the component D_1 of the entire matrix factor $\mathsf{D}_p = \mathsf{D}_1 + \lambda \mathsf{D}_2 + \lambda^2 \mathsf{D}_3$ is used. If the radial distortion λ were known, then one could solve the normal equations $\mathsf{D}_p^\mathsf{T} \mathsf{D}_p \mathbf{f} = 0$ to obtain an eigenvector that minimizes the residual of Equation 4. The radial distortion λ is not known, however, and approximate normal equations $\mathsf{D}_1^\mathsf{T} \mathsf{D}_p \mathbf{f} = 0$ are solved instead. It is not surprising that this approximation obtains a biased result.

As a driver for RANSAC, one solves minimal problems, in which the matrices are already square, and the techniques of [3] are appropriate. However, in the case where an accurate F and λ is required directly from a large set of matchpoints, a new approach is desired.

2.2   An Algorithm for Overconstrained Estimation of F and λ

If we allow D_1, D_2, and D_3 to be rectangular, the problem is overconstrained and typically there will be no solution in the presence of noise. We therefore construct a minimization problem that defines a suitable approximate solution to the QEP of Equation 4. Because noise corrupts the entries of D_1, D_2, and D_3, it is reasonable to seek a solution which involves perturbing those noisy matrices (hopefully removing the noise) in such a way that an exact solution of the perturbed system does exist. This formulation is a constrained optimization problem in which the perturbed system must satisfy Equation 4 exactly (additionally there is the familiar constraint that the eigenvector $\mathbf{f}$ must be nontrivial). The metric to be minimized is the magnitude of the perturbation, given by $\|\tilde{\mathsf{D}}_1 - \mathsf{D}_1\|_F^2 + \|\tilde{\mathsf{D}}_2 - \mathsf{D}_2\|_F^2 + \|\tilde{\mathsf{D}}_3 - \mathsf{D}_3\|_F^2$, where the perturbed matrices are denoted by $\tilde{\mathsf{D}}_1, \tilde{\mathsf{D}}_2$, and $\tilde{\mathsf{D}}_3$, and $\| \cdot \|_F^2$ is the squared Fröbenius norm.

Obvious approaches to this problem, such as general-purpose minimization via e.g. iterative Levenberg-Marquadt or gradient descent, are unlikely to be satisfactory, because they would be equally suited to an error metric which better represents the statistics of observational error (e.g. the Euclidean reprojection error used in standard bundle adjustment). The expectation is that the above optimization problem, while more descriptive than the normal equations, is still simpler than bundle adjustment in a way that will admit a non-iterative algorithm, or a (more) globally convergent one, or one that is faster.

The rectangular QEP may be converted to a linear rectangular generalized eigenvalue problem through a technique similar to the linearization procedure for the square QEP. A new variable $\mathbf{u} = \lambda \mathbf{f}$ is introduced, obtaining the simultaneous linear matrix equations:

$$D_1 \mathbf{f} + \lambda \left(D_2 \mathbf{f} + D_3 \mathbf{u} \right) = 0$$
$$\mathbf{u} - \lambda \mathbf{f} = 0$$

This system of equations may be written equivalently as a single matrix equation

$$\left(\begin{bmatrix} D_1 \\ & I \end{bmatrix} - \lambda \begin{bmatrix} -D_2 & -D_3 \\ I & \end{bmatrix} \right) \begin{bmatrix} \mathbf{f} \\ \mathbf{u} \end{bmatrix} = 0 \tag{5}$$

Here I is the 9×9 identity matrix.

Recent work studying the eigenvalue problem in the case of non-square pencils has shown that this problem can be solved efficiently, and spurious eigenvalues are avoided [4]. We draw on these results to develop an algorithm that simultaneously estimates radial distortion and epipolar geometry while exploiting the additional information that matchpoints afford.

Let

$$A = \begin{bmatrix} D_1 \\ & I \end{bmatrix} ; \quad B = \begin{bmatrix} -D_2 & -D_3 \\ I & \end{bmatrix} ; \quad \mathbf{v} = \begin{bmatrix} \mathbf{f} \\ \mathbf{u} \end{bmatrix} \tag{6}$$

The problem may then be expressed as finding perturbed rectangular matrices $\tilde{A}$ and $\tilde{B}$, an eigenvector $\mathbf{v}$ encoding the fundamental matrix, and an eigenvalue λ determining the radial distortion, which minimizes the quantity $\|\tilde{A} - A\|_F^2 + \|\tilde{B} - B\|_F^2$ subject to the constraint encoded in Equation 6.

The algorithm is initialized with a choice of $\lambda = 0$. Given λ, an updated estimate of the eigenvector $\mathbf{v}$ is obtained by computing the right singular vector corresponding to the smallest singular value of $A - \lambda B$. A refinement of λ is then computed; following the result of [4], this refinement is given by the positive root of the scalar quadratic equation

$$\mathbf{v}^T \left(B^T + \lambda A^T \right) \left(A - \lambda B \right) \mathbf{v} = 0 \tag{7}$$

This procedure is repeated until convergence. See [4] for a proof that the procedure converges to a local minimum. In our experiments the algorithm has converged reliably and swiftly (typically in less than 20 iterations) to the true minimum.

2.3   Simultaneous Solution for Multiple View Pairs

Estimation of λ from a single view pair fails to exploit all of the available information in the common case where many views are available, all at the same fixed (unknown) lens distortion. Given n pairs of views, and their n sets of correspondences $(\{\hat{\mathbf{p}}_1\}, \{\mathbf{p}_1\}), \ldots, (\{\hat{\mathbf{p}}_n\}, \{\mathbf{p}_n\})$, then the n epipolar constraints may be expressed jointly with a single common lens distortion by the matrix equation

$$\left(\begin{bmatrix} A_1 & & \\ & \ddots & \\ & & A_n \end{bmatrix} - \lambda \begin{bmatrix} B_1 & & \\ & \ddots & \\ & & B_n \end{bmatrix} \right) \begin{bmatrix} v_1 \\ \vdots \\ v_n \end{bmatrix} = 0 \qquad (8)$$

Each A_i and B_i is obtained from Equation 6 as applied to the correspondence set $(\{\hat{p}_i\}, \{p_i\})$. Straightforward application of the algorithm of Section 2.2 to Equation 8 leads to a significant problem, however. If v_i is a non-trivial null-vector of $(A_i - \lambda B_i)$, then $[0 \cdots 0 \ v_i^T \ 0 \cdots 0]^T$ will be a nontrivial eigenvector of Equation 8, for all $i \in 1 \ldots n$, as will any linear combination of such eigenvectors. If the algorithm converges to one of these primitive eigenvectors, then the information present in A_j and B_j for all $j \neq i$ is ignored and has no impact on the estimation of the radial distortion parameter λ. It is desirable to force each of the v_i components of the eigenvector of Equation 8 to be individually normalized (and, hence, nonzero) in order to incorporate as much information as possible into the estimate of λ, and to simultaneously obtain a nontrivial estimate for each F_i, the fundamental matrix for each view pair.

In order to accomplish this task, the algorithm discussed in Section 2.2 is modified. Rather than explicitly constructing the large matrices in Equation 8, it suffices to keep track of the individual A_i and B_i. As before, λ is initialized to 0. The estimate for the eigenvector, however, is not taken from the SVD of the large system. Rather, each component v_i is estimated individually from A_i and B_i. Doing this applies the normalization constraint individually to each v_i. The subsequent update of λ is performed as before, in which the equation to be solved is obtained from the combined aggregate matrices and eigenvector.

It is worth noting that, in addition to the crucial property of ensuring that each F_i is nontrivial, this algorithm also exploits most of the sparse structure of Equation 8. Updating the eigenvector involves only the small, relatively dense matrices A_i and B_i, and the computational cost is linear in the number of image pairs. The other operation, defined in Equation 7, does formally involve the large sparse matrices, but the matrix-matrix and matrix-vector products may be implemented straightforwardly to take advantage of the block-diagonal structure of A and B. Again, the cost is linear in the number of image pairs.

3   Experimental Results

We initially study the algorithm using the controlled conditions of a synthetic dataset. In this dataset, feature points were distributed on a regular grid bounded by the unit cube. Two views, each of 640x480 pixels, of this cloud of feature points were synthetically generated and matchpoints between these views are therefore known. Each synthetic camera observed the origin from a distance of 4 units, and the baseline between the views was 30 degrees. The views were synthetically distorted with a known value of λ. The experiment was intended to serve as a baseline that does not involve potentially noisy estimates of feature location that result from feature extraction on real-world data.

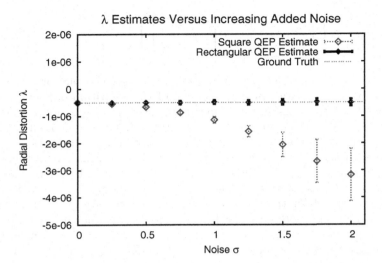

Fig. 1. Accuracy of λ estimation in the presence of increasing Gaussian positional noise. Ground truth is shown as dashed line. Both the rectangular method (solid line) and the square methods (dashed line) are shown for comparison.

The robustness of the estimator with respect to noise was explored by perturbing feature locations with zero mean additive Gaussian noise. Given 75 correspondences under these conditions, F and λ were estimated. Figure 1 compares the ground truth λ to the estimated λ as noise σ ranged from 0 to 2 pixels. For each noise level, 100 trials were performed and error bars depict one standard deviation. Both the technique described in this work and the method of [3] are shown for comparison.

Notice that the new method exhibits a great reduction in bias at one pixel of error, an amount not uncommon in typical computer vision applications. As error grows as large as two pixels the trend continues.

Given a fixed noise level of 1 pixel reprojection error, it is instructive to study the behavior of the new algorithm as the number of available matchpoints increases. Figure 2 plots λ accuracy as a function of the number of matchpoints used. In this case, random subsets of the available matchpoints were generated over 100 trials for each datapoint. Error bars correspond to one standard deviation.

For purposes of comparison, the new method is also compared to the previously known technique [3]. In order to do so, the earlier approach requires that the rectangular design matrices resulting from the overdetermined set of matchpoints be converted into a square system via the normal equations. Figure 2 shows the behavior of this approach (depicted as a dashed line) as compared directly to the new method (depicted as a solid line).

In the minimal case of 9 correspondences, the two methods produce identical distributions of λ estimates. This is a consequence of two things. First, corresponding trials for the square and rectangular methods received identical input

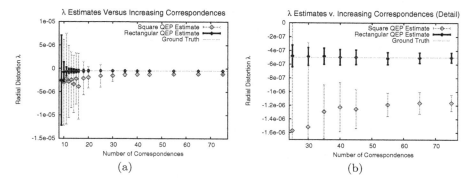

Fig. 2. Accuracy of λ with respect to increasing number of correspondences. (a) A comparison between square (dashed lines) and rectangular QEP (solid lines) from 9 to 75 correspondences. (b) A closeup view of the results. Accuracy from 25 to 75 correspondences.

corrupted by the same noise samples. Second, and more importantly, the rectangular algorithm produces an exact solution which is identical to the result for a square solver for a minimal data set.

Adding just a few additional correspondences dramatically reduces both the bias and variance of the rectangular method, while similar improvements in the results of the square method are not as dramatic. The rectangular method's variance drops significantly below the magnitude of the actual value λ at around 25 correspondences, a point at which the rectangular method's estimate could be said to provide meaningful information. The variance of the rectangular method decreases to about 15% of λ at 75 correspondences, while the square square method's variance is approximately 23% of λ at that point. This difference, while significant, is overshadowed by the dramatic differential in bias at high numbers of correspondences.

3.1   Multiple View-Pair Results

Experiments were performed to provide empirical validation for the case in which a single λ is estimated jointly for multiple view pairs. The setup was similar to the above, except that the baseline for image pairs was reduced to 4 degrees. In all, 8 successive views were generated, and each of the 7 view pairs was obtained via correspondences between adjacent views. Figure 3 shows a plot of the results. The first error bar denotes the mean and standard deviation of λ estimates obtained from 100 trials on the first view pair, each from 75 correspondences corrupted by iid positional Gaussian noise of $\sigma = 1$ pixel. The second error bar represents the results obtained from joint estimation for the first two view pairs; the third bar, from joint estimation for the first three, and so forth.

The variance of the estimates clearly decreases as more pairs are added. The benefits are most dramatic with the addition of the first few view pairs. Although these results may suggest that an online algorithm making use of our new technique could perform well with only a few views, there is no real computational

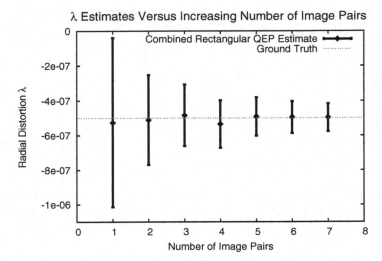

Fig. 3. Accuracy of λ using the rectangular QEP method with respect to increasing number of view pairs. Ground truth is shown as dashed line.

incentive to do so. The computational cost of a single iteration of the multiple view-pair algorithm applied to n pairs is equal to that of the independent algorithm applied separately to the n pairs.

3.2   Real-World Results

In order to obtain a sense for the algorithm's performance in a practical setting, an experiment was performed on a real image sequence generated from a handheld camera. Each image was captured at a resolution of 640x480 pixels, and the lens had a nominal focal length of 4 mm. The first and last images in the sequence are shown in Figure 4.

The same camera was also calibrated offline using a well-known method [1]. The iterative technique was constrained to compute the first radial coefficient of the standard multiplicative model. This was then converted to the division model (see Section 2) using standard least squares to obtain a ground-truth estimate of $\lambda = -8.5 \times 10^{-7}$ or a maximum of 54 pixels at the image corner.

The image data was then used to study the behavior of the new algorithm in a real-world context with respect to this ground truth distortion. Proposed matchpoints were generated [13], followed by RANSAC outlier detection based on a square QEP hypothesis generator. An inlier threshold of 1 pixel was employed resulting in an average of approximately 100 inliers from approximately 140 proposals per image pair.

These correspondences were provided to the new method to estimate λ and F for each image pair independently. In this case, the solution produced by the square method that was known to be closest to the ground-truth estimate was selected as a fair baseline comparison to the new technique. Figure 5 plots the

Fig. 4. First and last images of a real-world sequence used to study the new algorithm. The dataset is composed of six images total captured with a hand-held camera.

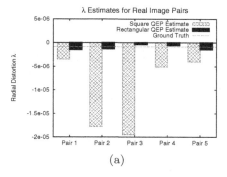
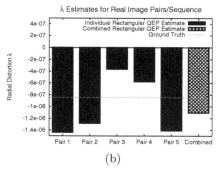

(a)   (b)

Fig. 5. Accuracy of λ as estimated from each neighboring pair in the real image sequence shown in Figure 4. (a) The square method consistently overestimates distortion, while the new rectangular method obtains dramatically better results. (b) A zoomed-in view of the rectangular estimates in (a), compared with the joint estimate for all 5 pairs, obtained via the multiple view-pairs algorithm of Section 2.3.

distortion estimate (shown as a bar graph for clarity) achieved by both techniques as compared to ground truth (shown as a dashed line).

The results appear to reflect what has already been observed in the simulations. The rectangular method exhibits a large reduction in bias compared to the square method. A close-up view of the results obtained by the new method are shown in Figure 4b. The global estimate of λ derived from all five pairs is also shown. This estimate is more accurate than any of the individual estimates.

4   Conclusion

We have developed a new approach to the simultaneous estimation of radial distortion and multi-view geometry. The method supports any number of correspondences arising from any number of views. In practice, this approach yields two new algorithms. The first exploits the redundancy of extra correspondences much more effectively than previous methods, while the second introduces an efficient method for estimating a single global λ simultaneously with multiple, independent, multi-view geometries.

These algorithms have been explored in the context of the epipolar geometry, in both simulated and real-world experiments. We find the results demonstrate the striking benefits of the new technique, and lead to more reliable and accurate camera calibration and motion estimation, with a reduced need for a priori knowledge of the scene or camera.

References

1. Tsai, R.: A Versatile Camera Calibration Technique for High-Accuracy 3D Machine Vision Metrology Using Off-the-Shelf TV Cameras and Lenses. IEEE Journal of Robotics and Automation **3** (1987) 323–344
2. Devernay, F., Faugeras, O.: Automatic calibration and removal of distortion from scenes of structured environments. In: SPIE. Volume 2567. (1995) 62–72
3. Fitzgibbon, A.W.: Simultaneous linear estimation of multiple view geometry and lens distortion. In: IEEE Conference on Computer Vision and Pattern Recognition. Volume 1. (2001) 125–132
4. Boutry, G., Elad, M., Golub, G.H., Milanfar, P.: The generalized eigenvalue problem for non-square pencils using a minimal perturbation approach. (To appear in SIAM Journal on Matrix Analysis and Applications)
5. Micusik, B., Pajdla, T.: Estimation of omnidirectional camera motion from epipolar geometry. In: IEEE Conference on Computer Vision and Pattern Recognition. (2001) 125–132
6. Thirthala, S., Pollefeys, M.: The radial trifocal tensor: A tool for calibrating the radial distortion of wide-angle cameras. In: IEEE Conference on Computer Vision and Pattern Recognition. Volume 1. (2005) 321–328
7. Stein, G.: Lens distortion calibration using point correspondences. In: IEEE Conference on Computer Vision and Pattern Recognition. (1997) 602–608
8. Claus, D., Fitzgibbon, A.W.: A rational function lens distortion model for general cameras. In: IEEE Conference on Computer Vision and Pattern Recognition. Volume 1. (2005) 213–219
9. Wright, T.G., Trefethen, L.N.: Eigenvalues and pseudospectra of rectangular matrices. IMA Journal of Numerical Analysis **22** (2002) 501–519
10. Longuet-Higgins, H.C.: A computer algorithm for reconstructing a scene from two projections. Nature **293** (1981) 133–135
11. Hartley, R.: In defense of the eight-point algorithm. IEEE Transactions on Pattern Analysis and Machine Intelligence **19** (1997) 580–593
12. Tisseur, F., Meerbergen, K.: The quadratic eigenvalue problem. SIAM Review **43** (2001) 235–286
13. Nister, D., Naroditsky, O., Bergen, J.: Visual odometry. In: IEEE Conference on Computer Vision and Pattern Recognition. Volume 1. (2004) 652–659

Camera Calibration with Two Arbitrary Coaxial Circles

Carlo Colombo, Dario Comanducci, and Alberto Del Bimbo

Dipartimento di Sistemi e Informatica,
Via S. Marta 3, 50139 Firenze, Italy
{colombo, comandu, delbimbo}@dsi.unifi.it

Abstract. We present an approach for camera calibration from the image of at least two circles arranged in a coaxial way. Such a geometric configuration arises in static scenes of objects with rotational symmetry or in scenes including generic objects undergoing rotational motion around a fixed axis. The approach is based on the automatic localization of a surface of revolution (SOR) in the image, and its use as a calibration artifact. The SOR can either be a real object in a static scene, or a "virtual surface" obtained by frame superposition in a rotational sequence. This provides a unified framework for calibration from single images of SORs or from turntable sequences. Both the internal and external calibration parameters (square pixels model) are obtained from two or more imaged cross sections of the SOR, whose apparent contour is also exploited to obtain a better calibration accuracy. Experimental results show that this calibration approach is accurate enough for several vision applications, encompassing 3D realistic model acquisition from single images, and desktop 3D object scanning.

1 Introduction

Camera calibration is a fundamental problem in computer vision and photogrammetry, whose solution allows relating 2D image coordinates to directions in the 3D space. The calibration methods proposed in the literature exhibit a trade-off between geometric accuracy and flexibility of use. Very high accuracies are typically required for laboratory applications, and obtained with special purpose 3D calibration patterns [1]. On the other hand, results from projective geometry were recently used to develop flexible and reasonably accurate calibration approaches for desktop vision applications exploiting scene constraints. A popular scene-based calibration approach uses the vanishing points of three mutually orthogonal directions [2], thus proving useful in the reconstruction of architectural environments [3], [4]. Images of spheres were used for desktop calibration purposes first in [5], and more recently in [6]; however, spherical calibration approaches are typically not robust w.r.t. noisy image features. The desktop calibration approach proposed in [7] uses a planar (2D) checkerboard to achieve a good trade-off between accuracy and flexibility. The same author proposed in [8] an approach based on linear (1D) artifacts that can be used for simultaneous calibration of multiple cameras with a

A. Leonardis, H. Bischof, and A. Pinz (Eds.): ECCV 2006, Part I, LNCS 3951, pp. 265–276, 2006.

partially overlapping field of view. Another desktop approach appears in [9]: by exploiting the image of two arbitrary coplanar circles, the focal length of the camera and its extrinsic parameters are obtained.

Being quite common in man-made environments, surfaces of revolution (SORs) were also proposed for desktop internal calibration purposes [10] and single view metric reconstruction [11], [12]. Thanks to their symmetry properties, SORs can be conveniently used as multiple camera calibration artifacts. The SOR features usable for calibration are the elliptical imaged cross-sections and the apparent contour. In [10], the apparent contour alone is used to calibrate the camera; this method requires that that two SORs are present in the same image, or that two or more images of SORs taken from the same camera are available. In [12] it is shown that the visible portions of two manually segmented imaged cross-sections are enough for calibrating from one view the focal length and the principal point provided that the camera has square pixels (a constraint always met by the modern devices), even when a single SOR object is present in the image.

In this paper, we present a desktop calibration approach based on the presence in the image of at least two coaxial circles. Such a geometric configuration often arises in practical applications, either in static scenes of a rotationally-symmetric object or in dynamic scenes of a generic object rotating on a turntable (Single

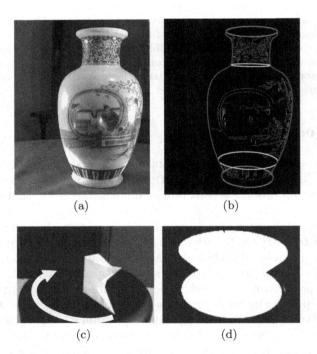

(a)   (b)

(c)   (d)

Fig. 1. (a): A real SOR object. (b): Characteristic curves (apparent contour, imaged cross sections) extracted from (a). (c): An object undergoing Single Axis Motion on a turntable. (d): The virtual SOR induced by the rotating object in (c).

Axis Motion, SAM). A unified framework is provided for both cases, by extracting a SOR object from image data, and using it as calibration artifact. However, while in the former case the SOR is a real object (Fig. 1(a, b)), in the latter case it is actually a "virtual surface," whose image is obtained by superposition of the difference between the current and the first frame of the sequence (Fig. 1(c, d)). As in [12], calibration of a square pixel camera is achieved from a single SOR view. However, that calibration approach is extended here to both internal and external parameters, and is completely automatic, thanks to a homology-based curve segmentation strategy. In addition, our approach combines both the calibration primitives exploited in [12] (imaged cross-sections) and those used in [10] (apparent contour) so as to add robustness and accuracy to the calibration task. Besides, the approach offers a new solution to the problem of camera calibration from turntable sequences, differing from previous solutions (see e.g. [13]) in that it doesn't require point tracking and can also deal with textureless objects. Experimental results provide a quantitative evaluation of calibration performance and demonstrate the use of the approach for the purpose of metric 3D reconstruction and texture acquisition in practical applications.

2   Automatic SOR Segmentation

A SOR can be parameterized as

$$\mathcal{P}(\vartheta, t) = (\rho(t)\cos(\vartheta), \rho(t)\sin(\vartheta), t) \ , \tag{1}$$

where $\vartheta \in [0, 2\pi]$ and $t \in [0, 1]$. The scaling function $\rho(z)$ controls the 3D shape of the SOR. The perspective projection of a SOR like the vase of Fig. 1(a) gives rise to two different kinds of image curves, namely the *apparent contour* and the *imaged cross sections* of Fig. 1(b). The former is the image of the points at which the surface is smooth and the projection rays are tangent to the surface. The shape of this curve is view dependent. On the other hand, imaged cross sections are view independent elliptical curves, which correspond to parallel coaxial circles in 3D and arise from surface normal discontinuities or surface texture content. Both the apparent contour and the imaged cross sections of a SOR are transformed onto themselves by a 4-dof harmonic homology

$$\mathbf{H} = \mathbf{I} - 2\frac{\mathbf{v}_\infty \mathbf{l}_s^\mathrm{T}}{\mathbf{v}_\infty^\mathrm{T} \mathbf{l}_s} \ , \tag{2}$$

where $\mathbf{l}_s$ and $\mathbf{v}_\infty$ are respectively the imaged axis of revolution and the vanishing point of the normal direction of the plane through $\mathbf{l}_s$ and the camera center [14].

The SOR segmentation problem concerns with automatically estimating from a SOR image the harmonic homology of Eq. 2 together with the imaged SOR curves (apparent contour, visible imaged cross sections) consistent with it. All of this geometric information will be exploited later to calibrate the camera. The segmentation strategy follows closely the two-phase approach proposed in [15]. The first phase is devoted to estimating the harmonic homology and *all* the

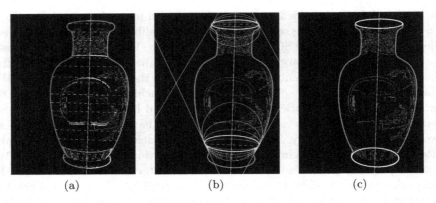

(a)   (b)   (c)

Fig. 2. Automatic SOR segmentation. (a): Homology estimation and curve segmentation. (b): Conic pencil-based curve classification. (c): The final result.

image curves (possibly including clutter) consistent with it. This is achieved by solving an optimization problem involving edge points extracted from the image according to a multiresolution scheme, where the RANSAC algorithm is used at the lowest resolution level to provide a first guess of the homology parameters. In Fig. 2(a) the final output of the first phase is shown.

The second phase is devoted to classifying the image curves obtained before respectively into (a) apparent contour, (b) imaged cross sections and (c) clutter. To this aim, the tangency condition between each imaged cross-section and the silhouette is exploited, allowing us to construct a conic pencil for each silhouette point pair (Fig. 2(b)), and to look, among all possible conic pencils, for the two ellipses receiving the largest consensus in a Hough-like voting procedure (Fig. 2(c)). Besides being of key importance for the purpose of SOR segmentation, the use of the apparent contour significantly improves the quality of the homology estimate, and hence of the calibration parameters estimated from it.

Automatic segmentation of the imaged virtual SOR arising from SAM sequences follows the same lines as above, but is significantly easier thanks to the fact that clutter is almost absent, and binary images (with the virtual SOR as the foreground) are used, instead of color images.

3   Camera Calibration

3.1   Internal Parameters

The imaged SOR fixed entities are strictly related to the calibration matrix K, which embeds information about the internal camera parameters. In particular it holds $\mathbf{l}_s = \omega \mathbf{v}_\infty$, where $\omega = K^{-T}K^{-1}$ is referred to as the image of the absolute conic (IAC) [16]. Moreover, since cross sections are parallel circles in 3D, they intersect at the circular points of the families of planes orthogonal to the SOR symmetry axis. Their projection in the image, $\mathbf{i}$ and $\mathbf{j}$, are also related to the image of the absolute conic as $\mathbf{i}^T \omega \mathbf{i} = 0$ and $\mathbf{j}^T \omega \mathbf{j} = 0$. The resulting system

$$\begin{cases} \mathbf{i}^{\mathrm{T}} \, \omega \, \mathbf{i} = 0 \\ \mathbf{j}^{\mathrm{T}} \, \omega \, \mathbf{j} = 0 \\ \mathbf{l}_s = \omega \mathbf{v}_\infty \end{cases} \tag{3}$$

provides four linear constraints on ω, whose coefficients can be computed from (the visible portions of) two imaged ellipses as shown in [12]. In that paper, it is demonstrated that only three out of the four constraints above are actually independent. Therefore, the system of Eq. 3 can be used to calibrate a square pixel camera (zero skew and unit aspect ratio: 3 dofs) from a single image.

3.2   External Parameters

In [17], external orientation is obtained from the imaged cross sections of a right straight homogeneous generalized cylinder (RSHGC) under orthographic viewing conditions. In the following we address the problem of external calibration under full perspective viewing conditions from the image of two cross sections of a SOR—this being a specialization of a RSHGC. Similarly to [18] and [9], our solution is based on the image of two circles, but with the important difference that in our case the circles are coaxial, and not coplanar. Our approach exploits the knowledge of (1) the imaged SOR symmetry axis $\mathbf{l}_s$; (2) the vanishing line $\mathbf{l}_\infty = \mathbf{i} \times \mathbf{j}$ common to all the planes orthogonal to the SOR symmetry axis, and (3) one or more imaged cross sections. We recall that the matrix K represents only the internal camera parameters; the complete projection matrix is

$$\mathtt{P} = \mathtt{K}\mathtt{R}[\mathtt{I}_{3\times3} \mid -\mathbf{c}],$$

where the 3-vector $\mathbf{c}$ is the camera center in (inhomogeneous) world coordinates, and R is the rotation between the world frame and the camera frame. Without loss of generality, we can take as world frame origin the center of the bottom cross section of the SOR, and as z axis the SOR symmetry axis; furthermore, we can impose that the camera center must lie on the half plane X > 0, Y = 0.

Rotation Matrix. The first step is the computation of the rotation matrix

$$\mathtt{R} = \begin{bmatrix} \mathbf{n}_X \ \mathbf{n}_Y \ \mathbf{n}_Z \end{bmatrix} \ , \tag{4}$$

where $\mathbf{n}_X$, $\mathbf{n}_Y$, $\mathbf{n}_Z$ are unit vectors. It is well known that, given a point image $\mathbf{p}$ in homogeneous coordinates, the inhomogeneous 3-vector $\mathtt{K}^{-1}\mathbf{p}$ represents the direction (with respect to the camera frame) of the ray passing through the camera center and $\mathbf{p}$ [16]. Therefore, if we choose any two points on the line $\mathbf{l}_s$, we can determine two vectors lying on the plane Y = 0, whose normalized cross product provides us with the unit vector $\mathbf{n}_Y$. (The sign of the cross product must be consistent with the definition of the world frame orientation given above—see also the example below.) The same procedure can be applied to compute the unit vector $\mathbf{n}_Z$ from two points properly chosen on the vanishing line $\mathbf{l}_\infty$. Finally, the unit vector $\mathbf{n}_X$ is computed as the cross product of $\mathbf{n}_Y$ and $\mathbf{n}_Z$. Fig. 3 shows three points which can be conveniently chosen for obtaining the rotation matrix. These are:

- the homology vertex $\mathbf{v}_\infty \in \mathbf{l}_\infty$, computed as shown in Section 2;
- the imaged center of the bottom cross section $\mathbf{x}_c$. This is the projection of the world origin in the image, and can be obtained from the pole-polar relationship between the imaged bottom cross-section (represented by the 3×3 symmetric matrix $\mathbf{C}_b$) and the vanishing line $\mathbf{l}_\infty$ as $\mathbf{x}_c = \mathbf{C}_b^{-1}\mathbf{l}_\infty$;
- the intersection $\mathbf{x}_i = \mathbf{l}_s \times \mathbf{l}_\infty$ between $\mathbf{l}_s$ and $\mathbf{l}_\infty$.

In Fig. 3, the imaged z axis ($\mathbf{l}_s$) is oriented from $\mathbf{x}_c$ to $\mathbf{x}_i$. Since the x coordinate of the camera center is positive, the vector

$$\mathbf{m}_Y = (\mathbf{K}^{-1}\mathbf{x}_c) \times (\mathbf{K}^{-1}\mathbf{x}_i) = \mathbf{K}^\top (\mathbf{x}_c \times \mathbf{x}_i) \tag{5}$$

must have the same direction as the Y axis, in order to obtain a right-hand world frame. The vector $\mathbf{m}_Z$ orthogonal to the plane $z = 0$ and directed as the z axis must then be obtained as

$$\mathbf{m}_Z = (\mathbf{K}^{-1}\mathbf{v}_\infty) \times (\mathbf{K}^{-1}\mathbf{x}_i) = \mathbf{K}^\top (\mathbf{v}_\infty \times \mathbf{x}_i) \ . \tag{6}$$

The unit vectors $\mathbf{n}_Y$ and $\mathbf{n}_Z$ are finally obtained by normalization of $\mathbf{m}_Y$ and $\mathbf{m}_Z$, respectively.

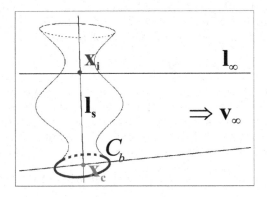

Fig. 3. Lines and points needed for rotation matrix computation

As the matrix R thus computed is seldom a rotation matrix, a final refinement step based on the SVD decomposition is carried out to obtain the best orthogonal approximation to R [7].

Camera Center. The last step is that of the computation of camera center. Although any visible cross section of known height z could be exploited, for the sake of simplicity, in what follows we will use the bottom cross section (at $z = 0$), the extension of the equations to the general case being straightforward. Let ρ be the radius of the bottom cross-section, and consider again the projection matrix P. Any point on the plane $z = 0$ is mapped onto the image by the homography $\mathbf{H}_0$ given by:

$$\mathbf{x} = P\,(X, Y, 0, 1)^{\top} =$$
$$= \begin{bmatrix} \mathbf{p}_1 \ \mathbf{p}_2 \ \mathbf{p}_4 \end{bmatrix} (X, Y, 1)^{\top} = \tag{7}$$
$$= H_0\,(X, Y, 1)^{\top}\ ,$$

where $\mathbf{p}_i$ is the i-th column of P. In particular, the center of the bottom cross section is projected onto the inhomogeneous point with pixel coordinates (x_c, y_c), whose corresponding homogeneous vector is

$$\sigma \mathbf{x}_c = \sigma \begin{pmatrix} x_c \\ y_c \\ 1 \end{pmatrix} = H_0 \begin{pmatrix} 0 \\ 0 \\ 1 \end{pmatrix} = \mathbf{p}_4\ . \tag{8}$$

More generally, the homography H_0 transforms any point of the bottom cross section into the homogeneous image point

$$\mathbf{x}_\vartheta = H_0 \begin{pmatrix} \rho \cos \vartheta \\ \rho \sin \vartheta \\ 1 \end{pmatrix} = \rho \cos \vartheta\ \mathbf{p}_1 + \rho \sin \vartheta\ \mathbf{p}_2 + \sigma \mathbf{x}_c\ , \tag{9}$$

with pixel coordinates $(x_\vartheta, y_\vartheta)$ such that

$$\frac{y_\vartheta}{x_\vartheta} = \frac{\rho \cos \vartheta\ p_{21} + \rho \sin \vartheta\ p_{22} + \sigma y_c}{\rho \cos \vartheta\ p_{11} + \rho \sin \vartheta\ p_{12} + \sigma x_c}\ , \tag{10}$$

where p_{ij} denotes the (i, j) element of P. Solving Eq. 10 for σ, we obtain

$$\sigma = \frac{(p_{21}x_\vartheta - p_{11}y_\vartheta) \cos \vartheta + (p_{22}x_\vartheta - p_{12}y_\vartheta) \sin \vartheta}{y_\vartheta x_c - x_\vartheta y_c}\ \rho\ . \tag{11}$$

Now, since by definition of the matrix P, the camera center C appears only in the fourth column:

$$\mathbf{p}_4 = -KRC\ , \tag{12}$$

by replacing Eq. 12 into Eq. 8 we finally obtain

$$C = (KR)^{-1}(-\sigma \mathbf{x}_c) = -\sigma R^{\top} K^{-1} \mathbf{x}_c\ . \tag{13}$$

Eqs. 11 through 13 show that, if the real size of the SOR is unknown, its distance w.r.t. the camera can be determined up to an arbitrary scale. Therefore, if the real dimensions of the SOR are not available, the radius ρ can arbitrarily be set to 1. The other parameters involved in Eqs. 11 and 13 can all be computed from the image. Specifically, the imaged world center $\mathbf{x}_c$ can be obtained as shown in the previous Section and, for any arbitrarily chosen ϑ, the point $(x_\vartheta, y_\vartheta)$ on the imaged cross section can be obtained as shown in [12].

4   Experimental Results and Applications

In order to assess the performance of the calibration algorithm, both synthetic and real-world tests were carried out. In the synthetic experiments, the reference SOR view of Fig. 3 was generated, corresponding to the following ground

Table 1. Calibration performance: focal length and principal point (ground truth: 750, (400, 300))

σ	avg(f)	std(f)	avg(x_p)	std(x_p)	avg(y_p)	std(y_p)
0.1	752.99	6.650	400.83	3.920	299.11	0.681
0.2	749.73	7.524	399.34	4.622	300.13	0.883
0.4	748.53	8.770	398.90	5.388	299.96	1.138
0.8	751.51	11.572	399.07	7.242	299.86	1.809
1.6	744.05	15.543	394.47	9.374	301.16	3.156

Table 2. External calibration estimates for increasing noise values. *Left*: Average value and standard deviation of the angle, in degrees, between each column of R and its estimate. *Right*: Camera center (ground truth: X = 1.6, z = 0.7), with $\vartheta = 0$.

σ	ROTATION						CAMERA CENTER			
	avg($\angle_X$)	std($\angle_X$)	avg($\angle_Y$)	std($\angle_Y$)	avg($\angle_Z$)	std($\angle_Z$)	avg(X)	std(X)	avg(Z)	std(Z)
0.1	0.210	0.121	0.127	0.102	0.146	0.111	1.605	0.014	0.704	0.0042
0.2	0.250	0.173	0.144	0.134	0.185	0.148	1.598	0.015	0.700	0.0044
0.4	0.300	0.227	0.186	0.140	0.213	0.212	1.597	0.018	0.696	0.0054
0.8	0.479	0.261	0.284	0.166	0.347	0.273	1.600	0.023	0.698	0.0088
1.6	0.675	0.346	0.419	0.295	0.455	0.349	1.583	0.033	0.696	0.0105

truth camera parameters: $f = 750$ (focal length), $(x_p, y_p) = (400, 300)$ (principal point), $c = (1.6, 0.0, 0.7)$ (camera center). Ground truth data were corrupted with increasing Gaussian noise values ranging from 0 to 1.6; for each of these values, 1000 Monte Carlo trials were performed.

Tab. 1 gives the internal calibration performance (average and standard deviation) for the focal length and principal point. The results show that performance undergoes a graceful degradation as the noise increases. Specifically, the average remains almost constant for all noise values considered, while the standard deviation proportionally increases with noise.

Tab. 2 provides calibration performance for external parameters. Results show that the rotation matrix is more sensitive than the camera center to image noise. Specifically, both the average and standard deviation values of the angle between homologous unit vectors increase with noise. Performance in terms of camera center follows instead the same pattern as with internal parameters, with almost constant average error values, and linearly increasing standard deviation values.

Real-world tests have concerned texture acquisition of a SOR object, and camera calibration for the SOR and SAM cases. As shown in [12], internal camera calibration permits both the 3D reconstruction and the texture acquisition of the imaged SOR. However, having computed also the external camera parameters, a much simpler method than the one proposed in that paper can be used to acquire the texture on the SOR. Indeed, for each visible pair (ϑ, t) in Eq. 1, the corresponding imaged point can be obtained directly via the projection matrix P. In Figs. 4(a,b), the reconstructed camera pose and a synthetic view of the

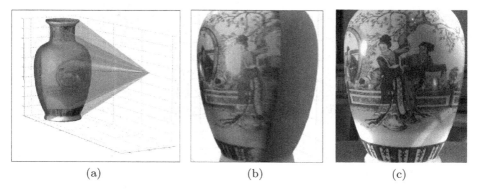

(a)   (b)   (c)

Fig. 4. (a): The reconstructed camera pose for the vase of Fig. 1(a). (b): A synthetic view of the reconstructed vase. (c): A real photo of the vase from the same viewpoint as in (b).

Table 3. Calibration with a real SOR object (*left*) and with a turntable (SAM) sequence (*right*). Two different cameras were used. Ground truth and estimated values are denoted respectively as v and $\hat{v}$. The percentage error $\varepsilon_\%$ is evaluated as $100 \cdot |v - \hat{v}|/v$.

	SOR			SAM		
parameter	v	$\hat{v}$	$\varepsilon_\%$	v	$\hat{v}$	$\varepsilon_\%$
f (focal length)	718.52	728.67	1.41	398.46	390.17	2.08
x_p (principal point)	320.01	343.27	7.27	167.22	186.62	11.60
y_p (principal point)	239.96	240.65	0.29	121.07	98.06	19.01
z (camera center)	217.82	198.26	8.98	240.01	217.37	9.43

textured model extracted from Fig. 1(a) are shown. The real photo in Fig. 4(c), obtained from the same viewpoint as in (b), confirms the good result obtained, despite the fact that the tree in the original image was highly foreshortened.

Tab. 3(left) reports the ground truth vs estimated values and the error percentage for each of the internal calibration parameters (in pixels) and one external parameter (the third component of the camera center, in mm). The ground truth was computed with a 3D calibration grid and the standard Tsai algorithm [1]—the camera had a negligible radial distortion and square pixels. A similar test was conducted for the case of a turntable sequence. Tab. 3(right) shows the comparison between the calibration results obtained by using, as calibration artifact, the virtual SOR segmented as in Fig. 5(a), with those obtained with the Tsai algorithm. For both the real cases addressed, results show a similar performance as for the noise sensitivity of the internal calibration parameters. Specifically, the principal point is more sensitive w.r.t. noise than the focal length. This may be explained by the fact, reported in the literature on SOR-based calibration (see e.g. [12]), that the accuracy of the principal point (but not that of the focal length) depends not only on image noise, but also on the relative position of the imaged SOR axis w.r.t. the principal point itself. In particular, the estimation

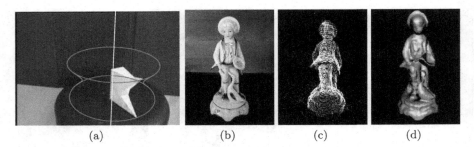

(a)   (b)   (c)   (d)

Fig. 5. (a): The segmented virtual SOR for the object rotating on a turntable. A medium-profile analog camera was used. (b): A complex object. (c,d): The 3D model (point cloud, solid) extracted from a turntable sequence of the object in (b).

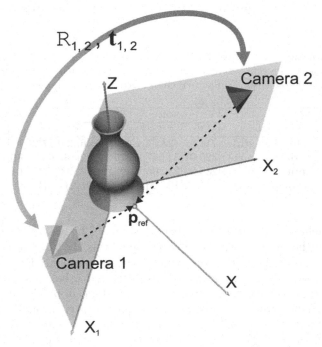

Fig. 6. View-dependent external calibration can be made view-independent using a common reference point p_{ref}, thus making it possible to compute the relative positioning transformation R_{12}, t_{12}. The x_i's are the view-dependent world axes, while x through p_{ref} is the absolute one.

uncertainty is bigger and bigger as imaged axis of symmetry get closer to the principal point.

Figs. 5(b,c,d) show the reconstruction results for a complex object obtained with a desktop 3D scanning system based on the calibration procedure described in this paper. The system is composed by a turntable, an square pixel camera and a laser stripe illuminator, which makes visible a vertical slice of the rotating object being acquired. After virtual SOR image extraction and camera calibration performed *by exploiting the same object being scanned*, shape acquisition is finally obtained by laser profile rectification and collation, as shown in [19]. The 3D model accurately reproduces the shape of the original object.

5   Conclusions and Future Work

A novel approach was proposed to automatically extract SOR-related image primitives and calibrate both internal and external camera parameters from coaxial circles, arising either from a single image of a SOR or from a turntable sequence featuring arbitrarily-shaped objects. The method has been employed successfully in a desktop 3D laser scanner based on SAM and laser profile rectification, obtaining good results.

Although the external calibration approach proposed is view-dependent (the x-axis of the world frame being required to lie on the plane through the SOR axis and the camera center), such 1-parameter dependence can be easily removed given an identifiable reference point on either coaxial circle. Absolute external calibration can be useful for the relative positioning of any pair of cameras having the SOR and the reference point in their fields of view (see Fig. 6).

As future work, we are trying to obtain 3D textured models of generic objects, extending the projection method developed for the SOR case. The idea is to project the model point cloud (obtained with the laser scanner) onto each frame of a video sequence of the real object undergoing SAM, after having registered frame by frame the projected point cloud with the blob (obtained by background subtraction) of the rotating object.

Acknowledgments. This work was funded, in part, by the Italian Ministry of University and Education (MIUR), in the context of the national project LIMA3D - "Low cost 3D imaging and modelling automatic system". The authors thank Mr. F. Pernici for his support in the preliminary phase of the project.

References

1. Tsai, R.Y.: A versatile camera calibration technique for high-accuracy 3D machine vision metrology using off-the-shelf TV cameras and lenses. IEEE Journal of Robotics and Automation **3** (1987) 323–344
2. Caprile, B., Torre, V.: Using vanishing points for camera calibration. The International Journal of Computer Vision **4** (1990) 127–140
3. Sturm, P., Maybank, S.: A method for interactive 3D reconstruction of piecewise planar objects from single images. In: British Machine Vision Conference. (1999) 265–274
4. Liebowitz, D., Criminisi, A., Zisserman, A.: Creating architectural models from images. In: EuroGraphics. Volume 18. (1999) 39–50
5. Daucher, N., Dhome, M., Lapreste, J.: Camera calibration from spheres images. In: 3rd European Conference on Computer Vision. (1994) 449–454

6. Agrawal, M., Davis, L.S.: Camera calibration using spheres: A semi-definite programming approach. In: 9th IEEE International Conference on Computer Vision. Volume 2. (2003) 782–789
7. Zhang, Z.: A flexible new technique for camera calibration. IEEE Transactions on PAMI **22** (2000) 1330–1334
8. Zhang, Z.: Camera calibration with one dimensional objects. In: 7th European Conference on Computer Vision. Volume IV. (2002) 161–174
9. Chen, Q., Wu, H., Wada, T.: Camera calibration with two arbitrary coplanar circles. In: European Conference on Computer Vision. (2004) 521–532
10. Wong, K.Y.K., Mendonça, P., Cipolla, R.: Camera calibration from surfaces of revolution. IEEE Transactions on PAMI **25** (2003) 147–161
11. Wong, K.Y.K., Mendonça, P.R.S., Cipolla, R.: Reconstruction of surfaces of revolution from single uncalibrated views. In: British Machine Vision Conference. Volume 1. (2002) 93–102
12. Colombo, C., Del Bimbo, A., Pernici, F.: Metric 3D reconstruction and texture acquisition of surfaces of revolution from a single uncalibrated view. IEEE Transactions on PAMI **27** (2005) 99–114
13. Jiang, G., Quan, L., Tsui, H.T.: Circular motion geometry by minimal 2 points in 4 images. In: IEEE International Conference on Computer Vision. (2003) 221–227
14. Abdallah, S.M.: Object Recognition via Invariance. PhD thesis, The University of Sydney, Australia (2000)
15. Colombo, C., Comanducci, D., Del Bimbo, A., Pernici, F.: Accurate automatic localization of surfaces of revolution for self-calibration and metric reconstruction. In: IEEE CVPR Workshop on Perceptual Organization in Computer Vision. (2004) (On CD-ROM.)
16. Hartley, R.I., Zisserman, A.: Multiple View Geometry in Computer Vision. Cambridge University Press (2000)
17. Xu, G., Tanaka, H.T., Tsuji, S.: Right straight homogeneous generalized cylinders with symmetric cross-sections: Recovery of pose and shape from image contours. In: IEEE International Conference on Computer Vision and Pattern Recognition. (1992) 692–694
18. Rothwell, C.A., Zisserman, A., Marinos, C.I., Forsyth, D., Mundy, J.L.: Relative motion and pose from arbitrary planar curves. Image and Vision Computing **10** (1992) 251–262
19. Colombo, C., Comanducci, D., Del Bimbo, A.: A desktop 3D scanner exploiting rotation and visual rectification of laser profiles. In: IEEE International Conference on Vision Systems. (2006) (On CD-ROM.)

Molding Face Shapes by Example

Ira Kemelmacher and Ronen Basri*

Dept. of Computer Science and Applied Math.,
The Weizmann Institute of Science,
Rehovot 76100, Israel

Abstract. Human faces are remarkably similar in global properties, including size, aspect ratios, and locations of main features, but can vary
considerably in details across individuals, gender, race, or due to facial
expression. We propose a novel method for 3D shape recovery of a face
from a *single* image using a *single* 3D reference model of a different person's face. The method uses the input image as a guide to mold the
reference model to reach a desired reconstruction. Assuming Lambertian
reflectance and rough alignment of the input image and reference model,
we seek shape, albedo, and lighting that best fit the image while preserving the rough structure of the model. We demonstrate our method by
providing accurate reconstructions of novel faces overcoming significant
differences in shape due to gender, race, and facial expressions.

1 Introduction

The 3-dimensional shape of a face and its reflectance properties contain important information that can be used for recognition and for predicting appearance
under novel viewing conditions. Recovering this information from a single image
is difficult, since shape from shading algorithms generally require knowledge of
the lighting conditions and the reflectance properties of the face [1, 2, 3, 4] (see
some attempts to relax these assumptions in [5, 6, 7]). People, in contrast, seem
to skillfully recognize faces from novel images overcoming significant viewpoint
and lighting variations. This ability is often attributed to familiarity with faces
as a class (e.g., [8]).

To address this difficulty, various algorithms use class information to restrict
the set of allowable reconstructions. One approach attempts to exploit the symmetry of faces [9, 10]. The advantage of using symmetry is that reconstruction
can rely on a mere single image without the need for additional examples of
face models. The disadvantage is that point-wise correspondence between the
two symmetric portions must be established, and this task is generally difficult.
Another approach is to learn the set of allowable reconstructions from a large
number of faces in a database. This can be achieved by embedding all 3D faces

* Research was supported in part by the Israel Science Foundation grant number
266/02 and by the European Commission Project IST-2002-506766 Aim Shape. The
vision group at the Weizmann Inst. is supported in part by the Moross Laboratory
for Vision Research and Robotics.

A. Leonardis, H. Bischof, and A. Pinz (Eds.): ECCV 2006, Part I, LNCS 3951, pp. 277–288, 2006.

in a linear space [11, 12, 13, 14, 15] (see also [16] where this approach is combined with symmetry) or by using a training set to determine a density function for faces [17, 18]. These methods can achieve accurate reconstructions, but they require a large number of face models as well as point-wise correspondence between all the models. Finally, [19] proposed a method for rendering faces in novel views assuming that different faces share the exact same shape while differ only in albedo.

In a global sense, different faces indeed are highly similar. Faces of different individuals share the same main features (eyes, nose, mouth) in roughly the same locations, and their sizes and aspect ratios do not vary much. However, locally, face shapes can vary considerably across individuals, gender, race, or as a result of facial expressions. Face recognition methods use this global similarity of faces, e.g., to estimate the pose of novel faces, for example by aligning a face image to a generic face model. In this paper we will demonstrate how this global similarity can be exploited to obtain a detailed shape reconstruction of novel faces.

Below we introduce a novel method for shape recovery of a face from a *single image* that uses only *a single reference 3D face model* of a different person in the training set. Intuitively, our method uses the input image as a guide to mold the reference model to reach a desired reconstruction. Specifically, the method modifies the shape and albedo of the model face to fit the image. Since in general selecting shape and albedo to fit an image is an ill posed problem, we will restrict the method to produce reconstructions that preserve the rough shape and albedo of the reference model.

Our method assumes Lambertian reflectance, light sources at infinity, and rough alignment between the input image and the reference model. It allows for multiple unknown light sources and attached shadows by using a spherical harmonic approximation to model reflectance (following [20, 21]). We cast the problem as an image irradiance equation [2] with unknown lighting, albedo, and surface normals. We then use the reference model to estimate lighting and provide initial estimate of albedo. We further introduce regularization terms to seek solutions that preserve the rough shape and albedo of the reference model. These terms will smooth the difference in shape and albedo between the reference model and the sought face. We show experiments demonstrating that the method can achieve accurate reconstructions of novel faces overcoming significant differences in shape due to gender, race, and facial expressions.

Although this paper emphasizes the use of a single model of a face to reconstruct another face, we note that this method can supplement methods that make use of multiple models in a database. In particular, we may select to mold the model from the database that best fits the image. Alternatively, we may choose the best fit model from a linear subspace spanned by the database, or we may choose a model based on probabilistic criteria. In all cases our method will try to improve the reconstruction by relying on the selected model.

The paper is divided as follows. Section 2 defines the optimization function. Section 3 describes the reconstruction algorithm. Experimental results are shown in Sect. 4.

2   Problem Statement

Consider an image $E(x, y)$ of a face defined on a compact domain $\Omega \subset \Re^2$, whose corresponding surface is given by $z(x, y)$. The surface normal at every point is denoted $\mathbf{n}(x, y)$ (boldface is used to denote vectors) with

$$\mathbf{n}(x, y) = \frac{1}{\sqrt{p^2 + q^2 + 1}} (p, q, -1)^T, \tag{1}$$

where $p(x, y) = \partial z / \partial x$ and $q(x, y) = \partial z / \partial y$. We assume that the face is Lambertian with albedo $\rho(x, y)$ and ignore the effect of cast shadows and interreflections. Under these assumptions, for an object illuminated by an arbitrary configuration of light sources at infinity, it has been shown [20, 21] that reflectance can be expressed in terms of spherical harmonics as

$$R(\mathbf{n}; \rho, \mathbf{l}) \approx \rho \sum_{i=0}^{K-1} l_i Y_i(\mathbf{n}), \tag{2}$$

where $\mathbf{l} = (l_0, ... l_{K-1})$ denote the harmonic coefficients of lighting and $Y_i(\mathbf{n})$ ($0 \leq i < K - 1$) include the spherical harmonic functions evaluated at the surface normal. Because the reflectance of Lambertian objects under arbitrary lighting is very smooth this approximation is highly accurate already when a low order harmonic approximation is used. Specifically, a second order harmonic approximation (including nine harmonic functions) captures on average at least 99.2% of the energy in an image. A first order approximation (including four harmonic functions) can also be used with somewhat less accuracy. It has been shown analytically that a first order harmonic approximation captures at least 87.5% of the energy in an image, while in practice, owing to the fact that only normals with $n_z \geq 0$ are observed, the accuracy seems to approach 95% [22]. Below we will model reflectance using a first order harmonic approximation and write this in vector notation as

$$R(\mathbf{n}; \rho, \mathbf{l}) \approx \rho \mathbf{l}^T \mathbf{Y}(\mathbf{n}), \tag{3}$$

with $\mathbf{Y}(\mathbf{n}) = (1, n_x, n_y, n_z)^T$ and n_x, n_y, n_z are the components of $\mathbf{n}^1$.

The image irradiance equation is then given by

$$E(x, y) = R(\mathbf{n}; \rho, \mathbf{l}). \tag{4}$$

In general, when ρ and $\mathbf{l}$ are provided this equation can be solved using shape from shading algorithms (e.g., [2, 3, 23, 24]), so we will need a method to estimate ρ and l.

To supply the missing information we will be assisted by a reference model of a face of a different individual. Let $z_{\text{ref}}(x, y)$ denote the surface of the reference

---

[1] Formally, we should set $\boldsymbol{Y} = (1/\sqrt{4\pi}, \sqrt{3/(4\pi)} n_x, \sqrt{3/(4\pi)} n_y, \sqrt{3/(4\pi)} n_z)$. For convenience we omit these constant factors and rescale the lighting coefficients to include these factors.

face with $\mathbf{n}_{\mathrm{ref}}(x,y)$ denoting the normal to the surface, and $\rho_{\mathrm{ref}}(x,y)$ denote its albedo. We will use this information to determine the lighting and provide initial guess for the sought albedo.

Finally, to regularize the problem we will define the difference shape as

$$d_z(x,y) = z(x,y) - z_{\mathrm{ref}}(x,y) \tag{5}$$

and the difference albedo as

$$d_\rho(x,y) = \rho(x,y) - \rho_{\mathrm{ref}}(x,y) \tag{6}$$

and require that these differences will be smooth. We are now ready to define our optimization function:

$$\min_{\mathbf{l},\rho,z} \int\!\!\int_\Omega \left((E - \rho\mathbf{l}^T\mathbf{Y}(\mathbf{n}))^2 + \lambda_1 \triangle g(d_z) + \lambda_2 \triangle g(d_\rho) \right) dxdy. \tag{7}$$

$\triangle g(.)$ denotes the Laplacian of a Gaussian function, and λ_1 and λ_2 are positive constants. Below we will refer to the first term in this integral as the "data term" and the other two terms as the "regularization terms". Note that we chose to regularize d_z and d_ρ rather than z and ρ in order to preserve the discontinuities in z_{ref} and ρ_{ref}.

3   Surface Reconstruction

Evidently, without regularization the optimization functional (7) is ill-posed. Specifically, for every choice of depth $z(x,y)$ and lighting l it is possible to prescribe albedo $\rho(x,y)$ to make the first term vanish. With regularization and appropriate boundary conditions the problem becomes well-posed.

We approach this optimization by solving for lighting, depth, and albedo separately. First, we recover the lighting coefficients l by finding the best coefficients that fit the reference model to the image. This is analogous to solving for pose by matching the features of a model face to the features extracted from an image of a different face. Next we solve for depth $z(x,y)$ using the recovered lighting coefficients and the albedo of the reference model. This in fact is the usual shape from shading problem. Finally, we use the lighting and the recovered depth to estimate the albedo $\rho(x,y)$. This procedure can be repeated iteratively, although in our experiments one iteration seemed to suffice. These three steps are described in detail in the next three subsections.

The use of the albedo of the reference model may seem restrictive since different people may vary significantly in skin color. Nevertheless, it can be readily verified that linearly transforming the albedo (i.e., $\alpha\rho(x,y) + \beta$, with scalar constants α and β) can be compensated for by scaling appropriately the light intensity and changing the ambient term l_0. Our albedo recovery, consequently, will be subject to this ambiguity. It is important to note that to make sure that marks on the reference face would not influence much the reconstruction we first smooth the albedo of the reference model by a Gaussian.

3.1 Lighting Recovery

In the first step we attempt to recover the lighting coefficients by fitting the reference model to the image. To this end, we substitute in (7) $\rho \rightarrow \rho_{\text{ref}}$ and $z \rightarrow z_{\text{ref}}$ (and consequently $\mathbf{n} \rightarrow \mathbf{n}_{\text{ref}}$). At this stage both regularization terms vanish, and only the data term remains:

$$\min_{\mathbf{l}} \int \int_{\Omega} \left(E - \rho_{\text{ref}} \, \mathbf{l}^T \mathbf{Y}(\mathbf{n}_{\text{ref}}) \right)^2 dx dy. \tag{8}$$

Substituting for $\mathbf{Y}$ and discretizing the integral we obtain

$$\min_{\mathbf{l}} \sum_{(x,y) \in \Omega} \left(E(x,y) - \rho_{\text{ref}}(x,y)(l_0 + \tilde{\mathbf{l}}^T \mathbf{n}_{\text{ref}}(x,y)) \right)^2, \tag{9}$$

where $\tilde{\mathbf{l}} = (l_1, l_2, l_3)^T$. This is a highly over-constrained linear least square optimization with only four unknowns (the components of $\mathbf{l}$) and can be solved simply using the pseudo-inverse.

The lighting coefficients recovered with this procedure will be used subsequently to recover depth. To examine whether the coefficients recovered indeed are close to the true lighting coefficients we have run the following experiment. Using a database of 56 3D faces from the USF database [26] we recovered the lighting from images of each of these models by comparing the image to all the other 3D models in the database. We calculated for each such pair the angle between the true lighting and the recovered one; this represents the error in lighting recovery. The result of the experiment is shown in Fig. 1. We observe that the mean angle is 11.3° with standard deviation of 6.2°. As our experiments demonstrate (Sec. 4), this error is sufficiently small allowing accurate reconstructions.

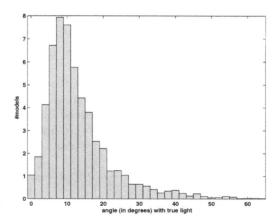

Fig. 1. Accuracy of the lighting recovered. We plot a histogram of the angle (in degrees) between the true lighting coefficients and the recovered coefficients using reference models of different individuals. The distribution was calculated over 56 face shapes.

3.2   Depth Recovery

At this stage we have obtained an estimate for $\mathbf{l}$. We continue using ρ_{ref} for the albedo and turn to recovering $z(x, y)$. As we mentioned above, z can be recovered by solving a shape from shading problem, since the reflectance function is completely determined by the lighting coefficients and the albedo. Below we will further exploit the resemblance of the sought surface to the reference face to linearize the problem.

We first handle the data term. Denote by $N(x, y) = \sqrt{p^2 + q^2 + 1}$, we will assume that $N(x, y) \approx N_{\text{ref}}(x, y)$. The data term in fact minimizes the difference between the two sides of the following equation system

$$E = \rho_{\text{ref}} \left(l_0 + \frac{1}{N_{\text{ref}}} \tilde{\mathbf{l}}^T (p, q, -1)^T \right), \tag{10}$$

with p and q as unknowns. With additional manipulation this becomes

$$E - \rho_{\text{ref}} \left(l_0 - \frac{1}{N_{\text{ref}}} l_3 \right) = \frac{\rho_{\text{ref}}}{N_{\text{ref}}} (l_1 p + l_2 q). \tag{11}$$

In discretizing this equation system we will use $z(x, y)$ as our unknowns, and replace p and q by the forward differences:

$$p = z(x + 1, y) - z(x, y)$$
$$q = z(x, y + 1) - z(x, y), \tag{12}$$

obtaining

$$E - \rho_{\text{ref}} \left(l_0 - \frac{1}{N_{\text{ref}}} l_3 \right) =$$
$$\frac{\rho_{\text{ref}}}{N_{\text{ref}}} (l_1 (z(x + 1, y) - z(x, y)) + l_2 (z(x, y + 1) - z(x, y))). \tag{13}$$

The data term thus provides one equation for every unknown. Note that by solving for $z(x, y)$ we in fact enforce integrability.

Next we treat the regularization term $\lambda_1 \triangle g(d_z)$ (the second regularization term vanishes at this stage). We implement this term as the difference between $d_z(x, y)$ and the average of d_z around (x, y) obtained by applying a Gaussian function to d_z (denoted $g(d_z)$). Consequently, this term minimizes the difference between the two sides of the following equation system

$$\lambda_1 (z(x, y) - g(z)) = \lambda_1 (z_{\text{ref}}(x, y) - g(z_{\text{ref}})). \tag{14}$$

It should be noted that to avoid degeneracies the input face must be lit by non-ambient light, since under ambient light intensities are independent of surface orientation. The assumption we used, that $N(x, y) \approx N_{\text{ref}}(x, y)$ further requires that there will be light coming from directions other than the camera direction. If a face is lit from the camera direction (e.g., flash photography) then $l_1 = l_2 = 0$

and the right-hand side of (11) vanishes. This degeneracy can be addressed by solving instead a usual nonlinear shape from shading algorithms (e.g., [3, 23, 24]).

Combining these two sets of equations we obtain a linear set of equations with two linear equations for every unknown. This system of equations is still rank deficient, and we need to add boundary conditions. We can use Dirichlet boundary conditions, but these will require us to know the depth values along the boundary of the face. We could use the depth values of the reference model, but these may be incompatible with the sought solution. Alternatively, we can constrain the derivatives of z along the boundaries using Neumann boundary conditions. One possibility is to assign p and q along the boundaries to match the corresponding derivatives of the reference model p_{ref} and q_{ref} so that the surface orientation of the reconstructed face along the boundaries will coincide with the surface orientation of the reference face. A less restrictive assumption is to assume that the surface is planar along the boundaries, i.e., that the partial derivatives of p and q in the direction orthogonal to the boundary $\partial\Omega$ vanish. (Note that this does not imply that the entire boundaries are planar.) This assumption will be roughly satisfied if the boundaries are placed in slowly changing parts of the face. It will not be satisfied for example when the boundaries are placed along the eyebrows, where the surface orientation changes rapidly. We use this type of Neumann boundary conditions in our experiments.

Finally, since all the equations we use for the data term, the regularization term, and the boundary conditions involve only partial derivatives of z, while z itself is absent from these equations, the solution can be obtained only up to an additive factor. We will rectify this by arbitrarily setting one point to $z(x_0, y_0) = z_0$.

3.3   Estimating Albedo

Once both the lighting and depths are recovered, we may turn to estimating the albedo. Using the data term the albedo is given by

$$\rho(x, y) = \frac{E(x, y)}{l_0 + \tilde{\mathbf{l}}^T \mathbf{n}(x, y)}. \tag{15}$$

The first regularization term is independent of ρ, and so it can be ignored, and the second term optimizes the following equations

$$\lambda_2 \triangle g(\rho) = \lambda_2 \triangle g(\rho_{\text{ref}}). \tag{16}$$

Again these provide a linear set of equations, in which the first set determines the albedo values, and the second set smoothes these values. Boundary conditions are placed by simply terminating the smoothing process at the boundaries.

4   Experiments

To test our method we performed several sets of experiments. For reference models we used the first set of the USF face database, which contains depth and texture

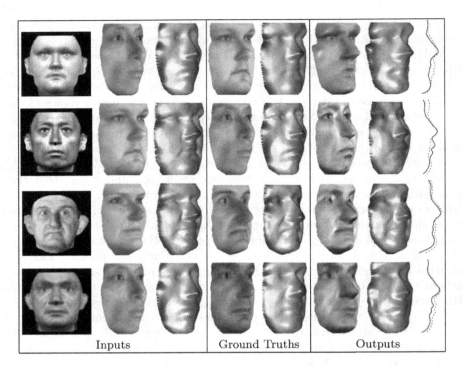

Fig. 2. Reconstruction from synthetic images. From left to right: Images rendered from the USF database, reference models (the surfaces are colored from blue to red according to $z(x,y)$), and albedo painted on the model. These were used as inputs to our method. Ground truth shapes and albedos. The output obtained includes the recovered 3D shape and the recovered albedo painted on the output shape. Finally a profile curve of the recovered shape (blue) overlayed on the profile curve of the ground truth shape (green) and the profile curve of the reference model (red, dashed).

maps of 56 real faces (male and female adult faces with a mixture of race and age) obtained with a laser scanner [26]. The texture maps provided in USF database are not identical to the real albedos of the faces, since they contain noticeable effects of the lighting conditions. To reduce these effects we averaged each texture map with its mirror image, and used the result as albedos of the reference models.

In all experiments we attempted to recover the shape of frontal facing faces. The following parameters were used throughout all our experiments. The reference albedo was kept in the range between 0 and 255. Both λ_1 and λ_2 were set to 110. We smoothed the reference albedo by a 2-D Gaussian with $\sigma_x = 3$ and $\sigma_y = 4$. The same smoothing parameters were used for the two regularization terms. Finally, to align the images with the reference models we marked five corresponding points on the image and the reference model, two at the centers of the eyes, one on the tip of the nose, one in the center of the mouth and one in the bottom of the chin (Fig. 4, right column). We then used these correspondences to determine a 2D rotation, translation, and scale to fit the image to the

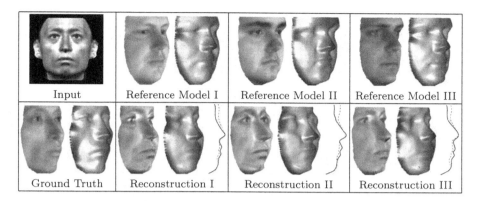

| Input | Reference Model I | Reference Model II | Reference Model III |
| Ground Truth | Reconstruction I | Reconstruction II | Reconstruction III |

Fig. 3. Reconstructions of the same face using several different reference models. The first row contains the input image (left column) and three different reference models used as input. The second row contains the ground truth shape (left column) and the three reconstructions obtained using each of the reference models. An overlay of profiles is shown on the right of the each reconstruction (the recovered profile in blue, the ground truth profile in green, and the reference profile in dashed red).

Fig. 4. Left column: The model used for reference in the experiments with real images (Fig. 5). Right column: Five points used for alignment (two at the centers of the eyes, one on the tip of the nose, one in the center of the mouth and one in the bottom of the chin).

reference model. After alignment all the images contained 150×200 pixels. To recover depth (Eqs. (13) and (14)) we directly solved a system of linear equations. Our non-optimized MATLAB implementation of the algorithm takes only 30 seconds on a Pentium IV PC.

The first set of experiments contain controlled experiments in which we artificially rendered faces from the USF database and then used our algorithm to recover their shapes and albedos from the rendered images. These experiments allow us to show comparisons of our reconstructions to the ground truth shapes. To produce an image we illuminated a model by 2-3 point sources from directions $\mathbf{l}_i$ and with intensity L_i. The intensities reflected by the surface due to this light are given by $I = \sum_{i=1}^{n} \rho L_i \max(\cos(\mathbf{n}^T \mathbf{l}_i), 0)$. Fig. 2 shows several images obtained this way. For each image we selected a reference model of a different individual and used the image and the reference model to recover the depth and albedo

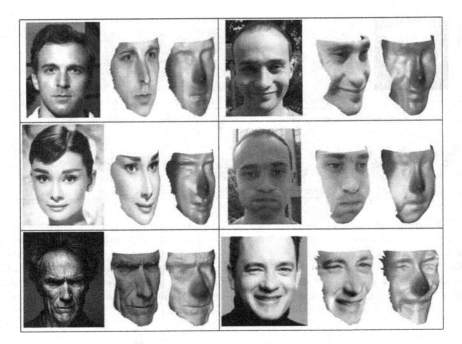

Fig. 5. Six experiments with real images. In each experiment, the input image and the reconstruction results are presented. Images were obtained from the YaleB database (top left), cropped from [12] (middle left), http://www.swirc.com (bottom left) and http://crazy4cinema.com/Actor/hanks.html (bottom right). The rest of the images were photographed by us.

of the rendered face. For comparison we show the reconstructed shapes and the laser scanned shapes. We show both the reconstructed and the scanned shapes in two ways, with albedo painted on the shape and in a colored representation with the color representing the depth values. The latter representation better displays the details of the shape independent of the variations in albedo. We further plot an overlay of the profile curves of the reconstructed shape (in blue), the ground truth model (green), and the reference model (red, dashed). It can be seen that fairly accurate reconstructions are obtained in spite of gender (third row) and race (top and bottom rows) differences between the faces in the input image and the reference model.

We further use the same setting to demonstrate the robustness of the algorithm. In Fig. 3 we present reconstructions of the same face using several different reference models. The face to be reconstructed differs quite significantly in shape from the reference faces due to difference in race. While there are some inaccuracies in the cheek areas, in general the recovered shapes are consistently very similar to the ground truth.

Finally, we applied the method to several real images, including some containing facial expressions. These images include one from the YaleB face database

[25], images photographed by us, and images that were downloaded from the worldwide web. For reference we used one of the 3D models from the USF database. The results are shown in Fig. 5. While we do not have the ground truth faces in these experiments, we can still see that fairly convincing reconstructions are obtained. Note in particular the reconstructions obtained with different facial expressions (right column) and the wrinkles present in the reconstruction (left column, last row).

To conclude, our experiments demonstrate that the method can accurately reconstruct faces under a large variety of uncontrolled lighting conditions and that differ from the reference face by gender, race, and expression.

5   Conclusion

In this paper, we have presented a novel algorithm for the recovery of 3D shape and albedo of faces from a single image by using a single reference model of different individual. Unlike existing methods, our method does not need to establish correspondence between symmetric portions of a face, nor does it require to store a database of many faces with point correspondences across the faces. Instead, our method exploits the global similarity of faces to fill in the information missing in order to apply shape recovery by solving a shape from shading problem. We tested our method by comparing the recovery obtained with rendered images to ground truth shapes and by applying the method to various real images.

Our experiments demonstrate that the method was able to accurately recover the shape of faces overcoming significant differences across individuals including differences in race, gender and variations in expressions. Furthermore we showed that the method can handle a variety of uncontrolled lighting conditions, and that it can achieve consistent reconstructions with different reference models. We hope in the future to further improve the accuracy of our method by taking an explicit account of the noise characteristics in the image and by better modeling the reflectance properties of a face (e.g., by using a second order harmonic approximation). Finally, we intend to further extend our method to handle non-frontal faces.

References

1. Horn, B.: Obtaining Shape from Shading Information. The Psychology of Computer Vision. McGraw-Hill, New York (1975)
2. Horn, B., Brooks, M., eds.: Shape from Shading. MIT Press: Cambridge, MA (1989)
3. Rouy, E., Tourin, A.: A viscosity solutions approach to shape-from-shading. SIAM Journal of Numerical Analysis **29**(3) (1992) 867–884
4. Zhang, R., Tsai, P., Cryer, J., Shah, M.: Shape from shading: A survey. PAMI **21**(8) (1999) 690–706
5. Pentland, A.: Finding the illuminant direction. Journal Optical Society of America (1982) 448–455

6. Zheng, Q., Chellappa, R.: Estimation of illuminant direction, albedo, and shape from shading. PAMI **13**(7) (1991) 680–702
7. Tsai, P., Shah, M.: Shape from shading with variable albedo. Optical Engineering (1998) 121–1220
8. Moses, Y., Edelman, S., Ullman, S.: Generalization to novel images in upright and inverted faces. Perception **25** (1996) 443–461
9. Shimshoni, I., Moses, Y., Lindenbaum, M.: Shape re-construction of 3d bilaterally symmetric surfaces. IJCV **39**(2) (2000) 97–100
10. Zhao, W., Chellappa, R.: Symmetric shape-from-shading using self-ratio image. IJCV **45** (2001) 55–75
11. Atick, J., Griffin, P., Redlich, A.: Statistical approach to shape from shading: Reconstruction of three-dimensional face surfaces from single two-dimensional images. Neural Computation **8**(6) (1996) 1321–1340
12. Blanz, V., Vetter, T.: A morphable model for the synthesis of 3d faces. SIGGRAPH **I** (1999) 187–194
13. Zhou, S., Chellappa, R., Jacobs, D.: Characterization of human faces under illumination variations using rank, integrability, and symmetry constraints. ECCV **1** (2004) 588–601
14. Smith, W., Hancock, E.: Recovering facial shape and albedo using a statistical model of surface normal direction. ICCV (2005) 588–595
15. Romdhani, S., Vetter, T.: Efficient, robust and accurate fitting of a 3d morphable model. ICCV (2003)
16. Dovgard, R., Basri, R.: Statistical symmetric shape from shading for 3d structure recovery of faces. ECCV (2004)
17. Sim, T., Kanade, T.: Combining models and exemplars for face recognition: An illuminating example. CVPR Workshop on Models versus Exemplars (2001)
18. Zhang, L., Samaras, D.: Face recognition under variable lighting using harmonic image exemplars. CVPR **I** (2003) 19–25
19. Shashua, A., Riklin-Raviv, T.: The quotient image: Class based re-rendering and recognition with varying illuminations. PAMI **23**(2) (2001) 129–139
20. Basri, R., Jacobs, D.: Lambertian reflectance and linear subspaces. PAMI **25**(2) (2003) 218–233
21. Ramamoorthi, R., Hanrahan, P.: On the relationship between radiance and irradiance: Determining the illumination from images of a convex lambertian object. JOSA **18**(10) (2001) 2448–2459
22. Frolova, D., Simakov, D., Basri, R.: Accuracy of spherical harmonic approximations for images of lambertian objects under far and near lighting. ECCV (2004) 574–587
23. Dupuis, P., Oliensis, J.: An optimal control formulation and related numerical methods for a problem in shape reconstruction. The Annals of Applied Probability **4**(2) (1994) 287–346
24. Kimmel, R., Sethian, J.: Optimal algorithm for shape from shading and path planning. Journal of Mathematical Imaging and Vision **14**(3) (2001) 237–244
25. Georghiades, A., Belhumeur, P., Kriegman, D.: From few to many: generative models for recognition under variable pose and illumination. PAMI **23**(6) (2001) 643–660
26. USF DARPA Human-ID 3D Face Database: Courtesy of Prof. Sudeep Sarkar, University of South Florida, Tampa, FL. http://marthon.csee.usf.edu/HumanID/

Reconstruction of Canal Surfaces from Single Images Under Exact Perspective

Vincenzo Caglioti and Alessandro Giusti

Politecnico di Milano
{caglioti, giusti}@elet.polimi.it

Abstract. This paper addresses the reconstruction of canal surfaces from single images. A canal surface is obtained as the envelope of a family of spheres of constant radius, whose center is swept along a space curve, called axis. Previous studies either used approximate relationships (quasi-invariants), or they addressed the recognition based on a geometric model. In this paper we show that, under broad conditions, canal surfaces can be reconstructed from single images under exact perspective. In particular, canal surfaces with planar axis can even be reconstructed from a single fully-uncalibrated image. An automatic reconstruction method has been implemented. Simulations and experimental results on real images are also presented.

1 Introduction

One of the prominent problems in computer vision is reconstruction of the shape of 3D objects from a single, bidimensional image. This work, in particular, deals with a *shape from contour* problem: reconstruction of a canal surface from a single perspective image. A canal surface is obtained as the envelope of a family of spheres of constant radius, whose center is swept along a space curve, called axis.

Circular cross section pipes and flexible wires can be modeled as canal surfaces, and reconstructed with this approach. Moreover, long-exposure photographs of a moving sphere (e.g. a kicked soccer ball) are images of canal surfaces as well, therefore we are also applying this technique to sport environments in order to analyze particular nonparabolic trajectories deriving from fast ball spin.

Some approaches about shape reconstruction of such objects are based on information about the surface normal [1], other approaches consist of shape from shading techniques based on Lambertian model [2]. Some other approaches are based on the use of stereoscopic vision [3]. Approximate relationships, as, e.g., quasi-invariants, are used in [4, 5, 6]. A reconstruction method for orthogonal projections, which requires that at least a cross section is visible, is presented in [7].

Other publications ([8, 9]) focus on the geometric properties of generalized cylinders, but do not deal with the reconstruction process. Likewise, works such as [10] aim at identifying the 2D perspective projection of the axis of revolution

A. Leonardis, H. Bischof, and A. Pinz (Eds.): ECCV 2006, Part I, LNCS 3951, pp. 289–300, 2006.

and do not return a full 3D reconstruction of the shape. An example of full 3D reconstruction of another class of generalized cylinders has been presented in [11], that deals with solids of revolution.

This work is entirely based on the geometric properties of canal surfaces and of their apparent contours in perspective images, and allows to find a full 3D reconstruction of the canal surface and its curvilinear axis. In particular, canal surfaces with planar axis can even be reconstructed from a single fully-uncalibrated image, while nonplanar-axis canal surfaces need a calibrated image. [12] provides a useful algorithm for contour tangent direction estimation.

Section 2 provides some basic definitions and properties, which are used in section 3 to derive the key relations used in the paper; section 4 describes how we deal with uncalibrated images; section 5 details the geometric considerations driving the actual reconstruction process; section 6 conveys a broad view of the complete reconstruction process, whereas section 7 describes the results obtained by our prototype implementation. Section 8 presents the conclusions and future directions of our work.

2   Definitions and Basic Properties

A canal surface can be defined as the envelope surface of a family of spheres with constant radius R, whose centers lie on a space curve called axis, such that, at any axis point, the axis curvature radius is strictly larger than R.

A planar-axis canal surface is a canal surface whose axis is a planar curve.

Property 1. A canal surface is equivalent to the union of circumferences with radius R, called cross sections, such that each cross section is centered on the axis. An axis point and the cross section centered on it are said to be associated. A cross section has a supporting plane perpendicular to the tangent to the axis at its associated point.

A canal surface projects a pair of facing apparent contours; our approach only considers the lateral contours of the canal surface, and does not require any cross section to be visible.

Two contour points are said to be coupled if they are the image of two points on the same cross section.

Property 2. Let P be a point on the canal surface, C be the cross section on which P lies, and P_s the associated axis point: Let T be the tangent plane to the canal surface in P: T is parallel to the tangent to the axis at P_s.

An immediate consequence is that the tangent plane is perpendicular to the plane supporting C.

For any point on the axis P_s, we can define a Tangent Cylinder (TC): The TC has radius R and axis tangent to the canal surface axis in P_s. The intersection between the TC and the canal surface contains the cross section centered on P_s. If the axis is rectilinear, the TC coincides with the canal surface.

3   Properties of Canal Surface Contours

A number of properties of the apparent contours are presented in this section.

3.1   Coupling Condition

First, we present a necessary condition[1] for the coupling of contour points which involves the camera parameters, but holds regardless of the geometry of the axis. The property is used to detect coupled points on contours, enabling us to reconstruct the axis shape when the camera parameters are known; it is also used in the opposite direction, generating constraints for camera parameters when two coupled points are known in advance: this allows to calibrate the camera when contour features presented in the following allow to detect pairs of coupled points.

Property 3. Let c_1 and c_2 be two facing contours on the image; let t_1 (t_2) be the tangent to c_1 (c_2) at point p_1 (p_2), and let v_h be the intersection between t_1 and t_2.

The points p_1 and p_2 are coupled only if the angle formed by $\overline{Op_1}$ and $\overline{Ov_h}$ coincides with the angle formed by $\overline{Op_2}$ and $\overline{Ov_h}$, where O is the camera viewpoint.

Proof. Now we prove the above necessary condition.

Let P_1 (P_2) be the point on the canal surface which projects to p_1 (p_2), let T_1 (T_2) be the plane tangent to the canal surface at P_1 (P_2); note that T_1 (T_2) is the interpretation plane of t_1 (t_2).

Let C be the cross section containing P_1 and P_2, and let P_s be the axis point, center of C. Let Π_{sym} be the plane bisecting T_1 and T_2: since both T_1 and T_2 are tangent to C (which is a circumference) and perpendicular to its supporting plane, C is symmetrical w.r.t. Π_{sym}; P_1 and P_2, intersection of symmetrical entities, are symmetrical as well. Let V be the intersection line between T_1 and T_2: V lies on Π_{sym}; The camera viewpoint O, which belongs to V, lies on Π_{sym} as well. Therefore, the angle formed by $\overline{OP_1}$ and V equals the angle formed by symmetrical entities $\overline{OP_2}$ and V. The thesis immediately follows.

This condition is necessary but not sufficient for the coupling of p_1 and p_2: however, if p_2 is constrained to lie on a curve c_2, and t_2 is constrained to be tangent to c_2 in p_2, few, sparse choices of p_2 satisfy the condition[2].

3.2   Properties of Planar-Axis Canal Surfaces

When the axis of the canal surface is constrained to lie on a plane, additional properties hold.

---

[1] See [10] for a similar property for surfaces of revolution; note that its extension to canal surfaces is not straightforward.

[2] An exception is the degenerate case where parts of c_2 coincide to an arc of an ellipse which is both tangent to t_1 in p_1 and image of a sphere.

In the following, three possible relations between the viewpoint position and the canal surface will be considered: consider the two planes parallel to the axis plane, at distance R from it; they are tangent to the canal surface at two diametric points for each cross section, and the canal surface is entirely enclosed between the two planes; the viewpoint can lie outside the space enclosed by the two planes (*configuration 1*), between the two planes (*configuration 2*), or on one of the two planes (degenerate *configuration 3*). If the axis is rectilinear, the canal surface is a cylinder, therefore the following considerations do not apply.

Inflection Points

Property 4. If a planar-axis canal surface is seen by a camera whose viewpoint is placed according to configuration 1 or configuration 2, an inflection point on one contour is always coupled to an inflection point on the facing contour, and the related axis point is an inflection point for the axis.

A proof is given in [6]; note that this property is independent of camera calibration.

3.3   Bitangents

Inflection points on contours are not the only useful feature: also bitangents to canal surface contours allow to determine coupled points regardless of the camera calibration parameters, by means of the following property (see figure 1):

Property 5. Let b_1 be a bitangent to contour c_1, and name p_1^a and p_1^b the two tangency points. If the viewpoint is placed according to configuration 1 or configuration 2, a bitangent (b_2) to the contour c_2 exists, and its tangency points p_2^a and p_2^b are coupled with p_1^a and p_1^b respectively[3].

Proof. Let P_1^a, P_1^b, P_2^a and P_2^b be the points on the canal surface which project to p_1^a, p_1^b, p_2^a and p_2^b respectively; let C^a be the cross section passing through by P_1^a and P_2^a, and C^b the cross section passing through P_1^b and P_2^b; call P_s^a (P_s^b) the axis point at the center of C^a (C^b), and D^a (D^b) the directions of the tangent to the axis in P_s^a (P_s^b).
    Let T_1 be the interpretation plane of b_1: T_1 is tangent to the canal surface in P_1^a and P_1^b; then, T_1 contains both D^a and D^b. Moreover, D^a and D^b are constrained to be parallel to the axis plane. Since T_1 and the axis plane are not parallel, D^a and D^b coincide; therefore C^a and C^b lie on parallel planes.
    Because C^a and C^b are two circumferences tangent to the same plane (T_1) and lying on parallel planes, their centers P_s^a and P_s^b lie on a plane parallel to T_1; moreover, being axis points, P_s^a and P_s^b must lie on the axis plane. Let Λ be the line connecting P_s^a and P_s^b: since T_1 and the axis plane are not parallel, Λ has direction $D^a = D^b$; Λ is a bitangent for the axis, with P_s^a and P_s^b as

---

[3] The property requires minor adjustments to deal with spines whose tangent orientation varies broadly.

tangency points; moreover, since C^a and C^b lie on planes perpendicular to Λ, they are cross sections of the right cylinder T_{cyl}, which is the tangent cylinder to the canal surface in both C^a and C^b.

Let T_2 be the other plane, besides T_1, tangent to T_{cyl} and passing through the viewpoint O: T_2 is also tangent to the canal surface in P_2^a (which belongs to C^a) and P_2^b (which belongs to C^b); therefore, T_2 projects to a single line b_2, which is a bitangent for c_2 in p_2^a and p_2^b; moreover, p_1^a is coupled with p_2^a, because they are images of points belonging to the same cross section; similarly, p_1^b is coupled with p_2^b.

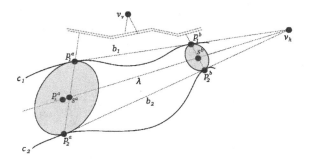

Fig. 1. Coupled bitangents and related vanishing points

Coupled bitangents also allow to find another constraint on camera calibration parameters: with relation to the entities defined above, the following property holds:

Property 6. Let v^a be the image line passing through p_1^a and p_2^a, v^b the image line passing through p_1^b and p_2^b, v_v the intersection of v^a and v^b, and O the viewpoint; let λ be the image of Λ; the direction identified by vanishing point v_v is orthogonal to the vector connecting O to any point on λ.

The property follows from the symmetry of P_1^a, P_1^b, P_2^a and P_2^b w.r.t. the plane containing Λ and O.

Three points on λ can be extracted from a a pair of coupled bitangents: v_h, intersection of b_1 and b_2; s^a, found using the cross ratio on p_1^a, s^a, p_2^a and v_v; and s^b, found similarly on the other cross section[4].

The maximum number of bitangents to a planar curve grows more than linearly with the number of inflection points: elaborate axis shapes are then likely to have a large number of bitangents; many meaningful bitangents can also be found bridging a number of canal surfaces with planar axis, which share the radius and axis plane: think of a set of identical torii placed on a planar surface.

Rectilinear parts on contours share the properties of bitangents; moreover, unlike bitangents they can also be exploited in the 3D-axis case.

---

[4] Note that s^a and s^b are not the images of the center of C^a and C^b.

4   Uncalibrated Camera

When an unknown canal surface is seen from an unknown camera, the contour properties presented in the previous section allow to define a number of constraints on the camera calibration parameters; if a sufficient number of constraints is defined, the camera can be calibrated, then the reconstruction can be carried out as detailed in the following section.

Although theoretically the camera could be calibrated even when the axis is not planar, provided that enough rectilinear parts on the canal surface contours allow to determine a sufficient number of coupled points pairs, we focus on the planar axis case. We can therefore use constraints originating from coupled inflection points on the contours and from coupled bitangents.

- Using property 3 in the reverse direction, a pair of coupled image points p_1 and p_2 enables us to enforce that

$$\frac{p_1^\top \omega v_h}{\sqrt{p_1^\top \omega p_1} \cdot \sqrt{v_h^\top \omega v_h}} = \frac{p_2^\top \omega v_h}{\sqrt{p_2^\top \omega p_2} \cdot \sqrt{v_h^\top \omega v_h}} \tag{1}$$

where p_1 and p_2 are expressed in homogeneous coordinates, and ω is the image of the absolute conic, related with the calibration matrix K by $\omega = K^{-\top} K^{-1}$. The pair of coupled points can be identified on the image by means of property 4 or property 5.
- In addition to the equations presented before, according to property 6 a pair of coupled bitangents or rectilinear parts allows us to enforce the following linear constraints on ω:

$$s_a^\top \omega v_v = 0 \tag{2}$$

$$s_b^\top \omega v_v = 0 \tag{3}$$

$$v_h^\top \omega v_v = 0 \tag{4}$$

where s_a and s_b have been defined in property 6. Two of these relations are independent.
- Regardless of inflection points and bitangents on contours, a valid camera calibration hypothesis allows a reconstruction where all found axis points and axis tangent directions lie on the same plane – the axis plane. The planarity of the axis tangent directions is easily checked by quantifying how well intersection points of coupled points' tangents fit to a line (the image of the line at the infinite of the axis plane). This constraint could be used in the absence of features such as bitangents or inflection points.

5   Canal Surface Reconstruction

For every pair of coupled points p_1 and p_2, the associated cross section in space can be reconstructed without ambiguity, provided that the radius of the canal surface is known.

The cross section orientation is represented by vanishing point v_h, intersection of tangents t_1 and t_2 (see figure 2). The angle α between T_1 and T_2 is computed; since the cross section radius R is known, and both T_1 and T_2 are tangent to C and perpendicular to its supporting plane, the distance between P_s and V is determined as a function of α alone. P_s is also constrained to lie on the plane bisecting T_1 and T_2. In conclusion, the cross section position is completely specified by constraining its tangency points to T_1 or T_2 to lie on the interpretation line of P_1 or P_2.

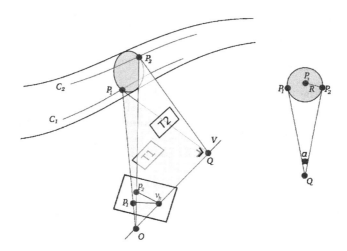

Fig. 2. Cross section reconstruction

Note that a scaled version of the canal surface can be reconstructed by using an arbitrary value for R.

When an ordered sequence of coupled point pairs along two facing contours is known, cross sections reconstructed from adjacent coupled point pairs can be joined in order to approximate the canal surface.

6   Implementation Notes

Starting from the input image, reconstruction requires to perform a number of sequential steps:

1. Edges on the input image are found using the Canny algorithm ([13]), and the edge points are localized with subpixel precision by fitting a gaussian curve to the gradient values around the found pixels; this allows to detect edges with enhanced precision.
2. Edge points are subdivided into chains, using an edge tracking algorithm biased towards smooth contours, which tolerates small discontinuities;

3. An estimate of the direction of the tangent to the contour in each of the edge points is computed, using the angle median method presented at [12];

4. If the camera calibration parameters are unknown and the axis is planar, inflection points and bitangents (section 6.1) are detected and coupled; the camera is then calibrated as described in section 4.

5. Contour points are coupled according to the procedures presented in section 6.3;

6. For each of the found couples, a cross section in space is reconstructed, exploiting the geometrical construction presented in section 5.

7. An optional postprocessing filter is used to mitigate the errors in the cross section localization.

6.1   Detecting Bitangents

Our input from the previous steps is a set of edge chains; each contour point is annotated with the orientation of the tangent to the contour, which is considered continuous along the contour[5] (except that around angular points).

A bitangent is defined between two edge points p^a and p^b if the contour tangent at p^a is collinear both with the contour direction at p^b, and with the direction of the vector connecting p^a to p^b.

Unfortunately, a threshold-based algorithm tends to detect clusters of many nearby bitangents if contours around tangency points have low curvature; therefore, we implemented an algorithm which filters out unwanted results, and has proved very effective in our tests:

1. A candidate bitangents list is populated with a threshold-based criterion;

2. The bitangents are ranked according to their alignment;

3. The highest ranked bitangent is extracted and returned, and all nearby bitangents are recursively discarded from the list; the step is repeated until the list is empty.

6.2   Coupling Inflection Points and Bitangents

Unpaired inflection points and bitangents are useless for camera calibration: we must determine which pairs of bitangents or inflection points are actually coupled, in order to determine the constraints presented at section 4.

Since the number of inflection points and bitangents in an image is usually limited, simple heuristics can be used in order to couple features; for example, a pair of coupled points must be near the tangency points of a circle, bitangent to the respective contours, confined inside the projection of the canal surface (i.e. not extending to overlap with the background)[6].

Moreover, several other rules based on simple geometric considerations allow to further constrain the possible solutions.

---

[5] Therefore, its range is not defined.

[6] Note that in the calibrated case we would be able to use an ellipse as the exact image of a sphere, instead of a circle.

6.3   Coupling Contour Points

As we noted previously, the condition stated in property 3 is a necessary condition for a pair of points to be coupled, but not a sufficient one: therefore, given a point on a contour, it does not usually allow to determine a single candidate coupled point, but suggests a set of possible candidates.

However, if a pair of coupled points is known, other pairs can be searched in the proximity on the facing contours: the two facing contours can also be given a consistent mutual orientation, in order to further reduce the search scope.

We define a fitness value $J_c(p_1, p_2)$ which quantifies how well a pair of contour points meets the condition stated in property 3, as the squared difference between the two angles $p_1 \widehat{O} v_h$ and $p_2 \widehat{O} v_h$:

The algorithm starts from an initial pair of coupled points, determined e.g. by property 3 or by a pair of bitangents, and, starting from this pair, other pairs are found incrementally by "walking" along the coupled contours, limiting the search of candidate coupled points to a very limited set at each iteration, and choosing the one minimizing J_c.

The processed contour parts are marked, then the algorithm is applied again with a different starting pair, ignoring contour parts already considered.

7   Experimental Results

We implemented the presented procedures in a Java-based prototype. Experimental results are presented with both simulated images and photographic ones; both planar-axis canal surfaces and nonplanar-axis canal surfaces are represented: several images with enough contour features for camera calibration have also been used.

To evaluate reconstruction results in photographic images, where the actual shape is not known, a preliminary qualitative evaluation has been carried out by

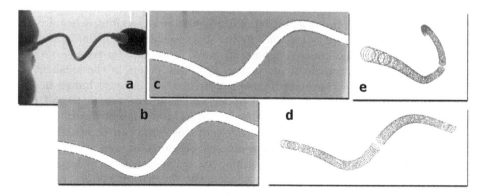

Fig. 3. Reconstruction of a 3D-axis canal surface from calibrated image: the object geometry (a), original image with edge detection (b), detection of coupled points and image of associated axis points (c), 3D view of reconstructed object (d, e)

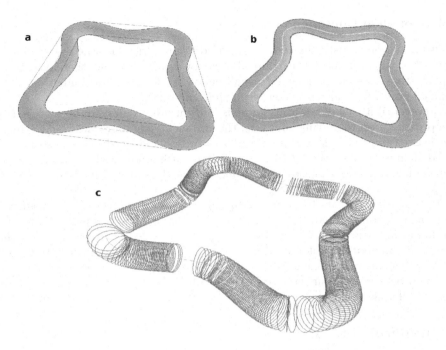

Fig. 4. A planar-axis canal surface (synthesized): original image with edge detection and detected bitangents and inflection points (a), detection of coupled points and image of associated axis points (b), 3D view of reconstructed object from different viewpoint (c)

reconstructing symmetrical canal surfaces seen from a generic viewpoint, then assessing the symmetry of the reconstructed shape; in this respect, we observed that the reconstruction is free of systematic errors; we also noted a remarkable robustness w.r.t. errors in given camera parameters.

Errors in placement and orientation of individual cross sections is heavily dependent on the quality of edges and on the distance between facing contours. We observed that when coupled points on facing contours are seen, from the viewpoint O, within an angle of more than 1/30 rad, errors in the localization of cross sections are acceptable; in particular, in the synthetic image in figure 4, where cross sections are viewed under an angle less than 1/10 rad, the average displacement error of the reconstructed cross section is within 1/10 of the cross section radius. Note that the effect of this error can be heavily mitigated by a moving average on neighboring cross sections, or more sophisticated techniques such as curve fitting. Also, the reconstruction quality heavily depends on the perspective effects: as these increase, the error decreases, and vice versa. It halves as the camera field of view is widened by 15°, it doubles as the canal surface radius is reduced by 1/3. In photographic images obtained with a standard 2Mpixel camera, we observed that the error variance increases by a factor between 2 and 4 w.r.t. a synthetic image with similar characteristics, depending on contour sharpness, precision in camera calibration, and nonidealities of the imaged canal surface objects (unavoidable with flexible wires, for example).

Although not tuned for computational efficiency, the actual point coupling and surface reconstruction phases always required less time than the preceding edge detection and tracking steps. The whole procedure for the 3D-axis canal surface represented in figure 3 takes about 8 seconds on a Pentium 4 system, but only about 1.8 seconds are due to the actual point coupling procedure and reconstruction.

The planar-axis uncalibrated case has been tested as well.

The test image of a planar-axis canal surface depicted in Figure 4 allowed to calibrate the camera with an 8% average error by using only the linear constraints (2), (3), (4): since most bitangents' endpoints were affected by rather large localization errors along the contours due to minimal curvature around the tangency points, the determination of their v_v has been quite imprecise; the results improve by adding the nonlinear constraint (1), which is robust w.r.t. this sort of error.

8   Conclusions and Future Work

We presented a technique for reconstructing a canal surface from a single perspective image. The developed technique allows to reconstruct a canal surface, having a nonplanar axis, from a calibrated image. Moreover, canal surfaces with planar axis can be reconstructed from a single, fully-uncalibrated image. The implemented technique has been validated through experiments with both simulated and real images.

The present version of the full-uncalibrated reconstruction technique is based on projective-invariant features such as inflection points of bitangents: ongoing activity is aimed at the extension of this technique to cases, where such invariant features are not visible in the image.

References

1. J. R. Kender, R.K.: On seing spaghetti: self-adjusting piecewise toroidal recognition of flexible extruded objects. IEEE Transactions on Pattern Analysis and Machine Intelligence **17** (1995)
2. A. D. Gross, T.E.B.: Recovery of shcgs from single intensity views. IEEE Transactions on Pattern Analysis and Machine Intelligence **18** (1996)
3. J. M. Chung, T.N.: Extracting parametric descriptions of circular generalized cylinders from a pair of contours for 3-d shape recognition. In: Proc. of the 1995 IEEE Conference on Robotics and Automations. (1995)
4. M. Zerroug, R.N.: Three-dimensional descriptions based on the analysis of the invariant and quasi-invariant properties of some curved-axis generalized cylinders. IEEE Transactions on Pattern Analysis and Machine Intelligence **18** (1996)
5. M. Zerroug, R.N.: Part-based 3d descriptions of complex objects from a single view. IEEE Transactions on Pattern Analysis and Machine Intelligence **21** (1999)

6. N. Pillow, S. Utcke, A.Z.: Viewpoint-invariant representation of generalized cylinders using the symmetry set. In: Proc. of the British Machine Vision Conference. (1994)
7. F. Ulupinar, R.N.: Shape from contour. IEEE Transactions on Pattern Analysis and Machine Intelligence **17** (1995)
8. J. Ponce, D.C.: Finding the limbs and the cusps of generalized cylinders. International Journal of Computer Vision **1** (1987)
9. J. Ponce, D. Chelberg, W.B.M.: Invariant properties of straight homogeneous generalized cylinders and their contours. IEEE Transactions on Pattern Analysis and Machine Intelligence, Vol. 11 **11** (1989)
10. R. Glachet, M. Dhome, J.T.L.: Finding the perspective projection of an axis of revolution. Pattern Recognition Letters **12** (1991)
11. Pernici, del Bimbo, C.: Metric 3d reconstruction and texture acquisition of surfaces of revolution from a single uncalibrated view. IEEE Transactions on Pattern Analysis and Machine Intelligence **27** (2005)
12. J. Matas, Z. Shao, J.K.: Estimation of curvature and tangent direction by median filtered differencing. In: Proc. of the 8 th Intl Conference on Image Analysis and Processing. (1995)
13. Canny, J.: A computational approach to edge detection. IEEE Trans. Pattern Anal. Mach. Intell. **8** (1986) 679–698

Subspace Estimation Using Projection Based M-Estimators over Grassmann Manifolds

Raghav Subbarao and Peter Meer

Department of Electrical and Computer Engineering,
Rutgers University, Piscataway, NJ 08854, USA
{rsubbara, meer}@caip.rutgers.edu

Abstract. We propose a solution to the problem of robust subspace estimation using the projection based M-estimator. The new method handles more outliers than inliers, does not require a user defined scale of the noise affecting the inliers, handles noncentered data and nonorthogonal subspaces. Other robust methods like RANSAC, use an input for the scale, while methods for subspace segmentation, like GPCA, are not robust. Synthetic data and three real cases of multibody factorization show the superiority of our method, in spite of user independence.

1 Introduction

The estimation of subspaces is a problem which occurs frequently in computer vision, e.g., in the analysis of dynamic scenes [5, 8, 14]. Given data lying in a N dimensional space, linear regression estimates a $N - 1$ dimensional hyperplane containing the inliers. If a regression algorithm is adapted to simultaneously estimate k *linearly independent* constraints which the inliers in the data satisfy, the intersection of the hyperplanes represented by these k constraints gives the required $N - k$ dimensional subspace.

We will generalize the robust projection based M-estimator (pbM) of [3, 13] to obtain a *user independent, robust, multiple subspace* estimation algorithm. As we discuss later, the parameter space is an algebraic structure known as the Grassmann manifold and we adapt the pbM algorithm to account for the geometry of this space [6].

If all the data points lie in the same subspace, then *Principal Component Analysis* (PCA) could be used to obtain the subspace. Standard PCA is not enough in practice because the data may contain multiple subspaces and/or outliers. Methods such as [1, 2] perform *robust PCA* to handle outliers. There are two problems with robust PCA algorithms which make them infeasible for multiple subspace estimation. Firstly, the methods of [1, 2] have breakdown points of 0.5, and secondly, the algorithms cannot handle structured outliers. These methods can only be used to estimate a single subspace and an example of this is shown in Section 4.

A number of multiple subspace estimation techniques have been developed in the vision community, e.g., subspace separation [5, 10] and generalized PCA

A. Leonardis, H. Bischof, and A. Pinz (Eds.): ECCV 2006, Part I, LNCS 3951, pp. 301–312, 2006.

(GPCA) [17, 16]. Much of the work done in this area was geared towards solving the problem of motion segmentation.

Most methods make simplifying assumptions about the data. Firstly, in [5, 10] it is assumed that the subspaces are orthogonal. Therefore, for degenerate motions where the subspaces share a common basis vector, the methods break down [20]. Secondly, the methods of [5, 10] require the data to be centered which is difficult to ensure in practice, especially in the presence of outliers. Finally, [5, 17] do not account for outliers. Outliers were partially accounted for in [16], but it is assumed that even in the presence of outliers the algorithm returns a rough estimate of the true subspaces *and* the scale of the noise corrupting the inliers is known. Both these assumptions are often not true in practice.

In this paper we propose a robust, pbM based, subspace estimation method. It does not suffer from the drawback of previous methods and can be used for multiple subspace estimation by iteratively estimating the 'dominant' subspace, treating all points *not* belonging to this subspace as outliers. After removing the points lying in the estimated subspace, the procedure can be repeated on the remaining points. We assume the dimension of the subspaces and the number of motions is known beforehand although the second assumption can be relaxed. Our method offers several advantages.

– No user input is required for the scale of noise affecting the inliers.
– Handles data sets with more outliers than inliers.
– Handles noncentered data and estimates the centroid of the inliers.
– Does not require orthogonal subspaces for the inliers.

The remainder of the paper is organized as follows. Section 2 gives an introduction to Grassmann manifolds and the conjugate gradient algorithm over Grassmann manifolds. In Section 3 we discuss robust subspace estimation with the pbM estimator. In Section 4 we validate our method on synthetic data and real data by comparing its performance with subspace separation [5, 10], GPCA [17, 16] and RANSAC [7].

2   Grassmann Manifolds

We discuss a few relevant concepts about Grassmann manifolds in this section. A more thorough introduction to Grassmann manifolds can be found in [6].

A manifold is a topological space that is locally similar (homeomorphic) to Euclidean space. The dimension of the Euclidean space to which the manifold is locally similar to, is also the dimension of the manifold. Every real manifold can be embedded in a higher dimensional Euclidean space which means that we can think of the manifold as a smooth surface lying in a higher dimensional Euclidean space, as illsutrated in Figure 1a.

We are concerned with a particular class of manifolds known as Grassmann manifolds. A point on the *Grassmann manifold*, $\mathbf{G}_{N,k}$, represents a k dimensional subspace of $\mathbb{R}^N$ and is numerically represented by an orthonormal basis as a $N \times k$ matrix, i.e., $\mathbf{Y}^T\mathbf{Y} = \mathbf{I}_{k \times k}$. Since many different basis span the same subspace,

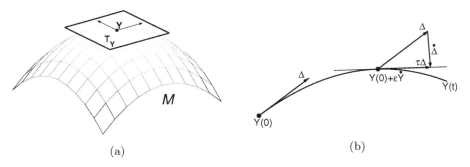

(a)   (b)

Fig. 1. Example of a manifold. (a) A two-dimensional manifold embedded in $\mathbb{R}^3$. The tangent space at the point $\mathbf{Y}$ is also shown. (b) Parallel transporting the vector Δ along the curve $\mathbf{Y}(t)$. The point moves along $\dot{\mathbf{Y}}$ and the component of $\dot{\Delta}$, which does not lie in the tangent space, is removed.

this representation of points on $\mathbf{G}_{N,k}$ is *not* unique [6]. $\mathbf{G}_{N,k}$ is a manifold of dimension $d = Nk - k(k+1)/2$ embedded in $\mathbb{R}^{Nk}$.

The *tangent space* $T_{\mathbf{Y}}$, at a point $\mathbf{Y}$, is the plane tangent to the surface of the manifold at that point. An example is shown in Figure 1a. For a d-dimensional manifold, the tangent space is a d-dimensional vector space. The tangent space is associated with an inner product g_c, such that for any two tangent vectors $\Delta_1, \Delta_2 \in T_{\mathbf{Y}}$ the inner product $g_c(\Delta_1, \Delta_2)$ lies in $\mathbb{R}$.

For a real function f defined on the manifold, the gradient at $\mathbf{Y}$ is defined to be that *unique* vector $\nabla f \in T_{\mathbf{Y}}$ which satisfies

$$tr(f_{\mathbf{Y}}^T \Delta) = g_c(\nabla f, \Delta) \tag{1}$$

where, $f_{\mathbf{Y}}$ is the Jacobian of f at $\mathbf{Y}$ and tr is the trace operator. For Grassmann manifolds the gradient vector is given by

$$\nabla f = f_{\mathbf{Y}} - \mathbf{Y}\mathbf{Y}^T f_{\mathbf{Y}}. \tag{2}$$

Since the tangent space of a manifold varies from point-to-point, if we move a tangent vector from one point to another point it generally does not lie on the tangent plane anymore. However, a tangent vector can be moved along paths on the manifold by taking infinitesimal steps along the curve $\mathbf{Y}(t)$, and at each step removing the component of the vector not in the tangent space. This process is known as *parallel transport*. Figure 1b shows a simple case of this idea.

A *geodesic* is defined to be the curve of shortest length between two point on the manifold. Parametric formulae can be derived for a geodesics on the Grassmann manifold, given the starting point and the tangent vector at that point [6].

Most function optimization techniques, e.g., Newton iterations and conjugate gradient, apply to functions defined over Euclidean spaces. Based on the theoretical concepts defined above, similar methods have been developed for Grassmann manifolds [6]. As we show in Section 3, the parameter space we consider is the direct product of a Grassmann manifold and a real space, $\mathbf{G}_{N,k} \times \mathbb{R}^k$. The rest of this section discusses conjugate gradient function minimization over this parameter space. The algorithm follows the same general structure as standard conjugate gradient but has some differences with regard to the movement of tangent vectors.

We now discuss a conjugate gradient algorithm for the minimization of a function $\mathbf{f}$ from the manifold $\mathbf{G}_{N,k} \times \mathbb{R}^k$ to $\mathbb{R}$. Conjugate gradient minimization requires the computation of $\mathbf{G}$ and $\mathbf{g}$, the gradients of f with respect to $\boldsymbol{\Theta}$ and $\boldsymbol{\alpha}$. To obtain the gradients at a point $(\boldsymbol{\Theta}, \boldsymbol{\alpha})$, compute the Jacobians $\mathbf{J}_{\boldsymbol{\Theta}}$ and $\mathbf{J}_{\boldsymbol{\alpha}}$ of f with respect to $\boldsymbol{\Theta}$ and $\boldsymbol{\alpha}$. The gradients are

$$\mathbf{G} = \mathbf{J}_{\boldsymbol{\Theta}} - \boldsymbol{\Theta}\boldsymbol{\Theta}^T \mathbf{J}_{\boldsymbol{\Theta}} \qquad\qquad \mathbf{g} = \mathbf{J}_{\boldsymbol{\alpha}}. \qquad (3)$$

Let $(\boldsymbol{\Theta}_0, \boldsymbol{\alpha}_0) \in \mathbf{G}_{N,k} \times \mathbb{R}^k$ be the point at which the algorithm is initialized. Compute the gradients $\mathbf{G}_0$ and $\mathbf{g}_0$, at $(\boldsymbol{\Theta}_0, \boldsymbol{\alpha}_0)$ and the search directions are $\mathbf{H}_0 = -\mathbf{G}_0$ and $\mathbf{h}_0 = -\mathbf{g}_0$.

The following iterations are done till convergence. Iteration $j+1$ now proceeds by minimizing f along the geodesic defined by the search directions $\mathbf{H}_j$ on the Grassmann manifold and $\mathbf{h}_j$ in the Euclidean component of the parameter space. This is known as *line minimization*. The parametric form of the geodesic is

$$\boldsymbol{\Theta}_j(t) = \boldsymbol{\Theta}_j \mathbf{V} \mathrm{diag}(\cos \lambda t)\mathbf{V}^T + \mathbf{U}\mathrm{diag}(\sin \lambda t)\mathbf{V}^T \qquad (4)$$
$$\boldsymbol{\alpha}_j(t) = \boldsymbol{\alpha}_j + t\mathbf{h}_j. \qquad (5)$$

where, t is the parameter, $\boldsymbol{\Theta}_j$ is the estimate from iteration j and $\mathbf{U}\mathrm{diag}(\lambda)\mathbf{V}^T$ is the compact SVD of $\mathbf{H}_j$ consisting of the k largest singular values and corresponding singular vectors. The *sin* and *cos* act element-by-element.

Denoting the value of the parameter t where the minimum is achieved by t_{min}, set $\boldsymbol{\Theta}_{j+1} = \boldsymbol{\Theta}_j(t_{min})$ and $\boldsymbol{\alpha}_{j+1} = \boldsymbol{\alpha}_j(t_{min})$. The gradient vectors are parallel transported to this point by

$$\mathbf{H}_j^\tau = [-\boldsymbol{\Theta}_j \mathbf{V}\mathrm{diag}(\sin \lambda t_{min}) + \mathbf{U}\mathrm{diag}(\cos \lambda t_{min})]\,\mathrm{diag}(\lambda)\mathbf{V}^T \qquad (6)$$
$$\mathbf{G}_j^\tau = \mathbf{G}_j - [\boldsymbol{\Theta}_j \mathbf{V}\mathrm{diag}(\sin \lambda t_{min}) + \mathbf{U}(\mathbf{I} - \mathrm{diag}(\cos \lambda t_{min}))]\,\mathbf{U}^T \mathbf{G}_j \qquad (7)$$

where, τ is the parallel transportation operator. No explicit parallel transport is required for the Euclidean component of the parameter space since parallel transport for Euclidean spaces is trivially achieved by moving the whole vector as it is. The new gradients $\mathbf{G}_{j+1}$ and $\mathbf{g}_{j+1}$ are computed at $(\boldsymbol{\Theta}_{j+1}, \boldsymbol{\alpha}_{j+1})$. The new search directions are chosen orthogonal to *all* previous search directions as,

$$\mathbf{H}_{k+1} = -\mathbf{G}_{k+1} + \gamma_k \mathbf{H}_k^\tau \qquad\qquad \mathbf{h}_{k+1} = -\mathbf{g}_{k+1} + \gamma_k \mathbf{h}_k \qquad (8)$$
$$\gamma_k = \frac{tr\left((\mathbf{G}_{k+1}-\mathbf{G}_k^\tau)^T \mathbf{G}_{k+1}\right)+(\mathbf{g}_{k+1}-\mathbf{g}_k)^T \mathbf{g}_{k+1}}{tr\left(\mathbf{G}_k^T \mathbf{G}_k\right)+\mathbf{g}_k^T \mathbf{g}_k} \qquad (9)$$

where, tr is the trace operator. The algorithm is summarized in Figure 2.

- Initialize at $(\boldsymbol{\Theta}_0, \boldsymbol{\alpha}_0) \in \mathbf{G}_{N,k} \times \mathbb{R}^k$,
  - Compute the gradients $\mathbf{G}_0$ and $\mathbf{g}_0$ at $(\boldsymbol{\Theta}_0, \boldsymbol{\alpha}_0)$ using (3).
  - Set $\mathbf{H}_0 = -\mathbf{G}_0$ and $\mathbf{h}_0 = -\mathbf{g}_0$.
- For $j = 0, 1, \ldots$
  - Minimize $f(\boldsymbol{\Theta}_j(t), \boldsymbol{\alpha}_j(t))$ over t where $\boldsymbol{\Theta}_j(t)$ and $\boldsymbol{\alpha}_j(t)$ are as in (4) and (5).
  - Set $\boldsymbol{\Theta}_{j+1} = \boldsymbol{\Theta}_j(t_{min})$ and $\boldsymbol{\alpha}_{j+1} = \boldsymbol{\alpha}_j(t_{min})$.
  - Compute the gradients $\mathbf{G}_{j+1}$ and $\mathbf{g}_{j+1}$ at $(\boldsymbol{\Theta}_{j+1}, \boldsymbol{\alpha}_{j+1})$ according to (3).
  - Parallel transport the vectors $\mathbf{H}_j$ and $\mathbf{G}_j$ to $(\boldsymbol{\Theta}_{j+1}, \boldsymbol{\alpha}_{j+1})$ using (6) and (7).
  - Set the new search directions according to (8) and (9).

Fig. 2. Conjugate gradient algorithm for minimization of $f(\boldsymbol{\Theta}, \boldsymbol{\alpha})$ on $G_{N,k} \times \mathbb{R}^k$

3   Robust Subspace Estimation

Robust methods, such as RANSAC and its variations, handle data corrupted with outliers by making assumptions about the scale of the noise corrupting the inliers. The pbM estimator [3, 13] is independent of a user supplied scale parameter and exploit the intrinsic relation between the optimization criteria and the data space.

3.1   Projection Based M-Estimators

The subspace estimation problem can be stated as follows. Let $\mathbf{y}_{io}$ be the true value of the given data points $\mathbf{y}_i$. Given $\mathbf{y}_i$, $i = 1, \ldots, n$, the problem of subspace estimation is to estimate $\boldsymbol{\Theta} \in \mathbb{R}^{N \times k}$, $\boldsymbol{\alpha} \in \mathbb{R}^k$

$$\boldsymbol{\Theta}^T \mathbf{y}_{io} - \boldsymbol{\alpha} = \mathbf{0}_k \qquad (10)$$
$$\mathbf{y}_i = \mathbf{y}_{io} + \delta \mathbf{y}_i \qquad\qquad \delta \mathbf{y}_i \sim GI(0, \sigma^2 \mathbf{I}_{N \times N})$$

where, σ the *unknown* scale of the noise. Handling non-identity covariances for heteroscedastic data, is a trivial extension of this problem e.g. [11]. The multiplicative ambiguity is resolved by requiring $\boldsymbol{\Theta}^T \boldsymbol{\Theta} = \mathbf{I}_{k \times k}$.

Given a set of k linearly independent constraints, they can be expressed by an equivalent set of *orthonormal* constraints. The $N \times k$ orthonormal matrix $\boldsymbol{\Theta}$ represents the k constraints satisfied by the inliers. The inliers have $N - k$ degrees of freedom and lie in a subspace of dimension $N - k$. Geometrically, $\boldsymbol{\Theta}$ is the basis of the k dimensional null space of the data and is a point on the Grassmann manifold $G_{N,k}$. Usually $\boldsymbol{\alpha}$ is taken to be zero since any subspace must contain the origin. However, for a robust formulation where the data is not centered, $\boldsymbol{\alpha}$ represents an estimate of the centroid of the inliers. Since we are trying to estimate both $\boldsymbol{\Theta}$ and $\boldsymbol{\alpha}$, the complete search space for the parameters is $G_{N,k} \times \mathbb{R}^k$. The projection of $\boldsymbol{\alpha}$ onto the column space of $\boldsymbol{\Theta}$ is given by $\boldsymbol{\Theta}\boldsymbol{\alpha}$ and this product should be independent of the basis used to represent the subspace.

The robust M-estimator formulation of the subspace estimation problem is

$$\left[\hat{\alpha}, \hat{\Theta}\right] = \arg\min_{\alpha, \theta} \frac{1}{n \left|\mathbf{S}_{\Theta}\right|^{1/2}} \sum_{i=1}^{n} \rho\left(\mathbf{x}_i^T \mathbf{S}_{\Theta}^{-1} \mathbf{x}_i\right) \tag{11}$$

where, $\mathbf{x}_i = \Theta^T \mathbf{y}_i - \alpha$, $\mathbf{S}_{\Theta}$ is a scale matrix and $\left|\mathbf{S}_{\Theta}\right|$ is its determinant. Note, that M-scores are usually not normalized by the determinant of the scale matrix. In our case, the scale matrix varies with the subspace Θ and this normalization is required [13]. The function $\rho(u)$ considered here is a *loss function* in u, i.e., it is nondecreasing with $|u|$, has a unique minimum at $\rho(0) = 0$ and a maximum of one as $|u| \to 1$. The M-estimator problem can be rewritten in terms of the function $\kappa(u) = 1 - \rho(u)$ which is referred to as the *M-kernel function*

$$\left[\hat{\alpha}, \hat{\Theta}\right] = \arg\max_{\alpha, \Theta} \frac{1}{n \left|\mathbf{S}_{\Theta}\right|^{1/2}} \sum_{i=1}^{n} \kappa\left(\mathbf{x}_i^T \mathbf{S}_{\Theta}^{-1} \mathbf{x}_i\right). \tag{12}$$

We use the redescending M-estimator with the biweight loss function [3].

Consider a set of points $\mathbf{x}_i \in \mathbb{R}^k$, $i = 1, \ldots, n$ which have been generated by some *unknown* probability distribution direction, $f(\mathbf{x})$. *Kernel density estimation*, also known as the Parzen window method in pattern recognition literature, returns an estimate of this unknown distribution as[1]

$$\hat{f}_{\Theta}(\mathbf{x}) = \frac{1}{n \left|\mathbf{H}\right|^{1/2}} \sum_{i=1}^{n} k\left((\mathbf{x}_i - \mathbf{x})^T \mathbf{H}^{-1} (\mathbf{x}_i - \mathbf{x})\right). \tag{13}$$

where, $\mathbf{H}$ is a bandwidth matrix, $k(u)$ is the *profile function* which decreases with increasing $|u|$.

The optimal choice for the bandwidth used is dependent on the true distribution. For one-dimensional kernel density estimation the following approximate bandwidth selection formula was derived in [18, Sec.3.2.2]

$$h = n^{-1/5} \operatorname*{med}_{j} \left|x_j - \operatorname*{med}_{i} x_i\right| \tag{14}$$

and we later discuss how we adapt this for data dependent bandwidth matrices.

There exist obvious similarities between (12) and (13). In (13), if we take the M-kernel function $\kappa(u)$ as the kernel $k(u)$, the projections $\Theta^T \mathbf{y}_i$ as the data points $\mathbf{x}_i$, replace $\mathbf{x}$ with α and the bandwidth matrix $\mathbf{H}$ with the scale matrix $\mathbf{S}_{\Theta}$, we get (12). The M-estimator problem can be rewritten as

$$\hat{\Theta} = \arg\max_{\Theta} \left[\max_{\mathbf{x}} \hat{f}_{\Theta}(\mathbf{x})\right] \tag{15}$$

---

[1] For $\hat{f}(x)$ to be a true density function and satisfy $\int_{\mathbb{R}} \hat{f}(x)dx = 1$ we should use $c\kappa(x)$ where c is chosen such that $c \int_{\mathbb{R}} \kappa(x)dx = 1$. However, this global scaling does not affect any of the further analysis and is ignored.

where, $\hat{f}_{\Theta}(x)$ refers to the estimate defined in (13). The formulation of (15) maximizes the value of the kernel density estimate at the mode. The inner maximization in (15) returns the intercept as the mode of $\hat{f}_{\Theta}(x)$, i.e., $\alpha = \max_x \hat{f}_{\Theta}(\mathbf{x})$. The pbM algorithm is based on this similarity between kernel density estimation and M-estimators.

3.2 The pbM Algorithm

The first part of each pbM iteration consists of *probabilistic sampling*. An elemental subset which uniquely defines a k-dimensional subspace of $\mathbb{R}^N$ is chosen to get an estimate of Θ.

Given Θ, the data points are projected into $\mathbb{R}^k$ and mean shift [4] is used find the mode of the projections in $\mathbb{R}^k$. The bandwidth matrix is taken to be diagonal, with the values for each direction independently chosen by (14). This method depends on the basis used and a rotation of the basis gives a bandwidth matrix which depends on the rotation in a complex manner. The pbM estimator exhibits a weak dependence on the exact form of the bandwidth, and this method is sufficient. Of the modes returned, the mode with highest density is retained as the intercept α and the density at α is assigned as the score of (Θ, α).

This score is now maximized in a neighborhood of Θ. In spite of the non-differentiable nature of (15), derivative based methods can be used for this optimization by ignoring the dependence of α and $\mathbf{S}_{\Theta}$ on Θ. To ensure $\Theta^T \Theta = I_{k \times k}$ continues to hold, conjugate gradient is adapted to the Grassmann manifold [6]. We include α in the search space and the complete parameter space is actually $G_{N,k} \times \mathbb{R}^k$. The algorithm is given in Figure 2. At the convergence of the minimization, the mode is refined again using mean shift initialized at the current estimate of $\hat{\alpha}$.

The procedure is repeated for each elemental subset and the (Θ, α) with the highest score is taken as $(\hat{\Theta}, \hat{\alpha})$. The inlier-outlier dichotomy estimation is user independent. Denote the i-th column of $\hat{\Theta}$ by $\hat{\theta}_i$ and consider the one-dimensional kernel density estimate of the projections along $\hat{\theta}_i$. The mode of this distribution is given by $\hat{\alpha}_i$, the i-th value of $\hat{\alpha}$. The first *strong minima* of this density on either side of the mode are used to define the limits of the inliers. Points with projections lying in this range for all the k basis vectors are declared to be inliers. Multiple subspaces are estimated by repeatedly running the above algorithm and removing the inliers at each stage from the data set.

4 Experimental Results

We compare the performance of our algorithm against various other estimators: robust PCA [1, 2], subspace separation [10], GPCA [17, 16] and RANSAC [7]. Most previous methods either try to handle multiple subspaces with no outliers e.g., GPCA, or estimate only one subspace in the presence of outliers e.g., robust PCA. RANSAC is the only previous method which can be used for estimating multiple subspaces even in the presence of outliers, but requires a user defined noise level. The superiority of pbM to RANSAC has also been experimentally verified before [3].

4.1   Synthetic Data

The synthetic data consisted of 100 points lying along two randomly chosen intersecting lines in 3D with 40 points on one line, 30 points on the other and 30 outliers. Zero mean Gaussian noise of increasing variance was added to the data and 1000 trials were run for each noise level. In each trial we considered four different estimation techniques, robust PCA, GPCA, RANSAC and the pbM estimator. The line with 40 points was estimated. Since robust PCA and GPCA do not account for noncentered data, the inliers are centered. Both RANSAC and pbM use 500 elemental subsets for estimation. Since the true scale of the noise corrupting the inliers is known, RANSAC was tuned to the optimal scale estimate as suggested in [15]. No user defined scale estimate is required for pbM.

The error between the true subspace Θ and estimated subspace $\hat{\Theta}$ is the geodesic length along the Grassmann manifold given by

$$e_{\Theta} = d_{gm}(\hat{\Theta}, \Theta) = \|\omega\|_2 \tag{16}$$

where, ω is the vector of angles between the basis of $\hat{\Theta}$ and Θ. These angles can be found by taking the SVD of $\hat{\Theta}^T \Theta = U\Sigma V^T$. The values along the diagonal of Σ are the cosines of the angles in ω. The elements of ω can be found by taking the inverse cosine of each diagonal elemnt of Σ.

σ	Mean				Standard Deviation			
	RPCA	GPCA	RANSAC	pbM	RPCA	GPCA	RANSAC	pbM
0.25	0.432	0.498	0.012	0.003	0.160	0.293	0.001	0.049
0.50	0.445	0.494	0.015	0.006	0.151	0.300	0.003	0.034
0.75	0.431	0.488	0.017	0.008	0.157	0.295	0.004	0.019
1.00	0.440	0.492	0.020	0.011	0.165	0.309	0.006	0.024
1.25	0.434	0.490	0.020	0.013	0.156	0.299	0.006	0.022
1.50	0.451	0.479	0.020	0.016	0.158	0.319	0.008	0.018
1.75	0.442	0.492	0.020	0.017	0.158	0.335	0.009	0.019
2.00	0.429	0.483	0.021	0.019	0.161	0.343	0.011	0.016

Fig. 3. For the synthetic data the line with 40 points is estimated. Robust PCA and GPCA break down due to the outliers. RANSAC performs almost as good as pbM but requires a user defined scale input which has been tuned to the optimal value.

The mean and standard deviation of the error e_{Θ} are shown in Figure 3. Robust PCA finds the direction which maximizes the variance of the projections and always estimates a line lying in between the two lines on the same plane, leading to a large mean error and relatively moderate standard deviation. GPCA breaks down because of the outliers. Even when applied only to the inliers, GPCA deteriorates with increasing noise levels. RANSAC is the only algorithm which is comparable to pbM.

4.2   Real Data: Multibody Factorization

For real data we consider the factorization problem [14], since it is well studied and the degeneracies are well understood [19, 20]. Factorization is based on the fact that if n rigidly moving points are tracked over f *affine* images, then $2f$ image coordinates are obtained which can be used to define feature vectors in $\mathbb{R}^{2f}$. These vectors lie in a four-dimensional subspace of $\mathbb{R}^{2f}$ [14]. If the data is centered then the dimension of the subspace is only three.

We compare pbM to subspace separation [10], GPCA [17, 16] and RANSAC [7]. Our sequences have large displacements between frames leading to more outliers. They also consist of few frames leading to more degeneracies, for e.g., with three motions over four frames it is impossible to have independent subspaces since only 8 independent vectors can exist in the space, while at least 9 linearly independent vectors are required for each motion subspace to have an independent basis.

In subspace separation [10], a similarity measure is defined for pairs of feature vectors and these are arranged in a $n \times n$ symmetric *shape interaction matrix*. The clustering is done by making this matrix block diagonal. In our implementation we use the similarity measure of [20] which is more appropriate for dependent subspaces. For block diagonalization we use the algorithm of [12]. Since outliers do not lie in any subspace they may have high interactions with the inliers and the result is not robust.

An analytic solution to the multiple subspace estimation problem, GPCA, was presented in [17, 16]. This method is fast and can handle dependencies among the subspaces, but it is not robust. RANSAC [7] requires a user defined estimate for the scale of the noise corrupting the inliers. The ground truth was found through manual inspection. Given the ground truth, we compute the scale of the inlier noise $\hat{\sigma}$, and the RANSAC scale input is optimally set to $1.96\hat{\sigma}$ [15].

We used the point matching algorithm of [9] to track points. For the real data sets, both RANSAC and pbM used 1000 elemental subsets for estimating the first subspace, and 500 elemental subsets for estimating each further subspace. An algorithm's performance is measured by its ability to cluster points correctly. This is measured by the ratio of the points declared as inliers to the number, among them, which are truly inliers. The closer this is to one the better.

We present our results on three progressively more complicated data sets. The *first sequence* consists of two moving bodies tracked over five frames. The motions subspaces are independent. Of the 158 features tracked, the two motions contained 52 and 30 points and 76 outliers. The results are shown in Figure 4. GPCA and subspace separation break down due to the outliers. GPCA randomly classifies the points into subspaces while subspace separation classifies all but one points into a single motion. Only on clean data, *with no outliers*, do GPCA and subspace separation give good results, but this never occurs in practice. The performance of RANSAC, when tuned to its optimal scale, is the same as pbM. A few of the mismatched points lie in the subspaces and are declared inliers.

The *second sequence* has three moving toys over four frames, with two of the motions having dependent subspaces. Of the 128 features tracked, the three motions contain 40, 30 and 21 inliers while 37 points were outliers. The results

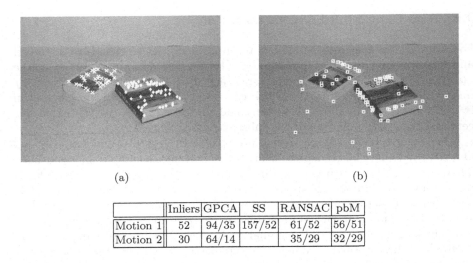

(a)   (b)

	Inliers	GPCA	SS	RANSAC	pbM
Motion 1	52	94/35	157/52	61/52	56/51
Motion 2	30	64/14		35/29	32/29

Fig. 4. *First Experiment.* (a) Segmented inliers returned by pbM for both motions, plotted on one of the frames. (b) Outliers returned by pbM. The table shows the results of the different estimators for the complete sequence.

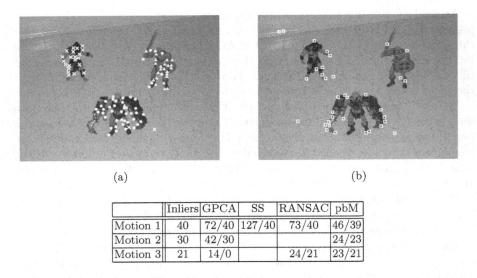

(a)   (b)

	Inliers	GPCA	SS	RANSAC	pbM
Motion 1	40	72/40	127/40	73/40	46/39
Motion 2	30	42/30			24/23
Motion 3	21	14/0		24/21	23/21

Fig. 5. *Second Experiment.* (a) Inliers returned by pbM for the three motions in the sequence. (b) Outliers returned by pbM. The table shows the results of the estimators.

are shown in Figure 5. GPCA and subspace separation break down due to the outliers. In fact, subspace separation also breaks down on the clean data set due to degeneracies. RANSAC is unable to separate between the two degenerate motions since it cannot differentiate between outliers and noisy inliers, and clas-

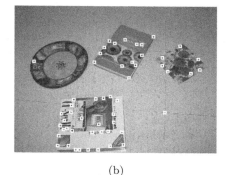

(a)   (b)

	Inliers	GPCA	SS	RANSAC	pbM
Motion 1	45	86/22	124/45	62/45	41/40
Motion 2	17	31/0			17/17
Motion 3	13	8/0		18/13	14/12

Fig. 6. *Third Experiment.* (a) Inliers returned by pbM for the three motions in the sequence. (b) Outliers returned by pbM. The table shows the results of the estimators.

sifies the inliers of both motions as a single motion. Only pbM is able to detect and segment all three motions.

The *third sequence* has three independent motions over four frames. The results are shown in Figure 6. The *plate* and *napkin* have the same motion, while the *book* and the *box* move independently. There are a large number of mismatches, and the motions subspaces are dependent. Among the 125 feature vectors the three motions contain 45, 17 and 13 inliers and there are 50 outliers. As before, GPCA and subspace separation break down. RANSAC cannot distinguish between two of the motions and combines both sets of inliers into one motion. Only pbM segments all motions correctly.

5   Conclusions

We proposed a robust subspace estimation algorithm based on the pbM estimator. The pbM algorithm required theoretical and computational modifications to estimate subspaces. For multiple structure estimation, currently, we recursively estimate the dominant subspace. We are working on methods which can simultaneously estimate the number of motions and segment them in a single step.

References

1. L. P. Ammann, "Robust singular value decompositions: A new approach to projection pursuit," *J. of Amer. Stat. Assoc.*, vol. 88, no. 422, pp. 505–514, 1993.
2. N. A. Campbell, "Robust procedures in multivariate analysis i: Robust covariance estimation," *Applied Statistics*, vol. 29, no. 3, pp. 231–237, 1980.

3. H. Chen and P. Meer, "Robust regression with projection based M-estimators," in *9th Intl. Conf. on Computer Vision*, (Nice, France), Oct 2003, pp. 878–885.

4. D. Comaniciu and P. Meer, "Mean shift: A robust approach toward feature space analysis," *IEEE Trans. Pattern Anal. Machine Intell.*, vol. 24, pp. 603–619, May 2002.

5. J. Costeira and T. Kanade, "A multi-body factorization method for motion analysis," in *Proc. 5th Intl. Conf. on Computer Vision*, Cambridge, MA, 1995, pp. 1071–1076.

6. A. Edelman, T. A. Arias, and S. T. Smith, "The geometry of algorithms with orthogonality constraints," *SIAM Journal on Matrix Analysis and Applications*, vol. 20, no. 2, pp. 303–353, 1998.

7. M. A. Fischler and R. C. Bolles, "Random sample consensus: A paradigm for model fitting with applications to image analysis and automated cartography," *Comm. Assoc. Comp. Mach*, vol. 24, no. 6, pp. 381–395, 1981.

8. C. W. Gear, "Multibody grouping from motion images," *International J. of Computer Vision*, vol. 29, no. 2, pp. 133–150, 1998.

9. B. Georgescu and P. Meer, "Point matching under large image deformations and illumination changes," *IEEE Trans. Pattern Anal. Machine Intell.*, vol. 26, pp. 674–689, 2004.

10. K. Kanatani, "Motion segmentation by subspace separation and model selection," in *8th Intl. Conf. on Computer Vision*, volume II, (Vancouver, Canada), July 2001, pp. 301–306.

11. B. Matei and P. Meer, "A general method for errors-in-variables problems in computer vision," in *2000 IEEE Conf. on Computer Vision and Pattern Recognition*, volume II, (Hilton Head Island, SC), June 2000, pp. 18–25.

12. J. Shi and J. Malik, "Normalized cuts and image segmentation," *IEEE Trans. Pattern Anal. Machine Intell.*, vol. 22, no. 8, pp. 888–905, 2000.

13. R. Subbarao and P. Meer, "Heteroscedastic projection based M-estimators," in *Workshop on Empirical Evaluation Methods in Computer Vision*, San Diego, CA in conjunction with *IEEE CVPR*, 2005.

14. C. Tomasi and T. Kanade, "Shape and motion from image streams under orthography: A factorization method," *Intl. J. of Computer Vision*, vol. 9, no. 2, pp. 137–154, 1992.

15. P. H. S. Torr and D. W. Murray, "The development and comparison of robust methods for estimating the fundamental matrix," *Intl. J. of Computer Vision*, vol. 24, no. 3, pp. 271–300, 1997.

16. R. Vidal, Y. Ma, and J. Piazzi, "A new GPCA algorithm for clustering subspaces by fitting, differentiating and dividing polynomials," in *Proc. IEEE Conf. on Computer Vision and Pattern Recognition*, Washington, DC, vol. I, 2004, pp. 510–517.

17. R. Vidal, Y. Ma, and S. Sastry, "Generalized principal component analysis (GPCA)," in *Proc. IEEE Conf. on Computer Vision and Pattern Recognition*, Madison, WI, vol. I, 2003, pp. 621–628.

18. M. P. Wand and M. C. Jones, *Kernel Smoothing*. Chapman & Hall, 1995.

19. Y.Sugaya and K. Kanatani, "Geometric structure of degeneracy for multi-body motion segmentation," in D.Comaniciu et al., editor, *The 2nd Workshop on Statistical Methods in Video Processing*, no. 3247 in LNCS, pp. 1–2, Springer-Verlag, Berlin, Dec 2004.

20. L. Zelnik-Manor and M. Irani, "Degeneracies, dependencies and their implications in multi-body and multi-sequence factorizations," in *Proc. IEEE Conf. on Computer Vision and Pattern Recognition*, Madison, WI, number 2, 2003, pp. 297–293.

Learning 2D Hand Shapes Using the Topology Preservation Model GNG

Anastassia Angelopoulou[1], José García Rodríguez[2], and Alexandra Psarrou[1]

[1] Harrow School of Computer Science, University of Westminster,
Harrow HA1 3TP, United Kingdom
{agelopa, psarroa}@wmin.ac.uk
[2] Departamento de Tecnología Informática y Computación, Universidad de Alicante,
Apdo. 99. 03080 Alicante, Spain
jgarcia@dtic.ua.es

Abstract. Recovering the shape of a class of objects requires establishing correct correspondences between manually or automatically annotated landmark points. In this study, we utilise a novel approach to automatically recover the shape of hand outlines from a series of 2D training images. Automated landmark extraction is accomplished through the use of the self-organising model the growing neural gas (GNG) network which is able to learn and preserve the topological relations of a given set of input patterns without requiring a priori knowledge of the structure of the input space. To measure the quality of the mapping throughout the adaptation process we use the topographic product. Results are given for the training set of hand outlines.

1 Introduction

Modelling the shape of a class of non-rigid objects in two-dimensions requires the recovery of their structure from a set of images. A common modelling approach is the observation and analysis of a set of examples of the object or class of objects using standard statistical methods such as principal component analysis (PCA). This approach has turned out to be very effective in image segmentation and interpretation. The basic idea of statistical shape modelling is to establish new unseen legal instances of shapes taken from a given set of training examples, using as few parameters as possible. Shape training sets usually come from manually annotated boundaries. The difficulty arises over the need to automate the process. For example, in a clinical setting the first stage in the post-processing step of a T1-weighted MRI technique is to segment out the ventricles, which can be difficult in many cases if the patient is not properly aligned in the scanner. These post-processing step is laborious and must be very accurate if the purpose of the scan is to help determine the extent of disease progression. In very overburdened medical facilities, performing this task manually may not be feasible. An automated procedure may provide the means of yielding objective and consistent results across various institutions. It is imperative therefore that an accurate, rapid and automated algorithm be developed and deployed.

A. Leonardis, H. Bischof, and A. Pinz (Eds.): ECCV 2006, Part I, LNCS 3951, pp. 313–324, 2006.

In literature, various attempts have been made to automate the process of landmark based image registration and correct correspondences among a set of shapes. Baumberg's *et al.* [3] method, which generates flexible shapes models by using equally spaced spline control points around the boundaries of walking pedestrians, is an example of arbitrary parameterisation. The process is automatic, but it is arbitrary since it uses properties of the specific shape being modelled (each shape has a principal axis) thus, not generally applicable.

Davies *et al.* [6] method of automatically building statistical shape models by re-paremeterising each shape from the training set and optimising an information theoretic function to assess the quality of the model has received a lot of attention recently. The quality of the model is assessed by adopting a minimum description length (MDL) criterion to the training set. The MDL is obtained from information theoretic considerations and recently has received a lot of attention due to its ability to locate dense correspondence between the boundaries [18, 6, 7]. This is a very promising method and the models that are produced are comparable to and often better than the manual built models. However, due to very large number of function evaluations and nonlinear optimisation the method is computationally expensive.

Cremer's *et al.* [5] method of automatically constructing statistical shapes from a training set by combining the external energy of the Mumford-Shah functional with the internal energy of the snakes in a single variational framework, has improved segmentation in cases where occlusion or strongly cluttered backgrounds occur. In the case of learning $2D$ shapes the method it's fully automatic as long as no open boundaries or contour splitting are emerged.

Recently, Fatemizadeh *et al.* [8] have used modified growing neural gas to automatically correspond important landmark points from two related shapes by adding a third dimension to the data points and by treating the problem of correspondence as a cluster-seeking method by adjusting the centers of points from the two corresponding shapes. This is a promising method and has been tested to both synthetic and real data, but the method has not been tested on a large scale for stability and accuracy of building statistical shape models.

In this work, we introduce a new and computationally inexpensive method for the automatic selection of landmarks along the contours of $2D$ hand shapes. The novelty in using the Growing Neural Gas method for unsupervised learning is that we can automatically construct statistical shape models independently of closed or open shapes in contrast to Kass *et al.* [11] "Active Contour Models - Snakes" which can be defined only for closed contours. Furthermore, the incremental neural network, the growing neural gas (GNG) is used to automatically annotate the training set without using *a priori* knowledge of the structure of the input patterns. Unlike other methods, the incremental character of the model avoids the necessity to previously specify a reference shape. To evaluate the accuracy of the method we have tested it with other self-organising models such as Kohonen maps and Neural Gas (NG) maps and we applied the topographic product [2] to measure the best topology preservation of the order-preserving map.

The remaining of the paper is organised as follows. Section 2 introduces the statistical shape models. Section 3 provides a detailed description of the topology learning algorithm GNG. Section 4 reviews the topographic product, an existing measure used to quantify the topography of neural maps. A set of experimental results along with qualitative analysis is presented in Section 5, before we conclude in Section 6.

2   Statistical Shape Models

When analysing deformable shapes like hands it is convenient and usually effective to describe them using statistical shape models. The most well known statistical shape models are Cootes *et al.* [4] 'Point Distribution Models' (PDMs) that models the shape of an object and its variation by using a set of n_p landmark points from a training set of S_i shapes. In this work, PDM represents the hands as a set of n_p automatically extracted landmarks (in our case 64, 100, 144 and 169 neurons) in a vector $\mathbf{x} = [x_{i0}, x_{i1}, ..., x_{in_{p-1}}, y_{i0}, y_{i1}, ..., y_{in_{p-1}}]^T$. In order to generate flexible shape models the S_i shapes are aligned (translated, rotated, scaled) and normalised (removing the centre-of-gravity and placing it at the origin) to a common set of axes. The modes of variations of the hands are captured by applying principal component analysis (PCA). The ith shape in the training set can be back-projected to the input space by a linear model of the form:

$$\mathbf{x} = \overline{\mathbf{x}} + \Phi\beta_i \tag{1}$$

where $\overline{\mathbf{x}}$ is the mean shape, Φ describes a set of orthogonal modes of shape variations, and β_i is a vector of weights for the ith shape. To ensure that the above weight changes describe reasonable variations we restrict the weight β_i to the range $-3\sqrt{\lambda} \leq \beta_i \leq 3\sqrt{\lambda}$ and the shape is back-projected to the input space using Equation (1). PCA works well as long as good correspondences exist. To obtain the correspondences and represent the contour of the hands a self-organising network GNG was used.

3   Topology Learning

One way of selecting points of interest along the contour of 2D shapes is to use a topographic mapping where a low dimensional map is fitted to a higher dimensional manifold, whilst preserving the topographic structure of the data. A common way to achieve this is by using self-organising neural networks where input patterns are projected onto a network of neural units such that similar patterns are projected onto units adjacent in the network and vice versa. As a result of this mapping a representation of the input patterns is achieved that in postprocessing stages allows one to exploit the similarity relations of the input patterns. Such models have been successfully used in applications such as speech processing [12], robotics [17, 14] and image processing [16]. However, most common approaches are not able to provide good neighborhood and topology preservation if the logical structure of the input patten is not known *a priori*. In fact, the most common approaches specify in advance the number of neurons in the network and a graph that represents topological relationships between them, for example, a two-dimensional grid, and seek the best match to the given input pattern manifold. When this is not the case the networks fail to provide good topology preserving as for example in the case of Kohonen's algorithm.

The approach presented in this paper is based on self-organising networks trained using the Growing Neural Gas learning method [9]. This is an incremental training algorithm where the number of units in the network are determined by the unifying measure for neighborhood preservation [10], the topographic product. The links between the units in the network are established through competitive hebbian learning [13]. As a result the algorithm can be used in cases where the topological structure of the input pattern is not known a *priori* and yields topology preserving maps of feature manifold [15].

3.1 Growing Neural Gas

With Growing Neural Gas (GNG) [9] a growth process takes place from minimal network size and new units are inserted successively using a particular type of vector quantisation [12]. To determine where to insert new units, local error measures are gathered during the adaptation process and each new unit is inserted near the unit which has the highest accumulated error. At each adaptation step a connection between the winner and the second-nearest unit is created as dictated by the competitive hebbian learning algorithm. This is continued until an ending condition is fulfilled, as for example evaluation of the optimal network topology based on the topographic product [10]. This measure is used to detect deviations between the dimensions of the network and that of the input space, detecting folds in the network and, indicating that is trying to approximate to an input manifold with different dimensions. In addition, in GNG networks learning parameters are constant in time, in contrast to other methods whose learning is based on decaying parameters.

The network is specified as:

- A set N of nodes (neurons). Each neuron $c \in N$ has its associated reference vector $w_c \in R^d$. The reference vectors can be regarded as positions in the input space of their corresponding neurons.
- A set of edges (connections) between pairs of neurons. These connections are not weighted and its purpose is to define the topological structure. The edges are determined using the competitive hebbian learning algorithm. An *edge aging scheme* is used to remove connections that are invalid due to the activation of the neuron during the adaptation process.

The GNG learning algorithm to approach the network to the input manifold is as follows:

1. Start with two neurons a and b at random positions w_a and w_b in R^d.
2. Generate at random an input pattern ξ according to the data distribution $P(\xi)$ of each input pattern. Since the input space is the contour, $1D$ manifold,

the input pattern is the (x, y) coordinate of the edges. Typically, for the training of the network we generated 1000 to 10000 input patterns depending on the complexity of the input space.

3. Find the nearest neuron (winner neuron) s_1 and the second nearest s_2 by:

$$s_1 = \arg \min {}_{c \in A} \| \xi - w_c \| \tag{2}$$

and

$$s_2 = \arg \min {}_{c \in A\{s_1\}} \| \xi - w_c \| \tag{3}$$

4. Increase the age of all the edges emanating from s_1:

$$age_{(s_1,i)} = age_{(s_1,i)} + 1 \ (\forall i \in N_{s1}) \tag{4}$$

5. Add the squared distance between the input signal and the winner neuron to a counter error of s_1 such as:

$$\Delta error(s_1) = \|w_{s_1} - \xi\|^2 \tag{5}$$

6. Move the winner neuron s_1 and its topological neighbours (neurons connected to s_1) towards ξ by a learning step ϵ_w and ϵ_n, respectively, of the total distance:

$$\Delta w_{s_1} = \epsilon_w(\xi - w_{s_1}) \tag{6}$$

$$\Delta w_{s_n} = \epsilon_w(\xi - w_{s_n}) \tag{7}$$

for all direct neighbours n of s_1.

7. If s_1 and s_2 are connected by an edge, set the age of this edge to 0.

$$age_{(s_1,s_2)} = 0 \tag{8}$$

If it does not exist, create it.

8. Remove the edges larger than a_{max}. If this results in isolated neurons (without emanating edges), remove them as well.

9. Every certain number λ of input patterns generated insert a new neuron as follows:

   - Determine the neuron q with the maximum accumulated error:

$$q = \arg \max {}_{c \in A} E_c \tag{9}$$

- Determine among the neighbours of q the neuron f with the maximum accumulated error:

$$f = \arg\max_{c \in N_q} E_c \tag{10}$$

- Insert a new neuron r between q and its further neighbour f:

$$w_r = 0.5(w_q + w_f) \tag{11}$$

- Insert new edges connecting the neuron r with neurons q and f, removing the old edge between q and f.

10. Decrease the error variables of neurons q and f multiplying them by a fraction α:

$$\Delta error_{(q)} = -\alpha E_q \tag{12}$$

$$\Delta error_{(f)} = -\alpha E_f \tag{13}$$

11. Initialize the error variable of r with the new value of the error variable of q and f.

$$E_r = \frac{(E_q + E_f)}{2} \tag{14}$$

12. Decrease all error variables by multiplying them with a constant γ:

$$\Delta error_{(c)} = -\gamma E_c \tag{15}$$

13. If the stopping criterion is not yet achieved (in our case the number of neurons), go to step 2.

The algorithm was tested with three different topology preserving networks so that evaluation of the best topological map can be achieved. The testing involved two cases were the number of neurons were too few or too excessive for the training set of the images. In the former the topological map is lost, not enough neurons to represent the contour of the hands and in the later an overfit is performed. The parameters used in all simulations were: $\lambda = 1000$, $\varepsilon_w = 0.1$, $\varepsilon_n = 0.001$, $\alpha = 0.5$, $\gamma = 0.95$, $\alpha_{max} = 250$.

3.2   Characterising Hand Shape Using GNG

Given an image $I(x, y) \in \Re$ of the object we perform the transformation $\Psi_\nabla(x, y) = \nabla(I(x, y))$ that associates to each one of the pixels its probability of belonging to the contour of the object (Figure 1A, 1B and 1C). If we consider $\xi = (x, y)$ and $P(\xi) = \Psi_\nabla(\xi)$ we can apply the learning algorithm of the GNG to the image I, so that the network adapts its topology to the contours. The result of the learning process is a list of non ordered neurons representing the contour of the

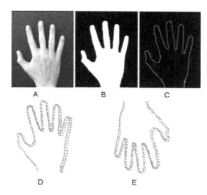

Fig. 1. Image A represents original image in grey level, in B threshold is applied that converts to B/W, in C the contour is obtained, and in D and E the neurons obtained from the adaptation process and the reordering of the neurons

hand. The list of neurons define a graph. To normalise the graph that represents the contour we must define a starting point, for example the neuron on the left-bottom corner. Taking that neuron as the first we must follow the neighbours until all the neurons had been added to the new list. The results of GNG reordering the neurons and the normalised neurons can be seen in Figure 1D and 1E. Since we want to apply the result of the neural network adaptation to the automatically annotation of the 2D contour, it is important that the result preserves the topology correctly. For this reason, we have used the topographic product as a measure to quantify this goal.

4   Measuring Topology Preservation

The topographic product [2] was one of the first attempts of quantifying the topology preservation of self-organizing neural networks. This measure is used to detect deviations between the dimensions of the network and that of the input space, detecting folds in the network and, indicating that is trying to approximate to an input manifold with different dimension.

In our case it is used to determine the optimum number of neural units that can be used to describe the 2D shape of a hand. This can be thought as an alternative to the MDL objective function introduced by Davies *et al.* [6].

4.1   Topographic Product

This measure compares the neighbourhood relationship between each pair of neurons in the network with respect to both their position on the map ($P_2(j,k)$) and their reference vectors ($P_1(j,k)$):

$$P_1(j,k) = [\prod_{l=1}^{k} \frac{d^V(w_j, w_{n_l^A(j)})}{d^V(w_j, w_{n_l^V(j)})}]^{1/l} \qquad (16)$$

$$P_2(j, k) = [\prod_{l=1}^{k} \frac{d^A(j, n_l^A(j))}{d^A(j, n_l^V(j))}]^{1/l} \qquad (17)$$

where j is a neuron, w_j is its reference vector, n_l^V is the l-th closest neighbour to j in the input manifold V according to a distance d^V and n_l^A is the l-th nearest neuron to j in the network A according to a distance d^A . Combining (6) and (7) a measure of the topological relationship between the neuron j and its k closer neurons is obtained:

$$P_3(j, k) = [\prod_{l=1}^{k} \frac{d^V(w_j, w_{n_l^A(j)})}{d^V(w_j, w_{n_l^V(j)})} \cdot \frac{d^A(j, n_l^A(j))}{d^A(j, n_l^V(j))}]^{1/2k} \qquad (18)$$

To extend this measure to all the neurons of the network and all the possible neighborhood orders, the topographic product P is defined as:

$$P = \frac{1}{N(N-1)} \sum_{j=1}^{N} \sum_{k=1}^{N-1} \log(P_3(j, k)) \qquad (19)$$

The sign of P indicates the topological relation of the input and the output space. $P < 0$ corresponds to a too low-dimensional input space, $P \approx 0$ indicates an approximate match, and $P > 0$ corresponds to a too high-dimensional input space [1]. In our case the negative values of the topographic product indicate the low-dimensionality of the input network.

5   Experiments

To illustrate the performance of the convergence algorithm described in Section 3, we present qualitative (Figure 3) and quantitative (Table 1) results for both manually and automatically generated models. The hand database, was composed of images of four individuals who contributed with four images of their right hand and at different poses (two of the fingers, the middle and the ring were captured at various displacements). We used 16 hand shapes which were extracted from the training set by thresholding. All images were of same size 395x500 pixels. The comparison was made by taking two reference models, a manually annotated hand model with 60 landmarks, and an automatic growing neural gas hand model with 144 neurons (Figure 2).

In Figure 3 two shape variations from the automatically generated landmarks were superimposed to the training set and the in between shape instances are drawn which shows the flexing of middle finger and hand rotation. These modes effectively capture the variability of the training set and present only valid shape instances. The quantitatively results (Table 1) show that the automatically generated models are more compact than the manual models since less variance is

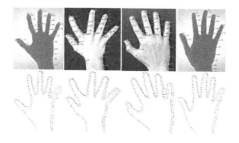

Fig. 2. First row manually annotated landmarks. Second row GNG with 144 neurons.

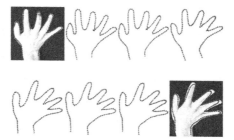

Fig. 3. Superimpose shape instances to the training set and taking the in between steps

Table 1. The results for the hand models

Mode	Manual model	Automatic model (144 neurons)
1	5.6718	1.5253
2	2.3005	1.1518
3	1.6976	0.9808
4	0.9896	0.3968
5	0.6357	0.3716
6	0.4713	0.1980
V_T	13.227	5.1783

captured per mode. It is interesting to note the big difference in the total variance between the two reference models. This may be because of errors in the manual annotation since all points were manually located and because of the difference of the number of points selected in the manual annotation. Table 2 shows the total variance achieved by maps containing varying number of neurons (25, 64, 100, 144, 169) used for the automatic annotation (Figure 4). The map of 144 neurons is the most compact since it achieves the least variance. This is constant with the optimal mapping selected by the topographic product. It is interesting to note that whilst there is significant difference between 25, 64 and 100 neurons (not enough neurons to represent the object) the mapping with

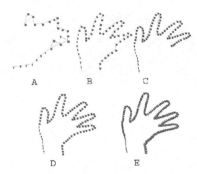

Fig. 4. Network size of 25 (A), 64 (B), 100 (C), 144 (D), and 169 (E), neurons

Table 2. A quantitative comparison of various neurons adapted to the hand model with variances for the first six modes, total variance and the topographic product

Mode	25 (neurons)	64 (neurons)	100 (neurons)	144 (neurons)	169 (neurons)
1	2.1819	4.2541	3.2693	1.5253	2.5625
2	1.2758	2.2512	1.4869	1.1518	0.9266
3	0.6706	0.5681	0.6154	0.9808	0.5734
4	0.4317	0.4645	0.4977	0.3968	0.3101
5	0.3099	0.2844	0.3532	0.3716	0.2491
6	0.2305	0.2489	0.1292	0.1980	0.1927
V_T	5.7486	8.6170	6.4108	5.1783	5.2470
T_P	0.0099	-0.018	-0.023	-0.024	-0.024

Table 3. The topographic product at different input patterns

Patterns	25 (neurons)	64 (neurons)	100 (neurons)	144 (neurons)	169 (neurons)
1000	0.013	-0.017	-0.021	-0.024	-0.025
5000	0.0099	-0.018	-0.023	-0.024	-0.024
10000	0.007	-0.018	-0.022	-0.021	-0.023

169 is good and has no significant difference with the mapping of 144 neurons. The reason is that for the current size of the images the distance between the neurons is short enough so adding extra neurons does not give more accuracy in placement. Thus, the topographic product for 144 and 169 neurons at 5000 input patterns is the same as can be seen from the Table 2. Table 3 shows the topographic product at different neurons and at different patterns. A qualitative representation of the topographic product is given in Figure 5. The introduction of extra neurons slows down the adaptation process. Figure 6 shows a comparative diagram of the learning time of various neurons and at different number of input pattern ξ. The adaptation with the 144 neurons is faster compared to the 169, and it takes 22 seconds at 5000 patterns to adapt to the contour of the hand.

Topographic product

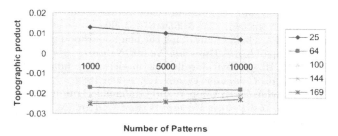

Fig. 5. Topographic product at different input patterns and at different number of neurons as a measure of the topology preservation of the network

Learning time

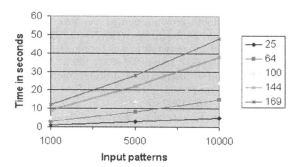

Fig. 6. Learning time for various neurons and at different input patterns

6   Conclusions

In this paper, we have used an incremental self-organising neural network (GNG) to automatically annotate landmark points on a training set of hand outlines. We have shown that the low dimensional incremental neural model (GNG) adapts successfully to the hand manifold, allowing good eigenshape models to be generated completely automatically from the training set. We have shown that these automatic models are more compact than manually landmark models as have been measured in terms of the total variance. Practically we have shown that the optimum number of neurons required to represent the contour depends mainly on the resolution of the input space and if it is not sufficient then the topology preservation is lost. In future work, the method needs to be tested to several sets of outlines since the number of neurons selected depends on the shape of the object.

References

1. H. Bauer, M. Herrman, and T. Villman. Neural maps and topographic vector quantization. *Neural Networks*, 12(4-5):659–676, 1999.
2. H.U. Bauer and K.R. Pawelzik. Quantifying the neighbourhood preservation of self-organizing feature maps. *IEEE Trans. on Neural Networks*, 3(4):570–579, 1992.
3. A. Baumberg and D. Hogg. Learning flexible models from image sequences. *3rd European Conference on Computer Vision*, 1:299–308, 1994.
4. T. F. Cootes, C. J. Taylor, D. H. Cooper, and Graham J. Training models of shape from sets of examples. *3rd British Machine Vision Conference*, pages 9–18, 1992.
5. D. Cremers, C. Schnorr, and J. Weickert. Diffusion-snakes: Introducing statistical shape knowledge into the mumford-shah functional. *International Journal of Computer Vision*, 50(3):295–313, 2002.
6. H. Rhodies Davies, J. Carole Twining, F. Tim Cootes, C. John Waterton, and J. Chris Taylor. A minimum description length approach to statistical shape modeling. *IEEE Transaction on Medical Imaging*, 21(5):525–537, 2002.
7. Anders Ericsson and Kalle Åström. Minimizing the description length using steepest descent. *In 14th British Machine Vision Conference*, 2, 2003.
8. E. Fatemizadeh, C. Lucas, and H. Soltania-Zadeh. Automatic landmark extraction from image data using modified growing neural gas network. *IEEE Transactions on Information Technology in Biomedicine*, 7(2):77–85, 2003.
9. B. Fritzke. A growing neural gas network learns topologies. *In Advances in Neural Information Processing Systems 7*, pages 625–632, 1995.
10. J. Geoffrey, F. Goodhill, and J. Terrence. A unifying measure for neighbourhood preservation in topographic mappings. *Proceedings of the 2nd Joint Symposium on Neural Computation*, 5:191–202, 1997.
11. M. Kass, A. Witkin, and D. Terzopoulos. Snakes: Active contour models. *International Journal of Computer Vision*, 4(1):321–331, 1987.
12. T. Kohonen. *Self-organising maps*. Springer Verlag, 2001.
13. T. Martinez. Competitive hebbian learning rule forms perfectly topology preserving maps. In *ICANN.*, 1993.
14. T. Martinez, H. Ritter, and K. Schulten. Three dimensional neural net for learning visuomotor-condination of a robot arm. *IEEE Transactions on Neural Networks*, 1:131–136, 1990.
15. T. Martinez and K. Schulten. Topology representing networks. *The Journal of Neural Networks*, 7(3):507–522, 1994.
16. M. Nasrabati and Y. Feng. Vector quantisation of images based upon kohonen self-organizing feature maps. In *Proc. IEEE Int. Conf. Neural Networks.*, pages 1101–1108, 1988.
17. H. Ritter and K. Schulten. Topology conserving mappings for learning motor tasks. In *Neural Networks for Computing, AIP Conf. Proc.*, 1986.
18. Hans Henrik Thodberg and Hildur Olafsdottir. Adding curvature to minimum description length shape models. *In 14th British Machine Vision Conference*, 2:251–260, 2003.

Towards Optimal Training
of Cascaded Detectors

S. Charles Brubaker, Matthew D. Mullin, and James M. Rehg

College of Computing and GVU Center,
Georgia Institute of Technology, Atlanta, GA 30332
{brubaker, mdmullin, rehg}@cc.gatech.edu

Abstract. Cascades of boosted ensembles have become popular in the object detection community following their highly successful introduction in the face detector of Viola and Jones [1]. In this paper, we explore several aspects of this architecture that have not yet received adequate attention: decision points of cascade stages, faster ensemble learning, and stronger weak hypotheses. We present a novel strategy to determine the appropriate balance between false positive and detection rates in the individual stages of the cascade based on a probablistic model of the overall cascade's performance. To improve the training time of individual stages, we explore the use of feature filtering before the application of Adaboost. Finally, we show that the use of stronger weak hypotheses based on CART can significantly improve upon the standard face detection results on the CMU-MIT data set.

1   Introduction

Object detection is one of the classic problems in computer vision, having applications to surveillance, robotics, multimedia processing, and HCI. Developing a generic object detection system is still an open problem, but there have been important successes over the past several years for some visual patterns such as faces [1], pedestrians [2], and cars [3]. Among the most influential systems is the face detector of Viola and Jones [1], which can be credited with the widespread popularity of cascaded detectors. We refer to detectors conforming to this general system architecture as cascades of boosted ensembles, or CoBEs.

The key elements of Viola and Jones' approach are:

- The cascade structure, which enables the detector to be simultaneously fast and accurate.
- The use of Adaboost [4] to combine weak hypotheses into a strong ensemble.
- Thresholding on single feature values to form weak hypotheses (threshold-based hypotheses).
- Feature selection from a large set of features, each of which might be only weakly discriminative in itself.

The large body of literature spawned by this seminal work has tended to focus on alternatives to Adaboost and on alternative feature sets, while other aspects

A. Leonardis, H. Bischof, and A. Pinz (Eds.): ECCV 2006, Part I, LNCS 3951, pp. 325–337, 2006.
© Springer-Verlag Berlin Heidelberg 2006

of the architecture have not received adequate attention. Here we focus on the false positive vs. detection trade-off in the individual stages of the cascade, faster ensemble learning, and the combination of Adaboost with CART [5] to improve detection performance.

The stages of the cascade are trained sequentially, as the output of one stage affects the training examples given to the next. Deciding when to stop training one stage and move on to the next and knowing the appropriate operating point on a stage's ROC curve are critical steps in the training of a cascade. Despite the guidelines provided in [1] and [6], however, obtaining state-of-the-art performance requires that these decisions be made by hand. We present a novel method for cascade learning, which uses a statistical model to predict the final cascade's performance and chooses the detection and false positive rates for the individual stages to meet a performance goal for the entire cascade. We show that the method is robust in the sense that a single set of parameters yields excellent performance over a variety of detection strategies and that it is capable of producing state of the art results.

One of the greatest obstacles to wider use of the CoBE architecture is that the detectors take a long time to train. We explore the use of feature filtering to reduce the feature pool available to Adaboost. Although this idea would seem to hold significant promise for speeding up the training process, we found it to be only moderately effective.

A remarkable aspect of the original Viola-Jones face detector is that it relies so heavily on Adaboost to produce the stage classifiers from such weakly discriminative individual features. We show that although this approach may be computationally efficient, combining Adaboost with CART-based weak learning can significantly improve the final detector's output.

In summary, we

- introduce a new criterion for cascade training, which provides a principled and robust mechanism for choosing stage thresholds and deciding when to stop training one stage and move onto the next,
- evaluate several feature filtering methods as ways to speed up the training process, and
- show that combining Adaboost with slightly stronger CART-based weak classifiers can improve the detector's performance over the standard practice of using threshold-based weak classifiers.

2   Previous Work

To make our discussion of previous work clear, we present a general framework for training a cascade of boosted ensembles in the LEARN-COBE procedure. The subroutines should be understood as placeholders for any number of solutions to the subproblem in question. Although not all changes made to the original Viola and Jones implementation strictly fit into this architecture, we believe it provides a useful abstraction of the CoBE approach.

*Let F be the set of features and E the set of examples. We denote the weights for E
as W. No more than L iterations of Adaboost are permitted. G refers to the goal cost
for the cascade, and $\langle \hat{f}_i, \hat{d}_i \rangle$ denotes the false positive and detection rate pair for the
ith stage.*

procedure LEARN-CoBE()

    $C \leftarrow \emptyset$ {Initialize an empty cascade.}

    for each stage i **do**

        $E \leftarrow$ BOOTSTRAP() {Acquire examples accepted by the current cascade.}

        $F' \leftarrow$ FILTER-FEATURES() {Reduce feature pool available to Adaboost.}

        $s_i \leftarrow \emptyset$ {Initialize current stage.}

        $W \leftarrow$ INITIALIZE-WEIGHTS() {Initialize example weights.}

        repeat

            $h \leftarrow$ WEAK-LEARN() {Learn a new hypothesis based on W.}

            $W \leftarrow$ REWEIGH-EXAMPLES() {Reweigh examples based on h.}

            $s_i \leftarrow s_i \cup h$ {Add the new hypothesis to the ensemble.}

            $\theta_i \leftarrow$ FIND-BEST-THRESHOLD() {Choose a threshold for the ensemble.}

            $\langle \hat{f}_i, \hat{d}_i \rangle \leftarrow$ VALIDATE() {Evaluate current ensemble on validation data.}

        until $|s_i| > L$ or PREDICT-COST() $\leq G$ {Is performance good enough?}

        $C \leftarrow C \cup \langle s_i, \theta_i \rangle$ {Add the stage to the cascade.}

    end for

Despite the critical importance of the FIND-BEST-THRESHOLD and PREDICT-COST functions to the performance of the final detector, they have received little attention. Our earlier work [7], is the only paper that addresses these questions directly in the CoBE context. In comparison, our new method of section 3.2 treats the actual cascade performance as a random variable, which is re-estimated during training stages.

Huitao Luo has recently published a method for adjusting the stage thresholds after the full cascade has been trained [8]. While the success of this method illustrates the importance of the stage thresholds for classification performance, it does not address how the thresholds should be chosen in the cascade training phase (FIND-BEST-THRESHOLD) – something that critically influences the bootstrapped data – or when it is appropriate to begin training a new stage (PREDICT-COST).

Šochman and Matas [9] use Waldboost to build a single boosted ensemble. When applying the detector to an instance, they decide whether to accept, reject, or continue evalutation after each weak hypothesis is calculated. This decision is based on an adaptation of Wald's sequential probability ratio test. Their test does not apply directly to our detectors, because each of our stage decisions is based on a new ensemble. In contrast to their method, we build an explicit probabilistic model of cascade performance based on validation data.

To improve the ensemble training time, we [10] showed how Adaboost with threshold-based weak learners can be replaced with Forward Feature Selection (FFS). Without any loss in detection performance, we were able to improve the training time of an ensemble over the original implementation of Adaboost. The key to the improved training time is that in FFS the best feature thresholds can be precomputed.

Leo Brieman once famously called Adaboost with trees "the best off-the-shelf classifier in the world" (NIPS workshop, 1996). Lienhart et al [11] explored the use of CART as a weak learner in the CoBE framework, but trees only produced moderate improvements over stumps in their experiments and did so only for low false positive rates, where the corresponding detection rate is less than 85%. In contrast, we find that CART trees result in significant improvements to the classification performance at all false positive rates. We hypothesize that this may be due in part to our strategy of adjusting both stage thresholds and post-processing when producing our ROC curves.

Much of the early research on the CoBE architecture focused on the boosting algorithm. In their 2002 paper, Viola and Jones observe that the goal of a stage in the cascade is not to minimize error, but to retain very high detection rates, while accepting modest false positive rates if necessary [6]. They propose Asymmetric Adaboost, which changes the REWEIGH-EXAMPLES routine to keep most of the weight on the positive examples (instead of treating positive and negative examples equally), ensuring that a high percentage is detected by each weak classifier. The problem of asymmetric learning is also addressed in [12], which introduces the Linear Asymmetric Classifier algorithm, a method to re-weigh hypotheses after they have been selected by other means.

Li and Zhang have applied another alternative boosting algorithm to face detection in their paper on FloatBoost [13], which instead of greedily adding hypotheses to the ensemble allows backtracking to eliminate the less useful or even hurtful hypotheses. In other respects, the algorithm proceeds as RealBoost.

Liu and Shum [14] found that using KL-boost combined with weak classifiers based on histograms of 1D projections in feature space improved detection performance over the original approach. However, it is not clear whether it is the changes to the weighing scheme or the means of forming the weak hypotheses that is critical to the improvement.

A more radical departure from the LEARN-COBE routine is due to Xiao et al [15]. Inspired by the observation that the operating point of a stage may not minimize error, they allow the hypothesis formed by the minimum error threshold of the previous stage to play the role of a weak hypothesis in the next stage of the cascade. Having thus produced a cascaded detector, they convert it to a single weighted voting scheme and train an SVM to relearn the confidence (vote) weights.

Others have changed the feature set while keeping the other key aspects of the CoBE architecture[11, 16]. A more detailed description of our work can be found in our technical report [17]. For a more comprehensive survey of face detection see [18].

3   Cascade Learning

Two of the most important decisions in building a cascade of boosted ensembles are:

1. When to stop training a stage and move on to the next one.
2. How to balance the detection versus false positive trade-off within a stage.

In terms of our LEARN-COBE algorithm, these decisions are determined by the function FIND-BEST-THRESHOLD, which chooses θ_i, fixing the stage's operating point, and by the function PREDICT-COST which determines when to move on to the next stage of the cascade.

3.1 Fixed Stage Goal

The standard approach outlined in [1, 6] is to choose a goal operating point $\langle F_g, D_g \rangle$ (a false positive and detection rate pair) and then take its Lth root to obtain $\langle f_g, d_g \rangle$, where L is the intended number of stages in the cascade. Each stage is constrained to achieve one of f_g or d_g (typically f_g works better) on a set of validation examples that have been accepted by all previous stages of the cascade. The training of the stage terminates when either the other goal criterion is achieved or the maximum number of boosting iterations is exceeded.

This goal-based strategy leaves something to be desired, however. First, it rigidly fixes the number of stages in the cascade before any training is done. Second, it does not permit any trade-off between the detection and false positive rates within the stages. For instance, when selecting the threshold of a stage, one might be able to significantly improve the false positive rate at a small expense to the detection rate, improving the chances of meeting the goal criteria. The extra leeway on the false positive criterion might also be used at a later stage to improve a stage's detection at the expense of the false positive rate. By fixing one element of the operating point, this strategy precludes taking advantage of such trade-offs.

3.2 Cascade Learning with Beta Variables

A key element of our approach is that the algorithm views the performance of the cascade $\langle F, D \rangle$ as a random variable and treats the empirical results on validation data for the individual stages, $\{\hat{f}_i\}$ and $\{\hat{d}_i\}$, as evidence. A statistical model estimates the distribution of full cascade operating points, and each stage is trained to use the minimum number of features that ensure that the probability of meeting the performance goals is sufficiently high.

The key assumption underlying the statistical model is that the results on the validation data for the current stage can be repeated at all subsequent stages. That is, for any $\langle \hat{f}_i, \hat{d}_i \rangle$ pair obtained by varying θ_i, it is possible to train the $(i + 1)$th stage and choose θ_{i+1} such $\langle \hat{f}_{i+1}, \hat{d}_{i+1} \rangle = \langle \hat{f}_i, \hat{d}_i \rangle$. We call this the "repeatability assumption". It is important to note that a similar assumption is implied in the fixed stage goal framework, where it is assumed that a particular operating point will be achieved in each stage. Although, the repeatability assumption is not strictly true in practice, it provides a guiding principle for applying our statistical model during training. The advantage of this model is that it affords a principled and practical way to make detection and false positive rate trade-offs in the individual stages.

The inputs to our new method are:

1. A goal operating point for the entire cascade $\langle F_g, D_g \rangle$.
2. A ratio η that reflects the relative importance of the false positive and detection criteria.
3. A maximum number of stages L.

The cascade learner then builds the fastest detector it can while achieving the goal performance with high probability.

Cost Function. Because a reasonable goal might not be known a priori, the algorithm must be robust to unattainable goals and produce results that are as close as possible. Depending on the attainability of the goal, therefore, we adjust our cost function. For simplicity, assume that $\eta > 1.0$, meaning that the false positive criterion is more important. We consider the following cases

1. If $\Pr[D < D_g] < \gamma$ and $\Pr[F > F_g] < \gamma$,
$$\text{cost} = \Pr[D < D_g] + \eta \Pr[F > F_g].$$
2. Else, if $\Pr[F > F_g] < \gamma$, then cost $= 2 + \eta - D$.
3. Otherwise, cost $= 2 + \eta + F$.

The first cost function is suitable when both goals are attainable with some substantial probability γ (0.95 was used our experiments). However, when this is not possible, then the function provides no incentive to trade a small decrease in the false positive rate for a large improvement in the detection rate (an analogous statement holds if $\eta < 1.0$, giving detection greater importance). Therefore, if both criteria cannot be met with probability γ, then we constrain the false positive rate to be met with probability γ and maximize the detection rate. Finally, if the criterion for false positive rate cannot be met with probability γ, we simply minimize the false positive rate. Typically, this means that the false positive rate is reduced to zero, effectively terminating the training process.

Cost Prediction. Minimizing this cost function requires the ability to compute $\Pr[D > D_g]$ and $\Pr[F < F_g]$. We will only treat the detection criterion, because the false positive one is analogous. Consider the likelihood $\Pr[\hat{d}_i | d_i]$, where $\hat{d}_i$ is the measured detection rate over M positive examples. Given the true detection rate d_i, the probability of m out of M examples being detected is just the binomial distribution
$$\binom{M}{m} (1 - d_i)^{M-m} d_i^m.$$
Taking a uniform prior $\Pr[d_i]$ over $[0, 1]$ and applying Bayes rule gives
$$\Pr[d_i | m, M] = \frac{\Pr[m | d_i, M] \Pr[d_i]}{\int_0^1 \Pr[m | p, M] \Pr[p] dp}$$
$$= \frac{(1 - d_i)^{M-m} d_i^m}{\int_0^1 (1 - p)^{M-m} p^m dp},$$
which is precisely the beta distribution with parameters $m + 1$ and $M - m + 1$.

Assume that the cascade has already been trained through stage i and that we are predicting the cost if the measured operating point of the next stage is $\langle \hat{f}_{i+1}, \hat{d}_{i+1} \rangle$.

PREDICT-COST-SAMPLE *maintains a set of sampled operating points for the currently trained cascade $\{\langle F_i^k, D_i^k \rangle\}_{k=1}^{K}$. All measurements are made with validation sets of M negative examples and the same number of positive examples.*

procedure PREDICT-COST-SAMPLE()
    for $j = i + 1$ to N **do**
        for $k = 1$ to K **do**
            $F_j^k \leftarrow F_{j-1}^k \cdot \beta_{\hat{f}_i}$, where $\beta_{\hat{f}_i}$ is a random beta deviate with parameters $\hat{f}_i M + 1$
            and $(1 - \hat{f}_i)M + 1$.
            $D_j^k \leftarrow D_{j-1}^k \cdot \beta_{\hat{d}_i}$, where $\beta_{\hat{d}_i}$ is a random beta deviate with parameters $\hat{d}_i M + 1$
            and $(1 - \hat{d}_i)M + 1$.
        end for
        $G_f \leftarrow |\{k : F_j^k > F_g\}|/M$
        $G_d \leftarrow |\{k : D_j^k < D_g\}|/M$
        $\text{cost}_j \leftarrow \text{COST}(G_f, G_d)$.
    end for
    return $\min_j \text{cost}_j$.

Therefore, conditioned on the validation measurements, D is the product of beta variables. The exact distribution only admits a clean analytic form in a few specialized cases [19], but it can easily be approximated. One strategy is to sample from the distribution for D by taking a sample from the distribution d_i for each stage and taking their product. The quantity $\Pr[D > D_g]$ can be estimated by counting the fraction of samples greater than D_g. This method is used in the PREDICT-COST-SAMPLE procedure. A final set of samples for a fully trained cascade is shown in Fig. 1.

Given the ability to estimate the cost for a (partially) trained cascade, we now describe its use in stage training. It is here that we apply the repeatability assumption; i.e., if we can achieve $\langle \hat{f}_i, \hat{d}_i \rangle$ on a validation set for the current stage, then we assume that we can achieve the same result for all subsequent stages. Therefore, as we are training the ith stage, we use the results on the validation set to estimate $\langle \hat{f}_j, \hat{d}_j \rangle$ for all previous stages ($j < i$), but we use the results for the ith stage on validation data for any subsequent stages ($j > i$). The operating point having the lowest cost according to this estimate is chosen for each stage, as shown in the FIND-BEST-THRESHOLD procedure.

3.3   Discussion

The main advantage of our new approach over the fixed stage goal approach is that it allows subtle tradeoffs between detection and false positive rates in the stages. Moreover, it can "remember" past trade-offs to help decide whether a new trade-off will improve the chances of achieving the cascade's goal operating point. Note that though we specify a maximum number of stages, we do not

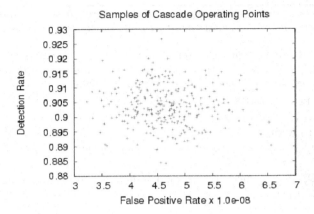

Fig. 1. Samples generated by PREDICT-COST-SAMPLE of the operating point for a fully trained twenty-stage cascade. The accumulation of error is significant even though a validation set of 1000 examples was used for both the positive and negative classes.

specify a minimum. If the learner predicts better performance with fewer stages, then it will plan for fewer stages.

As shown in Fig. 1, the variances in the distributions of F and D are significant for a twenty-stage cascade, even when one thousand examples are used at every stage. It is possible to account for this effect in the fixed stage goal approach simply by setting more ambitious goals than are necessary, so that even if the validation results are too optimistic, the desired performance may nevertheless be achieved. If forty stages are used instead of twenty, however, then the additional accumulation of error will change the distribution, and a new set of more ambitious goals may be required. Because we explicitly model the accumulation of errors, no such parameter retuning is necessary in our approach, making it well-suited for comparative studies.

To demonstrate the effectiveness and robustness of our improved cascade learning algorithm, we have conducted a set of experiments in which we automatically trained 35 detectors using a single set of parameters. This set of experiments ranges from a cascade using four level deep CART trees that achieves state of the art performance (see Sect. 5) to a cascade where the feature pool was reduced to 200 randomly selected features (see Sect. 4). Results for all of our experiments can be found in [17].[1]

4   Feature Selection

The primary computational cost in training the stage classifiers is that in every round of boosting the WEAK-LEARN routine examines every example for every

---

[1] Complete results and code are also available at http://www.cc.gatech.edu/cpl/cobe.

feature. Since reducing the example corpus weakens the generalization, the alternative of reducing the feature pool via the FILTER-FEATURES routine is an attractive option.

To actually improve the training time, however, the filtering algorithm itself must be faster than Adaboost. Unfortunately, few filtering algorithms offer an asymptotic improvement in training time. Nevertheless, asymptotically equivalent methods often admit implementation speed-ups, which make the actual run-time faster than the worst-case analysis time would indicate. Moreover, because Adaboost's greedy selection of features is not optimal, limiting the feature pool available to Adaboost may actually improve the results. The idea is that Adaboost may produce a better classifier when it is presented with a small set of features, all of which are good, rather than a large set containing these same good features in addition to many spurious ones.

For purposes of this discussion, therefore, we divide filtering techniques into two broad categories:

Fast Filters: This category consists primarily of ranking schemes which examine each feature once and sort according to some measure of the feature's discriminative power. These filters are typically much faster than Adaboost and run in $O(|F| \log |F|)$ time. From this category, we test random selection and ranking by mutual information. For the latter, we choose a feature threshold that maximizes the mutual information between the resulting binarized feature and the class label, and then select the features that have the most mutual information with the class label as individual features.

Slow Filters: This category includes methods that examine each feature in F before choosing the next feature to add to the selected pool F'. These filters run in $O(|F'||F||E|)$ time and are about as fast as Adaboost with a thresholding weak learner. From this category, we use the Conditional Mutual Information Maximization method of [20, 21] and Forward Feature Selection [10].

Notice that the running times given above assume that the examples have been sorted by their feature value for every feature in a precomputation step.[2] With this strategy, the evaluation of a feature, either for selection or for use in a weak classifier, can be performed in $O(|E|)$ time, where E is the set of examples. It is also important to realize that although these filtering methods sometimes choose a threshold value for the feature during the selection, the original feature values are retained for the boosting or ensemble learning phase of the training process.

In this context, our hope would be that filters from the first category would improve the training time significantly without diminishing the quality of the results and that filters from the second category would improve the quality of the results and offer a modest improvement in training time.

---

[2] This pre-sorting strategy has been previously noted in [22] and is explained in more detail in [23] and [17].

4.1   Analysis

We evaluate these methods by training a full cascade using the learning algorithm of Sect. 3.2 with a fixed set of parameters. To evaluate the classification performance, we apply the detector to the CMU-MIT data set and average the detection rate over a range of 0-130 false positives.[3] This roughly corresponds to the area under curve measure used for traditional ROC curves.

Fast Filters. Each of the fast methods was used to reduce the feature pool by 90% and 99% during the training of several detectors. As shown in table 1, in both cases random selection (RND) gives comparable performance to the ranking method (RANK). At first, this may seem counter-intuitive. The ranking method does, after all, include the most discriminative features. How can a random selection of features produce detectors that perform just as well or better? The answer is the well known redundancy problem [24]. The "best" features tend to misclassify the same examples, making it difficult for Adaboost to learn an ensemble of hypotheses that classifies these examples correctly. We discuss this phenomenon in greater detail in [17].

Table 1. Feature filtering results grouped by the number of features made available to the weak learner (Final Pool). Notice that the random filtering outperforms the ranking filter. Although CMIM and FFS are better than random filtering, they do not outperform the inherent feature selection strategy of Adaboost.

Filter	Initial Pool	Final Pool	Avg. Detection rate for [0-130] False Positives on CMU-MIT
RND	134736	13473	0.889
RANK	134736	13473	0.872
RND	134736	1347	0.874
RANK	134736	1347	0.834
RND	13473	200	0.829
CMIM	13473	200	0.870
FFS	13473	200	0.860

Slow Filters. To assess the asymptotically slower methods, Conditional Mutual Information Maximization (CMIM) and Forward Feature Selection (FFS), we first randomly selected 10% of the features and then used the methods to filter down to 200 features. For a baseline comparison we also trained a detector with 200 randomly selected features. Both the FFS and CMIM cascades produce ROC curves comparable to the one produced by a random 10% selection of features. That is, the detectors perform as well as they would if no filtering had been applied at all. Thus, although these methods offer a modest (factors of 2 or 3) improvement in training time, they do not outperform the greedy selection naturally employed by Adaboost.

---

[3] This upper bound of 130 false positives represents an average of one false positive per image.

5   Weak Learning

Although thresholding on a single feature has been the dominant practice in CoBEs for object detection, Adaboost does not restrict how the weak learning takes place. The thresholding strategy may be efficient in terms of training or execution time, but it seems doubtful that such a simple weak learner would give the best results. We therefore explore the use of CART-based weak hypotheses, which we found to significantly improve the cascade performance.

Our experiments show that CART-based detectors offer improved detection rates with only small drops in speed. The ROC curve of Fig. 2 shows the improvement coming from using CART trees of depth 2, 4, and 6, as opposed to stumps (i.e. threshold-based hypotheses) when discrete Adaboost is used. A more comprehensive set of results for RealBoost and GentleBoost can be found in [17]. These results are consistent with our findings for discrete Adaboost.

Table 2 gives a comparison to several other published cascade training methods. While a comprehensive comparison would include testing speed as well as classification performance, these numbers suggest that the current method produces results which are comparable to published work that is based on substantial mod-

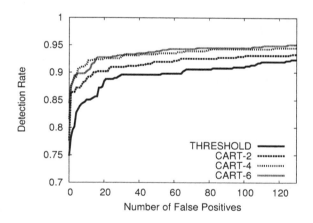

Fig. 2. CART depths up to 4 significantly and consistently improve performance

Table 2. A comparison of detection rates on the CMU-MIT data set for several standard detectors

Detector	False Positives							
	6	10	31	46	50	65	78	95
Viola-Jones [1]	–	0.761	0.884	–	0.914	0.920	0.921	0.929
Viola-Jones [1] (voting)	–	0.811	0.897	–	0.921	0.931	0.931	0.932
Luo [8]	0.866	0.874	0.903	–	0.911	–	–	–
Li-Zhang [13]	–	0.836	0.902	–	–	–	–	–
Schneiderman [25]	0.897	–	–	0.957	–	–	–	–
CART-4 w/ Realboost	0.891	0.905	0.931	0.935	0.935	0.943	0.948	0.951

ifications to the basic Adaboost learning method. Our results show that the basic method can yield excellent performance if stronger weak hypotheses are employed. Moreover these results can be obtained without hand-tweaking cascade parameters during training, as a consequence of our automatic global training method. Promising directions for future studies include an evaluation of these methods from the standpoint of testing speed and the use of our global training method of Sect. 3.2 in conjunction with previously-published stage learning algorithms.

6   Conclusion

We have described a novel algorithm for fully-automatic cascade training based on a probabilistic prediction of cascade performance. This method can take advantage of favorable trade-offs of detection and false positive rates for the individual stage and removes much of the guess-work associated with training cascades of boosted ensembles in the past. Because it takes into account the accumulation of error in the estimates of the overall cascade performance, it is well-suited for controlled experiments comparing cascaded detectors which are trained using a wide variety of stage learning algorithms.

A major barrier to the wider use of cascades of boosted ensembles is that they take a long time to train. We explore feature filters which can produce a moderate speed-up by reducing the set of features available to the ensemble learner.

Finally, we show that although thresholding on single features to form weak hypotheses may reduce training time and produce a faster detector, combining Adaboost with CART-based weak learning can significantly improve the detector's performance.

Acknowledgements

This material is based upon work which was supported in part by the National Science Foundation under NSF Award IIS-0133779.

References

1. Viola, P., Jones, M.J.: Robust real-time face detection. Int. J. Comput. Vision **57**(2) (2004) 137–154
2. Viola, P.A., Jones, M.J., Snow, D.: Detecting pedestrians using patterns of motion and appearance. In: Proc. ICCV. Volume 2. (2003) 734–741
3. Schneiderman, H., Kanade, T.: Object detection using the statistics of parts. Int. J. Comput. Vision **56**(3) (2004) 151–177
4. Freund, Y., Schapire, R.E.: A decision-theoretic generalization of on-line learning and an application to boosting. J. Comput. Syst. Sci. **55**(1) (1997) 119–139
5. Breiman, L., Friedman, J., Olshen, R., Stone, C.: Classification and Regression Trees. Wadsworth and Brooks, Monterey, CA (1984)
6. Viola, P., Jones, M.: Fast and robust classification using asymmetric AdaBoost and a detector cascade. In: NIPS 14. (2002) 1311–1318

7. Sun, J., Rehg, J.M., Bobick, A.F.: Automatic cascade training with perturbation bias. In: CVPR (2). (2004) 276–283
8. Luo, H.: Optimization design of cascaded classifiers. In: CVPR (1). (2005) 480–485
9. Sochman, J., Matas, J.: Waldboost-learning for time constrained sequential detection. In: CVPR (2). (2005) 150–157
10. Wu, J., Rehg, J.M., Mullin, M.D.: Learning a rare event detection cascade by direct feature selection. In: NIPS 16. (2004) 1523–1530
11. Lienhart, R., Kuranov, A., Pisarevsky, V.: Empirical analysis of detection cascades of boosted classifiers for rapid object detection. In: Pattern Recognition LNCS 2781. (2003) 297–304
12. Wu, J., Mullin, M., Rehg, J.: Linear asymmetric classifier for cascade detectors. In: Proc. 22nd International Conference on Machine Learning. (2005) 993–1000
13. Li, S.Z., Zhang, Z.Q.: Floatboost learning and statistical face detection. IEEE Trans. on PAMI **26**(9) (2004) 1112–1123
14. Liu, C., Shum, H.Y.: Kullback-leibler boosting. In: CVPR (1). (2003) 587–594
15. Xiao, R., Zhu, L., Zhang, H.J.: Boosting chain learning for object detection. In: Proc. ICCV. Volume 1. (2003) 709–715
16. Levi, K., Weiss, Y.: Learning object detection from a small number of examples: The importance of good features. In: CVPR (2). (2004) 53–60
17. Brubaker, S.C., Wu, J., Sun, J., Mullin, M.D., Rehg, J.M.: On the design of cascades of boosted ensembles for face detection. Technical Report GIT-GVU-05-28, Georgia Institute of Technology (2005)
18. Yang, M.H., Kriegman, D.J., Ahuja, N.: Detecting faces in images: A survey. IEEE Trans. on PAMI **24**(1) (2002) 34–58
19. Gupta, A.K., Nadarajah, S., eds.: Handbook of Beta Distribution and its applications. Marcel Dekker, Inc. (2004)
20. Vidal-Naquet, M., Ullman, S.: Object recognition with informative features and linear classification. In: Proc. ICCV. (2003) 281–288
21. Fleuret, F.: Fast binary feature selection with conditional mutual information. Journal of Machine Learning Research **5** (2004) 1531–1555
22. Opelt, A., Fussenegger, M., Pinz, A., Auer, P.: Weak hypotheses and boosting for generic object detection and recognition. In: ECCV (2). (2004) 71–84
23. Grossmann, E., Kale, A., Jaynes, C.: Towards interactive generation of "ground-truth" in background subtraction from partially labeled examples. In: Proc. ICCV VS-PETS workshop. (2005)
24. Guyon, I., Elisseeff, A.: An introduction to variable and feature selection. Journal of Machine Learning Research **3** (2003) 1157–1182
25. Schneiderman, H.: Feature-centric evaluation for efficient cascaded object detection. In: CVPR (2). (2004) 29–36

Learning and Incorporating Top-Down Cues in Image Segmentation

Xuming He, Richard S. Zemel, and Debajyoti Ray

Department of Computer Science, University of Toronto
{hexm, zemel, debray}@cs.toronto.edu

Abstract. Bottom-up approaches, which rely mainly on continuity principles, are often insufficient to form accurate segments in natural images. In order to improve performance, recent methods have begun to incorporate top-down cues, or object information, into segmentation. In this paper, we propose an approach to utilizing category-based information in segmentation, through a formulation as an image labelling problem. Our approach exploits bottom-up image cues to create an over-segmented representation of an image. The segments are then merged by assigning labels that correspond to the object category. The model is trained on a database of images, and is designed to be modular: it learns a number of image contexts, which simplify training and extend the range of object classes and image database size that the system can handle. The learning method estimates model parameters by maximizing a lower bound of the data likelihood. We examine performance on three real-world image databases, and compare our system to a standard classifier and other conditional random field approaches, as well as a bottom-up segmentation method.

1 Introduction

Shortcomings in the standard bottom-up approach to image segmentation, together with evidence from studies of human vision [1], suggest that prior knowledge about objects facilitates segmentation. Incorporating top-down information faces several challenges: (1) the appearance of objects in a class varies greatly in natural images; (2) shape also varies considerably, and is often corrupted by occlusion; (3) if the number of classes is large, local features may be insufficient to discriminate the class. The images in Figure 1 illustrate some of these difficulties.

In this paper we describe a segmentation scheme that integrates bottom-up cues with information about multiple object categories. Bottom-up cues are used to produce an over-segmentation that is assumed to be consistent with object boundaries but breaks large objects into small pieces. The problem then becomes how to group those segments into larger regions. We propose to use the top-down category-based information to help merge those segments into object components. We define this merging problem as an *image labelling* problem: the aim is to assign labels to the segments so that the segments belonging to the same object category have the same labels. The labels are assigned jointly to an image, taking into account interactions between segments.

A. Leonardis, H. Bischof, and A. Pinz (Eds.): ECCV 2006, Part I, LNCS 3951, pp. 338–351, 2006.
© Springer-Verlag Berlin Heidelberg 2006

Fig. 1. Lighting and background effects create highly variable appearances of objects. The animal shapes also vary considerably, due to viewpoint changes, articulation, and occlusion, as shown in the hippo images. Discriminating classes based on local cues is often hard, as can be seen by comparing local patches of the two images.

We adopt a learning approach to this labelling problem, learning the statistics of the correspondence between image features and labels, as well as the interactions between labels. We further decompose the problem by assigning images to contexts, and again use learning to define the contexts, and to find features that characterize the contexts. The resulting system produces a detailed segmentation of a test image into coherent regions, with a semantic label associated with each region in the image. The key contribution of this work is a modular, adaptive segmentation method that holds the potential for scaling up to large image databases and large numbers of object categories.

The rest of the paper is organized as follows. In Section 2 we describe related schemes for extending bottom-up cues for image segmentation to include top-down information. We then focus on the new combined approach in Section 3. Section 4 describes the learning and labeling algorithms. We compare our model with other approaches in Section 5.

2   Related Work

The primary methodological paradigm we employ is a discriminative learning approach, developed on a database of labeled images. A number of discriminative learning approaches have been developed utilizing labeled images for segmentation and related tasks. For example, conditional random field methods, originally defined for jointly labeling one-dimensional structures such as the parts-of-speech in a text string [2], have been extended to deal with two-dimensional images (e.g., [3]). In the domain of segmentation, Ren and Malik [4] propose a classification model using a number of low- and mid-level cues to define features of proposed segments, and training a classifier to discriminate good segments (based on human segmented natural images) from random ones. Our work aims to extend discriminative approaches to consider information about many different object classes.

Several recent segmentation approaches combine top-down knowledge with bottom-up information. These methods have generally focused on the figure-ground task, attempting to precisely delineate the boundaries of a single object in an image. One approach utilizes a deformable template to determine the boundary suggested by bottom-up cues [5], while another represents object knowledge as pairs of image fragments and their figure-ground labeling from a training set, and then segments a test image by covering it with a set of fragments whose appearances match the data and whose labeling is locally compatible [6]. These methods are highly class specific, working for a particular object type. A recent method extends the patch-based object knowledge to work with a wider variety of objects [7]. The approach proposed in this paper can be seen as attempting to incorporate more category-level rather than class-specific knowledge; the emphasis is on grouping image pixels into various categories across the whole image rather than a precise specification of a single figure-ground boundary.

The core of our approach is an image labelling method, in which the objective is formulated as classifying all pixels of an image using some vocabulary of labels. Recent related methods employ class-specific detectors, and jointly make use of information across objects to form a parse tree of an image [8], or to simultaneously detect multiple objects from a common context [9]. Methods that utilize image caption information to learn associations between image features and keywords are also relevant [10]. The training information provided by captions is considerably weaker than the labeled pixels we utilize; one would expect this to lead to less precision in the test image labels. Finally, the discriminative multi-class learning method proposed in [11], which we compare to our method below, utilizes a similar objective and training information. Their approach involved numerous rounds of stochastic sampling for each training image, and required the labeling to apply to individual pixels. The learning method proposed here is considerably simpler, and operates at a higher level than individual pixels, lending it the potential of scaling up to larger object databases and images.

3   Model Architecture

3.1   Super-Pixel Representation of Images

The segmentation process requires that an image is labelled at a pixel level so that the segments fully cover the image. However, a label algorithm operating at the pixel level will typically be highly redundant, due to the similarity between neighboring pixels within each object category. A pixel level model will also be

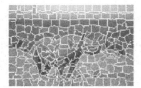

Fig. 2. An original image with 120x180 pixels becomes a 300 super-pixel image, where each contiguous region with a delineated boundary is a super-pixel

sensitive to, and limited by the resolution of an image. Instead, we build our model based on a higher level image representation than the pixel image, in which a small patch of similar pixels are grouped together to form a larger unit, a *super-pixel* [4]. Segmentation methods based on the bottom-up image cues can be utilized to generate such an image representation by over-segmenting the image into small but coherent regions. When the regions are small enough, their boundaries are usually consistent with the boundaries between object categories, and the potential error induced by such a decomposition will be relatively small. In this paper, we use a variant of the Normalized Cut segmentation algorithm [12], with a specific parameter setting to generate an over-segmentation of an image into super-pixels of a roughly consistent size, and build our approach on this superpixel representation.

The super-pixelization of an image can be viewed as a part of the bottom-up process in our system, while the labelling model discussed in the next section uses both top-down information and image cues to merge those super-pixels into segments with semantic meanings. Figure 2 shows an instance of super-pixel representation of image. Note that even if the size of a super-pixel is small, we significantly reduce the number of units to be labelled, which allows a compact model to be constructed without much sensitivity to the resolution of the image.

We also extract image features from the pixels grouped into super-pixels, providing a better description of input images for labelling. The resulting *image descriptor* of each super-pixel summarizes the statistics of the contained region with respect to features such as texture, edges, and color.

3.2   A Mixture of Conditional Random Fields

Our probabilistic model assigns labels to the super-pixels for a given input image by combining top-down category-based information with image cues. First, we introduce some notation. Let $\mathbf{X} = \{\mathbf{x}_i\}_{i \in S}$ be the input image, where S is a set of sites associated with the super-pixels and $\mathbf{x}_i$ is the image descriptor from the ith super-pixel. Each super-pixel $\mathbf{x}_i$ will be assigned a label $\mathbf{l}_i$ from a finite label set $\mathcal{L}$. The set of label variables $\{\mathbf{l}_i\}_{i \in S}$ for image $\mathbf{X}$ form a structural output $\mathbf{L}$.

We further decompose the labelling problem by assigning each image to a particular *context*; several recent approaches have demonstrated that the statistics of an image can be used to categorize the scene context (e.g., [13]). Suppose the images in a database can be grouped into several contexts. We denote the context set for the images in a database as $\mathcal{C}$, and c as the context variable for input image $\mathbf{X}$. Our model defines a conditional distribution over the output $\mathbf{L}$ given input $\mathbf{X}$:

$$P(\mathbf{L}|\mathbf{X}) = \sum_{c \in \mathcal{C}} P_M(\mathbf{L}|\mathbf{X}, c) P_G(c|\mathbf{X}) \tag{1}$$

where $P_M(\mathbf{L}|\mathbf{X}, c)$ is a conditional random field (CRF) for the context c, and $P_G(c|\mathbf{X})$ is a gating function which yields the probability distribution of context given the information from image $\mathbf{X}$. We refer to the model in Eqn. 1 as a Mixture of Conditional Random Fields (MoCRF). With CRFs as its mixture components, this model can be viewed as an extension of a mixture of experts model [14] by predicting a structural output from data. Below we describe the component CRF models in detail, followed by the gating function.

3.3   Context-Dependent Conditional Random Field

Given a context, the model captures the interactions between the labels of an image using a conditional random field of the labels $P_M(\mathbf{L}|\mathbf{X}, c)$. The random field is defined with respect to a graph G in which the label sites of neighboring super-pixels on the image plane are connected. We denote the neighbors of site i as $N(i)$.

The context-dependent CRF has three types of feature functions in its distribution, encoding the top-down contextual constraint of the labelling at three levels:

$$P_M(\mathbf{L}|\mathbf{X}, c) = \frac{1}{Z_c} \exp\{\sum_i f_a(\mathbf{l}_i, \mathbf{x}_i, c) + \sum_i \sum_{j \in N(i)} f_b(\mathbf{l}_i, \mathbf{l}_j, c) + f_c(\mathbf{L}, c)\}, \quad (2)$$

where $f_a(\mathbf{l}_i, \mathbf{x}_i, c)$ is a feature function describing the compatibility of the local image descriptor $\mathbf{x}_i$ at super-pixel i to a particular label variable $\mathbf{l}_i$; $f_b(\mathbf{l}_i, \mathbf{l}_j, c)$ accounts for pairwise interactions between labels of neighboring sites; and $f_c(\mathbf{L}, c)$ is a feature function for the global statistics of the label field $\mathbf{L}$ under context c. In our model, we implement those feature functions as follows:

(a) Local features $f_a(\mathbf{l}_i, \mathbf{x}_i, c)$**.** We utilize a classifier that independently predicts the label of every super-pixel to build the local feature function. The classifier provides a label distribution $\Phi_I(\mathbf{l}_i|\mathbf{x}_i, c)$ given input $\mathbf{x}_i$ and context c. The local feature $f_a(\mathbf{l}_i, \mathbf{x}_i, c)$ has the following form:

$$f_a(\mathbf{l}_i, \mathbf{x}_i, c, \gamma^c) = \alpha^c \sum_{k \in \mathcal{L}} \delta(\mathbf{l}_i = k) \log \Phi_I(\mathbf{l}_i = k|\mathbf{x}_i, c, \gamma^c), \quad (3)$$

where $\delta(x) = 1$ if x is true and 0 otherwise, α^c is a coefficient for modulating the entropy of the classifier output for context c, and γ^c represents the classifier parameters. The feature function describes the preference of different label configurations given the input. In this paper, we use a multilayer perceptron (MLP) as the classifier which takes color, edge magnitude and texture information from the ith super-pixel's descriptor as the input. Note that these feature functions may be able to find local image features that uniquely characterize a particular class, such as the combination of color, texture, and edges in a rhino's horn.

(b) Pairwise features $f_b(\mathbf{l}_i, \mathbf{l}_j, c)$**.** The pairwise feature functions exploit the local interactions between labels of neighboring super-pixels. We use a pairwise feature with a linear form in this model:

$$f_b(\mathbf{l}_i, \mathbf{l}_j, c) = \sum_{k \in \mathcal{L}} \sum_{k' \in \mathcal{L}} \delta(\mathbf{l}_i = k) \delta(\mathbf{l}_j = k') \log \Psi_{ij}^c(k, k'), \quad (4)$$

where Ψ_{ij}^c is a $|\mathcal{L}| \times |\mathcal{L}|$ compatibility matrix between label $\mathbf{l}_i$ and $\mathbf{l}_j$. The compatibility matrix incorporates both the statistics of neighboring label configurations and image descriptor information; it is defined as follows:

$$\Psi_{ij}^c(k,k') = \begin{cases} (1 - P_{ij}^b)\exp(\theta_{k,k'}^c) & k = k' \\ P_{ij}^b \exp(\theta_{k,k'}^c) & k \neq k' \end{cases} \tag{5}$$

where $\theta_{k,k'}^c$ is a scalar parameter for the compatibility of label values k, k' in context c. This formulation incorporates boundary information provided by a separate boundary classifier [15]: P_{ij}^b is the boundary probability between super-pixel i and j, which modulates the label pair compatibility, implementing the intuitive notion that the compatibility of labels of neighboring sites depends on the presence of a boundary between them. For example, one would expect that the likelihood of neighboring labels taking on the same value would decrease if there is a boundary between them, while the compatibility of taking on different values would decrease if no boundary exists. Therefore, $f_b(l_i, l_j, c)$ can be viewed as a data-dependent feature function specifying the regional context of labels.

(c) Global features $f_c(\mathbf{L}, c)$. The global feature function provide a coarse level constraint for the label configuration of the random field. In our model, the global features constrain the overall image label distribution to conform to a typical, average label distribution that characterizes the relative proportion of the various labels in a specific context. Assuming this average label distribution is $\mu^c = (\mu_1^c, ..., \mu_{|\mathcal{L}|}^c)$ for a given context c, we define a global feature that maximizes the match between the actual label distribution and the distribution μ^c:

$$f_c(\mathbf{L}, c) = \beta^c \sum_i \sum_{k \in \mathcal{L}} \delta(l_i = k) \log \mu_k^c, \tag{6}$$

where β^c is the weighting coefficient. This feature function is equivalent to the negative Kullback-Leibler divergence between the image label distribution and the target distribution for the given context. Note that this feature provides a global bias to the single node potential in the conditional random field.

3.4   Gating Function $P_G(c|\mathbf{X})$

The gating function is specified by a context classifier which generates a distribution of context c given an input image. The inputs to the classifier are the aggregate statistics of the image descriptors, including color, edge density and texture information. We use a multilayer perceptron as the context classifier in this model.

3.5   Model Summary

To summarize, our model has the following form:

$$P(\mathbf{L}|\mathbf{X}) = \sum_c \frac{P_G(c|\mathbf{X})}{Z_c} \exp\{\sum_{i,j} \mathbf{l}_i^T \log \Psi_{ij}^c \mathbf{l}_j + \alpha^c \sum_i \mathbf{l}_i^T \log \Phi_I + \beta^c \sum_i \mathbf{l}_i^T \log \mu^c\} \tag{7}$$

where the label variable $\mathbf{l}_i$ is represented as a vector with $|\mathcal{L}|$ elements, in which the kth element is 1 and the other elements are 0 when $\mathbf{l}_i = k$. Figure 3 provides

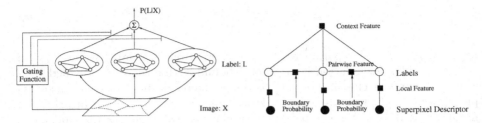

Fig. 3. Graphical model representation. **Left:** The superpixel descriptors are input to context-specific processing, with the gating function modulating the relevance of each context to a given image. **Right:** The context-specific processing combines local information based on super-pixel descriptor and specific label compatibility; pairwise interactions between labels of neighboring sites, modulated by the boundary probability; and global bias provided by the context-specific average label distribution.

an overview of the main components of the model. Note that the final label distribution can readily be used to define a segmentation of the image into coherent regions, where a segment corresponds to each contiguous group of pixels that are assigned the same label.

4   Image Labeling and Parameter Estimation

4.1   Inference and Learning Criterion

Given a new image $\mathbf{X}$, we predict its labelling based on the Maximum Posterior Marginals (MPM) criterion:

$$\mathbf{l}_i^* = \arg\max_{\mathbf{l}_i \in \mathcal{L}} \sum_{c \in \mathcal{C}} P_M(\mathbf{l}_i | \mathbf{X}, c) P_G(c | \mathbf{X}), \tag{8}$$

where the marginal label distributions of each super-pixel, $P_M(\mathbf{l}_i | \mathbf{X}, c)$, are computed by applying loopy belief propagation to every context-dependent CRF.

Given a set of labeled image data $\mathcal{X} = \{(\mathbf{L}^n, \mathbf{X}^n)\}$, we estimate the model's parameters based on the Conditional Maximum Likelihood criterion, that is,

$$\hat{\Theta} = \arg\max_{\Theta} \sum_{n} \log P(\mathbf{L}^n | \mathbf{X}^n), \tag{9}$$

where Θ denotes all the parameters in the model. Treating the context variable c as missing data, we could apply the EM algorithm to the learning problem. However, due to the partition functions in the mixture components, the posterior distribution $q(c | \mathbf{L}^n, \mathbf{X}^n)$ is intractable. Instead, we define a new cost function which is a lower-bound of the conditional data likelihood:

$$Q = \sum_{n} \sum_{c} P_G(c | \mathbf{X}^n) \log P_M(\mathbf{L}^n | \mathbf{X}^n, c). \tag{10}$$

Note that $Q \le \sum_n \log[\sum_c P_G(c | \mathbf{X}^n) P_M(\mathbf{L}^n | \mathbf{X}^n, c)] = \sum_n \log P(\mathbf{L}^n | \mathbf{X}^n)$.

4.2   A Modular Training Approach

Given the cost function in Eqn. 10, we can compute its gradient and estimate all the parameters using a gradient ascent method. However, training all parameters together becomes difficult in practice when we have a large label set, and large image database. In this work, we propose a modular approach to estimate the parameters, such that many components are learned separately and are then merged into the full system in a consistent way. This learning procedure may not produce an optimal system ultimately, but the approach leads to a more efficient learning process, capable of scaling up to large datasets.

The learning procedure is carried out as follows: (1). We cluster the training data, where each training image is represented by its aggregate label distribution, and define each cluster as a context. The clustering divides the training data into subsets, such that each image corresponds to a specific context. (2). Given this division of training data, we can train the gating function that predicts which context an image is in given its image features. (3). Within each subset, we estimate the parameters $\{\gamma^c\}$ of each context-dependent image classifier to independently predict the label distribution given the super-pixel descriptors as input. (4). Finally, we combine these components and jointly learn the remaining parameters in the model (the coefficients $\{\alpha^c, \beta^c\}$ and the compatibility parameters θ^c) by maximizing the cost function in Eqn. 10.

More specifically, in step 1, the clustering method is based on a mixture of unigram model for the labels: $P_u(\mathbf{L}) = \sum_c \prod_i P_u(\mathbf{l}_i|c)P_u(c)$, which we learn using the EM algorithm on the training data set. The conditional probability $P_u(\mathbf{l}_i|c)$ acts as the cluster center, or the prototype label distribution in context c, and is thus used as μ^c in the global feature function. In step 2, given the mixture of unigram model, we can compute the cluster responsibility of every image. Those responsibilities are used as training targets for the gating function $P_G(c|\mathbf{X})$. Step 3 can occur in parallel with step 2, as by sampling the responsibilities, we can form the context-dependent subsets from the training data, and learn the parameters γ^c of the local feature functions on the appropriate subsets.

Finally, in step 4, after parameters of the local and global feature functions as well as the gating function have been learned, we merge them into the model and optimize the remaining parameters with respect to the cost function. Note that the context-dependent CRFs are log-linear models with parameters $\{\theta^c, \alpha^c, \beta^c\}$, which can be estimated by gradient ascent:

$$\Delta\theta^c \propto P_G(c|\mathbf{X}^n) \sum_n \sum_{i,j \in N(i)} (\mathbf{l}_i^n \mathbf{l}_j^{nT} - \langle \mathbf{l}_i \mathbf{l}_j^T \rangle_{P_M(\mathbf{l}_i, \mathbf{l}_j|\mathbf{X}^n, c)}) \tag{11}$$

$$\Delta\alpha^c \propto P_G(c|\mathbf{X}^n) \sum_n \sum_i (\mathbf{l}_i^{nT} - \langle \mathbf{l}_i^T \rangle_{P_M(\mathbf{l}_i|\mathbf{X}^n, c)}) \log \Phi_I(\mathbf{l}_i|\mathbf{x}_i^n, c) \tag{12}$$

$$\Delta\beta^c \propto P_G(c|\mathbf{X}^n) \sum_n \sum_i (\mathbf{l}_i^{nT} - \langle \mathbf{l}_i^T \rangle_{P_M(\mathbf{l}_i|\mathbf{X}^n, c)}) \log \mu^c. \tag{13}$$

To avoid overfitting, we add a Gaussian prior on the parameters, which is equivalent to weight decay during learning. As the CRFs are defined on loopy graphs with intractable partition functions, the marginal distributions of the label variables in the gradient updates cannot be computed exactly. In this work, we approximate them by applying the loopy belief propagation algorithm. An alternative approach is to apply contrastive divergence [16] to each component CRF. The empirical results show that both of these approaches obtain similar and satisfactory performance in our model; below we report results using loopy belief propagation.

5   Experimental Evaluation

5.1   Data Sets

We applied our model to three different real data sets. In order to compare our method with an alternative approach, we utilized the two datasets used in our mCRF work [11], and used the same training and testing split as in that work. The first dataset is the Sowerby database, including a set of color images of outdoor scenes and their associated labels. The data set has a total of 104 images with 7 labels: 'sky', 'vegetation', 'road marking', 'road surface', 'building', 'street objects' and 'cars'. 60 of these images are used for training and the remaining 44 for testing. The second dataset is a 100-image subset of the Corel image database, consisting of African and Arctic wildlife natural scenes. It also has 7 classes: 'rhino/hippo', 'polar bear', 'vegetation', 'sky', 'water', 'snow' and 'ground'; and has a train/test split of 60/40.

To explore the scaling potential of our approach, we defined a third dataset by expanding this Corel dataset to include 305 manually labelled images with 11 classes: 'rhino/hippo', 'tiger', 'horse','polar bear', 'wolf/leopard', 'vegetation', 'sky', 'water', 'snow', 'ground' and 'fence'. The training set includes 229 randomly selected images and the remaining 76 are used for testing. We call this extended Corel data set CorelB, and refer to the smaller one as CorelA in the following sections.

Again, for comparison purposes, we use the same set of basic image features as in [11], including color, edge and texture information. For the color information, we transform the RGB values into CIE Lab* color space, which is perceptually uniform. The edge and texture are extracted by a set of filter-banks including a difference-of-Gaussian filter at 3 different scales, and quadrature pairs of oriented even- and odd-symmetric filters at 4 orientations $(0; \pi/4; \pi/2; 3\pi/4)$ and 3 scales. We also include the vertical and horizontal position of each pixel. Thus each pixel is represented by a 32 dimensional image feature vector. For super-pixels, we compute the normalized histograms of those image features extracted from the pixels in each super-pixel.

5.2   Model Specification

We use the normalized cut segmentation algorithm to build the super-pixel representation of the images, in which the segmentation algorithm is tuned to generate more than 300 segments for each image. Segments smaller than a minimum size (6 pixels) are merged into the neighboring super-pixels. This yields approximately 300 super-pixels per image on average. The boundary information is extracted using the algorithm in [15]. To avoid underflow, we convert the raw output of boundary probability into interval $[0.1, 0.9]$ by an affine transform.

The number of contexts in our experiments is specified based on the complexity of data set. For Sowerby and CorelA data sets, we use 2 contexts in clustering, and for CorelB, we use 4 contexts. The model selection issue is not explored here, and is left to future work.

The gating function is a MLP with 25 hidden units. It takes the normalized histograms of the image features in each image as input. We use 20 bins for each image feature. To avoid overfitting, the MLP is trained with Gaussian priors on weights. The local classifiers are also MLPs with 30 hidden units, using the histograms of the image features in each super-pixel as input. They are trained with cross-validation.

We compare our approach with a simple pixel-wise classifier and a CRF model. These comparisons provide insight into the utility of the pairwise compatibilities (CRF vs. classifier) and the contexts (MoCRF vs. CRF). The pixel-wise classifier is a MLP with one hidden layer, taking image features from a 3×3 window centered at each pixel and predicting the pixel's label. The CRF uses context-independent local feature and pairwise feature functions. The feature functions have the same form as our model. The distribution of label configuration $\mathbf{L}$ defined by the CRF has the following form:

$$P_{CRF}(\mathbf{L}|\mathbf{X}) = \frac{1}{Z} \exp\{\sum_{i,j} \mathbf{l}_i^T \log \Psi_{ij} \mathbf{l}_j + \alpha \sum_i \mathbf{l}_i^T \log \Phi_I(\mathbf{l}_i|\mathbf{x}_i)\} \qquad (14)$$

where Φ_I is a local classifier trained separately on all the data and Ψ_{ij} is the compatibility function including boundary information. We trained the CRF model using the pseudo-likelihood algorithm, and tested its performance using the same MPM criterion where the marginal distribution is calculated by the loopy belief propagation algorithm.

5.3   Results

We clustered the training images in each dataset as described above, yielding 2 clusters for the CorelA and Sowerby datasets, and 4 clusters for CorelB. In Fig. 4, we visualize the typical label distributions of the contexts from all three datasets. Note that these distributions usually have semantic meaning which is easy to interpret. For instance, the contexts in CorelA dataset represent the tropical and arctic environments, while the Sowerby dataset contexts are rural and suburban areas. CorelB dataset has 'tropic','field','jungle' and 'arctic' as its contexts. Given the context settings, we trained a context classifier as the gating function for each dataset. To evaluate those context classifiers, we use the largest cluster responsibility as the target context, and compute the accuracy of the classifier output. Based on that metric, the context classifiers we trained achieve 82%, 92% and 85% accuracy on Sowerby, CorelA and CorelB, respectively.

The performance of MoCRF is first evaluated according to the label error metric on the pixel level, i.e., the percentage of incorrectly labelled pixels. We

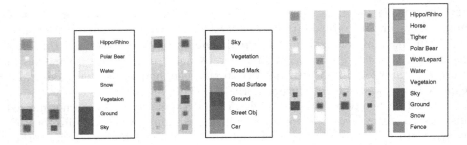

Fig. 4. The learned prototype label distribution for each of the three datasets: CorelA, Sowerby, and CorelB, is shown, with its associated key. See text for discussion.

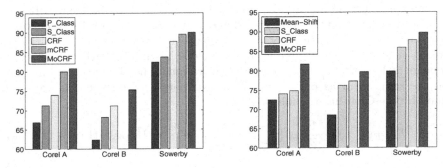

Fig. 5. A (left): Classification rates; B (right): Segmentation accuracy for the models

compared the performance of MoCRF to a simple pixel-wise classifier (P_Class), the super-pixel classifier in MoCRF considered alone (S_Class), and the CRF model over three datasets. We also include the performance of mCRF on the Sowerby and CorelA datasets [11]. The correct classification rates on the test sets of three datasets are shown in Figure 5A.

We can see that the super-pixel based classifiers alone provide a significant improvement over the pixel-wise classifiers. Built on the the same bottom-up cues, our model also has better performance over the super-pixel classifier and the conventional CRF model. Furthermore, it provides a slighter better performance than the mCRF model [11]. Note that our MoCRF model has a much simpler structure than the mCRF model: for the Sowerby and CorelA datasets, MoCRF has approximately 300 label variables, (equal to the number of super-pixels), no hidden variables, and approximately 120 parameters for training excluding the classifiers; while mCRF has about 2×10^4 label variables, 10^3 hidden variables and 10^3 free parameters. Learning is therefore quite slow in mCRF, and the model has poor scaling properties. Thus, although we only match this earlier model in terms of classification accuracy, our model can be applied to the problems with a considerably larger set of labels and larger image sizes.

Original	Hand-labeling	Classifier	MoCRF	Mean-Shift

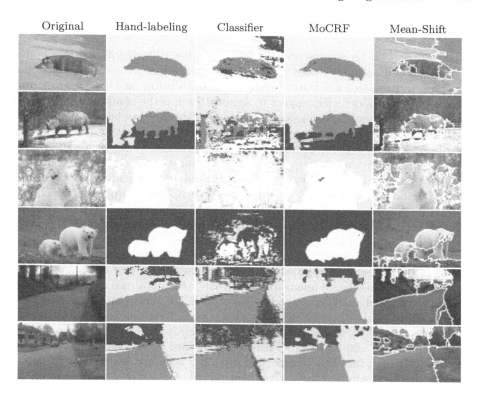

Fig. 6. Some labeling results for the Corel (4 top rows) and Sowerby (2 bottom rows) datasets, using the pixel-wise classifier, CRF, MoCRF, and Mean Shift segmentation. The color keys for the labels are the same as Fig. 4.

We compare the performance of the pixel-wise classifier, our model, and Mean-Shift segmentation in Figure 5B. We tune the parameters of Mean-Shift such that it generates the best results according to the manual labeling for a small set of randomly chosen images. The performance is measured according to a second metric used for evaluation, a segmentation metric which computes the percentage of pixel pairs that are correctly segmented. To reduce the computational burden, we randomly sampled 10% pixels from each image to estimate the accuracy. Again, we can see that our model obtains better results by adding top-down category information, and multi-level contextual constraints.

We also show the outputs of these methods on some test images in Figure 6. The figure shows the approaches based solely on low-level cues can be fooled, such that some single objects in the images are split. MoCRF works much better on those images by integrating the super-pixel representation and mixture of CRF framework. Note that the super-pixelization will cause some errors which cannot be corrected by the top-down information. Also, the model cannot use global spatial configuration to correct errors since no geometric information is included in the global feature functions.

6   Discussion

In this paper we have presented a discriminative framework that integrates bottom-up and top-down cues for image segmentation. We adopt a labelling approach to provide some purchase on the segmentation problem. A chief contribution of our model with respect to segmentation is the resulting extension of top-down cues to include a considerably wider range of object classes than earlier methods. The proposed framework is modular, in that images in a database are classified as to their context, and separate processes are learned for the different contexts. This modularity presents some promise of the system extending to large databases of images. While the top-down cues can be learned in a context-specific manner, the system integrates these with bottom-up cues, which are utilized in several ways: to define super-pixels in an image; to determine probabilities of local boundaries between super-pixels, which are used to constrain and guide labelling; and to enable context classification.

The results of applying our method to three different image datasets suggest that this integrated approach may extend to a variety of image types and databases. The labeling system consistently out-performs alternative approaches, such as a standard classifier and a standard CRF. Its performance matches that of an existing method, which operates at the pixel level and entails a considerably more involved training procedure, one which is unlikely to scale to larger images and image databases. Relative to a standard segmentation method, the segmentations produced by our method are more accurate, even when the standard method is optimized for a given test image. A relatively weak component in our model appears to be the gating function, as the images whose contexts are incorrectly classified contain a disproportionate number of label errors. We are currently evaluating other methods of summarizing the statistics of an image in order to facilitate more accurate context classification. Finally, a limitation of our model concerns its reliance on detailed training data. However, a growing effort to label images (e.g., [17]) should lead to a rapid growth in the volume of available labeled images.

Acknowledgments

We thank BAE Systems for letting us use their Sowerby Image Database. Funded by grants from Communications and Information Technology Ontario and NSERC.

References

1. Peterson, M., Gibson, B.: Shape recognition contributions to figure-ground organization in three-dimensional displays. Cognitive Psychology **25** (1993) 383–429.
2. Lafferty, J., McCallum, A., Pereira, F.: Conditional random fields: Probabilistic models for segmenting and labeling sequence data. In: Proc. 18th ICML. (2001).
3. Kumar, S., Hebert, M.: Discriminative random fields: A discriminative framework for contextual interaction in classification. In: ICCV. (2003).

4. Ren, X., Malik, J.: Learning a classification model for segmentation. In: ICCV. (2003).

5. Liu, L., Sclaroff, S.: Region segmentation via deformable model-guided split and merge. In: ICCV. (2001).

6. Borenstein, E., Sharon, E., Ullman, S.: Combining top-down and bottom-up segmentation. In: Proceedings IEEE Workshop of Perceptual Organization in Computer Vision. (2004).

7. Yu, S., Shi, J.: Object-specific figure-ground segregation. In: CVPR. (2003).

8. Tu, Z., Chen, X., Yuille, A., Zhu, S.C.: Image parsing: Unifying segmentation, detection, and object recognition. International Journal of Computer Vision **63** (2005) 113–140.

9. Murphy, K., Torralba, A., Freeman, W.: Using the forest to see the trees: A graphical model relating features, objects and scenes. In: NIPS-04. (2004).

10. Carbonetto, P., de Freitas, N., Barnard, K.: A statistical model for general contextual object recognition. In: ECCV. (2004).

11. He, X., Zemel, R., Carreira-Perpinan, M.: Multiscale conditional random fields for image labelling. In: CVPR. (2004).

12. Shi, J., Malik, J.: Normalized cuts and image segmentation. IEEE Trans. PAMI **22** (2000) 888–905.

13. Torralba, A., Oliva, A.: Statistics of natural image categories. Network: Computation in neural systems **14** (2003) 391–412.

14. Jacobs, R.A., Jordan, M.I., Nowlan, S., Hinton, G.E.: Adaptive mixtures of local experts. Neural Computation **3** (1991) 1–12.

15. Martin, D., Fowlkes, C., Malik, J.: Learning to detect natural image boundaries using local brightness, color and texture cues. IEEE Trans. PAMI. **26** (2003) 530–549.

16. Hinton, G.E.: Training products of experts by minimizing contrastive divergence. Neural Computation **14** (2002) 1771–1800.

17. Russell, B., Torralba, A., Murphy, K., Freeman, W.: LabelMe: A database and web-based tool for image annotation (2005).

Learning to Detect Objects of Many Classes Using Binary Classifiers

Ramana Isukapalli[1], Ahmed Elgammal[2], and Russell Greiner[3]

[1] Lucent Technologies, Bell Labs Innovations, Whippany, NJ 07981, USA
[2] Rutgers University, New Brunswick, NJ 08854, USA
[3] University of Alberta, Edmonton, CA T6G 2E8, CA

Abstract. Viola and Jones [VJ] demonstrate that cascade classification methods can successfully detect objects belonging to a single class, such as faces. Detecting and identifying objects that belong to any of a set of "classes", *many class detection*, is a much more challenging problem. We show that objects from each class can form a "cluster" in a "classifier space" and illustrate examples of such clusters using images of real world objects. Our detection algorithm uses a "decision tree classifier" (whose internal nodes each correspond to a VJ classifier) to propose a class label for every sub-image W of a test image (or reject it as a negative instance). If this W reaches a leaf of this tree, we then pass W through a subsequent VJ cascade of classifiers, specific to the identified class, to determine whether W is truly an instance of the proposed class. We perform several empirical studies to compare our system for detecting objects of any of M classes, to the obvious approach of running a *set* of M learned VJ cascade classifiers, one for each class of objects, on the same image. We found that the detection rates are comparable, and our many-class detection system is about as fast as running a *single* VJ cascade, and scales up well as the number of classes increases.

1 Introduction

The pioneering work of Viola and Jones [17, 16] has led to a successful face detection method based on "cascade classifiers", where each classifier is a binary classifier that is learned by applying Adaboost [3] (or some related algorithm [15, 18, 8, 13]) to a database of training images of faces and non-faces. The underlying principle in all these algorithms is to learn many binary classifiers during the training phase, then at performance time, run these classifiers as a "cascade" (*i.e.*, in a sequence one after another) on each region (at various resolutions) of the test image, eliminating non-faces at each stage. This work has also been used to detect objects of many other "classes" (like cars, motorbikes, etc.). Many researchers have extended the cascade detection method to solve several other related problems [7, 4, 9].

Our goal, however, is detecting and identifying objects (*i.e.*, assigning a class label) of *different* classes. One possible way to solve this problem is to build M different "single class Viola-Jones" (SC-VJ) cascades, one to detect objects of each class, then run them *all* at performance time to detect and identify objects of multiple classes. However, this does not scale up well; it requires running one cascade for each class of objects and is therefore expensive. Moreover, it can be ambiguous if more than one

A. Leonardis, H. Bischof, and A. Pinz (Eds.): ECCV 2006, Part I, LNCS 3951, pp. 352–364, 2006.

classifier labels a instance as positive. Another approach is to build one *many-class cascade* of classifiers and use it to detect objects of multiple classes. That is, let $T = T^+ \cup T^-$ be a training set images of positive examples (T^+) and negative examples (T^-), such that $T^+ = \cup_{i=1}^{M} T_i$ where T_i has images of class i and T^- does not have any images of any of the M classes. We can run the Viola-Jones algorithm on this set and produce N binary classifiers, such that each classifier can detect objects of *any* of the M classes (with a certain false positive rate) as a positive instance, but cannot assign a class label. We refer to each of these *binary* classifiers as a "many-class classifier" or, "MC-classifier". This approach has two problems: (1) Since MC-classifiers themselves are binary, during performance, they just label any object in T^+ as positive, but they cannot assign a more specific class label to it. (2) A single MC-classifier, built using objects of different classes as positive examples, can have a high false positive rate. This is not surprising: Many of these individual classes will naturally correspond to disjoint clusters (see below), and this MC-classifier corresponds to their *union*. Any algorithm that attempts to form a convex hull around such disjoint clusters is likely to include many extraneous instances.

In this paper, we present a "multi-class detector and identifier" that is built using MC-classifiers and several single-class cascades. We show that our *many-class detection algorithm* (MCDA) takes much less time than running M class-specific cascades, one for each of the M classes. We also show empirically that the accuracy of MCDA, in detecting and categorizing $M = 4$ diverse classes of objects, is similar to the detection rate of the class specific SC-VJ cascade.

Section 2 motivates and summarizes our framework. Section 3 explains the details of how we build our learning system and how we use it to detect objects of many classes. Section 4 provides empirical results in detecting objects of four classes and discusses how they compare with the SC-VJ cascade detection method, with respect to accuracy, efficiency and ROC curves. Section 5 discusses relevant work related to our research.

2   Motivation and Framework

The Viola-Jones learning algorithm "VJ" takes as input a set of images that are each correctly labeled as either a face or a non-face, and produces a cascade of boosted classifiers. Every classifier consists of many "linear separators", each built using one "rectangle feature", that is a rectangular sub-region in the (24×24 pixel) training images. The algorithm uses three kinds of rectangle features, each using rectangular regions of the same height and width adjacent to each other: (1) a two-rectangle feature (see Figure 1) that computes the difference between the sum of the intensities of the pixels of two adjacent rectangular regions; (2) a three-rectangle feature that computes the sum within two outside rectangles subtracted from the sum in a center rectangle; and (3) a four-rectangle feature that computes the difference between the diagonal pairs of rectangles. There are many (over a hundred thousand) possible combinations of rectangle features each of which can potentially be used as input for a linear separator. The learning algorithm chooses the best linear separators (those that can best separate faces in training data from non-faces, like the region across the mouth and nose; see the human face on the left in Figure 1) from these candidates, which are then used to build classifiers.

Let C_i be any classifier based on k linear separators. C_i classifies any sub-image W of a test image as a face if $\sum_{i=1}^{k} \alpha_i \cdot c_i(W) \geq \frac{1}{2} \sum_{i=1}^{k} \alpha_i$ where α_i is the weight[1] given to i^{th} linear separator c_i and $c_i(W)$ is the boolean classification result of c_i on W as a face or non-face (see [17] for details). We refer to the quantity $V_j(W) = \sum_{i=1}^{k} \alpha_j \cdot c_j^i(W)$, as the *SCO*-value ("sum of classifier output values") of C_i on W.

Fig. 1. Features of different classes on a rectangular region

VJ can be used to detect objects of classes other than faces. We use VJ to build N MC-classifiers using a training set of M different classes of classifiers, *i.e.*, $T = T^+ \cup T^-$ where $T^+ = \cup_{i=1}^{M} T_i$. Each of the N classifiers can detect objects of M classes (but cannot assign a class label). We define its "classifier space" as the N-dimensional space formed by using the *SCO*-value of each of N MC-classifiers as a dimension. That is, the N classifiers collectively map each input image to a point in the N-dimensional classifier space. We anticipate that the *SCO*-values of objects in a single class should be similar, and that objects from different classes should have different *SCO*-values. Our results show that this holds — in that each class will form a "cluster" in the classifier space; see Figure 2. For each cluster, we can assign the class label ℓ based on the number of images of each class in the cluster; see Section 3.1 for details.

Figure 2 shows various clusters of four classes of objects — cars, leaves, motorbikes and faces — plotted using the *SCO*-values of 2 of the MC-classifiers, on training images of these four classes of objects.[2] We selected the classifiers shown in Figure 2 ($C_1, C_2, \ldots, C_8$) manually to clarify our ideas. Of course, we do not anticipate that the *SCO*-values of *every* pair of MC-classifiers (or for that matter every set of $k \leq N$ classifiers) will form clusters.

Note that one *subset* of the N classifiers may be sufficient to distinguish class#1 from class#2; here, it would clearly be inefficient to consider all N classifiers. Unfortunately, a different subset may be necessary to separate class#1 from class#3, and a third subset for class#2 vs class#3, and so forth. There may be no small set of classifiers that is sufficient distinguish each class of objects from the others. That is why we use a dynamic process to find the most appropriate subset of classifiers: For each input image, this process sequentially decides which classifier to use next, based on the values observed from the classifiers previously executed on this window. The challenge is to *learn* the dynamic sequence of classifiers that can effectively distinguish the clusters corresponding to different classes.

---

[1] The weights for linear separators are learned during training.

[2] We presented clusters in two dimensions for clarity; in general there may be clusters in a p-dimensional space for $2 \leq p \leq N$.

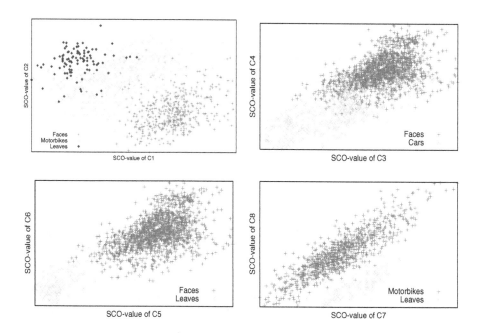

Fig. 2. Clusters of objects of the same class in cascade space

We use dynamic programming to find a sequence of MC-classifiers that optimally partition the training images into clusters. Our learning algorithm therefore builds a depth-d "decision tree classifier" (DTC, see Figure 3) that attempts to identify the appropriate label for each instance, using the learned MC-classifiers as features. Each DTC leaf, corresponding to one class of objects, also includes a further VJ cascade of classifiers, to verify an instance qualifies.

State representation: We can identify each node n in DTC with a state s. We represent s with the SCO-values of the classifiers on the path from the root of DTC to n (see Figure 3). That is, $s = \langle [V_{min,1}, V_{max,1}], \ldots [V_{min,k}, V_{max,k}] \rangle$, where for each i, $[V_{min,i}, V_{max,i}]$ is the range of SCO-values of C_i. We say two states are "δ-equivalent", written $s_1 \approx_\delta s_2$, iff

- s_1 and s_2 have applied the same set of classifiers, not necessarily in the same order
- For every classifier C_i used in s_1 and s_2, $|V_{min,i}^{(1)} - V_{min,i}^{(2)}| \leq \delta$ and $|V_{max,i}^{(1)} - V_{max,i}^{(2)}| \leq \delta$, where δ is a pre-defined constant. We set $\delta = 70$ in this work.

We use the equivalence property of states for two reasons: (1) during training, to merge all δ-equivalent states into one, and (2) during performance, to find the closest matching state from the training results and use the best classifier associated with it.

At run time, to classify a sub-image W within the current test image, MCDA basically follows DTC: it dynamically selects a classifier to apply to W, based on the responses of the previously run classifiers on W. If all the classifiers on the path from the root to

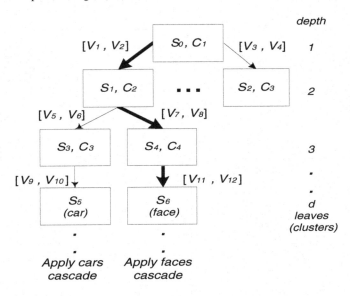

Fig. 3. Decision tree classifier. Each node is associated with a state, and every internal node with a particular classifier. Each leaf represents a cluster (*i.e.*, a single class), and has an associated cascade.

the leaf of DTC label W positively, we classify W with the class label ℓ of the corresponding leaf. We then apply a cascade, specific to this leaf, to W, to confirm that W is an instance of class ℓ. If any of the classifiers in DTC or the class specific cascade label W negatively, we stop processing W and proceed to the next sub-image. We can summarize the framework as follows:

- Use training data $T = T^+ \cup T^-$ to build N many-class boosted (binary) MC-classifiers, each designed to classify objects of any of the M classes as positive instances. (Note this does not distinguish these different classes).
- Use dynamic programming to build a DTC using these N MC-classifiers as binary "features", where each leaf corresponds to a cluster of a single class.
- For every leaf in DTC, find class label ℓ (explained in Section 3.1) and assign a cascade C of class ℓ to the leaf.
- At performance time, scan through each sub-image W of the test image. For each W, follow the decision tree DTC. If any of the classifiers encountered label W as negative, stop. Otherwise, if all label it as positive, tentatively assign W the class label ℓ associated with the leaf reached. Run the cascade associated with this leaf to confirm W is an instance of class ℓ.

We can contrast this approach with the other obvious algorithm for detecting M classes of objects: just use M class-specific cascades, each having N classifiers. We will call this "M-SC-VJ". This means classifying each instance would require running $M \times N$ classifiers. As our detection method chooses classifiers carefully in the first stage, we can assign a tentative class label using only $p \leq M$ classifiers (see clusters in Figure 2), then run *one* length-N cascade. Hence, we need only run a total of at most

$M + N$ classifiers for each image, which is clearly more efficient.[3] Section 4 presents empirical results confirming this.

3   Learning to Detect Objects of Many Classes

This section presents the details of using dynamic programming to construct a DTC of MC-classifiers, and then how we use this DTC to detect objects of many different classes.

3.1   Building DTC Classifier

Figure 4(a) presents the learning algorithm. We build N MC-classifiers using the images of T. We then produce a depth d decision tree (DTC) using these N classifiers.

Exploring sequences of classifiers: We explore every possible sequence of d MC-classifiers on the images of T^+ to find the sequence that yields the best clusters. That is, we first apply any MC-classifier C_1 on each image $w \in T^+$. We ignore all the images that C_1 labels as negatives. We sort the remaining images based on their SCO-values $V_1(w)$ of C_1 on these images, i.e., $\langle w_1, \ldots, w_{m/2}, w_{m/2+1}, \ldots, w_m \rangle$, where $V_1(w_j) > V_1(w_k)$ when $j > k$. We split them into two equal halves $\langle T_1^L \rangle$ and $\langle T_1^R \rangle$ (denoting the left and right branches), such that $\langle T_1^L \rangle$ contains $\{w_1, \ldots, w_{m/2}\}$ and $\langle T_1^R \rangle$ contains $\{w_{m/2+1}, \ldots, w_m\}$. We then apply another MC-classifier $C_2 \neq C_1$ on $\langle T_1^L \rangle$ and $\langle T_2^L \rangle$ separately resulting in (1) $\langle T_1^L, T_2^L \rangle$ and $\langle T_1^L, T_2^R \rangle$ that each represents one half of the classifiers of $\langle T_1^L \rangle$ that C_2 labeled as positives (2) $\langle T_1^R, T_2^L \rangle$ and $\langle T_1^R, T_2^R \rangle$ that each represents one half of the classifiers of $\langle T_1^R \rangle$ that C_2 labeled as positives.

We repeat the process for d steps, applying a sequence of d classifiers, $\langle C_1, \ldots, C_d \rangle$. The resulting 2^d leaves are clusters. Note that this is for one (random) sequence of d classifiers. When we consider $\binom{N}{d}$ different sequences of d classifiers, it leads to a total of $\binom{N}{d} \times 2^d$ clusters. While many clusters can have the same class, this is not be a problem. Any sub-image will now be matched to one of the smaller clusters. In general, we identify each node at depth i with a state s that is a list of ranges of SCO-values, of the form $\langle [V_{min}^1, V_{max}^1], \ldots, [V_{min}^i, V_{max}^i] \rangle$.

Computing the utilities of clusters: We want to determine the best decision tree within this tableau — the one that leads to the "purest" leaf nodes. Each leaf of the tree represents a cluster. We want the clusters that are as "pure" as possible, i.e., which group images of only one class together. For every cluster s_d, we compute the probability that images in s_d are of class i, weighted by the size of class i:

$$U(s_d) \quad = \quad \max_i \frac{P(T_i \mid s_d)}{|T_i|}$$

where of course $P(T_i \mid s_d)$ is the fraction of images of class i in s_d and $|T_i|$ is the number of images in training set T_i. Basically, we are computing the fraction of images

---

[3] While some classifiers are more expensive to apply than others, the difference in the cost of applying any two classifiers is negligible compared to the overall cost. So, running $M + N$ classifiers is better than running $M \times N$ classifiers.

Learn_DTC($T = T^+ \cup T^-$: TrainingSet)
- Build N MC-classifiers$\{C_1, C_2, \ldots C_N\}$ using images in T.
- Let All be the set of all $\binom{N}{d}$ sequences of d of MC-classifiers
- For every sequence of d classifiers $\langle C_1, \ldots, C_d \rangle$ from All
  - Let $\langle T_0 \rangle$ be set of all (+)images, i.e., T^+
  - For $i = 1$ to d do
    ○ Apply C_i separately on each partition $\langle T_{i-1} \rangle$
       produced by applying $\langle C_1, \ldots, C_{i-1} \rangle$
    ○ For each partition $\langle T_{i-1} \rangle$, remove all images that C_i labels as negatives
    ○ Split the rest of images into two (left and right) partitions
  - For each cluster s_d produced by applying the sequence of d classifiers
    ○ Assign maximum probable class label ℓ
    ○ Compute utility $U(s_d)$
  - For every state s_i resulting after applying $i < d$ classifiers
    ○ Compute utility $U(s_i) = max_j U(s_{i+1}^j)$
    ○ Let C_i^* be associated classifier that yielded max. utility when applied in s_i
    ○ Associate C_i^* with s_i, store $\langle s_i, C_i^* \rangle$
- Merge all the δ-equivalent states into one, store one classifier C_i^* with the max. utility
- The resulting $\langle s_i, C_i^* \rangle$ for $1 \leq i \leq d$ is DTC

MCDA (I_t : Test Image)
⋆ For each window W (of 24×24 pixels) within I_t
  ○ For $1 \leq i \leq d$,
    – Find state s_i "closest" to W,
    – Apply the C_i^* associated with s_i, to W
  ○ If all of $\langle C_1, C_2, \ldots C_d \rangle$ label W as a positive
    – Find the corresponding cluster, i.e., s_d,
    – Assign the mostly likely class ℓ associated with s_d, to W
    – Apply SC-VJ cascade $\langle C_1^\ell, C_2^\ell \ldots C_P^\ell \rangle$ to W
    – If class ℓ cascade also labels W as a positive, mark W as an instance of class ℓ
- Resize I_t by a factor of 0.8
- If I_t.length ≥ 24 and I_t.width ≥ 24, goto ⋆
- Return all windows marked as positive instances with class labels (and correct sizes)

Fig. 4. (a) Learning algorithm to produce DTC; (b) Dynamic classification algorithm

of each class i and normalizing it with the fraction of images in the training set, so that any class that has a high number of training images does not have an unfair advantage. We assign the class label ℓ that has the maximum utility to s_d. Recall this is after applying any sequence of d classifiers, $\langle C_1, C_2 \ldots C_d \rangle$. The idea is to assign high utility value to clusters that group images of the same class together. For any state s_i with possible "children" $\{s_{i+i}^j\}_j$, (each corresponding to the application of one other classifier), we compute the utility, $U(s_i) = \max_j \{U(s_{i+i}^j\}$ i.e., the maximum utility of any state produced by applying an additional $i + 1^{st}$ classifier.

Building DTC: We collect the $\langle s_i, C_i^* \rangle$ tuples and also the corresponding utilities, for all i, $1 \leq i \leq d$, where s_i denotes the state resulting after applying i classifiers, C_i^*

denotes the classifier that, when applied to s_i, transitions it to another state s_{i+1}^*, with the maximum utility among the states resulting after applying $(i+1)$ classifiers. For every two states s_i and s_j $(i \neq j)$ that are δ-equivalent we retain only one state that has higher utility and the corresponding classifier. Note that the $\langle s_i, C_i^* \rangle$ tuples for $1 \leq i \leq d$ tell us precisely the i classifiers applied so far, their individual SCO-values and the best classifier C_i^* to apply in s_i. This corresponds precisely to the DTC decision tree.

3.2 Detection

Our detection algorithm, MCDA shown in Figure 4(b), uses classifiers built by the cascade classifiers method [16, 18]. It examines each 24×24 pixel window in the image, then rescales by a factor 0.8 (*i.e.*, resizes the current height and width of the test image by a factor of 0.8) and repeats. For each window W, DTC first applies the classifier C_1^* associated with root (see Figure 3). This might reject W; if so the process terminates (*i.e.*, DTC continues with the next window). Otherwise, DTC computes the SCO-value associated with C_1^* on W and uses this value to decide which subsequent classifier C_2^* to apply. Again this could reject W, but if not, C_2^*'s SCO-value identifies the next classifier C_3^* to apply to W. This can continue for at most d steps, until W reaches a leaf (cluster). If all the d classifiers label W as a positive instance, DTC finds the class label ℓ associated with the cluster. We then run the SC-VJ cascade $\langle C_1^\ell, C_2^\ell, \ldots C_P^\ell \rangle$ associated with this leaf (of class ℓ) and declare W to be an object of class ℓ only if it passes all of these classifiers. Otherwise, we reject it as a negative instance.

4 Experimental Results

4.1 Experimental Setup

Data Used: We used four classes of objects in our experiments: faces, cars (rear view), leaves and motorbikes. We used a total of 1600 images of faces, collected from popular face image databases (including ones from Olivetti Research and AT&T, PIE, UMIST, Yale, etc.) in the training set of faces, T_F. We used the entire MIT-CMU database of faces, which has a total of 178 images with 532 faces, as the test set for faces. For the other three classes (cars, motorbikes and leaves), we used images from Caltech image database [1]. We split the 526 images of cars into two random sets of 476 and 50 images. We used the first set as the training set for cars, T_C, and the second set (with a total of 67 cars) as a test set. Similarly we split the 826 images of motorbikes into two random sets of 776 and 50 images and used the first set as the training set for motorbikes T_M and the second set of 50 images (with a total of 50 motorbikes) as the test set. Caltech database uses three different types of leaves (see Figure 5) and has a total of 186 images of leaves. We split this into two random sets of 156 and 30 images and used the first set as the training set for leaves T_L and the remaining set of 30 as the test set. We also used another 37 images of leaves (that we captured using a digital camera, with various backgrounds and sizes) in the test set. So, our entire test set for leaves has a total of 67 images, one leaf per image. Our training set for the negative examples, T^- has a total of 2320 images; none of these has any pictures of faces or cars or leaves or motorbikes.

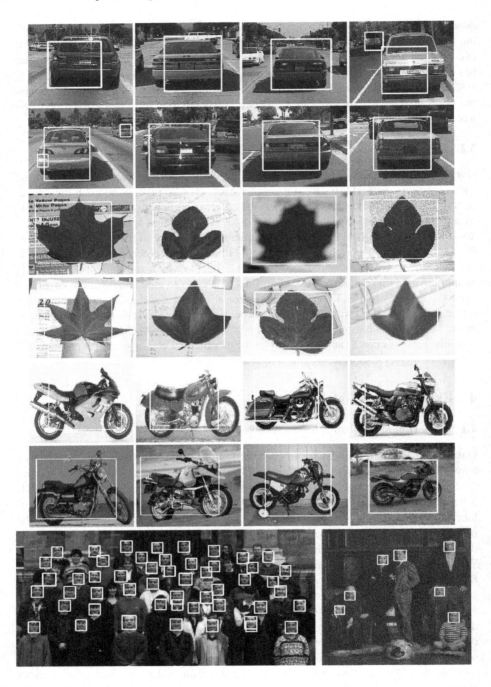

Fig. 5. Performance on test images of cars (rear view), leaves, motorbikes (side view) and faces

Building VJ Classifiers: We used T_C, T_L, T_M, T_F and T^- to build 4 SC-VJ cascade classifiers (one for each class), that involved $18, 17, 17$ and 21 classifiers for cars, leaves, motorbikes and faces, respectively. We also built $N = 10$ MC-classifiers that can detect objects of any of the four classes. Since we have four different classes, and with the application of each classifier (carefully, using DTC) we can distinguish between two classes, we set $d = 3$.[4] That is, we built a DTC upto a depth of 3 using our learning algorithm as explained in Section 3.1.

Training time: Our system required about 3 hours to build each of the 4 class specific cascades and another 1 hour to build the MC-classifiers[5]. It then required about 5 minutes to build DTC, so the total training time was approximately 18 hours.

Results: We compared MCDA to the standard set of $M = 4$ SC-VJ cascades, with respect to accuracy, ROC curves and efficiency. Note that MCDA applies d MC-classifiers (within DTC) to determine which class label to consider for each test sub-image, and then applies a cascade specific to that class. The SC-VJ detection algorithm has an easier task, as we explicitly identify which single class of objects it should seek for each image, which means it does not need to apply any MC-classifiers. This is why we do not expect the performance of MCDA to be better than SC-VJ, in terms of either efficiency or accuracy. However, our results indicate that MCDA does quite well in detecting objects as well as assigning class labels. In fact, our algorithm runs at least twice as fast as running M VJ cascades to detect $M = 4$ classes of objects; see Section 4.4.

4.2 Accuracy and Execution Time

Figure 5 shows some test images in which MCDA could successfully detect cars (rear view), leaves, motorbikes and faces. Table 1 compares MCDA with the SC-VJ cascade algorithm in terms of accuracy and efficiency. The peak accuracy, as we vary the number of cascade classifiers at the leafs,[6] for SC-VJ and MCDA are given in Table 1. These values are statistically indistinguishable at $p < 0.05$. While MCDA is slower than SC-VJ, by an additive 63%, 83.7%, 67.7% and 22.26%, we attribute this to: (1) the time needed to run the extra $d = 3$ classifiers using DTC and (2) the overhead involved in assigning a class label to each sub-image of any test image. Note that this is much better than the obvious M-SC-VJ alternative.

4.3 Number of Class-Specific Classifiers

We ran the following experiment to determine how these two approaches (MCDA and SC-VJ) each scale with the number d' of class-specific classifiers: We first applied $d = 3$ classifiers within DTC, then applied d' class-specific classifiers at each leaf, varying d' in the ranges [10–18], [10–17], [10–17] and [12–21] for cars, leaves, motorbikes and

---

[4] We tried larger values of d, but the results were not any better.

[5] 1. We use the Wu and Rehg [18] implementation of VJ.

  2. All results presented here were run on a 1 GHz. Intel Pentium processor with 256 Mbytes of memory running Windows-2000.

[6] We define "peak accuracy" as the accuracy value with negligible rate of increase with increasing values false positives.

Table 1. Comparison of test results for SC-VJ cascade, MCDA and MSC-VJ algorithms

Class	TestData			#Windows	Peak Accuracy		Av.Detcn.Time(sec)		
	#Images	#Objects	Av.Image Size		SC-VJ	MCDA	SC-VJ	MCDA	M-SC-VJ
Cars	50	65	265× 360	10,114,613	87.69%	86.15%	0.495	0.806	1.787
Leaves	67	67	318× 436	20,607,663	97.01%	95.52%	0.454	0.834	2.006
Motorbikes	50	50	279× 297	8,680,218	97.0%	92.0%	0.574	0.963	1.912
Faces	169	532	403× 402	76,957,710	92.11%	92.0%	1.541	1.883	4.558

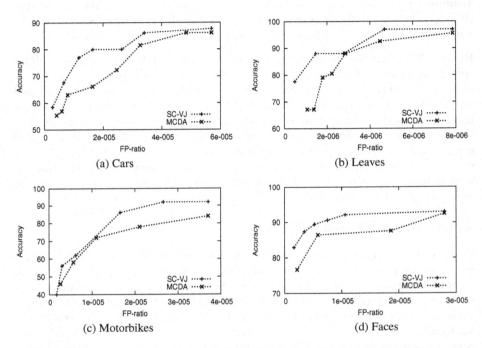

Fig. 6. ROC curves for SC-VJ cascade detection and MCDA for (a) Cars (rear); (b) Leaves; (c) Motorbikes; and (d) Faces

faces, respectively. For each value of d' we recorded the number of false positives and accuracy, as well as the total number of windows (24×24 pixel sub-images) processed. We also did this for SC-VJ. Each graph in Figure 6 plots accuracy against the number of false positives per window processed. We see that SC-VJ detection method performs better than MCDA, while the overall detection for MCDA is comparable to SC-VJ.

4.4 Comparison to M-SC-VJ

On the test set of each class, we ran each of the four cascade classifiers and recorded the execution time; see Table 1. As the execution time of this algorithm is linear in the number of classes, it does not scale as well as MCDA, which does not need to run multiple cascades.

5   Related Work

There has been a lot of interest in multiclass object detection recently. Torralba *et al.* [14] train binary classifiers "jointly" (for several classes) and use the common features to detect objects of the various classes. They show that feature sharing is a fundamental aspect of multiclass detectors that scale up well with the number of object classes. In our work, we use MC-classifiers that use features of multiple classes of objects to detect member of these classes. Different classes of objects have different features, *i.e.*, a classifier's *SCO*-value is different for different classes of objects. Using the *SCO*-values of the first d classifiers of DTC, we assign a class label to any sub-image of a test image. That is, using *SCO*-values, we reach some partition of the feature space where a single object class exists. Hence, our work implicitly utilizes feature sharing. But our learning and detection algorithms are significantly different. Fan [2] presents an algorithm that learns a hierarchical partitioning of the hypothesis space, which they use to do a coarse to fine search in the hypothesis space, pruning groups of hypotheses at every stage. Li, Fergus and Perona [6] use a generative probabilistic model to represent the shape and appearance of a constellation of features of an object. They learn the parameters of the model incrementally in a Bayesian manner. They test it on 101 different object categories. Lin and Liu [7] argue that face detection itself is a multiclass detection problem because of the variations in the appearance of a face caused by different poses, lighting conditions, expressions, occlusions, etc. They present a boosting algorithm to detect faces to account for all these variations. Our work is different from this as we try to assign a class label based on the clusters, and then detect objects using class specific cascades. We addressed related issues in a feature-based face-recognition system [5] by posing the task a "Markov Decision Problem (MDP)". We use dynamic programming to produce an optimal policy π^*, that maps "states" to "actions" (feature detectors) for that MDP, then used that optimal policy to recognize faces *efficiently*. We use similar techniques here in this work, as we again find the best sequence of classifiers. The current work differs because it considers *multiple* classes of objects.

6   Conclusions

This research provides a way to use learned binary classifiers to detect and identify objects in diverse classes. We first observe that images of each class can form clusters in the classifier space of MC-classifiers, and that different subsets of MC-classifiers may be sufficient to distinguish different pairs of classes. Hence, an efficient approach should select these classifiers dynamically. We present a learning algorithm that produces a decision tree, DTC, that first applies a dynamic sequence of classifiers to propose a possible class label for each sub-image of a test image, then applies a cascade of classifiers, specific to that class, that is effective for pruning away false positives.

We present empirical results to demonstrate that our approach is effective. In particular, we show that our implementation can detect and identify objects belonging to any of $M = 4$ classes, obtaining roughly the same accuracy and ROC-curve performance as the naive approach of simply running M different VJ systems. Moreover, our approach is about as fast as running a *single* VJ cascade, and will scale well as the number of object classes grows.

Acknowledgments

The authors thank Jianxin Wu and Jim Rehg for making the cascade detection code available. They also thank Caltech computational vision group and members of many other groups (including PIE, MIT/CMU, UMIST, Yale, Olivetti Research and AT&T) for making their image databases available.

References

1. R. Fergus, P. Perona and A.Zisserman Object class recognition by unsupervised scale-invariant learning In *CVPR*, 2003, pp. 264–271
2. X. Fan Efficient multiclass object detection by a hierarchy of classifiers In *CVPR*, 2003
3. Y. Freund and R.E. Schapire. A decision-theoretic generalization of on-line learning and an application to boosting. *Computational Learning Theory: Eurocolt*, 1995.
4. E. Grossmann. Adatree: boosting a weak classifier into a decision tree. In *IEEE Workshop on Learning in Computer Vision and Patter Recognition*, 2004.
5. R. Isukapalli and R. Greiner Use of Off-line Dynamic Programming for Efficient Image Interpretation *IJCAI*, Acapulco, Mexico, Aug 2003
6. F.F. Li, R.Fergus and P. Perona Learning generative visual models from few training examples: An incremental Bayesian approach tested on 101 object categories In *Proceedings of the Workshop on Generative Model Based Vision*, Washington, D.C., June 2004
7. Y. Lin and T. Liu Robust face detection with multi-class boosting In *CVPR* 2005, pp.680-687
8. C. Liu and H.Shum, Kullback-Leibler Boosting In *CVPR* 2003, pp.587–594
9. E-J. Ong and R. Bowden A boosted classifier tree for hand shape detection *International Conference on Automatic Face and Gesture Recognition*, 2004, pp.889–894
10. H. Rowley, S. Baluja and T. Kanade. Neural network-based face detection. *IEEE Transactions on Patten Analysis and Machine Intelligence (PAMI)*, 1998.
11. D. Roth, M. Yang and N. Ahuja. A snowbased face detector. In *NIPS*, 2000.
12. H. Schneiderman and T. Kanade. A statistical method for 3d object detection applied to faces and cars. In *ICCV*, 2000.
13. J. Sun, J.M. Rehg and A.Bobick Automatic cascade training with perturbation bias In *CVPR*, 2004
14. A. Torralba, K. Murphy and W.T. Freeman Sharing features: efficient boosting procedures for multiclass object detection In *CVPR*, 2004.
15. P. Viola and M. Jones. Fast and robust classification using asymmetric adaboost and a detector cascade. In *CVPR*, 2001.
16. P. Viola and M. Jones. Rapid object detection using a boosted cascade of simple features. In *CVPR*, 2001.
17. P. Viola and M. Jones. Robust real-time face detection. In *IJCV*, 2004.
18. J. Wu, J.M. Rehg and M.D. Mullin. Learning a rare event detection cascade by direct feature selection. In *NIPS*, 2003.

A Unifying Framework for Mutual Information Methods for Use in Non-linear Optimisation

Nicholas Dowson and Richard Bowden

Centre for Vision Speed and Signal Processing,
University of Surrey, Guildford, GU2 7JW, UK
{n.dowson, r.bowden}@surrey.ac.uk
http://www.ee.surrey.ac.uk/personal/n.dowson

Abstract. Many variants of MI exist in the literature. These vary primarily in how the joint histogram is populated. This paper places the four main variants of MI: Standard sampling, Partial Volume Estimation (PVE), In-Parzen Windowing and Post-Parzen Windowing into a single mathematical framework. Jacobians and Hessians are derived in each case. A particular contribution is that the non-linearities implicit to standard sampling and post-Parzen windowing are explicitly dealt with. These non-linearities are a barrier to their use in optimisation. Side-by-side comparison of the MI variants is made using eight diverse data-sets, considering computational expense and convergence. In the experiments, PVE was generally the best performer, although standard sampling often performed nearly as well (if a higher sample rate was used). The widely used sum of squared differences metric performed as well as MI unless large occlusions and non-linear intensity relationships occurred. The binaries and scripts used for testing are available online.

1 Introduction

Our aim is to place the common variants of Mutual Information (MI) into a single mathematical framework, and provide their analytic derivatives for use in non-linear optimisation methods. Furthermore an evaluation of the MI variants is provided allowing other researchers to choose a particular variant in an informed manner. We demonstrate that the four most commonly used variants, namely: standard sampling, Partial Volume Estimation, In-Parzen Windowing and Post-Parzen Windowing; vary primarily in how the joint histogram is sampled. The Jacobians and Hessians are derived for all these methods using an approach similar to that of Thevenaz and Unser [1], but who considered In-Parzen Windowing only. In the cases of standard sampling, post-Parzen window estimation and higher order partial volume estimation, this is novel. Using the established framework, the methods are compared in terms of computational cost, and convergence to the ground truth for eight data sets.

Generally papers using MI choose the method reported to best suit their application, without the scope to consider other methods. The obvious exceptions are several papers that discuss artefacts on the MI cost function surface [2, 3] and optimisation strategies [4]. However, only empirical analyses are made (unlike

A. Leonardis, H. Bischof, and A. Pinz (Eds.): ECCV 2006, Part I, LNCS 3951, pp. 365–378, 2006.
© Springer-Verlag Berlin Heidelberg 2006

the analytic comparisons here). Also, neither artefacts nor optimisation strategies are the focus here. Rather, we focus on providing a common framework and side by side comparison of MI methods, which to the authors' knowledge is currently unpublished elsewhere. The binaries and scripts used for testing are available online.

Registration, or aligning one image (template) relative to another image (reference), is a common problem in many machine vision applications: *e.g.* tracking, image mosaicking, object matching, and multi-modal registrations in medical imaging. A widespread strategy for registration is to minimise (or maximise) a similarity metric between a template and the region of overlap in a reference image using an optimisation algorithm. MI has proved to be superior to many other metrics. Since its concurrent introduction and popularisation by Viola and Wells [5], Studholme *et al.*[6] and Collignon *et al.*[7] it has been widely adopted.

Shannon proposed MI [8] in his theory of information as a measure of entropy of the information shared between two signals, with quantised *amplitudes* over a period of *time*. It is a simple extension to consider 2D or 3D images rather than 1D signals, which consist of quantised *intensities* over a 2D/3D *space*.

MI has been applied using many different optimisation methods with varying degrees of success, including the simplex algorithm [9], Powell's method [7, 10], Gradient Descent [11], hierarchical brute-force searches [12] hierarchical approaches [1, 13]. Pluim *et al.*'s survey [14] cites many more examples. Several optimisation methods were systematically compared by Maes in [15]. Due to space constraints, such a comparison is beyond the scope of this paper, but all the optimisation methods in [16] (Ch.10) and the Levenberg-Marquardt algorithm [17] have been implemented.

The advantages of MI include an invariance to changes in lighting conditions, robustness to noise, sharp maxima and computational simplicity [18]. In a comparative study of registration methods, an MI based algorithm outperformed 15 other algorithms [19]. However, MI is a non-linear function and is prone to artefacts in its cost function surface. To overcome this, other forms of MI have been developed. One approach, used by Wells *et al.*[11] is to convolve the histogram with a Parzen window [20], to account for uncertainty in the intensity values. Thevenaz and Unser have a more sophisticated Parzen windowing method using B-splines [1], which are applied during the construction of the histogram, giving more accurate results. In addition, Partial Volume Interpolation was introduced by Maes *et al.*[10], which increments several histogram bins for each sample based on the distance of the sample point from the surrounding pixels. Chen and Varshney extended this concept to Generalised Partial Volume Estimation, which uses extended spatial support [21].

The remainder of the paper is organised as follows. Section 2 reviews MI along with the four common sampling methods. After this, the first and second derivatives are derived in Section 3 and some analysis is performed in Section 4. Next, two example applications are discussed with a corresponding set of experiments in Section 5. The conclusion follows in Section 6.

2   Mutual Information

2.1   Registration

To start a brief formalisation of the registration process is required. Let f_R represent a reference image, and let f_T represent a template image. Both images are functions of position $\mathbf{x} \in \mathbb{R}^2$, although only trivial changes in the analysis below are required if the dimension of $\mathbf{x}$ is altered to represent volumetric data. Since f_R and f_T are represented as lattices of values at integral positions for $\mathbf{x}$, interpolation is used to obtain values at non-integral positions. There is insufficient space to discuss the choice of an interpolation method, but this is an important design issue. The interested reader is referred to a survey by Amidror [22].

For convenience and computational efficiency f_R is treated as infinite in extent and sampling is only performed within bounds of the lattice of f_T. Regions outside of the defined lattice of f_R are defined as 0. Hence f_T is considered constant with respect to any warp, and expensive boundary checking is avoided.

The registration process aims to align f_R and f_T, by minimising a distance function D for some warp function $\mathbf{w}$ with parameters $\mathbf{v}$: $\mathbf{v}_{reg} = \arg_{\mathbf{v}}\min D[f_R(\mathbf{x}), f_T(\mathbf{w}(\mathbf{x}, \mathbf{v}))]$. For computational reasons (because f_T is usually a smaller data set than f_R) it is easier to reformulate the problem as one of applying an inverse warp. Also, the function being minimised is MI, denoted by convention as I:

$$\mathbf{v}_{reg} = \arg_{\mathbf{v}}\min -I[f_R(\mathbf{w}^{-1}(\mathbf{x}, \mathbf{v})), f_T(\mathbf{x})]$$

To maintain notational clarity $\mathbf{w}^{-1}(\mathbf{x}, \mathbf{v})$ is referred to hereafter as $\mathbf{x_w}$. The negative sign is required because MI has larger values for better matches, and we wish to maintain the convention of referring to function minimisation.

2.2   Histogram Estimation

A measure of the information mutual to f_T and the corresponding region in f_R is obtained from the joint intensity histogram $h(r, t, \mathbf{v})$ of the two images. Here $r \in [0; r_{mx}] \in \mathbb{Z}$ and $t \in [0; t_{mx}] \in \mathbb{Z}$ index the intensities that f_R and f_T respectively consist of ($\mathbb{Z}$ is the set of integers). The histogram may be normalised to give an approximation of the probability distribution function (PDF) of intensities, i.e. $p(r, t, \mathbf{v}) = \frac{1}{N_\mathbf{x}}h(r, t, \mathbf{v})$, where $N_\mathbf{x}$ is the number of samples in the histogram. MI is defined here in terms of p rather than h for clarity, and the dependence on $\mathbf{v}$ is explicitly indicated:

$$I(\mathbf{v}) = \sum_{r,t} p_{rt}(r, t, \mathbf{v}) \log\left(\frac{p_{rt}(r, t, \mathbf{v})}{p_r(r, \mathbf{v})p_t(t)}\right) \tag{1}$$

A more common form of (1) has three entropy terms: $I = H_r + H_t - H_{rt}$. These are exactly the same and the more condensed form above is used for conciseness.

The PDF's p_r and p_t are easily obtained from the joint PDF, since $p_r = \sum_t p_{rt}$ and $p_t = \sum_r p_{rt}$. Note the treatment of r and t as discrete variables (or indices), indicating the finite bin-size of the histogram h from which p is derived. MI is *not* invariant to the bin-size Δi, which limits its bounds, as does the number of sample points: $I \leq \log(\min(\frac{r_{mx}}{\Delta i}, \frac{t_{mx}}{\Delta i}, k_{mx} N_{\mathbf{x}}))$, where k_{mx} indicates the number of histogram bins populated per sample. The joint histogram is defined in terms of two window functions $\psi()$, which act as membership functions:

$$h(r, t, \mathbf{v}) = \sum_{\mathbf{x}} \psi\left(r - \frac{f_R(\mathbf{x_w})}{\Delta i}\right) \psi\left(t - \frac{f_T(\mathbf{x})}{\Delta i}\right) \tag{2}$$

Where each sample taken from f_R and f_T is added to one histogram bin:

$$\psi(\epsilon) = \beta_0^-(\epsilon) = \begin{cases} 1 & 0 < \epsilon < 1 \\ 0 & \text{otherwise} \end{cases} \tag{3}$$

This kind of sampling is referred to as *standard sampling*. The $\beta()$ function in the above equation comes from the B-spline family of functions, and a brief digression describing these is now made.

2.3 B-Splines

B-spline functions are a family of functions with several useful properties, a brief description of which is given here. A more detailed description of B-spline functions and their numerical computation is given by Unser *et al.*in [23]. Firstly, the sum of a B-spline function for all integral distances from a real value is one, i.e. it has a portion of unity. This means that no renormalisation is required when histogramming. Secondly, the integral of a B-spline is one. Thirdly, order n B-splines are the convolution of any set of B-splines whose order sums to n. Lastly, the derivative of an order n B-spline is a function of two order $n - 1$ B-splines. These properties are summarised below.

$$\sum_{a \in \mathbf{Z}} \beta(\epsilon + a) = 1 \qquad \epsilon \in \mathbb{R}$$

$$\int_{\epsilon \in \mathbf{R}} \beta(\epsilon) = 1$$

$$\beta_n(\epsilon) = \beta_{n-1}(\epsilon) * \beta_0(\epsilon)$$

$$\frac{\partial \beta_n}{\partial \epsilon} = \beta_{n-1}(\epsilon + \frac{1}{2}) - \beta_{n-1}(\epsilon - \frac{1}{2})$$

The $0th$ order B-spline β_0 is simply a top hat function, centred about 0, i.e. $\beta_0(\epsilon) = 1$ when $|\epsilon| \leq \frac{1}{2}$ and 0 otherwise. We also define offset top-hat functions $\beta_0^- = \beta_0(\epsilon - \frac{1}{2})$ and $\beta_0^+ = \beta_0(\epsilon + \frac{1}{2})$.

2.4 Different Sampling Methods

For Standard Sampling (STD) we can see from (2) and (3) that for each of the $N_{\mathbf{x}}$ lattice points in f_T, each histogram in h_{rt} is incremented once. For reference the windowing function for STD is restated here in (4a), where f is an image,

i is an intensity index, Δi is the bin size of the histogram, and $\mathbf{x}$ is a sample point. An explanation of each functions below follows.

$$\psi_{std}(i - f(\mathbf{x})) = \beta_0^-(i - \frac{f(\mathbf{x})}{\Delta i}) \tag{4a}$$

$$\psi_{pve}^{(n)}(i) = \sum_{\mathbf{y} \in \mathbb{Z}^2} \beta_n(\mathbf{x} - \mathbf{y}) \beta_0^-(i - \frac{f(\mathbf{y})}{\Delta i}) \tag{4b}$$

$$\psi_{ppz}^{(n)}(i) = \beta_n^-(i - \frac{\text{floor}(f(\mathbf{x}))}{\Delta i}) \tag{4c}$$

$$\psi_{ipz}^{(n)}(i) = \beta_n^-(i - \frac{f(\mathbf{x})}{\Delta i}) \tag{4d}$$

Partial Volume Estimation (PVE), introduced by Maes as Partial Volume Interpolation in [10], aimed at making shifts between histogram bins smooth as the parameters of $\mathbf{v}$ varied. PVE has the added advantage of not adding any (possibly false) information other than the given data. The method involves populating the intensity histogram bins of the four lattice points surrounding each sample by a weighted amount. The weighting is proportional to the area of overlap between the square regions around the sample and lattice points. This is equivalent to integrating the region of each intensity for nearest neighbour interpolation: i.e. $h(i) = \int_{\mathbf{x}} \beta_0^-(i - f_{nn}(\mathbf{x}))$. Chen and Varshney extended partial volume interpolation to generalised Partial Volume Estimation (PVE) by using higher order B-splines to weight a larger region of pixels [21]. Although PVE has been treated as alternative *interpolation* methods, strictly speaking they are alternative *sampling* methods. Hence the term "PVE" being used.

The windowing function for PVE is given in (4b), where $\mathbf{y}$ are the coordinates of all lattice points in the image and n indicates the order in the sampling family. Note that (4b) collapses to (4a) with nearest neighbour interpolation for $n = 0$, since in that case only one valid value for $\mathbf{y}$ exists, that of the lattice point nearest to $\mathbf{x}$. For notational clarity, the first window function in (4b) is shown to take a vector as an input. This is simply a product of two window functions, one for each dimension of the vector, i.e. $\beta_n(\mathbf{x}) = \prod_{k=1}^K \beta_n(x_k)$, where K is the number of components in the vector $\mathbf{x}$.

The advantages of PVE are that it does not add information not explicitly given in the image, it is relatively inexpensive and has a smooth surface. The disadvantage is that for orders below 2, PVE is only C_1 smooth with cusps at points of $\mathbf{v}$ where grid-alignment between f_t and f_r occur. A strong bias towards these cusped positions exists. Also, a nearest neighbour model of the world ignores much of the information implicit to the image.

Two types of Parzen windowing routines exist: *Post-Parzen* Windowing (PPZ) and *In-Parzen* windowing (IPZ). In PPZ, the histogram is constructed before convolution with a Parzen window. In IPZ, each sample is convolved during histogram construction. This takes advantage of the information sample's intensity value before the information loss implicit to discretisation occurs.

The window equation for post-Parzen windowing is given in (4c), where floor($f(\mathbf{x})$) indicates reduction to the first integer value below $f(\mathbf{x})$. (4c) shows an nth order B-spline window function. In fact any window function may be used. B-splines were used here since they are inexpensive and their derivatives are easily obtainable [23]. The advantages of post-Parzen windowing are that it improves on the basic sampling method using a computationally cheap operation: $O(i_{\max}^2 w^2)$. However, there is information loss due to blurring of the histogram, and the function is not necessarily smooth. In-Parzen windowing differs slightly, in that it lacks the implicit discretisation of intensity values as shown in (4d). As a result, In-Parzen windowing has a guaranteed C_{n-1} smooth cost function surface and a more accurate histogram. Again some information loss occurs due to blurring of the histogram, and the method is comparatively expensive. Both (4c) and (4d) collapse to (4a) for $n = 0$.

3   Jacobians and Hessians

The Jacobian of MI may now be found by applying the product and chain rules to (1) and collecting the terms:

$$\frac{\partial I}{\partial \mathbf{v}} = \sum_{r,t} \frac{\partial p_{rt}}{\partial \mathbf{v}} \left(1 + \log\left(\frac{p_{rt}}{p_r}\right) - \log(p_t) \right) - \frac{p_{rt}}{p_r} \frac{\partial p_r}{\partial \mathbf{v}}$$

A more general definition of the above equation has been given by Thevenaz [1], where a non-constant $N_\mathbf{x}$ was accounted for. However their approach constructs the problem such that $N_\mathbf{x}$ is constant anyway, and making this assumption early on simplifies the following derivation considerably.

The summations in the fourth (last) term may be split to give $\sum_r \frac{1}{p_r} p_r' \cdot \sum_t p_{rt}$, since p_r and p_r' are not dependent on t. However $\sum_t p_{rt} = p_r$ since it is a sum of a joint histogram. So the fourth term becomes $\sum_r p_r'$, because p_r^{-1} and p_r cancel. However, because $N_\mathbf{x}$ is constant and p is based on a histogram, $\sum p$ always equals one, and therefore $\sum p'$ always equals zero, so this term disappears.

Also if the third term ($\sum_{r,t} p_{rt}' \log(p_t)$) is separated out, the summations may again be split to get $\sum_t \log(p_t) \sum_r p_{rt}'$. But $\sum_r p_{rt}' = p_t'$, which is zero as the template is constant. So the third term also disappears.

The remaining two terms are combined and the derivative of MI becomes:

$$\frac{\partial I}{\partial \mathbf{v}} = \sum_{r,t} \frac{\partial p_{rt}}{\partial \mathbf{v}} \log\left(\frac{e p_{rt}}{p_r}\right) \tag{5}$$

3.1   Derivative of Histogram Function

The derivative of the histogram function may be obtained using the chain rule:

$$\frac{\partial p_{rt}}{\partial \mathbf{v}} = \frac{\partial}{\partial \mathbf{v}} \frac{1}{N_\mathbf{x}} \sum_\mathbf{x} \psi[t - \frac{f_T(\mathbf{x})}{\Delta i}] \psi[r - \frac{f_R(\mathbf{x_w})}{\Delta i}] = \frac{1}{N_\mathbf{x}} \sum_\mathbf{x} \psi_T[t - \frac{f_T(\mathbf{x})}{\Delta i}] \frac{\partial}{\partial \mathbf{v}} \psi_R[r - \frac{f_R(\mathbf{x_w})}{\Delta i}]$$

$$= \frac{1}{N_\mathbf{x} \Delta i} \sum_\mathbf{x} \psi_T \frac{\partial \psi_R}{\partial \epsilon} \frac{\partial \epsilon}{\partial f_R} \frac{\partial f_R}{\partial \mathbf{w}} \frac{\partial \mathbf{w}}{\partial \mathbf{v}} = -\frac{1}{N_\mathbf{x} \Delta i} \sum_\mathbf{x} \psi_T \frac{\partial \psi_R}{\partial \epsilon} \nabla f_R \frac{\partial \mathbf{w}}{\partial \mathbf{v}}$$

The derivatives for the reference window functions differ for each sampling method. Here the intensities are indicated by r since only derivative for the reference image is required:

$$\frac{\partial \psi_{std}}{\partial \epsilon}(r) = \delta(r - \frac{f_R(\mathbf{x_w})}{\Delta i}) - \delta(r - 1 - \frac{f_R(\mathbf{x_w})}{\Delta i}) \tag{6a}$$

$$\frac{\partial \psi_{pve}^{(n)}}{\partial \epsilon}(r) = \sum_{\mathbf{y}} \left(\beta_{n-1}^+(\mathbf{x_w} - \mathbf{y}) - \beta_{n-1}^-(\mathbf{x_w} - \mathbf{y}) \right) \beta_0^-(r - \frac{f_R(\mathbf{y})}{\Delta i}) \tag{6b}$$

$$\frac{\partial \psi_{ppz}^{(n)}}{\partial \epsilon}(r) = \left(\beta_{n-1}^+(r - \frac{f_R(\mathbf{x_w})}{\Delta i}) - \beta_{n-1}^-(r - \frac{f_R(\mathbf{x_w})}{\Delta i}) \right) \sum_{m \in \mathbb{Z}} \delta(r - m) \tag{6c}$$

$$\frac{\partial \psi_{ipz}^{(n)}}{\partial \epsilon}(r) = \left(\beta_{n-1}^+(r - \frac{f_R(\mathbf{x_w})}{\Delta i}) - \beta_{n-1}^-(r - \frac{f_R(\mathbf{x_w})}{\Delta i}) \right) \tag{6d}$$

It should also be noted that for PVE the ∇f factor should be removed, since ψ_{pve} does not depend on $f_R(\mathbf{x_w})$, but on $\mathbf{x_w}$. Apart from this difference, note how similar the structure of all these equations are, showing their relationship. Note also how the δ functions in $\partial_\epsilon \psi_{std}$ and $\partial_\epsilon \psi_{ppz}$ imply that the gradient is constant, except at certain $\mathbf{v}$ positions on the cost function surface where a step change occurs. This exactly mirrors reality.

In these cases (STD and PPZ) the derivative function surface is a zero plane populated by impulse functions, the analytic derivative supplies almost no information to the optimisation function and convergence will fail. Hence it is better to use the approximate derivative $\frac{\partial \psi_R}{\partial \epsilon} \approx \frac{\Delta \psi_R}{\Delta \epsilon}$:

$$\frac{\partial \psi_{std}}{\partial \epsilon}(r) \approx \beta_0^-(r - \frac{f_R(\mathbf{x_w})}{\Delta i}) - \beta_0^-(r - 1 - \frac{f_R(\mathbf{x_w})}{\Delta i}) \tag{7a}$$

$$\frac{\partial \psi_{ppz}^{(n)}}{\partial \epsilon}(r) \approx \left(\beta_{n-1}^+(r - \frac{f_R(\mathbf{x_w})}{\Delta i}) - \beta_{n-1}^-(r - \frac{f_R(\mathbf{x_w})}{\Delta i}) \right) \sum_{m \in \mathbb{Z}} \beta_0^-(r - m) - \beta_0^-(r - m - 1) \tag{7b}$$

3.2 MI Hessian

The MI Hessian is approximated to:

$$\frac{\partial I^2}{\partial v_1 \partial v_2} = \sum_{r,t} \left(\frac{\partial p_{rt}}{\partial v_1} \frac{\partial p_{rt}}{\partial v_2} \frac{1}{p_{rt}} - \frac{\partial p_r}{\partial v_2} \frac{\partial p_{rt}}{\partial v_1} \frac{1}{p_r} + \frac{\partial p_{rt}^2}{\partial v_1 \partial v_2} \log \left(\frac{e p_{rt}}{p_r} \right) \right)$$

$$= \sum_{r,t} \left(\frac{\partial p_{rt}}{\partial v_1} \frac{\partial p_{rt}}{\partial v_2} \left(\frac{1}{p_{rt}} - \frac{1}{p_r} \right) \right) \tag{8}$$

because in the second term $\sum_t \frac{\partial p_{rt}}{\partial v_2} \frac{\partial p_r}{\partial v_1} \frac{1}{p_r} = \sum_t \frac{\partial p_{rt}}{\partial v_2} \frac{\partial p_{rt}}{\partial v_1} \frac{1}{p_r}$. The third term is approximately zero near the minimum. Its use only improves the speed of optimisation slightly at great computational expense.

3.3   Warp Functions, Their Jacobians and Hessians

Here we consider four types of warp functions $\mathbf{w}(\mathbf{x}, \mathbf{v})$: translation, Euclidean, similarity and affine. The equations for these warps are:

$$\mathbf{w}_{tx}(\mathbf{x}, \mathbf{v}) = \begin{pmatrix} x + v_1 \\ y + v_2 \end{pmatrix} \qquad \mathbf{w}_{eu}(\mathbf{x}, \mathbf{v}) = \begin{pmatrix} +x \cos v_3 + y \sin v_3 + v_1 \\ -x \sin v_3 + y \cos v_3 + v_2 \end{pmatrix}$$

$$\mathbf{w}_{af}(\mathbf{x}, \mathbf{v}) = \begin{pmatrix} xv_1 + yv_3 + v_5 \\ xv_2 + yv_4 + v_6 \end{pmatrix} \mathbf{w}_{si}(\mathbf{x}, \mathbf{v}) = \begin{pmatrix} +xv_4 \cos(v_3) + yv_4 \sin(v_3) + v_1 \\ -xv_4 \sin(v_3) + yv_4 \cos(v_3) + v_2 \end{pmatrix}$$

The Jacobians of each of these warps are:

$$\nabla f \frac{\partial \mathbf{w}_{tx}}{\partial \mathbf{v}} = \begin{pmatrix} f_x & f_y \end{pmatrix}$$

$$\nabla f \frac{\partial \mathbf{w}_{eu}}{\partial \mathbf{v}} = \begin{pmatrix} f_x & f_y & (f_x\,f_y)R'(x\,y)^T \end{pmatrix}$$

$$\nabla f \frac{\partial \mathbf{w}_{si}}{\partial \mathbf{v}} = \begin{pmatrix} f_x & f_y & (f_x\,f_y)v_4 R'(x\,y)^T & (f_x\,f_y)R(x\,y)^T \end{pmatrix}$$

$$\nabla f \frac{\partial \mathbf{w}_{af}}{\partial \mathbf{v}} = \begin{pmatrix} f_x x & f_y x & f_x y & f_y y & f_x & f_y \end{pmatrix}$$

where R is the standard rotation matrix. The Hessians for these warps are trivial to derive and are not shown here. Hereafter, warps are sometimes referred to by their Degrees of Freedom (DoF): e.g. 3DoF warp instead of Euclidean warp.

4   Analysis

4.1   Computational Costs

The computational costs of sampling methods are important when selecting which one to use for a particular application. Also, MI is sometimes regarded as an expensive option compared to say sum of square differences (SSD) or normalised correlation. This subsection shows that this is not necessarily true.

The SSD operation is $O(N_\mathbf{x})$: each operation requiring a warp, a template pixel access and multiple reference pixel accesses for interpolation. For MI, the only additional cost is to access each histogram bin after constructing it, i.e. MI is $O(N_\mathbf{x} + t_{mx} r_{mx})$. More sophisticated MI methods require multiple bin updates per sample, which can also increase computational cost. Theoretical estimates of costs for each function are given in Table 1.

The costs of calculating the Jacobian would appear to be substantially higher, since one histogram per warp parameter is required. However, there is some redundancy between the gradient and function evaluations, so this increase is not substantial. Likewise for the Hessian.

Some empirical tests were performed to verify the predictions of computational cost, the results of which are given in Fig. 1. As expected there is some overhead to the functions, which is indicated by an initial decrease in the cost per sample versus the number of samples before a steady state is reached.

Table 1. Computational complexity of various similarity methods

Function	Order	Interp. Method	Reads of f_t+f_r	Writes updates	Ancillary
SSD	n/a	NNI (Nearest Neighbour)	$N_\mathbf{x}(1+1)$	$N_\mathbf{x}$	
SSD	n/a	BLI (Bi-Linear)	$N_\mathbf{x}(1+4)$	$N_\mathbf{x}$	
SSD	n/a	BCI (Bi-Cubic)	$N_\mathbf{x}(1+16)$	$N_\mathbf{x}$	
MI(std)	n/a	NNI	$N_\mathbf{x}(1+1)$	$N_\mathbf{x}$	$t_{mx}r_{mx}$
MI(std)	n/a	BLI	$N_\mathbf{x}(1+4)$	$N_\mathbf{x}$	$t_{mx}r_{mx}$
MI(std)	n/a	BCI	$N_\mathbf{x}(1+16)$	$N_\mathbf{x}$	$t_{mx}r_{mx}$
MI(pve)	1st	n/a	$N_\mathbf{x}(1+4)$	$4N_\mathbf{x}$	$t_{mx}r_{mx}$
MI(pve)	2nd	n/a	$N_\mathbf{x}(1+9)$	$9N_\mathbf{x}$	$t_{mx}r_{mx}$
MI(pve)	3rd	n/a	$N_\mathbf{x}(1+16)$	$16N_\mathbf{x}$	$t_{mx}r_{mx}$
MI(ipz)	1st	BLI,BCI	$N_\mathbf{x}(1+(4,16))$	$4N_\mathbf{x}$	$t_{mx}r_{mx}$
MI(ipz)	2nd	BLI,BCI	$N_\mathbf{x}(1+(4,16))$	$9N_\mathbf{x}$	$t_{mx}r_{mx}$
MI(ipz)	3rd	BLI,BCI	$N_\mathbf{x}(1+(4,16))$	$16N_\mathbf{x}$	$t_{mx}r_{mx}$
MI(ppz)	1st	BLI,BCI	$N_\mathbf{x}(1+(4,16))$	$N_\mathbf{x}$	$4t_{mx}r_{mx}$
MI(ppz)	2nd	BLI,BCI	$N_\mathbf{x}(1+(4,16))$	$N_\mathbf{x}$	$9t_{mx}r_{mx}$
MI(ppz)	3rd	BLI,BCI	$N_\mathbf{x}(1+(4,16))$	$N_\mathbf{x}$	$16t_{mx}r_{mx}$

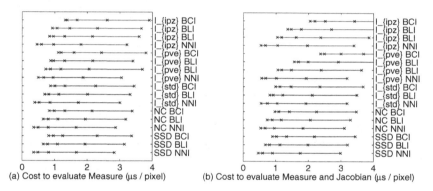

Fig. 1. Computational cost when evaluating (a) similarity functions and (b) their Jacobians as well. Efficiency increases with template size, reaching the minimum shown.

4.2   Artefacts

Although artefacts in the cost function surface of MI are beyond the scope of this paper, a brief mention is necessary since they can affect convergence of an optimisation algorithm to the correct minimum. The use of interpolation results in the appearance of artefacts in the cost function surface. Artefacts occur for all similarity functions, not just MI and there are two types of artefact, named for their appearance: *hiss* and periodic *glitches*.

Hiss appears as random high frequency shifts in the cost function surface. These random shifts are generally small compared to the overall value at a each position. The cause of hiss is non-linearities in the function, which cause discrete shifts as the warp parameters **v** vary. This behaviour is essentially random, since it depends on the numerous local shifts in value for each sample point.

Glitches are a periodic pattern in the cost function surface. They have a larger amplitude than hiss, although this is generally still smaller than the signal value. Glitches also have the more insidious effect of shifting global maxima to new positions or *bias*. Glitches are generally caused by a combination of synchronisation of sample positions in the reference and template image combined with biases caused by local correlations in the two sets of data. An example of this is the cusped pattern seen for first order PVE.

Of the MI families discussed, STD and PPZ are particularly prone to hiss due to their implicit non-linear floor functions. This is less of a problem than it might seem, since optimisation functions sample the cost function surface quite sparsely and the local trends in surface are not strongly affected by hiss. STD and first order PVE are somewhat prone to bias due to glitches [2], which can be more serious. The effect of glitches is seen in some results, but further discussion is not possible here due to space constraints.

5 Experiments

A series of experiments was performed to evaluate the ability of the MI families presented here to converge to a ground truth position. To provide a baseline measurement the same set of experiments was performed for sum of squared differences (SSD) and normalised correlation (NC). In all 13 functions were compared: SSD at 3 sample rates, NC, I_{std} at 3 sample rates, $I_{pve}^{(o)}$ (o=1,2,3), $I_{ipz}^{(o)}$ (o=1,2,3), where o denotes B-spline order. In all cases bi-linear interpolation was used. Similar results were obtained for bi-cubic interpolation, so these results are not shown. In general 1 sample/pixel was made. For SSD and I_{std} rates of 2 and 3 samples per pixel were tested as well to see if an increase to the equivalent computational expense of PVE and IPZ would give comparable results. PPZ was not tested because at the time of writing it was not yet implemented.

Eight reference and template image pairs were used to cover a variety of applications and not bias towards any particular method. Data-set 1 (**Brain**) used two simulated images of the same brain obtained using two different processes. The template was fairly large (71x89) and the intensities have different underlying functions. In addition the reference image was rotated by 5° and up-scaled by 3%. Similarity warps were allowed (i.e. 4 degrees of freedom DoF). Data-set 2 (**Satellite**) is an overhead image of an airport obtained from Google-earth^{TM}. The template was extracted directly from the image and is 41x41 pixels. Affine warps were allowed (i.e. 6DoF). Data-set 3 (**Hyena**) was taken from a noisy infra-red image of a Hyena. The image was shrunk by 75% without smoothing. The template was offset such that the ground truth is 0.25 off grid alignment. The template was also 41x41 pixels. Euclidean Warps were used for registration (3Dof). Data-set 4 (**Walk**) was extracted from a video supplied by the CAVIAR project (`http://homepages.inf.ed.ac.uk/rbf/CAVIAR/`) of Fisher *et al.*. There are 15 frames between the image and template, and the relationship between intensities is highly non-linear. The template was 19x37 pixels in size and 2DoF were used.

Fig. 2. The eight data sets used for testing the similarity metrics (numbered left to right top to bottom), with corresponding templates in the upper left corners

Data set 5 (**Rhino**) a baby rhinoceros is extracted 10 frames before the frame it is registered to. The baby rhino is occluded in many places by grass in the foreground, and the sequence is particularly noisy as it was taken at low resolution and highly compressed. The template was 17x33 pixels and 2DoF were used. Data-set 6 (**Hand**) was of a hand that changes in shape and in intensity over a large region of the template. The template was 33x33 pixels in size and 2DoF were used. Data-set 7 (**Claire**) was extracted from a clean motion sequence of a newscaster. The template was 11x11 and extracted from the preceeding frame. The 5% Gaussian noise was added to the image. 2DoF were used. Data-set 8 (**Sign**) was extracted from a sequence of a lady communicating using sign. Six frames separated the image and template and the (her) right eye was used as a feature. This data-set is notable for the large amount of occlusion. The template was 17x17 pixels in size and 2DoF were used.

These images were chosen for the large amounts of noise (Claire, Hyena), large occlusions (Sign, Rhino), nearby distractors (Satellite), and highly nonlinear relationships in intensity or structural variations (Walk, Brain, Hand). The data sets used are shown in Fig. 2.

Table 2 shows the mean error (μ), standard deviation (σ), and number of convergences to within 10% of the lower template dimension (N) for each data set and each similarity metric. In these tests, only the (x, y) positions were considered, since the other warp parameters are small compared to the (x, y) position. For the test-set, the ground truth was obtained using a brute force search of the cost function surface to an accuracy of 0.01 pixels. One thousand positions were randomly chosen uniformly from a region surrounding the ground truth. The region on each side of the ground truth was 30% of the minor template dimension, and where respectively relevant for rotation, scale and affine parameters: 15°, 10% and 0.1. Due to space constraints, only results using Levenberg-Marquardt are shown, but the other optimisation methods gave comparable results.

Since MI makes no assumptions about the template and reference intensities we expected it to perform somewhat better than SSD for many of the data-sets.

Table 2. Convergence to best match for 8 data sets and 13 similarity measures

Measure Sample Rate		SSD 1	SSD 0.5	SSD 0.33	NC 1	I_{std} 1	I_{std} 0.5	I_{std} 0.33	$I_{pve}^{(1)}$ 1	$I_{pve}^{(2)}$ 1	$I_{pve}^{(3)}$ 1	$I_{ipz}^{(1)}$ 1	$I_{ipz}^{(2)}$ 1	$I_{ipz}^{(3)}$ 1
1 Brain	μ	14.43	13.21	12.81	n/a	15.08	14.91	14.60	14.82	14.36	14.08	15.02	14.89	14.79
	σ	5.67	5.52	5.41	n/a	5.89	6.18	6.57	6.27	6.78	6.99	6.02	6.18	6.29
	N	0	0	0	0	7	15	26	22	42	49	13	16	21
2 Satellite	μ	13.83	8.73	7.41	9.16	8.56	6.71	5.91	6.87	5.11	4.78	7.69	6.70	6.28
	σ	162.48	28.52	15.16	3.51	4.35	5.65	6.04	5.56	6.12	6.23	5.12	5.69	5.90
	N	211	279	307	008	132	358	462	355	566	607	249	362	413
3 Hyena	μ	8.69	7.80	7.45	9.17	9.14	9.06	8.87	8.92	8.47	8.12	9.13	9.07	9.02
	σ	3.91	4.27	4.37	3.52	3.54	3.59	3.68	3.73	4.03	4.16	3.54	3.56	3.58
	N	57	119	146	8	10	11	16	25	53	68	8	8	15
4 Walk	μ	4.22	4.37	4.03	3.79	3.77	3.71	3.50	3.73	2.98	2.78	3.72	3.63	3.59
	σ	12.12	3.29	2.74	1.44	1.45	1.50	1.66	1.53	2.54	2.79	1.49	1.54	1.59
	N	94	146	129	37	41	56	114	37	379	450	50	66	69
5 Rhino	μ	2.49	2.40	2.22	3.77	2.93	1.84	0.81	2.80	0.62	0.60	2.56	2.39	2.32
	σ	1.42	1.32	1.14	1.37	1.73	1.74	1.42	1.84	1.38	1.42	1.56	1.60	1.70
	N	247	195	185	29	242	514	890	347	960	972	275	300	335
6 Hand	μ	7.43	6.71	6.14	7.76	7.65	7.22	7.15	7.41	6.86	6.39	7.41	7.19	7.07
	σ	3.25	4.34	4.82	2.75	2.91	3.60	3.88	3.35	4.79	5.06	3.25	3.63	3.72
	N	27	226	304	7	14	86	85	40	324	396	58	95	104
7 Claire	μ	2.17	2.10	1.74	2.33	2.26	2.06	2.03	2.31	2.34	2.41	2.17	2.11	2.03
	σ	0.93	0.91	1.01	0.85	0.96	1.28	1.49	1.04	2.08	2.13	1.09	1.21	1.27
	N	135	169	341	75	121	303	368	154	470	461	204	249	308
8 Sign	μ	7.29	7.46	7.41	3.76	4.37	5.02	5.08	4.14	5.60	5.53	4.92	5.30	5.52
	σ	0.66	0.70	0.65	1.43	1.44	1.57	1.50	1.47	1.75	1.75	1.51	1.56	1.60
	N	0	0	0	33	16	5	4	20	0	0	6	4	1

Particularly in the Hyena, Claire and Hand data-sets, SSD proved remarkably tolerant of noise and structural changes. Predictably, increasing the sampling rate only improved the results where there was high level detail or large amounts of noise. Normalised Correlation was generally the worst performer, except in the Sign and Walk sequences, where its tolerance of non-linear intensity relationships gave it an edge over SSD.

I_{std} performed better than SSD in about half the cases: where intensity relationships were highly non-linear. This could be due to a generally narrower basin of convergence than SSD and large amounts of hiss in the function surface of MI. Increasing the sampling rate usually improved performance substantially, since this decreases the amount of hiss in the surface. The exception was the Sign data-set, where the large occlusion created a large basin of convergence nearby.

Overall I_{pve} was the best performer when the order was above 2. Order 1 I_{pve} does not perform well due to the large number of glitches which often create local minima at points of grid alignment. This good performance was particularly noticeable in the Satellite, Walk, Hand and Rhino data sets, which either had much high frequency information or non-linear intensity relationships. This is probably due to the smooth function surface and wide but steep basin of convergence that PVE exhibits.

Surprisingly in most cases I_{ipz}, only outperformed I_{std} when the sample-rate was 1/pixel. Considering that sampling at 2 samples/pixel is equivalent in cost to first order IPZ, computational cycles would generally be better spent on using I_{pve} at higher sample rates for I_{std}.

In summary, in cases where the images have few occlusions, and lighting conditions do not change rapidly, SSD probably gives the best results per computational unit. SSD also proved surprisingly resilient to noise. Where lighting conditions vary and occlusions occur either I_{pve} (for $n \geq 2$) or I_{std} would be the methods of choice. A choice between these is difficult since the a higher sampling rate is necessary for I_{std} to work as well as I_{pve}, so the computational saving is not great. It is possible that I_{std} may outperform I_{pve} where the scales of the image and template are very different. This is left for future work.

6 Conclusion

This paper has introduced a single framework for the four main families of MI, namely: Standard sampling, Partial Volume Estimation, In-Parzen Windowing and Post Parzen Windowing. The analytic Jacobians and Hessians of these methods were also derived. A computational cost analysis was performed, which shows that STD MI is not much more expensive to compute than Sum of Squared Differences. The implementation was used to test the convergence of various image metrics using the Levenberg-Marquardt Method on a diverse array of images.

Despite its simplicity, SSD is the method of choice where the image is not occluded and the intensities of the template and reference image are linearly related. Where this does not occur I_{pve} (for $n \leq 2$) or I_{std} would be recommended.

Similarity functions (with Jacobians and Hessians) have been implemented in C++ for SSD, normalised correlation, and Mutual Information using standard sampling, partial volume estimation and in-Parzen windowing. The binaries and scripts used for testing are available online at the authors'URL.

Acknowledgements

Financial support from the CVSSP at Surrey University, the Department of Education and Skills, UK, and the EU FP6 Project "COSPAL", IST-2003-2.3.2.4, is gratefully acknowledged.

References

1. Thevenaz, P., Unser, M.: Optimization of mutual information for multi-resolution image registration. IEEE Trans. On Image Processing **9** (2000) 2083–2099
2. Pluim, J., Maintz, J., Viergever, M.: Interpolation artefacts in mutual information-based image registration. Computer Vision And Image Understanding **77** (2000) 211–232
3. Tsao, J.: Interpolation artifacts in multimodality image registration based on maximisation of mutual information. IEEE. Trans. Medical Imaging **22** (2003) 854–864

4. Maes, F.: Segmentation and registration of multimodal medical images: From theory, implementation and validation to a useful tool in clinical practice. PhD thesis, Dept. Elect. Eng. (ESAT/PSI), KU Leuven, Leuven, Belgium (1998)

5. Viola, P., Wells, W.: Alignment by maximization of mutual information. In: Proc. Int'l Conf. on Computer Vision, Boston, MA, USA (1995) 16–23

6. Studholme, C., Hill, D., Hawkes, D.: Automated 3d registration of truncated mr and ct images of the head. In: Proc. British Machine Vision Conference. (1995) 27–36

7. Collignon, A., Maes, F., Delaere, D., Vandermeulen, D., Suetens, P., Marchal, G.: Automated Multi-modality image registration based on information theory. In: Information Processing in Medical Imaging. Kluwer Academic (1995) 263–374

8. Shannon, C.: A mathematical theory of communication. The Bell System Technical Journal **27** (1948) 379–423, 623–656

9. Meyer, C., Boes, J., Kim, B., Bland, R., Wahl, P., Zasadny, K., Kison, P., Koral, K., Frey, K.: Demonstration of accuracy and clinical versatility of mutual information for automatic multimodality image fusion using affine and thin plate spline warped geometric deformations. Medical Image Analysis **1** (1997) 195–206

10. Maes, F., Collignon, A., Vandermeulen, D., Marchal, G., Suetens, P.: Multimodality image registration by maximisation of mutual information. IEEE. Trans. On Medical Imaging **16** (1997) 187–198

11. Wells, W.I., Viola, P., Atsumi, H., Nakajima, S., Kikinis, R.: Multi-modal volume registration by maximization of mutual information. Medical Image Analysis **1** (1996) 35–51

12. Studholme, C., Hill, D., Hawkes, D.: Automated 3-d registration of mr and ct images of the head. Medical Image Analysis **1** (1996) 163–175

13. Jenkinson, M., Smith, S.: A global optimisation method for robust affine registration of brain images. Medical Image Analysis **5** (2001) 143–156

14. Pluim, J., Maintz, J., Viergever, M.: Mutual-information-based registration of medical images: A survey. IEEE Trans. Medical Imaging **22** (2003) 986–1003

15. Maes, F., Vandermeulen, D., Seutens, P.: Comparative evaluation of multiresolution optimization strategies for multimodalitiy image registration by maximization of mutual information. Medical Image Analysis **3** (1999) 272–286

16. Press, W., Teukolsky, S., Vetterling, W., Flannery, B.: Numerical Recipes in C. 2nd edn. Cambridge University Press (1992)

17. Marquardt, D.: An algorithm for least-squares estimation of nonlinear parameters. Journal of the Society for Industrial and Applied Mathematics **11** (1963) 431–441

18. Viola, P., Wells, W.: Alignment by maximization of mutual information. Int'l Journal of Computer Vision **24** (1997) 137–154

19. West, J., Fitzpatrick, J.M., et.al., M.Y.W.: Comparison and evaluation of retrospective intermodality brain image registration techniques. J. Comput. Assisted Tomography **21** (1997) 554–566

20. Parzen, E.: On estimation of a probability density function and mode. The Annals of Mathematical Statistics **33** (1962) 1065–1076

21. Chen, H., Varshney, P.: Mutual information-based CT-MR brain image registration using generalised partial volume joint histogram estimation. IEEE. Trans. Medical Imaging **22** (2003) 1111–1119

22. Amidror, I.: Scattered data interpolation methods for electronic systems: A survey. Journal of Electronic Imaging **11** (2002) 157–176

23. Unser, M., Aldroubi, A., Eden, M.: B-spline signal processing: Part i–theory. IEEE. Trans. Signal Processing **41** (1993) 821–833

Random Walks, Constrained Multiple Hypothesis Testing and Image Enhancement[*]

Noura Azzabou[1,2], Nikos Paragios[1], and Frederic Guichard[2]

[1] MAS, Ecole Centrale de Paris,
Grande Voie des Vignes, Chatenay-Malabry, France
`noura.azzabou@certis.enpc.fr`, `nikos.paragios@ecp.fr`
`http://www.mas.ecp.fr`
[2] DxOLabs, 3, Rue Nationale, 92100 Boulogne, France
`{nazzabou, fguichard}@dxo.com`
`http://www.dxo.com`

Abstract. Image restoration is a keen problem of low level vision. In this paper, we propose a novel - assumption-free on the noise model - technique based on random walks for image enhancement. Our method explores multiple neighbors sets (or hypotheses) that can be used for pixel denoising, through a particle filtering approach. This technique associates weights for each hypotheses according to its relevance and its contribution in the denoising process. Towards accounting for the image structure, we introduce perturbations based on local statistical properties of the image. In other words, particle evolution are controlled by the image structure leading to a filtering window adapted to the image content. Promising experimental results demonstrate the potential of such an approach.

1 Introduction

In spite of the progress made in the field of image denoising, it is still an open issue. In fact, natural images contain various types of information such as texture, small details, noise, fine structure and homogeneous regions. Such conditions make image filtering a crucial and challenging task. Ideally, a denoising technique must preserve all image element except noise.

Prior art in image denoising consists of methods of various complexity. Local filter operators, image decomposition in orthogonal spaces, partial differential equations as well as complex mathematical models with certain assumptions on the noise model have been considered. The sigma filter method [15], the bilateral [22] filter, morphological operators [25] and the mean shift algorithm [5] are efficient local approaches to image denoising. The first two approaches compute a weighted average over the pixel neighborhood where weights reflect the spatial distance between pixels and also the difference between their intensities. Such methods account to a minimal extend for the image structure and introduce strong bias in process through the selection of the filter bandwidth.

Image decomposition in orthogonal spaces like wavelets [17], splines, fourier descriptors and harmonic maps is an alternative to local filtering. Images are represented through

---

[*] This work has been carried out during the affiliation of Ms. Azzabou and Prof. Paragios with CERTIS, Ecole Nationale des Ponts et Chaussees.

A. Leonardis, H. Bischof, and A. Pinz (Eds.): ECCV 2006, Part I, LNCS 3951, pp. 379–390, 2006.

a class of invertible transformations based on an orthogonal basis. Filtering consists of modifying the coefficients of the transformation space where often the most important ones are eliminated. Reconstruction of the image using the new set of coefficients leads to natural denosing. In their origin such methods failed to preserve boundaries a limitation that has been addressed through more careful selection of the orthogonal basis driven from the image structure [6, 13]. Such techniques have good performance when dealing with edges but they fail to preserve small details and texture.

Partial differential equations[1], higher order nonlinear operators [2], and functional optimization [19, 21, 23] have been also considered to address image denoising. The anisotropic diffusion [20] was a first attempt to incorporate image structure in the denosing process. Despite numerous advantages, theoretical justification [3] and numerous provisions of such a method one can claim that it remains myopic and cannot deal with image textures. The Mumford-Shah framework [19], the total variation minimization [21], the Beltrami flow [12], and other cost functionals of higher order [2] make the assumption that the image consists of a noise-free smooth component and the oscillatory pattern which corresponds to the random noise. Within such a concept constraints at limited scale are also introduced and image is reconstructed through the lowest potential of a cost function, that is often recovered in an iterative fashion through the calculus of variations. In the most general case such cost functions are not convex and therefore the obtained solution could correspond to a local minimum. Such methods are also myopic and still fail to account for texture patterns despite recent advances [24].

In order to account for image structure [18] an effort to understand the behavior of natural images when seen through a set of orientation and scale selective band-pass operators was made [14, 16]. Central assumption on this effort was that images exhibit differentially Laplacian statistics [16]. Such information is critical to an image denoising approach since it suggests the optimal way to regularize the problem and design the most efficient algorithm. Despite promising results, such simplistic modeling often fails to capture dependencies in a larger scale as well as account for the presence of repetitive patterns like texture.

To conclude, traditional state-of-the art techniques are often based on restoring image values based on local smoothness constraints within fixed bandwidth windows where image structure is not considered. Consequently a common concern for such methods is how to choose the most appropriate bandwidth and the most suitable set of neighboring pixels to guide the reconstruction process. In this context, the present work proposes a denoising technique based on multiple hypotheses testing. To this end, the reconstruction process is guided from multiple random walks where we consider a number of possible neighboring sites in the image and through a multiple hypotheses testing, we track the most suitable ones. Furthermore, image structure at a variable local scale is considered through a learning stage that consists of recovering probabilistic densities capturing co-occurrences of visual appearances at scale spaces. Kernels of fixed bandwidth are used to approximate such individual complex models for the entire visual spectrum. Random perturbations according to these densities guide the "trajectories"of a discrete number of walkers, while a weighted integration of the intensity through the random walks leads to the image reconstruction. Such a method is presented in [Fig. (1)].

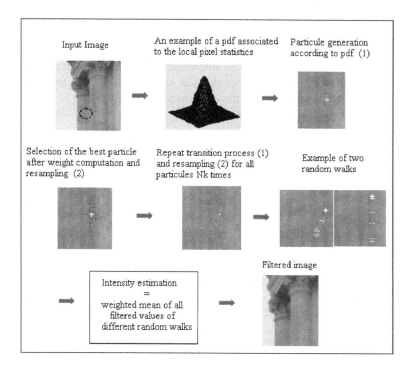

Fig. 1. Overview of Random Walks, Constrained Multiple hypotheses Testing and Image Enhancement

The reminder of this paper is organized in the following fashion; in section 2 we present density estimation of co-occurence for encoding the structure present in the image. Random walks and particle filters are presented in section 3. While section 4 is devoted to the application of the particle filtering to denoising as well as some experimental results and comparisons with the state of the art methods . Finally, we conclude in section 5.

2   Statistics of Natural Images

Understanding visual content has been a constant effort in computer vision with applications to image segmentation, classification, retrieval and coding. Statistical modeling of images aims to recover contextual information at a primitive stage of visual processing chain. Co-occurrence matrices [11] have been a popular method to classification and segmentation of texture images.

Such a matrix is defined by a distance and an angle, and aim to capture spatial dependencies of intensities. The formal mathematical definition of an element (m, n) for a pair (d, θ) is the joint probability on the image that a m-valued pixel co-occurs with a n-valued pixel, with the two pixels are separated by a distance d and an angle θ:

$$C_{d,\theta}(m, n) = p_{(\mathbf{x},\mathbf{y}) \in \Omega}(m, n) \left(I(\mathbf{x}) = m, I(\mathbf{y}) = n, \mathbf{y} - \mathbf{x} = de^{i\theta} \right)$$

with I being the observed image and Ω its domain. In the case of image denoising, the diagonal values of this matrix are of significant importance since implicitly they provide information on the geometric structure of the image. Inspired by such a concept, an intelligent denoising algorithm should be able to extract the most important correlations of local structure from the entire image domain, that is an ill-posed problem. Let us assume the absence of knowledge on the noise model. Then, in order to encode image structure we should seek for an estimate of the pdf.

$$p_f(d, \theta) = pdf(\{(d, \theta) \text{ where } \mathbf{x} \in \Omega, I(\mathbf{x}) = I(\mathbf{x} + de^{i\theta}) = f\})$$

To account for pixel values corrupted by noise, the constraint of exact matching could be relaxed, leading to:

$$p_{f,s}(d, \theta) = pdf(\{(d, \theta) \text{ where } \mathbf{x} \in \Omega, I(\mathbf{x}) = f, \left[\delta(\mathbf{x}, \mathbf{x} + de^{i\phi}) < \epsilon\right] \text{ and } [d < s]\})$$

where s is the scale considered for the pdf computation and $\delta(;)$ is a metric that reflects similarity between to pixels in the image. This metric can be a simple distance such as the L^1 or the L^2 norm or more complex measures like correlation, histogram matching, mutual information, etc. In our experiments, we integrated the local variance into the pdf expression. In fact local variance (noted $\sigma(.)$) is a simple primitive capable of describing texture at small scales. The new formulation of pdf is then as follows:

$$p_{f,\sigma,s}(d, \theta) = pdf(\{(d, \theta) \text{ where } \mathbf{x} \in \Omega, I(\mathbf{x}) = f,$$
$$\left[\delta(\mathbf{x}, \mathbf{x} + de^{i\theta}) < \epsilon_1\right] ; \left[\eta(\sigma(\mathbf{x}), \sigma(\mathbf{x} + de^{i\theta})) < \epsilon_2\right] \text{ and } [d < s]\})$$

As far as scale is concerned, different methods can be used to self-determine the scale like in the case of co-occurrence matrices. In the most general case we can assume scales of variable length that are self-adapted to the image structure. One can pre-estimate such *pdf* from the image using its empirical form.

However, $p_{f,s,\sigma}(d, \theta)$ aims to capture information of different structure, it describes spatial relation between similar patches in the image that may correspond to different population. To estimate $p_{f,s,\sigma}(d, \theta)$ non-parametric kernel-based density approximation strategies [26] like parzen windows were used.

Let $\{\mathbf{x}_i\}_{i=1}^{M}$ denote a random sample with probability density function p. The fixed bandwidth kernel density estimator consists of

$$\hat{p}(\mathbf{x}) = \frac{1}{M} \sum_{i=1}^{M} K_{\mathbf{H}}(\mathbf{x} - \mathbf{x}_i) = \frac{1}{M} \sum_{i=1}^{M} \frac{1}{\|\mathbf{H}\|^{1/2}} K\left(\mathbf{H}^{-1/2}(\mathbf{x} - \mathbf{x}_i)\right)$$

where $\mathbf{H}$ is a symmetric definite positive - often called a bandwidth matrix - that controls the width of the kernel around each sample point $\mathbf{x}_i$. Gaussian kernels are the most common selection of such an approach and that is what was considered in our case to approximate $p_{f,s,\sigma}(d, \theta)$. Once such pdf has been constructed from the image, we are able for a given image position $\mathbf{x}$ and an observation ($f = I(\mathbf{x}), \sigma$) to generate a number of hypotheses for the most prominent position of the related image structure ([Fig. 2]).

One can now reformulate the problem of image denoising for a given pixel as a tracking problem in the image domain. Thus, given a starting position (pixel itself),

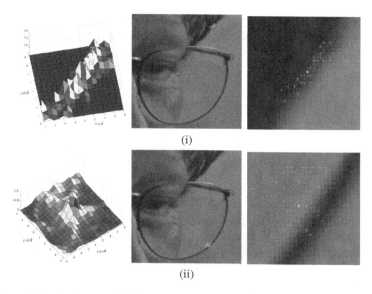

(i)

(ii)

Fig. 2. Two pdf distribution $p_{f,\sigma}(d,\theta)$ for different values of f ans σ (top ($f = 39, \sigma = 11.67$), bottom ($f = 96, \sigma = 3.55$), and sample generation according to these pdf (red pixel) for two different positions

the objective is to consider a feature vector that upon its successful propagation along similar image structure, is able to remove and recover the original image value. To this end, we define

- a feature vector, that defines the current state of the reconstruction process s_t,
- a measure of quality of a given hypothesis (feature vector) with respect to the image data.

with $\left[s_t = (\mathbf{x}_t, \hat{I}(\mathbf{x})) \right]$ being the state vector at a given time t. This state vector corresponds to the candidate site that can be used with in the filtering process and the reconstructed value induced by this site. The statistical interpretation of such an objective refers to the introduction of a probability density function (pdf) that uses previous states to predict possible new positions and image features to evaluate the new positions. The multiple hypotheses generation could be done in a number of fashions. Sequential Monte Carlo sampling is a well known technique that associates evolving densities to the different hypotheses, and maintains a number of them. Particle filters are popular techniques used to implement such a strategy.

3   Bayesian Tracking, Particle Filters and Multiple Hypotheses Testing

The Bayesian tracking problem can be simply formulated as the computation of the pdf relative to the present state s_t of a system, based on observations $z_{1:t}$ from time 1 to time t: $p(s_t|z_{1:t})$. Assuming that one can have access to the prior pdf $p(s_{t-1}|z_{1:t-1})$, the posteriori pdf $p(s_t|z_{1:t})$ can be computed using the Bayes' rule:

$$p(s_t|z_{1:t}) = \frac{p(z_t|s_t)p(s_t|z_{1:t-1})}{p(z_t|z_{1:t-1})},$$

where the prior pdf is computed via the Chapman-Kolmogorov equation

$$p(s_t|z_{1:t-1}) = \int p(s_t|s_{1:t-1})p(s_{t-1}|z_{1:t-1})ds_{t-1},$$

and

$$p(z_t|z_{1:t-1}) = \int p(z_t|s_t)p(s_t|z_{1:t-1})ds_t$$

The recursive computation of the prior and the posterior pdf leads to the exact computation of the posterior density. Nevertheless, in practical cases, it is impossible to compute explicitly the posterior pdf $p(s_t|z_{1:t})$, and therefore an approximation method is to be introduced.

Particle filters, which are sequential Monte-Carlo techniques, estimate the Bayesian posterior probability density function (pdf) with a set of samples. Sequential Monte-Carlo methods have been first introduced in [9, 27]. For a more complete review of particle filters, one can refer to [10, 7].

Particle filtering methods approximate the posterior pdf by M random state sample $\{s_t^m, m = 1..M\}$ associated to M weights $\{w_t^m, m = 1..M\}$, such that

$$p(s_t|z_{1:t}) \approx \sum_{m=1}^{M} w_t^m \delta(s_t - s_t^m).$$

Thus, each weight w_t^m reflects the importance of the sample s_t^m in the pdf.

The samples s_t^m are drawn using the principle of Importance Density [8], of pdf $q(s_t|s_{1:t}^m, z_t)$, and it is shown that their weights w_t^m are updated according to

$$w_t^m \propto w_{t-1}^m \frac{p(z_t|s_t^m)p(s_t^m|s_{t-1}^m)}{q(s_t^m|s_{t-1}^m, z_t)}. \tag{1}$$

This equation shows that particle weights are updated using two mainly informations : the observation pdf which reflects the likelihood of seeing an observation z_t knowing the state s_t and the transition model which control the evolution of a particle state. The *sampling importance resampling* algorithm (SIR) consists in choosing the prior density $p(s_t|s_{t-1})$ as importance density $q(s_t|s_{1:t}^m, z_t)$. Doing so, equation (1) becomes simply

$$w_t^m \propto w_{t-1}^m p(z_t|s_t^m), \tag{2}$$

To sum up particle filtering consists of three main steps:

- particle drawing according the transition law $p(s_t^m|s_{t-1}^m)$
- computation of the likelihood of observations generated by the particle $p(z_t^m|s_t^m)$
- weight updating according to $w_t^m \propto w_{t-1}^m p(z_t|s_t^m)$

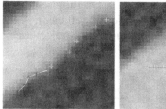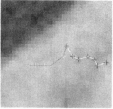

Fig. 3. Two different particle's random walks(in red and yellow) starting from the same origin pixel (in magenta) where origin pixel is on the border (left image) or in an homogeneous region (right image)

After several steps a degeneracy issue occurs, such that all weights but few become null. In order to keep as many samples as possible with respectful weights, a resampling is necessary. Different resampling processes exist. The SIR algorithm consists in selecting the most probable samples in a random way, potentially selecting several times the same sample. An example of propagation of multiple hypotheses is shown in [Fig. (3)] for two different situations according to the position of the origin pixel.

4   Random Walks and Image Denoising

We now consider the application of such a schema to image denoising. Thus, given an origin pixel $(\mathbf{x})$ reconstruction is equivalent to recover a number of "random" positions $(\mathbf{x} = \mathbf{x}_0, \mathbf{x}_1, ..., \mathbf{x}_\tau)$ with similar properties to $\mathbf{x}$ to reconstruct the corrupted origin value $(I(\mathbf{x}))$. The set of the obtained trajectories of each particle and their corresponding weights will represent the "filtering window". To this end, the use of "constrained" multiple hypotheses will be considered. This approach requires the definition of a perturbation model as well as a likelihood measure that reflects the contribution of a trajectory to the denoising process.

4.1   Likelihood Measure

Measuring similarities between image patches has been a well studied problem in computer vision. Within the proposed approach, filtering is done in a progressive fashion and therefore a need exists to measure the contribution of a new element in the filtering process. Parallel to that, each particle corresponds to a random walk where a certain number of pixels have been selected and contribute to the denoising process. Therefore, we define two metrics, one that accounts for the quality of potential additions and one for the intra-variability of the trajectories.

– The L^2 error-norm between local neighborhoods centered at the current position $\mathbf{x}_t$ and at the origin pixel $\mathbf{x}$.

$$D_{sim}(t) = \frac{1}{(2W+1)^2} \sum_{\mathbf{v} \in [-W,W] \times [-W,W]} |I(\mathbf{x} + \mathbf{v}) - I((\mathbf{x_t} + \mathbf{v})|^2$$

where W is the bandwidth which must be carefully selected to get a reliable measure of similarity while being computationally efficient.

- In order to account for the intra-variability of the trajectories, we consider the variance, centered at the origin value,

$$D_{intra}(t) = \frac{1}{t} \sum_{\tau=0}^{t} (I(\mathbf{x}_\tau) - I(\mathbf{x}))^2$$

that measures the "uniformity" of the trajectory and could also be determined within a larger neighborhood (not at the pixel level). This terms insures edges and fine structure enhancement since random walks with small intra-variability are favored.

These two metrics are considered within an exponential function to determine the importance of a new sample given the prior state of the walk.

$$w_t = e^{-(\frac{D_{sim}(t)}{2\sigma_g^2} + \frac{D_{intra}(t)}{2\sigma_v^2})} \tag{3}$$

The next step consists of defining an appropriate strategy for samples perturbation. This step is based on the statistical model for image structure introduced in the second section. The distribution $p_{f,\sigma}$ determines the transition model between particle at position $\mathbf{x}_t$ and $\mathbf{x}_{t+1}$. In fact similar patches have similar values of local mean and variance and our transition model guide particle to those patches, since displacements that guarantee this similarity are favored.

4.2   Implementation and Validation

In this section we will be concerned about the application of the particle filtering process to denoising. To this end, for each pixel $\mathbf{x}$ of the image, we generate N number of particles by applying N perturbations to the initial position $\mathbf{x}$. Then, each particle is propagated using a perturbation driven from the conditional distribution of the image statistics described in section (2). The process is repeated for (T) iterations. In each step of the process, we associate to each random walk a weight according to the likelihood measure defined in expression (3). We define then the walk value $\hat{I}_t^m(\mathbf{x})$ as the average value along the walk. It corresponds to the value used to reconstruct the original pixel according the "random walk" m :

$$\hat{I}_t^m(\mathbf{x}) = \frac{\sum_{\tau=0}^{t} D_{sim}(\tau) I(\mathbf{x}_\tau^m)}{\sum_{\tau=0}^{t} D_{sim}(\tau)}$$

Linear combination of the hypotheses weights and the corresponding denoised values is used to produce the current state of the process:

$$\hat{I}_t(\mathbf{x}) = \sum_{m=0}^{N} w_t^m \hat{I}_t^m(\mathbf{x})$$

In order to avoid degeneration of samples, as well as use with maximum efficiency all hypotheses, a frequent resampling process is used. In practice we use (N=30) particles,

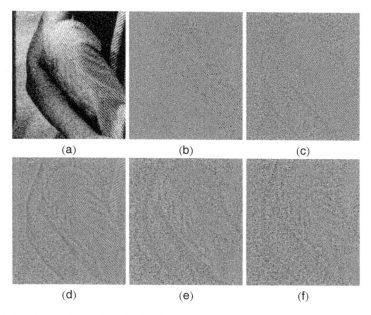

Fig. 4. Original image (a) and method noise of Total Variation (b), Anisotropic Diffusion (c), Bilateral Filter (d), Random Walks (e), Non Local Mean (f)

Table 1. PSNR values for denoised image (The PSNR of the image corrupted by gaussian noise of std=20 is equal to 22.15)

	TV	AD	Bilateral	NLmean	R.Walks
Barbara	26.18	26.45	26.75	29.46	28.77
Boat	27.72	28.06	27.82	28.70	28.53
FingerPrint	26.08	24.81	24.12	26.22	26.00
House	28.43	29.41	29.18	31.47	30.87
Lena	28.45	29.27	29.28	31.18	30.32

with (T=4) pixels contributing to each walk. To illustrate the random walks filtering an overview of the hole process is presented in [Fig. (1)].

Towards objective validation of the method, we used natural images corrupted by a synthetic gaussian noise (σ_n=20). We compared our approach to well known filtering techniques such as the bilateral filter [22], the Non Local Mean [4] approach, the total variation [21] and the anisotropic filtering [20] using an edge stopping function of the type $(1 + |\nabla I|^2 / K^2)^{-1}$. The parameters of different methods were tuned to get a good balance between texture preserving and noise suppression. As for qualitative criteria, we used the "method noise" criterion, which corresponds to the difference between the noisy image and the filtered one [Fig. (4)]. Ideally, the "method noise" should be free of all image information and must look like random noise. In case of the total variation, the anisotropic diffusion and the bilateral filter [Figs. (4.b), (4.c) and (4.d)]

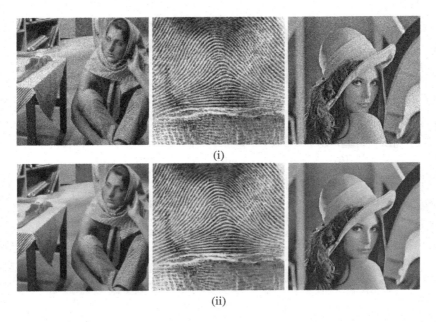

Fig. 5. Results of random walks filtering on natural images corrupted by additive gaussian noise; (i) Input image, (ii) Denoised Image

the method noise contains much more image details than our technique and the Non local mean. They fail to preserve the image texture because they are not based on patch comparison. Our Method has similar performance to the Non local mean filtering in terms of detail preservation. This is not surprising since particle weight is dependent on patch similarity. Thus, in homogeneous zones particles evolve in an isotropic fashion which is equivalent with considering a window with a fixed bandwidth. In textured regions, particles transitions rely on image structure where trajectories describing these structure are favored.

As far as quantitative validation is concerned we used the Peak Signal to Noise Ration criterion defined by

$$PSNR = 10log_{10}\frac{255^2}{MSE} \quad MSE = \frac{1}{\|\Omega\|}\sum_{\mathbf{x}\in\Omega}(I_0(\mathbf{x}) - \hat{I}(\mathbf{x}))^2$$

where I_0 is the noise free ideal image and $\hat{I}$ its estimation by the denoising process.

In table 1, we report experimental validation results for our method on image used ofently to evaluate performance of image denoising algorithms. Parameters of each method were selected to reach its best PSNR value. For our technique the following set of parameter (N=30, T=4, $\sigma_v=\sigma_g=15$, $W=4$) provides the best results. We can see that quantitative validation is in harmony with the qualitative one. The NLmean achieves the best result since it scans large width window (15×15 in our tests) to find similar patches. Our approach aims to introduce a technique where similar patch selection is guided by image structure. However, in the case of strong noise structures are not easily tractable which limits the performance of the method when compared to the Non local mean.

5 Conclusions

In this paper we have proposed a novel technique for image filtering. The core contribution of our method is the selection of an appropriate walk in the image domain towards optimal denoising. Such concept was implemented in a non-exclusive fashion where multiple hypotheses are maintained. The use of monte-carlo sampling and particle filters were considered to inherit such a property in the method. Furthermore, inspired by co-occurrence matrices we have modeled global image structure towards optimizing the selection of trajectories of the multiple hypotheses concept. To further adapt the method to the image structure such modeling was updated on line using local structure. Promising experimental results demonstrate the potentials of our approach.

Computational complexity is a major limitation of the method. The use of smaller number of hypotheses could substantially decrease the execution time. Improving the learning stage and guiding the particles to the most appropriate directions is a short term research objective. To this end, we would like to provide techniques capable of selecting the scales of each operator. Furthermore, we would like to consider kernels of variable bandwidth when recovering the non-parametric form of the learned distribution that are more efficient to capture image structure. More long term research objectives refer a better propagation of information within trajectories. Particle filters is a fairly simple approach that mostly propagates the mean value and the weights. The propagation of distributions can better capture the importance of the trajectories as well as the effect of new additions. In addition to that, geometric constraints on the '"walks"' could also improve the performance of the method in particular when texture is not present.

References

1. L. Alvarez, F. Guichard, P.-L. Lions, and J-M. Morel. Axioms and fundamental equations of image processing. *Archive for Rational Mechanics*, 123:199–257, 1993.
2. G. Aubert and P. Kornprobst. *Mathematical Problems in Image Processing: Partial Differential Equations and the Calculus of Variations*. Springer-Verlag, 2001.
3. M. Black, G. Sapiro, D. Marimont, and D. Heeger. Robust anisotropic diffusion. *IEEE Transactions on Image Processing*, 7:421–432, 1998.
4. A. Buades, B. Coll, and J.-M. Morel. A non-local algorithm for image denoising. In *CVPR*, pages 60–65, 2005.
5. Y. Cheng. Mean Shift, Mode Seeking, and Clustering. *IEEE Transactions on Pattern Analysis and Machine Intelligence*, 17:790–799, 1995.
6. M. Do and M. Vetterli. Pyramidal directional filter banks and curvelets. In *ICIP01*, pages III: 158–161, 2001.
7. A. Doucet, J. de Freitas, and N. Gordon. *Sequential Monte Carlo Methods in Practice*. Springer-Verlag, New York, 2001.
8. Arnaud Doucet. On sequential simulation-based methods for bayesian filtering. Technical Report CUED/F-INFENG/TR. 310, Cambridge University Department of Engineering, 1998.

9. N. Gordon. Novel Approach to Nonlinear/Non-Gaussian Bayesian State Estimation. *IEE Proceedings*, 140:107–113, 1993.

10. N. Gordon. A Tutorial on Particle Filters for On-line Non-linear/Non-Gaussian Bayesian Tracking. *IEEE Transactions on Signal Processing*, 50:174–188, 2002.

11. R.M. Haralick, K. Shanmugam, and I. Dinstein. Textural features for image classification. *SMC*, pages 610–621, 1973.

12. R. Kimmel, R. Malladi, and N. Sochen. Image processing via the beltrami operator. In *ACCV*, pages 574–581, 1998.

13. E. Le Pennec and S. Mallat. Sparse geometric image representations with bandelets. *IEEE Transactions on Image Processing*, pages 423– 438, 2005.

14. A. Lee, K. Pedersen, and D. Mumford. The nonlinear statistics of high-contrast patches in natural images. *International Journal of Computer Vision*, pages 83 – 103, 2003.

15. S. Lee. Digital image smoothing and the sigma filter. *CVGIP*, 24(2):255–269, November 1983.

16. A. Levin, A. Zomet, and Y. Weiss. Learning to perceive transparency from the statistics of natural scenes. In *NIPS*, 2002.

17. S. Mallat. A theory for multiscale signal decomposition: The wavelet representation. *IEEE Transactions on Pattern and Machine Intelligence*, pages 674–693, 1989.

18. P. Monasse and Guichard. Fast computation of a contrast invariant image representation. *IEEE Transactions on Image Processing*, 9:860–872, 2000.

19. D. Mumford and J. Shah. Optimal Approximation by Piecewise Smooth Functions and Associated Variational Problems. *Communications on Pure and Applied Mathematics*, 42: 577–685, 1989.

20. P. Perona and J. Malik. Scale space and edge detection using anisotropic diffusion. *IEEE Transactions on Pattern and Machine Intelligence*, 12:629–639, 1990.

21. L. Rudin, S. Osher, and E. Fatemi. Nonlinear Total Variation Based Noise Removal. *Physica D*, 60:259–268, 1992.

22. Carlo Tomasi and Roberto Manduchi. Bilateral filtering for gray and color images. In *ICCV*, pages 839–846, 1998.

23. D. Tschumperle and R. Deriche. Vector-valued image regularization with pde's : A common framework for different applications. *IEEE Transactions on Pattern Analysis and Machine Intelligence*, pages 506–517, 2005.

24. L. Vese and S. Osher. Modeling Textures with Total Variation Minimization and Oscillating Patterns in Image Processing. *Journal of Scientific Computing*, pages 553–572.

25. L. Vincent. Morphological grayscale reconstruction in image analysis: Applications and efficient algorithms. *IEEE Transactions on Image Processing*, 2:176–201, 1993.

26. M. Wand and M. Jones. *Kernel Smoothing*. Chapman & Hall,, 1995.

27. W. West. Modelling with mixtures. In J. Bernardo, J. Berger, A. Dawid, and A. Smith, editors, *Bayesian Statistics*. Clarendon Press, 1993.

From Tensor-Driven Diffusion to Anisotropic Wavelet Shrinkage

Martin Welk[1], Joachim Weickert[1], and Gabriele Steidl[2]

[1] Mathematical Image Analysis Group,
Faculty of Mathematics and Computer Science,
Saarland University, 66041 Saarbrücken, Germany
{welk, weickert}@mia.uni-saarland.de
http://www.mia.uni-saarland.de
[2] Faculty of Mathematics and Computer Science,
A5 University of Mannheim, 68131 Mannheim, Germany
steidl@math.uni-mannheim.de
http://kiwi.math.uni-mannheim.de

Abstract. Diffusion processes driven by anisotropic diffusion tensors are known to be well-suited for structure-preserving denoising. However, numerical implementations based on finite differences introduce unwanted blurring artifacts that deteriorate these favourable filtering properties. In this paper we introduce a novel discretisation of a fairly general class of anisotropic diffusion processes on a 2-D grid. It leads to a locally semi-analytic scheme (LSAS) that is absolutely stable, simple to implement and offers an outstanding sharpness of filtered images. By showing that this scheme can be translated into a 2-D Haar wavelet shrinkage procedure, we establish a connection between tensor-driven diffusion and anisotropic wavelet shrinkage for the first time. This result leads to coupled shrinkage rules that allow to perform highly anisotropic filtering even with the simplest wavelets.

1 Introduction

Anisotropy originates from physics where it decribes a direction-dependent behaviour of material properties. In image analysis, anisotropic filters that act direction-adaptive are an adequate framework to process oriented structures such as edges[1]. Since oriented features play a central role in many computer vision applications, it is not surprising that much research on anisotropic filtering has been carried out in the last decade.

One class of methods where anisotropy is used are anisotropic diffusion filters with a matrix-valued diffusion tensor instead of a scalar-valued diffusivity; see e.g. [25]. They include *edge-enhancing diffusion (EED)* that denoises images isotropically within regions and smoothes anisotropically along image edges, and *coherence-enhancing diffusion (CED)* that processes flow-like structures by smoothing along the flow direction.

---

[1] Sometimes the notion *anisotropic* is already used for space-variant filtering; see e.g. [18]. In our nomenclature, such a filter would be called *isotropic*.

A. Leonardis, H. Bischof, and A. Pinz (Eds.): ECCV 2006, Part I, LNCS 3951, pp. 391–403, 2006.

Also in the wavelet community many efforts have been made to incorporate anisotropy in order to represent and process oriented structures in a better way, e.g. by *contourlets* [9], *ridgelets* [12] and *curvelets* [4]. They take the form of frame elements that exhibit very high directional sensitivity and are highly anisotropic.

Initially, anisotropic concepts have been derived in a *continuous* setting where they can be described most elegantly. However, in order to apply anisotropic filters to digital images, one has to find adequate *discrete* representations for them. In practice this may create substantial problems with respect to rotation invariance, since the digital geometry allows to represent only a very restricted set of directions in a precise manner. If a filter is supposed to perform e.g. smoothing along an arbitrary one-dimensional structure, even slight directional errors can introduce blurring artifacts that severely deteriorate its performance. Therefore, research became necessary to find adequate discrete realisations of anisotropic filters, both in the diffusion setting [24, 26] and in the wavelet framework [3, 10].

The goal of the present paper is to address these problems by deriving novel discrete anisotropic filters that unify the concepts of tensor-driven diffusion and anisotropic wavelet shrinkage. We start by presenting a new scheme for anisotropic diffusion filtering that uses solutions of diffusion processes on 2×2 pixel images with a fixed diffusion tensor as building blocks. We show that this so-called *locally semi-analytic scheme (LSAS)* is absolutely stable, that it is simple to implement, that it gives an excellent approximation of rotation invariance, and that it hardly suffers from numerical blurring artifacts. Afterwards we interpret this scheme as a new strategy for anisotropic shift-invariant Haar wavelet shrinkage on a single scale. This leads to novel, anisotropic shrinkage rules with coupling of the coefficients.

Our paper is organised as follows. In Section 2 we derive our method as a novel scheme for anisotropic diffusion filtering, while Section 3 is devoted to its interpretation in the wavelet context. Experimental results are presented in Section 4, and the paper is concluded with a summary in Section 5.

Related work. Early schemes for anisotropic, tensor-driven diffusion such as [14, 19, 25] did not pay specific attention to the problem of rotation invariance and avoidance of blurring artifacts. Weickert and Scharr [26] addressed these problems by a scheme for coherence-enhancing diffusion filtering that uses optimised, Sobel-like approximations of all first order spatial derivatives. However, no stability theory was presented, and experiments showed only conditional stability. The same holds for the modified scheme of Wang [24] who used Simoncelli's derivative approximations [21] instead. Moreover, both schemes require stencil sizes of at least 5×5 pixels, while the scheme in the present paper is absolutely stable and comes down to a more local 3×3 stencil.

We notice that constructing numerical methods for diffusion filters from analytic solutions of simpler systems is also a feature of the method of short-time kernels, see e.g. [22], where a locally linearised diffusion equation is solved by Gaussian convolution.

Much research on relations between PDE-based filters and wavelets has been carried out in the *continuous* setting; see e.g. [1, 2, 5, 6, 15, 20]. Work on the relations between wavelet shrinkage and PDE-based denosing in the *discrete* framework include a paper by Coifman and Sowa [8] where they proposed total variation (TV) diminishing flows that act along the direction of Haar wavelets. Weickert et al. describes connections between (semi-)discrete diffusion filtering and Haar wavelet shrinkage, including a locally analytic four-pixel scheme, but focussed on the 1-D or the isotropic 2-D case with a scalar-valued diffusivity; see [27] and the references therein. To the best of our knowledge, however, nobody has found connections between nonlinear diffusion and wavelet shrinkage in the practically relevant anisotropic case so far. With respect to its four-pixel building blocks, our scheme can be regarded as an anisotropic, 2-D extension of the 1-D two-pixel scheme of Steidl et al. [23], and the 2-D isotropic four-pixel scheme of Welk et al. [28]. It is also an anisotropic extension of the equivalence results between discrete diffusion filtering and single scale Haar wavelet shrinkage that have been established by Mrázek and Weickert in the 1-D case [17] and in the isotropic setting [16].

2   A Local Discretisation of Anisotropic Diffusion with Low Numerical Blurring

We consider a nonlinear anisotropic diffusion equation [25]

$$\partial_t u = \text{div} \left(D(J) \cdot \nabla u \right) \tag{1}$$

where $D(J)$ is an anisotropic diffusion tensor which depends on the image via the so-called *structure tensor* [13]

$$J = J_\varrho(\nabla u_\sigma) := K_\varrho * \left(\nabla (K_\sigma * u) \, \nabla (K_\sigma * u)^{\text{T}} \right). \tag{2}$$

Here, K_ϱ and K_σ are Gaussian convolution kernels. This equation can model a wide variety of anisotropic diffusion processes, including EED and CED, by adjusting the parameters ϱ, σ, and the dependence of D on the structure tensor J.

In order to discretise (1) and (2) in a way that introduces as little numerical blurring artifacts as possible, we will base our discretisation of J on *four-pixel cells* consisting of 2×2 pixels. Furthermore, our discretisation of the divergence expression will allow for a decomposition into approximations on these cells.

2.1   Discretisation of the Diffusion Tensor

Discretising the diffusion tensor D means to discretise the structure tensor J. The main step herein is the discretisation of the gradients ∇v of the given pre-smoothed image $v := K_\sigma * u$. As for nonlinear isotropic diffusion [28] a good location to discretise these quantities most locally is in the centre of a four-pixel cell. We aim therefore at discretising $\nabla v = (\partial_x v, \partial_y v)^{\text{T}}$, and thus $\nabla v \nabla v^{\text{T}}$, at the centre $(\frac{3}{2}, \frac{3}{2})$ of a four-pixel cell $\{v_{ij}\}_{i,j=1,2}$ from a sampling of the spatial function v.

First, $\partial_x v$ and $\partial_y v$ can be approximated from the given pixels $v_{11}, v_{12}, v_{21}, v_{22}$ by central differences at midpoints between neighbouring pixel positions. By considering a quadratic grid with grid size 1 and taking arithmetic means of these expressions, we obtain approximations for the derivatives at $(\frac{3}{2}, \frac{3}{2})$:

$$(\partial_x v)_{\frac{3}{2},\frac{3}{2}} \approx \frac{1}{2}(v_{2,2} + v_{2,1} - v_{1,2} - v_{1,1}),$$

$$(\partial_y v)_{\frac{3}{2},\frac{3}{2}} \approx \frac{1}{2}(v_{2,2} - v_{2,1} + v_{1,2} - v_{1,1}).$$

(3)

Having discretised the gradient ∇v, one computes the outer product $\nabla v \nabla v^{\mathrm{T}}$. The structure tensor field results from smoothing this componentwise by the Gaussian of standard deviation ϱ.

2.2   Discretisation of Anisotropic Diffusion with Given Diffusion Tensor Field

We turn now to consider the anisotropic diffusion equation

$$\partial_t u = \mathrm{div}\,(D \cdot \nabla u)$$

(4)

with an arbitrary diffusion tensor field represented by positive semidefinite symmetric matrices $D = \begin{pmatrix} a & c \\ c & b \end{pmatrix}$. We assume that u is sampled at the integer pixel positions (i, j) while D is sampled at inter-pixel positions $(i + \frac{1}{2}, j + \frac{1}{2})$.

In discretising the right-hand side of (4) at some pixel position (i, j), we will use the values of u at positions $(i + \varepsilon_1, j + \varepsilon_2)$ where $\varepsilon_1, \varepsilon_2 \in \{-1, 0, +1\}$, and the diffusion tensors at $(i \pm \frac{1}{2}, j \pm \frac{1}{2})$. For abbreviation we set

$$D_{i-\frac{1}{2},j-\frac{1}{2}} := \begin{pmatrix} a_{--} & c_{--} \\ c_{--} & b_{--} \end{pmatrix}, \qquad D_{i-\frac{1}{2},j+\frac{1}{2}} := \begin{pmatrix} a_{-+} & c_{-+} \\ c_{-+} & b_{-+} \end{pmatrix},$$

$$D_{i+\frac{1}{2},j-\frac{1}{2}} := \begin{pmatrix} a_{+-} & c_{+-} \\ c_{+-} & b_{+-} \end{pmatrix}, \qquad D_{i+\frac{1}{2},j+\frac{1}{2}} := \begin{pmatrix} a_{++} & c_{++} \\ c_{++} & b_{++} \end{pmatrix}.$$

(5)

To obtain a discretisation which is "as local as possible", we decompose the differential operators div and ∇ herein according to the $45°$-rotated coordinates ξ, η where

$$\begin{pmatrix} \xi \\ \eta \end{pmatrix} := H \begin{pmatrix} x \\ y \end{pmatrix}, \qquad H := \frac{1}{\sqrt{2}} \begin{pmatrix} 1 & 1 \\ 1 & -1 \end{pmatrix}.$$

(6)

Note that $H = H^{\mathrm{T}} = H^{-1}$. To express the diffusion tensor in the ξ-η coordinates, D must be transformed by

$$HDH^{\mathrm{T}} = \frac{1}{2} \begin{pmatrix} a+b+2c & a-b \\ a-b & a+b-2c \end{pmatrix}.$$

(7)

Then we have

$$\left(\mathrm{div}\,(D\,\nabla u) \right)_{i,j} = \left((\partial_\xi, \partial_\eta)(HDH(\partial_\xi u, \partial_\eta u)^{\mathrm{T}}) \right)_{i,j}$$

$$= \frac{1}{2} \Big(\partial_\xi((a+b+2c)\partial_\xi u + (a-b)\partial_\eta u)$$

$$+ \partial_\eta((a-b)\partial_\xi u + (a+b-2c)\partial_\eta u) \Big)_{i,j}$$

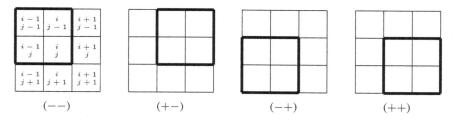

$i-1$ i $i+1$ / $j-1$ $j-1$ $j-1$ ... (figure grid)

Fig. 1. The four-pixel cells contributing to $\dot{u}_{i,j}$

$$\approx \frac{1}{2\sqrt{2}}\Big(\big((a+b+2c)\partial_\xi u + (a-b)\partial_\eta u\big)_{i+\frac{1}{2},j+\frac{1}{2}}$$
$$-\big((a+b+2c)\partial_\xi u + (a-b)\partial_\eta u\big)_{i-\frac{1}{2},j-\frac{1}{2}}$$
$$+\big((a-b)\partial_\xi u + (a+b-2c)\partial_\eta u\big)_{i+\frac{1}{2},j-\frac{1}{2}} \tag{8}$$
$$-\big((a-b)\partial_\xi u + (a+b-2c)\partial_\eta u\big)_{i-\frac{1}{2},j+\frac{1}{2}}\Big).$$

Expanding $\partial_\xi u$ and $\partial_\eta u$ finally yields the dynamical system

$$\dot{u}_{i,j} = \frac{1}{4}\big((a_{++}+b_{++}+2c_{++})(u_{i+1,j+1}-u_{i,j})$$
$$+(a_{++}-b_{++})(u_{i+1,j}-u_{i,j+1})$$
$$-(a_{--}+b_{--}+2c_{--})(u_{i,j}-u_{i-1,j-1})$$
$$-(a_{--}-b_{--})(u_{i,j-1}-u_{i-1,j})$$
$$+(a_{+-}-b_{+-})(u_{i+1,j}-u_{i,j-1}) \tag{9}$$
$$+(a_{+-}+b_{+-}-2c_{+-})(u_{i+1,j-1}-u_{i,j})$$
$$-(a_{-+}-b_{-+})(u_{i,j+1}-u_{i-1,j})$$
$$-(a_{-+}+b_{-+}-2c_{-+})(u_{i,j}-u_{i-1,j+1})\big),$$

where the dot denotes differentiation with respect to the time t. One observes that each summand on the right-hand side contains only quantities from one of the four-pixel cells

$$(--):\ \{i-1,i\}\times\{j-1,j\},\qquad (+-):\ \{i,i+1\}\times\{j-1,j\},$$
$$(-+):\ \{i-1,i\}\times\{j,j+1\},\qquad (++):\ \{i,i+1\}\times\{j,j+1\} \tag{10}$$

which allows to split up (9) into the average of four dynamical systems each of which only contains interactions within one four-pixel cell. For illustration see Figure 1. With $D = \begin{pmatrix} a & c \\ c & b \end{pmatrix}$ denoting the diffusion tensor discretised in $(\frac{3}{2},\frac{3}{2})$, one such four-pixel dynamical system for the cell $\{1,2\}\times\{1,2\}$ reads as follows:

$$\dot{u}_{1,1} = (a+b+2c)(u_{2,2}-u_{1,1}) + (a-b)(u_{2,1}-u_{1,2}),$$
$$\dot{u}_{2,1} = (a+b-2c)(u_{1,2}-u_{2,1}) + (a-b)(u_{1,1}-u_{2,2}),$$
$$\dot{u}_{1,2} = (a+b-2c)(u_{2,1}-u_{1,2}) + (a-b)(u_{2,2}-u_{1,1}), \tag{11}$$
$$\dot{u}_{2,2} = (a+b+2c)(u_{1,1}-u_{2,2}) + (a-b)(u_{1,2}-u_{2,1}).$$

2.3 Semi-analytical Solution of the Four-Pixel System

Next we want to solve the system (11) analytically where we assume that the diffusion tensors D are kept fixed during the image evolution[2]. To this end it is useful to introduce new variables $w_{i,j}$ by

$$W := HUH , \tag{12}$$

where $U := \begin{pmatrix} u_{1,1} & u_{2,1} \\ u_{1,2} & u_{2,2} \end{pmatrix}$, $W := \begin{pmatrix} w_{1,1} & w_{2,1} \\ w_{1,2} & w_{2,2} \end{pmatrix}$, and H happens to be the same matrix

as introduced by (6). Then we can rewrite (11) in terms of the new variables as

$$
\begin{aligned}
\dot{w}_{1,1} &= 0 , \\
\dot{w}_{2,1} &= -4aw_{2,1} - 4cw_{1,2} , \\
\dot{w}_{1,2} &= -4cw_{2,1} - 4bw_{1,2} , \\
\dot{w}_{2,2} &= 0 .
\end{aligned}
\tag{13}
$$

While $w_{1,1}$ and $w_{2,2}$ are constant, the dynamical system for $\mathbf{w} := (w_{2,1}, w_{1,2})^{\mathrm{T}}$ can be rewritten as

$$\dot{\mathbf{w}} = -4D\mathbf{w} . \tag{14}$$

Let the eigendecomposition of D be given by $D = \lambda_1 \mathbf{e}_1 \mathbf{e}_1^{\mathrm{T}} + \lambda_2 \mathbf{e}_2 \mathbf{e}_2^{\mathrm{T}}$ with eigenvalues $\lambda_{1,2} = \frac{1}{2}(a + b \pm \sqrt{(a - b)^2 + 4c^2})$ and orthonormal eigenvectors $\mathbf{e}_1, \mathbf{e}_2$. Then, remembering that D is kept constant, the solution of (14) is

$$\mathbf{w}(t) = e^{-4\lambda_1 t}(\mathbf{e}_1^{\mathrm{T}} \mathbf{w}(0))\mathbf{e}_1 + e^{-4\lambda_2 t}(\mathbf{e}_2^{\mathrm{T}} \mathbf{w}(0))\mathbf{e}_2 . \tag{15}$$

By the inverse transform of (12),

$$U(t) = H W(t) H , \tag{16}$$

this analytical solution can be expressed with respect to the original variables.

2.4 Numerical Scheme for Anisotropic Diffusion

We use now the explicit solution (15) of our four-pixel system as a building block for a numerical scheme for anisotropic diffusion. Because of the aforementioned splitting of (9) into the contributions from the four cells (10), the solution of (9) can be approximated by averaging the solutions of systems of the type (11). These solutions have been studied in Subsection 2.3. A time step will then be executed by computing the analytical solution (15) (resp. its back-transformed analog) for the desired evolution time, i.e. the time step size τ.

For the anisotropic diffusion processes that we are interested in, the diffusion tensor D depends on the structure tensor J_ϱ which arises from smoothing the outer product matrices $\nabla v \nabla v^{\mathrm{T}}$ with a suitable convolution kernel, as seen in (2). To evaluate (15) requires therefore to compute D from the current data u, and to determine the eigendecomposition of D.

---

[2] In analogy to semi-implicit schemes that keep the nonlinear diffusion fixed at the previous time level while discretising the remainder in an implicit fashion, we call a method semi-analytic if it freezes the diffusion tensor and searches for an analytic solution.

LSAS Algorithm for Anisotropic Diffusion

- **Compute the pre-smoothed image $v := K_\sigma * u^k$ by convolution.**

- **For each four-pixel cell $\{i, i + 1\} \times \{j, j + 1\}$, compute the approximation of the gradient ∇v according to (3), and the tensor product $\nabla v \nabla v^{\mathrm{T}}$.**

- **Compute the structure tensor field $J = K_\varrho * (\nabla v \nabla v^{\mathrm{T}})$ by convolution.**

- **For each four-pixel cell, compute the diffusion tensor $D = D(J)$.**

- **For each four-pixel cell, compute one time step of anisotropic diffusion via the analytical solution (12), (15), (16).**

- **For each pixel ($*$) with coordinates (i, j), consider the four cells**

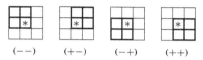

$$(--) \qquad (+-) \qquad (-+) \qquad (++)$$

which lead to four approximations

$$u_{i,j,--}^{k+1}, \ u_{i,j,+-}^{k+1}, \ u_{i,j,-+}^{k+1}, \ u_{i,j,++}^{k+1} .$$

Average:

$$u_{i,j}^{k+1} = \tfrac{1}{4}(u_{i,j,--}^{k+1} + u_{i,j,+-}^{k+1} + u_{i,j,-+}^{k+1} + u_{i,j,++}^{k+1}) .$$

Fig. 2. One time step of the locally semi-analytic scheme for anisotropic diffusion, where u^k, u^{k+1} refer to the old and new time step, respectively

We have therefore arrived at a *locally semi-analytic scheme (LSAS)* for anisotropic diffusion, one time step of which is summarised in Figure 2. The use of our analytical solution ensures that the resulting scheme for our four-pixel cell is stable in the Euclidean norm for any time step size (note that $\lambda_1, \lambda_2 \geq 0$). Since solutions from four-pixel cells are combined by simple averaging, this *absolute stability* transfers to the discretised anisotropic diffusion on the entire grid[3].

3   Anisotropic Wavelet Shrinkage

In [23], it was shown that one-dimensional nonlinear diffusion on two-pixel signals coincides with Haar wavelet shrinkage if the shrinkage function is chosen in accordance with the diffusivity and the threshold parameter is equal to the diffusion time. A generalisation of this result to isotropic two-dimensional nonlinear diffusion was proposed

---

[3] As for all known explicit diffusion schemes with unconditional stability, this favourable stability property is always in conjunction with conditional consistency: For fixed spatial grid size and a time step size tending to infinity, our scheme approaches a local averaging on a checkerboard decomposition of our grid.

in [28] where the shrinkage step was based on a diffusion inspired shrinkage function introduced in [16]. This shrinkage function couples the individual wavelet coefficients which leads to an improved rotation invariance of the procedure. Here we want to extend these promising results to the anisotropic setting.

The key for the connection between our four-pixel scheme and Haar wavelet shrinkage is the fact that the two-dimensional Haar wavelet transform acts naturally on subsequent 2×2-pixel tiles of an image. Let us choose one such tile, say $F := \begin{pmatrix} f_{1,1} & f_{2,1} \\ f_{1,2} & f_{2,2} \end{pmatrix}$, and explain how it changes under two-dimensional Haar wavelet shrinkage. One cycle of Haar wavelet shrinkage consists of three steps: the analysis step, the shrinkage step and the synthesis step.

In the *analysis step*, the four-pixel image F image is transformed into the wavelet domain. To this end, the low and high pass Haar filters are applied to the rows and columns of F. More precisely, F is multiplied from the left and the right by the matrix H from (6) which results in an image

$$C := HFH . \tag{17}$$

Obviously, with $U = F$ and $W = C$, this coincides with our variable transform (12).

The *shrinkage step* modifies the high-pass coefficients $c_{2,1}$, $c_{1,2}$ and $c_{2,2}$ of C by applying a shrinkage function S_θ depending on a threshold parameter θ. Let us consider two examples first before introducing a shrinkage rule inspired by anisotropic diffusion.

In ordinary wavelet shrinkage the thresholding depends on the individual coefficients. For example, *soft shrinkage* [11] shrinks the coefficients towards 0 by an amount that is given by a threshold parameter θ:

$$S_\theta(c_{i,j}) := \begin{cases} c_{i,j} - \theta \operatorname{sgn}(c_{i,j}) & \text{if } |c_{i,j}| \geq \theta , \\ 0 & \text{otherwise} . \end{cases} \tag{18}$$

In [16] a shrinkage function inspired by *isotropic* nonlinear diffusion filtering was introduced that leads to a *coupled* shrinking of the coefficients. More precisely, the thresholding applies with respect to $\gamma(C) := (c_{2,1}^2 + c_{1,2}^2 + c_{2,2}^2)^{\frac{1}{2}}$. For a soft shrinkage and $(i,j) \in \{(2,1), (1,2), (2,2)\}$ this comes down to

$$S_\theta(c_{i,j}) := \begin{cases} c_{i,j} - \frac{\theta}{\gamma(C)} \operatorname{sgn}(c_{i,j}) & \text{if } \gamma(C) \geq \theta , \\ 0 & \text{otherwise} . \end{cases} \tag{19}$$

Now we want to introduce an *anisotropic shrinkage* procedure with respect to a diffusion tensor D. In accordance with (13) and (15), we set $S_\theta(c_{2,2}) := c_{2,2}$ and define a coupled shrinkage of the antidiagonal coefficients $c_{1,2}$ and $c_{2,1}$ by

$$S_\theta\left(\begin{pmatrix} c_{2,1} \\ c_{1,2} \end{pmatrix}\right) := Q \begin{pmatrix} e^{-4\lambda_1\theta} & 0 \\ 0 & e^{-4\lambda_2\theta} \end{pmatrix} Q^{\mathrm{T}} \begin{pmatrix} c_{2,1} \\ c_{1,2} \end{pmatrix} , \tag{20}$$

where $Q := (e_1, e_2)$ denotes the eigenvector matrix of D, and the threshold parameter θ was identified with the diffusion time t. This shows that besides the low-pass coefficient $c_{1,1}$ also the high-pass coefficient $c_{2,2}$ remains unaffected, while the antidiagonal coefficients $c_{1,2}$ and $c_{2,1}$ are shrunken in a coupled way. Let us abbreviate this anisotropic shrinkage procedure by $S_\theta(C)$.

Finally, the *synthesis step* leads us from the wavelet domain back to the original image domain. To this end we perform the inverse transform of step 1,

$$F^{(1)} = HS_\theta(C)H \tag{21}$$

on the shrunken coefficients. This is just the analog of (16).

In summary, one cycle of the above anisotropic Haar wavelet shrinkage coincides with the solution of (11) with initial condition $U(0) = F$, where the threshold parameter plays the role of the diffusion time.

Expressing an image in terms of Haar wavelets leads to a natural decomposition into tiles of 2×2 pixels (decimated wavelet transform). Shrinking these tiles separately according to the preceding procedure is not translationally invariant. Fortunately this is cured by the averaging procedure (9). It can be interpreted as a so-called *cyclic spinning* [7] that is related to a shift-invariant undecimated wavelet transform.

Apart from shift invariance, the LSAS algorithm can also be seen as a simple approach to create *rotationally invariant* anisotropic Haar wavelet shrinkage: Since our novel anisotropic shrinkage rules are a numerical scheme for a rotationally invariant continuous diffusion filter, rotation invariance is approximated at no additional expense.

4   Experiments

In our first experiment (Fig. 3) we use our scheme to perform edge-enhancing diffusion [25]. In this case, there is no integration over the outer products, so $\varrho = 0$. The diffusion tensor D has the same eigenvectors as the outer product $J = \nabla v \nabla v^\mathrm{T}$, namely ∇v and its orthogonal $\nabla v^\perp$. The eigenvalue in direction ∇v is given by $g(|\nabla v|^2)$ where $g(s^2) = 1 - \exp(-3.31488\lambda^8/s^8)$ with a given threshold parameter $\lambda > 0$, which

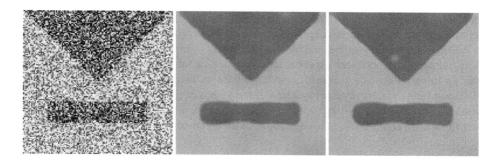

Fig. 3. Left to right: (a) Test image with noise. **(b)** Denoised by edge-enhancing diffusion with standard explicit scheme, $\lambda = 5$, $\sigma = 1.8$, $\varrho = 0$, $\tau = 0.166$, $N = 200$ iterations. **(c)** Denoised by edge-enhancing diffusion with LSAS, $\lambda = 5$, $\sigma = 1.8$, $\varrho = 0$, $\tau = 1$, $N = 200$ iterations.

Fig. 4. Left to right: (a) One quadrant of a rotationally invariant test image, 64×64 pixels. **(b)** Exact solution for coherence-enhancing diffusion with $\alpha = 0.001$, $C = 1$, $\sigma = 0.5$, $\varrho = 4$ and $t = 250$. **(c)** Filtered with the nonnegativity scheme [25] with $\tau = 1/6$, and $N = 1500$ iterations. Average absolute error: 17.99. **(d)** Processed with our LSAS algorithm, same parameters. Average absolute error: 3.81.

Fig. 5. Left to right: (a) Fingerprint image, 100×100 pixels. **(b)** Filtered with the nonnegativity scheme [25] for CED with $C = 1$, $\sigma = 0.5$, $\varrho = 4$, $\tau = 1/6$, and $N = 60$ iterations. **(c)** Processed with our LSAS algorithm for CED, same parameters. **(d)** LSAS algorithm with $\tau = 1$ and $N = 10$ iterations.

means that g is applied to the first eigenvalue of J. The eigenvalue of D in direction ∇v^{T} is fixed to 1. – The noisy image (Fig. 3a) is denoised with a standard explicit scheme with central spatial differences, and with the locally semi-analytic scheme. It is observed that the denoising result with our new scheme is slightly sharper. Moreover, a look at the parameters shows that the effective evolution time used by the new scheme is six times larger than with the explicit scheme which demonstrates how much the latter is indeed dominated by numerical blurring artifacts.

In our second experiment we consider coherence-enhancing diffusion (CED) [25]. It uses an integration scale ϱ that is considerably larger than σ, thereby introducing into J a smoothing over eigenvector systems. If the structure tensor has the eigendecomposition $J = \mu_1 \mathbf{e}_1 \mathbf{e}_1^{\mathrm{T}} + \mu_2 \mathbf{e}_2 \mathbf{e}_2^{\mathrm{T}}$ with $\mu_1 \geq \mu_2$, then the diffusion tensor $D(J)$ has the decomposition $D(J) := \lambda_1 \mathbf{e}_1 \mathbf{e}_1^{\mathrm{T}} + \lambda_2 \mathbf{e}_2 \mathbf{e}_2^{\mathrm{T}}$ with eigenvalues

$$\lambda_1 := \alpha,$$

$$\lambda_2 := \begin{cases} \alpha & \text{if } \mu_1 = \mu_2, \\ \alpha + (1-\alpha) \exp\left(\frac{-C}{(\mu_1 - \mu_2)^2} \right) & \text{else,} \end{cases} \tag{22}$$

some small regularisation parameter $\alpha > 0$ and a contrast parameter $C > 0$. This process smoothes along flow-like structures. For a rotationally invariant test image such as the one in Figure 4, only radial linear diffusion with diffusivity α takes place. Hence, the exact solution at time t is given by a convolution with a Gaussian of standard deviation $\sqrt{2\alpha t}$. By comparing the solutions of the so-called nonnegativity discretisation from [25] with our LSAS algorithm and the exact solution, we see that the LSAS does not suffer from visible blurring artifacts. It preserves rotation invariance very well and creates significantly lower errors than the nonnegativity scheme.

These quantitative findings are also confirmed in the fingerprint example in Figure 5. We observe that the LSAS gives much sharper results, and that it yields still realistic results for time step sizes far beyond the stability limit $1/6$ of the nonnegativity scheme.

5 Conclusions

The contributions in our paper are twofold: Firstly we have presented a novel scheme for anisotropic diffusion with a high degree of rotation invariance and practically invisible blurring artifacts. It is absolutely stable in the Euclidean norm and simple to implement due to its explicit nature. Therefore it can serve as the method of choice whenever a well-founded, highly accurate scheme for anisotropic, tensor-driven diffusion is required. Secondly, we have clarified the diffusion-wavelet connection in the anisotropic case for the first time in the literature. This has led to novel, anisotropic shrinkage rules with coupling of the coefficients. More importantly, it also demonstrates that sophisticated concepts such as ridgelets and curvelets are not the only way to perform advanced anisotropic wavelet-based shrinkage: Even the most elementary class of wavelets, namely Haar wavelets, are sufficient for implementing highly anisotropic filters in a rotationally invariant fashion. We hope that this novel connection can help to fertilise further research on simple, structure-adaptive anisotropic wavelet concepts and to gain new insights in the design of coupled shrinkage rules.

References

1. Y. Bao and H. Krim. Towards bridging scale-space and multiscale frame analyses. In A. A. Petrosian and F. G. Meyer, editors, *Wavelets in Signal and Image Analysis*, volume 19 of *Computational Imaging and Vision*, chapter 6. Kluwer, Dordrecht, 2001.
2. K. Bredies, D. A. Lorenz, P. Maaß, and G. Teschke. A partial differential equation for continuous non-linear shrinkage filtering and its application for analyzing MMG data. In F. Truchetet, editor, *Wavelet Applications in Industrial Processing*, volume 5266 of *Proceedings of SPIE*, pages 84–93. SPIE Press, Bellingham, 2004.
3. E. Candés, L. Demanet, D. Donoho, and L. Ying. Fast discrete curvelet transform. Technical report, Applied and Computational Mathematics, Caltech, Pasadena, CA, 2005.
4. E. J. Candés and D. L. Donoho. Curvelets: A surprisingly effective nonadaptive representation of objects with edges. In A. Cohen, C. Rabut, and L. L. Schumaker, editors, *Curve and Surface Fitting*, Saint-Malo, 2000. Vanderbilt University Press.
5. A. Chambolle and B. L. Lucier. Interpreting translationally-invariant wavelet shrinkage as a new image smoothing scale space. *IEEE Transactions on Image Processing*, 10(7):993–1000, 2001.

6. A. Cohen, W. Dahmen, I. Daubechies, and R. DeVore. Harmonic analysis in the space BV. *Revista Matematica Iberoamericana*, 19:235–262, 2003.

7. R. R. Coifman and D. Donoho. Translation invariant denoising. In A. Antoine and G. Oppenheim, editors, *Wavelets in Statistics*, pages 125–150. Springer, New York, 1995.

8. R. R. Coifman and A. Sowa. New methods of controlled total variation reduction for digital functions. *SIAM Journal on Numerical Analysis*, 39(2):480–498, 2001.

9. M. N. Do and V. Vetterli. Contourlets. In J. Stöckler and G. Welland, editors, *Beyond Wavelets*, pages 1–27. Academic Press, New York, 2003.

10. D. Donoho and A. Flesia. Digital ridgelet transform based on true ridge functions. In J. Stöckler and G. Welland, editors, *Beyond Wavelets*, pages 1–33. Academic Press, New York, 2003.

11. D. L. Donoho. De-noising by soft thresholding. *IEEE Transactions on Information Theory*, 41:613–627, 1995.

12. D. L. Donoho. Orthonormal ridglets and linear singularities. *SIAM Journal on Mathematical Analysis*, 31(5):1062–1099, 2000.

13. W. Förstner and E. Gülch. A fast operator for detection and precise location of distinct points, corners and centres of circular features. In *Proc. ISPRS Intercommission Conference on Fast Processing of Photogrammetric Data*, pages 281–305, Interlaken, Switzerland, June 1987.

14. B. Jawerth, P. Lin, and E. Sinzinger. Lattice Boltzmann models for anisotropic diffusion of images. *Journal of Mathematical Imaging and Vision*, 11:231–237, 1999.

15. Y. Meyer. *Oscillating Patterns in Image Processing and Nonlinear Evolution Equations*, volume 22 of *University Lecture Series*. AMS, Providence, 2001.

16. P. Mrázek and J. Weickert. Rotationally invariant wavelet shrinkage. In B. Michaelis and G. Krell, editors, *Pattern Recognition*, volume 2781 of *Lecture Notes in Computer Science*, pages 156–163, Berlin, 2003. Springer.

17. P. Mrázek, J. Weickert, and G. Steidl. Diffusion-inspired shrinkage functions and stability results for wavelet denoising. *International Journal of Computer Vision*, 64(2/3):171–186, Sept. 2005.

18. P. Perona and J. Malik. Scale space and edge detection using anisotropic diffusion. *IEEE Transactions on Pattern Analysis and Machine Intelligence*, 12:629–639, 1990.

19. T. Preußer and M. Rumpf. An adaptive finite element method for large scale image processing. *Journal of Visual Communication and Image Representation*, 11(2):183–195, June 2000.

20. J. Shen. A note on wavelets and diffusion. *Journal of Computational Analysis and Applications*, 5(1):147–159, 2003.

21. E. P. Simoncelli. Design of multidimensional derivative filters. In *Proc. 1994 IEEE International Conference on Image Processing*, volume 1, pages 790–793, Austin, TX, Nov. 1994.

22. N. Sochen, R. Kimmel, and F. Bruckstein. Diffusions and confusions in signal and image processing. *Journal of Mathematical Imaging and Vision*, 14(3):195–210, May 2001.

23. G. Steidl, J. Weickert, T. Brox, P. Mrázek, and M. Welk. On the equivalence of soft wavelet shrinkage, total variation diffusion, total variation regularization, and SIDEs. *SIAM Journal on Numerical Analysis*, 42(2):686–713, 2004.

24. W. Wang. On the design of optimal derivative filters for coherence-enhancing diffusion filtering. In *Proc. 2004 International Conference on Computer Graphics, Imaging and Visualization*, pages 35–40, Penang, Malaysia, July 2004. IEEE Computer Society Press.

25. J. Weickert. *Anisotropic Diffusion in Image Processing*. Teubner, Stuttgart, 1998.

26. J. Weickert and H. Scharr. A scheme for coherence-enhancing diffusion filtering with op-timized rotation invariance. *Journal of Visual Communication and Image Representation*, 13(1/2):103–118, 2002.

27. J. Weickert, G. Steidl, P. Mrázek, M. Welk, and T. Brox. Diffusion filters and wavelets: What can they learn from each other? In N. Paragios, Y. Chen, and O. Faugeras, editors, *The Handbook of Mathematical Models in Computer Vision*. Springer, New York, 2005.

28. M. Welk, J. Weickert, and G. Steidl. A four-pixel scheme for singular differential equations. In R. Kimmel, N. Sochen, and J. Weickert, editors, *Scale-Space and PDE Methods in Computer Vision*, volume 3459 of *Lecture Notes in Computer Science*, pages 585–597, Berlin, 2005. Springer.

SURF: Speeded Up Robust Features

Herbert Bay[1], Tinne Tuytelaars[2], and Luc Van Gool[1,2]

[1] ETH Zurich
{bay, vangool}@vision.ee.ethz.ch
[2] Katholieke Universiteit Leuven
{Tinne.Tuytelaars, Luc.Vangool}@esat.kuleuven.be

Abstract. In this paper, we present a novel scale- and rotation-invariant interest point detector and descriptor, coined SURF (Speeded Up Robust Features). It approximates or even outperforms previously proposed schemes with respect to repeatability, distinctiveness, and robustness, yet can be computed and compared much faster.

This is achieved by relying on integral images for image convolutions; by building on the strengths of the leading existing detectors and descriptors (*in casu*, using a Hessian matrix-based measure for the detector, and a distribution-based descriptor); and by simplifying these methods to the essential. This leads to a combination of novel detection, description, and matching steps. The paper presents experimental results on a standard evaluation set, as well as on imagery obtained in the context of a real-life object recognition application. Both show SURF's strong performance.

1 Introduction

The task of finding correspondences between two images of the same scene or object is part of many computer vision applications. Camera calibration, 3D reconstruction, image registration, and object recognition are just a few. The search for discrete image correspondences – the goal of this work – can be divided into three main steps. First, 'interest points' are selected at distinctive locations in the image, such as corners, blobs, and T-junctions. The most valuable property of an interest point *detector* is its repeatability, i.e. whether it reliably finds the same interest points under different viewing conditions. Next, the neighbourhood of every interest point is represented by a feature vector. This *descriptor* has to be distinctive and, at the same time, robust to noise, detection errors, and geometric and photometric deformations. Finally, the descriptor vectors are *matched* between different images. The matching is often based on a distance between the vectors, e.g. the Mahalanobis or Euclidean distance. The dimension of the descriptor has a direct impact on the time this takes, and a lower number of dimensions is therefore desirable.

It has been our goal to develop both a detector and descriptor, which in comparison to the state-of-the-art are faster to compute, while not sacrificing performance. In order to succeed, one has to strike a balance between the above

A. Leonardis, H. Bischof, and A. Pinz (Eds.): ECCV 2006, Part I, LNCS 3951, pp. 404–417, 2006.
© Springer-Verlag Berlin Heidelberg 2006

requirements, like reducing the descriptor's dimension and complexity, while keeping it sufficiently distinctive.

A wide variety of detectors and descriptors have already been proposed in the literature (e.g. [1, 2, 3, 4, 5, 6]). Also, detailed comparisons and evaluations on benchmarking datasets have been performed [7, 8, 9]. While constructing our fast detector and descriptor, we built on the insights gained from this previous work in order to get a feel for what are the aspects contributing to performance. In our experiments on benchmark image sets as well as on a real object recognition application, the resulting detector and descriptor are not only faster, but also more distinctive and equally repeatable.

When working with local features, a first issue that needs to be settled is the required level of invariance. Clearly, this depends on the expected geometric and photometric deformations, which in turn are determined by the possible changes in viewing conditions. Here, we focus on scale and image rotation invariant detectors and descriptors. These seem to offer a good compromise between feature complexity and robustness to commonly occurring deformations. Skew, anisotropic scaling, and perspective effects are assumed to be second-order effects, that are covered to some degree by the overall robustness of the descriptor. As also claimed by Lowe [2], the additional complexity of full affine-invariant features often has a negative impact on their robustness and does not pay off, unless really large viewpoint changes are to be expected. In some cases, even rotation invariance can be left out, resulting in a scale-invariant only version of our descriptor, which we refer to as 'upright SURF' (U-SURF). Indeed, in quite a few applications, like mobile robot navigation or visual tourist guiding, the camera often only rotates about the vertical axis. The benefit of avoiding the overkill of rotation invariance in such cases is not only increased speed, but also increased discriminative power. Concerning the photometric deformations, we assume a simple linear model with a scale factor and offset. Notice that our detector and descriptor don't use colour.

The paper is organised as follows. Section 2 describes related work, on which our results are founded. Section 3 describes the interest point detection scheme. In section 4, the new descriptor is presented. Finally, section 5 shows the experimental results and section 6 concludes the paper.

2   Related Work

Interest Point Detectors. The most widely used detector probably is the Harris corner detector [10], proposed back in 1988, based on the eigenvalues of the second-moment matrix. However, Harris corners are not scale-invariant. Lindeberg introduced the concept of automatic scale selection [1]. This allows to detect interest points in an image, each with their own characteristic scale. He experimented with both the determinant of the Hessian matrix as well as the Laplacian (which corresponds to the trace of the Hessian matrix) to detect blob-like structures. Mikolajczyk and Schmid refined this method, creating robust and scale-invariant feature detectors with high repeatability, which they coined Harris-Laplace and Hessian-Laplace [11]. They used a (scale-adapted) Harris measure or the determinant of the Hessian matrix to select the location, and the Laplacian to select the scale. Focusing on speed, Lowe [12] approximated the Laplacian of Gaussian (LoG) by a Difference of Gaussians (DoG) filter.

Several other scale-invariant interest point detectors have been proposed. Examples are the salient region detector proposed by Kadir and Brady [13], which maximises the entropy within the region, and the edge-based region detector proposed by Jurie et al. [14]. They seem less amenable to acceleration though. Also, several affine-invariant feature detectors have been proposed that can cope with longer viewpoint changes. However, these fall outside the scope of this paper.

By studying the existing detectors and from published comparisons [15, 8], we can conclude that (1) Hessian-based detectors are more stable and repeatable than their Harris-based counterparts. Using the determinant of the Hessian matrix rather than its trace (the Laplacian) seems advantageous, as it fires less on elongated, ill-localised structures. Also, (2) approximations like the DoG can bring speed at a low cost in terms of lost accuracy.

Feature Descriptors. An even larger variety of feature descriptors has been proposed, like Gaussian derivatives [16], moment invariants [17], complex features [18, 19], steerable filters [20], phase-based local features [21], and descriptors representing the distribution of smaller-scale features within the interest point neighbourhood. The latter, introduced by Lowe [2], have been shown to outperform the others [7]. This can be explained by the fact that they capture a substantial amount of information about the spatial intensity patterns, while at the same time being robust to small deformations or localisation errors. The descriptor in [2], called SIFT for short, computes a histogram of local oriented gradients around the interest point and stores the bins in a 128-dimensional vector (8 orientation bins for each of the 4×4 location bins).

Various refinements on this basic scheme have been proposed. Ke and Sukthankar [4] applied PCA on the gradient image. This PCA-SIFT yields a 36-dimensional descriptor which is fast for matching, but proved to be less distinctive than SIFT in a second comparative study by Mikolajczyk et al. [8] and slower feature computation reduces the effect of fast matching. In the same paper [8], the authors have proposed a variant of SIFT, called GLOH, which proved to be even more distinctive with the same number of dimensions. However, GLOH is computationally more expensive.

The SIFT descriptor still seems to be the most appealing descriptor for practical uses, and hence also the most widely used nowadays. It is distinctive *and* relatively fast, which is crucial for on-line applications. Recently, Se et al. [22] implemented SIFT on a Field Programmable Gate Array (FPGA) and improved its speed by an order of magnitude. However, the high dimensionality of the descriptor is a drawback of SIFT at the matching step. For on-line applications on a regular PC, each one of the three steps (detection, description, matching) should be faster still. Lowe proposed a best-bin-first alternative [2] in order to speed up the matching step, but this results in lower accuracy.

Our approach. In this paper, we propose a novel detector-descriptor scheme, coined SURF (Speeded-Up Robust Features). The detector is based on the Hessian matrix [11, 1], but uses a very basic approximation, just as DoG [2] is a very basic Laplacian-based detector. It relies on integral images to reduce the computation time and we therefore call it the 'Fast-Hessian' detector. The descriptor, on the other hand, describes a distribution of Haar-wavelet responses within the interest point neighbourhood. Again, we exploit integral images for speed. Moreover, only 64 dimensions are used, reducing the time for feature computation and matching, and increasing simultaneously the robustness. We also present a new indexing step based on the sign of the Laplacian, which increases not only the matching speed, but also the robustness of the descriptor.

In order to make the paper more self-contained, we succinctly discuss the concept of integral images, as defined by [23]. They allow for the fast implementation of box type convolution filters. The entry of an integral image $I_\Sigma(\mathbf{x})$ at a location $\mathbf{x} = (x, y)$ represents the sum of all pixels in the input image I of a rectangular region formed by the point $\mathbf{x}$ and the origin, $I_\Sigma(\mathbf{x}) = \sum_{i=0}^{i \leq x} \sum_{j=0}^{j \leq y} I(i, j)$. With I_Σ calculated, it only takes four additions to calculate the sum of the intensities over any upright, rectangular area, independent of its size.

3   Fast-Hessian Detector

We base our detector on the Hessian matrix because of its good performance in computation time and accuracy. However, rather than using a different measure for selecting the location and the scale (as was done in the Hessian-Laplace detector [11]), we rely on the determinant of the Hessian for both. Given a point $\mathbf{x} = (x, y)$ in an image I, the Hessian matrix $\mathcal{H}(\mathbf{x}, \sigma)$ in $\mathbf{x}$ at scale σ is defined as follows

$$\mathcal{H}(\mathbf{x}, \sigma) = \begin{bmatrix} L_{xx}(\mathbf{x}, \sigma) & L_{xy}(\mathbf{x}, \sigma) \\ L_{xy}(\mathbf{x}, \sigma) & L_{yy}(\mathbf{x}, \sigma) \end{bmatrix}, \tag{1}$$

where $L_{xx}(\mathbf{x}, \sigma)$ is the convolution of the Gaussian second order derivative $\frac{\partial^2}{\partial x^2} g(\sigma)$ with the image I in point $\mathbf{x}$, and similarly for $L_{xy}(\mathbf{x}, \sigma)$ and $L_{yy}(\mathbf{x}, \sigma)$.

Gaussians are optimal for scale-space analysis, as shown in [24]. In practice, however, the Gaussian needs to be discretised and cropped (Fig. 1 left half), and even with Gaussian filters aliasing still occurs as soon as the resulting images are sub-sampled. Also, the property that no new structures can appear while going to lower resolutions may have been proven in the 1D case, but is known to not apply in the relevant 2D case [25]. Hence, the importance of the Gaussian seems to have been somewhat overrated in this regard, and here we test a simpler alternative. As Gaussian filters are non-ideal in any case, and given Lowe's success with LoG approximations, we push the approximation even further with box filters (Fig. 1 right half). These approximate second order Gaussian derivatives, and can be evaluated very fast using integral images, independently of size. As shown in the results section, the performance is comparable to the one using the discretised and cropped Gaussians.

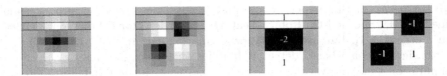

Fig. 1. Left to right: The (discretised and cropped) Gaussian second order partial derivatives in y-direction and xy-direction, and our approximations thereof using box filters. The grey regions are equal to zero.

The 9×9 box filters in Fig. 1 are approximations for Gaussian second order derivatives with $\sigma = 1.2$ and represent our lowest scale (i.e. highest spatial resolution). We denote our approximations by D_{xx}, D_{yy}, and D_{xy}. The weights applied to the rectangular regions are kept simple for computational efficiency, but we need to further balance the relative weights in the expression for the Hessian's determinant with $\frac{|L_{xy}(1.2)|_F |D_{xx}(9)|_F}{|L_{xx}(1.2)|_F |D_{xy}(9)|_F} = 0.912... \simeq 0.9$, where $|x|_F$ is the Frobenius norm. This yields

$$\det(\mathcal{H}_{\mathrm{approx}}) = D_{xx}D_{yy} - (0.9D_{xy})^2. \tag{2}$$

Furthermore, the filter responses are normalised with respect to the mask size. This guarantees a constant Frobenius norm for any filter size.

Scale spaces are usually implemented as image pyramids. The images are repeatedly smoothed with a Gaussian and subsequently sub-sampled in order to achieve a higher level of the pyramid. Due to the use of box filters and integral images, we do not have to iteratively apply the same filter to the output of a previously filtered layer, but instead can apply such filters of any size at exactly the same speed directly on the original image, and even in parallel (although the latter is not exploited here). Therefore, the scale space is analysed by up-scaling the filter size rather than iteratively reducing the image size. The output of the above 9×9 filter is considered as the initial scale layer, to which we will refer as scale $s = 1.2$ (corresponding to Gaussian derivatives with $\sigma = 1.2$). The following layers are obtained by filtering the image with gradually bigger masks, taking into account the discrete nature of integral images and the specific structure of our filters. Specifically, this results in filters of size 9×9, 15×15, 21×21, 27×27, etc. At larger scales, the step between consecutive filter sizes should also scale accordingly. Hence, for each new octave, the filter size increase is doubled (going from 6 to 12 to 24). Simultaneously, the sampling intervals for the extraction of the interest points can be doubled as well.

As the ratios of our filter layout remain constant after scaling, the approximated Gaussian derivatives scale accordingly. Thus, for example, our 27×27 filter corresponds to $\sigma = 3 \times 1.2 = 3.6 = s$. Furthermore, as the Frobenius norm remains constant for our filters, they are already scale normalised [26].

In order to localise interest points in the image and over scales, a non-maximum suppression in a $3 \times 3 \times 3$ neighbourhood is applied. The maxima of the determinant of the Hessian matrix are then interpolated in scale and

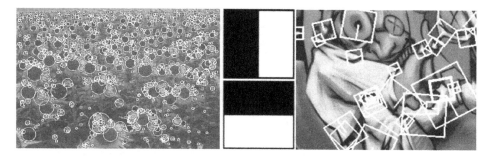

Fig. 2. Left: Detected interest points for a Sunflower field. This kind of scenes shows clearly the nature of the features from Hessian-based detectors. Middle: Haar wavelet types used for SURF. Right: Detail of the Graffiti scene showing the size of the descriptor window at different scales.

image space with the method proposed by Brown *et al.* [27]. Scale space interpolation is especially important in our case, as the difference in scale between the first layers of every octave is relatively large. Fig. 2 (left) shows an example of the detected interest points using our 'Fast-Hessian' detector.

4   SURF Descriptor

The good performance of SIFT compared to other descriptors [8] is remarkable. Its mixing of crudely localised information and the distribution of gradient related features seems to yield good distinctive power while fending off the effects of localisation errors in terms of scale or space. Using relative strengths and orientations of gradients reduces the effect of photometric changes.

The proposed SURF descriptor is based on similar properties, with a complexity stripped down even further. The first step consists of fixing a reproducible orientation based on information from a circular region around the interest point. Then, we construct a square region aligned to the selected orientation, and extract the SURF descriptor from it. These two steps are now explained in turn. Furthermore, we also propose an upright version of our descriptor (U-SURF) that is not invariant to image rotation and therefore faster to compute and better suited for applications where the camera remains more or less horizontal.

4.1   Orientation Assignment

In order to be invariant to rotation, we identify a reproducible orientation for the interest points. For that purpose, we first calculate the Haar-wavelet responses in x and y direction, shown in Fig. 2, and this in a circular neighbourhood of radius $6s$ around the interest point, with s the scale at which the interest point was detected. Also the sampling step is scale dependent and chosen to be s. In keeping with the rest, also the wavelet responses are computed at that current scale s. Accordingly, at high scales the size of the wavelets is big. Therefore, we use again integral images for fast filtering. Only six operations are needed to compute the response in x or y direction at any scale. The side length of the wavelets is $4s$.

Once the wavelet responses are calculated and weighted with a Gaussian ($\sigma = 2.5s$) centered at the interest point, the responses are represented as vectors in a space with the horizontal response strength along the abscissa and the vertical response strength along the ordinate. The dominant orientation is estimated by calculating the sum of all responses within a sliding orientation window covering an angle of $\frac{\pi}{3}$. The horizontal and vertical responses within the window are summed. The two summed responses then yield a new vector. The longest such vector lends its orientation to the interest point. The size of the sliding window is a parameter, which has been chosen experimentally. Small sizes fire on single dominating wavelet responses, large sizes yield maxima in vector length that are not outspoken. Both result in an unstable orientation of the interest region. Note the U-SURF skips this step.

4.2   Descriptor Components

For the extraction of the descriptor, the first step consists of constructing a square region centered around the interest point, and oriented along the orientation selected in the previous section. For the upright version, this transformation is not necessary. The size of this window is $20s$. Examples of such square regions are illustrated in Fig. 2.

The region is split up regularly into smaller 4×4 square sub-regions. This keeps important spatial information in. For each sub-region, we compute a few simple features at 5×5 regularly spaced sample points. For reasons of simplicity, we call d_x the Haar wavelet response in horizontal direction and d_y the Haar wavelet response in vertical direction (filter size $2s$). "Horizontal" and "vertical" here is defined in relation to the selected interest point orientation. To increase the robustness towards geometric deformations and localisation errors, the responses d_x and d_y are first weighted with a Gaussian ($\sigma = 3.3s$) centered at the interest point.

Then, the wavelet responses d_x and d_y are summed up over each subregion and form a first set of entries to the feature vector. In order to bring in information about the polarity of the intensity changes, we also extract the sum of the absolute values of the responses, $|d_x|$ and $|d_y|$. Hence, each sub-region has a four-dimensional descriptor vector $\mathbf{v}$ for its underlying intensity structure $\mathbf{v} = (\sum d_x, \sum d_y, \sum |d_x|, \sum |d_y|)$. This results in a descriptor vector for all 4×4 sub-regions of length 64. The wavelet responses are invariant to a bias in illumination (offset). Invariance to contrast (a scale factor) is achieved by turning the descriptor into a unit vector.

Fig. 3 shows the properties of the descriptor for three distinctively different image intensity patterns within a subregion. One can imagine combinations of such local intensity patterns, resulting in a distinctive descriptor.

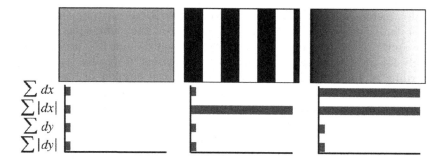

Fig. 3. The descriptor entries of a sub-region represent the nature of the underlying intensity pattern. Left: In case of a homogeneous region, all values are relatively low. Middle: In presence of frequencies in x direction, the value of $\sum |d_x|$ is high, but all others remain low. If the intensity is gradually increasing in x direction, both values $\sum d_x$ and $\sum |d_x|$ are high.

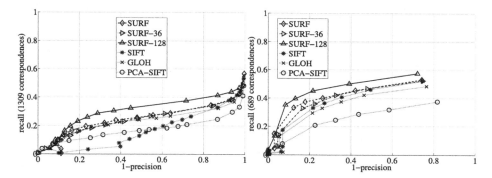

Fig. 4. The *recall* vs. *(1-precision)* graph for different binning methods and two different matching strategies tested on the 'Graffiti' sequence (image 1 and 3) with a view change of 30 degrees, compared to the current descriptors. The interest points are computed with our 'Fast Hessian' detector. Note that the interest points are not affine invariant. The results are therefore not comparable to the ones in [8]. SURF-128 corresponds to the extended descriptor. Left: Similarity-threshold-based matching strategy. Right: Nearest-neighbour-ratio matching strategy (See section 5).

In order to arrive at these SURF descriptors, we experimented with fewer and more wavelet features, using d_x^2 and d_y^2, higher-order wavelets, PCA, median values, average values, etc. From a thorough evaluation, the proposed sets turned out to perform best. We then varied the number of sample points and sub-regions. The 4×4 sub-region division solution provided the best results. Considering finer subdivisions appeared to be less robust and would increase matching times too much. On the other hand, the short descriptor with 3×3 subregions (SURF-36) performs worse, but allows for very fast matching and is still quite acceptable in comparison to other descriptors in the literature. Fig. 4 shows only a few of these comparison results (SURF-128 will be explained shortly).

We also tested an alternative version of the SURF descriptor that adds a couple of similar features (SURF-128). It again uses the same sums as before, but now splits these values up further. The sums of d_x and $|d_x|$ are computed separately for $d_y < 0$ and $d_y \geq 0$. Similarly, the sums of d_y and $|d_y|$ are split up according to the sign of d_x, thereby doubling the number of features. The descriptor is more distinctive and not much slower to compute, but slower to match due to its higher dimensionality.

In Figure 4, the parameter choices are compared for the standard 'Graffiti' scene, which is the most challenging of all the scenes in the evaluation set of Mikolajczyk [8], as it contains out-of-plane rotation, in-plane rotation as well as brightness changes. The extended descriptor for 4 × 4 subregions (SURF-128) comes out to perform best. Also, SURF performs well and is faster to handle. Both outperform the existing state-of-the-art.

For fast indexing during the matching stage, the sign of the Laplacian (i.e. the trace of the Hessian matrix) for the underlying interest point is included. Typically, the interest points are found at blob-type structures. The sign of the Laplacian distinguishes bright blobs on dark backgrounds from the reverse situation. This feature is available at no extra computational cost, as it was already computed during the detection phase. In the matching stage, we only compare features if they have the same type of contrast. Hence, this minimal information allows for faster matching and gives a slight increase in performance.

5   Experimental Results

First, we present results on a standard evaluation set, fot both the detector and the descriptor. Next, we discuss results obtained in a real-life object recognition application. All detectors and descriptors in the comparison are based on the original implementations of authors.

Standard Evaluation. We tested our detector and descriptor using the image sequences and testing software provided by Mikolajczyk [1]. These are images of real textured and structured scenes. Due to space limitations, we cannot show the results on all sequences. For the detector comparison, we selected the two viewpoint changes (Graffiti and Wall), one zoom and rotation (Boat) and lighting changes (Leuven) (see Fig. 6, discussed below). The descriptor evaluations are shown for all sequences except the Bark sequence (see Fig. 4 and 7).

For the detectors, we use the repeatability score, as described in [9]. This indicates how many of the detected interest points are found in both images, relative to the lowest total number of interest points found (where only the part of the image that is visible in both images is taken into account).

The detector is compared to the difference of Gaussian (DoG) detector by Lowe [2], and the Harris- and Hessian-Laplace detectors proposed by Mikolajczyk [15]. The number of interest points found is on average very similar for all detectors. This holds for all images, including those from the database used in

---

[1] http://www.robots.ox.ac.uk/~vgg/research/affine/

Table 1. Thresholds, number of detected points and calculation time for the detectors in our comparison. (First image of Graffiti scene, 800 × 640).

detector	threshold	nb of points	comp. time (msec)
Fast-Hessian	600	1418	120
Hessian-Laplace	1000	1979	650
Harris-Laplace	2500	1664	1800
DoG	default	1520	400

the object recognition experiment, see Table 1 for an example. As can be seen our 'Fast-Hessian' detector is more than 3 times faster that DoG and 5 times faster than Hessian-Laplace. At the same time, the repeatability for our detector is comparable (Graffiti, Leuven, Boats) or even better (Wall) than for the competitors. Note that the sequences Graffiti and Wall contain out-of-plane rotation, resulting in affine deformations, while the detectors in the comparison are only rotation- and scale invariant. Hence, these deformations have to be tackled by the overall robustness of the features.

The descriptors are evaluated using recall-(1-precision) graphs, as in [4] and [8]. For each evaluation, we used the first and the fourth image of the sequence, except for the Graffiti (image 1 and 3) and the Wall scene (image 1 and 5), corresponding to a viewpoint change of 30 and 50 degrees, respectively. In figures 4 and 7, we compared our SURF descriptor to GLOH, SIFT and PCA-SIFT, based on interest points detected with our 'Fast-Hessian' detector. SURF outperformed the other descriptors for almost all the comparisons. In Fig. 4, we compared the results using two different matching techniques, one based on the similarity threshold and one based on the nearest neighbour ratio (see [8] for a discussion on these techniques). This has an effect on the ranking of the descriptors, yet SURF performed best in both cases. Due to space limitations, only results on similarity threshold based matching are shown in Fig. 7, as this technique is better suited to represent the distribution of the descriptor in its feature space [8] and it is in more general use.

The SURF descriptor outperforms the other descriptors in a systematic and significant way, with sometimes more than 10% improvement in recall for the same level of precision. At the same time, it is fast to compute (see Table 2). The accurate version (SURF-128), presented in section 4, showed slightly better results than the regular SURF, but is slower to match and therefore less interesting for speed-dependent applications.

Table 2. Computation times for the joint detector - descriptor implementations, tested on the first image of the Graffiti sequence. The thresholds are adapted in order to detect the same number of interest points for all methods. These relative speeds are also representative for other images.

	U-SURF	SURF	SURF-128	SIFT
time (ms):	255	354	391	1036

Fig. 5. An example image from the reference set (left) and the test set (right). Note the difference in viewpoint and colours.

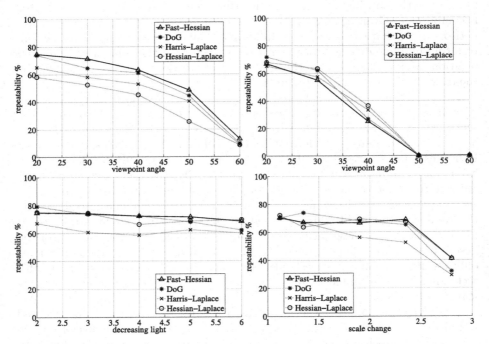

Fig. 6. Repeatability score for image sequences, from left to right and top to bottom, Wall and Graffiti (Viewpoint Change), Leuven (Lighting Change) and Boat (Zoom and Rotation)

Note that throughout the paper, including the object recognition experiment, we always use the same set of parameters and thresholds (see table 1). The timings were evaluated on a standard Linux PC (Pentium IV, 3GHz).

Object Recognition. We also tested the new features on a practical application, aimed at recognising objects of art in a museum. The database consists of 216 images of 22 objects. The images of the test set (116 images) were taken under various conditions, including extreme lighting changes, objects in reflecting

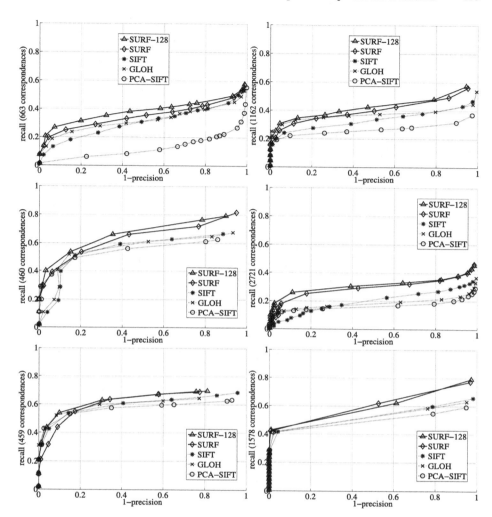

Fig. 7. Recall, 1-Precision graphs for, from left to right and top to bottom, Viewpoint change of 50 (Wall) degrees, scale factor 2 (Boat), image blur (Bikes and Trees), brightness change (Leuven) and JPEG compression (Ubc)

glass cabinets, viewpoint changes, zoom, different camera qualities, etc. Moreover, the images are small (320×240) and therefore more challenging for object recognition, as many details get lost.

In order to recognise the objects from the database, we proceed as follows. The images in the test set are compared to all images in the reference set by matching their respective interest points. The object shown on the reference image with the highest number of matches with respect to the test image is chosen as the recognised object.

The matching is carried out as follows. An interest point in the test image is compared to an interest point in the reference image by calculating the Euclidean distance between their descriptor vectors. A matching pair is detected, if its distance is closer than 0.7 times the distance of the second nearest neighbour. This is the nearest neighbour ratio matching strategy [18, 2, 7]. Obviously, additional geometric constraints reduce the impact of false positive matches, yet this can be done on top of any matcher. For comparing reasons, this does not make sense, as these may hide shortcomings of the basic schemes. The average recognition rates reflect the results of our performance evaluation. The leader is SURF-128 with 85.7% recognition rate, followed by U-SURF (83.8%) and SURF (82.6%). The other descriptors achieve 78.3% (GLOH), 78.1% (SIFT) and 72.3% (PCA-SIFT).

6 Conclusion

We have presented a fast and performant interest point detection-description scheme which outperforms the current state-of-the art, both in speed and accuracy. The descriptor is easily extendable for the description of affine invariant regions. Future work will aim at optimising the code for additional speed up. A binary of the latest version is available on the internet[2].

Acknowledgements. The authors gratefully acknowledge the support from Swiss SNF NCCR project IM2, Toyota-TME and the Flemish Fund for Scientific Research.

References

1. Lindeberg, T.: Feature detection with automatic scale selection. IJCV **30(2)** (1998) 79 – 116
2. Lowe, D.: Distinctive image features from scale-invariant keypoints, cascade filtering approach. IJCV **60** (2004) 91 – 110
3. Mikolajczyk, K., Schmid, C.: An affine invariant interest point detector. In: ECCV. (2002) 128 – 142
4. Ke, Y., Sukthankar, R.: PCA-SIFT: A more distinctive representation for local image descriptors. In: CVPR (2). (2004) 506 – 513
5. Tuytelaars, T., Van Gool, L.: Wide baseline stereo based on local, affinely invariant regions. In: BMVC. (2000) 412 – 422
6. Matas, J., Chum, O., M., U., Pajdla, T.: Robust wide baseline stereo from maximally stable extremal regions. In: BMVC. (2002) 384 – 393
7. Mikolajczyk, K., Schmid, C.: A performance evaluation of local descriptors. In: CVPR. Volume 2. (2003) 257 – 263
8. Mikolajczyk, K., Schmid, C.: A performance evaluation of local descriptors. PAMI **27** (2005) 1615–1630
9. Mikolajczyk, K., Tuytelaars, T., Schmid, C., Zisserman, A., Matas, J., Schaffalitzky, F., Kadir, T., Van Gool, L.: A comparison of affine region detectors. IJCV **65** (2005) 43–72

---

[2] http://www.vision.ee.ethz.ch/~surf/

10. Harris, C., Stephens, M.: A combined corner and edge detector. In: Proceedings of the Alvey Vision Conference. (1988) 147 – 151
11. Mikolajczyk, K., Schmid, C.: Indexing based on scale invariant interest points. In: ICCV. Volume 1. (2001) 525 – 531
12. Lowe, D.: Object recognition from local scale-invariant features. In: ICCV. (1999)
13. Kadir, T., Brady, M.: Scale, saliency and image description. IJCV **45(2)** (2001) 83 – 105
14. Jurie, F., Schmid, C.: Scale-invariant shape features for recognition of object categories. In: CVPR. Volume II. (2004) 90 – 96
15. Mikolajczyk, K., Schmid, C.: Scale and affine invariant interest point detectors. IJCV **60** (2004) 63 – 86
16. Florack, L.M.J., Haar Romeny, B.M.t., Koenderink, J.J., Viergever, M.A.: General intensity transformations and differential invariants. JMIV **4** (1994) 171–187
17. Mindru, F., Tuytelaars, T., Van Gool, L., Moons, T.: Moment invariants for recognition under changing viewpoint and illumination. CVIU **94** (2004) 3–27
18. Baumberg, A.: Reliable feature matching across widely separated views. In: CVPR. (2000) 774 – 781
19. Schaffalitzky, F., Zisserman, A.: Multi-view matching for unordered image sets, or "How do I organize my holiday snaps?". In: ECCV. Volume 1. (2002) 414 – 431
20. Freeman, W.T., Adelson, E.H.: The design and use of steerable filters. PAMI **13** (1991) 891 – 906
21. Carneiro, G., Jepson, A.: Multi-scale phase-based local features. In: CVPR (1). (2003) 736 – 743
22. Se, S., Ng, H., Jasiobedzki, P., Moyung, T.: Vision based modeling and localization for planetary exploration rovers. Proceedings of International Astronautical Congress (2004)
23. Viola, P., Jones, M.: Rapid object detection using a boosted cascade of simple features. In: CVPR (1). (2001) 511 – 518
24. Koenderink, J.: The structure of images. Biological Cybernetics **50** (1984) 363 – 370
25. Lindeberg, T.: Discrete Scale-Space Theory and the Scale-Space Primal Sketch, PhD, KTH Stockholm,. KTH (1991)
26. Lindeberg, T., Bretzner, L.: Real-time scale selection in hybrid multi-scale representations. In: Scale-Space. (2003) 148–163
27. Brown, M., Lowe, D.: Invariant features from interest point groups. In: BMVC. (2002)

Top-Points as Interest Points for Image Matching

B. Platel, E. Balmachnova, L.M.J. Florack*, and B.M. ter Haar Romeny

Technische Universiteit Eindhoven, P.O. Box 513,
5600 MB Eindhoven, The Netherlands
{B.Platel, E.Balmachnova, L.M.J.Florack,
B.M.terHaarRomeny}@tue.nl

Abstract. We consider the use of top-points for object retrieval. These points are based on scale-space and catastrophe theory, and are invariant under gray value scaling and offset as well as scale-Euclidean transformations. The differential properties and noise characteristics of these points are mathematically well understood. It is possible to retrieve the exact location of a top-point from any coarse estimation through a closed-form vector equation which only depends on local derivatives in the estimated point. All these properties make top-points highly suitable as anchor points for invariant matching schemes. By means of a set of repeatability experiments and receiver-operator-curves we demonstrate the performance of top-points and differential invariant features as image descriptors.

1 Introduction

Local invariant features are useful for finding corresponding points between images when they are calculated at invariant interest points. The most popular interest points are Harris points [1], extrema in the normalized scale-space of the Laplacian of the image [2] used in the popular SIFT keypoint detector [3] or a combination of both [4]. For an overview of different interest points the reader is referred to [5].

We propose a novel, highly invariant type of interest point, based on scale-space and catastrophe theory. The mathematical properties and behavior of these so-called top-points are well understood. These interest points are invariant under gray value scaling and offset as well as arbitrary scale-Euclidean transformations. The noise behavior of top-points can be described in closed-form, which enables us to accurately predict the stability of the points. For tasks like matching or retrieval it is important to take into account the (in)stability of the descriptive data.

For matching it is important that a set of distinctive local invariant features is available in the interest points. An overview of invariant features is given in [6]. The choice of invariant features taken in the top-points is free. Because of their simple and mathematically nice nature we have chosen to use a complete set of differential invariants up to third order [7, 8] as invariant features. A similarity measure between these invariant feature vectors based on the noise behavior of the differential invariants is proposed. By means of a set of repeatability experiments and receiver-operator-curves we demonstrate the performance of top-points and differential invariant features as image descriptors.

---

* The Netherlands Organization for Scientific Research (NWO) is gratefully acknowledged for financial support.

A. Leonardis, H. Bischof, and A. Pinz (Eds.): ECCV 2006, Part I, LNCS 3951, pp. 418–429, 2006.

2   Theory

We present an algorithm for finding interest points in Gaussian scale-space. As input we may use the original image, but we may also choose to use its Laplacian, or any other linear differential entity. The input for our algorithm will be referred to as $u(x, y)$.

2.1   Scale-Space Approach

To find interest points that are invariant to scaling we have to observe the input function at all possible scales. Particularly suitable for calculating the scale-space representation of the image (or any other linear differential entity of the image) is the Gaussian kernel [9]

$$\phi_\sigma(x, y) = \frac{1}{2\pi\sigma^2} e^{-\frac{1}{2}(x^2+y^2)/\sigma^2}.$$ (1)

The input function can now be calculated at any scale by convolution with the Gaussian

$$u(x, y, \sigma) = (\phi_\sigma * u)(x, y).$$ (2)

Derivatives of the input function can be calculated at any scale by

$$\mathcal{D}u(x, y, \sigma) = (\mathcal{D}\phi_\sigma * u)(x, y),$$ (3)

where $\mathcal{D}$ is any linear derivative operator with constant coefficients.

2.2   Catastrophe Theory

Critical points are points at any fixed scale at which the gradient vanishes. Catastrophe theory studies how such points change as certain control parameters change, in our case scale.

In the case of a generic 2D input function the catastrophes occurring in Gaussian scale space are creations and annihilations of critical points with opposite Hessian signature [10, 11], i.e. extrema and saddles. The movement of critical points through scale induces critical paths. Each path consists of one (or multiple) saddle branch(es) and extremum branch(es). The point at which a creation or annihilation occurs is referred to as a *top-point*[1]. A typical set of critical paths and top-points of an image is shown in Fig. 1. In a top-point the determinant of the Hessian of the input function becomes zero. A top-point is thus defined as a point for which

$$\begin{cases} u_x & = 0, \\ u_y & = 0, \\ u_{xx}u_{yy} - u_{xy}^2 & = 0. \end{cases}$$ (4)

The extrema of the normalized Laplacean scale space as introduced by Lindeberg [2], and used by Lowe [3] in his matching scheme, lie on the critical paths of the Laplacean image. Multiple of such extrema may exist on the extremum branch of a critical path, whereas there is only one top-point per annihilating extremum/saddle pair, Fig. 2a.

---

[1] This misnomer is reminiscent of the 1D case [12], in which only annihilations occur generically, so that a top-point is only found at the top of a critical path.

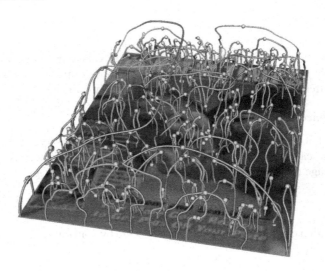

Fig. 1. Selection of critical paths and top-points of a magazine cover image

2.3 Invariance

Interest points are called invariant to transformation if they are preserved by the transformation. From their definition (4), it is apparent that top-points are invariant under gray value scaling and offset. Next to this the top-points are also invariant to scale-Euclidean transformations (rotation, scaling, translation).

The top-points however are in theory not invariant to affine or projective transformations just like the interest point detectors mentioned earlier, but in practice they show to be invariant under small affine or projective transformations.

2.4 Detection Versus Localization

Critical paths are detected by following critical points through scale. Top-points are found as points on the critical paths with horizontal tangents.

The detection of top-points does not have to be exact, since, given an adequate initial guess, it is possible to refine their position such that (4) holds to any desired precision. If (x_0, y_0, t_0) denotes the approximate location of a top-point we can calculate the position of the true top-point $(x_0 + \xi, y_0 + \eta, t_0 + \tau)$ in the neighborhood by:

$$\begin{bmatrix} \xi \\ \eta \\ \tau \end{bmatrix} = -\mathbf{M}^{-1} \begin{bmatrix} \mathbf{g} \\ \det\mathbf{H} \end{bmatrix}, \tag{5}$$

where

$$\mathbf{M} = \begin{bmatrix} \mathbf{H} & \mathbf{w} \\ \mathbf{z}^T & c \end{bmatrix}, \tag{6}$$

$$\mathbf{g} = \nabla u, \ \mathbf{H} = \nabla \mathbf{g}, \ \mathbf{w} = \partial_t \mathbf{g}, \ \mathbf{z} = \nabla\det\mathbf{H}, \ c = \partial_t \det\mathbf{H}, \tag{7}$$

in which **g** and **H** denote the image gradient and Hessian matrix, respectively, and in which all derivatives are taken in the point (x_0, y_0, t_0), cf. [11] for a derivation. This allows one to use a less accurate but fast detection algorithm.

2.5 Perturbative Approach in Scale Space

Given a set of measurements in scale space $v \in \mathbb{R}^n$ we can calculate the propagation of errors in a function $f : \mathbb{R}^n \to \mathbb{R}^m$ if the measurements are perturbed with noise n, $w = v + n \in \mathbb{R}^n$. The following equation describes how the perturbation affects f, using Einstein summation convention for repeated indices:

$$f_\alpha(w) - f_\alpha(v) \approx \delta f_\alpha \equiv \left. \frac{\partial f_\alpha}{\partial w_\beta} \right|_{w=v} n_\beta \tag{8}$$

The covariance matrix of f can be expressed as:

$$< \delta f_\alpha \delta f_\beta > = \frac{\partial f_\alpha}{\partial v_\gamma} \frac{\partial f_\beta}{\partial v_\delta} < n_\gamma n_\delta > \tag{9}$$

The noise matrix $< n_\gamma n_\delta >$ is given in [13] for the case when v denotes a partial derivative of the image obtained through convolution with a Gaussian derivative filter.

2.6 Stability

The stability of a top-point can be expressed in terms of the variances of spatial and scale displacements induced by additive noise. Since top-points are generic entities in scale space, they cannot vanish or appear when the image is only slightly perturbed. We assume that the noise variance is "sufficiently small" in the sense that the induced dislocation of a top-point can be investigated by means of a perturbative approach. By using eqn. (9) and substituting f with eqn. (5) we are able to calculate the effects of

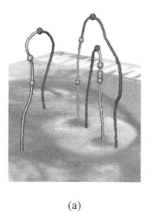

(a)	(b)

Fig. 2. a. A set of critical paths with corresponding top-points (topmost bullets), and extrema of the normalized Laplacian (remaining bullets). **b.** The ellipses schematically represent the variances of the scale-space displacement of each top-point under additive noise of known variance.

noise on the position of top-points in the form of a covariance matrix. It can be shown that the displacement depends on derivatives up to fourth order evaluated at the top-point, and on the noise variance. For detailed formulas (and experimental verifications) the reader is referred to [14].

The advantage of this approach is that variances of scale-space displacements can be predicted theoretically and in analytically closed-form on the basis of the local differential structure at a given top-point, cf. Fig. 2b for a schematic illustration. The ability to predict the motion of top-points under noise is valuable when matching noisy data (e.g. one may want to disregard highly instable top-points altogether).

2.7   Local Invariant Features

For matching it is important that a set of distinctive local invariant features is available in the interest points. It is possible to use any set of invariant features in the top-points. Mikolajcyck and Schmid [6] give an overview of a number of such local descriptors.

For our experiments we have used a complete set of differential invariants up to third order. The complete sets proposed by Florack et al. [8] are invariant to rigid transformations. By suitable scaling and normalization we obtain invariance to spatial zooming and intensity scaling as well, but the resulting system has the property that most low order invariants vanish identically at the top-points of the original (zeroth order) image, and thus do not qualify as distinctive features. Thus when considering top-points of the original image other distinctive features will have to be used. In [15] the embedding of a graph connecting top-points is used as a descriptor. This proved to be a suitable way of describing the global relationship between top-points of the original image. In this paper we use the Laplacian of the input function as input for our top-point detector. For this case the non-trivial, scaled and normalized differential invariants up to third order are collected into the column vector given by (10), again using summation convention:

$$
\begin{pmatrix}
\sigma\sqrt{u_i u_i}/u \\
\sigma u_{ii}/\sqrt{u_j u_j} \\
\sigma^2 u_{ij} u_{ij}/u_k u_k \\
\sigma u_i u_{ij} u_j/(u_k u_k)^{3/2} \\
\sigma^2 u_{ijk} u_i u_j u_k/(u_l u_l)^2 \\
\sigma^2 \varepsilon_{ij} u_{jkl} u_i u_k u_l/(u_m u_m)^2
\end{pmatrix}.
\tag{10}
$$

Here ε_{ij} is the completely antisymmetric epsilon tensor, normalized such that $\varepsilon_{12} = 1$. Note that the derivatives are extracted from the original, zeroth order image, but evaluated at the location of the top-points of the image Laplacian. This is, in particular, why the gradient magnitude in the denominator poses no difficulties, as it is generically nonzero at a top-point.

The resulting scheme (interest point plus differential feature vector) guarantees manifest invariance under the scale-Euclidean spatial transformation group, and under linear gray value rescalings.

2.8   Similarity Measure in the Feature Space

To compare features of different interest points a distance or similarity measure is needed. The most often used measures in literature are the Euclidean and Mahalanobis distance. If x_0 and x are two points from the same distribution which has covariance matrix Σ, then the Mahalanobis distance is given by

$$d(x_0, x) = (\mathbf{x} - \mathbf{x_0})^T \Sigma^{-1} (\mathbf{x} - \mathbf{x_0}) \qquad (11)$$

and is equal to the Euclidean distance if the covariance matrix Σ is the identity matrix. The advantage of the Mahalanobis distance is that it can be used to measure distances in non-Euclidean spaces. The drawbacks however are that the covariance matrix has to be derived by using a large training set of images, and that the covariance matrix is the same for every measurement. By using the perturbative approach from sec. 2.5 and using the set of differential invariants from (10) as functions f_α and the set of third order derivatives as v_β we can now calculate a covariance matrix for every single feature vector. This enables us to use (11) to calculate the similarity between two feature vectors using the covariance matrix Σ_{x_0} derived specifically for feature vector x_0, where $d(x_0, x)$ close to zero means very similar, and $d(x_0, x) \gg 0$ very dissimilar. Note that this makes the similarity measure asymmetric: $d(x_0, x) \neq d(x, x_0)$. Therefore we cannot speak of a distance measure. This however does not pose problems since we are only matching unidirectionally, viz. object to scene.

3 Experiments

3.1 Database

For the experiments we use a data set containing transformed versions of 12 different magazine covers. The covers contain a variety of objects and text. The data set contains rotated, zoomed and noisy versions of these magazine covers as well as images with perspective transformations. For all transformations the ground truth is known, which enables us to verify the performance of different algorithms on the database. Mikolajczyk's data set used in [4, 6] is not suitable for our purposes, as we require ground truth for genuine group transformations not confounded with other sources of image changes, such as changes in field of view. To our knowledge Mikolajczyk's data set does not provide this.

3.2 Repeatability

Schmid et al. [5] have introduced the so-called repeatability criterion to evaluate the stability and accuracy of interest points and interest point detectors. The repeatability rate for an interest point detector on a given pair of images is computed as the ratio between the number of point-to-point correspondences and the minimum number of interest points detected in the images ($\times 100\%$).

If the interest point in the perturbed image has moved less than a distance of ϵ pixels away from the position where it would be expected when following the transformation, we mark the point as a repeatable point (typically we set $\epsilon \approx 2$ pixels).

Experiments show the repeatability of top-points under image rotation (Fig. 4a) and additive Gaussian noise (Fig. 4b). Image rotation causes some top-points to be lost or created due to the resampling of the image. In the Gaussian noise experiment we

Fig. 3. A selection of data set images. From left to right: unchanged, rotated, added noise, scaled, changed perspective.

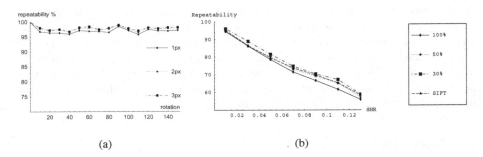

(a)   (b)

Fig. 4. a. The repeatability rate of the top-points for different angles of rotation for different ϵ. **b.** The repeatability rate of the top-points and SIFT interest points for additive Gaussian noise expressed in signal to noise ratio.

demonstrate that by using the stability variances described in Sec. 2.6 the repeatability of the top-points can be increased. The top-points are ordered on their stability variances. From this list 100%, 50% and 30% of the most stable top-points are selected for the repeatability experiment respectively. From Fig. 4b it is apparent that discarding instable points increases the repeatability significantly. We compare the repeatability of our interest point detector to the SIFT interest point detector by Lowe [3]. In Fig. 4b can be seen that when we apply a threshold on our stability measure (the SIFT keypoints have already been thresholded on stability) we slightly outperform the SIFT interest point detector for the noise case. Both algorithms perform worst for a rotation of 45 degrees. On the average taken over the entire database of 45 degree rotated images the repeatability of the SIFT interest points is 78%. Our top-point interest point detector showed a repeatability rate of 85% when thresholded on stability.

The high repeatability rate of the top-points enables us to match images under any angle of rotation and under high levels of noise.

3.3   Receiver Operator Characteristics

For the performance evaluation of the similarity measure we use a similar criterion as the one used in [6]. This criterion is based on Receiver Operating Characteristics (ROC) of detection rate versus false positive rate. Two points are said to be similar if the distance between their feature vectors is below a threshold t. The value of t is varied to obtain the ROC curves.

Given two images representing the same object the True Positive Rate TPR is the number of correctly matched points with respect to the number of possible matches:

$$TPR = \frac{\#\text{correct matches}}{\#\text{possible matches}} \qquad (12)$$

The condition for calling a match correct is the same as in sec. 3.2. The False Positive Rate FPR as defined in [6] is calculated as:

$$FPR = \frac{\#\text{incorrect matches}}{(\#\text{object points})(\#\text{scene points})} \qquad (13)$$

where the object is the original image and the scene a transformed version of the original image.

3.4 Performance of the Similarity Measure

To evaluate the performance of the similarity measure defined in sec. 2.8 we have calculated the ROC curves as described sec. 3.3 for a set of experiments. For comparison we have included the ROC curves for the Mahalanobis and Euclidean distance measures. The covariance matrix for the Mahalanobis distance was obtained by training on the data set itself. In Fig. 5 the mean ROC curves for three experiments are shown. In experiment a. the images in the database are matched to a 50% scaled down version of the same images. In experiment b. the images in the database are matched to noisy versions of the same images. In experiment c. the images in the database are matched to the 45 degree rotated versions of the same images. In all the experiments it is obvious that the new similarity measure greatly improves the performance of the matching algorithm.

3.5 Performance of the Descriptors

To evaluate the performance of the differential invariant features defined in sec. 2.7 we have calculated the ROC curves as described sec. 3.3 for a set of experiments. For comparison we have included the ROC curves of the SIFT algorithm for which a precompiled program is publicly available. The SIFT features consist of a 128 feature long vector containing information about the gradient angles in the neighborhood of the interest points. The experiments in Fig. 6 show superior performance of our differential invariant features over the SIFT features. The difference becomes even more evident if only stable top-points are used.

In a different set of experiments we have tested the performance of both algorithms under perspective change. For small perspective changes our algorithm performs slightly better than the SIFT algorithm. However this performance rapidly decreases for larger perspective changes. The SIFT features outperform our features in this case. This is probably due to the higher order information used in our feature vector which is more affected by perspective or affine changes than the first order information used in the SIFT feature vector.

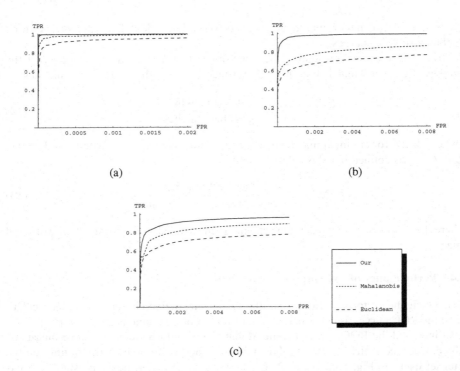

Fig. 5. a. mean ROC curve for 50% scaling. **b.** mean ROC curve for 5% additive Gaussian noise. **c.** mean ROC curve for 45 degree rotation.

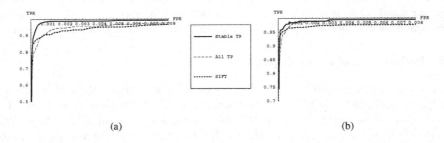

Fig. 6. a. ROC curve for 45 degree rotation. **b.** ROC curve for 5% additive Gaussian noise.

4   Retrieval Example

A simple example of an object retrieval task is demonstrated here. We have a set of magazine covers (of size 500×300 pixels) and a scene (of size 1000×700 pixels) containing a number of the magazines, distributed, rotated, scaled, and occluded.

The task is to retrieve a magazine from the scene image. For the query images we find approximately 1000 stable top-points per query image (which may be pre-computed off-line). For the scene image we find approximately 5000 stable top-points. In Fig. 8 the interest points are shown (above a certain scale), 782 points are matched correctly for the left image and 211 for the down-scaled right image. The objects can now easily be extracted from the scene by using a clustering algorithm as described in [3].

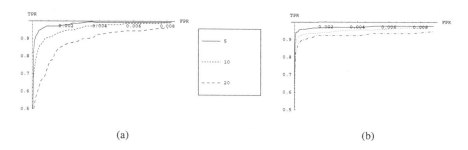

(a)   (b)

Fig. 7. ROC curves perspective change for 5, 10 and 20 degrees for: **a.** Our interest points and differential invariants **b.** SIFT interest points and features.

Fig. 8. Matching interest points (white) of a query object and a scene containing two rotated, scaled and occluded versions of the object. Interest points that do not match are shown in gray

5   Summary and Conclusions

We have introduced top-points as highly invariant interest points that are suitable for image matching. Top-points are versatile as they can be calculated for every generic function of the image.

We have pointed out that top-points are invariant under scale-Euclidean transformations as well as under gray value scaling and offset. The sensitivity of top-points to additive noise can be predicted analytically, which is useful when matching noisy images. Top-point localization does not have to be very accurate, since it is possible to refine its position using local differential image structure. This enables fast detection, without losing the exact location of the top-point.

The repeatability of the top-points has proven to be better than the widely used SIFT interest points in a set of experiments. In the future we strive to compare our top-points to other popular interest points like the Harris-Laplace points and descriptors like PCA-SIFT and GLOH.

As features for our interest points we use a feature vector consisting of only six normalized and scaled differential invariants. We have also introduced a similarity measure based on the noise behavior of our feature vectors. Thresholding on this similarity measure increases the performance significantly.

A similarity measure was derived based on the noise behavior of the differential invariant features. This measure significantly increases performance over the popular Mahalanobis and Euclidean distance measures.

For scale-Euclidean transformations as well as additive Gaussian noise our algorithm (6 features in vector) has proven to outperform the SIFT (128 features in vector) approach. However for large perspective changes the SIFT algorithm performs better probably due to the lower order derivatives used for the feature vector.

References

1. Harris, C., Stephens, M.: A combined corner and edge detector. In: Proc. 4th Alvey Vision Conf. (1988) 189–192
2. Lindeberg, T.: Scale-space theory: A basic tool for analysing structures at different scales. J. of Applied Statistics **21(2)** (1994) 224–270
3. Lowe, D.: Distinctive image features from scale-invariant keypoints. Int. J. Comput. Vision **60(2)** (2004) 91–110
4. Mikolajczyk, K., Schmid, C.: Scale and affine invariant interest point detectors. International Journal of Computer Vision **60(1)** (2004) 63–86
5. Schmid, C., Mohr, R., Bauckhage, C.: Evaluation of interest point detectors. Int. J. Comput. Vision **37(2)** (2000) 151–172
6. Mikolajczyk, K., Schmid, C.: A performance evaluation of local descriptors. IEEE Transactions on Pattern Analysis & Machine Intelligence **27(10)** (2005) 1615–1630
7. Florack, L.M.J., Haar Romeny, B.M.t., Koenderink, J.J., Viergever, M.A.: Scale and the differential structure of images. Image and Vision Computing **10(6)** (1992) 376–388
8. Florack, L.M.J., Haar Romeny, B.M.t., Koenderink, J.J., Viergever, M.A.: Cartesian differential invariants in scale-space. Journal of Mathematical Imaging and Vision **3(4)** (1993) 327–348
9. Koenderink, J.J.: The structure of images. Biological Cybernetics **50** (1984) 363–370

10. Damon, J.: Local Morse theory for solutions to the heat equation and Gaussian blurring. Journal of Differential Equations **115**(2) (1995) 368–401

11. Florack, L., Kuijper, A.: The topological structure of scale-space images. Journal of Mathematical Imaging and Vision **12**(1) (2000) 65–79

12. Johansen, P., Skelboe, S., Grue, K., Andersen, J.D.: Representing signals by their top points in scale-space. In: Proceedings of the 8th International Conference on Pattern Recognition (Paris, France, October 1986), IEEE Computer Society Press (1986) 215–217

13. Blom, J., Haar Romeny, B.M.t., Bel, A., Koenderink, J.J.: Spatial derivatives and the propagation of noise in Gaussian scale-space. Journal of Visual Communication and Image Representation **4**(1) (1993) 1–13

14. Balmachnova, E., Florack, L., Platel, B., Kanters, F., Haar Romeny, B.M.t.: Stability of top-points in scale space. (In: Proceedings of the 5th International Conference on Scale Space Methods in Computer Vision (Germany, April 2005)) 62–72

15. Platel, B., Fatih Demirci, M., Shokoufandeh, A., Florack, L., Kanters, F., Dickinson, S.: Discrete representation of top points via scale space tessellation. (In: Proceedings of the 5th International Conference on Scale Space Methods in Computer Vision (Germany, April 2005))

Machine Learning for High-Speed Corner Detection

Edward Rosten and Tom Drummond

Department of Engineering,
Cambridge University, UK
{er258, twd20}@cam.ac.uk

Abstract. Where feature points are used in real-time frame-rate applications, a high-speed feature detector is necessary. Feature detectors such as SIFT (DoG), Harris and SUSAN are good methods which yield high quality features, however they are too computationally intensive for use in real-time applications of any complexity. Here we show that machine learning can be used to derive a feature detector which can fully process live PAL video using less than 7% of the available processing time. By comparison neither the Harris detector (120%) nor the detection stage of SIFT (300%) can operate at full frame rate.

Clearly a high-speed detector is of limited use if the features produced are unsuitable for downstream processing. In particular, the same scene viewed from two different positions should yield features which correspond to the same real-world 3D locations[1]. Hence the second contribution of this paper is a comparison corner detectors based on this criterion applied to 3D scenes. This comparison supports a number of claims made elsewhere concerning existing corner detectors. Further, contrary to our initial expectations, we show that despite being principally constructed for speed, our detector significantly outperforms existing feature detectors according to this criterion.

1   Introduction

Corner detection is used as the first step of many vision tasks such as tracking, SLAM (simultaneous localisation and mapping), localisation, image matching and recognition. Hence, a large number of corner detectors exist in the literature. With so many already available it may appear unnecessary to present yet another detector to the community; however, we have a strong interest in real-time frame rate applications such as SLAM in which computational resources are at a premium. In particular, it is still true that when processing live video streams at full frame rate, existing feature detectors leave little if any time for further processing, even despite the consequences of Moore's Law.

Section 2 of this paper demonstrates how a feature detector described in earlier work can be redesigned employing a machine learning algorithm to yield a large speed increase. In addition, the approach allows the detector to be generalised, producing a suite of high-speed detectors which we currently use for real-time tracking [2] and AR label placement [3].

A. Leonardis, H. Bischof, and A. Pinz (Eds.): ECCV 2006, Part I, LNCS 3951, pp. 430–443, 2006.

To show that speed can been obtained without necessarily sacrificing the quality of the feature detector we compare our detector, to a variety of well-known detectors. In Section 3 this is done using Schmid's criterion [1], that when presented with different views of a 3D scene, a detector should yield (as far as possible) corners that correspond to the same features in the scene. Here we show how this can be applied to 3D scenes for which an approximate surface model is known.

1.1   Previous Work

The majority of feature detection algorithms work by computing a corner response function (C) across the image. Pixels which exceed a threshold cornerness value (and are locally maximal) are then retained.

Moravec [4] computes the sum-of-squared-differences (SSD) between a patch around a candidate corner and patches shifted a small distance in a number of directions. C is then the smallest SSD so obtained, thus ensuring that extracted corners are those locations which change maximally under translations.

Harris[5] builds on this by computing an approximation to the second derivative of the SSD with respect to the shift The approximation is:

$$\mathbf{H} = \begin{bmatrix} \widehat{I_x^2} & \widehat{I_x I_y} \\ \widehat{I_x I_y} & \widehat{I_y^2} \end{bmatrix}, \tag{1}$$

where $\widehat{}$ denotes averaging performed over the image patch (a smooth circular window can be used instead of a rectangle to perform the averaging resulting in a less noisy, isotropic response). Harris then defines the corner response to be

$$C = |\mathbf{H}| - k(\operatorname{trace} \mathbf{H})^2. \tag{2}$$

This is large if both eigenvalues of $\mathbf{H}$ are large, and it avoids explicit computation of the eigenvalues. It has been shown[6] that the eigenvalues are an approximate measure of the image curvature.

Based on the assumption of affine image deformation, a mathematical analysis led Shi and Tomasi[7] conclude that it is better to use the smallest eigen value of $\mathbf{H}$ as the corner strength function:

$$C = \min(\lambda_1, \lambda_2). \tag{3}$$

A number of suggestion have [5, 7, 8, 9] been made for how to compute the corner strength from $\mathbf{H}$ and these have been all shown [10] to be equivalent to various matrix norms of $\mathbf{H}$.

Zheng et al.[11] perform an analysis of the computation of $\mathbf{H}$, and find some suitable approximations which allow them to obtain a speed increase by computing only two smoothed images, instead of the three previously required.

Lowe [12] obtains scale invariance by convolving the image with a Difference of Gaussians (DoG) kernel at multiple scales, retaining locations which are optima in scale as well as space. DoG is used because it is good approximation for the Laplacian of a Gaussian (LoG) and much faster to compute. An approximation to DoG has been proposed which, provided that scales are $\sqrt{2}$ apart, speeds up computation by a factor of about two, compared to the striaghtforward implementation of Gaussian convolution [13].

It is noted in [14] that the LoG is a particularly stable scale-space kernel.

Scale-space techniques have also been combined with the Harris approach in [15] which computes Harris corners at multiple scales and retains only those which are also optima of the LoG response across scales.

Recently, scale invariance has been extended to consider features which are invariant to affine transformations [14, 16, 17].

An edge (usually a step change in intensity) in an image corresponds to the boundary between two regions. At corners of regions, this boundary changes direction rapidly. Several techniques were developed which involved detecting and chaining edges with a view to finding corners in the chained edge by analysing the chain code[18], finding maxima of curvature [19, 20, 21], change in direction [22] or change in appearance[23]. Others avoid chaining edges and instead look for maxima of curvature[24] or change in direction [25] at places where the gradient is large.

Another class of corner detectors work by examining a small patch of an image to see if it "looks" like a corner. Since second derivatives are not computed, a noise reduction step (such as Gaussian smoothing) is not required. Consequently, these corner detectors are computationally efficient since only a small number of pixels are examined for each corner detected. A corollary of this is that they tend to perform poorly on images with only large-scale features such as blurred images. The corner detector presented in this work belongs to this category.

The method presented in [26] assumes that a corner resembles a blurred wedge, and finds the characteristics of the wedge (the amplitude, angle and blur) by fitting it to the local image. The idea of the wedge is generalised in [27], where a method for calculating the corner strength is proposed which computes self similarity by looking at the proportion of pixels inside a disc whose intensity is within some threshold of the centre (*nucleus*) value. Pixels closer in value to the nucleus receive a higher weighting. This measure is known as the USAN (the Univalue Segment Assimilating Nucleus). A low value for the USAN indicates a corner since the centre pixel is very different from most of its surroundings. A set of rules is used to suppress qualitatively "bad" features, and then local minima of the, SUSANs, (Smallest USAN) are selected from the remaining candidates.

Trajkovic and Hedley[28] use a similar idea: a patch is not self-similar if pixels generally look different from the centre of the patch. This is measured by considering a circle. f_C is the pixel value at the centre of the circle, and f_P and $f_{P'}$ are the pixel values at either end of a diameter line across the circle. The response function is defined as

$$C = \min_P \ (f_P - f_C)^2 + (f_{P'} - f_C)^2. \tag{4}$$

This can only be large in the case where there corner. The test is performed on a Bresenham circle. Since the circle is discretized, linear or circular interpolation is used in between discrete orientations in order to give the detector a more isotropic response. To this end, the authors present a method whereby the minimum response function at all interpolated positions between two pixels can be efficiently computed. Computing the response function requires performing a search over all orientations, but any single measurement provides an upper bound on the response. To speed up matching, the response in the horizontal and vertical directions only is checked. If the upper bound on the response is too low, then the potential corner is rejected. To speed up the method further, this fast check is first applied at a coarse scale.

A fast radial symmetry transform is developed in [29] to detect points. Points have a high score when the gradient is both radially symmetric, strong, and of a uniform sign along the radius. The scale can be varied by changing the size of the area which is examined for radial symmetry.

An alternative method of examining a small patch of an image to see if it looks like a corner is to use machine learning to classify patches of the image as corners or non-corners. The examples used in the training set determine the type of features detected. In [30], a three layer neural network is trained to recognise corners where edges meet at a multiple of $45°$, near to the centre of an 8×8 window. This is applied to images after edge detection and thinning. It is shown how the neural net learned a more general representation and was able to detect corners at a variety of angles.

2   High-Speed Corner Detection

2.1   FAST: Features from Accelerated Segment Test

The segment test criterion operates by considering a circle of sixteen pixels around the corner candidate p. The original detector [2, 3] classifies p as a corner if there exists a set of n contiguous pixels in the circle which are all brighter than the intensity of the candidate pixel I_p plus a threshold t, or all darker than $I_p - t$, as illustrated in Figure 1. n was chosen to be twelve because it admits a high-speed test which can be used to exclude a very large number of non-corners: the test examines only the four pixels at 1, 5, 9 and 13 (the four compass directions). If p is a corner then at least three of these must all be brighter than $I_p + t$ or darker than $I_p - t$. If neither of these is the case, then p cannot be a corner. The full segment test criterion can then be applied to the remaining candidates by examining all pixels in the circle. This detector in itself exhibits high performance, but there are several weaknesses:

1. The high-speed test does not generalise well for $n < 12$.
2. The choice and ordering of the fast test pixels contains implicit assumptions about the distribution of feature appearance.
3. Knowledge from the first 4 tests is discarded.
4. Multiple features are detected adjacent to one another.

2.2   Machine Learning a Corner Detector

Here we present an approach which uses machine learning to address the first three points (the fourth is addressed in Section 2.3). The process operates in

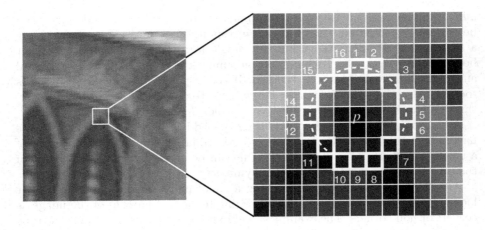

Fig. 1. 12 point segment test corner detection in an image patch. The highlighted squares are the pixels used in the corner detection. The pixel at p is the centre of a candidate corner. The arc is indicated by the dashed line passes through 12 contiguous pixels which are brighter than p by more than the threshold.

two stages. In order to build a corner detector for a given n, first, corners are detected from a set of images (preferably from the target application domain) using the segment test criterion for n and a convenient threshold. This uses a slow algorithm which for each pixel simply tests all 16 locations on the circle around it.

For each location on the circle $x \in \{1..16\}$, the pixel at that position relative to p (denoted by $p \to x$) can have one of three states:

$$S_{p \to x} = \begin{cases} d, & I_{p \to x} \leq I_p - t & \text{(darker)} \\ s, & I_p - t < I_{p \to x} < I_p + t & \text{(similar)} \\ b, & I_p + t \leq I_{p \to x} & \text{(brighter)} \end{cases} \tag{5}$$

Choosing an x and computing $S_{p \to x}$ for all $p \in P$ (the set of all pixels in all training images) partitions P into three subsets, P_d, P_s, P_b, where each p is assigned to $P_{S_{p \to x}}$.

Let K_p be a boolean variable which is true if p is a corner and false otherwise. Stage 2 employs the algorithm used in ID3[31] and begins by selecting the x which yields the most information about whether the candidate pixel is a corner, measured by the entropy of K_p.

The entropy of K for the set P is:

$$H(P) = (c + \bar{c}) \log_2(c + \bar{c}) - c \log_2 c - \bar{c} \log_2 \bar{c} \tag{6}$$

where $c = \big|\{p | K_p \text{ is true}\}\big|$ (number of corners)

and $\bar{c} = \big|\{p | K_p \text{ is false}\}\big|$ (number of non corners)

The choice of x then yields the information gain:

$$H(P) - H(P_d) - H(P_s) - H(P_b) \tag{7}$$

Having selected the x which yields the most information, the process is applied recursively on all three subsets i.e. x_b is selected to partition P_b in to $P_{b,d}$, $P_{b,s}$, $P_{b,b}$, x_s is selected to partition P_s in to $P_{s,d}$, $P_{s,s}$, $P_{s,b}$ and so on, where each x is chosen to yield maximum information about the set it is applied to. The process terminates when the entropy of a subset is zero. This means that all p in this subset have the same value of K_p, i.e. they are either all corners or all non-corners. This is guaranteed to occur since K is an exact function of the learning data.

This creates a decision tree which can correctly classify all corners seen in the training set and therefore (to a close approximation) correctly embodies the rules of the chosen FAST corner detector. This decision tree is then converted into C-code, creating a long string of nested if-then-else statements which is compiled and used as a corner detector. For full optimisation, the code is compiled twice, once to obtain profiling data on the test images and a second time with arc-profiling enabled in order to allow reordering optimisations. In some cases, two of the three subtrees may be the same. In this case, the boolean test which separates them is removed.

Note that since the data contains incomplete coverage of all possible corners, the learned detector is not precisely the same as the segment test detector. It would be relatively straightforward to modify the decision tree to ensure that it has the same results as the segment test algorithm, however, all feature detectors are heuristic to some degree, and the learned detector is merely a very slightly different heuristic to the segment test detector.

2.3   Non-maximal Suppression

Since the segment test does not compute a corner response function, non maximal suppression can not be applied directly to the resulting features. Consequently, a score function, V must be computed for each detected corner, and non-maximal suppression applied to this to remove corners which have an adjacent corner with higher V. There are several intuitive definitions for V:

1. The maximum value of n for which p is still a corner.
2. The maximum value of t for which p is still a corner.
3. The sum of the absolute difference between the pixels in the contiguous arc and the centre pixel.

Definitions 1 and 2 are very highly quantised measures, and many pixels share the same value of these. For speed of computation, a slightly modified version of 3 is used. V is given by:

$$V = \max \left(\sum_{x \in S_{\text{bright}}} |I_{p \to x} - I_p| - t \ , \ \sum_{x \in S_{\text{dark}}} |I_p - I_{p \to x}| - t \right) \tag{8}$$

with

$$S_{\text{bright}} = \{x | I_{p \to x} \geq I_p + t\}$$
$$S_{\text{dark}} = \{x | I_{p \to x} \leq I_p - t\} \tag{9}$$

2.4 Timing Results

Timing tests were performed on a 2.6GHz Opteron and an 850MHz Pentium III processor. The timing data is taken over 1500 monochrome fields from a PAL video source (with a resolution of 768×288 pixels). The learned FAST detectors for $n = 9$ and 12 have been compared to the original FAST detector, to our implementation of the Harris and DoG (difference of Gaussians—the detector used by SIFT) and to the reference implementation of SUSAN[32].

As can be seen in Table 1, FAST in general offers considerably higher performance than the other tested feature detectors, and the learned FAST performs up to twice as fast as the handwritten version. Importantly, it is able to generate an efficient detector for $n = 9$, which (as will be shown in Section 3) is the most reliable of the FAST detectors. On modern hardware, FAST consumes only a fraction of the time available during video processing, and on low power hardware, it is the only one of the detectors tested which is capable of video rate processing at all.

Examining the decision tree shows that on average, 2.26 (for $n = 9$) and 2.39 (for $n = 12$) questions are asked per pixel to determine whether or not it is a feature. By contrast, the handwritten detector asks on average 2.8 questions.

Interestingly, the difference in speed between the learned detector and the original FAST are considerably less marked on the Opteron processor compared to the Pentium III. We believe that this is in part due to the Opteron having a diminishing cost per pixel queried that is less well modelled by our system (which assumes equal cost for all pixel accesses), compared to the Pentium III.

Table 1. Timing results for a selection of feature detectors run on fields (768×288) of a PAL video sequence in milliseconds, and as a percentage of the processing budget per frame. Note that since PAL and NTSC, DV and 30Hz VGA (common for webcams) have approximately the same pixel rate, the percentages are widely applicable. Approximately 500 features per field are detected.

Detector	Opteron 2.6GHz		Pentium III 850MHz	
	ms	%	ms	%
Fast $n = 9$ (non-max suppression)	1.33	6.65	5.29	26.5
Fast $n = 9$ (raw)	1.08	5.40	4.34	21.7
Fast $n = 12$ (non-max suppression)	1.34	6.70	4.60	23.0
Fast $n = 12$ (raw)	1.17	5.85	4.31	21.5
Original FAST $n = 12$ (non-max suppression)	1.59	7.95	9.60	48.0
Original FAST $n = 12$ (raw)	1.49	7.45	9.25	48.5
Harris	24.0	120	166	830
DoG	60.1	301	345	1280
SUSAN	7.58	37.9	27.5	137.5

3   A Comparison of Detector Repeatability

Although there is a vast body of work on corner detection, there is much less on the subject of comparing detectors. Mohannah and Mokhtarian[33] evaluate performance by warping test images in an affine manner by a known amount. They define the 'consistency of corner numbers' as

$$CCN = 100 \times 1.1^{-|n_w - n_o|},$$

where n_w is the number of features in the warped image and n_o is the number of features in the original image. They also define accuracy as

$$ACU = 100 \times \frac{\frac{n_a}{n_o} + \frac{n_a}{n_g}}{2},$$

where n_g are the number of 'ground truth' corners (marked by humans) and n_a is the number of matched corners compared to the ground truth. This unfortunately relies on subjectively made devisions.

Trajkovic and Hedley[28] define stability to be the number of 'strong ' matches (matches detected over three frames in their tracking algorithm) divided by the total number of corners. This measurement is clearly dependent on both the tracking and matching methods used, but has the advantage that it can be tested on the date used by the system.

When measuring reliability, what is important is if the same real-world features are detected from multiple views [1] This is the definition which will be used here. For an image pair, a feature is 'detected' if is is extracted in one image and appears in the second. It is 'repeated' if it is also detected nearby in the second. The repeatability is the ratio of repeated features detected features. In [1], the test is performed on images of planar scenes so that the relationship between point positions is a homography. Fiducial markers are projected on to the planar scene to allow accurate computation of this.

By modelling the surface as planar and using flat textures, this technique tests the feature detectors' ability to deal with mostly affine warps (since image features are small) under realistic conditions. This test is not so well matched to our intended application domain, so instead, we use a 3D surface model to compute where detected features should appear in other views (illustrated in Figure 2). This allows the repeatability of the detectors to be analysed on features caused by geometry such as corners of polyhedra, occlusions and T-junctions. We also allow bas-relief textures to be modelled with a flat plane so that the repeatability can be tested under non-affine warping.

A margin of error must be allowed because:

1. The alignment is not perfect.
2. The model is not perfect.
3. The camera model (especially regarding radial distortion) is not perfect.
4. The detector may find a maximum on a slightly different part of the corner. This becomes more likely as the change in viewpoint and hence change in shape of the corner become large.

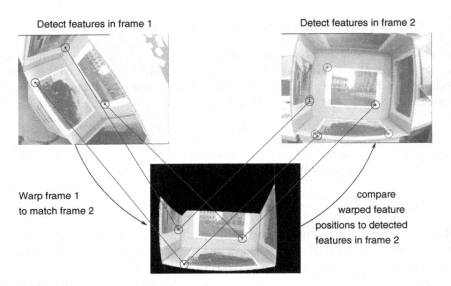

Fig. 2. Repeatability is tested by checking if the same real-world features are detected in different views. A geometric model is used to compute where the features reproject to.

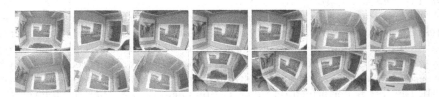

Fig. 3. Box dataset: photographs taken of a test rig (consisting of photographs pasted to the inside of a cuboid) with strong changes of perspective, changes in scale and large amounts of radial distortion. This tests the corner detectors on planar textures.

Instead of using fiducial markers, the 3D model is aligned to the scene by hand and this is then optimised using a blend of simulated annealing and gradient descent to minimise the SSD between all pairs of frames and reprojections.

To compute the SSD between frame i and reprojected frame j, the position of all points in frame j are found in frame i. The images are then bandpass filtered. High frequencies are removed to reduce noise, while low frequencies are removed to reduce the impact of lighting changes. To improve the speed of the system, the SSD is only computed using 1000 random points (as opposed to every point).

The datasets used are shown in Figure 3, Figure 4 and Figure 5. With these datasets, we have tried to capture a wide range of corner types (geometric and textural).

The repeatability is computed as the number of corners per frame is varied. For comparison we also include a scattering of random points as a baseline measure, since in the limit if every pixel is detected as a corner, then the repeatability is 100%.

Fig. 4. Maze dataset: photographs taken of a prop used in an augmented reality application. This set consists of textural features undergoing projective warps as well as geometric features. There are also significant changes of scale.

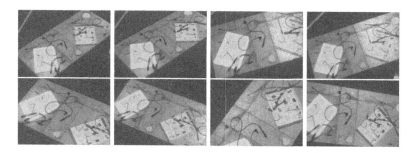

Fig. 5. Bas-relief dataset: the model is a flat plane, but there are many objects with significant relief. This causes the appearance of features to change in a non affine way from different viewpoints.

To test robustness to image noise, increasing amounts of Gaussian noise were added to the bas-relief dataset. It should be noted that the noise added is in addition to the significant amounts of camera noise already present (from thermal noise, electrical interference, and etc).

4   Results and Discussion

Shi and Tomasi [7], derive their result for better feature detection on the assumption that the deformation of the features is affine. In the box and maze datasets, this assumption holds and can be seen in Figure 6B and Figure 6C the detector outperforms the Harris detector. In the bas-relief dataset, this assumption does not hold, and interestingly, the Harris detector outperforms Shi and Tomasi detector in this case.

Mikolajczyk and Schmid [15] evaluate the repeatability of the Harris-Laplace detector evaluated using the method in [34], where planar scenes are examined. The results show that Harris-Laplace points outperform both DoG points and Harris points in repeatability. For the box dataset, our results verify that this is correct for up to about 1000 points per frame (typical numbers, probably commonly used); the results are somewhat less convincing in the other datasets, where points undergo non-projective changes.

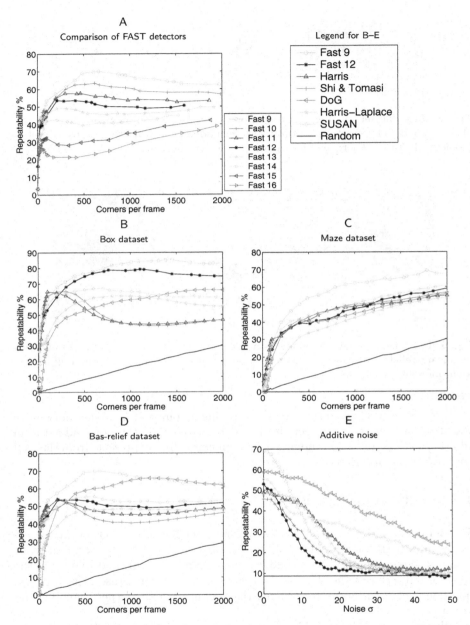

Fig. 6. A: A comparison of the FAST detectors shown that $n = 9$ is the most repeatable. For $n \leq 8$, the detector starts to respond strongly to edges. B, C, D: Repeatability results for the three datasets as the number of features per frame is varied. D: repeatability results for the bas-relief data set (500 features per frame) as the amount of Gaussian noise added to the images is varied. For FAST and SUSAN, the number of features can not be chosen arbitrarily; the closest approximation to 500 features per frame achievable is used.

In the sample implementation of SIFT[35], approximately 1000 points are generated on the images from the test sets. We concur that this a good choice for the number of features since this appears to be roughly where the repeatability curve for DoG features starts to flatten off.

Smith and Brady[27] claim that the SUSAN corner detector performs well in the presence of noise since it does not compute image derivatives, and hence, does not amplify noise. We support this claim: although the noise results show that the performance drops quite rapidly with increasing noise to start with, it soon levels off and outperforms all but the DoG detector.

The big surprise of this experiment is that the FAST feature detectors, despite being designed only for speed, outperform the other feature detectors on these images (provided that more than about 200 corners are needed per frame). It can be seen in Figure 6A, that the 9 point detector provides optimal performance, hence only this and the original 12 point detector are considered in the remaining graphs.

The DoG detector is remarkably robust to the presence of noise. Since convolution is linear, the computation of DoG is equivalent to convolution with a DoG kernel. Since this kernel is symmetric, this is equivalent to matched filtering for objects with that shape. The robustness is achieved because matched filtering is optimal in the presence of additive Gaussian noise[36].

FAST, however, is not very robust to the presence of noise. This is to be expected: Since high speed is achieved by analysing the fewest pixels possible, the detector's ability to average out noise is reduced.

5 Conclusions

In this paper, we have used machine learning to derive a very fast, high quality corner detector. It has the following advantages:

- It is many times faster than other existing corner detectors.
- High levels of repeatability under large aspect changes and for different kinds of feature.

However, it also suffers from a number of disadvantages:

- It is not robust to high levels noise.
- It can respond to 1 pixel wide lines at certain angles, when the quantisation of the circle misses the line.
- It is dependent on a threshold.

We were also able to verify a number of claims made in other papers using the method for evaluating the repeatability of corners and have shown the importance of using more than just planar scenes in this evaluation.

The corner detection code is made available from
`http://mi.eng.cam.ac.uk/~{}er258/work/fast.html`
and
`http://savannah.nongnu.org/projects/libcvd`
and the data sets used for repeatability are available from
`http://mi.eng.cam.ac.uk/~{}er258/work/datasets.html`

References

1. Schmid, C., Mohr, R., Bauckhage, C.: Evaluation of interest point detectors. International Journal of Computer Vision **37** (2000) 151–172
2. Rosten, E., Drummond, T.: Fusing points and lines for high performance tracking. In: 10th IEEE International Conference on Computer Vision. Volume 2., Beijing, China, Springer (2005) 1508–1515
3. Rosten, E., Reitmayr, G., Drummond, T.: Real-time video annotations for augmented reality. In: International Symposium on Visual Computing. (2005)
4. Moravec, H.: Obstacle avoidance and navigation in the real world by a seeing robot rover. In: tech. report CMU-RI-TR-80-03, Robotics Institute, Carnegie Mellon University & doctoral dissertation, Stanford University. Carnegie Mellon University (1980) Available as Stanford AIM-340, CS-80-813 and republished as a Carnegie Mellon University Robotics Institue Technical Report to increase availability.
5. Harris, C., Stephens, M.: A combined corner and edge detector. In: Alvey Vision Conference. (1988) 147–151
6. Noble, J.A.: Finding corners. Image and Vision Computing **6** (1988) 121–128
7. Shi, J., Tomasi, C.: Good features to track. In: 9th IEEE Conference on Computer Vision and Pattern Recognition, Springer (1994)
8. Noble, A.: Descriptions of image surfaces. PhD thesis, Department of Engineering Science, University of Oxford. (1989)
9. Kenney, C.S., Manjunath, B.S., Zuliani, M., Hewer, M.G.A., Nevel, A.V.: A condition number for point matching with application to registration and postregistration error estimation. IEEE Transactions on Pattern Analysis and Machine Intelligence **25** (2003) 1437–1454
10. Zuliani, M., Kenney, C., Manjunath, B.: A mathematical comparison of point detectors. In: Second IEEE Image and Video Registration Workshop (IVR), Washington DC, USA (2004)
11. Zheng, Z., Wang, H., Teoh, E.K.: Analysis of gray level corner detection. Pattern Recognition Letters **20** (1999) 149–162
12. Lowe, D.G.: Distinctive image features from scale-invariant keypoints. International Journal of Computer Vision **60** (2004) 91–110
13. James L. Crowley, O.R.: Fast computation of characteristic scale using a half octave pyramid. In: Scale Space 03: 4th International Conference on Scale-Space theories in Computer Vision, Isle of Skye, Scotland, UK (2003)
14. Mikolajczyk, K., Schmid, C.: An affine invariant interest point detector. In: European Conference on Computer Vision, Springer (2002) 128–142 Copenhagen.
15. Mikolajczyk, K., Schmid, C.: Indexing based on scale invariant interest points. In: 8th IEEE International Conference on Computer Vision, Vancouver, Canada, Springer (2001) 525–531
16. Brown, M., Lowe, D.G.: Invariant features from interest point groups. In: 13th British Machine Vision Conference, Cardiff, British Machine Vision Assosciation (2002) 656–665
17. Schaffalitzky, F., Zisserman, A.: Multi-view matching for unordered image sets, or How do I organise my holiday snaps? In: 7th Euproean Conference on Computer Vision, Springer (2002) 414–431
18. Rutkowski, W.S., Rosenfeld, A.: A comparison of corner detection techniques for chain coded curves. Technical Report 623, Maryland University (1978)
19. Langridge, D.J.: Curve encoding and detection of discontinuities. Computer Vision, Graphics and Image Processing **20** (1987) 58–71

20. Medioni, G., Yasumoto, Y.: Corner detection and curve representation using cubic b-splines. Computer Vision, Graphics and Image Processing **39** (1987) 279–290
21. Mokhtarian, F., Suomela, R.: Robust image corner detection through curvature scale space. IEEE Transactions on Pattern Analysis and Machine Intelligence **20** (1998) 1376–1381
22. Haralick, R.M., Shapiro, L.G.: Computer and robot vision. Volume 1. Adison-Wesley (1993)
23. Cooper, J., Venkatesh, S., Kitchen, L.: Early jump-out corner detectors. IEEE Transactions on Pattern Analysis and Machine Intelligence **15** (1993) 823–828
24. Wang, H., Brady, M.: Real-time corner detection algorithm for motion estimation. Image and Vision Computing **13** (1995) 695–703
25. Kitchen, L., Rosenfeld, A.: Gray-level corner detection. Pattern Recognition Letters **1** (1982) 95–102
26. Guiducci, A.: Corner characterization by differential geometry techniques. Pattern Recognition Letters **8** (1988) 311–318
27. Smith, S.M., Brady, J.M.: SUSAN - a new approach to low level image processing. International Journal of Computer Vision **23** (1997) 45–78
28. Trajkovic, M., Hedley, M.: Fast corner detection. Image and Vision Computing **16** (1998) 75–87
29. Loy, G., Zelinsky, A.: A fast radial symmetry transform for detecting points of interest. In: 7th Euproean Conference on Computer Vision, Springer (2002) 358–368
30. Dias, P., Kassim, A., Srinivasan, V.: A neural network based corner detection method. In: IEEE International Conference on Neural Networks. Volume 4., Perth, WA, Australia (1995) 2116–2120
31. Quinlan, J.R.: Induction of decision trees. Machine Learning **1** (1986) 81–106
32. Smith, S.M.: `http://www.fmrib.ox.ac.uk/~steve/susan/susan2l.c` (Accessed 2005)
33. Cootes, T.F., Taylor, C., eds.: Performenace Evaluation of Corner Detection Algorithms under Affine and Similarity Transforms. In Cootes, T.F., Taylor, C., eds.: 12th British Machine Vision Conference, Manchester, British Machine Vision Assosciation (2001)
34. Schmid, C., Mohr, R., Bauckhage, C.: Comparing and evaluating interest points. In: 6th IEEE International Conference on Computer Vision, Bombay, India, Springer (1998) 230–235
35. Lowe, D.G.: Demo software: Sift keypoint detector. `http://www.cs.ubc.ca/~lowe/keypoints/` (Accessed 2005)
36. Sklar, B.: Digital Communications. Prentice Hall (1988)

Smooth Image Segmentation by Nonparametric Bayesian Inference

Peter Orbanz and Joachim M. Buhmann

Institute of Computational Science, ETH Zurich
{porbanz, jbuhmann}@inf.ethz.ch

Abstract. A nonparametric Bayesian model for histogram clustering is proposed to automatically determine the number of segments when Markov Random Field constraints enforce smooth class assignments. The nonparametric nature of this model is implemented by a Dirichlet process prior to control the number of clusters. The resulting posterior can be sampled by a modification of a conjugate-case sampling algorithm for Dirichlet process mixture models. This sampling procedure estimates segmentations as efficiently as clustering procedures in the strictly conjugate case. The sampling algorithm can process both single-channel and multi-channel image data. Experimental results are presented for real-world synthetic aperture radar and magnetic resonance imaging data.

1 Introduction

Unsupervised data clustering and image segmentation models usually assume that an appropriate number of classes is either known a priori or specified by the data analyst. More sophisticated methods automatically select the number of clusters, e. g. by resampling strategies [1]. Recently, nonparametric Bayesian models based on Dirichlet processes have successfully been applied to machine learning problems such as natural language processing [2] and object categorization [3]. These models perform automatic model selection by supporting a range of prior choices for the number of classes; the different resulting models are then scored by the likelihood according to the observed data.

The question how automatic model selection can be performed in image segmentation for models such as Markov random fields plays an important role in computer vision; see e. g. [4] for recent work employing a Bayesian information criterion. Our approach, which is based on Dirichlet processes, combines spatial constraints on class labels with an estimate of a preferred number of clusters. The smoothness constraints are modeled as a Markov random field (MRF) on a neighborhood graph. To combine MRF image models for segmentation with a nonparametric selection of the segment number, the Dirichlet process prior is enhanced by a smoothness constraint on the label field. Local feature histograms are extracted from the image and grouped by histogram clustering. Adjacent image patches are assigned to the same cluster with high probability if they are neighbors with respect to the neighborhood graph of the MRF.

A. Leonardis, H. Bischof, and A. Pinz (Eds.): ECCV 2006, Part I, LNCS 3951, pp. 444–457, 2006.

The paper is organized as follows: Sec. 2 briefly reviews Dirichlet process mixture (MDP) models and their application to data clustering. We discuss their combination with MRFs in Sec. 3, and the histogram clustering model used for application to image segmentation in Sec. 4. Sec. 5 proposes a MCMC sampling algorithm to sample the combined model. Experimental results are given in Sec. 6.

2   Data Clustering with MDP Models

The statistical model considered in this work is a *Dirichlet process mixture* (MDP) model [5]. MDP approaches belong to a class of models referred to as *nonparametric Bayesian models*. A MDP clustering model consists of three principal ingredients: A parametric likelihood function F, a probability distribution G_0, which is referred to as the *base measure*, and a Dirichlet process DP (αG_0) parameterized by the base measure and a positive constant $\alpha \in \mathbb{R}_+$. In this article, the base measure G_0 will generally be assumed to be infinite. Under the MDP model, a set of distinct classes is assumed to generate the observed data $\mathbf{x}_1, \ldots, \mathbf{x}_n$. Each class has a generative distribution, described by the likelihood F. Each cluster (indexed by k) is characterized by a parameter value θ_k^*, so the data within the cluster is generated according to $\mathbf{x} \sim F(\,.\,|\theta_k^*)$. This makes MDP models conceptually similar to finite parametric mixture models. MDP models generate the parameter values θ_k^*, which characterize the classes, according to a Dirichlet process DP (αG_0). In contrast to parametric mixture models, the number of classes is not a constant, and will change during the sampling process.

Formally, models based on Dirichlet processes draw a distribution G at random from a stochastic process [5]. The sample values drawn by means of the DP, the mixture parameters $\theta_1, \ldots, \theta_n$, are assumed to be generated by the distribution G:

$$\theta_1, \ldots, \theta_n \sim G \quad \text{with} \quad G \sim \text{DP}(\alpha G_0) \ . \tag{1}$$

The practical applicability of the process, however, is based on the observation that the distribution G can be integrated out. Given a set of samples $\theta_1, \ldots, \theta_n$, a new sample θ_{n+1} has a closed-form conditional distribution:

$$\theta_{n+1}|\theta_1, \ldots, \theta_n \sim \frac{1}{n+\alpha} \sum_{i=1}^{n} \delta_{\theta_i}(\theta_{n+1}) + \frac{\alpha}{n+\alpha} G_0(\theta_{n+1}) \ , \tag{2}$$

where δ_θ denotes the Dirac measure concentrated at θ. Therefore, sampling the Dirichlet process generates random values in the domain of the base measure G_0, but with a different distribution than the one specified by G_0.

A draw from the distribution (2) will, with probability $\frac{n}{n+\alpha}$, yield a sample value which has already occurred. (Provided that G_0 is infinite, a draw from the second term in (2) will generate a previously unobserved value with probability one.) If any two samples θ_i, θ_j are identical, the corresponding Dirac measures coincide. One may therefore group the samples $\theta_1, \ldots, \theta_n$ into $N_c \leq n$ classes containing identical values. Each class $k \in \{1, \ldots, N_C\}$ is characterized by its associated sample value, denoted θ_k^*. Denoting the number of samples in group k by n_k, the distribution (2) may be rewritten as a sum over clusters rather than individual samples:

$$p_{n+1}(\theta_{n+1} | \theta_1, \ldots, \theta_n) := \sum_{k=1}^{N_C} \frac{n_k}{n + \alpha} \delta_{\theta_k^*}(\theta_{n+1}) + \frac{\alpha}{n + \alpha} G_0(\theta_{n+1}). \qquad (3)$$

The distribution may be regarded as a mixture model. It contains N_C finite (degenerate) components, which correspond to the clusters already created, and the base measure component, which is responsible for the creation of new classes. The probability of occurrence for each cluster is proportional to its size. The probability for a new class to be created is adjusted by means of the DP parameter α. Definition (3) also implies that DP (αG_0) can be sampled efficiently, if we provide an algorithm to sample the base measure G_0.

Data generation (of n data values $\mathbf{x}_1, \ldots, \mathbf{x}_n$) according to a MDP model can be summarized by

$$\mathbf{x}_i \sim F(\,.\,|\theta_i)$$
$$\theta_i \sim p_i(\theta_i | \theta_1, \ldots, \theta_{i-1}) \,. \qquad (4)$$

Inference of this model is not as straightforward as sampling (3), since the observed data is $\mathbf{x}_1, \ldots, \mathbf{x}_n$, whereas the DP distribution is conditional on $\theta_1, \ldots, \theta_n$. The generative model in (4) has to be sampled conditional on the observed data $\mathbf{x}_i$. A sampling algorithm as described in Sec. 5 obtains estimates of the parameters θ_i. MDP models perform automatic model selection, since the number of clusters is determined by the dynamics of the process, i.e., it is not an input parameter. New classes are generated during the sampling process. When sampling the parameter θ_i for a given data value $\mathbf{x}_i$, the data value may be assigned to an existing class k (by setting $\theta_i := \theta_k^*$). The probability for this to happen depends on the likelihood $F(\mathbf{x}_i | \theta_k^*)$ and on the number of points already assigned to the class in question (since large classes, with a large value of n_k, are more probable than small ones). If the cluster distribution provides a good description of the data, the probability of assignment is high, since the likelihood F assumes a large value. If this is not the case for any existing cluster, a new cluster is created for the data value with high probability. Generation of a new cluster corresponds to sampling from the base measure term in (3).

The applicability of MDP models to clustering problems in machine learning and computer vision may be best illustrated by the following observation: Any parametric mixture model of the form

$$m(\mathbf{x} | \mathbf{t}_1, \ldots, \mathbf{t}_K, c_1, \ldots, c_K) = \sum_{k=1}^{K} c_k r(\mathbf{x} | \mathbf{t}_k) \qquad (5)$$

can be used within the MDP clustering framework by setting $F = r$ and placing a suitable prior G_0 on the parameter t_k. The prior serves as the base measure.

The class parameters t_k are substituted by samples θ_k^* generated by a process $DP(\alpha G_0)$ as described above, and the cluster sizes n_k are analogous to the mixture weights c_k in the parametric case. Given a set of observed data values $\mathbf{x}_1, \ldots, \mathbf{x}_n$, sampling the MDP model will result in a set of estimates $\theta_1, \ldots, \theta_n$ for the corresponding class parameters. By grouping identical values, the parameter estimates implicitly determine the number of clusters, class assignments of the data and the mixture proportions of the model.

3   Markov Random Field Constraints and Dirichlet Process Models

This section describes how Markov random field models can be integrated with a MDP clustering approach. Our objective is to obtain a model capable of combining the clustering and model selection performed by the MDP with smoothness constraints on the class labels. The model is applicable to any clustering problem for which it is reasonable to assume a spatially coherent class structure, such as segmentation of noisy images: To obtain smooth segments, a MRF constraint encourages adjacent points in the image to be assigned to the same class.

Consider a clustering problem with vectorial input data $\mathbf{x}_1, \ldots, \mathbf{x}_n$. Each point $\mathbf{x}_i$ is assumed to be generated according to a parameter vector θ_i. Two points are considered to originate from the same cluster if their respective parameter vectors are identical. The cluster assignment of feature $\mathbf{x}_i$ is denoted by $S_i \in \{1, \ldots, N_c\}$. We will use the notation θ_{-i} (or S_{-i}) to denote the set of all parameters (or cluster assignments) with the value corresponding to feature i removed. The MDP clustering model for this problem is once again defined by a likelihood F and a base measure G_0 to parameterize the Dirichlet process.

To combine the MDP model with a MRF, we restrict the choice of MRF constraints to *pairwise difference priors* [6], which are commonly used to model spatial smoothness of the label field. The MRF definition is based on an undirected neighborhood graph $\mathcal{N}$ and we write $l \in \partial(i)$ to denote that the feature of index l is a neighbor of feature i. The MRF prior Π consists of two components,

$$\Pi(\theta) \propto P(\theta) M(\theta) . \tag{6}$$

P is a parametric prior on the parameter θ, which will be referred to as the *initial prior*. It is used to model initial beliefs about which parameter values are likely to occur. M is a MRF contribution term of the form $M(\theta_i) \propto \exp(-H(\theta_1, \ldots, \theta_n))$, H being a cost function defined on the neighborhood graph $\mathcal{N}$. The term M is used to model constraints such as smoothness, which are conditional on the neighborhood of a feature. M defines a pairwise difference prior if the cost function assumes the form $H(\theta_i|\theta_{-i}) = \sum_{l \in \partial(i)} w_{il} \Phi(\theta_i - \theta_l)$, where Φ is a non-negative, even function and w_{il} are weights associated with the edges of the graph. Conditional on θ_{-i}, the prior for θ_i is given by

$$\Pi(\theta_i|\theta_{-i}) \propto P(\theta_i|\theta_{-i}) \exp(-H(\theta_i|\theta_{-i})) . \tag{7}$$

In the above relations, normalization constants have been neglected, because in many practical cases, M will be improper.

The MDP approach and MRF constraints are combined by drawing the initial prior P in (6) from a DP. The resulting generative model is summarized by

$$
\begin{aligned}
\mathbf{x}_i &\sim F(\mathbf{x}_i|\theta_i) \\
\theta_i &\sim M(\theta_i|\theta_{-i})P(\theta_i) \\
P &\sim \mathrm{DP}\,(\alpha G_0) \ .
\end{aligned}
\tag{8}
$$

To obtain a conditional form of this model, i. e. a form in which the random measure P does not occur explicitly, the conditional MDP prior (3) is substituted into (7). For a fixed size data set $\mathbf{x}_1, \ldots, \mathbf{x}_n$, the sequential form (3) of the conditional prior is rewritten as a prior for θ_i given the remaining parameter values:

$$
p_n(\theta_i|\theta_{-i}) \propto \sum_{k=1}^{N_C} n_{-i}^k \delta_{\theta_k^*}(\theta_i) + \alpha G_0(\theta_i) \ ,
\tag{9}
$$

where n_{-i}^k denotes the number of observations assigned to cluster k when $\mathbf{x}_i$ is removed from the set. The conditional form of the combined MDP/MRF prior is then given by

$$
\Pi\,(\theta_i|\theta_{-i}) \propto p_n(\theta_i|\theta_{-i}) \exp\,(-H\,(\theta_i|\theta_{-i})) \ .
\tag{10}
$$

Smoothness constraints for clustering problems are formulated on the cluster assignments, so the MRF cost function is a function defined on labels. A cost function modeling spatial smoothness measures whether or not neighboring features are assigned to the same cluster. This binary notion of similarity between neighbors is expressed by cost functions of the general form

$$
H\,(S_i|S_{-i}) = \sum_{l \in \partial(i)} \delta_{S_i, S_l} \phi(S_1, \ldots, S_n) \ ,
\tag{11}
$$

as proposed by Geman e. a. [7]. A special property of the MDP setting is the one-to-one correspondence between cluster labels and cluster parameters (since two sites belong to the same cluster if and only if their class parameters θ are identical). The correspondence admits an equivalent formulation of the cost function (11) in terms of class parameters:

$$
H\,(\theta_i|\theta_{-i}) = \sum_{l \in \partial(i)} \delta_{\theta_i, \theta_l} \phi(\theta_1, \ldots, \theta_n) \ .
\tag{12}
$$

Combination of the resulting MRF with the conditional MDP prior (9) affects only the first, finite term, because the support of H is a subset $\{\theta_1, \ldots, \theta_n\}$. A random value $\theta \sim G_0$ drawn from an infinite base measure will be different from any value in $\mathrm{supp}\,(H)$ with probability one, and therefore

$$
M(\theta_i|\theta_{-i})G_0(\theta_i) = G_0(\theta_i)
\tag{13}
$$

almost surely. The relation holds irrespectively of any particular choice of G_0 and H. Intuitively, (13) expresses the modeling assumption that the MRF constraint should encourage uniform assignments of neighbors. The MRF contribution is non-trivial for a given label S_i only if one or more neighbors of $\mathbf{x}_i$ are assigned to the same class as $\mathbf{x}_i$. Since a draw from the base measure will always result in the creation of a new class, the MRF term does not affect the base measure term.

4   The Histogram Clustering Model

The primary focus of this article is on histogram clustering, with application to image segmentation. The input features are composed of a set of n histograms $\mathbf{h}_i = (h_{i1}, \ldots, h_{iN_{\text{bins}}})$, $h_{ij} \in \mathbb{N}_0$, representing local intensity distributions of a digital image. They replace the data values $\mathbf{x}_1, \ldots, \mathbf{x}_n$ in the previous sections. Each histogram is associated with a pixel location in the image, referred to as a *site*. All histograms contain an identical number N_{counts} of values.

Given a vector θ_i of bin probabilities, a random histogram $\mathbf{h}_i$ is multinomially distributed with density $F(\mathbf{h}_i|\theta_i) = 1/Z_M(\mathbf{h}_i) \exp\left(\sum_{j=1}^{N_{\text{bins}}} h_{ij} \log(\theta_{ij})\right)$. Each vector θ_i for is assumed to be drawn from the respective conjugate prior, a Dirichlet distribution $G_0(\theta_i|\beta, \boldsymbol{\pi}) = \frac{1}{Z_D(\beta, \boldsymbol{\pi})} \exp\left(\sum_{j=1}^{N_{\text{bins}}} (\beta\pi_j - 1) \log(\theta_{ij})\right)$, where $\beta \in \mathbb{R}_+$ and $\boldsymbol{\pi}$ is a vector representing a finite probability distribution on N_{bins} elements.

To apply MRF constraints to the image segmentation problem, two features are defined as neighbors in the MRF neighborhood graph $\mathcal{N}$ if their associated sites are neighbors in the image. These neighborhoods are either of size $D = 4$ (two horizontal and two vertical neighbors) or $D = 8$ (all direct neighbors), cropped at the image boundaries. The cost function is of the form (12). For the sake of simplicity, ϕ in (12) is chosen to depend only on a scale parameter λ (defined once for the whole image) and the size of the neighborhood:

$$H\left(\theta_i|\theta_{-i}\right) = \lambda \sum_{l \in \partial(i)} \left(D - \delta_{\theta_i, \theta_l}\right) , \tag{14}$$

where $D = 4$ or $D = 8$, respectively. Thus, $\exp(-H) = \exp(-\lambda D)$ for feature $\mathbf{h}_i$ if no neighbor is assigned to the same cluster. If one or more neighbors are assigned to the same class, $\exp(-H)$ will increase and thus favor the assignment.

The model may be extended to the case of multiple histograms available at each site. This extension makes the method applicable to color images, where a single one-dimensional histogram is drawn from each color channel at each site, and to radar images with multiple channels representing different frequency bands. Another possible application is the inclusion of additional filter information, by applying a filter transform to the image and drawing histograms from the filter response. For example, texture information may be included in the form of Gabor filter response histograms. Suppose that C histograms $\mathbf{h}_i^l = (h_{i1}^l, \ldots, h_{iN_{\text{bins}}}^l)$, $l = 1, \ldots, C$, are available at each site i. First consider the basic parametric Bayesian model without the DP, consisting of the multinomial likelihood and Dirichlet prior in the single-channel case. To model multiple channels, the different channels are assumed to be independent. Each marginal histogram $\mathbf{h}_i^l$ is parameterized by its own vector θ_i^l of bin probabilities, and we write $\theta_i := (\theta_i^1, \ldots, \theta_i^C)$. Due to independence, the joint likelihood $F(\mathbf{h}_i^1, \ldots, \mathbf{h}_i^C | \theta_i^1, \ldots, \theta_i^C)$ factors into a product over the channel likelihoods $F(\mathbf{h}_i^l | \theta_i^l)$. Each parameter vector θ_i^l is drawn from a Dirichlet distribution $G_0^l(\theta | \beta^l, \boldsymbol{\pi}^l)$, resulting in the model

$$F(\mathbf{h}|\theta)G_0(\theta) = \prod_{l=1}^{C} F(\mathbf{h}_i^l | \theta_i^l) G_0^l(\theta | \beta^l, \boldsymbol{\pi}^l) . \tag{15}$$

The MDP/MRF generative model for multichannel data is then obtained by substituting $F(\mathbf{h}|\theta)$ and $G_0(\theta)$ into the generative model (8).

5   Sampling

The algorithm proposed here to sample the combined MDP/MRF model is a Markov chain Monte Carlo procedure similar to the algorithm proposed MacEachern [8] for sampling MDP models with a conjugate likelihood/base measure pair. Each iteration samples a set of cluster assignments $S_1, \ldots, S_n$ for all sites. New estimates of the cluster parameters θ_k^* are then sampled conditional on the assignments S_i and the observed data. Due to the way in which the finitely supported cost function of the MRF acts on the MDP model, some key formulas reduce to the conjugate case. As a consequence, the sampling approach remains applicable despite the fact that the constrained model is not conjugate. It is easily extended to the case of multiple channels.

To sample a cluster assignment S_i given a current set of parameters $\theta_1, .., \theta_n$ and the datum $\mathbf{x}_i$, the posterior probability of occurrence for each class is computed by integrating the complete model over θ_i:

$$\int_{\Omega_\theta} \exp\left(-H(\theta_i|\theta_{-i})\right) F(\mathbf{x}_i|\theta_i) \left(\sum_{k=1}^{N_C} n_{-i}^k \delta_{\theta_k^*}(\theta_i) + \alpha G_0(\theta_i)\right) d\theta_i$$

$$= \sum_{k=1}^{N_C} n_{-i}^k \exp\left(-H(\theta_k^*|\theta_{-i})\right) F(\mathbf{x}_i|\theta_k^*) + \alpha \int_{\Omega_\theta} F(\mathbf{x}_i|\theta_i)G_0(\theta_i)d\theta_i . \tag{16}$$

Since $H(\theta|\theta_{-i}) \neq 0$ only if $\theta \in \{\theta_1^*, \ldots, \theta_{N_C}^*\}$, $\exp\left(-H(\theta|\theta_{-i})\right) \neq 1$ holds only on a set of Lebesgue measure zero. Such a set does not affect the value of the integral, and the MRF contribution term may therefore be neglected in the base measure integral, as we have done above. Each term in (16) corresponds to a single cluster (with the integral involving the base measure G_0 corresponding to the creation of a new group), and we define cluster proportions by setting

$$\tilde{q}_{i0} := \alpha \int_{\Omega_\theta} F(\mathbf{x}_i|\theta_i)G_0(\theta_i)d\theta_i$$

$$\tilde{q}_{ik} := n_{-i}^k \exp\left(-H(\theta_k^*|\theta_{-i})\right) F(\mathbf{x}_i|\theta_k^*) . \tag{17}$$

These proportions are transformed into cluster probabilities by normalization,

$$q_{ik} := \frac{\tilde{q}_{ik}}{\sum_{j=0}^{N_{\mathrm{C}}} \tilde{q}_{ij}} \ . \tag{18}$$

A cluster assignment S_i is sampled by sampling from the finite probability distribution defined by the vector $(q_{i0}, \ldots, q_{iN_{\mathrm{C}}})$. In the second step, new values for the cluster parameters θ_k^* are chosen by sampling from the class posterior, i. e. the posterior based on all data values currently assigned to the given class:

$$\theta_k^* \sim G_0\left(\theta_k^*\right) \prod_{i|S_i=k} F\left(\mathbf{x}_i|\theta_k^*\right) \ . \tag{19}$$

The combined MDP/MRF model is thus sampled by the following algorithm:

Algorithm 1 (MDP/MRF Sampling)
Initialize: Generate $\theta \sim G_0$ and set $\theta_i = \theta$ for $i = 1, \ldots, n$.
Repeat:

1. For $i = 1, \ldots, n$:
    (a) If $\mathbf{x}_i$ is the only feature assigned to its cluster $k = S_i$, remove this cluster.
    (b) For $k = 0, \ldots, N_{\mathrm{C}}$, compute the component probabilities $q_{i,k}$ according to eqs. (17) and (18).
    (c) Draw a random index k according to the finite distribution $(q_{i,0}, \ldots, q_{i,N_{\mathrm{C}}})$.
    (d) Assignment:
        $-$ If $k \in \{1, \ldots, N_{\mathrm{C}}\}$, assign $\mathbf{x}_i$ to cluster k.
        $-$ If $k = 0$, create a new cluster for $\mathbf{x}_i$.
2. For each cluster $k = 1, \ldots, N_{\mathrm{C}}$: Update the cluster parameters θ_k^* given the class assignments $S_1, \ldots, S_n$ by sampling

$$\theta_k^* \sim G_0\left(\theta_k^*\right) \prod_{i|S_i=k} F\left(\mathbf{x}_i|\theta_k^*\right) \ . \tag{20}$$

In the histogram clustering model introduced above for the single-channel case, F is a multinomial distribution, G_0 a Dirichlet distribution and the observed data $\mathbf{x}_i$ are the histograms $\mathbf{h}_i$. Due to the conjugacy of F and G_0, the integral required for the computation of q_{i0} may be solved analytically:

$$\tilde{q}_{i0} = \alpha \int_{\Omega_\theta} F(\mathbf{x}_i|\theta_i) G_0(\theta_i) d\theta_i = \alpha \frac{Z_D(\mathbf{h}_i + \beta\boldsymbol{\pi})}{Z_D(\beta\boldsymbol{\pi}) Z_M(\mathbf{h}_i)} \ . \tag{21}$$

Conjugacy also implies that the class posterior (20) is a Dirichlet distribution, with the prior parameters updated by the data assigned to the cluster:

$$G_0\left(\theta_k^*|\beta\boldsymbol{\pi}\right) \prod_{i|S_i=k} F\left(\mathbf{x}_i|\theta_k^*\right) = G_0\left(\theta_k^* \,\middle|\, \sum_{i|S_i=k} \mathbf{h}_i + \beta\boldsymbol{\pi}\right) \ . \tag{22}$$

Efficient sampling algorithms based on gamma samples are available for this distribution [9], which ensures the feasibility of step 2 of the algorithm.

In the case of multiple channels, products of multinomial and Dirichlet distributions have to be substituted for F and G_0 in the derivation above, assuming that the different channels are statistically independent. Since the MRF term is defined on class labels, it applies to all channels, rather than to each individual channel. The cluster proportions are computed according to

$$\tilde{q}_{i0} := \alpha \int_{\Omega_\theta} \prod_{l=1}^{C} \left(F(\mathbf{h}_i^l|\theta_i^l) G_0^l(\theta_i^l|\beta^l, \boldsymbol{\pi}^l) \right) d\theta_i = \prod_{l=1}^{C} \frac{Z_D(\mathbf{h}_i^l + \beta^l \boldsymbol{\pi}^l)}{Z_D(\beta^l \boldsymbol{\pi}^l) Z_M(\mathbf{h}_i^l)}$$

$$\tilde{q}_{ik} := n_{-i}^k \exp\left(-H(\theta_k^*|\theta_{-i}) \right) \prod_{l=1}^{C} F(\mathbf{x}_i^l|\theta_k^{*l}) . \tag{23}$$

The class posterior turns into a product of Dirichlet distributions, each of which may be sampled individually:

$$\prod_{l=1}^{C} \left(G_0^l \left(\theta_k^{*l}|\beta^l \boldsymbol{\pi}^l \right) \prod_{i|S_i=k} F\left(\mathbf{h}_i^l|\theta_k^{*l} \right) \right) = \prod_{l=1}^{C} G_0^l \left(\theta_k^{*l} \Big| \sum_{i|S_i=k} \mathbf{h}_i^l + \beta^l \boldsymbol{\pi}^l \right) . \tag{24}$$

Sampling of the Dirichlet process for the multichannel model is thus conducted by parallel Dirichlet process sampling procedures applied to the individual channels. The channels couple through the class assignments S_i, and through the MRF contribution defined on these labels.

6   Experimental Results

The experiments presented in this section were conducted on two classes of noisy images, synthetic aperture radar (SAR) and magnetic resonance imaging (MRI) data. Aside from the visual quality of the segmentations, we especially study two model selection questions: (i) How does the hyperparameter of the Dirichlet process influence the model selection (i. e. the number of segments selected)? (ii) How do results compare to other model selection methods?

The histograms used in the experiments shown here where extracted from a digital image by centering a square window around each pixel on an equidistant grid and sorting the intensity values of all pixels within the window into a histogram. Choosing the size of the histogram window generally results in a trade-off between regularity and detail: Using a large window will smooth segmentation results, but coarsen the resolution. Small windows preserve detail, but usually give less robust segmentation results. Using a model with a smoothness constraint permits the choice of small windows. For the experiments shown below, histograms were obtained from a five-by-five pixel sliding window, centered at each node of a rectangular grid of width two.

The nonparametric Bayesian model selection strategy introduced in the previous sections is compared with the stability method [10, 1], a competitive model

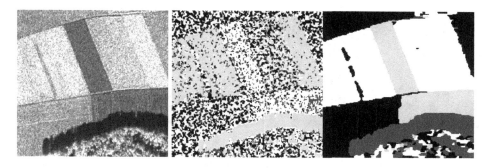

Fig. 1. Segmentation results on real-world radar data. Original image (left), unconstrained MDP segmentation (middle), MDP segmentation with smoothness constraint (right).

Fig. 2. A SAR image with a high noise level and ambiguous segments (left). Solutions without (middle) and with smoothing (right).

selection technique for clustering. Stability is a cross-validation based wrapper method for an arbitrary clustering algorithm chosen by the user. The method repeatedly computes clustering solutions on randomly chosen subsets of the input data, and evaluates the predictive power of the obtained cluster model on the remaining data. An instability index is computed for different number of clusters, which measures how unstable cluster solutions are under the random split procedure. The chosen model is the one for which the instability index is minimal. Usually, a local rather than the global minimum is chosen, since stability algorithms are known to preferentially estimate a global minimum for very simple solutions (often only two classes). Consider, for example, intensity-based image segmentation: A two-class segmentation, which simply splits the image into light and dark regions, tends to be highly stable with respect to the random split procedure, but is usually not the desired solution.

The MDP/MRF method applied for image segmentation employs a multinomial likelihood. To obtain a valid comparison, the algorithm chosen for use with stability is an EM algorithm which estimates a mixture of multinomial

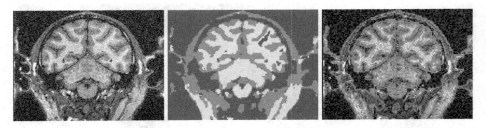

Fig. 3. MR frontal view image of a monkey's head. Original image (left), smoothed MDP segmentation (middle), original image overlaid with segment boundaries (right).

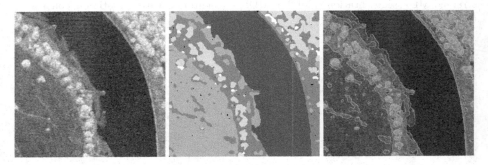

Fig. 4. Segmentation result for multichannel data: A SAR image with three channels (left), segmentation result obtained with the MDP/MRF model, and the original image overlaid with segment boundaries (right)

distributions (also known as the ACM algorithm [11]). Figs. 1 and 2 show results for two SAR images. Segments of the image in Fig. 1 are well separated. As the results show, segmentation quality for noisy data can be improved significantly by a smoothness constraint. Fig. 2 provides an example of ambiguous, poorly separated segments. In this case, both the unconstrained and constrained segmentation results are of limited quality. Another type of noisy data, a MR image, is shown in Fig. 3 together with its (constrained) segmentation result. Fig. 4 shows segmentation results obtained with the multichannel version of the algorithm on a SAR image consisting of three separate frequency bands.

The burn-in phase of the Gibbs sampling algorithm is assumed to have terminated once the number of assignments changed per iteration remains stable below 1% of the total number of sites. This condition is usually met after at most 500-1000 iterations. The behavior of the class assignments during the sampling process visualized by the plot in Fig. 5. In both cases, the algorithm takes about 600 iterations to stabilize (the curves become constant apart from fluctuations). The splitting behavior of the algorithm differs significantly between the two cases: In the unconstrained case, large batches of sites are reassigned at

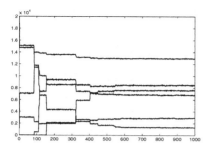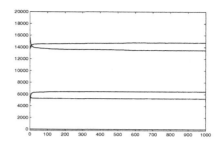

Fig. 5. Cluster sizes during the sampling process for the unconstrained and smoothed version of the MDP method. The number of sites assigned to each cluster (vertical) are drawn against the number of iterations (horizontal), with each graph representing a cluster. Left: Radar image (Fig. 1), no smoothing. Right: Same image, with smoothing.

Table 1. Number of clusters chosen by the algorithm on two radar images for different values of the hyperparameter

α		1e-10	1e-9	1e-8	1e-7	1e-6	1e-5	1e-4	1e-3
Image Fig. 1	MDP	2	4	4	6	5	4	5	6
	smoothed	2	2	3	4	4	4	4	4
Images Fig. 2	MDP	4	3	4	7	6	5	5	9
	smoothed	2	2	3	4	5	3	3	5

once to new clusters (visible as jumps in the diagram). In the constrained case, assignments change gradually.

The influence of the DP hyperparameter α is shown in Tab. 1. In general, the number of clusters increases for larger values of α (i. e. when the probability is high that a new cluster is created by the DP). When the smoothing constraint is activated, the number of clusters becomes more stable with respect to changes of α than without smoothing. We note that the number of clusters selected is more volatile for the poorly separated image in Fig. 2.

For comparison of the model selection results, the stability method has been applied to the two SAR images in Figs. 1 and 2. The resulting instability indices for two to nine clusters are given in Tab. 2. For the image in Fig. 1, the local minimum of the instability index is assumed for five clusters, with the solutions $N_{\mathrm{C}} = 3, 4, 5$ within range of the error bars. This outcome is comparable to the result of the smoothed MDP model, which (except for very small values of α) selects three or four clusters. The unconstrained MDP model tends to select a larger number of clusters. Since the instability index is obtained by averaging over results on random subsets, one should expect its results to be conservative. This is indeed the case, since the smoothed MDP approach produces a comparable number of segments as the stability method does without smoothing. Now consider the image in Fig. 2, for which MDP results, even in the smoothed case, are rather unstable (cf. Tab. 1). The local minimum

Table 2. Stability indices computed with ACM clustering on two radar images for different numbers of clusters

N_C	Stability index Image Fig. 1	Stability index Image Fig. 2	N_C	Stability index Image Fig. 1	Stability index Image Fig. 2
2	0.0012 ± 0.0009	0.0003 ± 0.3341	6	0.4740 ± 0.0867	0.2933 ± 0.3437
3	0.3359 ± 0.2324	0.1765 ± 0.2856	7	0.5164 ± 0.0434	0.2907 ± 0.3007
4	0.3204 ± 0.2113	0.1233 ± 0.3481	8	0.5598 ± 0.0728	0.3532 ± 0.2889
5	0.2947 ± 0.0884	0.1436 ± 0.1929	9	0.6637 ± 0.0512	0.3378 ± 0.2801

of the instability index is assumed at $N_C = 4$, but the whole range of computed solutions ($N_C = 2, \ldots, 9$) is within one standard deviation of the local minimum. Thus both the MDP/MRF approach and the stability method give unreliable results on an image with a high noise level and poorly discernible segments. Both methods are constructed around the same probabilistic model of the data (a multinomial histogram clustering model). We therefore conclude that the reliability of model selection results depends, for both approaches, on the ability of the clustering model to resolve differences between segment distributions.

7   Discussion

There exists a considerable number of DP-based models [12] with a wide range of applications in statistics and, more recently, natural language processing and document retrieval [13, 2]. To our knowledge, this paper summarizes the first attempt both to apply the Dirichlet nonparametric approach to image segmentation, and to combine it with Markov random fields, the standard Bayesian approach to image processing and spatial statistics.

We believe that a wide range of applications for MDP models may emerge in computer vision. Despite their mathematical intricacies, the fact that these models may be regarded as mixture distributions with a variable number of mixture components (cf. Sec. 2) makes them an intuitive and powerful tool for probabilistic modeling. Instead of the multinomial distribution employed in our histogram clustering approach, any type of parametric likelihood may be used with the MDP model. If the base measure is set to the respective conjugate prior, standard sampling algorithms are applicable. For example, a nonparametric analogue of the widely used k-means algorithm may be obtained by choosing a Gaussian of fixed, uniform covariance as the likelihood and a Gaussian prior on the mean parameter as the base measure. For applications requiring fast inference, sampling algorithms may be substituted by more efficient approximate methods [14].

We have shown how to combine the MDP clustering model with a spatial smoothness constraint. We like to emphasize that this nonparametric framework is applicable to any type of mixture component distribution and our sampling algorithm remains applicable for any conjugate likelihood/base measure pair.

Our experiments confirm what the structure of the model suggests: The ability of the parametric model used within the nonparametric framework to resolve differences between segments determines the quality of segmentation results. It also determines how stable model selection results are with respect to changes of the hyperparameter.

In summary, the MDP approach can be regarded as a model selection framework built in the style of a wrapper method around an application dependent parametric model. Additionally, it may be equipped with a smoothness constraint for image segmentation. The comparison with the stability framework based on cross-validation yields consistent results for the number of clusters.

References

1. Lange, T., Roth, V., Braun, M., Buhmann, J.M.: Stability-based validation of clustering solutions. Neural Computation **16** (2004) 1299–1323
2. Zaragoza, H., Hiemstra, D., Tipping, D., Robertson, S.: Bayesian extension to the language model for ad hoc information retrieval. In: Proc. SIGIR 2003. (2003)
3. Sudderth, E., Torralba, A., Freeman, W.T., Willsky, A.S.: Describing visual scenes using transformed dirichlet processes. In Weiss, Y., Schölkopf, B., Platt, J., eds.: Advances in Neural Information Processing Systems 18, MIT Press (2006)
4. Murtagh, F., Raftery, A.E., Starck, J.L.: Bayesian inference for multiband image segmentation via model-based cluster trees. Image and Vision Computing **23** (2005) 587–596
5. Antoniak, C.E.: Mixtures of Dirichlet processes with applications to bayesian nonparametric estimation. Annals of Statistics **2** (1974) 1152–1174
6. Besag, J., Green, P., Higdon, D., Mengersen, K.: Bayesian computation and stochastic systems. Statistical Science **10** (1995) 3–66
7. Geman, D., Geman, S., Graffigne, C., Dong, P.: Boundary detection by constrained optimization. IEEE Trans. on Pat. Anal. Mach. Intel. **12** (1990) 609–628
8. MacEachern, S.N.: Estimating normal means with a conjugate style Dirichlet process prior. Communications in Statistics: Simulation and Computation **23** (1994) 727–741
9. Devroye, L.: Non-uniform random variate generation. Springer (1986)
10. Breckenridge, J.: Replicating cluster analysis: Method, consistency and validity. Multivariate Behavioral Research **24** (1989) 147–161
11. Puzicha, J., Hofmann, T., Buhmann, J.M.: Histogram clustering for unsupervised segmentation and image retrieval. Pattern Recognition Letters **20** (1999) 899–909
12. MacEachern, S., Müller, P.: Efficient MCMC schemes for robust model extensions using encompassing Dirichlet process mixture models. In Ruggeri, F., Rios Insua, D., eds.: Robust Bayesian Analysis. Springer (2000)
13. Blei, D.M., Griffith, T.L., Jordan, M.I., Tenenbaum, J.B.: Hierarchical topic models and the nested chinese restaurant process. In Thrun, S., Saul, L., Schölkopf, B., eds.: Advances in Neural Information Processing Systems 16, MIT Press (2004)
14. Blei, D.M., Jordan, M.I.: Variational methods for the Dirichlet process. In: Proceedings of the 21st International Conference on Machine Learning. (2004)

Shape Analysis and Fuzzy Control for 3D Competitive Segmentation of Brain Structures with Level Sets

Cybèle Ciofolo and Christian Barillot

IRISA / CNRS, Team VisAGeS,
Campus de Beaulieu, 35042 Rennes Cedex, France
{Cybele.Ciofolo, Christian.Barillot}@irisa.fr
http://www.www.irisa.fr/visages/visages-eng.html

Abstract. We propose a new method to segment 3D structures with competitive level sets driven by a shape model and fuzzy control. To this end, several contours evolve simultaneously toward previously defined targets. The main contribution of this paper is the original introduction of prior information provided by a shape model, which is used as an anatomical atlas, into a fuzzy decision system. The shape information is combined with the intensity distribution of the image and the relative position of the contours. This combination automatically determines the directional term of the evolution equation of each level set. This leads to a local expansion or contraction of the contours, in order to match the borders of their respective targets. The shape model is produced with a principal component analysis, and the resulting mean shape and variations are used to estimate the target location and the fuzzy states corresponding to the distance between the current contour and the target. By combining shape analysis and fuzzy control, we take advantage of both approaches to improve the level set segmentation process with prior information. Experiments are shown for the 3D segmentation of deep brain structures from MRI and a quantitative evaluation is performed on a 18 volumes dataset.

1 Introduction

During the last decade, segmentation methods have become more and more sophisticated, in order to deal with very complex problems, such as texture segmentation, motion detection or medical imaging segmentation. Some approaches have now proved to be adapted to certain type of applications. In particular, the level set methods first proposed by Osher and Sethian [1] have become very common in the computer vision community and are now used in various contexts. The reason for such a broad field of applications is their implicit, intrisic, parameter and topology free formulation. In particular, they provide a very efficient framework for 3D image segmentation, where many 2D methods are difficult to apply.

A. Leonardis, H. Bischof, and A. Pinz (Eds.): ECCV 2006, Part I, LNCS 3951, pp. 458–470, 2006.

After the first contour-based algorithms [2, 3], more sophisticated methods have been proposed, using regional statistics [4] or both contour and region terms [5] to segment 3D structures, moving objects [6] or textured content of images [7]. But both contour and region constraints are generally derived from the grey levels of the image, and do not always provide enough information to segment complex structures with variable shapes, particularly if their borders do not appear clearly in the images, as it often occurs in medical imagery for example. For this reason, prior information in general and shape models [8] in particular have been widely associated with level sets for image segmentation.

For example, Rousson and Paragios propose an elegant introduction of shape priors in a variational framework to perform a level-set based segmentation of noisy or occluded data [9]. Tsai *et. al.* also take advantage of a shape model obtained by training to drive the evolution of a 3D contour [10], and Yang *et. al.* introduce a joint intensity-shape prior in a probalistic segmentation with level sets [11].

It sometimes happens however that the segmentation targets have very blurred borders, and that the grey levels inside these structures are not really homogeneous and even similar to that of neighboring objects. This phenomenon occurs for example in the deep grey structures of the brain, which may be difficult to distinguish from white matter. In this context, even shape information is sometimes not sufficient to achieve an accurate segmentation. A very useful framework is however provided by the fuzzy set theory, which is adapted to model non-precise knowledge, as, for instance, objects with ill-defined borders.

Consequently, the fuzzy sets theory has already been used in image segmentation, especially in medical imaging. Xu *et. al* use an adaptative fuzzy c-means algorithm that is combined with an isosurface algorithm and a deformable surface model to reconstruct the brain cortex [12]. Automatic segmentation methods for brain internal structures are also proposed [13], where the segmentation is based on a symbolic spatial description of the structures and finally refined with a deformable model.

In this article, our goal is to present a methodology which takes advantage of three approaches that have proved to give good results in different contexts: level set segmentation, shape modeling and fuzzy logic. The objective is to be able to segment several objects which borders do not appear clearly, and which can not be distinguished with only image statistics. As this is a very complex problem, which however occurs very often in medical imagery, the use of a single segmentation method would lead to a very complex mathematical modeling and difficult implementation. To avoid this, we combine a basic shape model and a very simple type of fuzzy decision system to locally drive the evolution of several level sets, which are simultaneously deformed to reach their respective targets. In previous work [14], we presented a preliminary version of this methodology which did not include any shape model, and applied it to the segmentation of brain structures. In this paper, we show how the use of a preliminary shape analysis strongly improves the robustness of the method. The algorithm is applied on a real Magnetic Resonance Images (MRI) dataset, in order to segment internal brain structures, which are of great interest for the quantitative morphological analysis of neurological pathologies.

This paper is organized as follows: Section 2 summarizes the principle of our level set segmentation driven with fuzzy control, Section 3 presents the construction of the shape model and experimental results are shown and discussed in Section 4. Finally, we conclude in Section 5.

2   Level Set Segmentation Driven by Fuzzy Control

In this section we briefly present how a fuzzy decision system tunes the terms of the evolution equations of several level sets. More details about this method can be found in [14].

2.1   General Principle

As we wish to segment simultaneously several structures in the same volume, we assign one level set (represented by one contour) to each target. As the level set formalism allows topological changes, a single target may be composed of several components, and the corresponding contour can split or merge. We use the level set equation evolution proposed in [15]:

$$F = g(P_T)(\rho\kappa - \nu), \tag{1}$$

where ν is a constant module force, whose sign leads the current contour toward the desired border; κ is the local curvature of the contour; ρ is the weight on curvature; g is a decreasing function; and P_T is the probability of transition between the inside and the outside of the structure to be segmented. Thus the role of the term $g(P_T)$ is to stop the evolution of the contour at the desired location.

The ν and P_T terms are computed according to a preliminary classification of tissues before the beginning of the level set evolution. The image intensities are viewed as samples of a Gaussian Mixture Model (GMM), whose parameters are estimated according to a Maximum A Posteriori principle, with a SEM algorithm [16]. The classes that are mainly represented inside the initialisation volume are automatically detected and determine the reduced GMM corresponding to the inside of the object to segment. For further details concerning the computation of these terms, see [15].

The advantages of the evolution force described in Eq. (1) is that it is very simple and directly derived from the original geometric active contour formulation [3]. It assigns a precise role to each term, while preserving the ability to modify each term according to geometrical constraints corresponding to visual requirements.

2.2   Non-overlapping Constraint

Each target has a physical meaning, which implies that they should not overlap. Consequently, the deformation of the contours needs to respect this non-overlapping constraint. This is generally done by using additional terms corresponding to an external force in the equation evolution of the level sets.

Recent approaches [4, 5] generally use energy minimization techniques to define the additional terms of the force. However, in medical imaging, the structures of interest are often very small compared to the image resolution and may have complex shapes. This makes it difficult to define energy constraints that remain both general and adapted to specific structures and pathologies. Another approach consists in translating the available information into decision rules that are directly used to drive the level set evolution. This can be done with the fuzzy set theory, which is very convenient to express rules in natural language.

We designed our method considering two main objectives: the implementation should be as simple as possible, and all the information provided by the data should be exploited. This lead us to use a particular type of fuzzy decision system: a fuzzy controller, both for its simplicity and ability to deal with precise measurements. The role of this fuzzy controller is to drive the different contours to their respective targets, while avoiding overlapping. This is directly related to Eq. (1), where the ν term determines the privileged evolution direction of the contour. Consequently, the output of the fuzzy controller is ν, and is calculated for each voxel, at each iteration of the evolution.

2.3   Fuzzy Controller

In [15], the proposed formulation for ν is given by:

$$\nu = \mathrm{Sign}(P(\lambda \in \Lambda_i | \mathbf{x}) - P(\lambda \in \Lambda_e | \mathbf{x})), \tag{2}$$

where $\mathbf{x}$ is the current voxel, λ is the class of the current voxel estimated from the volume histogram, and Λ_i and Λ_e are the reduced GMM representing respectively the inside and the outside of the structure to be segmented. As this equation doen not take into account the notion of segmentation target nor any non-overlapping constraint, the fuzzy controller replaces it by the following constraints:

1. Several contours that evolve in competition must not intersect even if each of them can split in several components;
2. Each contour must stay in the vicinity of the fuzzy label describing its segmentation target;
3. Eq. (2) is valid under Conditions 1 and 2.

Condition 1 is the non-overlapping constraint and may be related to some other methods, such as multiphase level sets [4]. However this approach is applicable if the regions can be distinguished by their statistics. In the case of regions presenting similar grey levels, such as the brain grey nuclei, one must use other features, like labels coming from an atlas, to guarantee that the different contours will not intersect. Another approach consists in using a repulsive evolution force [17, 7, 18]. Our method is similar to these ones, since the ν term defines a locally adaptive force. However, the advantage of the fuzzy controller is that this force can be defined even if homogeneous regions do not appear clearly in the image.

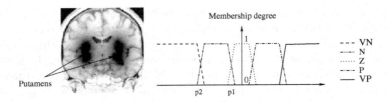

Fig. 1. Left: distance map from the putamens. Right: the five fuzzy states of $Dlab$: very negative (VN), negative (N), around zero (Z), positive (P) and very positive (VP).

Table 1. Fuzzy decision rules for the output variable ν. The states of $Dlab$ are very negative (VN), negative (N), around zero (Z), positive (P), and very positive (VP). The states of the variable Dc are null (N), too close (TC), close (C), rather close (RC) and far (F). The states of the variables Dp and ν are negative (N) and positive (P).

	$Dlab$=VN		$Dlab$=N		$Dlab$=Z		$Dlab$=P		$Dlab$=VP	
	Dp=N	Dp=P	Dp=N	Dp=P	Dp=N	Dp=P	Dp=N	Dp=P	Dp=N	Dp=P
Dc=N	N	N	N	N	N	N	N	N	N	N
Dc=TC	N	N	N	N	N	P	N	P	P	P
Dc=C	N	N	N	N	N	P	N	P	P	P
Dc=RC	N	N	N	N	N	P	N	P	P	P
Dc=F	N	N	N	N	N	P	N	P	P	P

In order to take the three conditions listed above into account, we define three fuzzy variables as inputs of the fuzzy controller:

1. Dc represents the distance from the current contour to the other ones.
2. $Dlab$ represents the signed distance from the current contour to the label corresponding to its segmentation target. An example of distance map, or fuzzy label map of the brain putamens is shown on Fig. 1.
3. Dp represents the difference of probability presented in Eq. (2).

These variables are then combined to define the fuzzy decision rules determined by the three conditions. The five states of each input and the rules are summarized in Table 1. They are used to assign a *positive* or *negative* state to ν, which respectively mean that the contour will locally expand or contract. We use only two states to caracterize ν, since it has been shown that only its sign has a real influence on the contour evolution [15].

Condition 2, which is related to the distance maps, is translated by a majority of P states in the right part of the table and N states in the left part. This means that if the processed voxel of the contour is far outside its label ($Dlab$=N or VN), it needs to contract (ν=N). On the contrary, if it is inside the label ($Dlab$=P or VP), it needs to expand (ν=P).

Condition 3 is mainly visible in the central part of the table ($Dlab$=Z and Dc=TC to F). This corresponds to the case where the contour is within the vicinity of its label and not too close to another one. Then the state of ν depends on the intensities of the volume only, as explained in Eq. (2).

This fuzzy controller is thus used to determine ν for each voxel, at each iteration of the segmentation process. Let us note that even if there are several contours, only one fuzzy controller is needed and used alternatively for each of them. Moreover, the expression of the propagation conditions in natural language avoids the use of weighting parameters in the evolution equation of the level sets, which is an advantage compared to many variational approaches. More details about the implementation are available in [14].

3   Shape Analysis for Level Set Segmentation

This part explains how a shape model is constructed and used to define the fuzzy variable $Dlab$, in order to be introduced in the segmentation process with level sets and fuzzy control.

3.1   Construction of the Shape Model

As many authors do, we use a principal component analysis (PCA) to construct the shape model. The main reason for this choice is that PCA provides the parameters of variation modes that are ordered according to their representativity. We thus take advantage of this property to define the fuzzy states of $Dlab$.

For each target, the PCA is performed on a population of n shapes that have previously been registered in the same referential as the processed volume and segmented. A shape is then represented by a vector $\mathbf{x_i}$, $i \in \{1, \ldots, n\}$, which components are the grey levels of the volume containing the shape. The mean shape $\bar{\mathbf{x}}$ is given by $\bar{\mathbf{x}} = \frac{1}{n} \sum_{i=1}^{n} \mathbf{x}_i$. The covariance matrix of the shape population is diagonalized in order to provide n eigenvalues $\lambda_1 \geq \cdots \geq \lambda_n$ and the associated eigenvectors, which constitute the matrix $\mathbf{\Phi}$. The variation modes represented by $\mathbf{\Phi}$ are ordered according to their respective eigenvalues. New samples $\tilde{\mathbf{x}}$ corresponding to the model can then be generated by using:

$$\tilde{\mathbf{x}} = \bar{\mathbf{x}} + \mathbf{\Phi_m b_m}, \tag{3}$$

where $\mathbf{\Phi_m}$ is a submatrix of $\mathbf{\Phi}$ representing m selected variation modes and $\mathbf{b_m}$ are the b_i weightings corresponding to each mode, $i \in \{1, \ldots, m\}$.

3.2   Introduction of the Shape Model in the Segmentation Process

Using a shape model to drive a segmentation method has become very common since the introduction of Active Shape Models [8]. However, these models strongly depend on the parametrisation of the shapes, which makes it difficult to use them in 3D. As we would like to avoid this dependance, we use a level set formalism instead of a parametric deformable model, as in [11, 10].

The shape model obtained by PCA is used for two purposes: (1) defining the segmentation target labels and (2) estimating the fuzzy states of the variable $Dlab$, which represents the distance to these labels. These two steps are now described for a given target.

Definition of the segmentation target label

A fuzzy label is used to approximately locate the target in the volume. It is created by applying a distance transformation [19] on the mean shape obtained by PCA.

Definition of the fuzzy states of *Dlab*

We assume that there is a relationship between the variation modes of the shape obtained by PCA and the area that is actually covered by the real target on the image. Indeed, let us consider the largest variation allowed by the shape model, by selecting large values of b_i in Eq. (3). They are likely to correspond to shapes which are very different from the mean shape, but remain realistic. Thus, the distance between these generated shapes and the label defined by the mean shape can be viewed as an indicator of which distance can be considered as *very negative* for *Dlab*.

We proceed as follows. First an appropriate number m of modes is selected in order to be able to generate shapes that correctly represent the variability of the structure. This is done by choosing m so that the cumulated variances of the first m modes are greater than 66% of the total variance. This is possible due to the ordering of modes provided by PCA.

Then we consider that small shape variations correspond to $|b_i| \leq \sqrt{\lambda_i}$ and large variations correspond to $|b_i| \leq 3\sqrt{\lambda_i}$, since $P(|b_i| \leq \sqrt{\lambda_i}) = 68\%$ and $P(|b_i| \leq 3\sqrt{\lambda_i}) = 99,7\%$. The corresponding "small variation" and "large variation" shapes are generated. An example is shown on Fig. 2.

Fig. 2. Areas covered by variations around the mean shape for both putamens. Dark grey: mean shape, light grey: small var. ($|b_i| = \sqrt{\lambda_i}$), white: large var. ($|b_i| = 3\sqrt{\lambda_i}$).

Finally, the mean distance between the mean shape and the "small variation" shape defines the point p_1 on Fig. 1, which distinguishes the *negative* and *around zero* states of *Dlab*. The mean distance between the mean shape and the "large variation" shape defines the point p_2 on Fig. 1, which is located between the *very negative* and *negative* states of *Dlab*. The points corresponding to the limits between the states *around zero*, *positive* and *very positive* are obtained by symmetry with respect to zero.

As there are several segmentation targets, this process is repeated for each of them, and we finally take the average p_1 and p_2 values to define *Dlab*. This averaging operation may be considered as information loss, since *Dlab* is not specific to each target. However, in practice, the structures to be segmented have approximately the same size, and their p_1 (respectively p_2) values are similar, which allows us to average them. The advantage of this approach is that we define a single fuzzy controller for all the targets, and thus reduce computation time and memory needs.

The main advantage of this method is that the fuzzy states of $Dlab$ are determined by the statistical analysis, instead of being estimated arbitrarily by an expert. This is a step forward in reducing the number of manually tuned parameters of the segmentation algorithm.

4   Application: Internal Brain Structures Segmentation

The method is applied to segment the brain grey nuclei, which are internal brain structures located in the deep grey matter. We focus on four segmentation targets: (1) left and right thalamus, (2) left and right caudate nucleus, (3) left and right pallidum and (4) left and right putamen. Each target is thus made of two parts, and we use four level sets for the segmentation, one for each target.

The grey nuclei are very difficult to segment, since their grey levels are not homogeneous and their borders with the surrounding white matter do not appear clearly on MRI. Consequently, even when they are segmented manually by experts, the results vary a lot according to the level of experience and the attention of the human observer. From a medical point of view, these structures are strongly involved in many neurological pathologies, which means that an automated segmentation method is critical to perform morphomotric analyses on large populations, without suffering from the variability of manual results. The grey nuclei are also a target for electro-stimulation in the treatment of Parkinson's disease. The segmentation is thus very useful to plan the surgical intervention.

4.1   Data

We test our method on a database provided on the Internet Brain Segmentation Repository (IBSR), and available at the Center for Morphometric Analysis, Massachusetts General Hospital (`http://www.cma.mgh.harvard.edu/ibsr`).

This database contains 18 real T1-weighted MR scans and the corresponding manual segmentation of 43 structures, performed by a trained expert. We consider this manual segmentation as the ground truth to assess our results. The MR scans are $256 \times 256 \times 128$ volumes, with slices of thickness 1.5mm, and pixel dimension going from 0.84mm to 1mm on each slice.

4.2   Experiments

In order to show the improvement brought by shape analysis, we present three different experiments:

— Exp. 1: segmentation of the grey nuclei without shape analysis,
— Exp. 2: segmentation of the grey nuclei with shape analysis for the propagation of the level sets (with the same initialisation as Exp. 1),
— Exp. 3: segmentation of the grey nuclei with shape analysis for the propagation and the initialisation of the level sets.

The first two experiments show the role of the shape analysis in the same conditions, and the third one demonstrates how the results can be improved by adding more prior information in the segmentation process.

Choice of the atlas and labels

For all experiments, an atlas is needed to define the fuzzy labels corresponding to the segmentation targets. For Exp. 1 (without shape analysis), one subject of the dataset is randomly chosen to be the atlas, and the segmentation is performed on the 17 other subjects. The fuzzy labels of the targets are then obtained from the manual segmentation associated to the atlas with a linear registration algorithm (12 parameters that maximise the mutual information are computed). As the manual results are subject to intra and inter-observer variability, it is likely that these labels are not accurate enough to drive the propagation of the contours properly. This motivates the use of a statistical analysis to construct a shape model which is used as an atlas. Consequently, for Exp. 2 and 3, a leave-one-out process is applied to construct the shape model of the targets as explained in Section 3. The statistical analysis is done from the manual segmentation associated with every subject but the processed one. To this end, the registration between the shapes is done with the same registration algorithm with 12 parameters. We select 5 modes, since this corresponds to a cumulated variance greater than 66% of the total variance, but in practice, we observe that the results are approximately the same for 3 modes or more.

Initialisation and results

For Exp. 1, the contours are initialised by doing a morphological erosion on the target labels. For Exp. 2, we use exactly the same initialisation to be able to compare the results with and without shape analysis. We also tried to use boxes roughly located in the center of the brain as initialisation. This lead to quite good results, but the computation time was larger and even if the final locations of the contours was satisfying, there were some inaccuracies along the borders, where the initialisation was not consistent with the location of the targets.

For Exp. 3, we include more prior information in the segmentation process, by using a better initialisation. This is done by performing a morphological erosion on the labels obtained by shape analysis, instead of the labels obtained by registration from one subject.

Let us stress that for comparison purposes, all the tests are run with the same set of parameters for all experiments and all subjects.

The segmentation takes approximately 15 to 20 minutes on a 3GHz Linux PC with 1GB memory. The results are good for 15 subjects. The registration does not perform very well for the 2 remaining subjects, and even if the segmentation process tempts to counteract this effect, the results are not accurate enough, which means that even if the global location is good, the borders of the target are not properly recovered. An example of results is shown on Fig. 3.

These results show that without shape analysis (top row), the grey nuclei, especially the putamens and pallida are over-segmented, while the global shape of the thalami is not completely realistic. This is corrected by the shape analysis, on

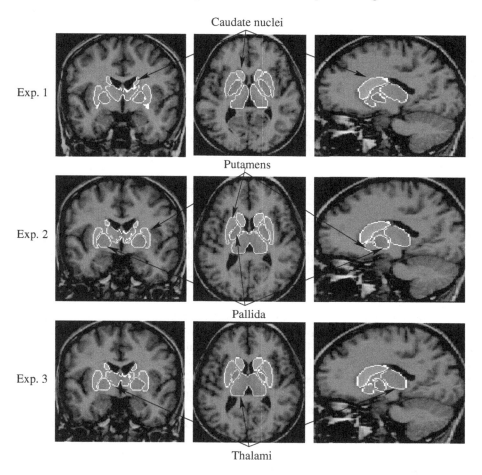

Fig. 3. Segmentation of the grey nuclei. Top row: without shape analysis, middle row: with shape analysis for the propagation of the level sets only, bottom row: with shape analysis for the propagation and the initialisation of the level sets.

the middle and bottom rows. Moreover, the segmentations shown on the middle and bottom rows look rather the same, which means that even if the initialisation used in Exp. 3 improves the results, this is an additional improvement that does not have as much influence as the use of the shape model to drive the propagation of the contours.

4.3   Quantitative Evaluation

In order to quantitatively assess our results on the IBSR dataset, we compute the mean distance M_d between our results and the ground truth provided by the manual segmentation. We also use the spatial accuracy index S, which is a similarity index based on the overlapping rate between the result and the truth [20]:

$$S = 2 \cdot \frac{\text{Card}(R \cap T)}{\text{Card}(R) + \text{Card}(T)} \quad M_d = \frac{\sum_{r \in R} \min_{t \in T} d(r,t)}{\text{Card}(R)},$$

where R is the segmentation result and T is the ground truth. Our results are summarized in Table 2. This table also contains the S and M_d values corresponding to the similarity between the 12-parameter registration result of the atlas structures and the ground truth.

Table 2. Similarity indice S and mean distance M_d for the segmentation of the thalami (Th.), caudate nuclei (CN), pallida (GP) and putamens (Pu.), with or without shape analysis (S.A.)

	Th.		NC		GP		Pu.	
	S	M_d	S	M_d	S	M_d	S	M_d
Registration	0.73	1.8	0.60	1.9	0.53	2.1	0.66	1.8
Exp. 1: Without shape analysis	0.77	1.7	0.60	2.1	0.56	2.0	0.62	1.9
Exp. 2: With S.A. for propagation	0.82	1.5	0.64	2.2	0.67	1.7	0.68	1.8
Exp. 3: With S.A. for prop. and init.	0.82	1.5	0.64	2.1	0.62	1.8	0.74	1.5

The table clearly shows that the segmentation results, especially with shape analysis, are better than the registration ones. The spatial accuracy index is good for the thalami. For the caudate nuclei, pallida and putamens, the lower values can be explained by the small size of the corresponding structures. Consequently, even a small difference between the result and the ground truth leads to a large variation in the spatial accuracy index. As an example, let us consider the result of a morphological erosion on the ground truth of one of these structures with a structuring element of size 1. The mean S value computed between the ground truth and the erosion result is only 0.77. This is the reason why, in literature, an S value greater than 0.7 is considered as a very good result [20]. Moreover, it is well-known that a manual segmentation performed by only one expert is not enough to be a real gold standard. An offset of one or two voxels with respect to the ground truth we use is thus acceptable.

Finally, the M_d values are low for all the grey nuclei, even the small ones which do not have very good S values. They are also significantly decreased by the use of the shape analysis for the propagation of the contours, and even more if the shape analysis is used for initialisation. As the quantitative results include the 2 cases on which the registration fails, these low M_d values show that the segmentation is more effective than registration only, and strongly improved by shape analysis. This is also demonstrated by the standard deviation of the mean M_d values, which is largely lower for segmentation with shape analysis (less than 0.3 voxels except for caudate nuclei) than for registration (around 0.5 voxels).

Moreover, as the segmentation parameters were the same for all the subjects in the dataset, it is obvious that these results are not optimal for each subject, but show the robustness of the method when used on several different volumes.

5   Conclusion and Future Work

We proposed a level set segmentation method which originally combines a statistical shape analysis and a fuzzy controller. Shape analysis and fuzzy control bring prior information in the segmentation process, while keeping the implementation of the method simple, which allows us to segment several structures simultaneously. The quantitative assessment of the experimental results show that the segmentation of small and blurred structures is strongly improved by shape analysis, and more accurate than registration.

Future work concerns the adaptation and application of the method to other small objects, using other types of prior information. In particular, the brain hippocampi and amygdala are particularly interesting to segment for medical purposes. This is a very difficult task since they are very small and their shape is highly variable, which makes their automated segmentation a challenge.

Acknowledgements

We thank the Center for Morphometric Analysis at Massachusetts General Hospital (http://www.cma.mgh.harvard.edu/ibsr/) for providing the MR brain data sets and their manual segmentations.

This work was supported by the CNRS and the Region Bretagne Council.

References

1. Osher, S., Sethian, J.A.: Fronts propagating with curvature dependant speed: algorithms based on Hamilton-Jacobi formulation. Jour. Comp. Phys. **79** (1988) 12–49
2. Caselles, V., Kimmel, R., Sapiro, G.: Geodesic active contours. Int. Jour. Comp. Vis. **22** (1997) 61–79
3. Malladi, R., Sethian, J.A., Vemuri, C.: Shape modeling with front propagation: a level set approach. IEEE Trans. Patt. Anal. Mach. Intell. **17** (1995) 158–175
4. Vese, L.A., Chan, T.F.: A multiphase level set framework for image segmentation using the Mumford and Shah model. Int. Jour. Comp. Vis. **50** (2002)
5. Paragios, N.: A variational approach for the segmentation of the left ventricle in cardiac image analysis. Int. Jour. Comp. Vis. **50** (2002) 345–362
6. Paragios, N., Deriche, R.: Geodesic active contours and level sets for the detection and tracking of moving objects. IEEE Trans. Patt. Anal. Mach. Intell. **22** (2000) 266–280
7. Paragios, N., Deriche, R.: Coupled geodesic active regions for image segmentation: a level set approach. In: Eur. Conf. Comp. Vis. (ECCV). (2000) 224–240
8. Cootes, T.F., Taylor, C.J., Cooper, D.H., Graham, J.: Active shape models - their training and application. Comp. Vis. Im. Underst. **61** (1995) 38–59
9. Rousson, M., Paragios, N.: Shape priors for level set representations. In: Eur. Conf. Comp. Vis. (ECCV). (2002) 78–92
10. Tsai, A., et. al.: A shape-based approach to the segmentation of medical imagery using level sets. IEEE Trans. Med. Imag. **22** (2003) 137–154

11. Yang, J., Duncan, J.S.: 3D image segmentation of deformable objects with joint shape-intensity prior models using level sets. Med. Image Anal. **8** (2004) 285–294
12. Xu, D.L., et. al.: Reconstruction of the human cerebral cortex from magnetic resonance images. IEEE Trans. Med. Imag. **18** (1999) 467–480
13. Colliot, O., Camara, O., Dewynter, R., Bloch, I.: Description of brain internal structures by means of spatial relations for MR image segmentation. In: Int. Soc. Opt. Eng. SPIE Med. Imag. (2004) 444–455
14. Ciofolo, C., Barillot, C.: Brain segmentation with competitive level sets and fuzzy control. In: Int. Conf. Inform. Proc. Med. Imag.(IPMI). (2005) 333–344
15. Baillard, C., Hellier, P., Barillot, C.: Segmentation of brain 3D MR images using level sets and dense registration. Med. Image Anal. **5** (2001) 185–194
16. Celeux, G., et. al.: L'algorithme SEM : un algorithme d'apprentissage probabiliste pour la reconnaissance de mélanges de densités. Rev. Stat. App. **34** (1986) 35–51
17. Zhao, H.K., Chan, T., Merriman, B., Osher, S.: A variational level set approach to multiphase motion. Jour. Comp. Phys. **127** (1996) 179–195
18. Samson, C., Blanc-Féraud, L., G., A., Zerubia, J.: A level set model for image classification. Int. Jour. Comp. Vis. **40** (2000) 187–197
19. Borgefors, G.: Distance transformations in digital images. Comp. Vis. Graph. Im. Proc. **34** (1986) 344–371
20. Zijdenbos, A.P., Dawant, B.M., Margolin, R.A., Palmer, A.C.: Morphometric analysis of white matter lesions in MR images: method and validation. IEEE Trans. Med. Imag. **13** (1994) 716–724

Variational Motion Segmentation with Level Sets

Thomas Brox[1], Andrés Bruhn[2], and Joachim Weickert[2]

[1] CVPR Group, Department of Computer Science, University of Bonn,
Römerstr. 164, 53113 Bonn, Germany
brox@mia.uni-saarland.de

[2] Mathematical Image Analysis Group, Faculty of Mathematics and Computer Science,
Saarland University, Building 27, 66041 Saarbrücken, Germany
{bruhn, weickert}@mia.uni-saarland.de

Abstract. We suggest a variational method for the joint estimation of optic flow and the segmentation of the image into regions of similar motion. It makes use of the level set framework following the idea of motion competition, which is extended to non-parametric motion. Moreover, we automatically determine an appropriate initialization and the number of regions by means of recursive two-phase splits with higher order region models. The method is further extended to the spatiotemporal setting and the use of additional cues like the gray value or color for the segmentation. It need not fear a quantitative comparison to pure optic flow estimation techniques: For the popular Yosemite sequence with clouds we obtain the currently most accurate result. We further uncover a mistake in the ground truth. Coarsely correcting this, we get an average angular error below 1 degree.

1 Introduction

Motion estimation and segmentation are strongly related topics that can benefit from each other. While motion information gives important hints on how to partition an image, the separation of regions releases motion estimation from the problem of ambiguities near motion boundaries.

Both tasks have a long tradition in computer vision. In motion estimation, especially variational techniques based on modifications of the method of Horn and Schunck [15] have yielded very convincing results. Important milestones on the way to today's state-of-the-art have been presented in [21, 5, 18, 1, 7].

Also in the scope of segmentation, variational methods perform fairly well. Pioneering works in this field include [20, 16, 29, 17, 11, 12, 24]. In recent years, variational segmentation techniques have often been based on level sets [14, 22], which offer many advantages, among others the convenient implicit representation of regions and their separating contours. For the same reason, also the work presented in this paper will make use of the level set framework.

In most cases, segmentation relies on the image gray value or color, sometimes extended by texture representations. In case of image sequences, however, also motion information has been a popular cue for segmentation over the past decades, e.g. in [26, 28, 6]. Most motion segmentation techniques thereby handle the optic flow, or just the image difference, as a precomputed feature that is fed into a standard segmentation method.

A. Leonardis, H. Bischof, and A. Pinz (Eds.): ECCV 2006, Part I, LNCS 3951, pp. 471–483, 2006.

In contrast to those methods, some more recent approaches embark on the strategy to solve the problems of optic flow estimation and segmentation simultaneously [27, 19, 13, 25, 2]. Cremers and Soatto introduced in [13] the level set based motion competition technique. The optic flow is estimated separately for each region by a parametric model, and the region contour is evolved directly by means of the fitting error of the optic flow. This idea has been adopted in [2], where the parametric model has been replaced by the better performing non-parametric optic flow model from [7].

Also the method proposed in the present paper follows the concept of motion competition where the fitting error of the optic flow drives the contour represented by level sets. Further on, the underlying optic flow model is also based on the technique from [7]. In this respect, our method is close to the approach in [2].

However, the method presented here is not restricted to two regions. The energy functional is inspired by the energy from [29] where also the number of regions is an unknown variable. Optimization of this energy is performed by means of a methodology suggested for texture segmentation in [8]: Starting with one region, regions are recursively split as long as this splitting decreases the total energy. For dealing with non-translational flow fields, we have to extend this idea by higher order region models. The recursive splitting yields the number of regions and appropriate initializations for the level set functions. These can then be evolved while the optic flow is simultaneously estimated within the regions. Moreover, our technique is not restricted to two frames but can also take more frames into account. In general, increasing the number of frames yields more accurate results.

The motion competition framework suffers from the fact that the optic flow is non-unique in those parts of the image with little or no structure. Although the smoothness term in variational techniques provides a dense flow field, it does not support the localization of the contour. Therefore, we also present a modification that allows the integration of additional cues like the gray value, color, or possibly even texture without the need to manually weight these different kinds of information.

Furthermore, we modify the underlying optic flow functional from [7]. Instead of matching only the gray value and gradient of a single pixel, we match a small Gaussian neighborhood around this pixel. It turns out that this matching of neighborhoods provides the variational model for the nonlinear version of the so-called CLG method from [10].

Apart from all these modelling aspects our paper also offers an experimental evaluation with excellent results. Thanks to the level set framework the precision at motion boundaries is so high that one can even notice a mistake in the ground truth of the popular Yosemite sequence. In fact, it turns out that the horizon is shifted one pixel towards the bottom. Correcting this, we obtain a further improvement of the results. However, even with the original ground truth, our method provides the most accurate flow fields in the literature.

Paper organization. The next section introduces the variational energy model that integrates motion estimation and multi-region segmentation. Section 3 then deals with the minimization of this energy. This includes the iterative scheme and the way how the level sets can be initialized. It is further described how the motion segmentation model can be extended by additional cues. Section 4 presents experimental results and a comparison to methods from the literature. The paper is concluded by a brief summary.

2 Model

The variational model is based on the optic flow functional in [7] and the segmentation model presented in [29]. It further makes use of the level set framework [14, 22, 12] in order to represent regions and their boundaries.

Given an image sequence $I(x, y, t) : \Omega \rightarrow \mathbb{R}$, we seek at each (spatiotemporal) point $\mathbf{x} := (x, y, t)$ the optic flow vector $\mathbf{w}(\mathbf{x}) := (u(\mathbf{x}), v(\mathbf{x}), 1)$ that describes the shift of the pixel at (x, y, t) to its new location $(x + u, y + v, t + 1)$ in the next frame. Additionally, we seek the set of level set functions $\Phi_i(x, y, t) : \Omega \rightarrow \mathbb{R}$, $i = 1, ..., N$, that represent the partitioning of the image domain Ω into disjoint regions Ω_i. The regions are represented such that $\mathbf{x} \in \Omega_i$ if and only if $\Phi_i(\mathbf{x}) > 0$, and region contours are represented by the zero-level lines of Φ_i. The number of regions N is also a free variable that is to be optimized.

In order to allow the motion estimation to benefit from the segmentation, we estimate a separate flow field $\mathbf{w}_i$ for each region. The final flow field $\mathbf{w}$ can then be assembled from $\mathbf{w}_i$ and the level set functions Φ_i.

Our model can be described by the spatiotemporal energy functional

$$E(\mathbf{w}, \Phi, N) =$$

$$\sum_{i=1}^{N} \int_{\Omega} H(\Phi_i) \Big(\Psi \big(\underbrace{|I(\mathbf{x} + \mathbf{w}_i) - I(\mathbf{x})|^2}_{\text{gray value constancy}} \big) + \gamma \Psi \big(\underbrace{|\nabla_2 I(\mathbf{x} + \mathbf{w}_i) - \nabla_2 I(\mathbf{x})|^2}_{\text{gradient constancy}} \big) \Big) \, \mathbf{dx} \quad (1)$$

$$+ \sum_{i=1}^{N} \int_{\Omega} \Big(\alpha \Psi \big(\underbrace{|\nabla_3 u_i|^2 + |\nabla_3 v_i|^2}_{\text{spatiotemporal smoothness}} \big) + \underbrace{\nu |\nabla_3 H(\Phi_i)|}_{\text{contour length}} + \lambda \Big) \, \mathbf{dx}$$

that is sought to be minimized under the constraint of disjoint regions. Thereby, ∇_3 denotes the spatiotemporal gradient $(\partial_x, \partial_y, \partial_t)^\top$, while ∇_2 stands for its spatial counterpart. Moreover, $H(s)$ denotes a regularized Heaviside function, which is in our case the error function. Its derivative $H'(\Phi)$ is a Gaussian with standard deviation 1.

The robust function $\Psi(s^2) := \sqrt{s^2 + 0.001^2}$ is applied in order to deal with outliers. In contrast to [7] we apply a separate robust function to both the gray value and the gradient constancy assumption, as suggested in [9]. This has the advantage that the relative importance of both terms is locally adjusted to the reliability of each term. The robust function applied to the smoothness term yields a model that allows for discontinuities. This is important, since although the level set framework captures the main motion discontinuies, there may be further smaller discontinuities within the regions. The parameter $\gamma \geq 0$ globally weights the influence of the gradient constancy assumption, whereas $\alpha \geq 0$ determines the penalty for non-smooth flow fields.

The energy in (1) follows the basic concept of motion competition [13, 2]. In comparison to the classic Chan-Vese model [12], the distance between the local value and the mean of the region is replaced by the local energy evoked by the data term of the optic flow model, i.e., it is tested how well the estimated optic flow fits the constancy assumptions. This energy drives the contour. Simultaneously, the model separates the estimation of the optic flow within the different regions. The parameter $\nu \geq 0$ weights the penalty for the length of the region contours.

In order to allow for more than two regions, the classic two-phase model is replaced by a level set based version of the segmentation functional from [29]. It handles not only more than two regions, but also optimizes the number of regions. The fixed penalty $\lambda = 0.1$ is added for each region in order to keep the number of regions small. The additional optimization variable increases the complexity of the segmentation task and, consequently, makes it more dependent on the initialization. How to find a good initialization will be an issue in Section 3.

2.1   Adding Color and Neighborhood Constraints

To further improve the quality of the estimated optic flow, the model can be extended by making use of color. For this purpose, the term from (1) that is responsible for the gray value constancy

$$E_1(\mathbf{x}) = \Psi\left(|I(\mathbf{x} + \mathbf{w}_i(\mathbf{x})) - I(\mathbf{x})|^2\right) \tag{2}$$

is replaced by a term that supposes a multi-channel image $\mathbf{I} = (I_1, I_2, I_3)$:

$$E_2(\mathbf{x}) = \Psi\left(\sum_{k=1}^{3} |I_k(\mathbf{x} + \mathbf{w}_i(\mathbf{x})) - I_k(\mathbf{x})|^2\right). \tag{3}$$

The gradient constancy assumption in (1) is changed in the same way. This simple extension motivates another idea. Instead of assuming only the gray value and gradient of the point itself to stay constant, one can suppose also the neighborhood around this point not to change during motion. This is the standard assumption for block matching approaches. Since it is well known that block matching methods suffer seriously under affine transformations and run into problems at motion boundaries, we consider only a very small Gaussian neighborhood $K_\rho(x, y) = \frac{1}{2\pi\rho^2} \exp\left(-\frac{x^2+y^2}{2\rho^2}\right)$ with $\rho = \sqrt{2}$. Consequently, we obtain additional constraints in the new term

$$E_3(\mathbf{x}) = \Psi\left(\int_{\mathbb{R}^2} K_\rho(\xi)\left(|I(\mathbf{x} - \xi + \mathbf{w}_i(\mathbf{x})) - I(\mathbf{x} - \xi)|^2\right) d\xi\right) \tag{4}$$

that can improve the robustness in the case of corrupted data. The gradient constancy assumption is extended in the same way. Minimization of the resulting energy functional in the next section will show that the latter extension comes down to the so-called *combined local-global (CLG)* method suggested in [10], which has been demonstrated to yield good results also in the presence of noise.

3   Optimization

In the optimization problem stated in (1), the optic flow field, the regions, and the number of regions are all unknown. Since variational approaches perform a local optimization, one has to take care of local optima. The initialization decides which optimum is hit by the method. For both optic flow estimation and segmentation techniques, coarse-to-fine strategies have proven their value in this respect. Coarse-to-fine strategies shift the problem of initialization to successively coarser scales. Starting with a scale where multiple optima are rare, one can use the coarse result as initialization for the next finer scale. In the iteration scheme described in Section 3.3 we also make use of this concept.

3.1   Initialization of the Regions at the Coarsest Scale

Before we minimize (1) by deriving the Euler-Lagrange equations, this section focuses on the initialization of the regions. Note that the number of regions N is an integer variable that cannot be optimized with a variational approach. For this purpose, we adopt a technique presented in the scope of texture segmentation in [8] that recursively splits the image domain for determining both N and good initializations for Φ_i. To this end, one needs a preliminary estimate of the optic flow, which is obtained by computing the optic flow without any partitioning.

The splitting works on the coarsest level, i.e., the flow is downsampled to this scale. The coarsest scale is chosen such that the image comprises at least 30 pixels in x and y-direction. At this scale, dominant regions are still visible and most disturbing structures have vanished. The scale of the temporal axis remains unchanged.

One starts with the whole image domain as one region, in which the level set function Φ is initialized by 8 horizontal stripes/boxes. The region is then split into two regions by minimizing the energy

$$E(\Phi) = \int_{\Omega} \left(- H(\Phi) \log p_1 - (1 - H(\Phi)) \log p_2 + \nu \, |\nabla_3 H(\Phi)| \right) \, \mathbf{dx} \tag{5}$$

which leads to the gradient descent

$$\partial_\tau \Phi = H'(\Phi) \left(\log \frac{p_1}{p_2} + \nu \operatorname{div} \left(\frac{\nabla_3 \Phi}{|\nabla_3 \Phi|} \right) \right). \tag{6}$$

At a first step, the two regions are modelled by the Gaussian probability densities

$$p_j(u, v) \propto \frac{1}{\sqrt{2\pi}(\sigma_u)_j} \exp \left(-\frac{(u - (\mu_u)_j)^2}{2(\sigma_u)_j^2} \right) \cdot \frac{1}{\sqrt{2\pi}(\sigma_v)_j} \exp \left(-\frac{(v - (\mu_v)_j)^2}{2(\sigma_v)_j^2} \right) \tag{7}$$

where $(\mu_{u/v})_j$ and $(\sigma_{u/v})_j$ are the means and the variances of the precomputed optic flow components u and v in the two regions. They are updated iteratively with the evolving contour. Since this model assumes constant flow fields in the regions, which is often unrealistic, the model is, after 500 iterations, extended to a linear approximation model $u(x, y, t) \approx a_j + b_j x + c_j y + d_j t$. Its parameters are estimated within the regions by least squares. With this model one can replace $(u - (\mu_u)_j)^2$ in (7) by $(u - a_j - b_j x - c_j y - d_j t)^2$ and $(\sigma_u)_j^2$ by $\int_{\Omega_j} (u - a_j - b_j x - c_j y - d_j t)^2 \, \mathbf{dx}/|\Omega_j|$. The values for v can be handled the same way. After again 500 iterations, we finally switch to a quadratic model, which can coarsely capture most smooth motion fields. The model parameters are again obtained by least squares, and the counterparts to the expressions in (7) are the deviation $(u - a_j - b_j x - c_j y - d_j t - e_j xx - f_j yy - g_j tt - h_j xy - r_j xt - s_j yt)^2$, the corresponding standard deviation, and the same for v. The successive increase of the model complexity avoids possible local optima that might disturb the partitioning when starting directly with the quadratic model.

The quadratic model is finally used to measure the energy according to (5), both in the original region and the separated regions. If the energy decrease is larger than $\lambda |\Omega|$, the region is split and the same process is repeated for the two new regions. When all further splits do not decrease the energy anymore, one has determined N. Moreover, a good initialization for Φ_i is available.

3.2 Euler-Lagrange Equations

With the abbreviations from [7]

$$
\begin{aligned}
(I_x)_i &:= \partial_x I(\mathbf{x} + \mathbf{w}_i), & (I_{xy})_i &:= \partial_{xy} I(\mathbf{x} + \mathbf{w}_i), \\
(I_y)_i &:= \partial_y I(\mathbf{x} + \mathbf{w}_i), & (I_{yy})_i &:= \partial_{yy} I(\mathbf{x} + \mathbf{w}_i), \\
(I_z)_i &:= I(\mathbf{x} + \mathbf{w}_i) - I(\mathbf{x}), & (I_{xz})_i &:= \partial_x I(\mathbf{x} + \mathbf{w}_i) - \partial_x I(\mathbf{x}), \\
(I_{xx})_i &:= \partial_{xx} I(\mathbf{x} + \mathbf{w}_i), & (I_{yz})_i &:= \partial_y I(\mathbf{x} + \mathbf{w}_i) - \partial_y I(\mathbf{x})
\end{aligned}
\tag{8}
$$

one can derive the following Euler-Lagrange equations from (1):

$$
H(\Phi_i)\Big(\Psi'\left((I_z)_i^2\right)(I_x)_i(I_z)_i + \gamma\,\Psi'\left((I_{xz})_i^2 + (I_{yz})_i^2\right)((I_{xx})_i(I_{xz})_i + (I_{xy})_i(I_{yz})_i)\Big)
$$
$$
-\alpha\operatorname{div}\left(\Psi'\left(|\nabla_3 u_i|^2 + |\nabla_3 v_i|^2\right)\nabla_3 u_i\right) = 0,
$$

$$
H(\Phi_i)\Big(\Psi'\left((I_z)_i^2\right)(I_y)_i(I_z)_i + \gamma\,\Psi'\left((I_{xz})_i^2 + (I_{yz})_i^2\right)((I_{yy})_i(I_{yz})_i + (I_{xy})_i(I_{xz})_i)\Big)
$$
$$
-\alpha\operatorname{div}\left(\Psi'\left(|\nabla_3 u_i|^2 + |\nabla_3 v_i|^2\right)\nabla_3 v_i\right) = 0,
$$

$$
H'(\Phi_i)\Big(-\Psi((I_z)_i^2) - \gamma\,\Psi\left((I_{xz})_i^2 + (I_{yz})_i^2\right) + \nu\operatorname{div}\left(\frac{\nabla_3\Phi_i}{|\nabla_3\Phi_i|}\right)\Big) = 0.
\tag{9}
$$

Obviously, the flow estimates $\mathbf{w}_i$ are only influenced by the image data in areas where $H(\Phi_i) > 0$, i.e., $\Phi_i > 0$. Thus they cannot be disturbed by data outside the region.

The contour evolution is driven by the fitting energy of the optic flow. Note that the corresponding Euler-Lagrange equation does not respect the additional constraint of disjoint regions yet. This has to be ensured in the gradient descent equation by establishing a competition between neighboring regions [8]:

$$
\partial_\tau \Phi_i = H'(\Phi_i)\left(e_i - \max_{\substack{H'(\Phi_j)>0.3 \\ j\neq i}} (e_j, e_i - 1)\right),
\tag{10}
$$

$$
e_k := -\Psi((I_z)_k^2) - \gamma\,\Psi\left((I_{xz})_k^2 + (I_{yz})_k^2\right) + \nu\operatorname{div}\left(\frac{\nabla_3\Phi_k}{|\nabla_3\Phi_k|}\right).
$$

Here, each region competes with the best performing neighboring region. This ensures that each pixel is part of exactly one region: the one where it fits best.

The extensions to color images and the matching of neighborhoods lead to simple adaptations in (9). Using (4) instead of (2) leads to replacing $(I_x)_i^2$ by $K_\rho * (I_x)_i^2$, $(I_y)_i^2$ by $K_\rho * (I_y)_i^2$, $(I_x)_i(I_y)_i$ by $K_\rho * ((I_x)_i(I_y)_i)$, and so on, where $K_\rho * (\cdot)$ denotes a convolution with K_ρ. One realizes that the resulting Euler-Lagrange equations coincide with those from the CLG method in [10]. The same way, one obtains the color case by replacing $(I_x)_i^2$ by $\sum_{k=1}^{3}((I_k)_x)_i)^2$ and so on.

3.3 Iteration Scheme

The iteration scheme for solving for $\mathbf{w}_i$ and Φ_i is similar to [7, 2] and consists of three nested iteration loops. Starting with the level set functions and the preliminary optic flow from Section 3.1 at the coarsest scale, the most outer iteration loop transfers the current flow estimates $\mathbf{w}_i$ and the level set functions Φ_i to the next finer scale before warping the second frame according to $\mathbf{w}_i$ towards the first one. Thus in each iteration, only an update $(du, dv)_i$ on $\mathbf{w}_i$ has to be computed; see [7]. The scaling factor between two successive levels is $\eta = 0.95$ like in [7]. Depending on the size of the image, it determines the number of outer iterations. The parameter ν is scaled at each level by $0.0002 \cdot A^{0.7}$ where A denotes the size of the image at the respective level. This scaling has been determined empirically in many segmentation experiments not restricted to the motion segmentation examples in this paper.

The central iteration loop is a fixed point iteration loop that removes the remaining nonlinearity in the optic flow equations. Furthermore it alternates the solution of the resulting linear equations and the update on Φ_i. We perform 10 of these central iterations, as suggested in [7].

There are two inner iteration loops, one for solving the linear equations on $(du, dv)_i$ via SOR with over-relaxation parameter $\omega = 1.95$, and one for evolving the level sets via (10). We perform 15 SOR iterations and 50 iterations on the level sets. The curvature term in (10) is implemented by mean curvature motion restricted to the narrow band given by $H'(\Phi_i) > 0.3$.

3.4 Integrating Additional Cues for Segmentation

The location of the contour can only be determined reliably by the data fitting error of the optic flow, if there is distinctive data available. In areas with little structure, the optic flow is not uniquely determined and hence cannot drive the contour. For such cases it is helpful to integrate cues besides motion for the contour evolution. This can be achieved by adding the term [29, 24, 8]

$$E_{\text{Image}} = -\sum_{i=1}^{N} \int_{\Omega} H(\Phi_i) \log p_i \, \mathbf{dx} \qquad (11)$$

to (1). It includes a statistical region model by means of the probability densities p_i. For making use of a color image $\mathbf{I} = (I_1, I_2, I_3)$, we model p_i as

$$p_i(\mathbf{I}) \propto \prod_{k=1}^{3} \frac{1}{\sqrt{2\pi}\sigma_{ik}} \exp\left(-\frac{(I_k - \mu_{ik})^2}{2\sigma_{ik}^2}\right) \qquad (12)$$

with the local means μ_{ik} and standard deviations σ_{ik} of channel k in region i.

Unfortunately, the contributions of the color channels and the optic flow can be different by some orders of magnitude and depend severely on the choice of the parameters in the optic flow model. A further weighting parameter seems necessary to balance the contributions. However, a manual choice of this parameter can be avoided.

One can verify that using a Gaussian model including the standard deviations like in (12) makes the model independent from a different scaling of each feature channel. The same independence from scaling can also be achieved for the motion channel by normalizing the fitting error in (10) by the average error in the whole image domain. Together with the contribution due to (11) one obtains:

$$e_k := \frac{\Psi((I_z)_k^2) + \gamma\,\Psi\left((I_{xz})_k^2 + (I_{yz})_k^2\right)}{\frac{1}{|\Omega|}\int_\Omega \left(\Psi(I_z^2) + \gamma\,\Psi\left(I_{xz}^2 + I_{yz}^2\right)\right)\mathbf{dx}} + \log p_k + \nu \operatorname{div}\left(\frac{\nabla_3 \Phi_k}{|\nabla_3 \Phi_k|}\right). \qquad (13)$$

The normalization factor, like the standard deviation in (12), can be regarded as an adaptive weight for the motion term that avoids a manual choice.

4 Experiments

4.1 Quantitative Evaluation

The Yosemite sequence with clouds, created by Lynn Quam, is currently still the most interesting test sequence for comparing motion estimation techniques, as it contains many typical challenges: One large discontinuity at the horizon and some smaller ones in the canyon, divergent and translational motion, relatively large displacements in the lower left, brightness changes in the sky, and small occlusions at the image boundaries. Furthermore, the ground truth and many published results from other methods are available.

Table 1 shows a comparison of our results to those from the literature using the angular error measure introduced in [4]. Obviously, modeling the sky and the canyon by separate regions yields a significant improvement in comparison to the method in [7, 23]. Also the changes in comparison to the method in [3] still have a large impact,

Table 1. Comparison between our results and those from the literature with 100% density for the Yosemite sequence with cloudy sky. AAE = average angular error. STD = standard deviation.

Technique	AAE ± STD
Alvarez et al. [1]	5.53° ± 7.40°
Mémin–Pérez [18]	4.69° ± 6.89°
Bruhn et al. [10]	4.17° ± 7.72°
Papenberg et al. (frames 8,9) [23]	2.44° ± 6.90°
Amiaz–Kiryati [2]	2.04° ± 7.83°
Papenberg et al. (all frames) [23]	1.78° ± 7.00°
Amiaz–Kiryati [3]	1.73° ± 5.85°
Bruhn–Weickert [9]	1.72° ± 6.88°
Our method (frames 8,9)	1.67° ± 6.30°
Our method (frames 7,8,9)	1.39° ± 6.32°
Our method (all frames)	1.22° ± 6.37°

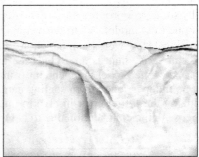

Fig. 1. Left: Frame 8 from the Yosemite sequence together with the estimated contour. **Right:** Angular error between the estimated flow field and the ground truth.

(151,64)   (183,59)   (215,66) (151,65)   (183,60)   (215,67)

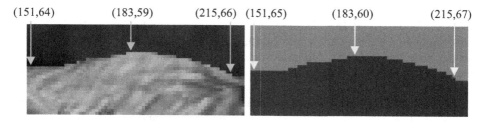

Fig. 2. Discrepancy between frame 8 and the ground truth. In the ground truth, the horizon is consistently 1 pixel too low, which cannot be explained by interpolation artifacts.

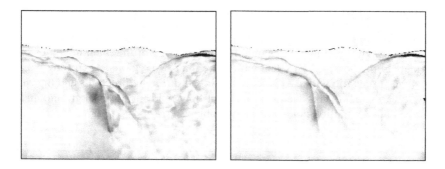

Fig. 3. Angular error with the corrected ground truth for the spatial (left) and the spatiotemporal method (right)

especially the spatiotemporal motion estimation in combination with 3-D level sets. Already taking one additional frame into account improves the result considerably. The parameters have been set to $\alpha = 5500$, $\gamma = 550$, and $\nu = 0.15$ for the variant with two frames, and $\alpha = 4000$, $\gamma = 550$, and $\nu = 0.15$ for the spatiotemporal version. The images have been presmoothed with a Gaussian kernel of size $\sigma = 1$ like in [7].

Fig. 1 depicts the resulting contour and the remaining error between the estimated flow and the ground truth. Only few areas with larger errors persist. One of these is still the horizon, which is actually very well estimated by the partitioning. The width of the error is almost exactly one pixel along the horizon, which is a good motivation to take a closer look at the ground truth.

Indeed it turns out that the ground truth delivered with the sequence is erroneous, as demonstrated in Fig. 2. Among other mistakes, the horizon is consistently one pixel too low. While this has not been decisive as long as the techniques had large errors at the horizon, it becomes quite important as soon as one is able to correctly estimate the flow there. We coarsely corrected the mistake by shifting the first 75 lines of the ground truth one pixel towards the top. We then obtained an average angular error of $1.40° \pm 3.69°$ for the method with two frames and $0.92° \pm 3.35°$ for the spatiotemporal version. In particular, the improvement of both statistical measures – the mean error and the standard deviation – confirms that our observation of an erroneous ground truth was right. This is also reflected in the corresponding error plots in Fig. 3. They show no more than a few misclassified pixels at the horizon. In fact, our results for the Yosemite sequence with clouds are so accurate that they even outperform the results obtained by the method in [7] for the much less challenging variant *without* cloudy sky.

The shifted horizon is the most significant mistake in the so-called ground truth, but unfortunately not the only one. The reader is invited to compare a zoomed version of frame 8 and the ground truth in order to realize further discrepancies in the canyon region that cannot be corrected so easily. In the near future, it may hence be necessary to have a good successor of this sequence.

4.2 Motion Segmentation with Multiple Objects

While the Yosemite sequence allows for comparing the quality of the estimated optic flow to that of other methods, it cannot demonstrate one of the main novelties of this paper, namely the possibility to deal with more than two regions. Therefore, we show in Fig. 4 a test scenario with two objects moving in different directions and the camera moving towards them. This yields a divergent flow field for the background and two nearly translational motion fields for the two objects.

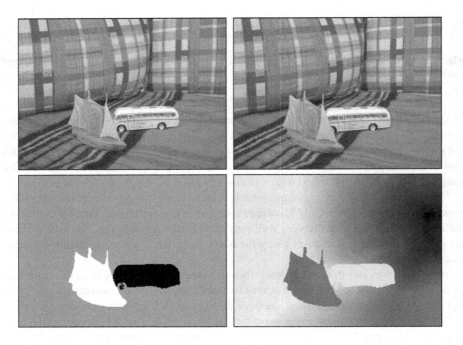

Fig. 4. Top row: Two input images with two moving objects. Both objects move straight forward. The camera moves into the scene. **Bottom left:** Segmentation result. **Bottom right:** Estimated motion. The color distinguishes the direction of the flow vector, the intensity its magnitude.

In this experiment, we also integrated the CIELAB color channels into the segmentation. They can help to improve the result in areas with little structure where the optic flow is not well-determined. Due to the implicit weighting, it was not necessary to put explicit weights to the optic flow term and the color channels. The free parameters were set to $\alpha = 550$, $\gamma = 50$, and $\nu = 0.5$, and the images were presmoothed with $\sigma = 1$ as above.

Fig. 4 shows the segmentation result and the estimated flow field where the hue represents the direction and the intensity the length of the flow vectors. With the same parameter $\lambda = 0.1$ as for the Yosemite sequence, three regions have been detected by the initialization part. The final contours are very precise and the estimated optic flow is not disturbed by the occlusions that appear near the object boundaries. Note the hull of the boat having basically no gradients in motion direction. Here, integrating color information helps significantly to determine the object boundary.

5   Summary

We have presented an approach for joint motion estimation and segmentation with a non-parametric motion model. It is capable to automatically detect and deal with an arbitrary number of regions, and it can take more than two frames into account. Moreover, it has been shown that it is possible to make use of further cues besides the motion information. To the best of our knowledge, our experiments yielded the currently most accurate results in the literature. The accuracy of the motion boundaries is so high that it is even possible to spot a mistake of a one-pixel shift in the ground truth of the Yosemite sequence. Obviously, today's motion estimation techniques are partially more accurate than certain presumably correct flow fields. To support further research, our next effort hence will be to provide a new, possibly also more challenging, synthetic test sequence with ground truth.

Acknowledgements

We thank Luis Garrido (University Pompeu Fabral, Barcelona, Spain) for raising the question if there is an error in the ground truth of the Yosemite sequence.

References

1. L. Alvarez, J. Weickert, and J. Sánchez. Reliable estimation of dense optical flow fields with large displacements. *International Journal of Computer Vision*, 39(1):41–56, Aug. 2000.
2. T. Amiaz and N. Kiryati. Dense discontinuous optical flow via contour-based segmentation. In *Proc. International Conference on Image Processing*, volume 3, pages 1264–1267, Genoa, Italy, Sept. 2005.
3. T. Amiaz and N. Kiryati. Piecewise-smooth dense optical flow via level sets. Technical Report VIA-2005-6-2, Vision and Image Analysis Laboratory, School of Electrical Engineering, Tel Aviv University, Israel, June 2005.
4. J. L. Barron, D. J. Fleet, and S. S. Beauchemin. Performance of optical flow techniques. *International Journal of Computer Vision*, 12(1):43–77, Feb. 1994.

5. M. J. Black and P. Anandan. The robust estimation of multiple motions: parametric and piecewise smooth flow fields. *Computer Vision and Image Understanding*, 63(1):75–104, Jan. 1996.

6. P. Bouthemy and E. François. Motion segmentation and qualitative dynamic scene analysis from an image sequence. *International Journal of Computer Vision*, 10(2):157–182, 1993.

7. T. Brox, A. Bruhn, N. Papenberg, and J. Weickert. High accuracy optical flow estimation based on a theory for warping. In T. Pajdla and J. Matas, editors, *Computer Vision - Proc. 8th European Conference on Computer Vision*, LNCS 3024, pages 25–36. Springer, May 2004.

8. T. Brox and J. Weickert. Level set based segmentation of multiple objects. In C. Rasmussen, H. Bülthoff, M. Giese, and B. Schölkopf, editors, *Pattern Recognition*, LNCS 3175, pages 415–423. Springer, Aug. 2004.

9. A. Bruhn and J. Weickert. Towards ultimate motion estimation: Combining highest accuracy with real-time performance. In *Proc. 10th International Conference on Computer Vision*. IEEE Computer Society Press, Beijing, China, pages 749–755, Oct. 2005.

10. A. Bruhn, J. Weickert, and C. Schnörr. Lucas/Kanade meets Horn/Schunck: Combining local and global optic flow methods. *Int. Journal of Computer Vision*, 61(3):211–231, 2005.

11. V. Caselles, R. Kimmel, and G. Sapiro. Geodesic active contours. *International Journal of Computer Vision*, 22:61–79, 1997.

12. T. Chan and L. Vese. Active contours without edges. *IEEE Transactions on Image Processing*, 10(2):266–277, Feb. 2001.

13. D. Cremers and S. Soatto. Motion competition: A variational framework for piecewise parametric motion segmentation. *Internatonal Journal of Computer Vision*, 62(3):249–265, 2005.

14. A. Dervieux and F. Thomasset. A finite element method for the simulation of Rayleigh–Taylor instability. In R. Rautman, editor, *Approximation Methods for Navier–Stokes Problems*, volume 771 of *Lecture Notes in Mathematics*, pages 145–158. Springer, Berlin, 1979.

15. B. Horn and B. Schunck. Determining optical flow. *Artificial Intelligence*, 17:185–203, 1981.

16. M. Kass, A. Witkin, and D. Terzopoulos. Snakes: Active contour models. *International Journal of Computer Vision*, 1:321–331, 1988.

17. S. Kichenassamy, A. Kumar, P. Olver, A. Tannenbaum, and A. Yezzi. Conformal curvature flows: from phase transitions to active vision. *Archive for Rational Mechanics and Analysis*, 134:275–301, 1996.

18. E. Mémin and P. Pérez. A multigrid approach for hierarchical motion estimation. In *Proc. 6th International Conference on Computer Vision*, pages 933–938, Bombay, India, 1998.

19. E. Mémin and P. Pérez. Hierarchical estimation and segmentation of dense motion fields. *International Journal of Computer Vision*, 46(2):129–155, 2002.

20. D. Mumford and J. Shah. Boundary detection by minimizing functionals, I. In *Proc. IEEE Computer Society Conference on Computer Vision and Pattern Recognition*, pages 22–26, San Francisco, CA, June 1985. IEEE Computer Society Press.

21. H.-H. Nagel and W. Enkelmann. An investigation of smoothness constraints for the estimation of displacement vector fields from image sequences. *IEEE Transactions on Pattern Analysis and Machine Intelligence*, 8:565–593, 1986.

22. S. Osher and J. A. Sethian. Fronts propagating with curvature-dependent speed: Algorithms based on Hamilton–Jacobi formulations. *Journal of Computational Physics*, 79:12–49, 1988.

23. N. Papenberg, A. Bruhn, T. Brox, S. Didas, and J. Weickert. Highly accurate optic flow computation with theoretically justified warping. Technical Report 124, Dept. of Mathematics, Saarland University, Saarbrücken, Germany, Jan. 2005. To appear in *International Journal of Computer Vision*.

24. N. Paragios and R. Deriche. Geodesic active regions: A new paradigm to deal with frame partition problems in computer vision. *Journal of Visual Communication and Image Representation*, 13(1/2):249–268, 2002.

25. N. Paragios and R. Deriche. Geodesic active regions and level set methods for motion estimation and tracking. *Computer Vision and Image Understanding*, 97(3):259–282, 2005.
26. J. L. Potter. Velocity as a cue to segmentation. *IEEE Transactions on Systems, Man and Cybernetics*, 5:390–394, 1975.
27. C. Schnörr. Determining optical flow for irregular domains by minimizing quadratic functionals of a certain class. *International Journal of Computer Vision*, 6(1):25–38, Apr. 1991.
28. W. B. Thompson. Combining motion and contrast for segmentation. *IEEE Transactions on Pattern Analysis and Machine Intelligence*, 2(6):543–549, 1980.
29. S.-C. Zhu and A. Yuille. Region competition: unifying snakes, region growing, and Bayes/MDL for multiband image segmentation. *IEEE Transactions on Pattern Analysis and Machine Intelligence*, 18(9):884–900, Sept. 1996.

Ellipse Fitting with Hyperaccuracy

Kenichi Kanatani

Department of Computer Science,
Okayama University, Okayama 700-8530, Japan
kanatani@suri.it.okayama-u.ac.jp

Abstract. For fitting an ellipse to a point sequence, ML (maximum likelihood) has been regarded as having the highest accuracy. In this paper, we demonstrate the existence of a "hyperaccurate" method which outperforms ML. This is made possible by error analysis of ML followed by subtraction of high-order bias terms. Since ML nearly achieves the theoretical accuracy bound (the KCR lower bound), the resulting improvement is very small. Nevertheless, our analysis has theoretical significance, illuminating the relationship between ML and the KCR lower bound.

1 Introduction

Circular and spherical objects in the scene are generally projected onto ellipses on the image plane, and their 3-D shapes and positions can be computed from their images [9]. For this reason, fitting ellipses (including circles) to a point sequence is one of the first steps of various vision applications, and numerous papers have been written on this subject. They are classified into two categories:

1. How can we judge whether a sequence of edge points entirely consists of points on an ellipse or it contains other points ("outliers")?
2. How can we fit the equation of an ellipse to a sequence of points known to be on an ellipse as accurately as possible?

For the first task, many algorithms and their efficient implementation techniques have been tested. There exists an abundance of literature on the second task, too. Most of the proposed methods were based on heuristics combining voting and least squares in many different forms [3, 4, 15, 20, 21, 22], but there are also theoretical treatments, mainly by statisticians, regarding the problem as statistical estimation [1, 2, 5, 16, 17, 19, 23]. However, their major concern is the consistency and efficiency of the estimator in the asymptotic limit as the number of points increases.

A contrasting approach was presented by Kanatani [11], who generalized ellipse fitting into an abstract framework, which he called *geometric fitting*. Having actual image processing in mind, he pursued fitting schemes whose accuracy rapidly increases as the noise level decreases for a fixed number of points. He asserted that such methods can tolerate larger image processing uncertainty for a desired accuracy level [13].

A. Leonardis, H. Bischof, and A. Pinz (Eds.): ECCV 2006, Part I, LNCS 3951, pp. 484–495, 2006.

In his framework, a lower bound on the covariance matrix of the estimator is obtained [11, 12]. Chernov and Lesort [6] called it the *KCR (Kanatani-Cramer-Rao) lower bound* and showed that it can be derived under a weaker assumption.

It can be shown that *ML (maximum likelihood)* can attain that bound except for higher order terms in the noise level [6, 11, 13]. It has turned out that all existing iterative linear computing schemes, such as *renormalization*[1] [10, 11, 14], *HEIV* [18], and *FNS* [7], has accuracy equivalent to ML [13]. It has been experimentally confirmed that these methods indeed attain high accuracy very close to the KCR lower bound.

We say that an estimation method has *hyperaccuracy* if it outperforms ML. In this paper, we demonstrate that there *does* exist a hyperaccurate method. Since ML nearly achieves the KCR lower bound, the accuracy improvement is very small. Nevertheless, our analysis has theoretical significance, illuminating the relationship between ML and the KCR lower bound.

2   KCR Lower Bound for Ellipse Fitting

We want to fit an ellipse to N points $\{(x_\alpha, y_\alpha)\}$, $\alpha = 1, ..., N$. An ellipse is represented by

$$Ax^2 + 2Bxy + Cy^2 + 2f_0(Dx + Ey) + Ff_0^2 = 0, \tag{1}$$

where f_0 is an arbitrary scaling constant[2]. If we define

$$\boldsymbol{u} = \begin{pmatrix} A\ B\ C\ D\ E\ F \end{pmatrix}^\top, \quad \boldsymbol{\xi} = \begin{pmatrix} x^2\ 2xy\ y^2\ 2f_0x\ 2f_0y\ f_0^2 \end{pmatrix}^\top, \tag{2}$$

eq. (1) is written as

$$(\boldsymbol{u}, \boldsymbol{\xi}) = 0. \tag{3}$$

Throughout this paper, we denote the inner product of vectors $\boldsymbol{a}$ and $\boldsymbol{b}$ by $(\boldsymbol{a}, \boldsymbol{b})$. Since the magnitude of the vector $\boldsymbol{u}$ is indeterminate, we adopt normalization $\|\boldsymbol{u}\| = 1$. Geometrically, eq. (3) describes a hyperplane in the 6-dimensional space $\mathcal{R}^6$ of the variable vector $\boldsymbol{\xi}$. The N points $\{(x_\alpha, y_\alpha)\}$, $\alpha = 1, ..., N$, can be regarded as points in $\mathcal{R}^6$ via the embedding $\boldsymbol{\xi} : \mathcal{R}^2 \to \mathcal{R}^6$ defined by the second of eqs. (2). Thus, ellipse fitting in $\mathcal{R}^2$ is converted to hyperplane fitting in $\mathcal{R}^6$.

Remark. Eq. (1) describes not necessarily an ellipse but also a parabola, a hyperbola, and their degeneracies (e.g., two lines), generically called a *conic*. For this reason, fitting a curve in the form of eq. (1) is often called *conic fitting* [9]. Even if the points $\{(x_\alpha, y_\alpha)\}$ are sampled from an ellipse, the fitted equation may define a hyperbola or other curves in the presence of large noise, and a technique for preventing this has been proposed [8]. Here, we do not impose any constraints to prevent non-ellipses, assuming that noise is sufficiently small.

---

[1] The program is available at http://www.suri.it.okayama-u.ac.jp

[2] One can set $f_0 = 1$ unless the data have too large magnitudes, in which case a large value of f_0 would stabilize numerical computation.

Suppose each point (x_α, y_α) is perturbed from its true position $(\bar{x}_\alpha, \bar{y}_\alpha)$ by Gaussian noise of mean 0 and standard deviation σ in each component independently. Then, the covariance matrix of $\boldsymbol{\xi}_\alpha$ has the form $4\sigma^2 V_0[\boldsymbol{\xi}_\alpha]$, where $V_0[\boldsymbol{\xi}_\alpha]$, which we call the *normalized covariance matrix*, is given, after omitting higher order terms[3] in σ, by

$$
V_0[\boldsymbol{\xi}_\alpha] = \begin{pmatrix}
\bar{x}_\alpha^2 & \bar{x}_\alpha \bar{y}_\alpha & 0 & f_0 \bar{x}_\alpha & 0 & 0 \\
\bar{x}_\alpha \bar{y}_\alpha & \bar{x}_\alpha^2 + \bar{y}_\alpha^2 & \bar{x}_\alpha \bar{y}_\alpha & f_0 \bar{y}_\alpha & f_0 \bar{x}_\alpha & 0 \\
0 & \bar{x}_\alpha \bar{y}_\alpha & \bar{y}_\alpha^2 & 0 & f_0 \bar{y}_\alpha & 0 \\
f_0 \bar{x}_\alpha & f_0 \bar{y}_\alpha & 0 & f_0^2 & 0 & 0 \\
0 & f_0 \bar{x}_\alpha & f_0 \bar{y}_\alpha & 0 & f_0^2 & 0 \\
0 & 0 & 0 & 0 & 0 & 0
\end{pmatrix}.
\tag{4}
$$

Since $\boldsymbol{\xi}_\alpha$ has only 2 degrees of freedom (i.e., x_α and y_α), $V_0[\boldsymbol{\xi}_\alpha]$ has rank 2.

Let $\hat{\boldsymbol{u}}$ be an estimator of $\boldsymbol{u}$ obtained by some means. Its accuracy is measured by the following covariance matrix:

$$
V[\hat{\boldsymbol{u}}] = E[(\boldsymbol{P}_{\mathbf{u}} \hat{\boldsymbol{u}})(\boldsymbol{P}_{\mathbf{u}} \hat{\boldsymbol{u}})^\top].
\tag{5}
$$

Here, $E[\cdot]$ denotes expectation with respect to the noise in the data $\{(x_\alpha, y_\alpha)\}$, and $\boldsymbol{P}_{\mathbf{u}}$ is the projection matrix ($\boldsymbol{I}$ denotes the unit matrix)

$$
\boldsymbol{P}_{\mathbf{u}} = \boldsymbol{I} - \boldsymbol{u}\boldsymbol{u}^\top,
\tag{6}
$$

which projects $\hat{\boldsymbol{u}}$ onto the hyperplane orthogonal to $\boldsymbol{u}$. Since the parameter vector $\boldsymbol{u}$ is normalized to unit norm, its domain is the unit sphere $\mathcal{S}^5$ in $\mathcal{R}^6$. Following the approach of Kanatani [11], we focus on the asymptotic limit of small noise and identify the domain of the errors with the tangent hyperplane to $\mathcal{S}^5$ at $\boldsymbol{u}$. Namely, we evaluate the error after projecting it onto that hyperplane. Thus, the covariance matrix $V[\hat{\boldsymbol{u}}]$ is a singular matrix of rank 5.

In this setting, Kanatani [11, 13] proved that if $\boldsymbol{\xi}_\alpha$ is regarded as an independent Gaussian random variable of mean $\bar{\boldsymbol{\xi}}_\alpha$ and covariance matrix $V[\boldsymbol{\xi}_\alpha]$, the following inequality holds for an arbitrary unbiased estimator $\hat{\boldsymbol{u}}$ of $\boldsymbol{u}$:

$$
V[\hat{\boldsymbol{u}}] \succ \left(\sum_{\alpha=1}^{N} \frac{\bar{\boldsymbol{\xi}}_\alpha \bar{\boldsymbol{\xi}}_\alpha^\top}{(\boldsymbol{u}, V[\boldsymbol{\xi}_\alpha]\boldsymbol{u})} \right)^{-}.
\tag{7}
$$

Here, $\succ$ means that the difference of the left-hand side from the right is positive semidefinite, and the superscript $-$ denotes the generalized inverse (of rank 5).

Chernov and Lesort [6] called the right-hand side of eq. (7) the *KCR* (*Kanatani-Cramer-Rao*) *lower bound* and showed that it holds except for terms of $O(\sigma^4)$ even if $\hat{\boldsymbol{u}}$ is not unbiased; it is sufficient that $\hat{\boldsymbol{u}}$ is "consistent" in the sense that $\hat{\boldsymbol{u}} \to \boldsymbol{u}$ as $\sigma \to 0$.

---

[3] We confirmed by experiment that inclusion of the omitted higher order terms has no noticeable effects in our numerical results shown later.

3 Maximum Likelihood Estimation

The best known method for solving the above problem is the *least squares* (or *algebraic distance minimization*), minimizing

$$J_{\mathrm{LS}} = \sum_{\alpha=1}^{N} (\boldsymbol{u}, \boldsymbol{\xi}_\alpha)^2. \tag{8}$$

This is a quadratic form $J_{\mathrm{LS}} = (\boldsymbol{u}, \boldsymbol{M}_{\mathrm{LS}} \boldsymbol{u})$ in $\boldsymbol{u}$ if we define

$$\boldsymbol{M}_{\mathrm{LS}} = \sum_{\alpha=1}^{N} \boldsymbol{\xi}_\alpha \boldsymbol{\xi}_\alpha^\top. \tag{9}$$

Hence, the solution $\hat{\boldsymbol{u}}_{\mathrm{LS}}$ is the unit eigenvector of $\boldsymbol{M}_{\mathrm{LS}}$ for the smallest eigenvalue. However, the solution $\boldsymbol{u}_{\mathrm{LS}}$ is known to have large statistical bias [11].

If $\boldsymbol{\xi}_\alpha$ is regarded as an independent Gaussian random variable of mean $\bar{\boldsymbol{\xi}}_\alpha$ and covariance matrix $V[\boldsymbol{\xi}_\alpha]$, *ML* (*maximum likelihood*) is to minimize the sum of the square Mahalanobis distances of the data points $\boldsymbol{\xi}_\alpha$ to the hyperplane to be fitted, minimizing

$$J = \sum_{\alpha=1}^{N} (\boldsymbol{\xi}_\alpha - \bar{\boldsymbol{\xi}}_\alpha, V_0[\boldsymbol{\xi}_\alpha]^-(\boldsymbol{\xi}_\alpha - \bar{\boldsymbol{\xi}}_\alpha)), \tag{10}$$

subject to the constraint $(\boldsymbol{u}, \bar{\boldsymbol{\xi}}_\alpha) = 0$, $\alpha = 1, ..., N$. We can use $V_0[\boldsymbol{\xi}_\alpha]$ instead of the full covariance matrix $4\sigma^2 V_0[\boldsymbol{\xi}_\alpha]$, because the solution is unchanged if $V_0[\boldsymbol{\xi}_\alpha]$ is multiplied by a positive constant. Introducing Lagrange multipliers for the constraint $(\boldsymbol{u}, \bar{\boldsymbol{\xi}}_\alpha) = 0$, we can reduce the problem to unconstrained minimization of the following function [7, 11, 18]:

$$J = \sum_{\alpha=1}^{N} \frac{(\boldsymbol{u}, \boldsymbol{\xi}_\alpha)^2}{(\boldsymbol{u}, V_0[\boldsymbol{\xi}_\alpha]\boldsymbol{u})}. \tag{11}$$

By differentiation with respect to $\boldsymbol{u}$, we have

$$\nabla_{\mathbf{u}} J = \sum_{\alpha=1}^{N} \frac{2(\boldsymbol{\xi}_\alpha, \boldsymbol{u})\boldsymbol{\xi}_\alpha}{(\boldsymbol{u}, V_0[\boldsymbol{\xi}_\alpha]\boldsymbol{u})} - \sum_{\alpha=1}^{N} \frac{2(\boldsymbol{\xi}_\alpha, \boldsymbol{u})^2 V_0[\boldsymbol{\xi}_\alpha]\boldsymbol{u}}{(\boldsymbol{u}, V_0[\boldsymbol{\xi}_\alpha]\boldsymbol{u})^2}. \tag{12}$$

The ML estimator $\hat{\boldsymbol{u}}$ is obtained by solving $\nabla_{\mathbf{u}} J = \boldsymbol{0}$, or

$$\boldsymbol{M}\boldsymbol{u} = \boldsymbol{L}\boldsymbol{u}, \tag{13}$$

$$\boldsymbol{M} = \sum_{\alpha=1}^{N} \frac{\boldsymbol{\xi}_\alpha \boldsymbol{\xi}_\alpha^\top}{(\boldsymbol{u}, V_0[\boldsymbol{\xi}_\alpha]\boldsymbol{u})}, \qquad \boldsymbol{L} = \sum_{\alpha=1}^{N} \frac{(\boldsymbol{\xi}_\alpha, \boldsymbol{u})^2 V_0[\boldsymbol{\xi}_\alpha]}{(\boldsymbol{u}, V_0[\boldsymbol{\xi}_\alpha]\boldsymbol{u})^2}. \tag{14}$$

The FNS of Chojnacki et al. [7] solves eq. (13) by iteratively computing eigenvalue problems; the HEIV of Leedan and Meer [18] iteratively computes generalized eigenvalue problems. In theory, the renormalization of Kanatani [11] also solves eq. (14) with the same accuracy as the FNS and the HEIV [13].

4   Error Analysis of ML

Substituting $\boldsymbol{\xi}_\alpha = \bar{\boldsymbol{\xi}}_\alpha + \Delta\boldsymbol{\xi}_\alpha$ in the matrix M in eqs. (14), we obtain

$$M = \bar{M} + \Delta_1 M + \Delta_2 M, \tag{15}$$

$$\Delta_1 M = \sum_{\alpha=1}^{N} \frac{\Delta\boldsymbol{\xi}_\alpha \bar{\boldsymbol{\xi}}_\alpha^\top + \bar{\boldsymbol{\xi}}_\alpha \Delta\boldsymbol{\xi}_\alpha^\top}{(\boldsymbol{u}, V_0[\boldsymbol{\xi}_\alpha]\boldsymbol{u})}, \qquad \Delta_2 M = \sum_{\alpha=1}^{N} \frac{\Delta\boldsymbol{\xi}_\alpha \Delta\boldsymbol{\xi}_\alpha^\top}{(\boldsymbol{u}, V_0[\boldsymbol{\xi}_\alpha]\boldsymbol{u})}, \tag{16}$$

where $\bar{M}$ is the value of the matrix M defined by the true values $\{\bar{\boldsymbol{\xi}}_\alpha\}$ of $\{\boldsymbol{\xi}_\alpha\}$. The matrix L in eqs. (14) is written as

$$L = \sum_{\alpha=1}^{N} \frac{(\bar{\boldsymbol{\xi}}_\alpha + \Delta\boldsymbol{\xi}_\alpha, \boldsymbol{u})^2 V_0[\boldsymbol{\xi}_\alpha]}{(\boldsymbol{u}, V_0[\boldsymbol{\xi}_\alpha]\boldsymbol{u})^2} = \sum_{\alpha=1}^{N} \frac{(\Delta\boldsymbol{\xi}_\alpha, \boldsymbol{u})^2 V_0[\boldsymbol{\xi}_\alpha]}{(\boldsymbol{u}, V_0[\boldsymbol{\xi}_\alpha]\boldsymbol{u})^2} = \Delta_2 L. \tag{17}$$

Letting $\boldsymbol{u}$ be the noise-free value of the solution, we expand the ML estimator $\hat{\boldsymbol{u}}$ in the form

$$\hat{\boldsymbol{u}} = \boldsymbol{u} + \Delta_1 \boldsymbol{u} + \Delta_2 \boldsymbol{u} + \cdots, \tag{18}$$

where $\Delta_k \boldsymbol{u}$ denotes terms which contain kth powers of the components of $\Delta\boldsymbol{\xi}_\alpha$ having a magnitude of $O(\sigma^k)$. Substituting eq. (18) into eq. (13), we obtain

$$(\bar{M} + \Delta_1 M + \Delta_1^* M + \Delta_2 M + \Delta_2^* M + \cdots)(\boldsymbol{u} + \Delta_1 \boldsymbol{u} + \Delta_2 \boldsymbol{u} + \cdots)$$
$$= \Delta_2 L(\boldsymbol{u} + \Delta_1 \boldsymbol{u} + \Delta_2 \boldsymbol{u} + \cdots), \tag{19}$$

where $\Delta_1^* M$ and $\Delta_2^* M$ are, respectively, the perturbation terms arising by replacing $\boldsymbol{u}$ in the denominator $(\boldsymbol{u}, V_0[\boldsymbol{\xi}_\alpha]\boldsymbol{u})$ in $\bar{M}$ and $\Delta_1 M$ by $\hat{\boldsymbol{u}}$ (the corresponding perturbation of $\Delta_2 M$ is of $O(\sigma^3)$). They have the form

$$\Delta_1^* M = -2 \sum_{\alpha=1}^{N} \frac{((\Delta_1 \boldsymbol{u}, V_0[\boldsymbol{\xi}_\alpha]\boldsymbol{u}) + O(\sigma^2))\bar{\boldsymbol{\xi}}_\alpha \bar{\boldsymbol{\xi}}_\alpha^\top}{(\boldsymbol{u}, V_0[\boldsymbol{\xi}_\alpha]\boldsymbol{u})^2}, \tag{20}$$

$$\Delta_2^* M = -2 \sum_{\alpha=1}^{N} \frac{((\Delta_1 \boldsymbol{u}, V_0[\boldsymbol{\xi}_\alpha]\boldsymbol{u}) + O(\sigma^2))(\Delta\boldsymbol{\xi}_\alpha \bar{\boldsymbol{\xi}}_\alpha^\top + \bar{\boldsymbol{\xi}}_\alpha \Delta\boldsymbol{\xi}_\alpha^\top)}{(\boldsymbol{u}, V_0[\boldsymbol{\xi}_\alpha]\boldsymbol{u})^2}. \tag{21}$$

Equating terms of $O(1)$, $O(\sigma)$, and $O(\sigma^2)$ on both sides of eq. (19), we obtain the following expressions (we omit the derivation):

$$\Delta_1 \boldsymbol{u} = -\bar{M}^- \Delta_1 M \boldsymbol{u} \tag{22}$$

$$\Delta_2 \boldsymbol{u} = -\bar{M}^- \Delta_2 M \boldsymbol{u} + \bar{M}^- \Delta_1 M \bar{M}^- \Delta_1 M \boldsymbol{u} + \bar{M}^- \Delta_1^* M \bar{M}^- \Delta_1 M \boldsymbol{u}$$
$$- \bar{M}^- \Delta_2^* M \boldsymbol{u} + \bar{M}^- \Delta_2 L \boldsymbol{u} - \|\bar{M}^- \Delta_1 M \boldsymbol{u}\|^2 \boldsymbol{u}. \tag{23}$$

From the first of eqs. (14), we have $\bar{M}\boldsymbol{u} = \boldsymbol{0}$ and hence $\bar{M}^- \boldsymbol{u} = \boldsymbol{0}$. It follows that terms on the right-hand sides of eqs. (22) and (23) are orthogonal to $\boldsymbol{u}$ except the last term $-\|\bar{M}^- \Delta_1 M \boldsymbol{u}\|^2 \boldsymbol{u}$, which is parallel to $\boldsymbol{u}$, accounting for the normalization $\|\boldsymbol{u}\| = 1$ (Fig. 1).

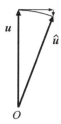

Fig. 1. The orthogonal and the parallel components of the error in $\hat{\boldsymbol{u}}$

It can be seen that the first order error $\Delta \boldsymbol{u}_1$ yields variations corresponding to the KCR lower bound. In fact, we have

$$E[\Delta_1 \boldsymbol{u} \Delta_1 \boldsymbol{u}^\top] = E[\bar{\boldsymbol{M}}^- \Delta_1 \boldsymbol{M} \boldsymbol{u} \boldsymbol{u}^\top \Delta_1 \boldsymbol{M} \bar{\boldsymbol{M}}^-]$$

$$= E[\bar{\boldsymbol{M}}^- \sum_{\alpha=1}^N \frac{\Delta \boldsymbol{\xi}_\alpha \bar{\boldsymbol{\xi}}_\alpha^\top + \bar{\boldsymbol{\xi}}_\alpha \Delta \boldsymbol{\xi}_\alpha^\top}{(\boldsymbol{u}, V_0[\boldsymbol{\xi}_\alpha] \boldsymbol{u})} \boldsymbol{u} \boldsymbol{u}^\top \sum_{\beta=1}^N \frac{\Delta \boldsymbol{\xi}_\beta \bar{\boldsymbol{\xi}}_\beta^\top + \bar{\boldsymbol{\xi}}_\beta \Delta \boldsymbol{\xi}_\beta^\top}{(\boldsymbol{u}, V_0[\boldsymbol{\xi}_\beta] \boldsymbol{u})} \bar{\boldsymbol{M}}^-]$$

$$= \bar{\boldsymbol{M}}^- \sum_{\alpha,\beta=1}^N \frac{(\boldsymbol{u}, E[\Delta \boldsymbol{\xi}_\alpha \Delta \boldsymbol{\xi}_\beta^\top] \boldsymbol{u}) \bar{\boldsymbol{\xi}}_\alpha \bar{\boldsymbol{\xi}}_\beta^\top}{(\boldsymbol{u}, V_0[\boldsymbol{\xi}_\alpha] \boldsymbol{u})(\boldsymbol{u}, V_0[\boldsymbol{\xi}_\beta] \boldsymbol{u})} \bar{\boldsymbol{M}}^-$$

$$= \bar{\boldsymbol{M}}^- \sum_{\alpha=1}^N \frac{4\sigma^2 \bar{\boldsymbol{\xi}}_\alpha \bar{\boldsymbol{\xi}}_\alpha^\top}{(\boldsymbol{u}, V_0[\boldsymbol{\xi}_\alpha] \boldsymbol{u})} \bar{\boldsymbol{M}}^- = 4\sigma^2 \bar{\boldsymbol{M}}^- \bar{\boldsymbol{M}} \bar{\boldsymbol{M}}^- = 4\sigma^2 \bar{\boldsymbol{M}}^-, \qquad (24)$$

where we have used the identity[4] $E[\Delta \boldsymbol{\xi}_\alpha \Delta \boldsymbol{\xi}_\beta^\top] = 4\sigma^2 \delta_{\alpha\beta} V_0[\boldsymbol{\xi}_\alpha]$, which is a consequence of our assumption that the noise in each $\boldsymbol{x}_\alpha$ is independent.

From the definition of $\bar{\boldsymbol{M}}$ and $V_0[\boldsymbol{\xi}_\alpha]$, we can see that eq. (24) coincides with the KCR lower bound. Adding the second order error $\Delta_2 \boldsymbol{u}$ affects this only by $O(\sigma^4)$, since expectation of odd powers of $\Delta \boldsymbol{\xi}_\alpha$ is 0 due to the symmetry of the noise distribution. Thus, as pointed out by Kanatani [11] and Chernov and Lesort [6], the covariance matrix of ML attains the KCR lower bound except for $O(\sigma^4)$. We now examine the effect of the second order error $\Delta_2 \boldsymbol{u}$.

5   Bias Evaluation for ML

Since $E[\Delta \boldsymbol{\xi}_\alpha] = \boldsymbol{0}$, we have $E[\Delta_1 \boldsymbol{M}] = \boldsymbol{O}$. Hence, the first order error $\Delta_1 \boldsymbol{u}$ is "unbiased". So, we evaluate the bias of the second order error $\Delta_2 \boldsymbol{u}$. The expectation of $\Delta_2 \boldsymbol{M}$ is

$$E[\Delta_2 \boldsymbol{M}] = \sum_{\alpha=1}^N \frac{E[\Delta \boldsymbol{\xi}_\alpha \Delta \boldsymbol{\xi}_\alpha^\top]}{(\boldsymbol{u}, V_0[\boldsymbol{\xi}_\alpha] \boldsymbol{u})} = \sum_{\alpha=1}^N \frac{4\sigma^2 V_0[\boldsymbol{\xi}_\alpha]}{(\boldsymbol{u}, V_0[\boldsymbol{\xi}_\alpha] \boldsymbol{u})} = 4\sigma^2 \boldsymbol{N}, \qquad (25)$$

where we define

$$\boldsymbol{N} = \sum_{\alpha=1}^N \frac{V_0[\boldsymbol{\xi}_\alpha]}{(\boldsymbol{u}, V_0[\boldsymbol{\xi}_\alpha] \boldsymbol{u})}. \qquad (26)$$

---

[4] The symbol $\delta_{\alpha\beta}$ is the Kronecker delta, taking on 1 for $\alpha = \beta$ and 0 otherwise.

The expectation of $\bar{M}^{-}\Delta_1 M\bar{M}^{-}\Delta_1 Mu$ is

$$
\begin{aligned}
&E[\bar{M}^{-}\Delta_1 M\bar{M}^{-}\Delta_1 Mu] \\
&= E[\bar{M}^{-}\sum_{\alpha=1}^{N}\frac{\bar{\xi}_\alpha\Delta\xi_\alpha^{\top}+\Delta\xi_\alpha\bar{\xi}_\alpha^{\top}}{(u,V_0[\xi_\alpha]u)}\bar{M}^{-}\sum_{\beta=1}^{N}\frac{\bar{\xi}_\beta\Delta\xi_\beta^{\top}+\Delta\xi_\beta\bar{\xi}_\beta^{\top}}{(u,V_0[\xi_\beta]u)}u] \\
&= \sum_{\alpha,\beta=1}^{N}\frac{\bar{M}^{-}\bar{\xi}_\alpha(\bar{M}^{-}\bar{\xi}_\beta)^{\top}E[\Delta\xi_\alpha\Delta\xi_\beta^{\top}]u+\bar{M}^{-}E[\Delta\xi_\alpha\Delta\xi_\beta^{\top}]u(\bar{\xi}_\alpha,\bar{M}^{-}\bar{\xi}_\beta)}{(u,V_0[\xi_\alpha]u)(u,V_0[\xi_\beta]u)} \\
&= 4\sigma^2\sum_{\alpha=1}^{N}\frac{(\bar{M}^{-}\bar{\xi}_\alpha,V_0[\xi_\alpha]u)\bar{M}^{-}\bar{\xi}_\alpha+(\bar{\xi}_\alpha,\bar{M}^{-}\bar{\xi}_\alpha)\bar{M}^{-}V_0[\xi_\alpha]u}{(u,V_0[\xi_\alpha]u)^2}.
\end{aligned}
\tag{27}
$$

The expectation of $\Delta_1^{*}M\bar{M}^{-}\Delta_1 Mu$ is

$$
\begin{aligned}
E[\Delta_1^{*}M\bar{M}^{-}\Delta_1 Mu] &= -2\sum_{\alpha=1}^{N}\frac{E[(\Delta_1 u,V_0[\xi_\alpha]u)\bar{\xi}_\alpha(\bar{\xi}_\alpha,\bar{M}^{-}\Delta_1 Mu)]}{(u,V_0[\xi_\alpha]u)^2} \\
&= -2\sum_{\alpha=1}^{N}\frac{E[(\bar{M}^{-}\Delta_1 Mu,V_0[\xi_\alpha]u)(\bar{\xi}_\alpha,\bar{M}^{-}\Delta_1 Mu)\bar{\xi}_\alpha]}{(u,V_0[\xi_\alpha]u)^2} \\
&= -2\sum_{\alpha=1}^{N}\frac{(\bar{M}^{-}V_0[\xi_\alpha]u,E[(\Delta_1 Mu)(\Delta_1 Mu)^{\top}]\bar{M}^{-}\bar{\xi}_\alpha)\bar{\xi}_\alpha}{(u,V_0[\xi_\alpha]u)^2}.
\end{aligned}
\tag{28}
$$

We can evaluate $E[(\Delta_1 Mu)(\Delta_1 Mu)^{\top}]$ as follows:

$$
\begin{aligned}
E[(\Delta_1 Mu)(\Delta_1 Mu)^{\top}] &= E[\sum_{\alpha=1}^{N}\frac{\bar{\xi}_\alpha(\Delta\xi_\alpha,u)}{(u,V_0[\xi_\alpha]u)}\sum_{\beta=1}^{N}\frac{\bar{\xi}_\beta^{\top}(\Delta\xi_\beta,u)}{(u,V_0[\xi_\beta]u)}] \\
&= \sum_{\alpha,\beta=1}^{N}\frac{(u,E[\Delta\xi_\alpha\Delta\xi_\beta^{\top}],u)\bar{\xi}_\alpha\bar{\xi}_\beta^{\top}}{(u,V_0[\xi_\alpha]u)(u,V_0[\xi_\beta]u)} = 4\sigma^2\sum_{\alpha=1}^{N}\frac{\bar{\xi}_\alpha\bar{\xi}_\beta^{\top}}{(u,V_0[\xi_\alpha]u)} = 4\sigma^2\bar{M}.
\end{aligned}
\tag{29}
$$

Thus, $E[\Delta_1^{*}M\bar{M}^{-}\Delta_1 Mu]$ is

$$
\begin{aligned}
E[\Delta_1^{*}M\bar{M}^{-}\Delta_1 Mu] &= 8\sigma^2\sum_{\alpha=1}^{N}\frac{(\bar{M}^{-}V_0[\xi_\alpha]u,\bar{M}\bar{M}^{-}\bar{\xi}_\alpha)\bar{\xi}_\alpha}{(u,V_0[\xi_\alpha]u)^2} \\
&= 8\sigma^2\sum_{\alpha=1}^{N}\frac{(V_0[\xi_\alpha]u,\bar{M}^{-}\bar{M}\bar{M}^{-}\bar{\xi}_\alpha)\bar{\xi}_\alpha}{(u,V_0[\xi_\alpha]u)^2} = 8\sigma^2\sum_{\alpha=1}^{N}\frac{(V_0[\xi_\alpha]u,\bar{M}^{-}\bar{\xi}_\alpha)\bar{\xi}_\alpha}{(u,V_0[\xi_\alpha]u)^2}.
\end{aligned}
\tag{30}
$$

The expectation of $\Delta_2^{*}Mu$ is

$$
E[\Delta_2^{*}Mu] = -2\sum_{\alpha=1}^{N}\frac{E[(\Delta_1 u,V_0[\xi_\alpha]u)\bar{\xi}_\alpha(\Delta\xi_\alpha,u)]}{(u,V_0[\xi_\alpha]u)^2}
$$

$$= 2 \sum_{\alpha=1}^{N} \frac{E[(\bar{M}^{-} \Delta_1 M u, V_0[\boldsymbol{\xi}_\alpha] u)(\Delta \boldsymbol{\xi}_\alpha, u) \bar{\boldsymbol{\xi}}_\alpha]}{(u, V_0[\boldsymbol{\xi}_\alpha] u)^2}$$

$$= 2 \sum_{\alpha=1}^{N} \frac{(\bar{M}^{-} V_0[\boldsymbol{\xi}_\alpha] u, E[\Delta_1 M u \Delta \boldsymbol{\xi}_\alpha^{\top} u]) \bar{\boldsymbol{\xi}}_\alpha}{(u, V_0[\boldsymbol{\xi}_\alpha] u)^2}. \tag{31}$$

We can evaluate $E[\Delta_1 M u \Delta \boldsymbol{\xi}_\alpha^{\top} u]$ as follows:

$$E[\Delta_1 M u \Delta \boldsymbol{\xi}_\alpha^{\top} u] = E[\sum_{\beta=1}^{N} \frac{(\Delta \boldsymbol{\xi}_\beta, u) \bar{\boldsymbol{\xi}}_\beta \Delta \boldsymbol{\xi}_\alpha^{\top} u}{(u, V_0[\boldsymbol{\xi}_\beta] u)}] = \sum_{\beta=1}^{N} \frac{\bar{\boldsymbol{\xi}}_\beta (u, E[\Delta \boldsymbol{\xi}_\beta \Delta \boldsymbol{\xi}_\alpha^{\top}] u)}{(u, V_0[\boldsymbol{\xi}_\beta] u)}$$

$$= 4\sigma^2 \frac{\bar{\boldsymbol{\xi}}_\alpha (u, V_0[\Delta \boldsymbol{\xi}_\alpha] u)}{(u, V_0[\boldsymbol{\xi}_\alpha] u)} = 4\sigma^2 \bar{\boldsymbol{\xi}}_\alpha. \tag{32}$$

Thus, $E[\Delta_2^{*} M u]$ is

$$E[\Delta_2^{*} M u] = 8\sigma^2 \sum_{\alpha=1}^{N} \frac{(\bar{M}^{-} V_0[\boldsymbol{\xi}_\alpha] u, \bar{\boldsymbol{\xi}}_\alpha) \bar{\boldsymbol{\xi}}_\alpha}{(u, V_0[\boldsymbol{\xi}_\alpha] u)^2} = 8\sigma^2 \sum_{\alpha=1}^{N} \frac{(V_0[\boldsymbol{\xi}_\alpha] u, \bar{M}^{-} \bar{\boldsymbol{\xi}}_\alpha) \bar{\boldsymbol{\xi}}_\alpha}{(u, V_0[\boldsymbol{\xi}_\alpha] u)^2}. \tag{33}$$

The expectation of $\Delta_2 L$ is

$$E[\Delta_2 L] = E[\sum_{\alpha=1}^{N} \frac{(\Delta \boldsymbol{\xi}_\alpha, u)^2 V_0[\boldsymbol{\xi}_\alpha]}{(u, V_0[\boldsymbol{\xi}_\alpha] u)^2}] = \sum_{\alpha=1}^{N} \frac{(u, E[\Delta \boldsymbol{\xi}_\alpha \Delta \boldsymbol{\xi}_\alpha^{\top}] u) V_0[\boldsymbol{\xi}_\alpha]}{(u, V_0[\boldsymbol{\xi}_\alpha] u)^2}$$

$$= 4\sigma^2 \sum_{\alpha=1}^{N} \frac{V_0[\boldsymbol{\xi}_\alpha]}{(u, V_0[\boldsymbol{\xi}_\alpha] u)} = 4\sigma^2 N. \tag{34}$$

The expectation of $\|\bar{M}^{-} \Delta_1 M u\|^2$ is

$$E[\|\bar{M}^{-} \Delta_1 M u\|^2] = E[(\bar{M}^{-} \Delta_1 M u, \bar{M}^{-} \Delta_1 M u)]$$

$$= E[(\sum_{\alpha=1}^{N} \frac{\bar{\boldsymbol{\xi}}_\alpha (\Delta \boldsymbol{\xi}_\alpha, u)}{(u, V_0[\boldsymbol{\xi}_\alpha] u)}, (\bar{M}^{-})^2 \sum_{\beta=1}^{N} \frac{\bar{\boldsymbol{\xi}}_\beta (\Delta \boldsymbol{\xi}_\beta, u)}{(u, V_0[\boldsymbol{\xi}_\beta] u)})]$$

$$= \sum_{\alpha,\beta=1}^{N} \frac{(u, E[\Delta \boldsymbol{\xi}_\alpha \Delta \boldsymbol{\xi}_\beta^{\top}] u)(\bar{\boldsymbol{\xi}}_\alpha, (\bar{M}^{-})^2 \bar{\boldsymbol{\xi}}_\beta)}{(u, V_0[\boldsymbol{\xi}_\alpha] u)(u, V_0[\boldsymbol{\xi}_\beta] u)}$$

$$= 4\sigma^2 \sum_{\alpha=1}^{N} \frac{(\bar{\boldsymbol{\xi}}_\alpha, (\bar{M}^{-})^2 \bar{\boldsymbol{\xi}}_\alpha)}{(u, V_0[\boldsymbol{\xi}_\alpha] u)} = 4\sigma^2 \mathrm{tr}(\sum_{\alpha=1}^{N} \frac{\bar{\boldsymbol{\xi}}_\alpha \bar{\boldsymbol{\xi}}_\alpha^{\top}}{(u, V_0[\boldsymbol{\xi}_\alpha] u)} (\bar{M}^{-})^2)$$

$$= 4\sigma^2 \mathrm{tr}(\bar{M}(\bar{M}^{-})^2) = 4\sigma^2 \mathrm{tr}(\bar{M}^{-} \bar{M} \bar{M}^{-}) = 4\sigma^2 \mathrm{tr}(\bar{M}^{-}). \tag{35}$$

From eqs. (25)~(35), the bias of the second order error $\Delta_2 u$ of eq. (23) is

$$E[\Delta_2 u] = 4\sigma^2 \Big[\sum_{\alpha=1}^{N} \frac{(\bar{M}^{-} \bar{\boldsymbol{\xi}}_\alpha, V_0[\boldsymbol{\xi}_\alpha] u) \bar{M}^{-} \bar{\boldsymbol{\xi}}_\alpha + (\bar{\boldsymbol{\xi}}_\alpha, \bar{M}^{-} \bar{\boldsymbol{\xi}}_\alpha) \bar{M}^{-} V_0[\boldsymbol{\xi}_\alpha] u}{(u, V_0[\boldsymbol{\xi}_\alpha] u)^2}$$

$$-\mathrm{tr}(\bar{M}^{-}) u \Big] + O(\sigma^4). \tag{36}$$

6   Hyperaccuracy Correction

The above analysis implies that we can obtain a hyperaccurate estimator by subtracting the bias $E[\Delta_2 u]$, or its estimate, from the ML estimator $\hat{u}$. Since the term $\mathrm{tr}(\bar{M}^-)u$ is for adjusting $\hat{u}$ to have unit norm (Fig. 1), we need not consider it if we normalize the solution in the end. So, we correct the ML estimator $\hat{u}$ in the form

$$\tilde{u} = N[\hat{u} - \Delta_c u], \tag{37}$$

where $N[\cdot]$ denotes normalization into unit norm. The correction term $\Delta_c u$ is given by

$$\Delta_c u = 4\hat{\sigma}^2 \sum_{\alpha=1}^{N} \frac{(M^- \xi_\alpha, V_0[\xi_\alpha]\hat{u})M^- \xi_\alpha + (\xi_\alpha, M^- \xi_\alpha)M^- V_0[\xi_\alpha]\hat{u}}{(\hat{u}, V_0[\xi_\alpha]\hat{u})}, \tag{38}$$

which is obtained from eq. (36) by omitting $O(\sigma^4)$, replacing u by $\hat{u}$, and replacing $\bar{M}$ by M defined by $\{\xi_\alpha\}$. The variance σ^2 in eq. (24) is estimated by

$$\hat{\sigma}^2 = \frac{(\hat{u}, M\hat{u})}{4(N-5)}. \tag{39}$$

The approximations involved in eq. (38) may introduce errors of $O(\sigma)$ or higher, but they do not affect the leading order of eq. (38).

7   Experiments

Fig. 2(a) shows $N = 20$ points $\{(\bar{x}_\alpha, \bar{y}_\alpha)\}$ taken on ellipse

$$\frac{x^2}{50^2} + \frac{y^2}{100^2} = 1 \tag{40}$$

with equal intervals. From them, we generated data points $\{(x_\alpha, y_\alpha)\}$ by adding Gaussian noise of mean 0 and standard deviation σ to the x and y coordinates

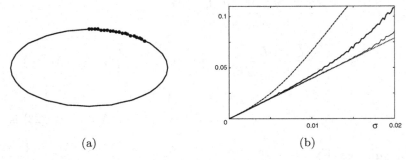

(a)   (b)

Fig. 2. (a) 20 points on an ellipse. (b) Noise level vs. fitting error: LS (broken line), ML (thick solid line), hyperaccuracy correction (thin solid line), KCR lower bound (dotted line).

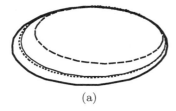 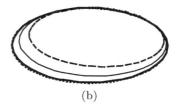

(a)   (b)

Fig. 3. Two instances of the fitted ellipse: LS (broken line), ML (thick solid line), hyperaccuracy correction (thin solid line), true ellipse (dotted line)

independently. Then, we fitted an ellipse by different methods. For computing ML, we used the FNS of Chojnacki et al. [7].

Fig. 2(b) plots for different σ the fitting error evaluated by the following root mean square over 10,000 independent trials:

$$E = \sqrt{\frac{1}{10000} \sum_{a=1}^{10000} \|P_u \hat{u}^{(a)}\|^2}. \tag{41}$$

Here, $\hat{u}^{(a)}$ is the ath value of $\hat{u}$. Since its sign is indeterminate, we chose the one for which $(\hat{u}^{(a)}, u) \geq 0$. The thick solid line is for ML; the thin solid line is the result of our hyperaccurate correction. For comparison, we also plot the LS (least squares) solution $\hat{u}_{LS}$ by the broken line. The dotted line is the square root of the lower bound on $E[\|P_u u\|^2]$ derived from eq. (7):

$$D = 2\sigma \sqrt{\text{tr}\Big(\sum_{\alpha=1}^{N} \frac{\bar{\xi}_\alpha \bar{\xi}_\alpha^\top}{(u, V_0[\xi_\alpha]u)}\Big)^-}. \tag{42}$$

As can be seen from Fig. 2(b), the LS solution is not very accurate, while ML is very accurate; it almost coincides with the KCR lower bound when the noise is small. As the noise increases, however, a small gap appears between ML and the KCR lower bound. After adding the hyperaccurate correction, the accuracy almost coincides with the KCR lower bound.

Fig. 3(a) shows one instance of the fitted ellipse ($\sigma = 0.009$). The dotted line is the true ellipse; the broken line is for LS; the thick solid line is for ML; the thin solid line is for our hyperaccurate correction. We can see that the fitted ellipse is closer to the true shape after the correction. Fig. 3(b) is another instance ($\sigma = 0.009$). In this case, the ellipse given by ML is already very accurate, and it slightly deviates from the true shape after the correction.

Thus, the accuracy sometimes improves and sometimes deteriorates. Overall, however, the cases of improvement is the majority; on average we observe slight improvement as shown in Fig. 2(b). After close examination, we have observed that the accuracy drop occurs almost always when the ellipse fitted by ML falls inside the true shape. However, the majority of the fitted ellipses are outside the true shape. Thus, the correction is effective on average.

We infer that ML is likely to produce ellipses outside the true shape because it is parameterized in the form of eq. (1). If the major or minor axis of the ellipse is a, the coefficient of x^2 or y^2 is proportional to $1/a^2$. If $1/a^2$ is "unbiased", a is biased to be larger than the true value, as can be easily seen from the shape of the graph of $y = 1/x^2$.

8   Conclusions

We have demonstrated the existence of "hyperaccurate" ellipse fitting which outperforms ML. This is made possible by error analysis of ML followed by subtraction of high-order bias terms. However, ML nearly achieves the KCR lower bound, meaning that even if the bias is eliminated, the solution still fluctuates with the magnitude corresponding to the KCR lower bound, which is theoretically impossible to reduce. Thus, the accuracy improvement by our method is almost unnoticeable in practice, compared to which removing outliers and stabilizing the computation have far more practical significance. Nevertheless, our analysis has theoretical significance, illuminating the relationship between ML and the KCR lower bound.

Acknowledgments. The author thanks Nikolai Chernov of the University of Alabama, U.S.A., for helpful discussions. He also thanks Junpei Yamada of Okayama University, Japan, and Yasuyuki Sugaya of Toyohashi University of Technology, Japan, for doing numerical experiments. This work was supported in part by the Ministry of Education, Culture, Sports, Science and Technology, Japan, under a Grant in Aid for Scientific Research C (No. 17500112).

References

1. D. A. Anderson, The circular structural model, *J. R. Statist. Soc.*, B-**43**-2 (1981), 131–141.
2. M. Berman and D. Culpin, The statistical behaviour of some least squares estimators of the centre and radius of a circle, *J. R. Statist. Soc.*, B-**48**-2 (1986), 183–196.
3. F. J. Bookstein, Fitting conic sections to scattered data, *Comput. Graphics Image Process.*, **9** (1979) 56–71.
4. J. Cabrera and P. Meer, Unbiased estimation of ellipses by bootstrapping, *IEEE Trans. Patt. Mach. Intelli.*, **18**-7 (1996-7), 752–756.
5. N. N. Chan, On circular functional relationships, *J. R. Statist. Soc.*, B-**27** (1965), 45–56.
6. N. Chernov and C. Lesort, Statistical efficiency of curve fitting algorithms, *Comput. Stat. Data Anal.*, **47**-4 (2004-11), 713–728.
7. W. Chojnacki, M. J. Brooks, A. van den Hengel and D. Gawley, On the fitting of surfaces to data with covariances, *IEEE Trans. Patt. Anal. Mach. Intell.*, **22**-11 (2000-11), 1294–1303.
8. A. Fitzgibbon, M. Pilu and R. B. Fisher, Direct least square fitting of ellipses, *IEEE Trans. Patt. Anal. Mach. Intell.*, **21**-5 (1999-5), 476–480.

9. K. Kanatani, *Geometric Computation for Machine Vision*, Oxford University Press, Oxford, U.K., 1993.

10. K. Kanatani, Statistical bias of conic fitting and renormalization, *IEEE Trans. Patt. Anal. Mach. Intell.*, **16**-3 (1994-3), 320–326.

11. K. Kanatani, *Statistical Optimization for Geometric Computation: Theory and Practice*, Elsevier Science, Amsterdam, The Netherlands, 1996, reprinted by Dover, New York, 2005.

12. K. Kanatani Cramer-Rao lower bounds for curve fitting, *Graphical Models Image Process.*, **60**-2, (1998-03), 93–99.

13. K. Kanatani, Further improving geometric fitting, *Proc. 5th Int. Conf. 3-D Digital Imaging and Modeling (3DIM 2005)*, June 2006, Ottawa, Ontario, Canada, pp. 2–13.

14. Y. Kanazawa and K. Kanatani, Optimal conic fitting and reliability evaluation, *IEICE Trans. Inf. & Sys.*, **E79-D**-9 (1996-9), 1323–1328.

15. D. Keren, D. Cooper and J. Subrahmonia, Describing complicated objects by implicit polynomials, *IEEE Trans. Patt. Anal. Mach. Intell.*, **16**-1 (1994-1), 38–53.

16. A. Kukush, I. Markovsky and S. Van Huffel, Consistent estimation in an implicit quadratic measurement error model, *Comput. Stat. Data Anal.*, **47**-1 (2004-8), 123–147.

17. A. Kukush and E. O. Maschlce, The efficiency of adjusted least squares in the linear functional relationship, *J. Multivariate Anal.*, **87**-2 (2003-10), 261–274.

18. Y. Leedan and P. Meer, Heteroscedastic regression in computer vision: Problems with bilinear constraint, *Int. J. Comput. Vision.*, **37**-2 (2000), 127–150.

19. M. Mühlich and R. Mester, Unbiased errors-in-variables estimation using generalized eigensystem analysis, *Proc. 2nd Workshop Statistical Methods in Video Processing*, May 2004, Prague, Czech, pp. 38–49.

20. P. D. Sampson, Fitting conic sections to "very scattered" data: An iterative refinement of the Bookstein algorithm, *Comput. Graphics Image Process.*, **18** (1982), 97–108.

21. G. Taubin, Estimation of planar curves, surfaces, and non-planar space curves defined by implicit equations with applications to edge and rage image segmentation, *IEEE Trans. Patt. Anal. Mach. Intell.*, **13**-11 (1991-11), 1115–1138.

22. G. Taubin, F. Cukierman, S. Sullivan, J. Ponce and D. J. Kriegman, Parameterized families of polynomials for bounded algebraic curve and surface fitting, *IEEE Trans. Patt. Anal. Mach. Intell.*, **16**-3 (1994-3), 287–303.

23. M. Werman and D. Keren, A Bayesian method for filtering parametric and nonparametric models to noisy data, *IEEE Trans. Patt. Anal. Mach. Intell.*, **23**-5 (2001-5), 528–534.

A Physically-Motivated Deformable Model Based on Fluid Dynamics

Andrei C. Jalba and Jos B.T.M. Roerdink

Institute for Mathematics and Computing Science,
University of Groningen, P.O. Box 800,
9700 AV, Groningen, The Netherlands
{andrei, roe}@cs.rug.nl

Abstract. A novel deformable model for image segmentation and shape recovery is presented. The model is inspired by fluid dynamics and is based on a flooding simulation similar to the watershed paradigm. Unlike most watershed methods, our model has a continuous formulation, being described by two partial differential equations. In this model, different fluids, added by placing density (dye) sources manually or automatically, are attracted towards the contours of the objects of interest by an image force. In contrast to the watershed method, when different fluids meet they may mix. When the topographical relief of the image is flooded, the interfaces separating homogeneous fluid regions can be traced to yield the object contours. We demonstrate the flexibility and potential of our model in two experimental settings: shape recovery using manual initializations and automated segmentation.

1 Introduction

A central problem in computer vision is image segmentation, the process of partitioning of an image into several constituent components. Among many segmentation techniques, deformable models, introduced in the 2.5-D case by Terzopoulos [1], specialized to the 2-D case by Kass *et al.* [2], and generalized to the 3-D case by Terzopoulos *et al.* [3], found applications in medical imaging (see [4, 5] for recent surveys), geometric modeling, computer animation, texture segmentation and object tracking. More recently, deformable models based on the level set framework [6, 7] have become extremely popular, since they can handle complicated topologies of the underlying shapes, unlike parametric snakes [2, 8].

Fluid models have been previously developed for medical image registration by Christensen *et al.* [9] and by Bro-Nielsen *et al.* [10]. Although Jain *et al.* [11] point out the connections between Christensen's work and active contours, the idea does not seem to have been explored in detail. Therefore, it is one of the goals of this paper to present a novel, physically-motivated deformable model for image segmentation and shape recovery based on a fluid simulation. The segmentation process implied by our method can be regarded as a flooding simulation of the topographical relief model of the gradient-magnitude image, similar to the

A. Leonardis, H. Bischof, and A. Pinz (Eds.): ECCV 2006, Part I, LNCS 3951, pp. 496–507, 2006.
© Springer-Verlag Berlin Heidelberg 2006

watershed paradigm [12, 13]. Similar to the watershed from markers, several density (dye) sources, placed automatically or manually, can be thought of as locations where the relief was pierced, and different fluids can enter as the relief is flooded. In contrast to the watershed method, when different fluids meet they are allowed to mix; this may happen at locations with weak response of the gradient operator. However, at locations with high gradient magnitudes, the advancing fluid-fronts will not mix. When the relief is completely flooded, the interfaces separating fluid regions with different densities can be traced to yield the contours of the objects present in the input image.

The proposed method needs an initialization step, but this step is less critical than in the active contour model, rendering the method suitable for automated segmentation. Unlike the active contour model, our model allows dye sources to be placed entirely inside an object, outside on one side of the object, or crossing over parts of boundaries. In contrast to attractive forces based on the squared gradient-magnitude image [2] which act only in small vicinities along boundaries of objects, the image force in our model exhibits increased capture range because of its long range attraction, and enhanced robustness against boundary leakage. Unlike the watershed method which needs to address the problem of severe over-segmentation, in our model this problem is dealt with intrinsically.

2   Formulation of the Proposed Deformable Model

2.1   Model Formulation

Mathematically, in the Eulerian (grid based) formulation, fluids are described by a velocity field $\mathbf{u}$, a density field ρ and a pressure field p. The evolution of these quantities is governed by the Navier-Stokes equations [14]

$$\frac{\partial \mathbf{u}}{\partial t} = -(\mathbf{u} \cdot \nabla)\mathbf{u} - \frac{1}{\rho}\nabla p + \nu \nabla^2 \mathbf{u} \tag{1}$$

$$\nabla \cdot \mathbf{u} = 0 \,, \tag{2}$$

where ν is the kinematic viscosity. The velocity causes the fluid to transport (advect) objects, densities, and other quantities along with the flow; in fact, the velocity of a fluid also carries itself; this is represented by the first term on the right-hand side of Eq. (1). The second term of Eq. (1), the pressure term, appears when an external force is applied to a fluid. The viscosity of a fluid measures the resistance of the fluid to the flow. In Eq. (1) viscosity is represented by diffusion of the velocity field. These equations have to be supplemented with boundary conditions, and here we will assume that the fluid lies in some bounded domain.

The Navier-Stokes equations can be adapted for image segmentation by (i) providing suitable external (image) forces, denoted by $\mathbf{F}$, which attract the fluid to the boundaries of the objects of interest; (ii) providing (manually or automatically) density (dye) sources, S_ρ, and (iii) defining appropriate initial and boundary conditions. In addition, we modify the equation for conservation of momentum by dropping the pressure term and by adding an additional damping term, such that the modified equation becomes

$$\frac{\partial \mathbf{u}}{\partial t} = -(\mathbf{u} \cdot \nabla)\mathbf{u} + \nu\nabla^2\mathbf{u} + \beta\,\nabla(\nabla \cdot \mathbf{u}) + \mathbf{F}\,, \qquad (3)$$

where β is the dynamic-viscosity coefficient of the fluid (see below). The rationale for removing the pressure term is that it is expensive to compute, since it involves solving a Poisson equation [14,15]. The new term in Eq. (3), the gradient of the divergence of the velocity field, is better suited for our purposes. Since $\nabla \cdot \mathbf{u}$ represents net change in velocity across a small region of space, following the gradient of this change tends to restore the initial velocity. Hence, it does act as a damping term, having a regularizing effect during the flow. Note that in our formulation we drop the incompressibility requirement, *i.e.*, Eq. (2).

The method should be able to represent objects (or boundaries) during and at the end of the simulation. Moreover, it should be possible during initialization to place density (dye) sources manually or automatically (similar to markers in watershed segmentation). Therefore, we supplement Eq. (3) by an additional equation for a density (dye) moving through the velocity field

$$\frac{\partial \rho}{\partial t} = -(\mathbf{u} \cdot \nabla)\rho + S_\rho\,, \qquad (4)$$

where S_ρ denotes density sources. Note that these quantities are only carried along (advected) by the fluid, and they do not affect its flow.

One still needs to devise suitable initial and boundary conditions. Analogous to our flooding paradigm, the initial fluid velocity is set to zero, *i.e.*, $\mathbf{u}(\mathbf{x}, t = 0) = \mathbf{u}_0(\mathbf{x}) = 0$, the initial density is set to some small constant ρ_0, $\rho(\mathbf{x}, t = 0) = \rho_0$. The same initialization is used at each grid location. Further, we assume that the resolution of the computational grid equals that of the input image. Then, dye sources S_ρ with equal density ($S_\rho = \rho_1$, with $\rho_1 > \rho_0$) are provided, which stop adding dye to the flow after a few time steps. An obvious choice for the external force $\mathbf{F}$ is some measure of the gradient of the input image I, such that the dye is attracted towards the contours of the objects of interest.

In our model sources can be placed far away from object boundaries, due to *self-advection* of velocities, which results in a *long-range attractive field*. The advantage of long-range attractive fields over attractive fields based on the squared gradient-magnitude image [2], is their increased capture range. Similar attractive fields have already been successfully used within the context of deformable models, see for example [16,17].

External forces. A suitable external force which guides the advancing fronts towards object boundaries is given by

$$\mathbf{F} = \mathbf{F}_{\mathbf{img}} + \mathbf{F}_{\mathbf{st}} + \mathbf{F}_{\mathbf{ct}} = \nabla(|\nabla I_\sigma|) - \kappa\mathbf{n} - \alpha\mathbf{n}\,, \qquad (5)$$

where $I_\sigma = I * G_\sigma$ denotes the input image, regularized by convolution with a Gaussian kernel of width σ, κ and $\mathbf{n}$ are the curvature and the unit normal at the *interface S* between fluids with different densities, and $\alpha \in (0, 1]$ is a constant weight. The term $\mathbf{F_{img}}$ represents the image force and attracts the dye towards object boundaries. The term $\mathbf{F_{st}}$ represents *surface tension* and ensures that homogeneous dye regions have smooth boundaries, since curvature is minimized. During the flow this term has a stabilizing effect and improves the behaviour of the model with respect to *boundary leakage*, a problem frequently encountered with active contours based on the level set formalism, see [17, 16, 6, 7]. The last term, $\mathbf{F_{ct}}$ plays the role of a pressure term, spreading the dye at constant speed, thus correcting the problem with densities being advected to the nearest object boundaries, see subsection 2.1. Note that this pressure force acts only at the interface between fluids, unlike the pressure force in Eq. (1). Similar pressure terms have been previously proposed both in the contexts of parametric active contours [18, 16] and level sets [6, 7]. All terms in Eq. (5) are scaled and/or normalized, such that they have the same magnitude.

Boundary conditions. For densities, Eq. (4), we simply assume continuity at the boundaries of the computational grid, *i.e.*, $\partial \rho / \partial \mathbf{n} = 0$. For velocities at the boundaries of the computational grid we use the so-called *no-slip* boundary condition [14], *i.e.*, $\mathbf{u} = 0$ at these locations. We could address the problem with the fluid spreading over object boundaries by defining boundary conditions similar to the no-slip condition. However, since the method should be also usable with grey-scale images, we use the rule

$$\mathbf{u} \leftarrow \mathbf{u}\, e^{-\gamma |\nabla I_\sigma|}, \tag{6}$$

where $\gamma > 0$ is a constant parameter controlling the "strength" of the stopping criterion used to update velocities at each time step of the simulation. According to this rule, the velocity is decreased exponentially in the presence of large image gradients, *i.e.*, near object boundaries. This rule along with the damping and viscosity terms of Eq. (3) greatly improves the behaviour of the model with respect to boundary leakage, see section 3.

2.2 Relation to Active Contours and Watersheds

Consider the interface S as a parametric curve that deforms in time, *i.e.*, $\mathbf{X}(s, t) = [x(s, t), y(s, t)]$ with $s \in [0, 1]$ is the arc-length parameter and t is the time. The dynamics of the curve is described by Newton's law,

$$\mu \frac{\partial^2 \mathbf{X}}{\partial t^2} + \gamma \frac{\partial \mathbf{X}}{\partial t} + \mathbf{F}_{int} = \mathbf{F}_{ext}, \tag{7}$$

where μ is mass density, γ is viscosity (damping) coefficient, and $\mathbf{F}_{int}$ and $\mathbf{F}_{ext}$ are internal and external forces. Since at the interface the forces are $\mathbf{F}_{int} = -(\alpha + \kappa)\, \mathbf{n}$ and $\mathbf{F}_{ext} = \nabla(|\nabla I_\sigma|)$, setting $\mu = 0$ in Eq. (7) as in [19], the equation of motion becomes

$$\gamma \frac{\partial \mathbf{X}}{\partial t} = (\alpha + \kappa)\, \mathbf{n} + \nabla(|\nabla I_\sigma|). \tag{8}$$

Note that since the particles are transported with the fluid, the advection equation, Eq. (4), can be discarded. Embedding the curve $\mathbf{X}$ as the zero level set of the scalar function $\phi(\mathbf{x}, t)$, the evolution becomes

$$\gamma \frac{\partial \phi}{\partial t} = (\alpha + \kappa) |\nabla \phi| + \nabla(|\nabla I_\sigma|) \cdot \nabla \phi. \tag{9}$$

The first three force terms from Eq. (3) (convection, diffusion and damping) have been ommited here since they act on the velocity field $\mathbf{u}$ in the proposed method. However, these terms have beneficial effects in our model (*e.g.* long-range attraction due to convection of velocities, regularization, etc.), which are lost in the level-set formulation from Eq. (9). Moreover, the flexibility in initialization will be lost and boundary-leakage problems specific to level sets will appear.

If we neglect the second term from Eq. (9), set $\kappa = 0$ and let $\alpha = \frac{1}{|\nabla I_\sigma|} \geq 0$, the level-set motion equation of the interface becomes

$$\gamma \frac{\partial \phi}{\partial t} = \frac{1}{|\nabla I_\sigma|} |\nabla \phi|, \tag{10}$$

which is a continuous formulation of the watershed method based on the Eikonal equation. Further, if sources (markers) are placed at regional minima of the gradient-magnitude image, the evolution becomes similar to the watershed from markers.

2.3   Method of Solution

Equations (3) and (4) can be solved using the *stable fluids* technique for solving Navier-Stokes equations developed by Stam [15]. The advantage of his technique is that it is easy to implement, allows the user to interact in real-time with three-dimensional simulations of fluids, and is stable, allowing for large time steps during the numerical integration. Although the model may not be accurate enough for certain engineering applications, its accuracy suffices for our purposes.

Eq. (3) is solved using a time step Δt. Assuming that the field is known at time t and we wish to advance the solution at time step $t + \Delta t$, we resolve Eq. (3) over the time step Δt in five steps. That is, the solution is found by composition of transformations on the state, *i.e.*, each transformation is a step that takes a field as input and produces a new field as output.

Force application. The gradient magnitude of the regularized image (see Eq. (5)) is computed using the Sobel operator. It was chosen because it is a difference-of-averages operator and because its response to diagonal edges is better than that of other operators such as the Prewitt operator. The surface-tension force, $\mathbf{F_{st}} = -\kappa\mathbf{n}$, is computed based on the following result. If the location of the interface at time t is given by a level set function $S(\mathbf{x}, t) = 0$, then its temporal evolution follows from

$$\frac{DS}{Dt} \equiv \frac{\partial S}{\partial t} + (\mathbf{u} \cdot \nabla)S = 0, \tag{11}$$

where DS/Dt is the material (advective) derivative. This equation simply states that the interface propagates with the fluid velocity. Comparing this equation with Eq. (4) it follows that the level sets $S(\mathbf{x}, t)$ can be tracked through the motion of densities by considering the graph $z = \rho(\mathbf{x}, t)$ and defining the interface in terms of level sets S as $S(\mathbf{x}, z, t) \equiv \rho(\mathbf{x}, t) - z = 0$. Then the normal to the interface, $\mathbf{n}$, can be computed by evaluating $\mathbf{n} \equiv \frac{\nabla S}{|\nabla S|}$, whereas the curvature is computed using $\kappa \equiv \nabla \cdot \mathbf{n}$. Finally, the pressure force, $\mathbf{F_{ct}}$, is evaluated using the previously computed normal, and the force application operator is given by

$$\mathbf{u}(\mathbf{x}, t + \Delta t) = \mathbf{u}(\mathbf{x}, t) + \Delta t\, \mathbf{F}(\mathbf{x}, t)\,. \tag{12}$$

Here we assume that the external force does not vary considerably during the time step Δt. Also, since the application of boundary conditions (see Eq. (6)) does not amplify the magnitudes of the velocity vectors, a stability requirement is that the total external force from Eq. (5) is bounded, which holds in our case.

Damping. Instead of solving the following equation $\frac{\partial \mathbf{u}}{\partial t} = \beta \nabla(\nabla \cdot \mathbf{u})$, to account for damping in Eq. (3), we simply consider the term $\beta \nabla(\nabla \cdot \mathbf{u})$ as a *damping force* and add its contribution to the velocity field as already done for the external force in Eq. (12).

Advection. The trajectory of the particle is traced back in time from each grid cell to its former position. Then the quantity q is copied from this position to the starting grid cell using some interpolation scheme. More formally, to update quantity q, the following equation is used

$$q(\mathbf{x}, t + \Delta t) \leftarrow q(\mathbf{x} - \Delta\mathbf{x}, t) = q(\mathbf{x} - \mathbf{u}(\mathbf{x}, t)\, \Delta t, t)\,. \tag{13}$$

As shown by Stam [15], the advantage of this method is that it results in an *unconditionally stable* advection solver.

Diffusion. The diffusion of velocity is modeled according to $\frac{\partial \mathbf{u}}{\partial t} = \nu \nabla^2 \mathbf{u}$. An obvious approach for solving this equation is to formulate an explicit, discrete form similar to Euler's method for integration of ordinary differential equations, see [20]. This method becomes unstable for large values of Δt and ν. Therefore, we prefer to use Stam's implicit method and solve the following equation

$$(\mathbf{I} - \nu \Delta t \nabla^2)\mathbf{u}(\mathbf{x}, t + \Delta t) = \mathbf{u}(\mathbf{x}, t)\,, \tag{14}$$

where $\mathbf{I}$ is the identity matrix. This formulation is stable for arbitrary time steps and viscosity coefficients.

2.4   Visualization

To steer the computations and to gain insight into the segmentation problem the user can interact with the simulation, for example, by adding or removing dye sources, adjusting parameters, etc., rendering the method suited for interactive segmentation. On the other hand, if the very purpose is automated segmentation, we will show in Section 3 that simple automatic initializations are also possible. To enable performing interactive segmentation, some method is needed to visualize either the concentration of the dye or the interfaces between different fluids. Since densities are readily available and can be easily visualized, we will only describe a method for tracing the interfaces between different fluids.

Using the density field ρ, for each grid cell $G_i(x_i, y_i)$ a weighted sum is computed at each corner of the current cell, i.e., at locations (x_i, y_i), (x_{i+1}, y_i), (x_i, y_{i+1}), (x_{i+1}, y_{i+1}). At each of these corners, the sum is computed by adding the densities of the (4-connected) neighbouring locations, weighted by forward and backward finite absolute differences between the current location and its neighbours; the resulting density value is normalized by dividing it by the sum of weights. Then, the average of the four density values, obtained by weighted summation at each corner of grid cell $G_i(x_i, y_i)$, is computed to obtain an estimate for the variation of the density $\rho_{a,i}$ inside the current cell. Finally, if the resulting value, $\rho_{a,i}$, is greater than zero, meaning that there is an interface between two fluids inside the current cell, it is traced using a 2-D polygonization method similar to the Marching Cubes algorithm [21]. All contours (fluid interfaces) found are then drawn superimposed on the input image.

3   Results

We will show several results on binary and grey-scale images obtained using the proposed deformable model. In particular, we will show that the new deformable model is (i) robust with respect to boundary leakage, (ii) insensitive to initialization, (iii) robust against noisy conditions, and (iv) can be used to perform automated segmentation.

Boundary leakage. The behaviour with respect to boundary leakage can be controlled by adjusting the viscosity parameter, ν, from Eq. (3), see Fig. 1. When setting $\nu = 1$, the fluid does not penetrate the thinner gaps of the object present in the image. In the remainder, we fix this value to $\nu = 0.1$.

Robustness to initialization. An important advantage of the proposed method over active contours is that it allows simple initializations, see Fig. 2. The initializations in Fig. 2 are very difficult (if not impossible) to handle by most snake methods, because some sources are placed inside objects, while others are outside. Besides, level-set snakes only accept closed contours. These initializations

Fig. 1. *Left*: Initialization superimposed on the initial image; *center*: no viscosity, $\nu = 0$; *right*: $\nu = 1.0$

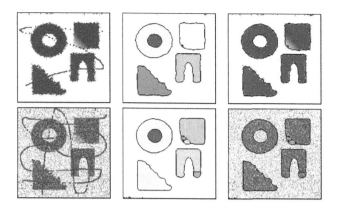

Fig. 2. *Left*: Initializations; segmentation results: *center* – dye regions with superimposed interfaces (boundaries), *right* – original images with superimposed contours

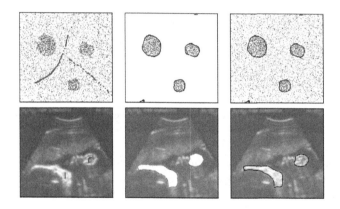

Fig. 3. Segmentation results on noisy images. *Left*: Initializations; segmentation results: *center* – dye regions with superimposed interfaces (boundaries), *right* – original images with superimposed contours.

pose also problems for the watershed method. As the number of markers does not change during the watershed evolution, a marker region lost during marker selection cannot be recovered later. Alternatively, more markers in one object result in over-segmentation.

Robustness to noise. The results in Fig. 3 show that the method copes quite well with respect to noisy images. As observed, the method is able to recover correctly the major shapes of the objects present in these noisy images.

Segmentation of medical images Results on several medical images are shown in Figs. 4 and 5. Although the image shown in the first figure (angiogram) is

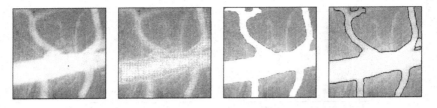

Fig. 4. *Left-to-right*: input image and initialization (a dot), velocity field **u**, detected regions, contours superimposed on the original image

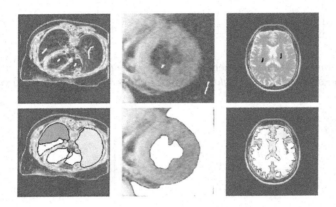

Fig. 5. *First row*: initializations (*left, center*: white segments, *right*: black segments); *second row*: results (regions)

quite noisy and difficult because of the thin and elongated structures, the method yields quite a good result, being able to recover the whole artery. Most important structures have been also correctly recovered for the objects in Fig. 5.

Automated segmentation. Our next experiment is automatic segmentation using a trivial automated method for initialization. To contrast our method to the watershed from markers, we placed dye sources at *all local minima* of the gradient magnitude image. This type of initialization usually results in over-segmentation using watershed from markers. However, this initialization poses no problem for our method, see Figs. 6 and 7. Since weak gradients do not stop the fluid from flowing, fluids with different densities will mix, but near equilibrium, different objects/regions reach different yet homogeneous densities. Note that, all major structures present in these images were correctly identified.

Missing and fuzzy boundaries. Although the proposed method can segment objects with missing boundaries (as shown in Fig. 1), the fluid may flow through larger gaps. A solution to this problem would be to integrate region-based energy terms in our model, similar to the minimal-variance term proposed by Chan and Vese [22]; such extensions are the subject of ongoing research. Our method can segment objects with fuzzy boundaries, provided that fluid sources are placed both inside and

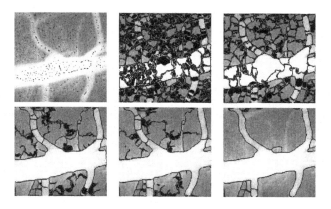

Fig. 6. *Left-to-right, top-to-bottom*: Successive snapshots

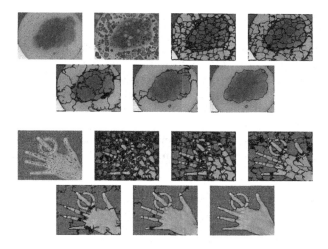

Fig. 7. *Left-to-right, top-to-bottom*: Successive snapshots

outside the object, see Fig. 8. However, when fluid sources are placed only outside (or inside) the object, the method may fail. We also performed experiments using the geodesic snake [6,7] augmented by the GVF field [16] to attract the contour towards the object boundaries, see Fig. 8, second row. Note that the geodesic snake fails to detect the boundary of the object even when the GVF field is used.

Parameter settings. In all our experiments we used the following parameter values: $\alpha = 0.2$, $\beta = 1.0$, $\gamma = 2.0$. Only the value of the viscosity parameter ν was adjusted when performing the boundary-leakage experiment. For the remaining experiments we also fixed the value of this parameter to $\nu = 0.1$. This indicates that the parameter setting of the proposed method is not critical.

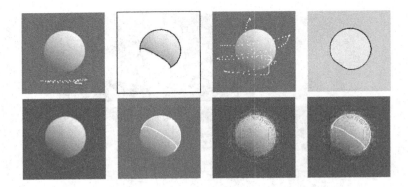

Fig. 8. Fuzzy boundaries. *First row*: Two different initializations and results by the proposed method; *second row*: results by the geodesic snake w/o attractive GVF field.

4   Conclusions

We have introduced a novel, physically-motivated deformable model for image segmentation, and demonstrated its flexibility and potential for shape recovery using manual initializations as well as automated segmentation. The proposed deformable model exhibits several important characteristics: (i) insensitivity to initialization, as opposed to snakes and watersheds, (ii) increased capture range of the attractive vector field, (iii) handling of topological changes, and (iv) good behaviour on noisy images. An important advantage is that the method can be used to perform automatic segmentation, with trivial initializations.

References

1. Terzopoulos, D.: Image analysis using multigrid relaxation methods. IEEE Trans. Pattern Anal. Machine Intell. **8** (1986) 129–139
2. Kass, M., Witkin, A., Terzopoulos, D.: Snakes: Active contour models. Int. J. Comput. Vis. **1** (1987) 321–331
3. Terzopoulos, D., Witkin, A., Kass, M.: Constraints on deformable models: Recovering 3D shape and nonrigid motion. Artificial Intelligence **36** (1988) 91–123
4. McInerney, T., Terzopoulos, D.: Deformable models in medical image analysis: a survey. Medical Image Analysis **1** (1996) 91–108
5. Suri, J., Liu, K., Singh, S., Laxminarayan, S., Zeng, X., Reden, L.: Shape recovery algorithms using level sets in 2-D/3-D medical imagery: A state of the art review. IEEE Trans. on Inf. Tech. in Biomed. **6** (2002) 8–28
6. Malladi, R., Sethian, J.A., Vemuri, B.C.: Shape modeling with front propagation: A level set approach. IEEE Trans. Pattern Anal. Machine Intell. **17** (1995) 158–175
7. Caselles, V., Kimmel, R., Sapiro, G.: Geodesic active contours. In: Proc. 5th Int. Conf. Computer Vision. (1995) 694–699
8. Terzopoulos, D., Platt, J., Barr, A., Fleischer, K.: Elastically deformable models. ACM Comput. Graph. **21** (1987) 205–214

9. Christensen, G.E., Ribbitt, R.D., Miller, M.I.: Deformable templates using large deformation kinematics. IEEE Trans. Image Processing **5** (1996) 1435–1447

10. Bro-Nielsen, M., Gramkow, C.: Fast fluid registration of medical images. In: Proc. of the 4th International Conference VBC '96, London, UK, Springer-Verlag (1996) 267–276

11. Jain, A.K., Zhong, Y., Dubuisson-Jolly, M.P.: Deformable template models: A review. Signal Processing **71** (1998) 109–129

12. Meyer, F., Beucher, S.: Morphological segmentation. J. Visual Commun. and Image Repres. **1** (1990) 21–46

13. Roerdink, J.B.T.M., Meijster, A.: The watershed transform: Definitions, algorithms and parallelization strategies. Fundamenta Informaticae **41**(1-2) (2000) 187–228

14. Chorin, A.J., Marsden, J.E.: A mathematical introduction to fluid mechanics. Second edn. Texts in Applied Mathematics 4. Springer-Verlag (1990)

15. Stam, J.: Stable fluids. In: SIGGRAPH'99, New York, NY, USA, ACM Press/Addison-Wesley Publishing Co. (1999) 121–128

16. Xu, C., Prince, J.L.: Snakes, shapes, and gradient vector flow. IEEE Trans. Pattern Anal. Machine Intell. **7**(3) (1998) 359–369

17. Jalba, A.C., Wilkinson, M.H.F., Roerdink, J.B.T.M.: CPM: A deformable model for shape recovery and segmentation based on charged particles. IEEE Trans. Pattern Anal. Machine Intell. **26** (2004) 1320–1335

18. Cohen, L.D.: On active contour methods and balloons. CVGIP: Image Understanding **53** (1991) 211–218

19. Cohen, L., Cohen, I.: Finite-element methods for active contour models and balloons for 2-D and 3-D images. IEEE Trans. Pattern Anal. Machine Intell. **15**(11) (1993) 1131–1147

20. Press, W.H., Flannery, B.P., Teukolsky, S.A., Vetterling, W.T.: Numerical Recipes in C: The Art of Scientific Computing. Cambridge Univ. Press, Cambridge (1988)

21. Lorensen, W.E., Cline, H.E.: Marching cubes: A high resolution 3D surface construction algorithm. In: SIGGRAPH'87. (1987) 1631–169

22. Chan, T., Vese, L.: Active contours without edges. IEEE Trans. Image Processing **10** (2001) 266–277

Video and Image Bayesian Demosaicing with a Two Color Image Prior

Eric P. Bennett[1], Matthew Uyttendaele[2], C. Lawrence Zitnick[2],
Richard Szeliski[2], and Sing Bing Kang[2]

[1] The University of North Carolina at Chapel Hill, Chapel Hill, NC*
[2] Microsoft Research, Redmond, WA

Abstract. The demosaicing process converts single-CCD color representations of one color channel per pixel into full per-pixel RGB. We introduce a Bayesian technique for demosaicing Bayer color filter array patterns that is based on a statistically-obtained two color per-pixel image prior. By modeling all local color behavior as a linear combination of two fully specified RGB triples, we avoid color fringing artifacts while preserving sharp edges. Our grid-less, floating-point pixel location architecture can process both single images and multiple images from video within the same framework, with multiple images providing denser color samples and therefore better color reproduction with reduced aliasing. An initial clustering is performed to determine the underlying local two color model surrounding each pixel. Using a product of Gaussians statistical model, the underlying linear blending ratio of the two representative colors at each pixel is estimated, while simultaneously providing noise reduction. Finally, we show that by sampling the image model at a finer resolution than the source images during reconstruction, our continuous demosaicing technique can super-resolve in a single step.

1 Introduction

Most digital cameras use a single sensor to record images and video. They use color filter arrays (CFAs) to capture one color band per pixel, and interpolate colors to produce full RGB per pixel. This interpolation process is known as demosaicing.

The Bayer filter is the most popular type of CFA used today. Demosaicing a raw Bayer image requires an underlying image model to guide decisions for reconstructing the missing color channels. At every pixel only one color channel is sampled, so we must use that information, combined with that of nearby samples, to reconstruct plausible RGB triples. An image model provides a prior for reconstructing the missing colors based on patterns of the surrounding samples. Demosaicing algorithms differ in how local spatial changes in a single color channel are used to propagate information to the other channels.

Demosaicing is inherently underspecified because there are no complete RGB triples anywhere in the image to learn an image specific prior from. Even worse,

---

* Research performed while an intern at Microsoft Research, Redmond.

A. Leonardis, H. Bischof, and A. Pinz (Eds.): ECCV 2006, Part I, LNCS 3951, pp. 508–521, 2006.
© Springer-Verlag Berlin Heidelberg 2006

if every pixel in an image has a random ratio of red, green, and blue, there is no hope of reconstructing the image. Only by assuming some local coherence between channels can we reasonably reconstruct the original image.

In this paper, we reduce the problem's complexity by developing an underlying statistical image model that treats all colors in a local area as a linear combination of no more than two representative colors. To use this model, we estimate the two representative colors for the local area centered at each pixel and find the linear blending for each pixel that determines its color.

Our two color model is motivated by the need to reconstruct accurate colors at edges. Current demosaicing algorithms can accurately reconstruct colors in image areas where only low frequencies are present. However, yellow or purple color fringing can appear at high frequency edges due to the edges in multiple color channels not being aligned in the reconstruction. By constraining the system to interpolate between fully specified RGB colors, there is less risk of misalignment. This constraint also provides noise reduction in smooth areas.

The underlying two colors at each pixel are estimated using K-Means clustering. The RGB colors used for clustering can come from any existing demosaicing algorithm. The final color at each pixel results from discovering the proper linear blending coefficient between the two representative colors.

Based on knowledge of a small set of CFA samples around each pixel, our problem is posed using Bayesian probabilities. Stating the problem statistically allows the model to include non-grid-aligned samples from multiple images or temporally adjacent video frames to increase color accuracy. Also, by sampling the demosaicer's output at an increased resolution, information from these additional samples exposes details between pixels, providing super-resolution in a single step.

2   Previous Work

There are many approaches to demosaicing. A simple technique for demosaicing a Bayer color filter array [1] (shown in Figure 1) is bilinear interpolation, which is able to reconstruct smooth and smoothly varying image areas. At the edges, bilinear interpolation risks creating aliasing or "zippering" artifacts where every other pixel along an edge alternates between being considered on or off the edge. Color fringing is the other significant artifact, where yellows, purples, and cyans appear along or on sharp edges. These artifacts result from bilinear interpolation incorrectly placing an edge in a color channel one pixel offset from the same edge in a different channel.

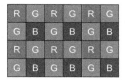

Fig. 1. The Bayer color filter array pattern

Solving the color fringing and zippering issues was the focus of much subsequent research. One approach is to bilinearly interpolate the green channel and then interpolate the red:green and blue:green ratios for the remaining samples [2]. This assumes there exists no green detail smaller than two pixels and that red and green locally vary in a fixed ratio with green. Median interpolation [3] assumes that bilinear interpolation can be repaired by median filtering the red-green and blue-green spaces. Both of these methods target fringing artifacts but can result in over-smoothing. Comparisons can be found in [4].

The approach for Vector Color Filter Array Demosaicing [5] uses filtering in a different way. It first generates pseudo-colors using the local combinations of R, G, and B CFA samples. The chosen color is the "median color" whose total distance to the other pseudo-colors is minimized.

Techniques sensitive to gradients were introduced to reduce over-smoothing by performing color interpolation only along sharp edges and not across them. Laroche and Prescott [6], Hamilton and Adams [7], and Chang et al. [8] presented algorithms with a chronologically increasing number of gradient directions evaluated and interpolated. Kimmel [9] modeled images as smooth surfaces separated by edge discontinuities which were enhanced with inverse diffusion.

There are also grid-based techniques that learn statistical image models. Malvar et al. [10] presents a fast linear interpolation scheme with color-specific kernels which were learned using a Wiener approach from the popular Kodak data set [11]. Another approach, independent of color filter array pattern, is Assorted Pixels [12] which constructs a kernel based on any multi-spectral array.

Hel-Or [13] modeled correlation between channels using Canonical Correlation Analysis. Bayesian statistical methods were applied to the demosaicing problem by Brainard [14] who modeled the base image priors as a set of sinusoids. Closer to our two color approach is Bayesian Matting [15], which finds the foreground and background colors from the surrounding areas. Using a Bayesian system, it finds a linear blending ratio between these two colors.

To perform super-resolution enhancement, additional resolution information must be acquired from somewhere. Zomet and Peleg [16] use information in multiple images taken from different sensors while Freeman et al. [17] inferred resolution from different resolution scalings of the same image. Demosaicing while providing super-resolution from multiple images was investigated by Fung and Mann [18]. Their approach places samples into a regularly spaced grid and each output pixel component is found using a nearest neighbor search of the registered inputs. Gotoh and Okutomi [19] generalized earlier super-resolution approaches to directly process Bayer samples from many frames. Their results used primarily synthetic frames (>20), and did not give quantitative results or consider single-image demosaicing.

To evaluate our results, we are interested in using a more perceptually valid measure than merely SNR or MSE. The S-CIELAB [20, 21] model provides an extension to the $L\alpha\beta$ color space that is aware of local contrast and can hint if the human visual system (HVS) cannot detect errors due to masking.

Also of interest is the iCAM [22] model which predicts the color the HVS perceives in the presence of nearby colors. Although we do not use such a complex model, there are methods that measure perceptual error considering more aspects of the HVS, such as the Multiscale Adaptation Model [23] and Visible Differences Predictor [24]. These and other models have proved useful in detecting HDR compression error and in allocating rendering tasks based on contrast [25, 26].

3   The Two Color Model

Central to our processing is the assumption that at most two representative colors exist within a local neighborhood. Every pixel within that neighborhood is either one of the representative colors or is a linear combination of both. This assumption is violated in areas where more than two different colors meet, but such occurrences are relatively rare. Assuming a Gaussian noise model, this distribution represents a cylindrical volume in color space which spans the two representative colors, as shown in Figure 2.

The two color model serves multiple purposes. Primarily, it serves as a constraint to the ill-conditioned demosaicing problem. With only a single channel reported from the sensor at each pixel, we rely on local color combinations from nearby samples to create RGB triples. To use information from neighboring pixels, an assumption of local coherence is made, as in Section 2. Our process, clustering Bayer samples into RGB triples, is discussed in Section 3.1.

Secondly, by snapping values to a consistent local, edge-preserving model, the amount of local variation is decreased, and therefore noise reduction is provided at no additional computational cost. Furthermore, model outliers can be readily identified and appropriately attenuated or preserved.

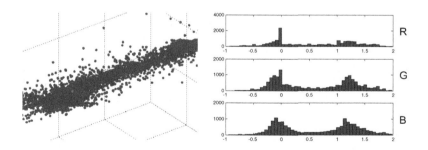

Fig. 2. Visualization of the two color model in a local neighborhood. For 100 randomly chosen pixels near edges in our calibration chart data set (shown in Table 1), the two representative colors were found and the 25 neighboring pixels of each were compared to the representative colors. On the left, a 3D color space plot of agreement with the two color model, as most nearby samples fall at or between the representative colors, shown in red. On the right, a histogram of the relative frequency for each channel, showing that the majority of pixels cluster near the representative colors (at 0 and 1).

Finally, previous approaches assume that when a single color channel changes, a similar change is likely reflected in all channels. This assumption can create sharp edges with color fringing. The yellow or purple edges of fringing result when a demosaicer makes an abrupt change in the value of one channel a single pixel before making a similar change in another channel. This is because edge boundaries cannot be reliably detected in a single color channel due to the sparse sampling of the Bayer grid. Because all three, just two, or only one channel may change, assuming simultaneous changes in all channels may create visible artifacts. However, once both representative colors are determined (i.e. the colors on each side of an edge), we can determine which channels actually vary.

3.1   Two Color Clustering

To discover the underlying two color model at each pixel, the neighborhood surrounding each pixel must be clustered into those two colors. The Bayer image provides only a single channel sample, leaving two unknown RGB triples and an unknown blending coefficient to specify the model.

To reduce the problem complexity, a preliminary demosaicing pass assigns each Bayer sample a fully specified RGB triple using any desired pre-existing demosaicer. Then, the demosaiced colors in the surrounding neighborhood of each pixel can be clustered. Using the K-Means algorithm evaluated in RGB space, two clusters can be computed, with their means being the representative colors. We use a weighted K-Means in which the weight is the inverse Euclidean distance from each sample to the center of the kernel. Note that cluster sizes are not balanced, so a single pixel detail in an otherwise smooth area can be preserved. Also, clustering can be performed in other color spaces, such as $L\alpha\beta$ or XYZ, but clustering in these spaces made little difference in regards to accuracy.

The neighborhood size of samples to cluster is a function of how large color details appear in the source image. We found a two pixel radius around the kernel's center to work well in all of our test cases. This supplies a sufficient number of samples from each of the Bayer color channels.

Because it is possible that more than two colors may exist in a local image area or that significant noise may be present, an outlier rejection stage is included. Using the mean and variance of the clusters, samples that lie outside of a single standard deviation of their closest cluster mean are rejected. K-Means is then repeated to obtain cleaner cluster means. This provides for better reproduction where color values change rapidly away from the kernel center.

The major factor in the quality of clustering is the choice of algorithm used for the "bootstrapping" demosaicing to make clustering tractable. Although any demosaicer could be used, there are qualities that improve performance. The first is preservation or accentuation of high frequency features. Algorithms such as bilinear interpolation and median interpolation have a tendency to low-pass filter, which should be avoided. Alternately, algorithms that preserve high frequencies are prone to generate edge fringing and aliasing. We obtained the best results using the Malvar et al.'s [10] demosaicer, which preserves high frequencies while not generating too many fringing artifacts.

4   Two Color Demosaicing

The two color model provides two RGB priors, $\bar{J}$ and $\bar{K}$, for each pixel x in the image. The color C of pixel x is assumed to be a linear combination these two colors, i.e.,

$$C = (1 - \alpha)\bar{J} + \alpha\bar{K}. \tag{1}$$

Within a neighborhood of our pixel x, our Bayer sensor gives us a set of samples $s_i \in S$. The index of the RGB color channel specified by sample s_i is denoted by t_i. If $\bar{J}_{t_i}$ specifies the t_ith color channel for color $\bar{J}$, and similarly for $\bar{K}$ and C, then we could compute the unknown value of α directly from the Bayer sample s_x at location x (the central pixel) as:

$$\alpha = \frac{s_x - \bar{J}_{t_x}}{\bar{K}_{t_x} - \bar{J}_{t_x}}. \tag{2}$$

However, if the difference between $\bar{J}_{t_x}$ and $\bar{K}_{t_x}$ is small, our estimate of α will be inaccurate due to discretization and image noise.

We compute a more robust estimate of α using the entire set of samples S. That is, we want to find the most likely value $\hat{\alpha}$ of α given our sample set S and color priors $\bar{J}$ and $\bar{K}$:

$$\hat{\alpha} = \arg\max_{\alpha} P(\alpha|S, \bar{J}, \bar{K}). \tag{3}$$

Using Bayes' theorem, and assuming $\bar{J}$ and $\bar{K}$ are independent of S and α, we can rearrange (3) to yield

$$P(\alpha|S, \bar{J}, \bar{K}) = \frac{P(S|\alpha, \bar{J}, \bar{K})P(\alpha)}{P(S)}. \tag{4}$$

Assuming all s_i are independent and $P(S)$ is a uniform distribution, we find

$$P(\alpha|S, \bar{J}, \bar{K}) \propto P(\alpha) \prod_i P(s_i|\alpha, \bar{J}, \bar{K}). \tag{5}$$

$\bar{J}$, $\bar{K}$, and α specify a predicted color $C^* = (1 - \alpha)\bar{J} + \alpha\bar{K}$ for pixel x. Assuming an independent identical distribution (i.i.d.) for neighboring color noise, the relationship between $C^*_{t_i}$ and s_i can be modeled using a normal distribution:

$$P(s_i|\alpha, \bar{J}, \bar{K}) \propto exp\left(-\frac{(s_i - C^*_{t_i})^2}{2\sigma_i^2}\right). \tag{6}$$

The distribution between neighboring pixels has been shown to be highly kurtotic [27], but for computational efficiency we assume a Gaussian distribution. The variance σ_i^2 is dependent on two factors: the global per-channel image noise σ_N and the pixel distance between x and s_i. We assume pixel colors are locally similar, and less similar farther away. Thus, the variance between s_i and C_{t_i} increases as their distance in image space increases. We compute the variance σ_i as

$$\sigma_i = \sigma_N(1 + \lambda\Delta_d), \tag{7}$$

where Δ_d is the pixel distance between x and s_i, and λ is empirically set to 6.

Since the value of s_i is known and we want to compute the value of α that maximizes equation (6), we find it useful to rearrange it as follows:

$$exp\left(-\frac{(s_i - ((1-\alpha)\bar{J}_{t_i} + \alpha\bar{K}_{t_i}))^2}{2\sigma_i^2}\right) = exp\left(-\frac{\left(\alpha - \frac{s_i - \bar{J}_{t_i}}{\bar{K}_{t_i} - \bar{J}_{t_i}}\right)^2}{2\left(\frac{\sigma_i}{\bar{K}_{t_i} - \bar{J}_{t_i}}\right)^2}\right). \qquad (8)$$

Equation (8) is a Gaussian over α with mean α_i and variance $\sigma_{\alpha_i}^2$:

$$\alpha_i = \frac{s_i - \bar{J}_{t_i}}{\bar{K}_{t_i} - \bar{J}_{t_i}} \text{ and } \sigma_{\alpha_i}^2 = \left(\frac{\sigma_i}{\bar{K}_{t_i} - \bar{J}_{t_i}}\right)^2. \qquad (9)$$

We can then combine equations (5) and (8) to yield

$$P(s_i|\alpha, \bar{J}, \bar{K}) \propto \prod_i exp\left(-\frac{(\alpha - \alpha_i)^2}{2\sigma_{\alpha_i}^2}\right). \qquad (10)$$

The optimal value of α for $P(s_i|\alpha, \bar{J}, \bar{K})$ is

$$\alpha^* = \frac{\sum_i (\sigma_{\alpha_i}^{-2}\alpha_i)}{\sum_i \sigma_{\alpha_i}^{-2}} \qquad (11)$$

In practice, we ignore the contribution of color components where the absolute difference between $\bar{J}_{t_i}$ and $\bar{K}_{t_i}$ is less than 2.0. When all color components are this close, only one color is present. Thus, α is set to perform a simple average of the cluster means.

Finally, to find our value of $\hat{\alpha}$ in (3), we need to define a prior over α, $P(\alpha)$. Given that most pixels within an image only get contribution from a single color, we bias α to have a value of 0 or 1:

$$P(\alpha) = \begin{cases} 1 & : \quad \alpha \in \{0, 1\} \\ \eta & : \quad \text{otherwise} \end{cases} \qquad (12)$$

where $\eta < 1$. The value of η depends upon the amount of smoothing desired. Given a large amount of image noise, $\eta \approx 1$.

Since the α prior function is flat with two impulses, we only need to examine the value of equation (3) at three points: 0, 1, and α^*, as shown in Figure 3.

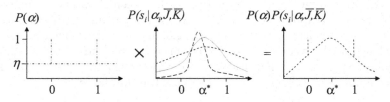

Fig. 3. Estimating the optimal value of α. Note that we only need to compare between α^* (see equation (11)), 0, and 1 because of our definition of the prior $P(\alpha)$.

Whichever is the maximum is assigned as the final value $\hat{\alpha}$ for our pixel, with a corresponding pixel color of $(1 - \hat{\alpha})\bar{J} + \hat{\alpha}\bar{K}$.

The quantitative error of this approach can be further decreased by forcing the red, green, or blue at a output pixel to be the value originally captured by the sensor, while setting the other two channels to be consistent with $\hat{\alpha}$. Because λ weights the central sample heavily, it is unlikely that these two values will be very different. Also, if the output sampling is done on a grid differing from the input grid, a source Bayer sample is not available at each pixel.

4.1   Multi-image Demosaicing

Using our gridless Baysian solution, information from multiple images can be introduced into the model without significantly altering the methodology. These supporting images are assumed to be similar, but not exactly the same, such as from subsequent video frames. Furthermore, these additional Bayer samples can be used without resampling them. To use supporting images, a per-image projective mapping must be computed to register each image to the first image.

As more images are added, we can shrink the neighborhood of samples used and still maintain sufficient samples to cluster into $\bar{J}$ and $\bar{K}$. By doing so, we can reduce the likelihood of it containing more than two representative colors.

If an R, G, and B sample each appear close to the sample we are reconstructing, nearest neighbor interpolation combination of Bayer samples could be used [18]. The notion of using weighted clustering and reconstruction remain the same as with a single input image. Once registered, even if the same color channel appears at the same pixel location, there is still a benefit: noise reduction.

By including supporting images, we risk introducing bad or misleading data. The global projective mapping does not account for all scene changes, such as lighting changes and moving objects. (It would be better to use robust local registration, but this is future work.) To avoid the effect of registration errors, we ensure that only data from the reference and supporting images that are locally similar are combined. Similarity is measured in RGB space using Sum of Absolute Differences (SAD) over a local window of 7×7, denoted as ϵ.

We handle multiple images by adjusting the definition of σ_i to include the correlation error between the reference and supporting images:

$$\sigma_i = \sigma_N(1 + \lambda\Delta_d)(1 + \tau\epsilon). \tag{13}$$

The term $(1 + \tau\epsilon)$ is the mismatch penalty, with $\tau = 0.1$ in our experiments.

To implement multi-image demosaicing, all that is required is adding nearby Bayer samples in the supporting images to the set S and using the above variance equation. Note that the samples in S are the Bayer sensor samples because using the original samples avoids the need for any resampling.

4.2   Super-Resolution

Another advantage of our statistical, grid-less approach is that any sampling grid can be used for the demosaicer's reconstruction, e.g., one with a greater resolution than the original images. Because floating-point Euclidean distances are used for the statistical measures, a continuous value of α can be generated anywhere in the image. Due to the alignment of samples from multiple images, the value of α may encode edges and sharpness between the pixels in the original grid. We can exploit this to handle super-resolution within our framework.

When super-resolving, the statistical clustering and local neighborhood sizes can be slightly shrunk to capture fine details. Other than that, the system operates similarly as it did in the multi-image demosaicing case.

5   Results

In this section, we discuss perceptual interpretation of demosaicing quality. To verify our system, multiple image sets have been tested.

5.1   Measuring Demosaicing Error

The standard way to benchmark demosaicers requires ground truth captured with a fully specified color at each sample. The Kodak PhotoCD [11] dataset is a popular source, but the image resolutions are low. As a result, we chose to use our own image data sets that are of significantly higher resolution. In our experiments, we sampled Bayer patterns from ground truth images by choosing one channel at each pixel. Although this may not reflect the optical process by which Bayer patterns are captured in cameras, it is common practice for benchmarking. After demosaicing, PSNR is computed against ground truth. We compute PSNR in the red channel, although all channels give similar results.

We believe that there are better metrics for measuring the quality of demosaicing. One metric is to test SNR only in areas near large gradients. This focuses the metric on edge reconstruction and does not carry a penalty for noise reduction in smooth areas. We implemented such a metric by thresholding the log-space gradient magnitude to form a mask, then dilating it by 2 pixels.

Another method is to choose a perceptual metric that accounts for perceptual contrast masking [24] and for the viewing distance. The S-CIELAB metric has these features and a MATLAB implementation is available. This metric returns a numerical score of 1 for any just-noticeable error, with 10 indicating very high error. We compute the percentages of pixels exceeding scores of 3, 5, and 10.

To test super-resolution, we create a reference by demosaicing a single image and bicubically upsampling it to have twice the horizontal and vertical resolution. We then perform three image demosaicings on the doubled resolution sampling grid to create the super-resolution output. By comparing results on calibration chart images, we can visually discern increased resolution.

5.2   Demosaicing Results

To test our algorithms, we chose three multi-image data sets and performed bilinear interpolation, High-Quality Linear Interpolation (HQLI) [10], and our method using a single image and using all three images. Both bilinear and HQLI

Table 1. Numerical analysis of demosaicing methods. We present three data sets and demosaic each with bilinear interpolation, high-quality linear interpolation, and our two color method using both a single input image and three input images. In addition to thumbnails of each input, edge masks (see Section 5.1) are also shown. PSNR is given for areas around edges and for the whole image. S-CIELAB statistics are stated as the percentage of the image with small (≥ 3), medium (≥ 5) and large (≥ 10) errors.

Crayons Data Set					
	Edges	Whole Image			
	PSNR	PSNR	$\geq$3CIE	$\geq$5CIE	$\geq$10CIE
Bilinear	28.305 dB	31.406 dB	9.036 %	2.537 %	0.272 %
High-Quality LI	30.784 dB	33.716 dB	5.294 %	1.439 %	0.168 %
2 Color - 1 Image	32.119 dB	35.204 dB	4.682 %	1.366 %	0.159 %
2 Color - 3 Images	32.914 dB	35.972 dB	3.988 %	1.128 %	0.122 %

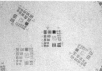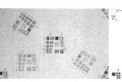

Calibration Charts Data Set					
	Edges	Whole Image			
	PSNR	PSNR	$\geq$3CIE	$\geq$5CIE	$\geq$10CIE
Bilinear	21.746 dB	32.554 dB	5.526 %	1.806 %	0.268 %
High-Quality LI	24.213 dB	34.857 dB	4.039 %	0.889 %	0.016 %
2 Color - 1 Image	24.583 dB	35.574 dB	2.507 %	0.437 %	0.012 %
2 Color - 3 Images	25.507 dB	36.519 dB	1.826 %	0.339 %	0.012 %

Ship Data Set					
	Edges	Whole Image			
	PSNR	PSNR	$\geq$3CIE	$\geq$5CIE	$\geq$10CIE
Bilinear	27.336 dB	34.263 dB	8.478 %	2.068 %	0.064 %
High-Quality LI	33.301 dB	39.047 dB	3.060 %	0.323 %	0.003 %
2 Color - 1 Image	34.458 dB	40.062 dB	2.428 %	0.262 %	0.005 %
2 Color - 3 Images	35.429 dB	40.770 dB	1.586 %	0.161 %	0.005 %

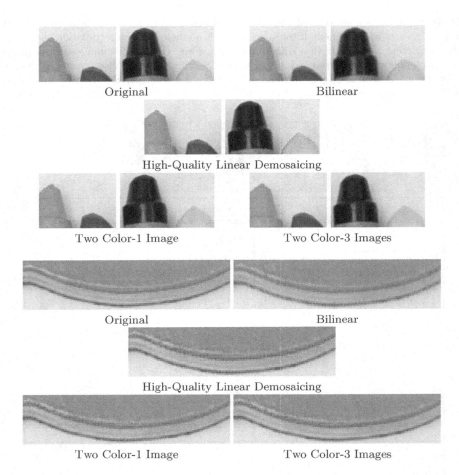

Fig. 4. Comparison of demosaicing two image regions using various demosaicing methods including bilinear, High-Quality Linear Demosaicing [10], and our method with one and three input images

were performed on a single image, as they are single Bayer image algorithms. HQLI was chosen as a representative algorithm both because of its visual performance and because it is our "bootstrap" algorithm. For a detailed comparison of HQLI results against many other previous algorithms, see [10]. The crayon and calibration chart datasets (Table 1) are static scenes taken with a moving camera, whereas the ship data set contains both scene and camera motion.

In Table 1, the PSNR, measured in dB, shows our single image method consistently outperforms the bilinear and HQLI methods for the entire image and for edges. The three image case further improves the results. Judging by the S-CIELAB metric, we also generally lower the number of offending pixels. Figure 5 shows a drop in pixel S-CIELAB error severity from the bilinear approach to our two color/three image technique.

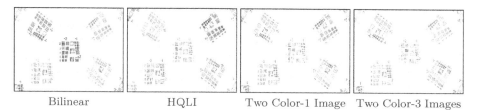

| Bilinear | HQLI | Two Color-1 Image | Two Color-3 Images |

Fig. 5. Comparison of error among demosaicing methods as measured by the S-CIELAB metric. The darker the pixel, the more perceivable the error is. Pixels highlighted in purple have an error greater than 10 CIE, or very noticeable error.

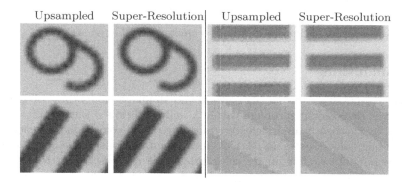

Upsampled   Super-Resolution | Upsampled   Super-Resolution

Fig. 6. Close-ups of our super-resolution results. For each image pair, the left is the result of our single image demosacing followed by bicubic up-sampling by a factor of two in each dimension. The right image is reconstructed using our three image demosaicing technique to directly get the up-sampled image. Notice our results are less blocky.

Figure 4 shows close-up views of the demosaiced crayon data. The bilinear method exhibits color fringing and aliasing for both examples, especially around the crayon tips and in the shadow of the red letter "Q". HQLI provides a cleaner result, but still has aliasing issues as well as difficulty handling the orange and yellow crayon edges. Our method provides sharper results with reduced artifacts in the single image and especially in the three image case.

The super-resolution results, shown in Figure 6, are good, but not dramatic. This is not surprising, because of the inherent limitations due to noise and discretization during image formation. Lin and Shum [28] showed that the practical limit is about 1.6 times the input resolution. Still, performing resolution enhancement with our method allows cleaner reconstruction using our image model.

6   Future Work

In Section 4, we assumed that all colors were equally likely to occur; this renders the denominator of equation (4) irrelevant. However, the system could be refined by substituting actual image statistics, derived either directly from the Bayer samples or from an initial demosaicing pass. Similarly, the neighborhood sizes, both for the clustering and reconstruction stages, are set based on experiments to maximize sharpness and accuracy. These variables could be tweaked or automatically configured to target image conditions and desired results.

In this paper, we focussed on demosaicing Bayer CCDs because the Bayer pattern is the most common CFA and we begin our processing by using the output of a Bayer demosaicer as a "bootstrap". Because our algorithm is inherently free of the necessity of samples falling on a grid, we can support any color filter array pattern given an initial demosaicing guess. Furthermore, it would also be beneficial to cluster without having to "bootstrap" the algorithm. One possible approach would be to first cluster the color channels independently, resulting in three sets of clusters (one each in R, G, and B). These sets of clusters would then have to be reconciled into only two clusters in RGB space.

7   Conclusions

We have presented a demosaicing method and an image model that solves the ill-conditioned demosaicing problem within a well-conditioned Bayesian framework based on local sensor samples clustered into two RGB color values at each pixel. By modeling colors across an edge as linear combinations of the colors on each side, the possibility of inducing color fringing is decreased. Furthermore, the proposed statistical model is not grid-based, thus easily allowing for extensions to both multi-image demosaicing for video processing and non-iterative super-resolution output sampling. By constraining the output image to a linear model, we also reduce visible noise in smooth areas while preserving sharp edges.

References

1. Bayer, B.: Color imaging array. In: U.S. Patent No. 3,971,065. (1976)
2. Cok, D.: Signal processing method and apparatus for producing interpolated chrominance values in a sampled color image signal. In: U.S. Patent No. 5,373,322. (1987)
3. Freeman, W.: Median filter for reconstructing missing color samples. In: U.S. Patent No 4,724,395. (1988)
4. Ramanath, R., Snyder, W., Bilbro, G., Sander, W.: Demosaicking methods for bayer color arrays. J. of Electronic Imaging 11(3) (2002) 306–315
5. Gupta, M., Chen, T.: Vector color filter array demosaicing. In: Procs. of SPIE, Sensors and Camera Systems for Scientific, Industrial, and Digital Photography Apps. II. Volume 4306. (2001) 374–382
6. Laroche, C., Prescott, M.: Apparatus and method for adaptively interpolating a full color image utilizing chrominance gradients. In: U.S. Patent No. 5,629,734. (1994)
7. Hamilton, J., Adams, J.: Adaptive color plane interpolation in single sensor color electronic camera. In: U.S. Patent No. 5,629,734. (1997)
8. Chang, E., Cheung, S., Pan, D.: Color filter array recovery using a threshold-based variable number of gradients. In: Procs. of SPIE/IS and T EI. Volume 3650. (1999)

9. Kimmel, R.: Demosaicing, image reconstruction from color CCD samples. IEEE Trans. on Image Processing **8** (1999) 1221–1228

10. Malvar, H., He, L., Cutler, R.: High-quality linear interpolation for demosaicing of bayer-patterned color images. In: Procs. of ICASSP. (2004)

11. Eastman Kodak Company: PhotoCD PCD0992 (http://r0k.us/graphics/kodak/)

12. Nayar, S., Narasimhan, S.: Assorted pixels: Multi-sampled imaging with structural models. In: ECCV. Volume 4. (2002) 189–205

13. Hel-Or, Y.: The canonical correlations of color images and their use for demosaicing. Technical Report HPL-2003-164R1, Hewlett Packard Labs. Israel (2004)

14. Brainard, D.: Bayesian method for reconstructing color images from trichromatic samples. In: Soc. for Imaging Science Technology Conf. (1995) 375–380

15. Chuang, Y., Curless, B., Salesin, D., Szeliski, R.: A bayesian approach to digital matting. In: CVPR. Volume 2. (2001) 264–271

16. Zomet, A., Peleg, S.: Multi-sensor super-resolution. In: Procs. IEEE Workshop on Apps. of Computer Vision. (2002) 27–31

17. Freeman, W., Jones, T., Pasztor, E.: Example-based super-resolution. IEEE Computer Graphics and Applications **22**(2) (2002) 56–65

18. Fung, J., Mann, S.: Projective demosaicing using multiple overlapping images. In: Procs. of the Int'l Symp. on Intelligent Multimedia, Video, and Speech Processing. (2004) 190–193

19. Gotoh, T., Okutomi, M.: Direct super-resolution and registration using raw CFA images. In: CVPR. Volume 2. (2004) 600–607

20. Zhang, X., Wandell, B.: A spatial extension of CIELAB for digital color image reproduction. In: Procs. of Soc. For Information Display. (1996) 731–734

21. Zhang, X., Wandell, B.: Color image fidelity metrics evaluated using image distortion maps. Signal Processing **70**(3) (1998) 201–214

22. Fairchild, M., Johnson, G.: The iCAM framework for image appearance, image differences, and image quality. J. of Electronic Imaging **13** (2004) 126–138

23. Pattanaik, S., Ferwerda, J., Fairchild, M., Greenberg, D.: A multiscale model of adaptation and spatial vision for realistic image display. In: ACM SIGGRAPH. (1998) 287–298

24. Daly, S.: The Visible Differences Predictor: An Algorithm for the Assessment of Image Fidelity. In: Digital Images and Computer Vision. MIT Press (1993) 179–206

25. Ramasubramanian, M., Pattanaik, S., Greenberg, D.: A perceptually based physical error metric for realistic image synthesis. In: ACM SIGGRAPH. (1999) 73–82

26. Walter, B., Pattanaik, S., Greenberg, D.: Using perceptual texture masking for efficient image synthesis. In: Procs. of Eurographics. (2002) 393–400

27. Lee, A., Mumford, D., Huang, J.: Occlusion models for natural images: A statistical study of a scale-invariant dead leaves model. IJCV **41** (2001) 35–59

28. Lin, Z., Shum, H.: Fundamental limits of reconstruction-based superresolution algorithms under local translation. IEEE Trans. PAMI **26**(1) (2004) 83–97

Generalized Multi-sensor Planning

Anurag Mittal

Dept of Computer Science and Engg*,
Indian Institute of Technology Madras,
Chennai-600036, India

Abstract. Vision systems for various tasks are increasingly being deployed. Although significant effort has gone into improving the algorithms for such tasks, there has been relatively little work on determining optimal sensor configurations. This paper addresses this need. We specifically address and enhance the state-of-the-art in the analysis of scenarios where there are dynamically occuring objects capable of occluding each other. The visibility constraints for such scenarios are analyzed in a multi-camera setting. Also analyzed are other static constraints such as image resolution and field-of-view, and algorithmic requirements such as stereo reconstruction, face detection and background appearance. Theoretical analysis with the proper integration of such visibility and static constraints leads to a generic framework for sensor planning, which can then be customized for a particular task. Our analysis can be applied to a variety of applications, especially those involving randomly occuring objects, and include surveillance and industrial automation. Several examples illustrate the wide applicability of the approach.

1 Introduction

Systems utilizing possibly multiple visual sensors have become essential in many applications. Surveillance and Monitoring, industrial automation, transportation and automotive, and medical systems are a few of the important application domains. Existing research has mainly focused on improving the algorithms deployed in these systems, while little focus has been given to the placement of sensors for optimal system performance. Each system also has its own set of requirements. In security systems, for instance, the captured video streams may be inspected either manually, or a more advanced computerized system may be utilized to detect spurious activity automatically. Furthermore, automated people detection and tracking systems may have different objectives. Some systems utilize multiple closely-spaced cameras for the purpose of accurate stereo matching. Others utilize widely separated cameras for maximizing the object visibility in a dense situation [14, 11]. Still others [23, 1, 4, 19], use multiple cameras for the main purpose of increasing the coverage area by utilizing non-overlapping field-of-view cameras. In this paper, we develop a generic formulation that can be customized to find good sensor configurations for any of these systems.

Sensor planning has been researched quite extensively, and there are several different variations depending on the application. A popular set of methods, called next-view

---

* This work was conducted while the author was with Siemens Corporate Research, Princeton, NJ USA.

A. Leonardis, H. Bischof, and A. Pinz (Eds.): ECCV 2006, Part I, LNCS 3951, pp. 522–535, 2006.

planning, attempt to build a model of the scene incrementally by successively sensing the unknown world from effective sensor configurations using the information acquired about the world up to this point [17, 25, 5, 13, 12, 2, 8]. A related set of methods [10] have focused on finding good sensor positions for capturing a static scene from desirable viewpoints assuming that some geometric information about the scene is available. Bordering on the field of graphics, the main contribution of such methods is to develop efficient methods for determining the view of the scene from different viewpoints.

Methods that are directly related to ours are those that assume that complete geometric information is available and determine the location of static cameras so as to obtain the best views of a scene. This problem was originally posed in the computational geometry literature as the "art-gallery problem" [18]. The traditional formulation of such problem assumes the simple assumption that two points are called visible if the straight line segment between them lies entirely inside the polygon. Even with such simple definition of visibility, the problem is NP-complete.

Some of the recent work has concentrated on incorporating a few more constraints like incidence angle and range into the problem and obtain an approximate solution to the resultant NP-complete problem via randomized algorithms [7]. Several researchers [6, 20, 24, 13, 26, 22] have studied and incorporated more complex constraints based on several factors not limited to (1) resolution, (2) focus, (3) field of view, (4) visibility, (5) view angle, and (6) prohibited regions. However, the problem becomes much more complex to be amenable to fast approximation solutions.

In addition to the "static" constraints considered so far, there are additional constraints that arise when dynamic obstacles are present. Such constraints are essential to analyze since system performance is a function of object visibility. In [3], it was proposed to combine visibility and static constraints via a weighted sum of the error due to the two factors. On the other hand, our earlier paper [15] proposed maximization of the visibility while static constraints were analyzed simply as *hard* constraints that would either be satisfied or not at a given location. In this work, we provide a more general approach towards integration of these two types of constraints. We utilize analysis of visibility constraints and determination of multi-camera visibility rates from [15]. Integration of such analysis with a variety of static constraints and application requirements leads to a generic formulation for sensor planning. Customization of the method for a given system allows the method to be utilized for a variety of different tasks and applications.

The paper is organized as follows. Section 2 briefly reviews prior work on estimating the probability of visibility of an object at a given location in a scene for a certain configuration of sensors. Section 3 describes the integration of static constraints with probabilistic visibility constraints. Maximization of the thus obtained quality measure over an entire region of interest will be considered in section 4. Section 5 concludes the paper with planning experiments for some synthetic and real scenes.

2   Visibility Analysis

In this section, we briefly review and generalize some visibility analysis results from [15] that are pertinent to this work.

Since the particular application domain might contain either two or three dimensions, we consider the general case of an m dimensional space. Let us assume that we have

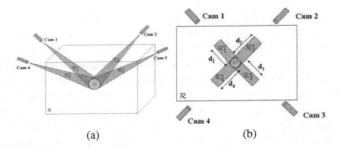

Fig. 1. Scene Geometry for (a) 3D case, (b) 2.5D case, where the sensors have finite heights

a region $\mathcal{R} \subset \mathbb{R}^m$ of *content* A observed by n sensors [Fig. 1]. Here, we use the term "content" in a general sense, such that it is the area of $\mathcal{R}$ if $m = 2$, and is the volume if $m = 3$. Let $\mathcal{E}_i$ be the event that a target object $\mathcal{O}$ at location $\mathcal{L} \in \mathcal{R}$ in angular orientation $\boldsymbol{\theta}$ is visible from sensor i. The definition of such "visibility" can be defined according to the application e.g visibility of only a part of the object might be sufficient. Then, it is useful to compute the following probabilities:

$$\{P(\mathcal{E}_i), i = 1..n\}, \quad \{P(\mathcal{E}_i \cap \mathcal{E}_j), i, j = 1..n\}, \dots, P(\bigcap_i \mathcal{E}_i) \tag{1}$$

In order to compute these probabilities, we first note that there exists a region of occlusion $\mathcal{R}_i^o$ for each sensor i such that the presence of another object in $\mathcal{R}_i^o$ would cause $\mathcal{O}$ to not be visible from i [1] [Fig. 1]. Now, let us assume that objects are located randomly in the scene with object density λ. Since λ is a function of the location and may also be influenced by the presence of nearby objects, let $\lambda(\mathbf{x_c}|\mathbf{x_O})$ be the density at location $\mathbf{x_c}$ given that visibility is being calculated at location $\mathbf{x_O}$. Then, it can be shown [16] that the probability that object $\mathcal{O}$ is visible from all of the sensors in a specified set $(i_1, i_2 \dots i_m)$ is [2]:

$$P(\bigcap_{i \in (i_1, \dots i_m)} \mathcal{E}_i) \approx \left(1 - \frac{b}{a}\right)^{1/b} \tag{2}$$

where

$$a = \frac{1}{\int_{\mathcal{R}_{(i_1, \dots i_m)}^o} \lambda(\mathbf{x_c}|\mathbf{x_0}) \, d\mathbf{x_c}}, \quad b = \frac{A_{ob} \cdot \lambda_{avg}}{\int_{\mathcal{R}_{(i_1, \dots i_m)}^o} \lambda(\mathbf{x_c}|\mathbf{x_0}) \, d\mathbf{x_c}} \tag{3}$$

Here, λ_{avg} is the average object density in the region, A_{ob} is the content of an occluding object, and $\mathcal{R}_{(i_1, \dots i_m)}^o$ is the combined region of occlusion for the sensor set $(i_1, \dots i_m)$ formed by the "geometric" union of the regions of occlusion $\mathcal{R}_{i_p}^o$ for the sensors in this set, i.e. $\mathcal{R}_{(i_1, \dots i_m)}^o = \bigcup_{p=1}^m \mathcal{R}_{i_p}^o$.

---

[1] Note that this region of occlusion is dependent on the application-specific definition of visibility. For instance, one may require that all of the object be visible, or one may require visibility of only the object center.

[2] Note that this is a better approximation than the one given in our earlier paper[15].

It may be noted that a is the effect on the probability due to the presence of an object, and b is a *correction* to such effect due to the finite object size.

3   Static Constraints and the Capture Quality

Several stationary factors affect the quality of the data acquired by a camera. We first describe such factors briefly and then discuss how they can be incorporated into a generic formulation that enables optimization of the sensor configuration with respect to a user-defined criteria.

3.1   "Static" Constraints

Some of the static constraints affecting the view of the camera are described next. Many of these constraints may be considered in either of two ways: *hard* constraints that *must* be satisfied at the given location for visibility, or *soft* constraints that may be measured in terms of a measure for the quality of the acquired data.

1. FIELD OF VIEW: Cameras have a limited field of view, and a constraint can be specified terms of a maximum angle from a central camera direction.
2. OBSTACLES: Fixed *high* obstacles like pillars block the view of a camera, and such constraint can be verified for a given object location.
3. PROHIBITED AREAS: There might also exist prohibited areas like desks or counterswhere people are not able to walk. These areas have a positive effect on the visibility in their vicinity since it is not possible for obstructing objects to be present within such regions.
4. IMAGE RESOLUTION: The resolution of an object in an image reduces as the object moves further away from the camera. Therefore, meaningful observations are possible only up to a certain distance from the camera.
5. ALGORITHMIC CONSTRAINTS: There are several algorithmic constraints that may exist. Such constraints may also be more complex involving inter-relationships between the views of several cameras. Stereo matching across two or more cameras is an example of such a constraint and involves a complex integration of several factors including image resolution, the maximum distortion of a view that can occur from one view to the other and the triangulation error.
6. VIEWING ANGLE: An additional constraint exists for the maximum angle α_{max} at which the observation of an object is meaningful. Such observation can be the basis for performing some other tasks such as object recognition. When the vertical viewing angle is considered, this constraint translates into a constraint on the minimum distance from the sensor that an object must be. The horizontal viewing angle can also be considered similarly by consideration of the angle between the object orientation and the camera direction.

3.2   The Capture Quality

In order to determine the quality or goodness of any given sensor configuration, the "static" constraints need to be integrated into a single *capture quality* function $q_l(\theta)$ that

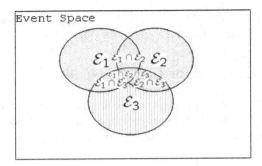

Fig. 2. The event space may be partitioned into disjoint event sets. Here, *only* $\mathcal{E}_i$, for instance, would only include event space that is not common with other events.

measures how well a particular object at location l in angular orientation θ is captured by the given sensor configuration. Due to occlusions, however, such quantity is a random variable that depends on the occurrence of events $\mathcal{E}_i$. The event space may be partitioned into the following disjoint sets [Fig. 2]:

$$\text{No} \mathcal{E}_i \text{ occurs, with quality:} \qquad 0$$
$$\text{Only} \mathcal{E}_i \text{ occurs, with quality:} \qquad q(\mathcal{E}_i)$$
$$\text{Only} \mathcal{E}_i \cap \mathcal{E}_j \text{occurs, with quality:} \quad q(\mathcal{E}_i \cap \mathcal{E}_j) \qquad \cdots$$
$$\bigcap_i \mathcal{E}_i \text{ occurs, with quality:} \qquad q(\bigcap_i \mathcal{E}_i)$$

Such separation allows one to specify the quality measure for each of such events separately. More specifically, such quality function needs to be specified for all of such events. In other words, one needs to specify for all possible sets, the quality measure $q_l(i_1, \ldots, i_m, \theta)$ that refers to the capture quality obtained if an object at the location l in angular orientation θ is visible from *all* of the sensors in the given m-tuple i.e. the event $(\bigcap_{i \in (i_1 \ldots i_m)} \mathcal{E}_i)$ occurs.

To give some insight into such specification of the quality function, one can consider the case of stereo matching. In such an application, since visibility from at least two sensors would be required for matching, the capture quality $\{q_l(i, \theta)\}, i = 1 \ldots n$ would be zero. For the terms involving two sensors, several competing requirements need to be considered. Under some simplifying assumptions, the error in the recovered depth due to image quantization may be approximated as being proportional to $\delta z \approx z^2/bf$, where z is the distance from the cameras, b is the baseline distance between the cameras, and f is the focal length. On the other hand, the angular distortion of the image of an object from one camera to the other may be approximated as $\theta_d \approx \tan^{-1}(b/z)$, and is directly related to the accuracy with which stereo matching may be performed. Furthermore, an increase in the distance from the cameras also decreases the size of the object view, which might further decrease the accuracy of stereo matching. Thus, in the perpendicular direction, the accuracy of stereo matching first increases with the distances from the cameras, and then decreases, while the quantization error increases with such distances. Thus, a quality function that peaks for some given distance and tapers off in either direction can be considered. Thus, for any given task requirement, a trade-off between different constraints is typically involved and it is up to the user to specify functions that define the desired behavior in such conditions.

Computation of probabilities of these disjoint events along with the specification of the capture quality associated with such events yields a probability function for the capture quality at a particular location (Fig. 5 illustrates an example where the function for a typical scene is averaged over the entire region of interest.). Given such a probability function, one can consider several integration measures of which the mean will be considered in this paper for simplicity purposes. The *mean* capture quality at a particular location for a particular object orientation θ may be written as:

$$q(\theta) = \sum_{\forall i} q(\mathcal{E}_i, \theta) P(\text{Only } \mathcal{E}_i) + \sum_{i < j} q(\mathcal{E}_i \cap \mathcal{E}_j, \theta) P(\text{Only } \mathcal{E}_i \cap \mathcal{E}_j) +$$

$$\cdots + q(\bigcap_i \mathcal{E}_i, \theta) P(\text{Only } \bigcap_i \mathcal{E}_i)$$

The probabilities $P(\text{Only } \bigcap_i \mathcal{E}_i)$ may be rewritten using the $P(\bigcap_i \mathcal{E}_i)$ terms that we had calculated earlier.

3.3 Integration of Quality Across Space

The analysis presented so far yields a function $q_s(\mathbf{x}, \theta)$, that refers to the capture quality of an object with orientation θ at location $\mathbf{x}$ given that the sensors have the parameter vector $\mathbf{s}$. Such parameter vector may include, for instance, the location, viewing direction and zoom of each camera. Given such a function, one can define a suitable *cost* function in order to evaluate a given set of sensor parameters w.r.t to the entire region to be viewed. Such sensor parameters may be constrained further due to other factors. For instance, there typically exists a physical limitation on the positioning of the cameras (walls, ceilings etc.). The sensor planning problem can then be formulated as a problem of constrained optimization of the cost function. Such optimization will yield the optimum sensor parameters according to the specified cost function.

Several cost functions may be considered. One may define a cost function that maximizes the minimum quality in the region. Another cost function, and perhaps the most reasonable one in many situations, is to define the cost as the negative of the average capture quality in a given region of interest:

$$C(\mathbf{s}) = - \int_{\mathcal{R}_i} \int_0^{2\pi} \lambda(\mathbf{x}, \theta) q_s(\mathbf{x}, \theta) \, d\theta \, d\mathbf{x} \tag{4}$$

This cost function has been utilized for obtaining the results in this paper. Note that we have added an additional parameter θ to the object density function in order to incorporate information about the object orientations into the density function. Since the orientation does not affect the occluding characteristics of an object, such parameter was integrated (and eliminated) for the visibility analysis presented previously.

4 Minimization of the Cost Function

The cost function defined by Equation 4 (as also other suitable ones) is highly complex and due to the variegated nature of the constraints, it is not possible to obtain a single method that optimizes such function in a very efficient manner. Furthermore, even for simple scenarios, it can be shown that the problem is NP-complete and not amenable to fast polynomial time solutions. Figure 3 illustrates the cost function for the scene shown in Figure 4 (b) where, for illustration purposes, only two of the nine parameters have been varied. Even in this two dimensional space, there are two global minima and several local minima. Furthermore, the gradient is zero in some regions.

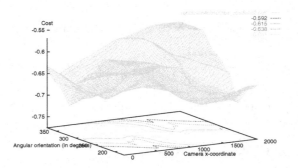

Fig. 3. The Cost Function for the scene in Figure [4 (b)] where, for illustration purposes, only the x-coordinate and direction of the second camera have been varied

Due to the generality and characteristics of the cost function, we propose to use a general method that is able to find the global minima of complex cost functions. Simulated Annealing and Genetic Algorithms are two classes of algorithms that may be considered[21]. For our experiments, we utilized a highly sophisticated simulated re-annealing software *ASA* developed by L. Ingber [9].

Using this algorithm, we were able to obtain extremely good sensor configurations in a reasonable amount of time (5min to a couple of hours on a Pentium IV 2.2GHz PC, depending on the desired accuracy of the result, the number of dimensions of the search space and complexity of the scene). For low dimensional spaces (< 4), where it was feasible to verify the results using full search, it was found that the algorithm quickly converged to a global minimum. For moderate dimensions of the search space (< 8), the algorithm was again able to obtain the optimum solution, but only after some time. Although the optimality of the solution could not be verified by full search, we assumed such solution to be optimum since running the algorithm several times from different starting points and different annealing parameters did not alter the final solution. For very high dimensional spaces (> 8), although the algorithm provided "good" solutions very quickly, it took several hours to converge to the best one. Some of the "optimal" solutions thus obtained will be illustrated in the next section.

5   Experiments

We will now demonstrate how the generic method developed so far may be customized for different task requirements. For simplicity, we will consider the specific $2.5D$ case of objects moving on a ground plane and sensors placed at some known heights H_i from this plane. The objects are also assumed to have the same horizontal profile at each height, such that the area of their profile onto the ground is A_{ob}. Examples of such objects include cylinders, cubes, cuboids, and square prisms.

We will also assume that we require only visibility of the center line of the object and only up to a length h from its top. Then, assuming that the average "radius" of the object is r, the region of occlusion is a rectangle of width $2r$ and a distance d_i from the object, that is proportional to the object's distance from sensor i:

$$d_i = (D_i - d_i)\mu_i = D_i \frac{\mu_i}{\mu_i + 1}, \quad \text{where} \quad \mu_i = \frac{h}{H_i} \tag{5}$$

Then, one may approximate the area of the region of occlusion R_i^o as $A_i^o \approx d_i(2r)$. These models enable one to reason about the particular application of people detection and tracking for objects moving on a plane. Using these assumptions, we first consider some synthetic examples.

5.1   Synthetic Examples

In the synthetic examples we consider, we use the following assumptions. The objects occur randomly with object density $\lambda = 1m^{-2}$, object height = 150cm, object radius r=15cm, minimum visibility height h=50cm and maximum visibility angle $\alpha_{max} = 45°$. The sensors are mounted H = 2.5m above the ground. The maps shown are capture quality maps scaled such that [0,1] maps onto [0,255]. First, we consider a rectangular room of size 10mX20m.

The first two examples [Fig. 4 a & b.] assume a simple quality function such that visibility from *any* direction is considered equally valid (i.e. the parameter θ is neglected) and fixed thresholds are put on the visibility distance from the camera based on camera resolution ($maxdist_{res}$) and maximum viewing angle α_{max} ($mindist_{view}$):

$$q_{\mathbf{x}}(\mathcal{E}_i, \theta) = \begin{cases} 1 \text{ if } mindist_{view} < d(\mathbf{x}, cam) < maxdist_{res} \\ 0 \text{ otherwise} \end{cases} \tag{6}$$

Furthermore, for multiple sensor terms, the quality is defined simply as the quality of the sensor having the best view:

$$q(\bigcap_{i \in (i_1, \dots i_m)} \mathcal{E}_i, \theta) = \max_{i \in (i_1, \dots i_m)} q(\mathcal{E}_i, \theta) \tag{7}$$

Using $mindist = 5m$ and $maxdist = 25m$, if the sensors have a field of view of 360° (omni-camera), configuration [a] was found optimum, while a field of view of 90° resulted in configuration [b]. The omni-camera is used for the rest of the examples in this scene.

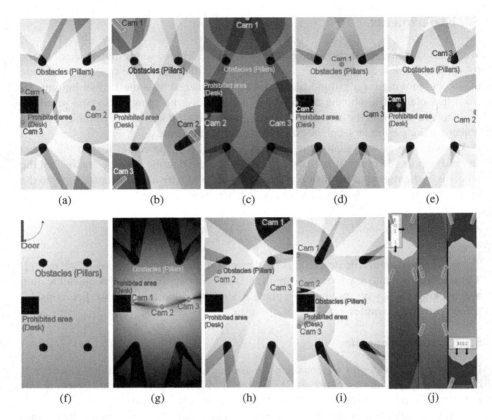

Fig. 4. Optimum configuration using: (a): a non-directional object visibility constraint and a uniform object density. [Eq. 4], (b): field of view restricted to 90°, (c): directional object visibility [Eq. 8], (d): directional object visibility, and a soft constraint on resolution and viewing angle [Eqs. 9 & 10], (e): non-directional object visibility, and using variable densities shown in Fig. (f), (g): stereo requirement, non-directional object visibility and uniform densities, (h): algorithmic constraint of no visibility with the top wall as background, (i): no visibility with the left wall as background, (j): Sensor Planning in a large "Museum", where several constraints are to be satisfied simultaneously.

Assuming that one requires visibility from *all* directions, one may alter the quality function as:

$$q_{\mathbf{x}}(\mathcal{E}_i, \theta) = \begin{cases} 1 \text{ if } \theta_{diff} < \theta^{max} \\ \quad \& \ d_{view}^{min} < d(\mathbf{x}, cam) < d_{res}^{max} \\ 0 \text{ otherwise} \end{cases} \tag{8}$$

where θ^{max} is the maximum angular orientation at which the observation of the object is still considered meaningful, and $\theta_{diff} = abs(\theta - dir(cam, \mathbf{x}))$ such that $dir(cam, \mathbf{x})$ is the angular direction of the camera from the point of view of $\mathbf{x}$ [Fig. 5 (a)]. Assuming that $\theta^{max} = 90°$, we obtain the sensor configuration shown in [c]. Note that the cameras are now more spread out in order to capture the objects from many directions.

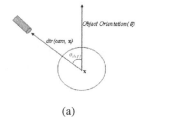 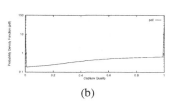

(a)   (b)

Fig. 5. (a): Computation of the viewing angle θ_{diff}, (b): The probability density function for the capture quality for Fig. 4 [d]. Note the unusually high values for zero and one due to the possibilities of complete object occlusion and perfect capture in certain conditions.

One may further expand the definition of the quality function in order to incorporate the *camera distance* constraints as soft constraints rather than hard ones. Furthermore, one may allow a soft constraint on the viewing orientation. Using one such possible quality function:

$$q_{\mathbf{x}}(\mathcal{E}_i, \theta) = H(\theta_{diff}) * \begin{cases} 1 & \text{if } d^{min}_{view} < d(\mathbf{x}, cam) < d^{max}_{res} \\ \frac{d(\mathbf{x}, cam)}{d^{min}_{view}} & \text{if } d(\mathbf{x}, cam) < d^{min}_{view} \\ exp\left(-\frac{d(\mathbf{x}, cam) - d^{max}_{res}}{d^{max}_{res}}\right) & \text{if } d(\mathbf{x}, cam) > d^{max}_{res} \end{cases}$$

(9)

where

$$H(\theta_{diff}) = \begin{cases} 1 & \text{if } \theta_{diff} < \theta^{min} \\ \frac{\theta_{diff} - \theta^{min}}{\theta^{max} - \theta^{min}} & \text{if } \theta^{min} < \theta_{diff} < \theta^{max} \\ 0 & \text{if } \theta_{diff} > \theta^{max} \end{cases}$$

(10)

and using $\theta^{min} = \pi/2$ and $\theta^{max} = \pi$, we obtained sensor configuration [d]. Note that camera one moves inwards compared to configuration [c] since the directional visibility requirement has been made a little less rigid. The probability distribution for the capture quality for this case is shown in Fig. [5 (b)]. Using such information, one may be able to utilize more complex capture requirements. For instance, one may be able to specify that a certain percentile of the capture quality be maximized.

Relaxing the assumption of uniform density, if variable density is assumed such that the density is highest near the door and decreases linearly with the distance from it[f], configuration [e] was found to be the best. Note that, compared to [a], the cameras move closer to the door in order to better capture the region with higher object density.

Next, we consider a stereo assumption such that matching across cameras and 3D reconstruction becomes an additional constraint. One can show that the error in triangulation for an omni-camera is proportional to:

$$e_{tr} \propto \sqrt{d_1^2 + d_2^2 + d_1 d_2 \cos(\alpha)}/\sin(\alpha)$$

(11)

where d_1 and d_2 are the distances of the object from the two cameras, and α is the angular separation between the two cameras as seen from the object. Although the error in matching is algorithm-dependent, a reasonable assumption is that:

$$e_m \propto d_1/cos(\alpha/2) + d_2/cos(\alpha/2) \qquad (12)$$

Considering a quality function that uses a weighted average of the two errors: $q = -(w_1 e_{tr} + w_2 e_m)$, configuration [g] was found to the best. Note that all the three cameras come closer to each other in order to be able to do stereo matching between any two of them.

In the final example for this scene, we consider a case where, because of algorithmic constraints, capture of an object with one of the walls as background is not useful. For instance, the wall may be painted a certain color and the objects may have a high probability of appearing in this color. Assuming that visibility with the top wall as background is not useful, we obtain configuration [h]. The same constraint with the left wall yields configuration [i]. Note that some cameras move close to the prohibited wall in order to avoid it as the background.

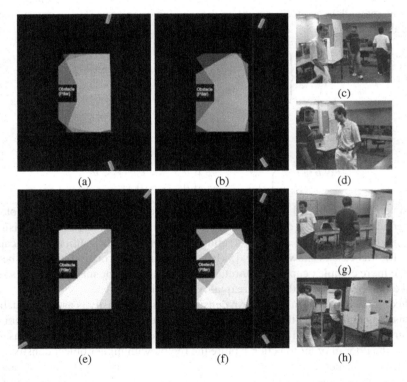

Fig. 6. (a): Configuration of two cameras for optimum face detection. (b): Configuration selected by a human operator. (c): An image from one of the cameras in (a). (d): An image from one of the cameras in (b). Note that one of the faces is not detected because of a large viewing angle. (e): Configuration of two cameras for person detection using background subtraction, where the top wall matches the color of people 33% of the time. (f): Configuration selected by a human operator. (g): An image from one of the cameras in (e). (h): An image from one of the cameras in (f). Note how the top portion of one person is not detected due to similarity with the background.

Next, we consider a more complex scene where several constraints are to be satisfied simultaneously. In Fig. 4 [j], the scene of a "museum" is shown where the entrance is on the left upper corner and the exit is on the bottom right corner. One is required to view

Distance	1.8m - 2.5m	2.5m - 3.1m	3.1m - 3.8m	3.8m - 4.5m	4.5m - 5.2m	5.2m - 6m	> 6m
Face Detection Rate	97.5%	94%	92.5%	85%	77%	40%	0 %

(a)

	Face Detection		Person Detection	
	w/ planning	w/o planning	w/ planning	w/o planning
Predicted	53.6%	48%	85%	81%
Actual	51.33%	42%	82%	76%

(b)

Fig. 7. (a): Face Detection rates for different distances from the cameras. Additionally, detection rates reduced by about 30% from frontal to the side view. This information was used by the sensor planner in the quality function. (b): Detection rates predicted by the algorithm compared with the actual rates obtained from experimental data.

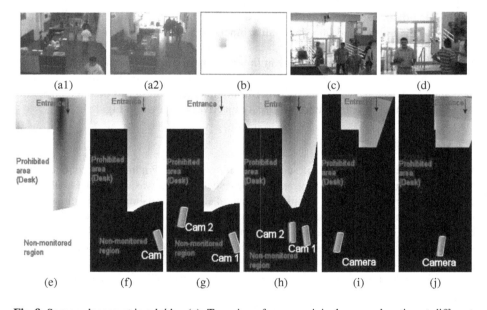

(a1)   (a2)   (b)   (c)   (d)

(e)   (f)   (g)   (h)   (i)   (j)

Fig. 8. Sensor placement in a lobby. (a): Two views from an original camera location at different times of the day. (b): Density map obtained via background subtraction (darker represents higher object density). (e): Mapping of the density map onto a plan view of the scene. (f): Optimal object visibility using one camera (72% visibility predicted, 78% obtained). (g): Optimal sensor placement using two cameras (91% visibility predicted, 93% obtained). (h): Optimal sensor placement using two cameras and a stereo requirement. (i): Optimization of face detection for people entering the building (46 % detection predicted, 43% obtained). An example of face detection using this sensor setting is shown in (c). (j): Optimization of face detection when the position of the camera cannot be changed (but the direction and zoom can) (33 % detection predicted, 35 % obtained). An example of face detection using this setting is shown in (d).

the faces of people as they enter or exit the scene. Additionally, 3D object localization is to be performed via stereo reconstruction for all parts of the scene. Note how the sensor placement varies in the three sections due to different combination of tasks.

5.2   Real Scenes

In real scenes, we first consider sensor planning in a small controlled environment [Fig. 6]. In the first experiment, face detection is maximized, while in the second one, we try to maximize person detection via background subtraction and grouping. We utilized an off-the-shelf face detector from OpenCV and characterized its performance over different camera distances and person orientations[Fig. 7 (a)]. This gives us the quality function that we need for our sensor planner. Cameras were then placed in the optimum sensor configuration thus obtained and face detection was performed on the video data. We also asked a human to try to position the cameras manually and the experiments were conducted with this configuration as well. Results of this experiment are presented in Fig.s [6(a),(b),(c),(d) & 7]. In the next experiment, we maximize person detection using background subtraction and grouping. An additional constraint we considered was that the appearance of one of the actors matched with one of the walls and the middle pillar/obstruction, thus making detection in front of them difficult. This condition was then integrated into the quality function. The results of this experiment are shown in Fig.s [6 (e),(f),(g),(h) & 7].

Next, we consider camera placement in the lobby of a building where we estimated the person densities over a period of time via a common background subtraction method [23] and a subsequent "foot finding" algorithm. This information was then fed back into the sensor planner to optimize for different objectives as shown in Fig. [8].

6   Conclusion

We have considered analysis of scenes that may contain dynamic objects occluding each other. Multi-view visibility analysis for such scenes was integrated with user-defined quality criteria based possibly on several static constraints such as image resolution, stereo matching and field of view. Apart from obtaining important performance characteristics of multi-sensor systems, such analysis was further utilized for obtaining optimal sensor configurations. The algorithm can be customized for optimum sensor placement for a variety of existing multi-sensor systems and has applications in several fields, including surveillance where it can be utilized in places such as museums, shopping malls, subway stations and parking lots. Future work includes specification of more complex cost functions, investigation of more efficient methods for optimization of the cost function and better estimation of the visibility probability by considering the effect of interaction between objects.

References

[1] Q. Cai and J.K. Aggarwal. Tracking human motion in structured environments using a distributed-camera system. *PAMI*, 21(11):1241–1247, November 1999.

[2] A. Cameron and H.F. Durrant-Whyte. A bayesian approach to optimal sensor placement. *IJRR*, 9(5):70–88, 1990.

[3] Xing Chen and James Davis. Camera placement considering occlusion for robust motion capture. Technical Report CS-TR-2000-07, Stanford University, December 2000.

[4] R.T. Collins, A.J. Lipton, H. Fujiyoshi, and T. Kanade. Algorithms for cooperative multi-sensor surveillance. *Proceedings of the IEEE*, 89(10):1456–1477, October 2001.

[5] D.J. Cook, P. Gmytrasiewicz, and L.B. Holder. Decision-theoretic cooperative sensor planning. *PAMI*, 18(10):1013–1023, October 1996.

[6] C. K. Cowan and P.D. Kovesi. Automatic sensor placement from vision tast requirements. *PAMI*, 10(3):407–416, May 1988.

[7] H. González-Banos and J.C. Latombe. A randomized art-gallery algorithm for sensor placement. In *SCG*, Medford, MA, June 2001.

[8] G. Hager and M. Mintz. Computational methods for task-directed sensor data fusion and sensor planning. *IJRR*, 10(4):285–313, August 1991.

[9] L. Ingber. Very fast simulated re-annealing. *Mathematical Computer Modeling*, 12:967–973, 1989.

[10] S.B. Kang, S.M. Seitz, and P.P. Sloan. Visual tunnel analysis for visibility prediction and camera planning. In *CVPR*, pages II: 195–202, Hilton Head, SC, June 2000.

[11] S. Khan and M. Shah. Consistent labeling of tracked objects in multiple cameras with overlapping fields of view. *PAMI*, 25(10):1355–1360, October 2003.

[12] K.N. Kutulakos and C.R. Dyer. Recovering shape by purposive viewpoint adjustment. *IJCV*, 12(2-3):113–136, April 1994.

[13] J. Maver and R.K. Bajcsy. Occlusions as a guide for planning the next view. *PAMI*, 15(5):417–433, May 1993.

[14] A. Mittal and L.S. Davis. M$_2$tracker: A multi-view approach to segmenting and tracking people in a cluttered scene. *IJCV*, 51(3):189–203, February 2003.

[15] A. Mittal and L.S. Davis. Visibility analysis and sensor planning in dynamic environments. In *ECCV*, page III: 543 ff., Prague, Czech Republic, May 2004.

[16] A. Mittal and L.S. Davis. A general method for sensor planning in multi-sensor systems: Extension to random occlusion. *Submitted to IJCV*, 2005.

[17] J. Miura and K. Ikeuchi. Task-oriented generation of visual sensing strategies. In *ICCV*, pages 1106–1113, Boston, MA, 1995.

[18] Joseph O'Rourke. *Art Gallery Theorems and Algorithms*. Oxford University Press, August 1987.

[19] A. Rahimi, B. Dunagan, and T.J. Darrell. Simultaneous calibration and tracking with a network of non-overlapping sensors. In *CVPR*, pages I: 187–194, 2004.

[20] M. K. Reed and P. K. Allen. Constraint-based sensor planning for scene modeling. *PAMI*, 22(12):1460–1467, December 2000.

[21] Yi Shang. *Global Search Methods for Solving Nonlinear Optimization Problems*. PhD thesis, University of Illinois at Urbana-Champaign, 1997.

[22] J. Spletzer and C.J. Taylor. A framework for sensor planning and control with applications to vision guided multi-robot systems. In *CVPR*, Kauai, Hawaii, 2001.

[23] C. Stauffer and W.E.L. Grimson. Learning patterns of activity using real-time tracking. *PAMI*, 22(8):747–757, August 2000.

[24] K. Tarabanis, R.Y. Tsai, and A. Kaul. Computing occlusion-free viewpoints. *PAMI*, 18(3): 279–292, March 1996.

[25] Y. Ye and J.K. Tsotsos. Sensor planning for 3d object search. *CVIU*, 73(2):145–168, February 1999.

[26] S.K. Yi, R.M. Haralick, and L.G. Shapiro. Optimal sensor and light-source positioning for machine vision. *CVIU*, 61(1):122–137, January 1995.

Variational Shape and Reflectance Estimation Under Changing Light and Viewpoints

Neil Birkbeck[1], Dana Cobzas[1], Peter Sturm[2], and Martin Jagersand[1]

[1] Computer Science, University of Alberta, Canada
{birkbeck, dana, jag}@cs.ualberta.ca
[2] INRIA Rhone-Alpes, France
peter.sturm@inrialpes.fr

Abstract. Fitting parameterized 3D shape and general reflectance models to 2D image data is challenging due to the high dimensionality of the problem. The proposed method combines the capabilities of classical and photometric stereo, allowing for accurate reconstruction of both textured and non-textured surfaces. In particular, we present a variational method implemented as a PDE-driven surface evolution interleaved with reflectance estimation. The surface is represented on an adaptive mesh allowing topological change. To provide the input data, we have designed a capture setup that simultaneously acquires both viewpoint and light variation while minimizing self-shadowing. Our capture method is feasible for real-world application as it requires a moderate amount of input data and processing time. In experiments, models of people and everyday objects were captured from a few dozen images taken with a consumer digital camera. The capture process recovers a photo-consistent model of spatially varying Lambertian and specular reflectance and a highly accurate geometry.

1 Introduction

The automatic computation of 3D geometric and appearance models from images is one of the most challenging and fundamental problems in computer vision. While a more traditional point-based method provides accurate results for camera geometry, a surface representation is required for modeling and visualization applications. Most surface-based approaches reconstruct the model based on stereo correlation data [1, 2, 3]. That works well for textured Lambertian surfaces but fails in the presence of specular highlights or uniform texture. Additionally, stereo-based techniques reconstruct only the shape and not the surface reflectance properties even though some approaches can handle specular objects using robust scores [4, 5].

We are proposing a surface reconstruction method that uses texture and shading information to successfully reconstruct both textured and non-textured objects with general reflectance properties. The similarity cost functional uses a parametric reflectance model that is estimated together with the shape. There exist other approaches that combine stereo for textured regions with shape from

A. Leonardis, H. Bischof, and A. Pinz (Eds.): ECCV 2006, Part I, LNCS 3951, pp. 536–549, 2006.

shading cues for texture-less regions [6, 7], but, in those works, the two scores are separate terms in the cost function and the combination is achieved either using weights [6] or by manually assigning regions [7]. Additionally, they only exploit diffuse objects whereas our method can also handle specular objects. Like photometric stereo, our method is able to reconstruct the surface of spatially varying or uniform material objects by assuming that the object is moving relative to the light source. Zhang et al. [8] and Weber et al. [9] also use light variation for reconstructing spatially varying albedo. But, in contrast to our approach, they do not consider the challenge of dealing with specular surfaces.

With respect to recovering specular surfaces, most of the approaches either filter or remove specularities and use only diffuse observations in the reconstruction [5]. Another option is to design similarity scores that account for specular highlights either by assuming a uniform surface material [10] or by enforcing dimensionality constraints on the observed intensity variations [11]. A more general approach is to explicitly model surface reflectance either with a parametric model [12] or a non-parametric model (BRDF map). Obtaining a BRDF map requires carefully calibrated lights and many samples [13]. For our system we made the choice of using a parametric model for reflectance as we are interested in reconstructing both shape and reflectance parameters.

Different representations have been proposed for shape reconstruction; they can be divided in two main classes - image-based (depth/disparity) and object-based (voxel grid, mesh, level set). Image-based representations are suitable for single view or binocular stereo techniques, but object based representations, which are not tied to a particular image, are more suitable for multi-view reconstruction. Mesh and level set techniques have the advantage over voxel representations that they give readily computable normals (essential in recovering shading). Additionally, the regularization terms can be easily integrated into a mesh or level set. An implicit level set representation leads to an elegant algorithm [2], but despite various efficient numerical solutions proposed for the level set methods [14], they are still slow compared to mesh based approaches that can take advantage of graphics hardware acceleration. We therefore decided to implement our method using an adaptive deformable mesh that allows for topological changes. The mesh is evolved in time based on a variational algorithm. Fua and Leclerc [6] and Duan et al. [15] have presented related variational mesh-based approaches but not as general as they only reconstruct diffuse objects.

Due to the high dimensionality, reconstruction can be difficult, slow and require lots of image data. To ameliorate these problems, we propose a multi-resolution algorithm that alternates between shape and reflectance estimation. Although in theory a general reflectance model can be estimated at every step, in practice we noticed that similar results are obtained more efficiently if the shape reconstruction is performed on filtered diffuse pixels assuming Lambertian reflectance. A Phong parametric model is then calculated using the final shape. Experiments show that the proposed method is able to reconstruct accurate and photo-realistic models that can be rendered in novel illumination conditions. To summarize, the main contributions of the paper are:

- We designed a photo-consistency functional suitable for surfaces with non-uniform general reflectance based on a parametric reflectance model;
- We present a variational method implemented as a PDE-driven mesh evolution interleaved with reflectance estimation. Our particular mesh implementation is robust to self-intersections while allowing topological changes;
- We designed a practical setup that provides the necessary light variation, camera and light calibration and requires only commonly available hardware: a light source, a camera, and a glossy white sphere.

2   Shape Refinement

We present the shape refinement problem beginning with a general continuous formulation that is then discretized on the mesh triangles. Next, we describe a numeric solution to the resultant optimization problem for an object with Lambertian or specular reflectance.

2.1   Problem Definition

The proposed capture setup consists of a single camera viewing an object placed on a turntable illuminated by a desk lamp. We take two sets of images of a full rotation, each with a different light position. Considering the proposed capture setup, the shape recovery problem takes the following as input:

- a set of n images $\mathcal{I} = \{I_i | i = 1 \cdots n\}$;
- the associated projection matrices P_i;
- the illumination information $L_i = (\mathbf{l}_i, l_i)$, assuming a single distant light source with direction $\mathbf{l}_i$ and color l_i;
- an initial shape S_0;

and computes a refined shape, S, and the corresponding reflectance parameters that best agree with the input images. A practical method for automatically calibrating the camera and the light is presented in Section 4.

Given the projection matrix $P_i = K[R_i, \mathbf{t}_i]$, the image coordinates $\mathbf{p}_i = (u_i, v_i, 1)^T$ for a 3D point $\mathbf{x}$ are expressed as $\mathbf{p}_i = \Pi(P_i \mathbf{x})$. Π represents the non-linear operator that transforms homogeneous coordinates into Cartesian ones (division with the homogeneous component).

We assume that surface reflectance is a parametric function implied by the surface (and surface normals) and imaging conditions. Therefore, the shape reconstruction problem is to recover a shape and its implied reflectance parameters that best agree with the input images. The shape and reflectance are estimated in an alternate fashion (see Section 4).

2.2   Shape Functional

We use a variational formulation for the shape recovery problem similar to the one from Faugeras and Keriven [2].

$$E(S) = \int_S g(\mathbf{x}, \mathbf{n}) dS = \int_v \int_u g(\mathbf{x}, \mathbf{n}) \|S_u \times S_v\| du dv \tag{1}$$

where $\mathbf{x} = (x(u, v), y(u, v), z(u, v))^T$ is a point on the surface and $\mathbf{n} = \frac{S_u \times S_v}{\|S_u \times S_v\|}$ is the surface normal at point $\mathbf{x}$.

The photo-consistency function g encodes the similarity between a point on the surface, and the images in which it is observed. We investigate a similarity function of the form:

$$g(\mathbf{x}, \mathbf{n}) = \sum_i h(\mathbf{x}, \mathbf{n}, P_i, L_i) \left(I_i(\Pi(P_i \mathbf{x})) - R(\mathbf{x}, \mathbf{n}, L_i)\right)^2 \qquad (2)$$

where R is a rendering equation returning the color of point $\mathbf{x}$ under light conditions L_i. The function h is a weighting function that accounts for visibility and discrete sampling effects. Refer to Fig. 1 for a explanation of our notations.

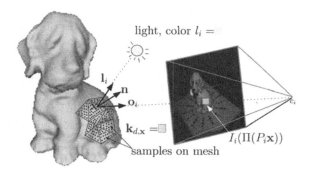

Fig. 1. An illustration of the sample points and the angles used in the shading equation

Rendering function. The function R encodes the reflectance model at a point $\mathbf{x}$ on the surface. In fact, R is a function of the entire surface as it should account for inter-reflections and shadowing of a point $\mathbf{x}$. In our capture setup we minimized self shadowing and inter-reflections and therefore ignored these subtleties. We model R with a parametric BRDF which is fitted to Eq. 2 (assuming known shape and imaging conditions).

For modeling the parametric BRDF we chose the Lambertian model to represent diffuse reflectance and the Phong model for the specular reflectance. The two models are briefly summarized below[1].

Lambertian model assumes constant BRDF and effectively models matte objects, such as clay, where the observed shading is a result of the foreshortening contribution of the light source. Integrating the Lambertian BRDF model into the reflectance equation we get the following expression for the observed color at a particular point $\mathbf{x}$ with normal $\mathbf{n}$:

$$R_{lamb}(\mathbf{x}, \mathbf{n}, L_i) = (\langle \mathbf{n}, \mathbf{l}_i \rangle l_i + a_i) k_{d,\mathbf{x}} \qquad (3)$$

---

[1] The proposed method works with color images but for simplicity reasons we present the theory for one color channel. In practice the colors are vectors in RGB space.

where $k_{d,\mathbf{x}}$ represents the Lambertian color (albedo). For better modeling of light effects in a normal room we incorporate an ambient term to capture the contribution of indirect light in each image a_i.

Specular reflectance is typically modeled as an additive component to the Lambertian model. We chose to represent the specular BRDF using the Phong model. Letting $\mathbf{o}_i$ be the outgoing direction from the point $\mathbf{x}$ to the center of the camera i (i.e., the view direction), and $\mathbf{h}_i$ the bisector of the angle between the view and the light directions $\mathbf{h}_i = \frac{\mathbf{o}_i + \mathbf{l}_i}{\|\mathbf{o}_i + \mathbf{l}_i\|}$ the shading model for a specular pixel is (refer to Fig. 1 for an illustration):

$$R_{spec}(\mathbf{x}, \mathbf{n}, L_i) = (\langle \mathbf{n}, \mathbf{l}_i \rangle l_i + a_i) k_{d,\mathbf{x}} + \langle \mathbf{n}, \mathbf{h}_{i,\mathbf{x}} \rangle^m l_i k_s. \qquad (4)$$

where k_s is the specular color and m is the specular exponent. The specular parameters are not indexed per point due to the fact that several observations are needed for reliably estimating the BRDF. Instead (as discussed in Section 3) we compute the specular parameters for groups of points having similar diffuse component, thus likely to have the same material.

Weight function. The similarity measure with respect to an image should be computed only for the visible points. This can be easily represented by setting the weight function, h, to the binary visibility function $V(\mathbf{x}, S, P_i)$.

To ensure that only relevant image information is used in evaluation of g, we use a subset of image observations for each point on the surface. In particular, we use the $n_{cameras}$ closest cameras to the median camera [5], where the median camera is chosen based on the azimuthal angle. This camera selection gives another binary weight function V'. Another sampling issue arises because a surface patch projects to a different area in each image. We compensate for this by giving more weight to observations that have frontal views and less weight to grazing views. This is accomplished by weighting the samples by $\langle \mathbf{n}, \mathbf{o}_i \rangle$. Cumulating visibility and sampling into the function h we get:

$$h(\mathbf{x}, \mathbf{n}, P_i, L) = \langle \mathbf{n}, \mathbf{o}_i \rangle V'(\mathbf{x}, S, P_i) \qquad (5)$$

2.3   Surface Evolution

Optimizing the photo-consistency function in Eq. 1 with respect to the surface S results in a surface evolution problem. The gradient flow PDE is derived from the Euler-Lagrange equation of Eq. 1. The PDE contains higher order terms [2] resulting from the general form of g being a function of $\mathbf{n}$. Instead of using the full PDE, complete with the higher order terms, we use a simplified PDE containing only the first order terms. This flow is accurate for a g that is only a function of surface position $\mathbf{x}$. Similar PDE's were used by [16, 15] but with different g functions.

$$\frac{\partial S}{\partial t} = (2g\kappa - \langle \nabla g, \mathbf{n} \rangle)\mathbf{n} \qquad (6)$$

where κ is the mean curvature. The flow will move each point along the current estimate for the normal. The first component of the motion in Eq. 6, $2g\kappa$, is

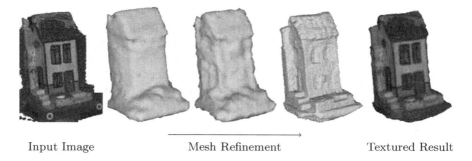

| Input Image | Mesh Refinement | Textured Result |

Fig. 2. An example of the mesh evolving to a refined shape

essentially a smoothing term, reducing the mean curvature of the object, whereas the second component ensures the evolution decreases the error function on the surface.

The shape refinement then proceeds by iteratively updating the initial shape, S_0, using Eq. 6 until convergence. We stop the evolution when there is no significant change in the error function for several steps. Fig 2 gives an example of our surface evolution algorithm starting from the visual hull.

2.4   Discretization on the Triangular Mesh

The numerical solution for the surface evolution depends on the chosen representation. As we explore the use of a mesh based representation, we must first break the integral into a sum of integrals over the triangles. Let $\Delta = (\mathbf{v}_1, \mathbf{v}_2, \mathbf{v}_3)$ be a triangle having vertices $\mathbf{v}_1, \mathbf{v}_2$ and $\mathbf{v}_3$. An interior point on the triangle can be expressed using the barycentric coordinates $\lambda_1, \lambda_2, \lambda_3$ satisfying $\lambda_1 + \lambda_2 + \lambda_3 = 1$ and $\lambda_k \geq 0$ for $k \in \{1, 2, 3\}$: $\mathbf{x} = \lambda_1 \mathbf{v}_1 + \lambda_1 \mathbf{v}_2 + \lambda_1 \mathbf{v}_3$. The triangle normal $\mathbf{n}$ is then computed by smoothly interpolating the normals $\mathbf{n}_1, \mathbf{n}_2, \mathbf{n}_3$ of the vertices: $\mathbf{n} = \lambda_1 \mathbf{n}_1 + \lambda_2 \mathbf{n}_2 + \lambda_3 \mathbf{n}_3$.

The integrals are then composed into a sum of regularly spaced sample points over the triangles, giving:

$$E(S) \approx \sum_{\{\mathbf{v}_1, \mathbf{v}_2, \mathbf{v}_3\} \in \Delta} \sum_{\{\lambda_1, \lambda_2, \lambda_3\}} g(\lambda_1 \mathbf{v}_1 + \lambda_2 \mathbf{v}_2 + \lambda_3 \mathbf{v}_3, \lambda_1 \mathbf{n}_1 + \lambda_2 \mathbf{n}_2 + \lambda_3 \mathbf{n}_3) \quad (7)$$

The method of computing the error on sampling points within the triangles relates our work to other mesh based approaches [6, 17, 10, 12]. An alternative approach, used in the work of Duan et al. [15], is to sample the error on the tangent plane of the mesh vertices.

Although a small number of samples points (e.g., using only the mesh vertices) may be sufficient for textureless surfaces, a textured surface may require a dense sampling that matches the image resolution. We use a dense sampling to ensure the method works on either textured or textureless surfaces.

One way to implement the gradient flow given by Eq. 6 is to derive the analytic gradient of g. But, there are several problems with the analytic gradient.

First, the visibility changes are not taken into account. While moving vertices it is possible that some parts of the surrounding triangles become occluded or visible (un-occluded), which is not taken into account by the analytic gradient. A second remark is that the formulas do not account for reflectance changes as the reflectance properties could only be computed after taking the step. Similar to the visibility case, moving a vertex results in changes in the shading. For these reasons we use a numerical computation for the gradient.

Numerical Gradient. The gradient of the similarity function along the direction of the normal, $\nabla g \cdot \mathbf{n}$, is computed numerically using central differences. Letting $g_{\mathbf{v}+}$ (resp. $g_{\mathbf{v}-}$) be the error computed on the mesh when a vertex $\mathbf{v}$ is replaced with $\mathbf{v}^+ = \mathbf{v} + \mathbf{n}\Delta n$ (resp. $\mathbf{v}^- = \mathbf{v} - \mathbf{n}\Delta n$), then:

$$\nabla g \cdot \mathbf{n} \approx \frac{g_{\mathbf{v}+} - g_{\mathbf{v}-}}{2\Delta n}$$

where $\Delta n = c_\Delta \sigma_{mesh}$ and $c_\Delta \in (0, 1]$, to ensure that the derivative step size is bounded by the minimum edge length (a tuning parameter σ_{mesh} explained in Section 4.1).

In order to compute the gradient efficiently, without displacing each vertex individually and computing the error over the entire mesh, we compute the gradient for a set of vertices simultaneously [18]. The idea is to partition the mesh into disjoint sets of vertices such that moving a vertex from a set does not influence the error for the rest of the vertices in that set. Ignoring visibility issues, displacing a vertex $\mathbf{v}$ affects all triangles within distance 2 from $\mathbf{v}$. Therefore, the gradient computation for a vertex $\mathbf{v}$ must do the reflectance fitting and error computation for these affected triangles. This means that we can displace other vertices at the same time as long as they do not both affect the same triangles.

3   Reflectance Fitting

As previously mentioned, we assume that the reflectance function is implied by the shape and imaging conditions. We experimented with two parametric reflectance models briefly introduced in Section 2.2 : Lambertian for diffuse and Phong for specular surfaces. We describe here how we practically recover the reflectance parameters from a set of images given a shape S, illumination conditions L_i and calibration parameters P_i.

3.1   Lambertian Reflectance

Lambertian reflectance has only one parameter per point $\mathbf{x}$ (the albedo $k_{d,\mathbf{x}}$). The albedo for each point $\mathbf{x}$ on the mesh with normal $\mathbf{n}$ is fit to the image observations for the current shape by minimizing

$$g_{lamb}(\mathbf{x}, \mathbf{n}) = \sum_i \langle \mathbf{n}, \mathbf{o}_i \rangle V'(\mathbf{x}, P_i) \left(I_i(\Pi(P_i\mathbf{x})) - (\langle \mathbf{n}, \mathbf{l}_i \rangle l_i + a_i)k_{d,\mathbf{x}} \right)^2 \quad (8)$$

which has a simple closed form solution using least squares.

3.2   Specular Reflectance

The parameters of the specular reflectance can be estimated given a set of input images, an object surface, and illumination information, by minimizing the similarity measure (Eq. 2). For a low parameter BRDF model, as the Phong model, given enough observations, the parameters can be estimated efficiently using an indirect iterated linear approach [19] or by a more direct non-linear method [20].

In practice, with only a limited number of input images, it is not always possible to fit a full reflectance model at each surface point. Instead of fitting the full model at each surface point, we chose to use an interpolation method that first attempts to fit the Phong model to the observations at each point. A reliable fitting is only possible when a point has several observations with a small angle between the surface normal and bisector of viewing and illumination direction. If there are not enough observations, the specular parameters will not be estimated correctly, leaving only a correctly fit Lambertian model. These points are assigned the specular parameters of a point where the specular fitting was successful. This assignment is based on the diffuse color of the point.

3.3   Filtering Specular Highlights

In practice, it is inefficient to fit a full reflectance model to each surface point during the optimization. Instead of fitting the full reflectance model, we choose to filter out the specular highlights during the optimization and perform the shape refinement only for diffuse observations.

It is known that specular highlights occur at points having a large $\langle \mathbf{n}, \mathbf{h}_i \rangle$. As a consequence, one approach is to give smaller weights (in the h function) to those observations [21]. But, for a surface estimation method it is not the best approach as it relies on the current estimate of $\mathbf{n}$. Another approach, and the one used in this work, is to use the fact that specular highlights typically cause a bright image observation. Therefore, a fraction of the samples having the brightest intensity (typically 1/3) are excluded from the computation of the albedo and the g measure for a point. This type of filtering is essentially another binary function, like the visibility function V.

4   System and Implementation Details

Recall that our formulation of the shape refinement problem requires calibrated input images, a calibrated light source, and an initial shape. We use a turntable based capture setup as an easy way to capture many views of an object, while automatically providing light variation, and allowing for an initial shape to be computed from the object's silhouette.

Our particular capture setup consists of a single camera viewing an object rotating on a turntable (see Fig. 3). Each set of images observes a full rotation of the object but has a different light position. In practice, the elevation of the light is varied between the two sets of images, and the light is positioned in a

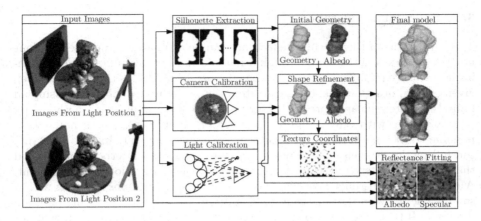

Fig. 3. Overview of the system used to scan objects

manner to avoid cast shadows (i.e., the source is placed close to the camera, implying that the camera also changes between the two sets of images).

The camera position is obtained through the automatic detection of a calibration pattern that is similar to the one used by Baumberg et al. [22]. A regular desk lamp is used as the light source and provides the majority of the illumination. The object rotates in front of a solid colored background, and a PCA based color segmentation is used to extract a set of silhouette images, which are used with shape from silhouette (SFS) to provide an initial shape.

The light source position and color are calibrated using a single glossy white sphere, which rotates along with the object on the turntable. Our approach is similar to other approaches that use a set of metallic spheres to calibrate a light source (e.g., [23]). The image of the specular highlight on the sphere in several views is used to triangulate the position of the source. As we used a white sphere, the non-specular pixels of the sphere are used to calibrate the light source color.

In order to make the recovered model useful in computer graphics applications, the reflectance model is represented in texture maps. As a prerequisite, we first need to obtain texture coordinates for the refined model. For this task, we have implemented a method similar to that of Lévy et al. [24].

4.1   Overview of the Shape Refinement Algorithm

The two components of the refinement in Eq. 6 are the gradient of the cost function and the regularizing component. The gradient is approximated per vertex using central differences, which was discussed in Section 2.4. The driving force behind the regularizing term is the mean curvature on the object, κ, which can be effectively approximated using a paraboloid method [25]. For a particular vertex, the mean curvature is computed by first finding the transformation taking the vertex to the origin and aligning its normal with the positive z axis. This transformation is applied to the neighboring vertices, and a paraboloid,

$z = ax^2 + bxy + cy^2$, is then fit to the transformed points. The mean curvature at the vertex is $\kappa = a + c$.

To handle topological changes in the mesh, we use the method proposed by Lachaud and Montanvert [26]. The mesh has a consistent global resolution, where edge lengths are confined to be within a certain range, i.e., if e is an edge in the mesh then $\sigma_{mesh} \leq \|e\| \leq 2.5\sigma_{mesh}$. A simple remesh operation ensures that the edges are indeed within this range and also performs the necessary operations related to topology changes. The global resolution of the mesh can be adjusted by altering this edge length parameter, σ_{mesh}.

The refinement starts with a low resolution mesh (i.e., large σ_{mesh}) and the corresponding low resolution images in a Gaussian pyramid. When the progress at a particular mesh resolution slows, the mesh resolution (and possibly the corresponding resolution in the Gaussian pyramid) is increased. This multi-resolution approach improves convergence, as there are fewer vertices (i.e., degrees of freedom), and enables the mesh to recover larger concavities.

5 Experiments

We have performed several experiments on synthetic and real image sequences to demonstrate the effectiveness of the method described in this paper. For the real sequences, the images were captured with either a consumer Canon Powershot A85 digital camera or a Point Grey Research Scorpion firewire camera. We used roughly 6 mesh resolutions during the refinement, and the total time for refinement was typically between 20 minutes and 1 hour. The captures contained roughly 60 input images and we found that using $n_{cameras} = 12$ simultaneous images provided sufficient results for many of the sequences. In the final stages of the refinement this parameter was increased to 24.

The first experiment demonstrates the refinement of an object that a standard correlation based method would have problems with: a 3D printout of the Stanford bunny model with uniform Lambertian reflectance. An initial shape obtained from SFS is a good approximation to the bunny, but several indentations near the legs of the bunny are not recovered (Fig. 4). These indentations are recovered by our method as illustrated by comparing the distance from the ground truth surface to the initial shape and the refined model (Fig. 5).

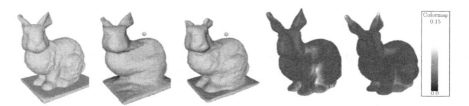

Fig. 4. From left to right a ground truth rendering, the recovered shape from SFS, and the refined model

Fig. 5. A portrayal of the distance from the ground truth object to the SFS model (left) and the refined model

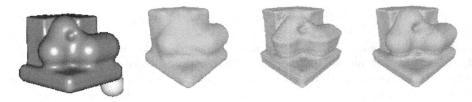

Fig. 6. From left to right, an input image of a synthetic specular object, the reconstruction from SFS, the reconstruction without specular filtering, and the reconstruction with specular filtering

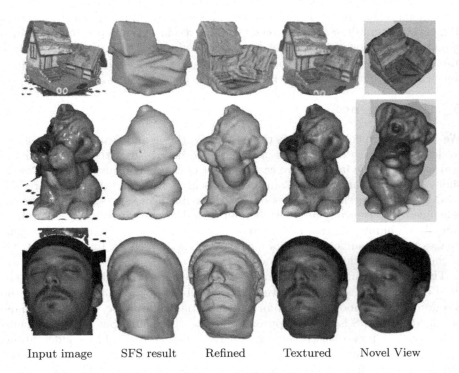

Input image   SFS result   Refined   Textured   Novel View

Fig. 7. Several reconstructed objects: a model house, a sad dog, and a human head

A second experiment, designed to test the effectiveness of the specular filtering, was performed on a synthetic object. The object has several concavities that were not reconstructed by the initial SFS shape (Fig. 6). The reconstruction obtained without specular filtering has artifacts. The most noticeable artifact is a sharp crease where the specularity was observed (second from the right of Fig. 6). On the other hand, the refinement that used specular filtering successfully recovered the indentations.

We have also tested the method on several real objects with both textured and glossy surfaces (Fig. 7). Our method was capable of recovering an accurate geometry on all the objects. Notice the large concavity that was recovered in the house sequence. The fitted specular parameters give realistic highlights on the reconstructed results (see the sad dog and human head results). Unfortunately, the reconstructed specular component was not always as sharp as the true specular component, which is noticeable on the sad dog object (a similar observation was made by Yu et al. [12]).

Fig. 8. An image of a real chess board (left), followed by a novel rendering of the captured models combined into a chess game

Our high quality results are easily integrated into realistic computer graphics applications. To illustrate this, we have captured several real models of a chess game and combined them into a computer chess game (Fig. 8).

6   Discussion

We have presented a variational method that alternatively reconstructs shape and general reflectance from calibrated images under known light. The surface evolution is implemented on a deformable mesh at multiple resolutions. We have demonstrated the usefulness of the proposed method on controlled sequences, where an object was rotated relative to a light source. The results are quite accurate, proving that the method is able to reconstruct a variety of objects.

The capture setup used in this work provides an efficient way to capture a 3D model of an object, but currently we need to be able to rotate this object in front of the camera. As future work, we would like to extend our method to work on objects where this form of light variation cannot be obtained. For small outdoor statues, it may be sufficient to use the flash on the camera, or capture images on a sunny day at different times to obtain the light variation on the object. A less restrictive method would be required for larger objects (e.g., buildings).

Other future directions include finding a more efficient way to utilize the information in specular highlights instead of filtering them out and to compare the advantages of a level set implementation. We would also like to have some guarantee that the recovered surface is at (or at least near) a global minimum of the functional.

References

1. Scharstein, D., Szeliski, R.: A taxonomy and evaluation of dense two-frame stereo correspondence algorithms. Int. J. Comput. Vision **47** (2002) 7–42
2. Faugeras, O., Keriven, R.: Variational principles, surface evolution, pde's, level set methods and the stereo problem. IEEE Trans. Image Processing **7** (1998) 336–344
3. Robert, L., Deriche, R.: Dense depth map reconstruction: A minimization and regularization approach which preserves discontinuities. In: ECCV '96. (1996) 439–451
4. Yang, R., Pollefeys, M., Welch, G.: Dealing with textureless regions and specular highlights - a pregressive space carving scheme using a novel photo-consistency measure. In: ICCV. (2003)
5. Esteban, C.H., Schmitt, F.: Silhouette and stereo fusion for 3d object modeling. Computer Vision and Image Understanding **96** (2004) 367–392
6. Fua, P., Leclerc, Y.: Object-centered surface reconstruction: combining multi-image stereo shading. In: Image Understanding Workshop. (1993) 1097–1120
7. Jin, H., Yezzi, A., Soatto, S.: Stereoscopic shading: Integrating shape cues in a variational framework. In: CVPR. (2000) 169–176
8. Zhang, L., Curless, B., Hertzmann, A., Seitz, S.M.: Shape and motion under varying illumination: Unifying structure from motion, photometric stereo, and multiview stereo. In: ICCV. (2003)
9. Weber, M., Blake, A., Cipolla, R.: Towards a complete dense geometric and photometric reconstruction under varying pose and illumination. In: BMVC. (2002)
10. Yu, T., Xu, N., Ahuja, N.: Shape and view independent reflectance map from multiple views. In: ECCV. (2004)
11. Jin, H., Soatto, S., Yezzi, A.: Multi-view stereo reconstruction of dense shape and complex appearance. IJCV **63** (2005) 175–189
12. Yu, T., Xu, N., Ahuja, N.: Recovering shape and reflectance model of non-lambertian objects from multiple views. In: CVPR. (2004)
13. Debevec, P.E., Malik, J.: Recovering high dynamic range radiance maps from photographs. In: Siggraph. (1997)
14. Sethian, J.: Level Set Methods. Cambridge University Press (1996)
15. Duan, Y., Yang, L., Qin, H., Samaras., D.: Shape reconstruction from 3d and 2d data using pde-based deformable surfaces. In: ECCV. (2004)
16. Caselles, V., Kimmel, R., Sapiro, G., Sbert, C.: Minimal surfaces based object segmentation. PAMI **19** (1997) 394–398
17. Zhang, L., Seitz, S.: Image-based multiresolution modeling by surface deformation. Technical Report CMU-RI-TR-00-07, Carnegie Mellon University (2000)
18. Zach, C., Klaus, A., Hadwiger, M., Karner, K.: Accurate dense stereo reconstruction using graphics hardware. In: Eurographics 2003. (2003) 227–234
19. Ikeuchi, K., Sato, K.: Determining reflectance properties of an object using range and brightness images. PAMI **13** (1991) 1139–1153
20. Lafortune, E.P., Foo, S.C., Torrance, K.E., Greenberg, D.P.: Non-linear approximation of reflectance functions. In: SIGGRAPH. (1997)
21. Marschner, S.R.: Inverse rendering for computer graphics. PhD thesis, Cornell University (1998)
22. Baumberg, A., Lyons, A., Taylor, R.: 3D S.O.M. - a commercial software solution to 3d scanning. In: Vision, Video, and Graphics (VVG'03). (2003) 41–48

23. Lensch, H.P.A., Goesele, M., Kautz, J., Heidrich, W., Seidel, H.P.: Image-based reconstruction of spatially varying materials. In: Eurographics Workshop on Rendering Techniques. (2001) 103–114
24. Lévy, B., Petitjean, S., Ray, N., Maillot, J.: Least squares conformal maps for automatic texture atlas generation. In: SIGGRAPH '02. (2002) 362–371
25. Surazhsky, T., Magid, E., Soldea, O., Elber, G., Rivlin, E.: A comparison of gaussian and mean curvatures triangular meshes. In: ICRA '03. (2003) 1021–1026
26. Lachaud, J.O., Montanvert, A.: Deformable meshes with automated topology changes for coarse-to-fine 3D surface extraction. Medical Image Analysis **3** (1999) 187–207

Specularity Removal in Images and Videos: A PDE Approach

Satya P. Mallick[1], Todd Zickler[2], Peter N. Belhumeur[3], and David J. Kriegman[1]

[1] Computer Science and Engineering, University of California at San Diego, CA 92093
[2] Engineering and Applied Sciences, Harvard University, Cambridge, MA 02138
[3] Computer Science, Columbia University, New York, NY 10027

Abstract. We present a unified framework for separating specular and diffuse reflection components in images and videos of textured scenes. This can be used for specularity removal and for independently processing, filtering, and recombining the two components. Beginning with a partial separation provided by an illumination-dependent color space, the challenge is to complete the separation using spatio-temporal information. This is accomplished by evolving a partial differential equation (PDE) that iteratively erodes the specular component at each pixel. A family of PDEs appropriate for differing image sources (still images vs. videos), differing prior information (e.g., highly vs. lightly textured scenes), or differing prior computations (e.g., optical flow) is introduced. In contrast to many other methods, explicit segmentation and/or manual intervention are not required. We present results on high-quality images and video acquired in the laboratory in addition to images taken from the Internet. Results on the latter demonstrate robustness to low dynamic range, JPEG artifacts, and lack of knowledge of illuminant color. Empirical comparison to physical removal of specularities using polarization is provided. Finally, an application termed *dichromatic editing* is presented in which the diffuse and the specular components are processed independently to produce a variety of visual effects.

1 Introduction

The reflectance of a wide variety of materials (including plastics, plant leaves, cloth, wood and human skin) can be described as a linear combination of specular and diffuse components. When this description is accurate, there are benefits to decomposing an image in this way. The diffuse reflectance component is often well-described by the Lambertian model, and by isolating this component, powerful Lambertian-based tools for tracking, reconstruction and recognition can be applied more successfully to real-world, non-Lambertian scenes. There is also evidence that specular reflectance plays a role in human perception, and there is a set of computer vision algorithms that rely solely on this component (e.g., [2, 5, 11]). Finally, in addition to image-analysis applications, specular/diffuse separation is important in image-based 3-D modeling, where (specular-free) diffuse texture maps are often desired, and in photo-editing, where the two components can be independently processed and recombined.

This paper addresses the separation of reflection components in images of general, possibly textured, scenes. We restrict our attention to surfaces that are well-represented by Shafer's dichromatic reflectance model [15], in which the spectral distribution of

A. Leonardis, H. Bischof, and A. Pinz (Eds.): ECCV 2006, Part I, LNCS 3951, pp. 550–563, 2006.

the specular component is similar to that of the illuminant while that of the diffuse component depends heavily on the material properties of the surface. The dichromatic model suggests the possibility of decomposing an image into its specular and diffuse components based on color information. Beginning with a single three-channel RGB image, the objective is to recover an RGB "diffuse image" and a monochromatic specular layer. This is an ill-posed problem, even when the illuminant color is known, and most existing methods operate by aggregating color information spatially across the image plane. We can differentiate between methods that are *global* and *local* in nature[1].

Klinker et al. [6] show that when the diffuse color is the same at each point on an object's surface, the color histogram of its image forms a T-shaped distribution, with the diffuse and specular pixels forming linear clusters. They use this information to estimate a single "global" diffuse color, and in principle, this approach can be extended to cases in which an image is segmented into several regions of homogeneous diffuse color. Results can be improved by exploiting knowledge of the illuminant color through transformations of color space [1, 18], but these methods also require an explicit segmentation of the scene into large regions of constant diffuse color. In recent work, R. Tan and Ikeuchi [16] avoid explicit segmentation by representing all of the diffuse colors in a scene by a global, low-dimensional, linear basis.

In addition to the global approaches mentioned above, there has been considerable interest in separating reflection components through purely local interactions. The advantage of this approach is that it admits highly textured scenes that do not contain piecewise constant diffuse colors. In most local methods, the illuminant color is assumed to be known *a priori*, which is not a severe restriction since it can often be estimated using established (global) methods (e.g., [7]). R. Tan and Ikeuchi [17] iteratively reduce the specular component of a pixel by considering one of its neighbors that putatively has a related diffuse component. P. Tan et al. [14] allow a user to specify a closed curve surrounding a specular region and then minimize an objective function based on local variations in diffuse chromaticity and specular intensity. One of the earliest local methods is that of Nayar et al. [10], which uses polarization as an additional cue to enable the recovery a spatially-varying source color.

The goal of this paper is to formalize the notion of "local interactions" for specular/diffuse separation, and thereby develop a general framework for achieving separation through local interactions in both images and videos. Unlike previous approaches[2], the method is developed in the continuous domain, with local interactions governed by partial differential equations (PDEs). This process selectively shares color information between nearby image points through multi-scale erosion [3] with structuring sets that vary over the image plane. We derive a family of PDEs that are appropriate for differing conditions, including images of both textured and untextured surfaces. We also show

---

[1] In addition to the color-based methods discussed here, there are a number of other methods that rely on multiple images and/or additional cues, such as variable lighting, variable polarization, and parametric reflectance. Readers are referred to [17] for a description of these methods.

[2] A notable exception is the work of P. Tan et al. [14], who use a *variational* PDE to separate manually-segmented highlight regions. Our work differs in that it uses *morphological* PDEs enabling separation without the need for manual segmentation.

how this framework extends naturally to videos, where motion information is available as an additional cue.

On the practical front, this paper presents results on high-quality images acquired in the laboratory (Fig. 3a, 3b), and shows that they compare favorably to ground-truth determined using cross polarization (Fig. 4). Results on 8-bit images downloaded from the Internet (Fig. 3d, 3e) suggest robustness to artifacts caused by low dynamic range, JPEG compression, and lack of knowledge of the illuminant color. The paper also provides results on videos (Fig. 5) for which explicit optical flow is not necessarily available. Finally, an application – *dichromatic editing* – is presented (Fig. 6).

2   Background and Notation

The dichromatic model of reflectance is a common special case of the bidirectional reflectance distribution function (BRDF) model, and it was originally developed by Shafer [15] for dielectrics. According to this model, the BRDF can be decomposed into two additive components: the interface (specular) reflectance and the body (diffuse) reflectance. The model assumes that each component can be factored into a univariate function of wavelength and a multivariate function of imaging geometry, and that the index of refraction of the surface is constant over the visible spectrum. These assumptions lead to the following expression for the BRDF of a dichromatic surface:

$$f(\lambda, \Theta) = g_d(\lambda)f_d + f_s(\Theta), \tag{1}$$

where λ is the wavelength of light and $\Theta = (\theta_i, \phi_i, \theta_r, \phi_r)$ parameterizes the directions of incoming irradiance and outgoing radiance. The function g_d is referred to as the *spectral reflectance* and is an intrinsic property of the material. The functions f_d (constant for Lambertian surfaces) and f_s are the diffuse and specular BRDFs, respectively. Taking into account the spectral power distribution of a light source $L(\lambda)$ and a camera sensitivity function $C_k(\lambda)$, the image formation equation for a surface element with surface normal $\hat{n}$, illuminated by a light source with direction $\hat{l}$ is written

$$I_k = (D_k f_d + S_k f_s(\Theta))\, \hat{n} \cdot \hat{l}, \tag{2}$$

$$\text{where } D_k = \int C_k(\lambda)L(\lambda)g_d(\lambda)d\lambda \text{ and } S_k = \int C_k(\lambda)L(\lambda)d\lambda.$$

An RGB color vector $\mathbf{I} = [I_1, I_2, I_3]^\top$ from a typical camera consists of three such measurements, each with a different sensitivity function with support in the visible spectrum. Note that S_k represents the effective source strength as measured by the kth sensor channel and is independent of the surface being observed. Similarly, D_k is the effective albedo in the kth channel. For notational simplicity, we define $\mathbf{S} = [S_1, S_2, S_3]^\top$ (with a corresponding definition for $\mathbf{D}$), and since scale can be absorbed by f_d and f_s, we assume $\|\mathbf{D}\| = \|\mathbf{S}\| = 1$.

3   Illuminant-Dependent Color Spaces

In the last few years there has been a burst of activity in defining color space transformations that exploit knowledge of the illuminant color to provide more direct access to the diffuse information in an image. While motivated by different applications, the transformations discussed here all share the same idea of linearly combining the three color channels of an RGB image to obtain one or two "diffuse channels".

R. Tan and Ikeuchi [17] obtain a one-channel diffuse image through the transformation

$$I_d = \frac{3 \max_k (I_k/S_k) - \sum_k (I_k/S_k)}{3\tilde{\lambda} - 1}, \tag{3}$$

where $k \in \{1, 2, 3\}$, and the bounded quantity $1/3 < \tilde{\lambda} \le 1$ is chosen arbitrarily. This transformation yields a positive monochromatic diffuse image, which can be seen by expanding Eq. 3 using Eq. 2 and assuming (for argument's sake) that $I_1/S_1 > I_2/S_2$, I_3/S_3. In this case,

$$I_d = \frac{2I_1/S_1 - I_2/S_2 - I_3/S_3}{3\tilde{\lambda} - 1} = \frac{(2D_1/S_1 - D_2/S_2 - D_3/S_3) f_d \hat{\mathbf{n}} \cdot \hat{\mathbf{l}}}{3\tilde{\lambda} - 1}. \tag{4}$$

Since this expression is independent of f_s and is directly related to $\hat{\mathbf{n}} \cdot \hat{\mathbf{l}}$, the positive image I_d is specular-free and depends directly on diffuse shading information.

An alternative transformation is proposed by Park [12], who isolates *two* predominantly diffuse channels while retaining a similarity to HSI color space. The transformation is composed of a linear transformation $\mathbf{L}_p$ and rotation $\mathbf{R}_p$, and is written

$$\mathbf{I}_p = \mathbf{R}_p \mathbf{L}_p \mathbf{I}, \quad \text{with} \quad \mathbf{R}_p \mathbf{L}_p \mathbf{S} = [\,0\;0\;2\,]^\top. \tag{5}$$

The matrices $\mathbf{R}_p$ and $\mathbf{L}_p$ are chosen such that the third color axis is aligned with the illumination color. As a result, that channel contains the majority of the specular component, leaving the other two channels to be predominantly diffuse.

A third transformation, proposed by Mallick et al. [8], defines a color space referred to as *SUV color space*. The transformation is written

$$\mathbf{I}_{SUV} = \mathbf{R} \mathbf{I}, \quad \text{with} \quad \mathbf{R} \mathbf{S} = [\,1\;0\;0\,]^\top. \tag{6}$$

Similar to Park's transformation, one of the transformed axes in SUV space is aligned with the illuminant color. Unlike Park's transformation, however, this channel includes *the complete* specular component, leaving the remaining two channels to be *purely diffuse*. To see this, we expand the expression for $\mathbf{I}_{SUV}$ using Eqs. 2 and 6 to obtain

$$\mathbf{I}_{SUV} = \left(\bar{\mathbf{D}} f_d + \bar{\mathbf{S}} f_s(\Theta) \right) \hat{\mathbf{n}} \cdot \hat{\mathbf{l}}, \tag{7}$$

where $\bar{\mathbf{D}} = \mathbf{R}\mathbf{D}$ and $\bar{\mathbf{S}} = \mathbf{R}\mathbf{S} = [1,\, 0,\, 0]^\top$. Letting $\mathbf{r}_i^\top$ denote the ith row of $\mathbf{R}$, the diffuse UV channels are

$$I_U = \mathbf{r}_2^\top \mathbf{D} f_d \hat{\mathbf{n}} \cdot \hat{\mathbf{l}}, \qquad I_V = \mathbf{r}_3^\top \mathbf{D} f_d \hat{\mathbf{n}} \cdot \hat{\mathbf{l}}, \tag{8}$$

which depend only on diffuse-shading and are specular-free. The S-channel is given by

$$I_S = \mathbf{r}_1^\top \mathbf{D} f_d \hat{\mathbf{n}} \cdot \hat{\mathbf{l}} + f_s(\Theta) \hat{\mathbf{n}} \cdot \hat{\mathbf{l}}. \qquad (9)$$

It contains all of the specular component in addition to an unknown diffuse component.

Each of the three transformations described in this section exploits knowledge of the illuminant to provide a partial dichromatic separation, which is an important step toward our stated goal. Of the three, the SUV color space defined in Eq. 6 is the best-suited for our purpose. Unlike Eq. 3, it is a linear transformation that yields two "diffuse" channels, and unlike Eq. 5, these two "diffuse" channels are in fact completely free of specularity. As described in the next section, these properties lead to a generalized notion of hue that can be used as a guide for local interactions, enabling the computation of a complete specular/diffuse separation even in cases of significant diffuse texture.

4 Specularity Removal and Differential Morphology

This section derives a family of non-linear PDEs for completing the partial specular/diffuse separation provided by a transformation to SUV color space. Intuitively, these PDEs define a series of local interactions in which color information is shared along curves (or surfaces) of constant "hue."

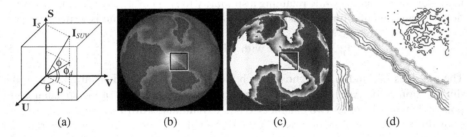

(a)   (b)   (c)   (d)

Fig. 1. (a) A color in the SUV color space is parameterized by (ρ, θ, ϕ). ρ and θ are independent of specularity, and θ generalizes the notion of "hue" for arbitrarily colored illuminants. The problem of removing specularity is reduced to finding ϕ_d, the diffuse part of ϕ. (b) A rendered RGB image of a textured sphere. (c) The value of θ at each pixel of the image. Notice that θ is constant in regions of constant diffuse color and is independent of specularity as well as shading. (d) Blown-up view of the iso-contours of θ in the rectangular region indicated in (b) and (c). White indicates regions of constant θ. In textured images, erosion of the specular component occurs along iso-contours of θ, which ensures that diffuse texture is preserved while the specularity is removed.

We begin by re-parameterizing SUV color space using a combination of cylindrical and spherical coordinates. As depicted in Fig. 1, suppressing the spatial dependence for notational simplicity, we define

$$\rho = \sqrt{I_U^2 + I_V^2}, \quad \theta = \tan^{-1}\left(\frac{I_U}{I_V}\right), \quad \phi = \tan^{-1}\left(\frac{I_S}{\rho}\right). \qquad (10)$$

This parameterization has the following properties:

1. Since they depend only on the diffuse UV channels, both ρ and θ are independent of the specular reflectance component.
2. Since the illuminant color is aligned with the S-axis, the angle θ parameterizes the pencil of dichromatic planes in an image. We refer to θ as *generalized hue*, since it reduces to the standard definition of hue in the special case of a white illuminant. It depends on the direction of the diffuse color vector but not the magnitude of the diffuse component.
3. ρ represents diffuse shading, since it is directly related to $\hat{\mathbf{n}} \cdot \hat{\mathbf{l}}$, and therefore, the magnitude of the diffuse component.
4. ϕ is a linear combination of specular and diffuse components, and we can write $\phi = \phi_s + \phi_d$, where ϕ_s and ϕ_d are the specular and diffuse contributions to ϕ.

According to these properties, the problem of computing a specular/diffuse separation is reduced to one of estimating $\phi_d(x, y)$, the diffuse contribution to ϕ at each image point. Once the scalar function $\phi_d(x, y)$ is known, the RGB diffuse component follow directly from inverting the transformations in Eqs. 10 and 6, with ϕ replaced by ϕ_d.

4.1 Multi-scale Erosion

Our goal is to compute a specular/diffuse separation through estimation of the scalar function $\phi_d(x, y)$ through purely local interactions. This section describes how this can be accomplished by evolving a PDE that iteratively "erodes" the specular contribution to ϕ and converges to an estimate of ϕ_d at each point. The erosion process is guided locally by the diffuse color information provided by ρ and θ, and is formulated in the continuous domain using one of a family of non-linear PDEs that define multi-scale erosion [3]. The theory presented in this section is related to the formulation of multi-scale erosion presented by Brockett and Maragos [3].

The multi-scale erosion $\varepsilon(\mathbf{x}, t)$ of a bivariate function $f \colon \mathbb{R}^2 \to \mathbb{R}$ by structuring set $B \subseteq \mathbb{R}^2$ at scale t is defined as

$$\varepsilon(\mathbf{x}, t) = (f \ominus tB)(\mathbf{x}) \triangleq \inf\{f(\mathbf{x} + \Delta\mathbf{x}) \colon \Delta\mathbf{x} \in tB\} \,,$$

where the set B is compact, and $tB \triangleq \{tb : b \in B\}$. Intuitively, $\varepsilon(\mathbf{x}, t)$ evaluated at a particular value of t corresponds to an erosion of the function $f(\mathbf{x})$, where the function value at $\mathbf{x} = (x, y)$ is replaced by the minimum of all function values in the "neighborhood" tB, which is a scaled replica of structuring set B. A multi-scale erosion is computed by considering the PDE

$$\frac{\partial \varepsilon}{\partial t}(\mathbf{x}, t) = \lim_{\Delta t \to 0} \frac{\varepsilon(\mathbf{x}, t + \Delta t) - \varepsilon(\mathbf{x}, t)}{\Delta t}. \tag{11}$$

When the structuring set is both compact and convex, the multi-scale erosion has a semigroup structure, allowing one to write [3]

$$\frac{\partial \varepsilon}{\partial t}(\mathbf{x}, t) = \lim_{\Delta t \to 0} \frac{\inf\{\nabla \varepsilon^\top \Delta\mathbf{x} : \Delta\mathbf{x} \in \Delta t B\}}{\Delta t}, \tag{12}$$

	Textureless	Texture 1	Texture 2	Video 1	Video 2
Set	2D Disk	2D Line	2D Ellipse	3D Disk	3D Line
Direction	Isotropic	Iso-cont. of θ	Iso-cont. of θ	Iso-surf. of θ	Optic Flow
$\mathbf{M}$	$\mathbf{I}_{2\times2}$	$\mathbf{I}_{2\times2} - \nabla\hat{\theta}\,\nabla\hat{\theta}^\top$	$\mathbf{A}\mathbf{A}^\top$	$\mathbf{I}_{3\times3} - \nabla\hat{\theta}\nabla\hat{\theta}^\top$	$\mathbf{F}\mathbf{F}^\top/\|\mathbf{F}\|^2$

Fig. 2. Summary of five cases from left to right: (1) image with uniform diffuse color, (2-3) textured image, (4) video, and (5) video with known optical flow. Rows depict: the structuring set used, the direction/surface of erosion, and the matrix $\mathbf{M}$ in the multi-scale erosion equation (Eq. 14.) $\mathbf{I}_{n\times n}$ is the identity matrix, and $\nabla\hat{\theta}$, $\mathbf{A}$ and $\mathbf{F}$ are as defined in Sec. 4.

where $\nabla\varepsilon$ is the two-dimensional spatial gradient of ε evaluated at t. Finally, as shown in [3], in the special case where B is disk-shaped, Eq. 12 becomes

$$\varepsilon_t = -\|\nabla\varepsilon\|. \tag{13}$$

Eq. 13 is an example of a PDE that can be used for specular/diffuse separation, albeit in the special case when the scene consists of a texture-less surface with uniform diffuse color. To see this, suppose we are given an input image with corresponding functions $\rho(\mathbf{x})$, $\theta(\mathbf{x})$ and $\phi(\mathbf{x})$, and suppose we define $\varepsilon(\mathbf{x},0) = \phi(\mathbf{x})$. The solution to Eq. 13 evaluated at scale t corresponds to the erosion of ϕ by a disk-shaped structuring set, meaning that the value of ϕ at each image point is replaced by the minimum value within a disk-shaped neighborhood of radius t. Since $\phi_d(\mathbf{x}) \le \phi(\mathbf{x})$, it follows that when the image contains at least one image point that is purely diffuse (that is, for which $\phi_s = 0$) then $\varepsilon(\mathbf{x},t)$ evaluated at t will converge to $\phi_d(\mathbf{x})$ as t is made sufficiently large. In the next three sub-sections, we develop more sophisticated PDEs for cases of multiple regions of uniform diffuse color, complex diffuse texture, and video. In all of these, the basic idea is the same: the value of ϕ_d at each image point is estimated by eroding the initial function ϕ. By changing the structuring set, however, the process can be controlled so that region boundaries and diffuse texture are preserved during the process. In particular, we show that the PDE governing the evolution of ϕ for three different cases – texture-less images, textured images, and video – can all be written as

$$\varepsilon_t = -g(\rho, \nabla\rho)\left(\nabla\varepsilon^\top\mathbf{M}\nabla\varepsilon\right)^{1/2}, \tag{14}$$

where $\mathbf{M}$ is a different matrix for each case. $g(\rho, \nabla\rho)$ is called the stopping function and is defined in the following section. Fig. 2 summarizes the cases we consider.

4.2 Texture-Less Surfaces: Isotropic Erosion

Eq. 13 describes a process in which the specular component of ϕ is eroded equally in all directions. This is desirable in cases of homogeneous diffuse color, but if regions of distinct color exist, there is a possibility that "color bleeding" may occur. To prevent this, we introduce a "stopping function" analogous to that used in anisotropic diffusion [13]. A stopping function is useful for attenuating the erosion process in two different cases

1. If a region of the surface is "white" (i.e., it reflects all wavelengths equally) or if the surface is the same color as the light source, the diffuse component of color cannot be isolated. Since $\rho = 0$ in this case, no diffuse color information is available, and erosion should be arrested.
2. Information about ϕ should not be shared across boundaries between regions of distinct color. Since these boundaries often coincide with large values of $\|\nabla\rho\|$, erosion should be attenuated when $\|\nabla\rho\|$ is large.

One possible stopping function that meets these guidelines is

$$g(\rho, \nabla\rho) = \left(\frac{1 - e^{-\rho}}{1 + e^{-\rho}}\right) \frac{e^{-(\|\nabla\rho\|-\tau)}}{1 + e^{-(\|\nabla\rho\|-\tau)}}, \tag{15}$$

where τ is a threshold on $\|\nabla\rho\|$, above which erosion is heavily attenuated. Incorporating this into Eq. 13 yields

$$\varepsilon_t = -g(\rho, \nabla\rho)\|\nabla\varepsilon\| = -g(\rho, \nabla\rho)\left(\nabla\varepsilon^\top \mathbf{I}_{2\times2}\nabla\varepsilon\right)^{1/2}. \tag{16}$$

The erosion process defined by this equation can be used for the specular/diffuse separation of images containing large regions of uniform diffuse color.

4.3 Textured Surfaces: Anisotropic Erosion

An example of a scene that does not contain regions of uniform diffuse color is shown in Fig. 1 (b). In this case, eroding the function ϕ isotropically would blur the diffuse texture. Instead, we need to erode ϕ anisotropically, only sharing information between neighboring image points for which ϕ_d is likely to be equal. Of course, we have no information about the diffuse color *a priori*, so it is impossible to know the correct neighborhood (if it even exists) with certainty. As depicted in Fig. 1 (c, d), since θ is independent of both specularity and shading information, the directions tangent to the iso-contours of $\theta(\mathbf{x})$ provide a good choice. In the absence of any additional information, they provide a good local predictor for the direction in which ϕ_d is constant.
We define

$$\nabla\hat{\theta} = \begin{cases} \nabla\theta/\|\nabla\theta\| & \|\nabla\theta\| > 0 \\ 0 & \|\nabla\theta\| = 0, \end{cases} \tag{17}$$

where $\nabla(\cdot)$ refers to the spatial gradient, and we denote the direction orthogonal to $\nabla\theta$ by $\mathbf{V}$.[3] The multi-scale erosion of ϕ with the spatially-varying, linear structuring sets $\mathbf{V}(\mathbf{x})$ is derived analogous to the isotropic (disk-shaped) case discussed previously.

$$\begin{aligned} \varepsilon_t &= \lim_{\Delta t\to 0} \frac{\inf\{\nabla\varepsilon^\top\Delta\mathbf{x} : \Delta\mathbf{x} \in \Delta t\mathbf{V}\}}{\Delta t} \\ &= \lim_{\Delta t\to 0} \frac{-\Delta t|\nabla\varepsilon^\top\mathbf{V}|}{\Delta t} = -|\nabla\varepsilon^\top\mathbf{V}|. \end{aligned} \tag{18}$$

---

[3] Since θ is periodic, a definition of distance is necessary for its gradient to be correctly computed. We define the distance between two angles θ_1 and θ_2 as $\min(|\theta_1 - \theta_2|, 2\pi - |\theta_1 - \theta_2|)$.

Using the fact that $\mathbf{V} = [\hat{\theta}_y \ -\hat{\theta}_x]^\top$ (or $[\hat{\theta}_y \ -\hat{\theta}_x]^\top$), and including the stopping function, we obtain

$$\varepsilon_t = -g(\rho, \nabla\rho) \left[\nabla\varepsilon^\top \left(\mathbf{I}_{2\times 2} - \nabla\hat{\theta}\nabla\hat{\theta}^\top \right) \nabla\varepsilon \right]^{1/2}. \tag{19}$$

Using similar arguments to that in the isotropic case, it can be shown that $\varepsilon(\mathbf{x}, t)$ evaluated at sufficiently large t will be equal to $\phi_d(\mathbf{x})$ (and will yield a correct specular/diffuse separation) if the iso-contour of θ passing through each point $\mathbf{x}$: 1) contains only points for which ϕ_d is constant; and 2) contains at least one point at which a purely diffuse observation ($\phi_s = 0$) is available. Note that in regions where the diffuse color is constant (i.e., $\nabla\hat{\theta} = [\,0\ \ 0\,]^\top$), this equation reduces to Eq. 16, and the erosion becomes isotropic as desired.

In practice, the transition from linear to disk-shaped structuring sets in Eq. 19 is controlled by a threshold on $\|\nabla\theta\|$. This discontinuous transition can be avoided by employing an elliptical structuring set with a minor axis aligned with the direction of $\nabla\theta$ and with an eccentricity that varies smoothly with $\|\nabla\theta\|$. To derive a PDE for the corresponding multi-scale erosion, we let E denote an elliptical structuring set, and we describe this set by the lengths of its major and minor axes (λ_1, λ_2) and the angle between its major axis and the x-axis (ψ). Points $\mathbf{x}$ on the boundary of E satisfy $\mathbf{x}^\top \mathbf{Q} \mathbf{x} = 1$ where $\mathbf{Q} = \mathcal{R}(-\psi)\boldsymbol{\Lambda}^{-2}\mathcal{R}(\psi)$, $\boldsymbol{\Lambda} = \mathrm{diag}(\lambda_1, \lambda_2)$ and $\mathcal{R}(\psi)$ is a clockwise rotation of the plane. As before, the multi-scale erosion defined by this set satisfies

$$\varepsilon_t = \lim_{\Delta t \to 0} \frac{\inf\{\nabla\varepsilon^\top \Delta\mathbf{x} : \Delta\mathbf{x} \in \Delta t E\}}{\Delta t}. \tag{20}$$

To simplify the right-hand side of this equation, we define the transformation $\mathbf{x} = \mathbf{A}\mathbf{x}'$, with $\mathbf{A} = \mathcal{R}(-\psi)\boldsymbol{\Lambda}\mathcal{R}(\psi)'$. The spatial gradient of ε with respect to $\mathbf{x}'$ is then given by the chain rule: $\nabla\varepsilon' = \mathbf{A}^\top\nabla\varepsilon$. The transformation $\mathbf{A}$ maps the set E to the unit disk (since $\mathbf{x}^\top \mathbf{Q} \mathbf{x} = \mathbf{x}^\top \mathbf{A}^\top \mathbf{Q} \mathbf{A} \mathbf{x} = \mathbf{x}'^\top \mathbf{x}' = 1$), and as a result, we can write $\inf\{\nabla\varepsilon^\top \Delta\mathbf{x} : \Delta\mathbf{x} \in \Delta t E\} = \inf\{\nabla\varepsilon'^\top \Delta\mathbf{x}' : \Delta\mathbf{x}' \in \Delta t B\}$. Substituting this into Eq. 20 and comparing with Eq. 13, we obtain $\varepsilon_t = -\|\nabla\varepsilon'\| = -\left(\nabla\varepsilon^\top \mathbf{A}\mathbf{A}^\top \nabla\varepsilon\right)^{1/2}$. Finally, the addition of the stopping function yields

$$\varepsilon_t = -g(\rho, \nabla\rho)\left(\nabla\varepsilon^\top \mathbf{A}\mathbf{A}^\top \nabla\varepsilon\right)^{1/2}. \tag{21}$$

4.4   Videos: Anisotropic Erosion in Three Dimensions

Thus far, we have dealt exclusively with still images, but the framework extends naturally to video, which can be treated as a 3D volume $\mathbf{I}(x, y, z)$ in which time is the third dimension (z). As in the case of textured images, the direction of $\nabla\theta$ is assumed to be a good local predictor for the direction (in 3D space-time) of maximum diffuse color change. We would like to preserve the component of $\nabla\phi$ along this direction during the erosion process, which is accomplished by restricting the erosion of ϕ to the iso-surfaces of θ. In the absence of additional information, there is no preferred direction within an iso-surface of θ, so a natural choice of structuring set is a circular disk contained within its tangent plane.

To compute the multi-scale erosion equation, we note that the structuring set described above consists of a disk (denoted C) whose surface normal is aligned with $\nabla\theta$. Thus, the maximum projection of $\nabla\phi$ onto the plane that contains this disk is given by $\left(\|\nabla\phi\|^2 - \|\nabla\hat{\theta}^\top \nabla\phi\|^2\right)^{1/2}$, and the evolution equation can be simply written as

$$\varepsilon_t = \lim_{\Delta t \to 0} \frac{\inf\{\nabla\varepsilon^\top \Delta\mathbf{x} : \Delta\mathbf{x} \in \Delta t C\}}{\Delta t} = \lim_{\Delta t \to 0} \frac{-\Delta t \left(\|\nabla\varepsilon\|^2 - \|\nabla\hat{\theta}^\top \nabla\varepsilon\|^2\right)^{1/2}}{\Delta t}$$

$$= -\left(\|\nabla\varepsilon\|^2 - \|\nabla\hat{\theta}^\top \nabla\varepsilon\|^2\right)^{1/2}, \text{ where } \nabla\varepsilon = [\,\varepsilon_x\ \varepsilon_y\ \varepsilon_z\,]^\top.$$

After some algebraic manipulations, and incorporating the stopping function, we obtain

$$\varepsilon_t = -g(\rho, \nabla\rho)\left[\nabla\varepsilon^\top(\mathbf{I}_{3\times 3} - \nabla\hat{\theta}\nabla\hat{\theta}^\top)\nabla\varepsilon\right]^{1/2}. \tag{22}$$

Note that the erosion equation for textured and texture-less surfaces are special cases of the erosion equation for videos.

As mentioned earlier, if some *a priori* information is known, better structuring sets can be designed. An interesting example is when optical flow estimates are available at each location in a video. We let $[\,u(x,y,z)\ v(x,y,z)\,]^\top$ represent the estimated optical flow at location (x,y,z) in the video, so that space-time points (x,y,z) and $(x+u, y+v, z+1)$ correspond to projections of the same surface element. It follows that ϕ_d can be estimated by eroding ϕ along the direction $\mathbf{F} = [u\ v\ 1]^\top$. Using the expression for erosion by a linear set derived in Eq. 19 we obtain

$$\varepsilon_t = -g(\rho, \nabla\rho)\left|\frac{\mathbf{F}^\top}{\|\mathbf{F}\|}\nabla\varepsilon\right| = -g(\rho, \nabla\rho)\left(\nabla\varepsilon^\top \frac{\mathbf{F}\mathbf{F}^\top}{\|\mathbf{F}\|^2}\nabla\varepsilon\right)^{1/2}. \tag{23}$$

5   Results

The methods were evaluated using images and videos acquired in the laboratory as well as those downloaded from the Internet. Using a known (or approximately known) illuminant color, each image is transformed into SUV space, and the functions ρ, θ and ϕ are computed. Specular/diffuse separation is achieved by numerically evolving the appropriate multi-scale erosion PDE with initial condition $\varepsilon(\mathbf{x}, 0) = \phi(\mathbf{x})$. The process is complete when the maximum change in ε is below a selected threshold, and this yields an estimate of $\phi_d(\mathbf{x})$, which completely defines the specular and diffuse components.

It is important to note that the non-linear PDEs governing erosion are defined at points where the partial derivatives exist. Even if this is satisfied by the initial data, however, at finite scales a multi-scale erosion generally develops discontinuities referred to as *shocks*. Shocks can be dealt with (as we do here) by replacing standard derivatives by morphological derivatives [3]. They can also be handled using viscosity solutions [4].

Fig. 3 (a, b) shows two 12-bit images[4] acquired in a controlled setting (with known illuminant color) along with the recovered specular and diffuse components. Both results

---

[4] All images in this section should be viewed on a monitor or high-quality color print. The images can be viewed at a higher resolution by zooming into the PDF document.

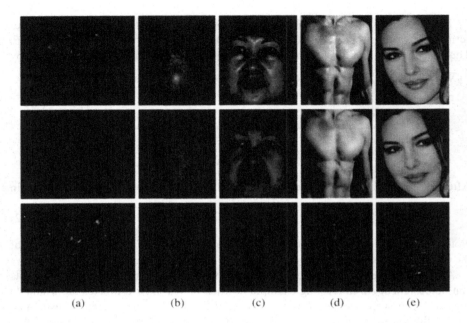

Fig. 3. Separation results for images. Top row: Input images. Middle row: Diffuse Component. Bottom row: Specular component. Equation 19 is used in all cases, since it naturally handles both textured and untextured surfaces. The 12-bit input images in (a, b) were acquired in the laboratory under known illuminant color. In (c), the illuminant color was not known and was assumed to be white. 8-bit JPEG images (d, e) were downloaded from the Internet, the illuminant was assumed to be white, and the gamma was assumed to be 2.2. Despite these sources of noise, diffuse and specular components are successfully recovered.

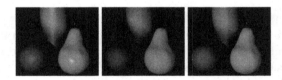

Fig. 4. Comparison to ground truth. Left: input image. Center: ground truth diffuse component obtained using linear polarizers. Right: diffuse component recovered using anisotropic multi-scale erosion.

were obtained using the anisotropic erosion defined in Eq. 19. The method correctly handles both regions of uniform color (e.g., the orange pepper Fig. 3 (a)) and regions with significant texture (e.g., the pear in Fig. 3 (b)). Looking closely at the pear, we notice that diffuse texture that is barely visible in the input image is revealed when the specularity is removed. Figure 3 (c) shows a 12-bit image of a human face in which the illuminant color was unknown and was assumed to be white. Again, diffuse texture is preserved, while the specular component is reduced. Pixels on the forehead between the eyebrows are saturated, and therefore violate the dichromatic model. The stopping

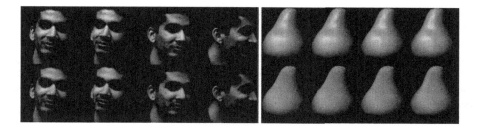

Fig. 5. Separation results for (12-bit) video. Top row: Frames from input sequences. Bottom row: Diffuse component recovered using Eq. 22. (Complete videos accompany this paper.)

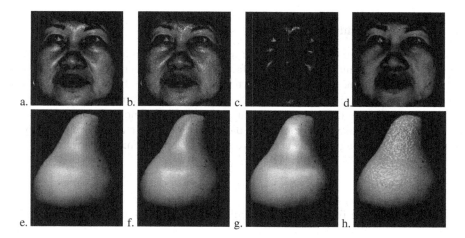

Fig. 6. Dichromatic editing examples. In each case a visual effect is simulated by independent processing of the recovered specular and diffuse components. (a) Input image. (b) Wetness effect by sharpening the specular component. (c) Skin color change by varying the intensity of the diffuse component. (d) Effect of make-up by smoothing the diffuse component and removing the specular component. (e) Input image. (f) Sharpened specular lobe, as would occur if the surface was more smooth. This is achieved by eroding the specular component using a disk-shaped structuring element and amplifying it. (g) Effect of an additional light source obtained by exploiting the object symmetry and reflecting the specular component about the vertical axis. (h) Avocado-like appearance by modulating the specular component.

function (Eq. 15) ensures that these pixels are implicitly identified and treated as outliers during the erosion process. While left here for illustrative purposes, these artifacts can be reduced by inpainting the diffuse and/or specular components in a post-process. (This is done, for example, by P. Tan et al. [14].)

Figure 4 compares the result of our algorithm with the ground truth obtained using polarization filters on the light source and camera. The polarizer in front of the light source is fixed while the polarizer in front of the camera is rotated to an orientation that produces an image with minimum specularity. The result of our algorithm is very close to the ground truth on both the textured surfaces (i.e., the vase and pear) and the untextured surfaces (i.e., the sphere).

Additional still-image results are shown in Fig. 3 (d, e). These images were downloaded from the Internet, so they exhibit low dynamic range (8-bit) and are corrupted by JPEG compression. Since illuminant color was not known, it was assumed to be white, and the gamma was assumed to be 2.2. Despite these sources of noise, the multi-scale erosion defined in Eq. 19 still succeeds in separating the diffuse and specular components. An animation of the erosion process accompanies this paper.

In addition to still images, we also evaluated the method on video sequences, some frames of which are shown in Fig. 5. In both cases, erosion is performed along iso-surfaces of θ using Eq. 22, and in both cases, texture is preserved while the specularity is removed. Complete videos accompany this paper.

5.1 Dichromatic Editing

To further demonstrate the efficacy of our approach, we use it as a means for *dichromatic editing* – the simulation of visual effects by the independent processing of reflection components. Some examples are shown in Fig. 6, where: 1) the specular and diffuse components are recovered using Eq. 19, 2) each component is processed individually, and 3) they are recombined. Since the diffuse and specular components often form two distinct components of visual perception, dichromatic editing can achieve a variety of visual effects, including the effects of make-up, surface roughening, and wetness.

6 Conclusion

This paper presents a framework for specular/diffuse separation in images and video that is based on local spatial (and spatio-temporal) interactions. Separation is framed in terms of differential morphology, which leads to a family of non-linear PDEs. By evolving these PDEs, we effectively erode the specular component at each image point. This erosion is guided by local color and shading information, so that diffuse texture is preserved without requiring an explicit segmentation of the image. By developing the problem in terms of morphological PDEs, we can benefit from existing robust numerical algorithms to solve them [9], which is an important advantage over purely discrete formulations. In addition, videos are naturally considered in this formulation, with the erosion equation for videos including the still-image equations as a special case.

The approach described in this paper relies purely on local color information, and is therefore limited to dichromatic surfaces for which the diffuse and specular colors are distinct. It requires the illuminant color to be known (at least approximately) *a priori*. In the future, we plan to overcome these limitations by exploiting additional cues, such as local shape, in addition to color.

Acknowledgment

The authors would like to thank Roger Brockett for helpful comments regarding the theoretical development in Sec. 4. This work was supported in part by the National Science

Foundation. S. Mallick and D. Kriegman were funded under IIS-03-08185 and EIA-02-24431, T. Zickler was funded under IIS-05-41173, and P. Belhumeur was funded under IIS-03-08185, EIA-02-24431, and ITR-00-85864.

References

1. R. Bajcsy, S. Lee, and A. Leonardis. Detection of diffuse and specular interface reflections and inter-reflections by color image segmentation. *IJCV*, 17(3):241–272, March 1996.
2. A. Blake and G. Brelstaff. Geometry from specularities. In *ICCV*, pages 394–403, 1988.
3. R. Brockett and P. Maragos. Evolution equations for continuous scale morphology. *IEEE trans. on Sig. Proc.*, 42:3377–3386, 1994.
4. M. G. Crandall, H. Ishii, and P. L. Lions. *User's Guide to Viscosity Solutions of Second Order Partial Differential Equations*, volume 26. July 1992.
5. G. Healey and T. O. Binford. Local shape from specularity. *CVGIP*, 42(1):62–86, 1988.
6. G. Klinker, S. Shafer, and T. Kanade. The measurement of highlights in color images. *IJCV*, 2(1):7–32, 1988.
7. H. S. Lee. Method for computing the scene-illuminant chromaticity from specular highlights. *JOSAA*, 3(10):1694–1699, 1986.
8. S. Mallick, T. Zickler, D. Kriegman, and P. Belhumeur. Beyond Lambert: Reconstructing specular surfaces using color. In *CVPR*, pages II: 619–626, 2005.
9. P. Maragos and M. A. Butt. Curve evolution and differential morphology. *Fundamenta Informaticae*, 41:91–129, 2000.
10. S. Nayar, X. Fang, and T. Boult. Separation of reflection components using color and polarization. *Int. Journal of Computer Vision*, 21(3):163–186, 1997.
11. M. Osadchy, D. Jacobs, and R. Ramamoorthi. Using specularities for recognition. In *ICCV*, pages 1512–1519, 2003.
12. J. B. Park. Efficient color representation for image segmentation under nonwhite illumination. In *SPIE, Volume 5267, pp. 163-174 (2003).*
13. P. Perona and J. Malik. Scale-space and edge detection using anisotropic diffusion. *PAMI*, 12(7):629–639, 1990.
14. T. Ping, S. Lin, L. Quan, and H.-Y. Shum. Highlight removal by illumination-constrained inpainting. In *ICCV*, pages 164–169, Nice, France, 2003.
15. S. Shafer. Using color to separate reflection components. *COLOR research and applications*, 10(4):210–218, 1985.
16. R. Tan and K. Ikeuchi. Reflection components decomposition of textured surfaces using linear basis functions. In *CVPR*, pages I: 125–131, 2005.
17. R. Tan and K. Ikeuchi. Separating reflection components of textured surfaces using a single image. *PAMI*, 27(2):178–193, February 2005.
18. T. Tan, R, K. Nishino, and K. Ikeuchi. Separating reflection components based on chromaticity and noise analysis. *PAMI*, 26(10):1373–1381, October 2004.

Carved Visual Hulls for Image-Based Modeling

Yasutaka Furukawa[1] and Jean Ponce[1,2]

[1] Department of Computer Science, University of Illinois at Urbana Champaign, USA
[2] Département d'Informatique, Ecole Normale Supérieure, Paris, France
{yfurukaw, ponce}@cs.uiuc.edu

Abstract. This article presents a novel method for acquiring high-quality solid models of complex 3D shapes from multiple calibrated photographs. After the purely geometric constraints associated with the silhouettes found in each image have been used to construct a coarse surface approximation in the form of a visual hull, photoconsistency constraints are enforced in three consecutive steps: (1) the rims where the surface grazes the visual hull are first identified through dynamic programming; (2) with the rims now fixed, the visual hull is carved using graph cuts to globally optimize the photoconsistency of the surface and recover its main features; (3) an iterative (local) refinement step is finally used to recover fine surface details. The proposed approach has been implemented, and experiments with six real data sets are presented, along with qualitative comparisons with several state-of-the-art image-based-modeling algorithms.

1 Introduction

This article addresses the problem of acquiring high-quality solid models[1] of complex three-dimensional (3D) shapes from multiple calibrated photographs, a process dubbed *image-based modeling*. A popular approach to image-based modeling is to acquire multiple depth maps with a laser range scanner, register them, and merge them into a single 3D model [4, 8, 14]. The relative accuracy of laser-based systems can be as high as 1/10,000 [14]. Comparable (and even higher) accuracy levels have been achieved using "ordinary" cameras in the close-range photogrammetry domain [22]. However, photogrammetric methods typically measure a rather sparse set of point (a few hundreds) and require markers. The accuracy levels currently achieved by automated, marker-less approaches to image-based modeling from calibrated photographs (e.g., [7, 10, 11, 15, 18, 23, 20]) are much lower. They are rarely quantified, often because of a lack of ground truth data, but it is probably fair to say that relative accuracies of about 1/200 are the state of the art. As a step toward higher accuracy, we present in this paper a method that combines the geometric and photometric constraints associated with multiple calibrated photographs to recover accurate solid object models in the form of *carved visual hulls* (see [7, 23, 20] for related approaches). The proposed algorithm has been implemented, and experiments with six real data sets are presented. As in previous studies, the lack of ground truth data has prevented us (so far) from conducting a quantitative assessment of the proposed method, but the qualitative results presented in Figs. 1 and 7 demonstrate the recovery of very fine surface details

---

[1] In the form of watertight surface meshes, as opposed to the partial surface models typically output by stereo and structure-from-motion systems.

A. Leonardis, H. Bischof, and A. Pinz (Eds.): ECCV 2006, Part I, LNCS 3951, pp. 564–577, 2006.
© Springer-Verlag Berlin Heidelberg 2006

Fig. 1. Overall flow of the proposed approach. Top: one of the 24 input pictures of a toy dinosaur (left), the corresponding visual hull (center), and the rims identified in each strip using dynamic programming (right). Bottom: the carved visual hull after graph cuts (left) and iterative refinement (center); and a texture-mapped rendering of the final model (right). Note that the scales on the neck and below the fin, as well as the undulations of the fin, are recovered correctly, even though the variations in surface height there is well below 1mm for this object about 20cm wide.

in all our experiments. Our technique also appears to fare rather well in preliminary —and once again qualitative— comparisons with several state-of-the-art image-based modeling algorithms (Fig. 8).

1.1 Background

Several recent approaches to image-based modeling attempt to recover *photoconsistent* models that minimize some measure of the discrepancy between the different image projections of their surface points. *Space carving* algorithms represent the volume of space around the modeled object by a grid of voxels, and erode this volume by carving away successive layers of voxels with high discrepancy [11, 18]. In contrast, *variational methods* explicitly seek the surface that minimize image discrepancy. Variants of this approach based on *snakes* iteratively deform a surface mesh until convergence [7, 21]. *Level-set* techniques, on the other hand, implicitly represent surfaces as the zero set of a time-varying volumetric density [6, 9]. The *graph cuts* global optimization technique can also be used to avoid local extrema during the search for the optimal surface [16, 23, 20]. The last broad class of image modeling techniques is the oldest one: The *visual hull*, introduced by Baumgart in the mid-seventies [1], is an outer approximation of the observed solid, constructed as the intersection of the visual cones associated with all input cameras. Many variants of Baumgart's original algorithm have also been proposed (e.g., [13, 15, 19]).

1.2 Approach

Hernández Esteban and Schmitt propose in [7] to use the visual hull to initialize the deformation of a surface mesh under the influence of photoconsistency constraints expressed by gradient flow forces [24] (see [9] for a related approach combining geometric and photometric approaches). Although this method yields excellent results, its reliance on snakes for iterative refinement makes it susceptible to local minima. In contrast, Vogiatzis, Torr and Cipolla use the visual hull to initialize the global optimization of a photometric error function [23]. The results are once again impressive, but silhouette consistency constraints are ignored in the minimization process, which may result in excessive carving. In fact, they add an *inflationary ballooning* term to the energy function of the graph cuts to prevent the over-carving, but this could still be a problem, especially in high-curvature regions (more on this in Section 5.2).

To overcome these problems, we propose in this paper a combination of global and local optimization techniques to enforce both photometric and geometric consistency constraints throughout the modeling process. The algorithm proposed by Lazebnik [13] is first used to construct a combinatorial mesh description of the visual hull surface in terms of polyhedral *cone strips* and their adjacency relations (see next section and [13] for details). Photoconsistency constraints are then used to refine this initial and rather coarse model while maintaining the geometric consistency constraints imposed by the visual hull. This is done in three steps: (1) the *rims* where the surface grazes the visual hull are first identified through dynamic programming; (2) with the rims now fixed, the visual hull is carved using graph cuts to globally minimize the image discrepancy of the surface and recover its main features, including its concavities (which, unlike convex and saddle-shape parts of the surface, are not captured by the visual hull); and (3) iterative (local) energy minimization is finally used to enforce both photometric and geometric constraints and recover fine surface details. While geometric constraints have been ignored in [23] in the global optimization process, our approach affords in its first two steps an effective method for enforcing hard geometric constraints during the global optimization process. As demonstrated in Section 5.2, the third step, similar in spirit to the local optimization techniques proposed in [7, 9], remains nonetheless essential in achieving high-quality results. The overall process is illustrated by Fig. 1, and the rest of this paper details each step and presents our implementation and its results, along with preliminary comparative experiments.

2   Identifying Rims on Visual Hull Surfaces

2.1   Visual Hulls, Cone Strips, and Rims

Let us consider an object observed by n calibrated cameras with optical centers $O_1, \ldots, O_n$, and denote by γ_i its apparent contour in the image I_i (Fig. 2(a)). The corresponding *visual cone* is the solid bounded by the surface Φ_i swept by the rays joining O_i to γ_i.[2] Φ_i grazes the object along a surface curve, the *rim* Γ_i. The *visual hull* is the solid formed by the intersection of the visual cones, and its boundary can be decomposed into a set of *cone strips* ϕ_i formed by patches from the cone boundaries that connect to each other at *frontier points* where two rims intersect (Fig. 2(b)). As illustrated by Fig. 2(c), each strip can be mapped onto a plane by parameterizing its boundary by the arc length

---

[2] We assume here for simplicity that γ_i is connected. As shown in Section 5, our algorithm actually handles apparent contours made of several nested connected components.

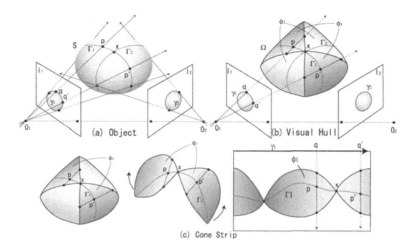

Fig. 2. A visual hull, cone strips and rims: (a) an egg-shaped object is viewed by 2 cameras with optical centers O_1 and O_2; the point x is a frontier point; (b) its visual hull is constructed from two apparent contours γ_1 and γ_2, the surface Ω of the visual hull consisting of two cone strips ϕ_1 and ϕ_2; (c) the cone strip ϕ_1 associated with the first image I_1 is stretched out along the apparent contour γ_1, so a point q on γ_1 corresponds to a vertical line in the right part of the diagram

of the corresponding image contour. In this figure, a viewing ray corresponds to a vertical line inside the corresponding strip, and, by construction, there must be at least one rim point along any such line (rim points are identified in [3] by the same argument, but the algorithm and its purpose are different from ours). Once the visual hull and the corresponding cone strips have been constructed using the algorithm proposed in [13], the next step is to identify the rim that runs "horizontally" inside each strip (Fig. 2(c)). Since rim segments are the only parts of the visual hull that touch the surface of an object, they can be found as the strip curves that minimize some measure of image discrepancy. The next section introduces such a measure, similar to that used in [6].

2.2 Measuring Image Discrepancy

Let us consider a point p on the visual hull surface. To assess the corresponding image discrepancy, we first use z-buffering to determine the images where it is visible, then select among these the τ pictures with minimal foreshortening. Next, a $\mu \times \mu$ grid is overlaid on a small patch of the surface's tangent plane at p, and τ $\mu \times \mu$ tangent plane "windows" $h_1, \cdots, h_\tau$ are retrieved from the corresponding input images. We normalize the intensity of each window h_i and compute the sum of squared differences (SSD) for each pair. Our final discrepancy measure is thus: $f(p) = \frac{2}{\tau(\tau-1)\mu^2} \sum_{i=1}^{\tau} \sum_{j=i+1}^{\tau} \text{SSD}(h_i, h_j)$. $\tau = 5$ and $\mu = 11$ in all our experiments.

2.3 Identifying a Rim in a Cone Strip

As noted earlier, the image discrepancy function should have small values along rims, thus these curves can be found as shortest paths within the strips, where path length

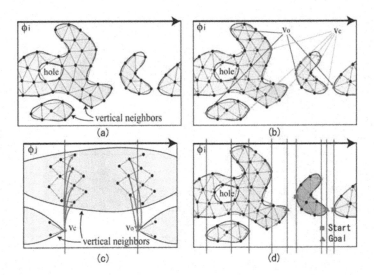

Fig. 3. (a) An undirected graph representing a cone strip ϕ_i. The two leftmost components are vertical neighbors. (b) The opening and closing vertices v_o and v_c of ϕ_i. (c) Illustration of the vertical edge creation process for a different strip ϕ_j. (d) After the horizontal and vertical edges of the directed graph G' associated with ϕ_i have been created, G' is split into two connected components, shown here in different shades of grey, with unique start and goal vertices each.

is determined by the image discrepancy function. In our visual hull implementation, a cone strip ϕ_i is represented by the undirected graph G with its polyhedral vertices V and edges E, and it is straightforward to find the shortest path by dynamic programming. However, the idealized situation in Fig. 2 rarely occurs in practice, and the rim may not be a continuous curve in its cone strip (Fig. 3(a)): As shown in [13], the boundaries of the cone strips often loose their singularities (frontier points) to measurement errors, resulting into multiple connected components. In practice, we can still apply dynamic programming to each connected component independently. Harder problems arise from the facts that (1) there may be multiple strip components intersecting the same vertical line (we call them *vertical neighbors*), with the rim being in any one of these; and (2) the rim can be discontinuous at any point inside the strip due to T-junctions. In this work, we assume for simplicity that rim discontinuities occur only at the following two types of strip vertices (Fig. 3(b)): an *opening* vertex v_o whose neighbors v' all verify $v_o \prec v'$, and a *closing* vertex whose neighbors v' all verify $v' \prec v_c$, where "$\prec$" denotes the circular order on adjacent vertices in G induced by the closed curve formed by the apparent contour. Under this assumption, dynamic programming can be still used to find the rim as a shortest path in the *directed* graph G' with vertices V and edges E', defined as follows. Firstly, for each edge (v_i, v_j) in E, we add to E' the *Horizontal* edge (v_i, v_j) if $v_i \prec v_j$, and the edge (v_j, v_i) otherwise. Secondly, to handle discontinuities, we add to E' the *Vertical* directed edges linking each opening (resp. closing) vertex to all vertices immediately following (resp. preceding) it in its vertical neighbors (Fig. 3(c)).

Next, we assign weights to edges in a directed graph G'. For horizontal edges, a weight is the physical edge length multiplied by the average image discrepancy of its two vertices. Vertical edges have weight 0. Then, we decompose the graph G' into connected components (Fig. 3(d)), and use dynamic programming to find the shortest path between the leftmost (start) vertex of each component and its rightmost (goal) vertex. At times, rim discontinuities may occur at other points than those selected by our assumptions. Accordingly, the simple approach outlined above may misidentify parts of the rim. Since the rims are used as hard constraints in the next global optimization step, we want to avoid false positives as much as possible. Among all the vertices identified as the rim points, we filter out false-positives by using the image discrepancy score $f(v)$ and the vertical strip size $g(v)$ at a vertex v. More concretely, a vertex v is detected as a false-positive if either $R/3 < g(v)$ or $R/15 < g(v)$ and $\eta < f(v)$ hold, where R is an average distance from all the vertices V' in the mesh to their center of mass $\sum_{v \in V'} v / |V'|$. η is a threshold for the image discrepancy score, and is selected for each data set in our experiments. Image discrepancy values are blurred along the identified rims before this filtering. Note that when the vertical strip size is small (at most $R/15$), there is little ambiguity in the location of the rim, and the corresponding vertex automatically passes the test according to the above rule.

The next two sections show how to carve the visual hull by combining photoconsistency constraints with the geometric *rim consistency* constraints associated with the identified rim segments. We start with a *global optimization* step by graph cuts to recover main surface features. A *local refinement* step is then used to reveal fine details.

3 Global Optimization

In this part of our algorithm, rim consistency is enforced as a hard constraint by fixing the location of the identified rim segments, which split the surface Ω of the visual hull into k connected components $\overline{G}_i$ $(i = 1, \ldots, k)$ (note that the rim segments associated with a single strip may not form a loop, so each graph component may include vertices from multiple strips). To enforce photoconsistency, we independently and iteratively deform the surface of each component $\overline{G}_i$ *inwards* to generate multiple layers forming a 3D graph, associate photoconsistency weights to the edges of this graph, and use graph cuts to carve the surface. [3] The overall process is summarized in Algorithm 1 and detailed in the next two sections.

3.1 Deforming the Surface

To construct the graph associated with each component $\overline{G}_i$ of the visual hull boundary, we first deform the surface *inwards* (remember that the visual hull is an *outer* object approximation) to create multiple offset layers. Note that the photoconsistency function is evaluated at all the vertices in each layer, and their surface normals are estimated by using the corresponding layer. At every iteration, we move every vertex v in $\overline{G}_i$ (except for the boundaries) along its surface normal $\mathbf{N}(v)$, and apply smoothing: $v \leftarrow v - \frac{\varepsilon}{\lambda}(\zeta_1 f(v) + \zeta_2)\mathbf{N}(v) + \mathbf{s}(v)$, where $\varepsilon, \zeta_1, \zeta_2$ are scalar constants, $f(v)$ is the

---

[3] The graph associated with a voxel grid serves as input in typical applications of graph cuts to image-based modeling (e.g., [2, 10, 16, 23]). The surface deformation scheme is proposed here instead to take advantage of the fact that the visual hull is already a good approximation.

Algorithm 1. Carving $\overline{G}_i$ with graph cuts

$J \leftarrow \overline{G}_i$; {$J$ will contain ρ layers of the mesh.}
for $j = 2$ to ρ **do**
  for $k = 1$ to λ **do** {Apply λ deformation steps to $\overline{G}_i$.}
    for each vertex $v \in \overline{G}_i$ except for the boundary **do**
      $v \leftarrow v - \frac{\varepsilon}{\lambda}(\zeta_1 f(v) + \zeta_2)\mathbf{N}(v) + \mathbf{s}(v)$;
    end for
  end for
  $J \leftarrow J \cup \overline{G}_i$; {Add a layer.}
end for
Add vertical, horizontal, and diagonal edges to J, and compute their weights;
Use graph cuts to find a minimum cut in J.

---

image discrepancy function defined earlier, $\mathbf{N}(v)$ is the unit surface normal, and $\mathbf{s}(v)$ is a smoothness term of the form $-\beta_1 \Delta v + \beta_2 \Delta \Delta v$ suggested in [5]. λ iterations are performed to generate each layer, and at total ρ layers are generated during the deformation process. Note that using $f(v)$ yields an adaptive deformation scheme: the surface shrinks faster where the image discrepancy function is larger, which is expected to provide better surface normal estimates. We use $\zeta_1 = 100$, $\zeta_2 = 0.1$, $\beta_1 = 0.4$, $\beta_2 = 0.3$, $\rho = 30$, and $\lambda = 20$ in all our experiments, which have empirically given good results for our test objects. On the other hand, ε, which determines an offset between adjacent layers, should depend on the depth of a surface from the visual hull boundary, and is set manually for each object, typically to about 0.3 times the average edge length in $\overline{G}_i$.

3.2   Building a Graph and Applying Graph Cuts

After a set of layers J has been created, three types of edges are added, as shown in Fig. 4. Vertical edges connect the offset instances of the same vertex in adjacent layers, horizontal edges connect vertices in the same layer, and diagonal edges connect vertices in adjacent layers. As before, photoconsistency values are computed at all the vertices in J, and a simple variant of the technique proposed in [2] is used to compute edge weights. Concretely, the weight of an edge (v_i, v_j) is computed as $w_{ij} = \frac{\alpha(f(v_i) + f(v_j))(\delta_i + \delta_j)}{d(v_i, v_j)}$, where $f(v_i)$ is the photoconsistency function value at a vertex v_i, $d(v_i, v_j)$ is the length of the edge, and δ_i is a measure of the sparsity of vertices around v_i, approximated

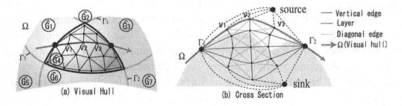

Fig. 4. Deforming the surface for graph cuts: (a) the surface Ω of the visual hull is decomposed into multiple independent components $\overline{G}_i$; (b) the deformation process is illustrated for the cross section of $\overline{G}_4$ that contains vertices v_1, v_2, and v_3

by the average distance to the adjacent vertices. Intuitively, weights should be large where vertices are sparse. We use $\alpha = 1, 10$, and 5 for horizontal, vertical, and diagonal edges, respectively, in all our experiments, which accounts for the fact that edges are not uniformly distributed around a vertex. Lastly, we connect all the vertices in the top (resp. bottom) layer to the source (resp. sink) node with infinite edge weights.

3.3 Practical Matters

For the global optimum provided by graph cuts to be meaningful, the edge weights must accurately measure the photoconsistency, which in turn requires good estimates of the normals in the vicinity of the actual surface. For parts of the surface far from the visual hull boundary, normal estimates computed at each vertex from neighbors in the same layer may be inaccurate. In practice, this suggests applying the surface deformation and graph cuts procedure to each component of the graph $\overline{G}_i$ several times, each iteration improving the accuracy of the normals and of the photoconsistency function, and therefore the quality of its global optimum. Note that after the pure inward deformation of the first iteration, the mesh is allowed to deform both inwards and outwards —while remaining within the visual hull— along the surface normals. Empirically, three iterations have proven sufficient to recover the main surface features in all our experiments.

4 Local Refinement

In this final step, we iteratively refine the surface while enforcing all available photometric and geometric information. At every iteration, we move each vertex v along its surface normal by a linear combination of three terms: an image discrepancy term, a smoothness term, and a rim consistency term. The image discrepancy term is simply the first derivative of $f(v)$ along the surface normal. The smoothness term is the same as in the previous section. The rim consistency term is similar to the one proposed in [7]: Consider an apparent contour γ represented by a discrete set of points q_j together with the corresponding viewing rays r_j. We add rim consistency forces to vertices as follows (Fig. 5): Let us define $d(v_k, r_j)$ as the distance between the vertex v_k and a viewing ray r_j; we find the *closest* viewing ray $r_k^* = \mathrm{argmin}_{r_j} d(v_k, r_j)$ to every vertex v_k. Next, if V_j denotes the set of all the vertices v_k whose closest viewing ray is r_j (i.e., $r_k^* = r_j$), we find the vertex v_j^* in V_j closest to r_j (i.e., $v_j^* = \mathrm{argmin}_{v_k \in V_j} d(v_k, r_i)$). Note that a surface satisfies the rim consistency conditions if and only if $d(v_j^*, r_j) = 0$ for all

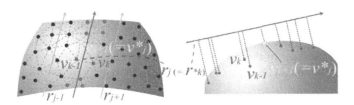

Fig. 5. The rim consistency force is computed for a viewing ray r_j, then distributed to all the vertices V_j whose closest ray is r_j. Here v_{k+1} is the closest vertex v_j^* to r_j.

viewing rays r_j. Therefore, we add an appropriately weighted force whose magnitude is proportional to $\overline{v_j^* r_j}$ to all vertices in V_j, where $\overline{v_k r_j}$ is the *signed* distance between the vertex v_k and a viewing ray r_j, with a positive sign when the projection of v_k lies inside the contour γ and negative otherwise. Concretely, we add to the vertex v_k in V_j the force $\mathbf{r}(v_k) = \overline{v_j^* r_j} \dfrac{\exp(-(\overline{v_k r_j} - \overline{v_j^* r_j})^2/2\sigma^2)}{\sum_{v_{k'} \in V_j} \exp(-(\overline{v_{k'} r_j} - \overline{v_j^* r_j})^2/2\sigma^2)} \mathbf{N}(v_k)$, where $\mathbf{N}(v_k)$ is the unit surface normal in v_k. The basic structure of the algorithm is simple. At every iteration, for each vertex v, we compute three terms and move v along its surface normal by their linear combinations: $v \leftarrow v + \mathbf{s}(v) + \mathbf{r}(v) - \kappa \nabla f(v) \cdot \mathbf{N}(v)$. κ is a scalar coefficient and is set depending on the object and the resolution of the mesh. After repeating this process until convergence—typically from 20 to 40 times, we remesh and increase the resolution, and repeat the same process until the image projections of the edges in the mesh become approximately 2 pixels in length. Typically, the remeshing operation is performed three times until the mesh reaches the final resolution.

5   Implementation and Results

5.1   Implementation

We have implemented the proposed approach in C++. The bottleneck of the computation is the global optimization and the local refinement steps, each of which takes about two hours for our large data sets such as the first toy dinosaur, the toy mummy, and the two human skulls, with a 3.0 GHz Pentium 4. The remaining steps including the visual hull construction and the rim identification take at most twenty minutes. Note that we have assumed so far that a single apparent contour is extracted from each input image. In fact, handling multiple nested components only requires a moderate amount of additional bookkeeping, whose description is omitted here for brevity. Note also that our algorithm does *not* require all silhouette holes to be found in each image: For example, silhouette holes are ignored for the human model shown in Fig. 7, while the apparent contour components associated with holes are explicitly used for the human skull models. In practice, the surface of an object may not be Lambertian. We identify and reject for each patch the input images where it may be highlighted by examining the mean intensity and color variance. The chain rule is used to compute the derivative of $f(v)$ along the surface normal as a function of image derivatives, which in turn are estimated by convolving the input images with the derivatives of a Gaussian function. Finally, the topology of an object's surface is not necessarily the same as that of its visual hull. We allow the topology of the deforming surface to change in the local refinement step, using a method similar to that of [12]: As resolution increases and edges are split, it may happen that three vertices in a shrinking area of the surface are connected to each other without forming a face. In this case, we cut the surface at the three vertices into two open components, and add a copy of the triangle to both components.

5.2   Results

We have conducted experiments with strongly calibrated cameras and six objects: two toy dinosaurs, two human skulls (modern man and *Homo Heidelbergensis*), a toy

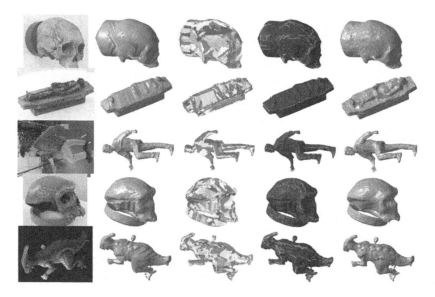

Fig. 6. From left to right, an input image, a visual hull, cone strips on the visual hull boundary, identified rim segments, and a surface after graph cuts for the remaining five objects

mummy, and a person. Four of the six data sets, captured in our laboratory, consist of 24 images, with an image size of about $2000 \times 2000 \text{pixel}^2$. The two exceptions are the person (courtesy of S. Sullivan), that only appears in 11 pictures, with an image size of roughly $2000 \times 1300 \text{pixel}^2$, and the second dinosaur (courtesy of S. Seitz) that appears in 21 images, with an image size of about $640 \times 480 \text{pixel}^2$. In all cases, contours have been extracted interactively.

Figure 1 illustrates the successive steps of our algorithm in a case of the first toy dinosaur. This object is about 20cm in diameter, with fine surface details including fin undulations, and scales in the neck. These details are well captured by the model, even though the corresponding height variations are a fraction of 1mm. Figure 6 shows input images and intermediate results for the remaining five objects. As can be seen in the figures, rim points have been successfully identified, especially at high-curvature parts of the surface. Our rim-discontinuity assumption (Section 2.3) breaks at the cloth of the standing human model, due to its complicated fold structure and the sparse input viewpoints, while the assumption rarely fails in the other data sets. Nonetheless, spurious rim points have been detected and filtered out by our conservative post-processing in all the data sets. With the help of the identified rim segments, the graph cuts step recovers the main surface structures rather well, including large concavities, while preserving high-curvature structural details, such as the fingernails of the first dinosaur, the fingers of the person, the cheekbones of the two skulls, and the metal bar sticking out from the second dinosaur. Figure 7 shows shaded and texture-mapped renderings of the final models including several close-ups. Note that some of the surface details are not recovered accurately. In some cases, this is simply due to the fact that the surface is not visible from any cameras: the bottom part of the first dinosaur, for example. In other

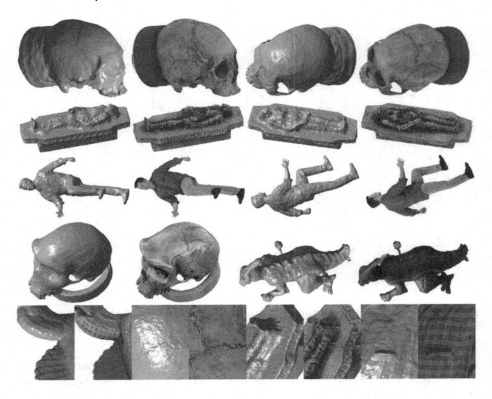

Fig. 7. Experimental results. See text for details, and the video submitted as supplemental material for animations.

cases, this is due to failures of our algorithm: For example, the eye sockets of the skulls are simply too deep to be carved away by graph cuts or local refinement. The human is a particularly challenging example, because of the extremely complicated folds of the cloth, and its high-frequency stripe patterns. Nonetheless, our algorithm has performed rather well in general, correctly recovering minute details such as the sutures of the skulls, the large concavity in the mummy's chest, much of the shirt fold structure in the human example, as well as the high-curvature structural details mentioned earlier.

To evaluate the contributions of each step in our approach, we have performed the following two experiments: First, we have implemented and added the ballooning term introduced in [23] to the energy function in the graph cuts step, while removing the hard constraints enforced by the identified rim segments to see its effects on the over-carving problem mentioned earlier (Fig. 8, first row). Note that the layer-based graph representation is still used in this experiment, instead of the voxel representation used in [23]. The leftmost part of the figure shows the result of our graph cuts step (with fixed rim segments), and the remaining three columns illustrate the effects of the ballooning term with three different weights associated with it, the weight being zero at the left and increasing to the right. As shown by the figure, high-curvature surface details have not been preserved with the ballooning term. Even in the third column of the figure, where

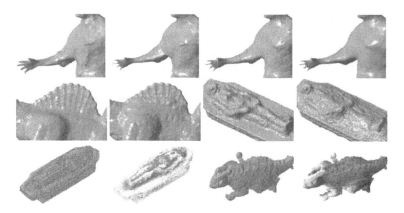

Fig. 8. A preliminary comparative evaluation of our algorithm. Top: comparison with our implementation of a variant of the method proposed by Vogiatzis *et al.* [23]. Middle: comparison with a purely local method initialized with the visual hull surface, akin to those proposed by Hernández Esteban and Schmitt [7], and Keriven [9]. Bottom: comparison with the voxel coloring method of Seitz [18]. See text for details.

Fig. 9. Assessing the accuracy of the reconstruction: α-blended surface textures backprojected from different images are shown for (from left to right) the visual hull, the surface obtained after graph cuts, and the final surface after local refinement for details of the dinosaur and shirt surfaces. See text for details.

Fig. 10. Preliminary results combining carved visual hulls with wide-baseline stereo. Large concavities such as eye sockets are successfully recovered.

the ballooning term is too high to preserve surface details in other parts of the surface, the fingers almost disappear. This may be due in part to the fact that photometric consistency measurements become unreliable at high-curvature parts of a surface which, on the other hand, tend to generate highly reliable rim consistency constraints. We have also tested our algorithm without its graph cuts phase, yielding a purely local method comparable to those proposed in [7, 9]. Figure 8 (second row) shows two examples: the graph cuts step being included in the left part of the diagram, and omitted in the right part. As expected, local minimum problems are apparent in the latter case. Of course, it would be highly desirable to conduct more comparisons with native implementations of the algorithms proposed in [7, 9, 23], but we do not have access to these (yet). In the mean time, we have tried an implementation of *voxel coloring* [11, 18], kindly provided by S. Seitz, on two of our examples (Fig. 8, bottom). The results appear rather noisy compared to ours (see Fig. 7), probably due to the lack of regularization, and several concavities are missed in the two objects (e.g., the chest of the mummy).

As noted before, we have been unable (so far) to conduct a quantitative assessment of our algorithm due to the lack of ground truth data. A qualitative assessment can be obtained by α-blending surface textures backprojected from different images: They will only appear consistent when the geometry is correct. Figure 9 shows the results of such an experiment. Blended textures on the surface after visual hull construction, global surface carving, and final local refinement are shown, from left to right, for the first dinosaur and the human figure. It is clear that the backprojected textures are consistent on the final surfaces.

6   Conclusions and Future Work

We have proposed a method for acquiring high-quality geometric models of complex 3D shapes by enforcing the photometric and geometric consistencies associated with multiple calibrated images of the same solid, and demonstrated the promise of the approach with six real data sets and some preliminary qualitative evaluation experiments. Next on our agenda is a quantitative assessment of our algorithm using a measuring device such as a laser theodolite to recover accurate ground truth at a number of key points. One of the limitations of our current approach is that it cannot handle concavities too deep to be carved away by the graph cuts or local refinement steps. To overcome this problem. we plan to combine our approach with recent work on sparse wide-baseline stereo from interest points (e.g., [17]) in order to incorporate stronger geometric constraints in the carving and local refinement stages, and Fig. 10 shows the results of a preliminary experiment. Attempting, as in [21], to explicitly handle non-Lambertian surfaces is of course of interest. Finally, we plan to follow the lead of photogrammetrists and add a final *simultaneous camera calibration* stage, where both the camera parameters and the surface shape are refined simultaneously using bundle adjustment [22].

Acknowledgments. This research was partially supported by the National Science Foundation under grant IIS-0312438, and the Beckman Institute. We thank Svetlana Lazebnik for providing the original visual hull software used in our implementation, and Steve Seitz for the toy dinosaur data set together with his voxel coloring software. We thank Jodi Blumenfeld and Steven R. Leigh for providing us with the two human skull data sets. Lastly, we want to thank Sariel Har-Peled and Theodore Papadopoulo for discussions on the global optimization method.

References

1. B.G. Baumgart. *Geometric modeling for computer vision*. Stanford University, 1974.
2. Y. Boykov and V. Kolmogorov. Computing geodesics and minimal surfaces via graph cuts. In *ICCV*, pages 26–33, 2003.

3. Kong Man Cheung, Simon Baker, and Takeo Kanade. Visual hull alignment and refinement across time: A 3d reconstruction algorithm combining shape-from-silhouette with stereo. In *CVPR*, June 2003.
4. B. Curless and M. Levoy. A volumetric method for building complex models from range images. In *SIGGRAPH*, pages 303–312. ACM Press, 1996.
5. H. Delingette, M. Hebert, and K. Ikeuchi. Shape representation and image segmentation using deformable surfaces. *IVC*, 10(3):132–144, 1992.
6. O. Faugeras and R. Keriven. Variational principles, surface evolution, PDE's, level set methods and the stereo problem. *IEEE Trans. Im. Proc.*, 7(3):336–344, 1998.
7. C. Hernández Esteban and F. Schmitt. Silhouette and stereo fusion for 3D object modeling. *CVIU*, 96(3):367–392, 2004.
8. D.F. Huber and M. Hebert. 3D modeling using a statistical sensormodel and stochastic search. In *CVPR*, volume 1, pages 858–865, 2003.
9. R. Keriven. A variational framework to shape from contours. Technical Report 2002-221, ENPC, 2002.
10. V. Kolmogorov and R. Zabih. Multi-camera scene reconstruction via graph cuts. In *ECCV*, volume 3, pages 82–96, 2002.
11. K.N. Kutulakos and S.M. Seitz. A theory of shape by space carving. *IJCV*, 38(3), 2000.
12. Jacques-Olivier Lachaud and Annick Montanvert. Deformable meshes with automated topology changes for coarse-to-fine 3d surface extraction. *Medical Image Analysis*, 3(2):187–207, 1999.
13. S. Lazebnik. Projective visual hulls. Technical Report MS Thesis, UIUC, 2002.
14. M. Levoy, K. Pulli, B. Curless, S. Rusinkiewicz, D. Koller, L. Pereira, M. Ginzton, S. Anderson, J. Davis, J. Ginsberg, J. Shade, and D. Fulk. The digital michelangelo project: 3D scanning of large statues. In *SIGGRAPH*, pages 131–144, 2000.
15. W. Matusik, H. Pfister, A. Ngan, P. Beardsley, R. Ziegler, and L. McMillan. Image-based 3D photography using opacity hulls. In *SIGGRAPH*, 2002.
16. S. Paris, F. Sillion, and L. Quan. A surface reconstruction method using global graph cut optimization. In *ACCV*, January 2004.
17. F. Schaffalitzky and A. Zisserman. Viewpoint invariant texture matching and wide baseline stereo. In *ICCV*, 2001.
18. S.M. Seitz and C.R. Dyer. Photorealistic scene reconstruction by voxel coloring. In *CVPR*, pages 1067–1073, 1997.
19. S. Sinha and M. Pollefeys. Visual hull reconstruction from uncalibrated and unsynchronized video streams. In *Int. Symp. on 3D Data Processing, Visualization & Transmission*, 2004.
20. S. Sinha and M. Pollefeys. Multi-view reconstruction using photo-consistency and exact silhouette constraints: A maximum-flow formulation. In *ICCV*, 2005.
21. S. Soatto, A.J. Yezzi, and H. Jin. Tales of shape and radiance in multiview stereo. In *ICCV*, pages 974–981, 2003.
22. V. Uffenkamp. State of the art of high precision industrial photogrammetry. In *Third International Workshop on Accelerator Alignment*, Annecy, France, 1993.
23. George Vogiatzis, Philip H.S. Torr, and R. Cipolla. Multi-view stereo via volumetric graph-cuts. In *CVPR*, pages 391–398, 2005.
24. C. Xu and J.L. Prince. Gradient vector flow: A new external force for snakes. In *CVPR*, pages 66–71, 1997.

What Is the Range of Surface Reconstructions from a Gradient Field?

Amit Agrawal[1], Ramesh Raskar[2], and Rama Chellappa[1]

[1] Center for Automation Research, University of Maryland,
College Park, MD, USA 20742
{aagrawal, rama}@cfar.umd.edu
[2] Mitsubishi Electric Research Labs (MERL),
201 Broadway, Cambridge, MA, USA 02139
raskar@merl.com

Abstract. We propose a generalized equation to represent a continuum of surface reconstruction solutions of a given non-integrable gradient field. We show that common approaches such as Poisson solver and Frankot-Chellappa algorithm are special cases of this generalized equation. For a $N \times N$ pixel grid, the subspace of all integrable gradient fields is of dimension $N^2 - 1$. Our framework can be applied to derive a range of meaningful surface reconstructions from this high dimensional space. The key observation is that the range of solutions is related to the degree of anisotropy in applying weights to the gradients in the integration process. While common approaches use isotropic weights, we show that by using a progression of spatially varying anisotropic weights, we can achieve significant improvement in reconstructions. We propose (a) α-surfaces using binary weights, where the parameter α allows trade off between smoothness and robustness, (b) M-estimators and edge preserving regularization using continuous weights and (c) Diffusion using affine transformation of gradients. We provide results on photometric stereo, compare with previous approaches and show that anisotropic treatment discounts noise while recovering salient features in reconstructions.

1 Introduction

Reconstruction from gradient fields is important in several applications such as photometric stereo (PS) and shape from shading (SfS) [1], mesh smoothing, retinex [2], high dynamic range compression [3], phase unwrapping, image editing, matting and fusion [4]. In gradient based algorithms, the gradient field of images is manipulated to achieve the desired goal and the final image is obtained by a 2D integration of the manipulated gradient field. In PS/SfS, surface normals/gradients are obtained first and the desired surface is obtained by integrating the gradient field. The gradient field of a surface should have zero curl or it should be integrable. The integral along any closed loop (path) should be equal to zero and the reconstruction should not depend on the choice of the integration path. In practice, the obtained gradient field is rarely integrable due to the inherent noise in the estimation process, or manipulation of gradient fields. In addition, ambiguities in the solution and ill-posed problems often lead to non-integrable gradient fields.

A. Leonardis, H. Bischof, and A. Pinz (Eds.): ECCV 2006, Part I, LNCS 3951, pp. 578–591, 2006.

Previous methods have used the integrability constraint during the estimation of surface (or surface normals) in PS, SfS and Shape from Texture as in [1][5]. In these methods, integrability is enforced as a constraint to regularize the solution or to remove the inherent ambiguities. For example, by enforcing integrability in uncalibrated PS, the ambiguity in shape estimation can be reduced to a generalized bas-relief transformation [6]. Another class of methods first estimate the gradient field and then apply integrability to estimate the surface as in [7][8][9][10]. We propose a general framework for surface reconstruction when a non-integrable gradient field is already provided.

Frankot & Chellappa [8] project the non-integrable gradient field on to a set of integrable slopes using the Fourier basis functions. Several variants of this approach have been proposed by either choosing a different basis function [11] (cosine functions) or using a redundant non-orthogonal set of basis functions (shapelets) [12]. In [7], a direct analytical solution based on solving a Poisson equation was proposed. Petrovic et al. [10] used a loopy belief propagation algorithm to obtain the integrable gradient field from a given non-integrable gradient field assuming Gaussian noise in the gradients. Most of these methods are based on minimizing a least square cost function, try to estimate a smooth surface and do not consider the effect of outliers in the given gradient field. A natural approach to overcome outliers and reduce noise would be to use a robust estimation like RANSAC. However, due to the high dimensionality, applying RANSAC is computationally prohibitive.

Noise reduction in images is a topic commonly addressed in image restoration techniques. Several PDE's based methods such as anisotropic diffusion [13], shock filters and energy based methods [14] (see [15] for detailed analysis and algorithms) have been proposed that try to restore an image while maintaining edges or sharp features. Inspired by the success of these approaches, we show how to incorporate robust estimation, regularization and anisotropic diffusion in the gradient integration problem.

Contributions: The contributions of our paper are as follows

- We present a generalized equation for surface reconstruction from non-integrable gradient fields. This unification results in a continuum of solutions based on the degree of anisotropy in assigning weights to the gradients during the integration.
- We show that common approaches such as Poisson solver and Frankot-Chellappa algorithm can be formulated as special cases of our framework at one end of the continuum and correspond to isotropic gradient weights.
- We derive new types of reconstructions using a progression of spatially varying anisotropic weights along the continuum. We propose a solution based on the general affine transformation of the gradients using diffusion tensors near the other end of the continuum and show that it produces better feature preserving reconstructions compared to previous methods.

The subspace of all integrable gradient fields for a $N \times N$ pixel grid is of dimension $N^2 - 1$ [16] and it is not possible (and practical) to characterize all the solutions. The solutions we propose constitute a range of *meaningful* solutions that might be close to the desired surface. Although we describe a range of solutions, the choice of using a particular algorithm for a given application remains an open problem. In general, for smooth surfaces without sharp discontinuities, least square approaches may give good solutions

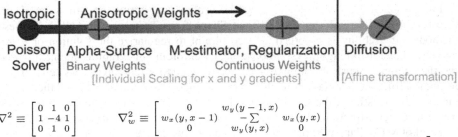

$$\nabla^2 \equiv \begin{bmatrix} 0 & 1 & 0 \\ 1 & -4 & 1 \\ 0 & 1 & 0 \end{bmatrix} \qquad \nabla_w^2 \equiv \begin{bmatrix} 0 & w_y(y-1,x) & 0 \\ w_x(y,x-1) & -\sum & w_x(y,x) \\ 0 & w_y(y,x) & 0 \end{bmatrix}$$

$$\nabla_D^2 \equiv \begin{bmatrix} 0 & d_{22}(y-1,x)+d_{21}(y-1,x) & -d_{21}(y-1,x) \\ d_{11}(y,x-1)+d_{12}(y,x-1) & -\sum & d_{11}(y,x)+d_{21}(y,x) \\ -d_{12}(y,x-1) & d_{22}(y,x)+d_{12}(y,x) & 0 \end{bmatrix}$$

∇^2: Isotropic kernel, ∇_w^2: Anisotropic kernel, ∇_D^2: Diffusion kernel

Fig. 1. A continuum of solutions can be derived using our framework by changing f_i's in (6). At one end is the Poisson solver which gives equal weight to all the gradients, resulting in a spatially invariant isotropic Laplacian kernel ∇^2. *Individual scaling* of the gradients using spatially varying weights (binary for α-surface, continuous for M-estimator and Regularization) results in anisotropic kernel ∇_w^2 ($\sum$ denotes the sum of neighboring values). In Diffusion, x and y gradients are scaled *and* linearly combined, resulting in an affine transformation of gradients. This results in diffusion kernel ∇_D^2.

while handling noise. With sharp features in surface, the proposed diffusion and alpha-surface methods produce better feature preserving reconstructions in the presence of noise and outliers.

2   Problem Statement

Consider a $H \times W$ rectangular grid (y, x) of image pixels. Let $\{p(y, x), q(y, x)\}$ denote the given non-integrable gradient field over this grid. Define the curl and divergence operators as: $\mathrm{curl}(p, q) = \frac{\partial p}{\partial y} - \frac{\partial q}{\partial x}$, $\mathrm{div}(p, q) = \frac{\partial p}{\partial x} + \frac{\partial q}{\partial y}$. Given $\{p, q\}$, the goal is to obtain a surface Z. Let $\{Z_x, Z_y\}$ denote the gradient field of Z. A common approach is to minimize the least square error function given by [7][1]

$$J(Z) = \int \int \left((Z_x - p)^2 + (Z_y - q)^2 \right) dx dy . \tag{1}$$

The Euler-Lagrange equation gives the *Poisson equation*: $\nabla^2 Z = \mathrm{div}(p, q)$. We will refer to this method as Poisson solver. One can always write $\{Z_x, Z_y\} = \{p, q\} + \{\epsilon_x, \epsilon_y\}$, where $\{\epsilon_x, \epsilon_y\}$ denote the *correction gradient field* which is added to the given non-integrable field to make it integrable. It was shown in [16] that integrable gradient fields form a subspace of dimension $HW - 1$ in the $2HW$-dimensional space of all gradient fields. By adding the correction gradient field, one can move from a point in the $2HW$-dimensional space corresponding to the given non-integrable gradient field to the subspace of valid integrable gradient fields. From (1), Poisson solver minimizes $J(Z) = \int \int (\epsilon_x^2 + \epsilon_y^2) dx dy$. Thus, Poisson solver finds that solution which minimizes the norm of the correction gradient field (see Fig. 2).

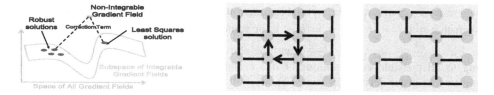

Fig. 2. Space of all solutions. (Left) Poisson solver finds the solution corresponding to the minimum norm correction gradient field, but this may not be robust. (Middle) We show that all gradients are not required for integration using a graph analogy. A 2D graph corresponding to a sample 4×4 grid. Nodes correspond to the value of the surface at the grid points and gradients correspond to the edges (Right) A spanning tree is the minimal configuration required for gradient integration. Using only those gradients which correspond to the edges in the spanning tree, all node values can be obtained up to a constant of integration.

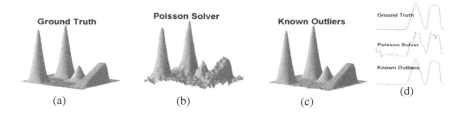

Fig. 3. Effect of outliers in 2D integration. (a) True surface (b) Gaussian noise ($\sigma = 0.02g$, g = maximum gradient magnitude) and uniformly distributed outliers were added to the gradients of this surface. Reconstruction using Poisson solver. Mean Square Error (MSE) = 10.81 (c) If the location of outliers were known, rest of the gradients can be integrated to obtain a much better estimate. MSE = 0.211 (d) One-D height plots for a scan line across the middle of grid.

It is well known that a least square solution does not perform well in the presence of outliers. Consider the surface shown in Figure 3(a), which consists of a ramp and several peaks. Gaussian random noise and uniformly distributed outliers were added to the gradient field of this surface. The reconstructed surface from the noisy gradient field using Poisson solver is shown in Figure 3(b). However, if we knew the locations of the outliers, we could use the rest of the gradients to perform the integration. The corresponding reconstruction is shown in Figure 3(c). It is clear that a better solution can be obtained by removing outliers. Thus, gradient integration can be thought of as a robust estimation problem. How can we find other meaningful solutions in the space of all solutions? In the next section, we put forward a framework to do so.

3   A General Framework

A general solution can be obtained by minimizing the following n^{th} order error functional

$$J = \int \int E(Z, p, q, Z_{x^a y^b}, p_{x^c y^d}, q_{x^c y^d}, \ldots) \, dxdy \, , \tag{2}$$

where E is a continuous differentiable function, a, b, c and d are non-negative integers such that $a + b = k$, $c + d = k - 1$ for some positive integer k, $Z_{x^a y^b} = \frac{\partial^k Z}{\partial x^a \partial y^b}$, $p_{x^c y^d} = \frac{\partial^{k-1} p}{\partial x^c \partial y^d}$, $q_{x^c y^d} = \frac{\partial^{k-1} q}{\partial x^c \partial y^d}$ and the above equation includes terms corresponding to all possible combinations of a, b, c and d for all k, $1 \leq k \leq n$. Restricting to first order derivatives $(n = 1)$, we will consider error functionals of the form $J = \int \int E(Z, p, q, Z_x, Z_y) dx dy$. The Euler-Lagrange equation gives

$$\frac{\partial E}{\partial Z} - \frac{d}{dx} \frac{\partial E}{\partial Z_x} - \frac{d}{dy} \frac{\partial E}{\partial Z_y} = 0 \quad \text{or} \quad \frac{\partial E}{\partial Z} = \text{div}\left(\frac{\partial E}{\partial Z_x}, \frac{\partial E}{\partial Z_y}\right). \tag{3}$$

Consider the following form for $\frac{\partial E}{\partial Z_x}$ and $\frac{\partial E}{\partial Z_y}$

$$\frac{\partial E}{\partial Z_x} = f_1(Z_x, Z_y) - f_3(p, q), \quad \frac{\partial E}{\partial Z_y} = f_2(Z_x, Z_y) - f_4(p, q), \tag{4}$$

where $f_i : \mathbf{R} \times \mathbf{R} \to \mathbf{C}, i = 1 \ldots 4$ are different functions. Note that these functions cannot be arbitrary as they should satisfy $\frac{\partial^2 E}{\partial Z_x \partial Z_y} = \frac{\partial^2 E}{\partial Z_y \partial Z_x}$. This implies that

$$\frac{\partial f_1(Z_x, Z_y)}{\partial Z_y} = \frac{\partial f_2(Z_x, Z_y)}{\partial Z_x}. \tag{5}$$

Substituting (4) into (3) and bringing all Z terms on one side, we get

$$\text{div}(f_1(Z_x, Z_y), f_2(Z_x, Z_y)) - \frac{\partial E}{\partial Z} = \text{div}(f_3(p, q), f_4(p, q)). \tag{6}$$

We first show that the previous solutions such as Poisson solver and Frankot-Chellappa algorithm (in general, projection onto continuous basis functions) can be derived using (6). We then propose other solutions using the above equation. In all solutions we assume Neumann boundary conditions given by $\nabla Z \cdot \hat{\mathbf{n}} = 0$.

Poisson Solver (Spatially Invariant Isotropic Weights): The Poisson equation $\text{div}(Z_x, Z_y) = \text{div}(p, q)$ can be obtained from (6) by substituting $\frac{\partial E}{\partial Z} = 0$, $f_1(Z_x, Z_y) = Z_x$, $f_2(Z_x, Z_y) = Z_y$, $f_3(p, q) = p$, $f_4(p, q) = q$ (see Table 1). (5) is satisfied as both sides are zero.

Numerical Solution: Let $u = \text{div}(p, q)$. Using finite differences and vectoring the 2D matrices in lexicographical ordering, the Poisson equation can be discretized to give $\mathbf{LZ} = \mathbf{u}$, where $\mathbf{u} = [u(1,1), \ldots, u(H, W)]^T$ and the matrix $\mathbf{L}$ is the sparse Laplacian matrix[1] of size $HW \times HW$. Each row of $\mathbf{L}$ has -4 at the diagonal entry and four 1's corresponding to the isotropic Laplacian kernel ∇^2. Z can be obtained as $\mathbf{Z} = \mathbf{L}^{-1}\mathbf{u}$.

Reconstruction using basis functions: Frankot-Chellappa (FC) algorithm reconstructs the surface Z by projecting $\{p, q\}$ on the set of integrable Fourier basis functions. Let $\mathcal{F}(s(x, y))$ denote the Fourier transform of $s(x, y)$[2]. Given $\{p, q\}$, Z is obtained as [8]

---

[1] The Laplacian matrix needs to be modified at the boundary according to the boundary conditions.

[2] $\mathcal{F}(s(x, y)) = \int_{-\infty}^{\infty} \int_{-\infty}^{\infty} s(x, y) e^{-j(\xi_x x + \xi_y y)} dx dy.$

Table 1. A continuum of solutions can be obtained by changing f_i's in (6), which control the anisotropy of the weights applied to the gradients. In weighted solutions, the Laplacian matrix is obtained using a *spatially varying anisotropic* kernel based on weights. This is in contrast with a spatially invariant isotropic kernel used in the Poisson equation. In M-estimators, the weights depend on the residual error, while in Diffusion and Regularization, they depend on the underlying surface.

Algorithm	\multicolumn{4}{c}{f_i's corresponding to (6), $\frac{\partial E}{\partial Z} = 0$}	Equation
	$f_1(Z_x, Z_y)$	$f_2(Z_x, Z_y)$	$f_3(p, q)$	$f_4(p, q)$	
Poisson solver	Z_x	Z_y	p	q	$\mathbf{LZ = u}$
Frank-Chell	$\mathcal{F}(Z_x)\phi$	$\mathcal{F}(Z_y)\phi$	$\mathcal{F}(p)\phi$	$\mathcal{F}(q)\phi$	(7)
α-surface	$b_x Z_x$	$b_y Z_y$	$b_x p$	$b_y q$	$\mathbf{L}_b\mathbf{Z = u}_b$
M-estimators	$w_x Z_x$	$w_y Z_y$	$w_x p$	$w_y q$	$\mathbf{L}_w\mathbf{Z = u}_w$
Regularization	$Z_x + \frac{\lambda}{2}\phi'(Z_x)$	$Z_y + \frac{\lambda}{2}\phi'(Z_y)$	p	q	$(\mathbf{L} + \lambda\mathbf{L}_w)\mathbf{Z = u}$
Diffusion	$d_{11}Z_x + d_{12}Z_y$	$d_{21}Z_x + d_{22}Z_y$	$d_{11}p + d_{12}q$	$d_{21}p + d_{22}q$	$\mathbf{L}_D\mathbf{Z = u}_D$

$$Z = \mathcal{F}^{-1}\left(-j\frac{\xi_x \mathcal{F}(p) + \xi_y \mathcal{F}(q)}{\xi_x^2 + \xi_y^2}\right) . \tag{7}$$

Let $\phi(x, y, \xi_x, \xi_y) = e^{j(\xi_x x + \xi_y y)}$. We have $\phi_x = j\xi_x\phi$, $\phi_y = j\xi_y\phi$. Substituting $\frac{\partial E}{\partial Z} = 0$, $f_1(Z_x, Z_y) = \mathcal{F}(Z_x)\phi$, $f_2(Z_x, Z_y) = \mathcal{F}(Z_y)\phi$, $f_3(p, q) = \mathcal{F}(p)\phi$, $f_4(p, q) = \mathcal{F}(q)\phi$ in (6), we get

$$\mathrm{div}(\mathcal{F}(Z_x)\phi, \mathcal{F}(Z_y)\phi) = \mathrm{div}(\mathcal{F}(p)\phi, \mathcal{F}(q)\phi) ,$$
$$\therefore \quad j\xi_x\mathcal{F}(Z_x) + j\xi_y\mathcal{F}(Z_y) = j\xi_x\mathcal{F}(p) + j\xi_y\mathcal{F}(q) ,$$
$$\therefore \quad -(\xi_x^2 + \xi_y^2)\mathcal{F}(Z) = j\left(\xi_x\mathcal{F}(p) + \xi_y\mathcal{F}(q)\right) .$$

which is equivalent to (7). The *projection* on the Fourier basis functions is implicit in the above definition of f_i's which transforms the domain as weighted basis functions ϕ, the weights being equal to the Fourier transform coefficients. One can generalize this approach to use any set of ortho-normal basis functions ϕ. Kovesi's [12] algorithm is in a similar spirit while using a redundant set of non-orthogonal basis functions.

In the next section, we show how the functions f_i's can be changed to obtain a continuum of solutions. Intuitively, in solving the Poisson equation, the Laplacian matrix $\mathbf{L}$ is obtained by using a *spatially invariant isotropic* kernel (∇^2) which gives equal weights to gradients. This results in Poisson solver being non-robust and favoring smoothness. To obtain robust solutions, we modify the Laplacian matrix by using *spatially varying anisotropic* kernel depending on local shape, or correction gradient field.

4   A Continuum of Solutions

Techniques for robust estimation includes the well-known RANSAC [17] algorithm and M-estimators. We first show that applying RANSAC to gradient integration is computationally prohibitive. To do that we need to find the minimum number m of gradients required for integration. For example, if we want to estimate a line from 2D points, we need $m = 2$ points. For a surface defined over a $H \times W$ grid, the minimum number of gradients required for integration is $m = HW - 1$. However, integration cannot be done using any such set of m gradients. These m gradients should form a spanning tree of the 2D planar graph defined on the grid. This can be seen as follows.

Define a 2D graph over the grid, where the nodes correspond to the value of the surface at each pixel (grid point) and the edges correspond to the gradients (see Fig. 2). To be able to integrate, each node should be reachable using some integration path. Since a spanning tree is a minimal configuration which spans all nodes, the gradients should be in that configuration. For HW nodes, the number of edges in any spanning tree is $HW - 1$, hence $m = HW - 1$.

4.1   RANSAC Gradient Integration (Computationally Prohibitive)

RANSAC works by randomly selecting a set of minimum data points m and finding the number of inliers using a given tolerance level τ. This is repeated T times and the set having the maximum number of inliers is used to estimate the parameters. A naive RANSAC based approach to surface reconstruction can be as follows:

- Find a random spanning tree of the 2D planar graph on the grid.
- Integrate using the gradients corresponding to the edges in the spanning tree. Find the number of gradient inliers using the solution given an error tolerance τ.
- Repeat T times and choose that spanning tree using which maximum number of inliers are obtained.

In [17], it was shown that to ensure with probability γ that at least one of the random selections is an error-free set of m data points, one must make at least T selections, where $T = \log(1 - \gamma)/\log(1 - w^m)$ and w is the probability that a particular data point is an inlier. However, T becomes extremely large as the size of grid is increased. For example, assuming $w = 0.95$, even for a 16×16 grid ($m = 255$), to ensure a probability $\gamma = 0.95$, $T = 1.43 * 10^6$. Thus, a random selection process for choosing the inliers set is practically impossible for decent grid sizes.

4.2 α-Surface: Anisotropic Scaling Using Binary Weights

As noted in [17], if there is a problem related rationale for choosing the set of inliers, one should use a deterministic selection process instead of a random one. In a general estimation problem like fitting a line, each data point is independent and there are no *structural constraints*. For 2D integration, integrability enforces a structural constraint. Also, since the goal is to fit a surface, there is an inherent smoothness involved (at regions separated by discontinuities). Thus, one can decide an initial spanning tree using a deterministic process.

Suppose we fix an initial spanning tree, claiming all gradients corresponding to the edges in this spanning tree to be inliers. We define α-surface as an iterative scheme, where at each iteration, based on the tolerance level α, all gradients for which the correction term is less than α are added to the inliers set. Formally, let S denote the set containing the gradients corresponding to the edges in the initial spanning tree. For an $\alpha \geq 0$, α-surface is given by

- Initialize: Integrate using the gradients in the set S to get Z^0. $k \leftarrow 1$.
- At iteration k: Compute Z_x, Z_y as the gradients of Z^{k-1}.
- If $|\epsilon_x| = |Z_x - p| \leq \alpha$ and Z_x not in S, add Z_x to set S. If $|\epsilon_y| = |Z_y - q| \leq \alpha$ and Z_y not in S, add Z_y to set S. Let n be the number of new additions to set S.
- Integrate using the gradients in S to obtain Z^k.
- Terminate if $n = 0$, else $k \leftarrow k + 1$.

Note that the gradients are not removed from S in the above scheme because the minimal configuration of spanning tree must be satisfied. The parameter α decides between outliers and inliers. If $\alpha = 0$, only the gradients corresponding to the initial spanning tree are considered as inliers and are used for integration. As α is increased, more gradients are used for integration. At a large value of α, all gradients will be treated as inliers and the solution becomes equivalent to that given by the Poisson solver. **By changing α, one can trace a path in the solution space**, where one end is the solution based on a minimal data configuration and the other end is the solution based on using all the data. Thus, α-surface is a weighted approach, where the weights are 1 for gradients in S (used for integration) and 0 otherwise. If we define

$$b_x(x,y) = 1 \quad \text{if } Z_x \in S, \quad 0 \quad \text{o.w.}, \quad b_y(x,y) = 1 \quad \text{if } Z_y \in S, \quad 0 \quad \text{o.w.}, \quad (8)$$

then the error functional J for each iteration of α-surface can be written as

$$J = \int \int b_x(Z_x - p)^2 + b_y(Z_y - q)^2 dx dy . \quad (9)$$

The corresponding Euler-Lagrange equation is $\text{div}(b_x Z_x, b_y Z_y) = \text{div}(b_x p, b_y q)$. Thus, the gradient fields $\{Z_x, Z_y\}$ and $\{p, q\}$ are *scaled* using the binary weights b_x and b_y in an anisotropic manner.

Determining initial spanning tree: An easy way to fix an initial spanning tree is to assign weights to each edge and find the minimum spanning tree (MST). In [18], an approach for curl correction was presented, where first all edges corresponding to non-zero curl were broken. The resulting graph was connected by finding the set of links with minimum total weight by assigning curl values as weights. We have experimented with two types of edge weights: one based on curl values and other based on gradient magnitude. In our experience, assigning gradient magnitude as weights gives better results compared to curl values. For results presented in Sect. 5, we use gradient magnitude as weights.

Determining α: Suppose that the gradients are corrupted by additive IID Gaussian noise $\mathbf{N}(0, \sigma^2)$. In discrete domain, curl values can be obtained by considering the smallest loop made up of 4 square connected pixels, $(y, x), (y, x+1), (y+1, x)$ and $(y+1, x+1)$ (see Fig. 2(middle)). The integral along this loop is

$$C_{p,q}(y, x) = p(y + 1, x) - p(y, x) + q(y, x) - q(y, x + 1) . \quad (10)$$

Using the above equation, the mean and variance of $C_{p,q}$ will be 0 and $4\sigma^2$ respectively (in practice, variance can be higher due to outliers). We estimate σ as $\sigma = \sqrt{(\sigma_C^2 - \mu_C^2)/4}$, where (μ_C, σ_C^2) denote the estimated mean and variance of $C_{p,q}$ using the given gradient field $\{p, q\}$. We use $\alpha = 1.5\sigma$.

Numerical Solution: Let $u_b = \text{div}(b_x p, b_y q)$. $\text{div}(b_x Z_x, b_y Z_y)$ can be written as $\nabla_b^2 Z$, where ∇_b^2 is the *weighted Laplacian kernel* (Fig. 1, ∇_w^2 with b's as weights). This weighted kernel is applied at each pixel to calculate the weighted Laplacian matrix $\mathbf{L}_b$ and the weighted divergence u_b. Z is obtained as $\mathbf{Z} = \mathbf{L}_b^{-1}\mathbf{u}_b$. Note that the matrix $\mathbf{L}_b$ is guaranteed to be invertible since the set S contains the gradients corresponding to some spanning tree (minimal configuration). Next we show how to generalize the inlier/outlier weighting scheme to approaches based on continuous weights.

4.3   Anisotropic Scaling Using Continuous Weights

In **M-estimators**, the effect of outliers is reduced by replacing the squared error residual $\rho(.) = (.)^2$ by another function of residuals. Here ρ is a symmetric, positive-definite function with a unique minimum at zero, and is chosen to be less increasing than square. Several functions such as Huber, Cauchy, Tuckey and those based on L^p norm have been proposed. M-estimators can be formulated as an iterative re-weighted least squares solution

$$J = \int\int w(\epsilon_x^{k-1})(Z_x - p)^2 + w(\epsilon_y^{k-1})(Z_y - q)^2 dxdy , \qquad (11)$$

where the weights $(w_x = w(\epsilon_x^{k-1}), w_y = w(\epsilon_y^{k-1}))$ at iteration k depends on the residual at iteration $k-1$ using the function ρ. The Euler-Lagrange equation of (11) gives $\mathrm{div}(w_x Z_x, w_y Z_y) = \mathrm{div}(w_x p, w_y q)$. This is similar to α-surface except that the weights are continuous. Z can be obtained as $\mathbf{Z} = \mathbf{L}_w^{-1}\mathbf{u}_w$.

Ill-posed problems (such as estimating optical flow) are often solved by **regularization**. The Poisson solver can be regularized by modifying the error function as

$$J(Z) = \int\int \left((Z_x - p)^2 + (Z_y - q)^2\right) + \lambda(\phi(Z_x) + \phi(Z_y))dxdy , \qquad (12)$$

where the second term is the regularization term using function ϕ. Common examples include $\phi(s) = \sqrt{1 + s^2}$ and $\phi(s) = \log(1 + s^2)$. The Euler-Lagrange equation of the above error functional gives: $\mathrm{div}(Z_x, Z_y) + (\lambda/2)\mathrm{div}(\phi'(Z_x), \phi'(Z_y)) = \mathrm{div}(p, q)$. In terms of (6), this corresponds to $\frac{\partial E}{\partial Z} = 0$, $f_1(Z_x, Z_y) = Z_x + \frac{\lambda}{2}\phi'(Z_x)$, $f_2(Z_x, Z_y) = Z_y + \frac{\lambda}{2}\phi'(Z_y)$, $f_3(p, q) = p$, $f_4(p, q) = q$ (Table 1). Minimizing the energy as above is difficult because of the above equation being non-linear. Using the principle of half-quadratic minimization (see [14] for details), one can introduce auxiliary variables $w = (w_x, w_y)$. Minimizing (12) is then equivalent to the following iterative minimization

- $Z^0 \equiv 0$. $k \leftarrow 1$. Repeat until convergence
- $w_x^k = \phi'(Z_x^{k-1})/(2Z_x^{k-1})$, $w_y^k = \phi'(Z_y^{k-1})/(2Z_y^{k-1})$
- Solve for Z^k: $\nabla^2 Z^k + \lambda \mathrm{div}(w_x^k Z_x^k, w_y^k Z_y^k) = \mathrm{div}(p, q)$

The equation for solving Z^k can be rewritten as $(\nabla^2 + \lambda\nabla_{w^k}^2)Z^k = \mathrm{div}(p, q)$, where $\nabla_{w^k}^2$ is the weighted Laplacian kernel (Fig. 1). The solution is given by $\mathbf{Z}^k = (\mathbf{L} + \lambda\mathbf{L}_{w^k})^{-1}\mathbf{u}$.

4.4   Affine Transformation of Gradients Using Diffusion Tensors

Image restoration from noisy images has been a classical problem in image processing. Anisotropic diffusion [13] and energy minimization methods [14][15] are some of the common approaches for image restoration. Weickert [19] proposed a generalization of divergence based equation for image restoration, given by $I_t = \texttt{div}(D\nabla I)$, where $D(y,x) = \begin{bmatrix} d_{11}(y,x) & d_{12}(y,x) \\ d_{21}(y,x) & d_{22}(y,x) \end{bmatrix}$ is a 2×2 symmetric, positive-definite matrix at each pixel (a field of diffusion tensors). We propose to generalize the Poisson solver using D as

$$\texttt{div}(D \begin{bmatrix} Z_x \\ Z_y \end{bmatrix}) = \texttt{div}(D \begin{bmatrix} p \\ q \end{bmatrix}) . \tag{13}$$

The above equation is the Euler-Lagrange equation of the following error functional: $J(Z) = \int \int d_{11}(Z_x - p)^2 + (d_{12} + d_{21})(Z_x - p)(Z_y - q) + d_{22}(Z_y - q)^2 dx dy$ and can be written as

$$\texttt{div}(d_{11}Z_x + d_{12}Z_y, d_{21}Z_x + d_{22}Z_y) = \texttt{div}(d_{11}p + d_{12}q, d_{21}p + d_{22}q) . \tag{14}$$

Note that (14) can be obtained from (6) by substituting $\frac{\partial E}{\partial Z} = 0$, $f_1(Z_x, Z_y) = d_{11}Z_x + d_{12}Z_y$, $f_2(Z_x, Z_y) = d_{21}Z_x + d_{22}Z_y$, $f_3(p,q) = d_{11}p + d_{12}q$, $f_4(p,q) = d_{21}p + d_{22}q$ (Table 1). Thus, Diffusion corresponds to the function f_i's being **affine** in their arguments. The gradients are scaled *and* linearly combined. The symmetry of the tensor D comes directly from the fact that (5) must be satisfied, leading to $d_{21} = d_{12}$. The positive-definiteness criteria is required to avoid ill-conditioning in the numerical solution obtained from discretization. Although we loosely call this scheme as Diffusion, there is no notion of time or iteration in this scheme.

Let $u_D = \texttt{div}(d_{11}p + d_{12}q, d_{21}p + d_{22}q)$. (14) can be written as $\nabla_D^2 Z = u_D$, where ∇_D^2 denote the weighted Laplacian kernel based on the diffusion tensor D (Fig. 1). The solution is given by $\mathbf{Z} = \mathbf{L}_D^{-1} \mathbf{u}_D$.

Obtaining diffusion tensor: Several schemes for obtaining diffusion tensor such as edge preserving [15](Eq. 3.60) and coherence preserving [19] have been proposed. We use an edge-preserving diffusion tensor obtained as follows. At each pixel, we find a 2×2 matrix H by convolving component wise $\begin{bmatrix} p^2 & p \times q \\ p \times q & q^2 \end{bmatrix}$ with a Gaussian kernel. Let $\mu_1 \geq \mu_2$ denote the eigen-values of H. We obtain new eigen values λ_1, λ_2 as: $\lambda_2 = 1$, $\lambda_1 = 1$ if $\mu_1 = 0$, $\lambda_1 = \beta + 1 - \exp(-3.315/\mu_1^4)$ if $\mu_1 > 0$. Here $\beta = 0.02$ to ensure positive-definiteness. D is obtained from the eigen-vectors of H and the new eigen-values.

In all the above solutions, $\frac{\partial E}{\partial Z} = 0$. Our framework could also be used when the Z values are known at some control points [20][21] by utilizing the $\frac{\partial E}{\partial Z}$ term.

Table 2. Mean square errors (MSE) for synthetic data sets

	Poisson-solver	FC		α-surface	M-estimator	Regularization	Diffusion
Ramp-Peaks	10.81		11.20	2.65	9.49	5.35	2.26
Vase	294.46		239.62	22.20	15.14	164.98	2.78
Mozart	2339.24		1316.66	219.72	359.12	806.85	373.72

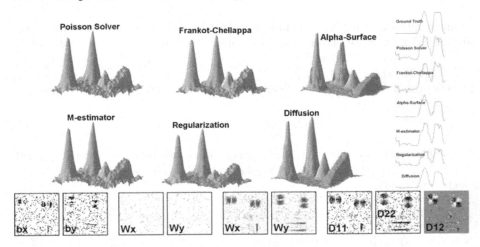

Fig. 4. Reconstruction in presence of noise and outliers (Ramp-Peaks): (Top two rows) (Left) Reconstructed surfaces using various algorithms (Right) One-D height plots for a scan line across the middle of grid for various solutions. (Bottom row) x and y gradient weights for the last iteration of α-surface, M-estimator & Regularization. Last three images shows d_{11}, d_{22} & d_{12} for Diffusion. (white= 1, black= 0) except for d_{12} (white= 0.5, black= -0.5). Notice that α-surface and Diffusion give much better results compared to other approaches.

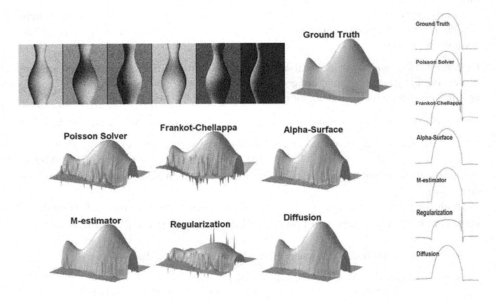

Fig. 5. Photometric Stereo on Vase: (Top row) Noisy input images and true surface (Next two rows) Reconstructed surfaces using various algorithms. (Right Column) One-D height plots for a scan line across the middle of Vase. Better results are obtained using α-surface, Diffusion and M-estimator as compared to Poisson solver, FC and Regularization.

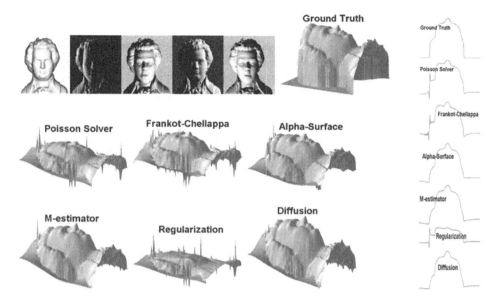

Fig. 6. Photometric Stereo on Mozart: Top row shows noisy input images and the true surface. Next two rows show the reconstructed surfaces using various algorithms. (Right Column) One-D height plots for a scan line across the Mozart face. Notice that all the features of the face are preserved in the solution given by α-surface, Diffusion and M-estimator as compared to other algorithms.

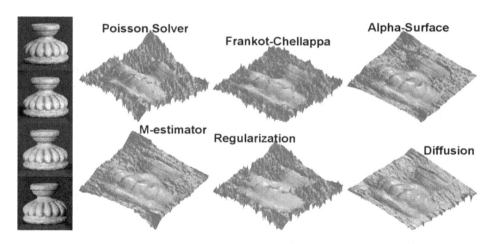

Fig. 7. Photometric Stereo on Flowerpot: Left column shows 4 real images of a flowerpot. Right columns show the reconstructed surfaces using various algorithms. The reconstructions using Poisson solver and Frankot-Chellappa algorithm are noisy and all features (such as top of flowerpot) are not recovered. Diffusion, α-surface and M-estimator methods discount noise while recovering all the salient features.

5   Results

We compare[3] Poisson solver, FC algorithm, α-surface, M-estimator using Huber function, Diffusion and Regularization using $\phi(s) = \sqrt{1 + s^2}$, $\lambda = 10$. Since the divergence of the given gradient field is not modified in the Regularization method, it usually does not perform as well as other approaches. Table 1 gives the summary of f_i's and the equation for each algorithm. Figure 4 shows the reconstructed surfaces using various algorithms from the noisy gradient field of the synthetic surface shown in Figure 3. Note that the surface reconstructed using α-surface and Diffusion are much better than those reconstructed using other approaches. We also present results on calibrated photometric stereo using synthetic and real sequences. The synthetic images were generated using the Lambertian reflectance model under distant point light sources. We first estimate the surface normals (n_x, n_y, n_z) at each pixel. The gradient field is then obtained as $p = -n_x/n_z$, $q = -n_y/n_z$. Pixels where the surface normal cannot be estimated (being in shadow in most of the images) give rise to outliers. Table 2 gives the MSE between the estimated surface and the true surface for various algorithms.

Vase: Six images generated using the Vase depth map are shown in Figure 5. We add Gaussian random noise ($\sigma = 10\%$ of maximum intensity) to the images. In addition, we also add small amount of uniformly distributed noise to the light source directions. The reconstructed surfaces using various algorithms are shown in Figure 5. α-surface, Diffusion and M-estimator gives better shape estimate compared to the rest of algorithms.

Mozart: Five images generated using the Mozart depth map are shown in Figure 6. Gaussian random noise ($\sigma = 5\%$ of maximum intensity) was added to the images. The reconstructed surfaces using various algorithms are also shown in Figure 6. While the discontinuities in the shape are smeared in Poisson solver, FC and Regularization, these are preserved in α-surface, Diffusion and M-estimator.

Flowerpot: Figure 7 shows results on calibrated photometric stereo using 4 real images of a flowerpot. Notice that least squares solutions (Poisson solver and FC algorithm) are noisy and do not recover all features (such as the top of the flowerpot). Diffusion, α-surface and M-estimator approaches recovers all salient features while discounting noise.

6   Conclusions

We proposed a general framework for surface reconstruction from gradient fields, based on controlling the anisotropy of weights for gradients during the integration. We showed that previous solutions such as Poisson solver and Frankot-Chellappa algorithm are special cases of our framework. We derived a continuum of solvers: α-surface (binary weights) where α allows tradeoff between smoothness and robustness, Regularization and M-estimators (continuous weights) and Diffusion (affine transformation on gradients). Results and comparisons showed that α-surface and Diffusion method give consistently better feature preserving reconstructions.

---

[3] Matlab code is available at http://www.cfar.umd.edu/~aagrawal

References

1. Horn, B.: Height and gradient from shading. Int'l J. Computer Vision **5** (1990) 37–75
2. Horn, B.: Determining lightness from an image. Comput. Graphics, Image Processing **3** (1974) 277–299
3. Fattal, R., Lischinski, D., Werman, M.: Gradient domain high dynamic range compression. ACM Trans. Graph. **21** (2002) 249–256
4. Agrawal, A., Raskar, R., Nayar, S., Li, Y.: Removing photography artifacts using gradient projection and flash-exposure sampling. ACM Trans. Graph. **24** (2005) 828–835
5. Forsyth, D.: Shape from texture and integrability. In: Proc. Int'l Conf. Computer Vision. (2001) 447–452
6. Belhumeur, P., Kriegman, D., Yuille, A.: The bas-relief ambiguity. Int'l J. Computer Vision **35** (1999) 33–44
7. Simchony, T., Chellappa, R., Shao, M.: Direct analytical methods for solving poisson equations in computer vision problems. IEEE Trans. Pattern Anal. Machine Intell. **12** (1990) 435–446
8. Frankot, R.T., Chellappa, R.: A method for enforcing integrability in shape from shading algorithms. IEEE Trans. Pattern Anal. Machine Intell. **10** (1988) 439–451
9. Yuille, A., Snow, D.: Shape and albedo from multiple images using integrability. In: Proc. Conf. Computer Vision and Pattern Recognition. (1997) 158–164
10. Petrovic, N., Cohen, I., Frey, B., Koetter, R., Huang, T.: Enforcing integrability for surface reconstruction algorithms using belief propagation in graphical models. In: Proc. Conf. Computer Vision and Pattern Recognition. Volume 1. (2001) 743–748
11. Georghiades, A.S., Belhumeur, P.N., Kriegman, D.J.: From few to many: Illumination cone models for face recognition under variable lighting and pose. IEEE Trans. Pattern Anal. Machine Intell. **23** (2001) 643–660
12. Kovesi, P.: Shapelets correlated with surface normals produce surfaces. In: Proc. Int'l Conf. Computer Vision. (2005) 994–1001
13. Perona, P., Malik, J.: Scale-space and edge detection using anisotropic diffusion. IEEE Trans. Pattern Anal. Machine Intell. **12** (1990) 629–639
14. Charbonnier, P., Blanc-Feraud, L., Aubert, G., Barluad, M.: Deterministic edge-preserving regularization in computed imaging. IEEE Trans. Image Processing **6** (1997) 298–311
15. Aubert, G., Kornprobst, P.: Mathematical Problems in Image Processing: Partial Differential Equations and the Calculus of Variations. Volume 147 of Applied Mathematical Sciences. Springer-Verlag (2002)
16. Karacali, B., Snyder, W.: Noise reduction in surface reconstruction from a given gradient field. Int'l J. Computer Vision **60** (2004) 25–44
17. Fischler, M.A., Bolles, R.C.: Random sample consensus: A paradigm for model fitting with applications to image analysis and automated cartography. Comm. of the ACM **24** (1981) 381–395
18. Agrawal, A., Chellappa, R., Raskar, R.: An algebraic approach to surface reconstruction from gradient fields. In: Proc. Int'l Conf. Computer Vision. Volume 1. (2005) 174–181
19. Weickert, J.: Anisotropic Diffusion in Image Processing. PhD thesis, University of Kaiserslautern, Germany (1996)
20. Horovitz, I., Kiryati, N.: Depth from gradient fields and control points: Bias correction in photometric stereo. Image and Vision Computing **22** (2004) 681–694
21. Kimmel, R., Yavneh, I.: An algebraic multigrid approach to image analysis. SIAM J. Sci. Comput. **24** (2003) 1218–1231

Practical Global Optimization for Multiview Geometry

Sameer Agarwal[1], Manmohan Krishna Chandraker[1], Fredrik Kahl[2],
David Kriegman[1], and Serge Belongie[1]

[1] University of California, San Diego, CA 92093, USA
{sagarwal, mkchandraker, kriegman, sjb}@cs.ucsd.edu
[2] Lund University, Lund, Sweden
fredrik@maths.lth.se

Abstract. This paper presents a practical method for finding the provably globally optimal solution to numerous problems in projective geometry including multiview triangulation, camera resectioning and homography estimation. Unlike traditional methods which may get trapped in local minima due to the non-convex nature of these problems, this approach provides a theoretical guarantee of global optimality. The formulation relies on recent developments in fractional programming and the theory of convex underestimators and allows a unified framework for minimizing the standard L_2-norm of reprojection errors which is optimal under Gaussian noise as well as the more robust L_1-norm which is less sensitive to outliers. The efficacy of our algorithm is empirically demonstrated by good performance on experiments for both synthetic and real data. An open source MATLAB toolbox that implements the algorithm is also made available to facilitate further research.

1 Introduction

Projective geometry is one of the success stories of computer vision. Methods for recovering the three dimensional structure of a scene from multiple images and the projective transformations that relate the scene and its images are now the workhorse subroutines in applications ranging from specialized tasks like matchmove in filmmaking to consumer products like image mosaicing for digital camera users.

The key step in each of these methods is the solution of an appropriately formulated optimization problem. These optimization problems are typically highly non-linear and finding their global optima in general has been shown to be NP-hard [1]. Methods for solving these problems are based on a combination of heuristic initialization and local optimization to converge to a *locally* optimal solution. A common method for finding the initial solution is to use a direct linear transform (for example, the eight-point algorithm [2]) to convert the optimization problem into a linear least squares problem. The solution then serves as the initial point for a non-linear minimization method based on the Jacobian and Hessian of the objective function, for instance, bundle adjustment. As has

A. Leonardis, H. Bischof, and A. Pinz (Eds.): ECCV 2006, Part I, LNCS 3951, pp. 592–605, 2006.

been documented, the success of these methods critically depends on the quality of the initial estimate [3].

In this paper we present the first practical algorithm for finding the globally optimal solution to a variety of problems in multiview geometry. The problems we address include general n-view triangulation, camera resectioning (also called cameras pose or absolute orientation) and the estimation of general projections $\mathbb{P}^n \mapsto \mathbb{P}^m$, for $n \geq m$. We solve each of these problems under three different noise models, including the standard Gaussian distribution and two variants of the bi-variate Laplace distribution. Our algorithm is provably optimal, that is, given any tolerance ϵ, if the optimization problem is feasible, the algorithm returns a solution which is at most ϵ far from the global optimum. The algorithm is a branch and bound style method based on extensions to recent developments in the fractional and convex programming literature [4, 5, 6]. While the worst case complexity of our algorithm is exponential, we will show in our experiments that for a fixed ϵ the runtime of our algorithm scales almost linearly with problem size, making this a very attractive approach for use in practice.

Recently there has been some progress made towards finding the global solution to a *few* of these optimization problems. An attempt to generalize the optimal solution of two-view triangulation [7] to three views was done in [8] based on Gröbner basis. However, the resulting algorithm is numerically unstable, computationally expensive and does not generalize for more views or harder problems like resectioning. In [9], linear matrix inequalities were used to approximate the global optimum, but no guarantee of actually obtaining the global optimum is given. Also, there are unsolved problems concerning numerical stability. Robustification using the L_1-norm was presented in [10], but the approach is restricted to the affine camera model. In [11], a wider class of geometric reconstruction problems was solved globally, but with L_∞-norm.

In summary, our main contributions are:

- A scalable algorithm for solving a class of multiview problems with a guarantee of global optimality.
- In addition to using the standard L_2-norm of reprojection errors, we are able to handle the robust L_1-norm for the perspective camera model.
- Introduction of fractional programming to the computer vision community.

We begin with an exposition on fractional programming in the next section along with an introduction to branch and bound algorithms. We describe in detail the construction of the lower bounds and present our initialization methods along with a novel bounds propagation scheme. This scheme exploits the special properties of structure and motion problems to restrict the branching process to a small, fixed number of dimensions independent of the problem size. Finally, we demonstrate that various structure and motion problems can indeed be formulated as fractional programs of the type we deal with and present the results of our experiments.

2 Fractional Programming

In its most general form, fractional programming seeks to minimize/maximize the sum of $p \geq 1$ fractions subject to convex constraints. Our interest from the point of view of multiview geometry, however, is specific to the minimization problem

$$\min_{x} \sum_{i=1}^{p} \frac{f_i(x)}{g_i(x)} \quad \text{subject to} \quad x \in D \tag{F1}$$

where $f_i : \mathbb{R}^n \to \mathbb{R}$ and $g_i : \mathbb{R}^n \to \mathbb{R}$ are convex and concave functions, respectively, and the domain $D \subset \mathbb{R}^n$ is a convex, compact set. Further, it is assumed that both f_i and g_i are positive with lower and upper bounds over D. Even with these restrictions the above problem is NP-complete [1], but we demonstrate that practical and reliable estimation of the global optimum is still possible for the multiview problems considered.

Let us assume that we have available to us upper and lower bounds on the functions $f_i(x)$ and $g_i(x)$, denoted by the intervals $[l_i, u_i]$ and $[L_i, U_i]$, respectively. Let Q_0 denote the $2p$-dimensional rectangle $[l_1, u_1] \times \cdots \times [l_p, u_p] \times [L_1, U_1] \times \cdots \times [L_p, U_p]$. Introducing auxiliary variables $t = (t_1, \ldots, t_p)^\top$ and $s = (s_1, \ldots, s_p)^\top$, consider the following alternate optimization problem:

$$\min_{x,t,s} \sum_{i=1}^{p} \frac{t_i}{s_i}$$

$$\text{subject to} \quad f_i(x) \leq t_i \qquad\qquad g_i(x) \geq s_i$$
$$x \in D \qquad\qquad (t, s) \in Q_0. \tag{F2}$$

We note that the feasible set for problem (F2) is a convex, compact set and that (F2) is feasible if and only if (F1) is. Indeed the following holds true [5]:

Theorem 1. $(x^*, t^*, s^*) \in \mathbb{R}^{n+2p}$ *is a global, optimal solution for* (F2) *if and only if* $t_i^* = f_i(x^*)$, $s_i^* = g_i(x^*)$, $i = 1, \cdots, p$ *and* $x^* \in \mathbb{R}^n$ *is a global optimal solution for* (F1).

Thus, Problems (F1) and (F2) are equivalent, and henceforth we shall restrict our attention to Problem (F2).

2.1 Branch and Bound Theory

Branch and bound algorithms are non-heuristic methods for global optimization in non-convex problems. They maintain a provable upper and/or lower bound on the (globally) optimal objective value and terminate with a certificate proving that the solution is ϵ-suboptimal (that is, within ϵ of the global optimum), for arbitrarily small ϵ.

Consider a non-convex, scalar-valued objective function $\Phi(x)$, for which we seek a global optimum over a rectangle Q_0 as in Problem (F2). For a rectangle $Q \subseteq Q_0$, let $\Phi_{\min}(Q)$ denote the minimum value of the function Φ over Q. Also, let $\Phi_{lb}(Q)$ be a function that satisfies the following conditions:

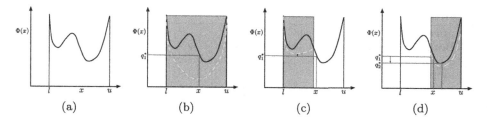

Fig. 1. This figure illustrates the operation of a branch and bound algorithm on a one dimensional non-convex minimization problem. Figure (a) shows the the function $\Phi(x)$ and the interval $l \leq x \leq u$ in which it is to be minimized. Figure (b) shows the convex relaxation of $\Phi(x)$ (indicated in yellow/dashed), its domain (indicated in blue/shaded) and the point for which it attains a minimum value. q_1^* is the corresponding value of the function Φ. This value is the best estimate of the minimum of $\Phi(x)$ is used to reject the left subinterval in Figure (c) as the minimum value of the convex relaxation is higher than q_1^*. Figure (d) shows the lower bounding operation in the right sub-interval in which a new estimate q_2^* of the minimum value of $\Phi(x)$.

(L1) $\Phi_{\mathrm{lb}}(Q)$ computes a lower bound on $\Phi_{\min}(Q)$ over the domain Q, that is, $\Phi_{\mathrm{lb}}(Q) \leq \Phi_{\min}(Q)$.
(L2) The approximation gap $\Phi_{\min}(Q) - \Phi_{\mathrm{lb}}(Q)$ uniformly converges to zero as the maximum half-length of sides of Q, denoted $|Q|$, tends to zero, that is

$$\forall\, \epsilon > 0,\ \exists\, \delta > 0 \text{ s.t. } \forall Q \subseteq Q_0,\ |Q| \leq \delta \Rightarrow \Phi_{\min}(Q) - \Phi_{\mathrm{lb}}(Q) \leq \epsilon.$$

The branch and bound algorithm begins by computing $\Phi_{\mathrm{lb}}(Q_0)$ and the point $q^* \in Q_0$ which minimizes $\Phi_{\mathrm{lb}}(Q_0)$. If $\Phi(q^*) - \Phi_{\mathrm{lb}}(Q_0) < \epsilon$, the algorithm terminates. Otherwise Q_0 is partitioned as a union of subrectangles $Q_0 = Q_1 \cup \cdots Q_k$ for some $k \geq 2$ and the lower bounds $\Phi_{\mathrm{lb}}(Q_i)$ as well as points q_i (at which these lower bounds are attained) are computed for each Q_i. Let $q^* = \arg\min_{\{q_i\}_{i=1}^k} \Phi(q_i)$. We deem $\Phi(q^*)$ to be the current best estimate of $\Phi_{\min}(Q_0)$. The algorithm terminates when $\Phi(q^*) - \min_{1 \leq i \leq k} \Phi_{\mathrm{lb}}(Q_i) < \epsilon$, else the partition of Q_0 is refined by further dividing some subrectangle and repeating the above. The rectangles Q_i for which $\Phi_{\mathrm{lb}}(Q_i) > \Phi(q^*)$ cannot contain the global minimum and are not considered for further refinement. A graphical illustration of the algorithm is presented in Figure 1.

Computation of the lower bounding functions is referred to as *bounding*, while the procedure that chooses a rectangle and subdivides it is called *branching*. The choice of the rectangle picked for refinement in the branching step and the actual subdivision itself are essentially heuristic. We consider the rectangle with the smallest minimum of Φ_{lb} as the most promising to contain the global minimum and subdivide it into $k = 2$ rectangles. Algorithm 1 uses the above-mentioned functions to present a concise pseudocode for the branch and bound method.

Although guaranteed to find the global optimum (or a point arbitrarily close to it), the worst case complexity of a branch and bound algorithm is exponential.

Algorithm 1. Branch and Bound

Require: Initial rectangle Q_0 and $\epsilon > 0$.

1: **Bound** : Compute $\Phi_{\text{lb}}(Q_0)$ and minimizer $q^* \in Q_0$.
2: $S = \{Q_0\}$ //Initialize the set of candidate rectangles
3: **loop**
4:     $Q' = \arg\min_{Q \in S} \Phi_{\text{lb}}(Q)$ //Choose rectangle with lowest bound
5:     **if** $\Phi(q^*) - \Phi_{\text{lb}}(Q') < \epsilon$ **then**
6:         **return** q^* //Termination condition satsified
7:     **end if**
8:     **Branch** : $Q' = Q_l \cup Q_r$
9:     $S = (S/\{Q'\}) \cup \{Q_l, Q_r\}$ //Update the set of candidate rectangles
10:    **Bound** : Compute $\Phi_{\text{lb}}(Q_l)$ and minimizer $q_l \in Q_l$.
11:    **if** $\Phi(q_l) < \Phi(q^*)$ **then**
12:        $q^* = q_l$ //Update the best feasible solution
13:    **end if**
14:    **Bound** : Compute $\Phi_{\text{lb}}(Q_r)$ and minimizer $q_r \in Q_r$.
15:    **if** $\Phi(q_r) < \Phi(q^*)$ **then**
16:        $q^* = q_r$ //Update the best feasible solution
17:    **end if**
18:    $S = \{\, Q \,|\, Q \in S, \Phi_{\text{lb}}(Q) < \Phi(q^*) \,\}$ //Discard rectangles with high lower bounds
19: **end loop**

However, we will show in our experiments that the special properties offered by multiview problems lead to fast convergence rates in practice.

2.2 Bounding

The goal of the **Bound** procedure is to provide the branch and bound algorithm with a bound on the smallest value the objective function takes in a domain. The computation of the function Φ_{lb} must possess three properties - crucial to the efficiency and convergence of the algorithm: (i) it must be easily computable, (ii) must provide as tight a bound as possible and (iii) must be easily minimizable. Precisely these features are inherent in the *convex envelope* of our objective function, which we define below.

Definition 1 (Convex Envelope). *Let $f : S \to \mathbb{R}$, where $S \subset \mathbb{R}^n$ is a non-empty convex set. The convex envelope of f over S (denoted* **convenv** f*) is a convex function such that (i)* **convenv** $f(x) \leq f(x)$ *for all $x \in S$ and (ii) for any other convex function u, satisfying $u(x) \leq f(x)$ for all $x \in S$, we have* **convenv** $f(x) \geq u(x)$ *for all $x \in S$.*

Finding the convex envelope of an arbitrary function may be as hard as finding the global minimum. To be of any advantage, the envelope construction must be cheaper than the optimal estimation.

In [4], it was shown that the convex envelope for a single fraction t/s, where $t \in [\,l, u\,]$ and $s \in [\,L, U\,]$, is given as the solution to the following *Second Order Cone Program* (SOCP):

$$\text{minimize} \quad \rho$$

$$\text{subject to} \quad \left\| \begin{matrix} 2\lambda\sqrt{l} \\ \rho' - s' \end{matrix} \right\| \leq \rho' + s' \qquad \left\| \begin{matrix} 2(1-\lambda)\sqrt{u} \\ \rho - \rho' - s + s' \end{matrix} \right\| \leq \rho - \rho' + s - s'$$

$$\lambda L \leq s \leq \lambda U \qquad\qquad (1-\lambda)L \leq s - s' \leq (1-\lambda)U$$

$$\rho' \geq 0 \qquad\qquad\qquad \rho - \rho' \geq 0$$

$$l \leq t \leq u \qquad\qquad\qquad L \leq s \leq U$$

where we have substituted $\lambda = \dfrac{u-t}{u-l}$ for ease of notation, and ρ, ρ', s' are auxiliary scalar variables.

It is easy to show that the convex envelop of a sum is always greater (or equal) than the sum of convex envelopes. That is, if $f = \sum_i t_i/s_i$ then **convenv** $f \geq \sum_i$ **convenv** t_i/s_i. It follows that in order to compute a lower bound on Problem (F2), one can compute the sum of convex envelopes for t_i/s_i subject to the convex constraints. Hence, this way of computing a lower bound $\Phi_{\mathrm{lb}}(Q)$ amounts to solving a convex SOCP problem which can be done efficiently [12]. It can be shown [5] that the convex envelope satisfies conditions (L1) and (L2), and therefore, is well-suited for our branch and bound algorithm.

2.3   Branching

Branch and bound algorithms can be slow, in fact, the worst case complexity grows exponentially with problem size. Thus, one must devise a sufficiently sophisticated branching strategy to expedite the convergence.

A general branching strategy applicable to fractional programs [5] is to branch along p dimensions corresponding to the denominators s_i of each fractional term t_i/s_i in Problem (F2). This limits the practical applicability to problems containing 10-12 fractions [13]. However, we demonstrate in Section 4.1 that for our class of problems, it is possible to restrict the branching to a *small* and *fixed* number of dimensions regardless of the number of fractions, which substantially enhances the number of fractions our algorithm can handle.

Algorithm 2. α-bisection

Require: A rectangle $Q \subset \mathbb{R}^{2p}$
 1: $j = \arg\max_{i=1,\ldots,p}(U_i - L_i)$
 2: $V_j = \alpha(U_j - L_j)$
 3: $Q_l = [\, l_1, u_1 \,] \times \cdots \times [\, l_p, u_p \,] \times [\, L_1, U_1 \,] \times \cdots \times [\, L_j, V_j \,] \times \cdots \times [\, L_p, U_p \,]$
 4: $Q_r = [\, l_1, u_1 \,] \times \cdots \times [\, l_p, u_p \,] \times [\, L_1, U_1 \,] \times \cdots \times [\, V_j, U_j \,] \times \cdots \times [\, L_p, U_p \,]$
 5: **return** (Q_l, Q_r)

After a choice has been made of the rectangle to be further partitioned, there are two issues that must be addressed within the branching phase - namely, deciding the dimensions along *which* to split the rectangle and *where* along a chosen dimension to split the rectangle. We pick the dimension with the largest interval and employ a simple spatial division procedure, called α-bisection (see Algorithm 2) for a given scalar α, $0 < \alpha \leq 0.5$. It can be shown [5] that the α-bisection leads to a branch-and-bound algorithm which is convergent.

3   Applications to Multiview Geometry

In this section, we elaborate on adapting the theory developed in the previous section to common problems of multiview geometry. In the standard formulation of these problems based on the Maximum Likelihood Principle, the exact form of the objective function to be optimized depends on the choice of noise model. The noise model describes how the errors in the observations are statistically distributed given the ground truth.

In the Gaussian noise model, assuming an isotropic distribution of error with a known standard deviation σ, the likelihood for two image points - one measured point x and one true x' - is

$$p(x|x') = (2\pi\sigma^2)^{-1} \exp(-\|x - x'\|_2^2/(2\sigma^2)) \ . \tag{1}$$

Thus maximizing the likelihood of the observed point correspondences and assuming iid noise, is equivalent to minimizing $\sum_i \|x_i - x_i'\|_2^2$, which we interpret as a combination of two vector norms - the first for the point-wise error in the image and the second that cumulates these point-wise errors. We call this the (L_2, L_2)-formulation.

The exact definition of the Laplace noise model depends on the particular definition of the multivariate Laplace distribution [14]. In the current work we choose two of the simpler definitions. The first one is a special case of the multivariate exponential power distribution giving us the likelihood function:

$$p(x|x') = (2\pi\sigma)^{-1} \exp(-\|x - x'\|_2/\sigma) \ . \tag{2}$$

An alternative view of the bivariate Laplace distribution is to consider it as the joint distribution of two iid univariate Laplace random variables, where $x = (u, v)^\top$ and $x' = (u', v')^\top$ which gives us the following likelihood function

$$p(x|x') = \frac{1}{2\sigma}e^{-\frac{1}{\sigma}|u-u'|} \frac{1}{2\sigma}e^{-\frac{1}{\sigma}|v-v'|} \ = \ (4\sigma^2)^{-1} \exp(-\|x - x'\|_1/\sigma) \ . \tag{3}$$

Maximizing the likelihoods in (2) and (3) is equivalent to minimizing $\sum_i \|x_i - x_i'\|_2$ and $\sum_i \|x_i - x_i'\|_1$, respectively. Again, in our interpretation of these expressions as a combination of two vector norms, we denote these minimizations as (L_2, L_1) and (L_1, L_1), respectively.

We summarize the classification of overall error under various noise models in Table 1.

Table 1. Different cost-functions of reprojection errors

Gaussian	Laplacian I	Laplacian II
$\sum_i \|x_i - x_i'\|_2^2$	$\sum_i \|x_i - x_i'\|_2$	$\sum_i \|x_i - x_i'\|_1$
(L_2, L_2)	(L_2, L_1)	(L_1, L_1)

3.1   Triangulation

The primary concern in triangulation is to recover the 3D scene point given measured image points and known camera matrices in $N \geq 2$ views. Let $P = [p_1 \quad p_2 \quad p_3]^\top$ denote the 3×4 camera where p_i is a 4-vector, $(u, v)^\top$ image coordinates, $X = (U, V, W, 1)^\top$ the extended 3D point coordinates, then the reprojection residual vector for this image is given by

$$r = \left(u - \frac{p_1^\top X}{p_3^\top X}, v - \frac{p_2^\top X}{p_3^\top X} \right)^\top \tag{4}$$

and hence the objective function to minimize becomes $\sum_{i=1}^{N} ||r_i||_p^q$ for the (L_p, L_q)-case. In addition, one can require that $p_3^\top X > 0$ which corresponds to the 3D point being in front of the camera. We now show that by defining $||r||_p^q$ as an appropriate ratio f/g of a convex function f and a concave function g, the problem in (4) can be identified with the one in (F2).

$(\boldsymbol{L_2, L_2})$. The norm-squared residual of r can be written $||r||_2^2 = ((a^\top X)^2 + (b^\top X)^2)/(p_3^\top X)^2$ where a, b are 4-vectors dependent on the known image coordinates *and* the known camera matrix. By setting $f = ((a^\top X)^2 + (b^\top X)^2))/(p_3^\top X)$ and $g = p_3^\top X$, a convex-concave ratio is obtained. It is straightforward to verify the convexity of f via the convexity of its epigraph:

$$\textbf{epi} f = \{(X, t) \,|\, t \geq f(X)\}$$
$$= \left\{ (X, t) \,|\, \frac{1}{2}(t + p_3^\top X) \geq \left\| \left(a^\top X, b^\top X, \frac{1}{2}(t - p_3^\top X) \right) \right\| \right\},$$

which is a second-order convex cone [6].

$(\boldsymbol{L_2, L_1})$. Similar to the (L_2, L_2)-case, the norm of r can be written $||r||_2 = f/g$ where $f = \sqrt{(a^\top X)^2 + (b^\top X)^2}$ and $g = p_3^\top X$. Again, the convexity of f can be established by noting that the epigraph $\textbf{epi} f = \{(X, t) \,|\, t \geq ||(a^\top X, b^\top X)||\}$ is a second-order cone.

$(\boldsymbol{L_1, L_1})$. Using the same notation as above, the L_1-norm of r is given by $||r||_1 = f/g$ where $f = |a^\top X| + |b^\top X|$ and $g = p_3^\top X$.

In all the cases above, g is trivially concave since it is linear in X.

3.2   Camera Resectioning

The problem of camera resectioning is the analogous counterpart of triangulation whereby the aim is to recover the camera matrix given $N \geq 6$ scene points and their corresponding images. The main difference compared to the triangulation problem is that the number of degrees of freedom has increased from 3 to 11.

Let $p = \left(p_1^\top, p_2^\top, p_3^\top \right)^\top$ be a homogeneous 12-vector of the unknown elements in the camera matrix P. Now, the squared norm of the residual vector r in (4) can be rewritten in the form $||r||_2^2 = ((a^\top p)^2 + (b^\top p)^2)/(X^\top p_3)^2$, where a, b are 12-vectors determined by the coordinates of the image point x and the scene point

X. Recalling the derivations for the (L_2, L_2)-case of triangulation, it follows that $||r||_2^2$ can be written as a fraction f/g with $f = ((a^\top p)^2 + (b^\top p)^2)/(X^\top p_3)$ which is convex and $g = X^\top p_3$ concave in accordance with Problem (F2). Similar derivations show that the same is true for camera resectioning with (L_2, L_1)-norm as well as (L_1, L_1)-norm.

3.3   Projections from $\mathbb{P}^n$ to $\mathbb{P}^m$

Our formulation for the camera resectioning problem is very general and not restricted by the dimensionality of the world or image points. Thus, it can be viewed as a special case of a $\mathbb{P}^n \mapsto \mathbb{P}^m$ projection with $n = 3$ and $m = 2$.

When $m = n$, the mapping is called a homography. Typical applications include homography estamation of planar scene points to the image plane, or inter-image homographies ($m = n = 2$) as well as the estimation of 3D homographies due to different coordinate systems ($m = n = 3$). For projections ($n > m$), camera resection is the most common application, but numerous other instances appear in the computer vision field [15].

4   Multiview Fractional Programming

4.1   Bounds Propagation

Consider a fractional program with p fractions. For all problems presented in Section 3, the denominator is a linear function in the unknowns. For example, in the case of triangulation, the unknown point coordinates $X = (U, V, W, 1)^\top$ are linear in $g_i(X) = p_{3i}^\top X$ for $i = 1, \ldots, p$. Suppose $p > 3$ and bounds are given on three denominators, say g_1, g_2, g_3 which are not linearly dependent. These bounds then define a convex polytope in $\mathbb{R}^3$. This polytope constrains the possible values of U, V and W which in turn induce bounds on the other denominators $g_4, \ldots, g_p$. The bounds can be obtained by solving a set of linear equations each time branching is performed.

Thus, it is sufficient to branch on three dimensions in the case of triangulation. Similarly, in the case of camera resectioning, the denominator has only three degrees of freedom and more generally, for projections $\mathbb{P}^n \mapsto \mathbb{P}^m$, the denominator has n degrees of freedom.

4.2   Coordinate System Independence

All three error norms (see Table 1) are independent of the coordinate system chosen for the scene (or source) points. In the image, one can translate and scale the points without effecting the norms. For all problem instances and all three error norms considered, the coordinate system can be chosen such that the first denominator g_1 is a constant equal to one. Thus, there is no need to approximate the first term in the cost-function with a convex envelope, since it is a convex function already.

4.3   Initialization

In the construction of the algorithm we assumed that initial bounds are available on the numerator and the denominator of each of the fractions. This initial rectangle Q_0 in $\mathbb{R}^{2p}$ is the starting point for the branch and bound algorithm.

Let γ be an upper bound on the reprojection error in pixels (specified by the user), then we can bound the denominators $g_i(x)$ by solving the following set of optimization problems:

$$\text{for } i = 1, \ldots, p, \qquad \min g_i(x) \qquad \max g_i(x)$$
$$\frac{f_j(x)}{g_j(x)} \leq \gamma \qquad \qquad \frac{f_j(x)}{g_j(x)} \leq \gamma \qquad j = 1, \ldots, p.$$

Depending on the choice of error norm, the above optimization problems will be instances of linear or quadratic programming. We will call this γ-initialization. While tight bounds on the denominators are crucial for the performance of the overall algorithm, we have found that the bounds on the numerators are not. Therefore, we set the numerator bounds to preset values.

5   Experiments

Both triangulation and estimation of projections $\mathbb{P}^n \mapsto \mathbb{P}^m$ have been implemented for all three error norms in Table 1 in the Matlab environment using the convex solver SeDuMi [12] and the code is publicly available[1]. The optimization is based on the branch and bound procedure as described in Algorithm 1 and α-bisection (see Algorithm 2) with $\alpha = 0.5$. To compute the initial bounds, γ-initialization is used (see Section 4.3) with $\gamma = 15$ pixels for both real and synthetic data. The branch and bound terminates when the difference between the global optimum and the underestimator is less than $\epsilon = 0.05$. In all experiments, the Root Mean Squares (RMS) errors of the reprojection residuals are reported regardless of the computation method.

5.1   Synthetic Data

Our data is generated by creating random 3D points within the cube $[-1, 1]^3$ and then projecting to the images. The image coordinates are corrupted with iid Gaussian noise with different levels of variance. In all graphs, the average of 200 trials are plotted. In the first experiment, we employ a weak camera geometry for triangulation, whereby three cameras are placed along a line at distances 5, 6 and 7 units, respectively, from the origin. In Figures 2(a) and (b), the reprojection errors and the 3D errors are plotted, respectively. The (L_2, L_2) method, on the average, results in a much lower error than bundle adjustment, which can be attributed to bundle adjustment being enmeshed in local minima due to the non-convexity of the problem. The graph in Figure 2(c) depicts the percentage

---

[1] See http://www.maths.lth.se/matematiklth/personal/fredrik/download.html.

number of times (L_2, L_2) outperforms bundle adjustment in accuracy. It is evident that higher the noise level, the more likely it is that the bundle adjustment method does not attain the global optimum.

In the next experiment, we simulate outliers in the data in the following manner. Varying numbers of cameras, placed 10° apart and viewing toward the origin, are generated in a circular motion of radius 2 units. In addition to Gaussian noise with standard deviation 0.01 pixels for all image points, the coordinates for *one* of the image points have been perturbed by adding or subtracting 0.1 pixels. This point may be regarded as an outlier. As can seen from Figure 3(a) and (b), the reprojection errors are lowest for the (L_2, L_2) and bundle methods, as expected. However, in terms of 3D-error, the L_1 methods perform best and already from two cameras one gets a reasonable estimate of the scene point.

In the third experiment, six 3D points in general position are used to compute the camera matrix. Note that this is a minimal case, as it is not possible to compute the camera matrix from five points. The true camera location is at a distance of two units from the origin. The reprojection errors are graphed in Figure 3(c). Results for bundle adjustment and the (L_2, L_2) methods are identical and thus, likelihood of local minima is low.

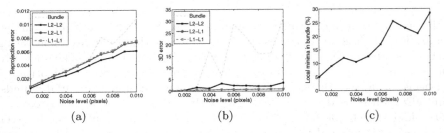

(a)   (b)   (c)

Fig. 2. Triangulation with forward motion. The performance of bundle adjustment degrades rapidly with increasing noise, while our algorithm continues to perform well, both in terms of (a) reprojection error and (b) 3D error. The plot in (c) shows percentage number of times our algorithm outperforms bundle adjustment.

Table 2. Mean and median runtimes (in seconds) for the three algorithms as the number of points for a resectioning problem is increased. MI is the percentage number of times the algorithm reached 500 iterations.

Points	(L_2, L_2)			(L_2, L_1)			(L_1, L_1)		
	Mean	Median	MI	Mean	Median	MI	Mean	Median	MI
6	42.8	35.5	0.5	41.6	31.5	1.5	7.9	4.7	0.0
10	51.8	41.9	0.5	105.8	66.6	3.5	20.3	13.5	0.5
20	72.7	50.5	2.5	210.2	121.2	9.0	46.8	28.2	1.0
50	145.5	86.5	4.5	457.9	278.3	8.5	143.0	75.9	2.5
70	172.5	107.8	3.5	616.5	368.7	7.5	173.0	102.8	1.5
100	246.2	148.5	4.5	728.7	472.4	4.0	242.3	133.6	2.0

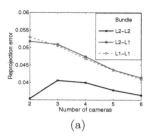 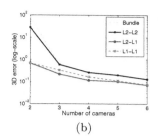 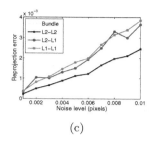

(a)   (b)   (c)

Fig. 3. (a) and (b) show reprojection and 3D erorrs, respectively, for triangulation with one outlier. Despite a higher reprojection error, the L_1-algorithms better bundle adjustment in terms of 3D error. (c) Reprojection errors for camera resectioning.

To demonstrate scalability, Table 2 reports the runtime of our algorithm over a variety of problem sizes for resectioning. The tolerance, ϵ, here is set to within 1 percent of the global optimum, the maximum number of iterations to 500 and mean and median runtimes are reported over 200 trials. The algorithm's excellent runtime performance is demonstrated by almost linear scaling in runtimes.

5.2   Real Data

We have evaluated the performance on two publicly available data sets as well - the dinosaur and the corridor sequences. In Table 3, the reprojection er-

Table 3. Reprojection errors (in pixels) for triangulation and resectioning in the Dinosaur and Corridor data sets. "Dinosaur" has 36 turntable images with 324 tracked points, while "Corridor" has 11 images in forward motion with a total of 737 points.

Experiment	Bundle		(L_2, L_2)		(L_2, L_1)		(L_1, L_1)	
	Mean	Std	Mean	Std	Mean	Std	Mean	Std
Dino (triangulation)	0.30	0.14	0.30	0.14	0.18	0.09	0.22	0.11
Corridor (triangulation)	0.21	0.16	0.21	0.16	0.13	0.13	0.15	0.12
Dino (resection)	0.33	0.04	0.33	0.04	0.34	0.04	0.34	0.04
Corridor (resection)	0.28	0.05	0.28	0.05	0.28	0.05	0.28	0.05

Table 4. Number of branch and bound iterations for triangulation and resectioning on the Dinosaur and Corridor datasets. More parameters are estimated for resectioning, but the main reason for the difference in performance between triangulation and resectioning is that several hundred points are visible to each camera for the latter.

Experiment	(L_2, L_2)		(L_2, L_1)		(L_1, L_1)	
	Mean	Std	Mean	Std	Mean	Std
Dino (triangulation)	1.2	1.5	1.0	0.2	6.7	3.4
Corridor (triangulation)	8.9	9.4	27.4	26.3	25.9	27.4
Dino (resection)	49.8	40.1	84.4	53.4	54.9	42.9
Corridor (resection)	39.9	2.9	49.2	20.6	47.9	7.9

rors are given for (1) triangulation of all 3D points given pre-computed camera motion and (2) resection of cameras given pre-computed 3D points. Both the mean error and the estimated standard deviation are given. There is no difference between the bundle adjustment and the (L_2, L_2) method. Thus, for these particular sequences, the bundle adjustment did not get trapped in any local optimum. The L_1 methods also result in low reprojection errors as measured by the RMS criterion. More interesting is, perhaps, the number of iterations on a standard PC (3 GHz), see Table 4. In the case of triangulation, a point is typically visible in a couple of frames. The differences in iterations are most likely due to the setup: the dinosaur sequence has circular camera motion which is a better-posed geometry compared to forward motion in the corridor sequence.

6 Discussions

In this paper, we have demonstrated that several problems in multiview geometry can be formulated within the unified framework of fractional programming, in a form amenable to global optimization. A branch and bound algorithm is proposed that provably finds a solution arbitrarily close to the global optimum, with a fast convergence rate in practice. Besides minimizing reprojection error under Gaussian noise, our framework allows incorporation of robust L_1 norms, reducing sensitivity to outliers. Two improvements that exploit the underlying problem structure and are critical for expiditious convergence are: branching in a small, constant number of dimensions and bounds propagation.

It is inevitable that our solution times be compared with those of bundle adjustment, but we must point out that it is producing a certificate of optimality that forms the most significant portion of our algorithm's runtime. In fact, it is our empirical observation that the optimal point ultimately reported by the branch and bound is usually obtained within the first few iterations.

A distinction must also be made between the accuracy of a solution and the optimality guarantee associated with it. An optimality criterion of, say $\epsilon = 0.95$, is only a worst case bound and does not necessarily mean a solution 5% away from optimal. Indeed, as evidenced by our experiments, our solutions consistently equal or better those of bundle adjustment in accuracy.

Acknowledgements

Sameer Agarwal and Serge Belongie are supported by NSF-CAREER #0448615, DOE/LLNL contract no. W-7405-ENG-48 (subcontracts B542001 and B547328), and the Alfred P. Sloan Fellowship. Manmohan Chandraker and David Kriegman are supported by NSF EIA 0303622 & NSF IIS-0308185. Fredrik Kahl is supported by Swedish Research Council (VR 2004-4579) & European Commission (Grant 011838, SMERobot).

References

1. Freund, R.W., Jarre, F.: Solving the sum-of-ratios problem by an interior-point method. J. Glob. Opt. **19** (2001) 83–102
2. Longuet-Higgins, H.: A computer algorithm for reconstructing a scene from two projections. Nature **vol.293** (1981) 133–135
3. Hartley, R.I., Zisserman, A.: Multiple View Geometry in Computer Vision. Cambridge University Press (2004) Second Edition.
4. Tawarmalani, M., Sahinidis, N.V.: Semidefinite relaxations of fractional programs via novel convexification techniques. J. Glob. Opt. **20** (2001) 137–158
5. Benson, H.P.: Using concave envelopes to globally solve the nonlinear sum of ratios problem. J. Glob. Opt. **22** (2002) 343–364
6. Boyd, S., Vandenberghe, L.: Convex Optimization. Cambridge University Press (2004)
7. Hartley, R., Sturm, P.: Triangulation. CVIU **68** (1997) 146–157
8. Stewénius, H., Schaffalitzky, F., Nistér, D.: How hard is three-view triangulation really? In: Int. Conf. Computer Vision. (2005) 686–693
9. Kahl, F., Henrion, D.: Globally optimal estimates for geometric reconstruction problems. In: Int. Conf. Computer Vision, Beijing, China (2005) 978–985
10. Ke, Q., Kanade, T.: Robust L_1 norm factorization in the presence of outliers and missing data by alternative convex programming. In: CVPR. (2005) 739–746
11. Kahl, F.: Multiple view geometry and the L_∞-norm. In: Int. Conf. Computer Vision, Beijing, China (2005) 1002–1009
12. Sturm, J.: Using SeDuMi 1.02, a Matlab toolbox for optimization over symmetric cones. Optimization Methods and Software **11-12** (1999) 625–653
13. Schaible, S., Shi, J.: Fractional programming: the sum-of-ratios case. Opt. Meth. Soft. **18** (2003) 219–229
14. Kotz, S., Kozubowski, T.J., Podgorski, K.: The Laplace distribution and generalizations. Birkhäuser (2001)
15. Wolf, L., Shashua, A.: On projection matrices $P^k \mapsto P^2$, $k = 3, \ldots, 6$, and their applications in computer vision. Int. Journal Computer Vision **48** (2002) 53–67

Perspective n-View Multibody Structure-and-Motion Through Model Selection

Konrad Schindler, James U, and Hanzi Wang

Institute for Vision Systems Engineering,
Monash University, Clayton, 3800 VIC, Australia
{Konrad.Schindler, James.U, Hanzi.Wang}@eng.monash.edu.au

Abstract. Multi-body structure-and-motion (MSaM) is the problem to establish the multiple-view geometry of an image sequence of a 3D scene, where the scene consists of multiple rigid objects moving relative to each other. So far, solutions have been proposed for several restricted settings, such as only two views, affine projection, and perspective projection of linearly moving points. We give a solution for sequences of several images, full perspective projection, and general rigid motion. It can deal with the fact that the set of correspondences changes over time, and is robust to outliers. The proposed solution is based on Monte-Carlo sampling and clustering of two-view motions, linking them through the sequence, and model selection to yield the best explanation for the entire sequence.

1 Introduction

Structure-and-motion recovery from images as the only source of information has been extensively studied in the last decade. For the case of static scenes, the problem of fitting a 3D scene compatible with the images is well understood and essentially solved [1, 2]. Soon after the main SaM-theory had been established, researchers turned to the more challenging case of *dynamic* scenes, where the segmentation into independently moving objects and the motion estimation for each object have to be solved simultaneously (see Fig. 1). Even in the case of rigidly moving scene parts, which we will call *multibody structure-and-motion* or MSaM, the geometric properties of dynamic scenes turned out to be non-trivial. So far, algebraic solutions exist for the case of 2 views [3, 4], for multiple affine views [5, 6], and for multiple affine views of linearly moving points [7]. Non-algebraic approaches have been presented for 2 views, which apply conventional SaM and search for different motions, either iteratively [8, 9], or simultaneously [10].

Here, we will examine the more realistic case of more than 2 views, perspective projection, and general rigid motion. The setting is the following: a scene with multiple rigidly moving objects is recorded with a camera with calibrated intrinsics. Calibration is convenient to avoid the degenerate cases of pure camera rotation or planar objects, and to reduce the number of points necessary to estimate a motion. However, the presented approach can be directly extended to an uncalibrated setting with different motion models for degenerate and non-degenerate cases, as shown for 2 views in [10]. Image correspondences are tracked

A. Leonardis, H. Bischof, and A. Pinz (Eds.): ECCV 2006, Part I, LNCS 3951, pp. 606–619, 2006.

  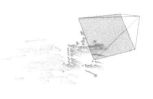

Fig. 1. The multibody structure-and-motion problem. From a number of tracked correspondences, estimate the number of moving objects, the segmentation into different objects, and the 3D motion of the objects.

through the captured sequence with a feature point tracker. Points may be lost (e.g., due to occlusion), new points may be detected to replace the lost ones, and the set of point tracks may contain outliers, which have been wrongly matched between frames. Furthermore, the number of motions present may vary throughout the sequence, e.g. when an object leaves the field of view.

An algebraic solution for the described case has so far proved elusive. Therefore, we face a chicken-and-egg problem: the motions are needed for clustering, but the clustering is needed to compute the correct motions. The method presented here follows a recover-and-select scheme. In a first step, motion models for pairs of consecutive frames are instantiated by Monte-Carlo sampling. Robust statistical analysis of the residuals is used to estimate the scale of the noise and the set of inliers for each such motion model. The motions are then clustered, so that similar candidates reinforce each other, and the resulting two-view motions are linked between consecutive image pairs to obtain a set of candidate motions through the sequence (section 2). Then, a model selection method is applied to this set to find the most likely set of motions *over the entire sequence* (section 3). An outline of the complete process is given in Algorithm 1. The method is demonstrated on several data sets (section 4).

Algorithm 1. Outline of n-view multibody structure-and-motion method

---

1. *Tracking: track feature points through the sequence*
2. *Generating candidates: for each pair of consecutive frames $(i, i+1)$*
   - *(a) Sample a set of epipolar geometries $\{E_j^i\}$*
   - *(b) For each E_j^i, estimate inlier set and standard deviation*
   - *(c) Cluster $\{E_j^i\}$ and re-estimate representatives $\{\overline{E}_k^i\}$ for each cluster*
3. *Motion linking: recursively link $\{\overline{E}_k^i\}$ through frames to obtain candidate motions*
4. *Model selection: build objective function for candidate motions and maximize*
5. *Postprocessing: enforce temporal consistency to clean up segmentation*
6. *(optional) Triangulation: triangulate 3D coordinates of feature points*

The original contribution of the paper is an extension of a recent method for two-view MSaM [10], which for the first time solves the MSaM problem for perspective image sequences and general rigid 3D motion. The problem is sometimes referred to as *3D motion segmentation*, however we prefer the term *multibody structure-and-motion*, to emphasize that points are not only segmented into rigidly moving sets, but also their tracks in 3D space are recovered.

2   Generating Candidate Motions

We start from a sequence of F frames recorded with a calibrated camera. With the point tracker, N points have been tracked through the sequence. Each of these points appears in at least 2 and at most F consecutive frames. Let an (unknown) 3D scene point be denoted by $\mathbf{x}$, and its image in the ith frame by a homogeneous 3-vector $\mathbf{v}^i$, with $\{i \in 1 \dots F\}$. Since the camera intrinsics are known, we can always pre-multiply the image points to obtain normalized image coordinates $\mathbf{u}^i = \mathsf{K}^{-1}\mathbf{v}^i$. At this point, it is unknown how many moving objects are visible in the sequence, and hence it is also unknown, which object a point belongs to, or whether the track for that point contains false matches.

The first step in a recover-and-select framework is to generate candidate motions. A candidate is a hypothetical object moving in 3D space, modeled as a number of scene points $\mathbf{x}$. The object moves through the field of view for a number of frames, and the points $\mathbf{x}$ gives rise to point tracks $\mathbf{u}$ through these frames, which satisfy an appropriate n-view relation. For two consecutive frames, points on the same rigid object have to satisfy the epipolar constraint $(\mathbf{u}^{i+1})^{\mathsf{T}}\mathsf{E}\mathbf{u}^i = 0$, where E denotes an essential matrix.

Candidate motions will be generated by randomly generating such essential matrices and linking them to longer motions. Since brute-force random sampling and linking leads to a combinatorial explosion, some care has to be taken: very improbable motions need to be pruned from the candidate set as early as possible, and redundant motions, which are very similar, need to be avoided. As will be seen, the important notion here is that in correspondence-based structure-and-motion, a moving object is modeled as a rigidly moving *set of points*. The common trait of the steps in this section is that they focus on this *inlier set*, rather than the motion parameters, to compare and judge tentative motions.[1]

2.1   Pairwise Sampling

As atomic hypotheses to start from, essential matrices between consecutive frames are generated by Monte-Carlo sampling: random 5-tuples of correspondences are drawn and an essential matrix is estimated for each 5-tuple using the

---

[1] We are aware that making hard inlier/outlier decisions at an early point is theoretically questionable from a statistical point of view. For the sake of simplicity, we will nevertheless explain the method using hard decisions. The described algorithms can easily be extended to fuzzy membership values by replacing the binary inlier/outlier index of each point with its inlier probability. However, the practical difference is small, and in our view does not warrant the additional complexity and computational burden.

Fig. 2. Local sampling scheme for tentative motion models. Samples are drawn from sub-regions of the image plane to exploit spatial coherence and reduce the required sample number.

five-point algorithm [11]. To increase the chance of finding an uncontaminated sample, it is advisable to exploit the spatial coherence of points belonging to the same motion. Except for special cases such as transparent objects, points belonging to the same rigid object will be clustered in the image plane, and a local sampling scheme will dramatically reduce the number of samples required to find an uncontaminated one. For the experiments in section 4, the image plane was subdivided into 3 overlapping rows and 3 overlapping columns, and samples were drawn from the entire image, each column, each row, and each of the 9 regions defined by a row-column intersection (see Fig. 2). This hierarchical scheme proved to be a reasonable compromise between local coherence and global extension, which works well for different images.

Note that for each moving object we only have to make sure good candidates are found in *one* of the sub-regions. If, as in most practical scenarios, the minimum image area covered by an object is known, it is easy to find such a subdivision. This means that the required sample number per frame is constant, independent of the number of motions, and the total number of samples grows linearly with the length of the sequence.

The inlier set and standard deviation for each candidate motion are computed in a robust way by estimating the probability density function of the residuals and discarding points outside the first mode of that density. Due to lack of space, we refer the interested reader to [10] for details. Having estimated the inlier set and standard deviation of all tentative epipolar geometries, the candidate set can be pruned for the first time: only plausible candidates in terms of inlier count and standard deviation are retained. The thresholds can be chosen conservatively, since they only serve to discard the most improbable candidates: an upper bound for the allowable standard deviation is the localization uncertainty of the tracked image points, which is easily obtained from the point tracker, while the minimum inlier number is set to some very low value, say 5% of all image points in a frame.

2.2   Motion Clustering

The set of epipolar geometries recovered at this point will be highly redundant. Many of the candidate motions will correspond to the same object and be similar. Conversely, it is improbable that there are many clusters of similar motions among the spurious candidates, which have survived to this point. Clustering the essential matrices will detect and remove as much as possible of the redundancy. This will both reduce the number of candidate motions further, and allow an improved estimation of the correct ones.

Clustering epipolar geometries in parameter space is difficult. Even similar sets of moving points may yield motions with very different parameters, due to correlations and to the non-linearity of the geometric relations. We therefore return to the definition of similarity as "explaining the same tracks", and resort to clustering based on the inlier sets, similar to [12]. Each epipolar geometry is represented by a binary vector of size N, with entries 1 for its inliers, and entries 0 for its outliers. The Hamming-distance d_H between these vectors (the number of differing bits) is then used as a similarity measure for clustering. $d_H = 0$ means that two inlier sets are identical, while $d_H = N$ means that the outliers of one set are exactly the inliers of the other. Our implementation uses simple average-linkage hierarchical clustering, however more sophisticated methods could potentially be used.

The new set of candidates is now given by the representative "mean" motions of all clusters. These "means" are obtained with a simple consensus mechanism: the inliers of the "mean" are all points, which are inliers to >50% of the cluster members, and its epipolar geometry is re-estimated from this inlier set. Optionally, one can discard very small clusters (say, with ≤2 members), which are likely to be spurious motions, in order to further reduce the candidate set.

2.3   Motion Linking

After clustering, we are left with a small number of essential matrices (in practice, <10 per frame), each representing the motion of a set of points from one frame of the sequence to the next. It is important to notice that we have not yet achieved an optimal set of epipolar geometries for each pair of consecutive frames. It is quite possible that some of the candidate motions only explain part of a moving object, or that they explain two objects, if their relative motion between the two frames is small. It is also quite likely that some spurious epipolar geometries accidentally are strong enough to survive up to this point.

The epipolar geometries now have to be concatenated to longer motion chains. It is not known, when each moving object has entered the field of view, and when it has left it, so all chains of ≥1 epipolar geometries are potential candidates. Again, exhaustively linking all possible chains of length ≤ F leads to a combinatorial explosion, and it disregards the temporal coherence of motions. Since sequence analysis only makes sense, if the scene changes slowly compared to the frame-rate, few tracks on each moving object will be lost per frame. Linking only essential matrices with similar inlier sets, thus enforcing the temporal coherence, greatly reduces the number of candidates. Only a loose threshold (say, 50%) should be used, so as not to eliminate motions with strong self-occlusions due to rotation.

At the linking stage, we can no longer avoid the inherent complexity of the problem. Unlike the previous steps, motion linking provokes a potentially exponential increase in the number of candidates. This is why great care has been taken to prune the candidate set as early as possible. Although the described measures for reducing the number of candidates are extremely simple, they are efficient. Experimentally, for sequences of up to 4 motions and 10 frames, the number of candidate motions is generally <1000.

Note that generating motions by linking epipolar geometries in this way does not impose any restrictions on the motion other than rigidity, so long as the inlier sets are consistent. Within the limitations of the feature tracker, irregular and jerky motions are not penalized compared to smooth ones, since there is no temporal prediction involved.

3   Selection of Motions

The result so far is a set $\mathcal{S}$ of candidates for object motions. The desired result is a minimal required set to explain the motion of the tracked image points. This can be viewed as a model selection problem: from the combinatorial set of explanations given by all subsets of $\mathcal{S}$, select the one with highest probability $\mathcal{P}$. Due to Shannon's theorem, maximizing the probability is equivalent to minimizing the codelength $\mathcal{L}$, since the two are related by $\mathcal{L} \sim -\log(\mathcal{P})$. We will derive the selection criterion using an MDL-like approach based on codelengths.

3.1   Codelength of Motion Data

Given is a sequence of F images. Points through the sequence have been tracked with a tracker, which may lose points (e.g., due to occlusions) and replace them by detecting new feature points. The search area for the tracker is usually restricted to a window of size $w \times w$ around a point's position in the previous image (for unrestricted matching, w is the image size).

Now let us assume that over a part of the sequence, which has $F^1 \leq F$ frames, a rigid object $\mathcal{M}_1$ has moved through the scene. The total number of tracked 3D points on the rigid object is N^1, of which only N_i^1 are visible in each frame $\{i \in 1 \dots F\}$ (if $F^1 < F$, then $N_i^1 = 0$ for some frames). Conversely, each 3D point $\mathbf{x}_j$ is only seen in F_j^1 of the F^1 frames. If we want to code these points without using their 3D structure, this has to be done by specifying their coordinates within the search window for each frame. Assuming uniform density over the search area, the coding length (the negative log-likelihood) is

$$\mathcal{L}_{1+} = \sum_{i=1}^{F} N_i^1 \log \frac{1}{w^2}. \tag{1}$$

On the other hand, if the 3D structure and motion is known, the approximate coordinates of each point can be constructed by projecting the corresponding 3D point $\mathbf{x}_j$ into the image, and only the residual r_{ij} with respect to this location has to be coded. Assuming that the residuals have a zero-mean normal distribution with standard deviation $\sigma_x = \sigma_y = \sigma$, the codelength for this is

$$\mathcal{L}_{1a-} = \frac{1}{2\sigma^2} \sum_{i=1}^{F} \sum_{j=1}^{N_i^1} r_{ij}^2 + \sum_{i=1}^{F} N_i^1 \log(2\pi\sigma^2). \tag{2}$$

However, we also have to encode the 3D structure and motion parameters. Generalizing Torr's GBIC approximation [13], their coding length can be estimated from the number of equations used to estimate the different parameters. Each coordinate of a *structure* point $\mathbf{x}_j$ is computed from $2F_j^1$ equations, and there are 3 coordinates for each of the N^1 points. Each *motion* parameter of the ith frame is computed from $2N_i^1$ equations, and for F^1 frames and calibrated intrinsics, there are $(6F^1 - 7)$ motion parameters. Taken together, the codelength is

$$\mathcal{L}_{1b-} = \frac{3}{2} \sum_{j=1}^{N^1} \log(2F_j^1) + \frac{1}{2} \left(6 - \frac{7}{F^1} \right) \sum_{i=1}^{F^1} \log(2N_i^1) . \tag{3}$$

The goal is to model multiple motions, so we need an index to store which points belongs to motion $\mathcal{M}_1$ in each frame of the sequence. To this end, we need (i) a binary index to indicate, which points belong to $\mathcal{M}_1$ in any of its frames, (ii) the first frame, in which $\mathcal{M}_1$ is visible, and (iii) the subset of the following F^1 frames in which each point is visible. The codelength for these together is

$$\mathcal{L}_{1c-} = N + \log(F) + N^1 \log \left(\frac{F^1(F^1 - 1)}{2} \right) . \tag{4}$$

Using the structure-and-motion representation, we reduce the codelength by $\mathcal{L}_{1+}$, but increase it by $(\mathcal{L}_{1a-} + \mathcal{L}_{1b-} + \mathcal{L}_{1c-})$. The total savings thus are

$$\mathcal{D}_1 = \log \frac{w^2}{2\pi\sigma^2} \sum_{i=1}^{F} N_i^1 - \frac{1}{2\sigma^2} \sum_{i=1}^{F} \sum_{j=1}^{N_i^1} r_{ij}^2 - \frac{3}{2} \sum_{j=1}^{N^1} \log(2F_j^1) -$$

$$- \left(3 - \frac{7}{2F^1} \right) \sum_{i=1}^{F^1} \log(2N_i^1) - N - \log(F) - N^1 \log \left(\frac{F^1(F^1 - 1)}{2} \right) . \tag{5}$$

If this value is positive, using the structure-and-motion representation reduces the total codelength, or equivalently, it increases the probability of the model.

If we also use a second motion $\mathcal{M}_2$, then a point $\mathbf{u}_i$ may be an inlier to both of them, and it is at this stage not possible to decide, which one it shall be assigned to. To assure the minimal codelength, we therefore have to make sure that the point is only coded once in each frame. Adding the savings $(\mathcal{D}_1 + \mathcal{D}_2)$ unjustly assumes that coding these points twice could reduce the codelength further. To remedy this, we must introduce a correction term, $(\mathcal{D}_1 + \mathcal{D}_2 - \mathcal{D}_{1\cap2})$, where

$$\mathcal{D}_{1\cap2} = \log \frac{w^2}{2\pi\sigma_1^2} \sum_{i=1}^{F} N'^1 + \log \frac{w^2}{2\pi\sigma_2^2} \sum_{i=1}^{F} N'^2 - \frac{1}{2\sigma_1^2} \sum_{i=1}^{F} \sum_{j=1}^{N'^1} r_{1j}^2 - \frac{1}{2\sigma_2^2} \sum_{i=1}^{F} \sum_{j=1}^{N'^2} r_{2j}^2 . \tag{6}$$

Here, N'^1 means the portion of the inliers to both, which have larger normalized residuals in $\mathcal{M}_1$, and similar for $\mathcal{M}_2$. It is important to understand that correct treatment of ambiguous points is a fundamental requirement in a scheme, which uses model selection to simultaneously recovers multiple motions. If it is neglected, any motion whose likelihood outweighs the complexity penalty will increase the total likelihood and be selected. As an extreme example look at the case where $\mathcal{M}_2$ consists of the first $(F^1 - 1)$ frames of $\mathcal{M}_1$, i.e., it is a subset of $\mathcal{M}_1$ representing the case that the object has left the field of view or become occluded in the last frame. If $\mathcal{M}_2$ reduces the codelength, then in most cases so does $\mathcal{M}_1$, and both will be selected, which clearly contradicts the desire to minimize the model complexity. If, on the contrary, we take care not to "explain the same points twice" by introducing $\mathcal{D}_{1\cap 2}$, then the two will never both be selected, because if one is a subset of the other, $\mathcal{D}_{1\cap 2} > \min(\mathcal{D}_1, \mathcal{D}_2)$.

3.2 Minimizing the Codelength

To minimize the codelength one must maximize the total savings $\mathcal{D}$. The question is, which motions to use, hence the variable is a boolean vector $\mathbf{b}$ of length M, which indicates the presence $(b_i = 1)$ or absence $(b_i = 0)$ of a motion in the model [14]. The total savings in codelength, as a function of which motions are used, are then given by the quadratic boolean expression $\mathcal{D}(\mathbf{b}) = \frac{1}{2}\mathbf{b}^\mathsf{T}\mathbf{Db}$, where $\mathbf{D}$ is a symmetric matrix of the following form:

$$\mathbf{D} = \begin{bmatrix} 2\mathcal{D}_1 & -\mathcal{D}_{1\cap 2} & \dots & -\mathcal{D}_{1\cap M} \\ -\mathcal{D}_{1\cap 2} & 2\mathcal{D}_2 & \dots & -\mathcal{D}_{2\cap M} \\ \vdots & \vdots & \ddots & \vdots \\ -\mathcal{D}_{1\cap M} & -\mathcal{D}_{2\cap M} & \dots & 2\mathcal{D}_M \end{bmatrix} \tag{7}$$

Note that no parameters have to be tuned in (5) and (6). The formulation as a quadratic problem is only possible, because the contributions of different motions to the codelength have been separated, and this is achieved by the simplification of only considering the joint probabilities of up to 2 motions.[2]

Maximizing $\mathcal{D}$ over $\mathbf{b}$ belongs to the class of quadratic 0-1 integer problems, which in general can only be solved through exhaustive evaluation of the 2^M possible solutions. For our problem, with off-diagonal elements $\mathbf{D}_{ij} \leq 0$ (i.e., $\mathcal{D}$ is a submodular set function), the situation is slightly better:

Lemma 1: *Let $\widehat{\mathbf{b}}$ be the vector, at which $\mathcal{D}$ attains the global maximum, and let $\mathbf{b}'$ be a subset of $\widehat{\mathbf{b}}$, $\{\forall i : \widehat{b}_i \geq b_i'\}$. Let $\mathbf{b}''$ be obtained by switching exactly one 0-element of $\mathbf{b}'$ to 1, $|\mathbf{b}'' - \mathbf{b}'| = 1$. Then, if $\mathcal{D}(\mathbf{b}'') \leq \mathcal{D}(\mathbf{b}')$, vector $\mathbf{b}''$ cannot be a subset of $\widehat{\mathbf{b}}$. If $\forall \mathbf{b}'' : \mathcal{D}(\mathbf{b}'') \leq \mathcal{D}(\mathbf{b}')$, then $\mathbf{b}' = \widehat{\mathbf{b}}$.*

Proof: *Switching **all** elements to 1, for which $\{\widehat{b}_i \neq b_i'\}$, must yield the largest possible increase of $\mathcal{D}$, since $\widehat{\mathbf{b}}$ is the global maximum. This implies that switching any one of them to 1 increases $\mathcal{D}$, because $\forall i \neq j : \mathbf{D}_{ij} = \mathbf{D}_{ji} \leq 0$.*

The lemma states that the path from any subset $\mathbf{b}'$ to $\widehat{\mathbf{b}}$ does not contain descent steps. Making use of the fact that the scene only contains a small number R of motions, and that the empty solution $\mathbf{b} = \mathbf{0}_{M \times 1}$ is a subset of $\widehat{\mathbf{b}}$, one

---

[2] If ≥ 3 motions share points, their joint use is over-penalized, e.g., for 3 motions the last term of the joint savings $\mathcal{D}_1 + \mathcal{D}_2 + \mathcal{D}_3 - \mathcal{D}_{1\cap 2} - \mathcal{D}_{1\cap 3} - \mathcal{D}_{2\cap 3} + \mathcal{D}_{1\cap 2\cap 3}$ is disregarded. However the influence of this approximation is small, because the number of affected points is small.

Algorithm 2. Multi-branch optimization for $\mathcal{D} = \frac{1}{2}\mathbf{b}^{\mathsf{T}}\mathbf{D}\mathbf{b}$.

---

1. **Level 0:** *Start from a scene without any motions:* $R = 0$, $\mathcal{D} = 0$, $\mathbf{b} = \mathbf{0}_{M \times 1}$.
2. **Level 1:** *Compute the value of $\mathcal{D}$ for all M possible solutions with $(R=1)$ motion*
3. *Discard all solutions with $\mathcal{D} \leq 0$, since adding motions to such a solution cannot lead to the maximum (Lemma 1)*
4. **Level 2:** *Build all pairwise combinations $(R=2)$ of the remaining motions, and compute $\mathcal{D}$ for them*
5. *Discard those pairs, which do not attain a higher value than any of the two motions alone (again, these cannot lead to the maximum)*
6. **Level 3:** *Join the remaining pairs to triplets $(R=3)$ and compute $\mathcal{D}$ for them (Note that based on the previous steps, computing $\mathcal{D}$ for an R-tuple of motions only requires R additions)*
7. **Level R:** *Keep discarding dead-end search paths and increasing R, until no $(R+1)$-tuple exceeds the previous maximum attainable with R motions*

---

can devise a multi-branch ascent method (see Algorithm 2). The method always leads to the global maximum, however it is still exponential in complexity. For larger sets of candidate motions, one has to resort to a heuristic version: for each level of the search, the solutions are sorted by the objective value $\mathcal{D}(\mathbf{b})$ and only the best ones for each branch are retained. The number of branches, which are retained for the next step, decreases in geometric progression from one level to the next, say $T = \{40, 20, 10, \ldots\}$, so that the total number of search paths is $\{40, 800, 8000, \ldots\}$. Retaining multiple sub-branches avoids getting stuck at a weak local minimum and only gradually focuses on the most promising branches. The complexity for M candidates and R actual motions is $\mathcal{O}\left((\frac{1}{2})^{(1+2+\ldots+R)} M^{(R+1)} \right)$. Theoretically, the heuristic does not guarantee a global maximum anymore. In practice it produces good solutions, and in our experiments it outperforms all-purpose search methods such as Tabu-search or multi-start gradient descent, which do not exploit the special structure of the problem to the same extent.

3.3   Motion Segmentation

Having recovered the motions and their respective inlier sets, segmentation reduces to the problem of disambiguating points, which change from one motion to the next over time, or satisfy more than one motion model. An obvious solution in the presence of multiple frames is to enforce temporal consistency. So far, temporal consistency has only been used to link motions between consecutive pairs of frames, but not at the multi-frame level. Since a scene point is located on a physical object, it cannot normally pass from one motion to another, except for the case that the tracker drifts, i.e., it wrongly matches a point between two frames, but then locks onto the new point and tracks it correctly.

If in a part of the sequence a point switches back and forth between motions or is an inlier to more than one motion, we form a consensus over time, such that it drifts at most once, while changing as few class memberships as possible. This will clean up any false assignments due to points accidentally satisfying the epipolar constraint (the vast majority of cases). Even in the case that a point truly drifts from one motion to the other, the heuristic will detect this behavior and try to fix it, but the transition may happen in the wrong frame. Note that by temporal consistency, we again mean consistent class membership, rather than smoothness of tracks. The effect of the consensus over time is illustrated on a practical example in Fig. 3.

Fig. 3. Enforcing temporal consistency to improve motion segmentation. The two rows show the same region of the "flowershirt" sequence, with several points satisfying both epipolar geometries. *Top row:* segmentation based on individual residuals without enforcing coherence over time. *Bottom row:* segmentation after building a consensus over time. ***All segmentation results are best viewed in color.***

The segmentation of correspondences *between motions* is almost perfect (i.e., very few points are assigned to the *wrong* motion). However, some points on moving objects are often miss-classified as outliers. This is an inherent difficulty of robust classification methods, which provide a rejection class for outliers. The parameters of each class are estimated at the same time as the class membership, therefore there exists the possibility of estimating slightly incorrect parameters based on a subset of the class, and assigning the remainder of it to the outliers. Methods without an outlier class do not encounter this problem, because all points *have* to be assigned to one of the motions.

4   Experimental Evaluation

A synthetic data set was generated with 5 views of 4 rotating planar objects. Each object has 50 tracks, and 50 outliers were added by randomly generating tracks with a displacement between adjacent frames, which is similar to the correct tracks. The method correctly recovers the 4 motions, and the segmentation into the 5 classes (including outliers) is 97.5% correct. See Tab. 1 and Fig. 4.

The method has been tested on various real data sets. The first example is a sequence of 10 frames showing two independently moving piles of boxes. 300 initial points were tracked with the KLT-tracker [15], lost points were immediately replaced, and points which could not be tracked for at least one frame

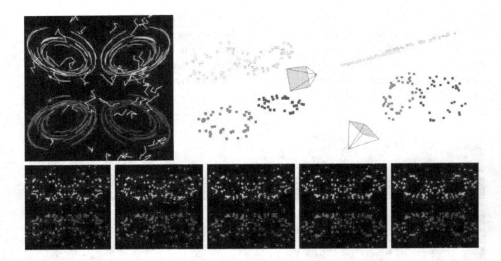

Fig. 4. Segmentation of the synthetic "spinning wheels" sequence. *Top:* Feature tracks (colors denote the ground truth segmentation), and two views of the recovered 3D points in the first frame. *Bottom:* Recovered segmentation through the sequence. Yellow dots are points classified as outliers.

Table 1. Segmentation results for "spinning wheels" sequence (4 moving objects with 50 points each, 50 outliers). False positives (FP) are outliers assigned to a motion, false negatives (FN) are points from the motion classified as outliers. No points were assigned to the wrong motion.

		frame 1	*frame 2*	*frame 3*	*frame 4*	*frame 5*
motion A	FP / FN	0 / 0	0 / 0	0 / 0	1 / 1	1 / 0
motion B	FP / FN	0 / 0	2 / 0	2 / 0	1 / 0	0 / 0
motion C	FP / FN	1 / 0	2 / 0	2 / 0	4 / 0	2 / 0
motion D	FP / FN	0 / 1	2 / 0	2 / 0	1 / 0	0 / 3

were removed, leading to a total of 350 tracks. The set of tracks includes several outliers on apparent contours. The method was applied and correctly recovered two motions. Figure 5 shows the first and last frame with the point tracks superimposed, and the recovered motions both in the image plane and in a top view to show the motion of the 3D scene.

The second scene is a sequence of 10 frames showing 3 objects moving on a table. 300 feature points per frame were tracked, resulting in a total of 439 tracks. The third object is not visible in the beginning, but enters the field of view later, and a part of the box on the upper right leaves the field of view towards the end of the sequence. Furthermore, the motion is not smooth, with two of the three objects stopping at some point.

The third scene consists of 11 frames from the movie "Groundhog Day" (courtesy of Josef Sivic and Andrew Zisserman). It shows a car moving diagonally

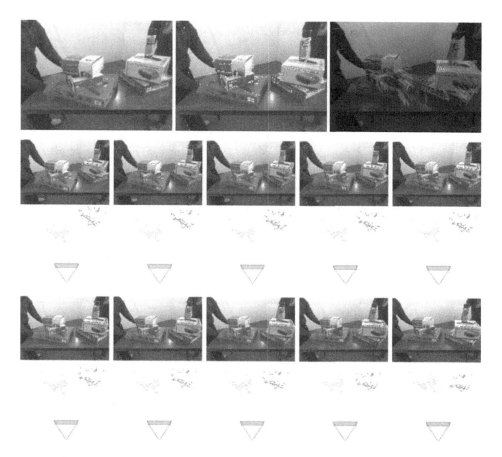

Fig. 5. Segmentation of the "boxes" sequence. *Top:* First frame, fifth frame with feature points superimposed, last frame with feature tracks superimposed. *Bottom:* Recovered segmentation and top view of 3D tracks through the sequence. Yellow dots are points classified as outliers.

towards the camera, while the camera itself pans to the right. 300 feature points per frame were tracked, resulting in a total of 524 tracks. The feature sets on both objects change a lot due to the fast motion, and there are several false matches due to strong motion blur. The background motion disappears at the ninth frame because the visible background becomes almost featureless.

5   Concluding Remarks

We have presented a scheme for multibody structure-and-motion of image sequences recorded with a perspective camera. The scheme is robust to outliers, can deal with unknown and varying number of moving objects, and with a set of correspondences, which changes over time. It recovers both the segmentation of

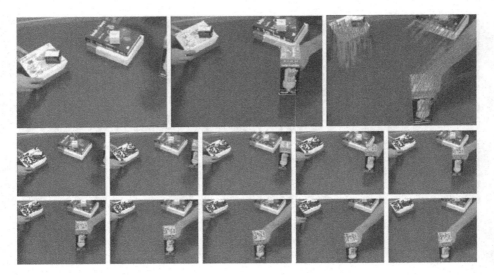

Fig. 6. Segmentation of the "lightbulb" sequence. *Top:* First frame, fifth frame with feature points superimposed, last frame with feature tracks superimposed. *Bottom:* Recovered segmentation through the sequence.

Fig. 7. Segmentation of the "delivery van" sequence. *Top:* First frame, fifth frame with feature points superimposed, last frame with feature tracks superimposed. *Bottom:* Recovered segmentation through the sequence.

the correspondences into different rigidly moving objects, and the feature tracks in 3D.

The method starts from atomic two-view motions and links them to tentative motions through the sequence, while constantly pruning redundant and overly unlikely motions to keep the size of the search space under control. In the final set of candidate motions, the best solution is found via model selection, and temporal coherence of the inlier sets is used to improve the segmentation.

An important limitation is that the method is based on a set of candidate motions generated by random sampling, therefore it can handle only a small number of moving objects, because of the exponentially growing number of required samples. In this context, it should be mentioned that multibody structure-and-motion, as opposed to 2D tracking, only makes sense for a relatively small number of moving objects, because the epipolar geometry can only be recovered reliably for objects which subtend a sufficiently large viewing angle, and hence cover a reasonable part of the image plane.

References

1. Hartley, R., Zisserman, A.: Multiple View Geometry in Computer Vision. Cambridge University Press (2000)
2. Faugeras, O., Luong, Q.T., Papadopoulo, T.: The geometry of multiple images. MIT Press (2001)
3. Wolf, L., Shashua, A.: Two-body segmentation from two perspective views. In: Proc. CVPR (2001) 263–270
4. Vidal, R., Soatto, S., Ma, Y., Sastry, S.: Segmentation of dynamic scenes from the multibody fundamental matrix. In: Proc. ECCV Workshop on Visual Modeling of Dynamic Scenes. (2002)
5. Costeira, J., Kanade, T.: A multi-body factorization method for motion analysis. In: Proc. 5th ICCV (1995) 1071–1077
6. Vidal, R., Hartley, R.: Motion segmentation with missing data using PowerFactorization and GPCA. In: Proc. CVPR (2004) 310–316
7. Han, M., Kanade, T.: Reconstruction of scenes with multiple linearly moving objects. In: Proc. CVPR (2000) 542–549
8. Torr, P.H.S.: Geometric motion segmentation and model selection. Philosophical Transactions of the Royal Society of London A **356** (1998) 1321–1340
9. Tong, W.S., Tang, C.K., Medioni, G.: Simultaneous two-view epipolar geometry estimation and motion segmentation by 4D tensor voting. IEEE TPAMI **26** (2004) 1167–1184
10. Schindler, K., Suter, D.: Two-view multibody structure-and-motion with outliers. In: Proc. CVPR (2005) 676–683
11. Nistér, D.: An efficient solution to the five-point relative pose problem. IEEE TPAMI **26** (2004) 756–770
12. Wills, J., Agarwal, S., Belongie, S.: What went where. In: Proc. CVPR (2003) 37–44
13. Torr, P.H.S.: Model selection for structure and motion recovery from multiple images. In Bab-Hadiashar, A., Suter, D., eds.: Data Segmentation and Model Selection for Computer Vision. Springer Verlag (2000)
14. Leonardis, A., Gupta, A., Bajcsy, R.: Segmentation of range images as the search for geometric parametric models. IJCV **14** (1995) 253–277
15. Tomasi, C., Kanade, T.: Detection and tracking of point features. Technical Report CMU-CS-91-132, Carnegie Mellon University (1991)

Confocal Stereo

Samuel W. Hasinoff* and Kiriakos N. Kutulakos*

Dept. of Computer Science, University of Toronto
{hasinoff,kyros}@cs.toronto.edu

Abstract. We present *confocal stereo*, a new method for computing 3D
shape by controlling the focus and aperture of a lens. The method is
specifically designed for reconstructing scenes with high geometric complexity or fine-scale texture. To achieve this, we introduce the *confocal
constancy* property, which states that as the lens aperture varies, the
pixel intensity of a visible in-focus scene point will vary in a scene-
independent way, that can be predicted by prior radiometric lens calibration. The only requirement is that incoming radiance within the cone
subtended by the largest aperture is nearly constant. First, we develop
a detailed lens model that factors out the distortions in high resolution
SLR cameras (12MP or more) with large-aperture lenses (e.g., f1.2).
This allows us to assemble an $A \times F$ aperture-focus image (AFI) for
each pixel, that collects the undistorted measurements over all A apertures and F focus settings. In the AFI representation, confocal constancy
reduces to color comparisons within regions of the AFI, and leads to focus metrics that can be evaluated separately for each pixel. We propose
two such metrics and present initial reconstruction results for complex
scenes.

1 Introduction

Recent years have seen many advances in the problem of reconstructing complex
3D scenes from multiple photographs [1, 2, 3]. Despite this progress, however,
there are many common scenes for which obtaining detailed 3D models is beyond
the state of the art. One such class includes scenes that contain very high levels of
geometric detail, such as hair, fur, feathers, miniature flowers, etc. These scenes
are difficult to reconstruct for a number of reasons—they create complex 3D
arrangements not directly representable as a single surface; their images contain
fine detail beyond the resolution of common video cameras; and they create
complex self-occlusion relationships. As a result, many approaches either side-
step the reconstruction problem [2], require a strong prior model for the scene
[4], or rely on techniques that approximate shape at a coarse level.

Despite these difficulties, the high-resolution sensors in today's digital cameras open the possibility of imaging complex scenes at a very high level of detail. With resolutions surpassing 12Mpixels, even individual strands of hair may

---

* Part of this work was done while the authors were visiting Microsoft Research Asia.

A. Leonardis, H. Bischof, and A. Pinz (Eds.): ECCV 2006, Part I, LNCS 3951, pp. 620–634, 2006.
© Springer-Verlag Berlin Heidelberg 2006

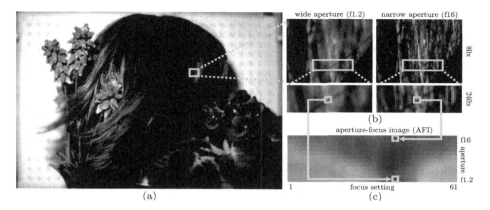

Fig. 1. (a) Wide-aperture image of a complex scene. (b) *Left:* Successive close-ups of a region in (a), showing a single in-focus strand of hair. *Right:* Narrow-aperture image of the same region, with everything in focus. Confocal constancy tells us that the intensity of in-focus pixels (e.g., on the strand) changes predictably between these two views. (c) The aperture-focus image (AFI) of a pixel near the middle of the strand. A column of the AFI collects the intensities of that pixel as the aperture varies with focus fixed.

be one or more pixels wide (Fig. 1a,b). In this paper, we explore the possibility of reconstructing such scenes with a new method called *confocal stereo*, which aims to compute depth maps at sensor resolution. The method is designed to exploit the capabilities of high-end digital SLR cameras and requires no special equipment besides the camera and a laptop. The only key requirement is the ability to actively control both the aperture and focus setting of the lens.

At the heart of our approach is a property we call *confocal constancy*, which states that as the lens aperture varies, the pixel intensity of a visible in-focus scene point will vary in a scene-*independent* way, that can be predicted by prior radiometric lens calibration. To exploit confocal constancy for reconstruction, we develop a detailed lens model that factors out the geometric and radiometric distortions observable in high resolution SLR cameras with large-aperture lenses (e.g., f1.2). This allows us to assemble an $A \times F$ *aperture-focus image (AFI)* for each pixel, that collects the undistorted measurements over all A apertures and F focus settings (Fig. 1c). In the AFI representation, confocal constancy reduces to color comparisons within regions of the AFI and leads to focus metrics that can be evaluated separately for each pixel.

Our work is closely related to depth-from-focus methods [5, 6, 7, 8], with the important difference that rather than defining our focus criterion over a spatial window, we consider pixels individually and manipulate a second, independent camera parameter (i.e., aperture). To our knowledge, aperture control has been considered only in the context of depth-from-defocus methods [9, 10, 11, 12], but these methods also rely on spatial windows and, hence, are unsuitable for reconstructing scenes at the resolutions we consider. Our work is also related to recent approaches employing finite or synthetic apertures for image-based rendering [13] and for 3D reconstruction [14, 15]. Unlike these methods, our approach requires only a single camera, and requires no special illumination or scene model.

Our work has five main contributions. First, unlike existing depth-from-focus or depth-from-defocus methods, our confocal constancy formulation shows that we can assess focus without modeling a pixel's spatial neighborhood or the blurring properties of a lens. Second, we show that depth-from-focus computations can be reduced to a pixel-matching problem, in the spirit of traditional stereo techniques. Third, we develop a method for the precise geometric and radiometric alignment of images taken at multiple focus and aperture settings, particularly suited for the case where the standard thin-lens model breaks down. Fourth, we introduce the aperture-focus-image representation as a basic tool for focus- and defocus-based 3D reconstruction. Fifth, we show that together, confocal constancy and accurate image alignment lead to a reconstruction algorithm that can compute depth maps at resolutions not attainable with existing techniques.

2   Confocal Constancy

Consider a camera whose lens contains multiple elements and has a range of known focus and aperture settings. We assume that no information is available about the internal components of this lens (e.g., the spacing of its elements). We therefore model the lens as a "black box" that redirects incoming light toward a fixed sensor plane, with the following idealized properties:

- **Negligible absorption:** light that enters the lens in a given direction is either blocked from exiting or is transmitted with no absorption.
- **Perfect focus:** for every 3D point in front of the lens there is a unique focus setting that causes rays through the point to converge to a single pixel on the sensor plane.
- **Aperture-focus independence:** the aperture setting controls only which rays are blocked from entering the lens; it does not affect the way that light is redirected.

These properties are well approximated by lenses used in professional photography applications, and we use such a lens to collect images of a 3D scene for A aperture settings, $\{\alpha_1, \ldots, \alpha_A\}$, and F focal settings, $\{f_1, \ldots, f_F\}$. This acquisition produces a 4D set of pixel data, $I_{\alpha f}(x, y)$, where $I_{\alpha f}$ is the image captured with aperture α and focal setting f.

Suppose that a 3D point $\mathbf{p}$ on an opaque surface is in perfect focus in image $I_{\alpha f}$ and suppose that it projects to pixel (x, y). In this case, the light reaching the pixel is restricted to a cone from $\mathbf{p}$ determined by the aperture setting (Fig. 2). For a sensor with a linear response, the intensity $I_{\alpha f}(x, y)$ at the pixel is proportional to the integral of outgoing radiance over the cone, i.e.,

$$I_{\alpha f}(x, y) = \kappa \int_{\omega \in \mathcal{C}_{xy}(\alpha, f)} L(\mathbf{p}, \omega) \, d\omega \, , \tag{1}$$

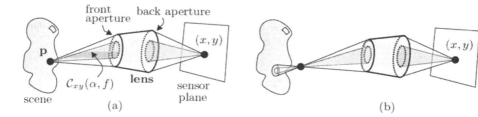

Fig. 2. Generic lens model. (a) At the ideal focus setting of pixel (x, y), the lens collects outgoing radiance from a scene point **p** and directs it toward the pixel. The 3D position of point **p** is uniquely determined by pixel (x, y) and its ideal focus setting. The shaded cone of rays, $\mathcal{C}_{xy}(\alpha, f)$, determines the radiance reaching the pixel. This cone is a subset of the cone subtended by **p** and the front aperture because some rays may be blocked by internal components of the lens, or by its back aperture. (b) For non-ideal focus settings, the lens integrates outgoing radiance from a region of the scene.

where ω measures solid angle, $L(\mathbf{p}, \omega)$ is the radiance for rays passing through **p**, κ is a constant that depends only on the sensor's response function [16], and $\mathcal{C}_{xy}(\alpha, f)$ is the cone of rays that reach (x, y). In practice, the apertures on a real lens correspond to a nested sequence of cones, $\mathcal{C}_{xy}(\alpha_1, f) \subset \ldots \subset \mathcal{C}_{xy}(\alpha_A, f)$, leading to a monotonically-increasing intensity at the pixel.

If the outgoing radiance at the in-focus point **p** remains constant within the cone of the largest aperture, and if this cone does not intersect the scene elsewhere, the relation between intensity and aperture becomes especially simple. In particular, the integral of Eq. (1) disappears and the intensity for aperture α is proportional to the solid angle subtended by the associated cone, i.e.,

$$I_{\alpha f}(x, y) \;=\; \kappa \, \| \mathcal{C}_{xy}(\alpha, f) \| \, L(\mathbf{p}) \;, \tag{2}$$

where $\| \mathcal{C}_{xy}(\alpha, f) \| = \int_{\mathcal{C}_{xy}(\alpha, f)} d\omega$. As a result, the ratio of intensities at an in-focus point for two different apertures becomes independent of the scene:

Confocal Constancy Property

$$\frac{I_{\alpha f}(x, y)}{I_{\alpha_1 f}(x, y)} \;=\; \frac{\| \mathcal{C}_{xy}(\alpha, f) \|}{\| \mathcal{C}_{xy}(\alpha_1, f) \|} \;\overset{\text{def}}{=}\; E_{xy}(\alpha, f) \;. \tag{3}$$

Intuitively, the constant of proportionality, $E_{xy}(\alpha, f)$, describes the relative amount of light received from an in-focus scene point for a given aperture. This constant, which we call the *relative exitance* of the lens, depends on lens internal design (front and back apertures, internal elements, etc.) and varies in general with aperture, focus setting, and pixel on the sensor plane.

Confocal constancy is an important property for evaluating focus for four reasons. First, it holds for a very general lens model that covers the lenses commonly used with high-quality SLR cameras. Second, it requires no assumptions about the appearance of out-of-focus points. Third, it holds for scenes with general reflectance properties, provided that radiance is nearly constant over the cone subtended by the largest aperture.[1] Fourth, and most important, it can be evaluated at *pixel resolution* because it imposes no requirements on the spatial layout (i.e., depths) of points in the neighborhood of **p**.

3   The Confocal Stereo Procedure

Confocal constancy allows us to decide whether or not the point projecting to a pixel (x, y) is in focus by comparing the intensities $I_{\alpha f}(x, y)$ for different values of aperture α and focus f. This leads to the following reconstruction procedure:

1. **(Relative exitance estimation)**   Compute the relative exitance of the lens for the A apertures and F focus settings (Sect. 4).
2. **(Image acquisition)**   For each of the F focus settings, capture an image of the scene for each of the A apertures.
3. **(Image alignment)**   Warp the captured images to ensure that a scene point projects to the same pixel in all images (Sect. 5).
4. **(AFI construction)** Build an $A \times F$ aperture-focus image for each pixel, that collects the pixel's measurements across all apertures and focus settings.
5. **(Confocal constancy evaluation)** For each pixel, process its AFI to find the focus setting that best satisfies the confocal constancy property (Sect. 6).

4   Relative Exitance Estimation

In order to use confocal constancy for reconstruction, we must be able to predict how changing the lens aperture affects the appearance of scene points that are in focus. Our approach is motivated by three basic observations. First, the apertures on real lenses are non-circular and the f-stop values describing them only approximate their true area (Fig. 3a,b). Second, when the aperture diameter is a relatively large fraction of the camera-to-object distance, the solid angles subtended by different 3D points in the workspace can differ significantly.[2] Third, vignetting and off-axis illumination effects cause additional variations in the light gathered from different in-focus points [17] (Fig. 3b).

To deal with these issues, we explicitly compute the relative exitance of the lens, $E_{xy}(\alpha, f)$, for all apertures α and for a sparse set of focal settings f. This can be thought of as a radiometric lens calibration step that must be performed just once for each lens. In practice, this allows us to predict aperture-induced intensity changes to within the sensor's noise level (i.e., within 1–2 gray levels).

To compute relative exitance for a focus setting f, we place a diffuse white plane at the in-focus position and capture one image for each aperture, $\alpha_1, \ldots, \alpha_A$. We then apply Eq. (3) to each pixel (x, y) to recover $E_{xy}(\alpha_i, f)$. To

---

[1] For example, a $70mm$ diameter aperture located $1.2m$ from the scene corresponds to 0.5% of the hemisphere, or a cone whose rays are less than $3.4°$ apart.

[2] For a $70mm$ diameter aperture, the solid angle subtended by scene points 1.1–1.2m away can vary up to 10%.

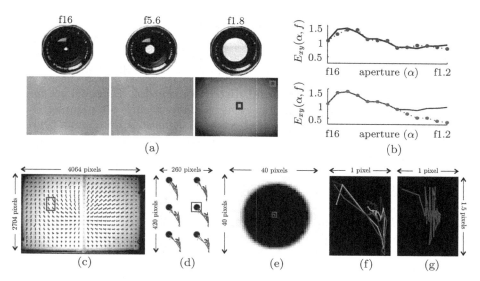

Fig. 3. (a) Images of an SLR lens showing variation in aperture shape with corresponding images of a diffuse plane. (b) *Top:* comparison of relative exitances for the central pixel indicated in (a), as measured using Eq. (3) (solid graph), and as approximated using the f-stop values (dotted) according to $E_{xy}(\alpha, f) = \alpha_1^2 / \alpha^2$ [16]. *Bottom:* comparison of the central pixel (solid) with the corner pixel (dotted) indicated in (a). The agreement is good for narrow apertures (i.e., high f-stop values), but for wider apertures, spatially-varying effects are significant. (c–g) To evaluate non-deterministic lens distortions, we computed centroids of dot features for images of a static calibration pattern. (c–f) Successive close-ups of a centroid's trajectory for three cycles (red, green, blue) of the 23 aperture settings. In (c–d) the trajectories are magnified by a factor of 100. As shown in (f), the trajectory, while stochastic, correlates with aperture setting. (g) Trajectory for the centroid of (e) over 50 images with the same lens settings.

obtain $E_{xy}(\alpha_i, f)$ for focus settings that span the entire workspace, we repeat the process for multiple values of f and use interpolation to compute the in-between values. Since Eq. (3) assumes that pixel intensity is a linear function of radiance, we linearize the images using the inverse of the sensor response function [16].

5   High-Resolution Image Alignment

The intensity comparisons needed to evaluate confocal constancy are only possible if we can locate the projection of the same 3D point in multiple images taken with different settings. The main difficulty is that real lenses map in-focus 3D points onto the image plane in a non-linear fashion that cannot be predicted by ordinary perspective projection. To enable cross-image comparisons, we develop an alignment procedure that reverses these non-linearities and warps the input images to make them consistent with a reference image.

Since our emphasis is on reconstructing scenes at the maximum possible spatial resolution, we aim to model real lenses with enough precision to ensure sub-pixel alignment accuracy. This task is especially challenging because at resolutions of 12MP or more, we begin to approach the optical and mechanical limits of the camera. In this domain, the commonly-used thin lens (i.e., magnification) model [6, 7, 8, 18, 15] is insufficient to account for observed distortions.

Deterministic second-order radial distortion model. To model geometric distortions caused by the lens optics, we use a model with $F + 5$ parameters for a lens with F focal settings. The model expresses deviations from an image with reference focus setting f_1 as an additive image warp consisting of two terms—a pure magnification term m_f that is specific to focus setting f, and a quadratic distortion term that amplifies the magnification:

$$\mathbf{w}_f^D(x, y) = \left[m_f + m_f(f - f_1)(k_0 + k_1 r + k_2 r^2) - 1 \right] \cdot \left[(x, y) - (x_c, y_c) \right] , \quad (4)$$

where k_0, k_1, k_2 are the quadratic distortion parameters, (x_c, y_c) is the estimated image center, and $r = \|(x, y) - (x_c, y_c)\|$ is the radial displacement. Note that when the quadratic distortion parameters are zero, the model reduces to pure magnification. Also note that the quadratic distortion term depends linearly on the focus setting as well. Empirically, we have found that the model of Eq. (4) is necessary to obtain sub-pixel registration at high resolutions.

Non-deterministic first-order distortion model. We were surprised to find that significant misalignments can occur even when the camera is controlled remotely without any change in settings, and is mounted securely on an optical table (Fig. 3g). While these motions are clearly stochastic, we also observed a reproducible, aperture-dependent misalignment of about the same magnitude (Fig. 3c–f). In order to achieve sub-pixel alignment, we approximate these motions by a global 2D translation, estimated independently for every image:

$$\mathbf{w}_{\alpha f}^{ND}(x, y) = \mathbf{t}_{\alpha f} . \quad (5)$$

Offline geometric lens calibration. We recover the full distortion model of Eqs. (4–5) in a single optimization step, using images of a calibration pattern taken over all F focus settings at the narrowest aperture, α_1. This optimization simultaneously estimates the $F + 5$ parameters of the deterministic model and the $2F$ parameters of the non-deterministic model. To do this, we solve a nonlinear least squares problem that minimizes the squared reprojection error over a set of features detected on the calibration pattern:

$$E(x_c, y_c, \mathbf{m}, \mathbf{k}, \mathbf{T}) = \sum_{(x,y)} \sum_f \|\mathbf{w}_f^D(x, y) + \mathbf{w}_{\alpha_1 f}^{ND}(x, y) - \Delta_{\alpha_1 f}(x, y)\|^2 , \quad (6)$$

where $\mathbf{m}$ and $\mathbf{k}$ are the vectors of magnification and quadratic parameters, respectively; $\mathbf{T}$ collects non-deterministic translations; and $\Delta_{\alpha_1 f}(x, y)$ is the displacement between a feature location at focus setting f and its location at the reference focus setting, f_1. To increase robustness, we fit the model iteratively, removing features whose reprojection error is more than 3.0 times the median.

Online alignment. While the deterministic warp parameters need only be computed once for a given lens, we cannot apply the non-deterministic translations computed during calibration to a different sequence. Thus, for a new capture we identify (potentially different) features in the scene and redo the optimization of Eq. (6), with all parameters except $\mathbf{T}$ fixed to the values computed offline.

6   Confocal Constancy Evaluation

Together, image alignment and relative exitance estimation allow us to establish a pixel-wise geometric and radiometric correspondence across all input images, i.e., for all aperture and focus settings. Given a pixel (x, y), we use this correspondence to assemble an $A \times F$ *aperture-focus image*, describing the pixel's intensity variations as a function of aperture and focus (Fig. 4a):

Aperture-Focus Image (AFI)

$$AFI_{xy}(\alpha, f) = \frac{1}{E_{xy}(\alpha, f)} \; \hat{I}_{\alpha f}(x, y) \; , \tag{7}$$

where $\hat{I}_{\alpha f}$ denotes the images after geometric image alignment.

AFIs are a rich source of information about whether or not a pixel is in focus at a particular focus setting f. We make this intuition concrete by developing two functionals that measure how well a pixel's AFI conforms to the confocal constancy property at f. Since we analyze the AFI of each pixel (x, y) separately, we drop subscripts and use $AFI(\alpha, f)$ to denote its AFI.

Direct Evaluation of Confocal Constancy. Confocal constancy tells us that when a pixel is in focus, its relative intensities across aperture should match the variation predicted by the relative exitance of the lens. Since Eq. (7) already corrects for these variations, confocal constancy at f implies constant intensity within column f of the AFI (Fig. 4b). Hence, to find the ideal focus setting we can simply find the column with minimum variance:

$$f^* = \arg\min_f \text{Var}\left\{ AFI(1, f), \ldots, AFI(A, f) \right\} \; . \tag{8}$$

The reason why the variance is higher at non-ideal focus settings is that defocused pixels integrate regions of the scene surrounding the true surface point (Fig. 2b), which generally contain "texture" in the form of varying geometric structure or surface albedo. Hence, for confocal constancy to be discriminative as a focus measure, such texture must be present in the scene.

Evaluation by AFI Model-Fitting. A disadvantage of the previous method is that most of the AFI is ignored when testing a given focus hypothesis f, since only one column participates in the calculation of Eq. (8). In reality, the 3D location of a scene point determines both the column of the AFI where confocal constancy holds as well as the degree of blur that occurs in the AFI's remaining, "out-of-focus" regions.[3] By taking these regions into account, we can create a focus detector with more resistance to noise and higher discriminative power.

---

[3] While not analyzed in the context of confocal constancy or the AFI, this is a key observation exploited by *depth-from-defocus* approaches [9, 10, 11, 12].

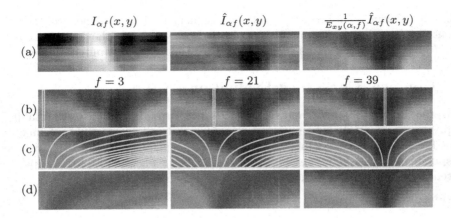

Fig. 4. (a) The $A \times F$ measurements for the pixel shown in Fig. 1. *Left:* prior to image alignment. *Middle:* after image alignment. *Right:* after accounting for relative exitance (Eq. (7)). Note that the AFI's smooth structure is discernible only after both corrections. (b) Direct evaluation of confocal constancy for three focus hypotheses. (c) Boundaries of the equi-blur regions, superimposed over the AFI (for readability, only a third are shown). (d) Results of AFI model fitting, with constant intensity in each equi-blur region, from the mean of the corresponding region in the AFI. Observe that for $f = 39$ the model is in good agreement with the measured AFI ((a), rightmost).

In order to take into account both in- and out-of-focus regions of a pixel's AFI, we develop an idealized, parametric AFI model that generalizes confocal constancy. This model is controlled by a single parameter—the focus hypothesis f—and is fit directly to a pixel's AFI measurements. The ideal focus setting is chosen to be the hypothesis that maximizes agreement with these measurements.

Our AFI model is based on two key observations. First, the AFI can be decomposed into a set of F disjoint *equi-blur* regions that are completely determined by the focus hypothesis f (Fig. 4c). Second, under mild assumptions on scene radiance, the intensity within each equi-blur region will be constant when f is the correct hypothesis. These observations suggest that we can model the AFI as a set of F constant-intensity regions whose spatial layout is determined by the focus hypothesis f. Fitting this model to a pixel's AFI leads to a focus criterion that minimizes intensity variance in every equi-blur region (Fig. 4d):

$$f^* = \arg\min_f \sum_{i=1}^{F} \left(w_i^f \operatorname{Var}\left\{ AFI(\alpha, \phi) \mid (\alpha, \phi) \in \mathcal{R}_i^f \right\} \right), \qquad (9)$$

where $\mathcal{R}_i^f$ is the i-th equi-blur region for hypothesis f, and w_i^f weighs the contribution of region $\mathcal{R}_i^f$ ($w_i^f = \operatorname{area}(\mathcal{R}_i^f)$ in our experiments).

To implement Eq. (9) we must compute the equi-blur regions for a given focus hypothesis f. Suppose that the hypothesis f is correct, and suppose that the current aperture and focus of the lens are α and f, respectively, i.e., a scene point $\mathbf{p}$ is in perfect focus for this setting. Now consider "defocusing" the lens by

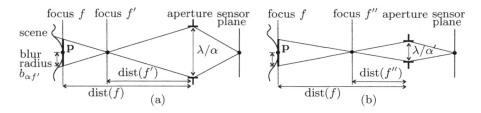

Fig. 5. (a) Quantifying the blur due to aperture α at a non-ideal focus setting f'. The aperture's diameter can be expressed in terms of its f-stop value α and the focal length λ. (b) A second aperture-focus combination with the same blur radius. In our AFI model, (α, f') and (α', f'') belong to the same equi-blur region.

changing its focus to f' (Fig. 5a). We represent the blur associated with the pair (α, f') by a circular disc centered on point **p** and parallel to the sensor plane. From similar triangles, the radius of this disc is equal to

$$b_{\alpha f'} = \frac{\lambda}{2\alpha} \frac{|\text{dist}(f) - \text{dist}(f')|}{\text{dist}(f')} , \tag{10}$$

where λ is the focal length of the lens and $\text{dist}(\cdot)$ converts focus settings to distances from the front aperture.

Given a focus hypothesis f, Eq. (10) assigns a "blur radius" to each point (α, f') in the AFI and induces a set of nested, wedge-shaped curves of equal blur radius (Figs. 4c and 5b). We quantize the possible blur radii into F bins associated with the widest-aperture settings, i.e., $(\alpha_A, f_1), \ldots, (\alpha_A, f_F)$, which partitions the AFI into F equi-blur regions, one per bin.

While Eq. (10) fully specifies our parametric AFI model, it is important to note that this model is approximate. We have implicitly assumed that once relative exitance and geometric distortion have been factored out (Sects. 4–5), defocusing is well-approximated by the thin-lens model [17]. Moreover, the intensity at two equi-blur positions in an AFI will be constant only if two conditions hold: (i) outgoing radiance remains constant within the cone of the largest aperture for *all* scene points contributing intensity to the pixel (i.e., the shaded region of the scene in Fig. 2b), and (ii) depth variations within this region do not significantly affect the defocus integral. In practice, we have found that this model matches the observed pixel variations quite well (Fig. 4d).

7   Experimental Results

To test our approach, we used a Canon EOS-1Ds digital SLR camera with a wide-aperture, fixed focal length lens (Canon EF$85mm$ 1.2L). The lens aperture was under computer control and its focal setting was adjusted manually using a printed ruler on the body of the lens. We operated the camera at its highest resolution, capturing 4604×2704-pixel images in RAW 12-bit mode. Each image was demosaiced using Canon software and linearized using the algorithm in

[16]. We used $A = 13$ apertures ranging from f1.2 to f16, and $F = 61$ focal settings spanning a workspace that was $17cm$ in depth and $1.2m$ away from the camera. Successive focal settings therefore corresponded to a depth difference of approximately $2.8mm$. We mounted the camera on an optical table in order to allow precise ground-truth measurements and to minimize external vibrations.

To enable the construction of aperture-focus images, we first computed the relative exitance of the lens (Sect. 4) and then performed offline geometric calibration (Sect. 5). Our geometric distortion model was able to align the calibration images with an accuracy of approximately 0.15 pixels, estimated from centroids of dot features (Fig. 3e). The accuracy of online alignment was about 0.5 pixels, i.e., higher than during offline calibration but well below one pixel. This penalty is expected since far fewer features are used for online alignment.

Quantitative evaluation: "Box" dataset. To quantify reconstruction accuracy, we used a tilted planar scene consisting of a box wrapped in newsprint (Fig. 6). The plane of the box was measured with a FaroArm Gold 3D touch probe whose single-point accuracy was $\pm 0.05mm$ in the camera's workspace. To relate probe coordinates to coordinates in the camera's reference frame we used the Matlab Camera Calibration Toolbox along with further correspondences between image features and 3D coordinates measured by the probe. A similar procedure was used to estimate the mapping between focal settings and the depth of in-focus points, i.e., the dist(·) function in Eq. (10).

We computed a depth map of the scene for three focus criteria: direct confocal constancy (Eq. (8)), AFI model-fitting (Eq. (9)), and a depth-from-focus (DFF) method, applied to the widest-aperture images, that chooses the focus setting with the highest variance in a 3×3 window centered at each pixel. The planar shape of the scene and its detailed texture can be thought of as a best-case scenario for such window-based approaches. The plane's footprint contained 2.8 million pixels, yielding an equal number of 3D measurements. As Table 1 shows, all three methods performed quite well, with accuracies of 0.37–0.45% of the object-to-camera distance. This performance is on par with previous quantitative studies (e.g., [12]) although few results with real images have been reported in the passive depth-from-focus literature. Significantly, AFI model-fitting slightly outperforms spatial variance (DFF) in both accuracy and number of outliers even though its focus computations are performed entirely at the pixel level and, hence, are of much higher resolution. Qualitatively, this behavior is confirmed by considering all three criteria for specific pixels (Fig. 6, top).

Table 1. Ground-truth accuracy results. The inlier threshold was set to $11mm$. All distances were measured relative to the ground-truth plane.

	median ABS dist. (mm)	inlier RMS dist. (mm)	% inliers	RMS % dist. to camera
confocal constancy evaluation	3.18	4.61	66	0.454
AFI model fitting	2.13	3.78	84	0.373
3×3 spatial variance (DFF)	2.16	3.79	80	0.374

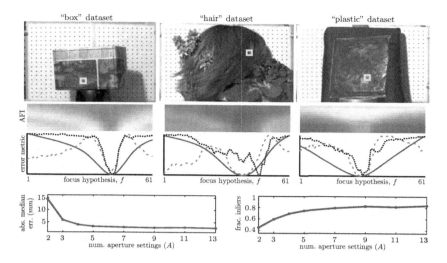

Fig. 6. *Top:* Behavior of focus criteria for a specific pixel (highlighted square) in three test datasets. The dotted graph is for 3×3 variance (DFF), dashed is for direct confocal constancy (Eq. (8)) and the solid graph is for AFI model-fitting (Eq. (9)). While all three criteria often have corresponding local minima near the ideal focus setting, AFI model-fitting varies much more smoothly and exhibits no spurious local minima in these examples. For the middle example, which considers the same pixel shown in Fig. 1, the global minimum for variance is at an incorrect focus setting. This is because the pixel lies on a strand of hair only 1–2 pixels wide, beyond the resolving power of variance calculations. *Bottom:* AFI model fitting error and inlier fraction as a function of A ("box" dataset, inlier threshold $= 11mm$).

As a final experiment with this dataset, we investigated how AFI model fitting degrades when a reduced number of apertures is used (i.e., for AFIs of size $A' \times F$ with $A' < A$). Our results suggest that reducing the apertures to five or six causes little reduction in reconstruction quality (Fig. 6, bottom).

"Hair" dataset. Our second test scene was a wig with a messy hairstyle, approximately $25cm$ tall, surrounded by several artificial plants (Figs. 1 and 6).[4] Reconstruction results for this scene (Fig. 7) show that our confocal constancy criteria lead to very detailed depth maps, at the resolution of individual strands of hair, despite the scene's complex geometry and despite the fact that depths can vary greatly within small image neighborhoods (e.g., toward the silhouette of the hair). By comparison, the 3×3 variance operator produces uniformly-lower resolution results, and generates smooth "halos" around narrow geometric structures like individual strands of hair. In many cases, these "halos" are larger than the width of the spatial operator, as blurring causes distant points to influence the results.

In low-texture regions, such as the cloth flower petals and leaves, fitting a model to the entire AFI allows us to exploit defocused texture from nearby

---

[4] For additional results, see `http://www.cs.toronto.edu/~hasinoff/confocal`.

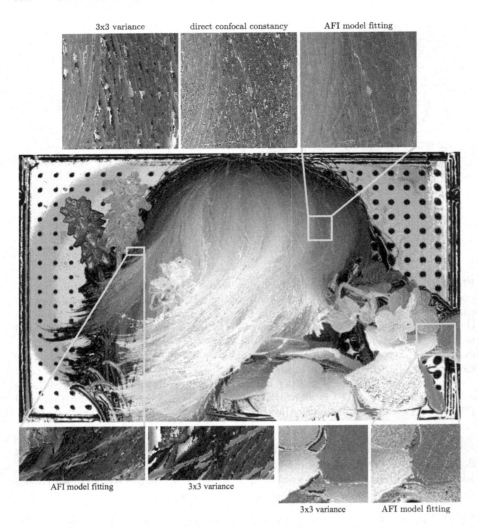

Fig. 7. *Center:* Depth map for the "hair" dataset using AFI model fitting. *Top:* Several distinctive foreground strands of hair are resolved in the AFI-based depth map. Direct evaluation of confocal constancy is also sharp but much noisier, making structure difficult to discern. By contrast, 3×3 variance (DFF) exhibits thick "halo" artifacts and fails to detect most of the foreground strands (see also Fig. 6, top). *Bottom right:* DFF yields smoother and more accurate depths for the low-texture leaves. *Bottom left:* Unlike DFF, AFI model fitting resolves structure amid significant depth discontinuities.

scene points. Window-based methods like variance, however, generally yield even better results in such regions, because they propagate focus information from nearby texture more directly. Like all focus measures, those based on confocal constancy are uninformative in extremely untextured regions, i.e., when the AFI is constant. Such pixels may be detected using a "confidence" measure (e.g., assessing the steepness of the minimum) or by processing the AFI further.

8   Concluding Remarks

The extreme locality of shape computations derived from aperture-focus images is both a key advantage and a major limitation of the current approach. While we have shown that processing a pixel's AFI leads to highly detailed reconstructions, this locality does not yet provide the means to handle large untextured regions or to reason about global scene geometry and occlusion [18, 19, 15]. To handle low texture, we are exploring the possibility of analyzing AFIs at multiple levels of detail and for multiple pixels simultaneously. We are also investigating a space-sweep approach to analyze occlusions, analogous to voxel-based stereo.

Acknowledgements. This work was supported in part by the Natural Sciences and Engineering Research Council of Canada under the RGPIN and CGS-D programs, by a fellowship from the Alfred P. Sloan Foundation, by an Ontario Premier's Research Excellence Award and by Microsoft Research.

References

1. Zitnick, C.L., Kang, S.B., Uyttendaele, M., Winder, S., Szeliski, R.: High-quality video view interpolation using a layered representation. In: SIGGRAPH. (2004) 600–608
2. Fitzgibbon, A., Wexler, Y., Zisserman, A.: Image-based rendering using image-based priors. IJCV **63** (2005) 141–151
3. Hertzmann, A., Seitz, S.M.: Example-based photometric stereo: Shape reconstruction with general, varying BRDFs. PAMI **27** (2005) 1254–1264
4. Wei, Y., Ofek, E., Quan, L., Shum, H.Y.: Modeling hair from multiple views. In: SIGGRAPH. (2005) 816–820
5. Darrell, T., Wohn, K.: Pyramid based depth from focus. In: CVPR. (1988) 504–509
6. Nayar, S., Watanabe, M., Noguchi, M.: Real-time focus range sensor. PAMI **18** (1996) 1186–1198
7. Favaro, P., Soatto, S.: Learning shape from defocus. In: ECCV (2). (2002) 735–745
8. Favaro, P., Osher, S., Soatto, S., Vese, L.A.: 3D shape from anisotropic diffusion. In: CVPR (1). (2003) 179–186
9. Pentland, A.P.: A new sense for depth of field. PAMI **9** (1987) 523–531
10. Subbarao, M., Surya, G.: Depth from defocus: A spatial domain approach. IJCV **13** (1994) 271–294
11. Farid, H., Simoncelli, E.P.: Range estimation by optical differentiation. J. Optical Society of America, A **15** (1998) 1777–1786
12. Watanabe, M., Nayar, S.K.: Rational filters for passive depth from defocus. IJCV **27** (1998) 203–225
13. Isaksen, A., McMillan, L., Gortler, S.J.: Dynamically reparameterized light fields. In: SIGGRAPH. (2000) 297–306

14. Levoy, M., Chen, B., Vaish, V., Horowitz, M., McDowall, I., Bolas, M.T.: Synthetic aperture confocal imaging. In: SIGGRAPH. (2004) 825–834
15. Favaro, P., Soatto, S.: Seeing beyond occlusions (and other marvels of a finite lens aperture). In: CVPR (2). (2003) 579–586
16. Debevec, P., Malik, J.: Recovering high dynamic range radiance maps from photographs. In: SIGGRAPH. (1997) 369–378
17. Smith, W.J.: Modern Optical Engineering. 3rd edn. McGraw-Hill, NY (2000)
18. Asada, N., Fujiwara, H., Matsuyama, T.: Seeing behind the scene: Analysis of photometric properties of occluding edges by the reversed projection blurring model. PAMI **20** (1998) 155–167
19. Schechner, Y.Y., Kiryati, N.: Depth from defocus vs. stereo: How different really are they? IJCV **39** (2000) 141–162

Author Index

Lecture Notes in Computer Science

For information about Vols. 1–3847

please contact your bookseller or Springer

Vol. 3897: B. Preneel, S. Tavares (Eds.), Selected Areas in Cryptography. XI, 371 pages. 2006.

Vol. 3896: Y. Ioannidis, M.H. Scholl, J.W. Schmidt, F. Matthes, M. Hatzopoulos, K. Boehm, A. Kemper, T. Grust, C. Boehm (Eds.), Advances in Database Technology - EDBT 2006. XIV, 1208 pages. 2006.

Vol. 3895: O. Goldreich, A.L. Rosenberg, A.L. Selman (Eds.), Theoretical Computer Science. XII, 399 pages. 2006.

Vol. 3894: W. Grass, B. Sick, K. Waldschmidt (Eds.), Architecture of Computing Systems - ARCS 2006. XII, 496 pages. 2006.

Vol. 3893: L. Atzori, D.D. Giusto, R. Leonardi, F. Pereira (Eds.), Visual Content Processing and Representation. IX, 224 pages. 2006.

Vol. 3891: J.S. Sichman, L. Antunes (Eds.), Multi-Agent-Based Simulation VI. X, 191 pages. 2006. (Sublibrary LNAI).

Vol. 3890: S.G. Thompson, R. Ghanea-Hercock (Eds.), Defence Applications of Multi-Agent Systems. XII, 141 pages. 2006. (Sublibrary LNAI).

Vol. 3889: J. Rosca, D. Erdogmus, J.C. Príncipe, S. Haykin (Eds.), Independent Component Analysis and Blind Signal Separation. XXI, 980 pages. 2006.

Vol. 3888: D. Draheim, G. Weber (Eds.), Trends in Enterprise Application Architecture. IX, 145 pages. 2006.

Vol. 3887: J.R. Correa, A. Hevia, M. Kiwi (Eds.), LATIN 2006: Theoretical Informatics. XVI, 814 pages. 2006.

Vol. 3886: E.G. Bremer, J. Hakenberg, E.-H.(S.) Han, D. Berrar, W. Dubitzky (Eds.), Knowledge Discovery in Life Science Literature. XIV, 147 pages. 2006. (Sublibrary LNBI).

Vol. 3885: V. Torra, Y. Narukawa, A. Valls, J. Domingo-Ferrer (Eds.), Modeling Decisions for Artificial Intelligence. XII, 374 pages. 2006. (Sublibrary LNAI).

Vol. 3884: B. Durand, W. Thomas (Eds.), STACS 2006. XIV, 714 pages. 2006.

Vol. 3882: M.L. Lee, K.-L. Tan, V. Wuwongse (Eds.), Database Systems for Advanced Applications. XIX, 923 pages. 2006.

Vol. 3881: S. Gibet, N. Courty, J.-F. Kamp (Eds.), Gesture in Human-Computer Interaction and Simulation. XIII, 344 pages. 2006. (Sublibrary LNAI).

Vol. 3880: A. Rashid, M. Aksit (Eds.), Transactions on Aspect-Oriented Software Development I. IX, 335 pages. 2006.

Vol. 3879: T. Erlebach, G. Persinao (Eds.), Approximation and Online Algorithms. X, 349 pages. 2006.

Vol. 3878: A. Gelbukh (Ed.), Computational Linguistics and Intelligent Text Processing. XVII, 589 pages. 2006.

Vol. 3877: M. Detyniecki, J.M. Jose, A. Nürnberger, C. J. '. van Rijsbergen (Eds.), Adaptive Multimedia Retrieval: User, Context, and Feedback. XI, 279 pages. 2006.

Vol. 3876: S. Halevi, T. Rabin (Eds.), Theory of Cryptography. XI, 617 pages. 2006.

Vol. 3875: S. Ur, E. Bin, Y. Wolfsthal (Eds.), Hardware and Software, Verification and Testing. X, 265 pages. 2006.

Vol. 3874: R. Missaoui, J. Schmidt (Eds.), Formal Concept Analysis. X, 309 pages. 2006. (Sublibrary LNAI).

Vol. 3873: L. Maicher, J. Park (Eds.), Charting the Topic Maps Research and Applications Landscape. VIII, 281 pages. 2006. (Sublibrary LNAI).

Vol. 3872: H. Bunke, A. L. Spitz (Eds.), Document Analysis Systems VII. XIII, 630 pages. 2006.

Vol. 3871: E.-G. Talbi, P. Liardet, P. Collet, E. Lutton, M. Schoenauer (Eds.), Artificial Evolution. XI, 310 pages. 2006.

Vol. 3870: S. Spaccapietra, P. Atzeni, W.W. Chu, T. Catarci, K.P. Sycara (Eds.), Journal on Data Semantics V. XIII, 237 pages. 2006.

Vol. 3869: S. Renals, S. Bengio (Eds.), Machine Learning for Multimodal Interaction. XIII, 490 pages. 2006.

Vol. 3868: K. Römer, H. Karl, F. Mattern (Eds.), Wireless Sensor Networks. XI, 342 pages. 2006.

Vol. 3866: T. Dimitrakos, F. Martinelli, P.Y.A. Ryan, S. Schneider (Eds.), Formal Aspects in Security and Trust. X, 259 pages. 2006.

Vol. 3865: W. Shen, K.-M. Chao, Z. Lin, J.-P.A. Barthès, A. James (Eds.), Computer Supported Cooperative Work in Design II. XII, 659 pages. 2006.

Vol. 3863: M. Kohlhase (Ed.), Mathematical Knowledge Management. XI, 405 pages. 2006. (Sublibrary LNAI).

Vol. 3862: R.H. Bordini, M. Dastani, J. Dix, A.E.F. Seghrouchni (Eds.), Programming Multi-Agent Systems. XIV, 267 pages. 2006. (Sublibrary LNAI).

Vol. 3861: J. Dix, S.J. Hegner (Eds.), Foundations of Information and Knowledge Systems. X, 331 pages. 2006.

Vol. 3860: D. Pointcheval (Ed.), Topics in Cryptology – CT-RSA 2006. XI, 365 pages. 2006.

Vol. 3858: A. Valdes, D. Zamboni (Eds.), Recent Advances in Intrusion Detection. X, 351 pages. 2006.

Vol. 3857: M.P.C. Fossorier, H. Imai, S. Lin, A. Poli (Eds.), Applied Algebra, Algebraic Algorithms and Error-Correcting Codes. XI, 350 pages. 2006.

Vol. 3855: E. A. Emerson, K.S. Namjoshi (Eds.), Verification, Model Checking, and Abstract Interpretation. XI, 443 pages. 2005.

Vol. 3854: I. Stavrakakis, M. Smirnov (Eds.), Autonomic Communication. XIII, 303 pages. 2006.

Vol. 3853: A.J. Ijspeert, T. Masuzawa, S. Kusumoto (Eds.), Biologically Inspired Approaches to Advanced Information Technology. XIV, 388 pages. 2006.

Vol. 3852: P.J. Narayanan, S.K. Nayar, H.-Y. Shum (Eds.), Computer Vision – ACCV 2006, Part II. XXXI, 977 pages. 2006.

Vol. 3851: P.J. Narayanan, S.K. Nayar, H.-Y. Shum (Eds.), Computer Vision – ACCV 2006, Part I. XXXI, 973 pages. 2006.

Vol. 3850: R. Freund, G. Păun, G. Rozenberg, A. Salomaa (Eds.), Membrane Computing. IX, 371 pages. 2006.

Vol. 3849: I. Bloch, A. Petrosino, A.G.B. Tettamanzi (Eds.), Fuzzy Logic and Applications. XIV, 438 pages. 2006. (Sublibrary LNAI).

Vol. 3848: J.-F. Boulicaut, L. De Raedt, H. Mannila (Eds.), Constraint-Based Mining and Inductive Databases. X, 401 pages. 2006. (Sublibrary LNAI).